- *If it is an annual project, ask who completed the job last time. Then contact that photographer to see what they charged.*

- *Find out who you are bidding against and contact those people to make sure you received the same information about the job. While agreeing to charge the same price is illegal, sharing information on prices is not.*

- *Talk to photographers not bidding on the project and ask them what they would charge.*

- *Finally, consider all aspects of the shoot, including preparation time, fees for assistants and stylists, rental equipment and other material costs. Don't leave anything out.*

— *For important business information, turn to the Business of Photography on page 5.*

1994 Photographer's Market

Distributed in Canada by McGraw-Hill,
300 Water Street,
Whitby Ontario L1N 9B6.
Also distributed in Australia by Kirby Books, Private Bag No. 19, P.O. Alexandria NSW 2015.

Managing Editor, Market Books Department:
Constance J. Achabal.

This 1994 hardcover edition of Photographer's Market *features a "self-jacket" that eliminates the need for a separate dust jacket. It provides sturdy protection for your book while it saves paper, trees and energy.*

*International Standard Serial Number
0147-247X
International Standard Book Number
0-89879-608-3*

1994
Photographer's Market

Where & How to Sell Your Photographs

Edited by
Michael Willins

WRITER'S DIGEST BOOKS
CINCINNATI, OHIO

Contents

The Markets

© Oscar Williams

© Dennis D. Savage

© Paul Natkin

Resources

© William Skutans

From the Editor

In photography, as well as everyday life, it is often difficult for people to step outside their comfort zones. Many artists would rather focus on techniques and subject matter they already understand without pushing and challenging themselves to develop better material. In this edition of *Photographer's Market* we challenged ourselves, and hopefully succeeded, to create a book that is more in tune with your needs. We have included a wealth of new information and made changes that should help in your marketing efforts.

As the industry continues to witness major technological advances we realized a detailed explanation of these changes was imperative. The article Riding the Wave of the Future starting on page 34 discusses these advances and shows how you can benefit from them. Along with the technological improvements of the past decade there has been a move by photographers toward stock photography. New agencies are popping up throughout the world and searching for photographers with stunning images. As a photographer you may wonder what to look for when being courted by an agency. This dilemma and many other questions can be answered in the article Exploring Your Stock Options on page 29.

If you own past editions of this book you will notice that feature articles of individuals switched from being called Close-ups to Insider Reports. Equipped with a new design these stories also provide more advice about selling work. These tips, developed from tougher interview questions, come from top photographers, such as Ira Lerner, Paul Natkin, Mark Downey, Lee Foster, Mary Ann Carter, Pat Goetzinger and Donna Jernigan. Designer Steven Sessions adds his suggestions along with gallery director Herbert Ascherman, Jr., Visuals Editor Jennifer Keane of Reidmore Books in Canada, and Rebecca Taylor of FPG International.

In piecing together the listings we felt it was essential to add our own thoughts whenever possible to give you more details when evaluating markets. As a new feature, these "editorial comments" are set off by bullets (●) and include information such as awards won, design changes or adopted policies that could affect you when dealing with certain markets.

One extremely important resource for anyone interested in working with magazine publishers is the new Subject Index at the back of this book. Separated into 24 categories, ranging from animals to travel, this index can help you find markets interested in the types of images you produce.

While some of the changes we have made are obvious, others are subtle.

We devised a more consistent and readable format for many sections throughtout the book and increased the point size in introductions and upfront material to make them easier to read. We also redesigned the Table of Contents, added to the number of photo samples and updated the Business of Photography.

Although we have made many modifications, we have not forgotten about those things that worked in the past. Introduced last year, you still will find the maple leaf symbol (✹) in front of all Canadian listings and the double dagger (‡) in front of markets outside the United States and Canada. An asterisk (*) still appears before all new listings and a black square (■) designates audiovisual markets. Following Recommended Books & Publications and the Glossary in the back of this book, you will again find the First Markets Index which assists new photographers in finding markets.

Now that we have pushed ourselves to make this edition better than ever, we are asking you to push yourself. Don't take the easy way out by merely collecting names and addresses and mailing off submissions. Inappropriate submissions will only alienate you from the very people you are trying to impress.

Instead, read through the material we have provided and follow the suggestions made by professionals working in the photo industry. Doing so will improve your chances for success and show you that it is better to test yourself rather than settle for second best.

How to Use Your Photographer's Market

Now that you have this book in your hands, what are you going to do with it? Unless you have owned past editions of *Photographer's Market* you may not feel comfortable flipping through these pages, finding markets and submitting work. There are nearly 2,500 listings in this book, not to mention the 11 Insider Reports, three indexes and loads of helpful business information. All of this can be overwhelming and understanding how best to proceed is important.

Before diving into the listings it is a good idea to turn to page 5 and read the Business of Photography. This feature gives you guidance on pricing images and negotiating sales, mailing submissions and understanding copyright laws. There also are several sample forms that can help you in day-to-day operations and contribute to a more professional appearance.

Anyone who has worked in the photo industry over the past five years, either buying or selling images, can tell you that the field has undergone some major changes. The move toward stock photography, and ways to choose a stock agency, are covered in detail beginning on page 29. Meanwhile, some of the more prominent technological changes, such as CD-ROM and computer manipulation, are discussed in the article Riding the Wave of the Future starting on page 34.

The bulk of the book is made up of markets interested in using images, but there are also dozens of listings in the Resources section which contain information about contests and workshops. While attending workshops can improve your skills as a photographer, entering contests can be a way for you to test those skills against others in the field.

Where to begin

With around 2,500 listings to review, it is easy to get lost when searching for a place to start. The first step is to thin out those sections which are of little or no use to you. If, for example, you are a professional who only wants to shoot product shots, there is little sense in spending all your time pouring over editorial listings. Advertising, Public Relations and Audiovisual Firms would be a natural for you as would Art/Design Studios, Businesses/Organizations and Stock Agencies.

If you are a beginner wanting to build a portfolio start with the Publications section, which includes consumer magazines, newspapers, special interest publications and trade publications. This, however, does not mean that other sections should be ignored, just prioritized. Most sections of the book contain markets whose needs "cross over."

For all newer or lesser-known photographers it is a good idea to use the First Markets Index in the back of the book. The index, which contains hundreds of buyers, is divided into categories to save you time in finding the markets you're interested in. This list also includes buyers at all points of the payscale and these listings contain the phrase, "Interested in receiving work from newer, lesser-known photographers."

This edition also contains a new Subject Index, designed to help you find buyers who are interested in the work you produce. This index can be found at the back of the book and it includes only those listings in the Publications section.

While payment is important for any businessperson, don't judge markets solely on the aspect of money. Through negotiations you may find that those payments are not set in stone. You also may find that one buyer who pays $500 for a magazine cover photo only buys one or two shots each year. On the other hand, a buyer who pays $35 for a magazine cover shot might buy 50 images annually. Obviously the odds of selling your work are greater if you contact markets which buy a lot of images. When reviewing the listings it is important to know how many photos a buyer purchases from freelancers each year. This usually is stated in this manner: "Uses 70 photos/issue; 80 percent supplied by freelancers." The numbers will change, but you get the idea. Some markets did not provide any payment information and those listings contain the code "NPI," which stands for "No payment information given."

While reading the book take a good look at this year's sample photos. These images are examples of photos buyers have purchased in the past and the cutline information will help you better understand the freelancing process. The captions also will explain the strengths of the photos and, in some cases, background information about images.

Probably the most important thing to remember when preparing to submit photos to a buyer is to know what the buyer wants. There is no sense in wasting time, effort and money submitting work to buyers who aren't interested in the subject matter. Each listing tells you what topics the buyer is interested in. In many cases a query letter and a stock photo list can give a book publisher or a paper product company a good idea what you have to offer.

This brings up another important point. Most listings have information regarding the submission process. Some may want to see unsolicited submissions along with a query letter. Others may just want photographers to submit stock photo lists. Follow these instructions in order to improve your chances for success.

The Business of Photography

As a photographer you may feel pretty confident in your ability to shoot pictures. You have made several sales to publishers or businesses and received positive feedback from editors regarding your talent. However, are you relying solely on photographic skills to make a name for yourself or are you succeeding because of the time you spend in the office, marketing images?

Numerous photographers struggle with the business end of the job. Although they produce tremendous images, they don't understand or feel comfortable with procedures such as negotiating prices, self promotion or record-keeping. However, those who succeed, more often than not, have mastered the dual role of photographer and businessman.

This section provides you with an opportunity to step back, review your everyday work habits and really examine ways to improve sales. This edition contains new information on pricing and negotiating, provides the latest material regarding copyright protection, and it examines the proper way to present a portfolio and submit images. Accompanying this material are several forms, provided by the American Society of Media Photographers (ASMP), which should serve as a foundation for daily operation. The forms, however, are meant to be used as guidelines and should be tailored to suit your specific needs.

At the end of this section you will find two articles that should answer a lot of questions in your mind. The first, beginning on page 29, is a detailed discussion of stock agencies. It explains how agencies operate and teaches you what to look for when choosing an agency to market your photos. The second article, starting on page 34, describes some technological changes that are affecting photography. You also will learn ways to benefit from these advances.

Prior to setting up your business, it's best to talk with other photographers about their professional habits. There also will be times, especially when searching for legal advice or tax guidance, when you should consult a professional. Such guidance is invaluable in preventing unexpected disasters. However, when you finish reading this material, you should have a better understanding of standard trade practices and feel more comfortable while building a solid business.

Pricing and negotiating

Whether you have been a professional photographer for 20 years or 20 minutes, there is a basic philosophy of pricing you must understand—*Never underestimate a photo's worth to a client, regardless of what you are told.*

Businesses routinely spend well over $100,000 on national advertising space in magazines. They set budgets for such advertising campaigns, keeping the high ad rates in mind, but they often restrict funds for photography. Photographers often are asked to provide images or job estimates, but during negotiations they are told by clients, "We have a very limited budget on this campaign." As a photographer in this type of situation, you have to ask yourself, "What's fair?" If the image is going to anchor a national advertisement and it conveys the perfect message for the client, why should you settle for a low rate?

When pricing a photo or job, the first thing you must do is consider the usage: "What is going to be done with the photo?" Too often, photographers shortchange themselves in negotiations because they do not understand how images will be used. Instead, they allow clients to set prices and prefer to accept lower fees rather than lose sales. Photographers argue that they would rather make the sale than lose it because they refused to lower their price.

Unfortunately, those photographers who look at short-term profits are actually bringing down the entire industry. Clients realize, if they shop around, they can find photographers willing to shoot assignments or sell image rights at very low rates. Therefore, prices stay depressed because buyers, not photographers, are setting usage fees.

However, there are ways to combat low prices. First, educate yourself about a client's line of work. If most of your clients are in the advertising field, acquire advertising rate cards for magazines so that you know what a client pays for ad space. Talk with seasoned photographers to find out what they charge in certain situations. This type of professionalism helps during negotiations because it shows buyers that you are serious about your work. The added knowledge also gives you an advantage when settling on fees because photographers are not expected to understand a client's profession.

Some photographers, at least in the area of assignment work, operate on day rates or half-day rates. Editorial photographers will typically quote fees in the low hundreds, while advertising and corporate shooters may quote fees in the low thousands. However, all photographers are finding that day rates by themselves are incomplete. As a result, they also bill clients for the number of finished pictures and rights purchased, as well as additional expenses, such as equipment rental and hiring assistants.

Keep in mind that there are all sorts of ways to negotiate sales. Some clients, such as paper product companies, prefer to pay royalties on the number of times a product is sold. Special markets, such as galleries and stock agencies, typically charge photographers a commission, from 20 to 50 percent, for displaying or representing their images. In these markets, payment on sales comes from the purchase of prints by gallery patrons, or from commission on the rental of photos by clients of stock agencies. Pricing formulas should be developed depending on your costs and current price levels in those markets, as well as on the basis of submission fees, commissions and other administrative costs charged to you.

Bidding a job

As you build your business you will encounter another aspect of pricing and negotiating that can be very difficult. Like it or not, clients often ask photographers to supply "bids" for jobs. In some cases, the bidding process is merely procedural and the assignment will go to the photographer who can best complete the assignment. In other instances, the photographer who submits the lowest bid will earn the job. When contacted, it is imperative to find out which bidding process is being used. Putting together an accurate estimate takes time and you do not want to waste a lot of effort if your bid is being sought merely to meet some quota.

However, correctly working through the steps is necessary if you want to succeed. You do not want to bid too much on a project and repeatedly get turned down, but you also don't want to bid too low and forfeit income. When a potential client calls to ask for a bid there are several dos and don'ts to consider:

- Always keep a list of questions by the telephone, so that you can refer to it when bids are requested. The questions should give you a solid understanding of the project and help you in reaching a price estimate.
- Never quote a price during the initial conversation, even if the caller pushes for a "ballpark figure." A spot estimate can only hurt you in the negotiating process.
- Immediately find out what the client intends to do with the photos and ask who will own copyrights to the images after they are produced. It is important to note that many clients believe, if they hire you for a job, they own all rights to the images you create. If they want all rights make sure the price they pay is worth it to you.
- If it is an annual project, ask who completed the job last time. Then contact that photographer to see what they charged.
- Find out who you are bidding against and contact those people to make sure you received the same information about the job. While agreeing to charge the same price is illegal, sharing information on prices is not.
- Talk to photographers not bidding on the project and ask them what they would charge.
- Finally, consider all aspects of the shoot, including preparation time, fees for assistants and stylists, rental equipment and other material costs. Don't leave anything out.

Copyright/rights

While negotiating prices there will be some discussion of rights: "Who will own the copyright once the images are used?" As mentioned earlier, buyers often want to keep all rights. They don't realize that you are selling usage rights of photos and not the images themselves. Buyers also see the technological advances that are taking place and they want to gain complete control of images that might end up in the ads of competitors. They also realize that photos can be manipulated and reused for similar campaigns.

There are certain terms photo buyers use when they seek ownership of copyrights. The most common terms are "work for hire" and "all rights." However, the basic concept can come in many other disguises as well, including, "buyout," "unlimited use," "world rights," "in perpetuity" and "no right of reversion." "Exclusive rights" also may be a signal that the client really wants all rights, but this is a term that usually can be negotiated for limited periods, such as one year.

Here is a list of image rights typically sold in the marketplace:

• One-time rights. These photos are "leased" on a one-time basis; one fee is paid for one use.

• First rights. This is generally the same as purchase of one-time rights, though the photo buyer is paying a bit more for the privilege of being the first to use the image. He may use it only once unless other rights are negotiated.

• Serial rights. The photographer has sold the right to use the photo in a periodical. It shouldn't be confused with using the photo in "installments." Most magazines will want to be sure the photo won't be running in a competing publication.

• Exclusive rights. Exclusive rights guarantee the buyer's exclusive right to use the photo in his particular market or for a particular product. A greeting card company, for example, may purchase these rights to an image with the stipulation that it not be sold to a competing company for a certain time period. The photographer, however, may retain rights to sell the image to other markets. Conditions should always be in writing to avoid any misunderstandings.

• Promotion rights. Such rights allow a publisher to use the photographer's photo for promotion of a publication in which the photo appeared. The photographer should be paid for promotional use in addition to the rights first sold to reproduce the image. Another form of this—agency promotion rights—is common among stock photo agencies. Likewise, the terms of this need to be negotiated separately.

• Work for hire. (See sidebar in this section for detailed definition.)

• All rights. This involves selling or assigning all rights to a photo for a specified period of time. This differs from work for hire, which always means the photographer permanently surrenders all rights to a photo and any claims to royalties or other future compensation. Terms for all rights — including time period of usage and compensation — should only be negotiated and confirmed in a written agreement with the client.

It is understandable for a client not to want a photo he used to appear in a competitor's ad. Skillful negotiation usually can result in an agreement between the photographer and the client that says the image(s) will not be sold to a competitor, but could be sold to other industries, possibly offering regional exclusivity for a stated time period as well.

The area of copyrights is one in which photographers can never be too careful, since it involves a complex set of terms and considerations that are frequently misunderstood by photographers and photo buyers alike. Even a knowledgeable photographer will find himself at risk when dealing with a misinformed or intentionally deceptive client. So, it's essential not only to know your rights under the Copyright Law but also to make sure that every photo buyer you deal with understands them.

In the past couple years, ASMP has lobbied hard for politicians to improve

Work for hire definition:

Under the Copyright Act of 1976, section 101, a "work for hire" is defined as:

"(1) a work prepared by an employee within the scope of his or her employment; or (2) a work . . .

- *specially ordered or commissioned for use as a contribution to a collective work**
- *as part of a motion picture or audiovisual work**
- *as a translation*
- *as a supplementary work**
- *as a compilation*
- *as an instructional text*
- *as a test*
- *as answer material for a test*
- *or as an atlas*

. . . if the parties expressly agree in a written instrument signed by them that the work shall be considered a work made for hire."

NOTE: The asterisk (*) denotes categories within the Copyright Law which apply to photography.

copyright protection for photographers. In 1993 ASMP pushed for approval of the Copyright Reform Act, designed to eliminate the requirement that work must be registered in the Copyright Office of the Library of Congress if copyright owners want to sue infringers for attorneys' fees and statutory damages. ASMP also contends that, with the registration requirement in place, photographers who have not registered their work often do not pursue legal battles against infringers. The Act could discourage infringements by making it easier for copyright owners to collect damages.

Copyright protection

Here are a few basic practices you can implement to ensure protection of your copyright. Primarily, you should mark each of your images with a copyright notice—copyright, copr. or ©—plus the year of creation as well as the name of the owner, which in most cases is the creator. Since the © symbol is universally accepted in most countries and it is becoming more common for photographers to work with clients overseas, it is best to settle on this designation as you establish your routine practices.

According to the Buenos Aires Convention, which covers many Western Hemisphere countries, copyright notices should also include the notation "All rights reserved." However, all rights are automatically reserved under U.S. Copyright Law. For convenience, you can have rubber stamps made or use a computer software package to create labels for your images. Such labeling is preferable to handmarking, since handwritten notices—especially those done in ink—can sometimes become unreadable or bleed through into printed images. If clients ever advise you not to include copyright information on your slides or prints, take this as a warning sign and do not do business with them.

In the event that you have to file suit against a photo buyer for copyright infringement, copyright registration is ordinarily necessary if you are a U.S. citizen. To do this, you should write to the Copyright Office of the Library of Congress, Washington DC 20559. Request the form titled Form VA (works of visual arts).

As a quick reference, here are several areas to remember when dealing with questions of copyright and rights:
- contracts
- licensing
- setting value and prices for images
- keeping records of all correspondence and submissions
- enforcement of rights

A valuable tool for any photographer dealing with the copyright language and various forms of the photography business is the *SPAR* Do-It-Yourself Kit*. This survival package includes sample forms, explanations and checklists of all terms and questions a photographer should ask himself when negotiating a job and pricing it. It's available from SPAR, the Society of Photographer and Artist Representatives, Inc., Suite 1166, 60 E. 42nd St., New York NY 10165, (212)822-1415. Price: $50 plus $3 shipping and handling. New York state residents pay in-state tax of $4.37.

Submissions

Marketing images is a very time consuming and often frustrating aspect of everyday business. Developing promotional pieces, making cold calls to art directors and setting up appointments are not the tasks creative people like to concentrate on. They would rather shoot pictures and often have a hard time understanding why editors reject submissions or refuse to review portfolios.

Editors reject submissions or portfolios for a variety of reasons. Some of these, such as editors not having enough time to review material, are out of your control. The key, however, is to cut down on your mistakes by giving editors what they want. Make it easier for them to accept your work, rather than reject it.

Before sending photo submissions out into the marketplace, be sure to stamp each print or transparency with your copyright notice, and a "Return to: (your name, address, phone number) and an identifying number." The address and identifying number will assist both you and the photobuyer in locating any images which may be misplaced. Also, computer software packages are available that help in both organizing images and printing out labels for them.

To ensure your images' safe arrival and return, pay attention to the way you package them. Insert 8×10 black-and-white photos into an $8\frac{1}{2} \times 11$ plastic jacket; transparencies should be stored in protective vinyl pages. Most camera stores carry these in a variety of format sizes. Never submit photos in mounted glass—the glass can break. Also, do not send slides in the "little yellow boxes"—many photo buyers consider them an inconvenience and will not even look at the slides.

Another highly recommended practice which helps to ensure the safe handling and return of your photos is the inclusion of a delivery memo. This is a form that summarizes the number and type of photos (slides or prints) and specifies the terms under which you are making the photos available. In particular, you can specify the value of the photos if they are damaged or lost. Then, by signing and returning a copy, the photo buyer confirms both the safe arrival of the images and his acceptance of the terms. Or if he declines to accept the photos on those terms, he simply returns the photos.

Be sure to include a return mailing label, adequate postage and an envelope with your submission. If you include a manila envelope, also pack two cardboard sheets to stiffen the envelope so your images aren't damaged. You can also buy heavy weight insulated envelopes that are reusable. These can be purchased at most office supply or stationery stores.

Send your submissions via first class mail. The service is quicker and handling tends to be less rough. Many photographers also use certified mail. Though a certified package travels a bit slower than first class mail because it is logged in at each enroute destination, it is much easier to trace in the event of a mishap. Also, to ensure the safe arrival of your submission, we recommend making a quick address check by phone. We make the effort to update all addresses every year, but businesses still move and go out of business after press time. Many photo buyers discourage phone calls, but your address check can be handled by a firm's receptionist without having to disturb the photo buyer.

There are still other ways to safeguard against losing an irreplaceable image; some involve a little pre-planning. When submitting black-and-white prints, never send out the negatives. If a photo buyer is interested in purchasing your image, but doesn't like a technical flaw such as contrast, offer to send a reprint. Transparencies are a bit trickier. It is ideal to send out dupes with an offer to send the original if the other party is interested in purchasing rights to the image. Some labs can produce high-quality dupes, though you may want to decide which are your most valuable (marketable) images since this can become costly. If you're shooting an image that you feel is going to be marketable, expose multiple images—in-camera dupes— (if this is possible) at the time you shoot your original. Using this method, you retain other "original" images should one be lost.

As more businesses and publications start to use facsimile transmission (fax) machines, more photographers have begun to submit trial images or proofs of assignments to clients by fax. We have added fax numbers to many of the listings in the various sections. However, since faxes are more or less considered a priority form of communication, it's advisable in terms of business etiquette not to use a fax to contact a listing until you have established a working relationship with them.

Cover letters/queries/resumes

The cover letter and query letter are slightly different approaches to the same goal—making a photo sale. You, as the photographer, use either of these "vehicles" as a means to convince the photo buyer that your photography will enhance his product or service. Be sure to have the point you wish to make clearly in mind before you begin writing.

A proper cover letter should include an itemization of what photos you are submitting and caption information pertinent to each image. Photo captions should explain who, what, where, why and how. Try to avoid offering "when" information so you don't date your image(s). Also, be sure to make clear what rights you are offering for sale, and where you can be reached during the day if the photo buyer wishes to reach you via phone or mail. Keep your cover letter brief and concise.

If you want to send a query letter, try to limit it to one page. In publishing, the purpose of the query letter is to propose a photo story idea or a photo/text package. Make the story idea sound exciting, yet maintain an overall business tone in the proposal. This is also an excellent time to provide a bit more information about your photographic specialty; such material will establish credibility prior to your requesting an assignment from the photo buyer. In the query letter you can either request the photo buyer's permission to shoot the assignment for his consideration, submit stock photos, or ask to be considered for an upcoming assignment.

Quite a few of the listings in *Photographer's Market* will be looking to buy stock photos for their future use, and will ask that photographers submit a stock photo list. A stock list is simply a summary of all the photos you have available on different subject matter or regions, whether black and white or color, in print or transparency form, and so on. You can either submit a stock list with your query letter to a market or send one when it is specifically recommended in a listing as the main method of contact.

Some photo buyers may ask you to shoot on speculation. Though this implies some interest on their part, if the material isn't used, you aren't compensated for your time and materials. If, however, you are hired on assignment and the material isn't used, you will sometimes be paid a "kill fee." Such a fee generally amounts to one-fourth to one-third of the agreed upon assignment fee. Be sure to negotiate the kill fee prior to taking an assignment.

Resumes also may be sent with your query letter to give the photo buyer more indepth information about your skills and previous experience. The resume should be attractive, and as complete as possible. Be sure to highlight past accomplishments beginning with photo experience (specify whether it's industrial, advertising, editorial, etc.). If you have any staff photo experience, include it, plus any photography-related education (including workshops attended), shows or exhibitions held, or awards and achievements earned in the photographic field. Professional memberships also are good to list.

Recordkeeping

When operating a business it is important to maintain an organized recordkeeping system. Photographers are constantly asked by clients to supply images at a moment's notice. If you plan to stay in business long your system must allow you to easily find and mail photographs without losing track of them. Otherwise, clients will start to find other photographers who can supply images faster.

Filing prints and transparencies

Each photographer must work out his own system of coding and filing images according to what is best for his needs. Talk to different photographers to see what method of photo filing and retrieval works for them. You can also refer to books such as *Sell & Re-Sell Your Photos* and *How to Shoot Stock Photos*, published by Writer's Digest Books, for good information on filing methods.

Transparencies can be coded by a letter that would stand for a general topic, such as "A" for aviation subjects, "B" for medical shots, "C" for children, and so on. Within these areas, simply assign a numerical code to each transparency. Rohn Engh, author of *Sell & Re-Sell Your Photos*, says the key to easy retrieval also lies in setting up a good 3×5 index card system that catalogs cross-over subjects, such as pediatric shots of medical personnel and children interacting. When you receive a photo request, it will be much easier to find the requested photo when you simply have to refer to your catalog system rather than rifle through large numbers of images. For easy storage, invest in some 20-slide capacity 35mm transparency sleeves (or whatever size image sleeve your work requires), then store those in a notebook by subject letter, and within the sleeve itself by image number.

A slight variation of this coding can be used for black-and-white prints. You would still use the letter code "A," for instance, to represent aviation subjects. The next number, however, would denote how many rolls of film have been shot in that subject heading, and the third number would represent which frame on a given roll of film was exposed. Such a coding system would read as A-35-26: "A" for aviation, "35" meaning this was the 35th roll of film shot, and "26" denoting the image to be pulled from the file is on the 26th frame. Black-and-white prints can be stored in a manila folder marked with this coding number, and a photocopy of that picture taken from the contact sheet. This latter step will help to more quickly identify the print in the folder, and if the folder is empty, will let you know at a glance what image to make more copies of. Cross referencing via 3×5 cards is important, too.

If you want to adapt the coding system previously described, you can use a numerical coding system in which "1" stands for negatives, "2" for transparencies, "3" for prints, etc. In this case 2-A-24 would stand for an aviation transparency assigned the number 24 for filing purposes. Don't forget the 3×5 card system here either. Many photographers are finding that use of a computer to store their image codes and captions is very helpful. Software packages which enable you to set coding in a label format have also become available. With these packages, labels can be printed from the computer and in turn, attached to your prints or slides.

If you are interested in going this route you will want to refer to Engh's book, which contains a chapter on use of the computer in a photography business. You will also want to watch photography publications for information about the best computers for photography-related business uses. Also, talk to other photographers about their good—or not-so-good—experiences with different computer models.

Use of a computer can also help you track images submitted to photo buyers for consideration, and record which ones have been purchased and how much was paid for them. The process of tracking photos also can be accomplished manually by maintaining separate 'project' folders that let you review the status of submissions easily. Your payment ledger can be a useful tool here as well. All you need to note is the date photo submissions were sent out, when they were returned, and when payment was made. The photo's code can be entered in the ledger, thereby providing handy information about the status of a specific image.

Once you get a system of photo filing and retrieving adapted to your special needs, the time investment needed to maintain and add to the system can be done easily and with a limited time expenditure.

When perfecting a recordkeeping system it also is vital to have forms similar to the ones beginning on page 16. These samples, reprinted from FORMS, which was produced by the American Society of Media Photographers, are mainly helpful in protecting your images. However, they also provide you with a solid tracking system, so that you know who has your images and when they are going to be returned. To order copies of FORMS write to ASMP, 419 Park Avenue S., New York NY 10016. Phone: (212)889-9144. Price: $19.95 plus $2 shipping and handling. New York state residents must pay sales tax.

Financial records

You won't know whether your business is making a profit unless you keep accurate financial records that allow you to determine profits and losses quickly. Browse around office supply stores to determine the type of ledger you feel can suit your business needs. Ideally, a ledger should include spaces for information such as job number, date of assignment, client name, expenses incurred, sales taxes and payments due. For tax purposes, be sure to retain all business receipts, invoices and cancelled checks to support ledger entries. For convenience, file these records in an envelope by month—it will be less time consuming when filling out income-tax forms each year. Using computer software which performs electronic spreadsheet functions is also a good way to organize your accounting records. If you set up basic ledgers on computer, then you can input sales, expenses and tax information daily, weekly or monthly, as needed.

Another business necessity you will want to look into is designing and printing business forms. These forms are useful when selling stock photography as well as when shooting on assignment. For assignment work such forms should

TERMS & CONDITIONS

1. "Photograph(s)" means all photographic material furnished by Photographer hereunder, whether transparencies, negatives, prints or otherwise.

2. Except as otherwise specifically provided herein, all photographs and rights therein, including copyright, remain the sole and exclusive property of Photographer. Any additional uses require the prior written agreement of Photographer on terms to be negotiated. Unless otherwise provided herein, any grant of rights is limited to one (1) year from the date hereof for the territory of the United States.

3. Client assumes insurer's liability (a) to indemnify Photographer for loss, damage, or misuse of any photograph(s), and (b) to return all photographs prepaid and fully insured, safe and undamaged, by bonded messenger, air freight, or registered mail, within thirty (30) days after the first use thereof as provided herein, but in all events (whether published or unpublished) within _____ after the date hereof. Client assumes full liability for its principals, employees, agents, affiliates, successors and assigns (including without limitation messengers and freelance researchers) for any loss, damage, or misuse of the photographs. Client will supply Photographer with two free copies of each use of the photographs.

4. Reimbursement by Client for loss or damage of each original transparency shall be in the amount of One Thousand Five Hundred Dollars ($1,500), or such other amount set forth next to said item on the front hereof. Reimbursement by Client for loss or damage of each other item shall be in the amount set forth next to said item on the front hereof. Photographer and Client agree that said amount represents the fair and reasonable value of each item, and that Photographer would not sell all rights to such item for less than said amount.

5. Photographer's copyright notice "©[YEAR OF FIRST PUBLICATION] [PHOTOGRAPHER'S NAME]" must accompany each use as an adjacent credit line. Invoice amount will be tripled if said credit is not provided.

6. Client will not make or permit any alterations, additions, or subtractions in respect of the photographs, including without limitation any digitalization or synthesization of the photographs, alone or with any other material, by use of computer or other electronic means or any other method or means now or hereafter known.

7. Client will indemnify and defend Photographer against all claims, liability, damages, costs, and expenses, including reasonable legal fees and expenses, arising out of any use of any photographs for which no release was furnished by Photographer, or any photographs which are altered by Client. Unless so furnished, no release exists. Photographer's liability for all claims shall not exceed in any event the total amount paid under this invoice.

8. Client assumes full risk of loss or damage to materials furnished by client hereunder and warrants that said materials are adequately insured against such loss or damage. Client shall indemnify Photographer against all claims, liability, damages and expenses incurred by Photographer in connection with any third party claim arising out of use of said material hereunder.

9. All expense estimates are subject to normal trade variance of 10%.

10. Time is of the essence for receipt of payment and return of photographs. No rights are granted until timely payment is made.

11. Client may not assign or transfer this agreement or any rights granted hereunder. This agreement binds and inures to the benefit of Photographer, Client, Client's principals, employees, agents and affiliates, and their respective heirs, legal representatives, successors and assigns. Client and its principals, employees, agents and affiliates are jointly and severally liable for the performance of all payments and other obligations hereunder. No amendment or waiver of any terms is binding unless set forth in writing and signed by the parties. However, the invoice may reflect, and Client is bound by, oral authorizations for fees or expenses which could not be confirmed in writing because of immediate proximity of shooting. This agreement incorporates by reference Article 2 of the Uniform Commercial Code, and the Copyright Act of 1976, as amended.

12. Except as provided in (13) below any dispute regarding this agreement shall be arbitrated in [PHOTOGRAPHER'S CITY AND STATE] under rules of the American Arbitration Association and the laws of [STATE OF ARBITRATION]. Judgment on the arbitration award may be entered in any court having jurisdiction. Any dispute involving $ _____ [LIMIT OF LOCAL SMALL CLAIMS COURT] or less may be submitted without arbitration to any court having jurisdiction thereof. Client shall pay all arbitration and court costs, reasonable legal fees, and expenses, and legal interest on any award or judgment in favor of Photographer.

13. Client hereby expressly consents to the jurisdiction of the Federal courts with respect to claims by Photographer under the Copyright Act of 1976, as amended.

14. In the event a shoot extends beyond eight (8) consecutive hours, Photographer may charge for such excess time of assistants and freelance staff at the rate of one-and-one-half their hourly rates.

15. Reshoots: Clients will be charged 100% fee and expenses for any reshoot required by Client. For any reshoot required because of an act of God or the fault of a third party, Photographer will charge no additional fee and Client will pay all expenses. If Photographer charges for special contingency insurance and is paid in full for the shoot, Client will not be charged for any expenses covered by insurance. A list of exclusions from such insurance will be provided on request.

16. Cancellations and postponements: Client is responsible for payment of all expenses incurred up to the time of cancellation, plus 50% of Photographer's fee. If notice of cancellation is given less than two (2) business days before the shoot date, Client will be charged 100% fee. Weather postponements: Unless otherwise agreed, Client will be charged 100% fee if postponement is due to weather conditions on location and 50% fee if postponement occurs before departure to location.

EDITORIAL ASSIGNMENT INVOICE

TO:

INVOICE #:
INVOICE DATE:
JOB #:
EDITOR:
STORY SLUG:

SS/FED. ID#:

DESCRIPTION/RIGHTS GRANTED/PERIOD OF USE

FEES

Photography Fees @ $ per day   _____
Prep Days @ $ per day   _____
Travel/Weather Days @ $ per day   _____
Usage Fees and Space Rates   _____

$ _____

EXPENSES

Assistants and Crew   _____
Film and Polaroids   _____
Photo Lab   _____
Locations   _____
Telephone   _____
Rentals and Props   _____
Shipping and Messengers   _____
Transportation   _____
Meals and Lodging   _____
Miscellaneous   _____

$ _____

Subtotal   _____
Sales Tax   _____
Less Advance   _____
Total Amount Due $_____

Time is of the essence for payment which is due upon receipt. Granting of right of usage is contingent upon full payment and is subject to the terms and conditions on the reverse side. Balance is subject to monthly rebilling charges applied thereafter. Adjustment of amount, or terms, must be requested within 14 days of invoice date. All expenses are subject to normal trade variance of 10% from estimated amounts.

EDITORIAL ASSIGNMENT ESTIMATE/CONFIRMATION

TO:

DATE:
JOB #:
EDITOR:
STORY SLUG:

SS/FED. ID#:

ASSIGNMENT DESCRIPTION/RIGHTS GRANTED/PERIOD OF USE

FEES

Photography Fees @ $ per day   _____
Prep Days @ $ per day   _____
Travel/Weather Days @ $ per day   _____
Usage Fees and Space Rates   _____
                                        $ _____

EXPENSES

Assistants and Crew   _____
Film and Polaroids   _____
Photo Lab   _____
Locations   _____
Telephone   _____
Rentals and Props   _____
Shipping and Messengers   _____
Transportation   _____
Meals and Lodging   _____
Miscellaneous   _____
                                        $ _____

Subtotal   _____
Sales Tax   _____
Total Estimated Fees and Expenses   _____
Cash Deposit Required Prior to Start of Assignment $ _____

ACKNOWLEDGED AND ACCEPTED   DATE
_____
PLEASE SIGN AND RETURN ONE COPY

Usage is limited to that specified above and is subject to all terms and conditions on the reverse side. Unless otherwise agreed to in writing, the Photographer retains ownership of all photographs resulting from this assignment. Additional usage requires negotiation of additional fees. Time in excess of a normal working day will be pro-rated and billed on an hourly basis as overtime. Payment of invoices regarding this assignment will be due upon receipt.

include columns for estimating services, assignment confirmation, and delivery of photos and invoicing. Photographers selling from stock will be concerned with delivery of photos and invoicing. When sending photos out in the marketplace be sure to itemize what images are being sent so the photo buyer and you will have a record. Business forms can be reproduced quickly and inexpensively at most quick-print services.

Also, either by purchasing or having access to a desktop publishing system and laser printer, you can design and produce forms specifically for your needs. With this kind of system, you can produce master forms to be duplicated or print them out for each client or sale. Not only does use of a business form help you keep track of your work, it presents a more professional appearance to the photo buyer who will perceive you as being organized and dependable.

Depending upon the size of your business and your sales volume, you may find professional assistance indispensable when it comes to accounting and preparing taxes. Many photographers do their own bookkeeping in the beginning and delegate these tasks as they become more successful and involved in other aspects of their business. However, some photographers will—right from the beginning—at least have their records reviewed periodically by experts to ensure their accuracy. Whenever possible, try to find someone who works primarily with creative people or similar small business operators. Such specialists are often more familiar with the needs and problems of business people such as photographers, as well as any laws governing them.

Such review—whether done by you or by an expert—is important, too, for the overall financial health of your business. Looking closely at your costs and cash flow helps you to identify both profitable and unprofitable areas of your business. In particular, a good rule of thumb is that earnings should be in the range of 25 to 40 percent of your billings. If not, then it would be helpful to go back and study your records to see where you may need to cut costs or raise prices.

For any specific questions about starting up or maintaining your business, contact the following: American Society of Media Photographers (ASMP), 419 Park Ave. S., New York NY 10016, (212)889-9144; Service Corps of Retired Executives Association (SCORE) at Suite 5900, 409 Third St. SW, Washington DC 20024-3212, (202)205-6762. SCORE is a 12,000-member group of business men and women who provide free management assistance to those requiring expert advice.

Model/property releases

Photographers should be attuned to the need for obtaining model and property releases. Such a release gives the photographer the right to use, sell and publish the photo in editorial or advertising matter without fear of de-

---

ADULT RELEASE

In consideration of my engagement as a model, and for other good and valuable consideration herein acknowledged as received, I hereby grant to _____ ("Photographer"), his/her heirs, legal representatives and assigns, those for whom Photographer is acting, and those acting with his/her authority and permission, the irrevocable and unrestricted right and permission to copyright, in his/her own name or otherwise, and use, re-use, publish, and re-publish photographic portraits or pictures of me or in which I may be included, in whole or in part, or composite or distorted in character or form, without restriction as to changes or alterations, in conjunction with my own or a fictitious name, or reproductions thereof in color or otherwise, made through any medium at his/her studios or elsewhere, and in any and all media now or hereafter known for illustration, promotion, art, editorial, advertising, trade, or any other purpose whatsoever. I also consent to the use of any printed matter in conjunction therewith.

I hereby waive any right that I may have to inspect or approve the finished product or products and the advertising copy or other matter that may be used in connection therewith or the use to which it may be applied.

I hereby release, discharge and agree to save harmless Photographer, his/her heirs, legal representatives and assigns, and all persons acting under his/her permission or authority or those for whom he/she is acting from any liability by virtue of any blurring, distortion, alteration, optical illusion, or use in composite form, whether intentional or otherwise, that may occur or be produced in the taking of said picture or in any subsequent processing thereof, as well as any publication thereof, including without limitation any claims for libel or invasion of privacy.

I hereby warrant that I am of full age and have the right to contract in my own name. I have read the above authorization, release, and agreement, prior to its execution, and I am fully familiar with the contents thereof. This release shall be binding upon me and my heirs, legal representatives, and assigns.

DATE	NAME

WITNESS	ADDRESS

Reprinted from FORMS with permission of the American Society of Media Photographers, Inc. (ASMP).

mands for additional financial compensation or legal reprisals. In this age of stock photo sales, it is unknown whether the photo buyer will use the image for editorial or advertising use. It is wise to have model releases on file; their existence may gain you additional sales from buyers who prefer the work they use to be model-released. The images can't ever be used in such a way as to embarrass or insult the subject, however.

Usually photo rights purchased for editorial use (i.e., public education purposes) are free from the need for a model release. Such markets include newspapers, textbooks, filmstrips, encyclopedias or magazines. An exception to this, however, is when the photo is used for a cover illustration. Photos used for advertising purposes always need model releases. If photographing children, remember that the guardian also must sign before the release is legally binding. Also, be aware that laws governing the use of releases vary from state to state.

Lawyers also are advising photographers to obtain property releases, especially if recognizable property—including pets—will be used for advertising purposes. Government property, facilities, park lands and so on also fall under this requirement. Since it is unclear exactly when property releases are needed in every case, it would be wise for your own protection to obtain one every time you shoot.

Agents and reps

Another avenue that some photographers take in promoting themselves as they become more established is to work through an agent or photographer's representative, or "rep." This can be especially valuable for photographers who are involved in highly competitive markets such as advertising and art/ design studios or who want to branch out on a regional or national basis. The primary value of having a rep is that it frees the photographer to spend as much of his time as possible shooting or planning for work.

Since some photographers are less comfortable with the marketing and negotiating aspects of their business, using a rep can be very attractive. However, many photographers either like to rep themselves, or split the repping duties with another person. It's quite common with husband and wife photography teams that either or both of them will handle repping for their business. Of course, one big plus to keeping it "in the family" is that you don't have to pay out the rep's commission every time you make a sale.

Photographer/rep relationships are of a limited nature and end for various reasons. So it's important when planning to work with a rep to consider also how you will handle the eventual termination. Such relationships are usually governed by a contract, which should include not only compensation for sales but also terms for severance. Also, the procedure for letting go of the rep— even if it's basically "at will"—needs to be spelled out. If you are not willing or able to offer a severance package, or you wish to reserve the right of termination on your terms, then having the agreement in writing will help to limit your liability when a rep presses the issue legally. For additional information— as well as names and addresses—on photo reps, see Writer's Digest Books' newest market book title, _A Guide to Literary Agents and Art/Photo Reps_.

Taxes

Whether you're a freelance photographer or a fulltime studio owner, taxes are an inevitable part of the territory for you as an operator of a small business.

The various types of taxes—income, payroll, social security and sales tax—all have a great deal of impact on your costs of doing business, and so must be considered as you are developing your pricing formulas. Accordingly, to keep your business profitable in both the short and the long term, it's best to learn what taxes are in effect in the area where you market your work and how to keep track of all tax-related information. It's also your responsibility.

Changes in the law

Once again, we want to remind you of one such change in federal tax law which is favorable to photographers and other creative people. This is the revision of the 1986 tax reform bill, the Technical Corrections Act. Under this revision, which just became effective on 1988 returns, photographers can now deduct any expenses accumulated in the production of images, within the same calendar year as they were produced. Previously, these expenses had to be spread out over a number of years until the image logged a profit. Without this revision, bookkeeping would have become unmanageable beyond a point for most photographers. The revision also relieved stock photographers, in particular, of the burden of projecting what the sales for certain images would be in the current year.

Another important related change under the 1986 Act has been a confusing new classification for individuals who incorporate as businesses. This is the Personal Service Corporation, or PSC classification. In most cases, individuals who incorporate their businesses in a number of professional areas automatically become classified as PSCs, and they are taxed at a very high rate of 34 percent. Though photography is not one of the professions that come under this category and is exempt from this tax rate, many individual photographers who incorporate have still been led to think that they must file as PSCs. As a result, the IRS has had to review claims by photographers and set some clearer guidelines.

Even though incorporated photographers were considered exempt from the PSC rate, they apparently qualified for another high tax rate. The catch was that according to UNICAP rules—the guidelines established under the original 1986 Act—incorporated photographers had been classified as manufacturers, and as such, were required to assign higher value to their inventories. Of course, this would often result in these photographers having to pay higher taxes. Lobbying efforts which led to the 1988 repeal of the UNICAP rules as they apply to photographers also made photographers effectively exempt from taxes on verifiable creative expenses. In other words, incorporated photographers are free of the obligation to both taxes. Nonetheless, all photographers are still subject to a number of taxes of which they must have a clear understanding and plan for accordingly.

Self-employment tax

If you are a freelancer—whether you have a primary source of income and photography serves as a sideline or photography is your fulltime pursuit—it's important to be aware of higher tax rates on self-employment income. All income you receive without taxes being taken out by an employer qualifies as self-employment income. Normally, when you are employed by someone else, your income is taxed at a lower rate and the employer shares responsibility for the taxes due. However, when you are self-employed, even if only part-time, you are taxed at a higher rate on that income, and you must pay the entire amount yourself. This also applies to social security tax.

Freelancers frequently overlook self-employment and social security taxes and fail to set aside a sufficient amount of money. They also tend to forget state and local taxes are payable. If the volume of your photo sales reaches a point where it becomes a substantial percentage of your income, then you are required to pay estimated tax on a quarterly basis. This requires you to project what amount sales you expect to generate in a three-month period. However burdensome this may be in the short run, it works to your advantage in that you plan for and stay current with the various taxes you are expected to pay.

Many other deductions can be claimed by self-employed photographers. It's in your best interest to be aware of them. Examples of 100 percent deductible claims include production costs of resumes, business cards and brochures; photographer's rep commissions; membership dues; costs of purchasing portfolios and educational/business-related magazines and books; insurance, legal and professional services; and office expenses. Be aware that if you take a client out to dinner or treat him to some form of entertainment as a business investment, you may only deduct 80 percent of the costs. Making the photographer pay more out-of-pocket for meals and entertainment is the IRS' way of reducing abuses which have occurred.

Other deductions

Additional deductions may be taken if your office or studio is home-based. The catch here is that your work area can be used only on a professional basis; your office can't double as a family room after hours. The IRS also wants to see evidence that you use the work space on a regular basis via established business hours and proof of actively marketing your work. If you can satisfy these criteria then a percentage of mortgage interests, real estate taxes, rent, maintenance costs, utilities, and homeowner's insurance, plus office furniture and equipment, can be claimed on your tax form at year's end. (Furniture and equipment can be depreciated over a seven-year period.) To figure the percentage of your home or apartment that is used for business, divide the total floor space of your home or apartment (e.g., 4,000 sq. ft.) by the percentage used for business (e.g., 400) to get your answer (10 percent). Next, divide your total home expenses (e.g., $1,000) by 10 percent, and you've got your deductible total of $100.

Be aware that the above-mentioned deductions are only available to "professional" photographers, not hobbyists. According to hearsay, anyone who deducts for use of home facilities and equipment automatically runs a higher risk of being audited, especially if the individual is late in filing. The burden of proof will be on you if the IRS questions any deductions claimed. To maintain professional status in the eyes of the IRS you will need to show a profit for three years out of a five-year period. If you are working out of your home, be sure to keep separate records and bank accounts for personal and business finances, as well as a separate business phone. Since the IRS can audit tax records as far back as seven years, it's vital to keep all paperwork related to your business. This includes invoices, vouchers, expenditures and sales receipts, canceled checks, deposit slips, register tapes and business ledger entries for this period.

Tax deferments

Fulltime photographers—especially those who have a high sales volume—may be interested in investments as a tax shelter for their income. However, as experts in the industry have noted, you should avoid deferring income in this way for the foreseeable future since tax rates are quite likely to rise. In the long run, such tax deferments would result in higher business taxes. So, it's advisable that if you are already doing this, or have considered it, you should consult with a tax advisor or investment counselor to get complete, accurate information about such shelters.

Sales tax

Sales taxes are deceptively complicated and need special consideration. For instance, if you are working in more than one state, use models or work with reps in one or more states, or work in one state and store equipment in another, you may be required to pay sales tax in each of the states that apply. In particular, if you are working with an out-of-state stock photo agency which has clients over a wide geographic area you will need to explore your tax liability with a tax professional.

As with all taxes, sales taxes must be reported and paid on a timely basis to avoid audits and/or penalties. In regard to sales tax, you should:

1) Always register your business at the tax offices with jurisdiction in your city and state.

2) Always charge and collect sales tax on the full amount of the invoice, unless an exemption applies.

3) If an exemption applies because of resale, you must provide a copy of the customer's resale certificate.

4) If an exemption applies because of other conditions, i.e., selling one-time reproduction rights or working for a tax-exempt, nonprofit organization, you must also provide documentation.

Background information and assistance

In general, to plan properly for your taxes—especially when the size of your business and volume of sales increase—you should seek out the advice of an accountant or a tax expert. As suggested before, it's best to work with someone familiar with the needs and concerns of small business people, particularly photographers. You can also obtain more background information about federal taxes and any recent changes in tax law for small business operators by contacting a local branch of the IRS. You can request a number of booklets which provide specific information on allowable deductions and rate structures. These include: 334—Tax Guide for Small Business; 463—Travel, Entertainment and Gift Expense; 505—Tax Withholding and Estimated Tax; 525—Taxable and Nontaxable Income; 533—Self-Employment Tax; 535—Business Expenses; 538—Accounting Periods and Methods; 587—Business Use of Your Home; 910—Guide to Free Tax Services; 917—Business Use of Car. Order by phone at (800)829-3676.

Insurance

Taxes are not the only responsibility that self-employed photographers must take for themselves. Setting up proper, comprehensive insurance coverage on their business and themselves is also an important task. When deciding on the types of insurance—liability, property, health, disability and life—and the amounts of coverage, it's best to look carefully at your needs and at which companies can provide you with the best policies.

Policies are not all the same and it's important to make sure every aspect of your business is covered. After examining his policy, a photographer who works out of his home may be surprised to find out that his home owner insurance does not cover his equipment. Separate coverage for a business owner is needed to guarantee that all phases of operation are covered.

Generally it's a good strategy to set up your business coverage with two main areas in mind—liability and property protection. Liability coverage aides you in the event a client or other individual is injured or suffers property damage as a result of using your products or services. Insurance for your equipment will cover you in the case of loss from fire, water damage, theft, vandalism, or for other stipulated reasons. It's important to read your policy closely and know what is covered. Some photographers find out too late that their property is covered only in the office, not out in the field. There also is the possibility that certain pieces of equipment, such as cameras, are covered in the case of theft, but a computer may not be included in the policy.

In order to safeguard against property loss many photographers find it helpful to keep some equipment in a different location. Duplicate transparencies of top images can be made and kept in a safety deposit box. The same storage procedure can be used for backup computer files or b&w and color print negatives. Other storage spaces can be used for larger pieces of equipment. Taking such precautions can insure that, if a disaster strikes at the office, all is not lost. Fireproof safes can protect equipment from fire damage, but film may melt inside during a sweltering blaze.

Worker's compensation, which applies to anyone you hire, is another form of insurance that is indispensable if you grow beyond being your only employee. This is available through most state governments or private insurance companies. In general, liability insurance covers members of the general public; worker's compensation insures employees. "Grey" areas come into the picture in many states because it's sometimes hard to determine according to labor and tax laws whether models, set builders or any other subcontractors are "employees." Therefore, a blend of liability coverage and worker's compensation should protect you in most cases.

Health and disability insurance are important to freelance photographers as well. With the high cost of hospitalization, health coverage is vital. You can't afford to live without it. Many professional or trade organizations such as the American Society of Media Photographers (ASMP) or Advertising Photographers of America (APA) offer health/disability packages to members. In some cases, a policy is even included as a membership benefit. But, in order to qualify for disability coverage, you will need to accumulate a track record of sales so the insurance agent can calculate an income-average measure to determine the appropriate amount of coverage for you.

When you select a disability plan, first consider how long you could survive on your income — should a long-term injury occur — before you would need to rely on disability payments. Self-employed photographers will ideally want to have three to four months worth of "liquid" income accrued, such as cash-value life insurance, money-market accounts or savings accounts that can be dipped into in an emergency.

Since you don't want to go bankrupt paying insurance premiums for every potential disaster, you will want to first determine what misfortunes you can afford to pay out-of-pocket. In other words, protect yourself from losses that would be "catastrophic" to you.

It's important to "shop around" until you find an agent with whom you're comfortable, and one who is well versed in the professional needs of photographers. Check with other photographers, or call some photography trade groups for recommendations of agents in your area. These groups will also be able to assist you in determining your insurance needs and recommend companies which offer specialized coverage to photographers. Also, take the time to carefully read all policy clauses to be certain you get the insurance coverage you need. Finally, when you're researching companies to do business with, select those licensed to do business in your state.

Exploring Your Stock Options

by Michael Willins

At times, photography seems like a desert—barren except for occasional mirages which show you glimpses of potential clients just before they vanish. But unlike a mirage in a desert, the clients have not disappeared. They have just been scooped up in a photo industry that is packed with professionals. However, despite the competition, there are ways to cultivate new clients. One method, in particular, is stock photography.

For some of you, stock has become an oasis, a place where you can survive the tough marketplace while building a list of impressive credits. Whatever your reasons for producing stock, you should consider the possibility of contracting with a stock agency. Stock can provide additional income when assignment work is thin, and it might serve as a stable investment when you begin to consider retirement. The difficulty lies in weeding out the good agencies from the bad and not getting roped into a contract with an agency that is disreputable.

How to proceed

Before you approach an agency, make sure you have a large body of work from which to choose. Initial submissions can range from 200-400 images and these should only be outstanding photos. Edit your material carefully *before* you submit it to an agency for review. Agency staff members are not interested in sifting through sloppy submissions to find a few worthwhile slides.

Remember, once you sign with an agency you must provide a large quantity of stunning, new images on a regular basis. Don't rely on your initial submission to make all your money. Shooting often and supplying a lot of images is one key to successful stock photography.

When mailing a submission, make sure it contains a self-addressed, stamped envelope (SASE) so that the material can be easily returned. If the agency is not within your own country, send a self-addressed envelope (SAE) with International Reply Coupons (IRC). It also is wise to protect your submission by sending it via certified mail. Agency employees must sign for certified packages and this way you will know if a submission gets lost in the mail.

Although stock agencies are reviewing your talent, remember that you are not the only one under the microscope. Set certain criteria for the type of agency *you* want to work with and make sure you can trust the agencies to which you submit material. This will require plenty of research, but the end result will be worth it. You do not want to sign a contract with a questionable agency and later discover you made a mistake.

One way to protect yourself is to ask for a list of photographers who work with the agency you are researching. The agency can, and should, provide such a list, although some agencies like to provide only a few names of their top money earners. Certainly those photographers will give you a glowing report of an agency, but their opinions may not always be accurate. Therefore, you should demand nothing less than a complete list.

Once you have the list in hand, search for photographers you know and trust, then contact those people to get an understanding of the agency. If the names are unfamiliar, contact numerous people listed; explain your situation and ask if they are satisfied with the agency. Find out if they are paid promptly and often. Ask if they are given complete information on statements, and the frequency of statements. A few probing questions such as these will help you determine if the agency is reputable.

It also is helpful to review agency catalogs so that you can see what images and categories are already offered. Then concentrate on subjects that are new and fill a void in the stock files. This will improve your chances of contracting with a stock house that needs your images.

Examining contracts

Once an agency shows an interest in your work, contract negotiations are soon to follow. Stock photographer Ann Purcell of Alexandria, Virginia, says it is imperative for photographers to review contracts before signing. "Most contracts are written by the lawyers and agencies to be good for the agencies. You have to go over those contracts extremely carefully," says Purcell, who, along with her husband, Carl, co-authored the book *Stock Photography: The Complete Guide* (Writer's Digest Books). If you are new to the process it is often wise to hire an attorney who can review contracts and give you sound advice.

One major point to consider is whether the contract requires exclusivity. Agencies want to have sole possession of certain images and, therefore, they prefer to sign photographers to exclusive contracts. As a photographer, however, you should never enter into such an agreement. After all, you certainly want to have the right to market your own images.

The Purcells, who work with 10 agencies worldwide, always demand non-exclusive contracts and find that most agencies are willing to negotiate this issue. As a way of pleasing both sides, the Purcells often guarantee exclusivity within a specific region surrounding the agency, says Ann. It is important, however, to make sure the "region" is spelled out in the contract.

She adds that many agencies typically include an automatic rollover clause in contracts. Such clauses state that when the original contract ends it will automatically renew for the same length of time unless the photographer cancels the agreement. Contracts often last three to five years, so it is best not to let the agreement rollover unless you are satisfied with the relationship. The Purcells normally change automatic rollover clauses to state that contracts will renew only after the couple has been contacted and approved the terms.

As more agencies adopt CD-ROM technology and digital manipulation becomes more commonplace, photographers also must include contract language that protects their image rights, says Ann. If an agency fails to include information in the contract prohibiting the use of images on clip art disks, the Purcells write it in. "Make sure the agency does not have all rights to your pictures and can't sell electronic rights to your work," she says.

Payment and fees

As mentioned before, you must find out the frequency of payment. Will you receive a check when usage rights are sold or will payment come on a monthly, quarterly, or worse, annual basis? Always be on the lookout for agencies with infrequent pay periods. If other photographers complain that they do not receive prompt payment from an agency, be suspicious. This may mean that an agency is lackadaisical in its treatment of photographers, or possibly it is having financial difficulties.

Besides frequency of payment, there are a variety of financial points to consider when examining an agency's business practices:
- Avoid agencies that sell usage rights at substantial discounts. This sometimes develops when photographers accept small commissions from sales. A typical commission is around 50 percent. If an agency receives a larger percentage it can succeed, even though it sells usage rights at a lower rate. While the agency prospers from such sales, the photographer suffers.
- Watch out for agencies that charge unreasonable fees. It is not uncommon for agencies to split promotional or duping fees with photographers, however some agencies take advantage of such agreements. For example, the Purcells were shocked to find out that one of the photo industry's leading agencies was charging photographers 30 cents per transparency dupe when it only cost the agency 15 cents to have a duplicate made. "In a year they were probably making close to a million dollars off their photographers who were paying for their own dupes. It's something you have to keep an eye on," says Ann Purcell.
- Steer clear of agencies that play favorites. In order to get top-notch photographers to sign contracts, some stock companies offer financial guarantees. However, in order to meet these guarantees agencies will promote the work of these top photographers, while providing limited marketing for others. This

reduces income for photographers not seen as agency stars.

• Some smaller agencies are run by photographers who are interested in promoting their own work. Be careful when dealing with such agencies because you do not want to have an owner marketing his own work and ignoring yours.

• Be cautious when dealing with agencies that have trouble handling large numbers of photographers. This can affect your income if an agency has too many photographers to promote. Larger agencies are fine if everyone is treated fairly.

• Look for agencies that permit you to audit account records to verify sales of your images. This is important if you ever feel an agency is being dishonest. For example, some agencies borrow money that is supposed to go to photographers and use those funds for operational expenses. The Picture Agency Council of America (PACA) and the American Society of Media Photographers (ASMP) issued a joint statement discouraging such practices. Before auditing, however, you should agree to give the agency proper notice.

Agency advantages

At this point you are probably wondering if contracting with an agency is more trouble than it's worth. However, there are more honest agencies than dishonest ones, so don't be discouraged. It just takes time to research stock houses and find those with which you are comfortable.

Although you may market your own work, and feel pretty confident as a business person, there are numerous advantages to having a stock agency promote your material. The most obvious bonus is that you can concentrate more on your photography and less on everyday business procedures. After all, isn't the creative work more fun and what you really want to do? It also allows you more time to seek out additional assignment work.

Next, stock agencies can provide expertise in negotiating. Often a photographer will not recognize the true value of an image and, as a result, negotiates fees well below a fair price. Good agencies, however, make a living negotiating and they know what clients should pay for specific usages. Overall, this will result in higher fees for images. Although you only receive a percentage of the income, your amount can equal the price which you would have negotiated. Therefore, you will receive approximately the same amount of money without having to handle any business tasks.

Another advantage lies in the marketing abilities of an agency. As an individual photographer with limited financial resources you probably cannot promote your work to many different places. An agency with a solid marketing scheme is invaluable. Stock houses also can reach clients that you otherwise might not reach. While you may concentrate on editorial sales to the magazine industry, you might want to contract with an agency that specializes in sales to paper product companies, advertising agencies and book publishers.

If you want to find out more about choosing a stock agency there are several places to look. As mentioned before, PACA and ASMP issued a joint statement on agency practices that they feel can improve the relationship between stock houses and photographers. Both of these organizations are interested in improving the photo industry and can guide you along the way. For information, write to PACA President Paul Henning, % Third Coast Stock Source Inc., PO Box 92397, Milwaukee WI 53202, or ASMP, 419 Park Avenue South, New York NY 10016.

66 Make sure the agency does not have all rights to your pictures and can't sell electronic rights to your work, **99**

—Ann Purcell

Riding the Wave of the Future
by Michael Willins

For many of you, words like pixels, gigabytes and bitmaps are as foreign as nuclear physics. They are words that exemplify a changing photo industry and, for that reason, should be despised. After all, how many photographers want to forfeit creative time behind the camera for time in front of a glowing computer screen? Certainly the idea of scanning three or four images into a Macintosh and combining them into one can make you nervous. Now anyone with the proper equipment, regardless of their artistic skills, can easily twist, rotate and flip images until they are unrecognizable.

However, photographers peering into the future of their profession can no longer loathe or ignore the technological advances that are taking place. The profession is in the midst of an exciting revolution.

"We're in a transitional period," says Paul Henning, president of the Picture Agency Council of America (PACA). "A lot of people in the stock industry are casting about trying to figure out what is the right direction to go in. What kinds of technologies should they invest in? Should they invest at all? Should they wait six months or twelve months until there is a clearer direction of what the standards are going to be?"

The land of CD-ROM

Technological advances are beginning to change the way stock agencies archive, select and distribute pictures. A handful of agencies have begun to market catalogs on CD-ROM, allowing clients to peruse disks to find images they want to use. In May 1993, for example, FPG International launched its first digital photo collection. The agency, which hopes to find users among art directors, graphic designers, art buyers and picture editors, included 5,700 images on CD-ROM. Once clients select images from the disk, they must contact FPG to acquire usage rights, negotiate licenses and obtain transparencies.

The CD-ROM technology allows a photographer's images to be digitized and then encoded onto compact disks. Thousands of images can be stored on a single disk and then viewed on TV with a special CD-ROM player, or on computers equipped with CD-ROM drives. The players sell for around $350 to $650 and it costs less than $3 per image to have them placed on disk.

"People don't seem to be talking too much about pictures anymore," says Henning, who serves as director for Third Coast Stock Source in Milwaukee, Wisconsin. "They are so caught up in this electronic imaging area. It's kind of sad in a way in that it's taking a lot of the emphasis away from the creation of images. They're simply looking at hardware. And that's becoming a crucial part of our business."

One concern regarding CD-ROM is the fact that some users may purchase disks, find images they need and use those photos without negotiating payment with copyright owners. However, some safeguards against such infringements have been taken.

Kodak's Pro Photo CD Master disk, for example, has several functions designed to guard against infringement. Photographers can protect images by including copyright information, placing a faint mark (such as a copyright symbol) over the photo or encoding work so that buyers must purchase special access codes to use images for desktop publishing applications.

While CD-ROM is a system on the rise, its success in the photo industry will depend on client usage. Currently, a large number of Kodak Photo CD buyers are advertising firms, universities, museums and various businesses who use CD-ROM for presentations and ads.

The entire photo industry, however, is banking on the number of CD-ROM users to increase. Not only are stock agencies producing their own disks, but photographers are taking advantage of the technology. One freelancer, Lee Foster of Berkeley, California, has a disk of travel images and articles and plans to produce three more. Foster discusses his move into CD-ROM as our Insider Report subject on page 280.

Jim Pickerell of Rockville, Maryland, who is considered an authority on stock photography, created the Digital Stock Connection (DSC) in 1993 to assist photographers in producing and distributing catalogs on CD-ROM. In his May 1993 newsletter, *TakingStock*, Pickerell says the DSC pools images from photographers, produces disks and then markets them to potential users. Each disk costs around $10. Photographers negotiate their own image sales, handle the delivery of film to clients and retain 100 percent of any negotiated fees, states Pickerell.

Despite low CD-ROM sales Pickerell believes there is a bright future for this technology. For that reason, he decided to start the DSC. "Those who wait for clear evidence that clients are heavily using CD-ROM disks could find that it costs them more to catch up and get up to speed than if they had begun to slowly educate and position themselves earlier," he says.

Creating your system

While CD-ROM is worth considering, there are other innovations photographers can explore. If you own a computer, or plan to get one, there are all kinds of image manipulation software packages from which to choose. Of course you will need the hardware to go along with the programs, but piecing together a system based on your knowledge and needs is a good way to get started.

Photographer Bob Hahn, owner of Digital Graphics Inc., in Bethlehem, Pennsylvania, says about five years ago he was using a computer for basic bookkeeping. As technology and his understanding of computers improved he realized that the system could help him with his corporate assignments. "It was a natural to use the computer to do computer graphics for slides shows, titling slides, things like that," says Hahn. He is often hired to produce slide shows for sales meetings, new product releases and training programs.

Operating on an IBM-compatible system that he constructed, Hahn uses various software for retouching, graphics, illustration and layout. Over the past four years he has invested around $50,000 in equipment, but he believes the money was well spent. "My actual time behind the camera has decreased, but I've greatly increased my time on the computer and, therefore, increased my income," he says.

Hahn and Alan Brown of Photonics Graphics Inc., in Cincinnati, Ohio, agree that photographers can no longer ignore the evolution that is taking place. Brown says design firms and advertising agencies are buying Macintosh computers and image manipulation programs so that they can do photo work in-house.

"There isn't a day that goes by that I don't hear a client saying, 'Gosh, you know, I can't wait to get (Adobe) Photoshop, because if I had Photoshop I could do all sorts of neat things with the stuff I do.' Those are clients saying that and I find that troubling and scary," says Brown. "As photographers, if we want to maintain any form of control over our images we're going to have to deal with that and gain that control back. But that means there's a whole bunch of new stuff out there that we're going to have to learn. I've learned more about separations, typesetting and production aspects than I ever thought I wanted to know. But I've had to do it."

Brown, who uses Photoshop and a variety of 3-D modeling programs, says the bulk of his work revolves around cover designs for brochures, annual reports and books. The design and production tasks he performs are completely different from his work five years ago when he would merely create images and drop them off to the client. "Life has become much more complex," he says. "Assignments are far more interesting and challenging than they were in the past. I find that I'm continually challenged and excited by what I do. That all makes it very worthwhile to me."

On-line networks

The complexity of the industry doesn't just stop with new software and different ways to store images. Two on-line computer networks, the Kodak

Picture Exchange (KPX) and Picture Network International (PNI), have been developed to showcase images to clients. Subscribers to each network can access image files, figure out which ones they want to use and then negotiate payment. The networks will be ideal for photographers and agencies who want to market images to clients.

PACA's Henning says such systems have a lot to offer, especially with small and medium size agencies. "On-line delivery of pictures is going to be the best method of allowing clients to search pictures and to deliver pictures to clients, but a lot of developments are going to have to take place for that to be viable," he says.

As Henning sees it, one of those important developments must be a truly fiber optic telephone system rather than one based on digital transmission. There also are many lingering questions that need answers before photographers and stock agencies can feel comfortable with on-line networks. "How viable are these systems going to be? How large is the customer base going to be? What are the costs involved to get onto either of the systems?" asks Henning.

"If you, as an agent, are going to put your pictures into a system with other people's pictures, who else are you going to be in with? What is the competition going to be like within the system? What quality standards are going to be established? Are there going to be people on the system whose images are vastly inferior to the ones that you're putting on there?"

Choosing the best system to produce, store and market images is not easy. And, with new products coming out monthly, such choices won't be any easier. The important thing is to educate yourself on the equipment that exists and figure out what works best for you. By doing this you will avoid the mistakes that others have made. "I think there are a lot of people who are really enamored by what they see as this incredible tool, but they don't understand the implications," says Brown. "There is a high learning curve. It takes a lot of time."

Brown says people often don't have the creative vision to produce outstanding work, even though they have the equipment. "I liken it to the autoexposure, autofocus camera syndrome. There are a lot of people out there who can pick up an autofocus camera and take adequate photographs," he says. "There will be a lot of people who will pick up a computer and be able to do something with it. It takes a lot more than that to do something successful and consistent, and to show your client that you know what you're talking about."

Important Information on Market Listings

● *The majority of markets listed in this book are those which are actively seeking new freelance contributors. Some important, well-known companies which have declined complete listings are included within their appropriate section with a brief statement of their policies. In addition, firms which for various reasons have not renewed their listings from the 1993 edition are listed in the "'93-'94 Changes" lists at the end of each section.*

● *Market listings are published free of charge to photography buyers and are not advertisements. While every measure is taken to ensure that the listing information is as accurate as possible, we cannot guarantee or endorse any listing.*

● Photographer's Market *reserves the right to exclude any listing which does not meet its requirements.*

● *Although every buyer is given the opportunity to update his listing information prior to publication, the photography marketplace changes constantly throughout the year and between editions. Therefore it is possible that some of the market information will be out of date by the time you make use of it.*

● *Market listings new to this edition are marked with an asterisk. These new markets are often the most receptive to new freelance talent.*

● *This book is edited (except for quoted material) in the masculine gender because we think "he/she," "she/he," "he or she," "him or her" in copy is distracting.*

Key to Symbols and Abbreviations

🍁 *Canadian Markets*
‡ *Markets located outside the United States and Canada*
■*Audiovisual Markets*
New Listings
●*Introduces special comments that were inserted by the editor of* Photographer's Market.
NPI no payment information given
SASE self-addressed stamped envelope
IRC International Reply Coupon, for use on reply mail in markets outside of your own country
Ms, Mss manuscript(s)
© *copyright*
FAX facsimile transmission
(for definitions and abbreviations relating specifically to the photographic industry, see the glossary in the back of the book.)

The Markets

Advertising, Public Relations and Audiovisual Firms

If you are eager to work with advertising agencies, public relations firms or audiovisual companies you must closely examine these fields and the outside forces that affect them. While there are conflicting opinions about how well these markets are recovering from the recession of the early 1990s, there is no doubt that these companies will be affected by the policies of a new presidential administration.

Leaders in the advertising field have numerous concerns regarding the present administration, particularly its role in promoting tax increases for corporations. According to published reports in *Advertising Age*, industry professionals believe corporate tax increases could force clients to tighten their advertising budgets. As a result, photographers may witness tougher negotiations with art directors who must adhere to budget constraints. This is extremely unfortunate given the fact that many photographers and agencies suffered severe losses during the recession and endured tighter advertising budgets. Rick Labs, of CL&B Advertising in Manlius, New York, says low budgets have already resulted in a thinning out of location crews, which reduces the amount of quality work.

However, the advertising picture is not all doom and gloom. Many magazine publishers witnessed advertising revenue increases in the early months of 1993. And, four months into 1993, agencies also were delighted by proposals for investment tax credits. As the industry continues to rebound, more and more work will arise for photographers attempting to prove themselves in the advertising world.

Think globally

As you search for advertising markets, or jobs in general, you should remember that advances in communication and overall technology have made this a more global economy. When putting together portfolios or self-promotion pieces be aware of governmental regulations, in the United States and abroad, which might affect your business as a freelancer. For example, in the early part of 1993 the Quebec Court of Appeals ruled in favor of Canadian lawmakers by upholding legislation banning tobacco advertising nationwide. Photographers who promote themselves should stay abreast of such regulations by reading trade journals. While sending tearsheets from cigarette ads to an agency in the United States may land you a job, such samples may hurt your chances of working with a Canadian firm.

Focus on the client

In order to succeed you must become more creative and offer images buyers can't resist. Some agencies are seeing tremendous growth in the number of computer manipulated photos they receive. They also see more hand-tinted work, gels and dramatic lighting. Call attention to your work by showing clients that you can offer more than other photographers. Do your own research and development by experimenting with various techniques and let agencies know that you have a unique vision.

Also, present yourself as a professional by studying potential markets and knowing what art directors like to see and have used in the past. When showing portfolios, get some feedback regarding your work. If an art director can provide some constructive criticism, listen and learn to improve your chances of attracting clients.

Once you are hired, it is important to stay focused on what the client wants. Too often photographers and art directors get so close to their work they forget the overall concept the client wants in an advertisement. By working hard to accommodate clients, you can cultivate repeat business and jobs from referrals.

One photographer who has adapted to demands of the advertising field is Ira Lerner, a fashion photographer from New York City. The subject of our Insider Report on page 70, Lerner began 10 years ago to develop his skills as an art director and he now offers such services along with his photographic talent.

Inside these markets

In this section you will find over 200 listings, including around 35 new ones. A new feature in this year's edition is the bulleted (●) comment found inside certain listings throughout the book. These editorial comments were written by the editor of *Photographer's Market* and typically point out awards a market has received, or share some special information about the listing.

Any listing with audiovisual, film or video needs has been designated with a special AV symbol—a solid, black square (■). These markets also contain detailed information under the subhead "Audiovisual Needs."

A number of factors go into the way advertising, public relations and audiovisual firms determine their rates of payment for photography. Many times rates are based on the overall budgets for projects. Nevertheless, you should certainly negotiate payment based on usage (see information on Pricing and Negotiating on page 6). We have attempted to obtain more specific information from listings regarding their rates of payment, but some firms only discuss those terms with photographers during negotiations. The code NPI, for "no payment information given" appears in listings which do not provide specific terms.

Any listing which is interested in working with newer, lesser-known photographers has been placed in the First Markets Index located in the back of this book. These markets also acknowledge this fact inside their listings.

Finally, some markets that were in the 1993 edition of *Photographer's Market* are not in this year's issue. These markets were omitted for a variety of reasons which can be found under '93-'94 Changes at the end of this section.

Alabama

■**BARRY HUEY, BULLOCK & COOK, ADVERTISING, INC.**, Suite 400, 3800 Colonnade Pkwy., Birmingham AL 35243. (205)969-3200. Fax: (205)969-3136. Art Directors: Mike Macon/Gracey Tillman. Estab. 1972. Ad agency. Types of clients: retail, food and sporting goods. Client list provided on request.
Needs: Works with 6-10 freelance photographers/month. Uses photos for consumer magazines, trade magazines, P-O-P displays, catalogs, posters and audiovisuals. Subjects include: fishing industry, water sports, can food products and golf equipment. Model release preferred. Captions preferred.
Audiovisual Needs: Uses AV for product introductions, seminars and various presentations.
Specs: Uses 5×7 b&w prints; 35mm, 2¼×2¼, 4×5 and 8×10 transparencies.
Making Contact & Terms: Submit portfolio for review. Provide resume, business card, brochure, flyer or tearsheets to be kept on file for possible future assignments. Works on assignment basis only. Pays $50-400/b&w photo; $85-3,000/color photo; $500-1,600/day; $150-20,000/job. Payment is made on acceptance plus 90 days. Buys all rights.
Tips: Prefers to see "table top product with new, exciting lighting."

■**J.H. LEWIS ADVERTISING, INC.**, 1668 Government St., Mobile AL 36604. (205)476-2507. President: Larry Norris. Creative Directors, Birmingham office: Spencer Till; Mobile office: Ben Jordan and Helen Savage. Ad agency. Uses billboards, consumer and trade magazines, direct mail, foreign media, newspapers, P-O-P displays, radio and TV. Serves industrial, entertainment, financial, agricultural, medical and consumer clients. Commissions 25 photographers/year.
Specs: Uses b&w contact sheet and 8×10 b&w glossy prints; uses 8×10 color prints and 4×5 transparencies; produces 16mm documentaries.
Making Contact & Terms: NPI. Pays per job, or royalties on 16mm film sales. Buys all rights. Model release preferred. Arrange a personal interview to show portfolio; submit portfolio for review; or send material, "preferably slides we can keep on file," by mail for consideration. SASE. Reports in 1 week.

■**TOWNSEND, BARNEY & PATRICK,** (formerly Barney & Patrick Inc.), 300 St. Francis St., Mobile AL 36602. (205)433-0401. Ad agency. Vice President/Creative Services: George Yurcisin. Types of clients: industrial, financial, medical, retail, fashion, fast food, tourism, packaging, super markets and food services.

The solid, black square before a listing indicates that the market uses various types of audiovisual materials, such as slides, film or videotape.

Needs: Works with 1-3 freelance photographers/month. Uses photographers for consumer magazines, trade magazines, direct mail, brochures, P-O-P displays, audiovisuals, posters and newspapers.
Audiovisual Needs: Works with freelance filmmakers to produce TV and audiovisuals.
Specs: Uses 8×10 and 11×17 glossy b&w prints; 35mm, 2¼×2¼, 4×5 and 8×10 transparencies; 16mm, 35mm film and videotape.
Making Contact & Terms: Arrange a personal interview to show portfolio or query with samples and list of stock photo subjects. Provide resume, business card, brochure, flyer or tearsheets to be kept on file for possible future assignments. Does not return unsolicited material. Reports as needed. NPI; payment "varies according to budget." Pays net 30. Buys all rights. Model release required.

Alaska

THE NERLAND AGENCY, 808 E St., Anchorage AK 99501. (907)274-9553. Ad agency. Art Director: James Ford. Types of clients: retail, hotel, restaurant, fitness, healthcare. Client list free with SASE.
Needs: Works with 1 freelance photographer/month. Uses photographers for consumer magazines, trade magazines, direct mail and brochures and collateral pieces. Subjects include Alaskan scenic shots.
Specs: Uses 11×14 matte b&w prints; 35mm, 2¼×2¼ and 4×5 transparencies.
Making Contact & Terms: Query with samples. Provide resume, business card, brochure, flyer or tearsheets to be kept on file for possible future assignments. Does not return unsolicited material. Pays $500-700/day or minimum $100/job (depends on job). Pays on receipt. Buys all rights or one-time rights. Model release and captions preferred.
Tips: Prefers to see "high technical quality (sharpness, lighting, etc). All photos should capture a mood. Simplicity of subject matter. Keep sending updated samples of work you are doing (monthly). We are demanding higher technical quality and looking for more 'feeling' photos than still life of product."

Arizona

■**ARIZONA CINE EQUIPMENT INC.**, 2125 E. 20th St., Tucson AZ 85719. (602)623-8268. Estab. 1972. AV firm. Types of clients: industrial and retail.
Needs: Works with 6 photographers, filmmakers and/or videographers/month. Uses photos for audiovisual. Model/property release required. Captions preferred.
Audiovisual Needs: Uses slides, film and videotape.
Specs: Uses color prints; 35mm, 4×5 transparencies.
Making Contact & Terms: Query with resume of credits. Query with list of stock photo subjects. Send unsolicited photos by mail for consideration. Query with samples. Works with freelancers on assignment only. Keeps samples on file. SASE. Reports in 3 weeks. Pays $15-30/hour; $250-500/day; or per job. Pays on receipt of invoice. Buys all rights; negotiable. Credit line sometimes given.

■**FARNAM COMPANIES, INC.**, Dept. PM, 2nd Floor, 301 W. Osborn, Phoenix AZ 85013-3928. (602)285-1660. Inhouse ad agency. Creative Director: Trish Spencer. Types of clients: animal health products, primarily for horses and dogs, some cattle.
Needs: Works with 2 freelance photographers/month. Uses photographers for direct mail, catalogs, consumer magazines, P-O-P displays, posters, AV presentations, trade magazines and brochures. Subject matter includes horses, dogs, cats, farm scenes, ranch scenes, cowboys, cattle and horse shows. Occasionally works with freelance filmmakers to produce educational horse health films and demonstrations of product use.
Specs: Uses 8½×10 glossy b&w and color prints; 35mm, 2¼×2¼ and 4×5 transparencies; 16mm and 35mm film and videotape.
Making Contact & Terms: Arrange a personal interview to show portfolio. Query with samples. Send unsolicited photos by mail for consideration. Provide resume, business card, brochure, flyer or tearsheets to be kept on file for possible future assignments. Works with freelance photographers on assignment basis only. SASE. Reports in 2 weeks or per photographer's request. Pays $25-75/b&w photo; $50-300/color photo. Pays on publication. Buys one-time rights. Model release required. Credit line given whenever possible.
Tips: "Send me a number of good, reasonably priced for one-time use photos of dogs, horses or farm scenes. Better yet, send me good quality dupes I can keep on file for *rush* use. When the dupes are in the file and I see them regularly, the ones I like stick in my mind and I find myself planning ways to use them. We are looking for original, dramatic work. We especially like to see horses, dogs, cats and cattle captured in artistic scenes or poses. All shots should show off quality animals with good conformation. We rarely use shots if people are shown and prefer animals in natural settings or in barns/stalls."

JOANIE L. FLATT AND ASSOC. LTD, Suite 2, 623 W. Southern Ave, Mesa AZ 85210. (602)835-9139. Fax: (602)835-9597. PR firm. CEO: Maggie Bruce. Types of clients: service, educational, insurance companies, developers, builders and finance.
Needs: Works with 2-3 photographers/month. Uses photographers for consumer magazines, brochures and group presentations. Subject matter varies.
Specs: Vary depending on client and job.
Making Contact & Terms: Query with list of stock photo subjects. Provide resume, business card, brochure, flyer or tearsheets to be kept on file for possible future assignments. Works with local freelance photographers only. Does not return unsolicited material. Reports in 3 weeks. NPI. Photographer bids a job in writing. Payment is made 30 days after invoice. Buys all rights and sometimes one-time rights. Model release required. Captions preferred. Credit line given if warranted depending on job.

■**PAUL S. KARR PRODUCTIONS,** 2949 W. Indian School Rd., Phoenix AZ 85017. (602)266-4198. Contact: Kelly Karr. Film & tape firm. Types of clients: industrial, business and education. Works with freelancers on assignment only.
Needs: Uses filmmakers for motion pictures. "You must be an experienced filmmaker with your own location equipment, and understand editing and negative cutting to be considered for any assignment." Primarily produces industrial films for training, marketing, public relations and government contracts. Does high-speed photo instrumentation. Also produces business promotional tapes, recruiting tapes and instructional and entertainment tapes for VCR and cable. "We are also interested in funded co-production ventures with other video and film producers."
Specs: Uses 16mm films and videotapes. Provides production services, including sound transfers, scoring and mixing and video production, post production, and film-to-tape services.
Making Contact & Terms: Query with resume of credits and advise if sample reel is available. NPI. Pays/job; negotiates payment based on client's budget and photographer's ability to handle the work. Pays on production. Buys all rights. Model release required.
Tips: Branch office in Utah: Karr Productions, 1045 N. 300 East, Orem UT 84057. (801)226-8209. Contact: Mike Karr.

WALKER AGENCY, #160, 15855 N. Greenway Hayden Loop, Scottsdale AZ 85260-1726. (602)483-0185. Fax: (602)948-3113. President: Mike Walker. Estab. 1982. Marketing communications. Types of clients: banking, marine industry and outdoor recreation products.
Needs: Uses photos for consumer and trade magazines, posters and newspapers. Subjects include outdoor recreation scenes: fishing, camping, etc. "We also publish a newspaper supplement 'Escape to the Outdoors' which goes to 11,000 papers." Model/property release required.
Specs: Uses 8×10 glossy b&w prints with borders; 35mm, 2¼×2¼, 4×5 and 8×10 transparencies.
Making Contact & Terms: Query with resume of credits. Query with list of stock photo subjects. Provide resume, business card, brochure, flyer or tearsheets to be kept on file for possible future assignments. Reports in 1 week. Pays $25/b&w or color photo; $150-500/day; also pays per job. Pays on receipt of invoice. Buys all rights; other rights negotiable.
Tips: In portfolio/samples, prefers to see a completely propped scene. "There is more opportunity for photographers within the advertising/PR industry."

Arkansas

BLACKWOOD, MARTIN, AND ASSOCIATES, P.O. Box 1968, 300 First Place, Fayetteville AR 72702. (501)442-9803. Ad agency. Creative Director: Gary Weidner. Types of clients: food, financial, medical, insurance, some retail. Client list provided on request.
Needs: Works with 3 freelance photographers/month. Uses photographers for direct mail, catalogs, consumer magazines, P-O-P displays, trade magazines and brochures. Subject matter includes "food shots—fried foods, industrial."
Specs: Uses 8×10 high contrast b&w prints; 35mm, 4×5 and 8×10 transparencies.
Making Contact & Terms: Arrange a personal interview to show portfolio; query with samples; provide resume, business card, brochure, flyer or tearsheets to be kept on file for possible future assignments. Works with freelance photographers on assignment basis only. Does not return unsolicited material. Reports in 1 month. NPI. Payment depends on budget—"whatever the market will bear." Buys all rights. Model release preferred.
Tips: Prefers to see "good, professional work, b&w and color" in a portfolio of samples. "Be willing to travel and willing to work within our budget. We are using less b&w photography because of newspaper reproduction in our area. We're using a lot of color for printing."

*■CEDAR CREST STUDIO, P.O. Box 28, Mountain Home AR 72653. (501)425-9377. Owner: Bob Ketchum. Estab. 1972. AV firm. Types of clients: industrial, financial, fashion, retail, food. Examples of recent projects: Mountain Home Public Schools (teacher recruitment); Arkansas State Police (TV/public service announcement); and "Days of Old," music video.
Needs: Works with 4 freelancers/month. Uses photos for covers on CDs and cassettes.
Audiovisual Needs: Uses slides, film and videotapes.
Specs: Uses ½", 8mm and ¾" videotape.
Making Contact & Terms: Works with local freelancers only. Does not keep samples on file. Cannot return material. NPI. Pays on publication. Credit line sometimes given.

■WILLIAMS/CRAWFORD/PERRY & ASSOCIATES, INC., P.O. Box 789, Ft. Smith AR 72901. (501)782-5230. Fax: (501)782-6970. Creative Director: Jim Perry. Estab. 1983. Types of clients: financial, healthcare, manufacturing, tourism. Examples of ad campaigns: Touche-Ross, 401K and Employee Benefits (videos); Cummins Diesel engines (print campaigns); and Freightliner Trucks (sales promotion and training videos).
Needs: Works with 2-3 freelance photographers—filmmakers—videographers/month. Uses photographers for consumer magazines, trade magazines, direct mail, P-O-P displays, catalogs, posters, newspapers and audiovisual uses. Subjects include: people, products and architecture. Reviews stock photos, film or video of healthcare and financial.
Audiovisual Needs: Uses photos/film/video for 30-second video and film TV spots, 5-10-minute video sales, training and educational.
Specs: Uses 5×7, 8×10 b&w prints; 35mm, 2¼×2¼ and 4×5 transparencies.
Making Contact & Terms: Query with samples, provide resume, business card, brochure, flyer or tearsheets to be kept on file for possible future assignments. Works with freelancers on assignment basis only. Cannot return material. Reports in 1-2 weeks. Pays $500-1,200/day. Pays on receipt of invoice and client approval. Buys all rights (work-for-hire). Model release required; captions preferred. Credit line given sometimes, depending on client's attitude (payment arrangement with photographer).
Tips: In freelancer's samples, wants to see "quality and unique approaches to common problems." There is "a demand for fresh graphics and design solutions." Freelancers should "expect to be pushed to their creative limits, to work hard and be able to input ideas into the process, not just be directed."

California

ADVANCE ADVERTISING AGENCY, #202, 606 E. Belmont, Fresno CA 93701. (209)445-0383. Manager: Martin Nissen. Ad and PR agency and graphic design firm. Types of clients: industrial, commercial, retail, financial. Examples of recent projects: Investors Thrift (direct mail); Windshield Repair Service (radio, TV, newspaper); and Mr. G's Carpets (radio, TV, newspaper).
Needs: Model release required.
Specs: Uses color and b&w prints.
Making Contact & Terms: Send unsolicited photos by mail for consideration. Provide business card, brochure, flyer to be kept on file for possible future assignments. Keeps samples on file. Reports in 1-2 weeks. NPI; payment negotiated per job. Pays 30 days from invoice. Credit line given. Buys all rights.
Tips: In samples, looks for "not very abstract or overly sophisticated or 'trendy.' Stay with basic, high quality material." Advises that photographers "consider *local* market target audience."

■AIRLINE FILM & TV PROMOTIONS, 13246 Weidner, Pacoima CA 91331. (818)899-1151. President: Byron Schmidt. Types of clients: major film companies.
Audiovisual Needs: Works with 4-5 freelance photographers/month. Uses freelance photographers for films and videotapes. Subjects include publicity and advertising.
Specs: "Specifications vary with each production." Uses 8×10 color prints; 35mm transparencies; VHS videotape.
Making Contact & Terms: Provide resume, business card, self-promotion piece or tearsheets to be kept on file for possible future assignments. Works on assignment only. Does not return unsolicited material. Payment varies per assignment and production: pays $250-500/b&w photo; $500-1,000/job.

Market conditions are constantly changing! If you're still using this book and it's 1995 or later, buy the newest edition of **Photographer's Market** *at your favorite bookstore or order directly from* **Writer's Digest Books.**

Pays on acceptance. Buys all rights. Model release required. Credit line sometimes given. Looks for work that shows "imagination."

AUSTIN ASSOCIATES, Suite 600, 2055 Gateway Place, San Jose CA 95111. (408)453-7776. Ad agency. Art Director: Meri Duffy. Serves high technology clients.
Needs: Works with 3 photographers/month. Uses work for billboards, consumer magazines, trade magazines, direct mail, P-O-P displays, newspapers. Subject matter of photography purchased includes: table top (tight shots of electronics products).
Specs: Uses 8×10 matte b&w and color prints; 35mm, 2¼×2¼, 4×5 or 8×10 transparencies.
Making Contact & Terms: Arrange a personal interview to show portfolio, send unsolicited photos by mail for consideration; provide resume, business card, brochure, flyer or tearsheets to be kept on file for possible future assignments. Works on assignment basis only. Does not return unsolicited material. Reports in 3 weeks. Pays $500-2,500/job. Pays on receipt of invoice. Buys all rights (work-for-hire). Model release required, captions preferred.
Tips: Prefers to see "originality, creativity, uniqueness, technical expertise" in work submitted. There is more use of "photo composites, dramatic lighting, and more attention to detail" in photography.

BENNETT, ALEON, AND ASSOCIATES, Suite 212, 13455 Ventura Blvd., Sherman Oaks CA 91423. (818)990-8070. President: Aleon Bennett. Estab. 1950. Types of clients: finance, industrial.
Needs: Works with varied number of freelance photographers/month. Uses photos for trade magazines and newspapers. Model release required. Captions preferred.
Specs: Uses b&w prints.
Making Contact & Terms: Query with resume of credits. Cannot return material. NPI. Pays per photo. **Pays on acceptance.** Buys all rights.

***JUDY GANULIN PUBLIC RELATIONS**, 1117 W. San Jose, Fresno CA 93711. (209)222-7411. Fax: (209)226-7326. Owner: Judy Ganulin. Estab. 1984. PR firm. Types of clients: general, nonprofit, political. Examples of recent projects: election for County Clerk, Susan B. Anderson (TV, brochure); publicity for annual conference, Central California Employment Round Table (TV and newspaper publicity and ads); San Joaquin Health Center, Blue Cross of California (special event).
Needs: Works with a varying number of freelancers/month. Uses photos for direct mail, newspapers and signage. Subjects include: portraits. Reviews stock photos, "varies according to client needs." Model release required. Captions preferred; include what, where and when.
Making Contact & Terms: Interested in receiving work from newer, lesser-known photographers. Query with samples. Provide resume, business card, brochure, flyer or tearsheets to be kept on file for possible future assignments. Keeps samples on file. SASE. Reports in 3 weeks. NPI; "subject to mutual agreement with photographer." Pays on receipt of invoice. Credit line sometimes given depending on use of photo and appropriateness of credit. Rights negotiable.
Tips: Looks for "ability to do many different kinds of photography, or specialty in one."

■**HAYES ORLIE CUNDALL INC.**, 46 Varda Landing, Sausalito CA 94965. (415)332-7414. Fax: (415)332-5924. Executive Vice President and Creative Director: Alan W. Cundall. Estab. 1991. Ad agency. Uses all media except foreign. Types of clients: industrial, retail, fashion, finance, computer and hi-tech, travel, healthcare, insurance and real estate.
Needs: Works with 1 freelance photographer/month on assignment only. Model release required. Captions preferred.
Making Contact & Terms: Provide resume, business card and brochure to be kept on file for future assignments. "Don't send anything unless it's a brochure of your work or company. We keep a file of talent—we then contact photographers as jobs come up." NPI. Pays on a per-photo basis; negotiates payment based on client's budget, amount of creativity required and where work will appear. "We abide by local photographer's rates."
Tips: "Most books are alike. I look for creative and technical excellence, then how close to our offices; cheap vs. costly; personal rapport; references from friends in agencies who've used him/her. Call first. Send samples and resume if I'm not able to meet with you personally due to work pressure. Keep in

The asterisk before a listing indicates that the market is new in this edition. New markets are often the most receptive to freelance submissions.

touch with new samples." Produces occasional audiovisual for industrial and computer clients; also produces a couple of videos a year.

THE HITCHINS COMPANY, 22756 Hartland St., Canoga Park CA 91307. (818)715-0510. President: W.E. Hitchins. Estab. 1985. Ad agency. Types of clients: industrial, retail (food) and auctioneers.
Needs: Uses photos for trade magazines, direct mail and newspapers. Model release required.
Specs: Uses b&w and color prints. "Copy should be flexible for scanning."
Making Contact & Terms: Provide resume, business card, brochure, flyer or tearsheets to be kept on file for possible future assignments. Works on assignment only. Cannot return material. NPI. Pays on receipt of invoice (30 days). Rights purchased negotiable; "varies as to project."
Tips: Wants to see shots of people and products in samples.

*RICHARD BOND LEWIS & ASSOCIATES, 1112 W. Cameron Ave., West Covina CA 91790. (818)962-7727. Creative Director: Dick Lewis. Estab. 1971. Ad agency. Types of clients: industrial, consumer products manufacturer, real estate, autos. Client list free with SASE.
Needs: Works with 1-2 freelance photographers/month. Uses photos for billboards, consumer and trade magazines, direct mail, catalogs and newspapers. Subjects include: product photos. Model release required. Captions preferred.
Specs: Uses 4×5 color prints and 4×5 transparencies.
Making Contact & Terms: Arrange a personal interview to show portfolio. Provide resume, business card, brochure, flyer or tearsheets to be kept on file for possible future assignments. Works on assignment only. Cannot return material. "Will return upon request." NPI; payment negotiable. Pays "usually 10 days from receipt of invoice—no later than 30 days." Credit line given "if client approves." Buys all rights; "we request negatives on completion of job."
Tips: Prefers to see a variety—people, industrial, product, landscape, some fashion. "Bring in portfolio and leave some samples which best describe your capabilities."

■MARKEN COMMUNICATIONS, Suite 130, 3600 Pruneridge, Santa Clara CA 95051. (408)296-3600. Fax: (408)296-3803. President: Andy Marken. Production Manager: Leslie Posada. Estab. 1977. Ad agency and PR firm. Types of clients: furnishings, electronics and computers. Examples of recent ad campaigns include: Burke Industries (resilient flooring, carpet); Boole and Babbage (mainframe software); Maxar (PCs).
Needs: Works with 3-4 freelance photographers/month. Uses photos for trade magazine, direct mail, publicity and catalogs. Subjects include: product/applications. Model release required.
Audiovisual Needs: Slide presentations and sales/demo videos.
Specs: Uses color and b&w prints; 35mm, 2¼×2¼ and 4×5 transparencies.
Making Contact & Terms: Arrange a personal interview to show portfolio. Query with samples. Submit portfolio for review. "Call." Works with freelancers on an assignment basis only. SASE. Reports in 1 month. Pays $50-1,000/b&w photo; $100-1,800/color photo; $50-100/hour; $500-1,000/day; $200-2,500/job. Pays 30 days after receipt of invoice. Credit line given "sometimes."

*■THE MARKET CONNECTION, Suite 203, 4020 Birch St., Newport Beach CA 92660. (714)851-6313. Fax: (714)833-0253. Communications Director: Sandy Kang. Estab. 1986. PR firm. Types of clients: food, consumer products. Examples of recent projects: sales meeting, Kwikset, division Black & Decker; video cookbook, Campbell Soup Company; and fitness walk media tours, All American Gourmet, division Kraft.
Needs: Works with 3 freelance photographers and 2 videographers/month. Uses photos for billboards, consumer and trade magazines, direct mail, P-O-P displays, posters, newspapers and audiovisual. Subjects include: recipes. Model/property release required. Captions preferred.
Audiovisual Needs: Uses slides and videotape.
Specs: Uses 8×10 glossy color and/or b&w prints; 35mm or 2¼×2¼ transparencies; ¾" SP or BETA SP videotape.
Making Contact & Terms: Interested in receiving work from newer, lesser-known photographers. Submit portfolio for review. Keeps samples on file. Cannot return material. Reports in 1-2 weeks. NPI. Pays on receipt of invoice. Credit line not given. Buys all rights; negotiable.

The code NPI (no payment information given) appears in listings that have not given specific payment amounts.

■**MORRIS MEDIA,** #105, 2730 Monterey St., Torrance CA 90503. (310)533-4800. Contact: Operations Manager.
Needs: Uses 4-6 freelancers per month to produce slide sets and videotapes. Subjects vary according to projects. Reviews stock photos. Model release required. Captions preferred.
Specs: Uses b&w and color prints, any size and format; 35mm and 2¼ × 2¼ transparencies; and ¾" and 1" NTSC videotape.
Making Contact & Terms: Submit portfolio/demo tape by mail. Query with samples. Provide resume and list of stock photo subjects with business card, self-promotion piece or tearsheets to be kept on file for possible future assignments. Works with local freelancers on assignment only. Cannot return materials. Reports in 1 week. NPI; payment negotiable. Pays on publication/delivery. Credit line given. Buys all rights (work-for-hire).
Tips: "Submit enough material initially to get acquainted." In samples/demos, wants to see creativity and fee range indicated.

*■**NATIONAL TELEVISION NEWS, INC.,** 6133 Kentland Ave., Woodland Hills CA 91367. (818)883-6121. President: Howard Back. Estab. 1961. Examples of recent clients: Mazda (employee video news magazine); Highway Users Federation (documentary video); and Coldwell-Banker (video news releases).
Needs: Works with one freelancer per month to produce videotapes. Usually needed to shoot location video or news/feature coverage.
Audiovisual Needs: Uses ¾" Beta videotapes.
Making Contact & Terms: Provide resume to be kept on file for possible future assignments. Works with freelancers on assignment only. Cannot return material. NPI; payment negotiable. Buys all rights.

■**NEW & UNIQUE VIDEOS,** 2336 Sumac Dr., San Diego CA 92105. (619)282-6126. Fax: (619)283-8264. Director of Acquisitions: Candace Love. Estab. 1981. AV firm. Types of clients: industrial, financial, fashion, retail and special interest video distribution. Examples of recent projects: "Ultimate Mountain Biking," Raleigh Cycle Co. of America (special interest video); "John Howard's Lessons in Cycling," John Howard (special-interest video); and "Battle at Durango: First-Ever World Mountain Bike Championships," *Mountain & City Biking Magazine* (special interest video).
Needs: Works with 2-6 photographers and/or videographers/year. Subjects include: mainly cycling and sports; anything that fits as "new and unique" in special interest realm. Reviews stock photos: cycling, sports, comedy, romance, "new and unique." Model/property release preferred.
Audiovisual Needs: Uses VHS videotape, ¾" and Betacam SP.
Making Contact & Terms: Query with list of stock photo (video) subjects. Works on assignment only. Keeps samples on file. SASE. Reports in 3 weeks. NPI; payment always negotiated." **Pays on acceptance.** Credit line given. Buys exclusive and nonexclusive rights.
Tips: In samples looks for "originality, good humor and timelessness. We are seeing an international hunger for action footage; good wholesome adventure; comedy, educational, how-to—special interest. The entrepreneurial, creative and original video artiste—with the right attitude—can always feel free to call us."

■**ON-Q PRODUCTIONS INC.,** 618 E. Gutierrez St., Santa Barbara CA 93103. (805)963-1331. President: Vincent Quaranta. Estab. 1984. Producers of multi-projector slide presentations and computer graphics. Types of clients: industrial, fashion and finance.
Needs: Buys 100 freelance photos/year; offers 50 assignments/year. Uses photos for brochures, posters, audiovisual presentations, annual reports, catalogs and magazines. Scenic, people and general stock. Model release required. Captions required.
Specs: Uses 35mm, 2¼ × 2¼ and 4 × 5 transparencies.
Making Contact & Terms: Provide stock list, business card, brochure, flyer or tearsheets to be kept on file for possible future assignments. Pays $100 minimum/job. Buys rights according to client's needs.
Tips: Looks for stock slides for AV uses.

PHOTEC, P.O. Box 20328, Long Beach CA 90801. (310)983-9732. Assignment photography and stock photo agency. Manager/Owner: Steve Potter. Estab. 1964. Clients: industrial, commercial, marine, maritime, public services, high-tech R&D, manufacturing, training, publishers and licensing agencies.

Can't find a listing? Check at the end of each market section for the " '93-'94 Changes" lists. These lists include any market listings from the '93 edition which were either not verified or deleted in this edition.

Needs: Uses photography stock for consumer and technical trade magazines, direct mail, catalogs, posters, signage, brochures, annual reports and manuals. Subjects include: boat living (people live-aboards); boats in design, manufacture and use; high-tech/aerospace technology and equipment. Reviews stock photos of boat living and cruising, boats in design, manufacture and use; boat operating, navigating and maintenance.

Specs: Uses 8×12 glossy b&w and color prints; 35mm, 120mm and 4×5 transparencies, S-VHS videotape.

Making Contact & Terms: Interested in receiving work from newer, lesser-known photographers "if they are talented, well trained. (No portrait, school, editorial or 'papparazi' types.)" Query with resumé of credits and education, list of photo subjects, samples, business card, brochure and flyer/tearsheets. SASE. NPI. Pays via contract/agreement only. Rights must be negotiable. Model/property release required for people and with privately owned boats/equipment. Photo captions preferred; include "who, what, when, where, why and how." Credit line usually given; negotiable.

Tips: "Technical photographic capabilities in all formats, knowledge of boats and operating uses and an artistic sense are essential, but you should be more technical than 'arty.' Also, know graphics methods/limitations, 'state-of-the-art' photo technology, films and materials." Sees a trend toward PC-CD-electronic scanning/storage/repro technology development; cost-effective equipment and training, i.e., hi-resolution and continuous tone/color eq. and transmission; and facsimile (Fax) at reasonable cost.

■**BILL RASE PRODUCTIONS, INC.**, 955 Venture Court, Sacramento CA 95825. (916)929-9181. Manager/Owner: Bill Rase. Estab. 1965. AV firm. Types of clients: industry, business, government, publishing and education. Produces filmstrips, slide sets, multimedia kits, motion pictures, sound-slide sets, videotapes, mass cassette, reel and video duplication. Photo and film purchases vary.

Needs: "Script recording for educational clients is our largest need, followed by industrial training, state and government work, motivational, etc." Freelance photos used sometimes in motion pictures. No nudes. Color only. Vertical format for TV cutoff only. Sound for TV public service announcements, commercials, and industrial films. Uses stock footage of hard-to-find scenes, landmarks in other cities, shots from the 1920s to 1980s, etc. Special subject needs include 35 mm and ¾-inch video shot of California landmark locations, especially San Francisco, Napa Valley Wine Country, Gold Country, Lake Tahoe area, Delta area and Sacramento area. "We buy out the footage—so much for so much," or ¾-inch video or 35 mm slides. Uses 8×10 prints and 35mm transparencies.

Making Contact & Terms: NPI. Payment depends on job, by bid. Pays 30 days after acceptance. Buys one-time rights or all rights; varies according to clients' needs. Model release required. Query with samples and resume of credits. Freelancers within 100 miles only. Does not return samples. SASE. Reports "according to the type of project. Sometimes it takes a couple of months to get the proper bid info."

Tips: "Video footage of the popular areas of this country and others is becoming more and more useful. Have price list, equipment list and a few slide samples in a folder or package available to send."

■**RED HOTS ENTERTAINMENT**, (formerly Winmill Entertainment), 813 N. Cordova St., Burbank CA 91505-2924. (818)954-0065. President/Creative Director: Chip Miller. Estab. 1987. Motion picture, music video, commercial, and promotional trailer film production company. Types of clients: industrial, fashion, entertainment, motion picture, TV and music.

Needs: Works with 2-6 freelance photographers/month. Uses freelancers for TV, music video, motion picture stills and production. Model release required. Property release preferred. Captions preferred.

Making Contact & Terms: Interested in receiving work from newer, lesser-known photographers. Provide business card, resume, references, samples or tearsheets to be kept on file for possible future assignments. NPI; payment negotiable "based on project's budget." Rights negotiable.

Tips: Wants to see minimum of 12 pieces expressing range of studio, location, style and model-oriented work. Include samples of work published or commissioned for production.

EDGAR S. SPIZEL ADVERTISING AND PUBLIC RELATIONS, C-31, 2610 Torrey Pines Rd., La Jolla CA 92037-3445. Ad agency and PR firm. President: Edgar S. Spizel. Types of clients: retail, finance, hotels, developers, arts, TV and radio.

Needs: Works with 2 freelance photographers/month. Uses photographers for consumer and trade magazines, direct mail, P-O-P displays, posters, signage and newspapers. Subjects include people, buildings, hotels, apartments, interiors.

Specs: Uses 8×10 glossy b&w and color prints; 35mm, 2¼×2¼, 4×5 transparencies.

Making Contact & Terms: Send unsolicited photos by mail for consideration; provide resume, business card, brochure, flyer or tearsheets to be kept on file for possible future assignments. Works with freelance photographers on an assignment basis only. Does not return unsolicited material. NPI; pays by the hour, day, or job. **Pays on acceptance.** Buys all rights. Model release required. Credit line sometimes given.

■**RON TANSKY ADVERTISING CO.**, Suite 111, 14852 Ventura Blvd., Sherman Oaks CA 91403. (818)990-9370. Fax: (818)990-0456. Consulting Art Directors: Van Valencia, Norm Galston. Estab. 1976. Ad agency and PR firm. Serves all types of clients.
Needs: Works with 2 freelance photographers/month. Uses photos for billboards, consumer and trade magazines, direct mail, P-O-P displays, brochures, catalogs, signage, newspapers and AV presentations. Subjects include: "mostly product—but some without product as well." Special subject needs include: consumer electronics, nutrition products and over-the-counter drugs. Model release required.
Audiovisual Needs: Works with freelance filmmakers to produce TV commercials.
Specs: Uses b&w or color prints; 2¼×2¼, 4×5 transparencies; 16mm and videotape film.
Making Contact & Terms: Query with resume of credits. Provide resume, business card, brochure, flyer or tearsheets to be kept on file for possible future assignments. SASE. Payment "depends on subject and client's budget." Pays $50-250/b&w photo; $100-1,500/color photo; $500-1,500/day; $100-1,500/complete job. Pays in 30 days. Buys all rights.
Tips: Prefers to see "product photos, originality of position and lighting" in a portfolio. "We look for creativity and general competence, i.e., focus and lighting as well as ability to work with models." Photographers should provide "rate structure and ideas of how they would handle product shots." Also, "don't use fax unless we make request."

■**DANA WHITE PRODUCTIONS, INC.**, 2623 29th St., Santa Monica CA 90405. (310)450-9101. Fax: (310)450-9101. AV firm. President: Dana White. Estab. 1977. Types of clients: corporate and educational. Examples of recent productions: MacMillan-McGraw-Hill (textbook illustrations); Pepperdine University (awards banquets, tribute to winners); St. Joseph Center (homelessness, multi-image).
Needs: Works with 2-3 freelance photographers/month. Uses photographers for catalogs, audiovisual and books. Subjects include: people, products and architecture. Interested in reviewing 35mm stock photos.
Audiovisual Needs: Uses all AV formats; also slides for multi-image slide shows using 1-9 projectors. "Photographer must be able to work well on his own and shoot to the style of our company."
Specs: Uses b&w prints; 35mm, 2¼×2¼ transparencies.
Making Contact & Terms: Interested in receiving work from newer, lesser-known photographers. Arrange a personal interview to show portfolio; query with samples, past credits. Works with freelancers on assignment only. Cannot return material. Report time depends on schedule. Pays $20-150/hour; $50-1,200/day; $25-100/color photo. **Pays on acceptance** and receipt of invoice. Buys one-time rights, exclusive product rights and all rights; negotiable, usually share in rights. Model release required; property release preferred for company logos and ID's. Credit line given sometimes.
Tips: In freelancer's portfolio or demos, wants to see "quality of composition, lighting, saturation, degree of difficulty and importance of assignment." The trend is toward "more video, less AV." To break in, freelancer should "diversify, negotiate, get the job. Don't get stuck in a fixed way of doing things. Work flexibly with producers."

■**WILSON & WILSON**, 970 Arnold Way, San Jose CA 95128-3476. (408)271-7900. Fax: (408)292-9595. Art Director: Erica K. Wilson. Ad agency, PR firm. Types of clients: industrial, finance, business to business, high-tech and distribution companies.
Needs: Works with 2-3 freelance photographers/month. Uses photos for trade magazines, direct mail, catalogs, posters, newspapers, trade shows and annual reports. Subjects include: technology and real estate. Reviews stock photos on technology and real estate, also b&w people shots. Model release preferred. Captions preferred.
Audiovisual Needs: Uses photos for slide shows, training and sales video.
Specs: Uses 3×5 to 11×16 (depends on job), glossy b&w prints; 35mm, 4×5 transparencies; 1″ videotape.
Making Contact & Terms: Query with samples. Provide resume, business card, brochure, flyer or tearsheets to be kept on file for possible future assignments, "follow with phone call for portfolio review." Keeps samples on file. Reports as needed. Pays $70-120/hour; $750-1,200/day; photographer's quote. Credit line sometimes given depending upon job. Rights negotiable.
Tips: In portfolio, wants to see "technical proficiency, ability to *show product* creatively. Variety preferred." One trend is that "Standards are continually improving." To break in with this firm, "flexibility is important. Be able to contribute to creative process. Have ability to work with tight deadlines."

Los Angeles

BEAR ADVERTISING, 1424 N. Highland, Los Angeles CA 90028. (213)466-6464. Vice President: Bruce Bear. Ad agency. Uses consumer magazines, direct mail, foreign media, P-O-P displays and trade magazines. Serves sporting goods, fast foods and industrial clients.

Needs: Works with 4 freelance photographers/month on assignment only. Prefers to see samples of sporting goods, fishing equipment, outdoor scenes, product shots with rustic atmosphere of guns, rifles, fishing reels, lures, camping equipment, etc.
Specs: Uses b&w and color photos.
Making Contact & Terms: Call to arrange interview to show portfolio. Provide business card and tearsheets to be kept on file for possible future assignments. SASE. Reports in 1 week. Pays $150-250/b&w photo; $200-350/color photo. Pays 30 days after billing to client. Buys all rights.

*BRAMSON & ASSOCIATES, 7400 Beverly Blvd., Los Angeles CA 90036. (213)938-3595. Fax: (213)938-0852. Principal: Gene Bramson. Estab. 1970. Ad agency. Types of clients: industrial, financial, retail, healthcare.
Needs: Works with 2-5 freelancers/month. Uses photos for trade magazines, direct mail, catalogs, posters, newspapers, signage. Subject matter varies. Reviews stock photos. Model/property release required. Captions preferred.
Making Contact & Terms: Interested in receiving work from newer, lesser-known photographers. Submit portfolio for review. Query with stock photo list. Send unsolicited photos by mail for consideration. Query with samples. Provide resume, business card, brochure, flyer or tearsheet to be kept on file for possible future assignments. Works with freelancers on assignment only. Keeps samples on file. SASE. Reports in 1-2 weeks. NPI. Payment varies depending on budget for each project. Credit line sometimes given. Buys all rights.
Tips: "If it's not great work don't bother."

*LEVINSON ASSOCIATES, Suite 650, 1440 Veteran Ave., Los Angeles CA 90027. (213)460-4545. Fax: (213)663-2820. Assistant to President: Jed Leland, Jr. Estab. 1969. PR firm. Types of clients: industrial, financial, entertainment. Examples of recent projects: DCC Compact Classics (record co.); Writers Guild Literacy Program (public service); Hollywood Press Club (award dinner gala).
Needs: Works with varying number of freelancers/month. Uses photos for trade magazines and newspapers. Subjects vary. Model release required. Property release preferred. Captions preferred.
Making Contact & Terms: Works with local freelancers only. Keeps samples on file. Cannot return material. NPI.

■MYRIAD PRODUCTIONS, Suite 402, 1314 N. Hayworth Ave., Los Angeles CA 90046. (213)851-1400. President: Ed Harris. Estab. 1965. Primarily involved with sports productions and events. Works with freelance photographers on assignment only basis.
Needs: Uses photos for portraits, live-action and studio shots, special effects, advertising, illustrations, brochures, TV and film graphics, theatrical and production stills. Model/property release required. Captions preferred; include name(s), location, date, description.
Specs: Uses 8 × 10 b&w glossy prints, 8 × 10 color prints and 2¼ × 2¼ transparancies.
Making Contact & Terms: Provide brochure, resume and samples to be kept on file for possible future assignments. Send material by mail for consideration. Cannot return material. Reporting time "depends on urgency of job or production." NPI. Credit line sometimes given. Buys all rights.
Tips: "We look for an imaginative photographer, one who captures all the subtle nuances, as the photographer is as much a part of the creative process as the artist or scene being shot. Working with us depends almost entirely on the photographer's skill and creative sensitivity with the subject. All materials submitted will be placed on file and not returned, pending future assignments. Photographers should not send us their only prints, transparencies, etc. for this reason."

San Francisco

PURDOM PUBLIC RELATIONS, 395 Oyster Point, San Francisco CA 94080. (415)588-5700. President: Paul Purdom. Estab. 1965. PR firm. Types of clients: industrial and financial. Examples of recent PR campaigns: Sun Microsystems, Varian Associates, Acuson Corporation (all showing computers and instruments systems in use).
Needs: Works with 4-6 freelance photographers/month. Uses photos for trade magazines, direct mail and newspapers. Subjects include: industrial and scientific topics. Model release preferred.
Specs: Uses 35mm and 2¼ × 2¼ transparencies; film: contact for specs.
Making Contact & Terms: Query with resume of credits, list of stock photo subjects. Provide resume, business card, brochure, flyer or tearsheets to be kept on file for possible future assignments. Works on assignment only. Does not return material. Reports as needed. Pays $50-150/hour, $400-1,500/day. Pays on receipt of invoice. Buys all rights.

*REDGATE COMMUNICATIONS CORPORATION, Suite 6300, 185 Berry St., San Francisco CA 94107. Associate Creative Director: Judi Muller. Estab. 1987. Marketing communications agency. Types of clients: hi tech and healthcare.

Needs: Works with 1-6 photographers/month. Uses photos for brochures and corporate magazines. Subjects include: portraits and conceptual still life. Model release required.

Specs: Uses b&w prints; 35mm 2¼×2¼, 4×5 transparencies.

Making Contact & Terms: Interested in receiving work from newer, lesser-known photographers. Provide business card and tearsheets to be kept on file for possible future assignments. Keeps samples on file. SASE. "We call when something applicable comes up." NPI. Pays on receipt of invoice (+45 days). Credit line sometimes given depending upon "corporate magazine, yes, otherwise no." Rights negotiable (depends on project).

Tips: "I am looking for interesting, conceptual, unique photography. We already have reliable people we use for standard shots."

■**VARITEL VIDEO**, 350 Townsend St., San Francisco CA 94107. (415)495-3328. Vice President of Marketing and Sales: Lori Anderson. Production Manager: Blake Padilla. Types of clients: advertising agencies.

Needs: Works with 10 freelance photographers/month. Uses freelance photographers for filmstrips, slide sets and videotapes. Also works with freelance filmmakers for CD Rom, Paint Box.

Specs: Uses color prints; 35mm transparencies; 16mm, 35mm film; VHS, Beta, U-matic ¾" or 1" videotape. Also, D2.

Making Contact & Terms: Provide resume, business card, self-promotion piece or tearsheets to be kept on file for possible future assignments. Does not return unsolicited material. Reports in 1 week. Pays $50-100/hour; $200-500/day. **Pays on acceptance.** Rights vary.

Tips: Apply with resume and examples of work to Julie Resing.

Colorado

■**FRIEDENTAG PHOTOGRAPHICS**, 356 Grape St., Denver CO 80220. (303)333-7096. Manager: Harvey Friedentag. Estab. 1957. AV firm. Serves clients in business, industry, government, trade and union organizations. Produces slide sets, motion pictures and videotape.

Needs: Works with 5-10 freelancers/month on assignment only. Buys 1,000 photos and 25 films/year. Provide flyer, business card and brochure and nonreturnable samples to show to clients. Reviews stock photos of business, training, public relations and industrial plants showing people and equipment or products in use. Model release required.

Audiovisual Needs: Uses freelance photos in color slide sets and motion pictures. No posed looks. Also produces mostly 16mm Ektachrome and some 16mm b&w; ¾" and VHS videotape. Length requirement: 3-30 minutes. Interested in stock footage on business, industry, education, recreation and unusual information.

Specs: Uses 8×10 glossy b&w prints; 8×10 glossy color prints; transparencies; 35mm or 2¼×2¼ or 4×5 color transparencies.

Making Contact & Terms: Send material by mail for consideration. SASE. Reports in 3 weeks. Pays $300/day for still; $500/day for motion picture plus expenses, or $25/b&w photo or $50/color photo. **Pays on acceptance.** Buys rights as required by clients.

Tips: "More imagination needed, be different and above all, technical quality is a must. There are more opportunities now than ever, especially for new people. We are looking to strengthen our file of talent across the nation."

Connecticut

■**AV DESIGN**, 1823 Silas Deane, P.O. Box 588, Rocky Hill CT 06067. (203)529-2581. Fax: (203)529-5480. President: Joseph Wall. Types of clients: industrial, finance, manufacturers, insurance and lecturers. Examples of ad campaigns: Pirelli Armstrong and Stanley Hardware, (multi-image presentations); also, Heublein, (product photography).

The solid, black square before a listing indicates that the market uses various types of audiovisual materials, such as slides, film or videotape.

Audiovisual Needs: Works with 3 freelance photographers/month. Uses photographers for slide sets, multimedia productions and videotapes. Subjects include industrial—manufacturing.
Specs: Uses 8×10 b&w and color prints; 35mm, 2¼×2¼ and 4×5 transparencies.
Making Contact & Terms: Query with samples, resume or stock photo list. Works with local freelancers on assignment basis only; interested in stock photos/footage. Reports in 1 month. NPI; payment varies according to client's budget. **Pays on acceptance.** Buys all rights. Captions and model release preferred.

■DISCOVERY PRODUCTIONS, 1415 King St., Greenwich CT 06831-2519. (203)531-6288. Proprietor: David Epstein. PR/AV firm. Serves educational and social action agencies. Produces 16mm and 35mm documentary, educational and industrial films.
Needs: Buys 2 films annually.
Making Contact & Terms: Query first with resume of credits. Provide resume to be kept on file for possible future assignments. Works with up to 2 freelance photographers/month on assignment only. Pays 25-60% royalty. Pays on use and 30 days. Buys all rights, but may reassign to filmmaker. Model release required.
Tips: Possible assignments include research, writing, camera work or editing. "We would collaborate on a production of an attractive and practical idea."

■DONAHUE ADVERTISING & PUBLIC RELATIONS, INC., 227 Lawrence St., Hartford CT 06106. (203)728-0000. Fax: (203)247-9247. Ad agency and PR firm. Creative Director: Rob Saelens. Estab. 1980. Types of clients: industrial and high-tech.
Needs: Works with 1-2 photographers and/or videographers/month. Uses photos for trade magazines, catalogs and posters. Subjects include: products.
Audiovisual Needs: Uses videotape—infrequently.
Specs: Uses 8×10 matte and glossy color or b&w prints; 4×5 transparencies.
Making Contact & Terms: Contact through rep. Arrange personal interview to show portfolio. Send unsolicited photos by mail for consideration. Provide resume, business card, brochure, flyer or tearsheets to be kept on file for possible future assignments. Keeps samples on file. Cannot return material. Reports in 1-2 weeks. Pays $1,200-1,500/day. Pays on receipt of invoice with purchase order. Buys all rights. Model/property release required. Credit line not given.

THE MORETON AGENCY, P.O. Box 749, East Windsor CT 06088. (203)627-0326. Art Director: Roy Kimball. Ad agency. Types of clients: industrial, sporting goods, corporate and consumer.
Needs: Works with 3-4 photographers/month. Uses photos for consumer and trade magazines, direct mail, catalogs, newspapers and literature. Subjects include: people, sports, industrial, product and fashion. Model release required.
Specs: Uses b&w prints; 35mm, 2¼×2¼, 4×5 and 8×10 transparencies.
Making Contact & Terms: Provide business card, brochure, flyer or tearsheets to be kept on file for possible future assignments. Works with freelance photographers on assignment only. Cannot return material. NPI. Credit line negotiable. Buys all rights.

Delaware

■LYONS MARKETING COMMUNICATIONS, 715 Orange St., Wilmington DE 19801. (302)654-6146. Ad agency. Senior Art Director: Erik Vaughn. Types of clients: consumer, corporate and industrial.
Needs: Works with 6 freelance photographers/month. Uses photos for consumer and trade magazine ads, direct mail, P-O-P displays, catalogs, posters and newspaper ads. Subjects vary greatly. Some fashion, many "outdoor-sport" type of things. Also, high-tech, business-to-business. Model release required; captions preferred.
Specs: Format varies by use.
Making Contact & Terms: Query with resume of credits and list of stock photo subjects. Provide resume, business card, brochure, flyer or tearsheets to be kept on file for possible future assignments. SASE. Reports in 3 weeks. NPI. Payment varies based on scope of job, abilities of the photographer. Pays on publication. Credit line given depending on job. Rights purchased vary.
Tips: "We consider the subjects, styles and capabilities of the photographer. Rather than guess at what we're looking for, show us what you're good at and enjoy doing. Be available on a tight and changing schedule; show an ability to pull together the logistics of a complicated shoot."

District of Columbia

■HILLMANN & CARR INC., 2121 Wisconsin Ave. N.W., Washington DC 20007. (202)342-0001. Art Director: Michal Carr. Estab. 1975. Types of clients: corporations, industrial, government, associations and museums.

Needs: Model releases required. Captions preferred.

Audiovisual Needs: Uses slides, films and videotapes for multimedia productions. "Subjects are extremely varied and range from the historical to current events. We do not specialize in any one subject area. Style also varies greatly depending upon subject matter."

Specs: Uses 35mm transparencies; 16mm and 35mm film.

Making Contact & Terms: Provide resume, business card, self-promotion pieces or tearsheets to be kept on file for possible future assignments. Works on assignment only. Cannot return material. "If material has been unsolicited and we do not have immediate need, material will be filed for future reference." NPI; payment and rights negotiable.

Tips: Looks for photographers with multi-image experience and artistic style. "Quality reproduction of work which can be kept on file is extremely important."

■WORLDWIDE TELEVISION NEWS (WTN), Suite 300, 1705 DeSales St. NW, Washington DC 20036. (202)835-0750. Fax: (202)887-7978. Bureau Manager, Washington: Paul C. Sisco. Estab. 1952. AV firm. "We basically supply TV news on tape, for TV networks and stations. At this time, most of our business is with foreign nets and stations."

Needs: Buys dozens of "news stories per year, especially sports." Works with 6 freelance photographers/month on assignment only. Generally hard news material, sometimes of documentary nature and sports.

Audiovisual Needs: Produces motion pictures and videotape.

Making Contact & Terms: Send name, phone number, equipment available and rates with material by mail for consideration. Provide business card to be kept on file for possible future assignments. Fast news material generally sent counter-to-air shipment; slower material by air freight. SASE. Reports in 2 weeks. Pays $100 minimum/job. Pays on receipt of material; nothing on speculation. Video rates about $500/half day, $900/full day or so. Negotiates payment based on amount of creativity required from photographer. Buys all video rights. Dupe sheets for film required.

Florida

BEBER SILVERSTEIN & PARTNERS, 3361 SW Third Ave., Miami FL 33145. (305)856-9800. Fax: (305)854-1932. Ad agency. Associate Creative Director: Joe Perz. Art Directors: James Hale, Bob Geffert. Estab. 1975. Types of clients: industrial, financial, fashion, retail and food. Examples of recent projects: Florida Power and Light and First Florida Bank.

Needs: Works with 6-10 freelance photographers/filmmakers/videographers/month. Uses photos for billboards, consumer magazines, trade magazines, direct mail, P-O-P displays, posters and newspapers.

Specs: Uses any size or finish color or b&w prints; 2¼×2¼, 4×5 or 8×10 transparencies and ¾" or ½" film.

Making Contact & Terms: Submit portfolio for review. Query with samples. Works with freelancers on assignment only. Samples kept on file. Does not return unsolicited material. Reports only if likes work. Pays $200-5,000/job. Pays in 30-60 days. Buys all rights and rights for usage over specific time; negotiable. Model and/or property release required. Credit line given sometimes, depending on price of photography.

■STEVEN COHEN MOTION PICTURE PRODUCTION, 4800 NW 96th Dr., Coral Springs FL 33076-2447. (305)346-7370. Contact: Steven Cohen. Examples of productions: TV commercials, documentaries, 2nd unit feature films and TV series - 2nd unit.

Needs: Model release required.

Specs: Uses 16mm, 35mm film; 1", ¾" U-Matic and ½" VHS, Beta videotape.

Making Contact & Terms: Query with resume, provide business card, self-promotion piece or tearsheets to be kept on file for possible future assignments. Works on assignment only. Cannot return material. Reports in 1 week. NPI. Pays on acceptance or publication. Credit line given. Buys all rights (work-for-hire).

The First Markets Index preceding the General Index in the back of this book provides the names of those companies/publications interested in receiving work from newer, lesser-known photographers.

COLEE SARTORY, Suite 405, 631 US Hwy. #1, North Palm Beach FL 33408. (407)844-7000. Ad agency. Art Director: Don Bolt. Types of clients: industrial, finance, residential.
Needs: Works with 2-3 photographers/month. Uses photographers for trade magazines, newspapers, brochures. Subjects include residential, pertaining to client.
Specs: Uses b&w and color prints; 35mm, 2¼×2¼ and 4×5 transparencies.
Making Contact & Terms: Arrange a personal interview to show portfolio. Submit portfolio for review. Provide resume, business card, brochure, flyer or tearsheets to be kept on file for possible future assignments. Works with local freelance photographers on an assignment only. Pays $50-100/hour and $250-1,000/day. Pays on receipt of invoice. Buys all rights. Model release required.

CREATIVE RESOURCES, INC., 2000 S. Dixie Highway, Miami FL 33133. (305)856-3474. Fax: (305)856-3151. Chairman and CEO: Mac Seligman. Estab. 1970. PR firm. Handles clients in travel (hotels, resorts and airlines).
Needs: Works with 1-2 freelance photographers/month on assignment only. Buys 10-20 photos/year. Photos used in PR releases. Model release preferred.
Specs: Uses 8×10 glossy prints; contact sheet OK. Also uses 35mm or 2¼×2¼ transparencies and color prints.
Making Contact & Terms: Provide resume to be kept on file for possible future assignments. Query with resume of credits. No unsolicited material. SASE. Reports in 2 weeks. Pays $50 minimum/hour; $200 minimum/day; $100/color photo; $50/b&w photo. Negotiates payment based on client's budget. For assignments involving travel, pays $60-200/day plus expenses. **Pays on acceptance.** Buys all rights.
Tips: Most interested in activity shots in locations near clients.

RICH FIELD ADVERTISING AGENCY, 2050 Spectrum Blvd., Ft. Lauderdale FL 33309. (305)938-7600. Fax: (305)938-7790. Inhouse ad agency for Interim Services. Advertising Director: Patrick Lockhart. Estab. 1946. Types of clients: temporary services.

© Mac Seligman

Mac Seligman of Creative Resources, Inc., in Miami, Florida, says there are thousands of photos of Rio de Janeiro, but this one from Sugar Loaf Mountain tells a story. The shot, taken by Seligman, was used to help promote a new hotel in Rio and Seligman liked the way the photo places the hotel "in the heart of it all."

Needs: Uses photographers for consumer magazines, trade magazines, direct mail, posters, newspapers and signage. Subjects include "People Helping People®." Reviews stock photos of people.
Specs: Uses color prints; 35mm, 2¼ × 2¼, 4 × 5 transparencies.
Making Contact & Terms: Query with resume of credits. Send unsolicited photos by mail for consideration. Cannot return material. Reports in 3 weeks or "as needed." Pays $1,000-1,500/day; other payment "depends on what service I'm going after." Pays on receipt of invoice. Buys all rights; "total buy-out only." Model release and photo captions required. Credit line given sometimes, "depending on usage."

HACKMEISTER ADVERTISING & PUBLIC RELATIONS, INC., Suite 204, 2631 E. Oakland, Ft. Lauderdale FL 33306. (305)568-2511. President: Dick Hackmeister. Estab. 1979. Ad agency and PR firm. Serves industrial, electronics manufacturers who sell to other businesses.
Needs: Works with 1 freelance photographer/month. Uses photos for trade magazines, direct mail, catalogs. Subjects include: electronic products. Model release and captions required.
Specs: Uses 8 × 10 glossy b&w and color prints and 4 × 5 transparencies.
Making Contact & Terms: "Call on telephone first." Does not return unsolicited material. Pays by the day and $200-2,000/job. Buys all rights.
Tips: Looks for "good lighting on highly technical electronic products – creativity."

RONALD LEVITT ASSOC. INC., Dept. PM, 141 Sevilla, Coral Gables FL 33134. (305)443-3223. PR firm. President: Ron Levitt. Types of clients: corporate, fashion, finance.
Needs: Works with 3-4 freelance photographers/month. Uses photos for consumer and trade magazines, direct mail, newspapers and brochures.
Specs: Uses b&w and color prints; 35mm transparencies.
Making Contact & Terms: Arrange a personal interview to show a portfolio. Provide resume, business card, brochure, flyer or tearsheets to be kept on file for possible future assignments. Works with freelance photographers on assignment only. Reports immediately. Pays $75 minimum/hour; $600 minimum/day. Pays on receipt of invoice. Buys all rights. Model release required; captions preferred. Credit line sometimes given.

■MYERS, MYERS & ADAMS ADVERTISING, INC., 938 N. Victoria Park Rd., Ft. Lauderdale FL 33304. (305)523-0202. Creative Director: Virginia Sours-Myers. Estab. 1986. Ad agency. Types of Clients: industrial, retail, fashion, finance, marine, restaurant, medical and real estate.
Needs: Works with 3-5 photographers, filmmakers and/or videographers/month. Uses photos for billboards, consumer and trade magazines, direct mail, P-O-P displays, catalogs, newspapers and audiovisual. Subjects include: marine, food, real estate, medical and fashion. Wants to see "all subjects" in stock images and footage.
Audiovisual Needs: Uses photos/film/video for slide shows, film and videotape.
Specs: Uses all sizes b&w/color prints; 35mm, 2¼ × 2¼, 4 × 5 transparencies; 35mm film; 1", ¾", but to review need ½".
Making Contact & Terms: Provide resume, business card, brochure, flyer or tearsheets to be kept on file for possible future assignments. Works with freelancers on assignment basis only. Cannot return material. Reports as needed. Pays $50-200/hour; $800-2,500/day; $50-10,000/job. Credit line given sometimes, depending on usage. Buys all rights (work-for-hire) and 1 year's usage.
Tips: "We're not looking for arty-type photos or journalism. We need photographers that understand an advertising sense of photography: good solid images that sell the product." Sees trend in advertising toward "computer-enhanced impact and color effects. Send samples, tearsheets and be patient. Please don't call us. If your work is good we keep it on file and as a style is needed we will contact the photographer. Keep us updated with new work. Advertising is using a fair amount of audiovisual work. We use a lot of stills within our commercials. Make portfolio available to production houses."

PRODUCTION INK, 2826 NE 19 Dr., Gainesville FL 32609. (904)377-8973. Fax: (904)373-1175. President: Terry Van Nortwick. Ad agency, PR firm. Types of clients: hospital, industrial, computer.
Needs: Works with 1 freelance photographer/month. Uses photos for ads, billboards, trade magazines, catalogs and newspapers. Reviews stock photos. Model release required.
Specs: Uses b&w prints and 35mm, 2¼ and 4 × 5 transparencies.
Making Contact & Terms: Arrange personal interview to show portfolio. Submit portfolio for review. Provide resume, business card, brochure, flyer or tearsheets to be kept on file for possible future assignments. Keeps samples on file. NPI. Pays on receipt of invoice. Credit line sometimes given; negotiable. Buys all rights.

*■SHERRY WHEATLEY SACINO, INC., 235 Central Ave., St. Petersburg FL 33701. (813)894-7273. Fax: (813)823-3895. Director of Client Services: Debbie Madden. Estab. 1983. PR firm. Types of clients: industrial, financial, fashion, retail and food. Examples of recent projects: Florida Power (brochures, posters); Paragon Cable (brochures, posters); Columbia Restaurants (video, brochures, posters).

Needs: Works with a varying number of freelancers/month. Photo usage depends on job and client. Subject matter varies.

Audiovisual Needs: Uses all types of audiovisual material, "depends on job and client."

Making Contact & Terms: Query with stock photo list. Query with samples. Provide resume, business card, brochure, flyer or tearsheets to be kept on file for possible future assignments. Works with local freelancers on assignment only. Keeps samples on file. Cannot return material. "Only contact when needed." NPI. Pays on receipt of invoice. Credit line sometimes given. Buys all rights; negotiable.

*SOUTHSHORE ADVERTISING INC., 5301 N. Federal Highway, Boca Raton FL 33487. (407)994-8530. Fax: (407)998-9203. Advertising Director: Todd Beitler. Estab. 1988. Ad agency. Types of clients: real estate.

Needs: Works with 1-2 freelancers/month. Uses photos for catalogs and newspapers. Subjects include: real estate, residential/commercial. Reviews stock photos on real estate. Model release preferred. Property release required. Captions preferred.

Specs: Uses color and/or b&w prints; 35mm transparencies.

Making Contact & Terms: Interested in receiving work from newer, lesser-known photographers. Arrange interview. Send unsolicited photos by mail for consideration. Works on assignment only. Keeps samples on file. SASE. Reports in 3 weeks. NPI. Pays on receipt of invoice. Credit line sometimes given depending on usage/placement. Rights negotiable.

■TEL–AIR INTERESTS, INC., 1755 NE 149th St., Miami FL 33181. (305)944-3268. Production Manager: Fred Singer. AV firm. Serves clients in business, industry and government.

Needs: Buys 10 filmstrips and 50 films/year. Uses photos for filmstrips, slide sets, multimedia kits, motion pictures, sound-slide sets and videotape. Model release required; captions preferred.

Specs: Uses b&w prints and 8 × 10 matte color prints; also 35mm transparencies.

Making Contact & Terms: Arrange a personal interview to show portfolio. Submit portfolio for review. SASE. Reports in 1 month. Pays $100 minimum/job. Pays on production. Buys all rights.

Georgia

■FRASER ADVERTISING, 1201 George C. Wilson Dr. #B, Augusta GA 30909. (706)855-0343. President: Jerry Fraser. Estab. 1980. Ad agency. Types of clients: automotive, industrial, manufacturing, residential.

Needs: Works with "possibly one freelance photographer every two or three months." Uses photos for consumer and trade magazines, catalogs, posters and AV presentations. Subject matter: "product and location shots." Also works with freelance filmmakers to produce TV commercials on videotape. Model release preferred. Property release preferred.

Specs: Uses glossy b&w and color prints; 35mm, 2¼ × 2¼ and 4 × 5 transparencies; videotape and film. "Specifications vary according to the job."

Making Contact & Terms: Interested in receiving work from newer, lesser-known photographers. Provide resume, business card, brochure, flyer or tearsheets to be kept on file for possible future assignments. Works with freelance photographers on assignment only. Cannot return unsolicited material. Reports in 1 month. NPI; payment varies according to job. Pays on publication. Buys exclusive/product and other rights; negotiable.

Tips: Prefers to see "samples of finished work – the actual ad, for example, not the photography alone. Send us materials to keep on file and quote favorably when rate is requested."

■PAUL FRENCH & PARTNERS, INC., 503 Gabbettville Rd., LaGrange GA 30240. (706)882-5581. Contact: Charles Hall. AV firm. Estab. 1969. Types of clients: industrial, corporate.

Needs: Works with freelance photographers on assignment only basis. Uses photographers for filmstrips, slide sets, multimedia. Subjects include: industrial marketing, employee training and orientation, public and community relations.

Specs: Uses 35mm and 4 × 5 color transparencies.

Making Contact & Terms: Query with resume of credits to be kept on file for possible future assignments. Pays $75-150 minimum/hour; $600-1,200/day; $150 up/job, plus travel and expenses. **Payment on acceptance.** Buys all rights, but may reassign to photographer after use.

The asterisk before a listing indicates that the market is new in this edition. New markets are often the most receptive to freelance submissions.

Tips: "We buy photojournalism . . . journalistic treatments of our clients' subjects. Portfolio: industrial process, people at work, interior furnishings product, fashion. We seldom buy single photos."

■**GRANT/GARRETT COMMUNICATIONS,** (formerly Garrett Communications), P.O. Box 53, Atlanta GA 30301. (404)755-2513. Fax: (404)755-2513. President/Owner: Ruby Grant Garrett. Estab. 1979. Ad agency. Types of clients: technical. Examples of ad campaigns: Simons (help wanted); CIS Telecom (equipment); Anderson Communication (business-to-business).
Needs: Uses photos for trade magazines, direct mail and newspapers. Interested in reviewing stock photos/video footage of people at work. Model/property release required. Photo captions preferred.
Audiovisual Needs: Uses stock video footage.
Specs: Uses 4×5 b&w prints; VHS videotape.
Making Contact & Terms: Interested in receiving work from newer, lesser-known photographers. Query with resume of credits. Query with list of stock photo subjects. Provide resume, business card, brochure, flyer or tearsheets to be kept on file for possible future assignments. Works with freelancers on an assignment basis only. SASE. Reports in 1 week. NPI; pays per job. Pays on receipt of invoice. Credit line sometimes given, depending on client. Buys one-time and other rights; negotiable.
Tips: Wants to see b&w work in portfolio.

Idaho

CIPRA AD AGENCY, 314 E. Curling Dr., Boise ID 83702. (208)344-7770. Ad agency. President: Ed Gellert. Estab. 1979. Types of clients: industrial and retail.
Needs: Works with 1 freelance photographer/month. Uses photos for trade magazines. Subjects include: electronic, industrial and scenic. Reviews general stock photos.
Specs: Uses matte and glossy 4×5, 8×10, 11×14, color, b&w prints; also 35mm and 4×5 transparencies.
Making Contact & Terms: Provide resume, business card, brochure, flyer or tearsheets to be kept on file for possible future assignments. Usually works with local freelancers only. Keeps samples on file. Cannot return material. Reports as needed. Pays $75/hour. Pays on publication. Buys all rights. Model release required.

Illinois

BRAGAW PUBLIC RELATIONS SERVICES, Suite 807, 800 E. Northwest Hwy., Palatine IL 60067. (708)934-5580. Contact: Richard S. Bragaw. Estab. 1981. PR firm. Types of clients: professional service firms, high-tech entrepreneurs.
Needs: Works with 1 freelance photographer/month. Uses photographers for trade magazines, direct mail, brochures, newspapers, newsletters/news releases. Subject matter "products and people." Model release preferred. Captions preferred.
Specs: Uses 3×5, 5×7 and 8×10 glossy prints.
Making Contact & Terms: Provide resume, business card, brochure, flyer or tearsheets to be kept on file for possible future assignments. Works with freelance photographers on assignment basis only. SASE. Pays $25-100/b&w photo; $50-200/color photo; $35-100/hour; $200-500/day; $100-1,000/job. Pays on receipt of invoice. Credit line "possible." Buys all rights; negotiable.
Tips: "Execute an assignment well, at reasonable costs, with speedy delivery."

JOHN CROWE ADVERTISING AGENCY, 1104 S. 2nd St., Springfield IL 62704. (217)528-1076. President: Bryan J. Crowe. Ad agency. Serves clients in industry, commerce, aviation, banking, state and federal government, retail stores, publishing and institutes.
Needs: Works with 1 freelance photographer/month on assignment only. Uses photos for billboards, consumer and trade magazines, direct mail, newspapers and TV. Model release required.
Specs: Uses 8×10 glossy b&w prints; also uses color 8×10 glossy prints and 2¼×2¼ transparencies.
Making Contact & Terms: Send material by mail for consideration. Provide letter of inquiry, flyer, brochure and tearsheet to be kept on file for future assignments. SASE. Reports in 2 weeks. Pays $50 minimum/job or $18 minimum/hour. Payment negotiable based on client's budget. Buys all rights.

■**EGD & ASSOCIATES, INC.,** 1801 H Hicks Rd., Rolling Meadow IL 60008. (708)991-1270. Fax: (708)991-1519. Vice President: Kathleen Williams. Estab. 1970. Ad agency. Types of clients: industrial, retail, finance. Example of ad campaigns: Gould, Bostick and Jiffy Print.
Needs: Works with 7-8 freelance photographers—videographers/month. Uses photos for billboards, consumer and trade magazines, direct mail, P-O-P displays, catalogs and audiovisual. Subjects include: industrial products and facilities. Reviews stock photos/video footage of "creative firsts." Model release required.

Audiovisual Needs: Uses photos/video for slide shows and videotape.

Specs: Uses 4×5, 8×10 b&w/color prints; 35mm, 2¼×2¼, 4×5, 8×10 transparencies; videotape.

Making Contact & Terms: Arrange personal interview to show portfolio. Provide resume, business card, brochure, flyer or tearsheets to be kept on file for possible future assignments. Works with local freelancers on assignment basis only. Cannot return material. Reports in 1-2 weeks. NPI; pays according to "client's budget." Pays on 30 days of invoice. Credit line sometimes given; credit line offered in lieu of payment.

Tips: Sees trend toward "larger budget for exclusive rights and creative firsts. Contact us every six months."

■**GOLDSHOLL DESIGN AND FILM**, Dept. PM, 420 Frontage Rd., Northfield IL 60093. (708)446-8300. Contact: Deborah Goldsholl. AV firm. Serves clients in industry and advertising agencies. Produces filmstrips, slide sets, multimedia kits, corporate brochures, merchandising material and motion pictures.

Needs: Works with 2-3 freelance photographers/month on assignment only basis. Buys 100 photos, 5 filmstrips and 25 films/year. General subjects. No industrial equipment. Length requirement: 30 seconds to 30 minutes. Reviews stock footage.

Specs: Uses 16mm and 35mm film for industrial, educational, TV, documentaries and animation. Uses contact sheet or 35mm, 2¼×2¼, 4×5 or 8×10 transparencies.

Making Contact & Terms: Query with resume. SASE. Reports in 1 week. Provide letter of inquiry and brochure to be kept on file for future assignments. NPI. Pays by the job or by the hour; negotiates payment based on client's budget, amount of creativity required from photographer, photographer's previous experience/reputation. Pays in 30 days. Buys all rights. Model release required.

OMNI ENTERPRISES, INC., 430 W. Roosevelt Rd., Wheaton IL 60187. (708)653-8200. Fax: (708)653-8218. Contact: Steve Jacobs. Estab. 1962. Ad agency and consultants.Types of clients: business, industrial, area development, economic development and financial. Examples of recent projects: capabilities brochure, Schweppes; brochure, Viking Travel Services; technical folders, ads, Thomas Engineering, Inc.

Needs: Works with an average of 3 freelance photographers/month on assignment only. Uses photos for consumer and trade magazines, direct mail, newspapers and P-O-P displays. Buys 100 photos annually. Prefers to see composites in b&w and color. Needs photos of "all varieties—industrial and machine products and human interest." Model release required.

Specs: Uses 5×7 and 8×10 glossy b&w prints; 8×10 glossy color prints. Uses 2¼×2¼, 4×5 and 8×10 transparencies. Rarely uses 35mm.

Making Contact & Terms: Provide resume, flyer, business card, brochure, composites and list of equipment to be kept on file for possible future assignments. Call for an appointment. Pays $50-500/b&w photo; $100-750/color photo; $50-200/hour; $400-2,000/day. Buys one-time, second (reprint) rights or all rights.

Tips: In portfolio or samples, wants to see "creative composition; technical abilities, (i.e., lighting, color balance, focus and consistency of quality). We need to see samples and have an idea of rates. Because we are loyal to present suppliers, it sometimes takes up to 6 months or longer before we begin working with a new photographer."

QUALLY & COMPANY, INC., Suite 3, 2238 Central St., Evanston IL 60201-1457. (708)864-6316. Creative Director: Robert Qually. Ad agency and graphic design firm. Types of clients: finance, package goods and business-to-business.

Needs: Works with 4-5 freelance photographers/month. Uses photos for billboards, consumer and trade magazines, direct mail, P-O-P displays, posters and newspapers. "Subject matter varies, but is always a 'quality image' regardless of what it portrays." Model release required.

Specs: Uses b&w and color prints; 35mm, 2¼×2¼, 4×5 and 8×10 transparencies.

Making Contact & Terms: Query with samples or submit portfolio for review. Provide resume, business card, brochure, flyer or tearsheets to be kept on file for possible future assignments. Works with local freelance photographers on assignment only. Cannot return material. Reports in 2 weeks. NPI; payment depends on circumstances. Pays on acceptance or net 45 days. Credit lines sometimes given, depending on client's cooperation. Rights purchased depend on circumstances.

■**VIDEO I-D, INC.**, 105 Muller Rd., Washington IL 61571. (309)444-4323. President: Sam B. Wagner. Types of clients: health, education, industry, cable and broadcast.

Needs: Works with 5 freelance photographers/month to shoot slide sets, multimedia productions, films and videotapes. Subjects "vary from commercial to industrial—always high quality." "Somewhat" interested in stock photos/footage. Model release required.

Specs: Uses 35mm transparencies; 16mm film; U-matic ¾" and 1" videotape, BETA SP.
Making Contact & Terms: Provide resume, business card, self-promotion piece or tearsheets to be kept on file for possible future assignments; "also send video sample reel." Works with freelancers on assignment only. SASE. Reports in 3 weeks. Pays $8-25/hour; $65-250/day. **Pays on acceptance.** Credit line sometimes given. Buys all rights.
Tips: Sample reel—indicate goal for specific pieces. "Show good lighting and visualization skills. Be willing to learn. Show me you can communicate what I need to hear — and willingness to put out effort to get top quality."

Chicago

GARFIELD-LINN & COMPANY, 142 E. Ontario Ave., Chicago IL 60611. (312)943-1900. Creative Director: Terry Hackett. Associate Creative Director: Ralph Woods. Art Director: Walter Brown. Ad agency. Types of clients: Serves a "wide variety" of accounts; client list provided upon request.
Needs: Number of freelance photographers used varies. Works on assignment only. Uses photographs for billboards, consumer and trade magazines, direct mail, brochures, catalogs and posters.
Making Contact & Terms: Arrange interview to show portfolio and query with samples. NPI. Payment is by the project; negotiates according to client's budget.

DRUCILLA HANDY CO., Suite 1500, 18 N. Stetson, Chicago IL 60601. (312)565-3900. PR firm. Executive Vice President: Susanne Wren. Handles public relations campaigns for home furnishings and products, retail, building products, other consumer products and services.
Needs: Works with one freelancer every two months. Uses photos for newspapers.
Specs: Uses 2¼ × 2¼ and 4 × 5 transparencies.
First Contact and Terms: Query with resume of credits. Works on assignment only. Does not return unsolicited material. Reports in 2 weeks. Pays $500-1,200/day "depending on assignment from client." Pays on receipt of invoice. Buys all rights. Model release and photo captions preferred. Credit line given sometimes, depending on magazine.
Tips: "Query first; mention other public relations firms and clients that you have worked with."

*■MSR ADVERTISING, INC., 1507 N. North Park Ave., Chicago IL 60610-1228. (312)440-7002. Fax: (312)440-9827. Vice President/Creative Director: Phillip Ogliore. Estab. 1983. Ad agency. Types of clients: industrial, financial, retail, food, aerospace, hospital and medical. Examples of recent projects: "Back to Basics," MPC Products; and "Throw Mother Nature a Curve," New Dimensions Center for Cosmetic Surgery.
Needs: Works with 1-2 freelance photographers, 1-2 videographers/month. Uses photos for billboards, consumer and trade magazines, direct mail, P-O-P displays, catalogs, posters and signage. Subject matter varies. Reviews stock photos. Model/property release required.
Audiovisual Needs: Uses slides and videotape for business-to-business seminars, consumer focus groups, etc. Subject matter varies.
Specs: Uses 35mm, 2¼ × 2¼, 4 × 5 and 8 × 10 transparencies.
Making Contact & Terms: Interested in receiving work from newer, lesser-known photographers. Submit portfolio for review. Send unsolicited photos by mail for consideration. Query with samples. Provide resume, business card, brochure, flyer or tearsheets to be kept on file for possible future assignments. Works on assignment only. Keeps samples on file. SASE. Reports in 1-2 weeks. NPI. Payment terms stated on invoice. Credit line sometimes given. Buys all rights; negotiable.

*RUDER FINN , 444 N. Michigan Ave., Chicago IL 60611. (312)644-8600. Executive Vice President: Hal Bergen. Estab. 1948. PR firm. Handles accounts for corporations, trade and professional associations, institutions and other organizations.
Needs: Works with 4-8 freelance photographers/month nationally on assignment only. Buys over 100 photos/year. Uses photos for publicity, AV presentations, annual stockholder reports, brochures, books, feature articles and industrial ads. Uses industrial photos to illustrate case histories; commercial photos for ads; and consumer photos—food, fashion, personal care products. Present model release on acceptance of photo.

Market conditions are constantly changing! If you're still using this book and it's 1995 or later, buy the newest edition of Photographer's Market *at your favorite bookstore or order directly from* Writer's Digest Books.

Making Contact & Terms: Provide resume, flyer, business card, tearsheets and brochure to be kept on file for possible future assignments. Query with resume of credits or call to arrange an appointment. Pays $25 minimum/hour, or $200 minimum/day. Negotiates payment based on client's budget and photographer's previous experience/reputation.
Tips: Prefers to see publicity photos in a portfolio. Will not view unsolicited material.

*SANDRA SANOSKI COMPANY, INC., 166 E. Superior St., Chicago IL 60611. (312)664-7795. President: Sandra Sanoski. Estab. 1974. Ad agency specializing in display and publication design, packaging. Types of clients: retail and consumer goods.
Needs: Works with 3-4 freelancers/month. Uses photos for catalogs and packaging. Subject matter varies. Reviews stock photos. Model/property release required.
Specs: Uses 35mm, 2¼×2¼, 4×5, 8×10 transparencies.
Making Contact & Terms: Interested in receiving work from newer, lesser-known photographers. Arrange personal interview to show portfolio. Works on assignment only. Keeps samples on file. SASE. NPI. Pays net 30 days. Credit line not given. Buys all rights.

*SELZ, SEABOLT AND ASSOCIATES, 221 N. LaSalle, Chicago IL 60601. (312)372-7090. Fax: (312)372-6160. Graphic Coordinator: Charles Hutchinson. Estab. 1927. PR firm. Types of clients: industrial, financial, fashion, retail and food.
Needs: Works with 3 freelance photographers and 4 videographers/month. Uses photos for trade magazines, direct mail, catalogs and newspapers. Subjects include people and product shots. Reviews all types stock photos. Model/property release preferred. Captions preferred.
Audiovisual Needs: Uses slides and videotape.
Specs: Uses color/b&w prints; 35mm 2¼×2¼, 4×5 transparencies.
Making Contact & Terms: Interested in receiving work from newer, lesser-known photographers. Query with resume of credits. Works with freelancers on assignment only. Keeps samples on file. Cannot return material. Reports in 3 weeks. Pays $75/hour; $40/b&w photo. Pays on receipt of invoice. Credit line sometimes given. Buys one-time and all rights.
Tips: Looks for strong technique and style.

*■THOMAS & JAMES ADVERTISING, INC., Suite 1407, 135 S. LaSalle St., Chicago IL 60603. (312)629-1500. Fax: (312)629-1501. Creative Director: Thomas J. Wolst. Estab. 1990. Ad agency. Types of clients: financial, fashion, retail and recycling. Examples of recent projects: "Gold of Africa," The Art Institute of Chicago (print/radio); "Ho Ho Holiday Sale," Rosalee Stores, Inc. (print/radio/TV); "Don't Throw Our World Away," Nu-Recycling Technology, Inc. (print).
Needs: Works with a varying number of freelance photographers and filmmakers/month. Uses photos for direct mail, catalogs, newspapers, and signage. Subject matter varies. Reviews stock photos. Model (for fashion models) and property release preferred. Captions preferred (title, medium, date, photographer).
Audiovisual Needs: Uses videotape for commercials.
Specs: Uses 4×5 gloss/matte, color and/or b&w prints; 4×5 transparencies; 1″ film and ½″ videotape.
Making Contact & Terms: Interested in receiving work from newer, lesser-known photographers. Arrange personal interview to show portfolio. Provide resume, business card, brochure, flyer or tearsheets to be kept on file for possible future assignments. Works on assignment only. Keeps samples on file. Cannot return material. Reporting time varies. NPI. Pays on receipt of invoice, 30 days. Credit line not given. Buys one-time rights; negotiable.
Tips: Looks for "fresh, new ideas. . . . sellable presentation. . . . bold, strong impact. Thomas & James tends to use simple images. We don't want to make a prospective buyer have to work to understand our message and that of the image."

Indiana

*HP DIRECT, 5561 W. 74th St., Indianapolis IN 46268. (317)328-4650. Fax: (317)328-4646. Creative Director: Polly McNeal. Estab. 1984. Ad agency. Types of clients: industrial, financial and nonprofit organizations. Examples of recent projects: "Remember When" (membership renewal program), The American Legion; "If only they could talk" (fall '92 fundraiser), Humane Society of Indianapolis.
Needs: Works with 2-3 freelance photographers and 1-2 videographers/month. Uses photos for consumer magazines, trade magazines, direct mail, P-O-P displays, catalogs, posters, signage and audiovisual. Subjects include: war era, war veterans, family, environmental, humanitarian efforts. Reviews stock photos. Model/property release required.
Audiovisual Needs: Uses slides and videotape for various projects.
Specs: Uses all sizes and finishes color/b&w prints; 35mm, 2¼×2¼ transparencies.
Making Contact & Terms: Interested in receiving work from newer, lesser-known photographers. Submit portfolio for review. Provide resume, business card, brochure, flyer or tearsheets to be kept on file for possible future assignments. Works with local freelancers on assignment only. Keeps samples

on file. SASE. Reports in 1 month. NPI. Pays on receipt of invoice. Credit line not given. Buys all rights.

■**KELLER CRESCENT COMPANY**, 1100 E. Louisiana, Evansville IN 47701. (812)426-7551 or (812)464-2461. Manager Still Photography: Cal Barrett. Ad agency, PR and AV firm. Serves industrial, consumer, finance, food, auto parts and dairy products clients. Types of clients: Old National Bank, Community Coffee and Eureka Vac's.
Needs: Works with 2-3 freelance photographers/month on assignment only basis. Uses photos for billboards, consumer and trade magazinmes, direct mail, newspapers, P-O-P displays, radio and TV. Model release required.
Specs: Uses 8×10 b&w prints; 35mm, 4×5 and 8×10 transparencies.
Making Contact & Terms: Query with resume of credits, list of stock photo subjects. Send material by mail for consideration. Provide business card, tearsheets and brochure to be kept on file for possible future assignments. Prefers to see printed samples, transparencies and prints. Cannot return material. Pays $200-2,500/job; negotiates payment based on client's budget, amount of creativity required from photographer and photographer's previous experience/reputation. Buys all rights.

■**OMNI COMMUNICATIONS**, 655 W. Carmel Dr., Carmel IN 46032. (317)844-6664. Senior President: Winston Long. AV firm. Types of clients: industrial, corporate, educational, governmental and medical.
Needs: Works with 6-12 freelance photographers/month. Uses photographers for AV presentations. Subject matter varies. Also works with freelance filmmakers to produce training films and commercials.
Specs: Uses b&w and color prints; 35mm transparencies; 16mm and 35mm film and videotape.
Making Contact & Terms: Provide resume, business card, brochure, flyer or tearsheets to be kept on file for possible future assignments. Works with freelance photographers on assignment basis only. Does not return unsolicited material. NPI. **Pays on acceptance.** Buys all rights "on most work; will purchase one-time use on some projects." Model release required. Credit line given "sometimes, as specified in production agreement with client."

Kansas

MARKETAIDE, INC., Dept. PM, 1300 E. Iron, P.O. Box 500, Salina KS 67402-0500. (913)825-7161. Fax: (913)825-4697. Production Manager: Kendi Carlgren. Creative Director: Ted Hale. Ad agency. Uses all media. Serves industrial, retail, financial, nonprofit organizations, agribusiness and manufacturing clients.
Needs: Needs industrial photography (studio and on site), agricultural photography, and photos of banks, people and places.
Making Contact & Terms: Call to arrange an appointment. Provide resume and tearsheets to be kept on file for possible future assignments. Reports in 3 weeks. SASE. Buys all rights. "We generally work on a day rate ranging from $200-1,000/day." Pays within 30 days of invoice.
Tips: Photographers should have "a good range of equipment and lighting, good light equipment portability, high quality darkroom work for b&w, a wide range of subjects in portfolio with examples of processing capabilities." Prefers to see "set-up shots, lighting, people, heavy equipment, interiors, industrial and manufacturing" in a portfolio. Prefers to see "8×10 minimum size on prints, or 35mm transparencies, preferably unretouched" as samples.

PAT PATON PUBLIC RELATIONS/PATON & ASSOCIATES, INC., P.O. Box 7350, Leawood KS 66207. (913)491-4000. Contact: N.E. (Pat) Paton, Jr. Estab. 1956. Ad agency. Clients: medical, financial, home furnishing, professional associations, vacations resorts, theatre and entertainment.
Needs: Uses photos for billboards, consumer and trade magazines, direct mail, newspapers, P-O-P displays and TV. Model release required. Captions required.
Making Contact & Terms: Interested in receiving work from newer, lesser known photographers. Call for personal appointment to show portfolio. Works on assignment only. NPI. Payment negotiable according to amount of creativity required from photographer.

Kentucky

■**BARNEY MILLERS INC.**, 232 E. Main St., Lexington KY 40507. (606)252-2216. Fax: (606)253-1115. Chairman: Harry Miller. Estab. 1922. Types of clients: retail, legal and government. Examples of recent projects: Bluegrass AAA (internal training); Bank One (internal training); and Renfro Valley (television promotion).

Needs: Works with 3-4 freelance photographers/month. Uses photographers for video transfer, editing and titling. Reviews stock photos/footage. Captions preferred.
Specs: Uses b&w and color prints; 35mm transparencies; 8mm, super 8, 16mm and 35mm film.
Making Contact & Terms: Arrange a personal interview to show portfolio or submit portfolio by mail. Provide resume, business card, self-promotion piece or tearsheets to be kept on file for possible future assignments. Works with local freelancers only. SASE. Reports in 1 week. Pays $35-200/hour. **Pays on acceptance.** Credit line given if desired.

■KINETIC CORPORATION, 240 Distillery Commons, Louisville KY 40206. (502)583-1679. Fax: (502)583-1104. Director of Creative Service: Stephen Metzger. Estab. 1968. Types of clients: industrial, financial, fashion, retail and food.
Needs: Works with freelance photographers and/or videographers as needed. Uses photos for audiovisual and print. Subjects include: location photography. Model and/or property release required.
Audiovisual Needs: Uses photos for slides and videotape.
Specs: Uses varied sizes and finishes color and b&w prints; 35mm, 2¼ × 2¼, 4 × 5, 8 × 10 transparencies; and ¾" Beta SP videotape.
Making Contact & Terms: Provide resume, business card, brochure, flyer or tearsheets to be kept on file for possible future assignments. Works with local freelancers only. Keeps samples on file. SASE. Reports only when interested. Pays $100-200/hour; $750-1,000/day. Pays within 30 days. Buys all rights.

*■PRATHER & ASSOCIATES INC., 208 Goldrush Rd., Lexington KY 40503. (606)278-5856. Fax: (606)278-5856. Creative Director: Doug Prather. Estab. 1982. Ad agency. Types of clients: industrial, financial, retail, commercial, equine and medical. Examples of recent clients: Valvoline, Long John Silvers and Kentucky Textiles.
Needs: Works with 2-4 freelance photographers/month. Uses photos for consumer and trade magazines, direct mail, P-O-P displays, catalogs, posters, annual reports and packaging. Subject matter varies. Reviews stock photos. Model release required. Property release negotiable. Captions negotiable.
Audiovisual Needs: Uses film.
Specs: Uses 11 × 14 glossy color prints; 2¼ × 2¼, 4 × 5, 8 × 10 transparencies; EPR, EPX, VPS videotape.
Making Contact & Terms: Interested in receiving work from newer, lesser-known photographers. Contact through rep. Submit portfolio for review. Query with stock photo list. Send unsolicited photos by mail for consideration. Query with samples. Provide resume, business card, brochure, flyer or tearsheets to be kept on file for possible future assignments. Works with freelancers on assignment only. Keeps samples on file. SASE. Reports in 1-2 weeks. Pays $75-125/hour; $750-1200/day. Pays on receipt of invoice. Credit line sometimes given depending on negotiations, publications and client. Buys all rights; negotiable.

Louisiana

RICHARD SACKETT EXECUTIVE CONSULTANTS, Suite 3400, 101 Howard Ave., New Orleans LA 70113. (504)522-4040. Ad agency. Creative Director: Ginger Legeai. Types of clients: industrial, optical, retail, real estate, hotel, shopping center management, marine. Client list free with SASE.
Needs: Works with 3 photographers/month. Uses photographers for billboards, consumer and trade magazines, direct mail, P-O-P displays, posters, newspapers. Subject matter includes merchandise, places, scenery of the city, scenery of the sites of construction, mood photos and food.
Specs: Uses 35mm, 4 × 5 and 8 × 10 transparencies.
Making Contact & Terms: Arrange a personal interview to show portfolio; send unsolicited photos by mail for consideration. Works with freelance photographers on an assignment basis only. SASE. Reports in 1 week. Pays $600-1,000/day and $3,000-40,000/job. Pays on publication or on receipt of invoice. Buys all rights. Model release required. Credit line given when appropriate.

Maryland

*■MARC SMITH COMPANY, INC., P.O. Box 5005, Severna Park MD 21146. (410)647-2606. Art Director: Ed Smith. Estab. 1963. Ad agency. Types of clients: industrial. Client list on request with SASE.
Needs: Uses photos for trade magazines, direct mail, catalogs, slide programs and trade show booths. Subjects include: products, sales literature (still life), commercial buildings (interiors and exteriors). Model release required for building owners, designers, incidental persons. Captions required.

Specs: Vary: b&w and color prints and transparencies.
Making Contact & Terms: Provide resume, business card, brochure, flyer or tearsheets to be kept on file for possible future assignments. Works with freelance photographers on assignment only. Cannot return material. Reports in 1 month. NPI; pays by the job. Pays when client pays agency, usually 30-60 days. Buys all rights.
Tips: Wants to see "proximity, suitability, cooperation and reasonable rates."

Massachusetts

■**CRAMER PRODUCTION CENTER**, Dept. PM, 355 Wood Rd., Braintree MA 02184. (617)849-3350. Fax: (617)849-6165. Film/video production company. Operations Manager: Maura MacMillan. Estab. 1982. Types of clients: industrial, financial, fashion, retail and food. Examples of recent projects: 3-D music video for Meditech; "Walktoberfest," National Diabetes (PSA broadcast); and New England Chevy campaign, Cuneo Sullivan Dolabany Wilgus (broadcast spot).
Audiovisual Needs: Works with 3-8 freelance filmmakers and/or videographers/month for P-O-P displays and audiovisual. Subjects include: industrial to broadcast/machines to people. Reviews stock film or video footage. Uses film and videotape.
Making Contact & Terms: Send demo of work, ¾″ or VHS videotape. Query with resume of credits. Works on assignment only. Keeps samples on file. Reports in 1 month. Pays $175-560/day, depending on job and level of expertise needed. Pays 30 days from receipt of invoice. Buys all rights. Model/property release required. Credit line sometimes given, depending on how the program is used.
Tips: Looks for experience in commercial video production. "Don't be discouraged if you don't get an immediate response. When we have a need, we'll call you."

■**FOREMOST COMMUNICATIONS**, (formerly Foremost Films & Video, Inc.), P.O. Box 823, Framingham MA 01701. (800)369-6527. Fax: (508)429-1065. President: David Fox. Estab. 1983. Video production/post production multi-media company. Types of clients: consumer, industrial and corporate. Examples of recent projects: Nahatan Medical (newsletter); The Smiling Lady (catalog); Enron Power/Jones Capital Corp. (marketing/documentation video project).
Needs: Works with 2-4 freelance photographers/videographers/month. Varied subjects. Reviews area footage. Model/property release required. Captions preferred.
Audiovisual Needs: Uses videotape; photos, all media related materials. "We are primarily producers of video, multimedia and photography."
Specs: Uses 35mm transparencies, slides and ½″, SVHS and all formats and standards of videotape.
Making Contact & Terms: Arrange personal interview to show portfolio. Provide resume, business card, brochure, flyer or tearsheets to be kept on file for possible future assignments. Works on assignment only. Keeps samples on file. Cannot return material. Reports in 1 month. NPI; payment depends on project, person's experience to match project—fee is negotiated. Pays within 30 days. Credit line sometimes given depending on situation and client. Buys all rights; negotiable.
Tips: Looks for style, abilities, quality and commitment and availability in reviewing freelancer's work. "We are expanding our commercial photography and audiovisual areas, including multimedia. We see a trend toward inclusion of photos with computer graphics and video. We tend to have more need in springtime and fall, than other times of the year. We're very diversified in our services—projects come along and we use people on an as-need basis."

MILLER COMMUNICATIONS, INC., Dept. PM, 607 Boylston, Copley Sq., Boston MA 02116. (617)536-0470. Supervisor: Marisa Tazzini. PR firm. Handles high technology/computer accounts, computer communication. Photos used in press kits, consumer and trade magazines.
Needs: Most interested in editorial type: photographs, head shots, creative product shots, user shots, equipment and press conference coverage.
Specs: Uses contact sheet; also 2¼×2¼ transparencies or color contact sheet and negatives.
Making Contact & Terms: Commissions 10 photographers/year. Pays $75 minimum/half day. Buys all rights. Model release preferred.
Tips: "Select a product the agency is representing and make up a portfolio showing this particular product from the simplest photography to the most sophisticated image-builder. Photographers we need must be thinkers, philosophers, not impulsive types who take 600 slides from which we can select 1 or 2 good pictures."

■**TR PRODUCTIONS**, 1031 Commonwealth Ave., Boston MA 02215. (617)783-0200. Executive Vice President: Ross P. Benjamin. Types of clients: industrial, commercial and educational.
Needs: Works with 1-2 freelance photographers/month. Uses photographers for slide sets and multimedia productions. Subjects include: people shots, manufacturing/sales and facilities.
Specs: Uses 35mm transparencies.
Making Contact & Terms: Provide resume, business card, self-promotion piece or tearsheets to be kept on file for possible future assignments. Works with local freelancers by assignment only; interested in stock photos/footage. Does not return unsolicited material. Reports "when needed." Pays $500-1,000/day. Pays "14 days after acceptance." Buys all AV rights.

Michigan

■CREATIVE HOUSE ADVERTISING, INC., Suite 301, 30777 Northwestern Hwy., Farmington Hills MI 48334. (313)737-7077. Senior Vice President/Executive Creative Director: Robert G. Washburn. Ad agency. Uses photos for brochures, catalogs, annual reports, billboards, consumer and trade magazines, direct mail, newspapers, P-O-P displays, radio and TV. Types of clients: retail, industry, finance and commercial products.
Needs: Works with 4-5 freelance photographers/year on assignment only. Also produces TV commercials and demo film. Model release required.
Audiovisual Needs: Uses 35mm and 16mm film.
Specs: Uses b&w and color prints; transparencies.
Making Contact & Terms: Arrange personal interview to show portfolio. Query with resume of credits, samples or list of stock photo subjects. Submit portfolio for review ("Include your specialty and show your range of versatility"). Send material by mail for consideration. Provide resume, business card, brochure, flyer and anything to indicate the type and quality of photos to be kept on file for future assignments. Local freelancers preferred. SASE. Reports in 2 weeks. Pays $100-200/hour or $800-1,600/day; negotiates payment based on client's budget and photographer's previous experience/reputation. Pays in 1-3 months, depending on the job. Does not pay royalties. Buys all rights.

*■ROBERT HUND INCORPORATED, 33505 State, Farmington MI 48335. (313)476-5555. Fax: (313)476-1630. President: Robert Hund. Estab. 1967. Ad agency, PR firm, Association Management. Types of clients: industrial and construction. Examples of recent projects: Marble Institute of America, Great Lakes Ceramic Tile Council, Water Control International.
Needs: Uses photos for trade magazines. Subjects include: construction/industrial. Reviews stock photos. Model/property release required.
Audiovisual Needs: Uses slides and videotape for presentation. Subjects include construction/industrial.
Making Contact & Terms: Query with resume of credits. Provide resume, business card, brochure, flyer or tearsheets. Does not keep samples on file. Cannot return material. Reporting time varies. NPI. Pays on receipt of invoice. Credit line sometimes given depending on project. Buys all rights.

*J.W. MESSNER, INC., Suite 403, 161 Ottawa NE, Grand Rapids MI 49503. (616)458-8384. Fax: (616)458-8786. Art Director: Pam Bogacz. Estab. 1977. Types of clients: industrial, retail, food and automotive.
Needs: Works with 6 freelance photographers and 10 videographers/month. Uses photos for billboards, consumer and trade magazines, direct mail, newspapers and audiovisual. Subjects include: animals, locations, people—healthcare, industrial. Model release required. Property release preferred.
Audiovisual Needs: Uses film or videotape. Subjects include: "depends on project."
Specs: 11×14 color/b&w prints; 2¼×2¼, 4×5, 8×10 transparencies.
Making Contact & Terms: Send unsolicited photos by mail for consideration. Provide resume, business card, brochure, flyer or tearsheets to be kept on file for possible future assignments. Works with freelancers on assignment only. Keeps samples on file. Cannot return material. Reports in 1 month. NPI; payment quoted per project. Pays on publication. Credit line not given. Buys all rights.
Tips: Likes to match photographer's style with the project.

■PHOTO COMMUNICATION SERVICES, INC., P.O. Box 508, Acme MI 49610. (616)922-3050. President: M'Lynn Hartwell Jackson. Estab. 1970. Commercial/Illustrative and AV firm. Types of clients: commercial/industrial, fashion, food, general, human interest. Examples of recent projects: Harper & Row, internal corporate AV communications; Zondervan Family Bookstores, a semiannual AV production for vendor recruitment/sales promotion; and General Electric Corp.
Needs: Works with variable number of freelance photographers/month. Uses photos for catalogs, P-O-P displays, AV presentations, trade magazines and brochures. Photos used for a "large variety of subjects." Sometimes works with freelance filmmakers. Model release required.

 The solid, black square before a listing indicates that the market uses various types of audiovisual materials, such as slides, film or videotape.

Audiovisual Needs: Primarily needs 35mm slides for industrial multi-image; also video and some film.

Specs: Uses 8 × 10 gloss and semigloss b&w and color prints (or larger); 35mm, 2¼ × 2¼, 4 × 5 and 8 × 10 transparencies; 16mm film; VHS/SVHS and ¾″ videotape.

Making Contact & Terms: Query with resume of credits, samples or list of stock photo subjects. Works with freelance photographers on assignment basis only. SASE. Reports in 1 month. Pays $25-150/hour, $100-1,000/day, or private negotiation. Pays 30 days from acceptance. Credit line given "whenever possible." Rights negotiated.

Tips: Looks for professionalism in portfolio or demos. "Be professional and to the point. If I see something I can use I will make an appointment to discuss the project in detail. We also have a library of stock photography."

ROSS ROY, INC., 100 Bloomfield Hills Parkway, Bloomfield Hills MI 48304. (313)433-6000. Ad agency. Contact: Art Director. Types of clients: Chrysler, K-Mart, FTD, Ameritech, La-Z-Boy, State of Michigan.

Needs: Uses freelance photographers for billboards, consumer and trade magazines, P-O-P displays, catalogs, posters, and newspapers. Subjects include retail, corporate, fashion, automotive, product.

Specs: Uses 8 × 10, 11 × 14 matte b&w prints; "all formats" transparencies.

Making Contact & Terms: Arrange a personal interview to show portfolio. Provide resume, business card, brochure, flyer or tearsheets to be kept on file for possible future assignments. Works with freelance photographers on assignment only. Does not return unsolicited material. Pays $250-1,500/ b&w photo; $300-2,500/color photo; $750-2,000/day. Pays on receipt of invoice. Buys all rights. Model release required.

Tips: Prefers to see lighting, design and a sense of style and individuality. Contact Jean Oliveri for list of art directors; contact art directors individually for interview, or send tearsheets, flyers, etc. if out-of-town. "We use photography extensively, but tend to use mostly local for advertising; out-of-town (location) for automotive. Be persistent in calling to set up the initial contact, but don't be pesky. Work looks best as a combination of laminated tearsheets and mounted transparencies."

■**SOUNDLIGHT PRODUCTIONS,** 1915 Webster, Birmingham MI 48009. (313)642-3502. Fax: (313)642-3502. Contact: Terry Keth Luke. Estab. 1972. Types of clients: corporations, industrial, businesses, training institutions, astrological and spiritual workshops and books and fashion magazines. Examples of productions: "Heavytruck Computer Stories," Rockwell International; and "What Can It Do?" Arcade Machine.

Needs: Works with 1-2 freelance photographers/month. Subjects include: city people in activities, business activities, industrial, scenic landscapes, animals, travel sites and activities, dance and models (glamour and nude). Reviews stock photos, film or video. Model release required, for models and advertising people. Captions preferred; include "who, what, where."

Audiovisual Needs: Uses freelance photographers for slide sets, multimedia productions and videotapes.

Specs: Uses 8 × 10 b&w prints, 5 × 7 and 8 × 10 glossy color prints, 35mm color slides; VHS, U-matic ¾″ and SVHS videotape.

Making Contact & Terms: Query with resume. Send stock photo list. Provide resume, slides, business card, self-promotion piece or tearsheets to be kept on file for possible future assignments. Works on assignment only. May not return unsolicited material. Reports in 2 weeks. Pays $5-100/b&w and color photo; $10-100/hour; $50-750/day; $2,000 maximum/job; sometimes also pays in "trades." Pays on publication. Credit line sometimes given. Buys one-time rights and various negotiable rights; depends on use.

Tips: In portfolios or demos, looks for "unique lighting, style, emotional involvement, beautiful, artistic viewpoint." Sees trend toward "more use of video, and manipulated computer images." To break into AV work, "join AV organizations, shoot stills of productions, volunteer your help, etc."

*****VARON & ASSOCIATES, INC.,** 31333 Southfield Rd., Beverly Hills MI 48025. (313)645-9730. Fax: (313)642-1303. President: Jerry Varon. Estab. 1963. Ad agency. Types of clients: industrial and retail.

Needs: Uses photos for trade magazines, catalogs and audiovisual. Subjects include: industrial. Reviews stock photos. Model/property release required. Captions preferred.

Audiovisual Needs: Uses slides and videotape for sales and training. Subjects include: industrial.

Specs: Uses 8 × 10 color prints; 4 × 5 transparencies.

Making Contact & Terms: Interested in receiving work from newer, lesser-known photographers. Arrange personal interview to show portfolio. Works with freelancers on assignment only. Keeps samples on file. Cannot return material. Reports in 1-2 weeks. Pays $1,000/day. **Pays on acceptance.** Credit line sometimes given. Buys all rights.

■**WALLER, COOK & MISAMORE ADVERTISING & PUBLIC RELATIONS,** Suite 100, 3001 Orchard Vista Dr. SE, Grand Rapids MI 49456. (616)940-0900. Ad agency. Art Director: Scott Scheerhorn. Types of clients: industrial, business-to-business. Client list free with SASE.
Needs: Works with 4-5 freelance photographers/month. Uses photographers for trade magazines, direct mail, P-O-P displays, catalogs, posters, AV presentations, case history articles. Subjects include products, illustrative, facilities, etc.
Specs: Uses all sizes b&w and color prints; 35mm, 2¼×2¼, 4×5, 8×10 transparencies, "all depending on situation."
Making Contact & Terms: Query with resume of credits and samples. Provide resume, business card, brochure, flyer or tearsheets to be kept on file for possible future assignments. Works with freelance photographers on assignment only. Does not return unsolicited material. Reports in 1 week. Pays $50-200/hour; $300-1,500/day; $150/b&w photo; $600/color photo. Pays within 30 days. Buys all rights. Model release required.
Tips: Prefers to see industrial, products and/or location photography. "Please send letter, credentials, and samples printed if available."

Minnesota

■**BUTWIN & ASSOCIATES ADVERTISING, INC.,** Suite 120, 7515 Wayzata Blvd., Minneapolis MN 55426. (612)546-0203. President: Ron Butwin. Estab. 1977. Ad agency. Types of clients: industrial, retail, corporate.
Needs: Works with 1-2 freelance photographers/month. Uses photos for billboards, direct mail, catalogs, newspapers, consumer magazines, P-O-P displays, posters, AV presentations, trade magazines, brochures and signage. Uses "a wide variety" of subjects and styles. Model release required.
Audiovisual Needs: Works with freelance filmmakers to produce TV commercials and training films.
Specs: Uses all sizes b&w or color prints; 35mm and 2¼×2¼, 4×5 and 8×10 transparencies; 16mm film and videotape.
Making Contact & Terms: Interested in receiving work from newer, lesser-known photographers. Provide resume, business card, brochure, flyer or tearsheets to be kept on file for possible future assignments. Cannot return material. NPI. Credit line sometimes given. Usually buys all rights.

■**CARMICHAEL-LYNCH, INC.,** 800 Hennepin Ave., Minneapolis MN 55403. (612)334-6000. Ad agency. Executive Creative Director: Jack Supple. Send info to: Kathy Dalager, Art Buyer. Types of clients: recreational vehicles, food, finance, healthcare, wide variety.
Needs: Uses many freelance photographers/month. Uses photographers for billboards, consumer and trade magazines, direct mail, P-O-P displays, brochures, posters, newspapers, and other media as needs arise. Also works with freelance filmmakers to produce TV commercials.
Specs: Uses all formats; 16mm and 35mm film and videotape.
Making Contact & Terms: Provide resume, business card, brochure, flyer or tearsheets to be kept on file for possible future assignments. Submit portfolio for review. Arrange a personal interview to show portfolio. Works with freelance photographers on assignment basis only. NPI. Pay depends on contract. Buys all rights or one-time rights, "depending on agreement." Model release required.
Tips: "No 'babes on bikes!' In a portfolio, we prefer to see the photographer's most creative work— not necessarily ads. Show only your most technically, artistically satisfying work."

*■**HP COMMUNICATIONS,** 13408 Oliver Ave. S., Burnsville MN 55337. (612)894-8352. Fax: (612)894-8352. President: Harry Prestanski. Estab. 1989. PR firm. Types of clients: industrial, fashion, retail and associations. Examples of recent projects: Cargill Salt, Solarchem Resources and Winnebago.
Needs: Works with 1 freelance photographer/month. Uses photos for consumer and trade magazines, posters, newspapers and audiovisual. Subject matter varies. Reviews stock photos. Model/property release required.
Audiovisual Needs: Uses slides and videotape. Subject matter varies.
Specs: Uses all formats. Videotape, Betacom preferred also ¾".
Making Contact & Terms: Interested in receiving work from newer, lesser-known photographers. Provide resume, business card, brochure, flyer or tearsheets to be kept on file for possible future assignments. Works with freelancers on assignment only. Keeps samples on file. Cannot return material. Reports back 1 month. Pays $50-150/hour; $200-800/day; $400-2,000/job. Pays on receipt of invoice. Credit line not given. Buys all rights.

The code NPI (no payment information given) appears in listings that have not given specific payment amounts.

MARTIN-WILLIAMS ADVERTISING INC., 10 S. 5th St., Minneapolis MN 55402. (612)340-0800. Fax: (612)342-9716. Production Coordinator/Buyer: Lyle Studt. Estab. 1947. Ad agency. Types of clients: industrial, retail, fashion, finance, agricultural, business-to-business and food. Client list free with SASE.

Needs: Works with 6-12 photographers/month. Uses photos for billboards, consumer and trade magazines, direct mail, catalogs, posters and newspapers. Subject matter varies. Model/property release required.

Specs: Uses 8 × 10 and larger b&w and color prints; 35mm, 2¼ × 2¼, 4 × 5 and 8 × 10 transparencies.

Making Contact & Terms: Arrange a personal interview to show portfolio. Provide resume, business card, flyer or tearsheets to be kept on file for possible future assignments. Works with freelance photographers on an assignment basis only. SASE. Reports in 2 weeks. Payment individually negotiated. Pays $500-2,400/b&w photo; $500-2,800/color photo; $100-350/hour; $800-2,800/day; $800-$12,000/complete job. Pays on receipt of invoice. Buys one-time rights or all rights.

Tips: Looks for "high quality work, imagination."

■**MEDIAWERKS**, 1400 Homer Rd., Winona MN 55987. (507)454-1400. Creative Director: Rich Hultman. Estab. 1975. Ad agency. Types of clients: industrial, retail, fashion, finance and landscape.

Needs: Works with 4 freelance photographers/month; various number of videographers/month. Photos used for billboards, consumer and trade magazines, direct mail, P-O-P displays, catalogs, posters, signage and newspapers. Subjects include: fashion, tabletop, and industrial. Model release required.

Audiovisual Needs: Recently added video editing (electronic) capabilities.

Specs: Uses b&w and color prints, and transparencies; all sizes.

Making Contact & Terms: Send unsolicited photos by mail for consideration. Provide resume, business card, brochure, flyer or tearsheets to be kept on file for possible future assignments. Works with freelance photographers on assignment basis only. Cannot return material. Pays $200-400/b&w photo; $400-700/color photo; $50-100/hour; $500-1,000/day. Pays on receipt of invoice. Buys exclusive product rights and one-time rights.

Tips: Prefers to see fashion, tabletop photos, stock, industrial, outdoor environment, archival. "Submit samples of best work which includes approximate costs and type of involvement."

Missouri

AARON D. CUSHMAN AND ASSOCIATES, INC., Suite 900, 7777 Bonhomme, St. Louis MO 63105. (314)725-6400. Executive Vice President/General Manager: Joseph B. McNamara. PR, marketing and sales promotion firm. Types of clients: real estate, manufacturing, travel and tourism, telecommunications, consumer products, corporate counseling.

Needs: Works with 3-5 freelance photographers/month. Uses photographers for news releases, special events photography, and various printed pieces. More news than art oriented.

Making Contact & Terms: Call for appointment to show portfolio. Pays $50-100/b&w photo; $50-250/color photo; $50-100/hour; $350-750/day.

Tips: "We are using increasing amounts of architecturally oriented and consumer product-related stills."

EVERETT, BRANDT & BERNAUER, INC., 1805 Grand Ave., Kansas City MO 64108. (816)421-0000. Contact: James A. Everett. Estab. 1967. Ad agency. Types of clients: construction, finance, industrial, auto dealership, agribusiness, insurance accounts. Examples of recent projects: Special-T-Metals, Independence School District and Missouri Valley Electric Company (all four-color brochures).

● This firm recently received an award from the Public Relations Society of America for work done on the *Organ Bank* newsletter. Also received the Commercial Media Award in 1992 for promotion of the Spina Bifida Association.

Needs: Works with 1-2 freelance photographers/month on assignment basis only. Buys 25 photos/year. Uses photos in brochures, newsletters, annual reports, PR releases, AV presentations, sales literature, consumer and trade magazines. Model release required.

Specs: Uses 5 × 7 b&w and color prints; transparencies.

Making Contact & Terms: Interested in receiving work from newer, lesser-known photographers. Arrange a personal interview to show portfolio. Provide resume and business card to be kept on file for possible future assignments. Prefers to work with local freelancers. SASE. Reports in 1 week. NPI; negotiates payment based on client's budget and amount of creativity required from photographer. Buys all rights; negotiable.

Tips: "We have a good working relationship with three local photographers and would rarely go outside of their expertise unless work load or other factors change the picture."

GGH&M ADVERTISING, Suite 136, 11500 Olive Blvd., St. Louis MO 63141. (314)991-5311. Fax: (314)991-5260. Contact: Art Director. Estab. 1968. Ad agency. Types of clients: retail, fashion and finance. Client list free with SASE.

Needs: Works with 2-3 photographers/month. Uses photos for consumer and trade magazines, posters and newspapers. Subjects include products to fashion shots. Model and property releases required. Photo captions required.

Making Contact & Terms: Interested in receiving work from newer, lesser-known photographers. Query with samples and outline of experience. Provide business card or flyer to be kept on file for possible future assignments. Works with freelance photographers on assignment only. SASE. NPI. Pays by the job. Buys all rights; rights negotiable. Photo captions required.

Tips: "More responsibility rests with photographer to suggest ideas, handle props and model accessories."

KUPPER PARKER COMMUNICATIONS INC., 6900 Delmar, St. Louis MO 63130. (314)727-4000. Fax: (314)727-3034. Advertising, public relations and direct mail firm. Creative Director: Peter A.M. Charlton. Senior Art Directors: Deborah Boggs, Michael Smith. Art Directors: William Tuttle, Jeff Twardoski, Anthony Patti. Graphic Designers: Lisa Taylor, John Mank. Estab. 1992. Types of clients: retail, fashion, automobile dealers, consumer, broadcast stations, health care marketing, sports and entertainment, business-to-business sales and direct marketing.

Needs: Works with 12-16 freelance photographers/month. Uses photographers for billboards, consumer and trade magazines, direct mail, P-O-P displays, catalogs, posters, signage and newspapers.

Making Contact & Terms: Query with resume of credits or with list of stock photo subjects. Provide resume, business card, brochure, flyer or tearsheets to be kept on file for possible future assignments. Works on assignment only. Does not return unsolicited material. Reports in 2 weeks. Pays $50-2,500/ b&w photo; $250-5,000/color photo; $50-300/hour; $400-2,500/day. Buys one-time rights, exclusive product rights, all rights, and limited-time or limited-run usage. Pays upon receipt of client payment. Model release required; captions preferred.

Montana

■CONTINENTAL PRODUCTIONS, (formerly Video International Publishers, Inc.), 118 Sixth St. S., Great Falls MT 59405. (406)761-5536. Executive in Charge of Production: Chuck Eastman. Types of clients: industrial, educational, retail and broadcast.

Needs: Works with 3-15 videographers/month. Uses video for films and videotapes. Subjects include: television commercials, educational/informational programs. All video is shot "film-style" (lighted for film, etc.). Reviews stock photos/footage. Model release required.

Specs: Uses U-matic ¾" SP, prefers 1" C-format or Beta SP.

Making Contact & Terms: Provide resume, business card, self-promotion piece or tearsheets to be kept on file for possible future assignments. Works with freelancers on assignment only. SASE. Reports in 1 month. NPI. Pays upon completion of final edit. Credit line not given. Buys all rights.

Tips: "Send the best copy of your work on ¾" cassette. Describe your involvement with each piece of video shown."

Nebraska

■J. GREG SMITH, Suite 102, 1004 Farnam, Burlington on the Mall, Omaha NE 68102. (402)444-1600. Art Director: Karen Kowalski. Ad agency. Types of clients: finance, banking institutions, national and state associations, agriculture, insurance, retail, travel.

Needs: Works with 10 freelance photographers/year on assignment only basis. Uses photographers for consumer and trade magazines, brochures, catalogs and AV presentations. Special subject needs include outer space, science and forest scenes.

Making Contact & Terms: Arrange interview to show portfolio. Looks for "people shots (with expression), scenics (well known, bright colors)." Pays $500/color photo; $60/hour; $800/day; varies/job. Buys all rights, one-time rights or others, depending on use.

Tips: Considers "composition, color, interest, subject and special effects when reviewing a portfolio or samples."

■SWANSON, RUSSELL AND ASSOCIATES, 1222 P St., Lincoln NE 68508. (402)475-5191. Creative Director: John Kloefkorn. Ad agency. Types of clients: primarily industrial, outdoor recreation and agricultural; client list provided on request.

Needs: Works with 10 freelance photographers/year on assignment only basis. Uses photographers for consumer and trade magazines, direct mail, brochures, catalogs, newspapers and AV presentations.
Making Contact & Terms: Query first with small brochure or samples along with list of clients freelancer has done work for. NPI. Negotiates payment according to client's budget. Rights are negotiable.

Nevada

■**DAVIDSON & ASSOCIATES**, 3940 Mohigan Way, Las Vegas NV 89119. (702)871-7172. President: George Davidson. Full-service ad agency. Types of clients: beauty, construction, finance, entertainment, retailing, publishing, travel.
Needs: Photos used in brochures, newsletters, annual reports, PR releases, AV presentations, sales literature, consumer and trade magazines.
Making Contact & Terms: Arrange a personal interview to show portfolio. Query with samples or submit portfolio for review. Provide resume, brochure and tearsheets to be kept on file for possible future assignments. Offers 150-200 assignments/year. Pays $15-50/b&w photo; $25-100/color photo; $15-50/hour; $100-400/day; $25-1,000 by the project. Pays on production. Buys all rights. Model release required.

■**TRI VIDEO TELEPRODUCTION–LAKE TAHOE**, P.O. Box 8822, Incline Village NV 89452-8822. (702)323-6868. Director: Jon Paul Davidson. Estab. 1978. Types of clients: corporate, documentary and government. Examples of recent projects: Grand Marnier Chefs Ski Race Western Regionals (publicity).
Needs: Uses 3-4 freelance photographers/year. Uses photographers and videographers for publicity photography on the set. Subjects include: video documentary, educational, motivational; b&w publicity photos. Model/property releases required.
Specs: Uses 5 × 7 SWG finish b&w prints; ¼" U-matic videotape; 1" and Betacam.
Making Contact & Terms: Interested in receiving work from newer, lesser-known photographers. Provide resume, business card, self-promotion piece or tearsheets to be kept on file for possible future assignments. Works with freelancers by assignment only. Cannot return material. Reports in 1 week. NPI. Pays by the hour and day. **Pays on acceptance.** Credit line given. Buys all rights; negotiable.
Tips: "We work in several cities–mostly western. We would like to know competent people for production assistance. In reviewing samples, we look for good clean composition, proper exposure–nothing exotic. We are seeing much greater video use by corporate clients. Publicity photos are always needed. Photographers interested in making the transition from film to videography should proceed with care. Composition is the same, electronics aren't!"

New Hampshire

■**PORRAS & LAWLOR ASSOCIATES**, 15 Lucille Ave., Salem NH 03079. (603)893-3626. Fax: (603)898-1657. Ad agency, PR and AV firm. Contact: Victoria Porras. Estab. 1980. Types of clients: industrial, educational, financial and service. Examples of recent projects: "You Can Get There from Here," MBTA; "Annual Giving," N.E. Telephone.
Needs: Works with 1-2 freelance photographers/month. Uses photographs for direct mail, catalogs, posters, signage and audiovisual uses. Subjects include: people and studio photography.
Specs: Uses all glossy and matte color and b&w prints; 35mm transparencies.
Making Contact & Terms: Interested in receiving work from newer, lesser-known photographers. Query with resume of credits, list of stock photo subjects and samples. Provide resume, business card, brochure, flyer or tearsheets to be kept on file for possible future assignments. Works with local freelancers on assignment only. Pays $800-1,500/day; $200-800/color photo; $150-500/b&w photo. Pays on receipt of invoice. Buys one-time and exclusive product rights; negotiable. Model release and captions preferred.
Tips: In sample, looks for "product photography, people, architectural, landscape, or other depending on brochure or promotion we are working on. We don't buy photos too often. We use photographers for product, architectural or diverse brochure needs. We buy stock photography for interior graphic projects and others–but less often." To break in with this firm, "stay in touch, because timing is essential."

Photographers Should Seek Dual Role

Ira Lerner has witnessed some disturbing things in his photographic career. He has seen art directors reject portfolios without giving them a glance. He has watched photographers repeatedly do good work for advertising agencies, only to have ensuing jobs go to other photographers. These ongoing problems have taught Lerner, of New York City, a lot since his days as a fine art student at Antioch College in Ohio. "I started to realize that photographers who are going to make big money in the nineties, and who control their careers and work all the time are going to be art directors," he says.

Ira Lerner

© Tania Mara

Around 10 years ago, Lerner began to transform himself into an established art director and today he no longer views himself as a "photographer." Instead, he considers himself a creative director who is able to take on larger projects and offer more to clients. "I realized, if you're a good photographer, you're already doing one of the most important aspects of an art director's job and that is visualizing an image. What you're usually not doing is combining that with client needs," says Lerner, who has shot fashion for clients such as Avon, Benetton, Anne Klein and Halston.

Lerner always felt he could supply outstanding images, but getting others to notice his work was not always easy. To combat the problem of having unreviewed portfolios returned to his office, he devised a special system. He started dropping off portfolios with notes in them about midway through the images. The messages would tell art directors to remove the notes if they reached that point in the portfolio. "I started getting back a number of portfolios with the notes still in them. So I knew the art directors hadn't looked at them," he recalls.

Rather than ask art directors why they hadn't looked at the portfolio, he would call a week or two later and ask how they liked it. He also would say he wanted to send the book back with some new photos. "Almost always the art director would say 'Yes.' An art director I'd have to work for weeks just to get him to let me drop off the book would turn around a week later and say 'Yes' because he knew that he didn't look at the book," says Lerner, adding that the note was usually gone the second time.

Lerner, who briefly worked on contract with *National Geographic* during his collegiate days, says he often sees very talented photographers who struggle. "You can't make it by picking up an account here and there. You want an account that's repeat business. If you have to go looking four days a week to find one job, and that's not a repeat customer, you're never going to build a business," he says.

One reason Lerner began to develop his skills as an art director is that he wanted to attract repeat clients. He found books that could teach him the different type faces and, while with *National Geographic,* he learned a lot about printing. As he developed his skills he found many art directors very receptive to his growing knowledge. He often made helpful suggestions regarding type faces or layout and they appreciated his input. He became a knowledgeable, "second opinion" for art directors, and they often hired him because of these skills. "If you think that you're going to get work by dropping off your portfolios at different agencies, you're living in a dream world. That is not the way business is being done," he says.

In tough economic times such as these it is imperative to offer additional services. "By 1995 photographers who are not doing their own art direction are not going to be in control of their careers. There are going to be too many people who can replace them. There are going to be too many people fighting for too few jobs. And the new electronic imaging is going to enable art directors to realize their own creative vision," he says.

—*Michael Willins*

© Ira Lerner

A humorous concept, a well trained dog, and a skilled actor to play Charlie Chaplin were crucial to the success of this ad for Charlie Chaplin Eyewear. Ira Lerner art directed and photographed this image, captured on Kodak Tri-X film using a Hasselblad camera with a Sonar 150mm lens.

New Jersey

■**AM/PM ADVERTISING, INC.**, 196 Clinton Ave., Newark NJ 07108. (201)824-8600. Fax: (201)824-6631. President: Robert A. Saks. Estab. 1962. Ad agency. Types of clients: food, pharmaceuticals and health and beauty aids.
Needs: Works with 6 freelance photographers/month. Uses photos for consumer and trade magazines, direct mail, P-O-P displays, catalogs, posters, newspapers and audiovisual. Subjects include: fashion, still-life and commercials. Reviews stock photos of food and beauty products. Model release required. Captions preferred.
Audiovisual Needs: "We use multi-media slide shows and multi-media video shows."
Specs: Uses 8×10, color and/or b&w prints; 35mm, 2¼×2¼, 4×5, 8×10 transparencies; 8×10 film; broadcast videotape.
Making Contact & Terms: Arrange personal interview to show portfolio. Send unsolicited photos by mail for consideration. Provide resume, business card, brochure, flyer or tearsheets to be kept on file for possible future assignments. Works on assignment only. Keeps samples on file. Reports in 1-2 weeks. Pays $150/hour; $1,000-2,000/day; $1,000-2,000/job; $1,000/color photo; $500/b&w photo. Pays on receipt of invoice. Credit line sometimes given depending upon client and use. Buys one-time rights.
Tips: In portfolio or samples, wants to see originality. Sees trend toward more use of special lighting.

ARDREY INC., 505 Main St., Metuchen NJ 08840. (908)549-1300. PR firm. Office Manager: Lisa Fania. Types of clients: industrial. Client list provided on request.
Needs: Works with 10-15 freelance photographers/month throughout US. Uses photographers for trade magazines, direct mail, brochures, catalogs, newspapers. Subjects include trade photojournalism.
Specs: Uses 4×5 and 8×10 b&w glossy prints; 35mm, 2¼×2¼ and 4×5 transparencies.
Making Contact & Terms: Provide resume, business card, brochure, flyer or tearsheets to be kept on file for possible future assignments. Works with freelance photographers on assignment basis only. SASE. Pays $150-450/day; "travel distance of location work—time and travel considered." Pays 30-45 days after acceptance. Buys all rights and negatives. Model release required.
Tips: Prefers to see "imaginative industrial photojournalism. Identify self, define territory you can cover from home base, define industries you've shot for industrial photojournalism; give relevant references and samples. Regard yourself as a business communication tool. That's how we regard ourselves, as well as photographers and other creative suppliers."

THE BECKERMAN GROUP, 35 Mill St., Bernardsville NJ 07924. (908)766-9238. Ad agency. Contact: Ilene Beckerman. Types of clients: industrial. Client list free with SASE.
Needs: Works with 3 photographers/month. Uses photos for catalogs, posters, corporate internal organs and brochures. Subject matter includes table top.
Specs: Uses b&w prints and 2¼×2¼ transparencies.
Making Contact & Terms: Arrange a personal interview to show portfolio. Provide resume, business card, brochure, flyer or tearsheets to be kept on file for possible future assignments. Works with freelance photographers on assignment only. Does not return unsolicited material. Reports as needed. Payment negotiable; maximum $1,500/day. Pays on receipt of invoice. Buys all rights. Model release required.
Tips: Looks for "the ability to think conceptually and solve a problem in a strong fresh way."

■**CREATIVE ASSOCIATES**, 44 Park Ave., Madison NJ 07940. (201)377-4440. Producer: Harrison Feather. Estab. 1975. AV firm. Types of clients: industrial, cosmetic and pharmaceutical.
Needs: Works with 1-2 photographers, filmmakers and/or videographers/month. Uses photos for trade magazines and audiovisual uses. Subjects include product and general environment. Reviews stock photos or videotape. Model release required. Property release preferred. Captions preferred.

Can't find a listing? Check at the end of each market section for the " '93-'94 Changes" lists. These lists include any market listings from the '93 edition which were either not verified or deleted in this edition.

Audiovisual Needs: Uses photos/video for slides and videotape.
Specs: Uses 35mm, 4×5 and 8×10 transparencies; videotape.
Making Contact & Terms: Provide resume, business card, brochure, flyer or tearsheets to be kept on file for possible future assignments. Works on assignment only. SASE. Reports as needed. Pays $500-1,000/day; $1,500-3,000/job. Pays on publication. Credit line sometimes given, depending on assignment. Rights negotiable; "depends on budget."

DIEGNAN & ASSOCIATES, Box 343 Martens, Lebanon NJ 08833. President: N. Diegnan. Ad agency/PR firm. Types of clients: industrial, consumer.
Needs: Commissions 15 photographers/year; buys 20 photos/year from each. Uses photos for billboards, trade magazines, and newspapers. Model release preferred.
Specs: Uses b&w contact sheet or glossy 8×10 prints. For color, uses 5×7 or 8×10 prints; also 2¼×2¼ transparencies.
Making Contact & Terms: Arrange a personal interview to show portfolio. Local freelancers preferred. SASE. Reports in 1 week. NPI. Negotiates payment based on client's budget and amount of creativity required from photographer. Pays by the job. Buys all rights.

■**INSIGHT ASSOCIATES**, 1293 Broad St., Bloomfield NJ 07003. (201)338-4730. President: Raymond Valente. Types of clients: major industrial companies.
Needs: Works with 4 freelancers/month. Uses freelancers for slide sets, multimedia productions, videotapes and print material—catalogs. Subjects include: industrial productions. Examples of clients: Matheson (safety), Witco Corp. (corporate image), Volvo (sales training), P.S.E.&G., Ecolab Inc. Interested in stock photos/footage. Model release preferred.
Specs: Uses 35mm, 2¼×2¼ and 4×5 transparencies.
Making Contact & Terms: Arrange a personal interview to show portfolio. SASE. Reports in 1 week. Pays $450-750/day on acceptance. Credit line given. Buys all rights.
Tips: "Freelance photographers should have knowledge of business needs and video formats. Also, versatility with video or location work. In reviewing a freelancer's portfolio or samples we look for content appropriate to our clients' objectives. Still photographers interested in making the transition into film and video photography should learn the importance of understanding a script."

■**INTERNATIONAL MEDIA SERVICES, INC.**, 718 Sherman Ave., Plainfield NJ 07060. (908)756-4060. AV firm/independent film and tape production company/media consulting firm. President/General Manager: Stuart Allen. Types of clients: industrial, advertising, print, fashion, broadcast and CATV.
Needs: Works with 0-25 freelance photographers/month; "depending on inhouse production at the time." Uses photographers for billboards, direct mail, catalogs, newspapers, consumer magazines, P-O-P displays, posters, AV presentations, trade magazines, brochures, film and tape. Subjects range "from scenics to studio shots and assignments"—varies with production requirements. Also works with freelance filmmakers to produce documentaries, commercials and training films.
Specs: Uses 8×10 glossy or matte b&w and color prints; 35mm, 2¼×2¼ and 8×10 transparencies; 16mm, 35mm film and ¾-1″ videotape.
Making Contact & Terms: Provide resume, business card, brochure, flyer or tearsheets to be kept on file for possible future assignments. Query with resume of credits. Query with list of stock photo subjects. Arrange a personal interview to show portfolio. SASE. Reporting time "depends on situation and requirements. We are not responsible for unsolicited material and do not recommend sending same. Negotiated rates based on type of work and job requirements." Usually pays $100-750/day, $25-2,500/job. Rights negotiable, generally purchases all rights. Model release required; captions preferred. Credit line given.
Tips: "Wants to see a brief book containing the best work of the photographer, representative of the type of assignment sought. Tearsheets are preferred but must have either the original or a copy of the original photo used, or applicable photo credit. Send resume and sample for active resource file. Maintain periodic contact and update file."

■**INTERTECH**, (formerly Unisource) 49 Brant Ave., Clark NJ 07066. Vice Pres./Creative Director: Les Aaron. Vice Pres./Client Services: Val Reisig. Vice Pres./Art Director: L. Friedlieb. Estab. 1970. Ad agency, PR firm. Types of clients: industrial, technical.
Needs: Works with 6-10 freelance photographers/month. Uses photos for trade magazines, direct mail, catalogs, signage, literature and PR. Subjects include: machinery. Model release required.
Audiovisual Needs: Uses freelancers to produce slides, film and videotape.
Specs: Uses 8×10 b&w prints; 4×5, 8×10 transparencies; film and videotape.
Making Contact & Terms: Arrange a personal interview to show portfolio. Query with resume of credits. Submit portfolio for review. Provide resume, business card, brochure, flyer or tearsheets to be kept on file for possible assignments. Works with freelance photographers on assignment basis only. Cannot return material. NPI. Pays per photo, per job. Pays on receipt of invoice. Buys all rights.

Tips: Prefers to see industrial, plant photography, studio work—all subjects. Amateurism is discouraged. "Impress us with talent, experience and offer value."

■**JANUARY PRODUCTIONS,** P.O. Box 66, 210 6th Ave., Hawthorne NJ 07507. (201)423-4666. Fax: (201)423-5569. Art Director: Karen Neulinger. Estab. 1973. AV firm. Types of clients: schools, teachers and public libraries. Audience consists of primary, elementary and intermediate-grade school students. Produces filmstrips. Subjects are concerned with elementary education—science, social studies, math and conceptual development.
Audiovisual Needs: Uses 35mm transparencies for filmstrips and pictures (slides) of products for company catalogs.
Making Contact & Terms: Interested in receiving work from newer, lesser-known photographers. Call or send resumé/samples of work. SASE. NPI. Payment amounts "depend on job." Buys all rights.
Tips: Wants to see "clarity, effective use of space, design, etc. We need clear photographs of our products for catalog use. The more pictures we have in the catalogs, the better they look and that helps to sell the product."

■**KJD TELEPRODUCTIONS, INC.,** 30 Whyte Dr., Voorhees NJ 08043. (609)751-3500. Fax: (609)751-7729. President: Larry Scott. Estab. 1989. AV firm. Types of clients: industrial, fashion, retail and food. Examples of recent projects: Marco Island Florida Convention, ICI Americas (new magazine show); "Kid Stuff," Whyte Light Syndications (TV broadcast); and "Rukus," Merv Griffin Productions (TV broadcast).
Needs: Works with 2 photographers, filmmakers and/or videographers/month. Uses photos for trade magazines and audiovisual. Model/property release required.
Audiovisual Needs: Primarily videotape, also slides and film.
Specs: Uses ½", ¾", Betacam/SP 1" videotape.
Making Contact & Terms: Send unsolicited photos by mail for consideration. Works on assignment only. Keeps samples on file. Reports in 1 month. Pays $50-300/day. **Pays on acceptance.** Credit lines sometimes given. Buys first rights.
Tips: "We are seeing more use of freelancers, less staff. Be visible!"

*■**KOLLINS COMMUNICATIONS, INC.,** (formerly R.J. Martin Co., Inc.), 425 Meadowlands Pkwy., Secaucus NJ 07094. (201)617-5555. Fax: (201)319-8760. Manager: R.J. Martin. Estab. 1992. Types of clients: Fortune 1000 pharmaceuticals, consumer electronics. Examples of projects: Sony (brochures); CBS Inc. (print ads); TBS Labs (slides).
Needs: Works with 2-4 freelance photographers/month. Uses photos for product shots, multimedia productions and videotapes. Subjects are various. Model release required.
Specs: Uses 35mm, 2¼ × 2¼, 4 × 5, 8 × 10 transparencies; Hi 8, ½" Betacam and 1" videotape.
Making Contact & Terms: Interested in receiving work from newer, lesser-known photographers. Submit portfolio by mail. Provide resume, business card, self-promotion piece or tearsheets to be kept on file for possible future assignments. Works on assignment only. Cannot return material. Reports in 2 weeks. NPI. Pays per day or per job. Pays by purchase order 30 days after work completed. Credit line given "when applicable." Buys all rights.
Tips: "Be specific about your best work (what areas), be flexible to budget on project—represent our company when on business."

LOHMEYER SIMPSON COMMUNICATIONS, 14 Pine St., Morristown NJ 07960. (201)267-0400. Purchasing Manager: Tony Grasso. Ad agency. Uses all media. Types of clients: automotive, electronic and industrial.
Needs: Works with freelance photographers on assignment only basis. Uses photos for cars, people, fashion and still life.
Specs: Uses semigloss prints and transparencies. Model release required.
Making Contact & Terms: Provide business card and tearsheets to be kept on file for possible future assignments. Model release required. Buys all rights, but may reassign to photographer. Negotiates payment based on client's budget, amount of creativity required, where the work will appear and photographer's previous experience and reputation. Pays $1,000/b&w photo; $2,000/color photo; or $2,000/day. Call to arrange an appointment. "Show samples of your work and printed samples." Reports in 2 weeks.
Tips: "Interested in cars (location/studio), still life (studio), location, editorial and illustration."

New Mexico

■**FOCUS ADVERTISING,** (formerly Mediaworks), 4002 Silver Ave. SE, Albuquerque NM 87108. (505)266-7795. President: Al Costanzo. Ad agency. Types of clients: retail, industry, politics, government, law. Produces overhead transparencies, slide sets, motion pictures, sound-slide sets, videotape, print ads and brochures.

Needs: Works with 1-2 freelance photographers/month on assignment only basis. Buys 70 photos and 5-8 films/year: health, business, environment and products. No animals or flowers. Length requirements: 80 slides or 15-20 minutes, or 60 frames, 20 minutes.

Specs: Produces ½" and ¾" video for broadcasts; also b&w photos or color prints and 35mm transparencies, "and a lot of 2¼ transparencies and some 4×5 transparencies."

Making Contact & Terms: Arrange personal interview or query with resume. Provide resume, flyer and brochure to be kept on file for possible future assignments. Prefers to see a variety of subject matter and styles in portfolio. Does not return unsolicited material. Pays $40-60/hour, $350-500/day, $40-800/job. Negotiates payment based on client's budget and photographer's previous experience/reputation. Pays on job completion. Buys all rights. Model release required.

New York

■**AUTHENTICATED NEWS INTERNATIONAL,** 34 High St., Katonah NY 10536-1117. (914)232-7726. Managing Editor: Mr. Sidney Polinsky. Types of clients: book publishers, media, newspapers, etc.

Needs: Works with approximately 25 freelance photographers/month. Uses photos for slide sets. Also uses high-quality slides for posters. Reviews stock photos/footage. Model release required. Captions required.

Specs: Uses 8×10 glossy b&w prints; 35mm, 2¼×2¼ and 4×5 transparencies.

Making Contact & Terms: Query with samples or resume. SASE. Reports in 1 month. Pays 50% commission to photographers. **Pays on acceptance.** Credit line given. Buys one-time rights.

■**CL&B ADVERTISING, INC.,** 100 Kinloch Commons, Manlius NY 13104-2484. (315)682-8502. Fax: (315)682-8508. President: Richard Labs. Creative Director: Adam Rozum. Estab. 1937. Advertising, PR and research. Types of clients: industrial, fashion, finance and retail. Examples of recent projects: "Charges, Choices and Familiar Faces," (ads and literature); "Girl, dogs, Volvo, fall foliage classics," (posters for retail); and "Glamor shots of donuts," (point of purchase).

Needs: Works with 4-6 freelance photographers/year. Uses photos for billboards, consumer and trade magazines, P-O-P displays, catalogs and newspapers. Subjects include: industrial, consumer, models, location and/or studio. Model/property release required.

Audiovisual Needs: "Wish we could find low cost, high quality 35mm panavision film team."

Specs: Uses all formats.

Making Contact & Terms: "Send bio and proof sheet (if available) first; we will contact you if interested." Works on assignment only. Also uses stock photos. Does not return unsolicited material. Pays $10-1,000/b&w photo; $10-2,500/color photo; $10-100/hour; $200-3,000/day; $100-10,000/job. Pays in 30 days. Credit line seldom given. Buys all rights.

Tips: "We review your work and will call if we think a particular job is applicable to your talents."

■**EDUCATIONAL IMAGES LTD.,** P.O. Box 3456, West Side Station, Elmira NY 14905. (607)732-1090. AV publisher. Executive Director: Dr. Charles R. Belinky. Types of clients: educational market, grades 6-12 and college; also serves public libraries, parks and nature centers. Produces filmstrips, slide sets, and multimedia kits.

Needs: Works with 12 freelance photographers/year. Buys 200-400 photos/year; film and video are "open." Subjects include: a heavy emphasis on natural history, ecology, anthropology, conservation, life sciences; also chemistry, physics, astronomy, math. "We are happy to consider any good color photo series on any topic that tells a coherent story. We need pictures and text." Model release preferred. Captions required.

Specs: Uses videotape; also buys any size transparencies, but 35mm preferred. Will consider buying photo collections, any subject, to expand files. Will also look at prints, "if transparencies are available."

Making Contact & Terms: Query with resume of credits. Submit material by mail for consideration. Prefers to see 35mm or larger transparencies and outline of related text in portfolio. Reports in 1 month. SASE. Pays $150 minimum/job, or on a per-photo basis. Buys all rights, but may reassign to photographer.

Tips: "Write for our catalog. Write first with a small sample. We want complete or nearly complete AV programs—not isolated pictures usually. Be reliable. Follow up commitments on time and provide only sharp, well-exposed, well-composed pictures. Send by registered mail."

■**FINE ART PRODUCTIONS,** 67 Maple St., Newburgh NY 12550. (914)561-5866. Director: Richie Suraci. Estab. 1989. Ad agency, PR firm and AV firm. Types of clients: industrial, financial, fashion, retail, food—all industries. Examples of recent projects: "Great Hudson River Revival," Clearwater, Inc. (folk concert, brochure); feature articles, Hudson Valley News (newspaper); and "Wheel and Rock to Woodstock," MS Society (brochure).

Needs: Uses photos for billboards, consumer and trade magazines, direct mail, P-O-P displays, catalogs, posters, newspapers, signage and audiovisual. Reviews stock photos. Model/property release required. Captions required; include basic information.
Audiovisual Needs: Uses slides, film (all formats) and videotape.
Specs: Uses color and b&w prints, any size or finish; 35mm, 2¼ × 2¼", 4 × 5, 8 × 10 transparencies; film, all formats; and ½", ¾" or 1" beta videotape.
Making Contact & Terms: Submit portfolio for review. Query with resume of credits. Query with list of stock photo subjects. Send unsolicited photos by mail for consideration. Query with samples. Provide resume, business card, brochure, flyer or tearsheets to be kept on file for possible future assignments. Keeps samples on file. SASE. Reports in 1 month or longer. NPI: "All payment negotiable relative to subject matter." Pays on acceptance, publication or on receipt of invoice; "varies relative to project." Credit line sometimes given, "depending on project or if they want it." Buys first, one-time and all rights; negotiable.
Tips: Looks for "all subjects, styles and capabilities."

HARRINGTON ASSOCIATES INC., 57 Fairmont Ave., Kingston NY 12401-5221. (914)331-7136. Fax: (914)331-7168. President: Gerard Harrington. Estab. 1988. PR firm. Types of clients: industrial, high technology, retail, fashion, finance, transportation, architectural, artistic and publishing. Examples of recent clinets include: Digital Equipment Corp. (story illustration); MCEP Dyames (P-O-P, catalogs, newspaper/magazine advertisiting, PR); and Bebee Ind., (trade show display).
• Winner of the Gold Eclat Award for public relations excellence, given out by the Hudson Valley Area Marketing Association.
Needs: Number of photographers used on a monthly basis varies. Uses photos for consumer and trade magazines, P-O-P displays, catalogs and newspapers. Subjects include: general publicity including head shots and candids. Also still lifes. Model release required.
Specs: Uses b&w prints, any size and format. Also uses 4 × 5 color transparencies; and ¾" videotape.
Making Contact & Terms: Interested in receiving work from newer, lesser-known photographers. Provide resume, business card, brochure, flyer or tearsheets to be kept on file for possible future assignments. Works with freelancers on assignment only. Cannot return material. Reports only when interested. NPI; payment negotiable. Pays on receipt of invoice. Credit line given whenever possible, depending on use. Buys all rights; negotiable.

KOPF, ZIMMERMANN, SCHULTHEIS, 898 Veterans Memorial Highway, Hauppauge NY 11788. (516)348-1440. Ad agency. Art Directors: Evelyn C. Rysdyk and Art Zimmermann. Estab. 1980. Types of clients: industrial (high-tech, medical, computers, software, etc.), business-to-business and consumer.
Needs: Works with 4 freelance photographers/month. Uses photos for billboards, consumer and trade magazines, catalogs, posters, newspapers. Subjects include: still life (technical products), office situations with models. Examples of ad campaigns: Philips Medical Systems and North Fork Bank.
Specs: Uses 35mm, 2¼ × 2¼, 4 × 5 and 8 × 10 transparencies.
Making Contact & Terms: Interested in receiving work from newer, lesser-known photographers. Query with samples. Provide resume, business card, brochure, flyer or tearsheets to be kept on file for possible future assignments. Works with freelance photographers on assignment only. Does not return unsolicited material. Pays $200-3,000/b&w photo; $200-5,000/color photo; $800-2,000/day; $200-5,000/job. Pays on receipt of invoice. Buys all rights; negotiable. Model/property release and captions required.
Tips: Prefers to see creative still life work and good people shots (annual report type); printed samples. Looks for good technical skills. Special note: "Show us something innovative. Fine art techniques also accepted." Seeks to work with "professionals only." Sees a trend in greater "use of highly creative, stylized, even gritty work."

■MCANDREW ADVERTISING CO., P.O. Box 254, 2125 St. Raymond Ave., Bronx NY 10462. (718)892-8660. Contact: Robert McAndrew. Estab. 1961. Ad agency, PR firm. Types of clients: industrial and technical. Examples of recent projects: Electronic Devices, Inc. (ad campaign); Yula Corp. (new photo series, brochure, trade show); and Wyssmont Co., Inc.
Needs: Works with 1 freelance photographer/month. Uses photos for trade magazines, direct mail, brochures, catalogs, newspapers, audiovisual. Subjects include: technical products. Reviews stock photos of science subjects. Model release required for recognizable people. Property release required. Captions preferred.
Audiovisual Needs: Uses slides and videotape.
Specs: Uses 8 × 10 glossy b&w or color prints; 34mm, 4 × 5 transparencies.
Making Contact & Terms: Interested in working with newer, lesser-known photograhers. Query with resume of credits. Provide resume, business card, brochure, flyer, tearsheets or non-returnable samples to be kept on file for possible future assignments. Works with local freelancers only. SASE. Reports in 1 month. Pays $65/b&w photo; $150/color photo; $700/day. "Prices dropping because

business is bad." Pays on receipt of invoice. Credit line sometimes given. Buys one-time rights.
Tips: Photographers should "let us know how close they are, and what their prices are. We look for photographers who have experience in industrial photography." In samples, wants to see "sharp, well-lighted" work.

MCCUE ADVERTISING & PR INC., 91 Riverside Dr., Binghamton NY 13905. (607)723-9226. President: Donna McCue. Ad agency and PR firm. Types of clients: industrial, retail, all types.
Needs: Works with 5 freelance photographers/month. Uses photos for consumer and trade magazines, direct mail, P-O-P displays, catalogs, signage and newspapers. Model release required.
Specs: Uses 8×10 prints; 35mm, 4×5 transparencies.
Making Contact & Terms: Provide resume, business card, brochure, flyer or tearsheets to be kept on file for possible future assignments. Cannot return material. Reports when assignment comes up. NPI; payment negotiable. Pays in 30 days. Credit line sometimes given. Buys all rights.

■NATIONAL TEACHING AIDS, INC., 1845 Highland Ave., New Hyde Park NY 11040. (516)326-2555. Fax: (516)326-2560. President: A. Becker. Estab. 1960. A.V. firm. Types of clients: schools. Produces filmstrips.
Needs: Buys 20-100 photos/year. Science subjects; needs photomicrographs and space photography.
Specs: Uses 35mm transparencies.
Making Contact & Terms: Cannot return material. Pays $50 minimum. Buys one-time rights; negotiable.

■ORGANIZATION MANAGEMENT, 7 Heather Lane, Gloversville NY 12078. (518)725-9714. President: Bill Dunkinson. Ad agency and PR firm. Types of clients: construction, credit and collections, entertainment, finance, government, publishing and travel accounts.
Needs: Photos used in brochures, newsletters, annual reports, PR releases, sales literature, consumer and trade magazines. Buys 200 photos/year.
Specs: Uses 5×7 and 8×10 glossy, matte and semigloss prints. NPI. Pays per job. Negotiates payment based on client's budget, amount of creativity required, where work will appear and photographer's previous experience/reputation. Credit line sometimes given.
Making Contact & Terms: No unsolicited material. Works with freelance photographers on assignment only; local freelancers preferred. Freelance filmmakers may query for assignment. SASE. Reports in 2 weeks.

*■PARAGON ADVERTISING, Suite 510, 220 Delaware Ave., Buffalo NY 14202. (716)854-7161. Fax: (716)854-7163. Senior Art Director: Leo Abbott. Estab. 1988. Ad agency. Types of clients: industrial, retail, food and medical.
Needs: Works with 0-5 photographers, 0-1 filmmakers and 0-1 videographers/month. Uses photos for billboards, consumer and trade magazines, P-O-P displays, catalogs, posters, newspapers, signage and audiovisual. Subjects include: location. Reviews stock photos. Model release required. Property release preferred.
Audiovisual Needs: Uses film and videotape for on air.
Specs: Uses 8×10 prints; 2¼×2¼ or 4×5 transparencies; 16mm film; and ¾", 1" Betacam videotape.
Making Contact and Terms: Interested in receiving work from newer, lesser-known photographers. Submit portfolio for review. Query with stock photo list. Send unsolicited photos by mail for consideration. Works on assignment only. Keeps samples on file. SASE. Reports in 1-2 weeks. Pays $500-2,000 day; $100-5,000 job. Pays on receipt of invoice. Credit line sometimes given. Buys all rights; negotiable.

PRO/CREATIVES, 25 W. Burda Pl., New City NY 10956-7116. President: David Rapp. Ad agency. Uses all media except billboards and foreign. Types of clients: package goods, fashion, men's entertainment and leisure magazines, sports and entertainment.
Specs: Send any size b&w prints. For color, send 35mm transparencies or any size prints.
Making Contact & Terms: Submit material by mail for consideration. Reports as needed. SASE. NPI. Negotiates payment based on client's budget.

■TOBOL GROUP, INC., 33 Great Neck Rd., Great Neck NY 11021. (516)466-0414. Fax: (516)466-0776. Ad agency/design studio. President: Mitch Tobol. Estab. 1981. Types of clients: high-tech, industrial, business-to-business and consumer. Examples of ad campaigns: Weight Watchers, (in-store promotion); Eutectic & Castolin; Mainco (trade ad); and Light Alarms.
Needs: Works with up to 4 photographers/videographers/month. Uses photos for billboards, consumer and trade magazines, direct mail, P-O-P displays, catalogs, posters, newspapers and audiovisual. Subjects are varied; mostly still-life photography. Reviews business-to-business and commercial video footage. Model release required.

Audiovisual Needs: Uses videotape.

Specs: Uses 4×5, 8×10, 11×14 b&w prints; 35mm, 2¼×2¼ and 4×5 transparencies; and ½" videotape.

Making Contact & Terms: Send unsolicited photos by mail for consideration. Query with samples. Provide resume, business card, brochure, flyer or tearsheets to be kept on file for possible future assignments: follow-up with phone call. Works on assignment only. SASE. Reports in 3 weeks. Pays $100-10,000/job. Pays net 30. Rights purchased depend on client. Credit line sometimes given, depending on client and price.

Tips: In freelancer's samples or demos, wants to see "the best they do—any style or subject as long as it is done well. Trend is photos or videos to be multi-functional. Show me your *best* and what you enjoy shooting. Get experience with existing company to make the transition from still photography to audiovisual."

■**VISUAL HORIZONS,** 180 Metro Park, Rochester NY 14623. (716)424-5300. Fax: (716)424-5313. President: Stanley Feingold. AV firm. Types of clients: industrial.

Audiovisual Needs: Works with 2 freelance photographers/month. Uses photos for AV presentations. Also works with freelance filmmakers to produce training films. Model release required. Captions required.

Specs: Uses 35mm transparencies and videotape.

Making Contact & Terms: Provide resume, business card, brochure, flyer or tearsheets to be kept on file for possible future assignments. Works on assignment only. Reports as needed. NPI. Pays on publication. Buys all rights.

HAROLD WARNER ADVERTISING, INC., 232 Delaware Ave., Buffalo NY 14202. (716)852-4410. Fax: (716)852-4725. Ad agency. Art Director: William Walsh. Estab. 1945. Types of clients: "We are the agency for 40 clients—all industrial."

Needs: Works with 3-4 photographers/month. Uses photographers for trade magazines, direct mail and catalogs. Subjects are varied—but all industrial. Reviews stock photos.

Specs: Uses 4×5 to 20×24 glossy and matte b&w and color prints; 35mm, 2¼×2¼, 4×5 and 8×10 transparencies.

Making Contact & Terms: Arrange personal interview to show portfolio. Query with resume of credits. Query with list of stock photo subjects. Provide resume, business card, brochure, flyer or tearsheets to be kept on file for possible future assignments. Works with freelancers on assignment only. Reports "as needed." Pays $500-800/day; specific rates negotiable. **Pays on acceptance.** Buys all rights. Model release required; captions preferred. No credit line given.

Tips: "Freelancers are few and far between who can deal with mundane, industrial topics such as machines and machine parts. Our work is largely industrial advertising, so we look for freelancers who can show experience and ability to shoot industrial subjects imaginatively."

■**ZELMAN STUDIOS, LTD.,** 623 Cortelyou Rd., Brooklyn NY 11218. (718)941-5500. General Manager: Jerry Krone. Estab. 1966. AV firm. Types of clients: industrial, retail, fashion, public relations, fundraising, education, publishing, business and government.

Needs: Works on assignment only. Uses photographers for slide sets, filmstrips, motion pictures and videotape. Subjects include: people, machines and aerial. Model release required. Property release preferred. Captions preferred.

Specs: Produces 16mm and 35mm documentary, educational and industrial video films and slide/sound shows. Uses 8×10 color prints; 35mm transparencies.

Making Contact & Terms: Interested in receiving work from newer, lesser-known photographers. Query with samples. Send material by mail for consideration. Submit portfolio for review. Provide resume, samples and calling card to be kept on file for possible future assignments. Pays $50-100/color photo; $250-800/job. **Pays on acceptance.** Buys all rights.

New York City

■**ALDEN GROUP-PUBLIC RELATIONS DIVISION,** 52 Zanderbilt Ave., New York NY 10017. (212)867-6400. Public Relations Director: Laura Baddish. Estab. 1955. PR firm. Photos used in newspapers, trade publications and general media. Types of clients: chemicals, health care, food/beverage, home furnishings, manufacturing and travel/resorts. Examples of ad campaigns: Gucci Eyewear (fashion), Sharp Watches (popular priced value). Most interested in product publicity by assignment; event/area coverage by assignment; portraits for publicity use; occasional use of models/props.

Audiovisual Needs: Assigns AV projects to filmmakers for industrial and commercial films.
Specs: Uses glossy b&w prints. For color, uses glossy prints and transparencies; contact sheet and negatives OK.
Making Contact & Terms: "Write first; describe your area of specialization and general abilities; access to models, props, studio; area/event/people coverage; equipment used; time and fee information; agency/commercial experience; and location and availability." SASE. Reports in 1 month or less. NPI. Buys all rights. Model release required.
Tips: "Work through our director." Also, "be able to respond quickly."

■**ANITA HELEN BROOKS ASSOCIATES**, 155 E. 55th St., New York NY 10022. (212)755-4498. Contact: Anita Helen Brooks. PR firm. Types of clients: beauty, entertainment, fashion, food, publishing, travel, society, art, politics, exhibits and charity events.
Needs: Photos used in PR releases, AV presentations and consumer and trade magazines. Buys "several hundred" photos/year. Most interested in fashion shots, society, entertainment and literary celebrity/personality shots. Model release preferred.
Specs: Uses 8×10 glossy b&w or color prints; contact sheet OK.
Making Contact & Terms: Provide resume and brochure to be kept on file for possible future assignments. Query with resume of credits. No unsolicited material; cannot return unsolicited material. Works on assignment only. Pays $50 minimum/job; negotiates payment based on client's budget. Credit line given.

■**COX ADVERTISING**, 379 W. Broadway, New York NY 10012. (212)334-9141. Fax: (212)334-9179. Ad agency. Associate Creative Director: Marc Rubin. Types of clients: industrial, retail, fashion and travel.
Needs: Works with 2 freelance photographers—videographers/month. Uses photographers for billboards, consumer magazines, trade magazines, direct mail, P-O-P displays, catalogs, posters, newspapers, signage and audiovisual. Reviews stock photos or video.
Audiovisual Needs: Uses photos for slide shows; also uses videotapes.
Specs: Uses 16×20 b&w prints; 35mm, 2¼×2¼, 4×5 and 8×10 transparencies.
Making Contact & Terms: Arrange personal interview to show portfolio. Works on assignment only. Cannot return material. Reports in 1-2 weeks. Pays minimum of $1,500/job; higher amounts negotiable according to needs of client. Pays within 30-60 days of receipt of invoice. Buys all rights when possible. Model release required. Credit line sometimes given.

■**RICHARD L. DOYLE ASSOC., INC.**, 15 Maiden Lane, New York NY 10038. (212)349-2828. Fax: (212)619-5350. Ad agency. Client Services: R.L. Stewart, Jr. Estab. 1979. Types of clients: primarily in insurance/financial services and publishers. Client list free with SASE.
Needs: Works with 5-6 freelance photographers/month. Uses photographers for consumer and trade magazines, direct mail, newspapers, audiovisual, sales promotion and annual reports. Subjects include people—portrait and candid.
Audiovisual Needs: Typically uses prepared slides—in presentation formats, video promotions and video editorials.
Specs: Uses b&w and color prints; 35mm and 2¼×2¼ transparencies.
Making Contact & Terms: Query with resume of credits and samples. Prefers resume, business card, brochure, flyer or tearsheets to be kept on file for possible future assignments. SASE. Reports in 2 weeks. NPI. **Pays on acceptance** or receipt of invoice. Buys all rights. Model release required; captions required.
Tips: Prefers to see photos of people; "good coverage/creativity in presentation. Be perfectly honest as to capabilities; be reasonable in cost and let us know you'll work *with us* to satisfy the client. Trends include more imaginative settings and composition in normally mundane situations."

■**EMMERLING POST INC., ADVERTISING**, (formerly John Emmerling Inc.), 135 E. 55th St., New York NY 10022. (212)751-7460. Executive Vice President/Associate Creative Director: Art Gilmore. Senior Vice President/Associate Creative Director: Stuart Cohen. Vice President/Art Director: Paul Shields. Types of clients: magazines, banks, aviation and computers. Current clients: *Readers' Digest*, IBM, Jet Aviation, Magazine Publishers of America and New York Eye Surgery Center.
Needs: Works with 5 photographers and videographers/month. Uses photographs for billboards, consumer and trade magazines, direct mail, P-O-P displays, posters, newspapers, audiovisual and other. Subjects include: reportage, people, still life.
Audiovisual Needs: Uses slides, film and videotape.
Specs: Uses b&w prints; 35mm, 2¼×2¼, 4×5 and 8×10 transparencies; 35mm film; 1", ¾", ½" videotape.
Making Contact & Terms: Mail samples. Local freelancers may call to arrange personal interview to show portfolio. Submit portfolio for review. Provide business card, brochure, flyer or tearsheets to be kept on file for possible future assignments. Keeps samples on file. Cannot return material. Reports

only as needed. NPI. Pays on receipt of invoice. Rights negotiable. Model release required. Credit line sometimes given depending upon fee schedule.
Tips: Looks for original work.

*EPSTEIN & WALKER ASSOCIATES, #5A, 65 W. 55 St., New York NY 10019. (212)246-0565. President/Creative Director: Lee Epstein. Ad agency. Types of clients: retail, publication, consumer and fashion. Examples of ad campaigns: *Woman's World Magazine,* (trade campaign to media buyers); Northville Gas, (radio/TV campaign to drivers); and Bermuda Shop, (woman's retail-image/fashion).
Needs: Works with 4-6 freelance photographers/year. Uses photos for consumer and trade magazines, direct mail and newspapers. Subjects include still life, people, fashion, etc.; "depends on concept of ads." Model release required.
Specs: Any size or format b&w prints; also 35mm, 2¼ × 2¼ transparencies.
Making Contact & Terms: Arrange personal interview to show portfolio. Provide resume, business card, brochure, flyer of tearsheets to be kept on file for possible future assignments. Works with local freelancers on assignment only. Cannot return material. Reports "as needed." Pays minimum of $300/ b&w photo or negotiates day rate for multiple images. Pays 30-60 days after receipt of invoice. No credit line given. Usually buys rights for "1 year usage across the board."
Tips: Trend within agency is "to solve problems with illustration, and more recently with type/copy only, more because of budget restraints regarding models and location expenses." Is receptive to working with new talent. To break in, show "intelligent conceptual photography with exciting ideas and great composition."

*■IMAGE ZONE, INC., #203, 19 W. 21st St., New York NY 10010. (212)924-8804. Fax: (212)924-5585. Managing Director: Doug Ehrlich. Estab. 1986. AV firm. Types of clients: industrial, financial, fashion. Examples of recent projects: Shearson Lehman Brothers (conference); Pfizer (exhibit); Bristol Myers (product launch).
Needs: Works with 1 freelance photographer, 2 filmmakers and 3 videographers/month. Uses photos for audiovisual projects. Subjects vary. Reviews stock photos. Model/property release preferred. Captions preferred.
Audiovisual Needs: Uses slides, film and videotape. Subjects include: "original material."
Specs: Uses 35mm transparencies; ¾" or ½" videotape.
Making Contact & Terms: Query with resume of credits. Provide resume, business card, brochure, flyer or tearsheets to be kept on file for possible future assignments. Works with local freelancers on assignment only. Keeps samples on file. Cannot return material. Reports when needed. Pays $500-1,500/job; also depends on size, scope and budget of project. Pays within 14 days of receipt of invoice. Credit line not given. Buys one-time rights; negotiable.

*JORDAN, MCGRATH, CASE & TAYLOR/DIRECT, 445 Park Ave., New York NY 10022. (212)326-9600. Contact: Karen Hochman. Ad agency. Uses all media. Types of clients: financial services, technology, package goods.
Needs: Still lifes and product photos. Buys 5-10 annually.
Specs: Uses b&w contact sheets for selection, then double-weight glossy or matte prints. Also uses transparencies. Determines specifications at time of assignment.
Making Contact & Terms: "Please do not call. Send promotional materials, which will be retained. Agency will call photographer or rep as appropriate assignments surface."

■KEYSTONE PRESS AGENCY, INC., 202 East 42nd St., New York NY 10017. (212)924-8123. Managing Editor: Brian F. Alpert. Types of clients: book publishers, magazines and major newspapers.
Needs: Uses photos for slide sets. Subjects include: photojournalism. Reviews stock photos/footage. Captions required.
Specs: Uses 8 × 10 glossy b&w and color prints; 35mm and 2¼ × 2¼ transparencies.
Making Contact & Terms: Cannot return material. Reports upon sale. NPI; payment is 50% of sale per photo. Credit line given.

KOEHLER IVERSEN ADVERTISING, 71 W. 23rd St., New York NY 10010. Fax: (212)645-6451. Creative Director: W. Peter Koehler. Estab. 1977. Ad agency. Types of clients: industrial, health care and pharmaceutical.

The asterisk before a listing indicates that the market is new in this edition. New markets are often the most receptive to freelance submissions.

Needs: Works with 2 photographers/month. Uses photos for trade magazines, direct mail, catalogs and newspapers. Subjects include: people/corporate. Model/property release required.
Specs: Uses b&w and color prints; 35 mm, 2¼×2¼, 4×5 transparencies.
Making Contact & Terms: Interested in receiving work from newer, lesser-known photographers. Query with samples, submit portfolio for review. Provide resume, business card, brochure, flyer or tearsheets to bc kept on file for possible future assignments. Works with freelance photographers on assignment only. Cannot return material. NPI; pays by the job or per photo. Payment made "30 days from receipt of invoice." Buys all rights. Model and property releases required.
Tips: Looks for "originality, composition and lighting" in work. Sees trends in increasing competition and flexible rates.

■**LIPPSERVICE**, 305 W. 52nd St., New York NY 10019. (212)956-0572. President: Ros Lipps. Estab. 1985. Celebrity consulting firm. Types of clients: industrial, financial, fashion, retail, food; "any company which requires use of celebrities." Examples of recent projects: "Remembering Felicia," Judy Kreston and David Lahm (cabaret action, tribute to Felicia Sanders); also projects for United Way of Tri-State and CARE; AIDS benefits.
Needs: Works with 6 freelance photographers and/or videographers/month. Uses photos for billboards, trade magazines, P-O-P displays, posters, audiovisual. Subjects include: celebrities. Model/property release required.
Audiovisual Needs: Uses videotape.
Specs: Uses videotape.
Making Contact & Terms: Provide resume, business card, brochure, flyer or tearsheets to be kept on file for possible future assignments. Works on assignment only. Keeps samples on file. Cannot return material. Reports in 3 weeks. NPI; pays per job. Credit line given. Rights purchased depend on job; negotiable.
Tips: Looks for "experience in photographing celebrities. Contact us by mail only."

■**MARSDEN**, 30 E. 33 St., New York NY 10016. (212)725-9220. Vice President/Creative Director: Stephen Flores. Types of clients: corporate, nonprofit, Fortune 500.
Needs: Works with 2-3 photographers/month. Uses photographers for filmstrips, slide sets, multimedia productions, films and videotapes. Subjects include industrial, technical, office, faces, scenics, special effects, etc.
Specs: Uses 35mm, 2¼×2¼, 4×5 and 8×10 transparencies; 16mm film; U-matic ¾", 1" and 2" videotapes.
Making Contact & Terms: Query with samples or a stock photo list. Provide resume, business card, self-promotion piece or tearsheets to be kept on file for possible future assignments. Works with local freelancers only; interested in stock photos/footage. "We call when we have a need—no response is made on unsolicited material." Pays $25-1,000/color photo; $150-600/day. **Pays on acceptance.** Buys one-time rights. Model release preferred. Credit line rarely given.

■**MATTHEW-LAWRENCE ADVERTISING & SALES PROMOTION INC.**, 322 8th Ave., New York NY 10011. (212)929-1313. Fax: (212)929-1396. Ad agency. President: Larry Danziger. Types of clients: industrial, fashion and finance. Examples of ad campaigns: Monsanto (ads and promotion programs); Dupont (collateral material and videos); and Federal Express (collateral materials).
Needs: Works with 2-3 freelance photographers/filmmakers/videographers per month. Uses photographers for consumer magazines, trade magazines, direct mail, P-O-P displays and audiovisual. Reviews stock photos and video.
Audiovisual Needs: Video.
Specs: Uses any size of format b&w prints; 35mm, 2¼×2¼, 4×5 and 8×10 transparencies; also VHS videotape.
Making Contact & Terms: Arrange personal interview to show portfolio. Provide resume, business card, brochure, flyer or tearsheets to be kept on file for possible future assignments. Works with freelancers on assignment only. Reports in 1-2 weeks. Pays $250-1,000/day. Pays on receipt of invoice. Buys all rights (work-for-hire). Model release required. Credit line sometimes given.
Tips: In freelancer's portfolio or demos, wants to see fashion and reportage.

MIZEREK ADVERTISING, 48 E. 43rd St., New York NY 10017. (212)986-5702. President: Leonard Mizerek. Estab. 1974. Types of clients: fashion, jewelry and industrial.
 ● Received a 1992 Readex Award for having the most recognized ad in a trade journal.
Needs: Works with 2 freelance photographers/month. Uses photographs for trade magazines. Subjects include: still life and jewelry. Reviews stock photos of creative images showing fashion/style. Model release required. Property release preferred.

Specs: Uses 8×10 glossy b&w prints; 4×5 and 8×10 transparencies.
Making Contact & Terms: Interested in receiving work from newer, lesser-known photographers. Submit portfolio for review. Provide resume, business, card, brochure, flyer or tearsheets to be kept on file for possible future assignments. SASE. Reports in 2 weeks. Pays $1,500-2,500/day; $500-1,000/job; $600/color photo; $300/b&w photo. **Pays on acceptance.** Credit line sometimes given. Buys all rights; negotiable.
Tips: Looks for "clear product visualization. Must show detail and have good color balance." Sees trend toward "more use of photography and expanded creativity."

■**MOLINO + ASSOCIATES, INC.**, Suite 2404, 245 Fifth Ave., New York NY 10016. (212)689-7370. Fax: (212)689-7448. PR firm. Production Manager: John Corrigan. Estab. 1989. Types of clients: nonprofit health care. Recent projects include General Motors Cancer Research Foundation, The Hebrew Home for the Aged at Riverdale and American Association for Cancer Research.
Needs: Works with 1-2 freelancers/month. Uses photos for direct mail, posters, newspapers and audiovisual. Subjects include: health care for the elderly.
Audiovisual Needs: Uses slides, film and videotape—"all, but not too often—once or twice a year."
Specs: Uses 5×7 and 8×10 color and b&w prints; 35mm transparencies.
Making Contact & Terms: Interested in receiving work from newer, lesser-known photographers. Submit portfolio for review. Provide resume, business card, brochure, flyer or tearsheets to be kept on file for possible future assignments. Works with local freelancers only. Keeps samples on file. SASE. Reports in 1-3 weeks. Pays $500-1,000/day; $12-16/b&w photo. Pays on receipt of invoice. Buys all rights and others; negotiable. Model release required for caregivers and patients. Captions preferred. Credit line sometimes given: "If the photo is used on an invitation, no; if in a brochure, yes."
Tips: Wants to see "subjects—people, styles—realistic. Capabilities: showing personality of subjects through lighting, etc. Mainly photos are used for fundraising and/or informational brochures. Photographer has to be good with people he/she's photographing—especially old people, have a good eye for composition and lighting."

■**RUTH MORRISON ASSOCIATES**, 19 West 44th St., New York NY 10036. (212)302-8886. Fax: (212)302-5512. Account Executive: Marinelle Hervas. Estab. 1972. PR firm. Types of clients: specialty foods, housewares, home furnishings and general business.
Needs: Works with 1-2 freelance photographers and/or videographers/month. Uses photos for consumer and trade magazines, P-O-P displays, posters, newspapers, signage and audiovisual.
Audiovisual Needs: Uses photos and videotape.
Specs: Specifications vary according to clients' needs. Typically uses b&w prints and transparencies.
Making Contact & Terms: Arrange personal interview to show portfolio. Provide resume, business card, brochure, flyer or tearsheets to be kept on file for possible future assignments. Works with freelancers on assignment only. Reports "as needed." Pays $100-1,000 depending upon client's budget. Credit line sometimes given, depending on use. Rights negotiable.

MOSS & COMPANY, INC., 49 W. 38th St., New York NY 10018. (212)575-0808. Executive Art Director: Anthony Micale. Ad agency. Serves clients in consumer products, manufacturing, utilities, insurance and packaged goods. Annual billing: $10,000,000.
Needs: Works with 2-3 freelance photographers/month. Uses photographers for billboards, consumer and trade magazines, direct mail, TV, brochures/flyers and newspapers.
Making Contact & Terms: Call for appointment to show portfolio. Negotiates payment based on client's budget: $300-3,000/job; $600/b&w photo; $2,000/color photo. Prefers to see samples of still life and people.
Tips: "Photographer must be technically perfect with regard to shooting still life and people."

NOSTRADAMUS ADVERTISING, #1128A, 250 W. 57th, New York NY 10107. (212)581-1362. President: Barry Sher. Estab. 1974. Ad agency. Types of clients: politicians, nonprofit organizations and small businesses.
Needs: Uses freelancers occasionally. Uses photos for consumer and trade magazines, direct mail, catalogs and posters. Subjects include: people and products. Model release required.
Specs: Uses 8×10 glossy b&w and color prints; transparencies, slides.
Making Contact & Terms: Provide resume, business card, brochure. Works with local freelancers only. Cannot return material. Pays $50-100/hour. Pays 30 days from invoice. Credit line sometimes given. Buys all rights (work-for-hire).

RICHARD H. ROFFMAN ASSOCIATES, Suite 6A, 697 West End Ave., New York NY 10025. (212)749-3647. Contact: Vice President. Estab. 1962. PR firm. Types of clients: all types of accounts, "everything from A to Z." Free client list available with SASE.

Needs: Photos used in public relations, publicity and promotion. Works with about 3 freelance photographers/month on assignment only.

Making Contact & Terms: Provide resume, flyer, business card or brochure to be kept on file for possible future assignments. Buys about 40 photos annually. Negotiates payment based on client's budget, amount of creativity required, where work will appear and photographer's previous experience/reputation. Pays $10-20/hour; $50-100/day; $50-100/job; $35/b&w photo; $85/color photo. Pays on delivery. Submit model release with photo.

Tips: "Nothing should be sent except a business card or general sales presentation or brochure. Nothing should be sent that requires sending back, as we unfortunately don't have the staff or time. We have assignments from time to time for freelancers."

*PETER ROTHHOLZ ASSOCIATES, INC., 380 Lexington Ave., New York NY 10168. (212)687-6565. Contact: Peter Rothholz. PR firm. Types of clients: pharmaceuticals (health and beauty), government, travel.

Needs: Works with 2 freelance photographers/year, each with approximately 8 assignments. Uses photos for brochures, newsletters, PR releases, AV presentations and sales literature. Model release required.

Specs: Uses 8 × 10 glossy b&w prints; contact sheet OK.

Making Contact & Terms: Provide letter of inquiry to be kept on file for possible future assignments. Query with resume of credits or list of stock photo subjects. Local freelancers preferred. SASE. Reports in 2 weeks. NPI; negotiates payment based on client's budget. Credit line given on request. Buys one-time rights.

Tips: "We use mostly standard publicity shots and have some 'regulars' we deal with. If one of those is unavailable we might begin with someone new—and he/she will then become a regular."

SCHORR, HOWARD AND MEGILL, 770 Lexington Ave., New York NY 10021. (212)935-5555. Principal: Martha Megill. Types of clients: industrial.

Needs: Works with 1-3 freelance photographers/month. Uses photographers for trade magazines. Subject matter includes manufacturing operations.

Specs: Uses b&w prints, 35mm and 2¼ × 2¼ transparencies (film and contact sheets).

Making Contact & Terms: Provide resume, business card, brochure, flyer or tearsheets to be kept on file for possible future assignments. Works on assignment only. Does not return unsolicited material. Reports in 1 week. Pays $500-1,500/day. Pays on receipt of invoice. Buys all rights. Model release required.

Tips: Wants to see in portfolio or samples "solid industrial photography experience, particularly in manufacturing processes and operations." To break in, "send b&w and color samples of industrial work. Send brochure, flyer, tearsheets; follow up with call."

■SPENCER PRODUCTIONS, INC., 234 5th Ave., New York NY 10001. General Manager: Bruce Spencer. Estab. 1961. PR firm. Types of clients: business, industry. Produces motion pictures and videotape.

Needs: Works with 1-2 freelance photographers/month on assignment only. Buys 2-6 films/year. Satirical approach to business and industry problems. Freelance photos used on special projects. Length: "Films vary—from a 1-minute commercial to a 90-minute feature." Model/property release required. Captions required.

Specs: 16mm color commercials, documentaries and features.

Making Contact & Terms: Interested in receiving work from newer, lesser-known photographers. Provide resume and letter of inquiry to be kept on file for possible future assignments. Query with samples and resume of credits. "Be brief and pertinent!" SASE. Reports in 3 weeks. Pays $50-150/ color and b&w photos (purchase of prints only; does not include photo session); $5-15/hour; $500-5,000/job; negotiates payment based on client's budget. Pays a royalty of 5-10%. **Pays on acceptance.** Buys one-time rights and all rights; negotiable.

Tips: "Almost all of our talent was unknown in the field when hired by us. For a sample of our satirical philosophy, see paperback edition of *Don't Get Mad . . . Get Even* (W.W. Norton), by Alan Abel which we promoted, or *How to Thrive on Rejection* (Dembner Books, Inc.) or rent the home video *Is There Sex After Death?*, an R-rated comedy featuring Buck Henry."

■TALCO PRODUCTIONS, 279 E. 44th St., New York NY 10017. (212)697-4015. President: Alan Lawrence. Vice President: Marty Holberton. Estab. 1968. Public relations agency and TV and audiovisual production firm. Types of clients: industrial and nonprofit organizations. Produces motion pictures and videotape.

Needs: Works with 1-2 freelancers/month. Model/property release required.
Audiovisual Needs: 16mm and 35mm film. Beta videotape. Filmmaker might be assigned "second unit or pick-up shots."
Making Contact & Terms: Query with resume of credits. Provide resume, flyer or brochure to be kept on file for possible future assignments. Prefers to see general work or "sample applicable to a specific project we are working on." Works on assignment only. SASE. Reports in 3 weeks. Payment negotiable according to client's budget and where the work will appear. Pays on receipt of invoice. Buys all rights.
Tips: Filmmaker "must be experienced—union member is preferred. We do not frequently use freelancers except outside the New York City area when it is less expensive than sending a crew." Query with resume of credits only—don't send samples. "We will ask for specifics when an assignment calls for particular experience or talent."

AL WASSERMAN COMPANY, % Merling Marx & Seidman, 5th Floor, 440 Park Ave S., New York NY 10016. Owner: Al Wasserman. Estab. 1991. Ad agency. Types of clients: industrial, finance, business-to-business, real estate, recruitment and fitness.
Needs: Uses photos for consumer and trade magazines, direct mail, catalogs, posters and newspapers. Subjects include: fitness and sports. Model release required. Captions preferred.
Specs: Uses 8×10 glossy b&w prints; 35mm, 2¼×2¼, 4×5, 8×10 transparencies.
Making Contact & Terms: Query with photocopies of samples. Provide resume, business card, brochure, flyer or tearsheets to be kept on file for possible future assignments. Works on assignment only. Cannot return material. Reports in 1 week. Pays $350-900/b&w photo; $350-900/color photo; $500-1,500/day; and $750-5,000/job. Pays on acceptance and receipt of invoice. Credit line sometimes given. Buys one-time rights or all rights.
Tips: Looks for originality. Send nonreturnable samples such as Xerox prints or shots.

North Carolina

■**EPLES ASSOCIATES,** 4819 Park Rd., Charlotte NC 28209. (704)522-1220. Graphics Manager: Barry Baker. Estab. 1968. Types of clients: industrial and others.
Needs: Works with 1-2 freelance photographers and/or videographers/month. Subjects include: photojournalism.
Audiovisual Needs: Uses slides and videotape.
Specs: "Specifications depend on situation."
Making Contact & Terms: Works on assignment only. NPI. Pays on receipt of invoice. Buys various rights. Model/property release required. Credit line sometimes given, "depends on client circumstance."

■**IMAGE ASSOCIATES,** 4314 Bland Rd., Raleigh NC 27609. (919)876-6400. Fax: (919)876-7064. AV firm. Estab. 1984. Creative Director: John Wigmore. Types of clients: industrial, financial and corporate. Examples of recent projects: "The American Dream," GECAP (multi-image); CTT (multi-image); and Exide Electronics (print).
Needs: Works with 3 freelance photographers/month for audiovisual uses. Interested in reviewing stock photos.
Audiovisual Needs: Uses photos for multi-image slide presentation and multimedia.
Making Contact & Terms: Interested in receiving work from newer, lesser-known photographers. Provide resume, business card, brochure, flyer or tearsheets to be kept on file for possible future assignments. Works with freelancers on assignment only. Cannot return material. Reports in 1 month. Pays $100 maximum/hour; $800 minimum/day; $50/color photo; $100/stock photo. Pays within 30 days of invoice. Buys all rights; negotiable. Model release, property release and captions required. Credit line given sometimes; negotiable.
Tips: "We have a greater need to be able to scan photos for multimedia computer programs."

*■**SMITH ADVERTISING & ASSOCIATES,** P.O. Drawer 2187, Fayetteville NC 28302. (919)323-0920. Fax: (919)323-3328. Creative Director: Ron Sloan. Estab. 1974. Ad agency. Types of clients: industrial, financial, retail, tourism, resort, real estate. Examples of recent projects: mild side-image, Sarasota Convention & Visitors Bureau, (newspaper/magazine/brochure); collateral-image, NC Ports Authority, (brochure); 401-K sign-ups, BB&T, (posters).
Needs: Works with 0-10 photographers, 0-3 filmmakers, 0-3 videographers/month. Uses photos for billboards, consumer and trade magazines, direct mail, P-O-P displays, catalogs, posters, newspapers, signage, audiovisual. Subjects include: area, specific city, specific landmark. Model release preferred. Property release preferred for identifiable people in photos for national publications. Photo captions preferred.

Audiovisual Needs: Uses slides, film, videotape for slide shows, TVC. Subjects include: archive, early years.
Specs: Uses 5×7 glossy color and b&w prints; 35mm, 2¼×2¼, 4×5 transparencies; ½" VHS fillm; ½"VHS videotape.
Making Contact & Terms: Interested in receiving work from newer, lesser-known photographers. Provide resume, business card, brochure, flyer or tearsheets to be kept on file for possible future assignments. Samples are kept on file "for limited time." SASE. Reports in 1-2 weeks. NPI; payment negotiable according to client's budget. Pays on publication. Credit lines sometimes given depending on subject and job. Buys all rights; negotiable.

North Dakota

KRANZLER, KINGSLEY COMMUNICATIONS LTD., P.O. Box 693, Bismarck ND 58502. (701)255-3067. Ad agency. Art Director: Scott Montgomery. Types of clients: wide variety.
Needs: Works with 1 freelance photographer/month. Uses photos for consumer and trade magazines, direct mail, P-O-P displays, catalogs, posters and newspapers. Subjects include local and regional. Model release required. Captions preferred.
Audiovisual Needs: Uses "general variety" of materials.
Specs: Uses 8×10 glossy b&w/color prints; 35mm, 2¼×2¼ and 4×5 transparencies.
Making Contact & Terms: Interested in receiving work from newer, lesser-known photographers. Query with list of stock photo subjects. Provide resume, business card, brochure, flyer or tearsheets to be kept on file for possible future assignments. Works with freelance photographers on assignment basis only; 90% local freelancers. SASE. Reports in 2 weeks. Pays $50/b&w photo; $50/color photo; $40/hour; $100/day. Pays on publication. Credit line given. Buys exclusive product and one-time rights; negotiable.
Tips: In reviewing a photographer's portfolio or samples, prefers to see "people—working, playing—various views of each shot, including artistic angles, etc., creative expressions using emotions." Looking for "small clean portfolio; basic skills; no flashy work. We are exclusively using photos in an electronic mode—all photos used are incorporated into our desktop publishing system."

Ohio

*■AD ENTERPRISE ADVERTISING AGENCY, 1450 SOM Center Road, Cleveland OH 44124. (216)461-5566. Fax: (216)461-8139. Art Director: Jim McPherson. Estab. 1953. Ad agency and PR firm. Types of clients: industrial, financial, retail and food.
Needs: Works with 1 freelance photographer, 1 filmmaker and 1 videographer/month. Uses photos for consumer and trade magazines, direct mail, P-O-P displays, catalogs and newspapers. Subjects vary to suit job. Reviews stock photos. Model release required with identifiable faces. Captions preferred.
Audiovisual Needs: Uses slides, film and videotape.
Specs: Uses 4×5, 8×10 glossy color/b&w prints; 35mm, 2¼×2¼ and 4×5 transparencies.
Making Contact & Terms: Interested in receiving work from newer, lesser-known photographers. Provide resume, business card, brochure, flyer or tearsheets to be kept on file for possible future assignments. Works with freelancers on assignment only. Keeps samples on file. SASE. Reports in 1-2 weeks. Pays $50-100/hour; $400-1,000/day. Pays after billing client. Credit line sometimes given, depending on agreement. Buys one-time rights and all rights; negotiable.
Tips: Wants to see industrial, pictorial and consumer photos.

■BARON ADVERTISING, INC., Suite 645, 1422 Euclid Ave., Cleveland OH 44115-1901. (216)621-6800. President: Selma Baron. Incorporated 1973. Ad agency. Types of clients: food, industrial and financial. In particular, serves various manufacturers of tabletop and food service equipment.
Needs: Uses 20-25 freelance photographers/month. Uses photos for direct mail, catalogs, newspapers, consumer magazines, P-O-P displays, posters, trade magazines, brochures and signage. Subject matter varies. Model/property release required.
Audiovisual Needs: Works with freelance filmmakers for AV presentations.
Making Contact & Terms: Interested in receiving work from newer, lesser-known photographers. Arrange a personal interview to show portfolio. Query with list of stock photo subjects. Provide resume, business card, brochure, flyer or tearsheets to be kept on file for possible future assignments. Works with freelancers on assignment only. Cannot return material. NPI. Payment "depends on the photographer." Pays on completion. Buys all rights.
Tips: Prefers to see "food and equipment" photos in the photographer's samples. "Samples not to be returned other than regional photographers."

■**ELITE VIDEO, INC.**, P.O. Box 2789, Toledo OH 43606. Fax: (419)537-0068. Director: David Thompson. Types of clients: advertising agencies, audiovisual firms, cable companies, home video distributors, closed circuit television firms, both domestic and international.
Needs: Works with 6-7 freelance photographers/month. Uses photos for audiovisual. Needs glamour, erotic, nude, bikini and humorous videos from snippets to full blown and edited features.
Specs: Needs clear VHS tape for initial samples. "The master should be professional quality."
Making Contact & Terms: Send sample footage via certified mail with a SASE. Keeps samples on file. Reports in 3 weeks. "Don't send a resume or listing of education. You can either produce this material, or you can't. If you can, we will call you quickly." Pays 50-67% commission for domestic sales and 50% for international sales. "We offer whatever rights the producer/videographer is willing to sell."
Tips: "This market is exploding. Don't sit on good material. Send it to us. If we return it, it will usually be with suggestions. If we like it, you will get a contract sent out and we will begin to aggressively market you and your work. In addition, we will happily make suggestions to help you improve the salability of your future work. Be professional."

■**FUNK/LUETKE, INC.**, Dept. PM, 12th Floor, 405 Madison Ave., Toledo OH 43604. (419)241-1244. Fax: (419)242-5210. PR firm. Project Manager: Kristin M. Paquette. Estab. 1985. Types of clients: corporate, industrial, finance, health/hospitals.
Needs: Works with 20 freelance photographers. Uses photographs for newspapers, audiovisual, employee newsletter. Subjects include: photojournalism (b&w), health-related-hospitals, corporate communications, industrial, location assignments and video newsletters.
Audiovisual Needs: Uses photos and/or film or video for broadcast quality videotape.
Specs: Uses 8×10, b&w prints; 35mm transparencies; BetaCam SP/broadcast quality.
Making Contact & Terms: Provide resume, business card, brochure, flyer or tearsheets to be kept on file for possible future assignments. Works with freelancers on assignment only. Keeps samples on file. Reports in 1-2 weeks. Pays $50-100/hour; $500-1,000/day; $50-1,500/job; $100/color photo; $75/b&w photo. Pays 45 days after receipt of invoice. Model release required or preferred depending on project. Credit line sometimes given depending upon project.
Tips: In samples and queries, wants to see "photojournalism (b&w), ability to cover location assignments, ability to work independently and represent firm professionally, enthusiasm for work, service-oriented, deadline oriented, available on short notice and willing to travel." Sees trend toward "more use of freelancers because of the need to match the right person with the right job." To break in with this firm, "be enthusiastic, eager to work and flexible. Be willing to research the client. Be a part of the assignment. Make suggestions; go beyond the assignment given. Be a partner in the job."

GRISWOLD INC., 101 Prospect Ave. W., Cleveland OH 44115. (216)696-3400. Executive Art Director: Bob Clancy. Ad agency. Types of clients: Consumer and industrial firms; client list provided upon request. Provide brochure to be kept on file for possible future assignments.
Needs: Works with freelance photographers on assignment only basis. Uses photographers for billboards, consumer and trade magazines, direct mail, P-O-P displays, brochures, catalogs, posters, newspapers and AV presentations.
Making Contact & Terms: Works primarily with local freelancers but occasionally uses others. Arrange interview to show portfolio. NPI. Payment is per day or project; negotiates according to client's budget. Pays on production.

■**THE JAYME ORGANIZATION**, One Corporate Exchange, 25825 Science Park Dr., Cleveland OH 44122. (216)831-0110. Fax: (216)464-2308. Contact: Associate Creative Director or Senior Art Director. Estab. 1947. Ad agency. Clients include: industrial, financial, food and business-to-business. Examples of recent campaigns: Dow Chemical (new business direct mail); Sherwin Williams (new business direct mail); and Interbold (new company introduction).
Needs: Works with 5-10 freelancers/year. Uses photos for trade magazines, direct mail, P-O-P displays, catalogs and audiovisual uses. Subject matter varies. Reviews stock photos and videotape footage. Model and property release required.
Audiovisual Needs: Uses slides and videotape as needed.
Specs: Uses 8×10 and 16×20 color and b&w prints; also uses 35mm, 2¼×2¼ and 4×5 transparencies. Occasionally uses videotape; formats not specified.
Making Contact & Terms: Submit portfolio for review. Provide resume, business card, brochure, flyer or tearsheets to be kept on file for possible future assignments. Works on assignment only. Keeps samples on file. Cannot return materials. Reports as needed; "we'll only call if interested in using them." NPI; payment determined by project budget. Pays on receipt of invoice. Credit lines sometimes given according to "project/client." Most rights negotiable; cases of buying all rights are negotiable, "depending upon client."
Tips: "We need to see a dynamite book."

■**JONES, ANASTASI, BIRCHFIELD ADVERTISING INC.**, 6065 Frantz Rd., Dublin OH 43017. (614)764-1274. Creative Director/VP: Joe Anastasi. Ad agency. Types of clients: telecommunications, hospitals, insurance, colleges, food and restaurants and industrial.
Needs: Works on assignment basis only. Uses photographers for billboards, consumer and trade magazines, brochures, posters, newspapers and AV presentations.
Making Contact & Terms: Arrange interview to show portfolio. NPI. Payment is per hour, per day, and per project; negotiates according to client's budget.

■**LIGGETT STASHOWER ADVERTISING, INC.**, 1228 Euclid Ave., Cleveland OH 44115. (216)348-8500. Fax: (216)736-8113. Contact: Linda M. Barberic. Estab. 1932. Ad agency. Types of clients: full service agency. Examples of recent projects: Sears Optical, Babcock and Wilcox, Evenflo and Teiarc.
Needs: Works with 50+ freelance photographers, filmmakers and/or videographers/month. Uses photos for billboards, consumer and trade magazines, direct mail, P-O-P displays, catalogs, posters, newspapers, signage and audiovisual. Interested in reviewing stock photos/film or video footage. Model/property release required.
Audiovisual Needs: Uses photos/film/commercials.
Specs: Uses b&w/color prints (size and finish varies); 35mm, 2¼×2¼, 4×5, 8×10, 16mm film; ¼-¾" videotape.
Making Contact & Terms: Interested in receiving work from newer, lesser-known photographers. Send unsolicited photos by mail for consideration. Query with samples. Provide resume, business card, brochure, flyer or tearsheets to be kept on file for possible future assignments. Works with local freelancers only. SASE. Reports in 1-2 weeks. Pays $100/b&w photo; $50-200/hour; $800-2,500/day. Pays within 45 days of acceptance. Credit line sometimes given, depending on usage. Buys one-time, exclusive product, all and other rights; negotiable.

LOHRE & ASSOCIATES INC., Suite 101, 2330 Victory Pkwy., Cincinnati OH 45206. (513)961-1174. Ad agency. President: Charles R. Lohre. Types of clients: industrial.
Needs: Works with 1 photographer/month. Uses photographers for trade magazines, direct mail, catalogs and prints. Subjects include: machine-industrial themes and various eye-catchers.
Specs: Uses 8×10 glossy b&w and color prints; 4×5 transparencies.
Making Contact & Terms: Query with resume of credits. Provide resume, business card, brochure, flyer or tearsheets to be kept on file for possible future assignments. Works with local freelancers only. SASE. Reports in 1 week. Pays $60/b&w photo; $250/color photo; $60/hour; $275/day. Pays on publication. Buys all rights.
Tips: Prefers to see eye-catching and thought-provoking images/non-human. Need someone to take 35mm photos on short notice in Cincinnati plants.

■**MIDWEST TALENT/CREATIVE TALENT**, 1102 Neil Ave., Columbus OH 43201. (614)294-7827. Fax: (614)294-3396. Talent Developer: Gary Aggas. Also 700 W. Pete Rose Way, Cincinnati OH 45203. (513)241-7827. Contact: Betty McCormick. Types of clients: talent and advertising agencies, production companies.
Needs: Works with 2-3 freelance photographers/month. Uses photographers for slide sets and video-tapes. Subjects include portfolios and promotional shots of models and actors.
Specs: Uses 5×7 and 11×14 b&w prints; 35mm transparencies; and U-matic ¾" videotape.
Making Contact & Terms: Query with samples or resume. Works with freelancers by assignment only. SASE. Reports in 2-3 weeks. Pays $4-10/b&w photo, $4-25/color photo, $25-65/hour and $100-275/job. **Pays on acceptance.** Buys all rights. Credit line given.
Tips: "Be concise, to the point and have good promotional package. We like to see well lit subjects with good faces."

*■**OLSON AND GIBBONS, INC.**, 2132 E. 9th St., Cleveland OH 44115-1245. (216)623-1881. Fax: (216)861-1790. Executive Vice-Presdient/Creative Director: Barry Olson. Estab. 1991. Ad agency, PR firm. Types of clients: industrial, financial, retail and food. Examples of recent projects: Rubbermaid (trade advertising); BF Goodrich (collateral); Providence Hospital (consumer advertising); Caterpillar and Pioneer-Standard Electronics (direct mail); March of Dimes (TV and radio); Custom Auto (outdoor).
Needs: Works with 2 freelancers/month. Uses photos for billboards, trade magazines, direct mail and P-O-P displays. Model/property release required.
Audiovisual Needs: Uses film and videotape.
Specs: Uses color and/or b&w prints; 35mm, 2¼×2¼, 4×5 transparencies; 16mm, 35mm film.
Making Contact & Terms: Interested in receiving work from newer, lesser-known photographers. Arrange personal interview to show portfolio. Provide resume, business card, brochure, flyer or tear-sheets to be kept on file for possible future assignments. Work with local freelancers on assignment only. Keeps samples on file. SASE. Reports in 1-2 weeks. NPI. Pays on receipt on invoice, payment by client. Credit line not given. Buys one-time or all rights; negotiable.

SMILEY/HANCHULAK, INC., 47 N. Cleveland-Massillon Rd., Akron OH 44333. (216)666-0868. Ad agency. Associate Creative Director: Dominick Sorrent, Jr. Clients: all types.
Needs: Works with 1-2 photographers/month. Uses freelance photographers for consumer and trade magazines, direct mail, P-O-P displays, catalogs, posters and sales promotion.
Specs: Uses 11 × 14 b&w and color prints, finish depends on job; 35mm or 2¼ × 2¼ (location) or 4 × 5 or 8 × 10 (usually studio) transparencies, depends on job.
Making Contact & Terms: Arrange a personal interview to show portfolio. Query with resume of credits, list of stock photo subjects or samples. Send unsolicited photos by mail for consideration or submit portfolio for review. Provide resume, business card, brochure, flyer or tearsheets to be kept on file for possible future assignments. If a personal interview cannot be arranged, a letter would be acceptable. Works with freelance photographers on assignment basis only. SASE. Report depends on work schedule. NPI. Pays per day or per job. Buys all rights unless requested otherwise. Model release required. Captions preferred.
Tips: Prefers to see studio product photos. "Jobs vary—we need to see all types with the exception of fashion. We would like to get more contemporary but photo should still do the job."

WATT, ROOP & CO., 1100 Superior Ave., Cleveland OH 44114. (216)566-7019. Vice President/Manager of Design Operations: Thomas Federico. Estab. 1981. PR firm. Types of clients: industrial, financial and medical. Examples of recent projects: Frances Payne Bolton School of Nursing (memorabilia shots for capabilities brochure); Cleveland Indians (marketing piece).
Needs: Works with 4 freelance photographers/month. Uses photos for trade magazines and corporate/capabilities brochures. Subjects include: corporate. Model release/property release preferred. Captions preferred.
Making Contact & Terms: Interested in receiving work from newer, lesser-known photographers. Provide resume, business card, brochure, flyer or tearsheets to be kept on file for possible future assignments. Works with local freelancers on assignment only. Reports "as needed." Pays $100-1,500/b&w photo; $400-2,000/color photo; $50-75/hour; $400-1,500/day. Pays on receipt of invoice. Credit line sometimes given. Buys all rights (work-for-hire); one-time rights; negotiable.
Tips: Wants to see "variety, an eye for the unusual. Be professional." Sees a trend in the way photographers are cutting their prices.

Oklahoma

ADVERTISING IN THREE-DIMENSION, 8921 E. 49th Place, Tulsa OK 74145. (918)664-1339. President: James W. Wray II. Types of clients: real estate, product advertisers, industrial, tourism, archaeology studies and medical.
Specs: Uses 3-D pictures taken with 35mm or larger format cameras. Accepts both b&w and color, but "no collectible stereoscopic cards."
Making Contact & Terms: Arrange interview to present work in person. Send list of 3-D photo subjects. NPI; payment negotiable according to usability.
Tips: "Our needs are very specialized and require very sharp, high-quality pictures in both standard and hyper-stereo."

■**JORDAN ASSOCIATES ADVERTISING & COMMUNICATIONS**, 1000 W. Wilshire, P.O. Box 14005, Oklahoma City OK 73113. (405)840-3201. Director of Photography: John Williamson. Ad agency. Types of clients: banking, manufacturing, food, clothing.
Needs: Generally works with 2-3 freelance photographers/month on assignment only. Uses photos for billboards, consumer and trade magazines, direct mail, foreign media, newspapers, P-O-P displays, radio and TV, annual reports and public relations. Model release required.
Specs: Uses b&w prints and transparencies. Works with freelance filmmakers in production of 16mm industrial and videotape, TV spots; short films in 35mm.
Making Contact & Terms: Arrange a personal interview to show portfolio (prefers to see a complete assortment of work in a portfolio). Provide flyer and business card to be kept on file for possible future assignments. SASE. Reports in 2 weeks. Pays $25-55 minimum/hour for b&w, $200-400 minimum/day for b&w or color (plus materials). Payment negotiable according to client's budget and where the work will appear. Buys all rights.

The solid, black square before a listing indicates that the market uses various types of audiovisual materials, such as slides, film or videotape.

Oregon

■**ADFILIATION ADVERTISING**, 323 W. 13th, Eugene OR 97401. (503)687-8262. Fax: (503)687-8576. Creative Director: Gary Schubert. Estab. 1976. Ad Agency. Types of clients: industrial, food, computer, medical.
Needs: Works with 2 freelance photographers, filmmakers and/or videographers/month. Uses photos for billboards, consumer and trade magazines, P-O-P displays, catalogs and posters. Interested in reviewing stock photos/film or video footage. Model/property release required. Captions preferred.
Audiovisual Needs: Uses slides, film and videotape.
Specs: Uses color and b&w prints and 35mm transparencies.
Making Contact & Terms: Submit portfolio for review. Query with resume of credits. Query with stock photo list. Provide resume, business card, brochure, flyer or tearsheets to be kept on file for possible future assignments. Works on assignment only. Keeps samples on file. SASE. Reports in 1-2 weeks. NPI; depends on job and location. Pays on receipt of invoice. Credit line sometimes given, depending on project and client. Rights purchased depends on usage; negotiable.

BEAR CREEK DIRECT, P.O. Box 906, Medford OR 97501. (503)776-2121, ext. 3404. Fax: (503)734-2901. Photo Coordinator: David Bjurstrom. In-house ad agency for mail order companies. Types of clients: mail order fruit, food, bakery, floral, gardening and gifts. Examples of recent projects: Harry & David and Jackson & Perkins Co. (catalogs, promotional literature and ads).
Needs: Works with 3 freelance photographers/month. Uses photos for direct mail, catalogs and brochures. Model/property release required for anything with identifiable people or locations.
Specs: Uses 35mm, 120mm and 4×5 transparencies.
Making Contact & Terms: Interested in receiving work from newer, lesser-known photographers. Provide resume, business card, brochure, flyer or tearsheets to be kept on file for possible future assignments. Cannot return material. Reports in 4 weeks. Pays $500-1,500/day; or $150-300/shot. Pays upon use. Buys one-time and all rights; negotiable.
Tips: "I want to see 'perfect' gardens with spectacular color, romantic feeling. Food shots must be warm and friendly—no blemishes or unsightly areas. Be able to provide large quantities of photography to choose from. We are very particular with all of the details of the shots. Look at our catalogs to see the kinds of photography we use."

■**CREATIVE COMPANY**, 3276 Commercial St. SE, Salem OR 97302. (503)363-4433. Fax: (503)363-6817. President/Creative Director: Jennifer L. Morrow. Estab. 1978. Ad agency. Types of clients: food products, health care, tourism, miscellaneous. Examples of recent projects: Supra Products, Oregon Fruit Products and Cherriots.
Needs: Works with 1-2 freelancers/month. Uses photos for direct mail, P-O-P displays, catalogs, posters, audiovisual and sales promotion packages. Model release preferred.
Specs: Uses 5×7 and larger glossy color or b&w prints; 2¼×2¼, 4×5 transparencies.
Making Contact & Terms: Arrange personal interview to show portfolio. Provide resume, business card, brochure, flyer or tearsheets to be kept on file for possible future assignments. Works with local freelancers only. SASE. Reports "when needed." Pays $50-300/b&w photo; $100-400/color photo; $20-75/hour; $400-1,200/day. Pays on publication or "when client pays." Credit line not given. Buys all rights.
Tips: In freelancer's porfolio, looks for "product shots, lighting, creative approach, understanding of sales message and reproduction." Sees trend toward "more special effect photography, manipulation of photos in computers." To break in with this firm, "do good work, be responsive and understand what color separations and printing will do to photos."

Pennsylvania

KEENAN-NAGLE ADVERTISING, 1301 S. 12th St., Allentown PA 18103-3814. (215)797-7100. Fax: (215)797-8212. Ad agency. Art Director: Donna Lederach. Types of clients: industrial, retail, finance, health care and high-tech.
Needs: Works with 7-8 freelance photographers/month. Uses photographers for billboards, consumer magazines, trade magazines, direct mail, posters, signage and newspapers.
Specs: Uses b&w and color prints; 35mm, 2¼×2¼, 4×5 and 8×10 transparencies.
Making Contact & Terms: Query with samples. Provide resume, business card, brochure, flyer or tearsheets to be kept on file for possible future assignments. Does not return unsolicited material. NPI. Pays on receipt of invoice. Model release required. Credit line sometimes given.

ROSEN-COREN AGENCY INC., 902 Fox Pavilion, Jenkintown PA 19046. (215)572-8131. Fax: (215)572-8139. Office Administrator: Ellen R. Coren. PR firm. Types of clients: industrial, retail, fashion, finance, entertainment.

Needs: Works with 4 freelance photographers/month. Uses photos for PR shots.

Specs: Uses b&w prints.

Making Contact & Terms: "Follow up with phone call." Works with local freelancers onlys. Reports when in need of service. Pays $35-65/hour; or /b&w and color photo. Pays when "assignment completed and invoice sent—45 days."

SCEPTER GROUP, INC., Box 265, Morgantown PA 19543. (215)286-6020. Ad agency. Art Director: Bruce Becker. Types of clients: industrial, retail, financial.

Needs: Works with 3-5 freelance photographers/month. Uses photographers for consumer and trade magazines, P-O-P displays, catalogs and newspapers. Subjects include people and products.

Specs: Uses 8×10 glossy prints; 2¼×2¼ and 4×5 transparencies.

Making Contact & Terms: Arrange a personal interview to show portfolio. Send unsolicited photos by mail for consideration. Does not return unsolicited material. Pays $500-2,000/day. Pays on receipt of invoice. Rights negotiable. Model release required.

Tips: Looks for "creativity, good product, situation, flair. Send samples, contact by phone."

■THE SLIDEING BOARD, 216 Blvd. of Allies, Pittsburgh PA 15222. (412)261-6006. Production Manager: Bob Fleck. Estab. 1979. Types of clients: consumer, industrial, financial and business-to-business.

Needs: Works with 5-6 photographers/month. Uses freelance photographers for slide sets, multimedia productions and videotapes. Prefers to work with local freelancers; works with national freelancers for stock, location and some video work. Subjects vary by assignment.

Specs: Uses 35mm, 4×5, 8×10 transparencies; also Betacam SP videotape.

Making Contact & Terms: Local freelancers call to arrange personal interview to show portfolio, slides or demo materials. All others provide resume, business card, self-promotion piece or tearsheets to be kept on file for possible future assignments. SASE. Reports in 2 weeks. NPI. Payment made upon acceptance. Buys one-time rights or all rights. Captions and model releases preferred. Credit line sometimes given.

Tips: Photographers must have knowledge of how to shoot for multi-image, be able to understand objectives of assignment and have ability to work unsupervised.

■STEWART DIGITAL VIDEO, 525 Mildred Ave., Primos PA 19018. (215)626-6500. Fax: (215)626-2638. Studio and video facility. Director of Sales: David Bowers. Estab. 1970. Types of clients: corporate, commercial, industrial, retail.

Audiovisual Needs: Uses 15-25 freelancers/month for film and videotape productions.

Specs: Reviews film or video of industrial and commercial subjects. Uses various film and videotape (specs).

Making Contact & Terms: Provide resume, business card, brochure, to be kept on file for possible future assignments. Works with freelancers on assignment basis only. Reports as needed. Pays $250-800/day; also pays "per job as market allows and per client specs." Photo captions preferred.

Tips: "The industry is really exploding with all types of new applications for film/video production." In freelancer's demos, "looks for a broad background with particular attention paid to strong lighting and technical ability." To break in with this firm, "be patient. We work with a lot of freelancers and have to establish a rapport with any new ones that we might be interested in before we will hire them." Also, "get involved on smaller productions as a 'grip' or assistant, learn the basics and meet the players."

V-GRAPH INC., P.O. Box 105, Westtown PA 19395. (215)399-1521. Multimedia firm. President: Rob Morris. Estab. 1986. Types of clients: industrial, financial and retail. Examples of recent projects: Bell Atlantic, Adria Labs and DuPont (trade shows).

Needs: Works with a few freelancers/month. Uses photos for direct mail, posters, audiovisual and computer graphics.

Audiovisual Needs: Uses videotape and computer graphics/digitized images.

Specs: Uses color prints.

Making Contact & Terms: Provide resume, business card, brochure, flyer or tearsheets to be kept on file for possible future assignments. Works with local freelancers only on assignment. Keeps samples on file. Cannot return material. Reports in 1 month. NPI; "rates determined by budget." Pays on receipt of invoice. Rights negotiable. Model/property release required. Credit line given sometimes, depending on the photographer.

Tips: Looks for "strength, imagination, skill. The use of photography is growing."

■**DUDLEY ZOETROPE PRODUCTIONS,** 19 E Central Ave., Paoli PA 19301. (215)644-4991. Producer: David Speace. Types of clients: corporate.
Needs: Works with 1-2 photographers/month. Uses freelance photographers for slide sets, multi-image productions, films and videotapes. Subject depends on client.
Specs: Uses 35mm transparencies; videotape; 16mm and 35mm film.
Making Contact & Terms: Arrange a personal interview to show portfolio. Provide resume, business card, self-promotion piece or tearsheets to be kept on file for possible future assignments. Works with freelancers on assignment only. Cannot return material. Reports in 1 week. NPI. Pays per day. Payment made on acceptance. Credit line sometimes given. Buys all rights.
Tips: "Make your approach straight forward. Don't expect an assignment because someone looked at your portfolio. We are interested in photographers who can shoot for AV. They must be able to shoot from varied angles and present sequences that can tell a story."

Rhode Island

■**MARTIN THOMAS, INC.,** Advertising & Public Relations, One Smith Hill, Providence RI 02903. (401)331-8850. Fax: (401)331-3750. President: Martin K. Pottle. Estab. 1987. Ad agency, PR firm. Types of clients: industrial and business-to-business. Examples of ad campaigns: DOS Plastics International (brochures, PR); Battenfeld of America (ad series); Hysol Adhesives (direct mail).
Needs: Works with 3-5 freelance photographers/month. Uses photos for trade magazines. Subjects include: location shots of equipment in plants and some studio. Model release required.
Audiovisual Needs: Uses videotape for 5-7 minute capabilities or instructional videos.
Specs: Uses 8×10 color and b&w prints; 35mm and 4×5 transparencies.
Making Contact & Terms: Send stock photo list. Provide resume, business card, brochure, flyer or tearsheets to be kept on file for possible future assignments. Send materials on pricing, experience. Works with local freelancers on assignment only. Cannot return material. Pays $1,000/day. Pays 30 days following receipt of invoice. Buys exclusive product rights; negotiable.
Tips: To break in, demonstrate you "can be aggressive, innovative, realistic and can work within our parameters and budgets. Be responsive, be flexible."

South Carolina

■**BROWER, LOWE & HALL ADVERTISING, INC.,** 215 W. Stone Ave., P.O. Box 3357, Greenville SC 29602. (803)242-5350. Art Director: Ken Howie. Estab. 1945. Ad agency. Uses billboards, consumer and trade magazines, direct mail, newspapers, P-O-P displays, radio and TV. Types of clients: consumer and business-to-business.
Needs: Commissions 6 freelancers/year; buys 50 photos/year.
Specs: Uses 8×10 b&w and color semigloss prints; also videotape.
Making Contact & Terms: Interested in receiving work from newer, lesser-known photographers. Arrange personal interview to show portfolio or query with list of stock photo subjects; will review unsolicited material. SASE. Reports in 2 weeks. NPI. Buys all rights; negotiable. Model release required.

LESLIE ADVERTISING AGENCY, 874 S. Pleasantburg Dr., Greenville SC 29607. (803)271-8340. Creative Coordinator: Marilyn Neves. Ad agency. Types of clients: industrial, retail, finance, food and resort.
Needs: Works with 1-2 freelance photographers/month. Uses photos for consumer and trade magazines and newspapers. Model release preferred.
Specs: Varied.
Making Contact & Terms: Query with resume of credits, list of stock photo subjects and samples. Submit portfolio for review "only on request." Provide resume, business card, brochure, flyer or tearsheets to be kept on file for possible future assignments. Occasionally works with freelance photographers on assignment basis only. SASE. Reports ASAP. Pays $150-3,000/b&w photo; $150-3,000/color photo; $500-3,000/day. Pays on receipt of invoice. Buys all rights or one-time rights.

The First Markets Index preceding the General Index in the back of this book provides the names of those companies/ publications interested in receiving work from newer, lesser-known photographers.

Tips: "We always want to see sensitive lighting and compositional skills, conceptual stengths, a demonstration of technical proficiency and proven performance. Send printed promotional samples for our files. Call or have rep call for appointment with creative coordinator. Ensure that samples are well-presented and that they demonstrate professional skills."

■**SOUTH CAROLINA FILM OFFICE**, State Development Board, Box 927, Columbia SC 29202. (803)737-0400. Director: Isabel Hill. Types of clients: motion picture and television producers.
Needs: Works with 8 freelance photographers/month. Uses photos to recruit feature films/TV productions. Subjects include: location photos for feature films, TV projects, and national commercials.
Specs: Uses 3×5 color prints; 35mm transparencies; 35mm film; VHS, U-matic ¾″ videotape.
Making Contact & Terms: Submit portfolio by mail. Provide resume, business card, self-promotion piece or tearsheets to be kept on file for possible future assignments. Works with local freelancers on assignment only. Does not return unsolicited material. NPI. Pays per yearly contract, upon completion of assignment. Buys all rights.
Tips: "Experience working in the film/video industry is essential. Ability needed to identify and photograph suitable structures or settings to work as a movie location."

Tennessee

■**ARNOLD & ASSOCIATES PRODUCTIONS, INC.**, 1204 16th Ave. S., Nashville TN 37212. (615)329-2800. President: John Arnold. Types of clients: Fortune 500.
Needs: Works with 4 freelance photographers/month. Uses photos for multimedia productions. Subjects include: national trade shows, permanent exhibits and national TV commercials. Model release required. Captions required.
Specs: Uses 35mm transparencies; 35mm film; U-matic ¾″ and 1″ videotape.
Making Contact & Terms: Query with resume. Works with freelancers by assignment only. Cannot return material. Reports in 2 weeks. Pays $300-1,200/day. Pays net 20 days. Buys all rights.
Tips: "We produce top-quality, award-winning productions working with top professionals able to provide highest quality work." Wants to see dramatic lighting, creative composition and sense of style in photos submitted.

■**K.P. PRODUCTIONS**, 3369 Joslyn St., Memphis TN 38128. (901)726-1928. Audiovisual firm. Creative Director: Michael Porter. Estab. 1990. Types of clients: industrial. Examples of recent projects: "Powership," for Federal Express, (training video); Redwing Grain Nozzle, for Redwing Technical Systems, (sales video); and Big Bend Ranch, for Kossman/Klein Advertising, (sales video).
Needs: Occasionally works with freelance filmmaker or videographer.
Audiovisual Needs: Uses film and videotape.
Specs: Uses 35mm motion picture film and Betacam videotape.
Making Contact & Terms: Arrange personal interview to present demo reels or cassettes. Works on assignment only. Keeps samples on file. SASE. Reports in 1-2 weeks. Pays $350-400/day. **Pays on acceptance** or receipt of invoice. Buys all rights; negotiable. Model/property release required. Credit line sometimes given.
Tips: Primarily looks for good composition and a "leading edge look." To break in with this firm, "have a good attitude and work within budget."

*■**LAVIDGE AND ASSOCIATES**, 409 Bearden Park Circ., Knoxville TN 37919. (615)584-6121. Fax: (615)584-6756. President: Arthur Lavidge. Estab. 1950. Ad agency. Types of clients: tourism, finance, food, resort, transportation, home furnishing. Examples of projects. Great Smoky Mountains (tourist brochure); Oldsmobile Dealer Assn. (ad campaign).
Needs: Works with freelancers "when need applies." Subjects include scenics and people. Interested in reviewing stock photos/video footage of people. Model release required. Captions preferred.
Audiovisual Needs: Uses slides and videotape.
Specs: Uses 35mm transparencies; videotape.
Making Contact & Terms: Provide resume, business card, brochure, flyer or tearsheets to be kept on file for possible future assignments. Works with freelancers on assignment only. Cannot return material. Reports in 1-2 weeks. Pays $50 minimum/b&w photo; $90 minimum/color photo; $95 minimum/hour; $490 minimum/day. Pays according to job and client's budget. Pays on publication or receipt of invoice. Credit line given sometimes, depending on client. Buys all rights (work-for-hire).
Tips: Wants to see "clear, sharp, realistic photos, and of course the beauty of the shot." Sees trend where "photos replace illustration more each day." Advises freelancers to be patient. "I work on a very busy schedule, but I'm always wanting to find new work, fresh ideas."

Texas

■**DYKEMAN ASSOCIATES INC.**, 4115 Rawlins, Dallas TX 75219. (214)528-2991. Fax: (214)528-0241. Contact: Production Manager. Estab. 1974. PR and AV firm. Types of clients: industrial, financial, sports, varied. Examples of recent projects: "Save Battleship Texas," Alcoa (publicity/documentation); and Medical Air Services Association.
Needs: Works with 4-5 photographers and/or videographers. Uses photos for publicity, billboards, consumer and trade magazines, direct mail, P-O-P displays, catalogs, posters, newspapers, signage, and audiovisual uses. Subjects include: photojournalism, brochures, PSAs. Reviews stock photos. "We handle model and/or property releases."
Audiovisual Needs: Uses photos for slides and videotape. "We produce and direct video. Just need crew with good equipment and people and ability to do part."
Specs: Uses 8½ × 11 and up glossy b&w or color prints; ¾" or Beta videotape.
Making Contact & Terms: Arrange personal interview to show portfolio. Provide resume, business card, brochure, flyer or tearsheets to be kept on file for possible future assignments. Works on assignment only. Cannot return material. Pays $800-1,200/day; $250-400/1-2 hours. "Currently we work only with photographers who are willing to be part of our trade dollar network. Call if you don't understand this term." Pays 30 days after receipt of invoice. Credit line sometimes given, "maybe for lifestyle publications—especially if photographer helps place." Buys exclusive product rights.
Tips: Reviews portfolios with current needs in mind. "If PSA, we would want to see examples. If for news story, we would need to see photojournalism capabilities. Show portfolio, state pricing, remember that either we or our clients will keep negatives or slide originals."

■**EDUCATIONAL VIDEO NETWORK**, 1401 19th St., Huntsville TX 77340. (409)295-5767. Fax: (409)294-0233. Chief Executive Officer: George H. Russell. Estab. 1953. AV firm. Types of clients: "We produce for ourselves in the education market."
Needs: Works with 2-3 videographers/month.
Audiovisual Needs: Uses videotape for all projects; slides.
Specs: Uses ½" videotape.
Making Contact & Terms: Query with program proposal. SASE. Reports in 3 weeks. NPI. Pays in royalties or flat fee based on length, amount of post-production work and marketability; royalties paid annually. Credit line given. Buys all rights; negotiable.
Tips: In freelancer's demos, looks for "literate, visually accurate, curriculum-oriented video programs that could serve as a class lesson in junior high, high school or college classroom. The switch from slides and filmstrips to video is complete. The schools need good educational material. Subjects that 'might' be appropriate usually are not."

GROUP 400 ADVERTISING, Suite 301, 8452 Fredericksburg, San Antonio TX 78229. (210)697-8055. Fax: (210)697-9744. General Manager: Gary T. Young. Estab. 1984. Ad agency. Types of clients: industrial. Examples of recent projects: Superior Auctioneers, renew auction (cover, inside); Thomas Daniel Productions, TV promo sheet (on-site photos); and Josie Ball Bakery, distributor brochure (product photos).
Needs: Works with 2-3 freelance photographers/month. Uses photos for trade magazines, direct mail and special projects (special effects photography). Subjects include auction activity/equipment. Model release required.
Specs: Uses 3 × 5 color prints; 35mm, 2¼ × 2¼ and 4 × 5 transparencies.
Making Contact & Terms: Interested in receiving work from newer, lesser-known photographers. Query with resume of credits and list of stock photo subjects. Provide resume, business card, brochure, flyer or tearsheets to be kept on file for possible future assignments. Works with freelance photographers on assignment basis only. SASE. Reports in 3 weeks. NPI; payment negotiable. Pays on receipt of invoice, usually net 30 days. Credit line sometimes given. Buys all rights; negotiable.
Tips: "Location is important for specific photo assignments. We use a substantial amount of photography for main auction company client—much internal production—freelance for special projects."

■**HANCOCK ADVERTISING AGENCY**, P.O. Box 630010, Nacogdoches TX 75963. (409)564-9559. Fax: (409)560-0845. Second office: 1418 Marshall, Houston TX 77006. (713)524-4424. Fax: (713)528-1257. Ad agency. Art Director: Judith Dollar. Types of clients: industrial, financial and retail.
Needs: Works with 6 freelance photographers/month. Uses photographs for billboards, trade magazines, direct mail, posters, newspapers, audiovisual, brochure/annual report/newsletter. Subjects include: people, product and still life. Model release preferred.
Audiovisual Needs: Uses photos for slides, film and videotape.
Specs: Uses b&w prints; 35mm, 2¼ × 2¼, 4 × 5 transparencies; ¾" videotape.
Making Contact & Terms: Submit portfolio for review. Query with resume of credits. Send stock photo list. Provide resume, business card, brochure, flyer or tearsheets to be kept on file for possible future assignments. Works on assignment only. Keeps samples on file. SASE. Reports in 1-2 weeks.

Pays $40-100/hour; $350-1,000/day. Pays on receipt of invoice. Credit line sometimes given depending upon usage. Buys all rights; negotiable.
Tips: Looks for "mood lighting and designer's eye." Also needs quick turn around. Sees trend toward "more use of photography in more markets, mainly Texas and South."

■**HEPWORTH ADVERTISING CO.**, 3403 McKinney Ave., Dallas TX 75204. (214)220-2415. Fax: (214)220-2416. President: S.W. Hepworth. Estab. 1952. Ad agency. Uses all media except P-O-P displays. Types of clients: industrial, consumer and financial. Examples of recent projects: Houston General Insurance, Holman Boiler, Hillcrest State Bank.
Needs: Uses photos for trade magazines, direct mail, P-O-P displays, newspapers and audiovisual. Model/property release required. Captions required.
Specs: Uses 8 × 10 glossy color prints, 35mm transparencies.
Making Contact & Terms: Submit portfolio by mail. Works on assignment only. Cannot return material. Reports in 1-2 weeks. Pays $350 minimum/job; negotiates payment based on client's budget and photographer's previous experience/reputation. **Pays on acceptance.** Credit line sometimes given. Buys all rights.
Tips: "For best relations with the supplier, we prefer to seek out a photographer in the area of the job location." Sees trend toward machinery shots. "Contact us by letter or phone."

*■**PENNY & SPEIER**, #400, 1800 W. Loop S., Houston TX 77027. (713)965-0331. Fax: (713)961-4128. Senior Art Director: Dean Narahara. Estab. 1969. Ad agency. Types of clients: industrial and real estate. Examples of recent projects: Friendswood Development, Ryland Homes, Citgo Petroleum.
Needs: Works with 4 freelance photographers, 1 filmmaker, 1 videographer/month. Uses photos for billboards, consumer and trade magazines, direct mail, catalogs, posters, signage and audiovisual. Subjects include: real estate and energy. Reviews stock photos. Model release required. Property release preferred. Captions preferred.
Audiovisual Needs: Uses slides, film, videotape.
Specs: Uses 8½ × 11 prints; 35mm, 2¼ × 2¼, 4x5 transparencies.
Making Contact & Terms: Contact through rep. Arrange personal interview to show portfolio. Send unsolicited photos by mail for consideration. Query with samples. Provide resume, business card, brochure, flyer or tearsheets to be kept on file for possible future assignments. Keeps samples on file. SASE. Reports in 1-2 weeks. Pays $1,000/day. Pays on receipt of invoice. Credit line sometimes given. Buys one-time or all rights; negotiable.

■**CARL RAGSDALE ASSOC., INC.**, 4725 Stillbrooke, Houston TX 77035. (713)729-6530. President: Carl Ragsdale. Types of clients: industrial and documentary film users.
Needs: Uses photographers for multimedia productions, films, still photography for brochures. Subjects include: industrial subjects—with live sound—interiors and exteriors.
Specs: Uses 35mm, 2¼ × 2¼, 4 × 5 transparencies; 16mm, 35mm film.
Making Contact & Terms: Provide resume to be kept on file for possible future assignments. Works on assignment only. Does not return unsolicited material. Reports as needed. Pays $350-800/day; negotiable. Pays upon delivery of film. Buys all rights.
Tips: "Do not call. We refer to our freelance file of resumes when looking for personnel. Swing from film to video is major change—most companies are now hiring inhouse personnel to operate video equipment. Resurgence of oil industry should improve the overall use of visuals down here." Photographer should have "ability to operate without supervision on location. Send samples of coverage of the same type of assignment for which they are being hired."

TED ROGGEN ADVERTISING AND PUBLIC RELATIONS, Suite 224, 1800 Augusta Dr. James Place, Houston TX 77057. (713)789-6216. Fax: (713)789-6216. Contact: Ted Roggen. Estab. 1945. Ad agency and PR firm. Types of clients: construction, entertainment, food, finance, publishing and travel.
Needs: Buys 25-50 photos/year; offers 50-75 assignments/year. Uses photos for billboards, direct mail, radio, TV, P-O-P displays, brochures, annual reports, PR releases, sales literature and trade magazines. Model release required. Captions required.
Specs: Uses 5 × 7 glossy or matte b&w prints; 4 × 5 transparencies; 5 × 7 color prints. Contact sheet OK.
Making Contact & Terms: Interested in receiving work from newer, lesser-known photographers. Provide resume to be kept on file for possible future assignments. Pays $75-250/b&w photo; $125-300/ color photo; $150/hour. **Pays on acceptance.** Rights negotiable.

■**SANDERS, WINGO, GALVIN & MORTON ADVERTISING**, Suite 100, 4110 Rio Bravo, El Paso TX 79902. (915)533-9583. Creative Director: Roy Morton. Ad agency. Uses photos for billboards, consumer and trade magazines, direct mail, foreign media, newspapers, P-O-P displays, radio and TV. Types of clients: retailing and apparel industries. Free client list.

Needs: Works with 5 photographers/year. Model release required.
Specs: Uses b&w photos and color transparencies. Works with freelance filmmakers in production of slide presentations and TV commercials.
Making Contact & Terms: Query with samples, list of stock photo subjects. Send material by mail for consideration. Submit portfolio for review. SASE. Reports in 1 week. Pays $65-500/hour, $600-3,500/day, negotiates pay on photos. Buys all rights.

TELEMEDIA INC., (formerly Pollaro Media Advertising & Productions), 400 W. Main, Denison TX 75020. (903)463-2294. Fax: (903)465-2372. Ad agency. Art Director: Greg Mack. Estab. 1972. Types of clients: retail. Examples of ad campaigns: country music video for Atlantic Records; "Bored with Ford," TV/print campaign for Regional Oldsmobile; and Jessie White Series, TV ads for Tri State Acura Dealers.
Needs: Works with 10 freelance photographers—videographers/month. Uses photographers for billboards, consumer magazines, trade magazines, direct mail, P-O-P displays, catalogs, posters, newspapers, signage and audiovisual uses. Subjects include: retail automotive and miscellaneous retail. Interested in reviewing stock photos/video footage of various retail subjects.
Audiovisual Needs: Uses film and videotape.
Making Contact & Terms: Query with samples. Provide resume, business card, brochure, flyer or tearsheets to be kept on file for possible future assignments. Works on assignment only. Cannot return material. Reports as needed. NPI. Pays within 30 days. Buys one-time rights. Model release required; photo captions preferred. Credit line given sometimes, depending on project.

■**EVANS WYATT ADVERTISING & PUBLIC RELATIONS,** 346 Mediterranean Dr., Corpus Christi TX 78418. (512)854-1661. Fax: (512)854-7722. Owner: E. Wyatt. Estab. 1975. Ad agency, PR firm. Types of clients: industrial, financial, healthcare, automotive, educational and retail.
Needs: Works with 3-5 freelance photographers and/or videographers/month. Uses photos for consumer and trade magazines, direct mail, catalogs, posters and newspapers. Subjects include: people and industrial. Reviews stock photos/video footage of any subject matter. Model release required. Captions preferred.
Audiovisual Needs: Uses slide shows and videos.
Specs: Uses 5×7 glossy b&w/color prints; 35mm, 2¼×2¼ transparencies; ½" videotape (for demo or review).
Making Contact & Terms: Query with resume of credits, list of stock photo subjects and samples. Submit portfolio for review. Provide resume, business card, brochure, flyer or tearsheets to be kept on file for possible future assignments. Works on assignment only. Reports in 1 month. Pays $400-1,000/day; $100-500/job; negotiated in advance of assignment. Pays on receipt of invoice. Credit line sometimes given, depending on client's wishes. Buys all rights.
Tips: Resolution and contrast are expected. Wants to see "sharpness, clarity and reproduction possibilities." Also, creative imagery (mood, aspect, view and lighting). Advises freelancers to "do professional work with an eye to marketability. Pure art is used only rarely." Video demo tape should be ½" VHS format.

■**ZACHRY ASSOCIATES, INC.,** 709 N. 2nd, Box 1739, Abilene TX 79604. (915)677-1342. Creative Director: Bob Nutt. Types of clients: industrial, institutional, religious service, commercial.
Needs: Works with 2 photographers/month. Uses photos for slide sets, videotapes and print. Subjects include: industrial location, product, model groups, lifestyle. Model release required.
Specs: Uses 5×7, 8×10 b&w prints; 8×10 color prints; 35mm, 2¼×2¼ transparencies; 4×5 transparencies; VHS videotape.
Making Contact & Terms: Query with samples and stock photo list. Provide resume, business card, self-promotion piece or tearsheets to be kept on file for possible future assignments. Works with freelancers by assignment only; interested in stock photos/footage. SASE. Reports as requested. NPI; payment negotiable. **Pays on acceptance.** Buys one-time and all rights.

Utah

EVANSGROUP, (formerly Evans/Salt Lake), 110 Social Hall Ave., Salt Lake City UT 84111. (801)364-7452. Ad agency. Art Director: Michael Cullis. Types of clients: industrial, finance.
Needs: Works with 2-3 photographers/month. Uses photographers for billboards, consumer and trade magazines, direct mail, P-O-P displays, posters and newspapers. Subject matter includes scenic and people.
Specs: Uses color prints and 35mm, 2¼×2¼ and 4×5 transparencies.
Making Contact & Terms: Query with list of stock photo subjects. Submit portfolio for review. Provide resume, business card, brochure, flyer or tearsheets to be kept on file for possible future assignments. Works with freelance photographers on assignment only. SASE. Reports in 1-2 weeks.

NPI; payment negotiable. Pays on receipt of invoice. Buys one-time rights. Model release required; captions preferred. Credit live given when possible.

■**HARRIS & LOVE, INC.**, Suite 1800, 136 E. S. Temple, Salt Lake City UT 84111. (801)532-7333. Fax: (801)532-6029. Senior Art Director: Preston Wood. Art Director: Rich Hansen. Estab. 1938. Types of clients: industrial, retail, tourism, finance and winter sports.
Needs: Works with 4 freelance photographers—filmmakers—videographers/month. Uses photos for billboards, consumer magazines, trade magazines, newspapers and audiovisual. Needs mostly images of Utah (travel and winter sports) and people. Interested in reviewing stock photos/film or video footage on people, science, health-care and industrial.
Audiovisual Needs: Contact Creative Director, Bob Wassom, by phone or mail.
Specs: Uses 35mm, 2¼ × 2¼, 4 × 5 transparencies.
Making Contact & Terms: Interested in receiving work from newer, lesser-known photographers. Send unsolicited photos by mail for consideration. Submit portfolio for review. Provide resume, business card, brochure, flyer or tearsheets to be kept on file for possible future assignments. Works with freelancers on assignment basis only. NPI. Buys all rights (work-for-hire); rights negotiable. Model and property releases required. Credit line given sometimes, depending on client, outlet or usage.
Tips: In freelancer's portfolio or demos, wants to see "craftsmanship, mood of photography and creativity." Sees trend toward "more abstract" images in advertising. "Most of our photography is a total buy out (work-for-hire). Photographer can only reuse images in his promotional material."

■**PAUL S. KARR PRODUCTIONS, UTAH DIVISION**, 1024 N. 250 East, Orem UT 84057. (801)226-8209. Vice President & Manager: Michael Karr. Types of clients: education, business, industry, TV-spot and theatrical spot advertising. Provides inhouse production services of sound recording, looping, printing and processing, high-speed photo instrumentation as well as production capabilities in 35mm and 16mm.
Needs: Same as Arizona office but additionally interested in motivational human interest material— film stories that would lead people to a better way of life, build better character, improve situations, strengthen families.
Making Contact & Terms: Query with resume of credits and advise if sample reel is available. NPI. Pays per job, negotiates payment based on client's budget and ability to handle the work. Pays on production. Buys all rights. Model release required.

■**SOTER ASSOCIATES INC.**, 209 N. 400 West, Provo UT 84601. (801)375-6200. Fax: (801)375-6280. Ad agency. President: N. Gregory Soter. Types of clients: industrial, financial and other. Examples of recent projects: cat ad, Dynix, Inc. (cats and computers, magazine ad); "Ready to Do This?" for Deseret Bank (construction loans, multiple media print); and Journal Writer campaign, Eagle Marketing (software, multiple media print).
Needs: Uses photos for consumer and trade magazines, direct mail and newspapers. Subjects include: product, editorial or stock. Reviews stock photos/videotape.
Audiovisual Needs: Uses photos for slides and videotape.
Specs: Uses 8 × 10 b&w prints; 2¼ × 2¼, 4 × 5 transparencies; videotape.
Making Contact & Terms: Arrange personal interview to show portfolio. Query with samples. Provide resume, business card, brochure, flyer or tearsheets to be kept on file for possible future assignments. Works on assignment only. Keeps samples on file. SASE. Reports in 1-2 weeks. NPI; payment negotiable. Pays on receipt of invoice. Buys all rights; negotiable. Model/property release required. Credit line not given.

Virginia

*■**BARKSDALE BALLARD & CO.**, #200, 8027 Leesburg Pike, Vienna VA 22183. (703)827-8771. Fax: (703)827-0783. Estab. 1987. PR firm. Types of clients: food. Examples of recent projects: Virginia Wineries Festival, Virginia Wineries Association (press materials); Virginia Wineries Association (press service); and Congressional Hearings (press service).

 The maple leaf before a listing indicates that the market is Canadian.

Needs: Uses photos for posters, newspapers and audiovisual.
Audiovisual Needs: Uses slides and film.
Making Contact & Terms: Interested in receiving work from newer, lesser-known photographers. Contact through rep. Provide resume, business card, brochure, flyer or tearshets to be kept on file for possible future assignments. Works with local freelancers only. Keeps samples on file. Reports in 1-2 weeks. NPI; cost depends on job and negotiation with photographer. Pays on receipt of invoice. "When possible we credit photos to photographer." Buys all rights; negotiable.
Tips: Photographers should have "good eye for true candid photography and be capable of staging 'natural' shots." Sees growth in "flat, computer-generated/manipulated artwork." Experience with special events a plus.

Washington

MATTHEWS ASSOC. INC., Suite 1018, 603 Stewart St., Seattle WA 98101. (206)340-0680. PR firm. President: Dean Matthews. Types of clients: industrial.
Needs: Works with 0-3 freelance photographers/month. Uses photographers for trade magazines, direct mail, P-O-P displays, catalogs and public relations. Frequently uses architectural photography; other subjects include building products.
Specs: Uses 8×10 b&w and color prints; 35mm, 2¼×2¼ and 4×5 transparencies.
Making Contact & Terms: Arrange a personal interview to show portfolio if local. If not, provide resume, business card, brochure, flyer or tearsheets to be kept on file for possible future assignments. SASE. Works with freelance photographers on assignment only. NPI. Pays per hour, day or job. Pays on receipt of invoice. Buys all rights. Model release preferred.
Tips: Samples preferred depends on client or job needs. "Be good at industrial photography."

West Virginia

■**CAMBRIDGE CAREER PRODUCTS**, 90 MacCorkle Ave., S.W., South Charleston WV 25303. (800)468-4227. Fax: (304)744-9351. President: E.T. Gardner, Ph.D.. Managing Editor: Amy Pauley. Estab. 1981.
Needs: Works with 2 still photographers and 3 videographers/month. Uses photos for multimedia productions, videotapes and catalog still photography. "We buy b&w prints and color transparencies for use in our 9 catalogs." Reviews stock photos/footage on sports, hi-tech, young people, parenting, general interest topics and other. Model release required.
Specs: 5×7 or 8×10 b&w prints; 35mm, 2¼×2¼, 4×5, and 8×10 transparencies and videotape.
Making Contact & Terms: Video producers arrange a personal interview to show portfolio. Still photographers submit portfolio by mail. SASE. Reports in 2 weeks. Pays $20-80/b&w photo, $250-850/color photo and $8,000-45,000 per video production. Credit line given. "Cover color transparencies used for catalog covers and video production, but not for b&w catalog shots." Buys one-time and all rights (work-for-hire).
Tips: "Still photographers should call our customer service department and get a copy of *all* our educational catalogs. Review the covers and inside shots, then send us appropriate high-quality material. Video production firms should visit our headquarters with examples of work. For still color photographs we look for high-quality, colorful, eye-catching transparencies. B&w photographs should be on sports, home economics (cooking, sewing, child rearing, parenting, food, etc.), and guidance (dating, sex, drugs, alcohol, careers, etc.). We have stopped producing educational filmstrips and now produce only full-motion video. Always need good b&w or color still photography for catalogs."

Wisconsin

BIRDSALL-VOSS & KLOPPENBURG, INC., 1355 W. Towne Square Rd., Mequon WI 53209. (414)241-4890. Ad agency. Art Director: Scott Krahn. Estab. 1984. Types of clients: travel, healthcare, financial, industrial and fashion clients such as Musebeck Shoes, Piedmont Vacations, Continental Vacations, WFSI-Milwaukee.
Needs: Uses 5 freelance photographers/month. Works with billboards, consumer magazines, trade magazines, direct mail, catalogs, posters and newspapers. Subjects include: travel and healthcare. Interested in reviewing stock photos of travel scenes in Carribean, California, Nevada, Mexico and Florida.
Specs: Uses 35mm, 2¼×2¼, 4×5, 8×10 transparencies.
Making Contact & Terms: Arrange a personal interview to show portfolio or query with resume of credits or list of stock photo subjects. Provide resume, business card, brochure, flyer or tearsheets to be kept on file for possible future assignments. Cannot return material. NPI. Pays 30 days on receipt of invoice. Buys all rights. Model release required.

Tips: Looks for "primarily cover shots for travel brochures; ads selling Florida, the Caribbean, Mexico, California and Nevada destinations."

WALDBILLIG & BESTEMAN, INC., 6225 University Ave., Madison WI 53705. (608)238-4767. Vice President/Senior Art Director: Gary Hutchins. Creative Director: Tom Senatori. Types of clients: industrial, financial and health care.
Needs: Works with 4-8 freelance photographers/month. Uses photos for consumer and trade magazines, direct mail, P-O-P displays, catalogs, posters, newspapers, brochures and annual reports. Subject matter varies. Model release required. Captions required.
Specs: Uses 8×9 glossy b&w and color prints; 35mm, 2¼×2¼, 4×5 transparencies.
Making Contact & Terms: Provide resume, business card, brochure, flyer or tearsheets to be kept on file for possible future assignments. Works with freelance photographers on assignment basis only. Reports in 2 weeks. Pays $100-200/b&w photo; $200-400/color photo. Pays on receipt of invoice. Buys all rights.
Tips: "Send unsolicited samples that do *not* have to be returned. Indicate willingness to do *any* type job. Indicate if you have access to full line of equipment."

Canada

■❋**JACK CHISHOLM FILM PRODUCTIONS LTD.,** #50, 99 Atlantic Ave., Toronto, Ontario M6J 3J8 Canada. (416)588-5200. Fax: (416)588-5324. President: Mary Di Tursi. Chief Librarian: Susanne Donato. Estab. 1956. Production house and stock shot, film and video library. Types of clients: finance and industrial.
Needs: Uses stock film and video footage.
Making Contact & Terms: Works with freelancers on an assignment basis only.

■❋**WARNE MARKETING & COMMUNICATIONS,** Suite 810, 111 Avenue Rd., Toronto, Ontario M5R 3MI Canada. (416)927-0881. Fax: (416)927-1676. President: Keith Warne. Estab. 1979. Ad agency. Types of clients: business-to-business.
Needs: Works with 5 photographers/month. Uses photos for trade magazines, direct mail, P-O-P displays, catalogs and posters. Subjects include: in-plant photography, studio set-ups and product shots. Special subject needs include in-plant shots for background use. Model release required.
Audiovisual Needs: Uses both videotape and slides for product promotion.
Specs: Uses 8×10 glossy b&w and color prints; 4×5 transparencies.
Making Contact & Terms: Send letter citing related experience plus 2 or 3 samples. Works on assignment only. Cannot return material. Reports in 2 weeks. Pays $1,000-2,000/day. Pays within 30 days. Buys all rights.
Tips: In portfolio/samples, prefers to see industrial subjects and creative styles. "We look for lighting knowledge, composition and imagination." Send letter and 3 samples, and wait for trial assignment.

Foreign

*‡**ALONSO Y ASOCIADOS, S.A.,** Lancaster #17 Col. Juarez, 06600 Mexico, D.F. Mexico. (525)525-1640/44. Vice President: Manuel Alonso Coratella. PR firm. Types of clients: industrial, fashion, financial. Client list free with SAE and IRC.
Needs: Works with 4 freelance photographers/month. Uses photos for consumer and trade magazines, P-O-P displays, catalogs, posters, signage and newspapers. Subjects include: client events or projects, portraits, models. Model release preferred. Captions preferred.
Specs: Uses 5×7 glossy color prints; 35 mm or 4×5 transparencies.
Making Contact & Terms: Send unsolicited photos by mail for consideration. Works with freelance photographers on an assignment basis only. SAE and IRCs. Reports in 2 weeks. NPI; payment depends on client budget. Payment made 15 days after receipt of invoice. Credit line sometimes given. Buys all rights.
Tips: Prefers to see portraits, product shots, landscapes, people. "Freelance photographers should provide recommendations, complete portfolio, good prices. Trends include journalism-type photography, audiovisuals."

 The double dagger before a listing indicates that the market is located outside the United States and Canada.

Advertising, Public Relations and Audiovisual Firms/'93-'94 changes

The following markets appeared in the 1993 edition of *Photographer's Market* but are not listed in the 1994 edition. They may have been omitted for failing to respond to our request for updated information, they may have gone out of business or they may no longer wish to receive freelance work.

AGS & R Communications (did not respond)

American International Meeting Makers (did not respond)

Anderson, Rothstein, Fuqua (did not respond)

Barrett Advertising (out of business)

Don Bosco Mulimedia (did not respond)

Broyles Allebaugh & Davis (did not respond)

Buyer Advertising Agency (did not respond)

Caldwell-Van Riper (did not respond)

Walter F. Cameron Advertising (did not respond)

Carden & Cherry Advertising Agency (did not respond)

Carlton Communications (did not respond)

Cleland, Ward, Smith & Associates (did not respond)

Corp Video Center (did not respond)

Covalt Advertising Agency (did not respond)

Creative Productions (did not respond)

CS&A Advertising (did not respond)

Darby Media Group (did not respond)

Data Command (did not respond)

Walt Disney Home Video (did not respond)

Documentary Films (inappropriate submissions)

Dallas C. Dort and Co. (did not respond)

Charles Duff Advertising Agency (did not respond)

Educational Filmstrips (did not respond)

EMC Publishing (did not respond)

EXPOtacular Industries (did not respond)

Fotheringham & Associates (did not respond)

The Garin Agency (did not respond)

Leon Shaffer Golnick Advertising (did not respond)

Gordon Gelfond Associates (did not respond)

Hancock Advertising Agency (did not respond)

Harding Productions (out of business)

Davis Harrison Advertising (did not respond)

Hart/Conway Co. (did not respond)

Hawbaker Communications (did not respond)

Hayes Publishing Co. (not reviewing freelance work)

Bernard Hodes Advertising (did not respond)

Holland Advertising (not reviewing freelance work)

Image Innovations (did not respond)

International Video Network (did not respond)

Jerryend Communications (did not respond)

George Johnson Advertising (not reviewing freelance work)

Keroff & Rosenberg Advertising (did not respond)

Klinger Group (did not respond)

Ladd Young & Laramore (unable to locate)

Leader Advertising Agency (did not respond)

Legasse Associates (unable to locate)

Levenson & Hill (did not respond)

MDK (unable to locate)

Meriwether Publishing (did not respond)

Warren Miller Entertainment (did not respond)

Motivation Media (not reviewing freelance work)

Muderick Media (did not respond)

Nationwide Advertising (did not respond)

Nissen Advertising (did not respond)

Phoenix Advertising (did not respond)

Pinne/Herbers Advertising (did not respond)

Praxis Media (did not respond)

Pierce Thompson & Associates (did not respond)

Premier Film, Video and Recording (did not respond)

Princeton Partners Advertising (did not respond)

Peter Rogers Associates (out of business)

Ronan, Howard, Associates (did not respond)

Roska Direct Marketing (did not respond)

Tamara Scott Productions (did not respond)

Sorin Productions (did not respond)

Lee Edward Stern Communications (out of business)

Stillpoint International (unable to pay freelancers)

Thompson & Company (did not respond)

Transtar Productions (not reviewing freelance work)

Wallack & Wallack Advertising (did not respond)

Winkler McManus (did not respond)

Wolf, Blumberg, Krody (did not respond)

Wolf Mansfield Bolling Advertising (did not respond)

World Wide Pictures (did not respond)

Wunderman Kato Johnson Chicago (did not respond)

Art/Design Studios

For photographers who think conceptually about projects, art/design studios can be exciting to work with and serve as bountiful sources of income. As with other markets, however, it pays to understand the workings of the design field and research the studios with which you hope to do business.

Typically, a design firm is hired to create a visual style for a company. Developing a corporate image is done through several mediums—annual reports, publication designs, direct marketing, catalogs and brochures, to name a few. Recently, however, design firms have moved into other areas of business, such as media buying, which used to be sacred to advertising firms. Agencies and design studios, which in the past worked hand-in-hand with each other on projects, are beginning to compete for jobs.

"There is still a lot of good work out there for photographers," says Laurel Harper, editor of *HOW,* one of the design industry's leading magazines. "Align yourself with a good design firm."

However, in an industry in which competition between studios is becoming more and more commonplace, this is not always easy to do. The field is filled with young designers who can't find jobs and attempt to make it as freelancers. Not only are young designers saturating the design field with new talent, but some are expanding into photography in order to offer a wider range of services.

"I had a friend tell me that the design profession is getting to be like acting. You do your waitressing during the day and you do your freelance work at night," says Harper, when discussing the young talent. Photographers should stay alert when working with freelance designers because they often don't acquire large paying assignments and they don't hire photographers on a regular basis. Therefore, photographers should not rely on freelance designers for the bulk of their work.

Questionable clients

Harper adds that clients are "wheeling and dealing more, pulling some things to get the work done cheaply." For example, clients may ask several designers to submit specs for potential jobs. Instead of hiring one of the studios, the client uses inhouse staff to compile a concept from the submitted specs. They also may hire cheaper design firms to do the work based on the specs from the other studios. These practices eventually affect photographers because designers get short-changed and cannot offer as much photo work.

As a photographer you should understand that some designers seek larger budgets for photography, but clients often tighten the purse strings when reviewing specs for projects. This poses a serious problem for studios that want to charge reasonable fees for their work, but end up getting undercut by other designers who are willing to work for lower wages. Clients realize they can get projects done for less and the entire industry suffers because of "low-balling" tactics.

Another problem is that business practices of some clients have kept design firms from climbing out of the recent recession. Many clients search for ways to cut corners and, quite often, this means less money for design projects. Designers also report that clients are taking a long time to pay.

Concentrate on strengths

For photographers, finding work with studios is much like seeking work with advertising agencies. When preparing your portfolio, concentrate on strengths and find those studios which have an interest in your area of expertise. Andy Snow, a photographer from Dayton, Ohio, who regularly works with over a dozen design firms, says whenever possible show originals or duplicate transparencies rather than printed pieces. Too often designers start looking at the layout of the printed artwork or the paper quality rather than the image, says Snow. Moreover, he advises freelancers to show medium or larger formats to potential clients rather than 35mm slides. There is still a belief among certain designers that "bigger is better," even though technological advances for 35mm cameras and film are increasing the quality of images. To combat this problem Snow dupes his 35mm slides into 5×8 transparencies.

Regardless of the format, it is important to show designers quality during portfolio reviews. "If you have good work and interesting stuff there's always a market for it," says Snow. "Designers are flooded with promo pieces. It's tough to stand out. Personal visits and being able to sit down and tell them about a shot or situation is a great way to do it." When giving a portfolio presentation, don't show large quantities of images. Narrow down your images to around a dozen top-quality shots.

Photographers who have mastered computer software, such as Adobe Photoshop or programs involving 3-D imaging, should seriously consider approaching design firms. Studios are quickly adapting these image manipulating programs to their everyday jobs and freelancers can benefit greatly from such computer knowledge.

More and more designers also are turning to stock as an alternative to assignment work, so if you shoot and market your own stock be sure to let designers know. However, carefully edit your files so that designers are not stuck looking at "generic" images.

To be successful with designers you must show them your style is unique.

Steven Sessions, of Steven Sessions Inc. in Houston, Texas, says he often matches photographers with clients because of the vision that certain artists can bring to projects. Sessions provides more details in our Insider Report on page 110.

*A.T. ASSOCIATES, 63 Old Rutherford Ave., Charlestown MA 02129. (617)242-6004. Fax: (617)242-0697. Partner: Annette Tucci. Estab. 1976. Design firm. Specializes in publication design, display design, packaging, signage. Types of clients: industrial, financial, retail, nonprofit.
Needs: Works with 3 freelancers/year. Uses photos for catalogs, posters, packaging and signage. Subjects vary. Model/property release preferred. Captions preferred.
Specs: Various sizes and finishes.
Making Contact & Terms: Interested in receiving work from newer, lesser-known photographers. Submit portfolio for review. Works with local freelancers only. Cannot return material. Reports in 1-2 weeks. NPI. Pays on receipt of invoice. Credit line sometimes given. Rights sometimes negotiable.

*ELIE ALIMAN DESIGN, INC., 134 Spring St., New York, NY 10012. (212)925-9621. Fax: (212)925-9621. Creative Director: Elie Aliman. Estab. 1981. Design firm. Specializes in annual reports, publication design, display design, packaging, direct mail. Types of clients: industrial, financial, publishers, nonprofit. Examples of recent projects: First Los Angeles Bank, Equitable Capital Investment and NYU State Business School.
Needs: Works with 1 freelancer/month. Uses photos for annual reports, consumer and trade magazines, direct mail, posters. Model release required. Property release preferred. Photo captions preferred.
Specs: Uses 35mm, 2¼ × 2¼, 4 × 5, 8 × 10 color transparencies.
Making Contact & Terms: Interested in receiving work from newer, lesser-known photographers. Query with resume of credits. Provide resume, business card, brochure, flyer or tearsheets to be kept on file for possible future assignments. Keeps samples on file. Cannot return material. Reports in 1-2 weeks. NPI. Pays on receipt of invoice. Credit line sometimes given. Buys first rights, one-time rights and all rights; negotiable.
Tips: Looking for "creative, new ways of visualization and conceptualization."

*BACHMAN DESIGN GROUP, 201 Bradenton Ave., Dublin OH 43017. (614)793-9993. Fax: (614)793-1607. Vice President/Creative: Deb Stilgenbauer Miller. Estab. 1988. Design firm. Specializes in display design, packaging, retail environments. Types of clients: financial, retail. Examples of recent projects: Corestates Financial Corp., Bancohio National Bank and Commonwealth Federal Savings Bank.
Needs: Works with 1 freelancer/month. Uses photos for P-O-P displays, posters. Subjects include: lifestyle, still. Reviews stock photos. Model/property release required. Photo captions preferred.
Specs: Uses color and/or b&w prints; 2¼ × 2¼, 4 × 5 transparencies.
Making Contact & Terms: Interested in receiving work from newer, lesser-known photographers. Query with resume of credits and samples. Provide resume, business card, brochure, flyer or tearsheets to be kept on file for possible future assignments. Works on assignment only. Keeps samples on file. Cannot return material. Reports in 1-2 weeks. NPI. Pays on receipt of invoice. Credit line sometimes given depending on clients needs/requests. Purchases one-time rights and all rights.

■AUGUSTUS BARNETT DESIGN & CREATIVE SERVICES, 632 St. Helens Ave. S., Tacoma WA 98402. (206)627-8508. Fax: (206)593-2116. President: Charlie Barnett. Estab. 1981. Ad agency, design firm. Specializes in industrial, business to business, retail, food and package design. Examples of recent projects: "Flavor of the Great Northwest," Bernstein's Salad Dressing, Light Fantastic (introduction), Tree Top Food Service (product expansion).
Needs: Works with 1-2 freelance photographers/month. Uses photographs for consumer and trade magazines, direct mail, P-O-P displays, newspapers and audiovisual. Subjects include: industrial, food-related, product photography. Model release required. Property release preferred for vine art, vintage cars, boats and documents. Captions preferred.

 The asterisk before a listing indicates that the market is new in this edition. New markets are often the most receptive to freelance submissions.

Audiovisual Needs: Reviews stock photos, slides and videotape. Uses "combo of 35mm (either simple or complex up to 15 projectors) plus either ¾" or ½" video, large projection system and some other special effects on occasion." Subjects include: "corporate video and slide shows for sales force and brokers."

Specs: Uses 5×7, 8×10, color and b&w glossy prints; 35mm, 2¼×2¼, 4×5 transparencies; VHS ½" videotape and some ¾" format, Betacam.

Making Contact & Terms: Call for interview or to drop off portfolio. Works on assignment only. Keeps samples on file. SASE. Reports in 1-2 weeks. Pays $90-150/hour; $600-1,500/day; negotiable. Pays on receipt of invoice. Credit line sometimes given "if the photography is partially donated for a nonprofit organization." Buys one-time and exclusive product rights; negotiable.

Tips: To break in "make appointment to leave portfolio and references/resumé to meet face-to-face."

BOB BARRY ASSOCIATES, Box H, Newtown Square PA 19073. Phone: (215)353-7333. Fax: (215)356-5759. Contact: Bob Barry. Estab. 1964. Design firm. Specializes in annual reports, publication design, displays, packaging, direct mail, signage, interiors and audiovisual installations. Types of clients: industrial, financial, commercial and government. Examples of recent projects: Corporate Profile brochure, Zerodec 1 Corporation (text illustration); Marketing program, Focht's Inc. (ads, brochures and direct mail); and Mavic Inc. exhibit (large color transparencies in display installations).

Needs: Works with 2-3 freelancers per month. Uses photos for annual reports, consumer and trade magazines, direct mail, P-O-P displays, catalogs, posters, packaging and signage. Subjects include: products, on-site installations, people working. Reviews stock images of related subjects. Model release preferred for individual subjects.

Specs: Uses matte b&w and color prints, "very small to cyclorama (mural) size;" 35mm, 2¼×2¼, 4×5, 8×10 transparencies.

Making Contact & Terms: Provide resume, business card, brochure, flyer or tearsheets to be kept on file for possible future assignments. Works on assignment only. Keeps samples on file. SASE. Reports as needed; can be "days to months." Pays $50-150/hour; $600-1200/day; other payment negotiable. Pays on variable basis, according to project. Credit lines sometimes given, depending upon "end use and client guidelines." Buys all rights; negotiable.

Tips: Wants to see "creative use of subjects, color and lighting. Also, simplicity and clarity. Style should not be too arty." Points out that the objective of a photo should be readily identifiable. Sees trend toward more use of photos within the firm and in the design field in general. To break in, photographers should "understand the objective" they're trying to achieve. "Be creative within personal boundaries. Be my eyes and ears and help me to see things I've missed. Be available and prompt."

*BERSON, DEAN, STEVENS, 65 Twining Lane, Wood Ranch CA 93065. (805)582-0898. Owner: Lori Berson. Estab. 1981. Design firm. Specializes in annual reports, display design, packaging and direct mail. Types of clients: industrial, financial and retail. Examples of recent projects: Hunt-Wesson, 3M National and Siemens.

Needs: Works with 1 freelancer/month. Uses photos for billboards, trade magazines, direct mail, P-O-P displays, catalogs, posters, packaging and signage. Subjects include: product shots and food. Reviews stock photos. Model/property release required.

Specs: Uses 8×10 b&w prints; 35mm, 2¼×2¼, 4×5, 8×10 transparencies.

Making Contact & Terms: Interested in receiving work from newer, lesser-known photographers. Provide resume, business card, brochure, flyer or tearsheets to be kept on file for possible future assignments. Works on assignment only. Keeps samples on file. SASE. Reports in 1-2 weeks. NPI. Pays within 30 days after receipt of invoice. Credit line not given. Rights negotiable.

BOB BOEBERITZ DESIGN, 247 Charlotte St., Asheville NC 28801. (704)258-0316. Owner: Bob Boeberitz. Estab. 1984. Graphic design studio. Types of clients: realtors, developers, retail, recording artists, mail-order firms, industrial, restaurants, hotels and book publishers.

Needs: Works with 1 freelance photographer every 2 or 3 months. Uses photos for consumer and trade magazines, direct mail, brochures, catalogs and posters. Subjects include: studio product shots, some location, some stock photos. Model release required.

Specs: Uses 8×10 b&w glossy prints; 35mm or 4×5 transparencies.

Making Contact & Terms: Interested in receiving work from newer, lesser-known photographers. Provide resume, business card, brochure, flyer or tearsheets to be kept on file for possible future assignments. Cannot return unsolicited material. Reports "when there is a need." Pays $50-200/b&w

The solid, black square before a listing indicates that the market uses various types of audiovisual materials, such as slides, film or videotape.

photo; $100-500/color photo; $50-100/hour; $350-1,000/day. Pays on per-job basis. Buys one-time and all rights.

Tips: "I usually look for a specific specialty. No photographer is good at everything. I also consider studio space and equipment. Show me something different, unusual, something that sets you apart from any average local photographer. If I'm going out of town for something it has to be for something I can't get done locally."

*BRAINWORKS DESIGN GROUP, 2335 Hyde St., San Francisco CA 94109. (415)474-6681. Fax: (415)776-2372. President: Al Kahn. Estab. 1986. Design firm. Specializes in publication design and direct mail. Types of clients: education.
Needs: Works with 2 freelancers/month. Uses photographs for direct mail, catalogs and posters. Wants conceptual images. Model release required.
Specs: Uses 35mm, 4×5 transparencies.
Making Contact & Terms: Interested in receiving work from newer, lesser-known photographers. Arrange personal interview to show portfolio. Send unsolicited photos by mail for consideration. Works with freelancers on assignment only. Keeps samples on file. Cannot return material. Reports in 1 month. Pays $500/day; $750/job. Pays on receipt of invoice. Credit line sometimes given, depending on client. Buys first rights, one-time rights and all rights; negotiable.

*CARLA S. BURCHETT DESIGN CONCEPT, 104 Main St., Box 5A Unadilla, NY 13849. (607)369-4709. Owner: Carla Burchett. Estab. 1972. Design firm. Specializes in packaging. Types of clients: houses and parks.
Needs: Works with "very few" freelancers. Uses photos for posters, packaging and signage. Subjects include: food. Interested in reviewing stock photos of children and animals. Model release required.
Specs: Uses 35mm, 4×5 transparencies.
Making Contact & Terms: Interested in receiving work from newer, lesser-known photographers. Send unsolicited photos by mail for consideration. Works with local freelancers only. Keeps samples on file. SASE. Will respond same week if not interested. NPI. Credit line given. Buys first rights; negotiable.

*CANETTI DESIGN GROUP THE PHOTO LIBRARY, 18 Sargent Place, Mt. Vernon NY 10550. (914)665-0601. Fax: (914)665-1156. Vice President: M. Berger. Estab. 1982. Design firm. Specializes in publication design, display design, packaging and direct mail. Types of clients: industrial, retail. Examples of recent projects: Canetti, Inc., Atwood Richards and Recyld Inc.
Needs: Works with 1-2 freelancers/month. Uses photos for annual reports, trade magazines and catalogs. Model/property release required. Captions required.
Making Contact & Terms: Interested in receiving work from newer, lesser-known photographers. Provide resume, business card, brochure, flyer or tearsheets to be kept on file for possible future assignments. Works with local freelancers only. NPI. Buys all rights.

*CAREW DESIGN, 200 Gate 5 Rd., Sausalito CA 94965. (415)331-8222. Fax: (415)331-7351. President: Jim Carew. Estab. 1977. Design firm. Specializes in publication design, packaging, direct mail and signage. Types of clients: industrial, publishers.
Needs: Works with 2 freelancers/month. Uses photos for consumer and trade magazines, catalogs and packaging. Reviews stock photos. Model/property release required. Captions preferred.
Specs: Uses 8×10, 11×17 semigloss color and/or b&w prints; 2¼×2¼, 4×5 transparencies.
Making Contact & Terms: Interested in receiving work from newer, lesser-known photographers. Provide resume, business card, brochure, flyer or tearsheets to be kept on file for possible future assignments. Works with local freelancers only. Keeps samples on file. SASE. Responds in 3 weeks. NPI. Credit line sometimes given depending on use. Buys first rights; negotiable.

*CSOKA/BENATO/FLEURANT, INC., Room 903, 134 W. 26th St., New York NY 10001. (212)242-6777. President: Bob Fleurant. Estab. 1969. Design firm. Specializes in annual reports, packaging and direct mail. Types of clients: industrial, financial and music. Examples of recent projects: "Wonders of Life," Met Life (Epcot Center souvenir); "Power of Music," RCA/BMG (sales kit); and "Booster Cables," Standard Motor Products (package design).
Needs: Uses photos for direct mail, packaging, music packages. Subjects include: still life, holidays, memorabilia, lifestyles and health care. Interested in reviewing stock photos of still life, holidays, memorabilia, lifestyles, and health care. Model release required for families, lifestyle business and health care. Property release preferred.
Specs: Uses 8×10 or larger color b&w prints; 35mm, 2¼×¼, 4×5, 8×10 transparencies.
Making Contact & Terms: Interested in receiving work from newer, lesser-known photographers. Query with stock photo list. Provide resume, business card, brochure, flyer or tearsheets to be kept on file for possible future assignments. "Only select material is kept on file." Works on assignment only. Keeps samples on file. Cannot return material. Reports only when interested. NPI. Pays 30 days

from receipt of invoice. Credit line sometimes given depending on client requirements, usage. Rights purchased depend on assignment; negotiable.

*❧DUCK SOUP GRAPHICS, INC., 257 Grandmeadow Crescent, Edmonton, Alberta T6L 1W9 Canada. (403)462-4760. Fax: (403)463-0924. Creative Director: William Doucette. Estab. 1980. Design firm. Specializes in annual reports, publication design, corporate literature/identity, packaging and direct mail. Types of clients: industrial, government, institutional, financial and retail.
Needs: Works with 2-4 freelancers/month. Uses photos for annual reports, billboards, consumer and trade mgazines, direct mail, posters and packaging. Subject matter varies. Reviews stock photos. Model release preferred.
Specs: Uses color and b&w prints; 35mm, 4×5, 8×10 transparencies.
Making Contact & Terms: Interested in receiving work from newer, lesser-known photographers. Provide resume, business card, brochure, flyer or tearsheets to be kept on file for possible future assignments. Works on assignment only. Keeps samples on file. SASE. Reports in 1-2 weeks. Pays $90-130/hour; $600-900/day; $500-6,000/job. Pays on receipt of invoice. Credit line sometimes given depending on number of photos in publication. Buys first rights; negotiable.

*GRAPHIC ART RESOURCE ASSOCIATES, 257 W. 10th St., New York NY 10014-2508. (212)929-0017. Fax: (212)929-0017 (phone first). Principal: Robert Lassen. Estab. 1980. Design firm, photography studio, ad agency, printing brokerage, etc. Specializes in publication design. Types of clients: industrial, financial and academic.
Needs: Works with 0-1 freelancers/year. Uses photos for books. Subjects include: people.
Specs: Uses 35mm b&w contact sheets or 11×14 color prints; 35mm transparencies.
Making Contact & Terms: "Just call. If I'm not too busy, I may see him or her. I'm not interested in dealing with reps." Works on assignment only. Keeps samples on file (but only a few). Cannot return material. "If I'm interested I'll call when I have something for them." Pays $40-60/hour. Pays "when I get paid." Credit lines sometimes given. Buys all rights, may negotiate, depends on client requirements.
Tips: "We supply all film and lab. I myself am a photographer, and virtually all photographic services are done in-house. Once in a while I need help." Looks for "professional competence, understanding of merchandising."

*GRAPHIC DESIGN CONCEPTS, Suite 2, 4123 Wade St., Los Angeles CA 90066. (310)306-8143. President: C. Weinstein. Estab. 1980. Design firm. Specializes in annual reports, publication design, display design, packaging, direct mail and signage. Types of clients: industrial, financial retail, publishers and nonprofit. Examples of recent projects: Cosmo Package, Amboy, Inc. (product/package photo); Aircraft Instruments, General Instruments, Inc. (product/package photo); and Retirement Residence, Dove, Inc. (pictorial brochure).
Needs: Works with 10 freelancers/month. Uses photos for annual reports, billboards, consumer and trade magazines, direct mail, P-O-P displays, catalogs, posters, packaging and signage. Subjects include: pictorial, scenic, product and travel. Reviews stock photos of pictorial, product, scenic and travel. Model/property release required for people, places, art. Captions required; include who, what, when, where.
Specs: Uses 8×10 glossy, color and b&w prints; 35mm, 2¼×2¼, 4×5, 8×10 transparencies.
Making Contact & Terms: Interested in receiving work from newer, lesser-known photographers. Provide resume, business card, brochure, flyer or tearsheets to be kept on file for possible future assignments. Works with freelancers on assignment only. Keeps samples on file. SASE. Reports as needed. Pays $15 minimum/hour; $100 minimum/day; $100 minimum/job; $50 minimum/color photo; $25 minimum/b&w photo. Pays on receipt of invoice. Credit line sometimes given depending upon usage. Buys rights according to usage.
Tips: In samples, looks for "composition, lighting and styling." Sees trend toward "photos being digitized and manipulated by computer."

*HAMMOND DESIGN ASSOCIATES, 79 Amherst St., Milford NH 03055. (603)673-5253. Fax: (603)673-4297. President: Duane Hammond. Estab. 1967. Design firm. Specializes in annual reports, publication design, display design, packaging, direct mail, signage and non-specialized. Types of clients: industrial, financial, publishers and nonprofit. Examples of recent projects: Fibercraft catalog, Fibercraft (product photos, cover); Christmas card, Transnational Travel (front of card); and Lester Lab brochure, Lester Labs (electronics).

 The maple leaf before a listing indicates that the market is Canadian.

Needs: Works with 1 freelancer/month. Uses photos for annual reports, trade magazines, direct mail, catalogs and posters. Subject matter varies. Reviews stock photos. Model release required. Property release preferred. Captions preferred.

Specs: Uses 8×10 and 4×5 matte or glossy, color and b&w prints; 35mm, 2¼×2¼, 4×5 transparencies.

Making Contact & Terms: Interested in receiving work from newer, lesser-known photographers. Send unsolicited photos by mail for consideration. Provide resume, business card, brochure, flyer or tearsheets to be kept on file for possible future assignments. Works with freelancers on assignment only. Cannot return unsolicited material. Pays $25-100/hour; $450-1,000/day; $25-2,000/job; $50-100/ color photo; $25-75/b&w photo. Pays on receipt of invoice net 30 days. Credit line sometimes given. Rights negotiable.

Tips: Wants to see creative and atmosphere shots, "turning the mundane into something exciting."

*DAVID HIRSCH DESIGN GROUP, INC., 205 W. Wacker Drive, Chicago IL 60606. (312)329-1500. Art Director: Peter Dugan. Estab. 1976. Design firm. Specializes in annual reports, publication design, direct mail and signage. Types of clients: industrial, financial and nonprofit. Examples of recent projects: employee annual report, Keebler Company; healthy children, Blue Cross/Blue Shield; and annual report, Baker Fentress Management Company.

Needs: Works with a various number of freelancers/month. Uses photographs for annual reports and catalogs. Subject matter varies. Model release required; property release preferred. Captions preferred.

Specs: Uses 8×10 color/b&w prints; 35mm, 2¼×2¼ and 4×5 transparencies.

Making Contact & Terms: Interested in receiving work from newer, lesser-known photographers. Send unsolicited photos by mail for consideration. Provide resume, business card, brochure, flyer or tearsheets to be kept on file for possible future assignments. Keeps samples on file. Sometimes returns material. "Reports as soon as we know something." NPI; pays by contract with photographer. Pays on receipt of invoice. Credit line not given. Buys all rights; negotiable.

■JOHN HOFFMAN DESIGN, 27 St. Joseph Ave., Long Beach CA 90803. (213)433-3343. Creative Director: John Hoffman. Estab. 1977. Ad agency, advertising design. Types of clients: industrial, retail, fashion and finance.

Needs: Works with 2-3 freelance photographers/month. Uses photographs for billboards, consumer and trade magazines, direct mail, P-O-P displays, catalogs, posters, newspapers, signage and audiovisual. Subjects include: food, package goods and autos. Reviews stock photos. Model/property release required.

Specs: Uses color and b&w prints; 35mm, 2¼×2¼, 4×5, 8×10 transparencies; film; videotape.

Making Contact & Terms: Interested in receiving work from newer, lesser-known photographers. Arrange personal interview to show portfolio. Query with resume of credits. Query with list of stock photo subjects. Send unsolicited photos by mail for consideration. Query with samples. Submit portfolio for review. Provide resume, business card, brochure, flyer or tearsheets to be kept on file for possible future assignments. Works with freelancers on assignment only. SASE. Reports in 3 weeks. NPI; "payment estimated only on job." Pays on receipt of invoice. Credit line sometimes given. Buys all rights.

*HULSEY GRAPHICS, 131 Green St., Gainesville GA 30501. (404)534-6624. Fax: (404)536-6858. President: Clay Hulsey. Estab. 1989. Design firm. Specializes in annual reports, publication design, packaging, direct mail. Types of clients: industrial, financial, retail.

Needs: Uses photographs for annual reports, consumer magazines, trade magazines, direct mail, catalogs, posters, packaging. Subject matter varies. Reviews stock photos. Model/property release required.

Specs: Uses 35mm, 4×5 transparencies.

Making Contact & Terms: Interested in receiving work from newer, lesser-known photographers. Query with resume of credits. Query with stock photo list. Provide resume, business card, brochure, flyer or tearsheets to be kept on file for possible future assignments. Works with freelancers on assignment. Keeps samples on file. Cannot return material. Reports only if interested. NPI. **Pays on acceptance.** Buys all rights.

*ELLIOT HUTKIN, INC., 2253 Linnington Ave., Los Angeles CA 90064. (310)475-3224. Fax: (310)446-4855. Art Director: Elliot Hutkin. Estab. 1982. Design firm. Specializes in publication design. Types of clients: industrial, financial, publishers. Examples of recent projects: *Benchmark* for Xerox Corp. (illustration); *Best of Korea* for IDI (illustration, info); and "Take Note!" brochure for Carlsberg Financial (illustration).

Needs: Works with 2-3 freelancers/month. Uses photos for consumer magazines, trade magazines, company magazines, brochures. Subject matter is "eclectic." Reviews stock photos; "eclectic material." Model release required. Property release preferred. Captions preferred; include location, subject (people), equipment shown.

Specs: Uses matte, glossy b&w prints; 35mm, 2¼×2¼, 4×5 transparencies.

Making Contact & Terms: Interested in receiving work from newer, lesser-known photographers. Query with stock photo list. Query with samples. Provide resume, business card, brochure, flyer or tearsheets to be kept on file for possible future assignments. Works on assignment only. Keeps samples on file. SASE. Reports only if assigning work. Pays $250-2,500/job. Pays 30 days after receipt of invoice. Credit line sometimes given (always in magazines; otherwise, depends on client). Rights vary with job/client; negotiable.

Tips: Wants to see an "editorial look; ability to work on the fly with available light, no pro models, very short time frames, and be able to shoot without disturbing ongoing work."

*PETER JAMES DESIGN STUDIO, Suite 203, 7520 NW 5th St., Ft. Lauderdale FL 33317. (305)587-2842. Fax: (305)587-2866. President: Jim Spangler. Senior Art Director: Kev Matney. Estab. 1980. Design firm. Specializes in display design, packaging, direct mail, signage and promotional ads. Types of clients: industrial, retail and nonprofit. Examples of recent projects: AcuraVision Reading Glasses, VSI International (catalog and applications); Arabel vertical blinds, Arabel (stock and product shots); Cellular USA, phone advertisements; and Alamo Rent A Car airline statement stuffers, Alamo Rent A Car (stock and assignments).

Needs: Works with 1-2 freelancers/month. Uses photos for consumer and trade magazines, direct mail, P-O-P displays, catalogs, posters and packaging. Subjects include: lifestyle shots and products. Reviews stock photos. Model release required. Captions preferred.

Specs: Uses 8×10, glossy, color prints; 35mm, 2¼×2¼, 4×5 transparencies.

Making Contact & Terms: Interested in receiving work from newer, lesser-known photographers. Arrange personal interview to show portfolio. Query with resume of credits. Query with samples. Provide resume, business card, brochure, flyer or tearsheets to be kept on file for possible future assignments. Works with freelancers on assignment only. Keeps samples on file. SASE. Reports as needed. Pays $150 minimum/hour; $1,200 minimum/day. Pays net 30 days. Credit line sometimes given depending upon usage.

Tips: Wants to see flexibility of subject and style, knowledge of the craft, innovative."

*JENSEN COMMUNICATIONS GROUP, INC., Penthouse, 145 6th Ave., New York NY 10013. (212)645-3115. Fax: (212)645-6232. Designer: Rya Kaufman. Estab. 1986. Design firm. Specializes in annual reports, publication design, direct mail. Types of clients: Fortune 500. Has done work for Philip Morris, The O'Connor Group and Warner-Lambert Co.

Needs: Works with 4 freelancers/year. Uses photos for annual reports, direct mail, posters. Subjects include: still lifes. Reviews stock photos; subjects are "broad, based on project need."

Specs: Vary based on project needs.

Making Contact & Terms: Interested in receiving work from newer, lesser-known photographers. Submit portfolio for review. Provide resume, business card, brochure, flyer or tearsheets to be kept on file for possible future assignments. Works on assignment only. Keeps samples on file. Cannot return material. Does not report; normally "up to photographer to follow-up." Pays by day rates based on project. Pays within 30 days of receipt of invoice. Credit line given sometimes, depending on project/client and use. Buys one-time rights most frequently.

BRENT A. JONES DESIGN, 328 Hayes St., San Francisco CA 94102. Phone: (415)626-8337. Contact: Brent A. Jones. Estab. 1983. Design firm. Specializes in annual reports and publication design. Types of clients: industrial, financial, retail, publishers and nonprofit.

Needs: Works with one freelancer/month. Uses photos for annual reports, consumer magazines, catalogs and posters. Reviews stock photos as needed. Model/property release required. Captions preferred.

Specs: Uses color and b&w prints; no format preference. Also uses 35mm, 4×5, 8×10 transparencies.

Making Contact & Terms: Query with resume of credits. Query with samples. Provide resume, business card, brochure, flyer or tearsheets to be kept on file for possible future assignments. Works with local freelancers only. Keeps samples on file. Cannot return material. Reports in 1 month. NPI; pays on per hour basis. Pays on receipt of invoice. Credit line sometimes given. Buys one-time rights; negotiable.

*JONES MEDINGER KINDSCHI BUSHKO INC., Fields Lane, North Salem NY 10560. (914)277-3715. Fax: (914)277-3744. Art Buyer: Wynn Medinger. Estab. 1980. Design firm. Specializes in annual reports and publication design. Types of clients: industrial, financial, retail and nonprofit. Examples of recent projects: Worked on brochures, magazines, etc. for IBM, GE and GTE.

Needs: Works with 10 freelancers/month. Uses photographs for annual reports, trade magazines, posters and product brochures. Subject matter varies. Model release required. Captions preferred.
Specs: Uses 35mm, 2¼ × 2¼ transparencies.
Making Contact & Terms: Interested in receiving work from newer, lesser-known photographers. Send unsolicited photos by mail for consideration. "No phone calls. Send tearsheets, samples only." Works with freelancers on assignment only. Keeps samples on file. SASE. Reporting time depends on projects. Pays $400-1,500/day. Pays 30 days after receipt of invoice. Credit line sometimes given. Rights negotiable.
Tips: Looking for corporate, environmental and portrait shots.

*LIEBER BREWSTER CORPORATE DESIGN, #2F, 324 W. 87th St., New York NY 10024. (212)874-2874. Fax: (212)877-6403. Principal: Anna Lieber. Estab. 1988. Design firm. Specializes in publication design, display design, packaging, direct mail, signage, corporate identity and capability brochures. Types of clients: industrial, financial, retail, publishers and nonprofit.
Needs: Works with 1 freelancer/month. Uses photos for direct mail, catalogs, posters, packaging, ads. Subjects include: food and wine, people and location. Reviews stock photos of food and wine.
Specs: Uses 8 × 10, b&w prints; 35mm, 2¼ × 2¼, 4 × 5, 8 × 10 transparencies.
Making Contact & Terms: Interested in receiving work from newer, lesser-known photographers. Provide resume, business card, brochure, flyer or tearsheets to be kept on file for possible future assignments. Works with freelancers on assignment only. Keeps samples on file. SASE. Reports only on solicited work. Pays $75-150/hour; $250-700/day; $500-2,000/job. **Pays on acceptance.** Pays on receipt of invoice. Credit line given. Rights negotiable.
Tips: Wants to see an "extremely professional presentation, well-defined style and versatility."

*MAUCK & ASSOCIATES, Suite 200, 303 Locust, Des Moines IA 50309. (515)243-6010. Fax: (515)243-6011. President: Kent Mauck. Estab. 1986. Design firm. Specializes in annual reports and publication design. Types of clients: industrial, financial, retail, publishers and nonprofit. Examples of recent projects: Meredith Corporation, annual report; Blue Cross Blue Shield, annual report; and Allied Group Insurance, annual report.
Needs: Works with 3 freelancers/month. Uses photographs for annual reports, billboards, consumer and trade magazines and posters. Subject matter varies. Reviews stock photos. Model release required.
Specs: Uses 35mm, 2¼ × 2¼, 4 × 5 transparencies.
Making Contact & Terms: Interested in receiving work from newer, lesser-known photographers. Arrange personal interview to show portfolio. Query with stock photo list. Query with samples. Provide resume, business card, brochure, flyer or tearsheets to be kept on file for possible future assignments. Keeps samples on file. SASE. Reports only when interested. Pays $700-900/day. Pays on receipt of invoice. Credit line given. Rights negotiable.

*MIRANDA DESIGNS INC., 745 President St., Brooklyn NY 11215. (718)857-9839. Owner: Mike Miranda. Estab. 1970. Design firm and publisher. Specializes in publication design, direct mail and product development. Types of clients: industrial, financial, retail and nonprofit.
Needs: Works with 1 freelancer/month. Uses photos for annual reports, consumer magazines, direct mail and catalogs. Subjects include: product and reportage. Model/property release required.
Specs: Uses 8 × 10, matte, b&w prints; 35mm transparencies.
Making Contact & Terms: Interested in receiving work from newer, lesser-known photographers. Provide resume, business card, brochure, flyer or tearsheets to be kept on file for possible future assignments. Works on assignment only. Keeps samples on file. Cannot return material. Reports in 1-2 weeks. NPI. Credit line sometimes given depending upon client. Rights bought depend on client's needs.

MITCHELL STUDIOS DESIGN CONSULTANTS, 1111 Fordham Lane, Woodmere NY 11598. (516)374-5620. Fax: (516)374-6915. Principal: Steven E. Mitchell. Estab. 1922. Design firm. Types of clients: corporations with consumer products. Examples of recent clients: Lipton Cup-A-Soup, Thomas J. Lipton, Inc.; Colgate Toothpaste, Colgate Palmolive Co.; and Chef Boy-Ar-Dee, American Home Foods—all three involved package design.

Needs: Works with variable number of freelancers/month. Uses photographs for direct mail, P-O-P displays, catalogs, posters, signage and package design. Subjects include: still life/product. Reviews stock photos of still life/people. Model release required. Property release preferred. Captions preferred.
Specs: Uses all sizes and finishes of color and b&w prints; 35mm, 2¼×2¼, 4×5, 8×10 transparencies.
Making Contact & Terms: Interested in receiving work from newer, lesser-known photographers. Submit portfolio for review, provide resume, business card, brochure, flyer or tearsheets to be kept on file for possible future assignments. Cannot return material. Reports as needed. Pays $35-75/hour; $350-1,500/day; $500 and up/job. Pays on receipt of invoice. Credit line sometimes given depending on client approval. Buys all rights.
Tips: In portfolio, looks for "ability to complete assignment." Sees a trend toward "tighter budgets." To break in with this firm, keep in touch regularly.

MORRIS BEECHER LORD, (formerly Morris Beecher), 1000 Potomac St. NW, Washington DC 20007. (202)337-5300. Fax: (202)333-2659. Contact: Diane Beecher. Estab. 1983. Ad agency. Specializes in publications, P-O-P, display design, direct mail, signage, collateral, ads and billboards. Types of clients: sports, health and nutrition, the environment, real estate, resorts, shopping centers and retail.
Needs: Works with 3-4 freelancers/month. Uses photos for billboards, direct mail, posters, signage, ads and collateral materials. Subjects include real estate, fashion and lifestyle. Reviews stock photos. Model release required. Captions preferred.
Specs: Uses any size or finish of color and b&w prints; 35mm transparencies.
Making Contact & Terms: Arrange personal interview to show portfolio. Provide business card, brochure, flyer or tearsheets to be kept on file for possible future assignments. Works on assignment only. Keeps samples on file. SASE. Usually pays per job. Credit line not given. Buys all rights.
Tips: Wants to see "very high quality work." Uses a lot of stock.

■**TOM NICHOLSON ASSOCIATES INC.**, 8th Floor, 295 Lafayette St., New York NY 10012. (212)274-0470. Fax: (212)274-0380. President: Tom Nicholson. Estab. 1987. Design firm. Specializes in interactive multimedia. Types of clients: industrial and publishers. Examples of recent projects: "History of Sailing," IBM (interactive multimedia); "Worldview," Worldview, Inc. (educational, physical sciences CD-ROM), and "Shopper's Express," Whittle Communications (interactive multimedia).
Needs: Works with 0-3 freelancers/month. Uses photos for CD-ROM multimedia. Subjects include: nature and sciences. Reviews stock photos of nature and sciences.
Specs: Uses various formats.
Making Contact & Terms: Interested in receiving work from newer, lesser-known photographers. Query with stock photo list. Provide resume, business card, brochure, flyer or tearsheets to be kept on file for possible future assignments. Cannot return material. NPI. Pays on publication. Credit line given. Buys one-time and all rights.
Tips: "The industry is moving toward electronic usage. Need realistic pricing to address this market."

*****O'MARA DESIGN GROUP, INC.**, Unit D, 1551 16th St., Santa Monica CA 90404. (310)315-0460. Fax: (310)315-0459. Contact: Dan O'Mara or Wil Conerly. Estab. 1983. Design firm. Specializes in annual reports, publication design and direct mail. Types of clients: industrial and financial.
Needs: Works with 2-3 freelancers/month. Uses photos for annual reports and catalogs. Reviews stock photos. Model release required.
Specs: Uses 35mm, 2¼×2¼, 4×5 transparencies.
Making Contact & Terms: Interested in receiving work from newer, lesser-known photographers. Send unsolicited photos by mail for consideration. Provide resume, business card, brochure, flyer or tearsheets to be kept on file for possible future assignments. Works with local freelancers only. Keeps samples on file. Cannot return material. Reports in 3-4 weeks. Pays $500-1,000/day. **Pays on acceptance.** Credit line sometimes given. Buys all rights.
Tips: Looks for "good working attitude, no prima donnas."

*****PIKE AND CASSELS, INC.**, Suite 100, 300 S. Liberty St., Winston-Salem NC 27101. (919)723-9219. Fax: (919)723-9249. Art Director: Keith Vest. Estab. 1985. Design and advertising firm. Specializes in publication design, display design, packaging, graphic standards and fashion. Types of clients: industrial, financial, retail and nonprofit.
Needs: Works with 1 freelancer/month. Uses photos for consumer and trade magazines, direct mail, P-O-P displays, catalogs, posters and packaging. Subjects include: tabletop-food and product. Model release preferred. Property release required. Captions preferred; include technique.
Specs: Uses color 35mm, 2¼×2¼, 4×5 transparencies.
Making Contact & Terms: Interested in receiving work from newer, lesser-known photographers. Provide resume, business card, brochure, flyer or tearsheets to be kept on file for possible future assignments. Works with freelancers on assignment only. Keeps samples on file. SASE. Reports in 1 month. NPI. Pays on receipt of invoice. Credit line not given. Buys all rights; negotiable.

Studios Demand Conceptual Thinking

The strength of outstanding design lies in the concepts that are created and the execution of ideas. Nobody knows this better than Steven Sessions, whose
studio thrives on the imagination of its workers and
the creative ideas of freelancers.

"It is not enough just to be different. We are in
the business of visual communication, whether literal
or emotional or symbolic," says Sessions. Based in
Houston, Steven Sessions, Inc., has earned numerous
regional and national awards from organizations such
as the New York Art Director's Club, The American
Institute of Graphic Arts and The American Advertising Federation. The studio also has been featured
in top design industry publications, such as *HOW,*
Print and *Communication Arts.*

Steven Sessions

There are many reasons why this 12-year-old com-
pany has been so successful. One reason is the implementation of computers into
the design process. Over the past five years employees have been scanning photos
into computers and using software, such as Adobe Photoshop, to manipulate and
create stunning designs. "It's not hard to do something different. It's hard, though,
to do something different that doesn't confuse the issue," says Sessions, who believes
understanding the client's needs is paramount to completing a successful project.

Photographers eager to work in the design industry should develop work that is
unique. Also, they should be aware of the demand for clever, high-quality images
that service the needs of clients. "Sometimes we get caught up in expressing ourselves
in the shot. We must remember that we're doing something for the client and not
for ourselves," he says.

While Sessions enjoys seeing strong angles, impressive lighting and solid composition in photographs, he is turned off by cliches and photos that are too literal. "Being
in Houston, I am completely bored by an oil rig with a sunset behind it. Forget it,"
he says. Trick lenses, such as fish eyes, also rank high on his list of unimpressive
works. "It says that this photographer is not very imaginative, and you're not likely
to get something special from somebody who is not imaginative."

Sessions says he receives many telephone calls and an average of one or two
portfolios each week from photographers. When reviewing portfolios he searches
for those artists who show they can shoot ordinary objects in a special way. "I prefer
to be a guide to the process," says Sessions, who gives photographers a lot of artistic
freedom. "Because I am not a photographer, I basically would prefer to rely on the
photographer for the photograph and just give them good guidance and direction
with regard to what we're trying to do with the image."

— *Michael Willins*

INTERIM

REPORT

1

THREE MONTHS

ENDED

MARCH 31, 1991

SOUTHDOWN, INC.

© photo by Jim Sims

Designer Steven Sessions likes to see images with impressive lighting and strong composition. Taken during construction of the Los Angeles Metro Rail, this photo displays both of these qualities. Shot by photographer Jim Sims of Vancouver, Washington, the image was used on the cover of an interim report by Southdown Inc., the nation's leading cement manufacturer.

Tips: Wants to see "flexibility in subjects and technique, fashion photography, processing control and organization of shoots."

ARNOLD SAKS ASSOCIATES, 350 E. 81st St., New York NY 10028. (212)861-4300. Fax: (212)535-2590. Director of Client Services: Timothy Coppins. Estab. 1968. Graphic design firm. Types of clients: industrial, financial, legal, pharmaceutical and utilities. Clients include: Bristol-Myers Squibb, Alcoa, Goldman Sachs and International Paper.
Needs: Works with approximately 15 photographers during busy season. Uses photos for annual reports and corporate brochures. Subjects include: corporate situations and portraits. Reviews stock photos; subjects vary according to the nature of the annual report. Model release required. Captions preferred.
Specs: Uses b&w prints; 35mm, 2¼ × 2¼, 4 × 5, 8 × 10 transparencies.
Making Contact & Terms: Interested in receiving work from newer, lesser-known photographers. "Appointments are set up during the spring for summer review on a first-come only basis. We have a limit of approximately 30 portfolios each season." Call Tim Coppins to arrange an appointment. Works on assignment only. Reports as needed. Payment negotiable, "based on project budgets. Generally we pay $1,250-2,250/day." Pays on receipt of invoice and payment by client; advances provided. Credit line sometimes given depending upon client specifications. Buys all rights; negotiable.
Tips: "Ideally a photographer should show a corporate book indicating his success with difficult working conditions and establishing an attractive and vital final product." This "company is well known in the design community for doing classic graphic design. We look for solid, conservative, straightforward corporate photography that will enhance these ideals."

JACK SCHECTERSON ASSOCIATES, 5316 251 Place, Little Neck NY 11362. (718)225-3536. Fax: (718)423-3478. Principal: Jack Schecterson. Estab. 1962. Design firm. Specializes in product, packaging and graphic design. Types of clients: industrial, consumer and product manufacturers.
Needs: "Depends on work in-house." Uses photos for annual reports, consumer and trade magazines, direct mail, P-O-P displays, catalogs and packaging. Subjects include: "depends on work in-house." Reviews stock photos. Model/property release required. Captions preferred.
Specs: Variety of size color/b&w prints; 35mm, 2¼ × 2¼, 4 × 5 and 8 × 10 transparencies.
Making Contact & Terms: Interested in receiving work from newer, lesser-known photographers. Works with local freelancers on assignment only. Cannot return material. Reports in 3 weeks. NPI; "depends upon job." Credit line sometimes given. Buys all rights.
Tips: Wants to see creative and unique images.

STEVEN SESSIONS, INC., Suite 500, 5177 Richmond Ave, Houston TX 77056. Phone: (713)850-8450. Fax: (713)850-9324. President: Steven Sessions. Estab. 1982. Design firm. Specializes in annual reports, packaging and publication design. Types of clients: industrial, financial, women's fashion, cosmetics, retail, publishers and nonprofit.
Needs: Always works with freelancers. Uses photos for annual reports, consumer and trade magazines, P-O-P displays, catalogs and packaging. Subject matter varies according to need. Reviews stock photos. Model/property release preferred.
Specs: Uses b&w and color prints; no preference for format or finish. Also uses 35mm, 2¼ × 2¼, 4 × 5, 8 × 10 transparencies.
Making Contact & Terms: Submit portfolio for review. Send unsolicited photos by mail for consideration. Provide resume, business card, brochure, flyer or tearsheets to be kept on file for possible future assignments. Keeps samples on file. SASE. Reports in 1-2 weeks. Pays $1,800-5,000/day. Pays on receipt of invoice. Credit line given. Sometimes buys all rights; negotiable.

DEBORAH SHAPIRO DESIGNS, 150 Bentley Ave., Jersey City NJ 07304. (201)432-5198. Contact: Deborah Shapiro. Estab. 1979. Design firm. Specializes in annual reports, publication design, direct mail and signage. Types of clients: industrial, financial, publishers and nonprofit organizations.
Needs: Occasionally works with freelancers. Typically needs still lifes and people shots. Reviews stock photos. Model release required.
Specs: Uses color prints and 35mm transparencies.
Making Contact & Terms: Send unsolicited photos by mail for consideration. Works with local freelancers only. Keeps samples on file. Cannot return material. Reports in 1 month. NPI; amount of payment "depends upon the photographer's ability and the client's budget." Pays on receipt of invoice. Credit line sometimes given depending upon client's usage. Buys one-time rights.

*SIGNATURE DESIGN, 20 Southmoor, Clayton MO 63105. (314)725-1935. Owner/Art Director: Therese McKee. Estab. 1988. Design firm. Specializes in packaging, signage and exhibit and corporate identity. Types of clients: nonprofit groups, museums and corporations. Examples of recent projects: membership brochure, friends of the St. Louis Public Library; how to festival poster and brochure friends of the St. Louis Public Libarary; and composting kiosk exhibit, Missouri Botanical Garden.

Needs: Works with 2 freelancers/month. Uses photographs for catalogs, posters, copy shots and brochures. Subjects are specific to brochures. Reviews stock photos.
Specs: Uses prints and 35mm, 2¼×2¼ and 4×5 transparencies.
Making Contact & Terms: Interested in receiving work from newer, lesser-known photographers. Arrange personal interview to show portfolio. Send unsolicited photos by mail for consideration. Provide resume, business card, brochure, flyer or tearsheets to be kept on file for possible future assignments. Keeps samples on file. Reports in 1-2 weeks. NPI. Pays on receipt of invoice. Credit line sometimes given. Buys all rights; negotiable.

SMART ART, 1077 Celestial St., Cincinnati OH 45202. (513)241-9757. President: Fred Lieberman. Estab. 1979. Design firm, advertising art. Specializes in annual reports, display design, packaging, direct mail, signage and advertising art. Types of clients: industrial, retail and health. Examples of recent projects: Western Produce Sales Annual (Chiquita); Vennite Corporate Sales Brochure (Neyra Industries); and Corporate Capabilities Brochure (Leonard Insurance).
Needs: Uses photographs for consumer and trade magazines, direct mail, P-O-P displays, catalogs, posters, packaging and signage for a wide diversity of clients. Reviews stock photos "on a wide variety of subjects; client list varies." Model/property release required. Captions preferred.
Specs: Uses 8×10 color and b&w prints; 2¼×2¼, 4×5, 8×10 transparencies.
Making Contact & Terms: Query with list of stock photo subjects. Provide resume, business card, brochure, flyer or tearsheets to be kept on file for possible future assignments. Works with local freelancers only. Keeps samples on file. Cannot return material. Reporting time "depends entirely on kinds of projects planned." Pays $50-200/hour; $350-1,500/day. Pays on receipt of invoice. "Generally client pays directly upon receipt of invoice." Buys all rights; negotiable. Credit lines sometimes given depending on what might be negotiated.

*TRIBOTTI DESIGNS, 22907 Bluebird Dr., Calabasas CA 91302. (818)591-7720. Fax: (818)591-7910. Contact: Bob Tribotti. Estab. 1970. Design firm. Specializes in annual reports, publication design, display design, packaging, direct mail and signage. Types of clients: industrial, financial, retail, publishers and nonprofit. Examples of recent projects: school catalog, South Western University School of Law; newsline, LA Daily News; and annual report, AM West Bank.
Needs: Uses photos for annual reports, consumer and trade magazines, direct mail, catalogs and posters. Subjects vary. Reviews stock photos. Model/property release required.
Specs: Uses 8×10, glossy, color and b&w prints; 35mm, 2¼×2¼, 4×5, 8×10 transparencies.
Making Contact & Terms: Interested in receiving work from newer, lesser-known photographers. Contact through rep. Query with resume of credits. Provide resume, business card, brochure, flyer or tearsheets to be kept on file for possible future assignments. Works with local freelancers only. Keeps samples on file. Cannot return material. Reports in 3 weeks. Pays $600-750. Pays on receipt of invoice. Credit line sometimes given. Buys one-time rights; negotiable.

*UNIT ONE, INC., Suite 101, 616 Washington St., Denver CO 80203. (303)863-7810. Fax: (303)863-7812. President: Chuck Danford. Estab. 1968. Design firm. Specializes in annual reports, publication design, display design, corporate identity, corporate collateral and signage. Types of clients: industrial, financial, nonprofit and construction/architecture. Examples of recent projects: A.B. Hirschfeld Press, identity and brochure; Western Mobile, corporate identity and corporate brochure; Denver International Airport, magazine; and The Neenan Company, corporate brochure.
Needs: Works with 1-2 freelancers/month. Uses photos for annual reports, trade magazines, direct mail, P-O-P displays, catalogs, posters and corporate brochures/ads. Subjects include: construction, architecture, engineering, people and oil and gas. Reviews stock photos "when needed." Model/property release required.
Specs: Reviews 2¼×2¼, 4×5 transparencies.
Making Contact & Terms: Interested in receiving work from newer, lesser-known photographers. Query with resume of credits. Provide resume, business card, brochure, flyer or tearsheets to be kept on file for possible future assignments. Works with local freelancers only. Keeps samples on file. SASE. Reports as needed. Pays $500-1,500/day; $300-450/location for 4×5 building shots. Pays within 30-45 days of completion. Credit line sometimes given, depending on the job, client and price. Buys all rights; negotiable.
Tips: Looks for "quality, style, eye for design, color and good composition."

*WEYMOUTH DESIGN INC., 332 Congress St., Boston MA 02210. (617)542-2647. Fax: (617)451-6233. Office Manager: Judith Hildebrandt. Estab. 1973. Design firm. Specializes in annual reports, publication design, packaging and signage. Types of clients: industrial, financial, retail and nonprofit.
Needs: Works with 1-2 freelancers/month. Uses photos for annual reports and catalogs. Subjects include executive portraits, people pictures or location shots. Subject matter varies. Model/property release required. "Photo captions are written by our corporate clients."

Specs: Uses 35mm, 2¼×2¼, 4×5 transparencies.
Making Contact & Terms: Interested in receiving work from newer, lesser-known photographers. Submit portfolio for review. Portfolio reviews only April-June; otherwise send/drop off portfolio for review. Works with freelancers on assignment only. Keeps samples on file. SASE. Pays $25 minimum/hour; $250 minimum/day. Pays on receipt of invoice. Buys one-time rights; negotiable.

CLARENCE ZIERHUT, INC., 2014 Platinum, Garland TX 75042. Phone: (214)276-1722. Fax: (214)272-5570. President: Clarence Zierhut. Estab. 1956. Design firm. Specializes in displays, packaging and product design. Types of clients: industrial.
Needs: Uses photos for direct mail, catalogs and packaging. Subjects usually are "prototype models." Model/property release required.
Specs: Uses 8×10 color prints, matte finish; 35mm transparencies.
Making Contact & Terms: Provide resume, business card, brochure, flyer or tearsheets to be kept on file for possible future assignments. Works with local freelancers only. Keeps samples on file. Cannot return material. Reports in 1-2 weeks. NPI; payment negotiable on bid basis. Pays on receipt of invoice. Credit line sometimes given depending upon client. Buys all rights.
Tips: Wants to see product photos showing "color, depth and detail."

Art/Design Studios/'93-'94 changes

The following markets appeared in the 1993 edition of *Photographer's Market* but are not listed in the 1994 edition. They may have been omitted for failing to respond to our request for updated information, they may have gone out of business or they may no longer wish to receive freelance work.

Art Etc.(did not respond)
Jack Barnes & Associates (did not respond)
Centro Arte (did not respond)
Comark Group (did not respond)
Contours Consulting Design Group (did not respond)
Jamie Davison Design (did not respond)
Designworks (did not respond)
Dina Designs (did not respond)
Drawing Board Graphic Design (did not respond)
Maureen Erbe Design (did not respond)
Franz-Hatlem Design Group (did not respond)
Fullmoon Creations (did not respond)
Fusion International (did not respond)
Eric Gluckman Communications (did not respond)
Graphics Studio (did not respond)
Hutchinson Associates (did not respond)
Innovative Design and Advertising (did not respond)
Innovative Design & Graphics (did not respond)
Lawrence Design Group (did not respond)
M. Designs (did not respond)
McKenzie & Company (did not respond)
MTC Design Communications (unable to locate)
Louis Nelson Associates (did not respond)
Oden & Associates (did not respond)
Print Group (unable to locate)
Sherin & Matejka (unable to locate)
Spiker Communications (did not respond)
Spot Design (did not respond)
Studio Q (did not respond)
Suissa Design (did not respond)
Traver Company, Graphic Designers (did not respond)
Winter Graphics (did not respond)

Book Publishers

After a period of mergers, buy-outs and consolidations, all in response to economic pressure, the book publishing industry is looking forward (cautiously) to better times ahead. Yet the changes instituted during the past decade will remain in effect for a long time. Some of these changes have had a direct impact on how publishers buy and use freelance photography.

"We are buying down, negotiating harder, shopping around, anything to save money," says Ruth Mandel, photo editor for W.W. Norton. Many publishers say they are seeking photographers willing to negotiate payment. Whether publishers deal directly with photographers (to avoid the cost of a stock agency) or with stock agencies, the bottom line is they are looking for more ways to stretch their purchasing dollars.

Publishers also are cutting costs by buying less photography or opting for smaller photo sizes, says Harvey Stein, a New York City-based freelance photographer who frequently lectures on the book publishing market. "Publishers may be buying the same number of photos, but making them smaller because photographers often are paid by photo size," he explains.

Stein has noticed other changes in the market. "Risk taking has declined," he says. "The trend is toward publishing safer books, avoiding difficult topics." Photography books with complicated or sophisticated themes, popular in the 1970s, have become increasingly difficult to sell to larger publishers, he says.

On the other hand, publishers are paying more attention to cover photography, because they've discovered covers are important selling tools. Thanks to this new awareness of the role visuals play in selling a book and to recent improvements in technology, publishers are using more color photography as both illustration and cover art.

How the industry works

The book publishing market for photography can be roughly divided into two sectors. In the first sector, publishers buy individual or groups of photographs for cover art and to illustrate books, especially textbooks, travel books and nonfiction subject books. For more on how book publishers select the work of freelancers, see the interview with Jennifer Keane starting on page 140. Keane is visuals editor for Reidmore Books, one of western Canada's leading textbook publishers.

For illustration, photographs may be purchased from a stock agency or from a photographer's stock or the publisher may make assignments. Publishers usually pay for photography used in book illustration or on covers on a per-image or per-project basis. Some pay photographers on hourly or day rates. No matter how payment is made, however, the competitive publishing market requires freelancers to remain flexible.

To approach book publishers for illustration jobs, send a query letter and photographs or slides and a stock photo list with prices, if available. If you have published work, tearsheets are very helpful in showing publishers how your work translates to the printed page.

The second sector is created by those publishers who produce photography books. These are usually themed and may feature the work of one or several photographers. It is not always necessary to be well-known to publish your photographs as a book. What you do need, however, is a unique perspective, a saleable idea and quality work.

For entire books, publishers may pay in one lump sum or with an advance plus royalties (a percentage of the book sales). When approaching a publisher for your own book of photographs, query first with a brief letter describing the project and samples. If the publisher is interested in seeing the complete proposal, photographers can send additional information in one of two ways depending on the complexity of the project.

Prints placed in sequence in a protective box, along with an outline, will do for easy-to-describe, straight-forward book projects. For more complex projects, you may want to create a book dummy. A dummy is basically a book model with photographs and print arranged as they will appear in a finished book form. Book dummies show exactly how a book will look including the sequence, size, format and layout of photographs and accompanying text. The quality of the dummy is important, but keep in mind the expense can be prohibitive.

To find the right publisher for your work, start by reading the listings in this section carefully. Send for catalogs and guidelines for those publishers that interest you. It is also a good idea to become familiar with your local bookstore. By examining the books already published, you can find those publishers who produce your type of work. Check for both large and small publishers. While smaller firms may not have as much money to spend, they are often more willing to take risks, especially on the work of new photographers.

A.D. BOOK CO., 6th Floor, 10 E. 39th St., New York NY 10016. (212)889-6500. Fax: (212)889-6504. Art Director: Van Aaron. Estab. 1949. Publishes trade books for advertising visual professionals. Photos used for text illustration, book covers and dust jackets. Photo guidelines free with SASE.
Needs: Buys 20 freelance photos; offers 5-10 assignments annually. Wants to see current advertising. Model release and photo captions required.
Making Contact & Terms: Provide resume, business card, brochure, flyer or tearsheets to be kept on file for possible future use. Uses 8×11 b&w prints; 35mm transparencies. SASE. Reports in 1 month. Pays $100-350/color photo; $50-100/b&w photo. Credit line given sometimes. Buys book rights.

ALLYN AND BACON PUBLISHERS, 160 Gould St., Needham MA 02194. (617)455-1265. Fax: (617)455-1294. Art Director: Linda Dickinson. Textbook publisher (college). Photos used in textbook covers and interiors. Examples of recent uses: *Teaching Children Science* (cover, 35mm); *Modern Management* (cover, 8 × 10 transparency); *Becoming a Teacher* (cover, 4 × 5 transparency).
Needs: Offers 4 assignments plus 80 stock projects/year. Multiethnic photos in education, business, social sciences and good abstracts. Reviews stock photos. Model/property release required.
Making Contact & Terms: Provide resume, business card, self-promotion piece or tearsheets to be kept on file for possible future assignments. "Do not call." Uses 8 × 10 or larger, matte b&w prints; 35mm, 2¼ × 2¼, 4 × 5, 8 × 10 transparencies. Keeps samples on file. Cannot return material. Reports back in "24 hours to 4 months." Pays $100-500/job; $300-500/color photo; $50-200/photo. Pays on usage. Credit line given on back cover. Buys one-time rights; negotiable.
Tips: "Watch for our photo needs listing in photo bulletin. Send tearsheet and promotion pieces. Don't send stock lists. Need bright, strong, clean abstracts and unstaged, nicely lit people photos."

AMERICAN ARBITRATION ASSOCIATION, 140 West 51st St., New York NY 10020-1203. (212)484-4000. Editorial Director: Jack A. Smith. Publishes law-related materials on all facets of resolving disputes in the labor, commercial, construction and insurance areas. Photos used for text illustration. Examples of recently published titles: *The Arbitration Journal*, cover and text; *Arbitration Times*, text; and *AAA Annual Report*, text.
Needs: Buys 10 photos annually; assigns 5 freelance projects annually. General business and industry-specific photos. Reviews stock photos. Model release and photo captions preferred.
Making Contact & Terms: Provide resume, business card, brochure, flyer or tearsheets to be kept on file for possible future assignments. Uses 8 × 10 glossy b&w prints; 35mm transparencies. SASE. Reports "as time permits." Pays $250-400/color photo, $75-100/b&w photo, $75-100/hour. Credit lines given "depending on usage." Buys one-time rights. Also buys all rights "if we hire the photographer for a shoot." Simultaneous submissions and previously published work OK.

*AMERICAN BIBLE SOCIETY, 1865 Broadway, New York NY 10023. (212)408-1235. Fax: (212)408-1435. Product Manager: Charles Houser. Estab. 1816. Publishes Bibles, New Testaments and illustrated scripture booklets and leaflets on religious and spiritual topics. Photos used for text illustration, promotional materials and book covers. Examples of recently published titles: *The Lord's Love is a Treasure* scripture calendar (cover); *God Is Always With You* booklet on homelessness (cover and text); and *God's Love for Us is Sure and Strong* on Alzheimer's disease (cover and text).
Needs: Buys 10-50 photos annually; offers 1-5 freelance assignments annually. Needs scenic photos, people (multicultural), religious activities. Reviews stock photos. Model release required. Property release preferred. Releases needed for portraits and churches. Captions preferred; include location and names of identifiable persons.
Making Contact & Terms: Interested in receiving work from newer, lesser-known photographers. Query with samples. Provide resume, business card, brochure, flyer or tearsheets to be kept on file for possible future assignments. Uses any size glossy color and/or b&W prints; 35mm, 2¼ × 2¼, 4 × 5, 8 × 10 transparencies. Keeps samples on file. SASE. Reports in 1 month. Pays $100-800/color photo; $50-500/b&w photo. Pays on receipt of invoice. Credit line sometimes given depending on nature of publication. Buys one-time and all rights; negotiable. Simultaneous and/or previously published work OK.
Tips: Looks for "special sensitivity to religious and spiritual subjects; contemporary, multicultural people shots are especially desired."

AMPHOTO BOOKS, 1515 Broadway, New York NY 10036. (212)764-7300. Senior Editor: Robin Simmen. Publishes instructional and how-to books on photography. Photos usually provided by the author of the book.
Needs: Submit model release with photos. Photo captions explaining photo technique required.
Making Contact & Terms: Query with resume of credits and book idea, or submit material by mail for consideration. SASE. Reports in 1 month. NPI. Pays on royalty basis. Buys one-time rights. Simultaneous submissions and previously published work OK.
Tips: "Submit focused, tight book ideas in form of a detailed outline, a sample chapter, and sample photos. Be able to tell a story in photos and be aware of the market."

APPLEZABA PRESS, P.O. Box 4134, Long Beach CA 90804. (213)591-0015. Publisher: D.H. Lloyd. Estab. 1977. Publishes adult trade books. Photos used for promotional materials and book covers. Recently published *A Weeb for all Seasons* (front & back covers).
Needs: Buys 1-2 photos annually; offers 1-2 freelance assignments annually. Photo needs depend on book. Model release and photo captions preferred.
Making Contact & Terms: Submit portfolio for review. Provide resume, business card, brochure, flyer or tearsheets to be kept on file for possible future assignments. Uses 8 × 10 b&w prints. SASE. Reports in 1 month. Pays $25-50/b&w photo. Credit line given. Buys all rights; negotiable.

Tips: In portfolio, wants to see photocopies or prints of samples. One trend is that "we are tending to use a greater percentage for our book covers rather than straight graphic art. Photos must illustrate title or content of book."

*ARCsoft PUBLISHERS, P.O. Box 179, Hebron MD 21830. (410)742-9009. President: Anthony R. Curtis. Publishes "books in personal computing and electronics, trade paperbacks, space science and journalism." Photos used for book covers.
Needs: Buys 10 photos annually; offers 10 freelance assignments annually. Action shots of personal computer/human interaction and electronics and space science close-up. Captions required.
Making Contact & Terms: Query with resume of credits. Query with samples. Query with list of stock photo subjects. Provide business card, brochure, flyer, tearsheets to be kept on file for possible future assignments. Uses 35mm, 2¼ × 2¼ and 4 × 5 slides. SASE. Reports in 1 month. NPI; payment per color photo or by the job; varies. Credit line given. Buys one-time and book rights.
Tips: "Send query and limit lists or samples of subjects in which we have an interest. We also publish the monthly news magazine *Space Today* and the annual *Space Almanac*."

ARJUNA LIBRARY PRESS, 1025 Garner St., D, Space 18, Colorado Springs CO 80905. Director: Joseph A. Uphoff, Jr. Estab. 1979. Publishes proceedings and monographs, surrealism and metamathematics (differential logic, symbolic illustration) pertaining to aspect of performance art (absurdist drama, martial arts, modern dance) and culture (progressive or mystical society). Photos used for text illustration and book covers. Example of recently published titles: *Died; Not Yet*, the graphic works of Mark Neville.
Needs: Surrealist (static drama, cinematic expressionism) suitable for a general audience, including children. Model release and photo captions preferred.
Making Contact & Terms: Interested in receiving work from newer, lesser-known photographers. Query with samples. Send unsolicited photos by mail for consideration. Submit portfolio for review. Provide resume, business card, brochure, flyer or tearsheets to be kept on file for possible future assignments. Uses 5 × 7 glossy (maximum size) b&w and color prints. Cannot return material. Reports in "one year." Payment is one copy of published pamphlet. Credit line given. Rights dependent on additional use. Simultaneous submissions and previously published work OK.
Tips: "We are not soliciting the stock photography market. We are searching for examples that can be applied as illustrations to conceptual and performance art. These ideas can be research in the contemporary context, new media, unique perspectives, animate (poses and gestures), or inanimate (landscapes and abstracts). Our preference is for enigmatic, obscure or esoteric compositions. This material is presented in a forum for symbolic announcements, *The Journal of Regional Criticism*. We prefer conservative and general audience compositions." It's helpful "to translate color photographs in order to examine the way they will appear in black and white reproduction of various types. Make a photocopy. It is always a good idea to make a photocopy of a color work for analysis."

ART DIRECTION BOOK CO., 6th Floor, 10 E. 39th St., New York NY 10016. (212)889-6500. Fax: (212)889-6504. Art Director: William Brooks. Estab. 1939. Publishes advertising art, design, photography. Photos used for dust jackets.
Needs: Buys 10 photos annually. Needs photos for advertising. NPI; payment depends on quality of work and needs at time of job. Credit line given. Buys all rights.
Making Contact & Terms: Submit portfolio for review. Uses photos by assignment only. SASE. Reports in 1 month. Pays $200 minimum/b&w photo; $500 minimum/color photo. Buys one-time rights.

*ASHLEY BOOKS, INC., 4600 W. Commercial Blvd., Ft. Lauderdale FL 33319. (305)739-2221. Fax: (305)485-2287. Vice President: Joan Calder. Estab. 1971. Publishes trade books and occasional cookbooks. Sometimes needs photos for text illustration. Examples of recently published titles: *The Quarterback*, *Literacy Development Through Family Reading* and *Almost Famous*. In all three, photos used in text.
Needs: Number of freelance photos bought varies annually; assigns about 25 freelance projects annually. Illustrations—sometimes food, wines and the like. Model release required. Captions preferred.
Making Contact & Terms: Query with resume of credits. Query with samples (do not send samples that need to be returned). Provide resume, business card, brochure, flyer or tearsheets to be kept on file for possible future assignments. Always send query first. Deals with local freelancers only. Uses 5½ × 8½, 6 × 9 b&w and color prints. Reports in 3 weeks; may be a little longer if work is seriously

The asterisk before a listing indicates that the market is new in this edition. New markets are often the most receptive to freelance submissions.

considered. NPI; payment depends on quality of work and needs at time of job. Credit line given. Buys all rights. Simultaneous submissions and previously published work OK.

Tips: "We are only looking for photographers for our cookbooks or book jackets. Don't send valuable material. If you take exceptional photos your work should generally speak for itself. If your work is rejected, don't be discouraged. Different jobs require different needs." Looks for "movement—nothing static; imagination, originality."

AUGSBURG FORTRESS, PUBLISHERS, Publication Services, P.O. Box 1209, Minneapolis MN 55440. (612)330-3300. Fax: (612)330-3455. Publishes Protestant/Lutheran books (mostly adult trade), religious education materials, audiovisual resources and periodicals. Photos used for text illustration, book covers, periodical covers and church bulletins. Guidelines free with SASE.

Needs: Buys 1,000 color photos and 250 b&w photos annually. No assignments. People of all ages, variety of races, activities, moods and unposed. "Always looking for church scenarios—baptism, communion, choirs, acolytes, ministers, Sunday school, etc." In color, wants to see nature, seasonal, church year and mood. Model release required.

Making Contact & Terms: Send material by mail for consideration. "We are interested in stock photos." Provide tearsheets to be kept on file for possible future assignments. Uses 8×10 glossy or semiglossy b&w prints, 35mm and 2¼×2¼ color transparencies. SASE. Reports in 6-8 weeks. "Write for guidelines, then submit on a regular basis." Pays $25-75/b&w photo; $40-125/color photo. Credit line nearly always given. Buys one-time rights. Simultaneous submissions and previously published work OK.

By taking advantage of an ordinary situation, Oscar Williams of San Jose, California, snapped this happy and saleable shot. Taken at his grandson's birthday party, the shot was purchased by Augsburg Fortress and used in a church bulletin. The publisher printed one million copies and Williams says he uses the tearsheets for other submissions.

© Oscar Williams

*AVE MARIA PRESS, University Campus, Notre Dame IN 46556. (219)287-2831. Production Manager: Paul J. Waddy. "We are primarily publishers of Catholic/Christian religious materials with emphasis on religious education, the sacraments, prayer, devotional books, the liturgy, children's books, etc." Photos used for text illustrations, promotional materials, book covers, dust jackets and audio cassette boxcards. Examples of recently published titles: *Your Family in Focus*, *Growing with Jesus*, and *Together as Parish* (all photos for cover art). Send SASE for photo guidelines and rate card (1 page).

Needs: Buys 20-40 freelance photos annually. "Individuals, couples, families and groups—meaningful, real-life situations, not obviously posed or overly dramatic; also scenic, still life and nature." In particular, wants to see "imaginative, new presentations of familiar subjects . . . photos that *suggest* a strong spiritual sense, or lack of it." Interested in stock photos.

Making Contact & Terms: "Provide up to 10 samples of best work for us to maintain in our 'permanent' file." Uses b&w prints, 8×10 preferred, glossy finish. SASE. Reports within 2 months. Book jackets and paperback covers $50; inside book illustrations $30; miscellaneous use in catalogs, ads, etc. $10; cassette boxcards and slip cases $20. "Rates listed are subject to increase for an exceptional piece of work or to meet an exceptional need." Credit line given on copyright page. Buys one-time rights. Simultaneous submissions and previously published work OK.

AVON BOOKS, 1350 Avenue of the Americas, New York NY 10019. (212)261-6800. Fax: (212)261-6925. Photo Editor: Julie Siegel. Publishes adult and juvenile fiction. Photos used for book covers. Examples of recently published titles: *How to Survive in the Jungle, The New Emperors* and *Confident Collector-Art Deco.*
Needs: Buys approximately 50 photos/year; offers approximately 2 assignments/year. Subject matter varies according to title. Model/property release required.
Making Contact & Terms: Interested in receiving work from newer, lesser-known photographers. Submit portfolio for review. Query with samples. Uses b&w prints; 35mm, 2¼×2¼, 4×5, 8×10 transparencies. Samples kept on file. Pays $500-750/job. Pays on receipt of invoice. Credit line given. Buys book rights; negotiable.

*BEACON PRESS, 25 Beacon St., Boston MA 02108. (617)742-2110. Fax: (617)742-2290. Design & Production Manager: Lori Foley. Estab. 1854. Publishes adult nonfiction trade and scholarly books; African-American, Jewish, Asian, Native American, gay and lesbian studies; anthropology; philosophy; women's studies; environment/nature. Photos used for book covers and dust jackets. Examples of recently published titles: *Straight Talk about Death for Teenagers* (½-pg cover photo, commissioned); *The Glory and the Power* (full-bleed cover photo, stock); and *Finding Home* (full-bleed cover photo, stock).
Needs: Buys 5-6 photos annually; offers 1-2 freelance assignments annually. "We look for photos for specific books, not any general subject or style." Model/property release required. Captions preferred.
Making Contact & Terms: Interested in receiving work from newer, lesser-known photographers. Provide resume, business card, brochure, flyer or tearsheets to be kept on file for possible future assignments. Uses 8×10 glossy b&w prints; 35mm, 2¼×2¼ transparencies. Keeps samples on file. SASE. Reports in 1 month. Pays $500-750/color photo; $150-250/b&w photo. Pays on receipt of invoice. Credit line given. Buys English-language rights for all (paperback & hardcover) editions; negotiable. Previously published work OK.
Tips: "I only contact a photographer if their area of expertise is appropriate for particular titles for which I need a photo. I do not 'review' portfolios because I'm looking for specific images for specific books. Be willing to negotiate. We are a nonprofit organization, so our fees are not standard for the photo industry."

BEAUTIFUL AMERICA PUBLISHING COMPANY, 9725 SW Commerce Circle, P.O. Box 646, Wilsonville OR 97070. (503)682-0173. Librarian: Andrea Tronslin. Estab. 1986. Publishes nature, scenic, pictorial and history. Photos used for text illustration, pictorial. Examples of recently published titles: *California—Vanishing Habitats & Wildlife* (photos and text); *The Rockies—Canada's Magnificent Wilderness* (scenic photos); and *Beautiful America's San Diego* (scenic photos).
Needs: Assigns 4-8 freelance projects annually; buys small number of additional freelance photos. Nature and scenic. Model release required. Captions required; include location, correct spelling of topic in caption.
Making Contact & Terms: Provide resume, business card, brochure, flyer or tearsheets to be kept on file for possible future assignments. Uses 35mm, 2¼×2¼, 4×5, and 8×10 transparencies. Payment varies based on project; $100 minimum/color photo. Credit line given. Buys one-time rights. Simultaneous submissions and previously published work OK.
Tips: "Do not send unsolicited photos!! Please do not ask for guidelines. We are using very little freelance, other than complete book or calendar projects."

BEDFORD BOOKS OF ST. MARTIN'S PRESS, 29 Winchester St., Boston MA 02116. (617)426-7440. Fax: (617)426-8582. Advertising and Promotion Manager: George Scribner. Estab. 1981. Publishes college textbooks (freshman composition, literature and history). Photos used for text illustration, promotional materials and book covers. Examples of recently published titles: *Our Times/3: Readings from Recent Periodicals; The Bedford Introduction to Drama, Second Edition;* and *The Winchester Reader.*
Needs: Buys 12 photos annually; offers 6 freelance assignments annually. Artistic, abstract, conceptual photos; nature or city; people—America or other cultures, multiracial often preferred. Also uses product shots for promotional material. Reviews stock photos. Model/property release required.
Making Contact & Terms: Interested in receiving work from newer, lesser-known photographers. Query with samples. Query with list of stock photo subjects. Provide resume, business card, brochure, flyer or tearsheets to be kept on file for possible future assignments. Works with local freelancers only for product shots. Uses 8×10 b&w and color prints; 35mm, 2¼×2¼, 4×5 transparencies. Keeps

Rochester, New York photographer Don Franklin wanted to portray a family as a cohesive unit when he snapped this image. The concept proved appealing to Ave Maria Press, which used the shot on the cover of its paperback, Your Family in Focus. *"It reinforced the theme of the book by suggesting a family firmly planted in an unstable world," says Paul Waddy, production manager at Ave Maria Press.*

samples on file. SASE. Reports in 3 weeks. Pays $50-500/color photo; $50-200/b&w photo; $250-1,000/job; $500-1,500/day. Credit line sometimes given; "always covers, never promo." Buys one-time rights and all rights; depends on project; negotiable. Simultaneous submissions and/or previously published work OK.

BEHRMAN HOUSE INC., 235 Watchung Ave., West Orange NJ 07052. (201)669-0447. Editor: Ms. Ruby G. Strauss. Estab. 1921. Publishes Judaica textbooks. Photos used for text illustration, promotional materials and book covers. Recently published title: *My Jewish Year*.
Needs: Interested in stock photos of Jewish content, particularly holidays, with children. Model/property release required.
Making Contact & Terms: Interested in receiving work from newer, lesser-known photographers. Query with samples. Query with resume of credits. Provide resume, business card, brochure, flyer or tearsheets to be kept on file for possible future assignments. Interested in stock photos. SASE. Reports in 3 weeks. Pays $50-500/color photo; $20-250/b&w photo. Credit line given. Buys one-time rights; negotiable.
Tips: Company trend is increasing use of photography.

BENFORD BOOKS, 27 W. 20th St., New York NY 10011. (212)206-9093. Fax: (212) 206-8978. Editorial Director: Elizabeth Loonan. Estab. 1991. Publishes books for all markets and subjects, nonfiction. Photos used for text illustration, book covers and dust jackets. Examples of recent titles: *California Indians, Indians of the Plains* and *Indians of the Southwest*.
Needs: Buys over 400 stock photos/year. Looks for a variety of subjects. Reviews stock photos. Model/property release preferred. Captions required.
Making Contact & Terms: Query with list of stock photo subjects. Uses all sizes of b&w prints; 35mm, 2¼×2¼, 4×5, 8×10 transparencies. Pays $50-250/color photo; $25-100/b&w photo. Credit line given. Buys one-time and book rights; negotiable. Simultaneous submissions and previously published work OK. "No unsolicited material accepted."

The First Markets Index preceding the General Index in the back of this book provides the names of those companies/publications interested in receiving work from newer, lesser-known photographers.

Tips: "We do not review portfolios."

*BLUE BIRD PUBLISHING, 1713 E. Broadway #306, Tempe AZ 85282. (602)968-4088. Publisher: Cheryl Gorder. Estab. 1985. Publishes adult trade books on home education, home business, social issues (homelessness), etc. Photos used for text illustration. Examples of recently published titles: *Homeless: Without Addresses in America* and *Green Earth Resource Guide.* In both, photos used for text illustration.
Needs: Buys 40 photos annually; offers 3 freelance assignments annually. Types of photos "depends on subject matter of forthcoming books." Reviews stock photos. Model release required; photo captions preferred.
Making Contact & Terms: Query with list of stock photo subjects. Provide resume, business card, brochure, flyer or tearsheets to be kept on file for possible future assignments. SASE. Reports in 1 month. Pays $25-150/color photo, $25/150/b&w photo; also pays flat fee for bulk purchase of stock photos. Buys book rights. Simultaneous submissions and previously published work OK.
Tips: "We will continue to grow rapidly in the coming years and will have a growing need for stock photos and freelance work. Send a list of stock photos for our file. If a freelance assignment comes up in your area, we will call."

*BLUE DOLPHIN PUBLISHING, INC., P.O. Box 1255, 13386 N. Bloomfield Rd., Nevada City CA 95959. (916)265-6925. Fax: (916)265-0787. President: Paul M. Clemens. Estab. 1985. Publishes comparative spiritual traditions, self-help, lay psychology, humor, cookbooks, children's books, natural living and healing. Photos used for text illustration, promotional materials, book covers and dust jackets. Examples of recently published titles: *Beyond Gurus, Tastes of Tuscany* and *The Land of the Living.* All photos used throughout text.
Needs: Buys 1-25 photos annually; offers 1-3 freelance assignments annually. Subject needs New Age, spiritual/psychological or regional. Model/property release preferred. Captions preferred.
Making Contact & Terms: Interested in receiving work from newer, lesser-known photographers. Query with a few samples. Provide resume, business card, brochure, flyer or tearsheets to be kept on file for possible future assignments. Works on assignment only. Uses 3×5, 5×7 color and/or b&w prints; 35mm, $2\frac{1}{4}\times2\frac{1}{4}$, 4×5, 8×10 transparencies. Keeps samples on file. SASE. Reports in 1 month. Pays $20/hour, or by arrangement per project. Pays on receipt of invoice. Credit line given. Buys one-time and book rights; prefers all rights; negotiable. Simultaneous submissions and previously published work OK.
Tips: Looks for "clarity, composition. Do 'different' things in life. Shoot the unique perspective. We're getting more electronic—looking for the unusual perspective."

DON BOSCO MULTIMEDIA, P.O. Box T, New Rochelle NY 10802. (914)576-0122. Fax: (914)654-0443. Production Director: John A. Thomas. Estab. 1956. Publishes educational/religious books for teachers, children and parents. Photos used for text illustration, promotional materials and book covers. Examples of recently published titles: *Faith & Families* (cover); *1993 Catalog* (cover); *On the Move* (interior illustration). Photo guidelines free on request.
Needs: Buys 20 photos annually; offers 2 freelance assignments annually. Photos of youths, families and religiously symbolic. Reviews stock photos. Model release required. Property release preferred.
Making Contact & Terms: Interested in receiving work from newer, lesser-known photographers. Query with resume of credits. Query with samples. Query with stock photo list. Uses 5×7 b&w and color glossy prints, transparencies. Uses slides and videos for prayer resources, documentaries. Samples kept on file. SASE. Reports in 3 weeks. Pays $25-300/b&w photo; $50-600/color photo; $30/hour; $100/day. Rights negotiable. Simultaneous submissions and previously published work OK.
Tips: "Style tends to be realistic or religiously symbolic." Interested in "scanned photos for direct input into Macintosh applications."

*⟡BOSTON MILLS PRESS, 132 Main St., Erin, Ontario N0B 1T0 Canada. (519)833-2407. Fax: (519)833-2195. Publisher: John Denison. Estab. 1974. Publishes coffee table books, local guide books. Photos used for text illustration, book covers and dust jackets. Examples of recently published titles: *Georgian Bay* (cover/text); *Credit River Valley* (cover/text); and *Ontario's Heritage Quilts* (cover/text).
Needs: "We're looking for book length ideas *not* stock. We pay a royalty on books sold plus advance."
Making Contact & Terms: Interested in receiving work from newer, lesser-known photographers. Query with resume of credits. Uses 35mm transparencies. Does not keep samples on file. SASE and IRC. Reports in 3 weeks. NPI; payment negotiated with contract. Credit line given. Simultaneous submissions OK.

The maple leaf before a listing indicates that the market is Canadian.

BROOKS/COLE PUBLISHING COMPANY, 511 Forest Lodge Rd., Pacific Grove CA 93950. (408)373-0728. Photo Coordinator: Larry Molmud. Publishes college textbooks only—child development, social psychology, family, marriages, chemistry, computers, etc. Photos used for text illustration, book covers and dust jackets.

Needs: Interested in stock photos. Model release preferred.

Making Contact & Terms: Query with list of stock photo subjects. Provide resume, business card, brochure, flyer or tearsheets to be kept on file for possible future assignments. "Also looking for photo researchers." Uses 8×10 glossy b&w prints; also transparencies, any format. SASE. Reports in 2-3 months. Pays $75-200/b&w or color photo. Credit line given. Buys one-time rights.

WILLIAM C. BROWN COMMUNICATIONS INC., (formerly William C. Brown Co. Publishers), 2460 Kerper Blvd., Dubuque IA 52001. (319)588-1451. Contact: Photo Research Department. Estab. 1944. Publishes college textbooks for most disciplines (music, computer and data processing, education, natural sciences, psychology, sociology, physical education, health, biology, art). In all cases, photos used for covers and/or interiors.

Making Contact & Terms: Submit material by mail for consideration. Provide business card, brochure or stock list to be kept on file for possible future use. Direct material to photo research. Uses 8×10 glossy or matte prints; also transparencies. Reports in 1-2 months. SASE. Pays up to $90/b&w interior photo; up to $135/color interior photo. Cover photos negotiable. **Pays on acceptance.** Buys one-time rights; also all editions and derivative works. Previously published work OK.

Tips: "We prefer to note your areas of specialties for future reference. We need *top quality* photography. To break in, be open to lower rates."

CAPSTONE PRESS, INC., 2440 Fernbrook Lane, Minneapolis MN 55447. (507)387-4992. Fax: (612)551-0511. Contact: Photo Research Editor. Estab. 1991. Publishes educational library books. Photos used for text illustration and book covers. Examples of published titles: *Sky Diving* (text illustration); *Monster Vehicles* (text illustration); and *The White House* (text illustration).

Needs: Buys 250 photos annually. Interested in stock photos. Model/property release and captions preferred.

Making Contact & Terms: Query with stock photo list. SASE. Reports in 1 month. Uses 35mm, 2¼×2¼ transparencies. Pays $10-50/color photo. Credit line given. Buys one-time rights.

Tips: "We like to use about 20 photos from same source for each book that requires photos. Send a listing of your subject areas so that we can review whenever we have a photo book."

CASCADE GEOGRAPHIC SOCIETY, P.O. Box 398, Rhododendron OR 97049. (503)622-4798 or (503)622-4994. Curator: Michael P. Jones. Estab. 1979. "Our photographs are for exhibits, educational materials, fliers, posters, etc., including historical artifact catalogs." Photo guidelines free with SASE.

Needs: Buys 200 photos annually; offers 200 freelance assignments annually. American history, wildlife, old buildings, living history, nature and environmental. Reviews stock photos of American history and nature subjects. Model release and captions preferred.

Making Contact & Terms: Interested in receiving work from newer, lesser-known photographers. Query with resume of credits. Query with samples. Query with stock photo list. Send unsolicited photos by mail for consideration. Submit portfolio for review. Provide resume, business card, brochure, flyer or tearsheets to be kept on file for possible future assignments. Works with local freelancers only. Uses 5×7, 8×10 b&w or color prints; 35mm, 2¼×2¼, 4×5, 8×10 transparencies; videotape. SASE. Reports in 1-2 weeks. Offers copies of published images in place of payment. Credit line given. Buys one-time rights. Simultaneous submissions and previously published work OK.

Tips: "We are primarily interested in American history and nature subjects that tell a story. We want the photos to come alive. Be flexible and remember that we are nonprofit. We can put your work in exhibits that will be viewed by the public."

CHINA BOOKS & PERIODICALS, 2929 24th St., San Francisco CA 94110. (415)282-2994. Fax: (415)282-0994. Art Director: Linda Revel. Estab. 1960. Publishes fiction, travel, health, language learning, art, history, culture and contemporary affairs. Photos used for text illustration, book covers and dust jackets. Examples of recently published titles: *SF Chinatown: A Walking Tour*, *China on the Edge* and *Mooncakes and Hungry Ghosts: Festivals of China*.

Needs: Photos with a China-related theme. Reviews stock photos. Model release required. Property release preferred. Captions preferred.

Making Contact & Terms: Interested in receiving work from newer, lesser-known photographers. Query with resume of credits. Query with samples. Keeps samples on file. Uses b&w and color prints; 35mm, 2¼×2¼, 4×5, 8×10 transparencies. SASE. Reports in 1 month. Photo guidelines free with SASE. Pays $25-100/b&w photo; $50-300/color photo; $15-50/hour. Credit line given. Buys one-time rights; negotiable. Simultaneous submissions and previously published work OK.

Tips: Sample photos "must be related to China, Southeast Asia or Chinese-Americans." To break into the publishing field, "learn as much as you can about the specific needs of the publishers and what field each one concentrates in."

CHRISTIAN BOARD OF PUBLICATION, Box 179, St. Louis MO 63166. (314)231-8500. Fax: (314)231-8524. Director of Product Development Design and Promotion: Nancy Dothage. Estab. 1910. Publishes religious curriculum, books and program materials. Photos used for text illustration and book covers. Examples of recently published titles: *A Mini-history of the Christian Church* (Disciples of Christ) (inside); *Curriculum for All Age Levels* (inside) and *Camp and Conference Materials* (inside). Photo guidelines free with SASE.
Needs: Buys 5-10 photos annually. Photos with people. Model/property release required; photo captions preferred.
Making Contact & Terms: Send unsolicited photos by mail for consideration. Keeps samples on file. SASE. Reports in 1 month. Pays $25/inside; $50/cover. Simultaneous submissions OK.
Tips: "Prefer photos of people interacting with each other."

CLEANING CONSULTANT SERVICES, 1512 Western Ave., P.O. Box 1273, Seattle WA 98111. (206)682-9748. Publisher: William R. Griffin. "We publish books on cleaning, maintenance and self-employment. Examples are related to janitorial, housekeeping, maid services, window washing, carpet cleaning, etc." Photos are used for text illustration, promotional materials, books covers and all uses related to production and marketing of books. Photo guidelines free with SASE. Sample issue $3.
Needs: Buys 20-50 freelance photos annually; offers 5-15 freelance assignments annually. Photos of people doing cleaning work. Reviews stock photos. Model release and captions preferred.
Making Contact & Terms: Query with resume of credits, samples, list of stock photo subjects or send unsolicited photos by mail for consideration. Provide resume, business card, brochure, flyer or tearsheets to be kept on file for possible future assignments. Uses 5×7 and 8×10 glossy b&w and color prints. SASE. Reports in 3 weeks. Pays $5-50/b&w photo; $5/color photo; $10-30/hour; $40-250/job; negotiable depending on specific project. Credit lines generally given. Buys all rights; depends on need and project; will negotiate rights purchased. Simultaneous submissions and previously published work OK.
Tips: "We are especially interested, in color photos of people doing cleaning work in other countries. For use on the covers of our quarterly magazine, *Cleaning Business.* Be willing to work at reasonable rates. Selling two or three photos does not qualify you to earn top-of-the-line rates. We expect to use more photos, but they must be specific to our market, which is quite select. Don't send stock sample sheets. Send photos that fit our specific needs. Call if you need more information or would like specific guidance."

*COMPASS AMERICAN GUIDES, 6051 Margarido Dr., Oakland CA 94618. (510)547-7233. Fax: (510)547-2145. Creative Director: Christopher C. Burt. Estab. 1990. Publishes travel guide series for every state in the U.S. and 15 major cities, also Canadian provinces and cities. Photos used for text illustration and book covers. Examples of recently published titles: *Discover America: Hawaii, Discover America: Los Angeles* and *Discover America: New Mexico.*
Needs: Buys 1,000-1,500 photos annually; offers 8-10 freelance assignments annually. Reviews stock photos (depends on project). Model release required. Property release preferred. Captions preferred.
Making Contact & Terms: Interested in receiving work from newer, lesser-known photographers. Provide resume, business card, brochure, flyer or tearsheets to be kept on file for possible future assignments. "Do not phone, fax OK." Works on assignment only. Uses 35mm, 2¼×2¼, 4×5, 8×10 transparencies. Keeps samples on file. Cannot return material. Reports in one week to five years. Pays $5,000+/job. Pays ⅓ advance, ⅓ acceptance, ⅓ publication. Credit line not given. Buys one-time and book rights. Photographer own copyright to images. Simultaneous submissions and previously published work OK.
Tips: "Our company works only with photographers native to, or currently residing in, the state or city in which we are publishing the guide. We like creative approaches that capture the spirit of the place being covered. We need a mix of landscapes, portraits, things and places."

Market conditions are constantly changing! If you're still using this book and it's 1995 or later, buy the newest edition of Photographer's Market *at your favorite bookstore or order directly from* Writer's Digest Books.

CONSERVATORY OF AMERICAN LETTERS, P.O. Box 298, Thomaston ME 04861. (207)354-0998. President: Robert Olmsted. Estab. 1986. Publishes "all types of books except porn and evangelical." Photos used for promotional materials, book covers and dust jackets. Examples of recently published titles: *Dan River Anthology* (cover); *After the Light* (cover).
Needs: Buys 2-3 photos annually. Model release required if people are identifiable. Photo captions preferred.
Making Contact & Terms: Interested in receiving work from newer, lesser-known photographers. Query with list of stock photo subjects. Send unsolicited photos by mail for consideration. Uses 3×5 to 8×10 b&w glossy prints, also 5×7 or 6×9 color prints. SASE. Reports in 1 week. Pays $5-40/ b&w photo; $35-150/color photo; per job payment negotiable. Credit line given. Buys one-time rights; negotiable.

DAVID C. COOK PUBLISHING CO., Dept. PM, 850 N. Grove, Elgin IL 60120. (708)741-2400. Fax: (708)741-0595. Director of Design Services: Randy Maid. Photo Acquisitions Administrator: Ruthie Corcoran. Publishes books and Sunday school material for pre-school through adult readers. Photos used primarily in Sunday school material for text illustration and covers, particularly in *Sunday Digest* and *Understanding the Bible* (for adults), *ID* (for senior highs) and *The Rock* (for junior highs). Younger age groups used, but not as much.
Needs: Buys 200 photos minimum/year; gives 20 assignments/year. Uses more color than b&w photos. Prefers to see Sunday school, church activities, social activities, family shots, people, action, sports. SASE. Previously published work OK. Mostly photos of junior and senior high age youth of all races and ethnic backgrounds, also adults and children under junior high age, and some preschool. Model/ property release required.
Making Contact & Terms: Interested in receiving work from newer, lesser-known photographers. Send query with samples. Unsolicited submissions can be sent no more than one time per month. Uses glossy b&w and semigloss prints; 8×10 prints are copied or kept on file for ordering at a later date; 35mm and larger transparencies; contact sheet OK; glossy b&w prints and 35mm and larger color transparencies for cover. NPI. Rights negotiated.
Tips: "Make sure your material is identified as yours. Send duplicate slides or color transparencies. Do not send original photos or negatives. "We claim no liability for unsolicited submissions."

As photography grows more competitive photographers must develop their own style to attract clients. Ruthie Corcoran, photo acquisitions administrator for David C. Cook Publishers, says photographer Dan Stultz, of West Chicago, Illinois, brings a unique vision to most projects. "He's very creative and offers ideas (such as painting with light, as in this photo) which we may not think of," says Corcoran.

© Dan Stultz

CRAFTSMAN BOOK COMPANY, 6058 Corte Del Cedro, Carlsbad CA 92008. (619)438-7828. Fax: (619)438-0398. Art Director: Bill Grote. Estab. 1957. Publishes construction books. Photos used for text illustration, promotional materials, and book covers. Examples of published titles: *National Repair and Remodeling Estimator*, *National Construction Estimator* and *Electrical Construction Estimator*.
Needs: Buys 60 freelance photos annually; offers 10 freelance assignments annually. Photos of construction contractors and carpenters at work. Reviews stock photos. Model release required.
Making Contact & Terms: Interested in receiving work from newer, lesser-known photographers. Query with samples/slides. Provide resume, business card, brochure, flyer or tearsheets to be kept on file for possible future assignments. Uses 5×7 b&w prints; 35mm transparencies. SASE. Reports in 2

weeks. Pays $35-45/b&w photo; $100-150/color photo. Buys one-time rights; negotiable. Simultaneous submissions and previously published work OK.

Tips: Wants to see "subjects interacting in residential construction. We look for unusual, brightly colored shots that are artistic and capture attention. We especially need shots of construction workers on rooftops with lots of sky visible."

*DEATH VALLEY NATURAL HISTORY ASSOCIATION, P.O. Box 188, Death Valley CA 92328. (619)786-2331. Fax: (619)786-2236. Executive Director: Esy Fields. Estab. 1953. Publishes adult, juvenile educational, science, history books, limited fiction. Photos used for text illustration and dust jackets. Examples of recently published titles: *Proceedings Third Death Valley Conference on History and Prehistory* (cover, illustrate text); *Death Valley Discovery* (text illustration); and *Titus Canyon Road Guide* (cover text).

Needs: Photos purchased varies with projects. Photos of Death Valley National Monument and surrounding Mojave Desert. Reviews stock photos. Model release required. Captions preferred (include name of location or subject matter).

Making Contact & Terms: Interested in receiving work from newer, lesser-known photographers. Query with samples. Provide resume, business card, brochure, flyer or tearsheets to be kept on file for possible future assignments. Works on assignment only. Uses any sized, any finish color and/or b&w prints. Does not keep samples on file. Reports only when interested. NPI. Pays on receipt of invoice. Credit line given. Buys all rights; negotiable.

DUTTON CHILDREN'S BOOKS, 375 Hudson St., New York NY 10014. (212)366-2600. Fax: (212)366-2011. Executive Editor: Donna Brooks. Associate Editor: Karen Lotz. Photos used for text illustration and book covers. Examples of recently published titles: *Atlantic Salmon* and *WASPS at Home.*

Needs: Offers 2 freelance assignments annually. Nature material, events on subjects of interest to children. Uses very few stock photos.

Making Contact & Terms: Query with samples. Query with stock photo list. Provide resume, business card, brochure, flyer or tearsheets to be kept on file for possible future assignments. Uses color/b&w prints; 35mm transparencies. Keeps samples on file. Reports in 3 months. Pays advance against royalties and expenses. Credit line given. Buys book rights. Buys all rights; negotiable. Simultaneous submissions and previously published work OK.

Tips: "We look for photos that portray a child's vision of the world, that capture a subject with the wonder and creativity that appeal to children. Photo essays are essential to the nonfiction market for children."

EAST COAST PUBLISHING, P.O. Box 2829, Poughkeepsie NY 12603. (800)327-4212. Contact: Vice President. Publishes adult trade, nonfiction, textbooks involving law and business. Photos used for text illustration, promotional materials, book covers and dust jackets. Examples of recently published titles: *Notary Public Handbook: A Guide for New York, Second Ed.* and *Notary Public Handbook: A Guide for New Jersey* (illustrations).

Needs: Buys 6 photos annually. Varies with assignment. Reviews stock photos. Model/property release required. Captions required.

Making Contact & Terms: Query with list of stock photo subjects. Provide resume, business card, brochure, flyer or tearsheets to be kept on file for possible future assignments. Uses 8×10 glossy b&w and color prints; 35mm, 4×5 transparencies. Keeps samples on file. SASE. Reports in 1 month. Pays $35-50/color or b&w photo. Credit line given. Buys all rights; negotiable. Simultaneous submissions and previously published work OK.

Tips: "We utilize photographs in the editorial functions and in the marketing phase of book publishing."

*ELLIOTT & CLARK PUBLISHING, Suite 21, 1638 R Street NW, Washington DC 20009. (202)387-9805. Fax: (202)483-0355. Vice President: Carolyn Clark. Estab. 1991. Looking for illustrated book projects, not single stock images.

Needs: Interested in natural history, Americana, history and music. Does not want to see "cute and fuzzy" subjects. Model/property release preferred. Captions preferred.

Making Contact & Terms: Interested in receiving work from newer, lesser-known photographers. Query with samples. Provide resume, business card, brochure, flyer or tearsheets to be kept on file for possible future assignments. Uses 35mm, 2¼×2¼, 4×5 transparencies. Keeps samples on file. SASE. Reports in 4-6 weeks. Royalties paid on gross sales of books. Single photographers get cover credit. Buys one-time rights and rights for hard and soft covers, and foreign language editions; negotiable.

Tips: "We like to feature one photographer's work. The photography must tell a story and the photographer must be able to relay the concept and know possible markets."

ELYSIUM GROWTH PRESS, 700 Robinson Rd., Topanga CA 90290. (310)455-1000. Fax: (310)455-2007. Editor: Ed Lange. Estab. 1961. Publishes adult trade books on nudist/naturist/clothing-optional resorts, parks and camps. Photos used for text illustration, promotional, book covers and dust jackets. Examples of recently published titles: *Nudist Nudes, Shameless Nude* and *Fun in the Sun Book III*. Photos used for cover and text in all three. Photo guidelines free with SASE; catalog, with SASE, 45¢ postage.
Needs: Buys 50 photos annually. Reviews stock photos. Model release, photo captions required.
Making Contact & Terms: Provide resume, business card, brochure, flyer or tearsheets to be kept on file for possible future assignments. Uses 5×7 glossy b&w and color prints; 35mm and 2¼×2¼ transparencies. SASE. Reports in 2 weeks. Pays $50-100/color photo, $35-50/b&w photo. Credit line given. Buys all rights; negotiable. Simultaneous submissions OK.
Tips: In samples, looking for "nudist/naturist lifestyle photos only."

EMC PUBLISHING, 300 York Ave., St. Paul MN 55101. (612)771-1555. Design and Production Manager: Eileen K. Slater. Publishes educational textbooks. Photos used for text illustration and book covers.
Needs: Variable. Reviews stock photos.
Making Contact & Terms: Query with resume of credits. Provide resume, business card, brochure, flyer or tearsheets to be kept on file. Uses 35mm and 4×5 transparencies. Does not return unsolicited material. Reports only as needed. NPI; payment negotiable. Credit line given. Rights negotiable.

ENTRY PUBLISHING, INC., 27 W. 96th St., New York NY 10025. (212)662-9703. President: Lynne Glasner. Estab. 1981. Publishes education/textbooks, secondary market. Photos used for text illustrations.
Needs: Number of freelance photos bought and freelance assignments given vary. Often looks for shots of young teens in school settings. Reviews stock photos. Model release required. Captions preferred.
Making Contact & Terms: Interested in receiving work from newer, lesser-known photographers. Query with list of stock photo subjects. Provide resume, business card, brochure, flyer or tearsheets to be kept on file for possible future assignments. Uses b&w prints. SASE. Reports in 3 weeks. NPI; payment depends on job requirements. Credit line given if requested. Buys one-time rights; negotiable. Simultaneous submissions and previously published work OK.
Tips: "Have wide range of subject areas for review and use. Stock photos are most accessible and can be available quickly during production of book."

J.G. FERGUSON PUBLISHING CO., 200 West Monroe, Chicago IL 60606. Editorial: Carol Summerfield. Publishes vocational guidance works for high schools and college, subscriptions, reference books and corporate histories. Photos used for text illustration. Examples of recently published titles: *Career Discovery Encyclopedia*, elementary school 6 volume set with jobs explained and illustrated by b&w photos and *Encyclopedia of Careers and Vocational Guidance*, high school/college level.
Needs: Buys several hundred freelance photos biannually. Persons at work in various occupational settings only. Reviews stock photos. Model release and captions preferred.
Making Contact & Terms: Send stock list and resume. Uses 8×10 glossy b&w prints; 35mm transparencies. NPI; payment negotiable. Credit line given. Buys book rights. Simultaneous submissions and previously published work OK.
Tips: Wants to see "encyclopedia style black and white photos of people in their jobs with good caption information. We search mainly for specific career images, so a list indicating what a photographer has that may fulfill our needs is the single best method of getting work with us."

*✦FITZHENRY & WHITESIDE LIMITED, 195 Allstate Parkway, Markham, Ontario L3R 4T8 Canada. (416)477-9700. Fax: (416)477-9179. Senior Vice President: Robert W. Read. Estab. 1966. Publishes general text and trade, nonfiction. Photos used for text illustration and book covers. Examples of recently published titles: *Canada Exploring New Directions, Fred Penner Treasury* and *Contemporary Canadian Architecture.*

Can't find a listing? Check at the end of each market section for the " '93-'94 Changes" lists. These lists include any market listings from the '93 edition which were either not verified or deleted in this edition.

Needs: Buys 100-200 photos annually; offers 5-10 freelance assignments annually. Interested in photos of people and places, narratives. Reviews stock photos. Model release and captions preferred.
Making Contact & Terms: Interested in receiving work from newer, lesser-known photographers. Query with samples. Query with stock photo list. Provide resume, business card, brochure, flyer or tearsheets to be kept on file for possible future assignments. Offers some assignments for product shots, mostly stock photos. Uses 8×10 b&w prints; 35mm transparencies. Keeps samples on file. SASE. Reports in 1 month. NPI, "varies too greatly." Pays on publication. Credit line given. Buys one-time and book rights; negotiable. Simultaneous submissions and previously published work OK.

J. FLORES PUBLICATIONS, P.O. Box 830131, Miami FL 33283. Editor: Eli Flores. Estab. 1982. Publishes adult trade, nonfiction only: military, firearms and current events. Uses photos for text illustration, promotional materials and book covers. Examples of recently published titles: *The Force Option* (cover); *Unlikely Assassins* and *Wings for the Valiant* (both cover/inside).
Needs: Action oriented, on-the-spot photographs. Reviews stock photos. Model release required; captions preferred.
Making Contact & Terms: Interested in receiving work from newer, lesser-known photographers. Query with samples and list of stock photo subjects. Uses any size glossy b&w prints, also color transparencies. SASE. Reports in 1 month. Pays $50-150/color photo; $30-100/b&w photo. Credit line given. Buys one-time rights; negotiable. Simultaneous submissions and previously published work OK.
Tips: "We look for stock that matches our need for a particular book or ad. The photographer should study the subject matter of books published by a particular publisher and submit photos that match. Photos are being used more than ever by book publishers. There are many books in which photographs play a more important role than the text."

MICHAEL FRIEDMAN PUBLISHING GROUP, INC., 15 W. 26th St., New York NY 10010. (212)685-6610. Photography Director: Christopher Bain. Estab. 1979. Publishes adult trade: science and nature series; sports; food and entertainment; design; and gardening. Photos used for text illustration, promotional materials, book covers and dust jackets.
Needs: Buys 7,500 freelance photos annually; offers 20-30 freelance assignments annually. Reviews stock photos. Captions preferred.
Making Contact & Terms: Query with specific list of stock photo subjects. Uses 35mm, 2¼×2¼, 4×5 and 8×10 transparencies. Pays $50-100/color stock photo; $350-500/day. Payment upon publication of book for stock photos; within 30-45 days for assignment. Credit line always given (95% of time, on page). Buys rights for all editions. Simultaneous submissions and previously published work OK.

FRIENDSHIP PRESS, National Council of the Churches of Christ in the U.S.A., Room 552, 475 Riverside Dr., New York NY 10115. (212)870-2280. Art Director: E. Paul Lansdale. Publishes adult and juvenile textbooks on social consciousness, especially of US and Third World. Photos used for text illustration, promotional material, book covers, dust jackets and PR work. Examples of recently published titles: *All A We A One*; *The Caribbean: Culture of Resistance, Spirit of Hope*; *Choices and Other Stories from the Caribbean* (guide). Photos used for covers and/or text.
Needs: Buys 10+ freelance photos annually. Social consciousness, people and places. Has yearly themes. Reviews stock photos. Model release and captions required.
Making Contact & Terms: Interested in receiving work from newer, lesser-known photographers. Arrange personal interview to show portfolio. Query with resume of credits, samples or list of stock photo subjects. Submit portfolio for review. Provide resume, business card, brochure, flyer or tearsheets to be kept on file for possible future assignments. Works on assignment only. Cannot return unsolicited material. Uses 8×10 glossy b&w and color prints; 2¼×2¼, 4×5 and 8×10 transparencies. Pays $25-400/b&w photo; $300-500/color photo. Buys one-time rights; negotiable.
Tips: "Do not send anything without a SAE and return postage. I like photocopies for my files with names, address and phone number."

GRAPEVINE PUBLICATIONS, INC., P.O. Box 2449, Corvallis OR 97339. (503)754-0583. Managing Editor: Chris Coffin. Estab. 1983. Publishes adult trade, textbooks and how-to books. Occasionally uses photos for promotional materials and book covers.
Needs: Model release required; photo captions preferred.
Making Contact & Terms: Provide resume, business card, brochure, flyer or tearsheets to be kept on file for possible future assignments. Works on assignment only. "Cannot guarantee returns or replies to queries/submittals." Pays $100-200/color photo; $50-100/b&w photo. Buys all rights. Simultaneous submissions and previously published work OK.
Tips: Just beginning to use photos.

GRAPHIC ARTS CENTER PUBLISHING COMPANY, P.O. Box 10306, Portland OR 97210. (503)226-2402. Editorial Director: Douglas A. Pfeiffer. Publishes adult trade photographic essay books. Photos used for photo essays.

Needs: Offers 5 freelance assignments annually. Landscape, nature, people, historic architecture and other topics pertinent to the essay. Captions preferred.

Making Contact & Terms: Uses 35mm, 2¼ × 2¼ and 4 × 5 transparencies (35mm as Kodachrome 25 or 64). NPI; pays by royalty—amount varies based on project; minimum, but advances against royalty are given. Credit line given. Buys book rights. Simultaneous submissions OK.

Tips: "Photographers must be previously published in book form, and have a minimum of five years full-time professional experience to be considered for assignment. Prepare an original idea as a book proposal. Full color essays are expensive to publish, so select topics with strong market potential. We see color essays as being popular compared to b&w in most cases."

GROLIER, INC., Sherman Turnpike, Danbury CT 06816. Chief Photo Researcher: Ann Eriksen. Estab. 1829. Publishes encyclopedias and yearbooks. Photos used for text illustration. Examples of recently published titles: *The New Book of Knowledge Annual* (encyclopedia); *The Americana Annual* and *The New Book of Popular Science Annual*. All photo use is text illustration unless otherwise negotiated. (Other uses are very rare!)

Needs: Buys 2,000 freelance photos/year; offers 5 assignments/year. "Encyclopediac." Interested in photos that aren't posed, of the subject in its natural habitat that are current and clear. Model release preferred for any photos used in medical articles, education articles, etc. Photo captions required; natural history subjects should carry latin identifications.

Making Contact & Terms: Interested in working with newer, lesser-known photographers. Query with list of stock photo subjects. Provide resume, business card, brochure, flyer or tearsheets to be kept on file for possible future assignments. Uses 8 × 10 glossy b&w/color prints; 35mm, 2¼ × 2¼, 4 × 5, 8 × 10 (originals preferred) transparencies. Cannot return unsolicited material. "Will contact when needed." Pays $50-100/b&w photo; $150-200/color photo; $700-1,000/day. Very infrequent freelance photography is negotiated by the job. Credit line given "either under photo or in back of book." Buys one-time rights; negotiable. Occasional foreign language rights. Simultaneous submissions and previously published work OK.

Tips: "Send subject lists and small selection of samples for file. Photocopy or printed samples *only* please. We do not return unsolicited photographs. In reviewing samples we consider the quality of the photographs, range of subjects and editorial approach. Keep in touch but don't overdo it. We continue to use about 50% b&w photos but have an increasingly hard time finding good photos in our price range. Quality often looks like bad conversions from color instead of good b&w original. Color use will increase and we see a trend toward increasing use of computerized images."

***GUERNICA EDITIONS, INC.**, P.O. Box 633, Station N.D.G., Montreal, H4A 3R1 Canada. (514)987-7411. Fax: (514)982-9793. Editor: Antonio D'Alfonso. Estab. 1978. Publishes adult trade (literary). Photos used for book covers. Examples of recently published titles: *Arrangiarsi* (cover); *The Other Shore* (cover); and *Fabio* (cover).

Needs: Buys various number of photos annually; "often" assigns work. Life events, including characters; houses. Photo captions required.

Making Contact & Terms: Interested in receiving work from newer, lesser-known photographers. Query with samples. Uses color and/or b&w prints. Sometimes keeps samples on file. Cannot return material. Reports in 1-2 weeks. Pays $100-150 for cover. Pays on publication. Credit line given. Buys book rights. "Photo rights go to photographers. All we need is the right to reproduce the work."

HANCOCK HOUSE PUBLISHERS, 1431 Harrison Ave., Blaine WA 98230. (206)354-6953. Fax: (604)538-2262. President: David Hancock. Estab. 1968. Publishes trade books. Photos used for text illustration, promotions, book covers. Examples of recently published titles: *Working with Dr. Schweitzer, Pheasants of the World* (350 color photos). Photos used for text illustration.

Needs: Birds/nature. Model release and photo captions preferred. Reviews stock photos.

Making Contact & Terms: SASE. Reports in 1 month. NPI. Credit line given. Buys non-exclusive rights. Simultaneous submissions and previously published work OK.

HARMONY HOUSE PUBLISHERS, 1008 Kent Rd., Goshen KY 40026. (502)228-4446. Owner: William Strode. Estab. 1984. Publishes photographic books on specific subjects. Photos used for text illustration, promotion materials, book covers and dust jackets. Recent book titles: *Country U.S.A., Emblems of Southern Valor* and *Georgia Tech.*

The code NPI (no payment information given) appears in listings that have not given specific payment amounts.

Needs: Number of freelance photos purchased varies. Assigns 30 shoots each year. Captions required.
Making Contact & Terms: Query with resume of credits along with business card, brochure, flyer or tearsheets to be kept on file for possible future assignments. Query with samples or stock photo list. Submit portfolio for review. Works on assignment mostly. Uses 35mm, 2¼ × 2¼, 4 × 5 or 8 × 10 transparencies. NPI; payment negotiable. Credit line given. Buys one-time rights and book rights. Simultaneous submissions and previously published work OK.
Tips: To break in, "send in book ideas to William Strode, with a good tray of slides to show work."

*D.C. HEATH AND COMPANY, 125 Spring St., Lexington MA 02173. (617)860-1468. Fax: (617)860-1259. Art and Photo Coordinator: Billie L. Ingram. Estab. 1875. Publishes college texts—all disciplines, but the majority are in hard sciences, history, politics, foreign language, English and math. Photos used for text illustration and book covers. Examples of recently published titles: *Biology: Discovering Life, The Enduring Vision* and *Introduction to Physical Science.* Photo guidelines available.
Needs: Buys "several hundred" photos annually; offers 20 freelance assignments annually. Wants editorial photos for all disciplines, plus artistic photos for covers. Reviews stock photos. Photo captions required "if subject matter is from field of natural sciences or hard sciences."
Making Contact & Terms: Interested in receiving work from newer, lesser-known photographers. Query with resume of credits. Query with stock photo list. Provide resume, business card, brochure, flyer or tearsheets to be kept on file for possible future assignments. Uses 8 × 10 b&w prints; 35mm, 2¼ × 2¼, 4 × 5 and 8 × 10 transparencies. Keeps samples on file. SASE. Reporting time depends on project. NPI. "We are constrained by low budgets and must keep costs down." Pays on receipt of invoice. Credit line given. Buys one-time rights. Simultaneous and/or previously published work OK.
Tips: "We use stock almost exclusively but do occasional set-up or assignment shots. I want original photos with good contrast, and composition. Interested in imaginative treatment of abstracts for math texts, computer texts and economics texts. We are not using more photos, but are using them in more ways as we move toward production of more supplements and alternative text presentations, such as slide sets, videocassettes, video disks and CDRom interactive software."

*HERALD PRESS, 616 Walnut Ave., Scottdale PA 15683. (412)887-8500. Fax: (412)887-3111. Contact: James Butti. Estab. 1908. Photos used for book covers and dust jackets. Examples of recently published titles: *Lord, Teach Us to Pray, Starting Over* and *Amish Cooking* (all cover shots).
Needs: Buys 5 photos annually; offers 10 freelance assignments annually. Subject matter varies. Reviews stock photos of people and other subjects. Model/property release required. Captions preferred (identification information).
Making Contact & Terms: Interested in receiving work from newer, lesser-known photographers. Query with samples. Provide resume, business card, brochure, flyer or tearsheets to be kept on file for possible future assignments. Works on assignment only or select from file of samples. Uses varied sizes of glossy color and/or b&w prints; 35mm transparencies. Keeps samples on file. SASE. Reports in 1 month. Pays $150-200/color photo. **Pays on acceptance.** Credit line given. Buys book rights; negotiable. Simultaneous submissions and previously published work OK.
Tips: "Put your resume and samples on file."

HOLT, RINEHART AND WINSTON, 1120 Capital of Texas Hwy. So., Austin TX 78746. (512)314-6500. Fax: (512)314-6590. Manager of Photo Research: Debra Saleny. Estab. 1866. "The Photo Research Department of the HRW School Division in Austin obtains photographs for textbooks in subject areas taught in secondary schools." Photos are used for text illustration, promotional materials and book covers. Examples of recently published titles: *Elements of Writing, Science Plus, People and Nations, World Literature, Biology Today* and *Modern Chemistry.*
Needs: Buys 3,500 photos annually. Photos to illustrate mathematics, the sciences—life, earth and physical, chemistry, history, foreign languages, art, English, literature, speech and health. Reviews stock photos. Model/property releases preferred. Photo captions required that include scientific explanation, location and/or other detailed information.
Making Contact & Terms: Interested in receiving work from newer, lesser-known photographers. Query with resume of credits. Query with stock photo list. Query with samples. Uses any size glossy b&w prints and color transparencies. Cannot return unsolicited material. Reports as needed. Pays $125-180/b&w photo; $150-225/color photo; $75-125/hour and $700-1,000/day. Credit line given. Buys one-time rights.
Tips: "We use a wide variety of photos, from portraits to studio shots to scenics. We like to see slides displayed in sheets. We especially like photographers who have specialties . . . limit themselves to one/two subjects." Send a letter and printed flyer with a sample of work and a list of subjects in stock. Do not call! Looks for "natural looking, uncluttered photographs, labeled with exact descriptions, technically correct, and including no evidence of liquor, drugs, cigarettes or brand names." Photography should be specialized, with photographer showing competence in one or more areas.

HOME PLANNERS, INC., Suite 110, 3275 W. Ina Road, Tucson, AZ 85741. (602)297-8200. Fax: (602)297-6219. Art Director: Cindy J. Coatsworth. Estab. 1946. Publishes material on home building and planning and landscape design. Photos used for text illustration, promotional materials and book covers. Examples of recently published titles: *The Home Remodeler, The Backyard Landscaper* and *Deck Planner.* In all three, photos used for cover and text illustrations.
Needs: Buys 50 freelance photos; offers 5 freelance assignments annually. Homes/houses—"but for the most part, it must be a specified house built by one of our plans." Property release preferred.
Making Contact & Terms: Provide resume, business card, brochure, flyer or tearsheets to be kept on file for possible assignments. Works on assignment only. Uses 4×5 transparencies. SASE. Reports in 1 month. Pays $25-100/color photo; $500-750/day; maximum $500/4-color cover shots. Credit line given. Buys all rights. Simultaneous submissions and previously published work OK.
Tips: Looks for "ability to shoot architectural settings and convey a mood. Looking for well-thought, professional project proposals."

HOMESTEAD PUBLISHING, Box 193, Moose WY 83012. Editor: Carl Schreier. Publishes 7-10 titles per year in adult and children's trade, natural history, Western American and art. Photos used for text illustration, promotional, book covers and dust jackets. Examples of recently published titles: *Yellowstone: Selected Photographs, Field Guide to Yellowstone's Geysers, Hot Springs and Fumaroles* and *Field Guide to Wildflowers of the Rocky Mountains.*
Needs: Buys 100-200 photos annually; offers 3-4 freelance assignments annually. Natural history. Reviews stock photos. Model release preferred. Photo captions required; accuracy very important.
Making Contact & Terms: Query with samples. Provide resume, business card, brochure, flyer or tearsheets to be kept on file for possible future assignments. Uses 8×10 glossy b&w prints; 35mm, 2¼×2¼, 4×5 and 6×7 transparencies. SASE. Reports in 3-4 weeks. Pays $70-300/color photo, $50-300/b&w photo. Credit line given. Buys one-time and all rights; negotiable. Simultaneous submissions and previously published work OK.
Tips: In freelancer's samples, wants to see "top quality—must contain the basics of composition, clarity, sharp, in focus, etc. Looking for well-thought out, professional projects proposals."

HOWELL PRESS, INC., Bay 2, 1147 River Road, Charlottesville VA 22901. (804)977-4006. Fax: (804)971-7204. President: Ross A. Howell, Jr. Estab. 1985. Publishes illustrated books, calendars and posters. Examples of recently published titles: *Shield of Zion: The Israel Defense Forces, Jungle Warriors: Defenders of the Amazon* and *Photographing Airplanes.*
Needs: Aviation, military history, gardening, maritime history, motorsports, cookbooks only. Reviews stock photos. Model/property release preferred. Captions preferred.
Making Contact & Terms: Interested in receiving work from newer, lesser-known photographers. Query. Uses b&w and color prints. Keeps samples on file. SASE. Reports in 1-2 weeks. NPI; payment varies. Buys one-time rights. Simultaneous submissions and previously published work OK.
Tips: When submitting work, please "provide a brief outline of project, including cost predictions and target market for project. Be specific in terms of numbers."

ILR PRESS, NY State School of Industrial and Labor Relations, Cornell University, Ithaca NY 14853-3901. (607)255-3061. Marketing and Promotion Manager: Andrea Fleck Clardy. Publishes books about all aspects of work and labor relations for academics, practitioners and the general public. Photos used for book covers and catalog of publications.
Needs: Buys 5-10 freelance photos annually. People at work in a wide variety of contexts, with high human interest and excellence in photo design. Reviews stock photos.
Making Contact & Terms: Query with samples. Uses b&w prints. SASE. Reports in 1 month. Pays $25-100/b&w photo. Credit line given. Buys one-time rights or book rights. Simultaneous submissions and previously published work OK.
Tips: Prefers to see "b&w prints of high human interest, images of people in the workforce. Particularly interested in photos that include women and people of color, high-tech professions and worker/manager groups."

*INITIATIVES PUBLISHING CO., #101, 800 Sailview Rd., Knoxville TN 37922. (615)966-1293. President: Gary Smith. Estab. 1988. Publishes how-to, self-help, motivational, personal finance, consumer affairs, financial planning and prosperity. Photos used for text illustration, promotional materials, book covers and dust jackets. Examples of recently published titles: *Save Your Home: How to Prevent Foreclosure* (text); *Career-Switcher!* (cover, promotion); *Bankruptcy: How It Really Affects You* (cover and text, promotion). Photo guidelines free with SASE.
Needs: Buys 12 or more photos annually; offers 6 or more freelance assignments annually. Relaxed people situation shots (paying bills, with family, in house, etc.). Reviews stock photos of couples at work or home, family at home. Model release required. Property release preferred.

Making Contact & Terms: Interested in receiving work from newer, lesser-known photographers. Query with resume of credits and samples. Provide resume, business card, brochure, flyer or tearsheets to be kept on file for possible future assignments. Works on assignment only. Uses 2¼×2¼ or 4×5 transparencies. Keeps samples on file. Cannot return material. Reports in 1 month. Pays $75-150/hour; $500-1,500/day; $250-3,000/job; $15-30/color photo; $5-15/b&w photo. Pays on acceptance. Credit line sometimes given depending on usage. Buys book rights, collateral and promo material; negotiable. Previously published work OK ("if outside our subject area").
Tips: Looks for "intimate, friendly style showing couples or families at home, couples in discussion. High degree of technical quality required (lighting, makeup, styling). Query for upcoming needs. Then submit accordingly. Keep marketability in mind, always." Plans to "use more in our direct mail marketing pieces. More set shots in place of stock."

INTERNATIONAL MARINE PUBLISHING COMPANY, P.O. Box 220, Camden ME 04843. (207)236-6046. Production Director: Molly Mulhern. Publishes how-to books on nautical subjects. Photos used for text illustration, book covers and dust jackets. Examples of recently published titles: *A Cruising Guide to the Maine Coast, Water Shots* and *Fiberglass Boat Repair Manual* (photos used for cover and text in all three).
Needs: Buys 100 freelance photos annually; offers 5 freelance assignments annually. Any nautically-related photos. Sometimes reviews stock photos. Model release preferred. Photo captions required.
Making Contact & Terms: Query with samples. Uses transparencies, any size. Cannot guarantee return of unsolicited material. Reports in 1 month. Pays $30-100/color photo, $10-50/b&w photo and $15-30/hour. Credit line given. Buys book rights. Previously published work OK.
Tips: "We do not supply photo guidelines—please do not request them."

JAMESTOWN PUBLISHERS, P.O. Box 9168, Providence RI 02940. Courier Delivery: 544 Douglas Ave., Providence RI 02908. (401)351-1915. Fax: (401)331-7257. Production Supervisor: Diane Varone. Estab. 1969. Publishes reading developmental textbooks. "We need photos to illustrate covers and text material, covering a wide range of photo matter." Examples of recently published titles: *Topics for the Restless*; all photos used for text illustrations.
Needs: Buys 10-20 photographs annually. "We use a wide variety of photos: biographical subjects, illustrative photos for covers, historical photos, nature, science, people, etc."
Making Contact & Terms: Query with list of stock photo subjects. Provide resume, business card, brochure, flyer or tearsheets to be kept on file for possible future assignments. Uses 8×10 glossy b&w prints; 35mm, 4×5 transparencies. Does not return unsolicited material. Reports in 1 month. Pays $100-150/b&w photo; $135-350/color photo. Credit line given. Buys one-time rights. Previously published work OK.
Tips: Looks for "creativity, high contrast (for our b&w texts), plus diversity. Send stock lists. I keep all stock sources on a computer file. Keep sending updated lists."

*JSA PUBLICATIONS, INC., P.O. Box 37175, Oak Park MI 48237. (313)932-0090. Fax: (313)932-8763. Art Director: Elena Panto. Estab. 1984. Publishes trade paperbacks on travel, humor and general nonfiction topics. Examples of recently published titles: *Mexico: A Colorful & Concise History, The I Love to Hate Madonna Joke Book* and *The Politically Incorrect Joke Book.*
Needs: Buys 25-40 photos annually. Does not offer freelance assignments. Interested in humorous photos. Model release required. Property release preferred. Captions preferred.
Making Contact & Terms: Interested in receiving work from newer, lesser-known photographers. Query with stock photo list. Does not keep samples on file. Reports in 3 weeks. Pays $40-70/b&w photo. Pays on receipt of invoice. Credit line given. Buys one-time and book rights; negotiable. Simultaneous submissions and previously published work OK.
Tips: Looks for strong clarity and composition and variety of subject matter. "Offer a product that is different than those photos carried by stock firms."

KALMBACH PUBLISHING COMPANY, 21027 Crossroads Circle, Waukesha WI 53187. (414)796-8776. Fax: (414)796-0126. Editor: Bob Hayden. Estab. 1942. Publishes how-to, hobby books on radio control model line, model railroading and model building (planes, tanks). Photos used for text illustration. Examples of recently published titles: *The Spirit Of Railroading* and *Steel Rails Across America.*
Needs: Needs photos of prototype locomotives, planes and tanks. Photo captions preferred.
Making Contact & Terms: Query with samples. Works on assignment only. Uses 5×7 or 8×10 glossy b&w prints; and 4×5 transparencies. Keeps samples on file. SASE. Reports in 1 month. Pays $20-25 minimum. Credit line given. Buys all rights. Simultaneous submissions OK.
Tips: "Since we deal with books and modeling magazine, we need photos of tanks, planes, etc. that include detail."

*B. KLEIN PUBLICATIONS., P.O. Box 8503, Coral Springs FL 33075. (305)752-1708. Fax: (305)752-2547. President: Bernard Klein. Estab. 1953. Publishes adult trade, reference and who's who. Photos used for text illustration, promotional materials, book covers, dust jackets. Examples of recently pub-

lished titles: *1933 Chicago Worlds Fair, 1939 NY Worlds Fair* and *Presidential Ancestors*.
Needs: Reviews stock photos.
Making Contact & Terms: Interested in receiving work from newer, lesser-known photographers. Query with resume of credits. Query with samples. Send unsolicited photos by mail for consideration. Works on assignment only. Cannot return material. Reports in 1-2 weeks. NPI.

KREGEL PUBLICATIONS, P.O. Box 2607, Grand Rapids MI 49501. (616)451-4775. Fax: (616)459-6049. Director of Publications: Al Bryant. Publishes textbooks for Christian and Bible colleges, reference works and commentaries, sermon helps and adult trade books. Photos used for book covers and dust jackets.
Needs: Buys 12-40 photos annually. Scenic and/or biblical (i.e., Holy Land, etc.). Reviews stock photos. Model release preferred.
Making Contact & Terms: Query with resume of credits. Query with samples. Send stock photo list. Uses 35mm and 2¼×2¼ transparencies. Keeps samples on file. SASE. Reports in 1 month. Pays $100-400/color photo. Credit line given. Buys book rights. Previously published work OK.
Tips: "We are tending to use more color photos on covers."

LAYLA PRODUCTION INC., 310 E. 44, New York NY 10017. (212)697-6285. Fax: (212)949-6267. Manager: Lori Stein. Estab. 1980. Publishes adult trade, how-to gardening and cooking books. Photos used for text illustration and book covers. Examples of recently published titles: *Roses of America* (commissioned 300 new editorial photos); *Bugs Bunny* (assigned photographers to shoot artworks); and *Tweety & Sylvester* (assigned shooting of artwork and memorabilila).
Needs: Buys over 150 photos annually; offers 6 freelance assignments annually. Gardening and cooking. Buys all rights.
Making Contact & Terms: Provide resume, business card, brochure, flyer or tearsheets to be kept on file for possible future assignments. Specifications for submissions are very flexible. SASE. Reports in 1 month; prefers no unsolicited material. Pays $20-200/color photo, $10-100/b&w photo, $25-100/hour. Other methods of pay depends on job, budget and quality needed. Simultaneous submissions and previously published work OK.
Tips: "We're usually looking for a very specific subject. We *do* keep all resumes/brochures received on file—but our needs are small, and we don't often use unsolicited material. We will be working on a series of gardening books through 1995."

LOOMPANICS UNLIMITED, P.O. Box 1197, Port Townsend WA 98368. Editorial Director: Steve O'Keefe. Estab. 1975. Publishes how-to and nonfiction for adult trade. Photos used for book covers. Examples of recently published titles: *Serial Slaughter: What's Behind America's Murder Epidemic* (cover), *The Big House: How American Prisons Work* (cover) and *Techniques of Safecracking* (inside).
Needs: Buys 2-3 photos annually; offers 1-2 freelance assignments annually. "We're always interested in photography documenting crime and criminals." Reviews stock photos. Model/property release preferred. Captions preferred.
Making Contact & Terms: Query with samples. Query with stock photo list. Provide tearsheets to be kept on file for possible future assignments. Uses b&w prints. Samples kept on file. SASE. Reports in 1 month. Pays $10-250 for cover photo; $5-20 interior photo. Credit lines given. Buys book rights; negotiable. Simultaneous submissions and previously published work OK.
Tips: "We look for clear, high contrast b&w shots that *clearly* illustrate a caption or product. Find out as much as you can about what we are publishing and tailor your pitch accordingly."

MCGRAW-HILL, College Division, 27 Floor, 1221 Avenue of the Americas, New York NY 10020. Manager: Safra Nimrod. Estab. 1889. Photos used for college textbooks. Examples of recently published titles: *Keller: Physics, 2nd edition* (300, color and b&w); *Pelczar: Microbiology* (400, color and b&w); and *Patterson: American Democracy, 2nd edition* (250, color and b&w). "Forget about photo guidelines; we don't have any."
Needs: Subjects include editorial, reportage, news, sociology, psychology, special effects, natural history, science, micrography—all college subjects. Reviews stock photos. Model/property release preferred. Captions required; include location, date, activities and points of interest.
Making Contact & Terms: Interested in receiving work from newer, lesser-known photographers. Provide resume, business card, self-promotion piece or tearsheets to be kept on file for possible future stock use. Do not send unsolicited photos. Uses 8×10 repro quality b&w prints; also transparencies

The asterisk before a listing indicates that the market is new in this edition. New markets are often the most receptive to freelance submissions.

or repro-quality dupes. No research fees. NPI; payment varies. **Pays on acceptance** after sizes are determined. Credit line given. Buys one-time rights.

Tips: "We look for professionalism in presentation, well edited work, consistent high quality. If there's one bad shot, we question the photographer's judgment." Looks for "editorial approach, clean, sharp images, unposed people and an interesting angle on a familiar subject. Send tearsheets or copies. Be willing to negotiate prices. There is continuing lack of good, new b&w photography."

McKINZIE PUBLISHING COMPANY, P.O. Box 241777, 11000 Wilshire Blvd., Los Angeles CA 90024-9577. (213)934-7685. Fax: (213)931-7217. Personnel Manager: Samuel P. Elliott. Estab. 1969. Publishes adult trade, "how-to," description and travel, sports, adventure, fiction and poetry. Photos used for text illustration, promotional materials and book covers.

Needs: Offers 4 or 5 freelance assignments annually. Shots of sports figures and events. Reviews stock photos. Model/property release required.

Making Contact & Terms: Arrange personal interview to show portfolio. Query with samples. Uses 3×5 glossy b&w/prints. SASE. Reports in 3 weeks. Pays $10-50/b&w photo; $50/hour. Credit line not given. Buys all rights; negotiable.

MACMILLAN PUBLISHING COMPANY, 445 Hutchinson Ave., Columbus OH 43235. Photo editor: Anne Vega. (800)228-7854, ext. 3704. Publishes college textbooks. Photos used for text illustration with emphasis in education, special education, physical education, counseling, management and personnel, health and nutrition, fashion merchandising, and clothing and textiles. Cover Design: Russ Maselli (800)228-7854, ext. 3688. Photos for book covers with emphasis in education, special education, physical education, counseling, management and personnel, health and nutrition, fashion merchandising, clothing and textiles, computer science, business marketing, criminal justice, geography and geology.

Needs: Professionally lighted, cover quality, color and b&w photos of lively and unique general K-12 education activities with ethnic mix; special education students, mainstreamed students; computer usage in K-12, college, business and home; world geography with and without people; and oceanography, including surface and underwater shots. Reviews stock photos only after inquiry and authorization to submit material with SASE and phone number. Model release required.

Making Contact & Terms: Inquire by sending a list of stock photo subjects, business card, brochure, flyer or tearsheets. Uses 8×10 glossy b&w prints with minimum ¼″ border, 35mm transparencies. Averages 1-3 months return time for rejected or considered work, 3-9 months return time for published work. Competitive textbook prices paid on publication. In-text photos pays $65-115/b&w photo; $80-175/color photo; $800-1,000/day; $400-800/cover photo. Pay scale depends on rights and priority level of book. Credit line given. Buys one-time, North American, world and limited exclusive rights. All photos for cover should be in color and addressed to Russ Maselli. Majority of photos used by Anne Vega are b&w and of education orientation. Previously published work in competing college textbooks not acceptable.

Tips: "If you don't have a promo piece, we prefer to receive duplicate slides and sample prints. Will accept quality photocopies to keep on file upon approving the quality from submissions of actual glossy prints/slides."

METAMORPHOUS PRESS, Box 10616, Portland OR 97210. (503)228-4972. Editor: Lori Stephens. "We publish books and tapes in the subject areas of communication, health and fitness, education, business and sales, psychology, women and children. Photos used for text illustration, promotional materials, book covers and dust jackets. Examples of recently published titles: *The Challenge of Excellence*; *Re-Creating Your Self*; and *The Professional ACT: Acting, Communication, Technique*. Photos used for cover and/or text illustration.

Needs: Reviews stock photos.

Making Contact & Terms: Query with list of stock photo subjects. Provide resume, business card, brochure, flyer or tearsheets to be kept on file for possible future assignments. Works on assignment only. Cannot return material. Reports as soon as possible. NPI; payment negotiable. Credit line given. Buys one-time and book rights. Also buys all rights, but willing to negotiate. Simultaneous submissions and previously published work OK.

Tips: "Let us have samples of specialties so we can match contents and styles to particular projects."

MILKWEED EDITIONS, 528 Hennepin Ave., Suite 505, Minneapolis MN 55403-1810. (612)332-3192. Fax: (612)332-6248. Art Director: R.W. Scholes. Estab. 1979. Publishes fiction, nonfiction and poetry. Photos used for text illustration, book covers and dust jackets. Examples of recently published titles: *Minnesota Gothic*, (counter poems throughout); *Twin Sons of Different Mirrors* (b&w photos used for text illustration) and *The Freedom of History* (color photo used for cover art).

Needs: Interested in high-quality photos, able to stand on own; "should not be journalistic." Model release required; photo captions preferred.
Making Contact & Terms: Arrange personal interview to show portfolio. Query with samples. Provide resume, business card, brochure, flyer or tearsheets to be kept on file. Uses 10×12 b&w glossy prints and 35mm transparencies. SASE. Reports in 1 month. Pays $10-100/b&w photo; $20-150/color photo; $10-650/job. "We buy piece work. We are a nonprofit organization." Credit line given. Buys one-time rights. Simultaneous submissions and previously published work OK.
Tips: Would like to see series works, usually b&w. "Look at our books for use. Then send in a fairly good copy (or original) to keep on file, plus a slide sheet with address and SASE." Sees trend in company toward "an increased use (of photos) compared to past graphic works." The same is generally true among book publishers.

*MILLIKEN PUBLISHING COMPANY, 1100 Research Blvd., St. Louis MO 63132. (314)991-4220. Fax: (314)991-4807. Managing Editor: Kathy Hilmes. Estab. 1960. Clients: teachers. Examples of recently published titles: *Space Exploration*, *Life in the Desert* and *Me and My Body* (all cover photos).
Needs: Works with very few photographers. Photos are needed occasionally for covers. Needs vary widely from shots of children to landscapes, other countries, monuments and science-related photos. Captions preferred; model release required.
Making Contact & Terms: Interested in receiving work from newer, lesser-known photographers. Send stock photo list and samples if available. Provide resume, business card, self-promotion piece or tearsheets to be kept on file for possible future assignments. Works mainly with local freelancers. Uses 8×10 glossy b&w and color prints; also 35mm and 4×5 transparencies. SASE. Reports in 1 month. Pays $25-100/b&w photo; $50-250/color photo; and $500-1,000/job. **Pays on acceptance.** Credit line given. Buys all rights; negotiable.
Tips: In portfolios or samples, looks for "clarity and interest of subject. We have used very little photography in the last five years, and I don't foresee much need in the coming year."

MOON PUBLICATIONS, INC., P.O. Box 3040, Chico CA 95927-3040. (916)345-5473. Fax: (916)345-6751. Photo Buyer: Carey Wilson. Estab. 1973. Publishes travel material. Photos used for text illustration, promotional materials and book covers. Examples of recently published titles: *Vacation Handbook (4th Ed.)*, *Cancun Handbook (3rd Ed.)* and *Texas Handbook (2nd Ed.)*. All photos used for cover and text illustration. Photo guidelines free with SASE.
Needs: Buys 12 photos annually. People, clothing and activity typical of area being covered, landscape or nature. Reviews stock photos. Photo captions preferred; include location, description of subject matter.
Making Contact & Terms: Interested in receiving work from newer, lesser-known photographers. Query with stock photo list. Provide resume, business card, brochure, flyer or tearsheets to be kept on file for possible future assignments. Uses 35mm, 2¼×2¼, 4×5, 8×10 transparencies. Keeps samples on file. SASE. Reports in 1 month. Pays $200-300/color photo. Pays on publication. Credit line given. Buys book rights; negotiable. Previously published work OK.
Tips: Wants to see "sharp focus, visually interesting (even unusual) compositions portraying typical activities, styles of dress and/or personalities of indigenous people of area covered in handbook. Unusual land or seascapes. Don't send snapshots of your family vacation. Try to look at your own work objectively and imagine whether the photograph you are submitting really deserves consideration for the cover of a book that will be seen worldwide. We continue to refine our selection of photographs that are visually fascinating, unusual."

MOTORBOOKS INTERNATIONAL, 275 South Third St., Stillwater MN 55082. (612)439-6001. Fax: (612)439-5627. Publisher: Tim Parker. Estab. 1965. Publishes trade and specialist and how-to, automotive, aviation and military. Photos used for text illustration, book covers and dust jackets. Examples of recently published titles: *Porsche Legends*, *American Farm Tractor* and *Bandits: Pictorial History of Aggressors*.
Needs: Buys 30 freelance photos and offers 12 assignments annually. Anything to do with transportation (not sailboats), tractors, cycles or airplanes. Reviews stock photos. Model release and captions preferred.
Making Contact & Terms: Works mostly on assignment. Any size prints or transparencies. SASE. Reports in 2 weeks. NPI; payment negotiable. Credit line given. Rights negotiable. Simultaneous submissions and previously published work OK.

MOUNTAIN AUTOMATION CORPORATION, P.O. Box 6020, Woodland Park CO 80866. (719)687-6647. President: Claude Wiatrowski. Estab. 1976. Publishes souvenir books. Photos used for text illustration, promotional materials and book covers. Examples of recently published titles: *Colorado's Black Canyon* (throughout); *Pike's Peak By Rail* (extra illustrations in video) and *Georgetown Loop RR* (extra illustrations in video).

Needs: Complete projects for illustrated souvenir books, not individual photos. Model release required. Property release preferred. Captions required.
Making Contact & Terms: Interested in receiving work from newer, lesser-known photographers. Query with book project. Uses 35 mm, 2¼ × 2¼, 4 × 5 transparencies. Keeps samples on file. SASE. Reports in 1 month. NPI; royalty on complete book projects. Credit lines given. Buys all rights. Simultaneous submissions OK.
Tips: "We *only* are interested in complete illustrated book projects for the souvenir market with very targeted markets."

MUSEUM OF NORTHERN ARIZONA, Route 4, Box 720, Flagstaff AZ 86001. (602)774-5211. Fax: (602)779-1527. Editor: Diana Lubick. Estab. 1928. Publishes biology, geology, archaeology, anthropology and history. Photos used for book covers. Examples of recently published titles: *The Sinagua, The San Juan River* and *Canyon Country*. Forty b&w and color photos used for text in each.
Needs: Buys approx. 80 photos annually. Biology, geology, history, archaeology and anthropology — subjects on the Colorado Plateau. Reviews stock photos. Photo captions preferred, include location and definition.
Making Contact & Terms: Interested in receiving work from newer, lesser-known photographers. Uses 8 × 10 glossy b&w prints; also 35mm, 2¼ × 2¼, 4 × 5 and 8 × 10 transparencies. Prefers 2¼ × 2¼ transparencies or larger. SASE. Reports in 1 month. Pays $35-250/color photo; $35-250/b&w photo. Credit line given. Buys one-time and all rights; negotiable. Simultaneous submissions and previously published work OK.
Tips: Wants to see top-quality, natural history work. To break in, send only pre-edited photos.

***NEW LEAF PRESS, INC.**, Box 311, Green Forest AR 72638. (501)438-5288. President: Tim Dudley. Publishes adult trade, cooking, fiction of religious nature, catalogs and general trade. Photos used for book covers and dust jackets. Example of recently published title: *When Your Dreams Don't Come True*.
Needs: Buys 20 freelance photos annually. Landscapes, dramatic outdoor scenes, "anything that could have an inspirational theme." Reviews stock photos. Model release required; captions preferred.
Making Contact & Terms: Query with samples and list of stock photo subjects. Does not assign work. Uses 6 × 8 glossy color prints. SASE. Reports in 4-6 weeks. Pays $100-175/color photo and $50-100/b&w photo. Credit line given. Buys one-time and book rights. Simultaneous submissions and previously published work OK.
Tips: In order to contribute to the company, send "quality, crisp photos." Trend in book publishing is toward much greater use of photography.

NORTHWORD PRESS, INC., Box 1360, Minocqua WI 54548. (715)356-9800. Fax: (715)356-9762. Directors of Photography: Robert Baldwin, Larry Mishkar. Estab. 1983. Photos used for text illustration, promotional materials, book covers and dust jackets. Examples of published titles: *Wild Wisconsin, Spirit of the North* and *Elk Country*.
Needs: Buys 500 photos annually. Wildlife, nature and outdoor activity. Reviews stock photos. Model/property release and captions required.
Making Contact & Terms: Query with stock photo list. Uses 35mm, 2½ × 2½, 4 × 5 and 8 × 10 transparencies. Keeps samples on file. Cannot return materials. Reports in 3 weeks. Photo guidelines free with SASE. Pays $50-500/color photo. Credit line given. Buys one-time rights and project rights. Simultaneous submissions and previously published work OK.
Tips: "Please submit only extremely high quality, well composed, 'razor sharp' focused images. Edit your submissions carefully. Do not include multiples of the same image. We look for creativity and imagination. Give your work that extra 'nudge' to make the shot unique."

***W.W. NORTON AND COMPANY**, 500 Fifth Ave., New York NY 10110. (212)354-5500. Fax: (212)869-0856. College Department: Ms. Ruth Mandel. Estab. 1923. Publishes college textbooks. Photos used for text illustration, book covers and dust jackets. Examples of recently published titles: *Biological Science (5th edition), The Swamproot Chronicle* and *The Anxious Decades*.
Needs: Variable. Photo captions preferred.
Making Contact & Terms: Interested in receiving work from newer, lesser-known photographers. Send stock photo list. Do not enclose SASE. Reports as needed. NPI. Credit line given. Buys one-time rights; negotiable. Simultaneous submissions and previously published work OK.
Tips: Views photo rates as too high. "We are buying down, negotiating harder, shopping around — anything to save money."

C. OLSON & CO., P.O. Box 5100-PM, Santa Cruz CA 95063. (408)458-3365. Editor: C. L. Olson. Estab. 1977.
Needs: Uses 2 photos/year — b&w or color; all supplied by freelance photographers. "Looking for color photos of glaciers — from land, sea and air. Photos of well-known Natural Hygienists. Also, photos of fruit and nut trees (in blossom with fruit) in public access locations like parks, schools,

churches, streets, businesses. You should be able to see the fruits up close with civilization in the background." Model/property release required for posed people and private property. Captions required.

Making Contact & Terms: Interested in receiving work from newer, lesser-known photographers. Query with samples. SASE, plus #10 window envelope. Reports in 2 weeks. NPI; "all rates negotiable." Pays on acceptance or publication. Credit line given on request. Buys all rights. Simultaneous submissions and previously published work OK.

Tips: Open to both amateur and professional photographers. "To ensure that we buy your work, be open to payment based on a royalty for each copy of a book we sell."

*OUR SUNDAY VISITOR, INC., 200 Noll Plaza, Huntington IN 46750. (219)356-8400. Fax: (219)356-8472. Managing Editor: Richard G. Beemer. Estab. 1912. Publishes religious (Catholic) periodicals, books and religious educational materials. Photos used for text illustration, promotional materials, book covers and dust jackets. Examples of recently published titles: *The Making of Saints* (b&w on cover); *Spanish Roots of America* (color on cover); and *Operation Rescue* (color on cover).

Needs: Buys 15-20 photos annually; offers 5 freelance assignments annually. Interested in family settings, "anything related to Catholic Church." Reviews stock photos. Model/property release required. Captions preferred.

Making Contact & Terms: Interested in receiving work from newer, lesser-known photographers. Query with samples. Works with freelancers on assignment only. Uses 8 × 10 glossy, color and/or b&w prints; 35mm transparencies. Keeps samples on file. SASE. Reports in 1 month. NPI. Pays on acceptance, receipt of invoice. Credit line given. Buys one-time rights.

OUTDOOR EMPIRE PUBLISHING, INC., Box C-19000, Seattle WA 98109. (206)624-3845. Human Resource Director: Margaret Durante. Publishes how-to, outdoor recreation and large-sized paperbacks. Photos used for text illustration, promotional materials, book covers and newspapers.

Needs: Buys 6 photos annually; offers 2 freelance assignments annually. Wildlife, hunting, fishing, boating, outdoor recreation. Model release preferred. Captions preferred.

Making Contact & Terms: Query with samples or send unsolicited photos by mail for consideration. Provide resume, business card, brochure, flyer or tearsheets to be kept on file for possible future assignments. Works on assignment only. Uses 8 × 10 glossy b&w and color prints; 35mm, 2¼ × 2¼ and 4 × 5 transparencies. SASE. Reports in 3 weeks. NPI; payment "depends on situation/publication." Credit line given. Buys all rights. Simultaneous submissions and previously published work OK.

Tips: Prefers to see slides or contact sheets as samples. "Be persistent; submit good quality work. Since we publish how-to books, clear informative photos that tell a story are very important."

PAPIER-MACHÉ PRESS, 795 Via Manzana, Watsonville CA 95076. (408)726-2933. Fax: (408)726-1255. Editor: Sandra Haldeman Martz. Estab. 1984. Publishes adult trade paperbacks focusing on issues of interest to mid-life and older women. Photos used for text illustration and promotional materials. Examples of recently published titles: *Palm Coast* (12 photos); *When I Am an Old Woman I Shall Wear Purple* (18 photos) and *If I Had My Life to Live Over I Would Pick More Daisies* (17 photos). "Guidelines for current theme anthologies are available with #10 SASE."

● At the 1991 American Booksellers Association this publisher won Book of the Year honors for its title *When I Am an Old Woman I Shall Wear Purple*.

Needs: Buys 60-80 photos annually; offers 2-3 freelance assignments annually. Human interest, usually women in "doing" role; sometimes couples, families, etc. Sometimes reviews stock photos. Model/property release preferred. "Generally we do not caption photos except for photographer's name."

Making Contact & Terms: Interested in receiving work from newer, lesser-known photographers. Query with samples (including photocopies). Provide resume, business card, brochure, flyer or tearsheets to be kept on file for possible future assignments. Uses 8 × 10 glossy b&w prints. Keeps samples on file. SASE. Reports in 3-6 months. "Guidelines for current theme anthologies are available with #10 SASE." Pays $25-50/b&w photo; $300-500/job; photographers also receive "copies of books, generous discount on books." Credit line given. Buys one-time rights and rights to use photos in promo material for books, e.g. flyers, ads, etc.; negotiable. Simultaneous submissions and previously published work OK.

Tips: "We are generally looking for photos to complement a specific theme anthology or poetry collection. It is essential for photographers to know what those current themes are."

*PELICAN PUBLISHING CO., 1101 Monroe St., Gretna LA 70053. (504)368-1175. Fax: (504)368-1195. Production Manager: Dana S. Bilbray. Publishes adult trade, juvenile, textbooks, how-to, cooking, fiction, travel, science and art books. Photos used for book covers. Examples of recently published titles: *Maverick Hawaii* (cover), *Maverick Berlin* and *Coffee Book*.

Needs: Buys 8 photos annually; offers 3 freelance assignments annually. Wants to see travel (international) shots of locations and people and cooking photos of food. Reviews stock photos of travel subjects. Model/property release required. Captions required.

Making Contact & Terms: Interested in receiving work from newer, lesser-known photographers. Query with stock photo list. Provide resume, business card, brochure, flyer or tearsheets to be kept on file for possible future assignments. Uses 8×10 glossy color prints; 35mm, 4×5 transparencies. Keeps samples on file. SASE. Reports as needed. Pays $100-500/color photo; negotiable with option for books as payment. **Pays on acceptance.** Credit line given. Buys one-time rights and book rights; negotiable.
Tips: "Be flexible on price. Keep publisher up on new materials."

THE PHOTOGRAPHIC ARTS CENTER, 163 Amsterdam Ave. #201, New York NY 10023. (212)838-8640. Fax: (212)873-7065. Publisher: Robert S. Persky. Estab. 1980. Publishes books on photography and art, emphasizing the business aspects of being a photographer, artist and/or dealer. Photos used for book covers. Examples of recently published titles: *Publishing Your Art As Cards & Posters* (cover illustration); and *The Photographer's Complete Guide To Exhibition & Sales Spaces* (text illustration).
Needs: Business of photography and art. Model release required.
Making Contact & Terms: Query with samples and text. Uses 5×7 glossy b&w or color prints; 35mm transparencies. SASE. Reports in 3 weeks. Pays $25-100/color photo, $25-100/b&w photo. Credit line given. Buys one time rights.
Tips: Sees trend in book publishing toward "books advising photographers how to maximize use of their images by finding business niches such as gallery sales, stock and cards and posters." In freelancer's submissions, looks for "manuscript or detailed outline of manuscript with submission."

PLAYERS PRESS INC., P.O. Box 1132, Studio City CA 91614. (818)789-4980. Vice President: David Cole. Estab. 1965. Publishes entertainment books including theater, film and television. Photos used for text illustration, promotional materials book covers and dust jackets. Examples of recently published titles: *Playing the Game*, (cover/text illustration); *Period Costume* (Vols. 1&2, text illustration); and *The Bear* (production photos of play).
Needs: Buys 50-1,000 photos annually. Entertainers, actors, directors, theatres, productions, actors in period costumes, scenic designs and clowns. Reviews stock photos. Model release required for productions/personalities. Photo captions preferred for names of principals and project/production.
Making Contact & Terms: Query with list of stock photo subjects. Send unsolicited photos by mail for consideration. Uses 8×10 glossy or matte b&w prints; 5×7 glossy color prints; 35mm, 2¼×2¼ transparencies. SASE. Reports in 3 weeks. Pays $5-500/color photo; $1-200/b&w photo. Credit line sometimes given, depending on book. Buys all rights; negotiable in "rare cases." Simultaneous submissions and previously published work OK.
Tips: Wants to see "photos relevant to the entertainment industry. Do not telephone; submit only what we ask for."

POCKET BOOKS, 1230 Avenue of the Americas, New York NY 10020. (212)698-7000. Contact: Art Director. Estab. 1939. Publishes hardcover, mass market and trade paperbacks. Photos used for book covers—uses mostly people and still lifes.
Needs: Reviews stock photos. Model release required.
Making Contact & Terms: Submit portfolio for review any day but Friday. Provide tearsheets to be kept on file for possible future assignments. SASE. Previously published work OK.
Tips: "I look for people who are conceptual as well as technically skilled. Please do not call. Drop off portfolio with us regularly with a variety of tearsheets to show us new work."

*THE PRESERVATION PRESS, NATIONAL TRUST FOR HISTORIC PRESERVATION, 1785 Massachusetts Ave. N.W., Washington DC 20036. (202)673-4252. Fax: (202)673-4172. Managing Editor: Janet Walker. Estab. 1975. Publishes travel guides, calendars, architectural history, historic preservation, cultural preservation, neighborhoods and communities, children's books. Photos used for text illustration, book covers, dust jackets and calendars. Examples of recently published titles: *Historic America 1994 desk calendar* (one photo for each week), *Guide to New York City Landmarks* (cover) and *Past Meets Future* (cover).
Needs: Buys 60 photos annually; offers 1 freelance assignment annually. Wants shots of architecture, homes, people shots with architecture or in neighborhoods, communities. Property release preferred. Captions preferred.
Making Contact & Terms: Interested in receiving work from newer, lesser-known photographers. Provide resume, business card, brochure, flyer or tearsheets to be kept on file for possible future assignments. Uses 8×10 glossy b&w prints; 35mm, 2¼×2¼, 4×5 transparencies. Does not keep samples on file. SASE. Reports "as necessary and always if SASE is enclosed." NPI. Pays on receipt of invoice. Credit line given. Buys one-time rights.
Tips: "We look for straight-forward photography of architectural subjects and people in settings showing buildings for use in our books. However, a photographer can present us with a book idea based on his or her photographic work."

PRINCETON BOOK COMPANY, PUBLISHERS/DANCE HORIZONS, P.O. Box 57, Pennington NJ 08534. (609)737-8177. Fax: (609)737-1869. Managing Editor: Debi Elfenbein. Estab. 1975. Publishes dance books for college, trade and specialty markets. All aspects of dance—ballet, jazz, modern, folk, social, etc. Photos used for text illustration and book covers. Examples of recently published titles: *Dance Film and Video Guide*, *Dance as a Theatre Art*, Second Edition and *Dance: Rituals of Experience*.
Needs: Buys 40-50 photos annually. Black and white photos of specific dance, sometimes specific performers, specific choreographers or companies. Model/property release required. Photo captions required; include names of performers, date of photo, date of copyright and holder of copyright.
Making Contact & Terms: Interested in receiving work from newer, lesser-known photographers. Provide resume, business card, brochure, flyer or tearsheets to be kept on file for possible future assignments. Works on assignment only. Uses 8 × 10 b&w prints. Keeps samples on file. SASE. Reports in 3 months. Pays $25-75/b&w photo. Credit line given. Buys all rights; negotiable. Simultaneous submissions and previously published work OK.
Tips: Looks for "exciting and realistic portraits of dancers performing, perhaps photos of demonstrations of ballet positions or exercises as needed. Always stamp name, phone and address on every sample photo, also copyright date and holder."

*‡QUARTO PUBLISHING PLC., 6 Blundell St., London N79BH England. (071)700-8043. Fax: (071)700-4191. Picture Manager: Rebecca Horsewood. Publishes adult books. Photos used for text illustration and book covers. Examples of recently published titles: *Geography Facts* (text illustration, covers); *Videoschool* (text illustration, covers); and *Golf Facts*. Photo guidelines free when projects come up.
Needs: Buys 1,000 + photos annually. "Depends on books being worked on." Model/property release required. Photo captions required; include full details of subject and name of photographer.
Making Contact & Terms: Interested in receiving work from newer, lesser-known photographers. Provide resume, business card, brochure, flyer or tearsheets to be kept on file for possible future assignments. Uses all types of prints. Does not keep samples on file. Cannot return material. Pays $50/color photo. Pays on publication. Credit line given. Buys book rights; negotiable. Simultaneous submissions and/or previously published work OK.
Tips: "Make sure material being sent in is relevant to project."

*RAGGED MOUNTAIN PRESS, P.O. Box 220, Camden ME 04843. (207)236-6046. Fax: (207)236-6314. Director of Art and Production: Molly Mylhern. Estab. 1991. Publishes how-to books for outdoor market. Photos used for text illustration, book covers and dust jackets. "We do not supply photo guidelines."
Needs: Buys approximately 25 photos annually. Model release required.
Making Contact & Terms: Interested in receiving work from newer, lesser-known photographers. Query with samples. Provide resume, business card, brochure, flyer or tearsheets to be kept on file for possible future assignments. Uses 35mm 2¼ × 2¼ transparencies. Keeps samples on file. Cannot return material. Reports in 1 month. Pays $100-400/job. **Pays on acceptance.** Buys all rights; negotiable. Previously published work OK.

REDBIRD PRESS, INC., P.O. Box 11441, Memphis TN 38111. (901)323-2233. Editor: Virginia McLean. Estab. 1984. Publishes juvenile and travel books. Photos used for text illustration. Examples of recently published titles: *Chasing the Moon to China* and *Kenya, Jambo!* (text illustration).
Needs: "Have only bought 1 freelance photo; thinking of using freelance in future." Children, lifestyles in India, Greece, Turkey, Peru, Saudi Arabia, Italy and England. Reviews stock photos. Model/property release preferred.
Making Contact & Terms: Interested in receiving work from newer, lesser-known photographers. Query with list of stock photo subjects. Provide resume, business card, brochure, flyer or tearsheets to be kept on file for possible future assignments. Uses 35mm and 4 × 5 transparencies. Keeps samples on file. Cannot return material. Reports in 3 weeks. Pays $10-50/color photo. Credit line given. Buys all rights; negotiable. Simultaneous submissions and previously published work OK.
Tips: "We have not used freelance work in past but are considering it."

✿REIDMORE BOOKS INC., Suite 1200, 10109 106th St., Edmonton, Alberta T5J 3L7. (403)424-4420. Fax: (403)441-9919. Contact: Visuals Editor. Estab. 1979. Publishes textbooks for K-12; textbooks published cover all subject areas. Photos used for text illustration and book covers. Examples of

The double dagger before a listing indicates that the market is located outside the United States and Canada.

Gain an Edge by Knowing What Publishers Need

"We're known for producing very visual books with high-quality photos. And we're well aware how crucial this is to our success," says Jennifer Keane, visuals editor for Reidmore Books. The company, located in Edmonton, Alberta, is "the largest educational publisher (by sales) west of Toronto," she says.

Reidmore publishes books for kindergarten through grade 12 and most books must be approved by the various Canadian Departments of Education for classroom use in different provinces. Some of Reidmore's titles are used in the U.S. as well. The company publishes 10 to 15 textbooks and, occasionally, one trade title each year.

Jennifer Keane

Geography and history books require the most artwork, says Keane. Photographs are used in copy when a visual further enhances students' understanding of the material, such as with landscapes or examples of Greek architecture. Yet, photographs also are used to illustrate intangible principles such as the economics or social dynamics of a country, she says.

Keane looks for photographs of active people and is particularly interested in shots set in countries other than the U.S. and Canada. "It's more difficult to find good photos of England or Russia, for example," she says. She'd like to find more freelance photographers who travel and keep a good stock of shots set in other countries.

Keane uses an equal amount of freelance photography and stock photos, but there are certain advantages to working directly with freelancers, she says. The photographers she works with know the company and are constantly on the lookout for shots that fit her needs.

Textbook approval in Canada can take a long time, sometimes up to a year or more. Keane urges photographers to allow her to hold onto their photographs until a book is complete. At times, a photograph will not meet approval of the Department of Education and she will have to obtain a new photograph on short notice. She returns to the original freelancer for a more suitable shot whenever possible.

As with U.S. educational publishers, Canadian publishers are increasing their involvement in multimedia publishing. Keane expects to find more publishers involved in "just-in-time" publishing in the next few years. This is a publishing program in which the publisher keeps a large data base of information on a particular subject. Teachers and others can request specific information and obtain just what they need. If publishers do get into this form of publishing in any big way, it may have an impact on print runs, says Keane. She's quick to add, however, there always will be a need for visuals, particularly photography.

There are, of course, some differences between Canadian and U.S. textbook publishing. The size of the population, and therefore the market, results in much smaller print runs for Canadian books. So, in general, rates for photographs tend to be lower for Canadian publishers. This is another reason Keane likes to work with freelancers directly. There's more room to negotiate and she can offer more by avoiding the middle step of going through a stock agency first.

"Another thing I like about working with freelance photographers is the insight they can give me. It's nice to be able to call the photographer and get something interesting to use in the written copy or caption," Keane explains.

When working on a trade book last summer, Keane hired a freelance photographer to work on assignment, but this is a very rare occurrence, she says. For the most part, she buys photos from the stock freelancers have on hand.

"If you have no experience with textbooks, find at least one of our textbooks. Examine it and try to figure out why we've chosen a particular photo."

Initially, Keane likes to see only duplicate slides and tearsheets. "Five images are plenty for me to get the idea about your work. You can put across your best work with five examples and still show a variety. It doesn't matter whether the work is all color, all black and white or a mix. I prefer tearsheets and what I'm really looking for is what you feel is your best work."

She sees about 10 portfolios each week, but some weeks are even heavier. "One thing I look for is a well-put-together stock list, complete and itemized but not too specialized. One that is direct and to-the-point and fits easily into my file."
—by Robin Gee

© Lorraine O. Schultz

Jennifer Keane of Reidmore Books, Inc., chose this photo of the Temple of Hephaestus as the closing shot for a textbook on Greece. Keane liked the image because it combined the ancient culture with newer buildings of today.

recently published titles: *Greece: Discovering the Past*, *China: Our Pacific Neighbour* and *Canada's Atlantic Neighbours*. Photo guidelines available.

● This publisher received the 1991 Alberta Educational Book Award from the Book Publishers Association of Alberta for its book *Canadians Responding to Change*.

Needs: Buys 250 photos annually; offers 1-3 freelance assignments annually. "Photo depends on the project, however, images should contain unposed action." Reviews stock photos. Model/property release preferred. Captions required; "include scene description and photographer's control number." **Making Contact & Terms:** Interested in receiving work from newer, lesser-known photographers. Arrange personal interview to show portfolio. Submit portfolio for review. Query with resume of credits. Query with samples. Query with stock photo list. Provide resume, business card, brochure, flyer or tearsheets to be kept on file for possible future assignments. Keeps samples of tearsheets, etc. on file. Cannot return material. Reports in 1 month. Pays $50-200/color photo; $50-200/b&w photo. Credit line given. Buys one-time rights and book rights; negotiable. Simultaneous submissions and previously published work OK.

Tips: "I look for unposed images which show lots of action. Please be patient when you submit images for a project. The editorial process can take a long time and it is in your favor if your images are at hand when last minute changes are made."

RESOURCE PUBLICATIONS, INC., Suite 290, 160 E. Virginia St., San Jose CA 95112. Editorial Director: Kenneth Guentert. Publishes imaginative resources for professionals in ministry, counseling and education. Photos used for text illustration and promotional materials.

Tips: "We are not a market for spot photos. However, we are interested in photographers who have ideas for books in our field."

◆ST. REMY PRESS, INC., Maison Bagg, 682 William, Montreal, Quebec H3C 1N9 Canada. (514)871-9696. Fax: (514)871-2230. Picture Editor: Chris Jackson. Estab. 1984. Publishes adult trade. "We are a publisher that creates both one-shot trade books and series books for such publishers as Time-Life Books, Reader's Digest General Books, Smithsonian Press, among others." Photos used for text illustration and covers. Examples of recently published titles: *Wildest Places on Earth* (photo book), *The Art of Woodworking* (series), *Backroads & Scenic Drives* (part of *Explore America* series).

Needs: Travel and technology. Reviews stock photos. Captions required.

Making Contact & Terms: Interested in receiving work from newer, lesser-known photographers. Arrange personal interivew to show portfolio. Provide resume, business card, brochure, flyer or tearsheets to be kept on file for possible future assignments. Uses 35mm, 2¼×2¼, 4×5, 8×10 transparencies. SASE. Reports in 2 months. NPI; payment negotiable. Credit line given. Buys one-time rights; negotiable. Previously published work OK.

Tips: "We're in the middle of a USA travel series, book on boating, woodworking series, and many others. Please send new tearsheets so I can see your style. DO NOT SEND PIX without calling first."

*SALEM PRESS, 131 El Camino, Pasadena, CA 91331. Contact: Photo Editor. Publishes reference books, encyclopedias, biographies, historical series — mostly biographical, scientific. Photos used for text illustration, book covers. Examples of recently published titles: *African American Encyclopedia* (b&w, most ¼ page); biographies for middle school students (b&w and color); and *20th Century Events* (b&w).

Needs: Needs multicultural, Asian and Hispanic-American culture and lifestyle. Model release preferred for famous people.

Making Contact & Terms: Interested in receiving work from newer, lesser-known photographers. Query with stock photo list. "I use small amounts of color stock material from all areas, rare small assignments." Uses 5×7 or 8×10 prints; all sizes of transparencies. Cannot return material. Reports in 1-2 weeks. Pays $75-100/color photo; $45-50/b&w photo. Pays on publication. Credit line given. Buys one-time rights; negotiable ("depends on situation"). Simultaneous submissions and/or previously published work OK.

Tips: Looks for "clarity, composition, unposed, natural looking, filters used to compensate for fluorescent lighting." Interested in "can-do, responsive photographers with good quality. We use photo researchers also, especially experienced researchers in Washington DC for access to public domain material."

The maple leaf before a listing indicates that the market is Canadian.

SANDHILL CRANE PRESS, INC., P.O. Box 147050, Gainesville FL 32614. (904)375-6610. Acquisitions Editor: Ross H. Arnett. Publishes nature books (natural history, conservation, etc.). Photos used for text illustration, book covers and dust jackets. Examples of recently published titles: *Florida Butterflies*; *In Search of Reptiles and Amphibians* and *Biogeography of the West Indies*.
Needs: "We use only author-supplied illustrations."
Making Contact & Terms: Query with book proposal only. Uses 8×10 glossy b&w prints; 35mm transparencies. SASE. Reports in 2 weeks. NPI.
Tips: "Fill frame with subject."

❋SELF-COUNSEL PRESS, 1481 Charlotte Rd., Vancouver, British Columbia V7J 1H1 Canada. (604)986-3366. Fax: (604)986-3947. Designer: Rod Poland. Estab. 1971. Publishes adult trade, self-help books, legal, business, reference, financial, retirement, psychology and travel series. Photos used for promotional materials (book dummies, blurbs, posters) and book covers. Examples of published titles: *The Body Image Trap, The Minute Takers Handbook* and *Assertiveness for Managers*. All photography used as cover art.
Needs: Buys 6 photos and offers 6 freelance assignments annually. Needs photos of business and people (business, seniors), architecture (interior and exterior). Reviews stock photos. Model/property releases required.
Making Contact & Terms: Interested in receiving work from newer, lesser-known photographers. Arrange a personal interview to show portfolio if possible. Query with samples or with stock photo lists. Provide resume, business card, brochure, flyer or tearsheets to be kept on file for possible future assignments. Cannot return material. Uses color prints; 35mm and 2¼×2¼ transparencies. Pays $100-200/b&w photo; $100-400/color photo; $400/day. Credit line sometimes given depending on agreed price, other circumstances. Buys all rights; negotiable. Simultaneous submissions and previously published work OK, depending on circumstances.
Tips: "Send samples but not originals. Generally unsolicited phone calls are not well-received since product is visual."

SIERRA PRESS, INC., P.O. Box 430, El Portal CA 95318. (209)379-2330. Fax: (209)379-2455. General Manager: Jim Wilson. Estab. 1984. Publishes color photography books, postcard books, posters and prints of national parks and monuments. Photos used for illustration and book covers. Examples of published titles: *Windows of the Past* (visual essay on ruins of the Southwest); *Islands in the Sky* (visual essay on the Colorado Plateau); and *Art on the Rocks* (postcard book on rock art).
Needs: Uses 300 photos annually. Brilliant and colorful landscapes utilizing dramatic lighting and intimate details of nature. Photo captions required; include location, subject, time of year.
Making Contact & Terms: Interested in receiving work from newer, lesser-known photographers. Query with stock photo list. Call for current projects. Uses 35mm, 2¼×2¼, 4×5, 8×10 transparencies; they must be sharp, clear and concise. SASE. Pays $50-250/color photo. Credit line given. Buys one-time rights. Simultaneous submissions and previously published work OK.
Tips: "Send stock list by location. If you indicate you have work from areas we're looking for, we will contact you. We keep a computerized file of photographers and the regions of which they have work."

THE SPEECH BIN INC., 1965 25th Ave., Vero Beach FL 32960. (407)770-0007. Fax: (407)770-0006. Senior Editor: Jan J. Binney. Estab. 1984. Publishes textbooks and instructional materials for speech-language pathologists, audiologists and special educators. Photos used for book covers, instructional materials and catalogs. Examples of recently published titles: *Talking Time* (cover); also catalogs.
Needs: Children; children with adults; school scenes; elderly adults; handicapped persons of all ages. Model release required.
Making Contact & Terms: Interested in receiving work from newer, lesser-known photographers. Provide resume, business card, brochure, flyer or tearsheets to be kept on file for possible future assignments. Works on assignment plus purchases stock photos from time to time. Uses 8×10 glossy b&w prints. Full color for catalog. SASE. Reports in 3 weeks. NPI; negotiable. Credit line "sometimes" given. Buys all rights; negotiable. Previously published work OK.

ST PUBLICATIONS, 407 Gilbert Ave., Cincinnati OH 45202. (513)421-2050. Fax: (513)421-5144. Publisher: Todd Swormstedt. Estab. 1906. Publishes professional books for the sign, screen printing and visual merchandising and store design industries. "Mostly how-to books." Photos used for text illustration, book covers and advertisements. Examples of recently published titles: *Practical Sign Shop Operation* and *Gold Leaf Techniques*.
Needs: Buys 3 or 4 photos annually; offers 3 or 4 freelance assignments annually. Model/property release required.
Making Contact & Terms: Query with resume of credits. Query with samples. Works on assignment only. Uses 5×9 color/b&w prints; 35mm, 2¼×2¼ transparencies. Reports in 3 months. NPI; payment negotiable according to job. Credit line given. Buys book rights; negotiable. Simultaneous submissions and previously published work OK.

Tips: Judges the "quality of the photo, as well as the care given to capture the subject in a communicative way. Most of our work is with book authors. We need photos for illustrations. We will need to use more freelance photography in the future."

STANDARD EDUCATIONAL CORP., 200 W. Monroe St., Chicago IL 60606. (312)346-7440. Fax: (312)580-7215. Picture Editor: Irene L. Ferguson. Publishes the New Standard Encyclopedia. Photos used for text illustration. To see style/themes used, look at encyclopedias in library, especially New Standard Encyclopedia.
Needs: Buys 300 photos annually (stock photos only). Major cities and countries, points of interest, agricultural and industrial scenes, plants and animals. Model release preferred. Captions required.
Making Contact & Terms: Query with stock photo list. Do not send unsolicited photos. Uses 8×10 glossy b&w prints; contact sheet OK; uses transparencies. SASE. Reports in 1 month. Pays $75-125/ b&w photo; $135-300/color photo. Credit line given. Buys one-time rights. Simultaneous submissions and previously published work OK.

STANDARD PUBLISHING, 8121 Hamilton Ave., Cincinnati OH 45231. (513)931-4050. Editor: Richard Briggs. Estab. 1866. Publishes adult trade books, journals, religious curriculum for all ages and children's books. Photos used for text illustration and book covers.
Needs: Buys 300 freelance photos annually. Pictures of human interest—people of all ages, individuals and small groups involved in activities and family situations. People should have a natural appearance, not an artificial, posed, "too perfect" look. Pictures with a definite Christian connotation, such as a church, cross, a still life composed of a Bible, communion cup and bread, grapes, wheat, candle, lamp, etc., and other inspirational scenes and symbols. Pictures of landscapes, seascapes and natural forms or elements. Reviews stock photos. Model release required.
Making Contact & Terms: Interested in receiving work from newer, lesser-known photographers. Query with samples/I.D. list. Uses 8×10 b&w and color prints, also b&w and color transparencies. SASE. Reports in 6-8 weeks. Pays $25-50/b&w photo; $50-150/color inside; $120-200/color cover. Credit line usually given. Buys one-time and book rights. Simultaneous submissions and previously published work OK "if known where."

STAR PUBLISHING COMPANY, 940 Emmett Ave., Belmont CA 94002. (415)591-3505. Managing Editor: Stuart Hoffman. Estab. 1978. Publishes textbooks, regional history, professional reference books. Photos used for text illustration, promotional materials and book covers. Recently published: *Microbiology Techniques* (cover and text illustration); *Keyboarding with Computer Applications* (text illustration); and *Principles and Practices of Anaerobic Bacteriology* (text illlustration).
Needs: Biological illustrations, photomicrographs, business, industry and commerce. Reviews stock photos. Model release required. Captions required.
Making Contact & Terms: Query with samples and list of stock photo subjects. Provide resume, business card, brochure, flyer or tearsheets to be kept on file for possible future assignments. Uses 5×7 minimum b&w and color prints; 35mm transparencies. SASE. Reports within 90 days when a response is appropriate. NPI; payment variable "depending on publication, placement and exclusivity." Credit line given. Buys one-time rights; negotiable. Previously published submissions OK.
Tips: Wants to see photos that are technically (according to book's subject) correct, showing photographic excellence.

STONE WALL PRESS, INC., 1241 30th St. NW, Washington DC 20007. President: Henry Wheelwright. Estab. 1972. Publishes national outdoor/conservation books and nonfiction. Photos used for text illustration, book covers and dust jackets. Example of recently published title: *Wildlife Extinction* (cover and text).
Needs: Dramatic color cover shots; very occasionally representative text illustrations. Reviews stock photos. Model release required. Captions preferred.
Making Contact & Terms: Provide resume, business card, brochure, flyer or tearsheets to be kept on file for possible future assignments. Uses 7×9 glossy color prints. Cannot return material. NPI. Credit line given. Buys one-time rights. Simultaneous submissions and previously published work OK.

*TEACHERS COLLEGE PRESS, COLUMBIA UNIV., 1234 Amsterdam Ave., New York NY 10027. (212)678-3929. Fax: (212)678-4149. Graphic Arts Manager: Dave Strauss. Estab. 1904. Publishes educational materials of all kinds, particularly early childhood, higher education and feminist literature. Photos are used for text illustration, promotional materials and book covers. Examples of recently published titles: *Literacy Events in a Community of Young Writers*, *Physical Knowlege in Preschool Education* and *Making Violence Sexy: Feminist Views on Pornography* (all photos used for book covers).
Needs: Buys 1-50+ photos annually. Interested in photos of racially mixed groups of children, shots of educational settings and details (columns, classrooms, etc). Reviews stock photos. Model release preferred for "any subject who will sue for rights." Property release preferred. Captions preferred; include name of photographer.

Making Contact & Terms: Interested in receiving from newer, lesser-known photographers. Query with samples. Send unsolicited photos by mail for consideration. Uses min. 5×7 glossy b&w prints. Keeps samples on file. SASE. Reports 1-2 weeks "or faster." Pays $50-100/b&w photo. Pays on receipt of invoice. Credit line sometimes given (book covers, yes—mailers, usually not). Buys one-time rights; negotiable. Simultaneous submissions and/or previously published work OK.

Tips: "Subjects must be realistic (i.e., not obvious model) with emphasis on mood." Sees two main problems with stock or freelance photos: "dead" poses or technicals flaws and "slick" models which look airbrushed and groomed.

TRANSPORTATION TRAILS, 9698 W. Judson Rd., Polo IL 61064. (815)946-2343. Editor: Larry Plachmo. Estab. 1977. Publishes historical transportation titles. Photos used for text illustration, promotional materials, book covers, dust jackets and condensed articles in magazines. Examples of recently published titles: *The Longest Interurban Charter* (text and cover); *Sunset Lines—The Story of The Chicago Aurora & Elgin Railroad* (text); *The Steam Locomotive Directory of North America* (text).

Needs: Buys over 500 photos annually. Transportation, mainly bus or interurban, mainly historical.

Making Contact & Terms: Query with samples of historical transportation photos. Uses glossy b&w prints; 35mm transparencies. SASE. Reports in 1 week. Rates vary depending on needs; $2.50-150/b&w photo. Credit line given. Buys one-time, book and all rights; negotiable. Simultaneous submissions and previously published work OK.

Tips: In photographer's samples, "quality is not as important as location and date." Looks for "historical photos of buses and interurbans. Don't bother us with photos less than 30 years old."

THE TRINITY FOUNDATION, Box 700, Jefferson MD 21755. (301)371-7155. President: John Robbins. Estab. 1978. Publishes religion and philosophy and adult trade paperbacks. Photos used for book covers.

Needs: Reviews stock photos. Model release and photo captions preferred.

Making Contact & Terms: Query with samples. Uses any size color transparencies. SASE. Reports in 1 month. NPI. Credit line given. Buys book rights. Simultaneous submissions and previously published work OK.

Tips: Looks for "sharp, clear pictures related to Christianity and philosophy."

2M COMMUNICATIONS LTD., 121 W. 27 St., New York NY 10001. (212)741-1509. Fax: (212)691-4460. President: Madeleine Morel. Estab. 1982. Publishes adult trade biographies. Photos used for text illustration. Examples of previously published titles: *Diane Keaton, Magic and the Bird* and *The Princess and the Duchess;* all for text illustration.

Needs: Buys approximately 200 photos annually. Candids and publicity. Reviews stock photos. Model release required. Captions preferred.

Making Contact & Terms: Query with stock photo list. Uses b&w prints; 35mm transparencies. Reports in 1 month. Pays $100-200/color photo, $50-100/b&w photo. Credit line given. Buys one-time, book and world English language rights. Simultaneous submissions OK.

TYNDALE HOUSE PUBLISHERS, 351 Executive Dr., Wheaton IL 60189. (708)668-8300. Fax: (708)668-6885. Purchase Agent, Design Dept: Marlene Muddell. Estab. 1962. Publishes adult trade, children and juvenile fiction, Bibles and Bible reference, calendars and videos for children. Photos used for text illustration, promotional materials, book covers, dust jackets, calendar and video boxes. Examples of recently published titles: *Seven Secrets for Effective Fathers* (cover); *Life Application Bible for Students* (interior/editorial photos); and *Live Long and Love It!* (cover).

Needs: Buys 75-100 photos annually; offers 25 assignments annually. Nature, conservation and people, especially families of mixed ages and backgrounds, Holy Land. Especially needed are color photos of various ethnics working together. Reviews stock photos. Model/property release required for shots in which faces are identifiable, private property.

Making Contact & Terms: Interested in receiving work from newer, lesser-known photographers. Arrange personal interview to show portfolio. Submit portolio for review. Query with samples. Query with stock photo list. Works on assignment only. Uses 8×10 glossy b&w or color prints; 35mm; 2¼×2¼, 4×5 transparencies. Keeps samples on file. SASE. Reports in 3 weeks. Pays $250-1500/color photo; $75-200/b&w photo. The upper-end figures are offered for high-quality work. **Pays on acceptance.** Credit line given. Buys book rights, world reproduction rights, English language, unless

---

Market conditions are constantly changing! If you're still using this book and it's 1995 or later, buy the newest edition of Photographer's Market *at your favorite bookstore or order directly from* Writer's Digest Books.

otherwise negotiated. Simultaneous submissions and/or previously published work OK.

Tips: "We look for people shots which convey as much universality as possible. We want pictures that tell a story, especially of helping and working together situations; marriage and family (must have wedding bands), as well as contemplative scenics; contemporary urban issues. We like ethnic shots. Be concerned about backgrounds. Often it's helpful to have quiet, neutral areas where type can be placed easily. Because of our Christian orientation, Biblical allusions and Holy Land shots are also useful. We want to be able to manipulate photo images with our Macintosh computer system within ethical boundaries. We're sometimes ghosting images as backgrounds."

*ULYSSES PRESS, P.O. Box 3440, Berkeley CA 94703. (510)601-8301. Fax: (510)601-8307. Publisher: Leslie Henriques. Estab. 1983. Publishes trade paperbacks and travel material. Photos used for book covers. Examples of recently published titles: *Hidden Hawaii* (cover photos on front and back), *New Key to Costa Rica* (color signature) and *Hidden Southwest* (cover photos).

Needs: Buys 30 photos annually. Wants scenic photographs of destinations covered in guidebook. Some use of portraits for back cover. Model release required. Property release preferred.

Making Contact & Terms: Interested in receiving work from newer, lesser-known photographers. Query with stock photo list. Provide resume, business card, brochure, flyer or tearsheets to be kept on file for possible future assignments. Uses 35mm, 2¼×2¼ transparencies. Does not keep samples on file. Cannot return material. Reports as needed. Payment depends on placement and size of photo: $150-350 non-agency. Pays on publication. Credit line given. Buys one-time rights. Simultaneous submissions and previously published work OK.

UNIVELT, INC., P.O. Box 28130, San Diego CA 92198. (619)746-4005. Manager: Robert H. Jacobs. Estab. 1970. Publishes technical books on astronautics. Photos used for text illustration, book covers and dust jackets. Examples of recently published titles: *Men & Women of Space* and *History of Rocketry and Astronautics*.

Needs: Uses astronautics; most interested in photographer's concept of space, and photos depicting space flight and related areas. Reviews stock photos; space related only. Captions required.

Making Contact & Terms: Interested in receiving work from newer, lesser-known photographers. Query with resume of credits. Provide business card and letter of inquiry to be kept on file for possible future assignments. Uses 6×9 or 4½×6 b&w photos. SASE. Reports in 1 month. Pays $25-100/b&w photo. Credit line given, if desired. Buys one-time rights. Simultaneous submissions and previously published work OK.

Tips: "Photos should be suitable for front cover or frontispiece of space books."

UNIVERSITY PUBLICATIONS OF AMERICA, Suite 800, 4520 East-West Hwy., Bethesda MD 20814-3389. (301)657-3200, ext. 625. Print Production Manager: Doris Brown. Publishes mostly foreign intelligence and history-type books—some subjects include *The Secret War in Central America*—current history; also Indian Documents; some books on Apartheid are upcoming. Uses photos for promotional materials and dust jackets.

Needs: Buys no photos at present. Portraits, actual scenes of the important events. Model release and captions preferred.

Making Contact & Terms: Query with list of stock photo subjects. Send unsolicited photos by mail for consideration. Provide resume, business card, brochure, flyer or tearsheets to be kept on file for possible future assignments. Uses 5×7 or 8×10 matte b&w prints. SASE. Reporting time depends on project. NPI. Buys one-time rights or book rights. Simultaneous submissions and previously published work OK.

Tips: "Since we have not yet used services like these we have no information; we are 'shopping' to see how cost effective it would be for us to use freelance photography."

VICTIMOLOGY, INC., 2333 N. Vernon St., Arlington VA 22207. (703)528-3387. Photography Director: Sherry Icenhower. Publishes books about victimology focusing on the victims not only of crime but also of occupational and environmental hazards. Examples of recently published titles: *Spouse Abuse, Child Abuse, Fear of Crime* and *Self-defense*. Photos used for text illustration.

Needs: Buys 20-30 photos/year. Submit model release with photo. Captions required.

Making Contact & Terms: "We will look at color photos only if part of an essay with text." Send b&w contact sheet or 8×10 glossy prints; color contact sheet or 5×7 or 8×10 glossy prints; 35mm transparencies. SASE. Reports in 6 weeks. Pays $30-150/color photos. Buys all rights, but may reassign to photographer after publication. Simultaneous submissions and previously published work OK.

J. WESTON WALCH, PUBLISHER, 321 Valley St., P.O. Box 658, Portland ME 04104-0658. (207)772-2846. Fax: (207)772-3105. Contact: Acquisitions. Estab. 1927. Publishes supplementary educational materials for grades 6-12 and adult education. All subject areas. Photos used for text illustration, promotional materials and book covers. Examples of recently published titles: *True Adventure Readers*

(3 Art series) (cover photos); *Steps to Good Grammar* (cover photo) and *Science and Social Issues* (text illustration).
Needs: Buys 30-40 or more photos/year; varies widely. Offers up to 5 freelance assignments annually. Black and white and color photos of middle school and high school students, ethnically diverse, in-school, library or real-life situations, historical photos, current events photos, special needs students and chemistry, ecology and biology. Reviews stock photos. Model release required. Captions preferred.
Making Contact & Terms: Interested in receiving work from newer, lesser-known photographers. Provide resume, business card, brochure, flyer or tearsheets to be kept`on file for possible future assignments. Uses 8×10 glossy b&w prints; also 35mm, 2¼×2¼, 4×5 and 8×10 transparencies. SASE. Pays $35-100/b&w; $100-500/color photo. Credit line sometimes given depending on photographer's request. Buys one-time rights.
Tips: One trend with this company is a "growing use of b&w and color photos for book covers." Especially wants to see "subjects/styles suitable for use in secondary schools."

WARNER BOOKS, 9th Floor, 1271 Avenue of the Americas, New York NY 10020. (212)522-7200. Creative Director: Jackie Merri Meyer. Publishes "everything but text books." Photos used for book covers and dust jackets.
Needs: Buys approximately 20 freelance photos annually; offers approximately 30 assignments annually. People, food still life, glamourous women and couples. Reviews stock photos. Model release required. Captions preferred.
Making Contact & Terms: Submit portfolio for review. Send brochure, flyer or tearsheets to be kept on file for possible future assignments. Cannot return unsolicited material. Uses color prints/transparencies; also some b&w and hand-tinting. Pays $800 and up/color photo; $1,200 and up/job. Credit line given. Buys one-time rights. Simultaneous submissions and previously published work OK.
Tips: "Printed and published work (color copies are OK, too) are very helpful. Do not call, we do not remember names—we remember samples—be persistent. Drop book off as often as possible and leave samples."

✦**WEIGL EDUCATIONAL PUBLISHERS LIMITED**, 2114 College Ave., Regina, Saskatchewan S4P 1C5 Canada. (306)569-0766. Fax: (306)757-4721. Attention: Editorial Department. Estab. 1979. Publishes textbooks and educational resources: social studies, life skills, environment/science studies, multicultural, language arts and geography. Photos used for text illustration and book covers. Example of recently published title: *Citizenship in Action*.
Needs: Buys 15-25 photos annually; offers 2-3 freelance assignments annually. Social issues and events, politics, education, technology, people gatherings, multicultural, environment, science, agriculture, life skills, landscape, wildlife and people doing daily activities. Reviews stock photos. Model/property release required. Captions required.
Making Contact & Terms: Query with samples. Query with stock photo list. Provide tearsheets to be kept on file for possible future assignments. Tearsheets or samples that don't have to be returned are best. Keeps samples on file. Uses 5×7, 3×5, 4×6, 8×10 color/b&w prints; 35mm, 2¼×2¼ transparencies. SASE. "We generally get in touch when we actually need photos." Pays $15 or more for images used in publication, including publication fee. Price is negotiable. Credit line given (photo credits as appendix). Buys one-time, book and all rights; negotiable. Simultaneous submissions and previously published work OK.
Tips: Need "clear, well-framed shots that don't look posed. Action, expression, multicultural representation are important, but above all, education value is sought. People must know what they are looking at. Please keep notes on what is taking place, where and when. As an educational publisher, our books use specific examples as well as general illustrations."

SAMUEL WEISER INC., P.O. Box 612, York Beach ME 03910. (207)363-4393. Art Director: Sandy Montgomery. Estab. 1956. Publishes books on esoterica, oriental philosophy, alternative health and mystery traditions. Photos used for book covers. Examples of published titles: *Heisler: Path to Power* (cover), *Durkheim: Japanese Cult of Tranquility* (cover) and *Bennett: Idiots in Pan's* (cover). Photo guidelines free with SASE.
Needs: Buys 2-6 photos annually. Photos of flowers, abstracts (such as sky, paths, roads, sunsets) and inspirational themes. Reviews stock photos.
Making Contact & Terms: Query with samples. Send unsolicited photos by mail for consideration. Provide resume, business card, brochure, flyer or tearsheets to be kept on file for possible future assignments. "We'll take color snapshots to keep on file, or color copies." Keeps samples on file. Uses color prints, 2¼×2¼ and 4×5 transparencies. SASE. Reports in 1 month. Pays $100-200/color photo. Credit line given. Buys book rights; negotiable. "We pay once for life of book because we do small runs." Simultaneous submissions and previously published work OK.
Tips: "We like to keep inexpensive proofs because we may see a nice photo and not have anything to use it on now. We search our files for covers, usually on tight deadline. We don't want to see goblins and halloween costumes."

THE WHEETLEY COMPANY, INC., Suite 1100, 4709 Golf Rd., Skokie IL 60076. (708)675-4443. Fax: (708)675-4489. Art Manager: Carol Stutz. Estab. 1986. Produces elementary and high school textbooks in all subjects. Photos used for text illustration and book covers. Examples of recently produced books: *World Geography* (photos used for text and cover illustration, Scholastic); *Mathematics of Money* (photos used for text and cover illustration, South-Western).

Needs: Subject matter depends upon the book being produced. Most photos used are "unposed." Photos frequently call for pictures of children and young people, including minorities. Reviews stock photos. Model release required. Photo captions preferred.

Making Contact & Terms: Interested in receiving work from newer, lesser-known photographers. Query with list of stock photo subjects. Provide resume, business card, brochure, flyer or tearsheets to be kept on file for possible future assignments. Cannot return unsolicited material. Uses glossy b&w prints; 35mm, 2¼×2¼, 4×5 transparencies. Reports in 1 month. Pays $135-165/quarter page of color photos; $60-120/quarter page of b&w photos. Credit line sometimes given depending on the "style established for the book." Buys one-time, exclusive product, North American or world rights; negotiable. Simultaneous submissions and previously published OK.

Tips: Send all information attention: Linda Rogers, Human Resources Manager.

JOHN WILEY & SONS, INC., 605 3rd Ave., New York NY 10158. (212)850-6731. Photo Research Director: Stella Kupferberg. Estab. 1807. Publishes college texts in all fields. Photos used for text illustration. Examples of recently published titles: *Geography* by deBlij, *Physics* by Halliday, *Psychology* by Huffman and *Computers* by Stern.

Needs: Buys 4,000 photos/year; 200+ photos used for text and cover illustration. Uses b&w and color photos for textbooks in psychology, business, computer science, biology, chemistry, geography, geology and foreign languages. Captions required.

Making Contact & Terms: Query with list of stock photo subjects. Uses 8×10 glossy and semigloss b&w prints; also 35mm and large format transparencies. SASE. "We return all photos securely wrapped between double cardboard by UPS." Pays $75-125/b&w print and $100-175/color transparency. Credit line given. Simultaneous submissions and previously published work OK.

Tips: "Initial contact should spell out the material photographer specializes in, rather than a general inquiry about our photo needs. Tearsheets and flyers welcome."

*WINDSOR PUBLICATIONS, INC., P.O. Box 2500, 21827 Nordhoff St., Chatsworth CA 91311. (818)700-0200, ext. 2525. Acquisitions Photo Editor: Michael Nugwynne. Publishes historical/editorial books of cities, counties and states throughout Northern America including Alaska, also publishes directory. Photos used for text illustration, book covers and dust jackets. Examples of recently published titles: *Los Angeles - Realm of Possibility* (text illustration); *Bear Down - University of Arizona Sports* (photographic chronicle); *San Francisco & Bay Area - California Gateway to the Future* (text illustration); and *Washington DC & Potomac Region - A Contemporary Portrait* (text illustration).

Needs: Buys "thousands" of photos and offers 30 freelance assignments annually. General shots, people, historical landmark, skyline, rurals, countryside, buildings, downtown, media, network, housing, economy, banking, medical, special events, transportation, recreation and leisure, cultural, shopping and education. Reviews stock photos. Model release preferred; captions required.

Making Contact & Terms: Query with samples and stock photo list. Provide resume, business card, brochure, flyer or tearsheets to be kept on file for possible future assignments. Uses 35mm, 2¼×2¼ and 4×5 transparencies. SASE. Reports in 1 month. Pays $50-75/color photo (higher for dust jacket — $250-500 maximum); $15/b&w photo. Credit line given. Buys one-time rights. Previously published work OK.

Tips: Looks for "color and composition of scenics, skyline and people."

WISCONSIN TRAILS BOOKS, P.O. Box 5650, Madison WI 53705. (608)231-2444. Photo Editor: Nancy Mead. Estab. 1960. Publishes adult nonfiction, guide books and photo essays. Photos used for text illustration and book covers. Recently published: *Ah Wisconsin* (all photographs) and *Best Wisconsin Bike Trips* (cover and ⅓ inside-photos). Photo guidelines free on request with SASE.

● This publisher also needs material for calendars and a bimonthly magazine. Check the Wisconsin Trails' listings in the Paper Products and Consumer Publications sections.

Needs: Buys many photos and gives large number of freelance assignments annually. Wisconsin nature and historic scenes and activities. Captions preferred, include location information.

Making Contact & Terms: Query with samples or stock photo list. Send unsolicited photos by mail for consideration. Provide resume to be kept on file for possible assignments. Uses 5×7 or 8×10 b&w prints and any size transparencies. SASE. Reports in 1 month. Pays $25-75/b&w photo; $50-200/color photo. Credit line given. Buys one-time rights. Simultaneous submissions and previously published work OK.

Tips: "See our products and know the types of photos we use."

WORD PUBLISHING, 5221 N. O'Connor, Irving TX 75239. (214)556-1900. Design Director: Tom Williams. Estab. 1951. Publishes Christian books. Photos used for book covers, publicity, brochures, posters, product advertising and stock photos. Examples of recently published titles: *The New World Order* by Pat Robertson; *Storm Warning* by Billy Graham and *Miracle Man: Nolan Ryan Autobiography*. Photos used for covers. "We do not provide want lists or photographer's guidelines."
Needs: Nature, people, studio shots and special effects. Model release required; property release preferred.
Making Contact & Terms: Provide brochure, flyer or tearsheets to be kept on file for possible future assignments. Please don't call. SASE. Reports in 1 month. Assignment photo prices determined by the job. Pays for stock $350-900. Credit line given. Rights negotiable.
Tips: In portfolio or samples, looking for strikingly lighted shots, good composition, clarity of subject. Something unique and unpredictable. "We use the same kinds of photos as the secular market. I don't need crosses, church windows, steeples, or wheat waving in the sunset. We are very busy with internal schedules. Don't send just a letter. Send your best work only. Give me something to look at, not to read about." Opportunity is quite limited: "We have hundreds of photographers on file, and we use about 3% of them."

WRITERS PUBLISHING SERVICE CO., 1512 Western Ave., Seattle WA 98101. (206)284-9954. Publisher: William R. Griffin. "We publish all types of books for independent authors, plus 10 to 15 books under our own imprint." Photos used for text illustration, promotional materials, book covers and dust jackets.
Needs: Uses 80-100 freelance photos and offers 50 freelance assignments annually. Open to all types of material. Separate division of company especially interested in photos of cleaning- and maintenance-related duties. Model release preferred; captions required.
Making Contact & Terms: Query with samples or stock photo list. Submit portfolio for review. Contact regarding ideas. Works with local freelancers on assignment only. Uses 5 × 7 and 8 × 10 glossy b&w and color prints. SASE. Reports within 30 days. Pays $5-50 per b&w photo. Credit line given. Buys one-time, book or all rights; negotiable. Simultaneous submissions and previously published work OK.
Tips: Prefers "original, creative, clear shots. Contact publishers to find out what they want, then shoot to fill that need. Be willing to pay your dues. Don't give up, but be realistic about income potential in early phases of career. There is more use of photos and illustrations by book publishers. Don't just send us standard sample shots. Send items that relate specifically to our market and needs. If you don't know what a publisher wants, ask! It's a lot better than having your letters and samples go in the trash because we don't want or can't use it."

*WRS GROUP, INC., P.O. Box 21207, Waco TX 76702. (817)776-6461. Fax: (817)757-1454. Art Director: Linda Filgo. Publishes non-fiction, health education material and inspirational work. Photos used for text illustration, promotional materials, book covers, dust jackets and catalogs. Examples of recently published titles: *Climbing Back*, *Blind Courage* and *Young At Heart*.
Needs: Buys 200-1,000 photos annually; offers 10 freelance assignments annually. Interested in anything dealing with lifestyles. Model/property release preferred.
Making Contact & Terms: Interested in receiving work from newer, lesser-known photographers. Submit portfolio for review. Send unsolicited photos by mail for consideration. Provide resume, business card, brochure, flyer or tearsheets to be kept on file for possible future assignments. Works with freelancers on assignment only. Keeps samples on file. SASE. Reports "only when needed." NPI; payment negotiable. **Pays on acceptance.** Buys one-time, book rights; negotiable. Simultaneous submissions and previously published work OK.
Tips: "Keep in touch. We always have new projects."

*ZOLAND BOOKS, 384 Huron Ave., Cambridge MA 02138. (617)864-6252. Fax: (617)661-4998. Design Director: Lori K. Pease. Publishes adult trade, some juvenile, mostly fiction, some photography, poetry. Photos used for book covers and dust jackets. Examples of recently published titles: *Art in Its Own Terms* by Fairfield Porter (cover), *Augusta Cotton* by Margaret Erhart (cover) and *Secret Words* by Jonathon Strong (author photo). Photo guidelines free with SASE.
Needs: Buys 3-5 photos annually; offers 3-5 freelance assignments annually. Subject matter varies greatly with each project. "We do like a painterly style and always need author photos, nature, people." Subject matter depends on book. Captions preferred.
Making Contact & Terms: Interested in receiving work from newer, lesser-known photographers. Query with samples. Provide resume, business card, brochure, flyer or tearsheets to be kept on file for possible future assignments. Mostly work with freelancers only. Use 4 × 5 glossy, b&w prints; 2¼ × 2¼, 4 × 5 transparencies. Keeps samples on file. SASE. Reports in 1-2 months. NPI. **Pays on acceptance.** Credit lines given. Rights vary with project; negotiable. Simultaneous submissions and previously published work OK.

Tips: Looks for work with a unique vision. Hand-painted work is of interest, as is nature, people. "We are a literary publishing company, not looking for commercial-advertising sorts of photography."

Book Publishers/'93-'94 changes

The following markets appeared in the 1993 edition of *Photographer's Market* but are not listed in the 1994 edition. They may have been omitted for failing to respond to our request for updated information, they may have gone out of business or they may no longer wish to receive freelance work.

And Books (did not respond)

Asian Humanities Press (did not respond)

Bonus Book (did not respond)

Cambridge University Press (did not respond)

Celo Valley Books (did not respond)

Chatham Press (did not respond)

Chatsworth Press (asked to be deleted)

Cleis Press (unable to locate)

Contemporary Books (did not respond)

CPI Group (not reviewing freelance work)

Delmar Publishers (did not respond)

Glencoe Publishing/Macmillan/McGraw Hill (did not respond)

Harpercollins Children's Books (did not respond)

Here's Life Publishers (not reviewing freelance work)

Hobby House Press (did not respond)

Imagine (moved to Businesses and Organizations)

Just Us Books (did not respond)

Kaleidoscopix (not reviewing freelance work)

Klutz Press (inappropriate submissions)

Knowledge Unlimited (did not respond)

Lebhar-Friedman (did not respond)

Liberty Publishing Company (did not respond)

Little, Brown & Co. (did not respond)

Llewellyn Publications (did not respond)

Lodestar Books (asked to be deleted)

Lucent Books (did not respond)

McDougal, Littell and Company (did not respond)

Macmillan Publishing Company (New York) (not reviewing freelance work)

Milady Publishing Corporation (did not respond)

Music Sales Corp. (did not respond)

New Society Publishers (did not respond)

Nordicpress (did not respond)

Peanut Butter Publishing (did not respond)

Prakken Publications (did not respond)

G.P. Putnam & Sons (did not respond)

William H. Sadlier (did not respond)

M.E. Sharpe (did not respond)

Theosophical Publishing House (did not respond)

Thorndike Press (did not respond)

Van Patten Publishing (did not respond)

Wasatch Publishers (asked to be deleted)

Wieser & Wieser (not reviewing freelance work)

Businesses and Organizations

With more than 3 million businesses and many more organizations in this country, freelance photographers interested in working directly with clients have many potential prospects. This section in *Photographer's Market* offers just a sampling of many different types of for-profit businesses as well as nonprofit associations or institutions. While many companies and organizations may already be working with advertising or public relations firms for promoting their products and activities, the listings in this section also welcome direct contact from freelancers.

While searching through these listings, concentrate on businesses that are receptive to your area of expertise. By focusing on your strengths and knowing what potential clients want to see, you will be able to make sales and earn assignments. As you acquire jobs, work hard to build on your successes. Once you complete a shoot for a major corporation, let other companies know about it. Send them promotional pieces containing shots that were used by the well-known firms. Doing so will show prospective clients that top-notch companies are confident in your abilities.

In all, there are 68 listings in this section and just less than half are new this year. It is extremely important to remember that these markets want to work with photographers who can get the job done. Some are still struggling to rebound from the recession and they don't want to waste their time with disorganized freelancers. Photographer Pat Goetzinger, of Milwaukee, Wisconsin, says one key to success when dealing with corporations is to maintain a professional appearance. Goetzinger supplies more information as the subject of our Insider Report beginning on page 162.

You will find a wide range of markets, from major corporations such as insurance companies to public interest and trade associations to universities and arts organizations. The types of photography which these listings usually require overlap somewhat with advertising markets. However, unlike that work which is largely directed toward external media or audiences, the photography for listings in this section tends to be more for specialized applications. Among these are employee or membership commmunications, annual reports, and documentary purposes such as recording meetings, group functions or theatrical presentations.

A fair number of these listings are receptive to stock images, while many have rather specific needs for which they assign photographers. These projects will sometimes require studio-type skills (again similar to the advertising/PR market), particularly in shooting corporate interiors and portraits of executives for annual reports. However, much of the coverage of meetings, events and performances calls for a different set of skills involving use of available light and fill flash. In particular, coverage of sporting events or theatrical performances may require agility with extreme or rapidly changing light conditions.

Unless these businesses and organizations are active at the national level, they typically prefer to work with local freelancers. Rates will vary widely depending upon the individual client's budget. We have tried to list current rates of payment where possible, but some listings have still only indicated "negotiable terms," or a per-shot, per-hour or per-day basis. Listings which have not provided a specific dollar amount include the code NPI, for "no payment information given." When quoting a price, especially for assigned work, remember to start with a basic day rate plus expenses and negotiate for final number of images, types of usage and time period for usage.

In particular, many of these clients wish to buy all rights to the images since they are often assigned for specific needs. In such cases, be sure to negotiate your terms in such a way that these clients get all the rights they need but that you also ultimately retain the copyrights.

*■ABBY LOU ENTERTAINMENT, 456 Glen Holly Dr., Pasadena CA 91105. (818)799-3537. Fax: (818)799-9849. President: George LeFave. Estab. 1987. Children's TV, toys, video production. Photos used in brochures, posters, catalogs and video production.
Needs: Buys 10-110 photos/year; offers 5-10 freelance assignments/year. Uses freelancers for children, toys. Examples of recent uses: video, catalog, brochure. Model/property release required. Captions preferred.
Audiovisual Needs: Uses slides and videotape. Subjects include: children and toys.
Making Contact & Terms: Interested in receiving work from newer, lesser-known photographers. Query with samples. Provide resume, business card, brochure, flyer or tearsheets to be kept on file for possible future assignments. Works with local freelancers only. Uses transparencies and videotape. Keeps samples on file. Cannot return material. Reporsts in 1 month. NPI. **Pays on acceptance** or usage. Credit lines sometimes given; "depends on job." Buys all rights; negotiable.
Tips: "Know your craft. Be flexible in negotiations." Concerned that "quality is not what it used to be."

*AIR-CONDITIONING & REFRIGERATION WHOLESALERS, Suite B, 10251 W. Sample Rd., Coral Springs FL 33065-3939. (305)755-7000. Fax: (305)755-4103. Manager of Communications: James McMullen.
Needs: Buys 40-60 photos/year; offers 2 or 3 assignments/year. Photos used in brochures, newsletters, newspapers, annual reports and PR releases. "Grip and grin shots, award presentations, groups at social and educational functions." Captions preferred, identification of individuals only.
Making Contact & Terms: Interestered in receiving work from newer, lesser-known photographers. Provide resume, business card, brochure, flyer or tearsheets to be kept on file for possible future assignments. Solicits photos by assignment only. Uses 5×7 glossy b&w and color prints; b&w and color contact sheets; b&w and color negatives. SASE. Reports as soon as selection of photographs is made. Pays $4-5/b&w photo; $5-8/color photo; $50-75/hour; and $300-375/day. Buys all rights; negotiable.
Tips: "Basically a freelance photographer working with us should use a photojournalistic approach, and have the ability to capture personality and a sense of action in fairly static situations. With those photographers who are equipped, we often arrange for them to shoot couples, etc., at certain functions on spec, in lieu of per-day or per-job fee."

*ALLIED INT'L CORP., P.O. Box 898, Newington VA 22122. (703)550-5507. Fax: (703)550-5063. Vice President: Simon Zebarjadi. Estab. 1980. Import/export confectionery/food products. Photos used in brochures, catalogs and labels of products.
Needs: Buys 10-20 photos/year; offers 10+ freelance assignments/year. Uses freelancers for fresh fruits, confectionery, cookies, etc. Reviews stock photos. Model/property release required. Captions preferred.
Making Contact & Terms: Interested in receiving work from newer, lesser-known photographers. Query with samples. Query with stock photo list. Work with local frelancers only. Uses 2¼×2¼ transparencies. Keeps samples on file. Cannot return material. Reports in 1-2 weeks. NPI. "Negotiable." **Pays on acceptance.** Buys all rights.
Tips: "Be flexible. Pay attention to requirements and instructions."

ALLRIGHT CORPORATION, Suite 1300, 1111 Fannin St., Houston TX 77002. (713)222-2505. Fax: (713)222-6833. National Director of Public Relations: H. M. Sinclair. Estab. 1926. Company operates in 87 cities in the US and Canada. Uses photos of parking facilities, openings, before and after shots, unusual parking situations, and Allright facilities in brochures, newsletters, newspapers, audiovisual presentations and catalogs.
Needs: Model release preferred.
Making Contact & Terms: Arrange a personal interview to show portfolio. Provide resume, brochure, flyer and tearsheets to be kept on file for future assignments. Uses 8×10 glossy b&w prints; also 35mm transparencies or 8×10 glossy color prints. SASE. Does not notify photographer if future assignments can be expected. Reports in 2 weeks. Pays $25 minimum/hour or on a per-photo basis. Buys all rights.
Tips: "We hire local photographers in our individual operating cities through the local manager, or directly by phone with photographers listed at national headquarters, or by prints, etc. sent in with prices from local cities to national headquarters or through local city headquarters."

AMATEUR SOFTBALL ASSOCIATION, 2801 NE 50th St., Oklahoma City OK 73111. (405)424-5266. Director of Publications and Communications: Ronald A. Babb. Media/PR Director: Bill Plummer III. Promotion of amateur softball. Photos used in newsletters, newspapers, association magazines.
Needs: Buys 10-12 photos/year; offers 5-6 assignments annually. Subjects include action sports shots. Model release required. Captions required.
Making Contact & Terms: Contact ASA National office first before doing any work. Uses prints or transparencies. SASE. Reports in 2 weeks. Pays $25 for previously published photo. Assignment fees negotiable. Credit line given. Buys all rights.

■AMERICAN ALLIANCE FOR HEALTH, PHYSICAL EDUCATION, RECREATION AND DANCE, 1900 Association Dr., Reston VA 22091. (703)476-3400. Fax: (703)476-9527. Director of Publications: Debra H. Lewin. Estab. 1885. Photos used in brochures, newsletters, magazines and catalogs.
Needs: Buys 50 photos/year; offers 2-3 assignments/year. Wants photos of sports, recreation, outdoor activities, health practices, physical education and other education specific settings; also interested in handicapped and special populations. Reviews stock photos. Model/property release preferred, especially for children and handicapped.
Audiovisual Needs: Uses slides.
Making Contact & Terms: Query with stock photo list. Provide resume, business card, self-promotion piece or tearsheets to be kept on file for possible future assignments. Call. Keeps samples on file. SASE. Reports in 1-2 weeks. Pays $100/color photo; $25/b&w photo. Pays upon usage. Credit line given. Buys one-time rights; negotiable.
Tips: "We are always looking for strong action or emotion. We usually need vertical formats for magazine covers with color work."

AMERICAN FUND FOR ALTERNATIVES TO ANIMAL RESEARCH, Suite 16-G, 175 W. 12th St., New York NY 10011. (212)989-8073. Contact: Dr. E. Thurston. Finances research to develop research methods which will not need live animals. Also informs the public of this and about current methods of experimentation. Photos used in reports, advertising and publications.
Needs: Buys 10+ freelance photos/year; offers 5+ freelance assignments/year. Needs b&w or color photos of laboratory animal experimentation and animal use connected with fashions (trapping) and cosmetics (tests on animals). Model release preferred.

 The asterisk before a listing indicates that the market is new in this edition. New markets are often the most receptive to freelance submissions.

Making Contact & Terms: Arrange a personal interview to show portfolio. Query with samples and list of stock photo subjects. Provide brochure and flyer to be kept on file for possible future assignments. Notifies photographer if future assignments can be expected. Uses 5×7 b&w prints; also uses 16mm film for educational films. SASE. Reports in 2 weeks. Pays $5 minimum/b&w photo; $5 or more/color photo; $30 minimum/job. Credit line given. Buys one-time rights and exclusive product rights; arranged with photographer.

Tips: In portfolios or samples wants to "see clear pictures of animals in cosmetic tests or testing labs, or fur ranches, and in the wilds."

AMERICAN MUSEUM OF NATURAL HISTORY LIBRARY, PHOTOGRAPHIC COLLECTION, Library Services Department, Central Park West, 79th St., New York NY 10024. (212)769-5419. Fax: (212) 769-5009. Manager, Special Collections: Joel Sweimler. Estab. 1869. Provides services for advertisers, authors, film and TV producers, general public, government agencies, picture researchers, publishers, scholars, students and teachers who use photos for brochures, newsletters, posters, newspapers, annual reports, catalogs, magazines, books and exhibits.

Needs: Model release required. Captions required.

Making Contact & Terms: Interested in receiving work from newer, lesser-known photographers. "We accept only donations with full rights (non-exclusive) to use; we offer visibility through credits." Credit line given. Buys all rights.

Tips: "We do not review portfolios. Unless the photographer is willing to give up rights and provide images for donation with full rights (credit lines are given), the museum is not willing to accept work."

AMERICAN RED CROSS, Photographic Services, 431 18th St. NW, Washington DC 20006. (202)639-3560. Photographic Manager: Joseph Matthews. Photos used to illustrate annual reports, articles, slide shows, ads and brochures.

Needs: "We need pictures of Red Cross volunteers working to provide the range of service to the public that the organization does, especially dramatic scenes at disasters. The ability to capture a 'moment' or the interaction between people is important. Never present yourself as shooting for the Red Cross unless you are currently under contract to do so." "We use people in action pictures and do not want to see scenic, travel, art, portraits or generic photographs. Quality should be very high." Model release must accompany photo.

Making Contact & Terms: Query by mail to describe material available. *Do not send unsolicited photographs.* "Because of small staff size we can only respond to specific queries. No general mailings will be answered." Assignments vary according to type and length of assignment and rights purchased. Send b&w contact sheet or 8×10 glossy prints. For color, send 35mm or larger transparencies. Payment depends on applications to Red Cross and rights purchased. "We distribute photographs to all chapters nationally and cannot control use. We normally buy unlimited, nonexclusive rights."

Tips: "We have photographers on staff, so we use freelancers infrequently. We are interested in knowing photojournalists in other areas of the U.S. who could provide coverage there if the need should arise. Send an introductory letter stating the type of work you do best and some samples of your published work. Take the time to research the type of work the Red Cross does; if you have the skill and the interest to help us support the goals of the Red Cross, contact me. Please also contact your local chapter. Many need newsletter and annual report photography, although this is best for 'new' photographers since many chapters have little or no budget for pictures. Volunteering time and work can sometimes get you published. Edit yourself more critically. Also, get opinion of someone whom you trust about your portfolio *before* you show it around."

AMERICAN SOCIETY FOR THE PREVENTION OF CRUELTY TO ANIMALS (ASPCA), 424 E. 92nd St., New York NY 10128. (212)876-7700 Ext. 3249. Fax: (212) 348-3031. Visual Arts Editor: Dave McMichael. Estab. 1866. Photos used in quarterly newsletters, pamphlets, booklets.

Needs: Photos of animals (domestic and wildlife): farm, domestic, lab, stray and homeless animals, endangered, trapped, injured, fur animals, marine and wildlife. Also, rain forest scenes and wildlife. Example of recent uses: *Traveling With Your Pet* and *ASPCA Animal Watch Magazine.* Model/property release preferred.

Making Contact & Terms: Interested in receiving work from newer, lesser-known photographers. Provide brochure and resume to be kept on file for possible future assignments. Please send a detailed, alphabetized stock list that can be kept on file for future reference. SASE. Reports when needed. Pays $30/b&w photo (inside use); $35/color photo (inside use); $100 for cover use. Credit line given. Buys one-time rights; negotiable.

Tips: "I like exciting pictures: strong colors, interesting angles, etc."

AMERICAN SOUVENIR & NOVELTY COMPANY, P.O. Box 9, Lebanon OR 97355. (503)259-1471. President: Edward Black. Manufactures souvenirs. Uses photos for souvenir photo products.
Needs: Buys about 100 freelance photos annually. Scenics, wildlife, sports and attractions. Reviews stock photos. Model release preferred. Captions preferred.
Making Contact & Terms: Query with stock photo list first. Uses 35mm color prints, negatives or transparencies. Does not return unsolicited material. Reports in 1 month. Pays $10-50/color photo, depending on subject and our manufacturing requirements. Buys "rights in our products only."
Tips: "We have strict format guidelines that must fit our products. We like to review many shots of one subject to find one or two that may be suitable for our needs since we add graphics to some products."

*AQUINO PRODUCTIONS., P.O. Box 15760, Stamford CT 06901. (203)967-9952. Fax: (203)975-1119. Publisher: Andres Aquino. Estab. 1983. Publishes posters, magazines and calendars. Photos used in posters, newspapers, magazines and catalogs.
Needs: Uses freelancers for travel, nature, business, glamour, people. Examples of recent uses: Westchester County Limousine (brochure); Bella Magazine (cover). Reviews stock photos. Model/property release required for people and private property. Captions required; include location and year (if applicable).
Making Contact & Terms: Query with stock photo list. Uses 8×10 glossy or matte b&w prints; 35mm, 2¼×2¼, 4×5 transparencies. Keeps samples on file. SASE. Reports in 3 weeks. NPI. "We buy photos in bulk." Credit line given. Buys all rights; negotiable.
Tips: "Become familiar with our publications. We offer a complete set of guidelines, sample photo requests and catalog of publications for $4." Looking for "sharp, well-exposed images from uncommon perspective covering people and places around the world." Sees trend toward more "computer-enhanced images."

*ARGUS COMMUNICATIONS, 200 E. Bethany, Allen TX 75002. (214)248-6300. Fax: (214)727-2175. Contact: Photo Department. Estab. 1963. Publishes posters, postcards, calendars and other "socially expressive" products.
Needs: Buys at least 200 photos/year, usually purchases stock photography. Subjects include animals, sports, the arts and contemporary shots (such as still lifes, abstracts). Reviews stock photos. Model release required. Captions required; include photo identification, name, address, phone number, subject description.
Making Contact & Terms: Interested in receiving work from newer, lesser-known photographers. Request guidelines. Works on assignment only. Send 35mm, 2¼×2¼, 4×5, 8×10 duplicate transparencies. Does not keep samples on file. SASE. Reports in 1 month to 6 weeks. "Do not phone." Pays flat fee per image beginning at $350/photo. Pays on acceptance. Credit line given. Rights vary depending on needs; negotiable.
Tips: "Please request our guidelines before submitting work so that you may cater your submission to our needs." Sees a trend toward "innovative work, soft focus, grain or b&w with color tinting."

*ARISTOPLAY, 334 E. Washington St., Ann Arbor MI 48104. (313)995-4353. Fax: (313)995-4611. Product Development Director: Lorraine Hopping Egan. Estab. 1979. Publishes educational board and card games. Photos used for catalogs and board and card games.
Needs: Bought 50-100 photos in last two years; purchase volume varies depending on game subjects. Offers 6-10 freelance assignments/year for local photographers. Has assigned photos dealing with science, kids playing our games, product shots and others. Reviews stock photos. "We will send out wish lists. Do not send unsolicited photos and please do not call; fax with questions or queries." Model release required for children; get permission from parents. Photo captions preferred; identify science subjects.
Making Contact & Terms: Interested in receiving work from newer, lesser-known photographers. Query with stock photo list. Provide resume, business card, self-promotion piece or tearsheets to be kept on file for possible future assignments. Works on assignment only. Uses 35mm, 2¼×2¼ transparencies. Keeps samples on file. Cannot return material. Reports in 1 month. Pays $35-65/color photo; other rates vary. Credit line given. Buys one-time rights.
Tips: "We publish 2-9 products per year. Each one is very different and may or may not require photos. If you are local, tell us your hourly, half day and day rate, and whether you've worked with children. Science games are big right now and the tendency is to use photos over artwork."

*BEDOL INTERNATIONAL GROUP, INC., P.O. Box 2847, Rancho Cucamonga CA 91729-2847. (909)948-0668. President: Mark A. Bedol. Estab. 1982. Produces stationery items, picture frames, calculators, calendars, etc. Photos used in brochures, press releases and picture frames.
Needs: Buys 300 photos/year; offers 6 freelance assignments/year. Uses freelancers for "photos of female models, female models with children and babies, cars." Examples of recent uses: catalog sheet, frame, product picture. Reviews stock photos. Model release required. Property release preferred.

Making Contact & Terms: Interested in receiving work from newer, lesser-known photographers. Provide resume, business card, brochure, flyer or tearsheets to be kept on file for possible future assignments. Work on assignment only. Uses various size color, b&w prints; 2¼×2¼ transparencies; 2¼×2¼ color film. Keeps samples on file. Cannot return material. Reports only when needed. Pays $50-85/hour; $50-100/color photo; $50-100/b&w photo. Pays on usage. Credit line not given. Buys all rights.
Tips: "Please send work in for review."

CALIFORNIA REDWOOD ASSOCIATION, Suite 200, 405 Enfrente Dr., Novato CA 94949. (415)382-0662. Fax: (415)382-8531. Contact: Pamela Allsebrook. Estab. 1916. "We publish a variety of literature, a small black and white periodical, run color advertisements and constantly use photos for magazine and newspaper publicity. We use new, well-designed redwood applications—residential, commercial, exteriors, interiors and especially good remodels and outdoor decks, fences, shelters."
Needs: Gives 40 assignments/year. Prefers photographers with architectural specialization. Model release required.
Making Contact & Terms: Send query material by mail for consideration for assignment or send finished speculation shots for possible purchase. Uses b&w prints. For color, uses 2¼×2¼ and 4×5 transparencies; contact sheet OK. Reports in 1 month. NPI; payment based on previous use and other factors." Credit line given whenever possible. Usually buys all but national advertising rights. Simultaneous submissions and previously published work OK if other uses are made very clear.
Tips: "We like to see any new redwood projects showing outstanding design and use of redwood. We don't have a staff photographer and work only with freelancers. We generally look for justified lines, true color quality, projects with style and architectural design, and tasteful props. Find and take 'scout' shots or finished pictures of good redwood projects and send them to us."

*M.W. CARR & CO., INC., 373 Highland Ave., Somerville MA 02144. (800)289-2277 or (617)623-0300, Ext. 371. Fax: (800)444-6927. Senior Graphic Designer: Tami O'Leary. Photo frame manufacturer. Photos used in photo frames.
Needs: Buys 10+ photos annually; offers 10+ freelance assignments annually. Wants portraits and American families. Review stock photos of people. Model release preferred. Property release required. Photographers can be fully responsible.
Making Contact & Terms: Interested in receiving work from newer, lesser-known photographers. Provide resume, business card, brochure, flyer or tearsheets to be kept on file for possible future assignments. Uses 8×10 glossy color and b&w prints; 35mm, 4×5 transparencies. Keeps samples on file. SASE. Reports in 1-2 weeks. Pays $200+/color photo; $200+/b&w photo; royalties possible. **Pays on acceptance.** Credit line sometimes given depending upon uniqueness. Buys all rights; negotiable.
Tips: "Be patient, send as much as you can, as often as you can. We select talent three times a year for major product intros."

CHICAGO COMPUTER & LIGHT, INC., 5001 N. Lowell Ave., Chicago IL 60630. (312)283-2749. President: Larry Feit. Estab. 1976. Photos used in newsletters, magazines, catalogs and press releases.
Needs: Offers 2 freelance assignments/year. New computer products for special sections and ads in trade journals. Model release required. Captions preferred.
Making Contact & Terms: Provide resume, business card, self-promotion piece or tearsheets to be kept on file for possible future assignments. Uses 35mm transparencies. SASE. Reports in 1-2 weeks. Pays $2,000/job. **Pays on acceptance.** Credit line sometimes given. Buys all rights; negotiable.
Tips: In freelancer's samples, looks for simplicity and uniqueness.

CHILD AND FAMILY SERVICES OF NEW HAMPSHIRE, 99 Hanover St., P.O. Box 448, Manchester NH 03105. (603)668-1920. Fax: (603)668-1937. Public Relations Coordinator: Renée Robertie. Estab. 1850. Statewide social service agency providing counseling to children and families. Photos used in brochures, newspapers, posters, annual reports, news releases, and displays and exhibits.
Needs: Buys 15-20 photos/year. Uses photos of children, teenagers and families and the elderly; "pictures depicting our services, such as an unwed mother, teenager on drugs or emotionally upset, couples and/or families—possibly indicating stress or conflict. Also looking for photos depicting healthy, happy children and families." Reviews stock photos. Model release required.

The First Markets Index preceding the General Index in the back of this book provides the names of those companies/ publications interested in receiving work from newer, lesser-known photographers.

Making Contact & Terms: Send material by mail for consideration. Provide business card and tear-sheets to be kept on file for future assignments. Uses 8×10 glossy b&w prints. SASE. Reporting time not specified. Pays $10-50/b&w photo. Credit line given on request. Buys one-time and all rights.
Tips: "Submit a few copies of applicable photos in which we might be interested rather than just a letter or form telling us what you have done or can do." Looks for "someone who can compose a photo that achieves an expression of feeling, emotion. Because we are primarily a service agency we want our artwork to reflect the clients we serve—people working on problems or solving them. We are looking for a range of emotions."

*M. CORNELL IMPORTERS, INC., 1462 18th St. N.W., St. Paul MN 55112. (612)633-8690. Fax: (612)636-3568. Merchandise Manager: Henry Cornell. Estab. 1958. Distributor of European-made giftware. Photos used in brochures, posters, magazines, press releases and catalogs.
Needs: Buys 30 photos/year; offers 10 freelance assignments/year. Uses stills of products. Examples of recent uses: catalogs and advertisements. Reviews stock photos of wildlife and nautical (particularly Florida). Property release preferred. Captions preferred.
Making Contact & Terms: Interested in receiving work from newer, lesser-known photographers. Query with samples. Query with stock photo list. Works with local freelancers on assignment only. Uses 4×5 transparencies. Reports in 1 month. Pays $50-300/color photo. **Pays on acceptance.** Buys all rights; negotiable.
Tips: "Offer quality, offer a studio or have access to a studio with all necessary equipment. Base quotes on long-term relationship."

*■COST OF WISCONSIN, INC., W172, N13050 Division Rd., Germantown WI 53022. (414)255-4220. Fax: (414)255-0096. Project Administrator: Jack Beatty. Estab. 1957. Designers/contractors for zoos, amusement parks, museums. Photos used in brochures, magazines, press releases, catalogs, trade shows and presentations.
Needs: Offers 5-6 freelance assignments/year. Uses freelancers for brochure/magazine for advertising (2¼ or larger); mounted 16×20 prints for trade shows (2¼ or larger); 8×10 prints for photocopying for hand-outs, advertising (2¼ or larger). Model/property release preferred; person where face is very distinguishable.
Audiovisual Needs: Videotape for presentations, seminars. Subjects include: amusement park construction, development.
Making Contact & Terms: Interested in receiving work from newer, lesser-known photographers. Provide resume, business card, brochure, flyer or tearsheets to be kept on file for possible future assignments. Work on assignment only. Uses contact sheets of color prints; 2¼×2¼, 4×5 transparencies; ½" videotape. Keeps samples on file. SASE. Reports only when interested in 5-6 weeks. NPI. **Pays on acceptance.** Credit line given. Buys all rights.
Tips: "We do very specialized work throughout the US. We will direct the type of shots required for our use. Color is very important. We try to create a mood."

*CREATIF LICENSING®., 31 Old Town Crossing, Mt. Kisco NY 10549. (914)241-6211. Vice President Marketing: Paul Cohen. Estab. 1975. License artwork to manufacturers. Photos of general merchandise in the gift industry.
Needs: Examples of recent uses: posters, bookmarks, address books, calendars. Reviews stock photos. Model/property release required for any copyright or protected design.
Making Contact & Terms: Query with samples and SASE. Uses 35mm, 4×5 transparencies. Samples kept on file. Reports in 3 weeks. NPI. Pays royalties on sales. Pays upon receipt of royalties, advances, guarantees. Rights purchased are "license for contracted time period for specific merchandising categories."
Tips: "We look for designs that would work well on calendars, posters and printed media for the gift and stationery market."

*DALOIA DESIGN., P.O. Box 268, Howard Beach NY 11414. (718)835-7641. Owner/Creative Director: Peter Daloia. Estab. 1983. Design, develop and market novelty and gift products. Photos used in posters, paper, novelty and gift items; display.
Needs: Use freelancers for humorous, abstract, odd shots, good composition, collage, montage, patterns, textures. Reviews stock photos. Model/property release required "whenever appropriate."
Making Contact & Terms: Interested in receiving work from newer, lesser-known photographers. Query with samples. Provide resume, business card, brochure, flyer or tearsheets to be kept on file for possible future assignments. Works with freelancers on assignment only. Uses 5×7, 4×5 color and b&w prints; 35mm, 2¼×2¼, 4×5 transparencies. Keeps samples on file. Cannot return material. Reports only when interested. NPI; pays "prevailing rates or royalties." Pays upon usage. Credit line sometimes given depending on use. Buys all rights; negotiable.
Tips: "Let the buyer decide on the best images." Sees trend toward "electronic manipulation of images."

*EPIC PRODUCTS, INC., 17395 Mt. Herrmann, Fountain Valley CA 92708. (714)641-8194. Fax: (714)641-8217. President: Steve DuBow. Estab. 1978. Housewares manufacturing company. Photos used in brochures, newsletters, press releases and catalogs.
Needs: Buys 100+ photos/year; offers 10 freelance assignments/year. Uses freelancers for product shots. Examples of recent uses: catalogs and product release.
Making Contact & Terms: Interested in receiving work from newer, lesser-known photographers. Provide resume, business card, brochure, flyer or tearsheets to be kept on file for possible future assignments. Work with local freelancers only. Uses color and b&w prints; 4×5 transparencies. Reports in 3 weeks. NPI. **Pays on acceptance.** Credit line given. Buys all rights.

■SCOTT EVANS PRODUCTIONS, MUSIC & ENTERTAINMENT, 660 NE 139th St., N. Miami FL 33161. (305)891-4449 or 891-0158. General Manager: Ted Jones. Estab. 1979. Entertainment services, party planning, producing and directing. Photos used in brochures, newsletters, newspapers, magazines, press releases, audiovisual, catalogs, model shoots, production shots and location shoots.
Needs: Buys 25-50 photos/year. Interview shots for promotional publications. Reviews stock photos; variety, entertainment related. Model release required. Captions required.
Audiovisual Needs: "We frequently videotape shows and performances for promotional purposes (demos) as well as for rehearsal purposes or selling products not readily available for quick viewing."
Making Contact & Terms: Provide resume, business card, self-promotion piece or tearsheets to be kept on file for possible future assignments; each circumstance is unique. Works with local freelancers on assignment only. Uses 35mm, b&w prints; 3×5, 8×10, color prints; ½" and ¾", videotape. Cannot return material. Reports as needed. NPI. Pays on acceptance, usage. Credit line given. Buys all rights; negotiable.
Tips: "Put together a simple, concise, sample resume demo as needed to project artist's skills to buyers in a manner/format that can be kept on file for quick reference." In samples or demos wants to see versatility, composition, sharpness, creativity, easy interpretation.

*FOTOFOLIO., 536 Broadway, New York NY 10012. (212)226-0923. Fax: (212)226-0072. Editorial and Art Director: Ron Schick. Estab. 1976. Photos used in posters, postcards, note cards and calendars.
Needs: Uses freelancers for all subjects, especially holiday, seasonal, urban and romance. Reviews stock photos. Model release required; celebrities, all identifiable subjects; include title, date, place.
Making Contact & Terms: Interested in receiving work from newer, lesser-known photographers. Query with samples. Provide resume, business card, brochure, flyer or tearsheets to be kept on file for possible future assignments. Uses any format. Keeps samples on file. SASE. Reporting time varies. Pays royalties. Pays upon usage and publication. Credit line given. Buys exclusive rights in format purchased.
Tips: "For review, edit tightly. No oversized prints. There is a monthly portfolio review on drop-off basis. Call for next date."

GARY PLASTIC PACKAGING CORP., 530 Old Post Rd., No. 3, Greenwich CT 06830. (203)629-1480. Marketing Director: Marilyn Hellinger. Estab. 1963. Manufacturers of custom injection molding; thermoforming; and stock rigid plastic packaging. Photos used in brochures, catalogs and flyers.
Needs: Buys 10 freelance photos/year; offers 10 assignments/year. Product photography. Model release required.
Making Contact & Terms: Query with resume of credits or with samples. Follow up with a call to set up an appointment to show portfolio. Prefers to see b&w and color product photography. Solicits photos by assignment only. Provide resume to be kept on file for possible future assignments. Works with local freelancers only. Uses 8×10 b&w and color prints; 2¼×2¼ slides; and b&w or color negatives. Notifies photographer if future assignments can be expected. Does not return unsolicited material. Reports in 2 weeks. Pays up to $150/color photo; up to $900/day. Pays by the job and the number of photographs required. Buys exclusive product rights.
Tips: The photographer "has to be willing to work with our designers."

*GEI INTERNATIONAL, INC., P.O. Box 6849, 100 Ball St. Syracuse NY 13217. (315)463-9261. Fax: (315)463-9034. Sales Manger: William Parker. Estab. 1988. Manufacturer of stainless steel rulers and graphic accessories. Photos used in brochures, press releases and catalogs.
Needs: Buys 18,000 photos/year. Uses freelancers for photos of "our stocked items."
Making Contact & Terms: Provide resume, business card, brochure, flyer or tearsheets to be kept on file for possible future assignments. Work with local freelancers only. Uses various size glossy b&w photos. Does not keep samples on file. SASE. Reports in 1-2 weeks. NPI. Pays upon usage. Buys all rights.

*GENERAL STORE INC., 7920 NW 76 Ave., Medley FL 33166. (305)885-7670. Fax: (305)888-7616. President: Joe Santa Marie. Estab. 1988. Decorative accessories, furniture. Photos used in press releases, catalogs and source material for design work.

Needs: Buys 100-120 photos/year; offers 2-4 freelance assignments/year. Uses freelancers for art objects, subjects for art work, etc. Examples of recent uses: Gift Decorative Accessories, Atlanta Highlights, Furniture Today (advertising). Reviews stock photos of farm animals, florals. Property release preferred. Captions required.

Making Contact & Terms: Interested in receiving work from newer, lesser-known photographers. Query with samples. Query with stock photo list. Work with local freelancers only. Uses 5×7 glossy, color prints and transparencies. SASE. Reports in 1-2 weeks. Pays $85-180/color photo; $85-180/b&w photo. Also pays royalties on sales. **Pays on acceptance.** Credit line not given. Buys "rights to use in our field our product or industry." Negotiable.

Tips: "Be flexible."

*■GREAT SMOKY MOUNTAINS NATURAL HISTORY ASSOCIATION, 115 Park Headquarters Rd., Gatlinburg TN 37738. Fax: (615)436-6884. Publications Specialist: Steve Kemp. Estab. 1953. Produces publications on Great Smokies. Photos used for brochures, newsletters, newspapers and books.

Needs: Buys 150 photos/year; offers 2 freelance assignments/year. Wants to see b&w of people enjoying park, transparencies of plants and animals. Examples of recent uses: *Smokies Guide* (park newspaper) b&w; and *Trees of Smokies* (field guide) color slides. Reviews stock photos. Model/property release preferred. Captions preferred; include location of shot.

Audiovisual Needs: Uses slides for slide shows given by park rangers. Subjects include: Great Smoky Mountains.

Making Contact & Terms: Interested in receiving work from newer, lesser-known photographers. Query with stock photo list. Provide resume, business card, self-promotion piece or tearsheets to be kept on file for possible future assignments. Uses 5×7 b&w prints; 35mm, 2¼×2¼ transarencies. Does not keep samples on file. SASE. Reports in 1 month. Pays $50-80/color photo; $30/b&w photo; sometimes works on royalties. Pays upon usage. Credit line given. Buys one-time rights.

Tips: "Take b&w photos of people hiking, looking at wildflowers, big trees, waterfalls in Great Smokies. We always need nature b&w's; nobody shoots b&w."

HILLSDALE COLLEGE, 33 College St., Hillsdale MI 49242. (517)437-7341. Fax: (517)437-0160. Director of Public Affairs: Bill Koshelnyk. Publishes alumni magazine, political/social action newsletter, brochures, books, etc. Photos used for text illustration, promotional materials, book covers and dust jackets.

Needs: Buys 20-30 photos/year; assigns 5-10 shoots/year. Recently published *Hillsdale Magazine* and assorted brochures. Looking for photos "that deal with the college's national outreach programs, athletics or alumni." Reviews stock photos. Model release preferred. Captions required.

Making Contact & Terms: Send unsolicited photos by mail for consideration. Uses 5×7 glossy b&w prints; 35mm, 2¼×2¼ transparencies. SASE. Reports in 2 weeks.Pays $50-100/color or b&w photo. Additional rates vary according to assignment. Credit lines given where possible. Buys all rights; negotiable. Simultaneous submissions and previously published work OK.

Tips: "Photos must have something to do with the activities of Hillsdale College or prominent figures who participate in our programs. Our needs are rapidly growing."

■HORIZONS MAGAZINE, P.O. Box 2467, Fargo ND 58108. (701)237-9461. Fax: (701)237-9463. Editor: Sheldon Green. Estab. 1971. Quality regional magazine. Photos used in magazines, audiovisual and calendars.

Needs: Buys 50 photos/year; offers 25 assignments/year. Scenics of North Dakota events, places and people. Examples of recent uses: "Scenic North Dakota" calendar, *Horizons Magazine* (winter edition) and "North Dakota Bad Lands." Model/property release preferred. Captions preferred.

Audiovisual Needs: Uses slides and videotape.

Making Contact & Terms: Query with samples. Query with stock photo list. Works on assignment only. Uses 8×10 glossy b&w prints; 35mm, 2¼×2¼, 4×5 transparencies. Does not keep samples on file. SASE. Reports in 1-2 weeks. Pays $150-250/day; $200-300/job. Pays on usage. Credit line given. Buys one-time rights; negotiable.

Tips: "Know North Dakota events, places. Have strong quality of composition and light." Sees trend developing in scanning of photos on disc. "Multiple use of original image."

■HUBBARD MILLING COMPANY, 424 N. Riverfront Dr., P.O. Box 8500, Mankato MN 56002. (507)388-9528. Fax:(507)388-9453. Supervisor, Marketing Communications: Scott W. Roemhildt. Estab. 1878. The Hubbard Feed Division manufactures animal feeds, pet foods and animal health products. Photos used in brochures, newsletters, posters and audiovisual presentations.

Needs: Buys 20 freelance photos/year; offers 10 freelance assignments/year. Livestock—beef cattle, dairy cattle, pigs, horses, sheep, dogs, cats. Model release required.

Making Contact & Terms: Query with samples. Query with list of stock photo subjects. Submit portfolio for review. Provide resume, business card, brochure, flyer or tearsheets to be kept on file for possible future assignments. Works on assignment only. Uses 3×5 and 5×7 matte b&w and color

A candid view of hikers walking through the Great Smoky Mountains served as a perfect illustration for the Golden Bell Guidebook of Gatlinburg, produced by the Great Smoky Mountains Natural History Association. Photographer Art Lavidge, of Knoxville, Tennessee, received $100 plus travel expenses for the shot which portrays the beauty of the outdoors.

prints; 2¼×2¼ and 4×5 transprarencies; and b&w and color negatives. SASE. Reports in 2 weeks. Pays $50-100/b&w photo; $200/color photo; $50-300/job. Buys one-time and all rights; negotiable.
Tips: Prefers "to see the types of work the photographer does and what types of subjects done. We look for lots of agricultural photos in a more serious setting. Keep up with modern farming methods and use confinement shots when deemed necessary. Stay away from 'cutesy' shots."

*ICART VENDOR GRAPHICS, 8568 W. Pico Blvd., Los Angeles CA 90035. (310)659-1023. Fax: (310)659-1025. Owner/President: John R. Pace. Estab. 1972. Manufactures art deco and contemporary decorative art posters. Photos used in brochures, posters, catalogs and magazines.
Needs: Buys 2 freelance photos/year; offers 2-4 freelance assignments/year. Art deco and contemporary subjects with universal appeal.
Making Contact & Terms: Interested in receiving work from newer, lesser-known photographers. Send unsolicited photos by mail for consideration. Provide resume, business card, brochure, flyer or tearsheets to be kept on file for possible future assignments. Open to solicitations from anywhere. Uses color prints. SASE. Reports in 1 month. NPI. Credit line given. Buys one-time rights.

*IMAGINE INC., P.O. Box 9674, Pittsburgh PA 15226. (412)921-8274. Fax: (412)921-8777. Special Projects Manager: Jim Lynn. Estab. 1982. Photos used in text illustration, promotional materials, trading card sets.
Needs: Wants glamour shots, bikini, lingerie. "No frontal nudity published but will review as samples of work." Examples of recent uses: Adult trading card sets "Scream Queens II" "Fantasy Girls," and "Scream Queens III." Reviews stock photos (glamour, bikini, lingerie). Model release required. Captions preferred.
Making Contact & Terms: Interested in receiving work from newer, lesser-known photographers. Query with stock photo list. Provide resume, business card, brochure, flyer or tearsheets to be kept on file for possible future assignments. Send unsolicited photos by mail for consideration. Uses all

sizes of color prints; 35mm, 2¼×2¼, 4×5 transparencies. Keeps samples on file. SASE (include cost of certified mail). Reports in 1 month. Pays $20-50/color photo; pays $20-50/b&w photo; also pays percentage of gross sales. Pays on publication. Credit line given. Buys one-time and promotional rights; negotiable.

Tips: "We publish trading card sets for adult collectors. Sets are high quality. Good taste and limited production runs help maintain high collector values. Submit work that is suitable for reproduction in 2½×3½ frame."

*IN-PLANT MANAGEMENT ASSOCIATION, 1205 W. College St., Liberty MO 64068-3733. (816)781-1111. (816)781-2790. Editor: Barbara Schaaf Petty. Membership association for in-house print/mail managers. Photos used in brochures and newsletters.

Needs: Buys 5-10 photos/year. Subject needs: equipment photos, issues (i.e., soy ink, outsourcing), people. Reviews stock photos. Captions preferred (location).

Making Contact & Terms: Interested in receiving work from newer, lesser-known photographers. Query with stock photo list. Provide resume, business card, brochure, flyer or tearsheets to be kept on file for possible future assignments. Uses 4×6, 5×7 b&w prints. Keeps samples on file. SASE. Reports in 3 weeks. NPI. Pays on usage. Credit line given. Buys one-time rights.

■INTERNATIONAL RESEARCH & EDUCATION (IRE), 21098 IRE Control Center, Eagan MN 55121-0098. (612)888-9635. Fax: (612)888-9124. IP Director: George Franklin, Jr. IRE conducts in-depth research probes, surveys, and studies to improve the decision support process. Company conducts market research, taste testing, brand image/usage studies, premium testing, and design and development of product/service marketing campaigns. Photos used in brochures, newsletters, posters, audiovisual presentations, annual reports, catalogs, press releases, and as support material for specific project/survey/reports.

Needs: Buys 75-110 photos/year; offers 50-60 assignments/year. "Subjects and topics cover a vast spectrum of possibilities and needs." Model release required.

Audiovisual Needs: Uses freelance filmmakers to produce promotional pieces for 16mm or videotape.

Making Contact & Terms: Provide resume, business card, brochure, flyer or tearsheets to be kept on file for possible future assignments. "Materials sent are put on optic disk for options to pursue by project managers responsible for a program or job." Works on assignment only. Uses prints (15% b&w, 85% color), transparencies and negatives. Cannot return material. Reports when a job is available. NPI; pays on a bid, per job basis. Credit line given. Buys all rights.

Tips: "We look for creativity, innovation and ability to relate to the given job and carry out the mission accordingly."

JUVENILE DIABETES FOUNDATION INTERNATIONAL, 432 Park Ave. S., New York NY 10016. (212)889-7575. Publications Manager: Sandy Dylak. Estab. 1970. Produces 4-color, 32-page quarterly magazine to deliver research information to a lay audience; also produces brochures, pamphlets, annual report and audiovisual presentations.

Needs: Buys 40 photos/year; offers 20 freelance assignments/year. Needs "mostly portraits of people, but always with some environmental aspect." Reviews stock photos. Model release preferred. Captions preferred.

Making Contact & Terms: Query with samples. Provide resume, business card, brochure, flyer or tearsheets to be kept on file for possible future assignments. Uses 2¼×2¼ transparencies. Cannot return material. Reports as needed. Pays $500/color photo; $500-700/day. Also pays by the job—payment "depends on how many days, shots, cities, etc." Credit line given. Buys one-time rights.

Tips: Looks for "a style consistent with commercial magazine photography—upbeat, warm, personal, but with a sophisticated edge. Call and ask for samples of our publications before submitting any of your own samples so you will have an idea what we are looking for in photography. Nonprofit groups have seemingly come to depend more and more on photography to get their message across. The business seems to be using a variety of freelancers, as opposed to a single inhouse photographer."

*■LA CROSSE AREA CONVENTION & VISITOR BUREAU, Box 1895, P.O. Box 1895, Riverside Park, La Crosse WI 54602-1895. (608)782-2366. Director of Marketing: Pamela Solberg. Estab. 1975. Provides "promotional brochures, trade show and convention planning, full service for meetings and conventions." Photos used in brochures, newspapers, audiovisual presentations and magazines.

Needs: Buys 8+ photos/year; offers "several" assignments/year through conventions. Conventions also buy photos. "Scenic photos of local area; local points of interest to tourists, etc. Will be increasing slide file." Model release required. Captions preferred.

Audiovisual Needs: May use videos of local scenery attractions.

Making Contact & Terms: Provide resume, business card, brochure, flyer or tearsheets to be kept on file for possible future assignments. Works with local freelancers on assignment only. Uses 5×7 glossy b&w prints, and color slides. Cannot return material. Reports in 3 weeks. Payment depends on

INSIDER REPORT

Success with Corporate Clients Requires Professional Attitude

Photographers who act professionally and consistently produce strong images can build solid client bases within the corporate field, according to Pat Goetzinger, of Milwaukee, Wisconsin. "I am constantly promoting myself, and not necessarily with mailers or phone calls, but every time I'm out on assignment, that is a promotion," says Goetzinger, who has been shooting professionally for over 10 years.

Whether he is working on an assignment for major accounts, such as Exxon, Miller Brewing Company or Philip Morris, or shooting at social gatherings, he takes advantage of every opportunity to prove his worth. "I've got to make myself look good all the time because all around me are potential clients. I think 90 percent of what I do is referral work," he says.

Pat Goetzinger

Goetzinger normally shoots corporate photos for press releases and internal publications, but he often branches out into other areas. He likes to shoot special assignments, such as conferences, conventions and even bike races, and over the last year he has moved into social events, such as weddings and parties. Some of this transition unfortunately is the result of a shrinking corporate marketplace, due to a sluggish economy and a new presidential administration that is tougher on big business. "Actually, I'm seeing the results already with cutbacks on budgets," he says.

To combat the tighter budgets, he feels it is essential to make his work stand out and eliminate a lot of idle time. He plans ahead for assignments so that he is not carrying unnecessary equipment, and he likes to schedule quarter-day jobs. When he is not shooting he completes endless business tasks. "For every hour of shooting pictures there is three hours of administrative stuff to do," says Goetzinger, referring to the daily planning, conferences and paperwork.

He believes it is essential that photographers have strong business skills, as well as photographic talent, if they are going to be successful. Lack of this knowledge frequently hurts newcomers to the field. "I have the feeling that 95 percent of the people coming out of photography schools are never going to make a living as photographers. I think it's because they come out of school with this lights-camera-action attitude," he says. "I've gone through a lot of assistants and they just aren't realistic about what they're going to have to do, and the sacrifices they're going to have to make, to get where they want to go."

Although Goetzinger works with a variety of cameras, he likes the latitude offered with the 35mm format. "With the zoom lenses you can move quicker. You can get so much more done in a shorter period of time than with larger formats," he says. This is particularly important when dealing with top executives who do not want to spend hours with photographers. Because of the time constraints, he often uses assistants as stand-ins to complete test shots. "Nothing ever goes the way you plan it. So you have to be flexible and think fast."

Part of maintaining a professional appearance is showing clients that you are concentrating on the subjects rather than the technical aspects of a shoot, such as new equipment and lighting. "You can't go out on a job with an idea that you've never tried. You have to work through the technical aspects and that's something I'm always doing," he says. "I'm always trying to make it easier because the easier the technical thing is the more you can concentrate on the subject and on your presentation. If you're too caught up in the technical, your subjects aren't at ease."

Goetzinger says one big mistake some photographers make is that they concentrate so much on what they are trying to do photographically that they do not pay attention to the needs and desires of the client. "Service is paramount. Quality and service are so much more important than price, especially when you're dealing with corporations," he says. "The customer wants you to file things. They want you to be able to pull a negative out of a file and make a print while they wait. I've gotten several accounts from people who used to work with some of my competition. They charged one third of what I charge, but they weren't professional in appearance or in actuality. People would say 'Gee, we loved their prices, but that's all we loved.'"
— *Michael Willins*

❝I've gone through a lot of assistants and they just aren't realistic about what they're going to have to do, and the sacrifices they're going to have to make, to get where they want to go.❞

— Pat Goetzinger

size/scope of project. Credit line given "where possible." Buys all rights.

MID AMERICA DESIGNS, INC., P.O. Box 1368, Effingham IL 62401. (217)347-5591. Fax: (217)347-2952. Operations Manager: Jeff Bloemker. Estab. 1975. Provides mail order catalog for Corvette parts & accessories.
Needs: Buys 300 freelance photos/year; offers 6 freelance assignments/year. Apparel and automotive parts. Reviews stock photos. Model release required. Property release preferred.
Making Contact & Terms: Provide resume, business card, brochure, flyer or tearsheets to be kept on file for possible future assignments. Works on assignment. Uses 2¼×2¼, 4×5 and 8×10 transparencies. Cannot return material. Reports in 2 weeks. Pays $65/b&w or color photo. Buys all rights; negotiable.

*BRUCE MINER POSTER CO. INC., Box 709, Peabody MA 01960. (508)741-3800. Fax: (508)741-3880. President: Bruce Miner. Estab. 1971. Photos used in posters.
Needs: Number of photos bought "varies." Wildlife photos. Reviews stock photos of wildlife. Model release preferred.
Making Contact & Terms: Interested in receiving work from newer, lesser-known photographers. Query with stock photo list. Provide resume, business card, brochure, flyer or tearsheets to be kept on file for possible future assignments. Uses 8×10 prints; 2¼×2¼ transparencies. Keeps samples on file. SASE. Reports in 1 month. NPI. Pays advance against royalties. Pays on usage. Credit line given. Buys one-time and all rights; negotiable.
Tips: Looking for "quality" submissions.

*THE MINNESOTA OPERA, 620 N. First St., Minneapolis MN 55401. (612)333-2700. Marketing: Nancy Bindas. Produces five opera productions, including several new works each year. Photos used in brochures, posters and press releases/publicity.
Needs: Buys 50 photos/year; offers 10 assignments/year. Operatic productions. Model release preferred. Captions required.
Making Contact & Terms: Send unsolicited photos by mail for consideration. Provide resume, business card, brochure, flyer or tearsheets to be kept on file for possible future assignments. Works with local freelancers only. Uses 5×7 glossy b&w prints and 35mm slides. Cannot return material. Reporting time depends on needs. Pays $6-12/b&w photo; $8-15/color photo; $60-85/hour. Credit line given. Buys all rights; negatives remain with photographer.
Tips: "We look for photography that dynamically conveys theatrical/dramatic quality of opera with clear, crisp active pictures. Photographers should have experience photographing theater and have a good sense of dramatic timing."

MIRACLE OF ALOE, 521 Riverside Ave., Westport CT 06880. (203)454-1919. Fax: (203)226-7333. Vice President: Jess F. Clarke, Jr. Estab. 1980. Manufacturers for mail order buyers of healthcare products. Photos used in newsletters, catalogs, direct mail and consumer magazines.
Needs: Works with 2 freelancers per month. Uses testimonial photos and aloe vera plants. Model release preferred.
Making Contact & Terms: Provide resume, business card, self-promotion piece or tearsheets to be kept on file for possible future assignments. Works on assignment only. Uses 4×5 b&w or color prints and 35mm transparencies. SASE. Reports in 1 month. Pays $30-45/photo. Pays on receipt of invoice. Credit line given. Buys one-time rights.
Tips: In freelancer's samples, looks for "older folks, head shots and nice white-haired ladies. Also show Aloe Vera plants in fields or pots; shoot scenes of Southern Texas aloe farms."

■NATIONAL ASSOCIATION OF DISPLAY INDUSTRIES (NADI), 470 Park Ave. S., New York NY 10016. (212)213-2662. Fax: (212)889-0727. Marketing Communications Director: Patricia Vitsky. Estab. 1943. Photos used for NADI trade shows. "Our 300 exhibitors use them as well."
Needs: Offers 2 assignments/year. Freelancers are used to photograph exhibitors' booths at trade show. Examples of recent uses: videotape for promo at trade show and videotape for awards dinner.
Audiovisual Needs: Uses slides and videotape.
Making Contact & Terms: Provide resume, business card, self-promotion piece or tearsheets to be kept on file for possible future assignments. Works with local freelancers on assignment only. Uses 5×7 b&w prints. Does not keep samples on file. SASE. NPI. Rights negotiable.

The solid, black square before a listing indicates that the market uses various types of audiovisual materials, such as slides, film or videotape.

NATIONAL BLACK CHILD DEVELOPMENT INSTITUTE, Suite 600, 1023 15th St. NW, Washington DC 20005. (202)387-1281. Deputy Director: Vicki D. Pinkston. Estab. 1970. Photos used in brochures, newsletters, newspapers, annual reports and annual calendar.
Needs: Candid action photos of black children and youth. Reviews stock photos. Model release required.
Making Contact & Terms: Query with samples. Send unsolicited photos by mail for consideration. Uses 5×7 or 8×10 glossy b&w prints and b&w contact sheets. SASE. Reports in 1 month. Pays $25/ cover photo and $15/inside b&w photo. Credit line given. Buys one-time rights.
Tips: "Candid action photographs of one black child or youth or a small group of children or youths. Most photographs selected are used in annual calendar and are placed beside an appropriate poem selected by organization. Therefore, photograph should communicate a message in an indirect way. Other photographs are used in quarterly newsletter and reports. Obtain sample of publications published by organization to see the type of photographs selected."

NEW EXPOSURE—A Catalog of Fine Art Photography, 8150 E. Smokehouse Tr., Scottsdale AZ 85262. (602)488-2831. Executive Director: Susan Brachocki. Estab. 1987. Specializes in marketing original fine art photographic prints.
Needs: Consigns approximately 80 freelance photos/year. Specializes in "a wide variety of b&w and color photographs, including landscapes, urban scenes, portraits and abstracts. We are interested in photographers who have exhibited a long-term commitment to their craft and produce *unique* images." No "commercial work, depressing or violent images." Does not want stock photos.
Making Contact & Terms: Query with samples. Reviews color or b&w prints and contact sheets; also slides. SASE. Reports in 1 month. Pays 50% royalty on retail print sales. Pays on completion of sale. Simultaneous submissions and previously published work OK.
Tips: "We are interested in fine-art b&w and color photography, not commercial stock work. Unique perspectives, superior print quality, experience are all important. Ability to provide prints of an image on a timely basis is key as well. Prints are reproduced in a high-quality mail-order catalog; and displayed in gallery exhibitions at various locations."

PHI DELTA KAPPA, P.O. Box 789, 8th & Union Sts., Bloomington IN 47402. Design Director: Carol Bucheri. Estab. 1915. Produces Kappan magazine and supporting materials. Photos used in magazine, flyers, and subscription cards.
Needs: Buys 10 photos/year; offers 1 assignment/year. Teachers, classrooms and high school students. Reviews stock photos. Model release required. Photo captions required; include who, what, when, where.
Making Contact & Terms: Query with list of stock photo subjects. Provide photocopies, brochure or flyer to be kept on file for possible future assignments. Uses 8×10 b&w prints, b&w contact sheets. SASE. Reports in 3 weeks. Pays $20-100/b&w photo; $30-400/color photo; $30-500/job. Credit line and tearsheets given. Buys one-time rights.
Tips: "Don't send photos that you wouldn't want to hang in a gallery. Just because you do a photo for publications does not mean you should lower your standards. Spots should be touched up (not with a ball point pen), the print should be good and carefully done, subject matter should be in focus. Send me photocopies of your b&w prints that we can look at. We don't convert slides and rarely use color."

*POSEY SCHOOL OF DANCE, INC., Box 254, Northport NY 11768. (516)757-2700. President: Elsa Posey. Estab. 1953. Sponsors a school of dance and a regional dance company. Photos used in brochures and newspapers.
Needs: Buys 10-12 photos/year; offers 4 assignments/year. Special subject needs include children dancing, ballet, modern dance, jazz/tap (theater dance) and classes including women and men. Reviews stock photos. Model release required.
Making Contact & Terms: Interested in receiving work from newer, lesser-known photographers. "Call us." Works on assignment only. Uses 8×10 glossy b&w prints. SASE. Reports in 1 week. NPI; payment negotiable. Pays $25-200/b&w or color photo. Credit line given if requested. Buys one-time rights; negotiable.
Tips: "We need photos of REAL dancers doing, not posing, dance. We need photos of children dancing. We receive 'cute' photos often portraying dancers as shadows!"

*■PULPDENT, 80 Oakland St., Watertown MA 02272. (617)926-6666. Fax: (617)343-4342. Advertising Manager: Jane Berk. Estab. 1947. Provides dental supplies. Photos used in brochures, press releases and catalogs.

Needs: Number of photos purchased varies. Number of freelance assignments varies. Photos feature products. Example of recent use: catalog. Reviews stock photos. Model/property release required.
Audiovisual Needs: Uses slides, film, videotape for marketing purposes.
Making Contact & Terms: Interested in receiving work from newer, lesser-known photographers. Arrange a personal interview to show portfolio. Query with samples. Work with local freelancers only. Uses color and b&w prints; 35mm, 2¼×2¼, 4×5 transparencies. Does not keep samples on file. SASE. Reports in 1 month. Pays $65/color photo; $65/b&w photo. Pays upon usage or within 30 days. Credit line given depending on use. Buys all rights.

*THE QUARASAN GROUP, INC., 214 W. Huron, Chicago IL 60610-3616. Contact: Randi Brill. A complete book publishing service and design firm. Offers design of interiors and covers to complete editorial and production stages, art and photo procurement. Photos used in brochures, books and other print products.
Needs: Buys 1,000-5,000 photos/year; offers 75-100 assignments/year. "Most products we produce are educational in nature. The subject matter can vary. For textbook work, male-female/ethnic/handicapped/minorities balances must be maintained in the photos we select to ensure an accurate representation." Reviews stock photos. Model release required.
Making Contact & Terms: Query with stock photo list or nonreturnable samples (photocopies OK). Provide resume, business card, brochure, flyer or tearsheets to be kept on file for possible future assignments. Prefers 8×10 b&w prints; 35mm, 2¼×2¼, 4×5, or 8×10 transparencies, or b&w contact sheets. Cannot return material. "We contact once work/project requires photos." NPI; payment based on final use size. Pays on a per photo basis or day rate. Credit line given, but may not always appear on page. Usually buys all rights or sometimes North American rights.
Tips: "Learn the industry. Analyze the products on the market to understand *why* those photos were chosen. Clients still prefer work-for-hire, but this is changing. Be organized and professional and meet the agreed upon schedules and deadlines. We are always looking for experienced photo researchers and top-notch photographers local to the Chicago area."

RECREATION WORLD SERVICES, INC., Drawer 17148, Pensacola FL 32522. (904)944-7864. Executive Vice President: K.W. Stephens. Estab. 1983. Serves publishers and membership service organizations including recreation, leisure and travel industries. Photos used in brochures, newsletters, newspapers, magazines and press releases.
Needs: Buys 5-10 photos/year; gives 2-5 assignments/year. Recreation type. Model release required. Property release preferred.
Making Contact & Terms: Send unsolicited photos by mail for consideration. Provide resume, business card, brochure, flyer or tearsheets to be kept on file for possible future assignments. Uses 3×4 prints. SASE. Reports in 2 weeks. NPI. "We request photographers to state their price." Buys all rights; negotiable.

REPERTORY DANCE THEATRE, P.O. Box 510427, Salt Lake City UT 84151-0427. (801)534-6345. Fax: (801)534-6344. General Manager: Kathy Johnson. Uses photos of dance company for promotion. Photos used in brochures, newspapers, posters, news releases and magazines.
Needs: Prefers to see dance or movement photos.
Making Contact & Terms: Arrange a personal interview to show portfolio. Queries by mail OK. Uses 8×10 b&w glossy prints; contact sheet OK. SASE. Reports in 2 weeks. NPI; payment negotiable. Buys all rights.

*REVERE/LIFEDANCE CO. INC., 3479 NW Yeon Ave., Portland OR 97210. (503)228-9430. Fax: (503)228-5039. President: Morris McClellan. Estab. 1982. Record company and distribution company. Photos used in catalogs, CD and cassette packaging.
Needs: Buys 3-8 photos/year. Uses photos of "nature, mostly." Examples of recent use: annual catalog of recordings (cover), CD/cassette (cover). Reviews stock photos of nature subjects. Photo captions should include: description of subject matter.
Making Contact & Terms: Interested in receiving work from newer, lesser-known photographers. Query with samples. Uses color prints; 35mm, 2¼×2¼, 4×5 transparencies. SASE. Reports only when interested. Pays $300-500/color photo. Pays on usage. Credit line given. Buys one-time rights; negotiable.
Tips: "We require nature photos that reflect relaxation, peace and beauty."

■RIPON COLLEGE, P.O. Box 248, Ripon WI 54971. (414)748-8115. Contact: Director of College Relations. Estab. 1851. Photos used in brochures, newsletters, posters, newspapers, audiovisual presentations, annual reports, magazines and press releases.

Needs: Offers 3-5 assignments/year. Formal and informal portraits of Ripon alumni, on-location shots, architecture. Model/property release preferred. Captions preferred.

Making Contact & Terms: Interested in receiving work from newer, lesser-known photographers. Provide resume, business card, brochure, flyer or tearsheets to be kept on file for possible future assignments. Works on assignment only. SASE. Reports in 1 month. Pays $10-25/b&w photo; $10-50/color photo; $30-40/hour; $300-500/day; $300-500/job; negotiable. Buys one-time and all rights; negotiable.

RSVP MARKETING, INC., Suite 5, 450 Plain St., Marshfield MA 02050. President: Edward C. Hicks. Direct marketing consultant/agency. Photos used in brochures, catalogs and magazines.

Needs: Buys 50-100 photos/year; offers 5-10 assignments/year. Industrial equipment, travel/tourism topics and modeled, clothing, sports events. Reviews stock photos. Model release preferred.

Making Contact & Terms: Query with list of stock photo subjects. Provide resume, business card, brochure, flyer or tearsheets to be kept on file for possible future assignments. Works on assignment only. Uses 2×2 and 4×6 b&w and color prints, and transparencies. Reports as needed. NPI; payment negotiable per photo and per job. Buys all rights.

Tips: "We look for photos of industrial and office products, high-tech formats and fashion."

SAN FRANCISCO CONSERVATORY OF MUSIC, 1201 Ortega St., San Francisco CA 94122. (415)564-8086. Publications Editor: Daphne Powell. Estab. 1917. Provides publications about the conservatory programs, concerts and musicians. Photos used in brochures, posters, newspapers, annual reports, catalogs, magazines and news releases.

Needs: Buys 25 photos/year; offers 10-15 assignments/year. Musical photos—musicians. Prefers to see in-performance shots, and studio shots of musicians.

Making Contact & Terms: Interested in receiving work from newer, lesser-known photographers. "Contact us only if you are experienced in photographing performing musicians." Works with local freelancers only. Uses 5×7 b&w prints and color slides; color slides for publication only. Payment varies by photographer; "credit line" to $25/b&w photo; $200-700/job. Credit line given "most of the time." Buys one-time rights and all rights; negotiable.

■**SAN FRANCISCO OPERA CENTER,** War Memorial Opera House, San Francisco CA 94102. (415)565-6491. Fax: (415)255-6774. Company Manager: Russ Walton. Estab. 1982. Produces live performances of opera productions of both local San Francisco area performances and national touring companies. Photos used in brochures, newspapers, annual reports, PR releases and production file reference/singer resume photos.

Needs: Buys 2-3 photos/year; offers a minimum 1 assignment/year. Production and performance shots, and artist/performer shots.

Audiovisual Needs: "We produce some video documentaries of our cultural exchanges, opera productions and training programs. Slides and film may also be used to cover these events."

Making Contact & Terms: Interested in receiving work from newer, lesser-known photographers. Query with resume of credits. Provide resume, business card, brochure, flyer or tearsheets to be kept on file for possible future assignments. Uses 8×10 standard finish b&w prints and b&w negatives. SASE. Reports in 2 weeks. Pays $8/b&w photo, $8/color photo, and $50-500/complete job. Credit line given. Buys all rights; negotiable.

Tips: "In portfolio or samples wants to see live action shots in a wide variety of lighting—including stage and outdoor—and performance settings. We need live performance shots and action shots of individuals; scenery also. Photographers should have extensive experience in shooting live performances and be familiar with the opera product. Once good photographers are located, we contract them regularly for various production/social/public events."

*■SCAN VIDEO ENTERTAINMENT, P.O. Box 451, Willernie MN 55090-0451. (612)426-8492. Fax: (612)429-7639. President: Mats Ludwig. Estab. 1981. Distributors of Scandinavian video films, books, calendars, cards.

Needs: Buys 100 photos; 5-10 films/year. Wants any subject related to the Scandinavian countries. Examples of recent uses: travel videos, feature films and Scandinavian fairy tales, all VHS. Reviews stock photos. Model/property release required.

Audiovisual Needs: Uses videotape for marketing and distribution to retail and video stores. Subjects include everything Scandinavian: travel, history, feature, children's material, old fashion, art, nature etc.

Making Contact & Terms: Interested in receiving work from newer, lesser-known photographers. Query with stock photo list. Uses color prints; 35mm transparencies; film and videotape. Does not keep samples. Cannot return material. Replies only if interested. Pays royalties on sales. Pays upon usage. Credit line not given. Buys all rights; negotiable.

Tips: Wants professionally made and edited films with English subtitles or narrated in English. Seeks work which reflects an appreciation of Scandinavian life, traditions and history.

■**SCHWINN BICYCLE COMPANY,** 217 N. Jefferson St., Chicago IL 60661. Manager/Marketing Communications: Paul Chess. Estab. 1895. Products include bicycles and fitness equipment. Photos used in brochures, newsletters, posters, audiovisual presentations, catalogs, magazines and press releases.
Needs: Subjects include only "identifiable" Schwinn products in use. Not interested in stock photos. Model/property release required. Captions required.
Making Contact & Terms: Interested in receiving work from newer, lesser-known photographers. Send unsolicited photos by mail for consideration. Reports ASAP. NPI; payment negotiable. Credit line given if requested. Buys all rights.

■**THE SOCIETY OF AMERICAN FLORISTS,** 1601 Duke St., Alexandria VA 22314. (703)836-8700. Editor and Publisher: Kate Penn. Estab. 1894. National trade association representing growers, wholesalers and retailers of flowers and plants. Photos used in magazines and promotional materials.
Needs: Offers 3-5 assignments/year. Needs photos of personalities, greenhouses, inside wholesalers, flower shops and conventions, as well as studio photography. Reviews stock photos. Model release required. Captions preferred.
Audiovisual Needs: Uses slides (with graphics) for convention slide shows.
Making Contact & Terms: Interested in receiving work from newer, lesser-known photographers. Query with samples. Provide resume, business card, brochure, flyer or tearsheets to be kept on file for possible future assignments. Uses b&w prints, or transparencies. SASE. Reports in 1 week. Pays $600-800/cover shot; $75-150/hour; $125-250/job. Credit line given. Buys one-time rights.
Tips: "We shoot a lot of tightly composed, dramatic shots, so we look for these skills. We also welcome input from the photographer on the concept of the shot. Our readers, as business owners, like to see photos of other business owners. Therefore, people photography, on location, is particularly popular."

■**SPECIAL OLYMPICS INTERNATIONAL,** Suite 500, 1350 New York Ave. NW, Washington DC 20005. (202)628-3630. Fax: (202)737-1937. Media Production Coordinator: Jill Dixon. Estab. 1968. Provides sports training/competition to people with mental retardation. Photos used in brochures, newsletters, posters, annual reports and audiovisual.
Needs: Buys 300 photos/year; offers 5 assignments/year. Sports action and special events. Model/property release preferred for athletes and celebrities. Captions preferred.
Audiovisual Needs: Uses slides and videotape.
Making Contact & Terms: Interested in receiving work from newer, lesser-known photographers. Provide resume, business card, self-promotion piece or tearsheets to be kept on file for possible future assignments. Uses 3×5, 5×7 and 8×10, glossy color prints; 35mm transparencies; VHS, U-matic, Betacam, 1-inch videotape. Keeps samples on file. SASE. Reports in 2-4 weeks. Pays $50-100/hour; $300-500/job. Processing additional. "Many volunteer time and processing because we're a not-for-profit organization." **Pays on acceptance.** Credit line depends on the material it is used on (no credit on brochure/credit in magazines). Buys one-time and all rights; negotiable.
Tips: Specific guidelines can be given upon request. Looking for "good action shots. We use primarily video instead of film."

*RICHARD STAFFORD GROUP, INC.,** 224 Miracle Mile, P.O. Box 735, Miami FL 33144. (305)461-2770. Photo Editor/Researcher: Alex Gonzalez. Estab. 1991. Publisher. Photos used in magazines, catalogs.
Needs: Buys 3-6 photos/month. Subjects include fine art, b&w photos. Reviews stock photos. Model/property release preferred. Captions preferred; include technical data (i.e., camera, lens, aperture, film).
Making Contact & Terms: Interested in receiving work from newer, lesser-known photographers. Provide resume, business card, self-promotion piece or tearsheets to be kept on file for possible future assignments. Send unsolicited photos by mail for consideration. Uses b&w prints no larger than 8×10. Keeps samples on file. SASE. Reports in 1 month. Pays $35-500/b&w photo. Pays 2 months after publication. Buys one-time rights.
Tips: Wants to see "an artistic sense of design in composition and richness in tonal range. We are seldom impressed by shadow."

Market conditions are constantly changing! If you're still using this book and it's 1995 or later, buy the newest edition of Photographer's Market *at your favorite bookstore or order directly from Writer's Digest Books.*

*TOPS NEWS, % TOPS Club, Inc., Box 07360, Milwaukee WI 53207. Editor: Kathleen Davis. Estab. 1948. TOPS is a nonprofit, self-help, weight-control organization. Photos used in membership magazine.
Needs: "Subject matter to be illustrated varies greatly." Reviews stock photos.
Making Contact & Terms: Query with stock photo list. Provide resume, business card, brochure, flyer or tearsheets to be kept on file for possible future assignments. Uses any size transparency or print. SASE. Reports in 1 month. Pays $75-125/color photo. Buys one-time rights.
Tips: "Send a brief, well-composed letter along with a few selected samples with a SASE."

*■UNION INSTITUTE, 440 E. McMillan St., Cincinnati OH 45206. (513)861-6400. Fax: (513)861-0779. Contact: Anu Mitra. Provides alternative higher education, baccalaureate and doctoral programs. Photos used in brochures, newsletters, magazines, posters, audiovisual presentations, annual reports, catalogs and news releases.
Needs: Uses photos of the Union Institute community involved in their activities. Also, photos that portray themes. Model release required.
Making Contact & Terms: Arrange a personal interview to show portfolio. Uses 5×7 glossy b&w and color prints; b&w and color contact sheets. SASE. Reports in 3 weeks. NPI; payment negotiable. Credit line given.
Tips: Prefers "good closeups and action shots of alums/faculty, etc. Our quarterly alumni magazine reaches an international audience concerned with major issues. Illustrating its stories with quality photos involving our people is our constant challenge. We welcome your involvement."

*UNITED AUTO WORKERS (UAW), 8000 E. Jefferson Ave., Detroit MI 48214. (313)926-5291. Editor: David Elsila. Trade union representing 1 million workers in auto, aerospace, and agricultural-implement industries. Publishes *Solidarity* magazine. Photos used for brochures, newsletters, posters, magazines and calendars.
Needs: Buys 85 freelance photos/year and offers 12-18 freelance assignments/year. Needs photos of workers at their place of work and social issues for magazine story illustrations. Reviews stock photos. Model releases preferred. Captions preferred.
Making Contact & Terms: Arrange a personal interview to show portfolio. Query with samples and send material by mail for consideration. Provide resume and tearsheets to be kept on file for possible future assignments. Uses 8×10 prints; contact sheets OK. Notifies photographer if future assignments can be expected. SASE. Reports in 2 weeks. Pays $50-100/b&w or color photo; $250/half-day; $475/day. Credit line given. Buys one-time rights.
Tips: In portfolio, prefers to see b&w and color workplace shots; prefers to see published photos as samples.

UNITED STATES SAILING ASSOCIATION, P.O. Box 209, Newport RI 02840. (401)849-5200. Fax: (401)849-5208. Editor: Allison Peter. Estab. 1897. *American Sailor Magazine* provided to members of United States Sailing Association. Photos used in brochures, posters and magazines.
Needs: Buys 30-50 photos/year. Examples of recent uses: *American Sailor* (cover, color slide); "US Sailing Directory" (cover); and membership brochure, (b&w and color). Reviews stock photos, action sailing/racing shots; close-up face shots. Captions preferred; include boat type/name, regatta name.
Making Contact & Terms: Query with stock photo list. Uses 5×7 matte b&w prints; 8×10 glossy color prints; 35mm transparencies. SASE. Reports in 2-3 weeks. "Financial resources no longer available for cover or inside photography."

UNIVERSITY OF NEW HAVEN, 300 Orange Ave., West Haven CT 06516. (203)932-7243. Public Relations Director: Toni Blood. Photos used in brochures, newsletters, newspapers, annual reports, catalogs and news releases.
Needs: Uses University of New Haven campus photos.
Making Contact & Terms: Query with resume "and non-returnable samples for our files. We'll contact to arrange a personal interview to show portfolio." Local freelancers preferred. Uses 5×7 glossy b&w prints; 35mm transparencies; contact sheet OK. SASE. "Can't be responsible for lost materials." Reports in 1 week. Pays $2-9/b&w photo; $10-25/color photo; $10-20/hour; $100-200 and up/day; payment negotiable on a per-photo basis. Buys all rights.
Tips: Looks for good people portraits, candids, interaction, news quality. Overall good versatility in mixed situations. "Call first to see if we need additional photographers. If yes, send samples and rates. Make appointment to show portfolio. Be reasonable on costs (we're a nonprofit institution). Be a resident in local area available for assignment." Sees a "need for better and better quality photo reproduction."

YEARBOOK ASSOCIATES, P.O. Box 91, Millers Falls MA 01349. (413)863-8093. Fax: (413)863-2777. Director of Photography: Paul B. Burr. Estab. 1977. Provides portraits and candids for yearbooks. Photos used in yearbooks.

Needs: Offers 5,000 assignments/year.

Making Contact & Terms: Interested in receiving work from newer, lesser-known photographers. Provide resume with current address and phone number. Note: Although most assignments are on a national basis, YBA has local needs in Washington DC and the New England area. Works on assignment only. Cannot return material. Scheduling is set up during June, July and August. Shooting starts in September. Pays $35-160/day. Credit line sometimes given. Buys exclusive product rights and all rights.

Tips: "In addition to portrait photographers we need people with school group and environmental portrait experience. Photographer should like to work with people and be willing to follow our directions. Candid photographer should bring or send a roll of 35mm b&w undeveloped with group shots, action shots of sports, general candids of people."

Businesses and Organizations/'93-'94 changes

The following markets appeared in the 1993 edition of *Photographer's Market* but are not listed in the 1994 edition. They may have been omitted for failing to respond to our request for updated information, they may have gone out of business or they may no longer wish to receive freelance work.

Alfred Publishing (did not respond)

American Association for Vocational Instructional Materials (did not respond)

American Dental Hygienists' Association (no longer uses photos)

American Power Boat Association (did not respond)

American Youth Soccer Organization (did not respond)

ASBO International (did not respond)

Bankers Life & Casualty (did not respond)

Custom Studios (did not respond)

Dayton Ballet (did not respond)

E&B Marine (did not respond)

Green Mountain Power (did not respond)

Institute of Real Estate Management (did not respond)

International Photo Corporation (did not respond)

Helen Keller International (did not respond)

Metal Forming Magazine/PMA Services (did not respond)

National Glass Association (did not respond)

Overseas Development Council (did not respond)

Palm Springs Desert Resort Convention and Visitors Bureau (did not respond)

PGA of America (did not respond

Photo Marketing Association (did not respond)

Special Report (did not respond)

Thiel College (did not respond)

T-Shirt Gallery (no longer uses photos)

United States Chess Federation (did not respond)

United States Professional Tennis Association (did not respond)

Vac-U-Max (did not respond)

Walter Van Enck Design Limited (did not respond)

Worcester Polytechnic Institute (did not respond)

Galleries

For photographers interested in marketing their fine art photography, galleries offer an enticing combination of exposure, sales and career advancement. Yet galleries, like other retail outlets, were hit hard by the recession and some were forced to close their doors or struggle through a slow recovery. The competition also remains stiff for gallery space and attention.

Despite the competition, there is some good news as galleries start to recover. Many galleries have increased the variety of work they carry in order to tap into growing segments of the art market. Fortunately for photographers, galleries are adding photography as part of this expansion and are considering fine art photography for both exhibitions and permanent collections.

At one time, some considered black & white work the only true medium for art photography, but today galleries are including color shows as well. In addition, galleries have expanded their definition of what they consider photographic images to include almost any work that uses photography as a point of departure. Thus, the door has opened for experimental techniques, processes and combinations of photography and other media, including paint, textiles, metal and computer manipulation.

Often film, video and other audiovisual media are included with photography shows. Accordingly, information about galleries' interests in these media are included in our listings. Watch for the special AV symbol, a solid, black square (■), at the start of those listings interested in seeing this type of work.

Photographers need a combination of quality work and a professional attitude to attract interest from galleries. It's best to start with a working knowledge of how galleries operate. There are several different types of galleries, each with different modes of operation, different clientele and, quite often, different needs.

How galleries operate

Although there are a growing number of all-photography galleries, most are still primarily art galleries which may either hold annual photography shows or special solo and group photography exhibits throughout the year. Some also include photography as part of their permanent collections and exhibit photos at all times. One gallery that specializes in exhibiting photography is the Ascherman Gallery in Cleveland, Ohio. In our Insider Report on page 174, gallery owner Herbert Ascherman offers his insight into the complex industry.

The largest group of galleries are retail, for profit operations. These galleries usually cater to both private and corporate collectors. Depending on the location, the clientele may include everyone from tourists and first-time buyers to sophisticated, long-time collectors and professional interior designers. The emphasis is on what sells and these galleries are interested only in work they feel will fit the needs of their clientele. Before approaching a retail gallery, be sure you have a very clear understanding of their clientele's interests and needs.

Art consultancies work primarily with professional art buyers including interior decorators, interior designers, developers, architects and corporate art collectors. Some include a viewing gallery open to the public, but they are most interested in being able to show their clients a wide variety of work. Consultancies maintain large slide files to match the needs of their clients in almost any situation. Photographers interested in working with consultants must have a body of work readily available.

Nonprofit galleries and alternative spaces offer photographers the most opportunity, especially if their work is experimental. Often sponsored by an educational facility or by a cooperative, the aim of these galleries is to expose the public to a variety of art forms and new artists. Since sales are secondary, profits from sales in these galleries will be lower than in retail outlets. Cooperatives offer artists (and photographers) the opportunity to have a say in how the gallery is operated. Most require a small membership fee and a donation of time. In exchange they take a very low commission on works sold.

Read the listings carefully to determine which galleries interest you most. Some provide guidelines or promotional information about the gallery's recent exhibits for a self-addressed, stamped envelope. Whenever possible, visit those galleries that interest you to get a real feel for their particular needs and outlook. Do not, however, try to show a portfolio without first making an appointment. Most galleries will look at transparencies, prints, tearsheets, bios, résumés and other material first. If interested, they will request to see a portfolio.

Most galleries operate on a commission basis. Galleries take a percentage commission for works sold. Retail galleries usually take 40-50 percent commission, while nonprofits usually charge 20-30 percent. A few also take a rental fee for space used. Prices may be set by either the gallery or the artist, but quite often by mutual agreement.

Most galleries provide insurance on-site and will handle promotional costs. Shipping costs often are shared with the gallery paying for shipment one-way. Galleries also provide written contracts outlining their expectations. Photographers should study their contracts carefully and treat the gallery as any other business partner.

THE AFTERIMAGE PHOTOGRAPH GALLERY, The Quandrangle 115, 2828 Routh St., Dallas TX 75201. (214)871-9140. Owner: Ben Breard. Estab. 1971. Interested in any subject matter. Frequently sells landscapes.
Exhibits: Prefers Cibachrome "or other fade-resistant process" for color and "archival quality" for b&w. Examples of recent exhibitions: Color landscapes by Robert Glenn Ketchum; "Hollywood Starts from the 1950s" by Sid Avery; color landscapes by Christopher Burkett. Sponsors openings; "an opening usually lasts 2 hours, and we have several a year." Photographer should "have many years of experience and a history of publications and museum and gallery display; although if one's work is strong enough, these requirements may be negated."
Making Contact & Terms: Open to exhibiting work of newer photographers, "but that work is usually difficult to sell." Charges 50% sales commission on most pictures handled directly (photographer sets price). Price range: $40-10,000. Unframed work only. Query first with resume of credits and biographical data or call to arrange an appointment. SASE. Reports in 2 days-2 months.
Tips: Currently landscapes sell the best. "Work enough years to build up a sufficient inventory of, say, 20-30 superb prints, and make a quality presentation. Edit your work down to the strongest images." Sees trend toward more color, bigger sizes, and more hand-painted prints.

AKRON ART MUSEUM, 70 E. Market St., Akron OH 44308. (216)376-9185. Curator: Barbara Tannenbaum.
Exhibits: Requirements: To exhibit, photographers must possess "a notable record of exhibitions, inclusion in publications, and/or a role in the historical development of photography. We also feature local photographers (Akron area)." Interested in innovative works by contemporary photographers; any subject matter. Examples of recent exhibitions: "Ralph Eugene Meatyard: An American Visionary;" "The Cuyahoga Valley: Photographs by Robert Glenn Ketchum;" Cibachrome color photographs; "Czech Modernism: Photography," a historical survey of Czechoslovakian photography. Presents 3-5 exhibits/year. Shows last 2 months. Sponsors openings; provides light food, beverages and sometimes entertainment. Photographer's presence at opening preferred. Presence during show is not required, but willingness to give a gallery talk is appreciated.
Making Contact & Terms: NPI; buys photography outright. Annually awards Knight Purchase Award to living artist working with photographic media. Will review transparencies. Send material by mail for consideration. SASE. Reports in 1-2 months, "depending on our workload."
Tips: "Prepare a professional looking packet of materials including high-quality slides, and always send a SASE. Never send original prints."

THE ALBUQUERQUE MUSEUM, 2000 Mountain Rd. NW, Albuquerque NM 87104. (505)243-7255. Fax: (505)764-6546. Curator of Art: Ellen Landis. Estab. 1967.
Exhibits: Requirements: Send photos, resume and artist's statement. Interested in all subjects. Examples of recent exhibitions: "Gus Foster," by Gus Foster (panoramic photographs); "Santiago," by Joan Myers (b&w 16×20); and "Frida Kahlo," by Lola Alvaraz Bravo (b&w various sizes). Presents 3-6 shows/year. Shows last 8-12 weeks. Photographer's presence at opening preferred, presence during show preferred.
Making Contact & Terms: Buys photos outright. Reviews transparencies. Interested in framed or unframed work, mounted or unmounted work, matted or unmatted work. Arrange a personal interview to show portfolio. Submit portfolio for review. Send material by mail for consideration. "Sometimes we return material; sometimes we keep works on file." Reports in 1 month.

a.k.a. SKYLIGHT GALLERY OF BEACON HILL, 43 Charles St., Boston MA 02114. (617)720-2855. Director: John Chittick.
Exhibits: Requirements: All images framed or matted; rent of gallery space; produce a postcard. Open to all types of photography. Examples of recent exhibitions: personal photographs from the father of American documentary film, Richard Leacock; large architectural street scenes, by Roger Kingston; manipulated polaroids/pinhole photography, by Fay Breed. Shows last 1 month. Sponsors openings. Photographer's presence at opening preferred.
Making Contact & Terms: Photographer pays $1,650 for 4-week show. This includes all fees. No gallery commission. "We strive to publicize the photographers and their works in the most marketable way so that the reception brings in many buyers. Our gallery offers a complete gallery exhibition and marketing plan to the photographer." Rental package includes: 3,200 postcards of one of photographer's images on exhibit. Gallery mails out 1,700 to selected Boston list, photographer gets 1,500. Gallery handles all publicity and press kits to 80 local media (TV, radio and newspapers); gallery plans and pays for opening reception for 200 people with wine and cheese and live music; paid advertising in *Art New England* and *Gallery Guide* (national issue); $5,000 insurance. Will review transparencies. Interested in mounted work. Arrange a personal interview to show portfolio. SASE. Reports in 1 month.
Tips: "If the photographer is interested in a Boston exhibit, this is a good idea. Sales prospects are rather good. The public is looking for 'original' photos to fit in home or office."

INSIDER REPORT

Director Teaches, Learns from Budding Photographers

A gallery director with a knack for remembering images, Herbert Ascherman, Jr., sees himself in a dual role — part educator and part student of fine art photography. The student maintains a library of over 1,000 photography books and learns as much as he can about the always evolving fine art field. "I try to learn a little bit from every show," says Ascherman. "I'm in a remarkable position because I see so much that comes across my desk in terms of what is going on in photography and where it's coming from. As a consequence, I have a good visual education."

Meanwhile, the educator, who has taught photography classes at his gallery in Cleveland, Ohio, constantly provides internships for budding artists. By giving students the opportunity to assist at the gallery, he helps them improve their skills and enhances their chance for success. "We would rather give someone their first show than give someone their fiftieth show. I would rather teach someone what a gallery is all about and get them into the process than deal with someone who is an Ansel Adams. Those type of people don't need me," he says.

Herbert Ascherman, Jr.

© Christine Ascherman

It is this philosophy and an overall knowledge of the industry that makes Ascherman's gallery a true training ground for young talent. He has displayed early photographs of numerous U.S. and foreign artists, including Sal Lopes, whose exhibit contained many of the images which later appeared in his book, *The Wall: Images & Offerings from the Vietnam Veterans Memorial.*

Ascherman receives 30-50 submissions each year and, from those, he finds three or four photographers with whom he agrees to sponsor one-person exhibits. He also organizes a group show from other promising artists who submit work. "Basically everybody has a good shot or two. But when I do an exhibition I want to make sure they have 25 good shots," he says. For this reason, Ascherman requires photographers to submit portfolios of 25-50 prints. He wants to see substance, but he also wants to make sure an artist has a large body of work.

Because he reviews so many portfolios, Ascherman has noticed a return to high-quality imagery, "classic, elegant and dramatic." Among younger photographers he has found more aggressive, hostile styles meant to shock viewers. "It's sort of the punk rock of photography," he says.

"I'm looking for a long-term vision and content as opposed to a short-term, newspaper-style impact," says Ascherman. Although he has a rather eclectic taste, he does not want political or religious works unless they are part of large retrospectives.

"As popular as photography is, you're dealing with a very esoteric set of trading cards. Only in the last 10 years, basically since Ansel Adams' death, has photography come into its own as a collectible format. Up to that point, it was just pictures and anybody could do them," he says. Even with the recent recession, Ascherman sees higher prices for images and a greater appreciation for the art form amongst collectors.

However, photographers eager to succeed should not be driven by the desire to make a fortune off their work. Instead, they must hold a true passion for their profession. "In this business you cannot succeed unless you are obsessed, unless you are single purposed, unless you are focused," he says.

—*Michael Willins*

© Herbert Ascherman, Jr.

As a gallery director in Cleveland, Ohio, Herbert Ascherman, Jr., sees many different photographic styles, ranging from classic and elegant to new and aggressive. Ascherman, who doubles as a photographer, shows a humorous nature in his book, Voyage. The collection of photos includes this shot of two women in Venice, Italy, who appear on both sides of the camera.

AMERICAN SOCIETY OF ARTISTS, INC., Box 1326, Palatine IL 60078. (708)991-4748 or (312)751-2500. Membership Chairman: Helen Del Valle.
Exhibits: Members and nonmembers may exhibit. "Our members range from internationally known artists to unknown artists—quality of work is the important factor. We have about 25 shows throughout the year which accept photographic art."
Making Contact & Terms: NPI; price range varies. Interested in framed, mounted or matted work only. Send SASE for membership information and application (state media). Reports in 2 weeks. Accepted members may participate in lecture and demonstration service. Member publication: *ASA Artisan*.

*ART CENTER OF BATTLE CREEK, 265 E. Emmett St., Battle Creek MI 49017. (616)962-9511. Curator: Tim Norris. Estab. 1962.
Exhibits: Interested in "experimentation; technical/compositional skill; originality—avoid clichés, personal statement." Examples of recent exhibitions: "Focus '92," statewide competition of work by Michigan photographers. Ninety-eight artists accepted, 136 works. All subjects, formats and processes represented. Occasionally presents one-person exhibits and 1 competition every other year (on the even years). Shows last 6 weeks. Sponsors openings; press releases are mailed to area and appropriate media. Photographer's presence at opening is preferred.
Making Contact & Terms: Interested in receiving work from newer, lesser-known photographers. Charges 33.3% commission. "We also accept gifts of photography by Michigan artists into the collection." General price range: $100-500. Will review transparencies if artist wants a solo exhibit. Interested in seeing framed or unframed, mounted or unmounted, matted work only. Send material by mail for consideration. SASE. Reports after exhibits committee has met (1-2 months).
Tips: Sees trend toward "experimentation with older formats and processes, use of hand tinting and an increase in social commentary. All photographers are invited to apply for exhibitions. The Center has a history of showing the work of emerging artists. Send examples of your best and most recent work. Be honest in your work and in presentation." Traditional landscapes are most popular with buying public.

*ART GRAPHIC THIRTY, 415 Massachusetts Ave., Indianapolis IN 46204. (317)684-9855. Director: Linda Walsh. Estab. 1993.
Exhibits: Requirements: Wants "material that would appeal and be appropriate for the gallery clientele." Scenery, nature, flowers, points of interest. Examples of recent exhibitions: Robert Wallace (scenery, flowers, fruits); William Christoff (Florida scenery); Joan Rough (children's circus scenes); and Robert Cook (scenery, everyday scenes). Presents 2+ shows/year. Shows last 6 weeks. Sponsors openings. Photographer's presence at opening preferred.
Making Contact & Terms: Charges 30% commission. General price range: $75+. Reviews transparencies. Interested in framed or unframed, mounted and matted work only. Works should not be exceedingly large. Arrange personal interview to show portfolio. Send material by mail for consideration. SASE. Reports in 1-2 weeks.
Tips: "Be open and realistic about the pricing of the work."

*ART INSTITUTE OF PHILADELPHIA., 1622 Chestnut St., Philadelphia PA 19103. (215)567-7080. Fax: (215)246-3339. Gallery Director: Greg Walker. Estab. 1973.
Exhibits: Requirements: all work must be ready to hang under glass or plexiglass; no clip frames. Interested in fine art, commercial. Examples of recent exhibitions: George Krause (fine art, b&w); Lisa Goodman (commercial, b&w/color); Enrique Bostelmann (documentary, b&w/color). Presents 4 exhibits/year. Shows last 30 days. Sponsors openings; provides refreshments, mailing of announcements for well-known artists, printing of announcements. Photographer's presence at opening is preferred, presence during show is preferred.
Making Contacts & Terms: Interested in receiving work from newer, lesser-known photographers. Sold in gallery. General price range: $150-2,000. Reviews transparencies. Interested in matted or unmatted work. Query with samples. Include 10-20 slides and a resume. SASE. Reports in 1 month.
Tips: "The gallery's concern is that artist must demonstrate the ability to present a mature body of work in any photography genre. In this area there are currently very few commercial galleries that show photography. We are open to showing the best photographic work that is submitted."

The asterisk before a listing indicates that the market is new in this edition. New markets are often the most receptive to freelance submissions.

*ARTSPACE, INC., 201 East Davie St., Raleigh NC 27601. (919)821-2787. Fax: (919)839-6002. Art Director: Ann Tharrington. Estab. 1986.
Exhibits: Works are reviewed by the Artspace Gallery Committee for invitational exhibitions; Artspace sponsors juried shows periodically that are open to all artists and photographers. Send slide, resume and SASE." Interested in all types, styles and subjects. Examples of recent exhibitions: "1,001 Chairs," by Karl Larsen (b&w serial work, framed); "West Art and the Law," by Mary Ellen Marks (b&w, framed); "New Works," Doug van de Zande (color, framed). Presents 1 show/2-3 years. Shows last 5-7 weeks. Sponsors openings; provides reception, invitations, refreshments, publicity, exhibition, installation. Photographer's presence at opening is preferred, presence during show is preferred.
Making Contact & Terms: Interested in receiving work from newer, lesser-known photographers. Charges 30% commission. General price range: $100-600. Reviews transparencies. Send material by mail for consideration. SASE. Reports in 60 days.

ASCHERMAN GALLERY/CLEVELAND PHOTOGRAPHIC WORKSHOP, Suite 4, 1846 Coventry Village, Cleveland Heights OH 44118. (216)321-0054. Fax: (216)321-4372. Director: Herbert Ascherman, Jr. Estab. 1977. Sponsored by Cleveland Photographic Workshop. Subject matter: all forms of photographic art and production. "Membership is not necessary. A prospective photographer must show a portfolio of 40-60 slides or prints for consideration. We prefer to see distinctive work—a signature in the print, work that could only be done by one person, not repetitive or replicative of others."
Exhibits: Examples of recent exhibitions: color work of land- and cityscapes by Ted Davis; works in palladium-platinum by Bob Herbst; and an annual group show by 12 photographers. Presents 6 shows/year. Shows last about 8 weeks. Openings are held for some shows. Photographers are expected to contribute toward expenses of publicity. Photographer's presence at show "always good to publicize, but not necessary."
Making Contact & Terms: Interested in receiving work from newer, lesser-known photographers. Charges 25-40% commission, depending on the artist. Sometimes buys photography outright. Price range: $100-1,000. "Photos in the $100-300 range sell best." Will review transparencies. Matted work only for show.
Tips: "Photographers should show a sincere interest in photography as fine art. Be as professional in your presentation as possible; identify slides with name, title, etc.; matte, mount, box prints. We are a Midwest gallery and for the most part, people here respond to competent, conservative images more so than experimental or trendy work, though we are always looking for innovative work that best represents the artist (all subject matter). Know our gallery; call first; find out something about us, about our background or interests. Never come in cold."

THE BALTIMORE MUSEUM OF ART, Art Museum Dr., Baltimore MD 21218. (410)396-6345. Fax: (410)396-6562. Contact: Department of Prints, Drawings and Photographs.
Exhibits: Interested in work of quality and originality; no student work.
Making Contact & Terms: NPI. Interested in unframed and matted work only. Arrange a personal interview to show portfolio or query with resume of credits. SASE. Reports in 2 weeks-1 month.

*BANNISTER GALLERY., Dept. of Art, Rhode Island College, Providence RI 02908. (401)456-9765. Fax: (401)456-8379. Director: Dennis O'Malley. Estab. 1978.
Exhibits: Requirements: Photographer must pass review by Gallery Committee. The committee changes yearly; consequently interests/requirements change. Interested in socio-political documentary/manipulated darkroom images/large format. Examples of recent exhibitions: Photographs by Earl Dotter (American Labor/b&w, 11" × 14" and 16" × 20"); "Africa Viewed," by Belcher, Barbosa, Staniski (color and b&w, various formats) and "Moments Without Proper Names," by Gordon Parks (photos for *Life* magazine '49-'70). Presents usually at least 1/year. Shows last 3 weeks. Sponsors openings; provides modest amount of refreshments, as budget allows. Photographer's presence at opening is preferred, presence during show preferred.
Making Contact & Terms: Interested in receiving work from newer, lesser-known photographers. Sold in gallery. Buys photos outright occasionally. Exhibits are for teaching purposes. Reviews transparencies. SASE. Reports 1-3 months, held for review by committee.

*BATON ROUGE GALLERY, INC., 1442 City Park Ave., Baton Rouge LA 70808. (504)383-1470. Director: Anne Boudreau. Estab. 1966.
Exhibits: Professional artists with established exhibition history—must submit 20 slides and resume to programming committee for approval. Open to all types, styles and subject matter. Examples of recent exhibitions: "Southwest Louisiana Artists," by Lynda Frese (mixed media photo collage); photography by Tom Neff (b&w landscape) and "Suburban Photographs," by Deanna Dikeman (b&w). Presents approximately 3 exhibits/year. Shows last 4 weeks. Sponsors openings; provides publicity, liquid refreshments. Photographer's presence at opening is preferred.

Making Contact & Terms: Interested in receiving work from newer, lesser-known photographers. Charges 33.3% commission. General price range: $200-600. Reviews transparencies. Interested in "professional presentation." Send material by mail for consideration. SASE. Reports in 2-3 months. Accepts submissions in March and October.

*BC SPACE, 235 Forest Ave., Laguna Beach CA 92651. (714)497-1880. Director: Mark Chamberlain.
Exhibits: Interested only in contemporary photography. Presents 8 solo or group shows/year; 6 weeks normal duration.
Making Contact & Terms: Charges commission. General price range: $150-3,000. Collaborates with artists on special events, openings, etc. For initial contact submit slides and resume. Follow up by arranging personal portfolio review. SASE. Responds "as soon as possible—hopefully within a month, but show scheduling occurs several times a year. Please be patient."
Tips: "Keep in touch—show new work periodically. If we can't give a show right away, don't despair. It may fit another format later. The shows have a rhythm of their own which takes time. Salability of the work is important, but not the prime consideration. We are more interested in fresh, innovative work."

*MONA BERMAN FINE ARTS, 78 Lyon St., New Haven CT 06511. (203)562-4720. Fax: (203)787-6855. Director: Mona Berman. Estab. 1979.
Exhibits: Requirements: "Photographers must have been represented by us for over 2 years. Interested in all except figurative, although we do use some portrait work." Examples of recent exhibits: "Suite Juliette," by Tom Hricko (b&w still life). Presents 0-1 exhibits/year. Shows last 4 weeks. Sponsors openings; provides all promotion. Photographer's presence at opening is required.
Making Contact & Terms: Interested in receiving work from newer, lesser-known photographers. Charges 50% commission. General price range: $300 and up. Reviews 35mm transparencies only. Interested in seeing unframed, unmounted, unmatted work only. Submit portfolio for review (35mm slides only). Query with resume of credits. Send material by mail for consideration (35mm slides with retail prices and SASE). Reports in 1 month.
Tips: "Have a variety of sizes available and a good amount of work available. Please note: We are primarily art consultants serving corporations, architects and designers. We do have private clients also. We do very few exhibits, we mainly show work to our clients for consideration and do sell a lot of photographs."

*JESSE BESSER MUSEUM, 491 Johnson St., Alpena MI 49707. (517)356-2202. Chief of Resources: Robert Haltiner. Estab. 1965.
Exhibits: Interested in a variety of photos suitable for showing in general museum. Examples of exhibitions: "Infrascapes," b&w, landscapes and scenic views by Gene Hollander; "Floral Photographs," fill-flash color photography of flowers at sunrise by Edward Mistarka; "Ophthalmic Images," extreme color close-ups of the eye and its problems by Csaba L. Martonyi. Presents 1-2 shows/year. Shows last 6-8 weeks.
Making Contact & Terms: Very receptive to presenting newer, lesser-known photographers. Charges 20% sales commission. "However, being a museum, emphasis is not placed on sales, per se." Price range: $25-500. Reviews transparencies. Submit samples to Chief of Resources, Robert Haltiner. Framed work only. SASE for return of slides. Reports in 2 weeks. "All work for exhibit must be framed and ready for hanging. Send *good* slides of work with resume and perhaps artist's statement. Trend is toward manipulative work to achieve the desired effect."
Tips: Most recently, Northern Michigan scenes sell best.

*BRIDGEWATER/LUSTBERG., 529 Broadway, New York NY 10012. (212)941-6355. Directors: Paul Bridgewater, Jamie Lustberg.
Exhibits: Requirements: Be good. Interested in predominantly representational, sometimes manipulated. Examples of recent exhibits: "Vintage Modern," by John Dugdale (revivalist); "Across the Waters," British/American group show (manipulated); "Robert Mapplethorpe," same first posthumous exhibit (opened week of his death). Presents 1 or 2 exhibits/year. Shows last 5 weeks. Sponsors openings; "Artist is responsible to deliver ready to hang." Photographer's presence at opening is preferred, presence during show is preferred.

Can't find a listing? Check at the end of each market section for the " '93-'94 Changes" lists. These lists include any market listings from the '93 edition which were either not verified or deleted in this edition.

Making Contact & Terms: Interested in reviewing work from newer, lesser-known photographers. Charges 50% commission. General price range: $500-15,000. Reviews transparencies. Interested in seeing matted or unmatted work. Visit gallery: open day 1st Wednesday each month, 1-3 p.m. Reports in 3 weeks.

*BROMFIELD GALLERY, 107 South St., Boston MA 02111. (617)451-3605. Director: Christina Lanzl. Estab. 1974.
Exhibits: Requirements: Usually shows New England artists. Interested in "programs of diversity and excellence." Examples of recent exhibitions: "Process and Product" juried by Barbara Hitchcock and Jim Dow. Presents various number of shows/year. Shows last 4 weeks. Photographer's presence at opening required.
Making Contact & Terms: Interested in receiving work from newer, lesser-known photographers. Charges 40% commission. General price range: $200-2,000. Reviews transparencies. Interested in framed or unframed, mounted or unmounted, matted or unmatted work. Submit portfolio for review. Send material by mail for consideration. Reports in 1 month.
Tips: "We are looking to expand our presentation of photographers." There is a "small percentage of galleries handling photographers."

J.J. BROOKINGS GALLERY, P.O. Box 1237, San Jose CA 95108. (408)287-3311. Director: Timothy C. Duran.
Exhibits: Requirements: Professional presentation, realistic pricing, numerous quality images. Interested in photography created with a painterly eye. Examples of recent exhibitions: Ansel Adams, James Crable, Linda Gray, Duane Michals, Edward Curtis, Ben Schonzeit, Sandy Skoglund and Todd Watts. Presents 3+ shows (not including group shows)/year. Sponsors openings. Photographer's presence at opening preferred.
Making Contact & Terms: Charges 50% commission. General price range: $500-10,000+. Reviews transparencies. Send material by mail for consideration. Reports in 3 weeks; "if not acceptable, reports immediately."
Tips: Interested in "whatever the artist thinks will impress me the most. 'Painterly' work is best. No documentary, landscape or politically-oriented work."

*C.A.G.E., 344 W 4th St., Cincinnati OH 45202-2603. (513)381-2437. Director: Krista Campbell. Estab. 1978.
Exhibits: There is a yearly call for entries; proposals are due in mid-November. Interested in all types of work. Examples of recent exhibits: "Re: Membering the Member," by Brad Smith (silver print) and solo shows by Kathe Kowalski and Paul Winternitz. Presents 3-5 exhibits/year. Shows last 5 weeks. Sponsors openings; announcements sent to public and media. Photographer's presence at opening is preferred.
Making Contact & Terms: Interested in receiving work from newer, lesser-known photographers. Charges 25% commission. General price range: $100-500. Reviews transparencies. Send material by mail for consideration.
Tips: Proposals are considered yearly in November with report to artists in February. "Submit good quality slides with a clear proposal for show. Also, we are a nonprofit gallery and exhibition is more important than sales."

CALIFORNIA MUSEUM OF PHOTOGRAPHY, University of California, Riverside CA 92521. (714)787-4787. Director: Jonathan Green.
Exhibits: The photographer must have the "highest quality work." Presents 12-18 shows/year. Shows last 6-8 weeks. Sponsors openings; inclusion in museum calendar, reception.
Making Contact & Terms: Curatorial committee reviews transparencies and/or matted or unmatted work. Query with resume of credits. SASE. Reports in 90 days.
Tips: "This museum attempts to balance exhibitions among historical, technology, contemporary, etc. We do not sell photos but provide photographers with exposure. The museum is always interested in newer, lesser-known photographers who are producing interesting work. We can show only a small percent of what we see in a year. The CMP has moved into a renovated 23,000 sq. ft. building. It is the largest exhibition space devoted to photography in the West."

THE CAMERA OBSCURA GALLERY, 1309 Bannock St., Denver CO 80204. (303)623-4059. Director: Hal Gould. Estab. 1963.
Exhibits: Examples of recent exhibitions: Sebastiao Salgado, Jock Sturges, O. Winston Link and Jay Dunitz. Shows last 6 weeks. Sponsors openings. Photographer's presence at opening preferred.
Making Contact & Terms: Receptive to exhibiting work of newer, lesser-known photographers "if it is good enough." Charges 40-50% commission. Buys photos outright. General price range: $200-25,000. Requires exclusive representation within metropolitan area. Arrange a personal interview to show portfolio.

Tips: Sees trend toward "more traditional principles of photography."

CENTER FOR EXPLORATORY AND PERCEPTUAL ART, Fourth Floor, 700 Main St., Buffalo NY 14202. (716)856-2717. Fax: (716)855-3959. Curator: Robert Hirsch. Estab. 1974.
Exhibits: Requirements: Work must be photographically related (film, digital, installation, non-silver, etc.). Artist should have enough work to fill at least half of the space. The total space is approximately 225 working feet. Interested in political, culturally diverse, contemporary and conceptual works. Examples of recent exhibitions: "Point & Shoot," a show by photographers exploring point and shoot cameras; "Juchitan – A Town of Women," by Graciela Iturbide. Presents 5-6 shows/year. Shows last 6 weeks. Sponsors openings; reception with lecture. Photographer's presence at opening required, presence during show preferred.
Making Contact & Terms: Extremely interested in exhibiting work of newer, lesser-known photographers. NPI. Interested in framed or unframed work, mounted or unmounted. Arrange a personal interview to show portfolio. Submit portfolio for review. Send material by mail for consideration. SASE. Reports in 1 month.

CENTER FOR PHOTOGRAPHY AT WOODSTOCK, 59 Tinker St., Woodstock NY 12498. (914)679-9957. Exhibitions Director: Kathleen Kenyon.
Exhibits: Interested in all creative photography. Presents 12 shows/year. Shows last 6 weeks. Sponsors openings.
Making Contact & Terms: Send 20 slides plus resume by mail for consideration. SASE. Reports in 4 months. Charges 25% sales commission.
Tips: "Write us a brief letter, enclose resume, statement on the work, 20 slides, SASE. We are closed Mondays and Tuesdays. Interested in contemporary and emerging photographers."

CONCEPT ART GALLERY, 1031 S. Braddock, Pittsburgh PA 15218. (412)242-9200. Fax: (412)242-7443. Director: Sam Berkovitz. Estab. 1972.
Exhibits: Desires "interesting, mature work." Work that stretches the bounds of what is percieved as typical photography. Examples of recent exhibitions: "Home Earth Sky," by Seth Dickerman and "Luke Swank," selected photos. Presents 1-2 shows/year. Shows last 30-45 days. Sponsors openings; provides color mailer and installation services. Photographer's presence at opening preferred.
Making Contact & Terms: Very interested in receiving work from newer, lesser-known photographers. NPI. Reviews transparencies. Interested in unmounted work only. Requires exclusive representation within metropolitan area. Send material by mail for consideration. SASE. Reports in 1-2 weeks.
Tips: "Mail portfolio with SASE for best results. Will arrange appointment with artist if interested." Sees trend toward "crossover work."

THE CONTEMPORARY ARTS CENTER, Dept. PR, 115 E. Fifth St., Cincinnati OH 45202. (513)721-0390. Contact: Bronwen Howells. Nonprofit arts center.
Exhibits: Requirements: photographer must be selected by the curator and approved by the board. Interested in avant garde, innovative photography. Examples of recent exhibits: "Warhol/Makos," the work of New York photographer Christopher Makos; "Images of Desire," contemporary advertising photography; "The Perfect Moment: Robert Mapplethorpe"; and "Songs of My People." Presents 1-3 shows/year. Shows last 6 weeks. Sponsors openings; provides printed invitations, music, refreshments, cash bar. Photographer's presence at opening preferred.
Making Contact & Terms: Photography sometimes sold in gallery. Charges 10% commission. General price range: $200-500. Reviews transparencies. Send query with resume and slides of work. SASE. Reports in 2 months.

*THE COPLEY SOCIETY OF BOSTON, 158 Newbury St., Boston MA 02116. (617)536-5049. Gallery Manager: Jason M. Pechinski. Estab. 1879.
Exhibits: Requirements: Must apply and be accepted as an artist member. Once accepted, artists are eligible to compete in juried competitions. Guaranteed showing twice a year in small works shows. There is a possibility of group or individual shows, on an invitational basis, if merit exists. Interested in all styles. Examples of recent exhibitions: portraiture by Al Fisher (b&w, platinum prints); landscape/exotic works by Eugene Epstein (b&w, limited edition prints); and landscapes by Jack Wilkerson (b&w). Presents various number of shows/year. Shows last 2-4 weeks. Sponsors openings for juried shows by providing refreshments. Does not sponsor openings for invited artists. Photographer's presence at opening required. Photographer's presence during show required for invited artists, preferred for juried shows.
Making Contact & Terms: Interested in receiving work from newer, lesser-known photographers. Charges 40% commission. General price range: $100-10,000. Reviews transparencies. Interested in framed work only. Request membership application. Quarterly review deadlines.
Tips: Wants to see "professional, concise and informative completion of application. The weight of the judgment for admission is based on quality of slides. Only the strongest work is accepted."

CROSSMAN GALLERY, University of Wisconsin-Whitewater, 800 W. Main St., Whitewater WI 53190. (414)472-5708. Director: Susan Walsh. Estab. 1971.
Exhibits: Requirements: Resume, artist's statement, list insurance information, 10-20 slides, work framed and ready to mount and have 4×5 transparencies available. Interested in all types, especially cibachrome as large format and controversial subjects. Examples of recent exhibitions: "Color Photography Invitational," by Regina Flanagan, Leigh Kane and Janica Yoder. Presents 1 show/biannually. Shows last 3-4 weeks. Sponsors openings; provides food, beverage, show announcement, mailing, shipping (partial) and possible visiting artist lecture/demo. Photographer's presence at opening preferred.
Making Contact & Terms: Buys photos outright. General price range: $250-2,800. Reviews transparencies. Interested in framed and mounted work only. Send material by mail for consideration. SASE. Reports in 1 month.
Tips: "The Crossman Gallery's main role is to teach. I want students to learn about themselves and others in alternative ways; about social and political concerns through art."

*DE HAVILLAND FINE ART, 39 Newbury St., Boston MA 02116. (617)859-3880. Fax: (617)859-3973. Gallery Director: Nadia Georgiou. Estab. 1989.
Exhibits: Requirements: "We prefer work that is matted and framed. Shape and size is of no particular consideration." Interested in nudes, mixed media, photo manipulation, polaroid transfers, etc. Examples of recent exhibitions: Works by George Totskas (mixed media); Maurhn McCabe (mixed media); and Kevin Osborn (polaroid transfers). Presents 1 show/year. Shows last 2 weeks. Sponsors openings, artist must be gallery member. Photographer's presence at opening required. Photographer's presence during show preferred.
Making Contact & Terms: Interested in receiving work from newer, lesser-known photographers. Charges 40% commission. General price range: $100-800. Reviews transparencies. Interested in framed, mounted or matted work. No documentaries. Submit portfolio for review. SASE. Reports in 1 month.
Tips: "The public won't pay a lot for photography. It must be special to attract attention and that's the type of work we're interested in."

*CATHERINE EDELMAN GALLERY, 2nd Floor, 300 W. Superior, Chicago IL 60610. (312)266-2350. Fax: (312)266-1967. Director: Catherine Edelman. Estab. 1987.
Exhibits: "We exhibit works ranging from traditional landscapes to painted photo works done by artists who use photography as the medium through which to explore an idea." Requirements: "The work must be engaging and not derivative of a well-known photographer." Examples of recent exhibitions: "Silent Dramas II," landscapes by Michael Kenna and Richard Misrach; "Images of Jazz," portraits of great jazz artists from the 1940s and 1950s, by Herman Leonard. Presents 9-10 exhibits/year. Shows last 4 weeks. Sponsors openings; free drinks. Photographer's presence at opening preferred.
Making Contact & Terms: Charges 50% commission. General price range: $300-5,000. Reviews transparencies. Interested in matted or unmatted work. Requires exclusive representation within metropolitan area. Shows are limited to works no larger than 40×60. Send material by mail for consideration. SASE. Reports in 2 weeks.
Tips: Looks for "consistency, dedication and honesty. Try to not be overly eager and realize that the process of arranging an exhibition takes a long time. The relationship between gallery and photographer is a partnership—there must be open lines of communication."

ELEVEN EAST ASHLAND (Independent Art Space), 11 E. Ashland, Phoenix AZ 85004. (602)271-0831. Director: David Cook. Estab. 1986.
Exhibits: Requirements: Contemporary only (portrait, landscape, genre, mixed media in b&w, color, non-silver, etc.); photographers must represent themselves, complete exhibition proposal form and be responsible for own materials. Interested in "all subjects in the contemporary vein—manipulated, straight and non silver processes." Example of recent exhibitions: "Landscapes," by Paul Berkner; "European Vacation," by David Cook; "Merged Realities," by Gail Hewlett. Presents 13 shows/year. Shows last 1 month. Sponsors openings; two inhouse juried/invitational exhibits/year. Photographer's presence during show preferred.

Market conditions are constantly changing! If you're still using this book and it's 1995 or later, buy the newest edition of Photographer's Market *at your favorite bookstore or order directly from* Writer's Digest Books.

Making Contact & Terms: Very receptive to exhibiting work of newer, lesser-known photographers. Charges 25% commission. General price range: $100-500. Reviews transparencies. Interested in framed or unframed work, mounted or unmounted work, matted or unmatted work. Shows are limited to material able to fit through the front door and in the space (4' × 8' max.). Query with resume of credits. Query with samples. SASE. Reports in 2 weeks.

Tips: To break in, "be sincerely looking for a venue for your art, and follow through."

ETHERTON/STERN GALLERY, 135 S. 6th Ave., Tucson AZ 85701. (602)624-7370. Director: Terry Etherton. Estab. 1981.

Exhibits: Photographer must "have a high-quality, consistent body of work—be a working artist/ photographer—no 'hobbyists' or weekend photographers." Interested in contemporary photography with emphasis on artists in Western and Southwestern US. Examples of recent exhibitions: "Sign Language," cibachrome prints by Skeet McAuley; gelatin silver prints by Joel-Peter Witkin; and cibachrome prints by William Lesch. Presents 8-9 shows/year. Shows last 5 weeks. Sponsors openings; provides wine and refreshments, publicity, etc. Photographer's presence at opening preferred, presence during show preferred.

Making Contact & Terms: Charges 50% commission. Occasionally buys photography outright. General price range: $200-20,000. Reviews transparencies. Interested in matted or unmatted, unframed work. Arrange a personal interview to show portfolio or send material by mail for consideration. SASE. Reports in 3 weeks.

Tips: "You must be fully committed to photography as a way of life. You should be familiar with the photo art world and with my gallery and the work I show. Do not show more than 20 prints for consideration. Show only the best of your work—no fillers. Have work sent or delivered so that it is presentable and professional." Wants to see "cutting edge, issue-oriented photos. Not interested in classical or traditional work." Figurative and expressive styles currently popular with visitors. To break in, "be aware of current trends and issues."

*FAHEY/KLEIN GALLERY, 148 N. La Brea Ave., Los Angeles CA 90036. (213)934-2250. Fax: (213)934-4243. Director: David Fahey. Estab. 1986.

Exhibits: Requirements: Must be established for a minimum of 5 years; preferably published. Interested in rare vintage and contemporary photography. Examples of recent exhibitions: "Notorious" by Herb Ritts (silver gelatin/platinum photographs); and works by Irving Penn (silver gelatin/platinum photographs) and Joel-Peter Witkin (silver gelatin photographs). Presents 10 shows/year. Shows last 5 weeks. Sponsors openings; provides announcements and beverages served at reception. Photographer's presence at opening and during show preferred

Making Contact & Terms: Charges 50% commission. Buys photos outright. General price range: $600-200,000. Reviews transparencies. Interested in unframed, unmounted and unmatted work only. Requires exclusive representation within metropolitan area. Send material by mail for consideration. SASE. Reports in 6 weeks.

Tips: "Have a comprehensive sample of innovative work."

*FENWAY GALLERY, 14958 Lakeside Rd., Lakeside MI 49116. (616)469-2818. Fax: (616)469-2818. Director: Bruce Wood. Estab. 1990.

Exhibits: Interested in post-modern, experimental and pictoralist work dealing with landscape and/ or figure. Examples of recent exhibits: "Nude in Contemporary Photography," by Douglas W. Neal and others (mixed media); "Landscape Photography," by J. Anne Montgomery and others (mixed media); "Large Polaroid Photographs," by Barbara Grad (20 × 24 Polaroid photos).

Making Contact & Terms: Interested in seeing work from newer, lesser-known photographers. Charges 50% commission. Buys photography outright. General price range: $100-1,000. Reviews transparencies. Interested in unframed, matted or unmatted work. Largest is 30 × 36. Query with samples. Send material by mail for consideration. SASE. Reports in 1-2 months.

Tips: "Interested in photographers working with a fine-art orientation. No documentary/journalism. Must have a consistent body of work. Buyers are extremely conservative, looking for quality and unusual formats. Best subjects: landscapes, nudes."

FILM IN THE CITIES, 2388 University Ave., St. Paul MN 55114. (612)646-6104. Gallery Director: James Dozier. Estab. 1977.

Exhibits: "The main criterion for exhibiting work at Film in the Cities is a cohesive, mature body of work." Interested in "a wide variety of contemporary photographic styles from documentary to experimental to mixed media." Examples of recent exhibitions: "Convergence" by African-American Photographers; "Barrage" by Linda Swartz, Sunil Gupta, Young Soon Min, Gadi Gofbarg; and "Cuba-USA" by 12 Cuban-American photographers. Presents 9-10 shows/year. Shows last 4-5 weeks. Sponsors openings. "*We* host the opening receptions for gallery shows and the only requirement is the photographer's presence if possible."

Making Contact & Terms: Charges 10% commission. General price range: $75 and up. Reviews transparencies. Interested in framed or unframed, mounted or unmounted, matted or unmatted work. Send material by mail for consideration or submit portfolio for review. SASE. Reports in 1 month.

*FINE ARTS MUSEUM OF THE SOUTH, P.O. Box 8426, 4850 Museum Dr., Mobile AL 36689. (205)343-2667. Assistant Director: David McCann. Estab. 1964. Open to all types and styles.
Exhibits: Examples of recent exhibits: Robert Glenn Ketchum, (color and b&w landscape and large format); Alabama landscape photography, *In View of Home* (historic and contemporary), by Richard Frank Jr. Presents 1-2 shows/year. Shows last about 1 month. Sponsors openings; provide light hors d'oeuvres and wine. Photographer's presence at opening is preferred.
Making Contact & Terms: Photography sold in gallery. Charges 20% commission. Occasionally buys photos outright. Reviews transparencies. Interested in framed work only. Arrange a personal interview to show portfolio; send material by mail for consideration. Returns material when SAE is provided "unless photographer specifically points out that it's not required."

FLEISHER ART MEMORIAL, DENE M LOUCHHEIM GALLERIES, 709-721 Catharine St., Philadelphia PA 19147. (215)922-3456. Gallery Coordinator: Lanny Bergner.
Exhibits: Interested in contemporary, avant-garde and experimental. Applicant must enter the juried Challenge Competition. Categories include photography. February deadline. Call for entry form. Also, photographers must live within 50 mile radius of Philadelphia. Presents 2-4 shows/year. Shows last 1 month. Sponsors openings. Photographer's presence during show preferred.
Making Contact & Terms: Charges 20% commission. General price range: $200-2,000. Enter challenge competition only. SASE. Returns material submitted for "Challenge" exhibit approximately 6 weeks following February deadline.
Tips: To be exhibited, "abide by the guidelines of the Challenge Competition." Photographers should be aware that "there is limited representation in Philadelphia."

FOCAL POINT GALLERY, 321 City Island Ave., New York NY 10464. (718)885-1403. Photographer/Director: Ron Terner. Estab. 1974.
Exhibits: Open to all subjects, styles and capabilities. Nudes and landscapes sell best. Examples of recent exhibitions: Thomas Tulis (winner), Jose Arquimides Guzman, Amy Heller and Viviann Rose (finalists), in 3rd annual juried exhibition. Presents 9 shows/year. Shows last 1 month. Photographer's presence at opening preferred.
Making Contact & Terms: Very receptive to exhibiting work of newer, lesser-known photographers. Charges 30% sales commission. General price range: $175-700. Artist should call for information about exhibition policies.
Tips: Sees trend toward more use of alternative processes. "The gallery is geared toward exposure — letting the public know what contemporary artists are doing — and is not concerned with whether it will sell. If the photographer is only interested in selling, this is not the gallery for him/her, but if the artist is concerned with people seeing the work and gaining feedback, this is the place. Most of the work shown at Focal Point Gallery is of lesser-known artists. Don't be discouraged if not accepted the first time. But continue to come back with new work when ready."

*FOSTER GOLDSTROM, #303, 560 Broadway, New York NY 10012. (212)941-9175. Fax: (212)274-8759. Director: Foster Goldstrom.
Exhibits: Interested in fine art. Examples of recent exhibits: "Walden Pond," by Bill Kane (photo on canvas and mixed medium); "A Startling Look at Child Development," by Barbara Mensch (mixed media photography); and "Body Works," by Gretta Sarfaty (photo on canvas with collage). Presents 1-2 shows/year. Shows last one month. Sponsors openings; provides wine.
Making Contact & Terms: Interested in reviewing work from newer, lesser-known photographers. Charges 50% commission. Interested in seeing framed or unframed, matted or unmatted work. Send material by mail for consideration. Send SASE with your work. Reports in 3 weeks.

FREEPORT ART MUSEUM, 121 N. Harlem Ave., Freeport IL 61032. (815)235-9755. Director: Becky Connors. Estab. 1976.
Exhibits: Interested in general, especially landscapes, portraits, senior citizens and country life. Examples of recent exhibitions: "Photographs" by Michael Johnson (large b&w landscapes); "The Many Faces of Hull-House" by Wallace Kirkland (b&w). Presents 1 or 2 shows/year. Shows last 6 weeks. Sponsors openings, "usually on Friday evenings." Pays mileage. Photographer's presence at opening required.
Making Contact & Terms: "We exhibit works by established or lesser-known photographers." Charges 10% commission. Reviews transparencies. Interested in framed work only. Send material by mail for consideration. SASE. Reports in 2 months.

*FULLER LODGE ART CENTER AND GALLERY, 2132 Central Ave., Los Alamos NM 87544. (505)662-9331. Director: Patricia Chavez. Estab. 1977.
Exhibits: Requirements: juried shows; send for prospectus or deadline. Interested in all styles and genres. Examples of recent exhibitions: "Que Pasa: Art in New Mexico" by Marilyn Conway (hand-tinted); and "1991 Biennial" by Dick Wales (landscapes/portraits). Presents 1-2 shows/year. Shows last 4-5 weeks. Sponsors openings. Photographer's presence at opening and during show preferred.
Making Contact & Terms: Interested in receiving work from newer, lesser-known photographers. Charges 30% commission. General price range: $200-500. Reviews transparencies. Interested in framed or unframed, mounted or unmounted work. Arrange personal interview to show portfolio. Query with resume of credits. SASE. Reports in 3 weeks.
Tips: "Be aware that we never do one person shows—artists will be used as they fit into scheduled shows. Should show impeccable craftsmanship. Opportunities are increasing. Photography is becoming a popular form of fine art."

GALERIA MESA, P.O. Box 1466, 155 N. Center, Mesa AZ 85211-1466. (602)644-2242. Contact: curator. Estab. 1980.
Exhibits: Interested in contemporary photography as part of its national juried exhibitions in any and all media. Presents 7-9 national juried exhibits/year. Shows last 4-6 weeks. Sponsors openings; refreshments and sometimes slide lectures (all free).
Making Contact & Terms: Charges 25% commission. General price range: $300-800. Interested in seeing only slides of work to start. Must fit through a standard size door and be ready for hanging. Enter national juried shows. SASE. Reports in 1 month.
Tips: "We do invitational or national juried exhibits only. Only submit professional quality work."

GALESBURG CIVIC ART CENTER, 114 E. Main St., Galesburg IL 61401. (309)342-7415. Director: Paulette Thenhaus. Estab. 1965.
Exhibits: Interested in landscapes, still lifes, abstract color and b&w. "Do not send actual work." Examples of recent exhibitions: "Galex 27," and "Members and Friends Show." Presents one show every other year, but also features photography in general shows. Sponsors openings; provides advertising, receptions, space, insurance, etc. Photographer's presence during show is preferred.
Making Contact & Terms: Interested in exhibiting work of newer, lesser-known photographers. Charges 40% commission. General price range: $100-300. Reviews transparencies. Interested in framed, matted work only. Requires exclusive representation within metropolitan area. Query with resume of credits. "Unsolicited work will not be accepted." Submit slides to exhibition committee to consider along with resume. Requirements are forwarded upon receipt. SASE. Reports according to specified deadlines.
Tips: This space is "primarily an art center." Opportunities in this market are improving gradually. Sees trend toward more photographers participating in shows.

THE GALLERY AT CENTRAL BANK, Box 1360, Lexington KY 40590. In U.S. only (800)637-6884. In Kentucky (800)432-0721. Fax: (606)253-6244. Curator: John G. Irvin. Estab. 1987.
Exhibits: Requirements: No nudes and only Kentucky photographers. Interested in all types of photos. Examples of recent exhibitions: "Covered Bridges of Kentucky," by Jeff Rogers; "Portraits of Children in Black and White," by Jeanne Walter Garvey and "The Desert Storm Series," by Brother Paul of the Abbey of Gethsemane. Presents 2-3 photography shows/year. Shows last 3 weeks. Sponsors openings. "We pay for everything, invitations, receptions and hanging. We give the photographer 100 percent of the proceeds."
Making Contact & Terms: Charges no commission. General price range: $75-1,500. Mounted, matted or unmatted work only. "If you can get it in the door we can hang it." Query with telephone call. Reports back probably same day.

GALLERY ONE, % New England School of Photography, 537 Commonwealth Ave., Boston MA 02215. (617)437-1868. Gallery Director: Samantha McCarthy. Estab. 1972.
Exhibits: Interested in commercial, art, photojournalism, documentary and mixed media. Examples of recent exhibitions: "Beyond Mothers and Children: New Feminist Photographers," a juried exhibition; "Images of Russia," street and still-life in Odessa, Ukraine by Sergei Rogozkin; and "An Intimate Vastness," b&w landscapes in Southwest by J.D. Marston. Sponsors openings. Supplies food and shares cost of postcard invitations to 500 names. "There is no opening if artist is not present."

The code NPI (no payment information given) appears in listings that have not given specific payment amounts.

Making Contact & Terms: Interested in reviewing work from newer, lesser-known photographers. Charges 20% commission. Reviews at least 20 transparencies. Work must be matted consistently, preference for framed work, but will accept unframed. Send slides, resume, artist statement by mail during June, July and August for consideration. SASE. Reports ASAP.
Tips: "Gallery is very receptive to new photographers, as well as, experimental photography."

*GALLERY 1114, 1114 N. Big Spring, Midland TX 79701. (915)685-9944. President: Travis Beckham. Estab. 1983.
Exhibits: Requirements: Work judged by exhibit committee. Interested in "work showing a coherent, innovative direction." Examples of recent exhibitions: "Mixed Metaphors" by Timothy Tracz (incongruities in reality); group show with Michael Banschbach (large format). Presents an average of 1 show/year. Shows last 6 weeks. Sponsors openings; provides publicity, invitations and refreshments. Photographer's presence at opening is preferred.
Making Contact & Terms: Interested in receiving work from newer, lesser-known photographers. Charges 40% commission. General price range: $50-400. Reviews transparencies. Interested in framed work only. Requires exclusive representation within metropolitan area. Send material by mail for consideration. SASE. Reports in 1-3 months.
Tips: "Send work that makes a statement, is formally interesting, shows direction."

GALLERY 614, #20, 0350 County Rd., Corunna IN 46730. (219)281-2752. Contact: Robert Green.
Exhibits: Interested only in carbro and carbon prints (nonsilver processes). Examples of recent exhibitions: carbro/carbon prints by Margaret Viles; and a tri-color/carbro prints by Robert Green. "The only limitations are the imagination." Sponsors openings.
Making Contact & Terms: Charges 30% commission. Buys photos outright. Price range: $750-3,000. Call to arrange an appointment. No unsolicited material. SASE. Mounted or matted work only. Also, teaches monochrome, tri-chrome carbro/carbon printing.
Tips: Open to the work of newer, lesser-known photographers, especially in nonsilver work. Sees "a return to style—classicism and b&w." Portraits and pictorials sell most frequently.

GALLERY TEN, 514 E. State St., Rockford IL 61104. (815)964-1743. Partner: Jean Apgar. Estab. 1985.
Exhibits: "We look for quality in presentation; will review any subject or style. However, Gallery Ten is in a conservative community so artists must consider that when submitting. We may show it, but it may not sell if it is of a controversial nature." Interested in fine art. Example of recent exhibitions: "Cyanotypes," by Joe Sarff. Number of exhibits varies. Shows last 6 weeks. Sponsors openings; provides publicity, mailer and opening refreshments. Photographer's presence at opening preferred.
Making Contact & Terms: Very receptive to exhibiting work of newer, lesser-known photographers. Charges 40% commission. General price range: $50-300. Reviews transparencies. Interested in mounted or unmounted work, matted work. "We prefer 20×24 or smaller." Send material by mail for consideration. SASE. Reports in 1 month.
Tips: "Quality in framing and presentation is paramount. We cannot accept work to sell to our clients that will self destruct in a few years."

*GALMAN LEPOW ASSOCIATES, INC., Unit #12, 1879 Old Cuthbert Rd., Cherry Hill NJ 08034. (609)354-0771. Fax: (609)428-7559. Principals: Elaine Galman and Judith Lepow. Estab. 1979.
Making Contact & Terms: Interested in reviewing work from newer, lesser-known photographers. General price range is open. Reviews transparencies. Interested in seeing matted or unmatted work. No size limit. Query with resume of credits. Visual imagery of work is helpful. SASE. Reports in 3 weeks.
Tips: "We are corporate art consultants and use photography for our clients."

STEPHEN GILL GALLERY, 135 E. 55th St., New York NY 10022. (212)832-0800. Vice President: Anne Gill. Estab. 1986.
Exhibits: Requirements: "Must be photography or photography used with mixed media." Conceptual work only. Shows last 120 days.
Making Contact & Terms: Very receptive to exhibiting work of newer, lesser-known photographers. Charges 50% commission. General price range: $250-2,500. Reviews transparencies. Send material by mail for consideration. SASE with slides only. Reports in 1-3 months.
Tips: Photographer must have an original vision. "Make me think, laugh or feel something. No copycats allowed." Opportunities for photographers with galleries are "excellent."

FAY GOLD GALLERY, 247 Buckhead Ave., Atlanta GA 30305. (404)233-3843. Fax: (404)365-8633. Owner/Director: Fay Gold. Estab. 1981.
Exhibits: Interested in surreal, nudes, allegorical, landscape (20th century); strong interest in contemporary color photography. The photographer must be inventive, speak a new language, and present something not seen before of quality, historical importance or corporate-oriented material. Examples

of recent exhibits: "Fantastic Voyage," a 20-year retrospective by Arthur Tress; "Notorious," celebrity photographs by Herb Ritts; "Untitled," recent photographs by George Tice. Presents 12 shows/year. Shows last 4 weeks. Sponsors openings; provides invitation, mailing, press releases to all media, serves wine, contacts all private and corporate collectors. Photographer's presence at opening preferred.

Making Contact & Terms: Very interested in receiving work from newer, lesser-known photographers. Charges 50% commission. General price range: $350-15,000. Reviews transparencies. Interested in unframed work, mounted work and matted work only. Generally requires exclusive representation within metropolitan area. Send slides and resume. SASE.

Tips: Interested in seeing "unusual, avant-garde" work.

HILLWOOD ART MUSEUM, Dept. PM, Long Island University, C.W. Post Campus, Brookville NY 11548. (516)299-2789. Director: Dr. Judy Collischan. Estab. 1974.

Exhibits: Interested in unconventional (not standard 8 × 10 format), three-dimensional, collage/montage and experimental. Examples of recent exhibitions: "Montage," by John Heartfield, Barbara Morgan and The Starn Twins; "Futurism and Photography," by Bragaglia; and "Photojournalism in the 80s," by Claudia Andujar. Presents exhibit "every few years." Shows last 6 weeks. Sponsors openings; provides announcement card, refreshments. Photographer's presence at opening and at show preferred.

Making Contact & Terms: Interested in reviewing work from newer, lesser-known photographers. Charges 10% commission. Reviews transparencies. No preferences as to matting, mounting or framing. Send material by mail for consideration; include slides or b&w prints and resume. SASE. Reports at earliest opportunity.

Tips: "We look for the originality of individual expression. Prepare the best possible slides and label them in a professional manner. Buying public interested in "photography of a more unconventional nature."

THE HOPKINS GALLERY, Main Street, Wellfleet MA 02667. (508)349-7246. Director: River Karmen. Estab. 1981.

Exhibits: "We accept varied work, seeking high quality and uniqueness." Examples of recent exhibitions: Works by Kristine Hopkins (hand colored), Karin Rosenthal (b&w nudes/landscapes) and Robin Winfield (photo collage). Presents 2 shows/year. Shows last 3 weeks. Sponsors openings; reception, invitations and press release. Photographer's presence at opening is preferred.

Making Contact & Terms: Charges 45% commission. General price range: $300-1,000. Reviews transparencies. Interested in framed work only. Send material by mail for consideration. SASE. Reports in 2 months.

Tips: Submit portfolio by March 1. "We have a very successful photography show each year and have cultivated a following with collectors."

HUGHES FINE ARTS CENTER, Dept. of Visual Arts, Box 8134, Grand Forks ND 58202-8134. (701)777-2257. Director: Brian Paulsen. Estab. 1979.

Exhibits: Interested in any subjects. Examples of recent exhibitions: Dana Sherman, Roger Sopher and Harley Strauss. All three exhibited b&w 35mm and 4 × 5 formats. Presents 1-3 shows/year. Shows last 2-3 weeks.

Making Contact & Terms: Very interested in receiving work of newer, lesser-known photographers. Does not charge commission; sales are between artist-buyer. Reviews transparencies. "Works should be framed and matted." No size limits or restrictions. Send transparencies only. SASE. Reports in 2 weeks.

Tips: "Send slides of work . . . we will dupe originals and return ASAP and contact you later." Needs "less photos imitating other art movements. Photographers should show their own inherent qualities."

*IMAGERY, 115 S. Columbus St., Lancaster OH 43130. (614)687-5121. Owner: Judy Smith. Estab. 1990.

Exhibits: Requirements: Archivally processed, mounted and matted work only. Slides must be submitted first. Interested in b&w, hand-tinted of any subject, type or style, except documentary. Examples of recent exhibitions: "Statements of Light," by Monte Nagler (4 × 5/b&w); and "from a Woman's Prospective," by Connie Imboden (2¼ × 2¼/b&w). Presents 5-6 exhibits/year. Shows last 1½ to 3 months. Sponsors openings; provides champagne opening, mailing. Photographer's presence at opening and during show preferred.

Making Contact & Terms: Interested in receiving work from newer, lesser-known photographers. Charges 40% commission. General price range: $50-1,600. Reviews transparencies. Interested in seeing framed or unframed mounted and matted work only. No restrictions; however, owner decides what pieces show. Send material by mail for consideration. SASE. Reports in 1 month.

Tips: "I'm interested in high-quality fine art b&w photography only. No class assignments. The public is buying tasteful nudes and landscapes."

In his "Guardian Series" displayed at Imagery gallery in Lancaster, Ohio, photographer Dennis Savage of Bloomingville, Ohio, wanted to show man's relationship with earth. Now part of the gallery's permanent collection, this image, with its strong side lighting and fine detail, beautifully portrays this concept. The shot won several regional awards and was included in the fall 1992 issue of the **Photo Review.**

*INTERNATIONAL MUSEUM OF PHOTOGRAPHY AT GEORGE EASTMAN HOUSE, 900 East Ave., Rochester NY 14607. (716)271-3361. Senior Curator, 19th and 20th Century: Will Stapp. "We are a museum housing one of the finest and largest collections of photographs. The collection consists of over 500,000 photographs spanning the entire history of photography, and represents the work of some 8,000 photographers from around the world."

Making Contact & Terms: May buy photos outright, but photos are not put up for sale. Interested in seeing unframed work only. Submit prints or slides by mail for consideration. SASE. Reports in 4-8 weeks.

Tips: Interested in photography on any subject; but "the works must be of aesthetic or historical ilmporatnce and the prints must be original and significant as objects."

JANAPA PHOTOGRAPHY GALLERY LTD., Dept. PM, #1D, 240 E. 4th St., New York NY 10009-7413. (212)777-1277. Director: Stanley Simon. Estab. 1980.

Exhibits: Photographers must be professional. Interested in contemporary, fine-art, avant-garde photography. Sponsors openings; provides press and public relations, mailing list, local newspaper listings and advertising, with all costs at photographer's expense. "We charge a fee of $250 for one-person show, or proportionate amount for more than one." Photographer's presence preferred at openings and during show. Photographer should be aggressive and willing to participate in own marketing.

Making Contact & Terms: Commission 25-50%, depending on artist. General price range: $150-250/b&w; $250-500/color, (16×20), archival work, matted and normally sold in portfolio groups. "We request exclusive area representation, if possible." Interviews are arranged by appointment for portfolio reviews. Mail queries including workprints, slides, resume and credits (incl. SASE). Reports ASAP.

Tips: "Exhibits are on hold for now. JANAPA has changed its concept toward becoming a consulting and resource organization, in which gallery viewing is arranged by appointment (except for openings). We are also seeking staff to work in sales, administrative and managerial career positions for expansion nationally. We look for exceptional work in composition, originality and technical concepts. We lean toward innovative styles, multi-imaging, abstracts, hand coloring, infrared toning. Fine art and contemporary photos sell most frequently. Submit good quality portfolio with cohesive body of work or a theme; could be style, technique or many things but must work together as a whole." Also, "learn more about galleries—how they work and what they do for you."

KENDALL CAMPUS ART GALLERY—MIAMI-DADE COMMUNITY COLLEGE, 11011 SW 104 St., Miami FL 33176-3393. (305)237-2322. Fax: (305)237-2658. Director: Robert J. Sindelir. Estab. 1970.
Exhibits: Requirements: Must be professional, creative and have an identifiable point of view. Interested in all types, styles and subjects. Example of recent exhibitions: "Images 3," by photogroup members. Presents 1-2 shows/year. Shows last 1 month. Sponsors openings; provides printing and sending of mailers and refreshments. Photographer's presence at opening preferred.
Making Contact & Terms: Interested in exhibiting work of newer, lesser-known photographers. Buys photos outright. Reviews transparencies. Interested in framed or unframed, mounted or unmounted, matted or unmatted work. Submit portfolio for review. Send material by mail for consideration. SASE. Reports in 1-2 weeks.

KIRKLAND ART CENTER, P.O. Box 213, East Park Row, Clinton NY 13323. (315)853-8871. Activities Coordinator: Elizabeth Hunt. Estab. 1960.
Exhibits: Interested in "all types/styles/subjects which are suitable for a community arts center. Only serious art, not work aimed at a commercial market, will be considered." Work "must be approved by the exhibition committee." Examples of recent exhibitions: "Photograms" by Judith Mohns; "Remembering: Women and Their Relationships" by Susan Landgraf; and "KAC Photography Annual." Presents 2-3 shows/year. Shows last 3½ weeks. Sponsors openings; "We send out and print black & white announcement cards, provide a wine and cheese reception, and encourage a talk by the artist." Photographer's presence at opening preferred.
Making Contact & Terms: Charges 25% commission. No size limits or restrictions on photography. Send material by mail for consideration. SASE. Reports within 2 months, "after review by exhibition committee."
Tips: The opportunities for photographers in galleries are "less than with other media such as painting/sculpture, but all artists are considered by the KAC. The quality of the work, not the resume, is the major consideration." Sees trend toward "more experimental works—combining photography with other media." Interest of public in buying photography "seems to remain stable . . . not great and yet not indifferent. People here are unwilling to pay high prices for any artwork."

LA MAMA LA GALLERIA, 6 E. First Street, New York NY 10003. (212)505-2476. Director/Curator: Lawry Smith. Estab. 1982.
Exhibits: Interested in all types of works. Looking for "movement, point of view, dimension." Examples of recent exhibitions: "Color Explosion," by Susan Islam (Turks); "Juxtaposed Gender," by Charles Justina (strongmen, nudes and lace); "Body Politic," by Don Gerron (people in bathtubs). Presents 2 shows/year. Shows last 3 weeks. Sponsors openings. Photographer's presence at opening required.
Making Contact & Terms: Very receptive to exhibiting work of newer, lesser-known photographers. Charges 20% commission. General price range: $200-2,000. Prices set by agreement between director/curator and photographer. Reviews transparencies. Interested in framed or unframed, mounted, matted or unmatted work. Requires exclusive representation within metropolitan area. Arrange a personal interview to show portfolio. Send material by mail for consideration. SASE. Reports in 1 month.
Tips: "Be patient; we are continuously booked 18 months-2 years ahead."

*LA PETITE GALERIE, 138 Church St., Burlington VT 05401. (802)865-3057. Owner: Jean Johnson. Estab. 1991.
Exhibits: Requirements: framed work only. Black and white or color, not over 3×5. Interested in scenic and wildlife. Examples of recent exhibitions: works by Al Stromerson, Dave Walsh, Stan Kirschner and Jim Sheehan. Presents 1 show/year. Shows last 30 days. Sponsors openings; provides publicity and reception. Photographer's presence preferred at opening and during show.
Making Contact & Terms: Interested in receiving work from newer, lesser-known photographers. Charges 40% commission. General price range: $100-500. Reviews transparencies. Interested in framed, matted or unmatted work only. Query with resume of credits. Query with samples. Send material by mail for consideration. "Or visit gallery." SASE. Reports in 3 weeks.
Tips: "Be a team player, these are group shows."

LEEDY-VOULKOS GALLERY, 1919 Wyandotte, Kansas City MO 64108. (816)474-1919. Director: Sherry Leedy. Estab. 1985.
Exhibits: Requirements: Photographer must have "an established exhibition record." Open to all styles and subject matter. Examples of recent exhibitions: Linda Robbennolt (Polaroids and Cibachromes); Peter Feldstein (cliches verre) and Michael Eastman. Shows last 6 weeks. Sponsors openings. Photographer's presence at opening preferred.
Making Contact & Terms: Charges 50% commission. General price range: $200-900. Reviews transparencies. Interested in framed or unframed work. Requires exclusive representation within metropolitan area. Send slides by mail for consideration. SASE. Reports in 1 month.
Tips: "Visit the gallery to get the general 'feel' of work exhibited."

LEWIS LEHR INC., Box 1008, Gracie Station, New York NY 10028. (212)288-6765. Director: Lewis Lehr. Estab. 1984. Private dealer.
Making Contact & Terms: Charges 50% commission. Buys photography outright. General price range: $500 plus. Reviews transparencies. Interested in mounted or unmounted work. Requires exclusive representation within metropolitan area. Query with resume of credits. SASE. Member AIPAD.
Tips: Vintage American color sells best. Sees trend toward "more color and larger" print sizes. To break in, "knock on doors." Do not send work.

■**THE LIGHT FACTORY PHOTOGRAPHIC ARTS CENTER**, P.O. Box 32815, Charlotte NC 28232. (704)333-9755. Contact: Gallery Manager. Nonprofit. Estab. 1972.
Exhibits: Requirements: Photographer must have a professional exhibition record for main gallery. Interested in contemporary and vintage art photography, documentary photography, any subject matter. Presents 8-10 shows/year. Presents 8-10 shows/year. Shows last 1-2 months. Sponsors openings; reception (3 hours) with food and beverages, artist lecture following reception. Photographer's presence at opening preferred.
Making Contact & Terms: Photography sold in the gallery. "Artists price their work." Charges 33% commission. Rarely buys photography outright. General price range: $500-12,000. Reviews transparencies. Write for gallery guidelines. Query with resume of credits and slides. Artist statement required. SASE. Reports in 2 months.
Tips: Among various trends such as fine art prints and documentary work, "we are seeing more mixed media using photography, painting, sculpture and videos. We have several smaller galleries to show work from up and coming photographers." Currently, documentary and landscape subjects are selling best through this gallery. "In general we are interested in the work as a whole and how the ideas have been expressed in the work. The photographs should also be a cohesive body of work which reflect the artist intent and purpose."

LIGHT IMPRESSIONS SPECTRUM GALLERY, 439 Monroe Ave., Rochester NY 14607. Gallery Director: Lance Speer. Estab. 1985.
Exhibits: Requirements: "Shows 19th and 20th century silver and non-silver photography by photographers of national reputation." Examples of exhibits: "Aaron Siskind: Photogravures & Platinum Prints," (large format gravures); "Duane Michals: The Nature of Desire," (silver photographic prints); "Italy by Armchair: Stereographs and Their Antecedents," (large format etchings, albumen prints, and stereographs, by multiple artists and photographers). Presents 8 shows/year. Shows last 4-6 weeks. Sponsors openings; provides invitations, press releases and food and beverage for the opening. Photographer's presence at opening preferred.
Making Contact & Terms: Charges 40% commission. General price range: $300-3,500.
Tips: Sees continued trend toward individual expressive directions, eclecticism and a rejection of some of the ideas of the Postmodern Aesthetic. Currently selling best are traditional high-focus landscapes as well as the untraditional and emerging technology based imagery.

*****LITE RAIL GALLERY**, 912 12th St., Sacramento CA 95814. (916)441-1013. Director: Michael Xepoleas. Estab. 1989.
Exhibits: Send slides, photographs and bio or resume along with $10 screening fee to gallery. Interested in "historical eventmaking, world history tragedies, abstract, realism photo collage. Examples of recent exhibits: "Lite Rail National," by Iona Datcu (mixed media, abstract); "Chernobyl Memories," by Igor Kostin; representational work by Robert Dolan. Presents 4 shows/year. Shows last 4 weeks. Sponspors openings on second saturday of each month. Photographer's presence at opening is not required, presence during show is not required.
Making Contact & Terms: "We exclusively deal with emerging talent." Charges 40-50% commission. General price range: $300-2,000. Reviews transparencies. Interested in seeing framed work only. Works are limited to 24 × 48 maximum. Submit portfolio for review material by mail for consideration. SASE. Reports in 1 month: "for juried exhibitions more time is required to review portfolios.

Tips: "Be prepared to send 1-3 pieces of artwork at any one time. Be patient with our screening process. Be prepared to ship artwork at artist's expense. We represent artists and help develop good marketing material. Tinted photographs are a big seller. The public likes the texture, styles and subject matter."

© Igor Kastin

This photo of workers at the Chernobyl nuclear plant in the former Soviet Union shows the devastation created after the plant exploded in 1986. The shot was included in an exhibition, Chernobyl Memories Not To Be Forgotten. Michael Xepoleas, owner of Lite Rail Gallery in Sacramento, California, says photographer Igor Kastin still shoots images at Chernobyl despite the fact that he has been diagnosed with leukemia.

*LOUISVILLE VISUAL ART ASSOCIATION,** 3005 Upper River Rd., Louisville KY 40207. (502)896-2146. Exhibition Coordinator: Al Gorman. Estab. 1909.
Exhibits: Requirements: Contemporary. Shows last 6 weeks. Sponsors openings; provides invitations, food, wine, press support. Photographer's presence at opening and during show preferred.
Making Contact & Terms: Charges 30% commission. General price range: $50-5,800. Reviews transparencies. No size limitations. Send material by mail for consideration. SASE.

*LYSOGRAPHICS FINE ART.,** 722 S. Meramec Ave., St. Louis MO 63105. (314)726-6140. Owner: Esther Lyss. Estab. 1970.
Making Contact & Terms: Interested in reviewing work from newer, lesser-known photographers. Reviews transparencies. Interested in seeing framed or unframed work. Arrange a personal interview to show portfolio. SASE. Reports in 1-2 weeks.
Tips: "Please call me and briefly describe your work. I am a private gallery and sell mostly 'on request.' When I do commercial installations, I do like to present photographs."

*M.C. GALLERY,** 400 1st Ave. N., Minneapolis MN 55401. (612)339-1480. Fax: (612)339-1480. Director: M.C. Anderson. Estab. 1984.
Exhibits: Interested in avant-garde work. Examples of recent exhibitions: works by Gloria Dephilips Brush, Ann Hofkin and Catherine Kemp. Shows last 6 weeks. Sponsors openings; attended by 2,000-3,000 people. Photographer's presence preferred at opening and during show.

Making Contact & Terms: Interested in receiving work from newer, lesser-known photographers. Charges 50% commission. General price range: $300-1,200. Reviews transparencies. Interested in framed or unframed work. Requires exclusive representation within metropolitan area. Submit portfolio for review. Query with resume of credits. Send material by mail for consideration. Material will be returned, but 2-3 times/year. Reports in 1-2 weeks if strongly interested, or it could be several months.

MARBLE HOUSE GALLERY, 44 Exchange Place, Salt Lake City UT 84111. (801)532-7332. Owner: Dolores Kohler. Estab. 1988.
Exhibits: Requirements: Professional presentation, realistic pricing and numerous quality images. Interested in painterly, abstract and landscapes. No documentary or politically-oriented work. No nudes. Examples of recent exhibitions: include the works of John Stevens and Dolores Kohler. Presents 2 shows/year. Shows last 1 month. As a member of the Salt Lake Gallery Association, there are monthly downtown gallery strolls. Also provide public relations, etc. Photographer's presence at opening preferred.
Making Contact & Terms: Interested in receiving work from newer, lesser-known photographers. Charges 50% commission. Buys photos outright. General price range: $50-1,000. Reviews transparencies. Interested in framed or unframed work, mounted or unmounted work, matted or unmatted work. Requires exclusive representation within metropolitan area. No size limits. Arrange a personal interview to show a portfolio. Submit portfolio for review. Query with resume of credits. Query with samples. Send material by mail for consideration. SASE. Reports in 1 month.

MARI GALLERIES OF WESTCHESTER, LTD., 133 E. Prospect Ave., Mamaroneck NY 10543. (914)698-0008. Director: Carla Reuben. Estab. 1966.
Exhibits: Requirements: "Must review work, a few originals to exhibition size and smaller photos or slides of body of work. Price list required." Interested in b&w and color exhibitions. "The works must have a cohesive theme or idea." Examples of recent exhibitions: Lange Mozian (colorized antique photographs); Arthur Goldenberg (color photography landscapes); and Gary Strausberg (nature photography). Presents 8 shows/year. Shows last 4-5 weeks. "We do a direct mailing to our customers and send a press release describing each artist to our press list. Beverage and food at opening reception for artists." Photographer's presence at opening required.
Making Contact & Terms: Charges 50% commission. General price range: $100-800. Reviews transparencies. Interested in framed or unframed work. Requires exclusive representation within metropolitan area. Arrange a personal interview to show a portfolio. SASE. Reports in 1-2 weeks.

MARSH ART GALLERY, University of Richmond, Richmond VA 23173. (804)289-8276. Fax: (804)287-6006. Director: Richard Waller. Estab. 1966.
Exhibits: Interested in all subjects. Examples of recent exhibitions: "Mountaineers to Main Streets: The Depression Years 1935-41"; "Builder Levy: Images of Appalachian Coalfields"; "The Encompassing Eye: Photography as Drawing." Presents 2-3 shows/year. Shows last 4 weeks. Photographer's presence at opening preferred.
Making Contact & Terms: Charges 10% commission. Reviews transparencies. Interested in framed or unframed, mounted or unmounted, matted or unmatted work. Work must be framed for exhibition. Query with resume of credits. Query with samples. Send material by mail for consideration. Reports in 1 month.
Tips: If possible, submit material which can be left on file and fits standard letter file. "We are a nonprofit university gallery interested in presenting contemporary art."

ERNESTO MAYANS GALLERIES, 601 Canyon Rd., Santa Fe NM 87501. (505)983-8068. Fax: (505)982-1999. Owner: Ernesto and Leonor Mayans. Estab. 1977.
Exhibits: Examples of recent exhibitions: "Cholos/East L.A.," by Graciela Iturbide (b&w); "Fresson Images," by Doug Keats (Fresson) and "Selected Works," by André Kertész (b&w). Publishes catalogs and portfolios."
Making Contact & Terms: Charges 50% commission. Buys photos outright. General price range: $200-5,000. Reviews transparencies. Interested in framed or unframed, mounted or unmounted work. Requires exclusive representation within area. Shows are limited to up to 16×20. Arrange a personal interview to show portfolio. Send material by mail for consideration. SASE. Reports back in 1-2 weeks. "Please call before submitting."
Tips: "Despite small exhibition space and large stable, we have theme invitationals."

MINOT ART GALLERY, P.O. Box 325, Minot ND 58701. (701)838-4445. Director: Judith Allen. Estab. 1970.
Exhibits: Examples of recent exhibitions: wildlife photos by Pat Gerlach; "Landscapes of Scotland," by Martin Guppy; and "The Color of Ireland," by Susan Hayden. Presents 3 shows/year. Shows last about 1 month. Sponsors openings; "the first Sunday of each month is usually when we have each exhibit's grand opening."

© Graciela Iturbide

Ernesto Mayans, president of Ernesto Mayans Gallery Ltd. in Santa Fe, New Mexico, says he appreciates the work of photographer Graciela Iturbide because of her direct treatment of subjects and the way she sees an image while creating it. Such was the case for this gelatin silver print, "Cuarto Pescaditos."

Making Contact & Terms: Very receptive to work of newer, lesser-known photographers. Charges 30% commission. General price range: $25-150. Submit portfolio or at least six examples of work for review. Prefer transparencies. SASE. Reports in 1 month.
Tips: "Wildlife, landscapes and floral pieces seem to be the trend in North Dakota. We get many slides to review for our 3 photography shows a year. Do something unusual, creative, artistic. Do not send postcard photos."

MONTEREY PENINSULA MUSEUM OF ART, 559 Pacific St., Monterey CA 93940. (408)372-5477. Fax: (408)372-5680. Director: Jo Farb Hernandez. Estab. 1969.
Exhibits: Interested in all subjects. Examples of recent exhibitions: "Morley Baer: 40 Years of Photographs," by Morley Baer; "People/Landscapes 1940s-1960s," by William Heick; "Photographic Views of Meiji: a Portrait of Old Japan"; and "Camera Work: Photographers 1903-1917." Presents 4-6 shows/year. Shows last approximately 6-12 weeks. Sponsors openings.
Making Contact & Terms: "Very receptive" to working with newer, lesser-known photographers. Buys photography outright. NPI. Reviews transparencies. Work must be framed to be displayed; review can be by slides, transparencies, unframed or unmatted. Send material by mail for consideration. SASE. Reports in 1 month.
Tips: Send 20 slides and resume at any time to the attention of the museum director.

THE MUSEUM OF CONTEMPORARY PHOTOGRAPHY, COLUMBIA COLLEGE CHICAGO, 600 S. Michigan Ave., Chicago IL 60605-1996. (312)663-5554. Fax: (312)360-1656. Director: Denise Miller-Clark. Assistant Director: Ellen Ushioka. Estab. 1984.
Exhibits: Interested in fine art, documentary, photojournalism, commercial, technical/scientific. "All high quality work considered." Examples of recent exhibitions: "Open Spain/Espana Abierta" (contemporary documentary Spanish photography/group show); "The Duane Michals Show," by Duane Michals (b&w narrative sequences, surreal, directorial); "Irving Penn: Master Images," by Irving Penn (b&w fashion, still life, portraiture). Presents 5 main shows and 8-10 smaller shows/year. Shows last 8 weeks. Sponsors openings, provides announcements.
Making Contact & Terms: "We do exhibit the work of newer and lesser known photographers if their work is of high professional quality." Charges 30% commission. Buys photos outright. General price range: $300-2,000. Reviews transparencies. Interested in reviewing unframed work only, matted or unmatted. Submit portfolio for review. SASE. Reports in 2 weeks. No critical review offered.
Tips: "Professional standards apply; only very high quality work considered."

MUSEUM OF PHOTOGRAPHIC ARTS, 1649 El Prado, Balboa Park, San Diego CA 92101. (619)239-5262. Assistant to the Director: Cathy Boemer. Estab. 1983.
Exhibits: "The criteria is simply that the photography be the finest and most interesting in the world, relative to other fine art activity. MoPA is a museum and therefore does not sell works in exhibitions. There are no fees involved." Examples of recent exhibitions: "Picturing California: A Century of Photographic Genius" (1851-1988, more than 70 photographers, b&w and color); "Seduced by Life: The Art of Lou Stoumen" (b&w); "Mary Ellen Mark: 25 Years" (b&w documentary). Presents 6-8 exhibitions annually from 19th century to contemporary. Each exhibition lasts approximately 2 months. Exhibition schedules planned 2-3 years in advance. The Museum holds a private Members' Opening Reception for each exhibition.
Making Contact & Terms: For space, time and curatorial reasons, there are few opportunities to present the work of newer, lesser-known photographers. Send resume of credits with a portfolio (unframed photographs) or slides. Portfolios may be submitted for review with advance notification. Files are kept on contemporary artists for future reference. Send return address and postage. Reports in 3 weeks.
Tips: "Exhibitions presented by the museum represent the full range of artistic and journalistic photographic works." There are no specific requirements."The executive director/curator makes all decisions on works that will be included in exhibitions. There is an enormous stylistic diversity in the photographic arts. The Museum does not place an emphasis on one style or technique over another."

NEIKRUG PHOTOGRAPHICA LTD., 224 E. 68th St., New York NY 10021. (212)288-7741. Fax: (212)737-3208. Owner/Director: Marjorie Neikrug. Estab. 1970.
Exhibits: Interested in "photography which has a unique way of showing the contemporary world. Special needs include photographic art for our annual Rated X exhibit." Examples of recent exhibitions: "A Guerrilla of Photography," by Stephan Lufino; "Intimate Impressions," by Marie-Claire Montanari. Sponsors openings "in cooperation with the photographer." Photographer's presence preferred.
Making Contact & Terms: Interested in receiving work from newer, lesser-known photographers. Charges 50% commission. Price range: $100-5,000. Requires exclusive representation in metropolitan area. Call to arrange an appointment or submit portfolio in person. SASE. Size: 11 × 14, 16 × 20 or 20 × 30.
Tips: "We are looking for meaningful and beautiful images—images with substance and feeling! Show us themes, organization of work, print interpretation and originality. Edit work carefully and make it easy for the viewer. Have neat presentation." Nudes and color landscapes currently sell best at this gallery.

NEVADA MUSEUM OF ART, (formerly Cassaza Graphics Gallery), 160 W. Liberty St., Reno NV 89501. (702)329-3333. Curator of Art: Howard Spencer. Estab. 1931.
Exhibits: Requirements: Nationally emerging photographers with art photography, 19th-20th century historic development, new trends. Examples of recent exhibitions: "Contemporary Basque Photography," group show organized in Spain; "Gus Bundy," artist's work from the permanent collection; "Selections From the Permanent Collection," featuring a number of recent photographic donations. Presents 10-12 shows/year in various media. Shows last 6-8 weeks. Sponsors openings; provides catered reception for up to 400 people, book signings, etc. Photographer's presence at opening preferred.
Making Contact & Terms: Charges 40% commission—not first priority. General price range: $75-2,000. Reviews transparencies. Interested in framed or unframed work. Does not require exclusive representation, but doesn't work with people who have already had recent exposure in the area. Query with samples. Send material by mail for consideration. SASE. Expect delay in reply.
Tips: "Be mature in style with consistent body of work." Opportunities are fair "if photographer prepares his work." Museum exhibits "a wide variety of art, including photography. It is a tax-exempt, not for profit institution."

*NEW GROUND GALLERY., 1286 Gilman St., Berkeley CA 94706. (510)525-7621. Fax: (510)234-6092. Owner: Brigitte Micmacker. Estab. 1992.
Exhibits: Must have a coherent body of work. Must offer something different, challenging in subject matter or in technique. Good technique. Adequate framing. Interested in art photography, abstract, maniuplated, mixed media, photo collage. Examples of recent exhibitions: works by Robin Lasser (b&w and color prints); Jeanne O'Connor (hand-painted film); and Merj Ross (b&w abstracted forms). Presents 2-3 shows/year. Shows last two months. Sponsors openings; provides reception for the artists, invitations sent, press release. Photographer's presence at opening is required.
Making Contact & Terms: Interested in reviewing work from newer, lesser-known photographers. Charges 50% commission. General price range: $150-800. Reviews transparencies. Interested in framed, mounted and matted work only. Works should be no smaller than 11 × 14. SASE. Reports in 1 month.
Tips: "We are not interested in journalistic or 'postcard' type photography."

NORTHERN ILLINOIS UNIVERSITY ART GALLERY IN CHICAGO, Suite 306, 212 W. Superior, Chicago IL 60610. (312)642-6010. Director: Peggy Doherty. Estab. 1985.
Exhibits: Requirements: Must be producing high-quality work in a series or within a theme. Interested in fine art, documentary and experimental. Examples of recent exhibitions: "Family Albums," by William Frederking & Martina Lopez; "A Portfolio," by Brad Temkin; "Formal Gardens," by Kate Roth. Presents 2-4 shows/year. Shows last 6 weeks. Photographer's presence at opening preferred.
Making Contact & Terms: Interested in reviewing work of newer, lesser-known photographers. Photographers may arrange sales with buyers, but gallery does not do the selling. General price range: $100-700. Reviews transparencies. Interested in matted or unmatted work. Send material by mail for consideration. SASE. Reports ASAP.
Tips: "Submit a body of cohesive work, at least 10-15 images on a theme."

*NYE GOMEZ GALLERY., 836 Leadenhall St., Baltimore MD 21230. (410)752-2080. Fax: (410)576-0418. Director: Lynn O'Sullivan. Estab. 1988.
Exhibits: Interested in work exploring human relationships or having psychological dimensions. Provocative work accepted. "We are a full-scope gallery (paintings, prints, sculpture, photography). One specialty is male and female figurative photography. Work must be innovative. We will not accept traditional nude or portraiture work." Examples of recent exhibitions: Abstract figurative, by Connie Imboden (gsp, 16×20); interpretation of figure, by Robert Flynt (color c and cibachrome, 11×14 to 30×40); "Gender Relationships," by Jim Long (gsp, 11×14). Presents 3-4 photo shows/year. Shows last 1 month. Sponsors openings; provides advertising, mailings, opening receptions. Photographer's presence at opening is required, presence during show is preferred.
Making Contact & Terms: Interested in reviewing work from newer, lesser-known photographers. Charges 50% commission. General price range: $150-2,000. "Initially will only review transparencies and resume; may later request to see actual work." Requires exclusive representation within metropolitan area or Mid-Atlantic region." No "walk-ins" please. SASE. Reports 1-2 months.
Tips: "We are looking for new work. If it's already been done, or is traditional nudes, or lacks a focus or purpose, we are not the gallery to contact! We find that more provocative figurative work sells best. For all our top figurative photographers, we are their top selling gallery in the world."

O.K. HARRIS WORKS OF ART, 383 W. Broadway, New York NY 10012. (212)431-3600. Director: Ivan C. Karp. Estab. 1969.
Exhibits: Requirements: "The images should be startling or profoundly evocative. No rock, dunes, weeds or nudes reclining on any of the above or seascapes." Interested in urban and industrial subjects and cogent photojournalism. Examples of recent exhibitions: "Chinatown" (color display transparencies) by Andrew Garn; "Montorgueil, Paris" (warm-tone b&w photos) by Arthur Gerbault; "Appalachian People" (gelatine silver prints) by Shelby Lee Adams. Presents 5-8 shows/year. Shows last 3 weeks.
Making Contact & Terms: Charges 40% commission. General price range: $350-1,200. Interested in matted or unmatted work. Appear in person, no appointment: Tuesday-Saturday 10-6. SASE. Reports back immediately.
Tips: "Do not provide a descriptive text."

OLIN FINE ARTS GALLERY, Washington & Jefferson College, Washington PA 15301. (412)222-4400. Contact: Paul Edwards. Estab. 1982.
Exhibits: Requirements: Photographer must be at least 18 years old, American citizen and artists assume most show costs. Interested in large format, experimental traditional photos. Examples of recent exhibitions: one-person show by William Wellman; "The Eighties" by Mark Perrott. Presents 1 show/year. Shows last 3 weeks. Sponsors openings; pays for non-alcoholic reception if artist attends. Photographer's presence at opening preferred.
Making Contact & Terms: Charges 20% commission. General price range: $50-1,500. Reviews transparencies. Interested in framed work only. Shows are limited to works that are no bigger than 6 feet; subject matter that is not for publication. Send material by mail for consideration. SASE. Reports in 1 month.

✿OPEN SPACE ARTS SOCIETY, 510 Fort St., Victoria, British Columbia V8W 1E6 Canada. (604)383-8833. Director: Sue Donaldson. Estab. 1972.
Exhibits: Interested in photographs as fine art in an experimental context, as well as interdisciplinary works involving the photograph. No traditional documentary, scenics, sunsets or the like. Examples

The asterisk before a listing indicates that the market is new in this edition. New markets are often the most receptive to freelance submissions.

of recent exhibitions: "Bed of Roses," (sexual imagery); "Companēras de Mexico," (Mexican women) and "Carnet Photographique," by Joanne Tremblay (female model). Presents 5 shows/year. Shows last 3-4 weeks. Sponsors openings.
Making Contact & Terms: Interested in receiving work from newer, lesser-known photographers. General price range: $100-1,000. Pays the C.A.R.F.A.C. fees; no commission. Query with transparencies of work. SASE. Reports 2 times a year.
Tips: "Submit 10-20 slides and artist statement of what the work is about or how you feel about it. Send for information about Open Space to give you an idea of how large the space is." Sees trend in multi-media installation work where photography is used as part of a larger artwork.

ORLANDO GALLERY, Dept. PM, 14553 Ventura Blvd., Sherman Oaks CA 91403. (818)789-6012. Directors: Robert Gino, Don Grant. Estab. 1958.
Exhibits: Interested in photography demonstrating "inventiveness" on any subject. Examples of recent exhibitions: landscapes by Kevin Lynch; figurative by Anthony Hall; figurative by Greg Gorman and Randee St. Nicholas. Shows last 4 weeks. Sponsors openings. Photographer's presence at opening and during show is preferred.
Making Contact & Terms: Very receptive to work of newer photographers. Charges 50% commission. Price range: $600-3,000. Query with resume of credits. Send material by mail for consideration. SASE. Framed work only. Reports in 1 month. Requires exclusive representation in area.
Tips: Make a good presentation.

PHOTOGRAPHIC IMAGE GALLERY, 208 SW First, Portland OR 97204. (503)224-3543. Director: Guy Swanson. Estab. 1984.
Exhibits: Interested in primarily mid-career to contemporary Master-Traditional Landscape in color and b&w. Examples of recent exhibitions: "Trains" by O. Winston Link; and "My Tibet" by Galen Rowell. Presents 12 shows/year. Shows last 1 month. Sponsors openings. Photographer's presence at opening preferred.
Making Contact & Terms: Charges 50% commission. General price range: $300-1,500. Reviews transparencies. Requires exclusive representation within metropolitan area. Query with resume of credits. SASE. Reports in 1 month.
Tips: Current opportunities through this gallery are fair. Sees trend toward "more specializing in imagery rather than trying to cover all areas."

■**PHOTOGRAPHIC RESOURCE CENTER**, 602 Commonwealth Ave., Boston MA 02215. (617)353-0700. Fax: (617)353-1662. Curator: John P. Jacob.
Exhibits: Interested in contemporary and historical photography and mixed-media work incorporating photography. "The photographer must meet our high quality requirements." Examples of recent exhibitions: "The Silence of the Passing Time," by Vistan (Wieslaw Brzoska); "Message Carriers," (Contemporary Native American); "Camera As Weapon: Worker Photography Between the Wars." Presents 5-6 group thematic exhibitions in the David and Sandra Bakalar Gallery and 8-10 one- and two-person shows in the Natalie G. Klebenov Gallery/year. Shows last 6-8 weeks. Sponsors openings; provides receptions with refreshments for the Bakalar Gallery shows.
Making Contact & Terms: Interested in receiving work from newer, lesser-known photographers. Will review transparencies. Interested in matted or unmatted work. Query with samples or send material by mail for consideration. SASE. Reports in 2-3 months "depending upon frequency of programming committee meetings."
Tips: "The PRC is a nonprofit gallery."

PHOTO-SPACE AT ROCKLAND CENTER FOR THE ARTS, 27 S. Greenbush Rd., West Nyack NY 10994. (914)358-0877. Executive Director: Julianne Ramos. Estab. 1947.
Exhibits: Requirements: Geographic Limits: Rockland, Westchester and Orange counties in New York and Bergen County in New Jersey. Interested in all types of photos. Examples of recent exhibitions: "Second Thoughts" by Ned Harris and "Photo Structures" by Gordon Rapp. Presents 4-5 shows/year. Shows last 2 months. Photographer's presence at opening preferred.
Making Contact & Terms: Charges 33% commission. General price range: $250-2,500. Reviews transparencies. Interested in matted or unmatted work. Shows are limited to 32×40. Query with samples. Send material by mail for consideration. SASE. Reports in 3 months.

 The maple leaf before a listing indicates that the market is Canadian.

PRAKAPAS GALLERY, #3C, 800 Prospect St., La Jolla CA 92037-4204. (619)454-1622. Fax: (619)454-9686. Director: Eugene J. Prakapas. Estab. 1976.

Exhibits: "Primary interest is Modernism of the 20s and 30s. But, we are interested in any work that is not just good or accomplished but remarkable – genuinely outstanding." Examples of recent acquisitions: Boris Ignatovich, Lazlo Moholy-Nagy and Raoul Ubac. "Our specialty is historical work and at the moment we are doing no exhibitions."

Making Contact & Terms: Commission received "depends entirely upon the situation." Buys photography outright. General price range: $500-100,000. Reviews transparencies, "but only if we request them – i.e., if prior arrangements are made." Requires exclusive representation within metropolitan area. Query with resume of credits. "We are not interested in seeing unsolicited material."

Tips: Opportunities offered photographers by galleries in general are "excellent, better than ever before. But in exhibiting a photographer's work, a gallery makes a substantial commitment in terms of reputation and money. If a photographer hopes for/expects such commitment, he should ensure that his submission reflects at least equal commitment on his part. All too often, submissions are sloppy, haphazard and unprofessional – an immediate turnoff."

QUEENS COLLEGE ART CENTER, Benjamin S. Rosenthal Library, Queens College, Flushing NY 11367-6701. (718)997-3770. Fax: (718)997-3753. Director: Suzanna Simor. Curator: Alexandra de Luise. Estab. 1952.

Exhibits: Requirements: Open to all types, styles, subject matter; decisive factor is quality. Photographer must be ready to deliver all the work in ready-to-be-exhibited condition and is responsible for installation, removal, transportation. Examples of recent exhibitions: "Three Mexican Photographers: Laura González, Salvador Lutteroth, Jesús Sánchez Uribe;" and "Agustín Víctor Casasola: Photographs of the Mexican Revolution . . ." Presents 2-4 shows/year. Shows last 1 month. Sponsors openings. Photographer is responsible for providing/arranging, refreshments and cleanup. Photographer's presence at opening required, presence during show preferred.

Making Contact & Terms: Charges 40% commission. General price range: $100-500. Interested in framed or unframed, mounted or unmounted, matted or unmatted work. Arrange a personal interview to show portfolio. Query with resume of credits. Query with samples. Send material by mail for consideration. Submit portfolio for review. SASE. Reports in 2-4 weeks.

RANDOLPH STREET GALLERY, 756 N. Milwaukee Ave., Chicago IL 60622. (312)666-7737. Exhibitions Director: Paul Brenner. Estab. 1979.

Exhibits: Exhibits work in all media, mostly in group exhibitions dealing with a specific topic, theme, social issue or asthetic concept. Examples of recent exhibitions: "Project Space," by Doug Ischar; "Who Discovers/Who Discolors," by Esther Parada. Presents 7 shows/year. Shows last 5 weeks. Sponsors openings; provides publicity brochure for exhibition. Photographer's presence at opening preferred.

Making Contact & Terms: NPI. Reviews slides. Interested in framed or unframed, mounted or unmounted, matted or unmatted work. Send material by mail for consideration. SASE. Reports in 1-4 months, depending on when the slides are received.

Tips: "We review quarterly and view slides only. We are a nonprofit exhibition space, therefore we do not represent artists, but can facilitate sales through the artist's gallery or directly through artist."

*RED MOUNTAIN GALLERY, Truckee Meadows Community College, 7000 Dandini Blvd., Reno NV 89512. (702)673-7084. Gallery Director: Erik Lavritzen. Estab. 1990.

Exhibits: Interested in all styles, subject matter, techniques – less traditional, more innovative and/or cutting edge. Examples of recent exhibits: "Tents," by Wendy Erickson (16 × 120 Cibachrome prints); recent work by Hal Honigbsburg (mixed media constructions). Number of photography exhibits presented each year depend on jury. Shows last 1 month. Sponsors openings; catered through school food service. Photographer's presence at opening is preferred.

Making Contact & Terms: Interested in reviewing work from newer, lesser-known photographers. Charges 20% commission. General price range: $100-700. Reviews transparencies. Interested in seeing matted work only. Send slides, material by mail for consideration (35mm glassless dupes). Work is reviewed once a year.

Tips: "Slides submitted should be sharp, accurate color and clearly labeled with name, title, dimensions, medium – the clearer the vitae the better. Statements not important!" Sees trend toward "less aesthetic concerns and explorations. Recession has dropped sales dramatically."

 The solid, black square before a listing indicates that the market uses various types of audiovisual materials, such as slides, film or videotape.

ROBINSON GALLERIES, 3514 Lake St., Houston TX 77098. (713)526-0761. Fax: (713)526-0763. Director: Thomas V. Robinson. Estab. 1969.
Exhibits: Requirements: Archivally framed and ready for presentation. Limited editions only. Work must be professional. Not interested in pure abstractions. Examples of recent exhibitions: Works by Pablo Corral (Cibachrome) and Ron English (b&w). Presents 1 show every other year. (Photographs included in all media exhibitions one or two times per year.) Shows last 4-6 weeks. Sponsors openings; provides invitations, reception and traditional promotion.
Making Contact & Terms: Charges 50% commission. General price range $100-400. Reviews transparencies. Interested in framed or unframed, matted or unmatted work. Requires exclusive representation within metropolitan area. Arrange a personal interview to show portfolio. Submit portfolio for review. Query with resume of credits. SASE. Reports in 1-2 weeks.
Tips: "Robinson Galleries is a fine arts gallery first, the medium is second."

*ROCKRIDGE CAFE, 5492 College Ave., Oakland CA 94618. (415)653-6806. Manager: Tom Hile. Estab. 1973.
Exhibits: "We show what we like, the only restrictions having to do with the fact that this is a family restaurant." Presents 10 exhibits/year. Shows last 6 weeks. "We will accommodate a reception."
Making Contact & Terms: Very interested in receiving work from newer, lesser-known photographers. NPI. Reviews transparencies. Interested in framed or unframed, mounted, matted or unmatted work. Accepts photos up to 3 × 6 feet. Query with samples. Send material by mail for consideration. Submit portfolio for review–"2 or 3 pieces as would be shown plus slides." SASE. Reports after receiving sample. Reports promptly.
Tips: Does not buy photos outright. Interested buyers will be referred to photographers. "Artists are responsible for hanging and taking down their work."

*THE ROSSI GALLERY., 2821 McKinney Ave., Dallas TX 75204. (214)871-0777. Fax: (214)871-1343. Owner: Hank Rossi. Estab. 1987.
Exhibits: Pay shipping both ways. Interested in black and white film noir. Challenging work and conceptual are preferred. Examples of recent exhibits: "Visions of the West," by Skeeter Hagler (b&w); photography by Natalie Caudill (mixed media photographs); "Spirit," by David Chasey (b&w). Presents 2 shows/year. Shows last 1 month. Sponsors openings; provides refreshments, invitations. Photographer's presence at opening required.
Making Contact & Terms: Interested in reviewing work from newer, lesser-known photographers. Charges 40% commission. General price range: $400-1500. Reviews transparencies. Interested in mounted, matted, or unmatted work only. Query with samples. SASE. Reports in 1 month.
Tips: "Be responsible and prompt. Figurative work is very strong."

SANTA BARBARA CONTEMPORARY ARTS FORUM, 2nd Floor, 653 Paseo Nuevo, Santa Barbara CA 93101. (805)966-5373. Fax: (805)962-1421. Director: Nancy Doll. Estab. 1976.
Exhibits: Requirements: Noncommercial photographers, although photojournalists are considered. Interested in works that deal with contemporary, aesthetic, critical and social issues. Examples of recent exhibitions: "Fire on Film," a group exhibition of the 1990 Santa Barbara Fire; "The Guiding Light," by Marta Peluso (b&w documentary); "Homeland," by Kathryn Clark (color installation-related work). Presents 1 or 2 shows/year, "but interested in more." Shows last 6-8 weeks. Sponsors openings; artist asked to give gallery talk. Photographer's presence at opening preferred.
Making Contact & Terms: NPI. Submit slides and resume for review. Send material by mail for consideration. Appointments *must* be arranged in advance. SASE. Reports in 4-6 weeks.
Tips: "Please note: CAF is a nonprofit alternative exhibition space."

MARTIN SCHWEIG STUDIO AND GALLERY, 4658 Maryland Ave., St. Louis MO 63108. (314)361-3000. Gallery Director: Cena Pohl.
Exhibits: Requirements: Photographs must be matted to standard frame sizes. Interested in all types, expecially interested in seeing work that pushes the boundaries of photography, in technique and subject. Examples of recent exhibitions: "Surfaces" by Yvette Drury Dubinsky and "Florence and Abroad" by Stan Strembicki. Presents 8 shows/year. Shows last 1 month. Sponsors openings. Photographer's presence at opening preferred.
Making Contact & Terms: Charges 40% commission. General price range: $100-700. Interested in mounted or matted work. Submit portfolio for review. Query with samples. SASE. Reports in 1 month.
Tips: "Our show schedule is decided by a panel of jurors. Usually a portfolio must be submitted twice."

SECOND STREET GALLERY, 201 Second St. NW, Charlottsville VA 22902. (804)977-7284. Executive Director: Paige Turner. Estab. 1973.
Exhibits: Requirements: Request exhibition guidelines. Presents 2-3 shows/year. Shows last 1 month. Sponsors openings. Photographer's presence at opening required.
Making Contact & Terms: Charges 30% commission. General price range: $250-2,000. Reviews transparencies. Interested in unmatted work only. Submit 10-12 slides for review. SASE. Reports in 6-8 weeks.

*MICHAEL SHAPIRO GALLERY, 3rd Floor, 250 Sutter St., San Francisco CA 94108. (415)398-6655. Owners: Michael Shapiro and Heather Shapiro. Estab. 1980.
Exhibits: Interested in "all subjects and styles. Superior printing and presentation will catch our atttention." Examples of exhibitions: Aaron Siskind (b&w); Andre Kertesz (b&w); and Vernon Miller (platinum). Shows last 4-6 weeks. Sponsors openings.
Making Contact & Terms: Very interested in receiving work from newer, lesser-known photographers. General price range: $500-50,000. Arrange a personal interview to show portfolio. SASE.
Tips: "Classic, traditional" work sells best.

THE SILVER IMAGE GALLERY, 318 Occidental Ave. S., Seattle WA 98104. (206)623-8116. Director: Dan Fear. Estab. 1973.
Exhibits: Interested in traditional landscapes, nudes and women photographers. Examples of recent exhibitions: "40 Women Photographers: An Historical Preview" (40 photographers); "the Classic Nude" (50 photographers); "Gordon Whitten: Abstract Journey—Visions into the Great American Desert" (color Cibachrome prints).
Making Contact & Terms: Somewhat interested in receiving work of newer, lesser-known photographers; constitutes 20% of work shown annually. General price range: $250 and up.
Tips: "A 'business-like' attitude is important. A good artist has mastered his/her technical skills and has a unique vision. I also try to figure out if the artist has any idea about the realities of selling photographs and making a living at it. Buying public is most interested in high quality, large format, beautiful prints and works by women photographers. Subjects include landscape, nudes, portraits, still lifes."

*SOUTH SHORE ART CENTER, INC., 119 Ripley Rd., Cohasset MA 02025. (617)383-9548. Executive Director: Lanci Valentine. Estab. 1954.
Exhibits: Interested in "all types of fine arts photography." Examples of recent exhibits: "Juried Photography" (all media, no theme), 100 selected from 350 entries; "Boone & Petit" (figurative sp. fx; silver prints) by Tom Boone/Tom Petit; "Beyond Photography" (special effects) by Kim DeNunzio, Linda Getger, Elaine Croce, Eleanor Gorman. Presents at least 2 shows/year—all New England (juried) and at least 1 invitational. Shows last 4 weeks. Sponsors openings; cost of announcements with photo (usually 5×7 b&w); all opening costs of juried shows. Artists pay part of costs of an invitational show (gallery rental). Photographer's presence at opening is preferred.
Making Contact & Terms: Very interested in receiving work from newer, lesser-known photographers. Charges 40% commission. Charges $8/piece for juried shows; $100/person for invitational group shows. General price range: $100-500. Reviews transparencies. Interested in exhibiting framed work only. Limitations: work "must be framed in wood or metal—no bare glass edges." Send resume and slide sheet.
Tips: "Traditional" work sells best.

*SPIRIT SQUARE CENTER FOR THE ARTS, 345 N. College St., Charlotte NC 28202. (704)372-9664. Fax: (704)377-9808. Curator of Exhibitions: Ken Bloom. Estab. 1975.
Exhibits: Requirements: must be able to present a cogent body of work and be responsible for effective presentation. Interested in wide ranging work; no tourism. Examples of recent exhibitions: documentary (b&w) by Robert Amberg; miscellaneous regional artists (experimental use and mixed media). Presents 6-8 shows/year. Shows last 6-8 weeks. Sponsors openings. Photographer's presence at opening preferred.
Making Contact & Terms: Interested in receiving work from newer, lesser-known photographers. Chares 40% commission. General price range: $80-1,500. Reviews transparencies. Interested in framed or unframed, mounted or unmounted. Submit portfolio for review. Send material by mail for consideration. SASE. Reports quarterly.
Tips: "The work has to be able to maintain its strength within the presence of other media—painting, sculpture, fiber arts."

Market conditions are constantly changing! If you're still using this book and it's 1995 or later, buy the newest edition of Photographer's Market *at your favorite bookstore or order directly from Writer's Digest Books.*

STATE OF ILLINOIS ART GALLERY, Suite 2-100, 100 W. Randolph, Chicago IL 60601. (312)814-5322. Director: Kent Smith. Assistant Director: Jane Stevens. Estab. 1985.
Exhibits: Requirements: Must be a resident of Illinois or have had a strong connection with Illinois. Interested in historic and contemporary art. Examples of recent exhibitions: "Life's Lessons," by Bea Nettles (b&w Polaroid); "Spirited Visions," by Patty Carroll (color portraits) and "A New Vision for Chicago," by Moholy-Nagy (b&w photograms). Presents 2 shows/year. Shows last 2 months. Sponsors openings; provides refreshments. Photographer's presence at opening and during show preferred.
Making Contact & Terms: NPI. "We do not sell photos, only exhibit work." Reviews transparencies. Send slides, "if we are interested we will arrange appointment." SASE. Work juried twice a year.

SUNPRINT CAFE & GALLERY, 638 State St., Madison WI 53703. (608)255-1555. Director: Rena Gelman. Estab. 1976.
Exhibits: Interested in all types of photography; 2-3 of 7-8 shows a year feature photography. "We get far more 'nature-photo' submissions than we could ever use. We look for a well-developed eye and a unique voice or statement." Professional quality—but not interested in slick comercially oriented work. Style and subjects can vary. "We are interested in non silver, color and/or b&w work." Examples of recent exhibitions: "Natural Extracts," by Erik Moshen (Cibachrome); handpainted archival and other photos by Dianne Francis and Andy Kraushaar; and "Poland," by Wendy Mukluk (b&w photos).
Making Contact & Terms: Very receptive to exhibiting the work of newer, lesser-known photographers. General price range: $100-400. Call for more information. Framed work only. "We need 1 month to view each portfolio; expect a follow-up letter from us. Include a SASE for return of slides."
Tips: "We have a restaurant and gallery business which encourages work to be viewed in a relaxed atmosphere. Lots of natrual light and track lighting. We schedule 6-week shows. Artists usually sell 0-3 pieces during show. Low-cost work sells more."

*SUNY PLATTSBURGH ART MUSEUM, SUNY College at Plattsburgh, Plattsburgh NY 12901. (518)564-2813 or (518)564-2178. Director: Edward Brohel. Estab. 1969.
Exhibits: "Professional work only." Presents "about 2 shows per year." Shows last 7 weeks. Sponsors openings. "Generally 4 gallery spaces have openings on the same day. One general reception, or tea, is held. It varies as to which gallery hosts." Photographer's presence at opening preferred.
Making Contact & Terms: Interested in receiving work from newer, lesser-known photographers. General price range: $25-200. Reviews transparencies. Interested in framed work only. Requires exclusive representation to a degree within metropolitan area. Send material by mail for consideration or submit portfolio for review. Returns material "if requested—some are kept on file." Reporting time "varies with gallery pressures."
Tips: "Be serious, be yourself and think."

UNION SQUARE GALLERY/ERNST HAAS VIEWING ROOM, 118 E. 17th St., New York NY 10003. (212)777-8393. Fax: (212)614-0688. Director: Todd Weinstein. Estab. 1980.
Exhibits: Interested in all types. "We show a lot of emerging artists." Examples of recent exhibitors: Ed Grazda (b&w photography); Maggie Steber (color photography); and Arlene Gottfried (color photography). Presents 6-7 shows/year. Shows last 6 weeks. Photographer's presence at opening required.
Making Contact & Terms: General price range: $250-1,200. Call. SASE.
Tips: "Get to know the gallery and follow shows."

*UNIVERSITY ART GALLERY NEW MEXICO STATE UNIVERSITY, Dept. 3572, P.O. Box 30001, Las Cruces NM 88003. (505)646-2545. Director: Karen R. Mobley. Extab. 1973.
Exhibits: Examples of recent exhibitions: permanent collection, by Graciela Iturbide (portrait photo); "Close to the Border" by Dellhah Montoya (portrait photo); permanent collection, by Celia Munoz (color photo/conceptual). Presents approx. 1 show/year. Shows last 6 weeks. Sponsors openings; provides curatorial, registration and shipping. Photographer's presence at opening required, presence during show preferred.
Making Contact & Terms: Buys photos outright. General price range: $100-1,000. Interested in framed or unframed work. Arrange a personal interview to show portfolio. Submit portfolio for review. Query with samples. Send material by mail for consideration. SASE. Reports in 1 month.
Tips: "The gallery does mostly curated, thematic exhibitions. Very few one-person exhibitions."

*VERED GALLERY, 68 Park Place, East Hampton NY 11937. (516)324-3303. Fax: (516)324-3303. Vice President: Janet Lehr. Estab. 1977.
Exhibits: Requirements: Submit slides with biography and SASE. Interested in avant-garde work. Examples of recent exhibitions: works by Duane Michal, Kelsey Lehr and Russell Munson. Shows last 3 weeks. Sponsors openings. Photographer's presence at opening preferred.
Making Contact & Terms: Charges 50% commission. General price range $350 ("vintage"). Reviews transparencies. Interested in slides or transparencies, then exhibition prints. Requires exclusive representation within metropolitan area. Query with resume of credits. SASE. Reports in 3 weeks.

VIRIDIAN GALLERY, 24 W. 57 St., New York NY 10019. (212)245-2882. Director: Kari Staubo. Estab. 1968.

Exhibits: Interested in eclectic. Member of Cooperative Gallery. Examples of recent exhibitions: works by Munk Abrahamson and Robert Smith. Presents 1-2 shows/year. Shows last 3 weeks. Photographer's presence at opening preferred.

Making Contact & Terms: Is receptive to exhibiting work of newer photographers "if members are cooperative." Charges 30% commission. General price range: $200-600. Will review transparencies only if submitted as membership application. Interested in framed or unframed, mounted, and matted or unmatted work. Request membership application details. Send materials by mail for consideration. SASE. Reports in 3 weeks.

Tips: Opportunities for photographers in galleries are "improving." Sees trend toward "a broad range of styles" being shown in galleries. "Cibachromes seem a 'given.' There are fewer hand-painted and altered types of work. More abstracts. The buying public seems open to this, too. The less 'complicated' and explicit pieces sell best. Presentation is vital! Initially, at least, offer less 'explicit' work. Be persistent!!"

VISION GALLERY INC., 1155 Mission St., San Francisco CA 94103. (415)621-2107. Fax: (415)621-5074. President: Joseph G. Folberg. Interested in contemporary and vintage 19th century. Estab. 1980.

Exhibits: Presents 8 shows/year. Shows last 6 weeks. Sponsors openings. Photographer's presence at opening is preferred.

Making Contact & Terms: Receives 50% commission. Buys photography outright. General price range: $200-15,000. Interested in mounted work only. Cannot return material. Arrange a personal interview to show portfolio. Submissions of slides only; must send SASE. Reports immediately.

Tips: "Landscapes, stills and nudes sell best."

■**WASHINGTON PROJECT FOR THE ARTS,** 400 Seventh St., NW, Washington DC 20004. (202)347-4813. Fax: (202)347-8393. Executive Director: Donald Russell. Estab. 1975.

Exhibits: Interested in still, video, film and installation exhibitions examining contemporary issues, community involvement, emphasizing innovation and risk; with a particular interest in work which examines the impact of cultural identity on the individual. "WPA primarily assists artists in the early stages of their careers, and gives recognition to talented mid-career artists who have been unable to gain exposure through more traditional venues." Examples of recent exhibitions: "Options 1993" (street photos & political issues) Ken Ashton & Mary Klein; "Gazing Into Fire" (photo montage-psychological) Joe Mills. Presents 4 shows/year. Shows last 6 weeks. Sponsors openings; "Artist honoraria ($200-1,000) provided to artists participating with WPA's exhibitions. The fees can be used for travel to the opening." Photographer's presence at opening preferred.

Making Contact & Terms: Interested in receiving work from newer, lesser-known photographers. NPI. Reviews transparencies. Send material by mail for consideration. SASE. Reports in 2 months.

Tips: In samples, looks for "good slides, clearly defined concept, unusual approaches, social impact."

WATERS GALLERY (formerly Wiesner Gallery, Ltd.), 425 W. 13th St., New York NY 10014. (212)675-8722. Acting Director: Craig Killy.

Exhibits: Requirements: Must have high quality works. Interested in all types of work. Examples of recent exhibitions: b&w works by John Milisenda; "Pictures From Here to There," by George Zimmermann (silver prints); and "Eye of a Camera," by Fred R. Tannery (silver prints). Presents 3-4 shows/year. Shows last 3-4 weeks. Sponsors openings; provides invitations and opening reception. Photographer's presence at opening and during show preferred.

Making Contact & Terms: Charges 50% commission. General price range: $200-10,000. Reviews transparencies. Interested in matted work only. Arrange a personal interview to show portfolio. Send material by mail for consideration. SASE. Reports in 1 month.

Tips: "Only serious photographers need to apply."

WESTCHESTER GALLERY, County Center, White Plains NY 10606. (914)684-0094. Fax: (914)684-0608. Gallery Coordinator: Jonathan G. Vazquez-Haight.

Exhibits: Requirements: submit 10 slides or actual work to be juried by panel of artists. Examples of recent exhibitions: works by Susi Dugaw, Ed Fausty and Howard Stern. Presents usually 2 photo shows/year. Shows last 1 month. Sponsors openings; gallery covers cost of space, light, insurance, mailers (printing and small mailing list) and modest refreshments. Photographer's presence at opening preferred.

Making Contact & Terms: Charges 33⅓% commission. General price range $150-5,000. Reviews transparencies. Interested in any presentable format ready to hang. Arrange a personal interview to show portfolio. Submit portfolio for review. Query with resume of credits. Send material by mail for consideration. SASE. Reports in 1 month.

Tips: "Most sales are at low end, $150. Gallery space is flexible and artists are encouraged to do their own installation."

CHARLES A. WUSTUM MUSEUM OF FINE ARTS, Dept. PM, 2519 Northwestern Ave., Racine WI 53404. (414)636-9177. Director: Bruce W. Pepich.
Tips: Interested in all fine art photography. It's regularly displayed in our Art Sales and Rental Gallery and the Main Exhibition Galleries. Sponsors biennial show limited to residents of Wisconsin; the sales and rental gallery is limited to residents of the Midwest. Many new and lesser-known photographers are featured. There is no limit to applicants for solo or group exhibitions, but they must apply in November of each year. Presents an average of 3 shows/year. Shows last 4-6 weeks. Sponsors openings. "We provide refreshments and 50 copies of the reception invitation to the exhibitor." Photographer's presence at opening preferred.
Making Contact & Terms: "Many of our exhibitors are emerging artists." Charges 40% commission from exhibitions, 40% from sales and rental gallery. General price range: $125-350. Will review transparencies. Interested in framed or unframed work. "Must be framed unless it's a 3-D piece. Sale prices for sales and rental gallery have a $1,000 ceiling." Query with resume of credits or send material by mail for consideration. SASE.
Tips: "Photography seems to fare very well in our area. Both the exhibitors and the buying public are trying more experimental works. The public is very interested in presentation and becoming increasingly aware of the advantage of archival mounting. They are beginning to look for this additional service. Our clients are more interested in work of newer (and more affordable) photographers. Landscapes currently sell best at our gallery." Sees trend toward "increasing uses of combinations of drawing and painting media with photography. We always look for the best quality in the photographs we exhibit. The technical process involved is not as important to us as the idea or message in the work."

Galleries/'93-'94 changes

The following markets appeared in the 1993 edition of *Photographer's Market* but are not listed in the 1994 edition. They may have been omitted for failing to respond to our request for updated information, they may have gone out of business or they may no longer wish to receive freelance work.

Alan Gallery (did not respond)
Alber Galleries (did not respond)
Art Museum of Southeast Texas (did not respond)
Artists Foundation Gallery at Cityplace (did not respond)
A-Space Gallery (unable to locate)
Barron Arts Center (did not respond)
Hank Baum Gallery (did not respond)
Berkshire Artisans Gallery (did not respond)
Bird-In-Hand Gallery (did not respond)
Blanden Memorial Art Museum (did not respond)
Brent Gallery (did not respond)
Broken Diamond (did not respond)
William Campbell Contemporary Art (did not respond)
Canton Art Institute (did not respond)
City of Los Angeles Photography Centers (did not respond)
Wilson W. Clark Memorial Library Gallery (did not resond)

David Clay Gallery (did not respond)
Converse College Milliken Gallery (did not respond)
Gallery at Cornerstone (did not respond)
Hyde Park Art Center (did not respond)
Images (out of business)
Jeb Gallery (did not respond)
Kent State University School of Art Gallery (did not respond)
Robert Klein Gallery (did not respond)
John Michael Kohler Arts Center (did not respond)
Lehigh University Art Galleries (did not respond)
Marlboro Gallery (did not respond)
Moreau Galleries (did not respond)
New Orleans Museum of Art (did not respond)
Northport/B.J. Spoke Gallery (did not respond)
Pace/MacGill Gallery (did not respond)
Palo Alto Cultural Center (did not respond)
Photo Gallery at Portland

School of Art (did not respond)
Photo Graphia Gallery (out of business)
Photography Gallery (did not respond)
Queen Emma Gallery (did not respond)
Quincy College/Gray Gallery (did not respond)
Real Art Ways (did not respond)
Holly Ross Assoc. (did not respond)
Rotunda Gallery (did not respond)
Somerstown Gallery (did not respond)
Tampa Museum of Art (did not respond)
University of Massachusetts Medical Center Gallery (did not respond)
Visual Studies Workshop Gallery (did not respond)
Edward Weston Fine Art (did not respond)
White Gallery-Portland State University (did not respond)
Woodstock Gallery of Art (did not respond)

Paper Products

If you want to sell photos and succeed in the greeting card industry, don't get discouraged if your work is not purchased by the three majors, which consistently corner over 80 percent of the market.

Although the greeting card industry is dominated by the big three producers, American Greetings, Gibson Greetings and Hallmark, there still is plenty of room for companies that focus on certain niches. Cards with regional appeal, humorous themes or those sold at extra low prices quite often are produced and marketed by smaller businesses, filling a void left by the larger companies. There are over 1,000 greeting card companies in the United States which sell over 7 billion cards annually. While there is a lot of competition for sales, opportunities do exist for freelancers who can consistently supply fresh ideas. Each year, for example, over 2 billion Christmas cards are sold. Success for one or two unique holiday images could develop into hefty royalty checks.

If you want to succeed in this field it is imperative that you research the marketplace and know what cards are displayed at retail shops. By examining the field you can cut down on the time and money you waste mailing inappropriate submissions. You also will improve your chances of making sales.

Within the paper products field there is a variety of potential buyers, including companies which produce greeting cards, posters and calendars. It is a field that uses a multitude of different images, from playful pets and children to nudes and boudoir.

Building a rapport

After your initial research, query to the companies you are interested in working with and send a stock photo list. Since these companies receive large volumes of submissions, they often appreciate knowing what is available rather than actually receiving it. This kind of query can lead to future sales even if your stock inventory doesn't meet their needs at the time because they know they can request a submission as their needs change. Some listings in this section advise sending quality samples along with your query while others specifically request only the list. As you plan your queries, it's important that you follow their instructions. It will help you establish a better rapport with the companies from the start.

Some larger companies have staff photographers for routine assignments, but also look to freelancers to supply images. Usually, this is in the form of stock images, and images are especially desirable if they are of unusual subject matter or remote scenic areas for which assignments — even to staff shooters — would be too costly. Freelancers are usually offered assignments once they have established a track record with a company and demonstrate a flair for certain techniques, subject matters or locations. Also, smaller companies are more receptive to working with freelancers, though they are less likely to assign work because of smaller budgets for photography.

The pay in this market can be quite lucrative if you can provide the right image at the right time for a client desperately in need of it, or if you develop a working relationship with one or a few of the better paying markets. You should be aware, though, that one reason for higher rates of payment in this market is that these companies may want to buy all rights to images. With changes in the copyright law, many companies are more willing to negotiate sales which specify all rights for limited time periods or exclusive product rights rather than complete surrender of copyright.

Another key consideration is that an image with good market value is effectively taken out of the market during the selection process. Many paper products companies work on lead times of up to two years before products are ready to market. It can be weeks, months or as much as a year before they report to photographers on their interest in using their images. In addition, some companies will pay only on publication or on a royalty basis after publication. For these reasons as well as the question of rights, you may want to reconsider selling images with high multiple resale potential in this market. Certainly, you will want to pursue selling to companies which do not present serious obstacles in these ways or which offer exceptionally good compensation when they do.

One tendency within this market which photographers should also keep in mind is varying degrees of professionalism among the companies. For instance, some smaller companies can be a source of headaches in a number of ways, including failing to report in a timely manner on submissions, delaying return of submissions or using images without authorization. This sometimes happens with the seemingly more established companies, too, though it's less common. Typically, many smaller companies have started as one- or two-person operations, and not all have acquired adequate knowledge of industry practices which are standard among the more established firms.

Since smaller firms usually offer the freelancer more opportunity in terms of breaking in and learning the industry, it's best not to write them off entirely but study them sufficiently before doing business with them.

One final note for those of you interested in this field. The Greeting Card Creative Network (GCCN) is an organization designed to help photographers, writers and artists in the greeting card field. The group provides access to a network of industry professionals, including publishers and licensing agents and acts as a clearinghouse for information on design and marketing trends, and legal and financial concerns within the industry. Annual membership fees in GCCN range from $40 (students) to $70 (professional artists). For more information, contact GCCN, Suite 760, 1200 G Street NW, Washington DC 20005. (202)393-1780.

ACME GRAPHICS, INC., Box 1348, Cedar Rapids IA 52406. (319)364-0233. Fax: (319)363-6437. President: Stan Richardson. Estab. 1913. Specializes in printed merchandise for funeral directors.
Needs: Religious, nature. Reviews stock photos.
Making Contact & Terms: Interested in receiving work from newer, lesser-known photographers. Query with samples. Send unsolicited photos by mail for consideration. Uses 35mm transparencies; color contact sheets; color negatives. SASE. Reports in 2 weeks. Pays $50/b&w photo; $50/color photo. Also, pays according to price set by photographer. **Pays on acceptance.** Buys all rights.

ADVANCED GRAPHICS, (see Angel Graphics).

AFRICA CARD CO., INC., Box 91, New York NY 10108. (718)672-5759. President: Vince Jordan. Specializes in all occasion cards.
Needs: Buys 25 photos annually. Submit seasonal material 2 months in advance. Submit model release with photo.
Making Contact & Terms: Call to arrange an appointment. Query with resume of credits. Submit material by mail for consideration. Uses 5×7 color glossy prints; 35mm, 2¼×2¼ transparencies. SASE. Reports in 6-10 weeks. Pays $15 minimum/color photo. Buys all rights.
Tips: "Do an assortment of work and try to be as original as possible."

ALASKA WILD IMAGES, P.O. Box 13149, Trapper Creek AK 99683. (907)733-2467. Editorial Director: Rollie Ostermick. Estab. 1976. Specializes in greeting cards, postcards and posters. Photo guidelines free with SASE.
Needs: Assigns minimum of 5 freelance photos/year. Alaskan and Canadian wildlife and wilderness. Does not want non-Alaska/Canadian material. Reviews stock photos. Model release preferred. Seldom uses people in photos; if they are recognizable must have release. Captions preferred.
Making Contact & Terms: Interested in receiving work from newer, lesser-known photographers. Query with stock photo list. Uses 35mm, 2¼×2¼ or 4×5 transparencies. SASE. Reports in 1 month. Pays $100 and up/color photo. Pays on publication. Credit line given. Buys exclusive product rights; negotiable. Simultaneous submissions and previously published work OK.
Tips: Looking for "dramatic close-ups of wildlife, wildflowers and awesome scenics, especially with pleasant mood lighting. We print primarily once a year and contact photographers to request submissions and to discuss actual needs prior to this time."

AMERICAN ARTS & GRAPHICS, INC., 10915 47th Ave. W., Everett WA 98117. (206)353-8200. Fax: (206)348-6296. Licensing Director: Shelley Pedersen. Estab. 1948. Specializes in posters. Photo guidelines free with SASE.
Needs: Works with 3-4 freelance photographers/month. Humorous, cute animals, exotic sports cars, male and female models (no nudes), some scenic. Images that would be appealing to our 12-20-year-old poster market. Submit seasonal material 5 months in advance. Reviews stock photos. Model release required.
Making Contact & Terms: Contact by phone to request guidelines. Uses 2¼×2¼, 4×5, 8×10 transparencies. SASE. Reports in 2 weeks. Pays $500 or more/color photo. **Pays on acceptance.** Credit line given. Buys poster rights only. Simultaneous submissions and previously published work OK (if not posters).
Tips: "Subject and style must appeal to our young, teenage market. A good way to get a feel for what we do is to look at our poster rack in your area."

*AMERICAN GREETINGS, 10500 American Rd., Cleveland OH 44144. (Prefers not to share information.)

ANGEL GRAPHICS, division of Angel Gifts Inc., P.O. Box 530, Fairfield IA 52556. (515)472-5481. Fax: (515)472-7353. Photo Editor: Jay Kreider. Estab. 1982. Specializes in posters, framing prints and wall decor.
Needs: Buys 100 photos/year. Assigns 10-15 photos/year. Seeks photos of wildlife, including endangered species, humorous, religious and inspirational, cute cats, dogs, scenics, celebrities, American Indians, African-American ethnic, florals and still life. Does not want risque or abstract photos. Model/property release preferred. Captions preferred.

Making Contact & Terms: Submit portfolio for review. Query with samples with SASE. Uses 35mm, 2¼×2¼, 4×5, 8×10 transparencies. "Bigger is better." Samples kept on file. "Do not send originals." Reports in 1 month. Pays $100-600/color photo; $100-500/b&w photo; negotiable. Pays upon usage. Credit line "depends on artist's needs." Buys exclusive product rights; negotiable. Simultaneous submission and previously published work OK.
Tips: "Must have sharp focus. We like colorful pieces. We need pieces that appeal to the general public (mall-type shoppers). Any piece that is well done, that all your friends would love to put on their walls is what we want to put in our catalog. We see a trend toward earth awareness."

ANGLER'S CALENDARS, 4955 E. 2900 N., Murtaugh ID 83344. (208)432-6625. Fax: (208)432-6625. Editor: Barbara Wolverton. Estab. 1975. Specializes in calendars.
 • This company received a Silver Award in 1992 from the Calendar Marketing Association in the category of Best Theme and a Gold Award in the category of Most Creative Marketing Application.
Needs: Buys 60 photos/year. Fly fishing, decoys, saltwater fishing, wildlife, waterfowl, deer and bass fishing. Examples of recently published calendars: "Angler's Calendar," "Decoy Calendar" and "Saltwater Fishing Calendar" (monthly photos). Reviews stock photos. Model release preferred. Captions required—include location and species of fish or animal.
Making Contact & Terms: Query with stock photo list. Uses 35mm, 2¼×2¼ and 4×5 transparencies. SASE. Reports in 2 weeks. Pays $50-200/color photo. Pays on publication. Credit line given. Buys one-time rights. Previously published work OK if advised of previous publication and date.
Tips: Interested in action shots; no dead fish or animals. "Look at past calendars to see style and format." In portfolios or samples, make a "neat presentation—clean and insured."

ART RESOURCE INTERNATIONAL LTD./BON ART, Fields Lane, Brewster NY 10509. (914)277-8888. Fax: (914)277-8602. Vice President: Robin Bonnist. Estab. 1980. Specializes in posters and fine art prints. Photo guidelines free with SASE.
Needs: Buys 500 images/year. Interested in all types but does not wish to see regional. Accepts seasonal material anytime. Model release required. Captions preferred.
Making Contact & Terms: Interested in receiving work from newer, lesser-known photographers. Send unsolicited photos by mail for consideration. Submit portfolio for review. Works on assignment only. Uses 35mm, 4×5 and 8×10 transparencies. SASE. Reports in 1 month. Pays $50-250/photo. Pays on publication. Credit line given if required. Buys all rights; exclusive reproduction rights. Simultaneous submissions and previously published work OK.
Tips: Looks for "new and exciting material; subject matter with universal appeal."

*ATLANTA MARKET CENTER, 240 Peachtree St. NW, Atlanta GA 30303. (404)220-2000. Creative Director: Peter Gordy. Estab. 1960. Specializes in wholesale gifts, apparel.
Needs: Buys 10 images annually. Offers 3 assignments/year. Interested in fashion, furniture. Reviews stock photos: sports. Model/property release required. Captions required.
Making Contact & Terms: Interested in receiving work from newer, lesser-known photographers. Query with samples. Works on assignment only. Uses 8×10 matte color and b&w prints; 35 mm transparencies. Keeps samples on file. Pays $500-1,000/day; $250-500/job. **Pays on acceptance.** Buys all rights; negotiable. Considers simultaneious sumbissions.
Tips: "Our needs vary a lot."

*AVANTI PRESS, #602, 84 Wooster St., New York NY 10012. (212)941-9000. Fax: (212)941-8008. Picture Researcher: Nathalie Goldstein. Specializes in greeting cards. Photo guidelines free with SASE.
Needs: Buys approximately 250 images annually; all supplied by freelancers. Offers 50 assignments annually. Interested in humorous, narrative, colorful, simple, to the point; also babies, children, animals (in humorous situations). Has specific deadlines for seasonal material. Does not want travel, sunsets, landscapes, nudes, high-tech. Reviews stock photos. Model/property release required.
Making Contact & Terms: Interested in receiving work from newer, lesser-known photographers. Submit portfolio for review. Uses color and b&w prints; 35mm, 2¼×2¼, 4×5, 8×10 transparencies. SASE. Reports in 1 month. NPI. Pays on license. Credit line given. Buys 5-year worldwide, exclusive card rights.
Tips: "Know our product. Think outside of the dots."

A bullet has been placed within some listings to introduce special comments by the editor of **Photographer's Market.**

© Allan Teger

An overriding piece of advice offered by editors and art directors is for photographers to create niches for themselves if they plan to be successful. Art Resources International liked the hand-tinted photographs of Allan Teger, of Newton, Massachusetts, and reproduced some of his work as open edition lithographs, including this shot of a French storefront.

CAROLYN BEAN PUBLISHING, LTD., 1129 N. McDowell Blvd., Petaluma CA 94954. President/Creative Director: Bruce Wilson. Specializes in greeting cards and stationery.
Needs: Buys 50-100 photos/year for the Sierra Club Note card and Christmas card series and new line of ASPCA cards. Sierra Club—wilderness and wildlife; ASPCA—cats, dogs, puppies, kittens. Submit seasonal material 1 year in advance; all-year-round review "include return postage." Publishes Christmas series December; everyday series January and May. Reviews stock photos. Prefers to see dramatic wilderness and wildlife photographs "of customary Sierra Club quality." Model release required.
Making Contact & Terms: Submit by mail. Provide business card and tearsheets to be kept on file for possible future assignments. Uses 35 mm, 2¼×2¼, 4×5 transparencies. SASE. Reports in 1 month. Simultaneous submissions and previously published work OK. Pays $250/color photo. Credit line given. Buys exclusive product rights. Anticipates marketing broader product lines for Sierra Club and may want to option other limited rights.
Tips: "Send only your best—don't use fillers."

BEAUTYWAY, Box 340, Flagstaff AZ 86002. (602)526-1812. President: Kenneth Schneider. Estab. 1979. Specializes in postcards, note cards and posters.
Needs: Buys 300-400 freelance photos/year (fee pay and joint venture). "Joint Venture is emphasized and is a program within Beautyway in which the photographer invests in his own images and works more closely in overall development. Through Joint Venture, photographers may initiate new lines or subjects with Beautyway which emanate from the photographer's strongest images." Interested in (1) Nationwide landscapes, emphasizes subjects of traveler interest and generic scenes of sea, lake and river. (2) Animals, birds and sealife, with particular interest in young animals, eyes and interaction. (3) Air, water and winter sports, as well as hiking, fishing and hunting. (4) The most important attractions and vistas of major cities, emphasizing sunset, storm, cloud and night settings. Model release required.

Making Contact & Terms: Interested in receiving work from newer, lesser-known photographers. Query with samples, stock list and statement of interests or objectives. All transparency formats OK. Ship in protective sleeves with photographer name, title and location on frame. SASE. First report averages two weeks, others vary. Pays $30 per each 2400 units printed. Usual minimum is $120 after publication. Previously published work OK if not potentially competitive.

Tips: Looks for "very sharp photos with bright colors and good contrast. Subject matter should be easily identified at first glance. We seek straightforward, basic scenic or subject shots. Obvious camera manipulation such as juxtaposing shots or unnatural filter use is almost always rejected. When submitting transparencies, the person's name, address and name and location of subject should be upon each transparency sleeve."

BOKMON DONG COMMUNICATIONS, P.O. Box 75358, Seattle WA 98125. Photo Editor: Jean Haner. Estab. 1983. Specializes in greeting cards. Send SASE for photographer's guidelines. For a sample card, send a 5×7 or larger SASE and include $1 in loose postage stamps (don't send cash or checks).

Needs: "The subject matter is not as important as the treatment. We are looking for a strong, original image that creates a mood and evokes positive feelings. It is essential that the photograph be unusual and innovative in style. A good balance of foreground and background interest, strong color, composition and lighting are important. Avoid cliches; no pictures of people. Special needs for 1994 include animals or flowers in uncommon situations." Submit seasonal material 8-12 months in advance. Reviews stock photos. Model/property release required. Captions required; include information about name of flower, animal, location of landscape.

Making Contact & Terms: Interested in receiving work from newer, lesser-known photographers. Uses any size transparencies. Reports in 2 weeks on queries; 2 months on photos. Payment negotiable; depends on purchase, $150 minimum. Pays on publication. Credit line given. Buys exclusive product rights. Simultaneous and previously published submissions OK "but not if submitted, published or sold to another card publisher."

Tips: "Read guidelines carefully! The photographer must remember the function of a greeting card—to communicate positive feelings from one person to another. The image must create a mood and have strong visual impact. The kinds of photographs we are looking for are ones that: you can recall without having to look through your files, people remember you by, are hanging on your walls." To break in, "be persistent. Study market to see what is selling. Keep submitting with our needs in mind. Avoid copying previously published material."

CATCH AMERICA, INC., 32 S. Lansdowne Ave., Lansdowne PA 19050. (215)626-7770. President: Michael Markowicz. Estab. 1988. Specializes in postcards and posters.

Needs: Contemporary. Model release required. Captions preferred.

Making Contact & Terms: Query with samples. Send unsolicited photos by mail for consideration. Uses 8×10 b&w prints and 35mm transparencies. SASE. NPI. Pays quarterly or monthly on sales. Credit line given. Rights purchased vary, but usually exclusive.

*CEDCO PUBLISHING CO., 2955 Kerner Blvd., San Rafael CA 94960. (415)457-3893. Fax: (415)457-3967. Contact: Art Dept. Estab. 1980. Specializes in calendars and picture books. Photo guidelines free with SASE.

Needs: Buys 1,500 images/year; 1,000 supplied by freelancers. Wild animals, domestic animals, nature, America, Ireland, inspirational, beaches, islands, whales, stock general and studio stock. East Coast 4×5 photos especially needed. New ideas welcome. East Coast beaches, studio ballet, music flowers. Model/property release required. Captions required.

Making Contact & Terms: Interested in receiving work from newer, lesser-known photographers. Query with non-returnable samples and a list of stock photo subjects. "Do not send any returnable material unless requested." Uses 35mm, 2¼×2¼, 4×5, 8×10 transparencies. Keeps samples on file. Reports as needed. Pays royalties on sales if whole calendar done by 1 photographer. Pays $200/b&w photo; $200/color photo; payment negotiable. Pays the December prior to the year the calendar is dated (i.e., if calendar is 1995, photographers are paid in December 1994). Credit line given. Buys one-time rights. Simultaneous submissions and previously published work OK.

Tips: No phone calls.

CHILDREN'S DEFENSE FUND, 25 E St. NW, Washington DC 20001. (202)628-8787. Fax: (202)662-3530. Production Manager: Janis Johnston. Specializes in calendars and books.

Needs: Buys 20 photos/year. Buys stock and assigns work. Wants to see children of all ages and ethnicity, serious, playful, poor, middle class, school setting, home setting and health setting. Does not want to see studio portraits. Domestic photos only. Model/property release required.

Making Contact & Terms: Provide resume, business card, self-promotion piece or tearsheets to be kept on file for possible future assignments. Uses b&w prints; 35mm, 2¼×2¼, 4×5, 8×10 transparencies. Keeps samples on file. SASE. Reports in 1-2 weeks. Pays $50-75/hour; $125-500/day; $50-150/

© photo by Dick Dietrich

Editors at DaySpring Greeting Cards appreciated the strong depth of field portrayed in this mountain scene by photographer Dick Dietrich, of Phoenix, Arizona. The peaceful setting fit in well with the overall design and meaning of this birthday card.

b&w photo. Pays on usage. Credit line given. Buys one-time rights. Previously published work OK.
Tips: Looks for "good, clear focus, nice composition, variety of settings and good expressions on faces."

CLASS PUBLICATIONS, INC., 71 Bartholomew Ave., Hartford CT 06106. (203)951-9200. Contact: Scott Moynihan. Specializes in posters.
Needs: Buys 50 images/year. Creative photography, especially humorous, cars, semi-nudes, guys, girls, etc. Interested in stock photos. Model release preferred. Captions preferred.
Making Contact & Terms: Query with samples. Submit portfolio for review. Uses b&w and color prints, contact sheets, negatives; 35mm, 2¼×2¼, 4×5 and 8×10 transparencies. SASE. Reports in 2 weeks. NPI. Pays per photo or royalties on sales. Pays on acceptance or publication. Credit line sometimes given. Buys one-time and exclusive poster rights. Simultaneous submissions and previously published work OK.
Tips: Looks for "creativity that would be widely recognized and easily understood."

COMSTOCK CARDS, #15, 600 S. Rock Blvd., Reno NV 89502. (702)856-9400. Fax: (702)856-9400. Production Manager: Gene Romaine. Estab. 1986. Specializes in greeting cards, invitations, notepads, magnets. Photo guidelines free with SASE.
Needs: Buys/assigns 20+ photos/year. Wild, outrageous and shocking adult humor only! "Do not waste our time, or yours, submitting hot men or women images." Definitely does not want to see traditional, sweet, cute, animals or scenics. "If it's appropriate to show your mother, we don't want it!" Submit seasonal material 9-10 months in advance. Model/property release required.
Making Contact & Terms: Interested in receiving work from newer, lesser-known photogaphers. Query with samples. Uses 35mm 6cm×6cm, 6cm×7cm, or 4×5 color transparencies. SASE. Reports in 3 weeks. Pays $50-150/color photo. **Pays on acceptance.** Credit line given if requested. Buys all rights; negotiable. Simultaneous submissions OK.
Tips: "Submit with SASE if you want material returned."

DAYSPRING GREETING CARDS (formerly Outreach Publications: Dayspring & Joyfully Yours Cards), P.O. Box 1010, Siloam Springs AR 72761. (501)524-9381. Fax: (501)524-8959. Research Manager: Becky Flory. Estab. 1971. Specializes in Christian greeting cards, calendars, postcards and stationery. Photo guidelines free with SASE.

Needs: Works on assignment only. Approximately 8 out of 12 images on calendars are photographs; cards and stationery, 100-200. Nature, seasonal, atmosphere, Bible still lifes (warm, not "high church"), good Victorian still lifes, wildlife, florals, water/seascapes, birds, children, cats, dogs, action sports. Submit seasonal material one year in advance. Model release required. Property release preferred.

Making Contact & Terms: Interested in receiving work from newer, lesser-known photographers. Submit portfolio for review. Provide resume, business card, self-promotion piece or tearsheets to be kept on file for possible future assignments. Uses 35mm, 2¼ × 2¼ transparencies. SASE. Reports in 3 weeks. Pays $100-300/b&w photo; $200-600/color photo. Credit line given. Buys one-time rights; negotiable.

*DeBOS PUBLISHING COMPANY, P.O. Box 36182, Canton OH 44735. (216)830-0872. Fax: (216)830-0872. Operations Director: Jennifer F. Rohl. Estab. 1990. Specializes in calendars and posters. Photo guidelines free with SASE.
Needs: Buys 24 images/year. Offers 24 assignments/year. Interested in civilian and military helicopters, in operation, all seasons. "We promote public interest in the helicopter industry." Submit seasonal material 6 months in advance. Reviews stock photos. Any helicopter photo relating to historical or newsworthy events. Model/property release required (owner of the helicopter, property release; pilot of aircraft, model release). Captions preferred; include name and address of operation and pilot; date and location of photograph(s) are recommended. DeBos Publishing Company will supply all releases.
Making Contact & Terms: Interested in receiving work from newer, lesser-known photographers. Provide resume, business card, self-promotion piece or tearsheets to be kept on file for possible future assignments. Works with freelancers on assignment only. Uses color prints; 35mm 2¼ × 2¼ and 4 × 5 transparencies. Keeps samples on file. SASE. Reports in 3 weeks. Pays $35-150/color photo. Pays when proper releases returned. Credit line given. Buys all rights; negotiable.
Tips: "Every company in the market for photography has its own view on what photographs should look like. Their staff photographers have their favorite lens, angle and style. The freelance photographer is their answer to a fresh look at the subject. Shoot the subject in your best point-of-view, and shoot it in a different way, a way people are not used to seeing. Everyone owns a camera, but the one who puts it to use is the one who generates the income. Quantity of money made should not take priority at first, but the quality and amount of work published should be your goal. If your work is good, your client will call on you time and again. Due to today's economy, companies like ourselves are keeping less photographers on staff. *Photographer's Market* allows us to successfully do so, using freelance photographers for our work. This also gives experience and income to photographers who like to work independently and on numerous subjects. This is an essential tool to both employer and employee."

DESIGN DESIGN, INC., P.O. Box 2266, Grand Rapids MI 49501. (616)774-2448. Fax: (616)774-4020. Art Director: Don Kallil. Estab. 1986. Specializes in greeting cards, calendars and gift wrap.
Needs: Buy stock images from freelancers and assigns work. Specializes in humorous, seasonal and traditional topics. Submit seasonal material one year in advance. Model/property release required. Captions preferred.
Making Contact & Terms: Submit portfolio for review. Provide resume, business card, self-promotion piece or tearsheets to be kept on file for possible future assignments. Uses color prints. Samples kept on file. SASE. Reports in 3 weeks. NPI. Pays royalties. Pays upon sales. Credit line given. Buys exclusive product rights; negotiable.

DIEBOLD DESIGNS, P.O. Box 236, High Bridge Rd., Lyme NH 03768. (603)795-4422. Fax: (603)795-4222. Owner: Peter D. Diebold. Estab. 1978. Specializes in greeting cards (Christmas).
Needs: Buys stock and assigns work. Nautical scenes which make appropriate Christmas card illustrations. Model/property release preferred.
Making Contact & Terms: Interested in receiving work from newer, lesser-known photographers. Provide self-promotion piece to be kept on file for possible future assignments. Uses color prints; 35mm, 4 × 5, 8 × 10 transparencies. Keeps samples on file. SASE. Reports in 3 weeks. Pays $100+/b&w and color photos. **Pays on acceptance.** Credit line negotiable. Buys exclusive product rights and all rights; negotiable. Simultaneous submissions and previously published work OK.
Tips: "We are seeking photos primarily for our nautical Christmas card line but would also be interested in any which might have potential for business to business Christmas greeting cards. Emphasis is on humorous situations. We have yet to acquire/publish designs using photos but are very actively in the market presently."

EPCONCEPTS, P.O. Box 363, Piermont NY 10968. (914)359-7137. President: Steve Epstein. Estab. 1983. Specializes in greeting cards, calendars, postcards, posters, stationery, gift wrap, prints.
Needs: Buys 20-30 photos/year. Children 2-5 years old and only 1-2 children in each picture. Child's face must be showing and in sharp focus. Child must be looking into the camera and engaged in childhood activity such as playing with a pet or collecting shells on a beach. Child must not be playing

The overhead view of a helicopter in flight near Niagara Falls served as a great advertisement for Rotorhead Helicopter Calendars published by DeBos Publishing Company. DeBos President Darrell DeBos says the shot was purchased for $150 from a photographer he met at an airshow. The photographer submitted numerous helicopter photos and his persistence in marketing eventually helped him make the sale.

with man-made toys. No religious. Submit seasonal material 3-6 months in advance. Reviews stock photos. Model release required.

Making Contact & Terms: Interested in receiving work from newer, lesser-known photographers. Query with samples. Send unsolicited photos by mail for consideration. Uses any size glossy or matte b&w or color prints; 35mm, 2¼ × 2¼ and 4 × 5 transparencies; b&w or color contact sheets; b&w or color negatives. SASE. Reports in 2 weeks. Pays $25/b&w or color photo. **Pays on acceptance.** Buys all rights. Previously published work OK.

Tips: Absolute must to include SASE or samples will not be returned.

FLASHCARDS, INC., 1136 N. Flagler Dr., Fort Lauderdale FL 33304. (305)467-1141. Photo Researcher: Micklos Huggins. Estab. 1980. Specializes in postcards, greeting cards, notecards and posters.

Needs: Buys 500 images/year. Humorous, human interest, animals in humorous situations, nostalgic looks, male nudes, Christmas material, valentines, children in interesting and humorous situations. No traditional postcard material; no florals or scenic. "If the photo needs explaining, it's probably not for us." Submit seasonal material 8 months in advance. Reviews stock photos. Model release required.

Making Contact & Terms: Interested in receiving work from newer, lesser-known photographers. Query with sample. Send photos by mail for consideration. Provide resume, business card, brochure, flyer or tearsheets to be kept on file for possible future assignments. Uses any size color or b&w prints, transparencies and color or b&w contact sheets. SASE. Reports in 5 weeks. Pays $100 for exclusive product rights. Pays on publication. Credit line given. Buys exclusive product rights. Simultaneous and previously published submissions OK.

GALISON BOOKS, 36 W. 44th St., New York NY 10036. (212)354-8840. Fax: (212)391-4037. Editorial Director: Sharon Kalman. Estab. 1980. Specializes in greeting cards, address bbooks, jigsaw puzzles.

Needs: Buys 50 photos/year. Sierra Club-like images, nature, animals, wild flowers, gardening. Reviews stock photos. Captions required; include location information.

Making Contact & Terms: Interested in receiving work from newer, lesser-known photographers. Query with stock photo list. Uses 2¼ × 2¼, 4 × 5 transparencies. "Do not send slides!" SASE. Pays $250 maximum/color or b&w photo. Pays on publication. Credit line given. Buys one-time rights. Previously published work OK.

*GIBSON GREETINGS INC., 2100 Section Road, Cincinnati OH 45222. (Prefers not to share information.)

GLENN ELLEN PRESS, 2 Seton Rd., Irvine CA 92715. (714)552-4295. Fax: (714)552-4170. Art Director: Robert Hutchinson. Estab. 1988. Specializes in greeting cards, calendars, framing prints. Photo guidelines free with SASE.

Needs: Buys/assigns 50-150 photos/year. Transparencies of religious art works, churches and cathedrals, archaeology, Israel, ancient Greece (ruins), monks, nature and religious subjects. Submit seasonal material 6 months to 1 year in advance. Reviews stock photos. Model release preferred. Captions preferred.

Making Contact & Terms: Query with samples. Query with list of stock photo subjects. Uses 35mm, 2¼×2¼, 4×5, 8×10 transparencies and b&w contact sheets. SASE. Reports in 1 month. Pays $25-50/b&w photo; $50-200/color photo; $25-50/hour; $100-1,500/job. Royalties negotiable. Pays on acceptance and publication. Credit line given. Buys one-time rights. Simultaneous submissions and previously published work OK.

Tips: Wants to see "one sheet of the photographer's best work in 35mm format." Sees trend toward "better color saturation and computer graphics."

© Richard Nowitz

Glenn Ellen Press Owner/President Robert Hutchinson enjoyed the clarity and framing of this city view of Jerusalem by photographer Richard Nowitz. The shot was used on the cover of a 1992 calendar Land of the Bible, as well as on an inside page. "We looked at the work of five other photographers and his was the best," says Hutchinson of Nowitz.

*GLITTERWRAP, INC., 40 Carver Ave., Westwood NJ 07679. (201)666-9700. Fax: (201)666-5444. Art Director: Danielle Grassi. Estab. 1987. Specializes in gift wrap, tote bags and accessories.

Needs: Buys 20-40 images annually for product design; buys 200+ images annually for catalog shots. Product design shots supplied by freelancers. Offers 2-3 catalog assignments, 2-4 flysheets annually. Interested in seasonal material; currently purchases only product photography; interested in expanding line to include photo subjects (i.e., wedding/Valentine's/Christmas/baby shower). Submit seasonal material 6-8 months in advance. Reviews stock photos. Model/property release required.

Making Contact & Terms: Interested in receiving work from newer, lesser-known photographers. Query with samples. Provide resume, business card, self-promotion piece or tearsheets to be kept on file for possible future assignments. Works on assignment only. Uses 4×5, 8×10 transparencies. Keeps samples on file. SASE. Reports in 3 weeks. Requires estimates based on job for product flyers;

and pays $200-500 for product designs. Pays upon usage for totes and wraps; within 30 days for catalog and flysheet work. Credit line given "if used on totes or wrap." Buys all rights; negotiable. Simultaneous submissions and/or previously published work OK.

Tips: "We generally purchase a few multi-purpose designs (i.e., party, floral). The remainder are occasion specific: juvenile birthday, adult birthday, baby showers, wedding anniversaries. Design must fit within the overlook the company is projecting. For instance, our focus is towards contemporary, fresh. Regarding product design, we're interested in finding work applicable to our line, something that will evoke emotion, strike a common chord. Regarding catalog photography, we want to see an ability to photograph a variety of surfaces, including highly reflective items."

GOES LITHOGRAPHING CO., 42 W. 61st St., Chicago IL 60621. (312)684-6700. Fax: (312)684-2065. Art Buyer: Barbara Habich. Estab. 1879. Specializes in calendars. Photo guidelines available.

Needs: Western and Eastern seaboard harbors, such as Camden Bay; fall scenes, covered bridges, period churches, Western scenes (mountains, scenics, rodeos), coastal scenes, historic sights, country, Americana; forests, streams, lakes, festivals—cultural costumes, activities and family gatherings. Does not wish to see people in any scenes submitted.

Making Contact & Terms: Send unsolicited transparencies by mail for consideration. Uses 2¼ × 2¼, 4×5 and 8×10 transparencies only; primarily 4×5's. No photographs. Always enclose envelope and return postage/insurance. Reports in 2 weeks. Pays $50-200/transparency. Buys all rights for certain lines and usage rights. "We purchase rights to republish in future years with original purchase."

Tips: "Send horizontal work. A vertical can usually be taken out of horizontal work. We seldom use veriticals. Be sure the transparencies you send have good lighting. This enhances all colors throughout the slide. Many submissions that we receive have colors which are washed out. If the subject is a desirable subject for our calendar line and the colors are flat and washed out, it will be rejected. Deep shadows are definitely discouraged for our use."

GRAND RAPIDS CALENDAR CO., 906 S. Division Ave., Grand Rapids MI 49507. Photo Buyer: Rob Van Sledright. Specializes in retail druggist calendars. Photo guidelines free with SASE.

Needs: Buys 10-12 images/year. Baby shots, family health, medical/dental (doctor/patient situations), pharmacist/customer situations, vacationing shots, family holiday scenes, winter play activities, senior citizen, beauty aids and cosmetics. No brand name of any drug or product may show. Model release required

Making Contact & Terms: Submit material January through June. Uses 5×7 and 8×10 glossy prints. SASE. Pays $10-20/photo. **Pays on acceptance.** Simultaneous submissions and previously published work OK.

‡GREETWELL, D-24, M.I.D.C., Satpur., Nasik 422 007 India. Phone: 30181. Chief Executive: Ms. V.H. Sanghavi. Estab. 1974. Specializes in greeting cards and calendars.

Needs: Buys approx. 100 photos/year. Landscapes, wildlife, nudes. No graphic illustrations. Submit seasonal material anytime throughout the year. Reviews stock photos. Model release preferred.

Making Contact & Terms: Query with samples. Uses any size color prints. SASE. Reports in 1 month. Pays $25/color photo. Pays on publication. Credit line given. Previously published work OK.

Tips: In photographer's samples, "quality of photo is important; would prefer nonreturnable copies. No originals please."

HALLMARK CARDS, INC., 2501 McGee, Drop #152, Kansas City MO 64108. (Prefers not to share information.)

IMPACT, 4961 Windplay Dr., El Dorado Hills CA 95630. (916)939-9333. Fax: (916)939-9334. Estab. 1975. Specializes in calendars, postcards, posters and books for the tourist industry. Photo guidelines free with SASE.

Needs: Buys stock and assigns work. Buys 3,000 photos/year. Offers 10-15 assignments/year. Wildlife, scenics, US travel destinations, national parks, theme parks and animals. Submit seasonal material 4-5 months in advance. Model/property release required.

Making Contact & Terms: Query with samples. Query with stock photo list. Provide resume, business card, self-promotion piece or tearsheets to be kept on file for possible future assignments. Uses 35mm, 2¼ × 2¼, 4×5, 8×10 transparencies. Keeps samples on file. SASE. Reports in 1 month. Pays $75/color photo. Pays on usage. Credit line given. Buys exclusive product rights; negotiable. Simultaneous submissions and previously published work OK.

 The double dagger before a listing indicates that the market is located outside the United States and Canada.

ARTHUR A. KAPLAN CO., INC., 460 W. 34th St., New York NY 10001. (212)947-8989. Art Director: Elizabeth Randazzo. Estab. 1956. Specializes in posters, wall decor and fine prints and posters for framing.
Needs: Buys 50-100 freelance photos/year. Flowers, scenes, animals, ballet, still life, oriental motif, musical instruments, abstracts, Americana, hand-colored and unique imagery. Reviews stock photos. Model release required.
Making Contact & Terms: Send unsolicited photos or transparencies by mail for consideration. Uses any size color prints; 35mm, 2¼×2¼, 4×5 and 8×10 transparencies. Reports in 1-2 weeks. Royalty 5-10% on sales. Offers advances. Pays on publication. Buys all rights, exclusive product rights. Simultaneous submissions OK.
Tips: "Our needs constantly change, so we need diversity of imagery. We are especially interested in images with international appeal."

KOGLE CARDS, INC., 1498 S. Lipam, Denver CO 80223. (303)795-3090. President: Patricia Koller. Estab. 1982. Specializes in greeting cards and postcards.
Needs: Buys about 12 photos/year. Thanksgiving and Christmas holiday; also humorous. Submit seasonal material 9 months in advance. Reviews stock photos. Model release required.
Making Contact & Terms: Query with samples. Will work with color only. SASE. Reports in 4 weeks. NPI; works under royalty with no advance. "The photographer makes more that way." Monthly royalty check. Buys all rights; negotiable.

LANDMARK CALENDARS, P.O. Box 6105, 51 Digital Drive, Novato CA 94948-6105. (415)883-1600. Fax: (415)883-6725. Contact: Photo Editor. Estab. 1979. Specializes in calendars. Photo guidelines free with SASE.
• Images for this market must be super quality. Newcomers should be certain that their work is strong enough to submit.
Needs: Buys/assigns 3,000 photos/year. Interested in scenic, nature, travel, sports, automobiles, collectibles, animals, food, people, miscellaneous. Does not want to see unfocused, grainy, under- and over-exposed photos; no nudes. "We accept all photos from November through February two years prior to the calendar product year. Send photos only within the terms of our guidelines." Reviews stock photos. Model release required. Captions required.
Making Contact & Terms: Unsolicited submissions are not accepted. Uses transparencies from 35mm to 8×10. Generally pays $100/photo. Pays in April of year preceding product year (i.e. would pay in April 1994 for 1995 product). Credit line given. Buys one-time and exclusive product rights, plus rights to use photo in sale material and catalogs. Previously published work OK.
Tips: Looks for "tack-sharp focus, good use of color, interesting compositions, correct exposures. Most of our calendars are square or horizontal, so work should allow cropping to these formats. For 35mm slides, film speeds higher than ASA 100 are generally unacceptable due to the size of the final image (up to 12×12)."

LOVE GREETING CARDS, INC., 1717 Opa Locka Blvd., Opa Locka FL 33054. (305)685-LOVE. Vice President: Norman Drittel. Specializes in greeting cards, postcards and posters.
Needs: Buys 75-100 photos/year. Nature, flowers, boy/girl (contemporary looks). Submit seasonal material 6 months in advance. Reviews stock photos. Model release preferred.
Making Contact & Terms: Query with samples or stock photo list. Send unsolicited photos by mail for consideration. Provide resume, business card, brochure, flyer or tearsheets to be kept on file for possible future assignments. Uses 5×7 or 8×10 color prints; 35mm, 2¼×2¼ and 4×5 transparencies; color contact sheets, color negatives. SASE. Reports in 1 month. Pays $75-150/color photo. Pays on publication. Credit line given. Buys exclusive product rights. Previously published work OK.
Tips: "We are looking for outstanding photos for greeting cards and new age posters." There is a "larger use of photos in posters for commercial sale."

McCLEERY-CUMMING COMPANY, INC., 915 E. Tyler St., Washington IA 52353. (319)653-2185. Fax: (319)653-4424. Art Director: Sandy Burns. Estab. 1903. Specializes in calendars. Photo guidelines free with SASE.
Needs: Buys stock images from freelancers. Buys 150 photos/year. Kittens and puppies (posed); hunting dogs (adult or pups, posed situation with hunting equipment); cheesecake (girls no younger than 17, in negligee or swimsuit); juvenile (4-8 years old, with or without pets); African-Americans (children doing something interesting, family, glamor); Spanish/Mexican (dancers in colorful cos-

A bullet has been placed within some listings to introduce special comments by the editor of Photographer's Market.

tumes); home interior (prefer living room or family room); cars (collectibles). Does not want to see medical, business, abstract, technology or babies. Submit seasonal material beginning in October of each year. Reviews stock photos. Model release required for people. Captions preferred.
Making Contact & Terms: Interested in receiving work from newer, lesser-known photographers. Submit resume, stock photo list, credits and tearsheets by mail. Uses 35mm, 2¼×2¼, 4×5, 8×10 sharp, bright transparencies. Samples kept on file. SASE. Reports in 1-2 weeks. NPI; negotiable. Buys one year exclusive, four year nonexclusive rights; negotiable.

NEW HEIGHTS, a division of Museum Graphics, Dept. PM, 703 Sandoval Way, Hayward CA 94544. (510)429-1452. President: Alison Jaques. Estab. 1988. Specializes in greeting cards, postcards and framing prints. Photo guidelines free with SASE.
Needs: Buys 40 photos/year. Humorous, seasonal, colorful, contemporary or cute photos. No scenic shots. Submit seasonal material 6-8 months in advance for printing. Reviews stock photos. Model release and captions required.
Making Contact & Terms: Send unsolicited photos by mail for consideration. Submit portfolio for review. Provide resume, business card, brochure, flyer or tearsheets to be kept on file for possible future assignments. Uses 8×10 b&w and color prints. SASE. Reports in 1 month. Pays 10% royalties on sales. Credit line given. Buys 10-year exclusive product rights for stationery usage. Simultaneous submissions and previously published work OK.
Tips: "New Heights is now looking for contemporary photographers to contribute to our card line. We are interested in fine art photography that is technically excellent and embodies a fresh, creative and humorous approach."

■**NORTHWORD PRESS INC.,** P.O. Box 1360, Minocqua WI 54548. (715)356-9800. Fax: (715)356-9762. Director of Photography: Robert W. Baldwin. Estab. 1984. Specializes in calendars, books, audio and videotapes. Photo guidelines free with SASE.
Needs: Buys 500+ photos/year. North American nature and wildlife, fishing, outdoor related sports such as canoeing, camping, etc. and scenics. "Do not submit anything that is even slightly soft focus. Submit only top quality originals. Do not send a lot of similars." Model/property release required. Captions required.
Making Contact & Terms: Interested in receiving work from newer, lesser-known photographers. Query with detailed stock photo list. SASE. Provide resume, business card, brochure, flyer or tearsheets to be kept on file for possible future assignments. Uses 35mm, 2¼×2¼, 4×5, 8×10 transparencies. SASE. Cannot return material. Reports in 1 month. Pays $50-500/color photo. Pays on publication. Credit line given. Buys one-time rights. Simultaneous submissions and previously published work OK.
Tips: Always looking for a different angle or point of view. Edit slides carefully. Prefer large format and Kodachrome slides. "We notify photographers by mail or phone of upcoming projects. I want to see a professional, well-presented submission that is well packaged, properly researched, and is pertinent to our product line. Be very critical, because we are."

*****P.S. GREETINGS, INC., D/B/A FANTUS PAPER PRODUCTS,** 4459 W. Division St., Chicago IL 60651. (312)384-0234. Fax: (312)384-0502. Art Director: Kevin Lahvic. Estab. 1979. Specializes in greeting cards. Photo guidelines free with SASE.
Needs: Buys 50-100 photos/year. Everyday—photo floral, photo pets, photo anniversary, photo scenery and photo religious. Christmas photos: winter scenes, religious, candles, bells, ornaments, etc. Submit Christmas and Easter material 1 year in advance. Reviews stock photos.
Making Contact & Terms: Query with resume of credits, samples and stock photo list. Send unsolicited photos by mail for consideration. Submit portfolio for review. Provide resume, business card, brochure, flyer or tearsheets to be kept on file for possible future assignments. Uses 35mm or 2¼×2¼ transparencies. SASE. Reports in 3-4 weeks. Pays $50-150/color photo. **Pays on acceptance.** Buys all rights.

PALM PRESS, INC., 1442A Walnut St., Berkeley CA 94709. (510)486-0502. Fax: (510)486-1158. Assistant Photo Editor: Theresa McCormick. Estab. 1980. Specializes in greeting cards.
Needs: Buys stock images from freelancers. Buys 100 photos/year. Wildlife, humor, nostalgia, unusual and interesting b&w and color, Christmas. Does not want abstracts or portraits. Submit seasonal material 1 year in advance. Model/property release required.
Making Contact & Terms: Query with resume of credits. Query with samples. Uses b&w and color prints; 35mm transparencies. SASE. Reports in 1-2 weeks. NPI; pays royalty on sales. Pays on usage. Credit line given. Buys exclusive product rights.
Tips: Sees trend in increased use of "occasion" photos.

PEMBERTON & OAKES, Dept. PM, 133 E. Carrillo St., Santa Barbara CA 93101. (805)963-1371. Photo Editor: Marian Groff. Specializes in limited edition lithographs and collector's porcelain plates. Photo guidelines free on request.

Needs: Buys 20-25 photos/year. Interested only in photos of children ages 2-4, with 1 or 2 children in each photo. Focus on high emotional appeal—"eye-catching, heart-stopping pictures of happy, pensive, curious, joyful children. Pictures that make one say 'I've seen my children looking just like that.' Children with pets/farm animals; out in nature a plus. Children with man made toys/objects only if child is using the object in a non-traditional, spontaneous way. Photos used as inspirations for original oils by nationally-acclaimed artist."

Making Contact & Terms: Uses any size or finish color or b&w prints; any size transparencies. Pays $1,000 minimum/color or b&w photo. Payment on acceptance. Buys all rights.

Tips: "Submit as many photos as you wish but please follow precise guidelines. We're always looking for holiday pictures—Christmas, Valentine's, Thanksgiving, Easter. No adults in picturers, only children. Candid photos best—children involved in activity, rather than looking at the camera. Will work one on one with photographers."

PORTAL PUBLICATIONS LTD., Dept. PM, Suite 400, 770 Tamalpais Dr., Corte Madera CA 94925. (415)924-5652. Fax: (415)924-7439. Art Production Coordinator: Mary Bennette. Estab. 1954. Specializes in greeting cards, calendars, posters, wall decor, framing prints, stationery, gift bags, T-shirts and note cards. Photo guidelines free with SASE.

Needs: Gives up to 400 or more assignments annually. Contemporary photography (florals, landscapes, black & white and hand-tinted black & white). Nostalgia, nature and wildlife, endangered species, humorous, animal photography, scenic, inspirational, tinted b&w children's photography, still life, garden themes and dance. Sports, travel, food and youth-oriented popular icons such as celebrities, movie posters and cars. Nothing too risque. Reviews stock photos. Model release required; captions preferred.

Making Contact & Terms: Query with samples. Submit portfolio for review. "Please limit submission to a maximum of 40 images showing the range and variety of work. All slides and transparencies should be clearly labeled and marked." Works with local freelancers on assignment only. Uses 35mm, 2¼ × 2¼, 4 × 5 and 8 × 10 transparencies. No originals; dupes only. SASE. Reports in 3 months. NPI. Payment determined by the product format. Pays on acceptance or publication. Credit line given. Buys one-time and exclusive product rights. Simultaneous submissions and previously published work OK.

Tips: "Ours is an increasingly competitive business, so we look for the highest quality and most unique imagery that will appeal to our diverse market of customers."

PRODUCT CENTRE-S.W. INC., THE TEXAS POSTCARD CO., P.O. Box 860708, Plano TX 75086. (214)423-0411. Art Director: Susan Hudson. Estab. 1980. Specializes in postcards, melamine trays and coasters.

Needs: Buys approximately 100 freelance photos/year. Texas, Oklahoma, Louisiana, Arkansas and Mississippi towns/scenics; regional (Southwest only) scenics, humorous, inspirational, nature (including animals), staged studio shots—model and/or products. No nudity. Submit seasonal material 1 year in advance. Model release required.

Making Contact & Terms: Interested in receiving work from newer, lesser-known photographers. Send insured samples with return postage/insurance. Include Social Security number and telephone number. Uses "C" print 8 × 10; 35mm, 2¼ × 2¼, 4 × 5 transparencies. SASE. No material returned without postage. Reports usually 3-4 months, depending on season. Pays up to $100/photo. Pays on publication. Buys all rights.

Tips: "Submit slides only for viewing. Must be in plastic slide sleeves and each labeled with photographer's name and address. Include descriptive material detailing where and when photo was taken. Follow the guidelines—9 out of 10 submissions rejected are rejected due to non compliance with submission guidelines."

RENAISSANCE GREETING CARDS, INC., P.O. Box 845, Springvale ME 04083-0845. (207)324-4153. Art Director: Janice Keefe. Estab. 1977. Photo guidelines free with SASE.

Needs: Buys/assigns 20-30 photos/year. "We're interested in nature photographs as well as images that are artsy, nostalgic, dramatic, innovative and humorous. Special treatment such as hand tinted b&w images are also of interest." No animals in clothing, risqué or religious. Submit seasonal material 1 year in advance. Reviews stock photos. Model release preferred.

Making Contact & Terms: Uses b&w, color prints; 35mm, 2¼ × 2¼, 4 × 5 transparencies; b&w, color contact sheets. SASE. Reports in 1 month. NPI; negotiates advance against royalties or flat fee. Pays 50% on acceptance, 50% on publication. Credit line given. Buys all rights or exclusive product rights; negotiable.

Tips: "It helps to start with our guidelines, which indicate what we're looking for at various times during the year."

ROCKSHOTS, INC., 632 Broadway, New York NY 10012. Fax: (212)353-8756. Art Director: Bob Vesce. Estab. 1978. Specializes in greeting cards.

Needs: Buys 20-50 photos/year. Sexy (including nudes and semi-nudes), outrageous, satirical, ironic, humorous photos. Submit seasonal material at least 6 months in advance. Model release required.

Making Contact & Terms: Interested in receiving work from newer, lesser-known photographers. Send SASE requesting photo guidelines. Provide flyer and tearsheets to be kept on file for possible future assignments. Uses b&w and color prints; 35mm, 2¼×2¼ and 4×5 slides. "Do not send originals!" SASE. Reports in 8-10 weeks. Pays $50-125/b&w, $125-300/color photo; other payment negotiable. **Pays on acceptance.** Rights negotiable. Simultaneous submissions and previously published work OK.

Tips: Prefers to see "greeting card themes, especially birthday, Christmas, Valentine's Day. Remember, nudes and semi-nudes are fantasies. Models should definitely be better built than average folk. Also, have fun with nudity, take it out of the normal boundaries. It's much easier to write a gag line for an image that has a theme and/or props. We like to look at life with a very zany slant, not holding back because of society's imposed standards."

THE RYTEX CO., Dept. PM, 5850 W. 80th, Indianapolis IN 46278. (317)872-8553. Product Development Manager: Mary Ann Sisson. Specializes in stationery and wedding invitations.

Needs: Buys 80-120 photos/year. Shots of personalized stationery. Submit seasonal material 8 months in advance. Model release required.

Making Contact & Terms: Query with samples. Provide resume, business card, brochure, flyer or tearsheets to be kept on file for possible future assignments. Works with local freelancers only. Uses 4×5 or 8×10 transparencies. SASE. Reports in 1 week. Pays $100-250/color photo, "open"/hour or job. **Pays on acceptance.** Buys all rights.

SACRED MOUNTAIN ASHRAM, 10668 Gold Hill Rd., Boulder CO 80302-9716. (303)459-3538 or 447-1637. Editor: Bob Comrow. Estab. 1974. Specializes in books and calendars.

Needs: Buys/assigns 30-35 photos/year. Religious (universal); prayer/meditation. "Devotional and reverential mood plus spontaneity are important." Submit seasonal material 3 months in advance. Reviews stock photos. Model release preferred. Captions preferred.

Making Contact & Terms: Query with stock photo list. Uses b&w, color prints; 35mm, 2¼×2¼, 8×10 transparencies; color contact sheets; color negatives. SASE. Reports in 3 weeks. Pays $25-100/b&w; $50-200/color photo. "Rates are negotiable, depending on photograph and specific publication." **Pays on acceptance.** Credit line given. Buys one-time rights. Simultaneous submissions and previously published work OK.

Tips: Wants to see shots of "people in prayer or meditation."

SCAFA-TORNABENE PUBLISHING CO., 100 Snake Hill Rd., West Nyack NY 10994. (914)358-7600. Contact: Susan Murphy. Specializes in unlimited edition offset reproductions for framers, commercial art trade, and manufacturers worldwide.

Needs: Interested in photography with decorative appeal for the wall decor market. Model release required.

Making Contact & Terms: Query with slides or photos. Call approximately two weeks from contact. Uses 35mm, 2¼×2¼, 4×5 and 8×10 camera ready prints. SASE. Reports in 3-4 weeks. Pays $150-250 flat fee for some accepted pieces. Royalty arrangements with advance against 5-10% royalty is standard. Buys only reproduction rights (written contract). Artist maintains ownership of original photograph. Requires exclusive publication rights to all accepted work.

Tips: "Send a good cross sampling of subjects that you shoot. Appropriate subject matter would be as follows: floral still lifes, dramatic landscapes, wildlife, domestic animals, sexy women and automobiles, to name a few. Colored, hand colored, black and white, and sepia tone photography are all considered."

SEABRIGHT PRESS, P.O. Box 7285, Santa Cruz CA 95061. (408)457-1568. Photo Editor: Jim Thompson. Estab. 1990. Specializes in greeting cards.

Needs: Buys stock images from freelancers. Buys 25-35 photos/year. Nature, landscapes, seasonal and any California images. Submit seasonal material 6 months in advance. Model/property release preferred. Captions preferred.

Making Contact & Terms: Query with samples. Uses 4×6 glossy color prints; 35mm transparencies. Samples kept on file. SASE. Reports in 3 weeks. Pays $35-100/color photo; royalties on sales may be negotiated. **Pays on acceptance.** Buys exclusive product rights; negotiable. Simultaneous submissions and previously published work OK.

Tips: "Submit only your best photos; photos with exceptional lighting are most likely to be of interest to us."

SIERRA CLUB BOOKS, 100 Bush St., San Francisco CA 94104-7813. Specializes in nature calendars. Send for free photo guidelines (mailed in February of every year).
Needs: Buys more than 140 photos annually. Needs photos of wildlife, natural history, scenery, hiking, etc. Calendars: nature/scenic; wildlife; "Trail" (mountaineering); engagement (nature and wildlife). No animals in zoos; no people engaged in outdoor recreation with machines. "We accept submissions *only* March 1 to April 30 of each year for calendars covering the year after the following" (i.e., photos for the 1995 calendar will be reviewed in the spring of 1993). Captions required.
Making Contact & Terms: Request guidelines by postcard only. Submit material by mail for consideration. Uses transparencies. Reports in 6-10 weeks. Pays $225-450. Pays on publication. Buys exclusive calendar rights for the year covered by each calendar. Simultaneous submissions OK.
Tips: "We're using international, as opposed to strictly North American, subjects in some of the calendars. We get lots of good scenics, but not as many good wildlife shots or shots appropriate for the 'Trail' calendar. *Be selective*. Don't submit more than 100 transparencies. Follow the guidelines in the spec sheet. We're looking for strong images and seasonal appropriateness."

SOUNDYCARDS, Box 420007, Naples FL 33942. (813)566-8343. President: William Leverick. Specializes in greeting cards with accompanying compact disc of nature sounds.
Needs: Buys 50+ photos/year. Nature photos only, featuring water (lakes, rivers, streams, waterfalls, rain, oceans, beaches etc.). Animals in photos OK. Also needs sources for the accompanying sound recordings if avaiable.
Making Contact & Terms: Mail submissions insured. Uses 35mm, 2¼×2¼, 4×5 and 8×10 transparencies. No color prints. SASE. Pays $150/color photo on publication. Credit line given. Buys exclusive and non-exclusive rights. Previously publised work is OK.
Tips: "Make sure to include pre-stamped and addressed return envelope for return of photos."

*SUNRISE PUBLICATIONS, INC., P.O. Box 4699, Bloomington IN 47402. (812)336-9900. Fax: (812)336-8712. Administrative Assistant: Kathy Christman. Estab. 1974. Specializes in greeting cards, posters, stationery. Photo guidelines free with SASE.
Needs: Buys approx. 30 images/year supplied by freelancers. Interested in nature, animals, endangered species, children (hand-tinted b&w photography). Does not want to see sexually suggestive industry/ business photos. Reviews stock photos. Model release required. Property release preferred.
Making Contact & Terms: Interested in receiving work from newer, lesser-known photographers. Submit portfolio for review. Works on assignment only. Uses 35mm; 4×5 transparencies. Keeps samples on file. Reports in 4-6 weeks. Pays $350/job; pay advance against royalties or flat fees. **Pays on acceptance.** Credit line given. Buys exclusive product rights; negotiable. Simultaneous submissions and previously published work OK.
Tips: "Look for Sunrise cards in stores, familiarize yourself with quality and designs before making a submission." Sees trend toward subjects involving tropical rainforest, endangered species, water (sea).

TIDE MARK PRESS, Box 280311, East Hartford CT 06128-0311. Editor: Scott Kaeser. Art Director: C. Cote. Estab. 1979. Specializes in calendars.
Needs: Buys 400-500 photos/year; few individual photos; all from freelance stock. Complete calendar concepts which are unique, but also have identifiable markets; groups of photos which could work as an entire calendar; ideas and approach must be visually appealing and innovative but also have a definable audience. No general nature or varied subjects without a single theme. Submit seasonal material in spring for next calendar year. Reviews stock photos. Model release preferred. Captions required.
Making Contact & Terms: "Contact us to offer specific topic suggestion which reflect specific strengths of your stock." Uses 35mm, 2¼×2¼, 4×5 and 8×10 transparencies. SASE. Reports in 1 month. Pays $125-150/color photo; royalties on sales if entire calendar supplied. Pays on publication or per agreement. Credit line given. Buys one-time rights.
Tips: "We tend to be a niche publisher and we rely on niche photographers to supply our needs."

WEST GRAPHICS, 238 Capp St., San Francisco CA 94110. (415)621-4641. Fax: (415)621-8613. Art Director: Tom Drew. Specializes in greeting cards, calendars, gift bags and humorous note pads. Photo guidelines free with SASE.
Needs: Buys 24-48 freelance photos/year. Humorous, animals, people in humorous situtions or anything of an unusual nature; prefers color. Does not want to see scenics. Submit seasonal material 1 year in advance. Model release required.
Making Contact & Terms: Interested in receiving work from newer, lesser-known photographers. Query with samples. Send unsolicited photos by mail for consideration. Submit portfolio for review. Uses 8×10 b&w glossy prints; 35mm, 2¼×2¼ and 4×5 transparencies. SASE. Reports in 1 month. Pays $200/color or b&w photo and/or 5% royalty on sales. Pays 30 days after publication. Credit line given. Buys 5-year greeting card rights. Simultaneous submissions and previously published work OK.
Tips: "Humor is our primary concern."

*WILLIAMHOUSE-REGENCY, INC., 28 W. 23rd St., New York NY 10010. (212)691-2000. Executive Art Director: Nancy Boecker. Estab. 1955. Specializes in greeting cards, stationery, invitations and announcements. Photo guidelines free with SASE.

Needs: Offers 15 assignments annually.

Making Contact & Terms: Interested in receiving work from newer, lesser-known photographers. Provide resume, business card, self-promotion piece or tearsheets to be kept on file for possible future assignments. Works with local freelancers on assignment only. Uses 4×5 and 8×10 transparencies. Keeps samples on file. SASE. Reports in 3 weeks. Pays $500-750/day. **Pays on acceptance.** Credit line not given. Buys all rights.

Tips: "We are interested in photographers who have photographed paper products that use embossing, foil leaf and subtle colors."

WISCONSIN TRAILS, Box 5650, Madison WI 53705. (608)231-2444. Photo Editor: Nancy Mead. Estab. 1960. Calendar portraying seasonal scenics, some books and activities from Wisconsin.

Needs: Buys 35 photos/issue. Needs photos of nature, landscapes, wildlife and Wisconsin activities. Makes selections in January for calendar 6 months ahead for issues; "we should have photos by December." Captions required.

Making Contact & Terms: Submit material by mail for consideration or submit portfolio. Uses 35mm, 2¼×2¼ and 4×5 transparencies. Reports in 1 month. Pays $25-100/b&w photo; $50-200/color photo. Buys one-time rights. Simultaneous submissions OK "if we are informed, and if there's not a competitive market among them." Previously published work OK.

Tips: "Be sure to inform us how you want materials returned and include proper postage. Calendar scenes must be horizontal to fit 8½×11 format, but we also want vertical formats. See our magazine and books and be aware of our type of photography. Submit only Wisconsin scenes."

*ZEPHYR PRESS, P.O. Box 1213, New York NY 10011. (212)633-8859. Publisher: Tobin Fraley. Estab. 1983. Specializes in calendars. Photo guidelines free with SASE.

Needs: American/nostalgia. Does not want to see skin/soft porn. "Material is best submitted February to June." Model release preferred. Captions required.

Making Contact & Terms: Provide resume, business card. Reports in 1 month. Pays $250/b&w photo; $250/color photo. Pays on royalty basis only if entire calendar is by single photographer. **Pays on acceptance.** Usually buys one-time rights, but it varies. Simultaneous submissions and previously published submissions OK.

Tips: "Just a few samples (such as show exhibit cards) are fine as a start." Generally "prefer to work with one photographer per calendar. We are open to ideas submitted by photographers."

Paper Products/'93-'94 changes

The following markets appeared in the 1993 edition of *Photographer's Market* but are not listed in the 1994 edition. They may have been omitted for failing to respond to our request for updated information, they may have gone out of business or they may no longer wish to receive freelance work.

Dayrunner (did not respond)
The Duck Press (did not respond)
Encore Studios (did not respond)
Fern-Wood Designs and Photo Marketing Agency (did not respond)
Freedom Greetings (did not respond)
Intercontinental Greetings (did not respond)
Lasercraft (did not respond)
Nature Company (asked to be deleted)
Nature's Design (did not respond)
Normally Marketing Systems (did not respond)
Nostalgia Company (did not respond)
One Sun Communications (out of business)
Quadriga Art (did not respond)
Recycled Paper Products (did not respond)
Scandecor (did not respond)
Starmakers Publishing (unable to locate)
Syracuse Cultural Workers (did not respond)
Vagabond
Vital Images (did not respond)

Publications

For many of you this is the section in which hopes and dreams can come true. When you decided to shoot and sell photographs your eyes probably twinkled at the thought of visiting exotic locations on assignment for a high-profile travel magazine. Flipping through the pages of *Life* or *National Geographic* you became attracted to photography because such shots are so breathtaking. In your mind, nothing could be better than circling the world, photographing wildlife or incredible landscapes and getting paid for it. If these are your beliefs, you're right. Those types of assignments are magical. If you think success like this will come overnight, you're wrong.

Editors from many of the top magazines are inundated daily with material from eager photographers. Susan White of *Vanity Fair* estimates that she receives around 40 promotional pieces every day and she only keeps about five. If your work is not top-notch and presented professionally don't expect editors to look at it for very long.

It is important to do your homework and know what a magazine editor prefers from freelancers. Some editors have strict policies when it comes to reviewing portfolios. They may only review photos on certain days of the week. Find out if the editor prefers small, medium or large formats. Do they want to see a mix of color and b&w photography? Do they want to see tearsheets or prints?

Whenever possible try to get some feedback regarding your work. Even if they hated the images in your portfolio, ask them why they disliked the shots. Also, try not to take a love-it-or-leave-it attitude regarding your work. Be willing to accept criticism and learn from the suggestions of editors. However, if you ask for an assessment of your work and an editor gives you a vague response, be a little suspicious. There are times when editors are too busy and don't look at portfolios. Without being too confrontational, see if you can submit your portfolio again in the near future.

The important thing is to be persistent without being a pest. Sending a new promotional piece often can be enough to keep your name in the mind of an editor. Constant phone calls from freelancers often bother editors who may be working on deadlines and don't have time to talk. If you get on an editor's bad side your chances of making a sale or getting an assignment for that publication drastically decrease.

If you are a new photographer it is often better to start with smaller publications to build your portfolio. This section is the largest in *Photographer's Market* and consists of four main categories—Consumer Publications, Newspapers & Newsletters, Special Interest Publications and Trade Publications. You should be able to find dozens of markets that are interested in the work you produce.

To make this search for markets easier we have created a Subject Index, located at the back of this book. This index is divided into 23 topics, and markets are listed according to the types of photographs they want to see. For example, if you shoot environmental photos there are numerous markets wanting to receive this type of material and they are listed in the index.

At the back of this book we also have a First Markets Index, which provides the names of those publications interested in receiving work from newer, lesser-known photographers. If you are just getting started this is an excellent place to look for potential markets.

Throughout this section you also will find bullets (•) inside some listings. These comments were written by the editor of the *Photographer's Market* and they are designed to provide additional information about the listing. The comments usually center on awards won by markets, design changes that have taken place, or they provide specific submission requirements.

Consumer Publications

In recent years technology has begun to change the way photographers and magazine publishers do business. Many of these technological advances are discussed in detail at the front of this book. Photographer Lee Foster, of Berkeley, California, who is featured in our Insider Report on page 280, tells how he has benefited from these changes by producing his own CD-ROM for travel writing and photography.

If you are interested in working in the consumer magazine market you should realize that some companies are taking a good look at the way information is presented. For example, some, like *Audubon* and *Cosmopolitan,* are examining ways to offer paperless magazines. As the general public gets more acquainted with on-line systems, publishers are sure to switch to such technology. Photos eventually will be viewed by editors on a computer screen rather than on a light table. Be prepared for such advances and do what you can to protect your copyright.

While consumer publications are advancing technologically they still are rebounding from poor newsstand sales and limited advertising dollars. According to an article in the February 22, 1993 issue of *Advertising Age,* 234 of 456 consumer magazines reported lower single-copy newsstand sales in the second half of 1992 than during the same period in 1991.

Because of the tough economy many publications still are not ready to spend a lot of money on photography. Editors often purchase stock photography instead of making assignments, so if you want to sell your work consider stock as a viable option.

ABOARD MAGAZINE, Suite 220, 100 Almeria Ave., Coral Gables FL 33134. (305)441-9744. Fax: (305)441-9739. Editor: Gloria L. Shanahan. Photo Editor: Alex Sanchez. Circ. 110,000. Estab. 1976. Inflight magazine for 10 separate Latin American national airlines. Bilingual bimonthly. Emphasizes travel through Central and South America. Readers are mainly Latin American businessmen, and American tourists and businessmen. Sample copy free with SASE. Photo guidelines free with SASE.
Needs: Uses 50 photos/issue; 30 supplied by freelance photographers. Needs photos of travel, scenic, fashion, sports and art. Special needs include good quality pix of Latin American countries, particularly Chile, Guatemala, Ecuador, Bolivia, Rep. Dominicana, El Salvador, Peru, Nicaragua, Honduras, Paraguay. Model/property release preferred. Captions preferred.
Making Contact & Terms: Interested in receiving work from newer, lesser-known photographers. Query with samples. Provide business card, brochure, flyer or tearsheets to be kept on file for possible future assignments. SASE. Reports in 1 month. Payment varies; pays $20/color photo; $150 for photo/text package. Pays on publication. Credit line given. Buys one-time rights. Previously published work OK.
Tips: If photos are accompanied by an article, chances are much better of them being accepted.

ACCENT ON LIVING, P.O. Box 700, Bloomington IL 61702. (309)378-2961. Fax: (309)378-4420. Editor: Betty Garee. Circ. 20,000. Quarterly magazine. Emphasizes successful disabled young adults (18 and up) who are getting the most out of life in every way and *how* they are accomplishing this. Readers are physically disabled individuals of all ages and socioeconomic levels and professionals. Sample copy $3 with 5×7 SAE and $1.21 postage. Free photo/writers guidelines; enclose SASE.
Needs: Uses 15 photos/issue; 80 supplied by freelancers. Needs photos for Accent on People department, "a human interest photo column on disabled individuals who are gainfully employed or doing unusual things." Also uses occasional photo features on disabled persons in specific occupations: art, health, etc. Manuscript required. Photos depict handicapped persons coping with the problems and situations particular to them: how-to, new aids and assistive devices, news, documentary, human interest, photo essay/photo feature, humorous and travel. "All must be tied in with physical disability. We want essentially action shots of disabled individuals doing something interesting/unique or with a new device they have developed. Not photos of disabled people shown with a good citizen 'helping' them." Model release preferred. Captions preferred.
Making Contact & Terms: Interested in receiving work from newer, lesser-known photographers. Query first with ideas, get an OK, and send contact sheet for consideration. Uses glossy prints and color photos, transparencies preferred. Provide letter of inquiry and samples to be kept on file for possible future assignments. Cover is usually tied in with the main feature inside. SASE. Reports in 1-2 weeks. Pays $50-up/color cover; pays $15-up/color inside photo; pays $5-up/b&w inside photo. Pays on publication. Credit line given if requested. Previously published work OK.
Tips: "Concentrate on improving photographic skills. Join a local camera club, go to photo seminars, etc. We find that most articles are helped a great deal with *good* photographs—in fact, good photographs will often mean buying a story and passing up another one with very poor or no photographs at all." Looking for *good* quality photos depicting what article is about. "We almost always work on speculation."

ADIRONDACK LIFE, Rt. 86, Box 97, Jay NY 12941. (518)946-2191. Art Director: Ann Eastman. Circ. 50,000. Estab. 1970. Bimonthly. Emphasizes the people and landscape of the north country of New York State. Sample copy $4 with 9×12 SAE and $1.10 postage. Photo guidelines free with SASE.
Needs: "We use about 40 photos/issue, most supplied by freelance photographers. All photos must be taken in the Adirondacks and all shots must be identified as to location and photographer."
Making Contact & Terms: Send one sleeve (20 slides) of samples. Send b&w prints (preferably 8×10) or color transparencies in any format. SASE. Pays $300/cover photo; $50-200/color or b&w photo; $150/day plus expenses. Pays 30 days after publication. Credit line given. Buys first N.A. serial rights. Simultaneous submissions OK.
Tips: "Send quality work pertaining specifically to the Adirondacks. In addition to technical proficiency, we look for originality and imagination. We emphasize vistas and scenics. We are using more pictures of people and action."

AFRICA REPORT, Dept. PM, 833 UN Plaza, New York NY 10017. (212)949-5666. Editor: Margaret A. Novicki. Bimonthly magazine. Emphasizes African political and economic affairs, especially those significant for US. Readers are Americans with professional or personal interest in Africa. Circ. 12,000. Free sample copy.
Needs: Uses 20 photos/issue. Personality, documentary, photo feature, scenic, spot news, human interest, travel, socioeconomic and political. Photos must relate to African affairs. "We will not reply to 'How I Saw My First Lion' or 'Look How Quaint the Natives Are' proposals." Wants, on a regular basis, photos of economics, African international affairs, development, conflict and daily life. Captions required.

Making Contact & Terms: Provide samples and list of countries/subjects to be kept on file for future assignments. Query on accompanying ms. SASE. Pays $25-35/inside photo; $25-75/cover photo; $150-250/ms. Pays on publication. Credit line given. Buys one-time rights. Reports in 1 month. Simultaneous submissions and previously published work OK. Uses 8 × 10 glossy prints; vertical format preferred for cover.

Tips: "Live and travel in Africa; and make political, economic and social events humanly interesting."

AFTER FIVE MAGAZINE, P.O. Box 492905, Redding CA 96049. (800)637-3540 only from northern California, otherwise (916)335-4533. Publisher: Katie Harrington. Monthly tabloid. Emphasizes news, arts and entertainment. Circ. 24,207. Estab. 1986. Sample copy $1.

Needs: Uses 8-12 photos/issue; 25% supplied by freelance photographers. Needs photos of animal/wildlife shots, travel and scenics of Northern California. Model release and captions preferred.

Making Contact & Terms: Provide resume, business card, brochure, flyer or tearsheets to be kept on file for possible assignments. SASE. Reports in 1-2 weeks. Pays $50/color cover photo; $50/b&w cover photo; $20/b&w inside photo; $60/b&w page rate. Pays on publication. Credit line given. Buys one-time rights. Previously published work OK.

Tips: "Need photographs of subjects north of Sacramento to Oregon-California border, plus southern Oregon."

AIM MAGAZINE, P.O. Box 20554, Chicago IL 60620. (312)874-6184. Editor: Ruth Apilado. Circ. 7,000. Estab. 1974. Quarterly magazine. Magazine dedicated to promoting racial harmony and peace. Readers are high school and college students, as well as those interested in social change. Sample copy for $3.50 with 9 × 12 SAE and 4 first-class stamps.

Needs: Uses 10 photos/issue. Needs "ghetto pictures, pictures of people deserving recognition, etc." Needs photos of "integrated schools with high achievement." Model release required.

Making Contact & Terms: Send unsolicited photos by mail for consideration. Send b&w prints. SASE. Reports in 1 month. Pays $25/color cover photo; $10/b&w cover photo. **Pays on acceptance.** Credit line given. Buys one-time rights. Simultaneous submissions OK.

Tips: Looks for "positive contributions."

ALABAMA LITERARY REVIEW, 253 Smith Hall, Troy State University, Troy AL 36082. (205)670-3315. Editor: Theron Montgomery. Circ. 800 + . Estab. 1987. Semi-annual journal. Emphasizes short stories, poetry, essays, short drama, art and photography. Readers are anyone interested in literature and art of all ages. Sample copy for $4.50/issue and 9 × 12 SASE.

Needs: Uses 5-6 photos/issue; 100% supplied by freelance photographers, 10% on assignment, 90% from stock. Will consider all kinds of photos. Special needs include anything artistic or thought-provoking. Model release required. Property release preferred.

Making Contact & Terms: Interested in receiving work from newer, lesser-known photographers. Send 8 × 10 glossy b&w prints by mail for consideration. SASE. Reports in 1-3 months. Pays in copies. Pays on publication. Credit line given. Buys first rights; returned upon publication. Simultaneous submissions OK.

Tips: "We take pride in discovering amateur photographers and presenting their work to a serious audience across the U.S. *ALR* is a good place for a new photographer to break in." Looks for "playoff on b&w, people and forms. Also, something that tells a story." The trend is towards b&w art forms. "Think of the completeness, proportion and metaphoric implications of the pictures."

ALASKA, Suite 200, 808 E St., Anchorage AK 99501. Fax: (907)272-2552. Editor: Tobin Morrison. Managing Editor: Nolan Hester. Photo Editor: Roy Corral. Circ. 260,000. Estab. 1963. Monthly magazine. Readers are people interested in Alaska. Sample copy $4. Free photo guidelines.

Needs: Buys 400 photos annually, supplied mainly by freelancers. Captions required.

Making Contact & Terms: Interested in receiving work from newer, lesser-known photographers. Send carefully edited, captioned submission of 35mm, 2¼ × 2¼ or 4 × 5 transparencies. SASE. Reports in 4 weeks. Pays $300/full page; $500/cover. Buys one-time rights; negotiable.

Tips: "Each issue of *Alaska* features 8- to 10-page photo feature. We're looking for themes and photos to show the best of Alaska. We want sharp, artistically composed pictures. Cover photo always relates to stories inside the issue."

ALASKA GEOGRAPHIC, Dept. PM, P.O. Box 93370, Anchorage AK 99509. (907)562-0164. Editor: Penny Rennick. Quarterly magazine. Covers Alaska and Northwestern Canada only. Readers are professional men and women, ages 30 and up. Circ. 9,000. Estab. 1972. Guidelines free with SASE.

The Subject Index, located at the back of this book, can help you find publications interested in the topics you shoot.

Needs: Uses about 70 photos/issue; most supplied by freelancers. Needs photos of scenics, animals, natural history and people. Each issue covers a special theme. Model release preferred; captions required.

Making Contact & Terms: Interested in receiving work from newer, lesser-known photogaphers. Query with list of stock photo subjects. SASE. "We don't have time to deal with inappropriate submissions, so know the area and subjects very well to avoid wasting time." Pays $200/color cover photo; $100/inside full-page color; $50/inside half-page color. Pays on publication. Credit line given. Buys one-time rights. Simultaneous submissions and previously published work OK.

Tips: Do not send mss, "just photos. Our freelance writing is done by assignment only."

alive now! MAGAZINE, Dept. PM, 1908 Grand Ave., P.O. Box 189, Nashville TN 37202. (615)340-7218. Assistant Editor: Beth A. Richardson. Circ. 80,000. Estab. 1975. Bimonthly magazine published by The Upper Room. "*alive now!* uses poetry, short prose, photography and contemporary design to present material for personal devotion and reflection. It reflects on a chosen Christian concern in each issue. The readership is composed of primarily college-educated adults." Sample copy free with 6×9 SAE and 85¢ postage. Themes list free with SASE; photo guidelines available.

Needs: Uses about 25-30 b&w prints/issue; 90% supplied by freelancers. Needs b&w photos of "family, friends, people in positive and negative situations, scenery, celebrations, disappointments, ethnic minority subjects in everyday situations—Native Americans, Hispanics, Asians and blacks." Model release preferred.

Making Contact & Terms: Query with samples. Send 8×10 glossy b&w prints by mail for consideration. Submit portfolio for review. SASE. Reports in 2 months; "longer to consider photos for more than one issue." Pays $25-35/b&w inside photo; no color photos. Pays on publication. Credit line given. Buys one-time rights. Simultaneous and previously published submissions OK.

Tips: Looking for high reproduction, quality photographs. Prefers to see "a variety of photos of people in life situations, presenting positive and negative slants, happy/sad, celebrations/disappointments, etc. Use of racially inclusive photos is preferred."

ALOHA, THE MAGAZINE OF HAWAII, Suite 309, 49 S. Hotel St., Honolulu HI 96813. (808)523-9871. Fax: (808)533-2055. Assistant Editor: Chardra Quinlan. Circ. 65,000. Estab. 1978. Bimonthly. Emphasizes culture, arts, history of Hawaii and its people. Readers are "affluent, college-educated people from all over the world who have an interest in Hawaii." Sample copy $2.95 with 9×11 SAE and $2.40 postage. Photo guidelines free with SASE.

Needs: Uses about 50 photos/issue; 90% supplied by freelance photographers. Needs "scenics, travel, people, florals, strictly about Hawaii. We buy primarily from stock. Assignments are rarely given and when they are it is to one of our regular local contributors. Subject matter must be Hawaiian in some way. A regular feature is the photo essay, 'Beautiful Hawaii,' which is a 6-page collection of images illustrating that theme." Model release required if the shot is to be used for a cover. Captions required.

Making Contact & Terms: Interested in receiving work from newer, lesser-known photographers. Submit portfolio for review. Query with stock photo list. Send unsolicited photos by mail for consideration. Provide resume, business card, brochure, flyer or tearsheets to be kept on file for possible future assignments. SASE. Reports in 3 weeks. Pays $10/b&w photo; $60/color transparency; $125/photo running across a two-page spread; $175/cover shot. Pays on publication. Credit line given. Buys one-time rights.

Tips: Prefers to see "a unique way of looking at things, and of course, well-composed images. Generally, we are looking for outstanding photos of Hawaii scenery that are not standard sunset shots printed in every Hawaii publication. We need to see that the photographer can use lighting techniques skillfully, and we want to see pictures that are sharp and crisp. Many photographers break in by submitting transparencies for Beautiful Hawaii. Competition is fierce, and it helps if a photographer can first bring in his portfolio to show to our art director. Then the art director can give him ideas regarding our needs."

AMELIA MAGAZINE, 329 "E" St., Bakersfield CA 93304. (805)323-4064. Editor: Frederick A. Raborg, Jr. Circ. 1,250. Quarterly magazine. Emphasizes literary: fiction, non-fiction, poetry, reviews, fine illustrations and photography, etc. "We span all age groups, three genders and all occupations. We are also international in scope. Average reader has college education." Sample copy $7.95 and SASE. Photo guidelines free with SASE.

Needs: Uses up to 4 photos/issue depending on availability; all supplied by freelance photographers. "We look for photos in all areas and try to match them to appropriate editorial content. Sometimes use photos alone; color photos on cover. We use the best we receive; the photos usually convince us." Model release required. Captions preferred.

Making Contact & Terms: Send unsolicited photos by mail for consideration. Send b&w or color, 5×7 and up, glossy or matte prints; 35mm or 2¼×2¼ transparencies. SASE. Reports in 2 weeks. Pays $100/color cover photo; $50/b&w cover photo; $5-25/b&w inside photo. **Pays on acceptance.**

Credit line given. Buys one-time rights or first N.A. serial rights. "We prefer first N.A., but one-time is fine." Simultaneous submissions OK.

Tips: In portfolio or samples, looks for "a strong cross-section. We assume that photos submitted are available at time of submission. Do your homework. Examine a copy of the magazine, certainly. Study the 'masters of contemporary' photography, i.e. Adams, Avedon, etc. Experiment. Remember we are looking for photos to be married to editorial copy usually."

AMERICA WEST AIRLINES MAGAZINE, Dept. PM, Suite 240, 7500 N. Dreamy Draw Dr., Phoenix AZ 85020. (602)997-7200. Art Director: Elaine Rettger. America West Airlines inflight magazine. Monthly. Emphasizes general interest—including: travel, interviews, business trends, food, etc. Readers are primarily business people and business travelers; substantial vacation travel audience. Circ. 125,000. Photo guidelines free with SASE. Sample copy $3.

Needs: Uses about 60-100 photos/issue; all supplied by freelance photographers. "Each issue varies immensely, we primarily look for stock photography of places, people, subjects such as animals, plants, scenics—we assign some location and portrait shots. We publish a series of photo essays with brief, but interesting accompanying text." Model release and captions required.

Making Contact & Terms: Provide resume, business card, brochure, tearsheets or color samples to be kept on file for possible future assignments. Pays $100-225/color inside photo, depends on size of photo and importance of story; $75-100/hour; $350/day+ film and expenses. Pays on publication. Credit line given. Buys one-time rights. Previously published work OK.

Tips: "We judge portfolios on technical quality, consistency, ability to show us that you can give us what we ask for with a certain uniqueness in style or design, versatility and creativity. Photographers we work with most often are those who are both technically and creatively adept, and who can take the initiative conceptually by providing new approaches or ideas."

AMERICAN CAGE-BIRD MAGAZINE, One Glamore Court, Smithtown NY 11787. (516)979-7962. Editor: Arthur Freud. Photo Editor: Anne Frizzell. Circ. 50,000. Estab. 1928. Monthly. Emphasizes care, breeding and maintenance of pet cage birds. Readers include bird fanciers scattered throughout the United States, Canada and other countries. Sample copy $3.

Needs: Uses about 15 photos/issue; 6 supplied by freelance photographers, 70% on assignment, 30% from stock. Needs sharp, clear b&w and color photos of budgies, cockatiels, canaries, parrots, toucans and people with such birds. Clever seasonal shots also good (Christmas, Fourth of July, etc.). "We choose photos which inform and/or entertain. Identification of the bird type or species is crucial." Model/property release preferred. Captions required.

Making Contact & Terms: Interested in receiving work from newer, lesser-known photographers. Send 5×7 glossy b&w prints, 35mm color slides or 2¼×2¼ transparencies by mail for consideration. SASE. Reports in 2 weeks. Pays $25/b&w photo; $25-100/color photo. "Vertical format color slides with dead space at top of slide are considered for cover with a higher payment." Pays on publication. Credit line given. Buys one-time rights. Previously published work OK.

AMERICAN DANE MAGAZINE, 3717 Harney St., Omaha NE 68131. (402)341-5049. Fax: (402)341-0830. Editor-in-Chief: Jennifer Denning-Kock. Circ. 7,000. Estab. 1916. Monthly magazine. For an audience of "primarily Danish origin, interested in Danish traditions, customs, etc." Sample copy $1 with 8½×11 SAE and 75¢ postage.

Needs: Buys approximately 6/year. Wants no scenic photos "unless they are identifiably Danish in origin." Avoid general material. Captions preferred.

Making Contact & Terms: Interested in receiving work from newer, lesser-known photographers. Send b&w contact sheet or 8×10 glossy or semigloss prints. SASE. Reports in 1-2 weeks. Pays $10-20/color photo; $20-40/photo/text package. Pays on publication. Buys first rights. Previously published work OK.

Tips: "Photos must be identifiably Danish in content and have the ability to capture Danish culture." Contact by mail.

AMERICAN HORTICULTURIST, 7931 E. Boulevard Dr., Alexandria VA 22308. (703)768-5700. Fax: (703)768-7533. Editor: Kathleen Fisher. Circ. 25,000. Estab. 1927. Monthly. "Alternate 4-color magazine with 2-color newsletter." Emphasizes horticulture. Readers are advanced amateur gardeners. Sample copy $3. Photo guidelines free with SASE.

Needs: Uses 25-30 (color/magazine), 5-10 (b&w/news edition) photos/issue; all supplied by freelancers. "Assignments are rare; 2-3/year for portraits to accompany profiles." Needs shots of people gardening, people engaged in horticulture research, public gardens, close-ups of particular plant species showing detail. "We only review photos to illustrate a particular ms which has already been accepted." Sometimes uses seasonal cover shots. Model release preferred. Captions required, include botanical names.

Making Contact & Terms: Interested in receiving work from newer, lesser-known photographers. Query with list of stock photo subjects, photo samples. Provide resume, business card, brochure, flyer or tearsheets to be kept on file for possible future assignments or requests. SASE. Reports in 3 weeks. Pays $50/color inside photo; $80/color cover photo; $25-50/b&w photo. Pays on publication. Buys one-time rights.

Tips: Wants to see "ability to identify precise names of plants, clarity and vibrant color."

AMERICAN SKATING WORLD, 1816 Brownsville Rd., Pittsburgh PA 15210-3908. (412)885-7600. Fax: (412)885-7617. Managing Editor: H. Kermit Jackson. Circ. 15,000. Estab. 1981. Monthly tabloid. Emphasizes ice skating—figure skating primarily, speed skating secondary. Readers are figure skating participants and fans of all ages. Sample copy $2.95 with 8×12 SAE and 3 first class stamps. Photo guidelines free with SASE.

Needs: Uses 20-25 photos/issue; 4 supplied by freelancers. Needs performance and candid shots of skaters and "industry heavyweights." Reviews photos with or without manuscript. Model/property release preferred for children and recreational skaters. Captions required; include name, locale, date and move being executed (if relevant).

Making Contact & Terms: Interested in receiving work from newer, lesser-known photographers. Query with resume of credits. Keeps samples on file. SASE. Report on unsolicited submissions could take 3 months. Pays $25/color cover photo; $5/b&w inside photo. Pays 30 days after publication. Buys one-time rights color; all rights b&w; negotiable. Simultaneous submissions and/or previously published work OK.

Tips: "Pay attention to what's new, the newly emerging competitors, the newly developed events. In general, be flexible!" Photographers should capture proper lighting in performances and freeze the action instead of snapping a pose.

AMERICAN SURVIVAL GUIDE, 774 S. Placentia Ave., Placentia CA 92670-6832. (714)572-2255. Fax: (714)572-1864. Editor: Jim Benson. Circ. 70,000. Extab. 1980. Monthly magazine. Emphasizes firearms, military gear, emergency preparedness, survival food storage and self-defense products. Average reader is male, mid-30s, all occupations and with conservative views. Sample copy $3.25 and SAE with $1.44 postage. Photo guidelines free with SASE.

Needs: Uses 100+ photos/issue; 50% supplied by freelance photographers. Photos purchased with accompanying manuscript only. Model release required. Captions required.

Making Contact & Terms: Interested in receiving work from newer, lesser-known photographers. Send written query detailing article and photos. Note: Will not accept text without photos or other illustrations. Pays $70/color and b&w page rate. Pays on publication. Credit line given. Buys all rights; negotiable.

Tips: Wants to see "professional looking photographs—in focus, correct exposure, good lighting, interesting subject and people in action. Dramatic poses of people helping each other after a disaster, riots or worn torn area. Wilderness survival too. Look at sample copies to get an idea of what we feature. We only accept photos with an accompanying manuscript (floppy disk with Word Perfect or Microsoft Word files). The better the photos, the better chance you have of being published."

AMERICANA MAGAZINE, Dept. PM, 29 W. 38 St., New York NY 10018. (212)398-1550. Editor: Sandra Wilmot. Bimonthly magazine. Emphasizes an interest in American history and how it relates to contemporary living. Circ. 200,000. Estab. 1973. Sample copy $3 and free photo guidelines.

Needs: Freelancers supply 95% of the photos; 50% stock, 50% assigned. Photos purchased with or without accompanying mss. Celebrity/personality (outstanding in the field of Americana—curator of White House, head of National Trust, famous painter, etc.); fine art; scenic (US—must relate to specific article); human interest; humorous; photo essay/photo feature (majority of stories); US travel; museum collections and old photography. "*Americana*'s stories should open the door on the past by giving the reader the opportunity to participate in the activity we are covering, be it crafts, collecting, travel or whatever. Travel, preservation, collecting and history are only a few of the subjects we cover. We often rely on contributors to point out new areas that are suitable for *Americana*. Many of the articles are very service-oriented, including practical advice and how-to information." Model release preferred. Captions required; include name, place, subject matter, date.

Making Contact & Terms: Send query with resume of credits. "Look at several issues of the magazine and then have story ideas before talking to us." SASE. "Make envelope large enough to hold material sent." Uses 8×10 b&w matte prints; color 35mm, 2¼×2¼, 4×5 and 8×10 transparencies; color covers only with vertical format. Previously published work OK. Reports in 3 months. Pays $25 minimum/b&w photo; $25-300/color photo; $350 maximum/day. Pays by assignment or on a per-photo basis. All payments negotiable. Pays on publication. Credit line given. Buys one-time rights and first NA. serial rights.

Tips: Wants to see "technical competence; artistic abilities; aptitude to shoot for an editorial assignment. Rarely accepts freelance work that does not relate to a specific story."

AMERICA'S EQUESTRIAN, P.O. Box 249, Huntington Station NY 11746. (516)549-0620. Fax: (516)423-0567. Publisher: Bill Bohn. Circ. 17,000. Estab. 1978. Publishes 7 issues/year: 6 bimonthly and 1 special calendar issue. Emphasizes horses. Sample copy $2 and 9 × 12 SAE with $1.50 postage. Photo guidelines free with SASE.
Needs: Uses 25-50 photos/issue; 2 supplied by freelance photographers. Needs photos of horse shots from specific events, and horse-related photos for special features. Reviews photos with or without accompanying ms. Special needs include "photos taken at major national and international equine events. We sometimes do photo essays tied in with our editorial themes." Model release preferred. Captions required; include name/address/phone on back of photo, no name on front of photo. No Polaroids.
Making Contact & Terms: Query with samples. Send unsolicited photos by mail for consideration. Must include cover letter. Provide resume, business card, brochure, flyer or tearsheets to be kept on file for possible future assignments. Uses b&w prints and color. SASE. Reports in 2 months. Pays $20/ inside photo; $100 for photo essays of 10-20 photos. Pays on publication. Credit line given. Buys first N.A. serial rights. "We keep photos published. No payment for unassigned photos, but will consider publishing for credit line."
Tips: Looks for people "who understand horse photography. Clear, crisp, good contrast and cropped so the subject fills the photo, a knowledge of how to shoot horses. We like to work with new people who want and need the exposure and would supply us with complimentary photos in exchange for a credit line."

*‡AMIGA FORMAT, 30 Monmouth St., Bath, Avon BA1 2BW England. (0225)442244. Fax: (0225)446019. Art Editor: Susan White. Circ. 161,000. Estab. 1989. Monthly magazine. Emphasizes leisure computing. Readers are males between 15 and 45 years old. Sample copy £4.
Needs: Uses 30-60 photos/issue. Needs photos of technology-concept editorial. Reviews photos with or without ms. Model/property release preferred. Captions preferred.
Making Contact & Terms: Interested in receiving work from newer, lesser-known photographers. Submit portfolio for review. Send unsolicited photos by mail for consideration. Provide resume, business card, brochure, flyer or tearsheets to be kept on file for possible assignments. Send 35mm, 2¼ × 2¼ transparencies. Keeps samples on file. SASE. Reports in 1 month. Pays $60/hour; $500/day; $600/color cover photo. Pays on publication. Credit line given. Buys one-time rights; negotiable.

ANYTIME TRAVEL GUIDE, Dept. PM, Box G3, Aspen CO 81612. (303)920-4040. Fax: (303)920-4044. Contact: Art Director. Bimonthly magazine. Emphasizes Aspen—lifestyle, sports, local issues. Readers are "Aspenites, both locals, part-time residents and lovers of the town wherever they live." Circ. 15,000. Estab. 1974. Sample copy free with 10 × 12 SAE and 6 first class stamps.
Needs: Uses "35 photos/issue; most supplied by freelancers, usually on assignment." Needs scenics, sports—skiing in winter and other mountain sports in summer—profiles, travel shots, etc. Model release preferred. "We're eager to see work of shooters who are in our area for work or pleasure."
Making Contact & Terms: Provide resume, business card, brochure, flyer or tearsheets. Does not keep samples on file. Cannot return material. Reports in 1 month. Pays $200, 30 days after publication. Credit line given. Buys exclusive rights in our market, one-time rights; negotiable.
Tips: Wants to see "technical proficiency, appropriate subject matter, vision and creative sensibility. We strive for the highest level of photography in all areas and design. Do *not* send inappropriate submissions that are unrelated to Aspen, CO. All our photography (and editorial text) are geared to our role as a 'city' magazine. When we do use stock shots they are usually from photographers who have worked extensively in our town, but we still like to see the work of others as long as they have shots *from our area. No general submissions please.*"

AQUARIUM FISH MAGAZINE, P.O. Box 6050, Mission Viejo CA 92690. (714)855-8822. Editor: Edward Bauman. Circ. 75,000. Estab. 1988. Monthly magazine. Emphasizes aquarium fish. Readers are both genders, all ages. Sample copy $3.50. Photo guidelines free with SASE.
Needs: Uses 30 photos/issue; all supplied by freelance photographers. Needs photos of aquariums and fish, freshwater and saltwater; ponds.
Making Contact & Terms: Query with list of stock photo subjects. Submit portfolio for review. Send 35mm, 2¼ × 2¼ transparencies by mail for consideration. SASE. Reports in 1 month. Pays $150/color cover photo; $50-75/color inside photo; $25/b&w inside photo; $75/color page rate; $25/b&w page rate. Pays on publication. Credit line given. Buys one-time rights. Previously published work OK.

ARIZONA HIGHWAYS, 2039 W. Lewis Ave., Phoenix AZ 85009. (Prefers not to share information.)

ASPEN MAGAZINE, Dept. PM, Box G3, Aspen CO 81612. (303)920-4040. Fax: (303)920-4044. Art Director: Elena Brown. Bimonthly magazine. Emphasizes Aspen—lifestyle, sports, local issues. Readers are "Aspenites, both locals, part-time residents and lovers of the town wherever they live." Circ. 15,000. Estab. 1974. Sample copy free with 10 × 12 SAE and 6 first class stamps.

Needs: Uses "35 photos/issue; most supplied by freelancers, usually on assignment." Needs scenics, sports—skiing in winter and other mountain sports in summer—profiles, travel shots, etc. Model release preferred. "We're eager to see work of shooters who are in our area for work or pleasure."
Making Contact & Terms: Provide resume, business card, brochure, flyer or tearsheets. Does not keep samples on file. Cannot return material. Reports in 1 month. Pays $200, 30 days after publication. Credit line given. Buys exclusive rights in our market, one-time rights; negotiable.
Tips: Wants to see "technical proficiency, appropriate subject matter, vision and creative sensibility. We strive for the highest level of photography in all areas and design. Do *not* send inappropriate submissions that are unrelated to Aspen, Colorado. All our photography (and editorial text) are geared to our role as a 'city' magazine. When we do use stock shots they are usually from photographers who have worked extensively in our town, but we still like to see the work of others as long as they have shots *from our area. No general submissions please.*"

ATLANTA JEWISH TIMES, Suite 470, 1575 Northside Dr., Atlanta GA 30318. (404)352-2400. Managing Editor: Fran Rothbard. Circ. 10,000+. Estab. 1925. Weekly tabloid. Emphasizes news of interest to Jewish community. Readers are well-educated, upscale and knowledgeable. Sample copy free with 9 × 13 SAE and 4 first-class stamps.
Needs: Uses approximately 15 photos/issue; 15% supplied by freelance photographers. Needs photos of Jewish holidays, personalities and events of interest (like rallies against the Klan, for example). Photo captions required.
Making Contact & Terms: Provide resume, business card, brochure, flyer or tearsheets to be kept on file for possible assignments. SASE. Reports in 1 month. Pays $75/color cover photo; $50/b&w cover photo; $25/b&w inside photo. Photo/text package negotiable. Pays on publication. Credit line given. Buys rights for use with 2 sister publications. Simultaneous and previously published work OK.
Tips: "Call us first if you have an idea so we can discuss options."

ATLANTIC CITY MAGAZINE, Dept. PM, Box 2100, Pleasantville NJ 08232. (609)272-7900. Editor: Ken Weatherford. Art Director: Michael Lacy. Circ. 50,000. Monthly. Sample copy $2 plus $1 postage.
Needs: Uses 50 photos/issue; all supplied by freelance photographers. Prefers to see b&w and color fashion, product and portraits, sports, theatrical. Model release required. Captions required.
Making Contact & Terms: Query with portfolio/samples. Cannot return material. Provide tearsheets to be kept on file for possible future assignments. Payment negotiable; usually $35-50/b&w photo; $50-100/color; $250-450/day; $175-300 for text/photo package. Pays on publication. Credit line given. Buys one-time rights.
Tips: "We promise only exposure, not great fees. We're looking for imagination, composition, sense of design, creative freedom and trust."

AUDUBON MAGAZINE, 950 3rd Ave., New York NY 10022. Picture Editor: Peter Howe. Bimonthly magazine. Circ. 475,000. Emphasizes wildlife. Sample copy $4. First-class $5.
Needs: Freelancers supply 100% of the photos. Photo essays of nature subjects, especially wildlife, showing animal behavior, unusual portraits with good lighting and artistic composition. Nature photos should be artistic and dramatic, not the calendar or post card scenic. Uses color covers only; horizontal wraparound format requires subject off-center. Also uses journalistic and human interest photos. Captions are required. Also seeks articles with accompanying photos on environmental topics, natural areas or wildlife, predominantly North America.
Making Contact & Terms: Important: Query first before sending material; include tearsheets or list previously published credits. SASE. Reports in 1 month. Portfolios should be geared to the magazine's subject matter. Must see original transparencies as samples. Uses 8 × 10 glossy b&w prints; 35mm, 2¼ × 2¼ and 4 × 5 transparencies. Plastic sheets only; no prints, no dupes. Pays $125-300/b&w and color inside; $700/color cover; $450/table of contents. Pays on publication. Credit line given. Buys one-time rights. No simultaneous sumbissions.
Tips: "Query first. Study recent issues (last 6 months). Do not send unsolicited material. If you do submit unsolicited material, it should be accompanied by return postage. We cannot assume the cost of sending back unsolicited material. All photos submitted must be accompanied by adequate captions or they will not be considered for publication."

AUTOGRAPH COLLECTOR MAGAZINE, 510-A So. Corona Mall, Corona CA 91720. (909)734-9636. Fax: (909)371-7139. Editors: Bill Miller and Darrell Talbert. Circ. 5,000. Extab. 1986. Magazine published 12 times/year. Emphasizes autograph collecting. Readers are all ages and occupations. Sample copy $6.
Needs: Uses 30-40 photos/issue; all supplied by freelancers. Needs photos of "autograph collectors with collections, autographs and VIPs giving autographs, historical documents in museums, etc." Model/property release required. Photo captions preferred.

Making Contact & Terms: Interested in receiving work from newer, lesser-known photographers. Send unsolicited photos by mail for consideration. Provide resume, business card, brochure, flyer or tearsheets to be kept on file for possible assignments. Send 4×5, 8×10 glossy b&w or color prints. SASE. Reports in 3 weeks. NPI. Pays on publication. Credit line given. Buys first N.A. serial rights; negotiable. Simultaneous submissions OK.

AUTOMOBILE MAGAZINE, 120 E. Liberty, Ann Arbor MI 48104. (313)994-3500. Art Director: Larry Crane. Circ. 500,000. Estab. 1986. Monthly magazine. Emphasizes automobiles. Readers are 97% male, $35,000-85,000/year income. Sample copy $5.
- This magazine recently won two silver Ozzie Awards and was listed as the third fastest growing magazine in America by *Advertising Age.*

Needs: Uses more than 100 photos/issue; all supplied by freelancers. Model release required. Property release preferred. "Our writers will write captions."

Making Contact & Terms: Interested in receiving work from newer, lesser-known photographers, but "it better be great." Query with resume. SASE. Reports in 1-2 weeks. Pays $900/color cover photo; $50-250/color inside photo; $750/day; $350/half day. **Pays on acceptance.** Credit line given. Buys one-time rights.

Tips: Looks for "car photos with an interesting twist—great compositions, super action, great ideas. Our photographers shoot on their own with little direction. Great ideas are *vital.* We need fewer photojournalists and more artists who can see."

BACK HOME IN KENTUCKY, P.O. Box 681629, Franklin TN 37068-1629. (615)794-4338. Fax: (615)790-6188. Editor: Nanci Gregg. Circ. 13,000. Estab. 1977. Bimonthly magazine. Emphasizes subjects in the state of Kentucky. Readers are interested in the heritage and future of Kentucky. Sample copy $2 with 9×12 SAE and $1.25 postage (first class).

Needs: Uses 25 photos/issue; all supplied by freelance photographers, less than 10% on assignment. Needs photos of scenic, specific places, events, people. Reviews photos with accompanying ms. Also seeking vertical cover (color) photos. Special needs include holidays in Kentucky; Christmas; the Kentucky Derby sights and sounds. Model release and captions required.

Making Contact & Terms: Interested in receiving work from newer, lesser-known photographers. Send any size, glossy b&w and color prints, 35mm transparencies by mail for consideration. Reports in 2 weeks. Pays $15/b&w photo; $20/color photo; $50+/cover photo; $15-100/text/photo package. Pays on publication. Credit line given. Usually buys one-time rights; also all rights; negotiable. Simultaneous submissions and previously published work OK.

Tips: "We look for someone who can capture the flavor of Kentucky—history, events, people, homes, etc. Have a great story to go with the photo—by self or another."

*BACKPACKER MAGAZINE, 33 E. Minor St., Emmaus PA 18098. (215)967-5171. Editor: John Viehman. Magazine published 9 times annually. Readers are male and female, ages 35-45. Photo guidelines free with SASE.

Needs: Uses 20-25 photos/issue; almost all supplied by freelancers. Needs photos of wildlife, scenics. Reviews photos with or without ms. Model/property release required.

Making Contact & Terms: Interested in receiving work from newer, lesser-known photographers. Query with resume of credits. Query with stock photo list. Provide resume, business card, brochure, flyer or tearsheets to be kept on file for possible assignments. SASE. Reports in 2 months. NPI; payment varies. Pays on publication. Credit line given. Rights negotiable. Sometimes considers simultaneous submissions and previously published work.

*BALL MAGAZINE, Side 'O' Fries Press 0775, Northampton MA 01061. (413)584-3076. Senior Editor: Douglas M. Kimball. Circ. 5,000-10,000. Estab. 1992. Quarterly magazine "hand bound." "Ball is interested in experimental, erotic, ethnic and class diversity photos." Readers are progressive, ages 18-40. Photo guidelines free with SASE.

Needs: Uses 2-8 photos/issue; all supplied by freelancers. Needs photos of experimental nature, erotica, grotesque, and in general, work which explores the dark or sinister side of American life. Reviews photos with or without ms. Model/property release preferred. Captions required; include date and format.

A bullet has been placed within some listings to introduce special comments by the editor of the Photographer's Market.

Making Contact & Terms: Interested in receiving work from newer, lesser-known photographers. Send unsolicited photos by mail for consideration. Uses b&w prints/transparencies. SASE. Reports in 1-2 weeks. Pays in contributor's copies. Pays on publication. Credit line given. Buys one-time rights. Simultaneous submissions OK.

Tips: "Give us work which reflects a working soul behind your technical proficiency that enhances the subject rather than abusing it. Our first priority is unique and diverse content. We encourage contributors to take chances stylistically."

BALLOON LIFE, 2145 Dale Ave., Sacramento CA 95815. (916)922-9648. Editor: Tom Hamilton. Circ. 4,000. Estab. 1986. Monthly magazine. Emphasizes sport ballooning. Readers are sport balloon enthusiasts. Sample copy free with 9 × 12 SAE and $2 postage. Photo guidelines free with 9 × 12 SASE.

Needs: Uses about 15-20 photos/issue; 90% supplied by freelance photographers, 5% on assignment. Needs how-to photos for technical articles, scenic for events. Model release preferred. Captions preferred.

Making Contact & Terms: Interested in receiving work from newer, lesser-known photographers. Send b&w or color prints; 35mm transparencies by mail for consideration. "We are now scanning our own color and doing color separations in house. As such we prefer 35mm transparencies above all other photos." SASE. Reports in 2 weeks. Pays $50/color cover photo; $15/b&w or color inside photo. Pays on publication. Credit line given. Buys first N.A. serial rights. Simultaneous submissions and previously published work OK.

Tips: "Photographs, generally, should be accompanied by a story. Cover the basics first. Good exposure, sharp focus, color saturation, etc. Then get creative with framing and content. Often we look for one single photograph that tells readers all they need to know about a specific flight or event. We're evolving our coverage of balloon events into more than just 'pretty balloons in the sky.' I'm looking for photographers who can go the next step and capture the people, moments in time, unusual happenings, etc. that make an event unique. Query first with interest in sport, access to people and events, experience shooting balloons or other outdoor special events."

BALLSTREET NEWS JOURNAL, (formerly *Ballstreet Journal*), 3768-C Hawkins NE, Albuquerque NM 87109. (505)343-1215. Fax: (505)343-1238. Editor: Marybeth Connelly. Circ. 25,000. Estab. 1991. Monthly magazine. Emphasizes sports card collections. Readers are male and female collectors, ages 25-60. Sample copy $6.95. Photo guidelines free with SASE.

Needs: Uses 18 photos/issue; all supplied by freelancers. Needs photos of basketball, football, hockey, baseball, auto racing in action. Amateur and professional athletes are used. Reviews photos with or without ms. Model/property release preferred. Captions preferred; include where and when photo was taken.

Making Contact & Terms: Interested in receiving work from newer, lesser-known photographers. Query with resume of credits. Provide resume, business card, brochure, flyer or tearsheets to be kept on file for possible assignments. Keeps samples on file. SASE. Reports in 2-3 weeks. Pays $200/color cover photo; $100/color inside photo. Pays on publication. Credit line given. Buys one-time rights; negotiable. Simultaneous submissions and/or previously published work OK.

Tips: "We are looking for action photos with plenty of border on all sides. In each issue there are shots of offensive and defensive plays, and a limited number of headshots. For the action photos, we look for a good angle on the player's face and evidence of action, like sprays of dirt from a player's shoes. Often we look at 10-12 photos of the same player before choosing the best shot. Take as many shots of an interesting scene as possible so you have several submissions to compare with others."

BASEBALL CARDS, Dept. PM, 700 E. State St., Iola WI 54990. (715)445-2214. Fax: (715)445-4087. Editor: Scott Kelnhofer. Monthly. Emphasizes sports memorabilia collecting. Readers are 12-45, male collectors. Circ. 310,000. Estab. 1981. Sample copy for 9 × 12 SAE with 5 first class stamps.

Needs: Uses about 10 photos/issue; all supplied by freelance photographers. Needs photos of baseball players, portrait and action. Model release and captions preferred.

Making Contact & Terms: Send color prints and 35mm and 2¼ × 2¼ transparencies. SASE. Reports in 2 weeks. Pays $25-50/b&w photo, $50-100/color photo. Pays on publication. Credit line given. Buys first and one-time reprint rights. Previously published work OK.

Tips: Seeing trend toward "more use of photographs. Since introducing a line of baseball cards bound in the publication, our photo needs are now 8-10 an issue." In portfolio or samples, "I'm looking for candid-portrait and action shots of baseball players, shots that capture a player's personality." To break in, "look at the magazine. See what we use. Then go out and shoot that sort of photo. And please don't ask us to credential you until you send us something we can use."

BASKETBALL DIGEST, Dept. PM, 990 Grove St., Evanston IL 60201-4370. (708)491-6440. Editor: Vince Aversano. Circ. 85,000. Monthly. Emphasizes pro-basketball.
Needs: Uses about 40 photos/issue; 100% supplied by freelance photographers. Needs sports action and portraits.
Making Contact & Terms: Provide resume, business card, brochure, flyer or tearsheets to be kept on file for possible future assignments. Uses 5×7 glossy b&w prints and 35mm transparencies. NPI. Pays on publication. Buys one-time rights.

BASSIN', Dept. PM, 15115 S. 76th East Ave., Bixby OK 74008. (918)366-4441. Managing Editor: Simon McCaffary. Published 8 times/year. Emphasizes bass fishing. Readers are predominantly male, adult; nationwide circulation with heavier concentrations in South and Midwest. Circ. 275,000 subscribers, 100,000 newsstand sales. Sample copy $2.50. Photo guidelines free.
Needs: Uses 50-75 photos/issue; "almost all of them" are supplied by freelance photographers. "We need both b&w and Kodachrome action shots of freshwater fishing; close-ups of fish with lures, tackle, etc., and scenics featuring lakes, streams and fishing activity." Captions required.
Making Contact & Terms: Query with samples. SASE. Reports in 6 weeks. Pays $250-300/color cover photo; $25/b&w inside photo; $35-150/color inside photo. Pays on publication. Credit line given. Buys first N.A. serial rights.
Tips: "Send lots of photos and give me a specific deadline in which to send them back. Don't send lists—I can't pick a photo from a grocery list. In the past, we used only photos sent in with stories from freelance writers. However, we would like higher quality stuff. I urge freelance photographers to participate."

♣BC OUTDOORS, 202-1132 Hamilton St., Vancouver, British Columbia V6B 2S2 Canada. (604)687-1581. Fax: (604)687-1925. Editor: George Will. Circ. 42,000. Estab. 1943. Emphasizes fishing, both fresh water and salt; hunting; RV camping; wildlife and management issues. Published 8 times/year (January/February, March, April, May, June, July/August, September/October, November/December). Free sample copy with $2 postage.
Needs: Uses about 30-35 photos/issue; 99% supplied by freelance photographers on assignment. "Fishing (in our territory) is a big need—people in the act of catching, or releasing fish. Hunting, canoeing and camping. Family oriented. By far most photos accompany mss. We are always on lookout for good covers—fishing, wildlife, recreational activities, people in the outdoors—horizontal and square format, primarily of British Columbia and Yukon. Photos with mss must, of course, illustrate the story. There should, as far as possible, be something happening. Photos generally dominate lead spread of each story. They are used in everything from double-page bleeds to thumbnails. Column needs basically supplied inhouse." Model/property release preferred. Captions or at least full identification required.
Making Contact & Terms: Send by mail for consideration actual 5×7 or 8×10 b&w prints; 35mm, 2¼×2¼, 4×5 or 8×10 color transparencies; color contact sheet. If color negative, send jumbo prints and negatives only on request. Query with list of stock photo subjects. SASE, Canadian stamps. Reports in 1-2 weeks normally. Pays $40-75/b&w photo; $50-300/color photo; and $150-up/cover photo. "Payment for photos when layout finalized so we know what we're using. We try to give 'photos-only' contributors an approximate publication date at time of acceptance. We reach an arrangement with the contributor in such cases (usually involving dupes)." Credit line given. Buys one-time rights inside; with covers "we retain the right for subsequent promotional use." Simultaneous submissions not acceptable if competitor; previously published work OK.
Tips: "We see a trend toward more environmental/conservation issues."

BETTER NUTRITION FOR TODAY'S LIVING, Dept. PM, 6151 Powers Ferry Rd., Atlanta GA 30339. (404)955-2500. Contact: Art Director. Circ. 450,000. Monthly magazine. Emphasizes "health food, healthy people." Readers are 30-40. Sample copy free with 9×12 SAE and 2 first-class stamps. Free guideline sheet with SASE.
Needs: Uses 8-10 photos/issue; 6 supplied by freelancers. Needs photos of "healthy people exercising (skiing, running, etc.) food shots, botanical shots." Model release preferred.
Making Contact & Terms: Send unsolicited photos by mail for consideration. Send 35mm transparencies. SASE. Reports in 1 month. Pays $400/color cover photo; $150/color inside photo. Pays on publication. Credit line given. Buys one-time rights. Simultaneous submissions and previously published work OK.

 The maple leaf before a listing indicates that the market is Canadian.

Tips: "We are looking for photos of healthy people (all ages) usually in outdoor settings. We work on a limited budget, so do not send submissions if you cannot work within it. Review past issues for photo style."

BICYCLING PLUS MT BIKE, 135 N. 6th St., Emmaus PA 18098. (215)967-5171. Editor and Publisher: James C. McCullagh. Photography Director: Mike Shaw. Publishes 10 monthly issues, 2 bimonthly issues. Circ. 300,000. Emphasizes touring, commuting, health, fitness and nutritional information, recreational riding and technical gearing for the beginning to advanced bicyclist. Sample copy $2; writer's/photo guidelines free with SASE.
Needs: Buys 10-20 photos/issue. Prefers photos with accompanying ms. Celebrity/personality, documentary, how-to, human interest, photo essay/photo feature, product shot, scenic, special effects and experimental, sport, spot news and travel. Seeks mss on any aspects of bicycling (nonmotorized); commuting, health, fitness and nutritional information, touring or recreational riding. Captions for destination, travel, race photography are required. Captioning on slide mounts is acceptable.
Making Contact & Terms: Send material by mail for consideration or query with resume of credits. SASE a must. Reports in 1 month. Uses b&w negatives; all formats of transparencies; vertical format required for *Mt Bike* cover. Pays $35-70/b&w photo; $75-300/color photo; $300/cover photo. Credit line given. Pays on publication. Buys one-time rights. Pays $25-300/ms.
Tips: "Major bicycling events (those that attract 500 or more) are good possibilities for feature coverage in the magazine. Use some racing photos. The freelance photographer should contact us and show examples of his/her work; then, talk directly to the editor for guidance on a particular shoot. For Mt Bike covers: Shoot vertical. The logo and blurbs run on every cover. These are constant; be aware of their location and what that means while shooting. A large single image that creates a simple cover often works best. Riding: While shooting people riding, be aware of the background. Watch out for wires, shadows, or other major distractions. Make sure people are riding in proper positions; must be wearing a helmet, dressed properly and on the correct side of the road. Models must be attractive, competent riders. A little color in their clothing helps lift them off the page. We are interested in receiving good, off-road, Mt Biking pictures. Singletrack riding through great landscapes is desirable, however, we do not want to see riders off the trail. Our photos comply with NORBA guidelines for off-road riding. Stay on trails, stay off delicate, living environments."

*BIKE JOURNAL INTERNATIONAL, 6 Prowitt St., Norwalk CT 06855. (203)855-0008. Fax: (203)853-9980. Art Director: Todd Mitchell. Circ. under 100,000. Estab. 1989. Monthly magazine. Emphasizes classic collectible motorcycles, hundreds of classifieds. Sample copy free with 8½ × 11 SAE and 3 first-class stamps. Photo guidelines free with SASE.
Needs: Uses 30-60 photos/issue; 90% supplied by freelancers. Needs photos of classic motorcycles with various, clean, clear, and attractive backgrounds, action shots. Will review photos with or without ms. Special photo needs include medium to large format, action shots. Captions preferred; include information on either the bike or the owner.
Making Contact & Terms: Interested in receiving work from newer, lesser-known photographers. Send unsolicited photos by mail for consideration. Provide resume, business card, brochure, flyer or tearsheets to be kept on file for possible assignments. Send color and b&w prints of various sizes; 35mm, 2¼ × 2¼, 4 × 5, 8 × 10 transparencies. Keeps samples on file. SASE. NPI. Pays on publication. Credit line not given. Buys one-time rights.
Tips: Looks for "creativity, clear action shots, detail, proper lighting."

BIRD TALK, P.O. Box 6050, Mission Viejo CA 92690. (714)855-8822. Photo Editor: Kathleen Etchepare. Monthly magazine. Emphasizes "better care of pet birds through informative and entertaining articles. Some birds of interest are: canaries, finches, parrots, parakeets, toucans, macaws, conures, lovebirds, cockatiels, cockatoos, mynahs." Readers are "owners of one pet bird or breeders of many." Sample copy $4.50. Photo guidelines free with SASE.
Needs: Uses 50-75 photos/issue; all by freelance photographers. Needs photos of "any and all pet birds either in portraits or in action—doing anything a bird is able to do." Model release and captions preferred.
Making Contact & Terms: Send 35mm, 5 × 7, 8 × 10 b&w prints; 35mm, 2¼ × 2¼, 4 × 5, 8 × 10 transparencies by mail for consideration. SASE. Reports in 4 weeks. Pays inside partial page: $15/b&w photo, $50/color photo; full pages: $25/b&w, $75/color; $150/cover and centerfold. Color prints acceptable but will often be used b&w. Pays on publication. Credit line given. Buys one-time rights.
Tips: Prefers to see "sharp feather focus. Cage bars acceptable, cages and perches must be clean. More b&w photos are used per issue than color. Send us clear shots of any pet birds with cover letter specifying *species* of bird. We also need a variety of shots of people interacting with their birds."

BIRD WATCHER'S DIGEST, Dept. PM, Box 110, Marietta OH 45750. (614)373-5285. Managing Editor/ Photography and Art: Bill Thompson III. Bimonthly. Circ. 99,000. Emphasizes birds and bird watchers. Readers are bird watchers/birders (backyard and field, veterans and novices). Digest size. Sample copy $3.50.
Needs: Uses 25-35 photos/issue; all supplied by freelance photographers. Needs photos of North American species. For the most part, photos are purchased with accompanying ms. Model release preferred.
Making Contact & Terms: Query with list of stock photo subjects and samples. SASE. Reports in 2 months. Pays $50-up/color inside. Pays on publication. Credit line given. Buys one-time rights. Previously published work in other bird publications should not be submitted.

BLADE MAGAZINE, Dept. PM, P.O. Box 22007, Chattanooga TN 37422. (615)894-0354. Fax: (615)892-7254. Managing Editor: Steve Shackleford. Circ. 100,000. Estab. 1973. Publishes 5 issues/ year. Specializes in handmade and factory knives. Readers are aged 30-70, blue collar, outdoors types, collectors. Sample copy free with 9×12 SAE and $2 postage. Photo guidelines free with SASE.
Needs: Uses 130 photos/issue; freelancer photography/issue—10% assignment and 60% freelance stock. Needs photos of how-tos on knifemaking, knife shots with artsy backgrounds, knives being used, knives on display, etc. Special needs include shots of the latest factory and handmade knives; any kind of colorful knife shot. Model release required. Captions required.
Making Contact & Terms: Send unsolicited photos by mail for consideration. Uses 4×5 or 5×7 color prints or 35mm transparencies. SASE. Reports in 1 month. Pays $50 up/b&w or color cover photo; $7/color or b&w inside photo. **Pays on acceptance.** Credit line given. Buys all rights; negotiable. Also publishes *Edges,* a pocketknife collector's tabloid. Black and white photos only used; read *Blade Magazine* listing for *Edges* information. Also publishes *Blade Trade,* b&w only; same rates and rules apply as for *Blade Magazine.*
Tips: Looks for "a true appreciation for the subtleties of knife design. Closeups of individual knife parts that tell more about the knife than any editorial can are also telling. Appreciation of appropriate props, ability to keep glare off blades (or to use glare in an artistic manner). Make the shot as animate as possible, even though knives are inanimate objects. Provide a variety of shots at reasonable prices and in plenty of time for each deadline."

THE BLOOMSBURY REVIEW, Dept. PM, 1028 Bannock St., Denver CO 80204. (303)892-0620. Art Director: Chuck McCoy. Editor: Tom Auer. Circ. 50,000. Published 6 times a year. Emphasizes book reviews, articles and stories of interest to book readers. Sample copy $3.50.
Needs: Uses 2-3 photos/issue; all supplied by freelance photographers. Needs photos of people who are featured in articles. Photos purchased with or without accompanying ms. Model release preferred. Captions preferred.
Making Contact & Terms: Provide brochure, tearsheets and sample print to be kept on file for possible future assignments. SASE. Reports in 1 month. NPI. Payment by the job varies. Pays on publication. Credit line and one-line bio given. Buys one-time rights.
Tips: "Send good photocopies of work to Art Director."

BLUE RIDGE COUNTRY, P.O. Box 21535, Roanoke VA 24018. (703)989-6138. Art Director: Rob Agee. Circ. 70,000. Estab. 1988. Bimonthly magazine. Emphasizes outdoor scenics of Blue Ridge Mountain region. Readers are upscale couples, ages 30-70. Sample copy free with 9×12 SAE and $2 postage. Photo guidelines free with SASE.
Needs: Uses up to 20 photos/issue; all supplied by freelance photographers; 10% assignment and 90% freelance stock. Needs photos of travel, scenics and wildlife. Future photo needs include themes of the Blue Ridge region. Model release preferred. Captions required.
Making Contact & Terms: Query with list of stock photo subjects. Send unsolicited photos by mail for consideration. Uses 35mm, 2¼×2¼, 4×5 transparencies. SASE. Reports in 1-2 months. Pays $100/color cover photo; $25-75/b&w photo; $25-100/color photo. Pays on publication. Credit line given. Buys one-time rights.
Tips: In photographer's samples looks for "photos of Blue Ridge region, color saturated, focus required and photo abilities. Freelancer should present him/herself neatly and organized."

THE B'NAI B'RITH INTERNATIONAL JEWISH MONTHLY, 1640 Rhode Island Ave. NW, Washington DC 20036. (202)857-6645. Editor: Jeff Rubin. Circ. 200,000. Estab. 1886. Monthly magazine. Emphasizes Jewish religion, cultural and political concerns worldwide.
Needs: Buys 100 photos/year, stock and on assignment. Occasionally publishes photo essays.
Making Contact & Terms: Present samples and text (if available). SASE. Reports in 6 weeks. Pays $25-300/b&w or color photo (cover); $300/day; $100-500/photo/text package. Pays on publicaiton. Buys first serial rights.
Tips: "Be familiar with our format and offer suggestions or experience relevant to our needs." Looks for "technical expertise, ability to tell a story within the frame."

BOAT PENNSYLVANIA, Dept. PM, Box 67000, Harrisburg PA 17106-1700. (717)657-4518. Editor: Art Michaels. Quarterly magazine. Published by the Pennsylvania Fish and Boat Commission. Emphasizes "non-angling boating in Pennsylvania: powerboating, canoeing, kayaking, sailing, personal watercraft and water skiing." Sample copy and guidelines free with 9 × 12 SAE and 4 first-class stamps.

• This publication only reviews original materials. Duplicates are not accepted.

Needs: Uses about 30 photos/issue; 80% supplied by freelance photographers. Model release required. Captions required.

Making Contact & Terms: Query with resume of credits. Send 35mm, 2¼ × 2¼ transparencies by mail for consideration. SASE. Reports in 1 week on queries; 3 months on submissions. NPI. **Pays on acceptance.** Credit line given. Buys variable rights, most often first rights.

Tips: "We are hungry for top-quality materials, but no matter how good a picture is, we insist on a few items. We feature subjects appropriate to Pennsylvania, so we can't use pictures with obviously non-Pennsylvania backgrounds. We prefer to show boats registered in Pennsylvania. If this is a problem, try to hide the boat registration completely. Finally, *Boat Pennsylvania* stresses safety, so pictures must show boaters accordingly. For instance, we would not publish a picture of a powerboat under way with people lying on the gunwale or leaning over the side. Submit a selection of cover possibilities. We look for verticals mostly, but we'd love to see horizontals for possible wraparounds."

*BODY, MIND & SPIRIT MAGAZINE, P.O. Box 701, Providence RI 02901. (401)351-4320. Fax: (401)272-5767. Editor-in-Chief: Paul Zuromski. Editor: Carol Kramer. Circ. 175,000. Estab. 1982. Bimonthly. Emphasizes New Age, natural living, metaphysical topics. Readers are split male/female interested in personal transformation and growth. Sample copy free with 9 × 12 SAE.

Needs: Uses 10-15 photos/issue; 5-10 supplied by freelance photographers. Needs special effects, inspirationals, paranormal photography; photos that are uplifting, spiritual (not religious) and illustrative of the New Age. Model release required. Captions required.

Making Contact & Terms: Interested in receiving work from newer, lesser-known photographers. Query with samples. Provide resume, business card, brochure, price requirements if available, flyer or tearsheets to be kept on file for possible future assignments. SASE. Reports in 1-3 months. Pays $20-100/b&w photo; $20-150/color photo. Pays on publication. Credit line given. Buys one-time rights. Previously published work OK.

Tips: Sees an increase in use of computer graphics. In portfolio or samples, wants to see "imagination, ability to portray abstract ideas." To break in, "be neat! Be clear and specific about expectations and requirements. Most photos are still purchased from stock because submissions are very pretty, but communicate nothing."

BOSTON MAGAZINE, Dept. PM, 300 Massachusetts Ave., Boston MA 02115. (617)262-9700. Art Director: Greg Klee. Associate Art Director: Lisa Puccio. Monthly magazine. Emphasizes a wide variety of subjects with Boston/New England focus. Readers are primarily residents of greater Boston metro area, and most of eastern Massachusetts, Cape Cod, southern New England; largely college-educated professionals who regard Boston as focal point of their lives. Circ. 140,000. Sample copy free with 9 × 12 SAE and $2.40 postage.

BOSTONIA MAGAZINE, 10 Lenox St., Brookline MA 02146. (617)353-9711. Editor: Keith Botsford. Art Director: Douglas Parker. Estab. 1900. Bimonthly. Circ. 150,000. Sample copy $3.50.

Needs: Uses 100 photos/issue; many photos are supplied by freelance photographers. Works with freelance photographers on assignment only basis. Provide resume, brochure and samples to be kept on file for possible future assignments. Needs include documentary photos and international travel photos; photo essay/photo features and human interest; and possibly art photos presented in long portfolio sections. Also seeks feature articles on people and the New England area accompanied by photos. Model releases and captions required.

Making Contact & Terms: Call for appointment or send photos by mail for consideration; send actual 5 × 7 b&w glossies for inside. SASE. Reports in 2 weeks. Pays on acceptance $50-400 for b&w photo; $300-600/color photo. 10¢/word or flat fee (depending on amount of preparation) for feature articles. Credit line given. Buys all rights, but may reassign to photographer after publication. No simultaneous submissions or previously published work.

BOW & ARROW HUNTING, Dept. PM, Box HH, Capistrano Beach CA 92624. (714)493-2101. Fax: (714)240-8680. Editor: Jack Lewis. Circ. 150,000. Bimonthly magazine. For archers and bowhunters. "We emphasize bowhunting—with technical pieces, how-tos, techniques, bowhunting tips, personality profiles and equipment tests." Writer's guidelines included with photo guidelines.

Needs: "We buy approximately 4 text/photo packages per issue." Technical pieces, personality profiles, humor, tournament coverage, how-to stories, bowhunting stories (with tips), equipment tests and target technique articles. Needs photos of animal (for bowhunting stories); celebrity/personality (if the celebrity is involved in archery); head shot (occasionally used with personality profiles, but we prefer a full-length shot with the person shooting the bow, etc.); how-to (must be step-by-step); human interest; humorous; nature, travel and wildlife (related to bowhunting); photo essay/photo feature; product shot (with equipment tests); scenic (only if related to a story); sport (of tournaments); and sport news. "No snapshots (particularly color snapshots), and no photos of animals that were not hunted by the rules of fair chase." Photos purchased with accompanying ms; rarely without. Captions required, include location, species and month taken.

Making Contact & Terms: Interested in receiving work from newer, lesser-known photographers. Query with samples OK, but prefers to see completed material by mail on speculation. Uses 5×7 or 8×10 glossy color and b&w prints; 35mm or 2¼×2¼ transparencies. SASE. Reports in 4-6 weeks. Pays $50-300 for text/photo package or on a per-photo basis for photos without accompanying ms. **Pays on acceptance.** Credit line given. Buys one-time rights.

Tips: "Send us a good, clean manuscript with good-quality b&w glossies (our use of color is limited). Most cover shots are freelance. Review the magazine before you submit anything."

❧BOWBENDER, Suite 200, 807 Manning Rd. NE, Calgary, Alberta T2E 7M8 Canada. (403)335-9445. Fax: (403)569-9590. Editor: Mrs. Kathleen Windsor. Five times/year. Emphasizes archery in Canada, especially bowhunting. Readership consists of married, professional males, 25-40 years of age with $20-40,000 annual income. Circ. 45,000. Estab. 1984. Sample copy for $2.50 and 9×12 SAE. Photo guidelines free with SASE; postage from U.S. must be submitted through Canadian mail order; postage from Canada, 39¢ stamp.

Needs: Uses 30 photos/issue; 100% supplied by freelance photographers; 99% comes from freelance stock and rest freelance photography from assignment. Uses big game animal shots only. Written release and captions preferred.

Making Contact & Terms: Query with list of stock photos or send unsolicited photos by mail for consideration. Send color and b&w, all sizes, all formats. SASE. Reports in 3 weeks maximum. Pays $200/color cover photo; $60/color inside photo; $30/b&w inside photo; 8-10¢ word/photo/text package (Canadian currency). Pays on publication. Credit line given. Buys first N.A. serial rights. Does not consider simultaneous submissions or previously published work.

Tips: Looking for shots of "any huntable big game for front cover: vertical shots clear, especially eyes. Close-up shots are best. Trend is mostly b&w inside shots. Submit samples first along with stock file. Label slides somehow. If photos are not catalogued by some code, at least label them. Slides especially are irreplaceable. We use as many photos as we can each issue. Look at a past issue before submitting."

BOWHUNTER, 6405 Flank Dr., P.O. Box 8200, Harrisburg PA 17105. (717)657-9555. Editor: M.R. James. Publisher/Editorial Director: Dave Canfield. Managing Editor: Richard Cochran. Circ. 250,000. Estab. 1971. Published 8 times/year. Emphasizes bow and arrow hunting. Sample copy $2. Writer's guidelines free with SASE.

Needs: Buys 50-75 photos/year. Scenic (showing bowhunting) and wildlife (big and small game of North America). No cute animal shots or poses."We want informative, entertaining bowhunting adventure, how-to and where-to-go articles." Photos purchased with or without accompanying ms.

Making Contact & Terms: Send material by mail for consideration. Query with samples. SASE. Reports on queries in 1-2 weeks; on material in 4-6 weeks. Uses 5×7 or 8×10 glossy b&w and color prints, both vertical and horizontal format; 35mm and 2¼×2¼ transparencies, vertical format; vertical format preferred for cover. Pays $35-100/b&w photo; $50-250/color photo; $300/cover photo, occasionally "more if photo warrants it." **Pays on acceptance.** Credit line given. Buys one-time publication rights.

Tips: "Know bowhunting and/or wildlife and study several copies of our magazine before submitting any material. We're looking for better quality and we're using more color on inside pages. Most purchased photos are of big game animals. Hunting scenes are second. In b&w we look for sharp, realistic light, good contrast. Color must be sharp; early, late light is best. We avoid anything that looks staged; we want natural settings, quality animals. Send only your best, and if at all possible let us hold those we indicate interest in. Very little is taken on assignment; most comes from our files or is part of the manuscript package. If your work is in our files it will probably be used."

BOWHUNTING WORLD, Dept. PM, Suite 101, 319 Barry Ave. S., Wayzata MN 55391. (612)476-2200. Editor: Tim Dehn. Published 11 times/year. "*Bowhunting World* is the oldest and most respected magazine in print for the hunting archer." It focuses editorially on all aspects of hunting with a bow and arrow in North America. Readers are primarily male, college-educated, avid bowhunters who participate in their sport year-round and who make an above-average income. Circ. 250,000. Estab. 1952. Free sample copy and photo guidelines.

Needs: Uses 10-25 photos/issue; most from freelancer stock. "We want to see wildlife subjects commonly hunted as big game and small game species in North America." Special needs include "big game species for cover selections."

Making Contact & Terms: Send 35mm by mail for consideration. SASE. Reports in 2-4 weeks. Pays $250/color cover photo; $40/b&w inside photo; $75-125 color/inside photo; and $200-500/text/photo package. Pays on publication. Credit line given. Buys one-time rights. Simultaneous submissions and previously published work OK "but please so state in cover letter."

Tips: "We look for technically excellent photos with trophy-class animals and/or unusual and beautiful settings. We're using more color than ever before, far less freelance b&w. And our covers are no longer limited to deer—we're using elk, bear and are open to moose, caribou and antelope as well. Send small, carefully screened submissions—not more than 60 slides. 20 excellent ones will get a far better reception than 20 excellent mixed with 40 average. Be prepared for us to hold your slides on file up to a year, and if there's a limit to the number we should hold, say so."

BOWLING DIGEST, 990 Grove St., Evanston IL 60201-4370. (708)491-6440. Editor: Vince Aversano. Circ. 150,000. Bimonthly. Emphasizes pro and amateur bowling.

Needs: Uses 50 photos/issue; all supplied by freelance photographers. Needs sports action and portraits.

Making Contact & Terms: Provide resume, business card, brochure, flyer or tearsheets to be kept on file for possible future assignments. NPI. Pays on publication. Buys one-time rights.

BRIDE'S & YOUR NEW HOME, Condé Nast Publications. 350 Madison Ave., New York NY 10017. (212)880-8829. Fax: (212)880-8331. Assistant to the Art Director: Ashley Thompson. Bimonthly magazine. Emphasizes weddings, marriage, honeymoon and setting up "your new home." Readers are engaged couples and their families reading for marriage advice and ideas at any age. Circ. 350,000-400,000. Estab. 1934. Sample copy free with SASE.

Needs: Uses photos of fashion, beauty, home interiors and stills, lifestyle, travel and scenics. Reviews photos with or without a ms. Model/property release required.

Making Contact & Terms: Contact through rep. Submit portfolio for review. Query with stock photo list. Provide resume, business card, brochure, flyer or tearsheets to be kept on file for possible assignments. Keeps samples on file. Reporting time depends on work and prospect of job. Pays $1,500/color cover photo; $250/color page rate; $200/b&w page rate; $200 & up/day. Pays day rate upon completion and page rate upon publication. Credit line given. Buys one-time rights and all rights (travel only); negotiable.

Tips: "Don't send us only examples of bridal fashion."

BRIGADE LEADER, P.O. Box 150, Wheaton IL 60189. (708)665-0630. Fax: (708)665-0372. Associate Editor: Deborah Christensen. Art Director: Robert Fine. Circ. 9,000. Estab. 1959. Quarterly magazine. For Christian men, age 20 and up. Seeks "to make men aware of their leadership responsibilities toward boys in their families, churches and communities." Sample copy $1.50 with 9×12 SAE and 98¢ postage. Photo guidelines free with SASE.

Needs: Buys 2-7 photos/issue; 50% freelance photography/issue comes from assignment and 50% from freelance stock. Needs photos of men in varied situations (alone, with their sons, with groups of boys or with one boy, with their families or at work), head shot, photo essay/photo feature and scenic.

Making Contact & Terms: Interested in receiving work from newer, lesser-known photographers. Arrange a personal interview to show portfolio or send photos for consideration. Send 8×10 glossy prints. Reports in 6 weeks. Pays $35/inside b&w photo; $75-100/b&w cover photo. Pays on publication. Buys first and second serial rights. Simultaneous submissions and previously published work OK.

Tips: "Do not send pornography or nudes. Study the magazine before submitting. Submit sharp and clear photos. We receive too much second-rate work."

BRITISH CAR, Dept. PM, P.O. Box 9099, Canoga Park CA 91309. (818)710-1234. Fax: (818)710-1877. Editor: Dave Destler. Circ. 30,000. Estab. 1985. Bimonthly magazine. Publication for owners and enthusiasts of British motor cars. Readers are U.S. citizens, male, 40 years old and owners of multiple cars. Sample copy $4.50. Photo guidelines free for SASE.

Needs: Uses 100 photos/issue; 50-75% (75% are b&w) supplied by freelancers. "Photos with accompanied manuscripts preferred. However, sharp uncluttered photos of different British marques may be submitted for file photos to be drawn on as needed." Photo captions required that include description of vehicles, owner's name and phone number, interesting facts, etc.

Making Contact & Terms: Send unsolicited photos by mail for consideration. Send 5×7 and larger, b&w prints. Does not keep samples on file unless there is a good chance of publication. SASE. "Publisher takes all reasonable precautions with materials, however cannot be held liable for damaged or lost photos." Reports in 6-8 weeks. Pays $25-100/color inside photo; $10-35/b&w inside photo. Payment negotiable, however standard rates will be paid unless otherwise agreed in writing prior to publication." Pays on publication. Buys world rights; negotiable.

Tips: "Find a journalist to work in cooperation with. Good photos submitted with a manuscript have a better chance of publication."

BRITISH HERITAGE, Cowles Magazines, Inc., P.O. Box 8200, Harrisburg PA 17105. (717)657-9555. Fax: (717)657-9552. Editor: Gail Huganir. Circ. 110,000. Estab. 1974. Bimonthly magazine. Emphasizes British history and travel. Readers are professional, middle-aged. Sample copy $4.85. Photographic guidelines available with SASE.
Needs: Uses about 50 photos/issue; 95% supplied by freelance photographers; 99% freelance stock and 1% assignment. Needs travel, scenic and historical photos. Captions required.
Making Contact & Terms: Provide resume, business card, brochure, flyer or tearsheets to be kept on file for possible future assignments. SASE. Reports in 4-6 weeks. Negotiates pay for cover photos. Pays $50-100/b&w inside photo; $75-250/color inside photo. Pays on publication. Credit line given. Buys one-time rights.
Tips: Looks for "good focal point, bright colors and sharp image. We prefer 2×2 or 2½×2¼ color transparencies. Call before submitting and for photographic guidelines."

*HUBIE BROWN'S PRO BASKETBALL, #204, 17962 Midvale Ave. N., Seattle WA 98133. (206)546-2461. Fax: (206)546-6015. Photo Editor: Eric Radovich. Circ. 200,000. Estab. 1983. Annual magazine. Emphasizes professional basketball. Readers are mostly college-educated males, ages 25-55. Sample copy $5.95.
Needs: Uses 100-150 photos/issue; all supplied by freelancers. Needs photos of sports action.
Making Contact & Terms: Interested in receiving work from newer, lesser-known photographers. Query with resume of credits. SASE. Reports in 3 weeks. Pays $100-150/color cover photo; $50-100/color inside photo; $20-50/b&w inside photo. Pays 60 days after on-sale date. Credit line given. Simultaneous submissions OK.

BUSINESS IN BROWARD, P.O. Box 7375, Ft. Lauderdale FL 33338-7375. (305)563-8805. Publisher: Sherry Friedlander. Circ. 20,000. Estab. 1986. Bi-monthly magazine. Emphasizes business. Readers are male and female executives, ages 30-65. Sample copy $4.
Needs: Uses 30-40 photos/issue; 75% supplied by freelancers. Needs photos of local sports, local people, ports, activities and festivals. Model/property release required. Photo captions required.
Making Contact & Terms: Contact through rep. Submit portfolio for review. Reports in 1-2 weeks. Pays $150/color cover photo; $75/color inside photo. Pays on publication. Buys one-time rights; negotiable. Previously published work OK.
Tips: "Know the area we service." Also publishes *Business in Palm Beach County.*

*BUSINESS PHILADELPHIA, 260 S. Broad St., Philadelphia PA 19102. (215)735-6971. Fax: (215)735-6965. Design Director: Nicole Fichera. Monthly magazine. Emphasizes business through the eyes of business people. Readers are CEO's, presidents, vice presidents and other top-level business executives.
Needs: Uses 20-25 photos/issue; 15 supplied by freelancers. Needs portrait photos, studio and location shots and still lifes. Reviews photos with or without a manuscript. Model release preferred.
Making Contact & Terms: Interested in receiving work from newer, lesser-known photographers. Submit portfolio for review. Provide resume, business card, brochure, flyer or tearsheets to be kept on file for possible assignments. Keeps samples on file. Reports in 1-2 weeks. Pays $75-200/job; $100-200/feature story, plus expenses. Pays 30 days after acceptance. Credit line given. Buys one-time rights; negotiable. Previously published work OK.
Tips: "Photographers should work well with CEO's, presidents and other executives whose portraits they are taking, while providing unique and avante garde concepts or styles to their photographs. While we do not offer much monetarily, *Business Philadelphia* offers photographers opportunities to experiment and create more artistic images than most business publications. Photographers should base the worth of an assignment using the amount of artistic control they have as well as the dollar amounts being offered."

BUXOM, 10th Floor, 801 Second Ave., New York NY 11217. (212)661-7878. Fax: (212)692-9297. Editor: Marc Medoff. Circ. 81,000. Estab. 1989. Bimonthly magazine. Emphasizes large-breasted women. Readers are young males, blue collar workers, over 18 years old. Sample copies free with 8½×11 SASE and 10 first class stamps. Photo guidelines free with SASE.
Needs: Uses 100-200 photos/issue; all supplied by freelancers. Needs photos of nude women with large breasts. Reviews photos with or without accompanying ms. Model/property release required, include copies of photo identification with date of birth over 18 years old.
Making Contact & Terms: Submit portfolio for review. Send unsolicited photos by mail for consideration. Provide resume, business card, brochure, flyer or tearsheets to be kept on file for possible future assignments. Send 35mm transparencies. Keeps samples on file. SASE. Reports in 1 month. Payment varies from $10/shot to $3,000/full set. **Pays on acceptance.** Credit line given. Buys one-time rights;

negotiable. Simultaneous submissions and previously published work OK.
Tips: "We require technical perfection. Focus, lighting, composition, etc. must be 100% perfect. Look at our magazine and competing titles."

BUZZWORM: The Environmental Journal, Suite 206, 2305 Canyon Blvd., Boulder CO 80302. (303)442-1969. Photo Editor: Christy Brennand. Circ. 100,000. Estab. 1988. Bimonthly magazine. Emphasizes environmental issues and worldwide conservation. Readers are affluent, educated, active, both sexes and a median age of 37. Sample copy $5. Photo guidelines free with SASE.
Needs: Uses 50 photos/issue; most are supplied by freelance photographers. Photo needs are specific to articles, mostly wildlife and environment. Model release preferred. Captions preferred.
Making Contact & Terms: Query with resume of credits and list of stock photo subjects. Provide resume, business card, brochure, flyer or tearsheets to be kept on file. No unsolicited calls or photos. SASE. Pays $400/color cover photo; $200/color page rate. Pays 60-90 days after publication. Credit line given. Buys one-time rights.
Tips: Wants to see photographer's tearsheets, stock lists, resume, specialties and future travel plans. "Send information requested and update us by mail as to your most recent photography, travels, etc."

*CABLE GUIDE MAGAZINE, 475 Fifth Ave., New York NY 10017. (212)683-6116. Fax: (212)683-8051. Photo Editor: Heather Alberts. Circ. 6 million. Monthly magazine. Emphasizes movie and TV personalities, sports figures, musicians, nature.
Needs: Uses 20-25 photos/issue; all supplied by freelancers. Needs photos of personalities or TV and movie coverage. Reviews photos with or without ms. Model/property release preferred. Captions preferred.
Making Contact & Terms: Interested in receiving work from newer, lesser-known photographers. Submit portfolio for review. SASE. Reports in 1-2 weeks. Pays $350-2,000/job. **Pays on acceptance.** Credit line given. Simultaneous submissions and/or previously published work OK.

CALIFORNIA ANGLER MAGAZINE, Dept. PM, Suite 3N, 1921 E. Carnegie St. N., Santa Ana CA 92705. (714)261-9779. Fax: (714)261-9853. Editor: Chuck Garrison. Circ. 30,000. Estab. 1985. Publishes 11 issues/year. Emphasizes fresh and saltwater fishing in California. Readers are 97% male, age 18-65 and dedicated California sport fishermen. Sample copy free with SAE and 3 first-class stamps. Photo guidelines free with SASE.
Needs: Uses 20-40 photos/issue; most supplied by freelance photographers. Needs shots depicting angling action rather than dead fish, and pictures illustrating angling how-to, technical skills. Special needs include underwater pictures of game fish, especially saltwater species and cover shots. Model release preferred. Captions required.
Making Contact & Terms: Interested in receiving work from newer, lesser-known photographers. Query with resume of credits and stock photo list. Send 35mm (Kodachrome or Fuji) or 2¼×2¼ transparencies by mail for consideration. SASE. Reports in 2 weeks. Pays $200-400/color cover photo; $25/b&w inside photo; $30-100/color inside photo; $300 for text/photo package. **Pays on acceptance** and on publication. Credit line given. Buys one-time rights; negotiable. Simultaneous submissions and previously published work sometimes OK.
Tips: Looks for "someone who has good action, scenic, supplemental, and people photos of fishing. Send samples. We get so little honestly good material, we hug the good stuff."

CALLIOPE, World History for Young People, 7 School St., Peterborough NH 03458. (603)924-7209. Fax: (603)924-7380. Picture Editor: Francelle Carapetyan. Circ. 7,000. Estab. 1990. Magazine published 5 times/year. Emphasis on Non-United States history. Readers are children, ages 8-14. Sample copies $3.95 with 7½×10½ or larger SASE and 5 first-class stamps. Photo guidelines free with SASE.
Needs: Uses 40-45 photos/issue; 15% supplied by freelancers. Needs contemporary shots of historical locations, buildings, artifacts, historical reenactments and costumes. Reviews photos with or without accompanying ms. Model/property release preferred. Captions preferred.
Making Contact & Terms: Query with stock photo list. Send unsolicited photos by mail for consideration. Provide resume, business card, brochure, flyer or tearsheets to be kept on file for possible future assignments. Send b&w or color prints; 35mm transparencies. Samples kept on file. SASE. Reports in 1 month. Pays on individual basis/color cover photo; $15-50/b&w inside photo. Pays on publication. Credit line given. Buys one-time rights; negotiable. Simultaneous submissions and previously published work OK.
Tips: "Given our young audience we like to have pictures which include people, both young and old. Pictures must be dynamic to make history appealing. Submissions must relate to themes in each issue."

CAMERA & DARKROOM, Suite 300, 9171 Wilshire Blvd., Beverly Hills CA 90210. (310)858-7155. Fax: (310)274-7985. Editor-in-Chief: Ana Jones. Executive Editor: Dave Howard. Circ. 40,000. Estab. 1979. Monthly publication. Circ. 80,000. Emphasizes darkroom-related and general photographic subjects. Free editorial guide.

© Steve Mulligan

While shooting an assignment for **Camera & Darkroom** *photographer Steve Mulligan of Moab, Utah, came across this slab of sandstone in Mill Creek Canyon, Utah. Shooting in black & white, Mulligan illuminated the rock with light while it peeked out of the shallow water. The image has sold three times and he received $100 from* **Camera & Darkroom** *for the unique shot.*

Needs: Uses 50% photos from stock; assigns 50%. Any subject if photography related. Model release required for covers, nudes, portraits. Property release preferred. Captions preferred; include camera, film, other technical information, title, date and location.

Making Contact & Terms: Interested in reviewing work from newer, lesser-known photographers. Query with samples. Send 8×10 or 11×14 glossy b&w prints and 35mm, 2¼×2¼, 4×5 or 8×10 color transparencies or 8×10 glossy color prints. Don't submit mounted prints. Uses color covers; vertical format required. SASE. Reports in 1 month-6 weeks. Pays $75-750/text/photo package, $30-75/b&w photo; $50 minimum/color photo and $200-350/cover; $500-750/portfolio. Pays on publication. Credit line given. Buys one-time rights.

CAMPUS LIFE, 465 Gundersen Dr., Carol Stream IL 60188. (708)260-6200. Fax: (708)260-0114. Editor: Jim Long. Photo Coordinator: Doug Johnson. Circ. 130,000. Estab. 1943. Monthly magazine except May/June and July/August. "*Campus Life* is a magazine for high school and college-age youth. We emphasize balanced living—emotionally, spiritually, physically and mentally." Sample copy $2. Photo guidelines free with SASE.

Needs: Buys 15 photos/issue. Head shots (of teenagers in a variety of moods); humorous, sport and candid shots of teenagers/college students in a variety of settings. "We want to see multiracial teenagers in different situations, and in every imaginable mood and expression, at work, play, home and school. No travel, how-to, still life, travel scenics, news or product shots. Shoot for a target audience of 18-year-olds." Photos purchased with or without accompanying ms. Model/property release preferred for controversial stories. Captions preferred.

Making Contact & Terms: Interested in reviewing work from newer, lesser-known photographers. Uses 8×10 glossy b&w prints and 35mm or larger transparencies. SASE. Reports in 4-6 weeks. Pays $70-100/b&w photo; $125-250/color photo. Pays on publication. Credit line given. Buys one-time rights; negotiable. Simultaneous submissions and previously published work OK.

Tips: "Ask for copies of past issues of campus life. Show work that fits our editorial approach. We choose photos that express the contemporary teen experience. We look for unusual lighting and color. Our guiding philosophy: that readers will 'see themselves' in the pages of our magazine." Looks for ability to catch teenagers in real-life situations that are well-composed but not posed. Technical quality, communication of an overall mood or emotion or action. "Look at a few issues to get a feel for what we choose. We're not interested in posed shots."

CANOE, Dept. PM, P.O. Box 3146, Kirkland WA 98083. (206)827-6363. Fax: (206)827-1893. Editor: Stephen Petit. Circ. 63,000+. Estab. 1973. Bimonthly magazine. Emphasizes a variety of paddle sports as well as how-to material and articles about equipment. For upscale canoe and kayak enthusiasts at all levels of ability. Also publishes special projects/posters. Free sample copy with 9 × 12 SASE.

Needs: Uses 30 photos/issue: 90% supplied by freelancers. Canoeing, kayaking, ocean touring, canoe sailing, fishing when compatible to the main activity, canoe camping but not rafting. No photos showing disregard for the environment, be it river or land; no photos showing gasoline-powered, multi hp engines; no photos showing unskilled persons taking extraordinary risks to life, etc. Accompanying mss for "Editorial coverage strives for balanced representation of all interests in today's paddling activity. Those interests include paddling adventures (both close to home and far away), camping, fishing, flatwater, whitewater, ocean kayaking, poling, sailing, outdoor photography, how-to projects, instruction and historical perspective. Regular columns feature paddling techniques, conservation topics, safety, interviews, equipment reviews, book/movie reviews, new products and letters from readers." Photos only occasionally purchased without accompanying ms. Model release preferred "when potential for litigation." Property release required. Captions are preferred, unless impractical.

Making Contact & Terms Interested in reviewing work from newer, lesser-known photographers. Query or send material. "Let me know those areas in which you have particularly strong expertise and/or photofile material. Send best samples only and make sure they relate to the magazine's emphasis and/or focus. (If you don't know what that is, pick up a recent issue first, before sending me unusable material.) We will review dupes for consideration only. Originals required for publication. Also, if you have something in the works or extraordinary photo subject matter of interest to our audience, let me know! It would be helpful to me if those with substantial reserves would supply indexes by subject matter." Uses 5 × 7 and 8 × 10 glossy b&w prints; 35mm, 2¼ × 2¼ and 4 × 5 transparencies; for cover uses color transparencies; vertical format preferred. SASE. Reports in 1 month. Pays $250/cover color photo; $150/half to full page color photos; $100/full page or larger b&w photos; $75/quarter to half page color photos; $50/quarter or less color photos; $75/half to full page b&w photos; $50/quarter to half page b&w photos; $25/less than quarter b&w photos. NPI for accompanying ms. Pays on publication. Credit line given. Buys one-time rights, first serial rights and exclusive rights. Simultaneous submissions and previously work OK, in noncompeting publications.

Tips: "We have a highly specialized subject and readers don't want just any photo of the activity. We're particularly interested in photos showing paddlers' *faces*; the faces of people having a good time. We're after anything that highlights the paddling activity as a lifestyle and the urge to be outdoors." All photos should be "as natural as possible with authentic subjects. We receive a lot of submissions from photographers to whom canoeing and kayaking are quite novel activities. These photos are often clichéd and uninteresting. So consider the quality of your work carefully before submission if you are not familiar with the sport. We are always in search of fresh ways of looking at our sport."

*CAPE COD LIFE INCLUDING MARTHA'S VINEYARD AND NANTUCKET, P.O. Box 767, Cataumet MA 02534-0767. (508)564-4466. Fax: (508)564-4470. Contact: Photo Editor. Circ. 35,000. Estab. 1979. Bimonthly magazine. Emphasizes Cape Cod lifestyle. "Readers are 55% female, 45% male, upper income, second home, vacation homeowners." Sample copy for $3. Photo guidelines free with SASE.

Needs: Uses 30 photos/issue; all supplied by freelancers. Needs "photos of Cape and Island scenes, people, places; general interest of this area." Model release required. Property release preferred. Photo captions preferred.

Making Contact & Terms: Interested in receiving work from newer, lesser-known photographers. Submit portfolio for review. Send unsolicited photos by mail for consideration. Send 35mm, 2¼ × 2¼, 4 × 5 transparencies. Keeps samples on file. SASE. Pays $200/color cover photo; $25-200/b&w photo; $25-150/color inside photo, depending on size. Pays 30 days after publication. Credit line given. Buys one-time rights; reprint rights for *Cape Cod Life* reprints; negotiable. Simultaneous submissions and previously published work OK.

Tips: Looks for "clear, somewhat graphic slides. Show us scenes we've seen hundreds of times with a different twist and elements of surprise."

THE CAPE ROCK, Southeast Missouri State University, Cape Girardeau MO 63701. (314)651-2156. Editor-in-Chief: Harvey Hecht. Circ. 1,000. Estab. 1964. Emphasizes poetry and poets for libraries and interested persons. Semiannual. Free photo guidelines.

Needs: Uses about 13 photos/issue; all supplied by freelance photographers. "We like to feature a single photographer each issue. Submit 25-30 thematically organized b&w glossies (at least 5×7), or send 5 pictures with plan for complete issue. We favor a series that conveys a sense of place. Seasons are a consideration too: we have spring and fall issues. Photos must have a sense of place: e.g., an issue featuring Chicago might show buildings or other landmarks, people of the city (no nudes), travel or scenic. No how-to or products. Sample issues and guidelines provide all information a photographer needs to decide whether to submit to us." Model release not required "but photographer is liable". Captions not required "but photographer should indicate where series was shot."
Making Contact & Terms: Send by mail for consideration actual b&w photos. Query with list of stock photo subjects. Submit portfolio by mail for review. SASE. Reporting time varies. Pays $100 and 10 copies on publication. Credit line given. Buys "all rights, but will release rights to photographer on request."
Tips: "We don't make assignments, but we look for a unified package put together by the photographer. We may request additional or alternative photos when accepting a package."

CAR COLLECTOR & CAR CLASSICS, P.O. Box 28571, Atlanta GA 30328. (404)998-4603. Editor: Westley D. Peterson. Circ. 54,000. Estab. 1977. Monthly. Emphasizes collector automobiles. Readers are 98% male, average age 41. Sample copy $2 postpaid. Photo and writers guidelines free with SASE.
Needs: Uses about 50-75 photos/issue; "nearly all" supplied by freelance photographers; 30% of photos on assignment per issue. Needs photos of "automobiles of the 1925-1965 era." Photos purchased with accompanying manuscript only. Model release required. Captions required.
Making Contact & Terms: Telephone first. Send b&w prints; 35mm, 2¼×2¼, 4×5 and/or 8×10 transparencies by mail for consideration. SASE. Reports ASAP, but no schedule. Pays $5/b&w inside photo; $10/color inside photo; $50-400/text/photo package. Pays on publication. Credit line always given. Buys all rights; negotiable.
Tips: "Do not submit photos to us without accompanying story and captions. Get connected with a writer so that a complete package can be offered. We are looking for cars shot from pleasing angles with good backgrounds. No 'fish-eye' or other 'trick lens' photos purchased."

CAR CRAFT MAGAZINE, 8490 Sunset Blvd., Los Angeles CA 90069. (310)854-2250. Fax: (310)854-2263. Editor: John Baechtel. Circ. 500,000. Estab. 1953. Monthly magazine. Emphasizes street machines, muscle cars and modern, high-tech performance cars. Readership is mostly males, ages 18-34. Sample copy free with SASE.
Needs: Uses 100+ photos/issue. Uses freelancers occasionally; all on assignment. Model/property release required. Captions preferred.
Making Contact & Terms: Interested in receiving work from newer, lesser-known photographers. Query with resume of credits. Provide resume, business card, brochure, flyer or tearsheets to be kept on file for possible assignments. Send 35mm and 8×10 b&w prints; 35mm and 2¼×2¼ transparencies by mail for consideration. SASE. Reports in 1 month. Pays $35-75/b&w photo; $75-250/color photo, cover or text; $60 minimum/hour; $250 minimum/day; $500 minimum/job. Payment for b&w varies according to subject and needs. Pays on publication. Credit line given. Buys all rights.
Tips: "We use primarily b&w shots. When we need something special in color or see an interesting color shot, we'll pay more for that. Review a current issue for our style and taste."

CAREER FOCUS, Dept. PM, 250 Mark Twain Tower, 106 W 11th St., Kansas City MO 64105. (816)221-4404. Fax: (816)221-1112. Circ. 500,000. Estab. 1988. Bimonthly magazine. Emphasizes career development. Readers are male and female African-American and Hispanic professionals, ages 21-45. Sample copy free with 9×12 SAE and 4 first class stamps. Photo guidelines free with SASE.
Needs: Uses approximately 40 photos/issue. Needs technology photos and shots of personalities; career people in computer, science, teaching, finance, engineering, law, law enforcement, government, hi-tech, leisure. Model release preferred. Captions required; include name, date, place, why.
Making Contact & Terms: Query with resume of credits and list of stock photo subjects. Keeps samples on file. SASE. Reports in 1 month. Pays $10-50/color photo; $5-25/b&w photo. Pays on publication. Credit line given. Buys one-time rights. Simultaneous submissions and previously published work OK.
Tips: "Freelancer must be familiar with our magazine to be able to submit appropriate manuscripts and photos."

CAREER WOMAN, Equal Opportunity Publications, Inc., Suite 420, 150 Motor Parkway, Hauppauge NY 11788-5145. (516)273-8743. Fax: (516)273-8936. Editor: Eileen Nester. Circ. 10,500. Estab. 1972. Published 3 times a year. Emphasizes career guidance and career opportunities for women at the college and professional level. Readers are college-age and entry-level professional women. Sample copy free with 9×12 SAE and 5 first-class stamps.
   • This publication received the 1992 Clarion Award for Most Improved Magazine from Women in Communications.

Needs: Uses at least one photo per issue (cover); planning to use freelance work for covers and possibly editorial; many photos come from freelance writers who submit photos with their articles. Contact for needs. Model release preferred. Captions required; include person's name and title.
Making Contact & Terms: Interested in receiving work from newer, lesser-known photographers. Query with list of stock photo subjects. Send unsolicited prints or 35mm transparencies by mail for consideration. SASE. Reports in 2 weeks. Pays $15/color and b&w photo; $100/cover shot. Pays on publication. Credit line given. Buys one-time rights. Simultaneous submissions and previously published work OK, "but not in competitive career-guidance publications."
Tips: "We are looking for clear color slides of women in a variety of professions and work environments. We are looking primarily for women (ages 25-35) who represent role models for our readers. They should be dressed and groomed in a professional manner. We've decided to use more cover photos than we have in the past. We are also open to using inside photos, but freelancers should contact us and discuss upcoming stories before sending photos. Read our magazine to get an idea of the editorial content. Contact us with ideas for cover shots. Cover photos do not have to tie in to any particular story in the magazine, but they have to be representative of the magazine's editorial content as a whole."

CARIBBEAN SPORTS & TRAVEL, 1995 NE 150th St., North Miami FL 33181. (305)945-7403. Fax: (305)947-6410. Editor: Kyle Stuart. Circ. 30,000. Estab. 1971. Emphasizes fishing, diving and golf in the Bahamas and the Caribbean. Readers are active, sports-minded travelers. Sample copy $2.50 and $1 for mailing and handling.
Needs: Uses about 35-40 photos/issue; most freelance photography comes from assignment. Needs photos of people fishing, cruising, diving and golfing in the Bahamas and Caribbean. Model release preferred. Captions required.
Making Contact & Terms: Interested in receiving work from newer, lesser-known photographers. Query with samples. Provide brochure to be kept on file for possible future assignments. SASE. Reports in 4 weeks. Pays $50/color photo; $300/photo/text package. Pays 30 days after publication. Credit line given. Buys one-time rights and all rights; negotiable. Simultaneous submissions OK.
Tips: Prefers 35mm slides, good quality. Prefers verticals, strong colors. "Contact editorial department by mail regarding photos available. Submit in envelope with stiffener for protection. Most freelance photography comes from assignment. Include SASE."

CARIBBEAN TRAVEL AND LIFE MAGAZINE, #830, 8403 Colesville Rd., Silver Spring MD 20910. (301)588-2300. Fax: (301)588-2256. Editorial Assistant: Stacy Small. Circ. 105,000. Estab. 1985. Published bimonthly. Emphasizes travel, culture and recreation in islands of Caribbean, Bahamas and Bermuda. Readers are male and female frequent Caribbean travelers, age 32-52. Sample copy $4.95. Photo guidelines free with SASE.
• In 1992 this publication received a bronze Ozzie Award for having the best overall design.
Needs: Uses about 100 photos/issue; 90% supplied by freelance photographers: 10% assignment and 90% freelance stock. "We combine scenics with people shots. Where applicable, we show interiors, food shots, resorts, water sports, cultural events, shopping and wildlife/underwater shots." Special needs include "cover shots—attractive people on beach; striking images of the region, etc." Captions preferred. "Provide thorough caption information. Don't submit stock that is mediocre."
Making Contact & Terms: Query with list of stock photo subjects. Uses 4-color photography. SASE. Reports in 3 weeks. Pays $400/color cover photo; $150/color full page; $125/color ¾ page; $100/color ½ page and $75/color ¼ page; $75-400/color photo; $1,200-1,500 per photo/text package. Pays after publication. Buys one-time rights. Does not pay research or holding fees.
Tips: Seeing trend toward "fewer but larger photos with more impact and drama. We are looking for particularly strong images of color and style, beautiful island scenics and people shots—images that are powerful enough to make the reader want to travel to the region; photos that show people doing things in the destinations we cover; originality in approach, composition, subject matter. Good composition, lighting and creative flair. Images that are evocative of a place, creating story mood. Good use of people. Submit stock photography for specific story needs, if good enough can lead to possible assignments. Let us know exactly what coverage you have on a stock list so we can contact you when certain photo needs arise."

Can't find a listing? Check at the end of each market section for the " '93-'94 Changes" lists. These lists include any market listings from the '93 edition which were either not verified or deleted in this edition.

CAROLINA QUARTERLY, Greenlaw Hall, CB#3520, University of North Carolina, Chapel Hill NC 27599-3520. (919)962-0244. Editor: Amber Vogel. Circ. 1,000. Estab. 1948. Emphasizes "current poetry, short fiction." Readers are "literary, artistic—primarily, though not exclusively, writers and serious readers." Sample copy $5.
Needs: Uses 1-8 photos/issue; all supplied by freelance photographers from stock. Often photos are chosen to accompany the text of the magazine.
Making Contact & Terms: Interested in receiving work from newer, lesser-known photographers. Send b&w prints by mail for consideration. SASE. Reports in 1-3 months, depending on deadline. NPI. Credit line given. Buys one-time rights.
Tips: "Look at a recent issue of the magazine to get a clear idea of its contents and design."

*CASINO PLAYER, 2524 Arctic Ave., Atlantic City NJ 08401. Photo Editor: Rick Greco. Circ. 200,000. Estab. 1988. Monthly magazine. Emphasizes casino gambling. Readers are frequent gamblers, age 35 and up. Sample copy free with 8½×11 SAE and $2 postage.
Needs: Uses 40-60 photos/issue; 5 supplied by freelancers. Needs photos of casinos, gambling, casino destinations, money, slot machines. Reviews photos with or without ms. Model release required for gamblers. Captions required; include name, hometown, titles.
Making Contact & Terms: Interested in receiving work from newer, lesser-known photographers. Query with resume of credits. Reports in 2-3 months. Pays $200/color cover photo; $40/color inside photo; $20/b&w inside photo. Pays on publication. Credit line given. Buys all rights; negotiable.
Tips: "Know the magazine before submission."

CAT FANCY, Fancy Publications, Inc., P.O. Box 6050, Mission Viejo CA 92690. (714)855-8822. Editor-in-Chief: Debbie Phillips-Donaldson. Circ. 303,000. Estab. 1965. Readers are "men and women of all ages interested in all phases of cat ownership." Monthly. Sample copy $4.50. Photo guidelines free with SASE.
Needs: Uses 20-30 photos/issue; all supplied by freelancers. "For purebred photos, we prefer shots that show the various physical and mental attributes of the breed. Include both environmental and portrait-type photographs. We also need good-quality, interesting b&w and color photos of mixed-breed cats for use with feature articles and departments." Model release required.
Making Contact & Terms: Send by mail for consideration actual 8×10 b&w photos; 35mm or 2¼×2¼ color transparencies. No duplicates. SASE. Reports in 6 weeks. Pays $35-100/b&w photo; $50-250/color photo; and $50-450 for text/photo package. Credit line given. Buys first N.A. serial rights.
Tips: "Nothing but sharp, high contrast shots, please. Send SASE for list of specific photo needs. We are using more color photos and prefer more action shots, fewer portrait shots. We look for photos of all kinds and numbers of cats doing predictable feline activities—eating, drinking, grooming, being groomed, playing, scratching, taking care of kittens, fighting, being judged at cat shows and accompanied by people of all ages."

CATHOLIC DIGEST, Dept. PM, St. Paul's Square, P.O. Box 64090, St. Paul MN 55164. (612)962-5000. Editor: Henry Lexau. Photo Editor: Susan Schaefer. Monthly magazine. Emphasizes religion, family life. Readers are mostly Catholic, mature with teenagers or grown children. Circ. 600,000. Sample copy free with SAE (6½×9½ envelope, $1.05 postage).
Needs: Uses 6-9 photos/issue; 1 supplied by freelance photographer. Needs photos of religious symbols and scenes, family life, senior citizens, middle-age, young adults, health, medical. Special needs include Catholic photos of all kinds, holiday/religious feasts. Model release required; captions preferred.
Making Contact & Terms: Send b&w and color prints, contact sheets, negatives or color slides by mail for consideration. SASE. Reports in 3 weeks. NPI. Pays on publication. Credit line given. Buys one-time rights. Previously published work OK.
Tips: "More of a demand for pictures which tell the thoughts and emotions of the people in them—pictures which draw the viewer into the 'private moment' of the shot." Looks for "candid, natural expressions of people in photos—limited use of (appropriate) props—classic, simple clothing—high contrast in b&w photos; rich harmony in 4-color. Seasonal photos should be received 4 to 5 months in advance of month of issue. Avoid clichés."

THE CATHOLIC WORLD, 997 Macarthur Blvd., Mahwah NJ 07430. (201)825-7300. Fax: (201)825-8345. Managing Editor: Laurie Felknor. Circ. 9,000. Estab. 1865. Bimonthly magazine.
Needs: Buys 5-10 photos/issue. Human interest, nature, religious (Roman Catholic).
Making Contact & Terms: Send material by mail for consideration. Uses 8×10 glossy b&w prints. SASE. Reports in 1 month. Pays $20-35/photo. Pays on publication. Credit line given. Buys one-time rights. Simultaneous submissions and previously published work OK.
Tips: Photos of people must reflect current hairstyles, clothing, etc. Each issue of *The Catholic World* is on a specific theme. Send query as to themes for the 6 issues per year.

CATS MAGAZINE, P.O. Box 290037, Port Orange FL 32129. (904)788-2770. Fax: (904)788-2710. Editor: Tracey Copeland. Circ. 150,000. Estab. 1945. Monthly magazine. For cat enthusiasts of all types. Free sample copy (must include $2 to cover postage and handling) and photo guidelines.
Needs: Buys 50-60 photos/year; 60% of photography per issue is assigned; 40% from freelance stock. Felines of all types: photos depicting cats in motion and capturing feline expression are preferred; celebrity/personality (with their cats); fine art (featuring cats); head shot (of cats); human interest (on cats); humorous (cats); photo essay/photo feature (cats); sport (cat shows); travel (with cats); and wildlife (wild cats). No shots of clothed cats or cats doing tricks. Model and property release preferred. Photo captions preferred.
Making Contact & Terms: Provide sample photos (portfolio) to be kept on file for possible future assignments. (Samples are filed for two years.) Send portfolio for consideration. Send to Roy Copeland, Art Director. 2¼×2¼ transparencies are preferred for feature photos as well as for the cover. Slides and 8×10 glossies are also accepted for editorial consideration, but 2¼ is preferred. SASE. Reports in 8-12 weeks. Pays $250/cover; $25-200/photo. Pays on publication. Buys first serial rights.
Tips: Label material clearly with name, address, phone, fax and breed/name of cats. If purebred cats are used as subjects, they must be representative specimens of their breed. Should be clear, sharp photographs of cats. "Our most frequent causes for rejection: not preferred format; cat image too small; backgrounds cluttered; too posed; too many props; uninteresting; poor quality purebred cats; dirty pet-type cats; shot wrong shape for cover; colors untrue; exposure incorrect. Cats should be portrayed in a realistic manner. Submit your specialty (ie: outdoor cat scenes, portraits or realistic shots)."

*CHANGES MAGAZINE, 3201 SW 15th St., Deerfield Beach FL 33442. (800)851-9100. Fax: (305)360-0034. Art Director: Iris Slones. Circ. 40,000. Estab. 1986. Bimonthly magazine. Emphasizes recovery and self-help. Readers are 80% women, ages 35-54, in recovery program or working on improving their lives. Photo guidelines free with SASE.
Needs: Uses 16 photos/issue; 14 supplied by freelancers. Needs photos of personalities, scenics, action shots, relationship pictures, animals, family photos. Reviews photos with or without ms. Special photo needs include conceptual cover shots, set-up shots. Model release required; photo captions preferred.
Making Contact & Terms: Query with stock photo list. Provide resume, business card, brochure, flyer or tearsheets to be kept on file for possible assignments. Keeps samples on file. Reports in 1-2 weeks. Pays $75-100/hour; $400-600/day; $250/color cover photo; $150/b&w cover photo; $100 color inside photo; $75/b&w inside photo; $100/color page rate; $75/b&w page rate; $75-250/photo/text package. Credit line given. Buys one-time rights; negotiable. Simultaneous submissions and/or previously published work OK.

CHANGING MEN: Issues in Gender, Sex & Politics, P.O. Box 305, 306 N. Brooks St., Madison WI 53715. Editor: Michael Biernbaum. Circ. 6,000. Estab. 1978. Biannual. Emphasizes men's issues, feminist, male politics, gay and heterosexual personal and political issues. Readers are anti-sexist men, feminists, gay and political activists. Circ. 6,000. Sample copy $6 (4-issue subscriptions $24).
Needs: Uses 6-8 photos/issue; all supplied by freelance photographers. Needs art photography; male body shots (not standard "nudes" or explicit sexual poses); images of men at work, play, in social and emotional relationships, etc.; journalism on gay and male feminist gatherings. Special needs include features on men's issues, AIDS, relationships with women, special issues of men of color, men's health, gay issues, antiporn, third world masculinities, gender, spirituality, etc. Model release preferred.
Making Contact & Terms: Interested in receiving work from newer, lesser-known photographers. Query with list of sample relevant stock photo subjects. Send b&w prints (photocopies acceptable) and contact sheets. SASE. Reports in 2 months. Pays $10-25/b&w inside photo; $35-50/covers; plus 2 sample copies. Pays after publication. Credit line given. Buys one-time rights.
Tips: "Display sensitivity to subject matter. Provide political photos showing conscience, strong journalism on feminist and gay issues." In samples, wants to see "emotional content of image; or strong statement about a man's situation; or humor/irony in 'changing' situations." To break in, shoot "well-composed images that stand on their own, by showing emotional feeling or mood or by making a statement."

CHARISMA MAGAZINE, 600 Rinehart Rd., Lake Mary FL 32746. (407)333-0600. Art Director: Eric T. Jessen. Circ. 200,000. Monthly magazine. Emphasizes Christians. General readership. Sample copy $2.50.
Needs: Uses approximately 20 photos/issue; all supplied by freelance photographers. Needs editorial photos—appropriate for each article. Model release required. Captions preferred.
Making Contact & Terms: Send unsolicited photos by mail for consideration. Provide brochure, flyer or tearsheets to be kept on file for possible assignments. Send color 35mm, 2¼×2¼, 4×5 or 8×10 transparencies. Cannot return material. Reports ASAP. Pays $300/color cover photo; $150/b&w inside photo; $50-150/hour or $400-600/day. Pays on publication. Credit line given. Buys all rights; negotiable. Simultaneous submissions and previously published work OK.

Tips: In portfolio or samples, looking for "good color and composition with great technical ability. To break in, specialize; sell the sizzle rather than the steak!"

THE CHESAPEAKE BAY MAGAZINE, 1819 Bay Ridge Ave., Annapolis MD 21403. (410)263-2662, (DC)261-1323. Art Director: Christine Gill. Circ. 35,000. Estab. 1972. Monthly. Emphasizes boating—Chesapeake Bay only. Readers are "people who use Bay for recreation." Sample copy available.
Needs: Uses "approximately" 21 photos/issue; 60% supplied by freelancers; 20% by freelance assignment. Needs photos that are Chesapeake Bay related (must); vertical powerboat shots are badly needed (color). Special needs include "vertical 4-color slides showing boats and people on Bay."
Making Contact & Terms: Interested in reviewing work from newer, lesser-known photographers. Query with samples or list of stock photo subjects. Send 35mm, 2¼×2¼, 4×5 or 8×10 transparencies by mail for consideration. SASE. Reports in 3 weeks. Pays $200/color cover photo; $25-75/b&w photo; $25-250/color photo; $150-1,000/photo/text package. Pays on publication. Credit line given. Buys one-time rights. Simultaneous submissions OK.
Tips: "We prefer Kodachrome over Ektachrome. Looking for: boating, bay and water-oriented subject matter. Qualities and abilities include: fresh ideas, clarity, exciting angles and true color. We're using larger photos—more double-page spreads. Photos should be able to hold up to that degree of enlargement. When photographing boats on the Bay—keep the 'safety' issue in mind. (People hanging off the boat, drinking, women 'perched' on the bow are a no-no!)"

CHICAGO LIFE MAGAZINE, P.O. Box 11311, Chicago IL 60611. Publisher: Pam Berns. Circ. 60,000. Estab. 1986. Bimonthly magazine. Emphasizes self-improvement. Readers are upscale men and women, ages 35-50, college-educated professionals, interested in improving their lifestyles through health, fitness, travel and business.
Needs: Uses 15 photos/issue; 80% supplied by freelancers. Uses photos for travel, health, food, cover and celebrity. Reviews photos with or without a manuscript. Model release required. Capstions required.
Making Contact & Terms: Provide resume, business card, brochure, flyer or tearsheets to be kept on file for possible assignments. Cannot return material. Reports in 1 week on queries. Pays $30/color cover and inside photos; $30/b&w inside photo. **Pays on acceptance.** Credit line given. Buys one-time rights. Simultaneous submissions and previously published work OK.

*CHICAGO RUNNER MAGAZINE, 7842 N. Lincoln Ave., Skokie IL 60077. (708)676-1900. Fax: (708)676-0063. Publisher: Eliot Wineberg. Circ. 45,000. Estab. 1991. Quarterly magazine. Emphasizes Chicago running. Readers are male and female, ages 25-55. Sample copies available.
Needs: Uses 40 photos/issue. 90% supplied by freelancers. Needs photos of people running in Chicago. Reviews photos with or without ms. Model/property release is preferred. Captions preferred.
Making Contact & Terms: Interested in reviewing work from newer, lesser-known photographers. Send unsolicited photos by mail for consideration. Send any size b&w prints. Keeps samples on file. SASE. Reports in 1-2 weeks. NPI. **Pays on acceptance.** Credit line given. Simultaneous submissions and/or previously published work OK.

♣CHICKADEE MAGAZINE, Suite 306, 56 The Esplanade, Toronto, Ontario M5E 1A7 Canada. (416)868-6001. Fax: (416)868-6009. Photo Researcher: Robin Wilner. Circ. 110,000. Estab. 1979. Published 10 times/year, 1 summer issue. A natural science magazine for children 3-9 years. Sample copy for $4.28 with 9×12 SAE and $1.50 money order to cover postage. Photo guidelines free.
Needs: Uses about 3-6 photos/issue; 2-4 supplied by freelance photographers. Needs "crisp, bright, close-up shots of animals in their natural habitat." Model/property release required. Captions required.
Making Contact & Terms: Request photo package before sending photos for review. Send 35mm transparencies. Reports in 6-8 weeks. Pays $325 Canadian/color cover; $200 Canadian/color page; text/photo package negotiated separately. **Pays on acceptance.** Credit line given. Buys one-time rights, nonexclusive, to reproduce in *Owl* and *Chickadee* in Canada and affiliated children's publications in remaining world countries. Previously published work OK.

CHILDREN'S DIGEST, P.O. Box 567, Indianapolis IN 46206. (317)636-8881. Editor: Elizabeth Rinck. Circ. 125,000. Estab. 1950. Magazine published 8 times/year. Emphasizes health and fitness. Readers are preteens—kids 10-13. Sample copy $1.25. Photo guidelines free with SASE.
Needs: "We have featured photos of wildlife, children in other countries, adults in different jobs, how-to projects." Reviews photos with accompanying ms only. "We would like to include more photo features." Model release preferred.
Making Contact & Terms: Send complete manuscript and photos on speculation; 35mm transparencies. SASE. Reports in 8-10 weeks. Pays $50-100/color cover photo; $20/color inside photo; $10/b&w inside photo. Pays on publication. Buys one-time rights.

NOVEMBER 1992 $2.95

CHESAPEAKE BAY
MAGAZINE

UNIQUELY
CHESAPEAKE

AUTUMN ON THE
POCOMOKE RIVER

TANGIER ISLAND
BY SMALL BOAT

THE MULTIHULL
LIFESTYLE

WILD THINGS—
LOONS, GREAT PINES,
ROCKFISH AND MORE

© photo by David Harp

Photographer David Harp of Baltimore, Maryland, has snapped over 20,000 images while exploring and documenting a vanishing lifestyle on Chesapeake Bay. This cover shot was an outtake from photos taken while Harp worked on a book, Water's Way: Life Along the Chesapeake. *Chris Gill, art director at* Chesapeake Bay Magazine, *says Harp has a brilliant eye for documenting the Bay and his cover shots often bring requests for reprints.*

CHILDREN'S MINISTRY MAGAZINE, % Group Publishing, Inc., P.O. Box 481, 2890 N. Monroe Ave., Loveland CO 80538. (303)669-3836. Fax: (303)669-3269. Art Director: Rich Martin. Circ. 30,000. Estab. 1991. Bimonthly magazine. Provides ideas and support to adult workers (professional and volunteer) with children in Christian churches. Sample copy $1 with 9 × 12 SAE. Photo guidelines free with SASE.

Needs: Uses 20-25 photos/issue; 3-6 supplied by freelancers. Needs photos of children (infancy—6th grade) involved in family, school, church, recreational activities; with or without adults; generally upbeat and happy. Reviews photos with or without a manuscript. Especially needs good portrait-type shots of individual children, suitable for cover use; colorful, expressive. Model release required when people's faces are visible and recognizable and could be used to illustrate a potentially embarrassing subject. Captions not needed.

Making Contact & Terms: Interested in reviewing work from newer, lesser-known photographers, "if they meet our stated requirements." Query with list of stock photo subjects. Send unsolicited photos by mail for consideration. Send 8 × 10 glossy b&w prints; 35mm, 2¼ × 2¼ transparencies. SASE. Reports in 1 month. Pays minimum $150/color cover photo; minimum $75/color inside photo; $40-60/b&w inside photo. Pays on publication. Credit line given. Buys one-time rights. Simultaneous submissions and previously published work OK.

Tips: Wants to see "sharp, well-composed and well-exposed shots of children from all walks of life; emphasis on the an active, upbeat colorful; ethnic mix is highly desirable." To be considered, "photos must appear current and contemporary. Professionalism must be evident in photos and their presentation. No under- or overexposed 'snapshot'-style photos, please."

CHILDREN'S PLAYMATE, Dept. PM, P.O. Box 567, Indianapolis IN 46206. (317)636-8881. Editor: Elizabeth A. Rinck. Circ. 115,000. Published 8 times/year. Emphasizes better health for children. Readers are children between the ages of 6-8. Sample copy $1.25 with 5 × 7 SASE. Photo guidelines free with SASE.

Needs: Number of photos/issue varies; all supplied by freelancers. Reviews photos with accompanying ms only. Model release required. Captions preferred.

Making Contact & Terms: Send unsolicited photos, accompanied by ms. Uses b&w prints and 35mm transparencies. SASE. Reports in 8-10 weeks. Pays $10/b&w inside photo; $20/color inside photo. Pays on publication. Credit line given. Buys one-time rights.

CHILE PEPPER, P.O. Box 4278, Albuquerque NM 87196. (505)266-8322. Fax: (505)266-0141. Art Director: Lois Bergthold. Bimonthly magazine. Emphasizes world cuisine, emphasis on hot, spicy foods and chile peppers. Readers are male and female consumers of spicy food, age 35-55. Circ. 70,000. Estab. 1986. Sample copy $2.95. Photo guidelines not available.

Needs: Uses 8-12 photos/issue; 10-20% supplied by freelancers. Needs photos of still life ingredients, location shots specifically of locales which are known for spicy cuisine, shots of chiles. Reviews photos with or without a manuscript. "We will be doing features on the cuisine of Louisiana, Mexico, Arizona and the Caribbean." Model/property preferred. Captions required; include location and species of chile (if applicable).

Making Contact & Terms: Query with stock photo list. Send unsolicited photos by mail for consideration. Provide resume, business card, brochure, flyer or tearsheets to be kept on file for possible assignments. Send b&w/color prints; 35mm, 4 × 5, 8 × 10 transparencies. Keeps samples on file. SASE. Reports in 3 weeks. Pays $150/color cover photo; $50/color inside photo; $25/b&w inside photo. Pays on publication. Credit line given. Buys one-time rights. Simultaneous submissions and/or previously published work OK.

Tips: "Looking for shots that capture the energy and exotica of locations, and still-life food shots that are not too classical, with a "fresh eye" and interesting juxtapositions."

THE CHRISTIAN CENTURY, 407 S. Dearborn St., Chicago IL 60605. (312)427-5380. Fax: (708)427-1302. Assistant Editor: Victoria Rebeck. Circ. 35,000. Estab. 1884. Weekly journal. Emphasis on religion. Readers are clergy, scholars, lay people, male and female, ages 40-85. Sample copy $2. Photo guidelines free with SASE.

Needs: Buys 50 photos/year; all supplied by freelancers. People of various races and nationalities; celebrity/personality (primarily political and religious figures in the news); documentary (conflict and controversy, also constructive projects and cooperative endeavors); scenic (occasional use of seasonal scenes and scenes from foreign countries); spot news; and human interest (children, human rights issues, people "in trouble," and people interacting). Photos with or without accompanying ms. For accompanying mss seeks articles dealing with ecclesiastical concerns, social problems, political issues and international affairs. Model release preferred. Captions preferred.

Making Contact & Terms: Interested in reviewing work from newer, lesser-known photographers. Send material by mail for consideration. Uses 8 × 10 b&w prints. Does not keep samples on file. SASE. Reports in 1 month. Pays $50/b&w cover photo; $25/b&w inside photo. Pays on publication. Credit line given. Buys one-time rights; negotiable. Simultaneous submissions and previously published work OK.

Tips: Looks for diverstiy in gender, race, age and religious settings. Photos should reproduce well on newsprint.

CHRISTIAN HISTORY, 465 Gundersen Dr., Carol Stream IL 60188. (708)260-6200. Fax: (708)260-0114. Art Director: Rai Whitlock. Quarterly magazine. Emphasizes history of Christianity. Readers are male, educated, history buffs. Sample copy free with SASE.
Needs: Uses 50 photos/issue; 40% supplied by freelancers. Needs photos of history. Special photo needs include The Crusades, The American Puritans, St. Francis Assisi. Captions required; include site and date, artist, subject.
Making Contact & Terms: Interested in reviewing work from newer, lesser-known photographers. Provide resume,business card, brochure, flyer or tearsheets to be kept on file for possible assignments. Does not keep samples on file. SASE. Reports in 1 month. Pays $100-200/color cover photo; $50-100/b&w cover photo; $50-75/color inside photo; $10-40/b&w inside photo. Pays on publication. Credit line given. Buys one-time rights.

THE CHRONICLE OF THE HORSE, P.O. Box 46, Middleburg VA 22117. (703)687-6341. Fax: (703)687-3937. Editor: John Strassburger. Cir. 23,000. Estab. 1937. Weekly magazine. Emphasizes English horse sports. Readers range from young to old. "Average reader is a college-educated female, middle-aged, well off financially." Sample copy for $2. Photo guidelines free with SASE.
Needs: Uses 10-25 photos/issue; 90% supplied by freelance photographers. Needs photos from competitive events (horse shows, dressage, steeplechase, etc.) to go with news story or to accompany personality profile. "A few stand alone. Must be cute, beautiful or news-worthy. Reproduced in b&w." Prefer purchasing photos with accompanying ms. Special photo needs include good photos to accompany our news stories, especially horse shows. Captions required with every subject identified.
Making Contact & Terms: Interested in receiving work from newer, lesser-known photographers. Query with idea. Send b&w and color prints (reproduced b&w). SASE. Reports in 3 weeks. Pays $15-30/photo/text package. Pays on publication. Credit line given. Buys one-time rights. Prefer first N.A. rights. Simultaneous submissions and previously published work OK.
Tips: "We do not want to see portfolio or samples. Contact us first, preferably by letter. Know horse sports."

THE CHURCH HERALD, 4500 60th St., Grand Rapids MI 49512. (616)698-7071. Editor: Jeffrey Japinga. Photo Editor: Christina Van Eyl. Circ. 100,000. Published 11 times/year. Emphasizes current events, family living, evangelism and spiritual growth, from a Christian viewpoint. For members and clergy of the Reformed Church in America. Sample copy $2 with 9 × 12 SAE.
Needs: Buys 1-2 photos/issue; 50% freelance photography/issue comes from assignment and 50% from freelance stock. Needs photos of life situations—families, couples, vacations, school; religious, moral and philosophical symbolism; seasonal and holiday themes.
Making Contact & Terms: Send photos for consideration. SASE. Reports in 4 weeks. Pays $35/b&w inside photo; $70/color inside photo; $150/color cover photo. **Pays on acceptance.** Buys first serial rights, second serial (reprint) rights, first N.A. serial rights or simultaneous rights. Simultaneous submissions and previously published work OK.
Tips: Looks for "good photo quality—photos that our readers will relate to in a positive way—a lot of what we get are junk photos we can't use. Have an understanding of the kinds of articles we run. I want to see interesting photos of good quality that depict real-life situations. We're using more color and commissioning more. Don't send me a list of what you have unless it's accompanied by a selection of photos. I'm happy to look at someone's work, but I'm frustrated by resumes and checklists."

CIRCLE K MAGAZINE, 3636 Woodview Trace, Indianapolis IN 46268. (317)875-8755. Executive Editor: Nicholas K. Drake. Circ. 15,000. Published 5 times/year. For community service-oriented college leaders "interested in the concept of voluntary service, societal problems, leadership abilities and college life. They are politically and socially aware and have a wide range of interests." Free sample copy.
Needs: Assigns 0-5 photos/issue. Needs general interest photos, "though we rarely use a nonorganization shot without text. Also, the annual convention requires a large number of photos from that area." Prefers ms with photos. Seeks general interest features aimed at the better-than-average college student. "Not specific places, people topics." Captions required, "or include enough information for us to write a caption."
Making Contact & Terms: Works with freelance photographers on assignment only basis. Provide calling card, letter of inquiry, resume and samples to be kept on file for possible future assignments. Send query with resume of credits. Uses 8 × 10 glossy b&w prints or color transparencies. Uses b&w and color covers; vertical format required for cover. SASE. Reports in 3 weeks. Pays up to $225-350 for text/photo package, or on a per-photo basis—$15 minimum/b&w print and $70 minimum/cover. **Pays on acceptance.** Credit line given. Previously published work OK if necessary to text.

*CITY SPORTS MAGAZINE, 2201 3rd St., San Francisco CA 94107. (415)626-1600. Fax: (415)621-2323. Art Director: Leslee Bassin. Circ. 144,000. Estab. 1974. Monthly magazine. Emphasizes individual sports. Readers are male and female professionals of all ages. Sample copy free with SASE.

Needs: Uses approximately 50 photos/issue; 50% supplied by freelancers. Needs photos of sports, travel. Reviews photos with or without ms. Special photo needs include San Francisco and Los Angeles Marathons, U.S. Open Tennis, Ironman Triathlon. Model/property release preferred. Captions preferred.

Making Contact & Terms: Interested in receiving work from newer, lesser-known photographers. Query with stock photo list. Does not keep samples on file. SASE. Reports in 1-2 weeks. Pays $200-250/color cover photo; $100-150/color inside photo; $75-100/b&w inside photo. Pays on publication. Credit line given. Buys one-time rights; negotiable.

Tips: Looks for strong "composition and lighting. Send what we ask for. We don't want an entire portfolio."

*CLASSIC AUTO RESTORER, P.O. Box 6050, Mission Viejo CA 92690. (714)855-8822. Fax: (714)855-3045. Managing Editor: Brian Mertz. Circ. 60,000. Estab. 1989. Bimonthly magazine. Emphasizes restoration of collector cars. Readers are male (91%), professional/technical/managerial, ages 35-55. Sample copy $5.50.

Needs: Uses 100 photos/issue; 95% supplied by freelancers. Needs photos of auto restoration projects and restored cars; related events such as tours, swap meets, auctions and vintage races. Reviews photos with accompanying ms only. Model/property release preferred. Captions required; include year, make and model of car; identification of people in photo.

Making Contact & Terms: Interested in receiving work from newer, lesser-known photographers. Submit portfolio for review. Provide resume, business card, brochure, flyer or tearsheets to be kept on file for possible assignments. Does not keep samples on file. SASE. Reports in 1 month. Pays $100-200/color cover photo; $100/color page rate; $100/b&w page rate; $100/page for photo/test package. Pays on publication. Credit line given. Buys first North American serial rights; negotiable. Simultaneous submissions OK.

Tips: Looks for "technically proficient photos of various automotive subjects, auto portraits, detail shots, action photos, good angles, composition and lighting, mostly 35mm, 2¼" format."

CLIMAX, 10th Floor, 801 Second Ave., New York NY 11217. (212)661-7878. Fax: (212)692-9297. Editor: Marc Medoff. Circ. 83,000. Estab. 1990. Bimonthly magazine. Emphasis on male and female relations between couples. Readers are young males, blue collar workers, over 18 years old. Sample copies free with 8½×11 SASE and 10 first class stamps. Photo guidelines free with SASE.

Needs: Uses 100-200 photos/issue; all supplied by freelancers. Needs photos of explicit sexuality involving couples only, "male-female, female-female." Reviews photos with or without accompanying ms. Model/property release required; include copies of photo identification with date of birth over 18 years old.

Making Contact & Terms: Submit portfolio for review. Send unsolicited photos by mail for consideration. Provide resume, business card, brochure, flyer or tearsheets to be kept on file for possible future assignments. Send 35mm transparencies. Keeps samples on file. SASE. Reports in 1 month. Payment varies from $10/shot to $3,000/full set. **Pays on acceptance.** Credit line given. Buys one-time rights; negotiable. Simultaneous submissions and previously published work OK.

Tips: "We require technical perfection. Focus, lighting, composition, etc., must be 100% perfect. Look at our magazine and competing titles."

COBBLESTONE: THE HISTORY MAGAZINE FOR YOUNG PEOPLE, Cobblestone Publishing, Inc., 7 School St., Peterborough NH 03458. (603)924-7209. Photo Editor: Francelle Carapetyan. Publishes 10 issues/year. Emphasizes American history; each issue covers a specific theme. Readers are children 8-14, parents, teachers. Sample copy for $3.95 and 8×10 SAE with $1.25 postage. Photo guidelines free with SASE.

Needs: Uses about 40 photos/issue; 5-10 supplied by freelance photographers. "We need photographs related to our specific themes (each issue is theme-related) and urge photographers to request our themes list." Model release required. Captions preferred.

Making Contact & Terms: Query with samples or list of stock photo subjects. Send 8×10 glossy b&w prints, or 35mm or 2¼×2¼ transparencies. SASE. "Photos must pertain to themes, and reporting dates depend on how far ahead of the issue the photographer submits photos. We work on issues 6 months ahead of publication." Cover photo negotiated; $15-50/inside photo. Pays on publication. Credit line given. Buys one-time rights. Simultaneous submissions and previously published work OK.

Tips: "In general, we use few contemporary images; most photos are of historical subjects. However, the amount varies with each monthly theme."

COLLAGES & BRICOLAGES, P.O. Box 86, Clarion PA 16212. (814)226-5799. Editor: Marie-José Fortis. Estab. 1986. Annual magazine. Emphasizes literary works, avant-garde, poetry, fiction, plays and nonfiction. Readers are educated people, writers, college professors in the U.S. and abroad. Sample copy $6.

Needs: Uses 5-10 photos/issue; all supplied by freelancers. Needs photos that make a social statement, surrealist photos and photo collages. Reviews photos with or without a manuscript. Photo captions preferred; include title of photo and short biography of artist/photographer.
Making Contact & Terms: Send unsolicited photos by mail for consideration. Send matte b&w prints. SASE. Reports in 2 weeks-3 months. Pays in copies. Simultaneous submissions and/or previously published work OK.
Tips: "*C&B* is primarily meant for writers. It will include photos if: a) they accompany or illustrate a story, a poem or an essay; b) they constitute the cover of a particular issue; or c) they make a statement (political, social, spiritual)."

COLONIAL HOMES MAGAZINE, Dept. PM, 1790 Broadway, New York NY 10019. (212)830-2950 or 830-2956. Editor: Jason Kontos. Bimonthly. Circ. 600,000. Emphasizes traditional architecture and interior design. Sample copy available.
Needs: All photos supplied by freelance photographers. Needs photos of "American architecture of 18th century or 18th century style—4-color chromes—no people in any shots; some food shots." Special needs include "American food and drink; private homes in Colonial style; historic towns in America." Captions required.
Making Contact & Terms: Submit portfolio for review. Send 4×5 or 8×10 transparencies by mail for consideration. Provide resume, business card, brochure, flyer or tearsheets to be kept on file for possible future assignments. SASE. Reports in 1 month. Pays $500/day. **Pays on acceptance.** Credit line given. Buys all rights. Previously published work OK.

*COLORADO HOMES & LIFESTYLES, 7009 S. Potomac, Englewood CO 80112. (303)397-7600. Fax: (303)397-7619. Art Director: Elaine St. Louis. Circ. 27,000. Estab. 1980. Bimonthly magazine. Emphasizes interior design and architecture of homes in Colorado. Primary readers are women, 35-55, the majority of them homeowners. Sample copies available.
Needs: Uses approximately 100 photos/issue; roughly one-third supplied by freelancers. Needs photos of home interiors, architecture, people (by assignment only), travel, food and entertaining, gardening, home products, etc. Reviews photos with accompanying ms only. "We will review photographers' books for possible future assignments." Model/property release preferred for private homes and people. Captions required; include what and where.
Making Contact & Terms: Interested in receiving work from newer, lesser-known photographers. Arrange personal interview to show portfolio. Send unsolicited photos by mail for consideration. Provide resume, business card, brochure, flyer or tearsheets to be kept on file for possible assignments. Send 5×7 or larger prints; 35mm, 2¼×2¼, 4×5, 8×10 transparencies. Keeps samples on file. SASE. Reports within 3 months. Pays $100-400/job for a feature story with 5+ shots; $50/color inside photo; $50/b&w inside photo. **Pays on acceptance.** Credit line given. Rights negotiable. Simultaneous submissions and/or previously published work OK.
Tips: "Our primary subject matter is homes. With very rare exceptions, subjects must be in Colorado. Particular attention to refined talent with subtle, controlled lighting, both tungsten and daylight/strobe. If you shoot homes for another (Colorado) client—interior designer, architect, etc.—consider submitting to us; that's a good way to break in because we don't have to pay, and we're *very* budget-conscious."

COLUMBUS MONTHLY, P.O. Box 29913, 5255 Sinclair Rd., Columbus OH 43229-7513. (614)888-4567. Editor: Lenore Brown. Assistant Editor: Jill Hawes. Art Director: Sharon Hunley. Circ. 38,000. Estab. 1975. Monthly magazine. Emphasizes local and regional events, including feature articles, personality profiles, investigative reporting, calendar of events, and departments on politics, sports, education, restaurants, books, media, food and drink, shelter and architecture and art. "The magazine is very visual. People read it to be informed and entertained." Sample copy $3.85.
Needs: Buys 150 photos/year. Celebrity/personality (of local or regional residents, or former residents now living elsewhere); fashion/beauty (local only); fine art (of photography, fine arts or crafts with a regional or local angle); head shot (by assignment); photo essay/photo feature on local topics only; product shot; and scenic (local or regional Ohio setting usually necessary, although once or twice a year a travel story, on spots far from Ohio, is featured). No special effects or "form art photography." Model/property releases required. Captions required.
Making Contact & Terms: Interested in receiving work from newer, lesser-known photographers. Arrange personal interview with art director to show portfolio or query with resume of credits. Works with freelance photographers on assignment only basis. Provide calling card, samples and tearsheet to be kept on file for possible future assignments. Uses 8×10 glossy b&w prints, contact proofsheet requested; 35mm, 2¼×2¼ or 4×5 transparencies, contact proof sheet requested for negative color; 2¼×2¼ or 4×5 color transparencies, vertical format required for cover. "Send mailer first with tearsheets or nonreturnable samples; follow up with phone call." SASE. Pays $20/b&w photo; $40/color photo; $45-80/assigned photo. Covers negotiated. **Pays on acceptance.** Credit line given. Buys one-time rights. Previously published work OK.

Tips: "Live in the Columbus area. Prior publication experience is not necessary. Call for an appointment. Need consistency, ability to make something as dull as a headshot a little more interesting. Should have ability to take 'news' type photos."

COMPLETE WOMAN, 1165 N. Clark, Chicago IL 60610. (312)266-8680. Art Director: Sheri L. Darnall. Estab. 1980. Bimonthly magazine. General interest magazine for women. Readers are "females, 21-40, from all walks of life."
Needs: Uses 50-60 photos/issue. Needs "how-to beauty shots, women with men, etc." Model release required. Captions preferred.
Making Contact & Terms: Query with list of stock photo subjects. Send unsolicited photos by mail for consideration. Provide resume, business card, brochure, flyer or tearsheets to be kept on file for possible assignments. Send b&w, color prints; 35mm transparencies. SASE. Reports in 1 month. Pays $75/color inside photo; $50/b&w inside photo. Pays on publication. Credit line given. Buys one-time rights. Simultaneous and previously published work OK.

*CONDE NAST TRAVELER, 360 Madison Ave., New York NY 10017. Has very specific needs and contacts a stock agency when seeking some shots.

CONFRONTATION: A LITERARY JOURNAL, English Dept., C.W. Post of L.I.U., Brookville NY 11548. (516)299-2391. Editor: Martin Tucker. Circ. 2,000. Estab. 1968. Semiannual magazine. Emphasizes literature. Readers are college-educated lay people interested in literature. Sample copy $3.
Needs: Reviews photos with or without a manuscript. Captions preferred.
Making Contact & Terms: Interested in reviewing work from newer, lesser-known photographers. Query with resume of credits. Query with stock photo list. Reports in 1 month. Pays $50-100/color cover photo; $20-40/b&w page rate. Pays on publication. Credit line given. Buys first N.A. serial rights; negotiable. Simultaneous submissions OK.

CONSERVATIONIST MAGAZINE, Dept. PM, NYSDEC, 50 Wolf Rd., Albany NY 12233. (518)457-5547. Contact: Photo Editor. Circ. 200,000. Estab. 1946. Bimonthly. Emphasizes natural history and environmental interests. Readers are people interested in nature and environmental quality issues. Sample copy $3 and 8½×11 SASE. Photo guidelines free with SASE.
Needs: Uses 40 photos/issue; 80% supplied by freelance photographers. Needs wildlife shots, people in the environment, outdoor recreation, forest and land management, fisheries and fisheries management, environmental subjects (pollution shots, a few), effects of pollution on plants, buildings, etc. Model release required. Captions required.
Making Contact & Terms: Interested in reviewing work from newer, lesser-known photographers. Query with samples. Send 35mm, 2¼×2¼, 4×5 or 8×10 transparencies by mail for consideration. Submit portfolio for review. Provide resume, business card, brochure, flyer or tearsheets to be kept on file for possible future assignments. SASE. Reports in 3 weeks. Pays $15/b&w or color photo. Pays on publication. Buys one-time rights. Simultaneous submissions and previously published work OK.
Tips: Looks for "artistic interpretation of nature and the environment," unusual ways of picturing environmental subjects (even pollution, oil spills, trash, air pollution, etc.); wildlife and fishing subjects from above and underwater at all seasons. "Try to have the camera see the subject differently."

*LEE CORSO'S COLLEGE FOOTBALL, #204, 17962 Midvale Ave. N., Seattle WA 98133. (206)546-2461. Fax: (206)546-6015. Photo Editor: Eric Radovich. Circ. 200,000. Estab. 1987. Annual magazine. Emphasizes college football. Readers are mostly college-educated males, ages 25-55. Sample copy $4.95.
Needs: Uses 100-150 photos/issue; all supplied by freelancers. Need photos of sports action.
Making Contact & Terms: Interested in receiving work from newer, lesser-known photographers. Query with resume of credits. SASE. Reports in 3 weeks. Pays $100-150/color cover photo; $50-100/color inside photo; $20-50/b&w inside photo. Pays 60 days after on-sale date. Credit line given. Simultaneous submissions OK.

COSMOPOLITAN, Dept. PM, 8th Floor, 224 W. 57th St., New York NY 10019. (212)649-3570. Art Director: Linda Cox. Photo Editor: Larry Mitchell. Monthly magazine.
Needs: Fashion, beauty, and still lifes of food and decorating. Model release required.
Making Contact & Terms: Arrange personal interview to show portfolio. "It's best to make appointment by phone for Tuesday or Thursday drop-off." Also, query with stock photo list. Provide resume, business card, brochure, flyer or tearsheets to be kept on file for possible future assignments. Keeps samples on file. SASE. Does not always report. "Feel free to call to check on status of material." Pays

$250/inside color photo or b&w page. Also covers expenses and any agent fees that apply. Credit line given. Buys one-time and all rights; negotiable.

COUNTRY, 5925 Country Lane, Greendale WI 53129. (414)423-0100. Fax: (414)423-1143. Editorial Assistant: Trudi Bellin. Estab. 1987. Bimonthly magazine. "For those who live in or long for the country." Readers are rural-oriented, male and female. "*Country* is supported entirely by subscriptions and accepts no outside advertising." Sample copy $2. Photo guidelines free with SASE.
Needs: Uses 150 photos/issue; 20% supplied by freelancers. Needs photos of scenics—country only. Model/property release required. Captions preferred; include season, location.
Making Contact & Terms: Interested in receiving work from newer, lesser-known photographers. Query with list of stock photo subjects. Send unsolicited photos by mail for consideration. Send 35mm, 2¼×2¼, 4×5 and 8×10 transparencies. Tearsheets kept on file but not dupes. SASE. Reports "as soon as possible; sometimes days, other times months." Pays $200/color cover photo; $50-125/color inside photo; $150/color page (full page bleed); $10-25/b&w photo. Pays on publication. Credit line given. Buys one-time rights. Previously published work OK.
Tips: "Technical quality is extremely important: focus must be sharp, no soft focus; colors must be vivid so they 'pop off the page.' Study our magazine thoroughly—we have a continuing need for sharp, colorful images, and those who can supply what we need can expect to be regular contributors."

COUNTRY JOURNAL, Dept. PM, P.O. Box 8200, 6405 Flank Dr., Harrisburg PA 17105. (717)657-9555. Art Editor: Sheryl O'Connell. Circ. 200,000. Estab. 1974. Bimonthly magazine. Emphasizes practical concerns and rewards of life in the country. Readers are mostly male, ages 35-55, occupations varied—most have good disposable income. Sample copy for $4. Photo guidelines free with SASE.
Needs: Uses 40 photos/issue; 95% supplied by freelance photographers. Needs photos of animal/wildlife, country scenics, vegetable and flower gardening, home improvements, personality profiles, environmental issues and other subjects relating to rural life. Model release required. Captions required.
Making Contact & Terms: Provide resume, business card, brochure, flyer or tearsheets to be kept on file for possible assignments. Send b&w prints and 35mm, 2¼×2¼, 4×5 and 8×10 prints with SASE by return mail for consideration. Reports in 1 month. Pays $500/color and b&w cover photo; $135/quarter page color and b&w page inside photo; $235/color and b&w page rate; $275-325/day. Pays on publication. Credit line given. Buys one-time rights. Simultaneous submissions OK.
Tips: "Know who you are submitting to. You can waste time, money and a possible opportunity by sending inappropriate samples and queries. If you can't find samples of the publication, call or send for them."

THE COVENANT COMPANION, 5101 N. Francisco Ave., Chicago IL 60625. (312)784-3000. Editor: James R. Hawkinson. Managing Editor: Jane K. Swanson-Nystrom. Art Director: David Westerfield. Circ. 23,500. Monthly denominational magazine of The Evangelical Covenant Church. Emphasizes "gathering, enlightening and stimulating the people of our church and keeping them in touch with their mission and that of the wider Christian church in the world."
Needs: Mood shots of nature, commerce and industry, home life, church life, church buildings and people. Also uses fine art, scenes, city life, etc.
Making Contact & Terms: "We need to keep a rotating file of photos for consideration." Send 5×7 and 8×10 glossy prints; color slides for cover only. SASE. Pays $15/b&w photo; $50-75/color cover. Pays within one month of publication. Credit line given. Buys one-time rights. Simultaneous submissions OK.
Tips: "Give us photos that illustrate life situations and moods. We use b&w photos which reflect a mood or an aspect of society—wealthy/poor, strong/weak, happiness/sadness, conflict/peace. These photos or illustrations can be of nature, people, buildings, designs and so on. Give us a file from which we can draw."

THE CREAM CITY REVIEW, University of Wisconsin-Milwaukee, English Dept., Box 413, Milwaukee WI 53201. (414)229-4708. Art Director: Laurie Buman. Circ. 2,000. Estab. 1975. Bienniel magazine. Emphasizes literature. Readers are mostly males and females with Ph. D's in English, ages 18-over 70. Sample copy $1.50-5. Photo guidelines free with SASE.

Needs: Uses 6-20 photos/issue; all supplied by freelancers. Needs photos of fine art and other works of art. Captions preferred.

Making Contact & Terms: Interested in reviewing work from newer, lesser-known photographers. Send unsolicited photos by mail for consideration. Send all sizes b&w and color prints; 35mm, 2¼×2¼, 4×5, 8×10 transparencies. SASE. Reports in 2 months. Pays $25/color cover photo; $25/ b&w cover photo; $5/b&w inside photo; $5/b&w page rate. Pays on publication. Credit line given. Buys one-time rights. Simultaneous submissions and/or previously published work OK.

Tips: "The artistic merit of submitted work is important. We have been known to change our look based on exciting work submitted. Take a look at *Cream City Review* and see how we like to look. If you have things that fit, send them."

CRUISE TRAVEL, 990 Grove St., Evanston IL 60201. (708)491-6440. Managing Editor: Charles Doherty. Circ. 160,000. Estab. 1979. Bimonthly magazine. Emphasizes cruise ships, ports, vacation destinations, travel tips, ship history. Readers are "those who have taken a cruise, plan to take a cruise, or dream of taking a cruise." Sample copy $3 with 9×12 SAE and $1.44 postage. Photo guidelines free with SASE.

Needs: Uses about 50 photos/issue; 75% supplied by freelance photographers. Needs ship shots, interior/exterior, scenic shots of ports, shopping shots, native sights, etc. Photos rarely purchased without accompanying ms. Model release preferred. Captions required.

Making Contact & Terms: Query with samples. "We are not seeking overseas contacts." Uses color prints; 35mm (preferred), 2¼×2¼, 4×5, 8×10 transparencies. SASE. Reports in 2 weeks. Pays variable rate for color cover; $25-150/color inside photo; $200-500/text/photo package for original work. Pays on acceptance or publication; depends on package. Credit line usually given, depends on arrangement with photographer. Buys one-time rights. Simultaneous submissions and previously published work OK.

Tips: "We look for bright colorful travel slides with good captions. Nearly every purchase is a photo/ ms package, but good photos are key. We prefer 35mm originals for publication, all color."

CRUISING WORLD MAGAZINE, 5 John Clark Rd., Newport RI 02840. (401)847-1588. Fax: (401)848-5048. Photo Editor: Paul F. Mirto. Circ. 130,000. Estab. 1974. Emphasizes sailboat maintenance, sailing instruction and personal experience. For people interested in cruising under sail. Sample copy free for 9×12 SAE.

Needs: Buys 25 photos/year. Needs "shots of cruising sailboats and their crews anywhere in the world. Shots of ideal cruising scenes. No identifiable racing shots, please." Also wants exotic images of cruising sailboats, people enjoying sailing, tropical images, different perspectives of sailing, good composition, bright colors. For covers, photos "must be of a cruising sailboat with strong human interest, and can be located anywhere in the world." Prefers vertical format. Allow space at top of photo for insertion of logo. Model release preferred. Property release required. Captions required; include location, body of water, make and model of boat.

Making Contact & Terms: Interested in receiving work from newer, lesser-known photographers "as long as their subjects are marine related." Send 35mm color transparencies. "We rarely accept miscellaneous b&w shots and would rather they not be submitted unless accompanied by a manuscript." For cover, "submit original 35mm Kodachrome slides. *No* duplicates. Most of our editorial is supplied by author. We look for good color balance, very sharp focus, the ability to capture sailing, good composition and action. Always looking for *cover shots*." Reports in 2 months. Pays $50-300/ inside photo; $500/cover photo. Pays on publication. Credit line given. Buys all rights, but may reassign to photographer after publication; first N.A. serial rights; or one-time rights.

CUPIDO, % Red Alder Books, P.O. Box 2992, Santa Cruz CA 95063. (408)426-7082. Photo Representative: David Steinberg. Monthly magazine. Emphasizes quality erotica. Circ. 60,000. Estab. 1984. Sample copy $10 (check payable to Red Alder Books).

Needs: Uses 50 photos/issue. Needs quality erotic and sexual photography, visually interesting, imaginative, showing human emotion, tenderness, warmth, humor OK, sensuality emphasized. Reviews photos only (no manuscripts, please).

Making Contact & Terms: Contact through rep. Arrange personal interview to show portfolio or submit portfolio for review. Query with stock photo list. Send unsolicited photos by mail for consideration. Send 8×10 or 11×14 b&w, color prints; 35mm, 2¼×2¼, 4×5, 8×10 transparencies. Keeps samples on file. SASE. Reports in 2-4 weeks. Pays $1,000-1,600/color cover photo; $60-120/color inside photo; $60-120/b&w inside photo. Pays on publication. Credit line given. Buys one-time rights. Simultaneous submissions and/or previously published work OK.

Tips: "Not interested in standard, porn-style photos. Imagination, freshness, emotion emphasized. Glamor OK, but not preferred."

CYCLE WORLD MAGAZINE, Dept. PM, 1499 Monrovia Ave., Newport Beach CA 92663. (714)720-5300. Editorial Director: Paul Dean. Monthly magazine. Circ. 350,000. For active motorcyclists who are "young, affluent, educated and very perceptive." For motorcycle enthusiasts.
Needs: "Outstanding" photos relating to motorcycling. Buys 10 photos/issue. Prefers to buy photos with mss. For Slipstream column see instructions in a recent issue.
Making Contact & Terms: Buys all rights. Send photos for consideration. Pays on publication. Reports in 6 weeks. SASE. Send 8×10 glossy prints. "Cover shots are generally done by the staff or on assignment." Uses 35 mm color transparencies. Pays $50-100/b&w photo; $150-225/color photo.
Tips: Prefers to buy photos with mss. "Read the magazine. Send us something good. Expect instant harsh rejection. If you don't know our magazine, don't bother us."

D MAGAZINE, Dept. PM, Suite 1200, 3988 North Central Expressway, Dallas TX 75204. (214)827-5000. Fax: (214)827-8844. Art Department: Liz Tindall, Jim Darilek. Consumer publication. Monthly magazine. Emphasizes Dallas issues and lifestyles. Circ. 120,000. Estab. 1975. Sample copy available for $2.50.
Needs: Uses 45 photos/issue; 95% supplied by freelancers. All photos are assigned. Subjects vary according to nature of story. Occasionally needs photo essay material. Model/property release required; photo captions preferred.
Making Contact & Terms: Submit portfolio for review. Provide business card, brochure, flyer or tearsheets to be kept on file for possible future assignments. Keeps samples on file. SASE. Reports in 1 month. Pays $650/color cover photo; $200/color inside photo. Credit line given. Buys one-time rights. Simultaneous submissions OK.
Tips: Expects to see "very creative work," but "it's very hard to find."

DAKOTA OUTDOORS, P.O. Box 669, Pierre SD 57501. (605)224-7301. Fax: (605)224-9210. Director of Operations and Production: Rachel Engbrecht. Circ. 6,500. Estab. 1978. Monthly magazine. Emphasizes hunting and fishing in the Dakotas. Readers are sportsmen interested in hunting and fishing, ages 35-45. Sample copy free for 9×12 SAE and 3 first-class stamps. Photo guidelines free with SASE.
Needs: Uses 15-20 photos/issue; 8-10 supplied by freelancers. Needs photos of hunting and fishing. Reviews photos with or without ms. Special photo needs include: scenic shots of sportsmen. Model/property release required. Captions preferred.
Making Contact & Terms: Interested in receiving work from newer, lesser-known photographers. Send 3×5 b&w prints; 35mm b&w transparencies by mail for consideration. Keeps samples on file. SASE. Reports in 3 weeks. Pays $50-150/b&w cover photo; $25-75/b&w inside photo; payment negotiable. Pays on publication. Credit line given. Usually buys one-time rights; negotiable.
Tips: "We want good quality outdoor shots, good lighting, identifiable faces, etc.—photos shot in the Dakotas. Use some imagination and make your photo help tell a story. Photos with accompanying story are accepted."

DALLAS LIFE MAGAZINE, DALLAS MORNING NEWS, Communications Center, P.O. Box 655237, Dallas TX 75265. (214)977-8433. Managing Editor: Mike Maza. Art Director: Lesley Becker. Circ. 850,000. Estab. 1842. Weekly magazine. Emphasizes Dallas. "We buy only Dallas-pegged material—this is a very locally-focused publication." Sample copy free with SASE.
Needs: Uses 20 photos/issue; 5% or less supplied by freelance photographers. Reviews photos with accompanying ms only. Captions required.
Making Contact & Terms: Query with resume of credits. Provide resume, business card, brochure, flyer or tearsheets to be kept on file for possible future assignments. SASE. Reports in 1 month. Pays $50-200/color photo. **Pays on acceptance.** Credit line given. Buys one-time rights.

DANCE MAGAZINE, 33 W. 60th St., New York NY 10023. (212)245-9050. Fax: (212)956-6487. Photo Editor: Jane Buchanan. Circ. 50,000. Estab. 1927. Monthly magazine. Emphasizes "all facets of the dance world." Readers are 85% female, age 18-40.
Needs: Uses about 60 photos/issue; almost all supplied by freelance photographers. Occasionally buys stock images; 95% of photos are assigned. Needs photos of all types of dancers—from ballroom to ballet. Dance, dancer, company and date of photo must accompany all submissions.

The First Markets Index preceding the General Index in the back of this book provides the names of those companies/ publications interested in receiving work from newer, lesser-known photographers.

Making Contact & Terms: Send query letter describing photos, slides, transparencies and how the work would suit the magazine's needs. Pays up to $285/color cover photo; $25-150/b&w inside photo; $60-200/color inside photo. Pays on publication. Credit line given. Buys one-time rights. Previously published work OK.

Tips: "We look for a photojournalistic approach to the medium—photos that catch the height of a particular performance or reveal the nature of a particular dancer. We occasionally will print a photo that is strikingly revealing of life backstage, or in rehearsal."

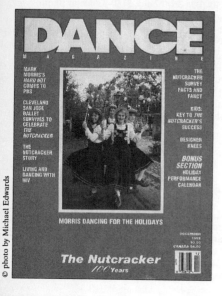

© photo by Michael Edwards

By querying Dance Magazine and explaining his image of English Morris dancers, English photographer Michael Edwards found a market for this shot. Edwards received $285 for the photo which tied in with a story on the subject. "We were looking for something about Morris dancing; we did not want another photo of the Christmas perennial 'Nutcracker,' " says Dance Magazine Editor Richard Philp.

DEER AND DEER HUNTING, P.O. Box 1117, Appleton WI 54912. (414)734-0009. Fax: (414)734-2919. Managing Editor: Al Hofacker. 8 issues/year. Distribution 200,000. Emphasizes whitetail deer and deer hunting. Readers are "a cross-section of American deer hunters—bow, gun, camera." Estab. 1977. Sample copy and photo guidelines free with 9 × 12 SAE with $2 postage.

Needs: Uses about 25 photos/issue; 20 supplied by freelance photographers. Needs photos of deer in natural settings. Model release and captions preferred.

Making Contact & Terms: Query with resume of credits and samples. "If we judge your photos as being usable, we like to hold them in our file. It is best to send us duplicates because we may hold the photo for a lengthy period." SASE. Reports in 2 weeks. Pays $500/color cover; $40/b&w inside; $75-250/color inside. Pays within 10 days of publication. Credit line given. Buys one-time rights. Simultaneous submissions and previously published work OK.

Tips: Prefers to see "adequate selection of b&w 8 × 10 glossy prints and 35mm color transparencies, action shots of whitetail deer only as opposed to portraits. We also need photos of deer hunters in action. We are currently using almost all color—very little b&w. Submit a limited number of quality photos rather than a multitude of marginal photos. Have your name on all entries. Cover shots must have room for masthead."

***DIR Communications,** 6198 Butler Pike, Blue Bell PA 19422. (215)653-0810. Fax: (215)653-0817. Creative Director: Scott Stephens. Publishes quarterly and annual magazines. Emphasizes education—medical, pre-natal, sports safety and job safety. Readers are high school males and females, medical personnel, pregnant women, new home owners. Sample copy free with 9 × 12 SASE and six first class stamps.

● This company produces numerous consumer publications: *First Baby, Student Aware, Job Search, Technology Education, Sports Safety, Medaware, America Moves, New Homeowner* and *Help Yourself.*

Needs: Uses 20-30 photos/issue; 90% supplied by freelancers. Needs photos of medical, teenage sports and fitness, pregnancy and lifestyle (of pregnant mothers), home interiors. Model/property release required. Captions preferred.

Making Contact & Terms: Interested in reviewing work from newer, lesser-known photographers. Submit portfolio for review. Send uncolicited photos by mail for consideration. Send 35mm, 2¼ × 2¼, 4 × 5, 8 × 10 transparencies. Keeps samples on file. SASE. Reports only when interested. Pays $400 + / color cover photo; $100 + /color inside photo. Pays on publication. Credit line given. Buys one time rights; negotiable. Simultaneous submissions and/or previously published work OK.

Tips: Looks for quality of composition and color sharpness. "Photograph pregnant women in all lifestyle situations. Do not stop shooting great looking models once they become pregnant!"

DIRT WHEELS, 10600 Sepulveda, Mission Hills CA 91345. (818)365-6831. Fax: (818)361-4512. Editor: Steve Casper. Circ. 50,000. Monthly magazine. Emphasizes ATVs (all-terrain vehicles), also known as 3&4 wheelers. Readers are young adult males. Sample copy free on request.
Needs: Uses 75-100 photos/issue; 25 supplied by freelance photographers. Needs photos of travel and scenic shots from different parts of the country; hunting and fishing (all with ATVs in the photos). Special photo needs include "unique spots to ride off-road vehicles." Photo captions preferred.
Making Contact & Terms: Interested in receiving work from newer, lesser-known photographers. Call and leave message. Reports in 1 month. Pays $50/color cover photo; $40/color inside photo; $20/ b&w inside photo; $100-300/photo/text package. Pays on publication. Credit line given. Buys one-time rights. Simultaneous submissions and previously published work OK.
Tips: "Go on a trip with a local ATV club—they'll probably be glad to put you up and show you a good time. Take great photos."

DOG FANCY, P.O. Box 6050, Mission Viejo CA 92690. (714)855-8822. Editor: Kim Thornton. Readers are "men and women of all ages interested in all phases of dog ownership." Monthly. Circ. 150,000. Estab. 1970. Sample copy $4.50; photo guidelines available with SASE.
Needs: Uses 20-30 photos/issue, 90% supplied from freelance stock. Specific breed featured in each issue. Prefers "photographs that show the various physical and mental attributes of the breed. Include both environmental and portrait-type photographs. We also have a major need for good-quality, interesting b&w photographs of any breed or mixed breed in any and all canine situations (dogs with veterinarians; dogs eating, drinking, playing, swimming, etc.) for use with feature articles." Model release required. Captions preferred (include dog's name and breed and owner's name and address).
Making Contact & Terms: Send by mail for consideration actual 8×10 b&w photos, 35mm or 2¼×2¼ color transparencies. Reports in 6 weeks. Pays $15-35/b&w photo; $50-150/color photo; $100-300 per text/photo package. Credit line given. Buys first N.A. serial rights; buys one-time rights.
Tips: "Nothing but sharp, high contrast shots. Send SASE for list of photography needs. We're looking more and more for good quality photo/text packages that present an interesting subject both editorially and visually. Bad writing can be fixed, but we can't do a thing with bad photos. Subjects should be in interesting poses or settings with good lighting, good backgrounds and foregrounds, etc. We are very concerned with sharpness and reproducibility; the best shot in the world won't work if it's fuzzy, and it's amazing how many are. Submit a variety of subjects—there's always a chance we'll find something special we like."

DOWN BEAT MAGAZINE, Dept. PM, Jazz Blues & Beyond, 180 W. Park Ave., Elmhurst IL 60126. (708)941-2030. Editorial Director: Frank Alkyer. Monthly. Emphasizes jazz musicians. Circ. 90,000. Estab. 1934. Sample copy available.
Needs: Uses about 30 photos/issue; 95% supplied by freelancers. Needs photos of live music performers/posed musicians/equipment, "primarily jazz and blues." Captions preferred.
Making Contact & Terms: Query with list of stock photo subjects; send 8×10 b&w prints; 35mm, 2¼×2¼, 4×5, 8×10 transparencies; b&w or color contact sheets by mail. Unsolicited samples for consideration will not be returned unless accompanied by SASE. Provide resume, business card, brochure, flyer or tearsheets to be kept on file for possible future assignments. "Send us two samples of your best work and a list of artists photographed." Reports only when needed. Pays $35/b&w photo; $75/color photo; $175/complete job. Credit line given. Buys one-time rights. Simultaneous submissions and previously published work OK.
Tips: "We prefer live shots and interesting candids to studio work."

*ELLE, 1633 Broadway, New York NY 10019. Uses very little freelance work.

ENTREPRENEUR, Dept. PM, 2392 Morse Ave., Irvine CA 92714. (714)261-2325. Fax: (714)755-4211. Photo Editor: Chrissy Borgatta. Publisher: Jim Fitzpatrick. Editor: Rieva Lesonsky. Design Director: Richard R. Olson. Cir. 360,000. Estab. 1977. Monthly. Emphasizes business. Readers are existing and aspiring small business owners.
Needs: Uses about 30 photos/issue; many supplied by freelance photographers; 60% on assignment; 40% from stock. Needs "editorially specific, conceptual and how-to, and industrial" photos. Model/ property release preferred. Captions required; include names of subjects.
Making Contact & Terms: Interested in reviewing work from newer, lesser-known photographers. Arrange a personal interview to show portfolio. Query with sample or list of stock photo subjects. Provide resume, business card, brochure, flyer or tearsheets to be kept on file for possible future assignments; "follow-up for response." Pays $75-200/b&w photo; $125-225/color photo. Pays "depending on photo shoot, per hour or per day. We pay $250-300 for all assignments." Pays on publication. Credit line given. Buys one-time rights; negotiable.

© Owen O'Rourke

An action-packed battle between two Huskies served as a great illustration for an article published by Dog Fancy on the aggressive behavior of some dogs. Photographer Owen O'Rourke of Woburn, Massachusetts, discovered the market through a newsletter and received $15 for the artwork.

Tips: "I am looking for photographers who use the environment creatively; I do not like blank walls for backgrounds. Lighting is also important. I prefer medium format for most shoots. I think photographers are going back to the basics—a good clean shot, different angles and bright colors. I am extremely tired of a lot of motion-blurred effect with gelled lighting. I prefer examples of your work—promo cards and tearsheets along with business cards and resumes. Portfolios are always welcome."

ENVIRONMENT, Dept. PM, 1319 18th St. NW, Washington DC 20036. (202)296-6267. Editor: Barbara T. Richman. Magazine published 10 times/year. Covers science and science policy from a national, international and global perspective. "We cover a wide range of environmental topics—acid rain, tropical deforestation, nuclear winter, hazardous waste disposal, worker safety, energy topics and environmental legislation." Readers include libraries, colleges and universities and professionals in the field of environmental science and policy. Circ. 12,500. Sample copy $4.50.

Needs: Uses 15 photos/issue; varying number supplied by freelance photographers. "Our needs vary greatly from issue to issue—but we are always looking for good photos showing human impact on the environment worldwide—industrial sites, cities, alternative energy sources, pesticide use, disasters, third world growth, hazardous wastes, sustainable agriculture and pollution. Interesting and unusual landscapes are also needed." Model release preferred; captions required.

Making Contact & Terms: Query with list of stock photo subjects. Send unsolicited photos by mail for consideration. Provide business card, brochure, flyer or tearsheets to be kept on file for possible future assignments. Send any size b&w print by mail for consideration. SASE. Reports in 2 months. Pays $35-100/b&w inside photo; $50-300/color photo. Pays on publication. Credit line given. Buys one-time rights. Simultaneous submissions and previously published work OK.

Tips: "We are looking for international subject matter—especially environmental conditions in developing countries."

✿EQUINOX MAGAZINE, 7 Queen Victoria Rd., Camden East, Ontario K0K 1J0 Canada. (613)378-6661. Editor: Bart Robinson. Bimonthly. Circ. 175,000. Emphasizes "Canadian subjects of a general 'geographic' and scientific nature." Sample copy $5 with 8½ × 14 SAE; photo guidelines free with SAE and IRC.
Needs: Uses 80-100 photos/issue; all supplied by freelance photographers. Needs "photo stories of interest to a Canadian readership as well as occasional stock photos required to supplement assignments. Story categories include wildlife, international travel and adventure, science, Canadian arts and architecture and Canadian people and places." Captions required.
Making Contact & Terms: Query with samples; submit portfolio for review. SASE. Reports in 6 weeks. "Most stories are shot on assignment basis—average $2,000 price. We also pay expenses for people on assignment. We also buy packages at negotiable prices and stock photography at about $250 a page if only one or two shots used." Pays on publication. Credit line given. Buys first N.A. serial rights.
Tips: We look for "excellence and in-depth coverage of a subject, technical mastery and an ability to work intimately with people. Many of the photographs we use are of people, so any portfolio should emphasize people involved in some activity. Stick to Kodachrome/Ektachrome transparencies."

EVANGELIZING TODAY'S CHILD, Child Evangelism Fellowship Inc., P.O. Box 348, Warrentown MO 63383. (314)456-4321. Editor: Mrs. Elsie Lippy. Circ. 23,000. Estab. 1942. Bimonthly magazine. Written for people who work with children, ages 5-12, in Sunday schools, Bible clubs and camps. Sample copy for $1. Photo guidelines free with SASE.
Needs: Buys 1-4 photos/issue; 50% from freelance asssignment; 50% from freelance stock. Children, ages 6-11; unique, up-to-date. Candid shots of various moods and activities. If full color needs to include good color combination. "We use quite a few shots with more than one child and some with an adult, mostly closeups. The content emphasis is upon believability and appeal. Religious themes may be especially valuable." No nudes, scenery, fashion/beauty, glamour or still lifes.
Making Contact & Terms: Interested in receiving work from newer, lesser-known photographers. Prefers to retain good-quality photocopies of selected glossy prints and duplicate slides in files for future use. Send material by mail with SASE for consideration; 8 × 10 b&w glossy prints or 35mm and larger transparencies. Publication is under no obligation to return materials sent without SASE. Pays on a per-photo basis. Pays $35 minimum/b&w photo; $45 minimum/color inside photo; $125/color cover shot. Credit line given. Buys one-time rights. Simultaneous submissions and previously published work OK.

✳✿EVENT, Douglas College, Box 2503, New Westminster, British Columbia V3L 5B2 Canada. (604)527-5293. Fax: (604)527-5095. Editor: Dale Zieroth. Visuals Editor: Ken Hughes. Circ. 1,000. Magazine published every 4 months. Emphasizes literature and fine art graphics (essays, short stories, plays, reviews, poetry, verse, photographs and drawings). Sample copy $5.
Needs: Buys 20 photos/issue. Animal, celebrity/personality, documentary, fine art, human interest, humorous, nature, nude, photo essay/photo feature, scenic, special effects/experimental, still life, travel and wildlife. Wants any "nonapplied" photography, or photography not intended for conventional commercial purposes. Needs excellent quality. Must be a series. Photos purchased with our without accompanying ms. Model release required. Captions required. "No unoriginal, commonplace or hackneyed work."
Making Contact & Terms: Send material by mail for consideration or submit portfolio for review. Send 8 × 10 b&w prints. Any smooth finish OK. "No color work unless the photographer agrees to reproduction in b&w and unless work is of a sufficient standard when in b&w." Vertical format preferred for cover. SAE and IRC or Canadian stamps. Pays $10-30/b&w photo. Pays on publication. Credit line given. Buys one-time rights. Simultaneous submissions OK.
Tips: "We prefer work that appears as a sequence: thematically, chronologically, stylistically. Individual items will only be selected for publication if such a sequence can be developed. Photos should preferably be composed for vertical, small format (6 × 9) and in b&w."

EXECUTIVE REPORT MAGAZINE, 3 Gateway Center, Pittsburgh PA 15222. (412)471-4585. Art/Production Director: Steve Karlovich. Circ. 26,000. Estab. 1981. Monthly magazine. Emphasizes business reporting. Readers are primarily male, average age 45-50, mid to upper management. Sample copy free with SASE. Photo guidelines not available.
Needs: Uses 4-15 photos/issue; all supplied by freelancers. Needs photos relating to business and business issues. Photo captions preferred.
Making Contact & Terms: Query with stock photo list. Provide resume, business card, brochure, flyer or tearsheets to be kept on file for possible assignments. Keeps samples on file. Cannot return material. "We will contact if interested." Pays $500/color cover photo; $50 "and up"/color and b&w inside photo and color and b&w page rate. **Pays on acceptance.** Credit line given.

EXPECTING MAGAZINE, Dept. PM, 685 3rd Ave., New York NY 10017. (212)878-8700. Art Director: Claudia Waters. Quarterly. Circ. 1,300,000. Emphasizes pregnancy and birth. Readers are pregnant women 18-40.

Needs: Uses about 12 photos/issue. Works with freelance photographers on assignment basis only for fashion, pregnant women and mothers with newborns; more than 50% of the issue comes from assignment. Provide card to be kept on file for future assignments. Occasionally uses stock color transparencies of women during labor and birth, and newborn babies, hospital or doctor visits. Model release required.

Making Contact & Terms: Arrange for drop-off to show portfolio. SASE. Do not send originals. No b&w photos used. Payment varies; $150-300/color photo. Pays on publication. Credit line given. Buys one-time rights. Previously published work OK.

Tips: In photographer's portfolio looks for "nice lighting, warm, friendly people, babies and candid lifestyle shots. Should not look too 'cataloguey.' Present a portfolio of transparencies and tearsheets of published work. I hire experienced professionals only."

FACES: The Magazine About People, 7 School St., Peterborough NH 03458. (603)924-7209. Fax: (603)924-7380. Picture Editor: Francelle Carapetyan. Circ. 13,000. Estab. 1984. Monthly (except June, July and August) magazine. Emphasizes cultural anthropology for young people ages 8-15. Sample copy $3.95 with 8×11 SASE and $1.25 postage.

Needs: Uses about 30-35 photos/issue; about 75% supplied by freelancers. "Photos (b&w use) for text must relate to themes; cover photos (color) should also relate to themes." Send SASE for themes. Photos purchased with or without accompanying ms. Model release preferred. Captions preferred.

Making Contact & Terms: Query with stock photo list and/or samples. SASE. Reports in 1 month. Pays $15-50/text photos; cover photos negotiated. Pays on publication. Credit line given. Buys one-time rights. Simultaneous submissions and previously published work OK.

Tips: "Photographers should request our theme list. Most of the photographs we use are of people from other cultures. We look for an ability to capture people in action—at work or play. We primarily need photos showing people, young and old, taking part in ceremonies, rituals, customs and with artifacts and architecture particular to a given culture. Appropriate scenics and animal pictures are also needed. All submissions must relate to a specific future theme."

*FAMILY MAGAZINE, 169 Lexington Ave., New York NY 10016. (212)545-9740. Circ. 500,000. Estab. 1960. Monthly magazine. Emphasizes military housewives, military family life, kids and moms. Readers are female homemakers, age 20-30, with military spouses. Sample copy $1.25. Photo guidelines free with SASE.

Needs: Uses 20 photos/issue; 15 supplied by freelancers. Needs photos that are family-oriented—travel, holidays, homemaking, moving, problem-solving, recreation, schooling, any real life activity. Reviews photos with or without ms. Model release required. Captions required; include names of specific places (travel) or items in shot.

Making Contact & Terms: Interested in receiving work from newer, lesser-known photographers. Send unsolicited photos by mail for consideration. Provide resume, business card, brochure, flyer or tearsheets to be kept on file for possible assignments. Send 35mm color transparencies. Keeps samples on file. Reports in 1 month. Pays $50/color inside photo. Pays on publication. Credit line given. Buys one-time rights; negotiable. Simultaneous submissions and/or previously published work OK.

Tips: "Never send original slides. We want only dupes to keep on file! A written request for return of photos will get your photos back to you. Otherwise, they stay on file. Also, along with written request, send SASE for photos' safe return."

FANTASY BASEBALL, 700 E. State St., Iola WI 54990. (715)445-2214. Fax: (715)445-4087. Editor: Greg Ambrosius. Bimonthly magazine. Emphasizes baseball. Readers are 99% male, ages 25-40, college-educated, professionals. Circ. 150,000. Estab. 1990. Sample copy free with 9×12 SASE. Photo guidelines free with SASE.

Needs: Uses 30 photos/issue; 90% supplied by freelancers. Needs photos of action game shots of major-league baseball. Reviews photos with accompanying ms only. Special needs include NFL and NBA photos.

Making Contact & Terms: Query with list of stock photo subjects. Send color slides. Does not keep samples on file. SASE. Reports in 1-2 weeks. Pays $100/color cover photo; $50/color inside photo; $25/b&w inside photo. Pays on publication. Buys one-time rights.

Tips: Wants "clear, precise action shots of top players. Have some great photos to show me."

The code NPI (no payment information given) appears in listings that have not given specific payment amounts.

FARM & RANCH LIVING, 5400 S. 60th St., Greendale WI 53129. (414)423-0100. Fax: (414)423-1143. Associate Editor: Trudi Bellin. Estab. 1978. Bimonthly magazine. "Concentrates on farming and ranching as a way of life." Readers are full-time farmers and ranchers. Sample copy $2. Photo guidelines free with SASE.
Needs: Uses about 130 photos/issue; about 30 from freelance photographers, 25% from stock. Needs agricultural and scenic photos. "We assume you have secured releases. If in question, don't send the photos." Captions should include season, location.
Making Contact & Terms: Interested in receiving work from newer, lesser-known photographers. Query with samples or list of stock photo subjects. Send 35mm, 2¼ × 2¼, 4 × 5, 8 × 10 transparencies by mail for consideration. SASE. "We only want to see one season at a time; we work one season in advance." Reporting time varies; "ASAP: can be a few days, may be a few months." Pays $200/color cover photo; $50-125/color inside photo; $150/color page (full-page bleed); $10-50/b&w photo. Pays on publication. Buys one-time rights. Previously published work OK.
Tips: "Technical quality extremely important. Colors must be vivid so they pop off the page. Study our magazines thoroughly. We have a continuing need for sharp, colorful images. Those who supply what we need can expect to be regular contributors."

FIELD & STREAM, 2 Park Ave., New York NY 10016. (212)779-5364. Photo Editor: Scott Wm. Hanrahan. This is a broad-based service magazine. The editorial content ranges from very basic "how it's done" filler stories that tell in pictures and words how an outdoor technique is accomplished or device is made, to feature articles of penetrating depth about national conservation, game management, and resource management issues; and recreational hunting, fishing, travel, nature and outdoor equipment. Writer's/photographer's guidelines available.
Needs: Photos using action and a variety of subjects and angles in color and occasionally b&w. "We are always looking for cover photographs, in color, which may be vertical or horizontal. Remember: a cover picture must have room at the left for cover lines." Needs photo information regarding subjects, the area, the nature of the activity and the point the picture makes.
Making Contact & Terms: Send 35mm and 2¼ × 2¼ transparencies. Will also consider 4 × 5 transparencies, but "majority of color illustrations are made from 35mm or slides." Submit photos by registered mail. Send slides in 8½ × 11 plastic sheets, and pack slides and/or prints between cardboard. SASE. Pays $75+/b&w photo, $450/color photo depending on size used on single page; $700/partial color spread; $900/full-color spread; $1,000+/color cover. Buys first N. A. serial rights returned after publication.

FIFTY SOMETHING MAGAZINE, Unit #E, 8250 Tyler Blvd., Mentor OH 44060. (216)974-9594. Editor: Linda L. Lindeman. Circ. 25,000. Estab. 1990. Bimonthly magazine. Emphasizes lifestyles for the fifty-and-better-reader. Readers are men and women age 50+. Sample copy free with 9 × 12 SAE and 4 first-class stamps. Photo guidelines free with SASE.
Needs: Uses 25-40 photos/issue; 30+ supplied by freelancers. Needs "anything pertaining to mature living—travel, education, health, fitness, money, etc." Model release preferred. Captions preferred.
Making Contact & Terms: Interested in receiving work from newer, lesser-known photographers. Query with list of stock photo subjects. Send unsolicited photos by mail for consideration. Submit portfolio for review. Provide resume, business card, brochure, flyer or tearsheets to be kept on file for possible assignments. Send b&w, color prints; 35mm, 2¼ × 2¼, 4 × 5, 8 × 10 transparencies. SASE. Reports in 6 months. Pays $100/color cover photo; $10/color inside photo; $5/b&w inside photo; $25-75/hour; $100-400/day; $25-125/photo/text package. Pays on publication. Credit line given. Buys one-time rights. Simultaneous submissions and previously published work OK.
Tips: "We are an upbeat publication with the philosophy that life begins at 50. Looking for stories/pictures that show this lifestyle. Also, use a lot of travel/photo essays."

FIGHTING WOMAN NEWS, 6741 Tung Ave. W., Theodore AL 36582. Editor: Debra Pettis. Quarterly. Circ. 5,000. Estab. 1975. Covers women's martial arts. Readers are "adult females actively practicing the martial arts or combative sports." Sample copy $3.50 postpaid. Photo guidelines free with SASE.
Needs: Uses several photos/issue; most supplied by freelance photographers. Needs powerful images of female martial artists; "action photos from tournaments and classes/demonstrations; studio sequences illustrating specific techniques and artistic constructions illustrating spiritual values. Obviously, photos illustrating text have a better chance of being used. We have little space for fillers. We are always short of photos suitable to our magazine." Model release preferred. Captions required; include identification information.
Making Contact & Terms: Interested in reviewing work from newer, lesser-known photographers. Query with resume of credits or with samples. Send 8 × 10 glossy b&w prints or b&w contact sheet by mail for consideration. Provide resume, business card, brochure, flyer or tearsheets to be kept on file for possible future assignments. SASE. Reports "as soon as possible." NPI. Payment for text/photo package to be negotiated." Pays on publication. Credit line given. Buys one-time rights. Simultaneous submissions and previously published work OK; "however, we insist that we are *told* concerning these

matters. We don't want to publish a photo that is in the current issue of another martial arts magazine."

Tips: Prefers to see "technically competent b&w photos of female martial artists in action; good solid images of powerful female martial artists. We don't print color. No glamour, no models; no cute little kids unless they are also skilled. Get someone knowledgeable to caption your photos or at least tell you what you have—or don't have if you are not experienced in the art you are photographing. We are a poor alternative publication chronically short of material, yet we reject 90% of what is sent because the sender obviously never saw the magazine and has no idea what it's about. Five of our last seven covers were live action photos and we are using fewer "enhancements" than previously. Best to present yourself and your work with samples and a query letter indicating that you have *seen* our publication. The cost of buying sample copies is a lot less than postage these days."

*FINAL FRONTIER: MAGAZINE OF SPACE EXPLORATION, #102, 1516 West Lake St., Minneapolis MN 55408. Art Director: C. Olson. Circ. 100,000. Estab. 1988. Biweekly magazine. Emphasizes space exploration and NASA's accomplishments. Readers are male professors ages 28-45. Sample copy $3.

Needs: Uses 25-35 photos/issue; 15 supplied by freelancers. Needs photos of space-related issues, space shuttles, space technologies (people involved in space exploration). Reviews photos with accompanying ms. only. Model/property release required for industry space technology photos. Captions required; include date, location, subject matter.

Making Contact & Terms: Interested in receiving work from newer, lesser-known photographers. Provide resume, business card, brochure, flyer or tearsheets to be kept on file for possible assignments. Keeps samples on file. Cannot return material. Reports in 1 month. Pays $150/color cover photo; $100/ b&w cover photo; $50/color inside photo; $35/b&w inside photo. Pays 30 days after publication. Credit line given. Buys one-time rights. Previous published work OK.

FINESCALE MODELER, 21027 Crossroads Circle, P.O. Box 1612, Waukesha WI 53187. (414)796-8776. Editor: Bob Hayden. Photo Editor: Paul Boyer. Circ. 82,000. Published 8 times/year. Emphasizes "how-to-do-it information for hobbyists who build nonoperating scale models." Readers are "adult and juvenile hobbyists who build nonoperating model aircraft, ships, tanks and military vehicles, cars and figures." Sample copy $2.95. Photo guidelines free with SASE.

Needs: Uses more than 50 photos/issue; "anticipates using" 10 supplied by freelance photographers. Needs "in-progress how-to photos illustrating a specific modeling technique; photos of full-size aircraft, cars, trucks, tanks and ships." Model release required. Captions required.

Making Contact & Terms: Provide resume, business card, brochure, flyer or tearsheets to be kept on file for possible future assignments. "Phone calls are OK." Reports in 8 weeks. Pays $25 minimum/ color cover photo; $5 minimum/b&w inside photo; $7.50 minimum/color inside photo; $30/b&w page; $45/color page; $50-500 for text/photo package. Pays for photos on publication, for text/photo package on acceptance. Credit line given. Buys one-time rights. "Will sometimes accept previously published work if copyright is clear."

Tips: Looking for "clear b&w glossy 5×7 or 8×10 prints of aircraft, ships, cars, trucks, tanks and sharp color positive transparencies of the same. In addition to photographic talent, must have comprehensive knowledge of objects photographed and provide copious caption material. Freelance photographers should provide a catalog stating subject, date, place, format, conditions of sale and desired credit line before attempting to sell us photos. We're most likely to purchase color photos of outstanding models of all types for our regular feature, FSM Showcase."

*FIRST VISIT, 8003 Old York Rd., Elkins Park PA 19117. (215)635-1700. Fax: (215)635-6455. Project Coordinator: Deana C. Jamroz. Circ. 2,250,000/year. Estab. 1991. Magazine published 3 times/year. Emphasizes postnatal care for infants. Readers are new parents who have just taken baby to first pediatrician visit. Sample copy free with 6×9 SAE and 2 first-class stamps. Photo guidelines free with SASE.

Needs: Uses 2-10 photos/issue; 80% supplied by freelancers. Needs photos of neonates, parents with new babies, grandparents with new babies, baby items/products, babies being fed, babies being bathed, etc. Reviews photo with or without ms. Model/property release required.

Making Contact & Terms: Interested in receiving work from newer, lesser-known photographers. Query with stock photo list. Does not keep samples on file. SASE. Pays $800/half day; $300-600/color inside photo; $100-500/b&w inside photo. **Pays on acceptance.** Credit line not given. Buys all rights.

Tips: "Payment for photos is negotiable depending upon degree of difficulty/technical difficulty of pictures."

FISHING WORLD, 51 Atlantic Ave., Floral Park NY 11001. (516)352-9700. Fax: (516)437-6841. Editor: Scott Shane. Circ. 250,000. Bimonthly magazine. Emphasizes techniques, locations and products of both freshwater and saltwater fishing. For men interested in sport fishing. Free sample copy and photo guidelines.

Needs: Buys 18-30/year; all freelance photography comes from freelance stock. Photos of "worldwide angling action." Photos purchased with accompanying ms; cover photos purchased separately. Captions required.

Making Contact & Terms: Send original transparencies. Send photos for consideration. SASE. Reports in 3 weeks. Pay rates for color: $300/cover; $50/quarter page; $75/half page; $100/three quarters page; $125/full page; $150/1½ page; $200/2-page spread. Black and white flat rate of $50. Pays on publication. Buys first N.A. serial rights.

Tips: "First, look at the magazine. In general, queries are preferred, though we're very receptive to unsolicited submissions accompanied by smashing photography." Inside photos are color. Trend is more boats. "Good-looking women are a plus."

FLOWER AND GARDEN MAGAZINE, Suite 310, 700 W. 47th St., Kansas City MO 64112. (816)531-5730. Fax: (816)531-3873. Editorial Assistant: Brent Shephard. Executive Editor: Kay Melchisedech Olson. Estab. 1957. "We publish 6 times a year and require several months of lead time." Emphasizes home gardening. Readers are male and female homeowners with a median age of 47. Sample copy $3.50. Photo guidelines free with SASE.

Needs: Uses 25-50 photos/issue; 75% supplied by freelancers. "We purchase a variety of subjects relating to home lawn and garden activities. Specific horticultural subjects must be accurately identified."

Making Contact & Terms: Interested in receiving work from newer, lesser-known photographers. To make initial contact, "Do not send great numbers of photographs, but rather a good selection of 1 or 2 specific subjects. We do not want photographers to call. We return photos by certified mail—other means of return must be specified and paid for by the individual submitting them. It is not our policy to pay holding fees for photographs." Pays $25-100/b&w photo; $100-500/color photo. Pays on publication. Buys one-time rights. Model/property release preferred. Captions preferred.

Tips: Wants to see "clear shots with crisp focus. Also, appealing subject matter—good lighting, technical accuracy, depictions of plants in a home garden setting rather than individual close-ups. Let us know what you've got, we'll contact you when we need it."

FLY FISHERMAN, Cowles Magazines, Inc., 6405 Flank Dr., P.O. Box 8200, Harrisburg PA 17112. (717)657-9555. Editor and Publisher: John Randolph. Managing Editor: Philip Hanyok. Circ. 130,000. Bimonthly. Emphasizes all types of fly fishing for readers who are "99% male, 79% college educated, 79% married. Average household income is $62,590 and 55% are managers or professionals; 85% keep their copies for future reference and spend 35 days a year fishing." Sample copy $3.50 with 9×12 SAE and $1 postage. Photo/writer guidelines for SASE.

Needs: Uses about 45 photos/issue, 70% of which are supplied by freelance photographers. Needs shots of "fly fishing and all related areas—scenics, fish, insects, how-to." Captions required.

Making Contact & Terms: Send 35mm, 2¼×2¼, 4×5 or 8×10 color transparenciesby mail for consideration. SASE. Reports in 4-6 weeks. NPI. Pays on publication. Credit line given. Buys one-time rights.

FLY ROD & REEL: THE MAGAZINE OF AMERICAN FLY-FISHING, Dept. PM, P.O. Box 370, Camden ME 04843. (207)594-9544. Fax: (207)594-7215. Managing Editor: Jim Butler. Magazine published 6 times/year, irregular intervals. Emphasizes fly-fishing. Readers are primarily fly fishermen ages 30-60. Circ. 44,000. Estab. 1979. Free sample copy with SASE. Photo guidelines free with SASE.

Needs: Uses 25-30 photos/issue; 15-20 supplied by freelancers. Needs "photos of fish, scenics (preferably with anglers in shot), equipment." Photo captions preferred that include location, name of model (if applicable).

Making Contact & Terms: Query with list of stock photo subjects. Send unsolicited photos by mail for consideration. Provide resume, business card, brochure, flyer or tearsheets to be kept on file for possible assignments. Send glossy b&w, color prints; 35mm, 2¼×2¼, 4×5 transparencies. Keeps samples on file. SASE. Reports in 1 month. Pays $500/color cover photo; $75/color inside photo; $75/b&w inside photo; $125/color page rate; $100/b&w page rate. Pays on publication. Credit line given. Buys one-time rights.

Tips: "Photos should avoid appearance of being too 'staged.' We look for bright color (especially on covers), and unusual, visually appealing settings. Trout and salmon are preferred for covers."

FOOD & WINE, Dept. PM, 1120 Avenue of the Americas, New York NY 10036. (212)382-5600. Art Director: Elizabeth Woodson. Monthly. Emphasizes food and wine. Readers are an "upscale audience who cook, entertain, dine out and travel stylishly." Circ. 850,000. Estab. 1978.

Needs: Uses about 25-30 photos/issue; freelance photography on assignment basis 85%, 15% freelance stock. "We look for editorial reportage specialists who do restaurants, food on location and travel photography." Model release and captions required.

Making Contact & Terms: Drop-off portfolio by appointment. Submission of flyers, tearsheets, etc. to be kept on file for possible future assignments and stock usage. Pays $450/color page; $100-450 color photo. **Pays on acceptance.** Credit line given. Buys one-time world rights.

FOOTBALL DIGEST, 990 Grove St., Evanston IL 60201-4370. (312)491-6440. Editor: Vince Aversano. Circ. 180,000. Published 10 times/year. Emphasizes pro football.
Needs: Uses about 40 photos/issue; all supplied by freelance photographers. Needs photos of sports action and portraits.
Making Contact & Terms: Provide resume, business card, brochure, flyer or tearsheets to be kept on file for possible assignments. Uses 5×7 glossy b&w prints and 35mm transparencies. NPI. Pays on publication. Buys one-time rights.

*FOR SENIORS ONLY, 339 N. Main St., New City NY 10956. (914)638-0333. Fax: (914)634-9423. Circ. 350,000. Estab. 1971. Biannual publication. Emphasizes career and college guidance—with features on travel, computers, etc. Readers are male and female, ages 16-19. Sample copy free with 6½×9½ SAE and 4 first-class stamps.
Needs: Uses various number of photos/issue; various number supplied by freelancers. Needs photos of travel, college-oriented shots and youths. Reviews photos with or without ms. Model/property release required.
Making Contact & Terms: Interested in receiving work from newer, lesser-known photographers. Query with stock photo list. Send unsolicited photos by mail for consideration. Send 5⅜×8⅜ color prints; 35mm transparencies. Cannot return material. Reports when needed. NPI. Pays on publication. Credit line given. Buys one-time rights; negotiable. Simultaneous submissions and/or previously published work OK.

FORTUNE, Dept. PM, Time-Life Bldg., New York NY 10020. (212)522-3803. Managing Editor: Marshall Loeb. Picture Editor: Michele F. McNally. Picture Editor reviews photographers' portfolios on an overnight drop-off basis. Emphasizes analysis of news in the business world for management personnel. Photos purchased on assignment only. Day rate on assignment (against space rate): $350; page rate for space: $400; minimum for b&w or color usage: $150.

*FOUR SEASONS, 930 Massachusetts Ave., Cambridge MA 02139. (617)876-6465. Fax: (617)864-3479. Executive Editor: Eric Lees. Estab. 1992. Consumer magazine. Emphasizes travel industry.
Needs: Needs photos of travel. Model/property release preferred. Captions required; information needed varies with articles.
Making Contact & Terms: Interested in receiving work from newer, lesser-known photographers. Send unsolicited photos by mail for consideration. Provide resume, business card, brochure, flyer or tearsheets to be kept on file for possible assignments. Send 35mm transparencies. Keeps samples on file. SASE. Reports in 3 weeks. Pays $50-200/color photo. Pays on publication. Credit line given. Buys one-time rights; first N.A. serial rights; all rights; negotiable.
Tips: "We are an international travel magazine interested in obtaining photos for editorial that may lack acceptable images. We cover 'the road less traveled.' "

FREEDOM MAGAZINE, #1200, 6331 Hollywood Blvd., Hollywood CA 90028. (213)960-3500. Editor: Tom Whittle. Production Manager: Geoff Brown. Bimonthly magazine. News magazine: Emphasizes investigative reporting, news and current events. Estab. 1968. Sample copy $2 with 9×12 SAE.
Needs: Uses 30-40 photos/issue; 70% supplied by freelance photographers. Needs photos of famous people, current politicians, legislators and public figures. Special photo needs include new current news stories—particular current issues in alignment with stories. Model release preferred. Captions required.
Making Contact & Terms: Query with list of stock photo subjects. Send nonreturnable photos or promotion. Unsolicited material sent will not be returned. Provide resume, business card, brochure, flyer or tearsheets to be kept on file for possible assignments. No specifications for samples. SASE. Reports in 1 month. Pays up to $150/b&w photo; up to $500/color photo; $100-1,500/complete job. Payment varies depending on photo. Pays on publication. Credit line given. Buys one-time rights.

FRONT PAGE DETECTIVE, Official Detective Group, 20th Floor, 460 W. 34th St., New York NY 10001. (212)947-6500. Editor-in-chief: Rose Mandelsberg-Weiss. Managing Editor: Christofer Pierson. Circ. 100,000. Magazine publised 7 times/year. Emphasizes factual articles and fact-based stories about crime. Readers are "police buffs, detective story buffs, law and order advocates." Sample copy $2.50. Photo guidelines for SASE.
Needs: "Only color covers are bought from freelance photographers. Situations must be crime, police, detective oriented; man and woman; action must portray impending disaster of a crime about to happen; *No bodies.*" Model release required. "Interesting weapons a plus."

Making Contact & Terms: Send by mail for consideration actual color photos, or 35mm, 2¼ × 2¼, 4 × 5 color transparencies. SASE. Reports in 1 month, after monthly cover meetings. Pays $200/color photo. **Pays on acceptance.** Credit line not given. Buys all rights.

GALLERY MAGAZINE, FOX MAGAZINE, POCKETFOX MAGAZINE, 401 Park Ave. S., New York NY 10016-8802. Photo Editor: Judy Linden. Estab. 1972. Emphasizes men's interests. Readers are male, collegiate, middle class. Photo guidelines free with SASE.
Needs: Uses 80 photos/issue; 10% supplied from freelancers (no assignments). Needs photos of nude women and celebrities, plus sports, adventure pieces. Model release required.
Making Contact & Terms: Send at least 100 35mm transparencies by mail for consideration. SASE. Reports in 4 weeks. Girl sets: pays $1,000-1,500; cover extra. Buys first N.A. serial rights plus nonexclusive international rights. Also operates Girl Next Door contest: $250 entry photo; $2,500 monthly winner; $25,000 yearly winner. Photographer: entry photo/receives 1-year free subscription, monthly winner $500; yearly winner $2,500. Send *by mail* for contest information.
Tips: In photographer's samples, wants to see "beautiful models and good composition. Trend in our publication is outdoor settings—avoid soft focus! Send complete layout."

GAME & FISH PUBLICATIONS, Suite 110, 2250 Newmarket Pkwy., Marietta GA 30067. (404)953-9222. Fax: (404)933-9510. Photo Editor: Tom Evans. Editorial Director: Ken Dunwoody. Combined circulation 525,000. Estab. 1975. Publishes 31 different monthly outdoors magazines: *Alabama Game & Fish, Arkansas Sportsman, California Game & Fish, Florida Game & Fish, Georgia Sportsman, Great Plains Game & Fish, Illinois Game & Fish, Indiana Game & Fish, Iowa Game & Fish, Kentucky Game & Fish, Louisiana Game & Fish, Michigan Sportsman, Mid-Atlantic Game & Fish, Minnesota Sportsman, Mississippi Game & Fish, Missouri Game & Fish, New England Game & Fish, New York Game & Fish, North Carolina Game & Fish, Ohio Game & Fish, Oklahoma Game & Fish, Pennsylvania Game & Fish, Rocky Mountain Game & Fish, South Carolina Game & Fish, Tennessee Sportsman, Texas Sportsman, Virginia Game & Fish, Washington-Oregon Game & Fish, West Virginia Game & Fish, Wisconsin Sportsman,* and *North American Whitetail.* All magazines (except *Whitetail*) are for experienced fishermen and hunters and provide information about where, when and how to enjoy the best hunting and fishing in their particular state or region, as well as articles about game and fish management, conservation and environmental issues. Sample copy $2.50 with 10 × 12 SAE. Photo guidelines free with SASE.
Needs: 50% of photos supplied by freelance photographers; 5% assigned. Needs photos of live game animals/birds in natural environment and hunting scenes; also underwater game fish photos and fishing scenes. Model release preferred. Captions required; include species identification and location. Number slides/prints. In captions, identify species and location.
Making Contact & Terms: Query with samples. Send 8 × 10 glossy b&w prints or 35mm transparencies (preferably Kodachrome) with SASE for consideration. Reports in 1 month. Pays $250/color cover photo; $75/color inside photo; $25/b&w inside photo. Pays 75 days prior to publication. Tearsheet provided. Credit line given. Buys one-time rights. Simultaneous submissions not accepted.
Tips: "Study the photos that we are publishing before sending submission. We'll return photos we don't expect to use and hold remainder in-house so they're available for monthly photo selections. Please do not send dupes. Photos will be returned upon publication or at photographer's request."

GARDEN DESIGN, Dept. PM, 4401 Connecticut Ave. NW, Washington DC 20008. (202)686-2752. Fax: (202)686-1001. Senior Editor: Cheryl Weber. Bimonthly. Emphasizes residential landscape architecture and garden design. Readers are gardeners, home owners, architects, landscape architects, garden designers and garden connoisseurs. Estab. 1982. Sample copy $5; photo guidelines free with SASE.
Needs: Uses about 80 photos/issue; nearly all supplied by freelance photographers; 80% from assignment and 20% from freelance stock. Needs photos of "public and private gardens that exemplify professional quality design." Needs to see both the design intent and how garden subspaces work together. Model release and captions required.
Making Contact & Terms: Submit proposal with resume and samples. Reports in 2 months or sooner if requested. Publishes color only, and uses original transparencies only for separation—do not send dupes. Pays $300/color cover photo; $150/inside photo over ⅓ page; $200/double page special; $75/⅓ page or smaller. Credit line given. Buys one-time first N.A. magazine publication rights. Previously published work may be acceptable but is not preferred.
Tips: "Show both detailed and comprehensive views that reveal the design intent and content of a garden, as well as subjective, interpretive views of the garden. A letter and resume are not enough—must see evidence of the quality of your work, in samples or tearsheets. Need excellent depth of field and superior focus throughout. Our trend is away from the large estate and/or public gardens, to smaller scale, well-conceived and executed residential ones."

*GATES: Magazine for College Students, 2200-A Hanover Ave., Richmond VA 23220. (804)355-0999. Editor-in-chief: C. Mason Gates. Circ. 50,000. Estab. 1991. Bimonthly magazine. Emphasizes college and the issues that pertain to college. Readers are male and female college students, ages 18-26. Free sample copy with 9×12 SASE and $2.90 postage.
Needs: Uses 10-15 photos/issue. 90% supplied by freelancers. Needs photos of personalities. Reviews photos with or without ms. Model/property release preferred. Captions preferred.
Making Contact & Terms: Interested in receiving work from newer, lesser-known photographers. Query with stock photo list. Provide resume, business card, brochure, flyer or tearsheets to be kept on file for possible assignments. Keeps samples on file. SASE. Reports in 3 weeks. NPI. Pays on publication. Buys one-time rights. Previously published work OK.

*‡GAY TIMES, 116-134 Bayham St. London NWI OBA United Kingdom (071)482-2576. Fax: (071)284-0329. International News Editor: Gillian Rodgerson. Circ. 30,000. Estab. 1983. Monthly magazine. Emphasizes news and culture from a lesbian and gay perspective. Readers are lesbians and gay men of all ages. Sample copy for £1.75.
Needs: Uses 50+ photos/issue. Needs photos of personalities, lesbian and gay news and events. Reviews photos with or without manuscript. Model release preferred. Captions required; include who it is, what they're doing, where, photographer's details.
Making Contact & Terms: Interested in receiving work from newer, lesser-known photographers. Send unsolicited photos by mail for consideration with introductory letter. Send 8×10 b&w prints; 35mm transparencies. Does not keep samples on file. SASE. Reports in 1 month. Pays £25 per photo and £25 commission. Pays on publication. Credit line given. Buys one-time rights; negotiable. Previously published work OK.
Tips: Looks for a "good grasp of news stories and ability to show this through photography. Unique coverage of lesbian and gay themes."

GENERAL LEARNING CORP., 60 Revere Dr., Northbrook IL 60062-1563. (708)205-3000. Photo Editor: Larry Glickman. Estab. 1969. Publishes four monthly school magazines running September through May. *Current Health I* is for children aged 9-12. *Current Health II*, *Writing!*, *Career World* are for high school teens. An article topics list and photo guidelines will be provided free with 9×12 SAE.
Needs: Color photos of children aged 9-12 and teens geared to our topic themes for inside use; 35mm or larger transparencies geared to our monthly focus article for cover use. Model release preferred. Captions preferred.
Making Contact & Terms: Interested in receiving work from newer, lesser-known photographers. Send 35mm transparencies or Xerox copies of photos. Label all photos with name and address for easy return. Pays $35/b&w; $75/color inside photo; $200/color cover photo. Pays on publication. Credit line given. Buys one-time rights; negotiable. Simultaneous submissions and previously published work OK.
Tips: "We are looking for contemporary photos of children and teens. Do not send outdated looking photos. Clothing and hairstyles should be current. We are always looking for ethnic children/teens. When sending photos for a specific article or magazine please specify which one and specify which month."

GENESIS MAGAZINE, 1776 Broadway, New York NY 10019. (212)265-3500. Fax: (212)265-8087. Art Director: Don Lewis. Circ. 500,000. Estab. 1973. Monthly magazine. Emphasizes nude women. Readers are male, ages 25-45. Photo guidelines free with SASE.
Needs: Uses 100 photos/issue. Needs photos of nudes. Special photo needs include surreal photojournalism and artistic nudes. Model release required (2 pieces of identification).
Making Contact & Terms: Send unsolicited photos by mail for consideration. Send color prints; 35mm, 2¼×2¼ transparencies. SASE. Reports in 1 month. Pays $1,000-3,000 per set. Pays 60 days after acceptance. Credit line given.
Tips: Needs "beautiful photos of beautiful women, no styled sets in historic costumes, or photos in poor taste."

*GENRE, #1, 8033 Sunset Blvd., Los Angeles CA 90046. (213)896-9778. Publisher: Richard Settles. Circ. 100,000. Estab. 1990. Bimonthly. Emphasizes gay life. Readers are gay men, ages 24-35. Sample copy $5.

 The double dagger before a listing indicates that the market is located outside the United States and Canada.

Needs: Uses 40 photos/issue. Needs photos of fashion, celebrities, scenics. Model/property release required. Captions preferred.

Making Contact & Terms: Interested in receiving work from newer, lesser-known photographers. Provide resume, business card, brochure, flyer or tearsheets to be kept on file for possible assignments. Cannot return material. Reports only if interested. "We pay only film processing." Pays on publication. Credit line given. Buys all rights; negotiable.

GENT, Suite 600, 2600 Douglas Rd., Coral Gables FL 33134. (305)443-2378. Editor: Steve Dorfman. Circ. 150,000. Monthly magazine. Showcases full-figured, D-cup nude models. Sample copy $5 (postpaid). Photo guidelines free with SASE.

Needs: Buys in sets, not by individual photos. "We publish mss on sex, travel, adventure, cars, racing, sports, gambling, grooming, fashion and other topics that traditionally interest males. Nude models must be extremely large breasted (minimum 38" bust line). Sequence of photos should start with woman clothed, then stripped to brassiere and then on to completely nude. Bikini sequences also recommended. Cover shots must have nipples covered. Chubby models also considered if they are reasonably attractive and measure up to our 'D-Cup' image." Model release and photocopy or photograph of picture ID required.

Making Contact & Terms: Send material by mail for consideration. Send transparencies. Prefer Kodachrome or large format; vertical format required for cover. SASE. Reports in 4-6 weeks. Pays 1st rights, $150/page; 2nd rights, $80/page; $300/cover photo; $250-400 for text and photo package. Pays on publication. Credit line given. Buys one-time rights or second serial (reprint) rights. Previously published work OK.

❧GEORGIA STRAIGHT, 2nd Floor, 1235 W. Pender St., Vancouver, BC V6E 2V6 Canada. (604)681-2000. Fax: (604)681-0272. Managing Editor: Charles Campbell. Circ. 85,000. Estab. 1976. Weekly tabloid. Emphasizes entertainment. Readers are generally well-educated people between 20 and 45 years old. Sample copy free with 10×12 SAE.

Needs: Uses 20 photos/issue; 35% supplied by freelance photographers. Needs photos of entertainment events and personalities. In particular looking for "portraits of high-profile movie stars." Captions preferred.

Making Contact & Terms: Query with list of stock photo subjects. Include resume, business card, brochure, flyer or tearsheets to be kept on file for possible assignments. Reports in 1 month. Pays $200/b&w cover photo and $85/b&w inside photo. Pays on publication. Credit line given. Buys one-time rights. Simultaneous submissions and previously published work OK.

Tips: In portfolio or samples, wants to see "portraits and concert photos. Almost all needs are for in-Vancouver assigned photos, except for high-quality portraits of film stars."

GIBBONS-HUMMS GUIDE: FLORIDA KEYS-KEY WEST, (formerly *Humm's Guide to the Florida Keys*), P.O. Box 2921, Key Largo FL 33037. (305) 451-4429. Fax: (305)451-5201. Art Director: Tricia Lay. Circ. 60,000 per quarter. Estab. 1972. Digest-sized quarterly. Emphasizes the Florida Keys. Readers are male and female visitors to the Keys, all ages. Sample copy free with 6×9 SASE. Photo guidelines free with SASE.

Needs: Uses approximately 30 photos/issue; approximately 1-5 supplied by freelancers. Needs photos of travel, tourists, wildlife, scenics, boating, watersports, nightlife. Reviews photos with or without ms. Model/property release required for close-ups of people, home interiors. Captions preferred; include specific location.

Making Contact & Terms: Interested in receiving work from newer, lesser-known photographers. Contact through rep. Arrange personal interview to show portfolio. Submit portfolio for review. Query with resume of credits. Query with stock photo list. Send unsolicited photos by mail for consideration. Provide resume, business card, brochure, flyer or tearsheets to be kept on file for possible assignments. Keeps samples on file. SASE. Reports in 1 month. Pays $100/color cover photo; $50/color inside photo; $50-100/photo/text package. Pays on publication. Credit line given. Buys one-time rights, first North American Serial rights, all rights, 2- or 3-time rights; negotiable. Simultaneous submissions and/or previously published work OK.

Tips: "We hate empty landscapes. Use lots of people, especially when shooting scenics."

GOLF DIGEST, Dept. PM, 5520 Park Ave., Box 0395, Trumbull CT 06611. (203)373-7000. Art Director/Graphic Administrator: Nick DiDio. Monthly magazine. Circ. 1,350,000. Emphasizes golf instruction and features on golf personalities and events. Free sample copy. Free photo guidelines with SASE.

Needs: Buys 10-15 photos/issue from freelance photographers. Needs celebrity/personality (nationally known golfers, both men and women, pros and amateurs); fashion/beauty (on assignment); head shot (golfing personalities); photo essay/photo feature (on assignment); product shot (on assignment); scenics (shots of golf resorts and interesting and/or unusual shots of golf courses or holes); and sport (golfing). Model release preferred; captions required. "The captions will not necessarily be used in print, but are required for identification."

Making Contact & Terms: Send 8 × 10 glossy b&w prints, no contact sheet; 35mm transparencies, no duplicates. Uses 35mm color transparencies for cover; vertical format required. Pays $100 minimum/job and also on a per-photo or per-assignment basis. Pays $75-200/b&w photo; $100-600/color photo; $500 minimum/cover photo. Credit line given. Pays on publication. Send material by mail for consideration. "The name and address of the photographer must appear on every slide and print submitted." SASE. Simultaneous submissions OK. Reports in 1 month.

Tips: "We are a very favorable market for a freelance photographer who is familiar with the subject. Most of the photos we use are done on specific assignment, but we do encourage photographers to cover golf tournaments on their own with an eye for unusual shots, and to let the magazine select shots to keep on file for future use. We are always interested in seeing good quality color and b&w work." Prefers Kodachrome-64 film; no Ektachrome.

A very creative approach in developing a humorous photo has brought in over $1,000 in royalties plus international exposure for Oakland, California, photographer Doug Keister. Originally submitted on spec, this image has been syndicated all over the world and was first used by Golf Digest *to illustrate an article on How to Have More Fun with Golf.*

GOLF MAGAZINE, Dept. PM, 2 Park Ave., New York NY 10016. (212)779-5000. Editor-in-Chief: George Peper. Art Director: Ron Ramsey. Monthly magazine. Emphasizes golf. Readers are male, ages 15-80, college educated, professional. Circ. 1,000,000. Free sample copy; photo and writer's guidelines free with SASE.

Needs: Celebrity/personality, head shot, golf travel photos, scenic, special effects and experimental, spot news, human interest, humorous and travel. Photos purchased with accompanying ms—golf related articles. Photos must be golf-related. Model release preferred; captions required. No cartoons.

Making Contact & Terms: Pays $50 minimum/job and on a per-photo basis. Pays $50 minimum/b&w photo; $50-600/color photo; $25-750/ms. **Pays on acceptance.** Buys first serial rights. Query with samples. SASE. Simultaneous submissions OK. Reports in 3 weeks. Send 8 × 10 glossy prints and transparencies. Uses 2¼ × 2¼ transparencies for cover; vertical format preferred.

GRAND RAPIDS MAGAZINE, 549 Ottawa Ave. NW, Grand Rapids MI 49503-1444. (616)459-4545. Fax: (616)459-4800. Publisher: John H. Zwarensteyn. Editor: Carole Valade Smith. Estab. 1963. Monthly magazine. Emphasizes community-related material of Western Michigan; local action and local people.

Needs: Animal, nature, scenic, travel, sport, fashion/beauty, photo essay/photo feature, fine art, documentary, human interest, celebrity/personality, humorous, wildlife, vibrant people shots and special effects/experimental. Wants on a regular basis western Michigan photo essays and travel-photo essays of any area in Michigan. Model release required. Captions required.

Making Contact & Terms: Interested in receiving work from newer, lesser-known photographers. Freelance photos assigned and accepted. Provide business card to be kept on file for possible future assignments; "only people on file are those we have met and personally reviewed." Arrange a personal interview to show portfolio. Query with resume of credits. Send material by mail for consideration. Submit portfolio for review. SASE. Reports in 3 weeks. Send 8×10 or 5×7 glossy b&w prints; contact sheet OK; 35mm, 120mm or 4×5 transparencies or 8×10 glossy color prints; Uses $2\frac{1}{4} \times 2\frac{1}{4}$ and 4×5 color transparencies for cover, vertical format required. Pays $25-35/b&w photo; $35-50/color photo; $100-150/cover photo. Buys one-time rights, exclusive product rights, all rights; negotiable.

Tips: "Most photography is by our local freelance photographers, so freelancers should sell us on the unique nature of what they have to offer."

*GRAND RAPIDS PARENT MAGAZINE, 549 Ottawa NW, Grand Rapids MI 49503. (616)459-4545. Fax: (616)459-4800. Editor: Carole Valade Smith. Circ. 12,000. Estab. 1989. Monthly magazine. Sample copy $2. Photo guidelines free with SASE.

Needs: Uses 20-50 photos/issue; all supplied by freelancers. Needs photos of families, children, education, infants, play, etc. Model/property release required. Captions preferred; include who, what, where, when.

Making Contact & Terms: Interested in receiving work from newer, lesser-known photographers. Query with resume of credits. Query with stock photo list. Sometimes keeps samples on file. SASE. Reports in 1 month. Pays $200/color cover photo; $35/color inside photo; $25/b&w inside photo; $50 +/ color page rate. Pays on publication. Credit line given. Buys one-time rights, all rights; negotiable. Simultaneous submissions and/or previously published work OK.

Tips: "We are not interested in 'clip art' variety photos. We want the honesty of photojournalism, photos that speak to the heart, that tell a story, that add to the story told."

GREAT LAKES FISHERMAN, 1432 Parsons Ave., Columbus OH 43201. (614)241-2313. Editor: Dan Armitage. Monthly. Circ. 41,000. Estab. 1976. Emphasizes fishing for anglers in the 8 states bordering the Great Lakes. Sample copy and photo guidelines free with SASE.

Needs: 12 covers/year supplied by freelance photographers; 100% from freelance stock. Needs transparencies for covers; 99% used are verticals. No full frame subjects; need free space top and left side for masthead and titles. Fish and fishermen (species common to Great Lakes Region) action preferred. Photos purchased with or without accompanying ms. "All b&w is purchased as part of ms package. Covers are not assigned but purchased as suitable material comes in." Model release required for covers; captions preferred.

Making Contact & Terms: Query with tearsheets or send unsolicited photos by mail for consideration. Prefers 35mm transparencies. SASE. Reports in 1 month. Provide tearsheets to be kept on file for possible future assignments. Pays $200/color photo; covers only. Pays on 15th of month preceding issue date. Credit line given. Buys one-time rights.

Tips: Sees trend toward: "More close-ups of *live* fish." To break in, freelancer should "look at 1993 covers" for insight.

*GUIDE FOR EXPECTANT PARENTS, 8003 Old York Rd., Elkins Park PA 19117. (215)635-1700. Fax: (215)635-6455. Project Coordinator: Deana C. Jamroz. Circ. 1,850,000/year. Estab. 1973. Biannual magazine. Emphasizes prenatal care for pregnant women and their partners. Sample copy free with 9×12 SAE and 4 first-class stamps. Photo guidelines free with SASE.

Needs: Uses 2-8 photos/issue; 80% supplied by freelancers. Needs photos of pregnant women with their spouses and physicians, nurses with pregnant women, pregnant women in classroom (prenatal) situations, pictures of new families. Reviews photos with or without ms. Model/property release required.

Making Contact & Terms: Interested in receiving work from newer, lesser-known photographers. Query with stock photo list. Does not keep samples on file. SASE. Reports in 3 weeks. Pays $300-600/ color inside photo; $100-500/b&w inside photo. **Pays on acceptance.** Credit line not given. Buys all rights.

GUIDEPOSTS ASSOCIATES, INC., Dept. PM, 21st Floor, 16 E. 34th St., New York NY 10016. (212)251-8124. Fax: (212)684-0679. Photo Editor: Courtney Reid-Eaton. Circ. 4,000,000. Estab. 1945. Monthly magazine. Emphasizes tested methods for developing courage, strength and positive attitudes through faith in God. Free sample copy and photo guidelines with 6×9 SAE and 65¢ postage.

Needs: 85% assignment, 15% stock (variable). "Photos mostly used are of an editorial reportage nature or stock photos, i.e., scenic landscape, agriculture, people, animals, sports. We work four months in advance. It's helpful to send stock pertaining to upcoming seasons/holidays. No lovers, suggestive situations or violence." Model release preferred.

Making Contact & Terms: Interested in receiving work from newer, lesser-known photographers. Send photos or arrange a personal interview. Send 35mm transparencies; vertical format required for cover, usually shot on assignment. SASE. Reports in 1 month. Pays by job or on a per-photo basis; pays $150-400/color photo; $750/cover photo; $400-600/day; negotiable. **Pays on acceptance.** Credit line given. Buys one-time rights. Simultaneous submissions OK.

Tips: "I'm looking for photographs that show people in their environment. I like warm, saturated color for portraits and scenics. We're trying to appear more contemporary. We want to stimulate a younger audience and yet maintain a homey feel. For stock—scenics; graphic images with intense color. *Guideposts* is an 'inspirational' magazine. NO violence, nudity, sex. No more than 60 images at a time. Write first and ask for a photo guidelines/sample issue; this will give you a better idea of what we're looking for. I will review transparencies on a light box or in a carousel. I am interested in the experience as well as the photograph. I am also interested in the photographer's sensibilities—Do you love the city? Mountain climbing? Farm life?"

GULF MARINER, P.O. Box 1220, Venice FL 34284. (813)488-9307. Editor: Thomas Kahler. Circ. 15,000+. Estab. 1984. Biweekly tabloid. Readers are recreational boaters, both power and sail. Sample copy free with 9×12 SAE and $1 postage.

Needs: Uses cover photo each issue—24 a year; 100% supplied by freelance photographers. Needs photos of boating related fishing, water skiing, racing and shows. Use of swimsuit-clad model or fisherman with boat preferred. All photos must have *vertical* orientation to match our format. Model release required. Captions preferred.

Making Contact & Terms: Interested in receiving work from newer, lesser-known photographers. Send 35mm transparencies by mail for consideration. SASE. Reports in 1-2 weeks. Pays $50/color cover photo. **Pays on acceptance.** Credit line optional. Rights negotiable. May use photo more than once for cover. Simultaneous submissions and previously published work OK.

Tips: "We are willing to accept outtakes from other assignments which is why we pay only $50. We figure that is better than letting an unused shot go to waste or collect dust in the drawer."

*GULFSHORE LIFE, Suite 400, 2900 S. Horseshoe Dr., Naples FL 33942. (813)643-3933. Creative Director: Mark May. Circ. 20,000. Estab. 1970. Monthly magazine. Emphasizes Southwest Florida. Readers are male and female, affluent, ages 40-65. Sample copy $3.95. Photo guidelines free with SASE.

- In 1992 this publication received a Charlie Award from the Florida Magazine Association for having the Best Overall Magazine with a circulation below 25,000. It also received a bronze Charlie Award for having the best use of photography and a silver award for Best Cover.

Needs: Uses 40-60 photos/issue; 80% supplied by freelancers. Needs "any type of photo which has some kind of connection to Southwest Florida." Special photo needs include wildlife. For accompanying mss seeks personalities, community activities, hobbies, boating, travel and nature. Model release required for people. Captions preferred; include location and names.

Making Contact & Terms: Interested in receiving work from newer, lesser-known photographers. Query with list of stock photo subjects and tearsheets. Send 5×7 glossy b&w prints; 35mm, 2¼×2¼, 4×5, 8×10 transparencies; vertical format required for cover. Does not keep samples on file. SASE. Reports only when interested. Rates for all photos negotiable, start at $50; $150 and up for cover; pays $300-600/day. Pays on publication. Credit line given. Buys one-time rights; negotiable. Simultaneous submissions and previously published work.

Tips: "A sample copy is helpful. No color prints are used. Well-composed and dramatic images are required for quality magazine reproduction." SASE required.

*HANDBALL MAGAZINE, 930 N. Benton Ave., Tucson AZ 85711. (602)795-0434. Fax: (602)795-0465. Editor: Vern Roberts. Circ. 8,500. Estab. 1951. Publication of the United States Handball Association. Bimonthly magazine. Emphasizes handball, health and fitness. Readers are male (mostly) and athletic. Sample copy $4.00.

A bullet has been placed within some listings to introduce special comments by the editor of the *Photographer's Market*.

Needs: Uses 50 photos/issue; 20 supplied by freelancers. Needs photos of sports—handball action, celebrities. Reviews photos with or without ms. Model/property release preferred for celebrities. Captions preferred.

Making Contact & Terms: Interested in receiving work from newer, lesser-known photographers. Send unsolicited photos by mail for consideration. Send 4×6 and larger glossy color and b&w prints. Keeps samples on file. SASE. Reports in 1-2 weeks. NPI. Pays on publication. Credit line given. Buys one-time rights. Simultaneous submissions and/or previously published work OK.

❀HARROWSMITH, 7 Queen Victoria Rd., Camden East ON K0K 1J0 Canada. (613)378-6661. Contact: Photo Editor. Estab. 1976. Magazine published 6 times/year. Circ. 154,000. Emphasizes alternative lifestyles, self-reliance, energy conservation, gardening, solar energy and homesteading. Sample copy $5 with 8½×14 SASE; free photo and writer's guidelines.

Needs: Buys 400 photos/year, 50 photos/issue; 40% assigned. Animal (domestic goats, sheep, horses, etc., on the farm); how-to; nature (plants, trees, mushrooms, etc.); photo essay/photo feature (rural life); horticulture and gardening; scenic (North American rural); and wildlife (Canadian, nothing exotic). "Nothing cute. We get too many unspecific, pretty sunsets, farm scenes and landscapes." Captions preferred. Photos purchased with or without accompanying ms and on assignment.

Making Contact & Terms: Interested in receiving work from newer, lesser-known photographers. Provide calling card, samples and tearsheets to be kept on file for possible future assignments. Uses 8×10 b&w glossy prints, contact sheet and negatives OK; 35mm and 2¼×2¼ transparencies and 8×10 glossy color prints. Query with samples and list of subjects. SAE. Reports in 4 weeks. Pays $50-500/job; $200-1,000 for text/photo package; $100-250/b&w photo; $100-300/color photo. **Pays on acceptance.** Credit line given. Buys first N.A. rights. Previously published work OK.

Tips: Prefers to see portfolio with credits and tearsheets of published material. Samples should be preferably subject oriented. In portfolio or samples, wants to see "clarity, ability to shoot people, nature and horticulture photo essays. Since there's a trend toward strong photo essays, success is more likely if a submission is made in a photo essay type package."

HAWAI'I REVIEW, % University of Hawai'i, 1733 Donaghho Rd., Dept. of English, Honolulu HI 96822. (808)956-8548. Editor-in-Chief: Tamara Moan. Circ. 2,000. Estab. 1973. Triannual journal. Literary and arts readership. Sample copy $5 with 9×12 SAE with 95¢ postage.

Needs: Freelance photography is all from stock. Prefers b&w experimental or "art" photos. No scenic or postcard-type shots. Special photo needs include cover photos. "Hawaii subjects are appreciated, but anything is considered." Model/property release required. Captions required; include artistic explanation and title.

Making Contact & Terms: Interested in receiving work from newer, lesser-known photographers. Send unsolicited photos by mail for consideration. Reports in 4 months. Pays $25-75/b&w or color photos. Pays on publication. Credit line given. Buys one-time rights; copyright reverts to artist upon publication. Simultaneous submissions OK if so noted in cover letter. *Must* include SASE.

Tips: "Photographs should make some kind of statement or be visually poetic. We use either 2-color or monochrome, so high-contrast b&w photos are best." To break in, "send a lot and often. Be professional in preparing your work and show as wide a variety as possible."

*‡HEALTH & BEAUTY MAGAZINE, 10 Woodford, Brewery Rd., Blackrock, Dublin Ireland. (01)2954095. Fax: (01)745682. Advertising Manager: David Briggs. Circ. 11,000. Estab. 1985. Bimonthly magazine. Emphasizes all body matters. Readers are male and female, ages 17-50 (all keen on body matters). Sample copy free with A4 SASE.

Needs: Uses approximately 40 photos/issue; 50% supplied by freelancers. Needs photos related to health, hair, fashion, beauty, food, drinks. Reviews photos with or without ms. Model/property release preferred. Captions preferred; include photo description.

Making Contact & Terms: Interested in receiving work from newer, lesser-known photographers. Send unsolicited photos by mail for consideration. Provide resume, business card, brochure, flyer or tearsheets to be kept on file for possible assignments. Send any size glossy color and b&w prints; 35mm, 2¼×2¼, 4×5, 8×10 transparencies; prints preferred. Keeps samples on file. SASE. Reports in 1 month. NPI. Credit line given. Buys all rights; negotiable. Simultaneous submissions and/or previously published work OK.

Tips: Looks for "male and female models of good body shape, shot in interesting locations with interesting body and facial features. Continue on a regular basis to submit good material for review."

HIGH SOCIETY MAGAZINE, 801 Second Ave., New York NY 10017. (212)661-7878. Fax: (212)692-9297. Photo Editor: Vivienne Maricevic. Circ. 400,000. Estab. 1976. Monthly magazine. Emphasis on "everything of sexual interest to the American male." Readers are young males, ages 21-40. Sample copies free with SASE. Photo guidelines available.

Needs: Uses 300 photos/issue; 50% supplied by freelancers. Needs sexually stimulating, nude photos of gorgeous women, ages 21-35. Reviews photos with or without accompanying ms. Special needs include outdoor and indoor scenes of nude women. Model/property release required. Captions preferred.

Making Contact & Terms: Interested in receiving work from newer, lesser-known photographers. Arrange personal interview to show portfolio. Send color prints; 35mm, 2¼ × 2¼ transparencies by mail for consideration. Does not keep samples on file. SASE. Reports in 1-2 weeks. Pays $300/color cover photo; $150/color inside photo; $100/b&w inside photo; $800/color page rate; $400/b&w page rate; $1,500/photo-text package. **Pays on acceptance.** Credit line given. Buys one-time rights; negotiable. Simultaneous submissions and previously published work OK.

Tips: Looks for "clear, concise color, interesting set preparation and props, strong contrast, backgrounds and settings, and knock-'em-out models. Look at our previous published issues and see what we buy."

HIGHLIGHTS FOR CHILDREN, Dept. PM, 803 Church St., Honesdale PA 18431. Photo Essay Editor: Kent L. Brown, Jr. Art Director: Rosanne Guararra. Circ. more than 3 million. Monthly magazine. For children, age 2-12. Free sample copy.

Needs: Buys 20 photos annually. "We will consider outstanding photo essays on subjects of high interest to children." Photos purchased with accompanying ms. Wants no single photos without captions or accompanying ms..

Making Contact & Terms: Send photo essays for consideration. Prefers transparencies. Send 8 × 10 glossy or matte b&w prints; 5 × 7 or 8 × 10 glossy or matte color prints. SASE. Reports in 3-7 weeks. Pays $30 minimum/b&w photo; $55 minimum/color photo; NPI on ms. Buys all rights.

Tips: "Tell a story which is exciting to children. We also need mystery photos, puzzles that use photography/collage, special effects, anything unusual that will visually and mentally challenge children."

ALFRED HITCHCOCK MYSTERY MAGAZINE, 1540 Broadway, New York NY 10036. Editor: Cathleen Jordan. Circ. 225,000. Estab. 1956. Published every four weeks. Emphasizes short mystery fiction. Readers are mystery readers, all ages, both sexes. Sample copy $3. Photo guidelines free with SASE.

Needs: Uses 1 photo/issue; all supplied by freelance photographers. Needs photographs that suggest a narrative element involving crime, should allow for a variety of possible interpretations. No gore; no accidents; no crime scenes. Model release required.

Making Contact & Terms: Interested in receiving work from newer, lesser-known photographers. Query with samples, "nonreturnable photocopies only." B&w photos only. Reports in 2 months if SASE is included. NPI; negotiated. **Pays on acceptance.** Credit line given. Buys one-time rights.

HOCKEY DIGEST, 990 Grove St., Evanston IL 60201-4370. (708)491-6440. Editor: Vince Aversano. Circ. 90,000. Monthly. Emphasizes pro hockey for sports fans.

Needs: Uses about 40 photos/issue; 100% supplied by freelance photographers. Needs photos of sports action and portraits.

Making Contact & Terms: Provide resume, business card, brochure, flyer or tearsheets to be kept on file for possible assignments. Uses 5 × 7 glossy b&w prints and 35mm transparencies. NPI. Pays on publication. Buys one-time rights.

HOCKEY ILLUSTRATED, 355 Lexington Ave., New York NY 10017. (212)949-6850. Fax: (212)986-5926. Editor: Stephen Ciacciarelli. Published 3 times/year, in season. Emphasizes hockey superstars. Readers are hockey fans. Circ. 50,000. Sample copy $2.50 with 9 × 12 SASE.

Needs: Uses about 60 photos/issue; all supplied by freelance photographers. Needs color slides of top hockey players in action. Captions preferred.

Making Contact & Terms: Query with action color slides. SASE. Pays $150/color cover photo; $75/ color inside photo. **Pays on acceptance.** Credit line given. Buys one-time rights.

HOME EDUCATION MAGAZINE, P.O. Box 1083, Tonasket WA 98855. (509)486-1351. Managing Editor: Helen Hegener. Circ. 4,700. Estab. 1983. Bimonthly magazine. Emphasizes homeschooling. Readers are parents of children, ages 2-18. Sample copy for $4.50. Photo guidelines free with SASE.

Needs: Number of photos used/issue varies based on availability; 25% supplied by freelance photographers. Needs photos of parent/child or children. Special photo needs include homeschool personalities and leaders. Model/property releases preferred. Captions preferred.

Making Contact & Terms: Interested in receiving work from newer, lesser-known photographers. Send unsolicited b&w prints by mail for consideration. Prefers b&w prints in normal print size (3 × 5). "Enlargements not necessary." Uses 35mm transparencies. SASE. Reports in 1 month. Pays $25/b&w cover photo; $5/b&w inside photo; $10-50/photo/text package. Pays on publication. Credit line given. Buys first N.A. serial rights; negotiable. Simultaneous submissions and previously published work OK.

Tips: In photographer's samples, wants to see "sharp clear photos of children doing things alone, in groups or with parents. Know what we're about! We get too many submissions that are simply irrelevant to our publication."

THE HOME SHOP MACHINIST, P.O. Box 1810, Traverse City MI 49685. (616)946-3712. Editor: Joe D. Rice. Circ. 25,000. Bimonthly. Emphasizes "machining and metal working." Readers are "amateur machinists, small commercial machine shop operators and school machine shops." Sample copy free with 9×12 SAE and 90¢ postage. Photo guidelines free with SASE.
Needs: Uses about 30-40 photos/issue; "most are accompanied by text." Needs photos of "machining operations, how-to-build metal projects." Special needs include "good quality machining operations in b&w."
Making Contact & Terms: Send 4×5 or larger glossy b&w prints by mail for consideration. SASE. Reports in 3 weeks. Pays $40/b&w cover photo; $9/b&w inside photo; $30 minimum for text/photo package ("depends on length"). Pays on publication. Credit line given. Buys one-time rights. Simultaneous submissions OK.
Tips: "Photographer should know about machining techniques or work with a machinist. Subject should be strongly lit for maximum detail clarity."

HORSEPLAY MAGAZINE, Dept. PM, P.O. Box 130, 11 Park Ave., Gaithersburg MD 20884. (301)840-1866. Associate Editor: Lisa Kiser. Circ. 50,000. Estab. 1972. Monthly magazine. Emphasizes English riding (show jumping, fox hunting, dressage, eventing). Readers are ages 15-35, female, middle to upper-middle class. Sample copy $3. Photo guidelines free with SASE.
Needs: Uses 45 photos/issue; 95% supplied by freelance photographers. Needs photos of horse shows, top riders, training photos and general horse care. Special photo needs include world championship events, major grand prix, major 3-day, major dressage competitions. Propety release required. Captions preferred; must identify horse and rider.
Making Contact & Terms: Interested in receiving work from newer, lesser-known photographers. Send b&w prints and 35mm transparencies by mail for consideration. Pays $200/color cover photo; $45/color inside photo; $22.50/b&w inside photo; $75 assignment fee. SASE. Buys one-time rights; negotiable. "Exclusive or first refusal photos only."
Tips: Wants to see "razor-sharp focus, good b&w contrast, uncluttered and colorful subjects/backgrounds."

HORSES MAGAZINE, Dept. PM, 21 Greenview, Carlsbad CA 92009. (619)931-9958. Fax: (619)931-0650. Managing Editor: Terry Reim. Circ. 6,500. Estab. 1961. Magazine published 6 times per year. Emphasizes show jumping and dressage. Readers are from teens to active seniors, primarily female with substantial number of males. Sample copy $5. Call for specs.
Needs: Uses approximately 134 photos/issue; 35% supplied by freelance photographers. Needs photos of people, ring, jumps and performance. "Send action photos or class winners for major international events." Special needs include "photos to accompany show reports of A-rated horse shows to which we do not send staff photographers." Captions required.
Making Contact & Terms: Send 4×5 and 8×10 glossy b&w and color prints; 35mm and 2¼×2¼ transparencies by mail for consideration. SASE. Reports in 1-2 weeks. Pays $15-25/color inside photo; $15-25/b&w inside photo. Pays 30 days after publication. Credit line given. Buys first N.A. serial rights.
Tips: "Prefer action photos to presentation photos." In photographer's samples "no proof sheets; 3×5, 5×7 and 8×10 b&w or color prints of action, people and win photos. Know the subject, do good work and look at what kinds of photos we publish."

HORTICULTURE MAGAZINE, 98 N. Washington St., Boston MA 02114. (617)742-5600. Fax: (617)367-6364. Photo Editor: Tina Schwinder. Circ. 250,000. Estab. 1904. Monthly magazine. Emphasizes gardening. Readers are all ages. Sample copy $2.50 with 9×12 SAE with $2 postage. Photo guidelines free with SASE.
Needs: Uses 25-30 photos/issue; 20-25 supplied by freelance photographers. Needs photos of gardening, individual plants. Model release preferred. Captions required.
Making Contact & Terms: Arrange a personal interview to show portfolio. Query with samples. Send 35mm color transparencies by mail for consideration. Submit portfolio for review. Provide resume, business card, brochure, flyer or tearsheets to be kept on file for possible future assignments. SASE. Reports in 1 month. Pays $500/color cover photo; $50-250/color page. Pays on publication. Credit line given. Buys one-time rights. Simultaneous submissions OK.
Tips: Wants to see gardening images, i.e., plants and gardens.

HOT ROD MAGAZINE, Dept. PM, 8490 Sunset Blvd., Los Angeles CA 90069. (213)854-2280. Editor: Jeff Smith. Monthly magazine. Circ. 850,000. For enthusiasts of high performance and personalized automobiles.

Needs: Typical subject areas include drag racing, street rods, customs, modified pickups, off-road racing, circle track racing. Will consider b&w and color photo features on individual vehicles; of race or event coverage with information; or b&w photos of technical or how-to subjects accompanied by text. However, best market is for "Roddin' at Random" section, which uses single photo and/or short copy on any "newsy" related subject, and "Finish Line," which runs short pieces on a wide variety of vehicular racing or other competition.

Making Contact & Terms: These sections pay $50-150 per photo or item used. Model release necessary. Buys all rights. Credit line given. **Pays on acceptance.** Reports in 2 weeks. Send 8×10 glossy prints or contact sheets with negs. Pays $50-250. Send transparencies. Pays $100-500.

Tips: "Look at the magazine before submitting material. Use imagination, bracket shots, allow for cropping, keep backgrounds clean. We generally need very sharp, crisp photos with good detail and plenty of depth of field. Majority of material is staff generated; best sell is out-of-area (non-Southern California) coverage or items for news/human interest/vertical interest/curiosity columns (i.e., 'Roddin' at Random' and 'Finish Line'). Again, study the magazine to see what we want."

HOUSE OF WHITE BIRCHES, 306 E. Parr Rd., Berne IN 46711. (219)589-8741. Fax: (219)589-8093. Editor: Beth Schwartz. Circ. 60,000. Estab. 1977. Bimonthly magazine. Emphasizes doll collecting. Readers are doll lovers—any type doll. Sample copy $2.

Needs: Uses 60 photos/issue; 25% supplied by freelance photographers on assignment. "We need romance and product shots of dolls with identification." Model release required. Captions required.

Making Contact & Terms: Interested in receiving work from newer, lesser-known photographers. Send color prints; 35mm, 2¼×2¼, 4×5, 8×10 transparencies by mail for consideration. Provide resume, business card, brochure, flyer or tearsheets to be kept on file for possible future assignments. SASE. Reports in 2 weeks. Pays $60/color cover photo; $15/color inside photo; $40/color page. Pays on publication. Credit line given. Buys one-time rights, all rights; negotiable. Previously published work OK.

Tips: In portfolio or samples wants to see "clear photos without sharp shadows."

HUDSON VALLEY MAGAZINE, Dept. PM, 297 Main Mall, Poughkeepsie NY 12601. (914)485-7844. Fax: (914)485-5975. Art Director: Lynn Hazelwood. Emphasizes contemporary living in the Hudson Valley. Readers are upscale, average age 45, average combined income $81,000. Circ. 26,000. Estab. 1986. Sample copy for 9×12 SASE.

Needs: Uses 30-40 photos/issue; 50% supplied by freelancers. Needs photos of scenic portraiture, architecture (all pertinent to the Hudson Valley). Model release and captions required.

Making Contact & Terms: Uses 8×10 glossy b&w and color prints; 35mm, 2¼×2¼, 4×5 and 8×10 transparencies. SASE. Reports in 1 month. Pays $50-250/b&w photo; $75-350/color photo; $350/day. Pays on publication. Credit line given. Previously published work OK.

Tips: Prefers to see "clear, sharp imagery capable of summing up the story at a glance; impact with subtlety and excellence! Initial contact should be an excellent quality color or b&w promotion piece with printed example of their work on it."

IDAHO WILDLIFE, P.O. Box 25, Boise ID 83707. (208)334-3748. Fax: (208)334-2114. Editor: Diane Ronayne. Circ. 27,000. Estab. 1978. Bimonthly magazine. Emphasizes wildlife, hunting, fishing. Readers are aged 25-70, 80% male, purchase Idaho hunting or fishing licenses; ⅔ nonresident, ⅓ resident. Sample copy $1. Photo guidelines free with SASE.

- This publication won 2 cover photography awards in 1992 from the Outdoor Writers Association of America. It also holds an annual photo contest which is described in the back of this book.

Needs: Uses 20-40 photos/issue; 30-60% supplied by freelancers. Needs shots of "wildlife, hunting, fishing in Idaho; habitat management." Photos of wildlife/people should be "real," not too "pretty" or obviously set up. Model release preferred. Captions required; include species and location.

Making Contact & Terms: Interested in receiving work from newer, lesser-known photographers. Query with list of stock photo subjects. SASE. Reports in 1 month. Pays $80/color cover photo; $40/color or b&w inside photo; $40/color or b&w page rate. Pays on publication. Credit line given. Buys one-time rights. Simultaneous submissions and previously published work OK.

Can't find a listing? Check at the end of each market section for the " '93-'94 Changes" lists. These lists include any market listings from the '93 edition which were either not verified or deleted in this edition.

Tips: "Write first for want list. 99% of photos published are taken in Idaho. Seldom use scenics. Love action hunting or fishing images but must look 'real' (i.e., natural light). Only send your *best* work. We don't pay as much as commercial magazines but our quality is as high or higher and we value photography and design as much as text."

IDEALS MAGAZINE, Ideals Publishing Corp., Suite 800, 565 Marriott Dr., Nashville TN 37214. (615)885-8270. Fax: (615)885-9578. Editor: Tim Hamling. Circ. 200,000. Estab. 1944. Magazine published 8 times/year. Emphasizes an idealized, nostalgic look at America through poetry and short prose, using "seasonal themes—bright flowers and scenics for Thanksgiving, Christmas, Valentine, Easter, Mother's Day, Friendship, Country and Home—all thematically related material. Issues are seasonal in appearance." Readers are "mostly college-educated women who live in rural areas, aged 50+." Sample copy $4. Photo guidelines free with SASE.
Needs: Uses 20-25 photos/issue; all supplied by freelancers. Needs photos of "bright, colorful flower close-ups, scenics, still life, children, pets, home interiors; subject-related shots depending on issue. We regularly send out a letter listing the photo needs for our upcoming issue." Model/property release required. No research fees.
Making Contact & Terms: Submit portfolio for review. Send unsolicited photos by mail for consideration. Provide resume, business card, brochure, flyer or tearsheets to be kept on file. Send b&w prints and 2¼×2¼, 4×5, 8×10 transparencies by insured mail. Does not keep samples on file. SASE. Reports in 1 month. NPI; rates negotiable. Pays on publication. Credit line given. Buys one-time rights. Simultaneous and previously published work OK.
Tips: "We want to see *sharp* shots. No moody or artsy photos, please. Would suggest the photographer purchase several recent issues of *Ideals* magazine and study photos for our requirements. *Ideals'* reputation is based on quality of its color reproduction of photos."

ILLINOIS ENTERTAINER, #150, 2250 E. Devon, Des Plaines IL 60018. (708)298-9333. Fax: (708)298-7973. Editor: Michael C. Harris. Circ. 80,000. Estab. 1975. Monthly magazine. Emphasizes music, video, theater, entertainment. Readers are male and female, 16-40, music/clubgoers. Sample copy $5.
Needs: Uses 20+ photos/issue; approximately 5 supplied by freelancers on assignment or from stock. Needs "live concert photos; personality head shots—crisp, clean, high-contrast b&ws." Model/property release required; "releases required for any non-approved publicity photos or pics with models." Captions required.
Making Contact & Terms: Interested in receiving work from newer, lesser-known photographers. Query with resume of credits and list of stock photo subjects. Send unsolicited photos by mail for consideration. Send 8×10 or 5×7 b&w prints. Does not keep samples on file. SASE. Reports in 1 month. Pays $100-125/color cover photo; $20-30/b&w inside photo. Pays no sooner than 60 days after publication. Buys one-time rights. Simultaneous submissions and previously published work OK.
Tips: Send high-contrast b&w photos. "We print on newsprint paper. We are seeing some more engaging publicity photos, though still fairly straightforward stuff abounds."

IN THE WIND, P.O. Box 3000, Agoura Hills CA 91376-3000. (818)889-8740. Fax: (818)889-1252. Photo Editor: Kim Peterson. Art Director: Rowan Johnson. Circ. 263,529. Estab. 1979. Bimonthly magazine. Emphasizes riding Harley-Davidson motorcycles and the enjoyment derived therein. Readers are 18-99, male/female working people. Sample copy $2 with 8×10 SASE. Photo guidelines free with SASE.
Needs: Uses hundreds of photos/issue; 75% supplied by freelance photographers, approximately 10% on assignment. Needs b&w or color prints and transparencies of riding and lifestyle situations. Always in need of action photos, bikes being ridden, no helmets if possible and people having fun with motorcycles worldwide. Model release required for nudes, posed photos. Property release preferred. Captions preferred; include location.
Making Contact & Terms: Interested in receiving work from newer, lesser-known photographers. Send 35mm glossy b&w and color prints; 35mm and 2¼×2¼ transparencies by mail for consideration. Provide resume, business card, brochure, flyer or tearsheets to be kept on file for possible assignments. Reports in 3 months. Pays $200/color cover photo, $35/color inside photo; $35/b&w inside photo; $50-500/photo/text package; and $35-1,500/job, for feature including cover, poster. Pays on publication. Buys all rights; negotiable.
Tips: "Read the magazine, be sure to include name and address on photos in Sharpie Permanent Marker ink. Not ball-point as it shows through. We want to see clarity, sharpness, feeling in work submitted. We are seeing more submissions of color prints—they are often converted to b&w.

*INDIANAPOLIS BUSINESS JOURNAL, 431 N. Pennsylvania St., Indianapolis IN 46204. (317)634-6200. Fax: (317)263-5060. Picture Editor: Robin Jerstad. Circ. 17,000. Estab. 1980. Weekly newspaper/monthly magazine. Emphasizes Indianapolis business. Readers are male 28 and up, middle management to CEO's.

Needs: Uses 15-20 photos/issue; 3-4 supplied by freelancers. Needs portraits of business people. Model release preferred. Captions required; include who, what, when and where.
Making Contact & Terms: Interested in receiving work from newer, lesser-known photographers. Query with resume and credits. Query with stock photo list. Cannot return material. Reports in 3 weeks. Pays $50-75/color inside photo; $25-50/b&w inside photo. Pays on publication. Credit line given. Buys one-time rights. Simultaneous submissions and/or previously published work OK.
Tips: "We generally use local freelancers (when we need them). Rarely do we have needs outside the Indianapolis area."

INSIDE DETECTIVE, Official Detective Group, 20th Floor, 460 W. 34th St., New York NY 10001. (212)947-6500. Editor-in-chief: Rose Mandelsberg-Weiss. Managing Editor: Christofer Pierson. Circ. 100,000. Magazine published 7 times/year. Readers are "police buffs, detective story buffs, law and order advocates." Sample copy $2.50. Photo guidelines free with SASE.
Needs: "Only color covers are bought from freelance photographers. Subjects must be crime, police, detective oriented, man and woman. Action must portray impending disaster of a crime about to happen. *No women in subservient positions.*" Model release required. "Interesting weapons a plus."
Making Contact & Terms: Send by mail for consideration color photos or 35mm, 2¼ × 2¼ or 4 × 5 color transparencies. SASE. Reports 1 month after monthly cover meetings. Pays $200/color photo. Pays on publication. Credit line not given. Buys all rights. No simultaneous or previously published submissions. Send all chromes to Editor-in-Chief: Rose Mandelsberg-Weiss.

INSIDE SPORTS, 990 Grove St., Evanston IL 60201-4370. (312)491-6440. Editor: Vince Aversano. Circ. 450,000. Monthly. Emphasizes pro and college sports. Readers are male; median age: 31, median income: $35,116.
Needs: Uses about 50 photos/issue; 100% supplied by freelance photographers. Needs photos of sports action and portraits.
Making Contact & Terms: Provide resume, business card, brochure, flyer or tearsheets to be kept on file for possible assignments. Uses 35mm and 2¼ × 2¼ transparencies. NPI. Pays on publication. Buys one-time rights.

*INSIDE THE BLACK HILLS, Box 9008, Rapid City SD 57709. (605)341-7080. Fax: (605)341-7180. Publisher: Janet Hagen. Circ. 20,000. Estab. 1990. Quarterly magazine. Emphasizes the Black Hills of South Dakota. Readers are male and female adults ages 21-80. Photo guidelines free with SASE.
Needs: Uses 12-14 photos/issue; all supplied by freelancers. Needs photos related to issued of the Black Hills of South Dakota. "May be any subject." Reviews photos with or without a ms. Model/property release required. Captions preferred.
Making Contact & Terms: Interested in receiving work from newer, lesser-known photographers. Provide resume, business card, brochure, flyer or tearsheets to be kept on file for possible assignments. Send b&w prints; 35mm, 2¼ × 2¼, 4 × 5, 8 × 10 transparencies. Does not keep samples on file. SASE. Reports in 1 month. Pays $50/color cover photo; $30/color inside photo; $20/b&w inside photo. Pays on publication. Buys one-time rights; negotiable.

INTERNATIONAL WILDLIFE, 8925 Leesburg Pike, Vienna VA 22184. (703)790-4419. Fax: (703)442-7332. Photo Editor: John Nuhn. Senior Photo Editor: Steve Freligh. Circ. 650,000. Estab. 1970. Bimonthly magazine. Emphasizes world's wildlife, nature, environment, conservation. Readers are people who enjoy viewing high-quality wildlife and nature images, and who are interested in knowing more about the natural world and man's interrelationship with animals and environment on all parts of the globe. Sample copy $3 from National Wildlife Federation Membership Services (same address); do not include order with guidelines request. Photo guidelines free with SASE.
Needs: Uses about 45 photos/issue; all supplied by freelance photographers; 30% on assignment, 70% from stock. Needs photos of world's wildlife, wild plants, nature-related how-to, conservation practices, conservation-minded people (tribal and individual), environmental damage, environmental research, outdoor recreation. Special needs include single photos for cover possibility (primarily wildlife but also plants, scenics, people); story ideas (with photos) from Canada, Europe, former Soviet republics, Pacific, China; b&w accompanying unique story ideas that have good reason not to be in color. Model release preferred. Captions required.
Making Contact & Terms: Send 35mm, 2¼ × 2¼, 4 × 5, 8 × 10 transparencies (magazine is 95% color) or 8 × 10 glossy b&w prints by mail for consideration. Query with samples, credits and stock listings. SASE. Reports in 3 weeks. Pays $800/color cover photo; $300-750/color inside photo; $100-400/day;

The Subject Index, located at the back of this book, can help you find publications interested in the topics you shoot.

$750-2,500/complete package. **Pays on acceptance.** Credit line given. Buys one-time rights with limited magazine promotion rights. Previously published work OK.
Tips: Looking for a variety of images that show photographer's scope and specialization, organized in slide sheets, along with tearsheets of previously published work. "Study our magazine; note the type of images we use and send photos equal or better. Think editorially when submitting story queries or photos. Assure that package is complete—sufficient return postage (no checks), proper size return envelope, address inside and do not submit photos in glass slides, trays or small boxes."

THE IOWAN MAGAZINE, Suite 350, 108 Third St., Des Moines IA 50309. (515)282-8220. Fax: (515)282-0125. Editor: Karen Massetti-Miller. Circ. 25,000. Estab. 1952. Quarterly magazine. Emphasizes "Iowa—its people, places, events and history." Readers are over 30, college-educated, middle to upper income. Sample copy $4.50 with 9×12 SAE and $2.25 postage. Photo guidelines free with SASE.
Needs: Uses about 50 photos/issue; 95% by freelance photographers on assignment and 5% freelance stock. Needs "Iowa scenics—all seasons." Model/property releases preferred. Captions required.
Making Contact & Terms: Interested in receiving work from newer, lesser-known photographers. Send b&w prints; 35mm, $2\frac{1}{4} \times 2\frac{1}{4}$ or 4×5 transparencies; or b&w contact sheet by mail for consideration. SASE. Reports in 1 month. Pays $25-50/b&w photo; $50-100/color photo; $200-500/day. Pays on publication. Credit line given. Buys one-time rights; negotiable.

ISLANDS, Dept. PM, 3886 State St., Santa Barbara CA 93105. (805)682-7177. Photo Editor: Zorah Krueger. Art Director: Albert Chiang. Bimonthly magazine. Emphasizes travel/islands. Readers are male, 40-60, affluent. Circ. 160,000. Sample copy $3.95. Photo guidelines free with SASE.
Needs: Uses 100 photos/issue; all supplied by freelancers. Needs travel shots and island photos. Model release preferred. Captions required.
Making Contact & Terms: Arrange a personal interview to show portfolio; query with resume of credits and list of stock photo subjects; submit portfolio for review; provide resume, business card, brochure, flyer or tearsheets to be kept on file for possible assignments. SASE. Reports in 1 month. Pays $500-1,000/color cover photo; $50-350/color inside photo. **Pays on acceptance.** Credit line given. Buys one-time rights. Simultaneous submissions OK.

JAZZ TIMES, 7961 Eastern Ave., Silver Spring MD 20910. (301)588-4114. Fax: (301)588-2009. Assignment Editor: Mike Joyce. Circ. 57,000. Estab. 1969. Monthly glossy magazine (10 times/year). Emphasizes jazz. Readers are jazz fans, record consumers and people in the music industry. Sample copy $2.95.
Needs: Uses about 50 photos/issue; 30 supplied by freelance photographers. Needs performance shots, portrait shots of jazz musicians. Captions preferred.
Making Contact & Terms: Interested in receiving work from newer, lesser-known photographers. Send 5×7 b&w prints by mail for consideration. SASE. Reports in 2 weeks. "If possible, we keep photos on file till we can use them." Pays $50/b&w for color; $15/b&w inside photo. Negotiates fees for cover photo. Pays on publication. Credit line given. Buys one-time or reprint rights; negotiable.
Tips: "Send whatever photos you can spare. Name and address should be on back."

*JAZZIZ MAGAZINE, Box 8309, Gainesville FL 32605-8309. (904)375-3705. Publisher: Michael Fagien. Circ. 95,000. Bimonthly magazine. Emphasizes "the spectrum of contemporary music." Sample copy $3.50 with $8\frac{1}{2} \times 11$ SAE and $1.15 postage. Photo guidelines free with SASE.
Needs: Uses about 35 photos/issue; 20 supplied by freelance photographers. Needs photos of "jazz and adult contemporary musicians, color and b&w, playing or posed."
Making Contact & Terms: Query with samples and list of stock photo subjects. Send color or b&w prints by mail for consideration. Submit portfolio for review. SASE. Reports in 1 month. NPI; negotiable by the job. Pays on publication. Credit line given. Rights negotiable.
Tips: Prefers to see "high quality photos with expression—photos which give the essence of inner feeling of the person photographed. Avoid resume shots. Unusual crops, angles and lighting always welcome."

JOURNEYMEN, 513 Chester Turnpike, Candia NH 03034. (603)483-8029. Editor: Paul S. Boynton. Estab. 1990. Quarterly magazine. Emphasizes male-oriented issues. Readers are male, ages 20-70. Sample copy $6. Photo guidelines available.
Needs: Uses 10-12 photos/issue; almost all supplied by freelancers. Needs photos of men: at work, at play, with children, friends and spouses. Model/property release preferred. Captions preferred.
Making Contact & Terms: Interested in receiving work from newer, lesser-known photographers. Submit portfolio for review. Send unsolicited photos by mail for consideration. Send 5×7 b&w prints. Keeps samples on file. SASE. Reports in 3 weeks. Pays $25-100/b&w cover photo. Pays on publication. Credit line given. Buys first N.A. serial rights; negotiable. Simultaneous submissions and/or previously published works OK.

Tips: "Almost all photos used are by freelancers. Guidelines and upcoming needs are available. Great opportunity for beginners. Happy to look at all submissions. We're interested in photos of men portrayed in positive images. We're interested in developing long-term relationships with freelancers from all over the U.S. to work on assignments."

JUNIOR SCHOLASTIC, 730 Broadway, New York NY 10003. (212)505-3071. Editor: Lee Baier. Senior Photo Researcher: Deborah Thompson. Circ. 600,000. Biweekly educational school magazine. Emphasizes junior high social studies (grades 6-8): world and national news, US history, geography, how people live around the world. Sample copy $1.75 with 9 × 12 SAE.
Needs: Uses 20 photos/issue. Needs photos of young people ages 11-14; non-travel photos of life in other countries; US news events. Reviews photos with accompanying ms only. Model release required. Captions required.
Making Contact & Terms: Arrange a personal interview to show portfolio. "Please do not send samples—only stock list or photocopies of photos. Nonreturnable." Reports in 1 month. Pays $200/color cover photo; $75/b&w inside photo; $100/color inside photo. **Pays on acceptance.** Credit line given. Buys one-time rights. Simultaneous submissions OK.
Tips: Prefers to see young teenagers; in US and foreign countries. "Personal interviews with teenagers worldwide with photos."

KALLIOPE, A Journal of Women's Art, 3939 Roosevelt Blvd., Jacksonville FL 32205. (904)381-3511. Contact: Art Editor. Circ. 1,000. Estab. 1978. Journal published 3 times/year. Emphasizes art by women. Readers are interested in women's issues. Sample copy $7. Photo guidelines free with SASE.
Needs: Uses 18 photos/issue; all supplied by freelancers. Needs art and fine art that will reproduce well in b&w. Needs photos of nature, people, fine art by excellent sculptors and painters, and shots that reveal lab applications. Model release required. Photo captions preferred. Artwork should be titled.
Making Contact & Terms: Interested in receiving work from newer, lesser-known photographers. Send unsolicited photos by mail for consideration. Send 5 × 7 b&w prints. SASE. Reports in 1 month. Pays contributor 3 free issues or free 1-year subscription. Buys one-time rights. Credit line given.
Tips: "Send excellent quality photos with an artist's statement (50 words) and resume."

KANSAS, Suite 1300, 700 SW Harrison, Topeka KS 66603. (913)296-3479. Editor: Andrea Glenn. Circ. 54,000. Estab. 1945. Quarterly magazine. Emphasizes Kansas scenery, arts, recreation and people. Photos are purchased with or without accompanying ms or on assignment. Free sample copy and photo guidelines.
Needs: Buys 60-80 photos/year; 75% from freelance assignment, 25% from freelance stock. Animal, human interest, nature, photo essay/photo feature, scenic, sport, travel and wildlife, all from Kansas. No nudes, still life or fashion photos. Model/property release preferred. Captions required.
Making Contact & Terms: Interested in receiving work from newer, lesser-known photographers. Send material by mail for consideration. No b&w. Transparencies must be identified by location and photographer's name on the mount. Uses 35mm, 2¼ × 2¼ or 4 × 5 transparencies. Photos are returned after use. Pays $50 minimum/color photo; $150 minimum/cover photo. **Pays on acceptance.** Credit line given. Not copyrighted. Buys one-time rights. Previously published work OK.
Tips: Kansas-oriented material only. Prefers Kansas photographers. "Follow guidelines, submission dates specifically. Shoot a lot of seasonal scenics."

KASHRUS MAGAZINE—The Guide for the Kosher Consumer, P.O. Box 204, Parkville Station, Brooklyn NY 11204. (718)336-8544. Editor: Rabbi Yosef Wikler. Circ. 10,000. Bimonthly. Emphasizes kosher food and food technology. Readers are kosher food consumers, vegetarians and producers. Sample copy for 9 × 12 SAE with $1.44 postage.
Needs: Uses 3-5 photos/issue; all supplied by freelance photographers. Needs photos of travel, food, food technology, seasonal nature photos and Jewish holidays. Model release preferred. Captions preferred.
Making Contact & Terms: Send unsolicited photos by mail for consideration. Provide resume, business card, brochure, flyer or tearsheets to be kept on file for possible future assignments. Uses 2¼ × 2¼, 3½ × 3½ or 7½ × 7½ matte b&w prints. SASE. Reports in 1 week. Pays $40-75/b&w cover photo; $25-50/b&w inside photo; $75-200/job; $50-200/text/photo package. Pays part on acceptance; part on publication. Buys one-time rights, first N.A. serial rights, all rights; negotiable. Simultaneous submissions and previously published work OK.

KEYBOARD, 20085 Stevens Creek Blvd., Cupertino CA 95014. (408)446-1105. Editor: Dominic Milano. Art Director: Richard Leeds. Monthly magazine. Circ. 82,000. Emphasizes "biographies and how-to feature articles on keyboard players (pianists, organists, synthesizer players, etc.) and keyboard-related material. It is read primarily by musicians to get background information on their favorite artists, new developments in the world of keyboard instruments, etc." Free sample copy and photographer's and writer's guidelines.

Needs: Buys 10-15 photos/issue. Celebrity/personality (photos of keyboard players at their instruments). Prefers shots of musicians with their instruments. Photos purchased with or without accompanying ms and infrequently on assignment. Captions required for historical shots only.

Making Contact & Terms: Query with list of stock photo subjects. Send first class to Richard Leeds. Uses 8×10 b&w glossy prints; 35mm color, 120mm, 4×5 transparencies for cover shots. Leave space on left-hand side of transparencies for cover shots. SASE. Reports in 2-4 weeks. Pays on a per-photo basis. Pays expenses on assignment only. Pays $35-150/b&w inside photo; $300-500/photo for cover; $75-250/ color inside photo. Pays on publication. Credit line given. Buys rights to one-time use with option to reprint. Simultaneous submissions OK.

Tips: "Send along a list of artist shots on file. Photos submitted for our files would also be helpful— we'd prefer keeping them on hand, but will return prints if requested. Prefer live shots at concerts or in clubs. Keep us up to date on artists that will be photographed in the near future. Freelancers are vital to us."

KIPLINGER'S PERSONAL FINANCE MAGAZINE, 1729 H St. NW, Washington DC 20006. (202)887-6492. Fax: (202)331-1206. Picture Editor: Douglas J. Vann. Circ. 1 million. Estab. 1935. Monthly magazine. Emphasizes personal finance.

Needs: Uses 15-25 photos/issue; 90% supplied by freelancers. Needs "business portraits and photo illustration dealing with personal finance issues (i.e. investing, retirement, real estate). Model release required. Captions required.

Making Contact & Terms: Contact through rep. Arrange personal interview to show portfolio. Query with list of stock photo subjects. Provide resume, business card, brochure, flyer or tearsheets to be kept on file for possible assignments. Keeps samples on file. SASE. Reports in 1-2 weeks. Pays $1,200/ color and b&w cover photo; $350/day against space rate per page. **Pays on acceptance.** Credit line given. Buys one-time rights.

KITE LINES, P.O. Box 466, Randallstown MD 21133-0466. (410)922-1212. Fax: (410)922-4262. Publisher-Editor: Valerie Govig. Circ. 13,000. Estab. 1977. Quarterly. Emphasizes kites and kite flying exclusively. Readers are international adult kiters. Sample copy $5. Photo guidelines free with SASE.

Needs: Uses about 45-65 photos/issue; "up to about 50% are unassigned or over-the-transom—but nearly all are from *kiter*-photographers." Needs photos of "unusual kites in action (no dimestore plastic kites), preferably with people in the scene (not easy with kites). Needs to relate closely to *information* (article or long caption)." Special needs include major kite festivals; important kites and kiters. Captions required. "Identify *kites* as well as people."

Making Contact & Terms: Query with samples or send 2-3 b&w 8×10 uncropped prints or 35mm or larger transparencies by mail for consideration. Provide relevant background information, i.e., knowledge of kites or kite happenings. SASE. Reports in "2 weeks to 2 months (varies with work load, but any obviously unsuitable stuff is returned quickly—in 2 weeks." Pays $0-30 per inside photo; $0-50 for color photo; special jobs on assignment negotiable; generally on basis of expenses paid only. "We provide extra copies to contributors. Our limitations arise from our small size. However, *Kite Lines* is a quality showcase for good work." Pays no later than on publication. Buys one-time rights; usually buys first world serial rights. Previously published work OK.

Tips: In portfolio or samples wants to see "ability to select important, *noncommercial* kites. Just take a great kite picture, and be patient with our tiny staff. Considers good selection of subject matter; good composition—angles, light, background and sharpness. But we don't want to look at 'portfolios'— just *kite* pictures, please."

LADIES HOME JOURNAL, Dept. PM, 100 Park Ave, New York NY 10017. (212)351-3563. Contact: Photo Editor. Monthly magazine. Features women's issues. Readership consists of women with children and working women in 30s age group. Circ. 6 million.

Needs: Uses 90 photos per issue; 100% supplied by freelancers. Needs photos of children, celebrities and women's lifestyles/situations. Reviews photos only without ms. Model release and captions preferred. No photo guidelines available.

Making Contact & Terms: Provide resume, business card, brochure, flyer or tearsheet to be kept on file for possible assignment. Reports in 3 weeks. Pays $185/b&w inside photo; $185/color page rate. **Pays on acceptance.** Credit line given. Buys one-time rights.

LAKE SUPERIOR MAGAZINE, Lake Superior Port Cities, Inc., P.O. Box 16417, Duluth MN 55816-0417. (218)722-5002. Fax: (218)722-4096. Editor: Paul L. Hayden. Circ. 20,000. Estab. 1979. Bimonthly magazine. "Beautiful picture magazine about Lake Superior." Readers are ages 35-55, male and female, highly educated, upper-middle and upper-management level through working. Sample copy $3.95 with 9×12 SAE and 5 first-class stamps. Photo guidelines free with SASE.

• In 1992 this publication received the Most Improved Magazine Award from a regional publishers association near the Great Lakes.

Needs: Uses 30 photos/issue; 70% supplied by freelance photographers. Needs photos of scenic, travel, wildlife, personalities, underwater, all photos Lake Superior-related. Photo captions preferred.

Making Contact & Terms: Interested in receiving work from newer, lesser-known photographers. Send unsolicited photos by mail for consideration. Provide resume, business card, brochure, flyer or tearsheets to be kept on file for possible assignments. Uses b&w prints; 35mm, 2¼×2¼, 4×5 transparencies. SASE. Reports in 3 weeks. Pays $75/color cover photo; $35/color inside photo; $20/b&w inside photo. Pays on publication. Credit line given. Buys first N.A. serial rights; reserves second rights for future use. Simultaneous submissions OK.

Tips: "Be aware of the focus of our publication—Lake Superior. Photo features concern only that. Features with text can be related. We are known for our fine color photography and reproduction. It has to be 'tops.' We try to use image large, therefore detail quality and resolution must be good. We look for unique outlook on subject, not just snapshots. Must communicate emotionally."

LAKELAND BOATING MAGAZINE, Suite 1220, 1560 Sherman Ave., Evanston IL 60201. (708)869-5400. Editor: Sarah D. Wortham. Circ. 45,000. Estab. 1945. Monthly magazine. Emphasizes powerboating in the Great Lakes. Readers are affluent professionals, predominantly men over 35. Sample copy $6 with 9×12 SAE and $2.80 postage.

Needs: Needs shots of particular Great Lakes ports and waterfront communities. Model release preferred. Captions preferred.

Making Contact & Terms: Query with list of stock photo subjects. Provide resume, business card, brochure, flyer or tearsheets to be kept on file for possible assignments. SASE. Pays $20-100/b&w photo; $25-100/color photo. **Pays on acceptance.** Credit line given. Buys one-time rights.

✹LEISURE WORLD, 1215 Ouellette Ave., Windsor, Ontario N9A 6N3 Canada. (519)971-3207. Fax: (519)977-1197. Editor-in-Chief: Doug O'Neil. Circ. 315,000. Estab. 1988. Bimonthly magazine. Emphasizes travel and leisure. Readers are auto club members, 50% male, 50% female, middle to upper middle class. Sample copy $2.

Needs: Uses 9-10 photos/issue; 25-30% supplied by freelance photographers. Needs photos of travel, scenics. Special needs include exotic travel locales. Model release preferred. Captions required.

Making Contact & Terms: Interested in receiving work from newer, lesser-known photographers. Send unsolicited photos by mail for consideration. Provide business card, brochure, flyer or tearsheets to be kept on file for possible assignments. Send b&w or color 35mm, 2¼×2¼, 4×5, or 8×10 transparencies. SASE. Reports in 2 weeks. Pays $50/color cover photo, $25/color inside photo, $25/b&w inside photo, or $100-150/photo/text package. Pays on publication. Credit line given. Buys one-time rights.

Tips: "We expect that the technical considerations are all perfect—frames, focus, exposure, etc. Beyond that we look for a photograph that can convey a mood or tell a story by itself. We would like to see more subjective and impressionistic photographs. Don't be afraid to submit material. If your first submissions are not accepted, try again. We encourage talented and creative photographers who are trying to establish themselves."

LETTERS, Dept. PM, 310 Cedar Lane, Teaneck NJ 07666. Associate Editor: Lisa Rosen. Monthly. Emphasizes "sexual relations between people, male/female; male/male; female/female." Readers are "primarily male, older; some younger women." Sample copy $3.

Needs: Uses 1 photo/issue; all supplied by freelance photographers. Needs photos of women in lingerie or scantily attired; special emphasis on shots of semi- or completely nude buttocks. Model release required.

Making Contact & Terms: Query with samples. Send 2¼×2¼ slides by mail for consideration. Provide brochure, flyer and tearsheets to be kept on file for possible future assignments. SASE. Reports in 2-3 weeks. Pays $150/color photo. Pays on publication. Buys all rights.

Tips: Would like to see "material germane to our publication's needs. See a few issues of the publication before you send in photos. Please send slides that are numbered and keep a copy of the list, so if we do decide to purchase we can let you know by the number on the slide. All of our covers are purchased from freelance photographers."

LIFE, Dept. PM, Time-Life Bldg., Rockefeller Center, New York NY 10020. (212)522-1212. Photo Editor: Barbara Baker Burrows. Monthly magazine. Emphasizes current events, cultural trends, human behavior, nature and the arts, mainly through photojournalism. Readers are of all ages, backgrounds and interests. Circ. 1,400,000.

Needs: Uses about 100 photos/issue. Prefers to see topical and unusual photos. Must be up-to-the minute and newsworthy. Send photos that could not be duplicated by anyone or anywhere else. Especially needs humorous photos for last page article "Just One More."

Making Contact & Terms: Send material by mail for consideration. SASE. Uses 35mm, 2¼×2¼, 4×5 and 8×10 slides. Pays $500/page; $600/page in color news section; $1,000/cover. Credit line given. Buys one-time rights.

Tips: "Familiarize yourself with the topical nature and format of the magazine before submitting photos and/or proposals."

LIVE STEAM MAGAZINE, Dept. PM, P.O. Box 629, Traverse City MI 49685. (616)941-7160. Editor-in-Chief: Joe D. Rice. Circ. 13,000. Monthly. Emphasizes "steam-powered models and full-size equipment (i.e., locomotives, cars, boats, stationary engines, etc.)." Readers are "hobbyists—many are building scale models." Sample copy free with 9×12 SAE and $1 postage. Photo guidelines free with SASE.

Needs: Uses about 80 photos/issue; "most are supplied by the authors of published articles." Needs "how-to-build (steam models), historical locomotives, steamboats, reportage of hobby model steam meets. Unless it's a cover shot (color), we only use photos with ms." Special needs include "strong transparencies of steam locomotives, steamboats or stationary steam engines."

Making Contact & Terms: Query with samples. Send 3×5 glossy b&w prints by mail for consideration. SASE. Reports in 3 weeks. Pays $40/color cover photo; $8/b&w inside photo; $30/page plus $8/ photo; $25 minimum for text/photo package (maximum payment "depends on article length"). Pays on publication—"we pay quarterly." Credit line given. Buys one-time rights. Simultaneous submissions OK.

Tips: "Be sure that mechanical detail can be seen clearly. Try for maximum depth of field."

LOS ANGELES MAGAZINE, Dept. PM, 1888 Century Park E., Los Angeles CA 90067. (213)557-7569. Editor: Lew Harris. Design Director: William Delorme. Executive Art Director: James Griglak. Assistant Art Director: Pamela Thornberg. Monthly magazine. Circ. 170,000. Emphasizes sophisticated Southern California personalities and lifestyle, particularly Los Angeles area.

Needs: Buys 45-50 photos/issue. Celebrity/personality, fashion/beauty, human interest, head shot, photo illustration/photo journalism, photo essay/photo feature (occasional), sport (occasional), food/ restaurant and travel. Most photos are assigned; occasionally purchased with accompanying ms. Free writer's guidelines.

Making Contact & Terms: Provide brochure, calling card, flyer, resume and tearsheets to be kept on file for possible future assignments. Submit portfolio for review. Send b&w contact sheet or contact sheet and negatives; 4×5, 2¼×2¼ or 35mm transparencies. All covers are assigned. Uses 2¼×2¼ color transparencies; vertical format required. SASE. Reports in 2 weeks. Pays $100 minimum/job; $100-300/b&w photo; $100-500/color photo; $450/cover photo. Pays 10¢/word minimum for accompanying ms. Pays on publication. Credit line given. Buys first serial rights. Simultaneous submissions and previously published work OK.

Tips: To break in, "bring portfolio showing type of material we assign. Leave it for review during a business day (a.m. or p.m.) to be picked up later. Photographers should mainly be active in L.A. area and be sensitive to different magazine styles and formats."

*LOTTERY PLAYER'S MAGAZINE, P.O. Box 5013, Cherry Hill NJ 08034. (609)779-8900. Fax: (609)273-6350. Editor: Denise Strub. Estab. 1981. Monthly tabloid. Emphasizes all aspects of gaming, especially lottery winners. Readers are male and female lottery players, usually between ages 35-65. Sample copy $2.50.

Needs: Uses 15-20 photos/issue; 1-2 supplied by freelancers. Needs photos of people buying lottery tickets, lottery winners, lottery and gaming activities. Reviews photos with or without ms. Captions required.

Making Contact & Terms: Interested in receiving work from newer, lesser-known photographers. Provide resume, business card, brochure, flyer or tearsheets to be kept on file for possible assignments. "Call with ideas." Keeps samples on file. SASE. Reports in 3 weeks. Pays $20-60/color cover photo; $20/b&w inside photo; rates vary. Pays 2 months after publication. Buys one-time rights, first North American serial rights, all rights; negotiable. Simultaneous submissions and/or previously published work OK.

Tips: "Photos should be clear, timely and interesting, with a lot of contrast."

LUTHERAN FORUM, P.O. Box 327, Delhi NY 13753. (607)746-7511. Editor: Paul Hinlicky. Circ. 4,500. Quarterly. Emphasizes "Lutheran concerns, both within the church and in relation to the wider society, for the leadership of Lutheran churches in North America."

Needs: Uses cover photo occasionally. "While subject matter varies, we are generally looking for photos that include people, and that have a symbolic dimension. We use *few* purely 'scenic' photos. Photos of religious activities, such as worship, are often useful, but should not be 'cliches'—types of photos that are seen again and again." Captions "may be helpful."

Tools of the Trade Help in Marketing Efforts

As a travel writer and photographer, Lee Foster of Berkeley, California, constantly searches for new ways to market his work. Foster's photos appear in the catalogs of several top stock agencies, including FPG International Corporation and Bruce Coleman Photo Library. For the past 10 years he has placed travel articles on the CompuServe computer network, and, in late 1992, he hooked up with a CD-ROM producer to create his own disk of travel photographs and stories.

Foster, who received a PhD in literature from Stanford University, says the decision to move into CD-ROM stemmed from a long-time desire to package his work. "All along I've been preparing myself to get this dual coverage of text and photos of destinations," he says. His first CD, which was produced by

Lee Foster

Ebook Inc. and distributed by Electronic Arts, contains over 1,000 images of California. The images accompany numerous articles, and he plans to produce three more disks highlighting other locations.

Although the compact disk is relatively new, Foster believes such technological advances will make products like his commonplace. Other photographers should seriously consider using such technology because the CD will become a vital piece of equipment for buyers who want to view, select and, hopefully, purchase images, he says.

In order for publishers to use the material on Foster's CD they must buy usage rights from him because he owns the copyright to the disk. Foster, who sells most of his work to consumer publications, is adamant about protecting copyright. While he believes photographers should take advantage of technological changes, he does not want to see the industry suffer because of poor business practices. "Every time a creative person's work is used that person should be paid," he says. One way to protect copyright is for photographers to not allow their work to get placed on clip art disks. When buyers purchase clip art disks they can use the photos for an indefinite period of time at no extra cost.

Foster estimates that his energy is spent equally in writing and photography, and he finds editors to be very receptive to the fact that he combines the two talents. "It's a double workload, but it's also a double opportunity," he says, adding that many editors will use an article if they have images to go with it.

The skill in providing text/photo packages lies in changing gears from note taking during an interview to photographing the situation. At times, this is difficult because you may see a perfect photo opportunity while you are in the middle of a gripping interview. You won't want to stop the conversation, but you also won't want to miss the shot. Foster says when this dilemma occurs he likes to take the photograph so that the moment is not lost.

By fulfilling a dual role Foster does not photograph a lot of different subjects. He does shoot a lot of film, however, because he likes to make at least six in-camera duplicates when he picks a subject. He gives one shot to each of his three stock agencies and then has three more for his own sales efforts.

Foster believes it is essential for photographers to generate sales on their own, even if they are on contract with stock agencies. "My advice generally to photographers is to market themselves vigorously in the specific direction that they are shooting. Then hope the stock agencies will help to cover them in the much larger markets that they may not be focused on," he says.

—*Michael Willins*

Over the last several years the photo industry has been bombarded with new ways of storing, manipulating and marketing images. Travel writer and photographer Lee Foster of Berkeley, California, has decided to market his work via CD-ROM, placing articles and images on the same disk. Foster maintains over 150,000 images from all over the world, including this one of the Terracotta Warrior site in Xian, China.

Making Contact & Terms: Query with list of stock photo subjects. SASE. Reports in 1-2 months. Pays $15-25/b&w photo. Pays on publication. Credit line given. Buys one-time rights. Simultaneous submissions or previously published work OK.

*THE MAGAZINE ANTIQUES, 575 Broadway, New York NY 10012. (212)941-2800. Fax: (212)941-2819. Editor: Allison E. Ledes. Circ. 56,700. Estab. 1922. Monthly magazine. Emphasizes art, antiques, architecture. Readers are male and female collectors, curators, academics, interior designers, ages 40-70. Sample copy $7.50.
Needs: Uses 60-120 photos/issue; 40% supplied by freelancers. Need photos of interiors, architectural exteriors, objects. Reviews photos with or without ms.
Making Contact & Terms: Interested in receiving work from newer, lesser-known photographers. Submit portfolio for review. Send 8 × 10 glossy prints; 4 × 5 transparencies. Does not keep samples on file. SASE. Reports in 1-2 weeks. NPI; rates negotiated on an individual basis. **Pays on acceptance.** Credit line given. Buys one-time rights; negotiable. Previously published work OK.

MAGICAL BLEND, 1461 Valencia St., San Francisco CA 94110. (415)821-9190. Art Directors: Matthew Courtway and Yuka Hirota. Circ. 57,000. Estab. 1980. Quarterly magazine. Emphasizes New Age consciousness, painting, collage and photography. Readers include people of "all ages interested in an alternative approach to spirituality." Sample copy $4.
Needs: Uses 1-12 photos/issue; 100% supplied by freelance photographers. Looks for creative, visionary and surreal work. Model release preferred if needed.
Making Contact & Terms: Interested in receiving work from newer, lesser-known photographers. Send unsolicited photos by mail for consideration. Send b&w or color prints; 35mm, 2¼ × 2¼, 4 × 5 and 8 × 10 transparencies. SASE. Reports in 3 weeks. Payment not given; credit line only. Buys one-time rights. If desired, print photographer's address with photo so readers can contact for purchases.
Tips: In portfolio or samples, looking for "images that are inspiring to look at that show people in celebration of life. Try to include positive images. The best way to see what we're interested in printing is by sending for a sample copy."

MAINSTREAM, Magazine of the Able-Disabled, 2973 Beech St., San Diego CA 92102. (619)234-3138. Managing Editor: William G. Stothers. Circ. 15,500. Estab. 1975. Published 10 times per year. Emphasizes disability rights. Readers are upscale, active men and women who are disabled. Sample copy $3 with 9 × 12 SAE with 6 first class stamps.
Needs: Uses 3-4 photos/issue. Needs photos of disabled people doing things, sports, travel, working, etc. Reviews photos with accompanying ms only. Model/property release preferred. Captions required.
Making Contact & Terms: Provide resume, business card, brochure, flyer or tearsheets to be kept on file for possible assignments. Keeps samples on file. SASE. Reports in 2 months. Pays $75/color cover photo; $35/b&w inside photo. Pays on publication. Credit line given. Buys all rights; negotiable. Previously published work OK "if not in one of our major competitors' publications."
Tips: "We definitely look for signs that the photographer empathizes with and understands the perspective of the disability rights movement."

MARLIN MAGAZINE, P.O. Box 2456, Winter Park FL 32790. (407)628-4802. Editor: David Ritchie. Photo Editor: Doug Olander. Circ. 30,000. Estab. 1981. Bimonthly magazine. Emphasizes offshore big game fishing for billfish, sharks and tuna. Readers are 94% male, 75% married, average age 43, businessmen. Free sample copy with 8 × 10 SAE. Photo guidelines free with SASE.
 • In mid-1992 *Marlin Magazine* was purchased by World Publications Inc., which has been more aggressive at marketing on the newsstands.
Needs: Uses 40-50 photos/issue; 98% supplied by freelancers. Needs photos of fish/action shots, scenics and how-to. Special photo needs include big game fishing action and scenics (marinas, landmarks etc.). Model release preferred. Captions required.
Making Contact & Terms: Send unsolicited photos by mail for consideration. Send b&w, color prints; 35mm transparencies. SASE. Reports in 1 month. Pays $500/color cover photo; $50-150/color inside photo; $35-150/b&w inside photo; $150-200/color page rate. Pays on publication. Buys first N.A. rights. Simultaneous submissions OK.

MARTIAL ARTS TRAINING, P.O. Box 918, Santa Clarita CA 91380-9018. (805)257-4066. Fax: (805)257-3028. Editor: Marian K. Castinado. Circ. 40,000. Bimonthly. Emphasizes martial arts training. Readers are martial artists of all skill levels. Sample copy free. Photo guidelines free with SASE.
Needs: Uses about 100 photos/issue; 90 supplied by freelance photographers. Needs "photos that pertain to fitness/conditioning drills for martial artists. Photos purchased with accompanying ms only. Model release required. Captions required.
Making Contact & Terms: Send 5 × 7 or 8 × 10 b&w prints; 35mm transparencies; b&w contact sheet or negatives by mail for consideration. SASE. Reports in 1 month. Pays $50-150 for text/photo package. Pays on publication. Credit line given. Buys all rights.

Tips: Photos "must be razor-sharp, b&w. Technique shots should be against neutral background. Concentrate on training-related articles and photos."

MASTER OF LIFE *WINNERS*, P.O. Box 38, Malibu CA 90265. (818)889-1575. Editor: Dick Sutphen. Circ. 120,000. Estab. 1976. Quarterly magazine. Emphasizes metaphysical, psychic development, reincarnation, self-help with tapes. Everyone receiving the magazine has attended a Sutphen Seminar or purchased Valley of the Sun Publishing books or tapes from a line of over 300 titles: video and audio tapes, subliminal/hypnosis/meditation/New Age music/seminars on tape, etc. Sample copy free with 12×15 SAE and 5 first-class stamps.
Needs: "We purchase about 20 photos per year for the magazine and also for cassette album covers. We are especially interested in surrealistic photography which would be used as covers, to illustrate stories and for New Age music cassettes. Even seminar ads often use photos that we purchase from freelancers." Model release required.
Making Contact & Terms: Interested in receiving work from newer, lesser-known photographers. Send b&w and color prints; 35mm transparencies by mail for consideration. SASE. Reports in 2 weeks. Pays $100/color photo; $50/b&w photo. Pays on publication. Credit line given if desired. Buys one-time rights; negotiable. Simultaneous submissions and previously published work OK.

MENNONITE PUBLISHING HOUSE, 616 Walnut Ave., Scottdale PA 15683. (412)887-8500. Photo Secretary: Debbie Cameron. Publishes *Story Friends* (ages 4-9), *On The Line* (ages 10-14), *Christian Living*, *Gospel Herald*, *Purpose* (adults).
Needs: Buys 10-20 photos/year. Needs photos of children engaged in all kinds of legitimate childhood activities (at school, at play, with parents, in church and Sunday School, at work, with hobbies, relating to peers and significant elders, interacting with the world); photos of youth in all aspects of their lives (school, work, recreation, sports, family, dating, peers); adults in a variety of settings (family life, church, work, and recreation); abstract and scenic photos. Model release preferred.
Making Contact & Terms: Send 8½×11 b&w photos by mail for consideration. Provide resume, business card, brochure, flyer or tearsheets to be kept on file for possible assignments. SASE. Reports in 1 month. Pays $20-50/b&w photo. Credit line given. Buys one-time rights. Simultaneous submissions and previously published work OK.

METAL EDGE, Dept. PM, 355 Lexington Ave., New York NY 10017. (212)949-6850. Fax: (212)986-5926. Editor: Gerri Miller. Monthly magazine. Emphasizes heavy metal music. Readers are young fans. Circ. 250,000. Estab. 1985. Sample copy free with large manila SASE.
Needs: Uses 125 photos/issue; 100 supplied by freelance photographers. Needs studio b&w and color, concert shots and behind-the-scenes (b&w) photos of heavy metal artists.
Making Contact & Terms: Arrange a personal interview to show portfolio. Query with samples and list of stock photo subjects. Reports ASAP. Pays $25-35/b&w inside photo; $75+/color; job. Pays on publication. Buys one-time rights for individual shots. Buys all rights for assigned sessions or coverage. Previously published work OK.
Tips: Prefers to see very clear, exciting concert photos; studio color with vibrancy and life that capture subject's personality.

*MEXICO EVENTS, P.O. Box 188037, Carlsbad CA 92009. (619)929-0707. Fax: (619)929-0714. Art Director: Jim Crandall. Circ. 180,000. Estab. 1992. Bimonthly magazine. Emphasizes travel to Mexico. Readers are avid travelers, 50/50 male and female, interested in Mexico. Sample copy $2. Photo guidelines free with SASE.
Needs: Uses 60-80 photos/issue; 90% supplied by freelancers. Needs photos of Mexican events and celebrations, travel, recreation in Mexico. Reviews photos with or without a ms. Model/property release preferred. Captions required; include names of people, identify area/locations, time of year/day.
Making Contact & Terms: Interested in receiving work from newer, lesser-known photographers. "Ask to be put on photographer's alert list. Submit photos as requested on alert bulletin." Does not keep samples on file. SASE. Reports in 1-2 months. Pays $100-200/color cover photo; $20-100/color inside photo. Pays on publication. Credit line given. Buys one-time rights. Previously published work OK. Do not send dupes.
Tips: "Photos must be taken in Mexico. Technically perfect. 35mm slides are fine. Larger format OK too. Build a photo file on Mexico events and celebrations. This is wide-open. Very few photographers have event photos."

MICHIGAN NATURAL RESOURCES MAGAZINE, P.O. Box 30034, Lansing MI 48909. (517)373-9267. Managing Editor: Richard Morscheck. Photo Editor: Gijsbert van Frankenhuyzen. Circ. 100,000. Estab. 1931. Bimonthly. Emphasizes natural resources in the Great Lakes region. Readers are "appreciators of the out-of-doors; 15% readership is out of state." Sample copy $4. Photo guidelines free with SASE.

Needs: Uses about 40 photos/issue; freelance photography in given issue—50% from assignment and 50% from freelance stock. Needs photos of Michigan wildlife, Michigan flora, how-to, travel in Michigan, outdoor recreation. Also, photos of people, especially minorities and handicapped, enjoying outdoor pursuits. Captions preferred.

Making Contact & Terms: Query with samples or list of stock photo subjects. Send original 35mm color transparencies by mail for consideration. SAE. Reports in 1 month. Pays $75-250/color page; $500/job; $800 maximum for text/photo package. **Pays on acceptance.** Credit line given. Buys one-time rights.

Tips: Prefers "Kodachrome 64 or 25 or Fuji 50 or 100, 35mm, *razor-sharp in focus!* Send about 20 slides with a list of stock photo topics. Be sure slides are sharp, labeled clearly with subject and photographer's name and address. Send them in plastic slide filing sheets. Looks for unusual outdoor photos. Flora, fauna of Michigan and Great Lakes region. Strongly recommend that photographer look at past issues of the magazine to become familiar with the quality of the photography and the overall content."

MICHIGAN OUT-OF-DOORS, P.O. Box 30235, Lansing MI 48909. (517)371-1041. Fax: (517)371-1505. Editor: Kenneth S. Lowe. Circ. 130,000. Estab. 1947. Monthly magazine. For people interested in "outdoor recreation, especially hunting and fishing; conservation; environmental affairs." Sample copy $2; free editorial guidelines.

Needs: Use 1-6 freelance photos/issue. Animal, nature, scenic, sport (hunting, fishing and other forms of noncompetitive recreation), and wildlife. Materials must have a Michigan slant. Captions preferred.

Making Contact & Terms: Send any size glossy b&w prints; 35mm or 2¼×2¼ transparencies. SASE. Reports in 1 month. Pays $15 minimum/b&w photo; $100/cover photo; $25/inside color photo. Credit line given. Buys first N.A. serial rights. Previously published work OK "if so indicated."

Tips: Submit seasonal material 6 months in advance. Wants to see "new approaches to subject matter."

*MINIATURES SHOWCASE, 21027 Crossroads Circle, Waukesha WI 53187. (414)796-8776. Fax: (414)796-1383. Editor: Geraldine Willems. Circ. 48,000. Estab. 1986. Bimonthly magazine. Emphasizes dollhouse miniatures. Readers are female, ages 40-70, collectors of miniatures. Sample copy $4 with 8×11 SASE. Photo guidelines free with SASE.

Needs: Uses 50 photos/issue; 20% supplied by freelancers. Needs photos of private collections. Reviews photos with or without ms. Special needs include private collections and handcrafters at work. Captions required; include description of what photo represents.

Making Contact & Terms: Interested in receiving work from newer, lesser-known photographers. Query with resume of credits. Keeps samples on file. SASE. Reports in 3 weeks. Pays $75-150/job. **Pays on acceptance.** Credit line given. Buys all rights.

Tips: Wants to see an "ability to photograph dollhouse miniatures without depth of field problem. Find an excellent, quality dollhouse collection in your area and query us."

*MIRABELLA, 8th Floor, 200 Madison Ave., New York NY 10016. (212)447-4600. Fax: (212)447-4708. Photography Director: Alison Morley. Circ. 600,000. Estab. 1989. Monthly magazine. Emphasizes fashion and also publishes features regarding news and talent. Readers are female, ages 20 and older.

Needs: Uses 100 photos/issue. Needs photos of personalities, fashion, travel, food, still lifes, beauty, photo illustrations. Reviews photos with or without ms. Special needs include great unseen photos of fascinating women of the world. Model release required. Captions required; include who, what, where, when, why.

Making Contact & Terms: Interested in receiving work from newer, lesser-known photographers. Submit portfolio for review. Query with stock photo list. Provide resume, business card, brochure, flyer or tearsheets to be kept on file for possible assignments. "Never send unsolicited photos." Keeps samples on file. SASE. Reports in 2 months. NPI; pays standard editorial rates. Pays on publication. Credit line given. Rights negotiable.

Tips: Likes photographers who portray a personal style, viewpoint and have strong technical skills. "Always look at a magazine and read it before submitting work to see that it is appropriate."

*MISSOURI ALUMNUS, Alumni Center, 407 Reynolds, Columbia MO 65211. (314)882-3049. Fax: 882-7290. Senior Information Specialist: Rob Hill. Circ. 125,000. Estab. 1912. Quarterly magazine. Emphasizes University of Missouri and its alumni. Readers are professional, educated, upscale alumni and friends of MU. Sample copy free with 9×12 SAE and 4 first-class stamps.

Needs: Uses 37-40 photos/issue; 10% supplied by freelancers. Needs photos of technology, personalities tied to MU alumni and professors. Reviews photos with or without ms. Model release preferred. Captions required.

Making Contact & Terms: Interested in receiving work from newer, lesser-known photographers. Query with resume of credits. SASE. Reports in 1-2 weeks. Pays 35/hour;$15-30/color inside photo; pays $15-30 b&w inside photo. Pays on publication. Credit line given. Buys one-time rights. Previously published works OK.

MODERN DRUMMER MAGAZINE, 870 Pompton Ave., Cedar Grove NJ 07009. (201)239-4140. Fax: (201)239-7139. Editor: Ron Spagnardi. Photo Editor: Scott Bienstock. Circ. 100,000. Magazine published 12 times/year. For drummers at all levels of ability: students, semiprofessionals and professionals. Sample copy $3.95.
Needs: Buys 100-150 photos annually. Needs celebrity/personality, product shots, action photos of professional drummers and photos dealing with "all aspects of the art and the instrument."
Making Contact & Terms: Submit freelance photos with letter. Send for consideration b&w contact sheet, b&w negatives, or 5 × 7 or 8 × 10 glossy b&w prints; 35mm, 2¼ × 2¼, 8 × 10 color transparencies. Uses color covers. SASE. Pays $200/cover; $50-150/color photo; $25-75/b&w photo. Pays on publication. Credit line given. Buys one-time international usage rights per country. Previously published work OK.

*MONDO 2000, PO Box 10171, Berkeley CA 94708. (510)845-9018. Fax: (510)649-9630. Art Director: Bart Nagel. Circ. 100,000. Estab. 1989. Quarterly magazine. Emphasizes lifestyle, high-tech computer and communication fields. Readers are professionals, 70 percent male, 30 percent female, median age of 29. Sample copies $7.
 • This publication lives on bizarre artwork and stories. Creativity is a must when submitting work to this market.
Needs: Uses approximately 25-30 photos/issue; around 70% supplied by freelancers. Needs photos of technology, portraits, fashion, experimental and bizarre art preferred. Computer manipulation encouraged. Reviews photos with or without ms. Model/property release preferred. No captions are necessary, provide description and details if they are not obvious.
Making Contact & Terms: Interested in receiving work from newer, lesser-known photographers. Submit portfolio for review. Provide resume, business card, brochure, flyer or tearsheets to be kept on file for possible assignments. Keeps samples on file. SASE. Reports in 3 weeks to 3 months. NPI. Pays 30 days to 3 months after publication. Buys one-time rights. Previously published work preferred.
Tips: "Put your name, address and phone number on everything. Call us a lot and tell us it's OK if we don't have a lot of money to pay." Wants to see sharp images with sound composition and lots of creativity. "We seek images from the darker side of the mind."

MONITORING TIMES, P.O. Box 98, Brasstown NC 28902. (704)837-9200. Fax: (704) 837-2216. Photo Editor: Beverly Berrong. Circ. 30,000. Estab. 1982. Monthly. Emphasizes radio communications, scanners and shortwave. Sample copy for $3 (postpaid).
Needs: Uses about 40 photos/issue; 50% supplied by freelance photographers. Needs photos of radio equipment, action scenes involving communications, individuals connected with story line. Special needs include b&w and color (cover) concerning radio, antennas, equipment, boats, planes, military exercises, anything dealing in radio communications. Model release preferred. Captions preferred.
Making Contact & Terms: Interested in receiving work from newer, lesser-known photographers. Query with samples or list of stock photo subjects. SASE. Reports in 2-4 weeks. Pays $35-75/color cover photo; $10-50/b&w inside photo; $50-200/text/photo package. **Pays on acceptance.** Credit line given if requested. Buys one-time rights.
Tips: "First, acquaint yourself with the publication and anticipate its reader profile. Product shots must be contrasty and sharp, suitable for camera-ready application. Action shots must revolve around story lines dealing with radio broadcasting (international), news events, scanner excitement: air shows, emergencies. We would prefer the photographer submit samples for us to keep on file, to be paid as used. A photocopy or contact print to be kept on file is also acceptable."

*MOPAR MUSCLE MAGAZINE, 3816 Industry Blvd., Lakeland FL 33811. (813)644-0449. Fax: (813)648-1187. Editor Greg Rager. Circ. 100,000. Estab. 1988. Bimonthly magazine. Emphasizes Chrysler products—Dodge, Plymouth, Chrysler (old and new). Readers are Chrysler product enthusiasts of all ages. Guidelines free with SASE.

The First Markets Index preceding the General Index in the back of this book provides the names of those companies/ publications interested in receiving work from newer, lesser-known photographers.

Needs: Uses approximately 120 photos/issue; 50% supplied by freelancers. Needs photos of automotive personalities, automobile features. Reviews photos with or without ms. Model release required. Property release preferred of automobile owners. Captions required; include all facts relating to the automotive subject.

Making Contact & Terms: Interested in receiving work from newer, lesser-known photographers. Send unsolicited photos by mail for consideration. Send 35mm, 4×5 color transparencies. Keeps samples on file. Reports in 3 weeks. NPI. Pays on publication. Credit line given. Buys all rights; negotiable.

MOTHERING MAGAZINE, P.O. Box 1690, Santa Fe NM 87504. (505)984-8116. Fax: (505)986-8335. Photo Editor: John Inserra. Estab. 1976. Quarterly magazine. Emphasizes parenting. Readers are progressive parents, primarily aged 25-40, with children of all ages, racially mixed. Sample copy $5.95. Free photo guidelines and current photo needs.

Needs: Uses about 40-50 photos/issue; nearly all supplied by freelance photographers. Needs photos of children of all ages, mothers, fathers, breastfeeding, birthing, education. Model/property release required.

Making Contact & Terms: Interested in receiving work from newer, lesser-known photographers. Please send duplicates of slides. Send 5×7 or 8×10 (preferred) b&w prints by mail for consideration. "Provide a well-organized, carefully packaged submission following our guidelines carefully. Send SASE please." Reports in 2 months. Pays $500/color cover photo; $50 for full page, $35 for less than full page/b&w inside photo. Pays on publication. Credit line given. Buys one-time rights.

Tips: "For cover: we want technically superior, sharply focused image evoking a strong feeling or mood, spontaneous and unposed; unique and compelling. Eye contact with subject will often draw in viewer; color slide only. For inside: b&w prints, sharply focused, action or unposed shots; 'doing' pictures—family, breastfeeding, fathering, midwifery, birth, reading, drawing, crawling, climbing, etc. No disposable diapers, no bottles, no pacifiers. We are being flooded with submissions from photographers acting as their own small stock agency—when the reality is that they are just individual freelancers selling their own work. As a result, we are using fewer photos from just one photographer, giving exposure to more photographers."

*MULTINATIONAL MONITOR, P.O. Box 19405, Washington DC 20036. (202)387-8030. Associate Editor: Holley Knaus. Circ. 3,500. Estab. 1978. Monthly magazine. "We are a political-economic magazine covering operations of multinational corporations." Emphasizes multinational corporate activity. Readers are in business, academia and many are activists. Sample copy free with 8½×11 SAE.

Needs: Uses 12 photos/issue; number of photos supplied by freelancers varies. "We need photos of industry, people, cities, technology, agriculture and many other business related subjects."

Making Contact & Terms: Query with list of stock photo subjects. SASE. Reports in 3 weeks. Pays in copies and in special circumstances will negotiate. Pays on publication. Credit line given. Buys one-time rights.

✤MUSCLE/MAG INTERNATIONAL, 6465 Airport Rd., Mississauga, Ontario L4V 1E4 Canada. (416)678-7311. Fax: (416)796-3563. Editor: Johnny Fitness. Circ. 260,000. Estab. 1974. Monthly magazine. Emphasizes male and female physical development and fitness. Sample copy $5.

Needs: Buys 2,000 photos/year; 50% assigned; 50% stock. Needs celebrity/personality, fashion/beauty, glamour, how-to, human interest, humorous, special effects/experimental and spot news. "We require action exercise photos of bodybuilders and fitness enthusiasts training with sweat and strain." Wants on a regular basis "different" pics of top names, bodybuilders or film stars famous for their physique (i.e., Schwarzenegger, The Hulk, etc.). No photos of mediocre bodybuilders. "They have to be among the top 20 in the world or top film stars exercising." Photos purchased with accompanying ms. Captions preferred.

Making Contact & Terms: Send material by mail for consideration; send $3 for return postage. Uses 8×10 glossy b&w prints. Query with contact sheet. Send 35mm, 2¼×2¼ or 4×5 transparencies; vertical format preferred for cover. Reports in 2-4 weeks. Pays $85-100/hour and $1,000-3,000 per complete package. Pays $15-35/b&w photo; $25-500/color photo; $300-500/cover photo; $85-300/accompanying ms. **Pays on acceptance.** Credit line given. Buys all rights.

Tips: Hulk image. "We would like to see photographers take up the challenge of making exercise photos look like exercise motion." In samples wants to see "sharp, color balanced, attractive subjects, no grain, artistic eye. Someone who can glamorize bodybuilding on film." To break in, "get serious: read, ask questions, learn, experiment and try, try again. Keep trying for improvement—don't kid yourself that you are a good photographer when you don't even understand half the attachments on your camera. Immerse yourself in photography."

*MUSTANG MONTHLY, P.O. Box 7157, Lakeland FL 33807-7157. (813)646-5743. Fax: (813)648-1187. Managing Editor: Rob Reaser. Circ. 80,000. Estab. 1978. Monthly magazine. Emphasizes 1964 through current model Mustangs. Readers are male and female ages 18-65 who span all occupations and income brackets. They have a deep passion for the preservation, restoration and enjoyment of all Mustangs, from the '60s classics to the current models. Free sample copy. Photo guidelines free.
Needs: 15% photos supplied by freelancers. Needs technical "how-to" and feature car photography. "Query first." Reviews photos with or without ms. Special photo needs include 1969-73 and 1979-current model Mustangs. Property release required for feature cars. Captions preferred.
Making Contact & Terms: Interested in receiving work from newer, lesser-known photographers. Currently looking to expand our freelance base. Submit portfolio for review. Query with stock photo list. Send unsolicited photos by mail for consideration. "Anything containing automobile subject matter." Send 35mm, 2¼×2¼, 4×5 transparencies. Does not keep samples on file. SASE. Reports in 1 month. Pays $200-250/color cover photo, $10/b&w inside photo; $150-300/photo/text package. Pays on publication. Credit line given. Buys one-time rights; first N.A. serial rights.
Tips: Wants to see "command of lighting and composition. *Mustang Monthly* is a showcase of the best Mustangs in the world. Photographer should have a working knowledge of Mustangs and automotive photography skills. We feature only pristine and correctly restored cars. Study past issues for style.

NATIONAL GEOGRAPHIC, (Prefers not to share information.)

NATIONAL GEOGRAPHIC TRAVELER, 1145 17th St. NW, Washington DC 20036. Senior Illustrations Editor: Winthrop Scudder. Circ. 850,000+. Bimonthly. Stories focus primarily on the U.S. and Canada with two foreign articles per issue on high interest, readily accessible areas. Minimal emphasis on rugged sporting themes. Occasional photographic essay with no text. Approximately 104 editorial pages, 8½×11, 6-7 articles per issue." Photo guidelines free with SASE. Sample copy available for $3.50 from Robert Dove, National Geographic Society, Gaithersburg MD 20760.
Needs: Uses approximately 80 photos per issue; 95% assigned to freelance photographers. Occasional needs for travel-related stock. Captions required. "Most main features are live assignments. 'Front & Back of the Book' features are using more stock. Ratios are probably 80% live; 20% stock."
Making Contact & Terms: Send only top quality portfolio of not more than 100 images. SASE. Reports in 1 month. Pays $100 minimum/b&w and color inside photo; $250-300/color or b&w page; $500/cover. Pays on publication. Credit line given. Buys one-time world rights. Does not piggyback on other assignments or accept articles previously published or commissioned by other magazines.
Tips: "The best approach is with a good story idea well presented in writing after submitting convincing sample of work. Do *not* telephone. Do not ask for appointment unless your work has been seen. Do not send form letters. We are looking for impact, atmosphere, human interest, involvement and a sense of place. We want pictures that will appeal to and motivate readers to visit the places profiled. *Study the magazine!* Be patient but realistic. Don't underestimate the difficulty or the competition. I'm looking for images that suggest technical ability and a strong aesthetic vision: photos should reflect strong visual architecture (a sense of how to use light and composition along with strong color palette sensibility). Photographs should also show an ability to work well with people."

NATIONAL GEOGRAPHIC WORLD, (Prefers not to share information.)

NATIONAL PARKS MAGAZINE, 1776 Massachusetts Ave. NW, Washington DC 20036. (202)223-6722. Editor: Sue Dodge. Circ. 285,000. Estab. 1919. Bimonthly magazine. Emphasizes the preservation of national parks and wildlife. Sample copy $3. Photo guidelines free with SASE.
Needs: Photos of wildlife and people in national parks, scenics, national monuments, national recreation areas, national seashores, threats to park resources and wildlife. Also seeks mss on national parks, wildlife with accompanying photos.
Making Contact & Terms: Send stock list with example of work if possible. *National Parks* does not accept unsolicited mss. or photos. Uses 4×5 or 35mm transparencies. SASE. Reports in 1 month. Pays $75-150/color photos; $200 full-bleed color covers. Pays on publication. Buys one-time rights.
Tips: "Photographers should be more specific about areas they have covered. We are a specialized publication and are not interested in extensive lists on topics we do not cover. Trends include 'more dramatic pictures.' "

NATIONAL WILDLIFE, 8925 Leesburg Pike, Vienna VA 22184. (703)790-4419. Fax: (703)442-7332. Photo Editor: John Nuhn. Senior Photo Editor: Steve Freligh. Circ. 850,000. Estab. 1962. Bimonthly magazine. Emphasizes wildlife, nature, environment and conservation. Readers are people who enjoy viewing high-quality wildlife and nature images, and who are interested in knowing more about the natural world and man's interrelationship with animals and environment. Sample copy $3; send to National Wildlife Federation Membership Services (same address). Photo guidelines free with SASE. Please keep requests for sample copies and guidelines separate.

Needs: Uses 45 photos/issue; all supplied by freelance photographers; 80% stock, 20% assigned. Needs photos of wildlife, wild plants, nature-related how-to, conservation practices, environmental damage, environmental research, outdoor recreation. Subject needs include single photos for cover possibility (primarily wildlife but also plants, scenics, people); b&w accompanying unique story ideas that have good reason not to be in color. Model release preferred. Captions required.

Making Contact & Terms: Interested in receiving work from newer, lesser-known photographers. Send 35mm, 2¼×2¼, 4×5, 8×10 transparencies (magazine is 95% color) or 8×10 glossy b&w prints by mail for consideration. Query with samples, credits and stock listings. SASE. Reports in 3 weeks. Pays $300-750/b&w inside photo; $800/color cover photo; $300-750/color inside photo; text/photo negotiable. **Pays on acceptance.** Credit line given. Buys one-time rights with limited magazine promotion rights. Previously published work OK.

Tips: Interested in a variety of images that show photographer's scope and specialization, organized in slide sheets, along with tearsheets of previously published work. "Study our magazine; note the types of images we use and send photos equal or better. We look for imagination (common subjects done creatively, different views of animals and plants); technical expertise (proper exposure, focusing, lighting); and the ability to go that one step further and make the shot unique. Think editorially when submitting story, queries or photos; assure that package is complete—sufficient return postage (no checks), proper size return envelope, address inside, and do not submit photos in glass slides, trays or small boxes."

NATURAL HISTORY MAGAZINE, Dept. PM, Central Park W. at 79th St., New York NY 10024. (212)769-5500. Editor: Alan Ternes. Picture Editor: Kay Zakariasen. Circ. 520,000. Monthly magazine. For primarily well-educated people with interests in the sciences. Free photo guidelines.

Needs: Buys 400-450 photos/year. Animal behavior, photo essay, documentary, plant and landscape. Photos used must relate to the social or natural sciences with an ecological framework. Accurate, detailed captions required.

Making Contact & Terms: Query with resume of credits. Uses 8×10 glossy, matte and semigloss b&w prints; and 35mm, 2¼×2¼, 4×5, 6×7 and 8×10 color transparencies. Covers are always related to an article in the issue. SASE. Reports in 2 weeks. Pays $100-350/b&w print, $100-500/color transparency and $500 minimum/cover. Pays on publication. Credit line given. Buys one-time rights. Previously published work OK but must be indicated on delivery memo.

Tips: "Study the magazine—we are more interested in ideas than individual photos. We do not have the time to review portfolios without a specific theme in the social or natural sciences."

NATURAL LIFE MAGAZINE, Dept. PM, 4728 Byrne Rd., Burnaby, British Columbia V5H 3X7 Canada. (604)435-1919. Photo Editor: Siegfried Gursche. Bimonthly magazine. Readers are health and nutrition, lifestyle and fitness oriented. Circ. 110,000. Sample copy $2.50 (Canadian) and 9½×11 SASE. Photo guidelines free with SASE.

Needs: Uses 12 photos/issue; 50% supplied by freelance photographers. Looking for photos of healthy people doing healthy things. Subjects include environment, ecology, organic farming and gardening, herbal therapies, vitamins, mineral supplements and good vegetarian food, all with a family orientation. Model release required. Captions preferred.

Making Contact & Terms: Send unsolicited photos by mail for consideration with resume, business card, brochure, flyer or tearsheets to be kept on file for possible assignments. Send color 4×5 prints and 35mm, 2¼×2¼, or 4×5 transparencies. SASE. Reports in 2 weeks. Pays $125/color cover photo; $60/color inside photo. Pays on publication. Credit line given. Buys all rights; will negotiate. Simultaneous submissions and previously published work OK.

Tips: "Get in touch with the 'Natural Foods' and 'Alternative Therapies' scene. Observe and shoot healthy people doing healthy things."

NATURE PHOTOGRAPHER, P.O. Box 2037, West Palm Beach FL 33402. (407)586-7332. Photo Editor: Helen Longest-Slaughter. Circ. 12,000. Estab. 1990. Bimonthly 4-color and b&w high quality magazine. Emphasizes "conservation-oriented, low-impact nature photography" with strong how-to focus. Readers are male and female nature photographers of all ages. Sample copies free with 10×13 SAE with 6 first-class stamps.

Needs: Uses 25-35 photos/issue; 90% supplied by freelancers. Needs nature shots of "all types—abstracts, animal/wildlife shots, flowers, plants, scenics, etc." Shots must be in natural settings; no setups, zoo or captive animal shots accepted. Reviews photos with or without ms. Captions required;

The maple leaf before a listing indicates that the market is Canadian.

include description of subject, location, type of equipment, how photographed. "This information published with photos."

Making Contact & Terms: Interested in receiving work from newer, lesser-known photographers. Query with resume of credits. Send stock photo list. Provide resume, business card, brochure, flyer or tearsheet to be kept on file for possible assignments. Prefers to see 35mm, 2¼×2¼ and 4×5 transparencies. Does not keep samples on file. SASE. Reports within 4 months, according to deadline. Pays $75/color cover photo; $30-40/color inside photo; $25/b&w inside photo; $75-150/photo/text package. **Pays on acceptance.** Credit line given. Buys one-time rights. Simultaneous submissions and previously published work OK.

Tips: Recommends working with "the best lens you can afford and slow speed slide film." Suggests editing with a 4× or 8× lupe (magnifier) on a light board to check for sharpness, color saturation, etc. Color prints are not used for publication in magazine.

*NATURIST LIFE INTERNATIONAL, 102 Oakwood Dr., S. Burlington VT 05403-6226. Editor-in-chief: Jim C. Cunningham. Circ. 2,000. Estab. 1987. Quarterly magazine. Emphasizes nudism. Readers are male and female nudists, age 30-80. Sample copy $5. Photo guidelines free with SASE.

Needs: Uses approx. 45 photos/issue; 80% supplied by freelancers. Needs photos depicting family-oriented, nudist/naturist work and recreational activity. Reviews photos with or without ms. Model release required. Property release preferred for recognizable nude subjects. Captions preferred.

Making Contact & Terms: Interested in receiving work from newer, lesser-known photographers. Query with resume of credits. Send unsolicited photos by mail for consideration. Provide resume, business card, brochure, flyer or tearsheets to be kept on file for possible assignments. Send 8×10 glossy color and b&w prints; 35mm, 2¼×2¼, 4×5, 8×10 (preferred) transparencies. Does not keep samples on file. SASE. Reports in 1-2 weeks. Pays $50 color photo; $25/color inside photo; $25/b&w inside photo. Only pays $10 if not transparency or 8×10 glossy. Pays on publication. Credit line given. "Prefer to own all rights but some times agree to one-time publication rights."

Tips: "The ideal NLI photo shows ordinary-looking people of all ages doing everyday activities, in the joy of nudism."

*NEIL SPERRY'S GARDENS, P.O. Box 864, McKinney TX 75069. (214)562-5050. Fax: (214)562-5053. Executive Editor: Mike Goldman. Circ. 26,000. Estab. 1986. Monthly magazine. Emphasizes Texas gardening and horticulture. Readers own their homes, are 30-55 years old and in upper income brackets. Sample copies free with 9×12 SASE. Photo guidelines free with SASE.

Needs: Uses 50-60 photos/issue. 85% supplied by freelancers. Needs photos of specific shots of Texas landscapes, plants. Reviews photos with accompanying ms only. Model/property release required. Captions required.

Making Contact & Terms: Interested in receiving work from newer, lesser-known photographers. Provide resume, business card, brochure, flyer or tearsheets to be kept on file for possible future assignments. Keeps samples on file. SASE. Reports in 3 weeeks. NPI. Pays on publication. Credit line given. Buys one-time rights.

Tips: "A good knowledge of horticulture and the specific needs of the Texas gardener must be evident in a photographer's work."

NEVADA MAGAZINE, Capitol Complex, Carson City NV 89710. (702)687-5416. Fax: (702)687-6159. Art Director: Paul Allee. Estab. 1936. Bimonthly. Circ. 130,000. State tourism magazine devoted to promoting tourism in Nevada, particularly for people interested in travel, people, history, events and recreation; age 30-70. Sample copy $1.50.

Needs: Buys 40-50 photos/issue; 30-35 supplied by freelance photographers. Buys 10% freelance on assignment, 20% from freelance stock. (Nevada stock photos only—not generic). Towns and cities, scenics, outdoor recreation with people, events, state parks, tourist attractions, travel, wildlife, ranching, mining and general Nevada life. Must be Nevada subjects. Captions required; include place, date, names if available.

Making Contact & Terms: Interested in receiving work from newer, lesser-known photographers. Send samples of Nevada photos. Send 8×10 glossy prints; 35mm, 2¼×2¼, 4×5, 8×10 transparencies; prefers vertical format for cover. Must be labeled with name, address and captions on each. SASE. Reports in 2-4 months. Pays $20-100/inside photo; $150/cover photo; $50 minimum/job. Pays on publication. Credit line given. Buys first N.A. serial rights.

Tips: "Send variety of good-quality Nevada photos, well-labeled. Self-edit work to 20-40 slides maximum. Increasing use of events photos from prior years' events. Real need for current casino shots. Label each slide or print properly with name, address and caption on each, not on a separate sheet. Send 35mm slides in 8×10 see-through slide sleeves."

NEW AGE JOURNAL, 342 Western Ave., Brighton MA 02135. (617)787-2005. Fax: (617)787-2879. Art Director: Linda Koury. Bimonthly magazine. Emphasizes new age, holistic health, spirituality, psychology, environment. Readers are 75% female. Circ. 160,000. Estab. 1975. Sample copy for $3.95 with SASE.
Needs: Uses 50-70 photos/issue; 75% supplied by freelancers. Needs personality/environmental portraits. Model release required. Captions preferred.
Making Contact & Terms: Interested in receiving work from newer, lesser-known photographers. Send unsolicited photos by mail for consideration. Provide resume, business card, brochure, flyer or tearsheets to be kept on file for possible assignments. Keeps samples on file. SASE. Pays $750-1,000/color cover photo; $300-700/color inside photo; $75-300/b&w inside photo. Pays on publication. Credit line given. Buys one-time rights. Simultaneous submissions and previously published work OK.
Tips: In samples wants to see dramatic environmental portraits. "We shoot a lot of people—photographer needs to capture attitude or personality of subject or setting. Send promo pieces that can be kept on file."

*NEW CHOICES FOR RETIREMENT LIVING, 28 W. 23rd St., New York NY 10010. (212)366-8817. Fax: (212)366-8899. Photo Editor: Christine Cancelli. Circ. 575,000. Estab. 1989. Monthly magazine. Emphasizes people over 50, retired or planning to retire. Readers are 50 plus years old, male and female, interested in retirement living.
Needs: Uses 40-50 photos/issue; 50% supplied by freelancers; 50% supplied by stock. Needs photos related to medical, food, money, environmental, travel, health and fitness. Reviews photos with or without ms. "No unsolicited photos please!" Model release required; property release preferred. Captions preferred.
Making Contact & Terms: Interested in receiving work from newer, lesser-known photographers. Provide resume, business card, brochure, flyer or tearsheets to be kept on file for possible assignments. Reports in 1 month. Pays $200/¼ color page rate; $150/¼ b&w page rate. **Pays on acceptance** and assignment within 30 days. Credit line given. Buys one-time rights; negotiable. Previously published work OK.
Tips: "I look for people in photos, a photojournalistic approach, but also a personal style. No landscapes, architecture or interiors without people. Respect portfolio review/submission guidelines of the people you contact. If you don't know what they are, call and ask, then comply with answer."

*NEW JERSEY MONTHLY, P.O. Box 920, 55 Park Place, Morristown NJ 07963. (201)539-8230. Fax: (201)538-2953. Art Director: Susan Amirian. Circ. 100,000. Monthly magazine. Emphasizes New Jersey.
Needs: Uses 20 photos/issue all supplied by freelancers. Special photo needs include New Jersey special interest, travel, politics, sports, entertainment, fashion.
Making Contact & Terms: Interested in receiving work from newer, lesser-known photographers. Submit potfolio for review. Query with stock photo list. Send unsolicited photos by mail. Provide resume, business card, brochure, flyer or tearsheets to be kept on file for possible future assignments. Send 35mm transparencies. Keeps samples on file. SASE. Reports in 1 month. NPI. **Pays on acceptance.** Credit line given. Buys one-time rights; negotiable. Previously published work OK.

NEW MEXICO MAGAZINE, Dept. PM, 495 Old Sante Fe Trail, Santa Fe NM 87503. (505)827-7447. Fax: (505)827-6496. Art Director: John Vaughan. Circ. 123,000. Monthly magazine. For affluent people age 35-65 interested in the Southwest or who have lived in or visited New Mexico. Sample copy $2.95 with 9×12 SASE and 75¢ postage. Photo guidelines free with SASE.
Needs: Uses about 60 photos/issue; 90% supplied by freelancers. Needs New Mexico photos only—landscapes, people, events, architecture, etc. "Most work is done on assignment in relation to a story, but we welcome photo essay suggestions from photographers." Cover photos usually relate to the main feature in the magazine. Model release preferred. Captions required; include who, what, where. Buys 40 photos/issue; 70% on assignment, 30% on stock.
Making Contact & Terms: Interested in receiving work from newer, lesser-known photographers. Submit portfolio to John Vaughan; uses transparencies. SASE. Pays $350/day; $150/color cover photo; $150/b&w cover photo; $50-90 color inside photo; $50-90/b&w inside photo. Pays on publication. Credit line given. Buys one-time rights.
Tips: Prefers transparencies submitted in plastic pocketed sheets. Interested in different viewpoints, styles not necessarily obligated to straight scenic. "All material must be taken in New Mexico. Representative work suggested. If photographers have a preference about what they want to do or where they're going, we would like to see that in their work. Transparencies or dupes are best for review and handling purposes."

NEW MEXICO PHOTOGRAPHER, Dept. PM, Box 2582–ENMU, Portales NM 88130. (505)562-2253. Publisher: Wendel Sloan. Biennial magazine. Emphasizes high-quality b&w photography taken anywhere in the world. Readers are photographers and patrons of high-quality photography. Circ. 2,000. Estab. 1989. Sample copy for $3. Photo guidelines free with SASE.
Needs: Uses 50 photos/issue; 100% supplied by freelancers. "We are devoted to all subject matters from b&w photographers everywhere." Likes to see seasonal photos for summer and winter issues; deadlines–April 15, October 15. Model release and captions preferred.
Making Contact & Terms: Send unsolicited b&w prints by mail for consideration. "Photos need not be mounted. However, the technical quality needs to be faultless. We've rejected great photos because of dust, water spots, etc." SASE. Reports after selections made, prior to publication. Photos selected on basis of semi-annual contest; photos are published and cash prizes also offered. Credit line given. Buys one-time rights. Simultaneous submissions and previously published work OK.
Tips: "Since we run very little advertising, we sponsor a contest for each issue to help pay for publication of the magazine. A $5 entry is charged for each entry, and all entrants in photo contest receive a copy of the magazine. Don't be fooled by our name. Although we do publish a lot of photography with a 'Southwestern' feel, *original* photography from anywhere excites us."

NEW YORK MAGAZINE, 755 Second Ave., New York NY 10017. (212)880-0829. Editor: Edward Kosner. Photography Director: Jordan Schaps. Picture Editor: Susan Vermazen. Circ. 430,000. Estab. 1968. Weekly magazine. Full service city magazine: national and local news, fashion, food, entertaining, lifestyle, design, profiles, etc. Readers are 28-55 years average with $90,000+ average family income. Professional people, family people, concerned with quality of life and social issues affecting them, their families and the community. Sample copy free with SASE.
Needs: Uses about 50 photos/issue; 85% assigned; 15% stock. Needs full range: photojournalism, fashion, food, product still lifes, conceptual and stock (occasionally). Always need great product still life, and studio work. "Model release and captions preferred for professional models; require model release for 'real' people." Captions required.
Making Contact & Terms: Arrange a personal interview to show portfolio. Submit portfolio for review, "as this is a *fast* paced weekly, phone appointments are *essential*, time permitting." Drop-offs, every Thursday. *Does not return unsolicited material.* Reports ASAP. Pays $1,000/color cover photo; $300/page of color; $125-200/photo spot; $150-300/b&w and color photo; $300/day. Pays on publication and receipt of original invoices. Credit line given. Buys one-time rights. "We reserve the right to reuse photography in context for house ads and self-promotion at no additional charge."
Tips: "We look for strong high-quality images that work with the text but tell their own story as well. We want the kind of photographer who can deliver images whether on his own or with spirited direction. You need to really get to know the magazine and its various departments ('Intelligencer,' 'Fast Track,' 'Hot Line,' 'Best Bets,' etc.) as well as the way we do fashion, entertaining, lifestyle, etc. *New York* is a great showcase for the talented newcomer looking for prestige exposure, the solid working photojournalist and the well-established advertising specialist looking for the creative freedom to do our kind of work. We lean toward traditional high-quality photographic solutions to our visual needs, but are ever mindful of and sensitive to the trends and directions in which photography is moving. Freelancers interested in working with us should: 1) make an appointment; 2) be prompt; 3) have materials geared to what we need and what you'd like to do in our pages; 4) leave a photo image with phone number; 5) not call frequently asking for work; 6) remember that this is a fast-paced weekly magazine. We're courteous, but on constant deadline."

NEW YORK OUTDOORS, 51 Atlantic Ave., Floral Park NY 11001. (516)352-9700. Fax: (516)437-6841. Editor: Gary P. Joyce. Associate Editor: Karen L. Silver. Published bimonthly. Covers the entire gamut of outdoor participatory recreation.
Needs: Quality "adventure" sports photography. Photos purchased with accompanying ms; cover and other purchased separately. Captions required.
Making Contact & Terms: Queries preferred. Send original transparencies. SASE. Reports in 3 weeks. Pay rates for color: $250/cover; $100/full page; $75/three quarter page; $50/half page; $25/quarter page. B&w flat rate $25. Pays on publication. Buys first N.A. serial rights.
Tips: "We're a regional with emphasis on New York action. Cover New Jersey, Connecticut, Rhode Island and Pennsylvania as well. Well stocked on fishing/hunting, interested in everything else relating to active outdoor sports."

NORTHERN OHIO LIVE, Dept. PM, 11320 Juniper Rd., Cleveland OH 44106. (216)721-1800. Art Director: Michael Wainey. Circ. 35,000. Estab. 1980. Monthly magazine. Emphasizes arts, entertainment, lifestyle and fashion. Readers are upper income, ages 25-60, professionals. Sample copy $2 with 9×12 SAE.
Needs: Uses 30 photos/issue; 20-100% supplied by freelance photographers. Needs photos of people in different locations, fashion and locale. Model release preferred. Captions preferred (names only is usually OK).

Making Contact & Terms: Arrange a personal interview to show portfolio. Send b&w and color prints; 35mm or 2¼ × 2¼ transparencies by mail for consideration. Provide resume, business card, brochure, flyer or tearsheet to be kept on file for possible assignments. Follow up phone call OK. SASE. Reports in 3 weeks. Pays $250/color cover photo; $250/b&w cover photo; $100/color inside photo; $50/b&w inside photo; $30-50/hour; $250-500/day. Pays on publication. Credit line given. Buys one-time rights. Previously published work OK.

Tips: In photographer's portfolio wants to see "good portraits, people on location, photojournalism strengths, quick turn-around and willingness to work on *low* budget. Mail sample of work, follow up with phone call. Portfolio review should be short — only *best quality* work!"

*NORTHWEST PARKS AND WILDLIFE, P.O. Box 18000, 1525 12th St., Florence OR 97439. (800)348-8401. Photo Coordinator: Barbara Grano. Circ. 20,000. Estab. 1991. Bimonthly magazine. Emphasizes state and national parks in Pacific Northwest — Oregon, Washington, Idaho, Alaska, Montana, Wyoming and British Columbia (southern). Readers are middle-age male and female, upper income/middle income. Sample copy $2.95 + $1.50 postage. Photo guidelines free with SASE.

Needs: Uses 8-12 (full page) photos/issue; all supplied by freelancers. Plans to publish b&w photo essays in the future. Needs photos of travel, scenics. Model release preferred. Photo captions required.

Making Contact & Terms: Send unsolicited photos by mail for consideration. Uses 35mm, 2¼ × 2¼, 4 × 5 transparencies. SASE. Reports in 1 month. Pays $250/color cover photo; $25-50/color inside photo; $25-50/b&w inside photo; $100-250/photo/text package. Pays on publication. Credit line given. Buys one-time rights.

Tips: "Mainly interested in scenics. Avoid colored filters. Use only film that can enlarge without graininess."

NORTHWEST TRAVEL, P.O. Box 18000, 1525 12th St., Florence OR 97439. (800)348-8401. Photo Coordinator: Barbara Grano. Circ. 50,000. Estab. 1991. Bimonthly magazine. Emphasizes Pacific Northwest travel — Oregon, Washington, Idaho and British Columbia (southern). Readers are middle-age male and female, upper income/middle income. Sample copy $2.95 + $1.50 postage. Photo guidelines free with SASE.

Needs: Uses 8-12 (full page) photos/issue; all supplied by freelancers. Needs photos of travel, scenics. Model release preferred. Photo captions required.

Making Contact & Terms: Send unsolicited photos by mail for consideration. Uses 35mm, 2¼ × 2¼, 4 × 5 transparencies. SASE. Reports in 1 month. Pays $250/color cover photo; $25-50/color inside photo; $25-50/b&w inside photo; $100-250/photo/text package. Pays on publication. Credit line given. Buys one-time rights.

Tips: "Mainly interested in scenics. Avoid colored filters. Use only film that can enlarge without graininess."

NUGGET, Suite 600, 2600 Douglas Rd., Coral Gables FL 33134. (305)443-2378. Editor-in-Chief: Christopher James. Circ. 100,000. Magazine published 8 times a year. Emphasizes sex and fetishism for men and women of all ages. Sample copy $5 postpaid; photo guidelines free with SASE.

Needs: Uses 100 photos/issue. Interested only in nude sets — single woman, female/female or male/female. All photo sequences should have a fetish theme (sadomasochism, leather, bondage, transvestism, transsexuals, lingerie, infantilism, wrestling — female/female or male/female — women fighting women or women fighting men, amputee models, etc.). Also seeks accompanying mss on sex, fetishism and sex-oriented products. Model release required.

Making Contact & Terms: Submit material for consideration. Buys in sets, not by individual photos. No Polaroids or amateur photography. Send 8 × 10 glossy b&w prints, contact sheet OK; transparencies, prefers Kodachrome or large format; vertical format required for cover. SASE. Reports in 2 weeks. Pays $250 minimum/b&w set; $300-400/color set; $200/cover photo; $250-350/ms. Pays on publication. Credit line given. Buys one-time rights or second serial (reprint) rights. Previously published work OK.

ODYSSEY, Science That's Out of This World, 7 School St., Peterborough NH 03458. (603)924-7209. Fax: (603)924-7380. Picture Editor: Francelle Carapetyan. Circ. 60,000. Estab. 1979. Monthly magazine. Emphasis on astronomy and space exploration. Readers are children, ages 8-15. Sample copy $3.95 with 8 × 11 or larger SAE and 5 first-class stamps. Photo guidelines available.

Needs: Uses 30-35 photos/issue. Needs photos of astronomy and space exploration from NASA and observatories, museum shots and others illustrating activities from various organizations. Reviews photos with or without ms. Model/property release required. Captions preferred.

Making Contact & Terms: Query with stock photo list. Send unsolicited photos by mail for consideration. Provide resume, business card, brochure, flyer or tearsheets to be kept on file for possible future assignments. Send color prints or transparencies. Samples kept on file. SASE. Reports in 1 month. Pays on individual basis/color cover photo; $25-75/inside color rate. Pays on publication. Credit line given. Buys one-time and all rights; negotiable.

Tips: "We like photos that include kids in reader-age range and plenty of action. Each issue is devoted to a single theme. Photos should relate to those themes."

OHIO FISHERMAN, 1432 Parsons Ave., Columbus OH 43207. (614)445-7506. Editor: Dan Armitage. Monthly. Circ. 41,000. Estab. 1974. Emphasizes fishing. Readers are the Buckeye State anglers. Sample copy and photo guidelines free with SASE.
Needs: Uses 10 covers/year supplied by freelance photographers. Needs transparencies for cover; 99% used are verticals with as much free space on top and left side of frame as possible. Fish and fishermen (species should be common to coverage area) action preferred. Photos purchased with or without accompanying ms. Model and property releases preferred; required for covers. Captions preferred.
Making Contact & Terms: Query with tearsheets or send unsolicited photos by mail for consideration. Requires 35mm transparencies. SASE. Reports in 1 month. Provide tearsheets to be kept on file for possible future assignments. Pays $200/color cover. Pays 15th of month prior to issue date. Credit line given. Buys one-time rights.
Tips: In reviewing photographs looks for clarity, action, color and suitability of format. "Study our covers to know where we need space for logos and cover blurbs. Don't give up easily, it sometimes takes a number of tries before you hit the right photo for us, as our needs are very specific."

OHIO MAGAZINE, 62 E. Broad St., Columbus OH 43215. (614)461-5083. Contact: Brooke Wenstrup. Estab. 1979. Monthly magazine. Emphasizes features throughout Ohio for an educated, urban and urbane readership. Sample copy $3 postpaid.
Needs: Travel, photo essay/photo feature, b&w scenics, personality, sports and spot news. Photojournalism and concept-oriented studio photography. Model/property releases preferred. Captions required.
Making Contact & Terms: Interested in receiving work from newer, lesser-known photographers. Send material by mail for consideration. Query with samples. Arrange a personal interview to show a portfolio. Send 8×10 b&w glossy prints; contact sheet requested. Also uses 35mm, 2¼×2¼ or 4×5 transparencies; square format preferred for covers. SASE. Reports in 1 month. Pays $30-250/b&w photo; $30-250/color photo; $350/day; and $150-350/job. Pays within 90 days after acceptance. Credit line given. Buys one-time rights; negotiable.
Tips: "Please look at magazine before submitting to get an idea what type of photographs we use." Send sheets of slides and/or prints with return postage and they will be reviewed. Dupes for our files are always appreciated—and reviewed on a regular basis. We are leaning more toward well-done documentary photography and less toward studio photography. Trends in our use of editorial photography include scenics, single photos that can support an essay, photo essays on cities/towns, more use of 180° shots. In reviewing a photographer's portfolio or samples we look for humor, insight, multi-level photos, quirkiness, thoughtfulness; stock photos of Ohio; ability to work with subjects (i.e., an obvious indication that the photographer was able to make subject relax and forget the camera—even difficult subjects); ability to work with givens, bad natural light, etc.; creativity on the spot—as we can't always tell what a situation will be on location."

OLD WEST, P.O. Box 2107, Stillwater OK 74076. (405)743-3370. Fax: (405)743-3374. Editor: John Joerschke. Circ. 30,000. Estab. 1964. Quarterly magazine. Emphasizes history of the Old West (1830 to 1915). Readers are people who like to read the history of the West, mostly male, age 45 and older. Sample copy free with 9×12 SAE and $2 postage.
Needs: Uses 100 or more photos/issue; "almost all" supplied by freelance photographers. Needs "mostly Old West historical subjects, some travel, some scenic (ghost towns, old mining camps, historical sites). Prefers to have accompanying ms. Special needs include western wear, cowboys, rodeos, western events. Captions required; include name and location of site.
Making Contact & Terms: Interested in receiving work from newer, lesser-known photographers. Query with samples, b&w only for inside, color covers. SASE. Reports in 1 month. Pays $75-150/color cover photos; $10/b&w inside photos. **Payment on acceptance;** cover photos on publication. Credit line given. Buys first N.A. serial rights.
Tips: "Looking for transparencies of existing artwork as well as scenics for covers, pictures that tell stories associated with Old West for the inside. Most of our photos are used to illustrate stories and come with manuscripts; however, we will consider other work (scenics, historical sites, old houses). Scenics should be free of modern intrusions such as buildings, power line, highways, etc."

OMNI MAGAZINE, 1965 Broadway, New York NY 10023. (212)496-6100. Art Director: Dwayne Flinchum. Monthly magazine. Emphasizes science. Circ. 850,000. Estab. 1978. Sample copy for contributors only (free). Photo guidelines free with SASE.
Needs: Uses 20-30 photos/issue; 100% supplied by freelancers. Needs photos of technology and portraiture. Mostly scientific or special-effect, "surreal" photography. Model/property release required. Captions preferred.

Making Contact & Terms: Send unsolicited photos by mail for consideration. Provide resume, business card, brochure, flyer or tearsheets to be kept on file for possible assignments. Send any format. Keeps samples on file. SASE. Reports in 1-2 weeks. Pays $800/color cover photo; $500/b&w cover photo; pays $300/color inside photo; $225/b&w inside photo; $450/color page rate; $350/b&w page rate; $500/day; $500-2,000/photo/text package. Pays on publication. Credit line given on opening spreads only. Buys one-time rights. Rights negotiable. Previously published work OK.

Tips: "We are always seeking surreal, graphic images for our cover, which are upbeat and will function well commercially on the newsstand. Have an understanding of our needs. Research our past 3 issues for an idea of what we commission. We assign a great deal of portraiture of leading scientists."

ON THE LINE, 616 Walnut Ave., Scottdale PA 15683. (412)887-8500. Contact: Editor. Circ. 8,500. Estab. 1875. Weekly magazine. For children, ages 10-14. Free sample copy and editorial guidelines.

Needs: Very little photography from assignment and 95%+ from freelance stock. "We need quality b&w photos only. Prefers vertical shots, use some horizontal. We need photos of children, age 10-14 representing a balance of male/female, white/minority/international, urban/country. Clothing and hair styles must be contemporary, but not faddish. Wants to see children interacting with each other, with adults and with animals. Some nature scenes as well (especially with kids)."

Making Contact & Terms: Send 8×10 b&w prints for consideration. SASE. Reports in 1 month. Pays $20-50/b&w (cover). **Pays on acceptance.** Buys one-time rights. Simultaneous submissions and previously published work OK.

© J.C. Allen and Son

Photographer Chester Allen of West Lafayette, Indiana, thought a young girl sitting on a wood fence holding a baby pig would make a nice photo portraying love for animals. But when the pig "kissed" the child on the cheek while squirming to break free the shutter captured a magical moment. After leafing through the Photographer's Market to find a buyer, Allen sold the shot to On the Line.

ON-DIRT MAGAZINE, P.O. Box 6246, Woodland Hills CA 91365. (818)340-5750. Fax: (818)348-4648. Photo Editor: Lonnie Peralta. Circ. 120,000. Estab. 1984. Monthly magazine. Emphasizes all forms of off-roading and racing. Readers are male and female off-road enthusiasts, ages 15-65. Sample copy $3.

Needs: Uses 100-135 photos/issue; 50% supplied by freelancers. Needs photos of off-road action from events, races or fun. Reviews photos with or without a manuscript. Special needs are "fun" drives, "jamborees" and how-to articles with photos. Model/property release preferred. Captions required.

Making Contact & Terms: Send unsolicited photos by mail for consideration. Send 5×7, 8×10 glossy with border b&w, color prints; 35mm transparencies. Keeps samples on file. SASE. Reports as needed. Pays $50/cover photo; $7/b&w inside photo; $7/color page rate; $7/b&w page rate; $7/hour. Pays on publication. Credit line given. Buys all rights; negotiable.

♦**ONTARIO OUT OF DOORS MAGAZINE,** 227 Front St. E., Toronto, Ontario M5A 1E8 Canada. (416)368-0185. Fax: (416)941-9113. Art Director: Yukio Yamada. Circ. 85,000. Estab. 1968. Monthly magazine. Emphasizes hunting and fishing in Ontario. Readers are male ages 20-65. Sample copies free with SAE, IRC. Photo guidelines free with SAE, IRC.
Needs: Uses 30 photos/issue; 50% supplied by freelancers, half on assignment, half from stock. Needs photos of game and fish species sought in Ontario; also scenics with anglers or hunters. Model/property releases required for photos used in advertising. Captions preferred.
Making Contact & Terms: Interested in receiving work from newer, lesser-known photographers. Query with list of stock photo subjects. Send b&w prints; 35mm transparencies. Keeps samples on file. Reports in 1 month. Pays $300-500/color cover photo; $100-200/color inside photo; $35-75/b&w inside photo. **Pays on acceptance.** Credit line given. Buys one-time rights. Previously published work OK.

OPEN WHEEL MAGAZINE, P.O. Box 715, 27 S. Main St., Ipswich MA 01938. (508)356-7030. Fax: (508)356-2492. Editor: Dick Berggren. Circ. 100,000. Estab. 1981. Monthly. Emphasizes sprint car, supermodified, Indy and midget racing. Readers are fans, owners and drivers of race cars and those with business in racing. Photo guidelines free for SASE.
Needs: Uses 100-125 photos/issue supplied by freelance photographers; almost all come from freelance stock. Needs documentary, portraits, dramatic racing pictures, product photography, special effects, crash. Photos purchased with or without accompanying ms. Model release required for photos not shot in pit, garage or on track. Captions required.
Making Contact & Terms: Send by mail for consideration 8×10 glossy b&w or color prints and any size slides. Kodachrome 64 preferred. SASE. Reports in 6 weeks. Pays $20/b&w inside; $35-250/color inside. Pays on publication. Buys all rights.
Tips: "Send the photos. We get dozens of inquiries but not enough pictures. We file everything that comes in and pull 80% of the pictures used each issue from those files. If it's on file, the photographer has a good shot."

OREGON COAST MAGAZINE, P.O. Box 18000, Florence OR 97439. (800)348-8401. Photo Coordinator: Barbara Grano. Circ. 62,000+. Estab. 1982. Bimonthly magazine. Emphasizes Oregon coast life. Readers are middle class, middle age. Sample copy $2.95 and $1.50 postage. Photo guidelines available with SASE with 52¢.
Needs: Uses 6-10 photos/issue; all supplied by freelancers. Needs scenics. Especially needs photos of typical subjects—waves, beaches, lighthouses—but from a different angle. Model release required. Captions required; include specific location and description. "Label all slides and transparencies with captions and photographer's name."
Making Contact & Terms: Interested in receiving work from newer, lesser-known photographers. Send unsolicited 35mm, 2¼×2¼, 4×5 transparencies by mail for consideration. SASE. Reports in 1 month. Pays $250/color cover photo; pays $100 for calendar usage; pays $25-50/color inside photo; $25-50/b&w inside photo; $100-250/photo/text package. Credit line given. Buys one-time rights.
Tips: "Send only the very best. Use only slide film that can be enlarged without graininess. An appropriate submission would be 20-60 slides. Don't use color filters. Protect slides with sleeves-put in plastic holders. Don't send in little boxes."

*****ORGANIC GARDENING,** 33 E. Minor St., Emmaus PA 18098. (215)967-8770. Fax: (215)967-8956. Photo Editor: Rob Cardillo. Circ. 800,000. Magazine publishes 9 issues/year. Emphasizes the entire range of gardening topics: annual/perennial flowers, vegetables, herbs, shrubs, trees/vines. Free photo guidelines/want lists with SASE.
Needs: Uses 80-100 photos/issue; 50% supplied by freelance photographers. Needs garden plants, close-ups of perfect, disease-free vegetables, fruits, nuts, herbs, and ornamentals growing in the garden; gardening techniques, organic methods in use (i.e. straw-mulched potatoes, row-covered winter squash, companion planting, plant protection); gardening activities, real gardeners performing various gardening tasks (i.e. turning compost, harvesting rutabagas, planting peas, dividing perennials, picking cherries, weeding, etc.). "These images are highly desired and often end up on a cover;" and garden wildlife, beneficial and pest insects in all stages, cats, dogs, gophers, moles, deer, frogs, birds, raccoons, etc. in recognizable garden settings. Model release required. Captions (as to species and variety) required.

Market conditions are constantly changing! If you're still using this book and it's 1995 or later, buy the newest edition of Photographer's Market *at your favorite bookstore or order directly from* Writer's Digest Books.

Making Contact & Terms: "Submissions should be sent in clear plastic slide pages with each item identified as to subject and photographer." Uses 35mm and larger transparencies (prefer Kodachrome or Fujichrome). Pays $75/quarter page; $125/half page; $200/page; $300/double page; $600/cover shot. Pays on publication. Credit line given. Buys one-time rights.

Tips: "Shoot using the entire range of lighting (especially early morning and late afternoon), under all weather conditions (after a frost or late spring snow, during a summer shower or early morning mist). Vary camera angles and focal lengths." To break in, "know the subject thoroughly. Know how to shoot people as well as plants. Don't shoot at high noon!"

THE OTHER SIDE, 300 W. Apsley St., Philadelphia PA 19144. (215)849-2178. Art Director: Cathleen Benberg. Circ. 12,000. Estab. 1965. Bimonthly magazine. Emphasizes social justice issues from a Christian perspective. Sample copy $2.

Needs: Buys 6 photos/issue; 95-100% from stock, 0-5% on assignment. Documentary, human interest and photo essay/photo feature. "We're interested in human-interest photos and photos that relate to current social, economic or political issues, both here and in the Third World." Model/property release preferred. Captions preferred.

Making Contact & Terms: Interested in receiving work from newer, lesser-known photographers. Send samples of work to be photocopied for our files and/or photos; a list of subjects is difficult to judge quality of work by. Send 8 × 10 glossy b&w prints; transparencies for cover, vertical format required. Materials will be returned on request. SASE. Pays $20-30/b&w photo; $50-100/cover photo. Credit line given. Buys one-time rights. Simultaneous submissions and previously published work OK.

Tips: In reviewing photographs/samples, looks for "sensitivity to subject and good quality darkroom work."

🍁**OUR FAMILY**, P.O. Box 249, Battleford Sasketchewan, S0M 0E0 Canada. Fax: (306)937-7644. Editor: Nestor Gregoire. Circ. 10,000. Estab. 1949. Monthly magazine. Emphasizes Christian faith as a part of daily living for Roman Catholic families. Sample copy $2.50 with 9 × 12 SAE and $1.08 Canadian postage. Free photo and writer's guidelines with SAE and 49¢ Canadian postage.

Needs: Buys 5 photos/issue; cover by assignment, contents all freelance. Head shot (to convey mood); human interest ("people engaged in the various experiences of living"); humorous ("anything that strikes a responsive chord in the viewer"); photo essay/photo feature (human/religious themes); and special effects/experimental (dramatic—to help convey a specific mood). "We are always in need of the following: family (aspects of family life); couples (husband and wife interacting and interrelating or involved in various activities); teenagers (in all aspects of their lives and especially in a school situation); babies and children; any age person involved in service to others; individuals in various moods (depicting the whole gamut of human emotions); religious symbolism; and humor. We especially want people photos, but we do not want the posed photos that make people appear 'plastic,' snobbish or elite. In all photos, the simple, common touch is preferred. We are especially in search of humorous photos (human and animal subjects). Stick to the naturally comic, whether it's subtle or obvious." Photos are purchased with or without accompanying ms. Model release required if editorial topic might embarrass subject. Captions required when photos accompany ms.

Making Contact & Terms: Send material by mail for consideration or query with samples after consulting photo spec sheet. Provide letter of inquiry, samples and tearsheets to be kept on file for possible future assignments. Send 8 × 10 glossy b&w prints; transparencies or 8 × 10 glossy color prints are used on inside pages, but are converted to b&w. SAE and IRC. (Personal check or money order OK instead or IRC.) Reports in 4 weeks. Pays $35/b&w photo; 7-10¢/word for original mss; 5¢/word for nonoriginal mss. **Pays on acceptance.** Credit line given. Buys one-time rights and simultaneous rights. Simultaneous submissions or previously published work OK.

Tips: "Send us a sample (20-50 photos) of your work after reviewing our Photo Spec Sheet. Looks for "photos that center around family life—but in the broad sense — i.e., our elderly parents, teenagers, young adults, family activities. Our covers (full color) are a specific assignment. We do not use freelance submissions for our cover."

*OUT MAGAZINE, Suite 800, 110 Greene St., New York NY 10012. (212)334-9119. Fax: (212)334-9227. Art Director: James Conrad. Circ. 150,000. Estab. 1992. Bimonthly magazine. Emphasizes gay and lesbian lifestyle. Readers are gay men and lesbians of all ages.

Needs: Uses 100 photos/issue; 50 supplied by freelancers. Needs photos of portraits, fashion, photojournalism. Reviews photos with or without ms. Model release required. Captions preferred.

Making Contact & Terms: Interested in receiving work from newer, lesser-known photographers. Submit portfolio for review. Send any size color and b&w prints; 35mm, 2¼ × 2¼, 4 × 5, 8 × 10 transparencies. Does not keep samples on file. SASE. Reports in 1 month. NPI. Pays on publication. Credit line given. Buys all rights; negotiable. Simultaneous submissions and/or previously published work OK.

Tips: "Don't ask to see layout. Don't call every 5 minutes. Turn over large portion of film."

★**OUTDOOR CANADA,** Suite 202, 703 Evans Ave., Toronto, Ontario M9C 5E9 Canada. (416)695-0311. Editor: Teddi Brown. Circ. 125,000. Estab. 1972. Magazine published 9 times a year. Free writers' and photographers' guidelines "with SASE or SAE and IRC only."
Needs: Buys 70-80 photos annually. Needs Canadian photos of people fishing, hunting, hiking, wildlife, cross-country skiing. Action shots. Captions required including identification of fish, bird or animal.
Making Contact & Terms: Interested in receiving work from newer, lesser-known photographers. Send transparencies for consideration. No phone calls, please. For cover allow undetailed space along left side of photo for cover lines. SAE and IRC for American contributors, SASE for Canadians *must* be sent for return of materials. Reports in 3 weeks; "acknowledgement of receipt is sent the same day material is received." Pays $400 maximum/cover photo; $30-225/inside color photo depending on size used. Pays on publication. Buys first serial rights.
Tips: "Study the magazine and see the type of articles we use and the types of illustration used" and send a number of pictures to facilitate selection. "We are using more photos. We are looking for pictures that tell a story. We also need photos of people in the outdoors. A photo that captures the outdoor experience and shows the human delight in it. Take more fishing photos. It's the fastest-growing outdoor pastime in North America."

OUTDOOR LIFE MAGAZINE, Dept. PM, 2 Park Ave., New York NY 10016. (212)779-5000. Art Director: Connie Lesko. Circ. 1,500,000. Monthly. Emphasizes hunting, fishing, shooting, camping and boating. Readers are "outdoorsmen of all ages." Sample copy "not for individual requests." Photo guidelines free with SASE.
Needs: Uses about 50-60 photos/issue; 75% supplied by freelance photographers. Needs photos of "all species of wildlife and fish, especially in action and in natural habitat; how-to and where-to." Captions preferred.
Making Contact & Terms: Send 5×7 or 8×10 b&w glossy prints; 35mm or 2¼×2¼ transparencies; b&w contact sheet by mail for consideration. No color prints—preferably Kodachrome 35mm slides." No duplicates. SASE. Reports in 1 month. Pays $35-275/b&w photo, $50-700/color photo depending on size of photos; $800-1,000/cover photo. Rates are negotiable. Pays on publication. Credit line given. Buys one-time rights.
Tips: "Have name and address clearly printed on each photo to insure return, send in 8×10 plastic sleeves. Multi subjects encouraged."

OUTDOOR PHOTOGRAPHER, Suite 1220, 12121 Wilshire Blvd., Los Angeles CA 90025. (310)820-1500. Art Director: Kurt R. Smith. Magazine published 10 times per year. Emphasizes professional and semi-professional scenic, travel, wildlife and sports photography. Readers are photographers of all ages and interests. Circ. 200,000+. Photo guidelines free with SASE.
Needs: Uses about 50-60 photos/issue; 90% supplied by freelance photographers. Model release and captions preferred.
Making Contact & Terms: Query with samples; send b&w prints or color transparencies by mail for consideration. SASE. Reports in 60 days. NPI. Payment for cover photos, inside photos and text/photo package to be arranged. Pays on publication. Credit line given. Buys one-time rights but will negotiate. Previously published work OK.

***OUTDOOR TRAVELER MID-ATLANTIC REGION,** P.O. Box 1788, Charlottesville VA 22902. (804)973-3952. Fax: (804)978-7449. Editor: Marianne Marks. Circ. 30,000. Estab. 1993. Quarterly magazine. Emphasizes outdoor recreation, travel, nature—all in the mid-Atlantic region. Readers are male and female outdoor enthusiasts and travelers, ages 20-50. Sample copy $3.
Needs: Uses 35 photos/issue; 95% supplied by freelancers. Needs photos of nature/wildlife, travel, scenics, outdoor recreation—all in the region. Reviews photos with or without ms. Special photo needs include seasonal photos related to outdoor recreation and scenery. Model release required. Property release is preferred. Captions required.
Making Contact & Terms: Interested in receiving work from newer, lesser-known photographers. Query with resume of credits. Keeps samples on file. SASE. Reports in 1-2 months. Pays $250/color cover photo; $15-50/color inside photo. Pays on publication. Credit line given. Buys one-time rights. Simultaneous submissions and previously published work OK.
Tips: Interested in "action-oriented, scenic photos of people engage in outdoor recreation (hiking, bicycling, skiing, rafting, canoeing, rock climbing, etc.)."

★**OWL MAGAZINE,** Suite 306, 56 The Esplanade, Toronto, Ontario M5E 1A7 Canada. (416)868-6001. Fax: (416)868-6009. Photo Researcher: Robin Wilner. Circ. 110,000. Estab. 1976. Published 10 times/year; 1 summer issue. A science and nature magazine for children ages 8-13. Sample copy $4.28 (incl. GST) and 9×12 SAE. Photo guidelines free with SAE.

Needs: Uses approximately 15 photos/issue; 10% supplied by freelancers. Needs photos of animals/ wildlife. Model/property release preferred. Captions required.

Making Contact & Terms: Request photo package before sending photos for review. Send 35mm transparencies. Keeps samples on file. SAE and IRCs. Reports in 6-8 weeks. Pays $325 Canadian/ color cover photo; $100 Canadian/color inside photo; $200 Canadian/color page rate. **Pays on acceptance.** Credit line given. Buys one-time rights. Previously published work OK.

Tips: "Photos should be sharply focused with good lighting showing animals in their natural environment. It is important that you present your work as professionally as possible. Become familiar with the magazine—look at back issues."

*PACIFIC NORTHWEST, #101, 701 Dexter Ave. N., Seattle WA 98109. (206)284-1750. Fax: (206)284-2550. Editor: Ann Naumann. Circ. 75,000. Estab. 1966. Magazine published 9 times/year. Emphasizes travel, food, outdoor recreation. Readers are active Northwesterners, ages 40-50, who like to travel. Sample copy $4. Photo guidelines free with SASE.

Needs: Uses 35 photos/issue; 25% supplied by freelancers. Needs photos of scenics (travel), profiles, interior/exterior home design. Reviews photos with or without ms. Model release required; property release preferred. Captions required; include place or person and date.

Making Contact & Terms: Query with stock photo list. Provide resume, business card, brochure, flyer or tearsheets to be kept on file for possible assignments. Keeps samples on file. SASE; "no guarantees." Reports in 6 weeks. Pays $475/color cover photo; $150-425/color inside photo; $150-425/ b&w inside photo; $250/color page rate. Pays on publication. Credit line given. Buys one-time rights. Previously published work OK.

PALM BEACH ILLUSTRATED MAGAZINE, 1016 N. Dixie Hwy., W. Palm Beach FL 33401. (407)659-0210. Fax: (407)659-1736. Editor: Judy Di Edwardo. Circ. 30,000. Estab. 1952. Magazine published 10 times a year. Emphasizes upscale, first-class living. Readers are highly influential, established people, ages 35-54. Sample copy free with SASE. Photo guidelines free.

Needs: Needs photos of travel. Reviews photos with or without a manuscript. Model/property release preferred. Captions preferred.

Making Contact & Terms: Send color prints; 35mm, 2¼ × 2¼ transparencies. SASE. Reports in 1 month. NPI; payment made on individual basis. Pays on publication. Credit line given. Buys one-time rights. Simultaneous submissions OK.

Tips: Looks for "travel and related topics such as resorts, spas, yacht charters, trend and lifestyle topics. Materials should appeal to affluent readers: budget travel is not of interest, for example. Editorial material on the latest best investments in the arts would be appropriate; editorial material on investing in a mobile home would not."

PALM BEACH LIFE, 265 Royal Poinciana Way, Palm Beach FL 33480. (407)837-4762. Design Director: Amy Woodcox. Circ. 30,000. Monthly magazine. Emphasizes entertainment, affluent lifestyle, travel, environment, personalities, decorating and the arts. For regional and general audiences. Sample copy $4.18.

• In 1992 this publication earned a Charlie Award from the Florida Magazine Association for having the Best Overall Design with a circulation over 25,000. It also earned a bronze award for having the Best Cover.

Needs: Freelance photographers supply 50% of the photos. Fine art, scenic, human interest and nature. Captions required.

Making Contact & Terms: Query or make appointment. Uses any size b&w glossy prints; 35mm, 2¼ × 2¼ and 4 × 5 transparencies; vertical or square format for cover. SASE. "*Palm Beach Life* cannot be responsible for unsolicited material." Reports in 4-6 weeks. Pays $200-600/job, or on a per-photo basis. Pays $25-50/b&w photo; $50-100/color photo; cover photo negotiable. **Pays on acceptance.** Credit line given. Simultaneous submissions OK.

Tips: "Don't send slides—make an appointment to show work. We have staff photographers and are only interested in something really exceptional or material from a location that we would find difficult to cover."

PALM SPRINGS LIFE MAGAZINE, P.O. Box 2724, 303 N. Indian Canyon Ave., Palm Springs CA 92263. (619)325-2333. Fax: (619)325-7008. Design Director: Bill Russom. Editor: Jamie Pricer. Circ. 24,000. Estab. 1957. Monthly magazine. Emphasizes Palm Springs/California desert area upscale resort living. Readers are extremely affluent, 35+ years old. "Primarily for our readers, Palm Springs may be second/vacation home." Sample copy $6. Photo guidelines free with SASE.

Needs: Uses 60+ photos/issue; 20% supplied by freelance photographers; 80% from assignment. Needs desert photos, scenic wildlife, gardening, fashion, beauty, interior design, travel, personalities and people (all local). Special needs include photo essays, art photography. Model release preferred. Property release required. Captions preferred; include who, what, when, where, why.

Making Contact & Terms: Interested in receiving work from newer, lesser-known photographers. Submit portfolio for review. Provide resume, business card, brochure, flyer or tearsheets to be kept on file for possible assignments. Uses 35mm, 2¼×2¼, 4×5 or 8×10 transparencies. SASE. Reports in 2 months. Pays $300-500/color cover photo; $25-200/color inside photo; $125/color page; $25-100/ b&w photo; $50-325/color photo; payment/job, negotiable. Pays on publication. Credit line given. Buys all rights; negotiable. Simultaneous submissions and previously published work OK.

Tips: In photographer's portfolio looks for published photographs, the "unusual" bend to the "usual" subject. "We will try anything new photographically as long as it's gorgeous! Must present professional-looking portfolio. Please don't submit photos of subjects I'd never use. Know your market!"

PARENTS MAGAZINE, 685 3rd Ave., New York NY 10017. (212)878-8700. Fax: (212)867-4583. Photo Editor: Meryl Levy. Emphasizes family relations and the care and raising of children. Readers are families with young children. Monthly. Circ. 1,800,000. Free photo guidelines.

Needs: Uses about 100 photos/issue; all supplied by freelance photographers. Needs family and/or children's photos. No landscape or architecture photos. Model release required.

Making Contact & Terms: Interested in receiving work from newer, lesser-known photographers. Some work with freelance photographers on assignment only basis. Arrange for drop off to show portfolio. "Clifford Gardener, Art Director, and Meryl Levy, Photo Editor. By looking at portfolios of photographers in whom we are interested we may assign a job." Reporting time depends on shooting schedule, usually 2-6 weeks. NPI. Payment depends on space usage, yearly standard rates and expenses. SASE. Credit line given. Buys one-time rights. No simultaneous submissions; previously published work OK.

Tips: Interested in seeing consistency within the work of photographers. "Don't be a jack of all trades, master of none. Send work that applies to parents' needs. Don't send samples of studio portraits."

*PASSENGER TRAIN JOURNAL, P.O. Box 379, Waukesha WI 53187. (414)542-4900. Fax: (414)542-7595. Editor: Carl Swanson. Circ. 13,000. Estab. 1968. Monthly magazine. Emphasizes rail passenger equipment and travel. Readers are mostly male, well-educated, ages 35-60. Photo guidelines free with SASE.

Needs: Uses 12-15 photos/issue; all supplied by freelancers. Needs photos of North American passenger trains, depots and rail transit systems in the United States. Reviews photos with or without ms. Special photo needs include general photos of Amtrak long-distance trains. Model/property release preferred for any recognizable person in the photo. Captions required; include name of train, direction of travel, date, location.

Making Contact & Terms: Interested in receiving work from newer, lesser-known photographers. Send unsolicited photos by mail for consideration. Send 5×7 glossy b&w prints; 35mm, 2¼×2¼ transparencies. Does not keep samples on file. SASE. Reports in 1 month. Pays $35/color cover photo; $35/b&w cover photo; $7-15/color inside photo; $7-15/b&w inside photo. Pays on publication. Credit line given. Buys one-time rights.

Tips: "We look for people who can convey the drama of passenger railroading through their pictures. Although our payment rates are fairly low, we feel this magazine is a good way for unknown photographers to see their work in print and get their name before the public."

PENNSYLVANIA, P.O. Box 576, Camp Hill PA 17011. (717)761-6620. Editor: Albert E. Holliday. Circ. 40,000. Bimonthly. Emphasizes history, travel and contemporary issues and topics. Readers are 40-60 years old, professional and retired; average income is $46,000. Sample copy $2.95. Photo guidelines free with SASE.

● If you want to work with this publication make sure you review several past issues and obtain photo guidelines.

Needs: Uses about 40 photos/issue; most supplied by freelance photographers. Needs include travel and scenic. All photos must be in Pennsylvania. Reviews photos with or without accompanying ms. Captions required.

Making Contact & Terms: Query with samples and list of stock photo subjects. Send 5×7 and up b&w prints; 35mm and 2¼×2¼ transparencies (duplicates only, no originals) by mail for consideration (4×5 or 4×6 color prints also OK). SASE. Reports in 2 weeks. Pays $100-150/color cover photo; $15-25/inside photo; $50-400/text/photo package. Credit line given. Buys one-time rights. Simultaneous submissions and previously published work OK.

PENNSYLVANIA GAME NEWS, Dept. PM, 2001 Elmerton Ave., Harrisburg PA 17110-9797. (717)787-3745. Editor: Bob Mitchell. Circ. 150,000. Monthly magazine. Published by the Pennsylvania Game Commission. For people interested in hunting, wildlife management and conservation in Pennsylvania. Free sample copy with 9×12 SASE. Free editorial guidelines.

Needs: Considers photos of "any outdoor subject (Pennsylvania locale), except fishing and boating." Photos purchased with accompanying ms.

Making Contact & Terms: Submit seasonal material 6 months in advance. Send 8×10 glossy b&w prints. SASE. Reports in 2 months. Pays $5-20/photo. **Pays on acceptance.** Buys all rights, but may reassign after publication.

*PENTHOUSE, 1965 Broadway, New York NY 10023. (Prefers not to share information.)

PETERSEN'S HUNTING MAGAZINE, Dept. PM, 8490 Sunset Blvd., Los Angeles CA 90069. (213)854-2184. Editor: Craig Boddington. Circ. 325,000. Monthly magazine. Readers are sport hunters who "hunt everything from big game to birds to varmints." Free photo guidelines.

Needs: Buys 4-8 color and 10-30 b&w photos/issue. "Good sharp wildlife shots and hunting scenes. No scenic views or unhuntable species." Present model release on acceptance of photo. Identify subject of each photo.

Making Contact & Terms: Send photos for consideration. Send 8×10 glossy b&w prints; transparencies. SASE. Reports in 3-4 weeks. Pays $35/b&w photo; $75-250/color photo; $500/color cover. Pays on publication. Buys one-time rights.

Tips: Prefers to see "photos that demonstrate a knowledge of the outdoors, heavy emphasis on game animal shots, hunters and action. Try to strive for realistic photos that reflect nature, the sportsman and the flavor of the hunting environment. Not just simply 'hero' shots where the hunter is perched over the game. Action—such as running animals, flying birds, also unusual, dramatic photos of same animals in natural setting. Submit a small selection of varied subjects for review—20-40 slides. Majority of photographs used are author-supplied; approx. 20% from outside photographers."

❀PETS MAGAZINE, Dept. PM, 10th Floor, 797 Don Mills Rd., Don Mills, Ontario M3C 355 Canada. (416)696-5488. Editor: Ed Zapletal. Estab. 1983. Bimonthly magazine. Emphasizes pets (mainly cats and dogs). Readers are about 85% female, 30 yrs.+, middle income and better. Circ. 67,000. Sample copy for 9×12 SASE. "Please use IRC or *Canadian* stamps."

Needs: Uses 10-15 photos/issue; 3-5 supplied by freelance photographers. Needs animal shots. Model release and captions preferred.

Making Contact & Terms: Provide resume, business card, brochure, flyer or tearsheets to be kept on file for possible assignments. SASE. Reports in 1-5 weeks (or more). Pays $25/color cover photo or b&w inside photo. Pays on publication. Credit line given. Buys all rights; will negotiate. Previously published work OK.

Tips: "To be frank, we rarely buy just photos—our writers (all freelance) send any photos needed for specific articles, or we use 'generic' photos from our (large) collection of photos (gathered through four photo contests)."

PHOENIX MAGAZINE, Dept. PM, 4707 N. 12th St., Phoenix AZ 85014. (602)248-8900. Executive Editor/Publisher: Dick Vonier. Art Director: James Forsmo. Monthly magazine. Circ. 50,000. Emphasizes "subjects that are unique to Phoenix: its culture, urban and social achievements and problems, its people and the Arizona way of life. We reach a professional and general audience of well-educated, affluent visitors and long-term residents." Buys 10-35 photos/issue.

Needs: Wide range, all dealing with life in metro Phoenix. Generally related to editorial subject matter. Wants on a regular basis photos to illustrate features, as well as for regular columns on arts. No "random shots of Arizona scenery, etc. that can't be linked to specific stories in the magazine." Photos purchased with or without an accompanying ms.

Making Contact & Terms: Query. Works with freelance photographers on assignment only basis. Provide resume, samples, business card, brochure, flyer and tearsheets to be kept on file for possible future assignments. SASE. Reports in 3-4 weeks. B&w: $25-75; color: $50-200; cover: $400-1,000. Pays within two weeks of publication. Payment for manuscripts includes photos in most cases. Payment negotiable for covers and other photos purchased separately.

Tips: "Study the magazine, then show us an impressive portfolio."

❀PHOTO LIFE, 130 Spy Court, Markham, Ontario L3R 5H6 Canada. (416)475-8440. Fax: (416)475-9246. Editor: Jerry Kobalenko. Circ. 55,000. Magazine published 8 times/year. Readers are advanced amateur and professional photographers. Circ. 55,000. Sample copy or photo guidelines free with SASE.

Needs: Uses 50 photos/issue; 80% supplied by freelance photographers. Needs animal/wildlife shots, travel, scenics and so on. Usually only by Canadian photographers or on Canadian subjects.

Making Contact & Terms: Query with resume of credits. SASE. Reports in 1 month. Pays $60/b&w photo; $75-100/color photo; $400 maximum/complete job; $700 maximum/photo/text package. Pays on publication. Buys first N.A. serial rights and one-time rights.

Tips: "Looking for good writers to cover any subject interesting to the advanced photographer. Fine art photos should be striking, innovative. General stock, outdoor and travel photos should be presented with a strong technical theme."

PHOTOGRAPHER'S MARKET, 1507 Dana Ave., Cincinnati OH 45207. (513)531-2690 ext. 286. Editor: Michael Willins. Circ. 40,000. Annual hardbound directory for freelance photographers.
Needs: Publishes 35-40 photos per year. Uses general subject matter. Photos must be work sold to listings in *Photographer's Market*, and photographer must own rights to the photos. Photos are used to illustrate to readers the various types of images being sold to photo buyers listed in the book. Captions should explain how the photo was used by the buyer, why it was selected, how the photographer sold the photo or got the assignment, how much the buyer paid the photographer, what rights were sold to the buyer and any self-marketing advice the photographer can share with readers. Look at book for examples.
Making Contact & Terms: Interested in reviewing work from newer, lesser-known photographers. Submit photos for inside text usage in fall and winter to ensure sufficient time to review them by spring deadline (late February to early March). Sponsors cover photo contest. All photos are judged according to subject uniqueness in a given edition, as well as technical quality and composition within the market section in the book. Photos are held and reviewed at close of deadline. Uses b&w glossy prints, any size and format; 5×7 or 8×10 preferred. Also uses tearsheets and 35mm transparencies. Reports are immediate if a photo is selected; photos not chosen are returned within 6-8 weeks of selection deadline. Pays $50 plus complimentary copy of books. Pays when book goes to printer. Book forwarded in September upon arrival from printer. Credit line given in descriptive caption. Buys second reprint rights and occasionally buys additional rights for promotional use. Promotional rights negotiable. Simultaneous submissions and previously published work OK.
Tips: "Send photos with brief cover letter describing the background of the sale. If sending more than one photo, make sure that photos are clearly identified with name and a code that corresponds to a comprehensive list. Slides should be enclosed in plastic slide sleeves, and original prints should be reinforced with cardboard. Cannot return material if SASE is not included. Tearsheets will be considered disposable unless SASE is provided and return is requested. Because photos are printed in black and white on newsprint stock, some photos, especially color shots, may not reproduce well. Photos should have strong contrast and not too much fine detail that will fill in when photo is reduced to fit our small page format. Usual reprint sizes are 2×3 and 3×4½. We prefer original photos whenever possible, but we will use tearsheets if photos are used in an interesting collage or striking cover layout."

PLANE & PILOT, Dept. PM, 12121 Wilshire Blvd., Los Angeles CA 90025. (310)820-1500. Contact: Art Director. Monthly magazine. Emphasizes personal, business and homebuilt aircraft. Readers are private, business and hobbyist pilots. Circ. 70,000-100,000.
Needs: Uses about 50 photos/issue; 90% supplied by freelance photographers. Needs photos of "production aircraft and homebuilt experimentals." Special needs include "air-to-air, technical, general aviation and special interest" photos. Written release and captions preferred.
Making Contact & Terms: Query with samples. Send 5×7 or 8×10 b&w glossy prints; 35mm transparencies; b&w contact sheets. SASE. Reports in 1 month. Pays $150-200 color cover photo; $25-50/ inside photo; $100-150/color inside photo; $500/job; $250-500/text/photo package. **Pays on acceptance.** Credit line given. Buys one-time rights. Simultaneous submissions and previously published work OK.
Tips: Prefers to see "a variety of well-shot and composed color transparencies and b&w prints dealing with mechanical subjects (aircraft, auto, etc.)" in samples. "Use good technique, a variety of subjects and learn to write well."

*PLAY MAGAZINE, 3620 NW 43rd St., Gainesville FL 32606. (904)375-3705. Fax: (904)375-7268. Art Director: Torne White. Circ. 90,000. Estab. 1992. Quarterly magazine. Emphasizes children's entertainment—music, education, play time, products. Readers are parents interested in "quality entertainment for their kids." Sample copy $4.
Needs: Uses 25-40 photos/issue; 50% supplied by freelancers. Needs photos of products, celebrities, children. Reviews photos with or without ms. Model release required. Property release preferred. Captions preferred.
Making Contact & Terms: Interested in reviewing work from newer, lesser-known photographers. Provide resume, business card, brochure, flyer or tearsheets to be kept on file for possible assignments. Keeps samples on file. Reports only if interested. NPI. Pays on publication. Credit line given. Buys one-time and stock usage rights. Previously published work OK.

*PLAYBOY, 680 N Lake Shore Drive, Chicago IL 60611. Rarely uses freelancers.

POLO MAGAZINE, Dept. PM, 656 Quince Orchard Rd., Gaithersburg MD 20878. (301)977-0200. Fax: (301)990-9015. Editor: Martha LeGrand. Circ. 7,000. Estab. 1975. Publishes monthly magazine 10 times/year with combined issues for January/February and June/July. Emphasizes the sport of polo and its lifestyle. Readers are primarily male; average age is 40. 90% of readers are professional/managerial levels, including CEO's and presidents. Sample copy free with 10 × 13 SASE. Photo guidelines free with SASE.

Needs: Uses 50 photos/issue; 70% supplied by freelance photographers; 20% of this by assignment. Needs photos of polo action, portraits, travel, party/social and scenics. Most polo action is assigned, but freelance needs range from dynamic action photos to spectator fashion to social events. Photographers may write and obtain an editorial calendar for the year, listing planned features/photo needs. Captions preferred, where necessary include subjects and names.

Making Contact & Terms: Query with list of stock photo subjects. Provide resume, business card, brochure, flyer or tearsheets to be kept on file for possible assignments. SASE. Reports in 2 weeks. Pays $25-150/b&w photo, $30-300/color photo, $150/half day, $300/full day, $200-500/complete package. Pays on publication. Credit line given. Buys one-time or all rights; negotiable. Simultaneous submissions and previously published work OK "in some instances."

Tips: Wants to see tight focus on subject matter and ability to capture drama of polo. "In assigning action photography, we look for close-ups that show the dramatic interaction of two or more players rather than a single player. On the sidelines, we encourage photographers to capture emotions of game, pony picket lines, etc." Sees trend toward "more use of quality b&w images." To break in, "send samples of work, preferably polo action photography."

✽POOL & SPA MAGAZINE, Unit 12, 270 Esna Park Drive, Markham, Ontario L3R 1H3 Canada. (416)752-2500. Editor: David Barnsley. Circ. 40,000. Quarterly. Emphasizes swimming pools, spas, hot tubs, outdoor entertaining, landscaping (patios, decks, gardens, lawns, fencing). Readers are homeowners and professionals 30-55 years old. Equally read by men and women.

Needs: Uses 20-30 photos/issue; 30% supplied by freelance photographers. Looking for shots of models dressed in bathing suits, people swimming in pools/spas, patios. Plans annual bathing suit issue late in year. Model release required.

Making Contact & Terms: Send unsolicited photos by mail for consideration. Send 8 × 10 glossy color prints; 35mm transparencies. SASE. Reports in 2 weeks. NPI; will negotiate payment. Pays on publication. Credit line given. Buys all rights; negotiable. Simultaneous submissions and previously published work OK.

Tips: Looking for "photos of families relaxing outdoors around a pool, spa or patio. We are always in need of visual material, so send in whatever you feel is appropriate for the magazine. Photos will be returned."

POPULAR ELECTRONICS, 500-B Bi-County Blvd., Farmingdale NY 11735. (516)293-3000. Fax: (516)293-3115. Editor: Carl Laron. Circ. 87,287. Estab. 1989. Monthly magazine. Emphasizes hobby electronics. Readers are hobbyists in electronics, amateur radio, CB, audio, TV, etc.—"Mostly male, ages 13-59." Sample copy free with 9 × 12 SAE and 90¢ postage.

Needs: Uses about 20 photos/issue; 20% supplied by freelance photographers. Photos purchased with accompanying ms only. Special needs include regional photo stories on electronics. Model/property release required. Captions preferred.

Making Contact & Terms: Arrange a personal interview to show portfolio. Query with samples. SASE. Reports in 2 weeks. Pays $250-400/color cover photo; $200-350 for text/photo package; $100-400/job. **Pays on acceptance.** Credit line given. Buys all rights; negotiable. Simultaneous submissions and previously published work OK.

✽POPULAR PHOTOGRAPHY, 1633 Broadway, New York NY 10019. (212)767-6578. Fax: (212)767-5629. Send to: Your Best Shot/Hard Knocks. Circ. 700,000. Estab. 1937. Monthly magazine. Readers are male and female photographers, amateurs to professionals of all ages. Photo guidelines free with SASE.

Needs: Uses many photos/issue; many supplied by freelancers. Uses photos for monthly contest feature, Your Best Shot, and in editorial critique of work, Hard Knocks.

Making Contact & Terms: Send unsolicited photos by mail for consideration. Send prints size 8 × 12 and under, color and b&w; any size transparencies. Does not keep samples on file. SASE. Reports in 8-12 weeks. Pays prize money for contest: $300 (first), $200 (second), $100 (third) and honorable mention. **Pays on acceptance.** Credit line given. Buys one-time rights.

✽PORTFOLIO, P.O. Box 3994, Walnut Creek CA 94598-3994. (510)935-7406. Fax: (510)935-7406. Director: Robert Devere. Circ. 5,000. Estab. 1992. Bimonthly journal. Emphasis on photography. Readers are mostly serious amateur and advanced photographers. Sample copies $3 with 9 × 12 envelope and 4 first-class stamps. Photo guidelines free with SASE.

Needs: Uses 6-10 photos/issue; almost all supplied by freelancers. Needs photos of nature, portraiture, scenics, people. Uses photos for how-to topics, but journal emphasizes people pictures. Reviews photos with accompanying ms only. Special photo needs include photographic illustrations with people or animals. Model/property release required for identifiable private property and portraits. Captions

required; include camera model, lens used, shutter speed, f/stop and lighting information if applicable.
Making Contact & Terms: Interested in receiving work from newer, lesser-known photographers. Query with resume of credits. Query with stock photo list. Send 3×5 to 8×10 glossy b&w prints by mail for consideration. Provide resume, business card, brochure, flyer or tearsheets to be kept on file for possible assignments. Keeps samples on file. SASE. Reports in 1 month. Pays $50/b&w inside photo; $100-200/photo/text package. **Pays on acceptance.** Credit line given. Buys one-time rights; negotiable. Simultaneous submissions and previously published work OK.
Tips: "We look for five basic characteristics by which we judge photographic materials: sharp exposures (unless the image was intended as a soft-focus shot), impact, easily identifiable theme or subject, emphasis of the theme or subject, and simplicity."

PORTLAND-THE UNIVERSITY OF PORTLAND MAGAZINE, 5000 N. Willamette Blvd., Portland OR 97203. (503)283-7202. Fax: (503)283-7110. Editor: Brian Doyle. Estab. 1985. 40-page magazine published quarterly.
• In 1992 this publication earned a gold medal for visual design from the Council for the Advancement and Support of Education.
Needs: Buys 20 photos/year; offers 3 assignments/year. Subjects include people. Model release preferred.
Making Contact & Terms: Interested in receiving work from newer, lesser-known photographers. Query with resume of credits. Query with list of stock photo subjects. Solicits photos by assignment only. Uses 8×10 glossy b&w prints; b&w contact sheets; 35mm and 2½×2½ transparencies. SASE. Reports in 2 weeks. Pays $100-300/b&w and color photo. Credit line given. Buys one-time rights.
Tips: "Our needs are fairly specific. Tell me how you can help me. We want strong, creative photos. No mugs and 'grip and grins.' " In portfolio of samples wants to see "interpretive ability more than photojournalistic work. Also show work with other magazines. Strong composition and color is important. Often buy already completed work. University magazines are a growing market for first-rate photography. Our best work in recent years has been on assignment. There are more than 500 university and college magazines—a little-known niche. Our needs are not extensive. A good promotional brochure gives me someone to contact in various areas on various subjects."

POWDER MAGAZINE, Dept. PM, Box 1028, Dana Point CA 92629. (714)496-5922. Managing Editor: Steve Casimiro. Published September through March. Emphasizes skiing. Circ. 150,000 plus. Sample copy $1; photo guidelines free with SASE.
Needs: Uses 70-80 photos/issue; 90% supplied by freelance photographers. Needs "ski action, ski action, ski action! Also scenics, personalities and humorous ski photos."
Making Contact & Terms: Query with samples or call to discuss requirements, deadlines, etc. SASE. Reports in 2 weeks. Pays $500/color cover photo; $200/color page, $50/color minimum. Pays on publication. Credit line given. Buys first N.A. serial rights. Simultaneous submissions OK.
Tips: "Our readers are advanced and expert skiers. Your submissions should reflect that. Be bold and exciting—lots of action. Avoid static, staged photos. Be creative (and weird). We *are* a market for experimental photos as well as 'traditional' action shots. We look for photographers who break the standards of ski photography."

PRAYING, P.O. Box 419335, Kansas City MO 64141. (800)821-7926. Editor: Art Winter. Photo Editor: Rich Heffern. Circ. 20,000. Estab. 1986. Bimonthly. Emphasizes spirituality for everyday living. Readers include mostly Catholic laypeople. Circ. 20,000. Estab. 1986. Sample copy and photo guidelines free with SASE.
Needs: Uses 3 photos/issue; all supplied by freelance photographers. Needs quality photographs which stand on their own as celebrations of people, relationships, ordinary events, work, nature, etc. Reviews photos with or without accompanying ms.
Making Contact & Terms: Query with samples. Send 8×10 b&w prints by mail for consideration. SASE. Reports in 2 weeks. Pays $50/b&w photo. Pays on publication. Credit line given. Buys one-time rights. Simultaneous submissions and previously published work OK.

A bullet has been placed within some listings to introduce special comments by the editor of the Photographer's Market.

Tips: Looking for "good *printing* composition. We get a lot of really *poor* stuff! Know how to take and print a quality photograph. Don't try to add holy element or reflective moment. Natural, to us, is holy. We have one rule: never to run a picture of someone praying."

Sometimes a very simple subject, such as this squash growing around the links in a fence, can be just what an editor is looking for. Praying Magazine Editor Art Winter found the spiritual nature of this image, taken by Peter Keegan of Cresskill, New Jersey, to be perfect for an article on meditation.

PREVENTION MAGAZINE, 33 E. Minor St., Emmaus PA 18098. (215)967-5171. Executive Art Director: Wendy Ronga. Circ. 2.5 million. Monthly magazine. Emphasizes health. Readers are mostly female, 35-50, upscale.
Needs: Uses 12-15 photos/issue; 60% on assignment, 40% from stock, but seeing trend toward "more assignment work than usual." Photo needs very specific to editorial, health, beauty, food. Model release required. Captions required.
Making Contact & Terms: Provide resume, business card, brochure, flyer or tearsheets to be kept on file for possible future assignments; tearsheets and/or dupes very important. Cannot return unsolicited material. Reports in 1 month. Pays $100-300/b&w photo; $150-600/color photo; $250-1,000/day. Pays on publication. Credit line given. Buys one-time rights.
Tips: Prefers to see ability to do one thing very well. "Good lighting technique is a must." Wants to see "something different, taking an unusual twist to an ordinary subject."

*PRE-VUE ENTERTAINMENT MAGAZINE, 7825 Fay Ave., La Jolla CA 92037. (619)456-5577. Fax: (619)542-0114. Photo Director/Editor: Penny Langford. Circ. 300,000. Estab. 1991. Monthly magazine. Emphasizes movies/celebrities. Readers are 91% male. Sample copy free with 6×9 SAE and 2 first-class stamps.
Needs: Uses 35 photos/issue; 10 supplied by freelancers. Needs photos of celebrities at play/events. Reviews photos with or without ms. Model release required. Captions required.
Making Contact & Terms: Interested in receiving work from newer, lesser-known photographers. Send unsolicited photos by mail for consideration. Provide resume, business card, brochure, flyer or tearsheets to be kept on file for possible assignments. Send any size, 3×3 and up, matte color and b&w prints; 35mm, 2¼×2¼, 4×5, 8×10 transparencies. Keeps samples on file. SASE. Reports in 1 month. NPI. Pays on publication. Credit line given. Buys all rights; negotiable. Simultaneous submissions and/or previously published work OK, "if I know where it was published previously."

PRIME TIME SPORTS & FITNESS, Dept. PM, P.O. Box 6097, Evanston IL 60204. (708)864-8113. Fax: (708)864-1206. Contact: Editor. Magazine publishes 8 times/year. Emphasizes sports, recreation and fitness. Readers are professional males (50%) and females (50%), 19-45. Sample copy free with SASE. Photo guidelines free with 10×12 SASE.

Needs: Uses about 70 photos/issue; 60 supplied by freelancers. Needs photos concerning women's fitness and fashion, swimwear and aerobic routines. Special photo needs include women's workout and swimwear photos. Upcoming short-term needs: summer swimwear, women's aerobic wear, portraits of women in sports. Model/property release required. Captions preferred; include names, the situation and locations.

Making Contact & Terms: Interested in reviewing work from newer, lesser-known photographers. Send unsolicited photos by mail for consideration. SASE. Reports in 6-8 weeks. Pays $200/color and b&w cover photo; $20/color and b&w inside photo; $20/color page rate; $50/b&w page rate; $30-60/hour. Time of payment negotiable. Credit line given. Buys all rights; negotiable. Simultaneous submissions and previously published work OK.

Tips: Wants to see "tight shots of personalities, people, sports in action, but only tight close ups." There are a "plethora of amateur photographers who have trouble providing quality action or fashion shots and yet call themselves professionals. However, bulk of photographers are sending in a wider variety of photos. Photographers can best present themselves by letting me see their work in our related fields (both published and unpublished) by sending us samples. Do not drop by or phone, it will not help."

THE PROGRESSIVE, 409 E. Main St., Madison WI 53703. Art Director: Patrick JB Flynn. Circ. 40,000. Estab. 1909. Monthly. Emphasizes "political and social affairs—international and domestic." Free sample copy and photo guidelines upon request.

Needs: Uses 5 or more b&w photos/issue; all supplied by freelance photographers and photo agencies. Looking for images documenting the human condition and the social/political structures of contemporary societies. Special photo needs include "Third World societies, labor activities, environmental issues and political resistance." Captions and credit information required.

Making Contact & Terms: Query with photocopies to be kept on file for possible future assignments. SASE. Reports once every month. Pays $300/color cover photo; $30-150/b&w inside photo; $150/b&w full-page. Pays on publication. Credit line given. Buys one-time rights. Simultaneous submissions and previously published work OK.

Tips: "Interested in photo essays and in images that make a visual statement."

THE QUARTER HORSE JOURNAL, P.O. Box 32470, Amarillo TX 79120. (806)376-4811. Fax: (806)376-8364. Executive Editor: Audie Rackley. Circ. 65,000. Estab. 1948. Monthly magazine. Emphasizes breeding and training of quarter horses. Free sample copy and editorial guidelines.

Needs: Photos purchased with accompanying ms only. "Materials should be current and appeal or be helpful to both children and adults." No photos of other breeds. Captions are required.

Making Contact & Terms: Write for details. Uses 5×7 or 8×10 glossy b&w prints; 35mm, 2¼×2¼, or 4×5 transparencies and 8×10 glossy color prints; "we don't accept color prints on matte paper." SASE. Reports in 2-3 weeks. Pays $50-250 for text/photo package. **Pays on acceptance.** Buys first N.A. serial rights and occasionally buys all rights.

*QUICK GUIDE, P.O. Box 4053, Woodland Hills CA 91364. Contact: Quick Guide Photo Editor. Estab. 1986. Quarterly and annual magazines. Emphasizes city specific photos for use in city guide books for hotel guests. Readers are hotel guests of all ages visiting a specific city. Photos guidelines free with SASE.

Needs: Uses 2-10 photos/issue; 90% supplied by freelancers. Needs photos of city specific events, attractions, recreational activities, scenics, regional food and animal/wildlife. "We are always interested in seeing fresh approaches to commonly photographed subjects." Model/property release preferred. "Get a release whenever possible, it will increase the sales power." Captions required; include exact street, building, public art and location names.

Making Contact & Terms: Interested in receiving work from newer, lesser-known photographers. Provide resume, business card, brochure, flyer or tearsheets to be kept on file for possible assignments. Make first contact by mail. Send transparencies. Reports in 1 month. Pays $250/color cover photo; $100/color inside photo; 50% reuse rate. Pays on publication. Credit line given. Buys one-time rights. Simultaneous submissions and/or previously published work OK.

Tips: "We prefer to see professional work by photographers who live in or near the cities in which Quick Guides are published: Baltimore, Boston, Chicago, Hawaii (Big Island), Houston, Long Beach, Maui, New York, Oahu, Philadelphia, Phoenix, San Diego, San Francisco, Seattle, St. Louis, Tucson and Washington DC. Make first contact by mail and include your phone number. If we like your work we'll contact you and send samples at that time. We only accept transparencies for consideration. Make sure that your name and address are on each slide along with accurate caption information. Make a note of how many slides you send on a delivery memo. Don't make excessive calls to the photo editor regarding your submission status, have patience."

RADIANCE, The Magazine for Large Women, P.O. Box 30246, Oakland CA 94604. (510)482-0680. Publisher/Editor: Alice Ansfield. Circ. 10,000. Estab. 1984. Quarterly magazine. "We're a positive/ self-esteem magazine for women all sizes of large. We have diverse readership, 90% women, ages 25-70 from all ethnic groups, lifestyles and interests." Sample copy $3.50. Writer's guidelines free with SASE. Photo guidelines not available.
Needs: Uses 20+ photos/issue; all supplied by freelance photographers. Needs portraits, cover shots, fashion photos. Model release preferred. Captions preferred.
Making Contact & Terms: Arrange a personal interview to show portfolio. Send unsolicited photos by mail for consideration. Provide resume, business card, brochure, flyer or tearsheets to be kept on file for possible assignments. SASE. Reports in 2-3 months. Pays $50-200/color cover photo; $15-25/ b&w inside photo; $8-20/hour; $400/day. Pays on publication. Credit line given. Buys one-time rights. Simultaneous submissions OK.
Tips: In photographer's portfolio or samples wants to see "clear, crisp photos, creativity, setting, etc." Recommends freelancers "get to know the magazine they're talking with. Work with the publisher (or photo editor) and get to know" her requirements. "Try to help the magazine with its goals."

RAG MAG, Box 12, Goodhue MN 55027. (612)923-4590. Editor: Beverly Voldseth. Circ. 200. Estab. 1982. Magazine. Emphasizes poetry and fiction, but is open to good writing in an genre. Sample copy $6 with 6¼×9¼ SAE and $1.05 postage.
• This publication has received very few freelance photos. For newcomers trying to build a portfolio of tearsheets this would be a good place to start.
Needs: Uses 3-4 photos/issue; all supplied by freelancers. Needs photos that work well in a literary magazine; faces, bodies, stones, trees, water, etc. Reviews photos without a manuscript. Uses photos on covers.
Making Contact & Terms: Interested in receiving work from newer, lesser-known photographers. Send unsolicited photocopies of photos by mail for consideration; include name on back of copies with brief bio. Does not keep samples on file. SASE. Reports in 2 weeks-2 months. Pays in copies. Pays on publication. Buys one-time rights. Simultaneous submissions and previously published work OK.
Tips: "I do not want anything abusive, sadistic or violent."

RAILROAD MODEL CRAFTSMAN, P.O. Box 700, Newton NJ 07860. (201)383-3355. Editor: W. Schaumburg. Circ. 75,000. Estab. 1930. Monthly. Emphasizes scale model railroading. Readers are adults interested in the hobby of model railroading. Sample copy $2.95. Photo guidelines free with SASE.
Needs: Uses 100+ photos/issue; 95% supplied by freelance photographers. Needs photos of creative and good railroad modeling, as well as photos accompanying "how-to" articles. Reviews photos with accompanying ms only. Model release preferred. Captions required.
Making Contact & Terms: SASE. Reports in 1 month. Pays $200/color cover photo. Pays on publication. Credit line given. Buys all rights; negotiable.

*RAND MCNALLY ROAD ATLAS, 8255 N. Central Park, Skokie IL 60076. (708)673-9100. Director, Art and Design: John Nelson. Estab. 1927. Annual. Emphasizes domestic auto travel. Readers are adults 25-65. Sample copy for 12×16 SASE. Photo guidelines free with SASE.
Needs: Uses 1 (cover) photo/issue. Needs photos of vacation-oriented summer scenery with paved road with later model auto(s) on it. No RVs, trucks; no heavy traffic shots. Other needs include several dozen line extensions of this product which require similar annual cover photo updates. Model release required. Captions required; location clearly identified.
Making Contact & Terms: Interested in receiving work from newer, lesser-known photographers. Query with samples. Send 4×5 color prints or 35mm transparencies by mail for consideration. Reports in 1 month. Pays up to $500/color cover photo. **Pays on acceptance.** Credit line given. Buys one-time rights. Simultaneous submissions and previously published work OK.
Tips: "Current shots are a must. For our travel guides and cover, we need clean, colorful 4×5 photos appropriate for destinations."

RANGER RICK, 8925 Leesburg Pike, Vienna VA 22184-0001. Photo Editor: Robert L. Dunne. Circ. 850,000. Estab. 1967. Monthly magazine. Readers are children, ages 6-12, interested in the natural world, wildlife, conservation and ecology. Sample copy $2. Photo guidelines free with SASE.

The asterisk before a listing indicates that the market is new in this edition. New markets are often the most receptive to freelance submissions.

Needs: Buys 400 photos annually; 90% supplied by freelancers; 0-10% on assignment. Needs photos of wild animals (U.S. and foreign birds, mammals, insects, reptiles, etc.); humorous (wild animals in funny poses or situations); photo essay/photo feature (with captions); celebrity/personality; and children (especially girls or racial minorities) doing things involving wild animals, outdoor activities, crafts, recycling and helping the environment. No plants, weather or scenics. No soft focus, grainy, or weak color shots. Reviews photos with or without accompanying ms, but query first on articles.

Making Contact & Terms: Interested in receiving work from newer, lesser-known photographers. Submit portofolio of 20-40 photos for review and a list of available material. Uses original color transparencies; vertical format on cover. "Allow space in upper left corner or across the top for insertion of masthead." SASE. Reports in 2 weeks. Pays $225/half page or less; $660/2-page spread; $500/color cover photo. Pays 3 months before publication. Buys first serial rights and right to reuse for promotional purposes at half the original price. Previously published work OK.

Tips: "Come in close on subjects." Wants no "obvious flash." Mail transparencies inside 20-pocket plastic viewing sheets, backed by cardboard, in a manila envelope. "Do your own editing. We don't want to see 20 shots of almost the same pose. We pay by reproduction size. Check printed issues to see our standards of quality, which are high. Looking for fresh, colorful, clean images. New approaches to traditional subject matter welcome."

REAL PEOPLE, 950 Third Ave., 16th Floor, New York NY 10022. (212)371-4932. Fax: (212)371-4932. Editor: Alex Polner. Circ. 130,000. Estab. 1988. Bimonthly magazine. Emphasizes celebrities. Readers are women 35 and up. Sample copy $3.50 with 6×9 SAE.

Needs: Uses 30-40 photos/issue; 10% supplied by freelancers. Needs celebrity photos. Reviews photos with accompanying ms. Model release preferred. Photo captions preferred.

Making Contact & Terms: Interested in receiving work from newer, lesser-known photographers. Query with resume of credits and/or list of stock photo subjects. Provide resume, business card, brochure, flyer or tearsheets to be kept on file for possible assignments. Send samples or tearsheets, perhaps even an idea for a photo essay as it relates to entertainment field. SASE. Reports only when interested. Pays $100-200/day. Pays on publication. Credit line given. Buys one-time rights.

*REASON MAGAZINE, 3415 S. Sepulveda, Los Angeles CA 90034. (310)391-2245. Fax: (310)391-4395. Art Director: Paula Brown. Circ. 32,000. Estab. 1968. Monthly magazine. Emphasizes political "think tank." Readers are 85% male, 20-40 years old, 15% female, 20-40 years old. Sample copy $4.

Needs: Uses approximately 6 photos/issue; 2 supplied by freelancers. Needs photos of political, environmental issues, current affairs, journalistic/editorial nature. Reviews photos with or without ms. Model/property release required. Captions preferred.

Making Contact & Terms: Interested in receiving work from newer, lesser-known photographers. Arrange personal interview to show portfolio. Submit portfolio for review. Provide resume, business card, brochure, flyer or tearsheets to be kept on file for possible assignments. Keeps samples on file. SASE. Reports in 3 weeks. NPI. Pays on publication. Credit line given. Buys one-time rights; negotiable. Simultaneous submissions and/or previously published work OK.

REDBOOK, 224 W. 57th St., New York NY 10019. Not reviewing freelance work.

RELIX MAGAZINE, P.O. Box 94, Brooklyn NY 11229. (718)258-0009. Fax: (718)692-4345. Editor: Toni A. Brown. Circ. 60,000. Estab. 1974. Bimonthly. Emphasizes rock and roll music. Readers are music fans, ages 13-50. Sample copy $3.

Needs: Uses about 50 photos/issue; "about 30%" supplied by freelance photographers; 20% on assignment; 80% from stock. Needs photos of "music artists—in concert and candid, backstage, etc." Special needs: "photos of rock groups, especially the Grateful Dead, San Francisco-oriented groups and sixties related bands." Captions preferred.

Making Contact & Terms: Interested in receiving work from newer, lesser-known photographers. Send 5×7 or larger b&w and color prints by mail for consideration. SASE. Reports in 1 month. "We try to report immediately; occasionally we cannot be sure of use." Pays $15-75/b&w photo; $25-300/color. Pays on publication. Credit line given. Buys all rights; negotiable. Simultaneous submissions and previously published work OK.

Tips: "B&w photos should be printed on grade 4 or higher for best contrast."

REMINISCE, 5400 S. 60th St., Greendale WI 53129. (414)423-0100. Fax: (414)423-1143. Editorial Assistant: Trudi Bellin. Estab. 1990. Bimonthly magazine. "For people who love reliving the good times." Readers are male and female, interested in nostalgia, ages 55+. "*Reminisce* is supported entirely by subscriptions and accepts no outside advertising." Sample copy $2. Photo guidelines free with SASE.

Needs: Uses 100 photos/issue; 35 supplied by freelancers. Needs photos with people interest—"we need high-quality color shots with nostalgic appeal." Model/property release required. Captions preferred; season, location.

Making Contact & Terms: Interested in receiving work from newer, lesser-known photographers. Query with list of stock photo subjects. Send unsolicited photos by mail for consideration. Send 35mm, 2¼×2¼, 4×5, 8×10 transparencies. Submit seasonally. Tearsheets filed but not dupes. SASE. Reports ASAP; "anywhere from a few days to a couple of months." Pays $200/color cover photo; $50-125/color inside photo; $150/color page rate; $10-50/b&w photo. Pays on publication. Credit line given. Buys one-time rights. Previously published work OK.

Tips: "Technical quality is extremely important; focus must be sharp, no soft focus; colors must be vivid so they 'pop off the page.' Color photos of nostalgic subjects stand the best chance of making our covers. Study our magazine thoroughly—we have a continuing need for sharp, colorful images, and those who can supply what we need can expect to be regular contributors."

REPTILE & AMPHIBIAN MAGAZINE, RD3, Box 3709-A, Pottsville PA 17901. (717)622-6050. Fax: (717)622-5858. Editor: Dr. Norman Frank. Circ. 10,000. Estab. 1989. Bimonthly magazine. Specializes in reptiles and amphibians only. Readers are college-educated, interested in nature and animals, familiar with basics of herpetology, many are breeders and conservation oriented. Sample copy $4. Photo guidelines with SASE.

Needs: Uses 20-30 photos/issue; 80% supplied by freelance photographers. Needs photos of related subjects. Photos purchased with or without ms. Model/property releases preferred. Captions required; clearly identify species with common and/or scientific name on slide mount.

Making Contact & Terms: Interested in receiving work from newer, lesser-known photographers. Send cover letter describing qualifications with representative samples. Must identify species pictured. Provide resume, business card, brochure, flyer or tearsheets to be kept on file for possible assignments. Send b&w and glossy prints; 35mm transparencies. Originals returned in 60-90 days. SASE. Reports in 1 month. Pays $25-50/color cover photo; $25/color inside photo; and $10/b&w inside photo. Pays on acceptance if needed immediately, or publication if the photo is to be filed for future use. Credit line given. Buys one-time rights. Previously published work OK.

Tips: In photographer's samples, looks for quality—eyes in-focus; action shots—animals eating, interacting, in motion. "Avoid field-guide type photos. Try to get shots with action and/or which have 'personality.' " All animals should be clearly identified with common and/or scientific name.

RICHMOND SURROUNDINGS MAGAZINE, Dept. PM, Suite 110, 7814 Carousel Lane, Richmond VA 23294. (804)346-4130. Managing Editor: Frances Helms. Art Director: John Hoar. Bimonthly magazine; "includes special newcomer annual edition." Emphasizes lifestyle, including business, health, education, leisure. Readers are upper income, college-educated, 30 and up. Circ. 20,000. Estab. 1979. Sample copy free with 8½×11 SASE and $1.50 postage.

Needs: Special photo needs, creative cover, editorial humor, advertising. 90% freelance photography in given issue from assignment and 10% from freelance stock. Model release and photo captions required.

Making Contact & Terms: Query with samples. Send unsolicited photos by mail for consideration. Provide resume, business card, brochure, flyer or tearsheets to be kept on file for possible future assignments. Send 5×7 glossy, 35mm transparencies, b&w contact sheet, color negatives. SASE. Reports in 4-6 weeks. Pays $150/b&w cover photo and $30-400/color cover photo, $25-150/b&w photo; $25-100/color photo; $10-100/hour; $100-500/day. Pays on publication. Credit line given. Buys all rights; willing to negotiate.

Tips: Looks for "creativity, photographs conveying emotion, as well as good technical quality. Be flexible. Be willing to accept lower fees for exposure and portfolio. Show versatility."

*RIDER, 29901 Agoura Rd., Agoura CA 91301. (818)991-4980. Editor: Mark Tuttle. Circ. 160,000. Monthly magazine. For dedicated motorcyclists with emphasis on long-distance touring, with coverage also of general street riding, commuting and sport riding. Sample copy $2.50 with 8½×11 SAE. Guidelines free.

Needs: Needs human interest, novelty and technical photos; color photos to accompany feature stories about motorcycle tours. Photos are rarely purchased without accompanying ms. Captions required.

Making Contact & Terms: Query first. Send 8×10 glossy or matte prints; 35mm transparencies. SASE. Reports in 4 weeks. NPI. Pay is inculded in total purchase price with ms. Pays on publication. Buys first-time rights.

Tips: "We emphasize quality graphics and color photos with good visual impact. Photos should be in character with accompanying ms and should include motorcyclists engaged in natural activities. Read our magazine before contacting us."

ROAD KING MAGAZINE, 23060 S. Cicero, Richton Park IL 60471. (708)481-9240. Editor: Rich Vurva. Photo Editor: Mary Beth Burns. Bimonthly magazine. Emphasizes trucks, truckers and trucking. Readers are over-the-road, long-haul truckers. Circ. 224,000. Sample copy free with 6×9 SAE and 85¢ postage.

Needs: Uses 20-25 photos/issue; 10-15 supplied by freelance photographers. Needs photos of trucks, truckstops and facilities, truckers. "We will need and use freelancers to accompany our reporters gathering stories. Our reporters also take back-up pictures simultaneously." Model release required.
Making Contact & Terms: Interested in receiving work from newer, lesser-known photographers. "Let us know who you are, where you are, if you are available for story assignments and your day rate." SASE. Pays $150-250/text/photo package. Buys all rights.

THE ROANOKER, P.O. Box 21535, Roanoke VA 24018. (703)989-6138. Fax: (703)989-7603. Editor: Kurt Rheinheimer. Circ. 14,000. Estab. 1974. Monthly. Emphasizes Roanoke and western Virginia. Readers are upper income, educated people interested in their community. Sample copy $2.
Needs: Uses about 40 photos/issue; most are supplied on assignment by freelance photographers. Needs "travel and scenic photos in western Virginia; color photo essays on life in western Virginia." Model/property releases preferred. Captions required.
Making Contact & Terms: Interested in receiving work from newer, lesser-known photographers. Send any size glossy b&w or color prints and transparencies by mail for consideration. SASE. Reports in 1 month. Pays $15-25/b&w photo; $20-35/color photo; $100/day. Pays on publication. Credit line given. Rights purchased vary; negotiable. Simultaneous submissions and previously published work OK.

ROBB REPORT For The Affluent Lifestyle, One Acton Place, Acton MA 01720. (508)263-7749. Design Director: Ilse Stryjewski. Circ. 50,000. Monthly. Emphasizes "the good life, e.g., yachting, exotic autos, investments, art, travel, lifestyle and collectibles." The magazine is aimed at the connoisseur who can afford an affluent lifestyle. Photo guidelines free with SASE.
Needs: Uses 30-50 photos/issue. Generally uses existing photography; freelance work is assigned once manuscripts have been reviewed for design treatment. Captions preferred.
Making Contact & Terms: Arrange a personal interview to show portfolio. Send promotional mailers to be kept on file for possible future assignments. Uses 35mm (Kodachrome preferred), 2¼ × 2¼, 4 × 5, 8 × 10 color transparencies. Reports within 1 month. NPI; pay is individually negotiated prior to assignment. Rates vary depending on whether photography purchased is stock or assigned. Pays on publication. Credit line given. Prefers to buy all rights; negotiable.

ROCK & ICE, P.O. Box 3595, Boulder CO 80307. (303)499-8410. Editor: George Bracksieck. Circ. 25,000. Estab. 1984. Bimonthly magazine. Emphasizes rock and ice climbing and mountaineering. Readers are predominantly professional, ages 17-50. Sample copy for $5. Photo guidelines free with SASE.
- Photos in this publication usually are outstanding action shots. Make sure your work meets the magazine's standards. Do not limit yourself to climbing shots from the U.S.
Needs: Uses 90 photos/issue; all supplied by freelance photographers; 20% on assignment, 80% from stock. Needs photos of climbing action shots, personalities and scenics. Buys photos with or without ms. Captions required.
Making Contact & Terms: Interested in receiving work from newer, lesser-known photographers. Query with list of stock photo subjects. Send unsolicited photos by mail for consideration. Send b&w prints; 35mm, 2¼ × 2¼ and 4 × 5 transparencies. SASE. Pays $250/color cover photo; $150/color and b&w page rate. Pays on publication. Credit line given. Buys one-time rights and first N.A. serial rights. Previously published work OK.
Tips: "Samples must show some aspect of technical rock climbing, ice climbing, mountain climbing or indoor climbing, scenics of places to climb or images of people who climb or who are indigenous to the climbing area. Climbing is one of North America's fastest growing sports."

ROLLING STONE, Dept. PM, 1290 Avenue of the Americas, New York NY 10104. (212)484-1616. Photo Editor: Laurie Kratochvil. Associate Photo Editor: Jodi Peckman. Emphasizes all forms of entertainment (music, movies, politics, news events).
Making Contact & Terms: "All our photographers are freelance." Provide brochure, calling card, flyer, samples and tearsheet to be kept on file for future assignments. Needs famous personalities and rock groups in b&w and color. No editorial repertoire. SASE. Reports immediately. Pays $150-350/day.
Tips: "Drop off portfolio at front desk any Wednesday between 10 am and noon. Pickup same day between 4 pm and 6 pm or next day. Leave a card with sample of work to keep on file so we'll have it to remember."

RUNNER'S WORLD, Dept. PM, 135 N. 6th St., Emmaus PA 18049. (215)967-5171. Fax: (215)965-5670. Executive Editor: Amby Burfoot. Photo Editor: Chuck Johnson. Monthly magazine. Emphasizes running. Readers are median aged: 37, 65% male, median income $40,000, college-educated. Circ. 450,000. Photo guidelines free with SASE.

Needs: Uses 100 photos/issue; 55 supplied by freelance photographers; features are generally assigned; columns and departments often come from stock. Needs photos of action, features, photojournalism. Model release and captions preferred.

Making Contact & Terms: Query with samples. Send b&w and color prints, and 35mm transparencies by mail for consideration. Submit portfolio for review. Provide resume, business card, brochure, flyer or tearsheets to be kept on file for possible future assignments. SASE. Pays as follows: color—$200/full page, $125/half page, $75/quarter page, $300/spread; b&w—$100/full page, $60/half page, $35/quarter page, $150/spread. Cover shots are assigned. Pays on publication. Credit line given. Photographic rights vary with assignment. Simultaneous submissions and previously published work OK.

Tips: "Become familiar with the publication and send photos in on spec. Also send samples that can be kept in our source file. Show full range of expertise; lighting abilities—quality of light—whether strobe sensitivity for people—portraits, sports, etc.. Both action and studio work if applicable, should be shown." Current trend is non-traditional treatment of sports coverage and portraits. Call prior to submitting work. Be familiar with running as well as the magazine.

*RURAL HERITAGE, 281 Dean Ridge Lane, Gainesboro TN 38562-9685. (615)268-0655. Editor: Gail Damerow. Quarterly magazine. Readers live the rural lifestyle and maintain its traditional values in the modern world. Sample copy $5.50, ($6 outside the U.S.).

Needs: "Most of the photos we purchase illustrate stories or poems. One exception is a well-captioned, humorous scene related to rural life. Another exception is cover photography. Each year we use four cover shots of draft horses or mules in harness."

Making Contact & Terms: "We prefer horizontal shots, 5×7 glossy b&w (though we often take color)." Please include SASE for the return of your material, and put your name and address on the back of each piece. Pays $10/photo to illustrate a story or poem; $15/photo for captioned humor; $25/cover shot. Also provides 2 copies of issue in which work appears. Pays on publication.

Tips: "Animals usually look better from the side than from the front. We like to see all the animal's body parts, including hooves, ears and tail. For animals in harness, we want to see the entire implement or vehicle. We prefer action shots (plowing, harvesting hay, etc.). Look for good contrast that will print well in black and white; watch out for shadows across animals and people. Please include the name of any human handlers involved, the farm, the town (or county), state, and the animal's names (if any) and breeds."

SACRAMENTO MAGAZINE, Dept. PM, 1021 Second St., Sacramento CA 95814. (916)446-7548. Managing Editor: Karen Coe. Art Director: Rebecca McKee. Circ. 30,000. Monthly magazine. Emphasizes business, government, culture, food, outdoor recreation and personalities for middle to upper middle class, urban-oriented Sacramento residents.

Needs: Uses about 40-50 photos/issue; most supplied by freelance photographers. "Photographers are selected on the basis of experience and portfolio strength. No work assigned on speculation or before a portfolio showing. Photographers are used on an assignment only basis. Stock photos used only occasionally. Most assignments are to area photographers and handled by phone. Photographers with studios, mobile lighting and other equipment have an advantage in gaining assignments. Darkroom equipment desirable but not necessary." Needs news photos, essay, avant-garde, still life, landscape, architecture, human interest and sports. All photography must pertain to Sacramento and environs. Captions required.

Making Contact & Terms: Send slides, contact sheets (no negatives) by mail or arrange a personal interview to show portfolio. Also query with resume of photo credits or mail portfolio. SASE. Reports up to 4 weeks. Pays $5-45/hour. Average payment is $15-20/hour; all assignments are negotiated to fall within that range. **Pays on acceptance.** Credit line given. Buys one-time rights. Will consider simultaneous submissions and previously published work, providing they are not in the northern California area.

SAILING, Dept. PM, 125 E. Main St., Box 248, Port Washington WI 53074. (414)284-3494. Editor: Micca L. Hutchins. Circ. 40,000. Monthly magazine. Emphasizes sailing. Our theme is "the beauty of sail." Readers are sailors with great sailing experience—racing and cruising. Sample copy free with 11×15 SAE and $2.40 postage. Photo guidelines free with SASE.

Needs: "We are a photo journal-type publication so about 50% of issue is photos." Needs photos of exciting sailing action, onboard deck shots; sailor-type boat portraits seldom used. Special needs include largely b&w, some inside color—mainly good *sailing* (not simply sailboats) shots. Captions required. "We must have area sailed, etc. identification."

Making Contact & Terms: Query with samples. Send 8×10 glossy b&w prints; 35mm transparencies by mail for consideration. "Request guidelines first—a big help." SASE. Reports in 1 month. Pays $100/color cover photo; $15-50/b&w inside photo; $50-100/color inside photo (depends on size used); text/photo package by arrangement. Pays 30 days after publication. Credit line given. Buys one-time rights. Simultaneous submissions and previously published work OK "if not with other sailing publications who compete with us."

Tips: "We are looking for good, clean, sharp photos of sailing action—exciting shots are for us. No 'fly-spec' sails against the horizon. We use close work from a sailor's perspective. Please request a sample copy to become familiar with format. Knowledge of the sport of sailing a requisite for good photos for us."

SAILING WORLD, 5 John Clarke Rd., Newport RI 02840. (401)847-1588. Fax: (401)848-5048. Editor: John Burnham. Art Director: Rachel Cocroft. Circ. 62,000. Estab. 1962. Monthly magazine. Emphasizes sailboat racing and performance cruising for sailors, upper income. Sample copy $5. Photo guidelines free with SASE.
Needs: "We will send an updated photo letter listing our needs on request. Freelance photography in a given issue: 20% assignment and 80% freelance stock. "We are using more 4-color photos and need high-quality work." Covers most sailing races.
Making Contact & Terms: Uses 35mm and 2¼×2¼ transparencies for covers. Vertical and square (slightly horizontal) formats. Reports in 1 month. Pays $500 for cover shot; regular color $50-300 (varies with use). Pays on publication. Credit line given. Buys first N.A. serial rights.
Tips: "We look for photos that are unusual in composition, lighting and/or color that feature performance sailing at its most exciting. We would like to emphasize speed, skill, fun and action. Photos must be of high quality. We prefer Kodachrome 64 or Fuji Velvia film. We have a format that allows us to feature work of exceptional quality. A knowledge of sailing and experience with on-the-water photography is really a requirement." Please call with specific questions or interests. "We cover current events and generally only use photos taken in the past 30-60 days."

SALT WATER SPORTSMAN, 280 Summer St., Boston MA 02111. (617)439-9977. Fax: (617)439-9357. Editor: Barry Gibson. Circ. 140,000. Estab. 1939. Monthly magzine. Emphasizes all phases of salt water sport fishing for the avid beginner-to-professional salt water angler. "Only strictly marine monthly sport fishing magazine in the U.S." Sample copy free with 9×12 SAE and $2 postage. Free photo and writer's guidelines.
Needs: Buys 1-6 photos/issue (including covers) without ms; 20-30 photos/issue with ms. Needs salt water fishing photos. "Think scenery with human interest, mood, fishing action, storytelling close-ups of anglers in action. Make it come alive—and don't bother us with the obviously posed 'dead fish and stupid fisherman' back at the dock. Wants, on a regular basis, cover shots, vertical Kodachrome (or equivalent) original slides depicting salt water fishing action or 'mood.' " For accompanying ms needs fact/feature articles dealing with marine sportfishing in the US, Canada, Caribbean, Central and South America. Emphasis on how-to.
Making Contact & Terms: Send material by mail for consideration or query with samples. Provide resume and tearsheets to be kept on file for possible future assignments. Holds slides for 1 year and will pay as used. Uses 8×10 b&w and color glossy prints and 35mm or 2¼×2¼ transparencies; cover transparency vertical format required. SASE. Reports in 1 month. Pay included in total purchase price with ms, or pays $20-200/b&w photo; $50-400/color photo; $600 minimum/cover photo; $250-up/text photo package. **Pays on acceptance.** Buys one-time rights.
Tips: "Prefers to see a selection of fishing action or mood—no scenics, lighthouses, birds, etc.—must be sport fishing oriented. Be familiar with the magazine and send us the type of things we're looking for. Example: no horizontal cover slides with suggestions it can be cropped etc. Don't send Ektachrome. We're using more 'outside' photography—that is, photos not submitted with ms package. Take lots of verticals and experiment with lighting. Most shots we get are too dark."

SANTA BARBARA MAGAZINE, Dept. PM, Suite H, 226 E. Canon Perdido, Santa Barbara CA 93101. (805)965-5999. Fax: (805)965-7627. Editor: Daniel Denton. Photo Editor: Kimberly Kavish. Circ. 11,000. Estab. 1975. Bimonthly magazine. Emphasizes Santa Barbara community and culture. Sample copy $2.95 with 9×12 SASE.
Needs: Uses 50-60 photos/issue; 40% supplied by freelance photographers. Needs portrait, environmental, architectural, travel, celebrity, et al. Reviews photos with accompanying ms only. Model release required. Captions preferred.
Making Contact & Terms: Provide resume, business card, brochure, flyer or tearsheets to be kept on file for possible future assignments; "portfolio drop off Thursdays, pick up Fridays." Cannot return unsolicited material. Reports in 4-6 weeks. Pays $75-250/b&w or color photo. Pays on publication. Credit line given. Buys first N.A. serial rights.
Tips: Prefers to see strong personal style and excellent technical ability. "Work needs to be oriented to our market. Know our magazine and its orientation before contacting me."

THE SATURDAY EVENING POST SOCIETY, Dept. PM, Benjamin Franklin Literary & Medical Society, 1100 Waterway Blvd., Indianapolis IN 46202. (317)634-1100. Editor: Cory SerVaas, M.D. Photo Editor: Patrick Perry. Magazine published 9 times annually. For family readers interested in travel, food, fiction, personalities, human interest and medical topics—emphasis on health topics. Circ. 600,000. Sample copy $4; free photo guidelines with SASE.

Needs: Prefers the photo essay over single submission. Model release required.
Making Contact & Terms: Send photos for consideration; 8 × 10 b&w glossy prints; 35mm or larger transparencies. Provide business card to be kept on file for possible future assignments. SASE. Reports in 1 month. Pays $50 minimum/b&w photo or by the hour; pays $150 minimum for text/photo package; $75 minimum/color photo; $300/color cover photo. Pays on publication. Prefers all rights. Simultaneous submissions and previously published work OK.

SCIENCE OF MIND MAGAZINE, Dept. PM, 3251 W. Sixth St., Los Angeles CA 90020. (213)388-2181. Fax: (213)388-1926. Editor: Kathy Juline. Photo Coordinator: Randall Friesen. Circ. 100,000. Estab. 1927. Monthly. Emphasizes Science of Mind philosophy. Readers include positive thinkers, holistic healing, psychological thinkers. Sample copy and photo guidelines free with 6 × 9 SASE.
Needs: Uses 7-10 photos/issue; 4-8 supplied by freelance photographers. Needs inspirational nature and people shots. Also, symbolic images. Reviews with or without accompanying ms. Model/property release required. Captions preferred.
Making Contact & Terms: Send high-quality duplicate 35mm transparencies by mail for consideration. Include 6 × 9 SASE. Reports in 4 weeks. Pays $100/color cover photo; $25/inside b&w photo; $50/inside color photo. Pays 30 days after masthead date. Credit line given. Buys one-time rights unless otherwise specified. Simultaneous submissions and previously published work OK.
Tips: "Send duplicates only. On first contact, do not send more than 24 slides. The longer we keep images in our file, the more opportunities for usage."

*SCIENTIFIC AMERICAN, 415 Madison Ave., New York NY 10017. (212)754-0474. Fax: (212)755-0474. Photography Editor: Nisa Geller. Circ. 600,000. Estab. 1854. Emphasizes science technology and people involved in science. Readers are male ages 35-65. Samples copies $3.95.
Needs: Uses 28-50 photos/issue; 90% supplied by freelancers. Needs photos of animals, scenics, technology, personalities and how-to shots. Reviews photos only on request. Model release required. Property release preferred. Captions required.
Making Contact & Terms: Interested in receiving work from newer, lesser-known photographers. Submit portfolio for review. Query with stock photo list. Provide resume, business card, brochure, flyer or tearsheets to be kept on file for possible assignments. Does not keep samples on file. Cannot return material. Reports in 1 month. Pays $350/day; $1,000/color cover photo. Pays on publication. Credit line given. Buys one-time rights; negotiable.
Tips: Wants to see strong natural and artificial lighting. "Send business cards and promotional pieces frequently when dealing with magazine editors. Find a niche."

✹SCORE, Canada's Golf Magazine, 287 MacPherson Ave., Toronto, Ontario M4V 1A4 Canada. (416)928-2909. Fax: (416)928-1357. Managing Editor: Bob Weeks. Magazine published 7 times/year. Emphasizes golf. "The foundation of the magazine is Canadian golf and golfers." Readers are affluent, well-educated, 80% male, 20% female. Circ. 110,000. Estab. 1980. Sample copy $2 (Canadian). Photo guidelines free with SAE with IRC.
Needs: Uses between 10 and 15 photos/issue; approximately 95% supplied by freelance photographers. Needs "professional-quality, golf-oriented color and b&w material on prominent Canadian male and female pro golfers on the US PGA and LPGA tours, as well as the European and other international circuits, scenics, travel, close-ups and full-figure." Model releases (if necessary) and captions required.
Making Contact & Terms: Query with samples and with list of stock photo subjects. Send 8 × 10 or 5 × 7 glossy b&w prints and 35mm or 2¼ × 2¼ transparencies by mail for consideration. Provide resume, business card, brochure, flyer or tearsheets to be kept on file for possible future assignments. SASE with IRC. Reports in 3 weeks. Pays $75-100/color cover photo; $30/b&w inside photo; $50/color inside photo; $40-65/hour; $320-520/day; and $80-2,000/job. **Pays on acceptance.** Credit line given. Buys all rights. Simultaneous submissions OK.
Tips: "When approaching *Score* with visual material, it is best to illustrate photographic versatility with a variety of lenses, exposures, subjects and light conditions. Golf is not a high-speed sport, but invariably presents a spectrum of location puzzles: rapidly changing light conditions, weather, positioning, etc. Capabilities should be demonstrated in query photos. Scenic material follows the same rule. Specific golf hole shots are certainly encouraged for travel features, but wide-angle shots are just as important, to 'place' the golf hole or course, especially if it is located close to notable landmarks or particularly stunning scenery. Approaching *Score* is best done with a clear, concise presentation. A picture is absolutely worth a thousand words, and knowing your market and your particular strengths will prevent a mutual waste of time and effort. Sample copies of the magazine are available and any photographer seeking to work with *Score* is encouraged to investigate it prior to querying."

SCRIPTS AND SCRIBBLES, University Arts Resources, 141 Wooster, New York NY 10012. (212)473-6695. Contact: Larry Qualls. Estab. 1988. Journal. Emphasizes theater, dance, contemporary art and architecture. Readers are university professors. Sample copy available.
Needs: Reviews photos with or without a manuscript. Model/property release required. Captions required.
Making Contact & Terms: Query with resume of credits. Reports in 3 weeks. NPI. Pays on publication. Credit line given. Rights negotiable. Previously published work OK.

SCUBA TIMES MAGAZINE, Suite 16, 14110 Perdido Key Dr., Pensacola FL 32507. (904)492-7805. Fax: (904)492-7807. Art Director: Trish Russell. Circ. 40,000. Estab. 1972. Bimonthly magazine. Emphasizes scuba diving. Sample copy $3. Photo guidelines free with SASE. Provides an editorial schedule with SASE.
   • The editorial staff at this magazine likes to work with photographers who can write as well as shoot outstanding images. Don't be afraid to deviate from "blue" photos when submitting work. Other vibrant colors can make you stand out.
Needs: Uses 50-60 photos/issue; all supplied by freelance photographers. Needs animal/wildlife shots, travel, scenics, how-to, all with an underwater focus. Model release preferred. Captions preferred.
Making Contact & Terms: Interested in receiving work from newer, lesser-known photographers. "Send a sample (40-60 dupes) for our stock file with each slide labelled according to location rather than creature. Send a complete list of destinations you have photographed. We will build a file from which we can make assignments and order originals." Send 35mm transparencies. SASE. Reports in 1 to 2 months. Pays $150/color cover photo; $75/color page rate; $75/b&w page rate. Pays 30 days after publication. Credit line given. Buys one-time rights. Previously published work OK "under certain circumstances."
Tips: Looks for underwater and "topside" shots of dive destinations around the world, close-ups of marine creatures, divers underwater with creatures or coral. "We look for photographers who can capture the details that, when combined, create not only a physical description, but also capture the spirit of a dive destination. In portfolio or samples, likes to see "broad range of samples, majority underwater."

*SEA KAYAKER, 6327 Seaview Ave. NW, Seattle WA 98107. (206)789-1326. Fax: (206)789-6392. Editor: Christopher Cunningham. Circ. 12,000. Estab. 1984. Quarterly magazine. Emphasizes sea kayaking—kayak cruising on coastal and inland waterways. Sample copy $4.85. Photo guidelines free with SASE.
Needs: Uses 50 photos/issue; 85% supplied by freelancers. Needs photos of sea kayaking locations, coastal camping, paddling techniques. Reviews photos with or without ms. Always looking for cover images (to be translated into paintings, etc. Model/property release preferred. Captions preferred.
Making Contact & Terms: Interested in receiving work from newer, lesser-known photographers. Submit portfolio for review. Send unsolicited photos by mail for consideration. Send 5×7 color and b&w prints; 35mm transparencies. Keeps samples on file. SASE. Reports in 1 month. Pays $45-50/color cover photo; $25-50/color inside photo; $15-35/b&w inside photo. Pays on publication. Credit line given. Buys one-time rights, first N.A. serial rights.
Tips: Subjects "must relate to sea kayaking and cruising locations."

*SEATTLE WEEKLY, 1931 Second Ave., Seattle WA 98101. (206)441-5555. Fax: (206)441-6213. Art Director: Fred Andrews. Circ. 35,000. Estab. 1976. Weekly. Emphasizes Seattle politics and the arts. Sample copy 75¢.
Needs: Uses 6-12 photos/issue; half supplied by freelancers. Needs photojournalistic shots and portraits. Reviews photos with or without ms. Model/property release preferred. Captions preferred.
Making Contact & Terms: Interested in receiving work from newer, lesser-known photographers. Arrange personal interview to show portfolio. Query with resume of credits. Does not keep samples on file. SASE. Reports in 1 month. Pays $150-250/color cover photo; $75-150/b&w inside photo. Pays on publication. Credit line given. Buys one-time rights; negotiable. Previously published work OK.

*SECURE RETIREMENT, #800, 200 K St. NW, Washington DC 20006. (202)822-9459. Fax: (202)822-9612. Editor: Denise Fremeau. Circ. 2 million +. Estab. 1992. Publication of the National Committee to Preserve Social Security and Medicare. Magazine published 8 times yearly. Emphasizes aging and senior citizen issues. Readers are male and female retirees/non-retirees, ages 50-80. Sample copy free with 9×12 SASE.
Needs: Uses 20-25 photos/issue; 10-15 supplied by freelancers. Needs photos of generic, healthy lifestyle seniors, intergenerational families. Reviews photos with or without a ms. Model release required. Captions preferred.
Making Contact & Terms: Interested in receiving work from newer, lesser-known photographers. Arrange personal interview to show portfolio. Provide resume, business card, brochure, flyer or tearsheets to be kept on file for possible assignments. Keeps samples on file. SASE. Reports in 3 weeks.

Pays $100-400/day; $200-300/color inside photo. Pays on publication. Credit line given. Buys one-time rights; negotiable. Simultaneous submissions and/or previously published work OK.

Tips: "We are also interested in hiring freelancers to cover events for us across the nation (approximately 3-7 events/month)."

SEEK, 8121 Hamilton Ave., Cincinnati OH 45231. (513)931-4050, ext. 365. Publisher: Eugene Wigginton. Editor: Eileen H. Wilmoth. Circ. 60,000. Quarterly, in weekly issues; 8 pages per issue; bulletin size. Emphasizes religion/faith. Readers are church people—young and middle-aged adults. Free sample copy with 6×9 SAE and 39¢ postage.

Needs: Uses about 3 photos/issue; all supplied by freelance photographers. Needs photos of people, scenes and objects to illustrate stories and articles on a variety of themes. Must be appropriate to illustrate Christian themes. Model release required.

Making Contact & Terms: Send by mail for consideration actual 8×10 b&w photos or query with list of stock photo subjects. SASE. "Freelance photographers submit assortments of b&w 8×10 photos that are circulated among all our editors who use photos." Reports in 4 weeks. **Pays on acceptance.** Pays $15-25/b&w photo. Credit line given. Buys first N.A. serial rights. Simultaneous submissions and previously published work OK if so indicated.

Tips: "Make sure photos have sharp contrast. We like to receive photos of young or middle-aged adults in a variety of settings."

SELF, Dept. PM, 350 Madison Ave., New York NY 10017. (212)880-8864. Editor-in-Chief: Alexandra Penney. Monthly magazine. Emphasizes self-improvement and physical and mental well being for women of all ages. Circ. 1,091,000.

Needs: Needs photos emphasizing health, beauty, medicine, relationships and psychology relating to women. Uses up to 200 photos/issue; all supplied by freelancers.

Making Contact & Terms: Works with photographers on assignment basis only. Provide tearsheets to be kept on file for possible future assignments. Pays $200/b&w and color photos; $350/day.

SENIOR MAGAZINE, 3565 South Higuera, San Luis Obispo CA 93401. (805)544-8711. Publisher: Gary Suggs. Circ. 500,000. Estab. 1981.Monthly magazine, tabloid. Emphasizes "the wonderful life over 40." Readers are male and female, ages 40 and older. Sample copies for 9×12 SAE and $1.25 postage.

Needs: Uses 5-15 photos/issue; most supplied by freelance photographers. Needs mainly personality shots. Buys photos with or without ms. Special photo needs include WWII photos—people, planes and famous wartime people. Model release required.

Making Contact & Terms: Query with list of stock photo subjects. SASE. Reports in 1-2 weeks. Pays $100/b&w cover photo; $50-75/b&w inside photo. **Pays on acceptance.** Credit lines given. Buys one-time rights, also second reprint rights. Previously published work OK if not from competitive "senior" publications.

Tips: "We really need photos of the famous; photos of unknowns and people over 50 with ms, only."

*SHOUT! MAGAZINE, 619 S. Main St., Gainesville FL 32601. (904)375-8953. Fax: (904)375-8959. President: Dana P. Mansfield. Circ. 250,000. Estab. 1986. Monthly tabloid. Emphasizes college fashion and spring break. Readers are 18-25. Sample copy free with 11×14 SAE and 7 first-class stamps.

Needs: Uses 150 photos/issue; 140 supplied by freelancers. Needs photos of "colorful" fashion, crowd shots, woman in swimwear, volleyball. Reviews photos with or without ms. Special photo needs include fashion. Model/property release required for swimwear. Captions preferred.

Making Contact & Terms: Interested in receiving work from newer, lesser-known photographers. Send unsolicited photos by mail for consideration. Provide resume, business card, brochure, flyer or tearsheets to be kept on file for possible assignments. Send 3×5 color prints; 35mm transparencies. Keeps samples on file. SASE. Reports in 1 month. NPI. Pays on publication. Credit line given. Buys one-time rights; negotiable. Simultaneous submissions and/or previously published work OK.

Tips: "More photos means more options to choose from; send what you have, let us decide."

SHOWBOATS INTERNATIONAL, Suite 200, 1600 SE 17th St., Ft. Lauderdale FL 33316. (305)525-8626. Fax: (305)525-7954. Executive Editor: Marilyn Mower. Circ. 60,000. Estab. 1981. Bimonthly magazine. Emphasizes exclusively large yachts (100 feet or over). Readers are mostly male, 40 plus, incomes above $1 million, international. Sample copy $5.

● In 1992 this publication received a bronze Charlie Award from the Florida Magazine Association for having the best overall magazine with a circulation below 25,000.

Needs: Uses 90-150 photos/issue; 85% supplied by freelancers. Needs photos of very large yachts and exotic destinations. "Almost all shots are commissioned by us." Model/property releases required.

Making Contact & Terms: Arrange personal interview to show portfolio. Submit portfolio for review. Query with resume of credits. Provide resume, business card, brochure, flyer or tearsheets to be kept on file for possible assignments. Does not keep samples on file. SASE. Reports in 3 weeks. Pays $350-500/color cover photo; $300/color page rate; $350-750/day. Pays on publication. Credit line given. Buys

first N.A. serial rights, all rights; negotiable. Previously published work OK, however, exclusivity is important.
Tips: "Don't send pictures that need any excuses. The larger the format, the better."

SIMPLY SEAFOOD, Dept. PM, Second Floor, 850 N.W. 46th St., Seattle WA 98107. (206)547-6030. Fax: (206)548-9346. Photo Editor: Carolyn Cox. Estab. 1991. Quarterly magazine. Emphasizes seafood recipes, step-by-step cooking of seafood, profiles of chefs. Sample copy $1.95. Photo guidelines free with SASE.
• In 1991 this publication received a Maggie Award as the Best New Consumer Magazine.
Needs: Uses 40 photos/issue; 25% supplied by freelancers. Needs "mainly food shots, a few travel, historic and fishing shots, chefs in different locations." Model/property release preferred. Captions preferred.
Making Contact & Terms: Interested in receiving work from newer, lesser-known photographers. Query with list of stock photo subjects. Provide resume, business card, brochure, flyer or tearsheets to be kept on file for possible assignments. Keeps samples on file. SASE. Reports as needed. Pays $100/color cover photo; $50/color inside photo. Pays on publication. Credit line given. Buys one-time rights; negotiable. Simultaneous submissions and previously published work OK.
Tips: "Looking for two types of photographers: food photographers to shoot our recipes, and photographers who can go and shoot a chef or scene in different locales."

SINGLE PROFILE MAGAZINE, P.O. Box 6098, Delray Beach FL 33484. (305)974-6453. Editor: Darin Bosse. Circ. 60,000. Estab. 1989. Quarterly magazine. Readers are male and female business and professional single people, ages 18-65. Brochure free with SASE. Photo guidelines free with SASE.
Needs: Uses 120-450 photos/issue; 50% supplied by freelancers. Needs photos of attractive, interesting, single, eligible men and women, 18-65, showing them at work or at play. There should be a relaxed atmosphere with clear view of face. Photo should say something about the subject. Reviews photos with or without a manuscript. Model/property release required. Photo captions required; include first name, marital status, age, profession and interests.
Making Contact & Terms: Query with stock photo list. Send unsolicited photos by mail for consideration. Provide resume, business card, brochure, flyer or tearsheets to be kept on file for possible assignments. Send 4×5, 5×7, 8×10 glossy b&w, color prints; 35mm, 4×5, 8×10 transparencies. Keeps samples on file. SASE. Reports in 4-6 weeks. Pays $250-750/color cover photo; $25-250/color inside photo; $25-250/b&w inside photo; $150-400/day. Pays on publication. Credit line given. Buys first N.A. serial rights. Simultaneous submissions and previously published work OK within 1 year.
Tips: "Pick attractive, interesting subjects and locations that tell something about the subject."

SINGLELIFE MILWAUKEE, Dept. PM, 606 W. Wisconsin Ave., Milwaukee WI 53203. (414)271-9700. Art Director: Paul Rosanski. Bimonthly. Emphasizes recreation and special interests for single adults. Readers are single adults 18-70. Circ. 24,000. Sample copy $2.50.
Needs: Uses about 20 photos/issue; all supplied by freelance photographers. Need photos of skiing, biking, dining, dancing, picnics, sailing—single people, couples or groups of people in recreational settings. Model release and captions required.
Making Contact & Terms: Send b&w or color glossy prints, 2¼×2¼ transparencies, b&w contact sheet by mail for consideration. SASE. Pays $30-100/b&w photo; $40-300/color photo; $50-300/job. Pays on publication. Credit line given. Buys all rights. Previously published work OK.
Tips: "We look for recreational scenes (active and passive) of couples or individuals in a portfolio. We also are getting very active in fashion photography."

SINISTER WISDOM, P.O. Box 3252, Berkeley CA 94703. Contact: Editor. Circ. 3,000. Estab. 1976. Published 3 times/year. Emphasizes lesbian/feminist themes. Readers are lesbians/women, ages 20-90. Sample copy $6.50. Photo guidelines free with SASE.
Needs: Uses 3-6 photos/issue. Needs photos relevant to specific theme, by lesbians only. Reviews photos with or without a ms. Model/property release required. Captions preferred.
Making Contact & Terms: Send unsolicited photos by mail for consideration. Provide resume, business card, brochure, flyer or tearsheets to be kept on file for possible assignments. Send all sizes or finishes. Reports in 2-9 months. Pays in copies. Pays on publication. Credit line given. Buys one-time rights; negotiable.

The First Markets Index preceding the General Index in the back of this book provides the names of those companies/publications interested in receiving work from newer, lesser-known photographers.

Tips: "Read at least one issue of *Sinister Wisdom*."

*680 MAGAZINE, P.O. Box 2340, Walnut Creek CA 92595. (510)935-7673. Fax: (510)934-8277. Art Director: John Cornett. Circ. 20,000. Estab. 1991. Quarterly magazine. General interest, Bay Area magazine. Readers are male and female, ages 21-65. Sample copy $3 with 11×13 SAE and 6 first-class stamps. Photo guidelines free with SASE.
Needs: Uses 20-30 photos/issue; 75% supplied by freelancers. Needs photos of travel, personalities, attractive people. Reviews photos with or without ms. Special photo needs include fashion, b&w. Model release preferred. Captions required; include who, what, where.
Making Contact & Terms: Interested in receiving work from newer, lesser-known photographers. Arrange personal interview to show portfolio. Does not keep samples on file. SASE. Reports in 1 month. Pays $50-150/color cover photo; $50-150/b&w cover photo; $10-40/color inside photo; $10-40/b&w inside photo. Pays on publication. Credit line given. Buys one-time rights; negotiable. Simultaneous submissions and/or previously published work OK.
Tips: "Sexy, black and white fashion photos are needed. Starting out accept all publication opportunities."

SKI, Dept. PM, 2 Park Ave, New York NY 10016. (212)779-5000. (212)779-5469. Editor: Dick Needham. Circ. 440,000. Estab. 1936. Monthly. Emphasizes skiing for skiers.
Needs: All photos supplied by freelance photographers; 20% assigned, 80% freelance stock. Model release required. Captions required.
Making Contact & Terms: Send 35mm, 2¼×2¼ or 4×5 transparencies by mail (dupes OK) for consideration. SASE. Reports in 1 week. Pays $750 color cover photo; $50-250/b&w inside photo; $50-350/color inside photo; $75-100/b&w half page; $150 b&w page; $250/color page; $200-600/job; $75-750/b&w or color photo; $350/day; $500-850 for text/photo package. **Pays on acceptance.** Credit line given. Buys one-time rights.

❦SKI CANADA, Dept. PM, 10 Pote Ave., Toronto, Ontario 2S7 M4N Canada. (416)322-9606. Fax: (416)941-9113. Editor: Cathy Carl. Monthly magazine published 6 times/year, fall and winter only. Readership is 75% male, ages 19-40, with high income. Circ. 60,000. Sample copy free with SASE.
Needs: Uses 80 photos/issue; 100% supplied by freelance photographers. Needs photos of skiing—competition, equipment, travel (within Canada and abroad), instruction, news and trends. Model release required; photo captions preferred.
Making Contact & Terms: Send unsolicited photos by mail for consideration. Provide resume, business card, brochure, flyer or tearsheets to be kept on file for possible assignments. Send color and 35mm transparencies. SASE. Reports in 1 month. Pays $100/photo/page or smaller; $200/ photo larger than 1 page; cover $400; rates are for b&w or color. Pays on publication. Credit line given. Buys first N.A. serial rights. Simultaneous submissions OK.
Tips: In samples, wants to see "sharp, good action shots. Also, shots that depict ski areas accurately, in good variety. In addition to payment receives 1 issue of our summer magazine *SunSports*—on newsstands first week of May each year—all summer sports: tennis, golf, windsurfing, waterskiing, cycling, footwear, fashion, beach activities, triathlon, etc."

SKY (Inflight Magazine of Delta Air Lines), Suite 300, 600 Corporate Dr., Ft. Lauderdale FL 33334. (305)776-0066. (800)523-6809. Fax: (305)493-8969. Photo Editor: Coni Kaufman. Circ. 500,000 (print run). Estab. 1971. Monthly magazine. Emphasizes general interest and business/finance topics. Sample copy $3 and 9×12 SAE.
• This publication went through a recent redesign and has several past honors for outstanding designs, including bronze Ozzie Awards in 1991 and 1992, and a 1992 Charlie Award from the Florida Magazine Association.
Needs: Uses about 70 photos/issue; 35% supplied by freelance photographers. Needs photos of travel, consumer, entertainment, business, lifestyle, sports, technology, collectibles. Reviews photos with accompanying ms only unless submitting for "Places" department. "We are actively seeking materials for 'Places' department, our photo end page that features interesting perspectives on Delta destination cities (vertical format only)." Model release required. Captions required, include in travel photos.
Making Contact & Terms: Interested in receiving work from newer, lesser-known photographers. Send 35mm and 2¼×2¼ transparencies by mail for consideration. Provide resume, buisness card, brochure, flyer or tearsheets to be kept on file for possible future assignments. SASE. Reports in 1 month. Pays $450/color cover photo; $100-175/color inside photo; $1,000/text/photo package. Pays on publication. Credit line given. Buys one-time rights. Simultaneous submissions and previously published work OK.
Tips: Request guidelines and include SASE. Follow up and send samples. No posed travel shots.

Freelancer Mark Downey of Alameda, California, has traveled worldwide in search of beautiful images and this shot, used on the cover of Sky magazine, epitomizes the mystical culture of India. Downey says the photo also was used in an advertorial and a catalog. (For more on Downey and his work see the Insider Report on page 378.)

© photo by Mark Downey

*SMITHSONIAN, Arts & Industrial Building, 900 Jefferson Dr., Washington DC 20560. (Prefers not to share information.)

*SOAP OPERA DIGEST, 45 W 25th St., New York NY 10010. (212)645-2100. Fax: (212)645-0683. Editor-in Chief: Lynn Leahey. Art Director: Catherine Connors. Photo Editor: Christina Bonicki. Circ. 1 million. Estab. 1975. Biweekly. Emphasizes daytime and nighttime TV serial drama. Readers are mostly women, all ages. Sample copy free with 5 × 7 SAE and 73¢ postage.
Needs: Needs photos of people who appear on daytime and nighttime TV soap operas; special events in which they appear. Uses mostly color and some b&w photos.
Making Contact & Terms: Interested in receiving work from newer, lesser-known photographers. Query with resume of credits to photo editor. Provide business card and promotional material to be kept on file for possible future assignments. SASE. Reports in 4 weeks. Pays $50-175/b&w photo; $100-400/color photo; $350-1,000/complete package. **Pays on acceptance.** Credit line given. Buys all rights; negotiable.
Tips: "Have photos of the most popular stars and of good quality." Sharp color quality is a must. "I look for something that's unusual in a picture, like a different pose instead of head shots. We are not interested in people who happened to take photos of someone they met. Show variety of lighting techniques and creativity in your portfolio."

*SOCIETY, Rutgers University, New Brunswick NJ 08903. (201)932-2280. Fax: (201)932-3138. Editor: Irving Louis Horowitz. Circ. 31,000. Estab. 1962. Bimonthly magazine. Readers are interested in the understanding and use of the social sciences and new ideas and research findings from sociology, psychology, political science, anthropology and economics. Free sample copy and photo guidelines.
Needs: Buys 75-100 photos/annually. Human interest, photo essay and documentary. Needs photo essays—"no random photo submissions." Essays (brief) should stress human interaction; photos should be of people interacting (not a single person) or of natural surroundings. Include an accompanying explanation of photographer's "aesthetic vision."
Making Contact & Terms: Send 8 × 10 b&w glossy prints for consideration. SASE. Reports in 3 months. Pays $250/photo essay. Pays on publication. Buys all rights to one-time usage.

SOUNDINGS, Dept. PM, 35 Pratt St., Essex CT 06441. (203)767-3200. Editor-in-Chief: Narleah Ross. Monthly tabloid. Emphasizes recreational boating. Readers are men, ages 40-60, with approximately $70,000 annual income. Circ. 105,000. Sample copy free with 12 × 18 SASE and $2.50 postage. Photo guidelines free with SASE.

Needs: Uses 50 photos/issue; 40% supplied by freelance photographers. Needs photos for story illustrations, plus a few pictures of boating enterprises. Editorial calendar available. Model release preferred; captions required.

Making Contact & Terms: Send unsolicited photos by mail for consideration. Provide resume, business card, brochure, flyer or tearsheets to be kept on file for possible assignments. Send b&w prints, any size and format, or 35mm transparencies. SASE. Reports in 1 month. Pays $200-400/color cover photo, $35 and up/b&w inside photo and $400/day. Pays on publication. Credit line given. Buys one-time rights. Previously published work OK.

Tips: In portfolios, "looking for a range of skills: action, fill flash, portrait, etc."

SOUTHERN ACCENTS, 2100 Lakeshore Dr., Birmingham AL 35209. (205)877-6000. Fax: (205)877-6600. Art Director: Lane Gregory. Estab. 1977. 6 issues/year. Emphasizes interiors, gardens. Readers are "upper class." Circ. 500,000. Sample copy available for 9 × 12 SAE and $2.50 postage.

Needs: Uses 200 photos/issue, 75% supplied by freelancers. "Needs interior and garden photos exclusively; our choice of locations." Model release required.

Making Contact & Terms: Interested in receiving work from newer, lesser-known photographers. Provide resume, business card, brochure, flyer or tearsheets to be kept on file for possible future assignments. SASE. Reports in 1 month. Pays $500-1,000/job (day rate). Pays on publication. Credit line given. Buys rights for one year; will negotiate with photographer unwilling to sell all rights.

Tips: "Send only samples of interiors, table scapes and gardens—no food or fashion."

SOUTHERN BOATING, 1766 Bay Rd., Miami Beach FL 33139. (305)538-0700. Editorial Director: Andree Conrad. Circ. 26,000. Estab. 1972. Monthly magazine. Emphasizes "boating (mostly power, but also sail) in the Southeastern US and the Caribbean." Readers are "concentrated in 30-50 age group; male and female; affluent—executives mostly." Sample copy $4.

Needs: Number of photos/issue varies; all supplied by freelancers. Needs "photos to accompany articles about cruising destinations, the latest in boats and boat technology, boating activities (races, rendezvous); cover photos of a boat in a square format (a must) in the context of that issue's focus (see editorial calendar)." Model release preferred. Captions required.

Making Contact & Terms: Query with list of stock photo subjects. SASE. Reporting time varies. Pays $50 up/color cover photo; $25 up/color inside photo; $10 up/b&w inside photo; $75-150/photo/ text package. Pays on publication. Credit line given. Buys one-time rights. Simultaneous submissions and previously published work OK.

Tips: "Photography on the water is very tricky. We are looking for first-rate work, preferably Kodachrome or Fujichrome, and prefer to have story *and* photos together, except in the case of cover material."

SOUTHERN EXPOSURE, P.O. Box 531, Durham NC 27702. (919)419-8311. Managing Editor: Eric Bates. Estab. 1972. Quarterly. Emphasizes the politics and culture of the South, with special interest in women's issues, black affairs and labor. Sample copy $4 with 9 × 12 SASE. Photo guidelines free with SASE.

Needs: Uses 30 photos/issue; most supplied by freelance photographers. Needs news and historical photos; photo essays. Model release preferred. Captions preferred.

Making Contact & Terms: Query with samples. Send glossy b&w prints by mail for consideration. SASE. Reports in 3-6 weeks. Pays $100/color cover photo; $50/b&w inside photo. Credit line given. Buys all rights "unless the photographer requests otherwise." Simultaneous submissions and previously published work OK.

SPORT FISHING, 330 W. Canton, Winter Park FL 32789. (407)628-4802. Fax: (407)628-7061. Photo Editor: Doug Olander. Circ. 100,000. Estab. 1986. Publishes 9 issues/year. Emphasizes off-shore fishing. Readers are upscale boat owners and off-shore fishermen. Sample copy $2.50 with 9 × 12 SAE and $1.58 postage. Photo guidelines free with SASE.

Needs: Uses 50 photos/issue; 85% supplied by freelance photographers. Needs photos of off-shore fish and fishing—especially big boats/big fish, action shots. "We are working more from stock—good opportunities for extra sales on any given assignment." Model release preferred; releases needed for subjects (under "unusual" circumstances) in photo. Captions preferred.

Making Contact & Terms: Interested in receiving work from newer, lesser-known photographers. Query with samples. Send unsolicited photos by mail for consideration. Provide resume, business card, brochure, flyer or tearsheets to be kept on file for possible assignments. Send 35mm, 2¼ × 2¼ and 4 × 5 transparencies by mail for consideration. "Kodachrome 64 and Fuji 100 are preferred."

Reports in 3 weeks. Pays $20-100/b&w page; $50-500/color page. Buys one-time rights unless otherwise agreed upon. Simultaneous submissions OK.

Tips: "Tack-sharp focus critical; avoid 'kill' shots of big game fish, sharks; avoid bloody fish in/at the boat. The best guideline is the magazine itself. Get used to shooting on, in or under water. Most of our needs are found there. If you have first rate photos and questions: call."

SPUR, 13 W. Federal, P.O. Box 85, Middleburg VA 22117. (703)687-6314. Fax: (703)687-3925. Editor: Cathy Laws. Bimonthly magazine. Emphasizes Thoroughbred horses. Readers are "owners, breeders, trainers and enthusiasts in the sports of racing, steeplechasing, polo, fox hunting, horse showing and three-day eventing." Circ. 15,000 + . Sample copy $5. Photo guidelines free with SASE.

Needs: Uses about 45-55 photos/issue; all supplied by freelance photographers. Buys 40% on freelance assignment, 60% from freelance stock. Needs photos of "horses and action (racing, steeplechasing, polo), scenic shots, people involved in Thoroughbred sports." Special needs include "covers—colorful, original approaches." All photos must be identified including names of people and horses.

Making Contact & Terms: Interested in receiving work from newer, lesser-known photographers. Query with samples. Send transparencies, slides or prints by mail for consideration; prefers slides. Provide resume, business card, brochure, flyer or tearsheets to be kept on file for possible future assignments. SASE. Reports in 3 weeks. Pays $250-500/day; $300 up/color cover photo; $20-100/b&w inside photo; $50-250/color inside photo. Pays on publication. Buys one-time rights. Credit line given.

Tips: "We want good action shots, great color—not too dark—we sometimes have problems on press with darkness. There is a trend toward increased use of Fuji Velvia film—colors print rich. Send samples—it doesn't matter if subjects are not horse-related. We want to see good examples of outdoor action as well as well-lit interiors."

*SPY, The Spy Building, 5 Union Square West, New York NY 10003. (Prefers not to share information.)

STAR, 660 White Plains Rd., Tarrytown NY 10591. (914)332-5000. Editor: Richard Kaplan. Photo Director: Alistair Duncan. Circ. 3,102,000. Weekly. Emphasizes news, human interest and celebrity stories. Sample copy and photo guidelines free with SASE.

Needs: Uses 100-125 photos/issue; 75% supplied by freelancers. Reviews photos with or without accompanying ms. Model release preferred. Captions required.

Making Contact & Terms: Query with samples and with list of stock photo subjects. Send 8 × 10 b&w prints; 35mm, 2¼ × 2¼ transparencies by mail for consideration. SASE. Reports in 2 weeks. NPI. Pays on publication. Credit line sometimes given. Simultaneous submissions and previously published work OK.

THE STATE: Down Home in North Carolina, Suite 2200, 128 S. Tryon St., Charlotte NC 28202. (704)371-3265. Editor: Scott Smith. Circ. 21,000. Estab. 1933. Monthly magazine. Regional publication, privately owned, emphasizing travel, history, nostalgia, folklore, humor, all subjects regional to North Carolina for residents of, and others interested in, North Carolina. Sample copy $3. "Send for our photography guidelines."

Needs: Freelance photography used; 5% assignment and 5% stock. Photos on travel, history and human interest in North Carolina. Captions required.

Making Contact & Terms: Send material by mail for consideration. Uses 5 × 7 and 8 × 10 glossy b&w prints; also glossy color prints and slides. Uses b&w and color cover photos, vertical preferred. SASE. Pays $25/b&w photo; $25-125/color photo; $125-150/complete job. Credit line given. Pays on publication.

Tips: Looks for "North Carolina material; solid cutline information."

STOCK CAR RACING MAGAZINE, 27 S. Main St., P.O. Box 715, Ipswich MA 01938. (508)356-7030. Fax: (508)356-2492. Editor: Dick Berggren. Circ. 400,000. Estab. 1966. Monthly magazine. Emphasizes all forms of stock car competition. Read by fans, owners and drivers of race cars and those with racing businesses. Photo guidelines free with SASE.

Needs: Buys 50-70 photos/issue. Documentary, head shot, photo essay/photo feature, product shot, personality, crash pictures, special effects/experimental, technical and sport. No photos unrelated to stock car racing. Photos purchased with or without accompany ms and on assignment. Model release required unless subject is a racer who has signed a release at the track. Captions required.

Making Contact & Terms: Send material by mail for consideration. Uses 8 × 10 glossy b&w prints; 35mm or 2¼ × 2¼ transparencies. Kodachrome 64 or Fuji 100 preferred. Pays $20/b&w photo; $35-250/color photo; $250/cover photo. Pays on publication. Credit line given. Buys one-time rights.

Tips: "Send the pictures. We will buy anything that relates to racing if it's interesting, if we have the first shot at it, and it's well printed and exposed. Eighty percent of our rejections are for technical reasons—poorly focused, badly printed, too much dust, picture cracked, etc. We get far fewer cover submissions than we would like. We look for full bleed cover verticals where we can drop type into the picture and position our logo."

*STORM MAGAZINE, 202 E. Main, Reddick IL 60961. (815)365-2239. Publisher: Dave A. Curl. Circ. 50,000. Estab. 1993. Monthly magazine. Emphasizes adult entertainment served up with humor, sophistication and spice. Readers are mature males and females from all walks of life, ages 18-80. Photo guidelines free with SASE.
Needs: Uses 75-100 photos/issue; all supplied by freelancers. Needs sophisticated erotica (couples), travel, scenics, technology, how-to, glamour, auto shots, sports, humor, food and drink and personality shots. Reviews photos with or without accompanying ms. Special photo needs include photos that deal with indoor entertainment—wine, song, romance. Model/property release preferred. Captions required.
Making Contact & Terms: Interested in receiving work from newer, lesser-known photographers. Submit portfolio for review. Send unsolicited photos by mail for consideration. Provide resume, business card, brochure, flyer or tearsheets to be kept on file for possible assignments. Uses 8 × 10, 5 × 7 color/b&w prints; 35mm, 4 × 5, 8 × 10 transparencies. Keeps samples on file. SASE. Reports in 1-2 weeks. Pays $750 + / color cover photo; $350/b&w cover photo; $100/color inside photo; $100/b&w inside photo; $250/color page rate; $150/b&w page rate. Pays on publication. Credit line given. Buys one-time rights. Simultaneous submissions and previously published work OK.
Tips: "We are looking for a style similar to *Playboy* magazine from the 60's. *Storm Magazine* brings adult entertainment to both sexes. This is not a magazine devoted to just sex, but the sophisticated enjoyment of life's romances. Be breezy and imaginative. Controversy and originality are sought-after products."

THE STRAIN, P.O. Box 330507, Houston TX 77233-0507. (713)733-6042. For articles contact: Alicia Adler; for columns, Charlie Mainze. Circ. 1,000. Estab. 1987. Monthly magazine. Emphasizes interactive arts and 'The Arts'. Readers are mostly artists and performers. Sample copy $5 with 9 × 12 SAE and 7 first class stamps. Photo guidelines free with SASE.
Needs: Uses 5-100 photos/issue; 95% supplied by freelance photographers. Needs photos of scenics, personalities, portraits. "During the upcoming year we will be concentrating on portraiture." Model release required. Captions preferred.
Making Contact & Terms: Send any format b&w and color prints or transparencies by mail for consideration. SASE. The longer it is held, the more likely it will be published. Reports in 1 year. Pays $50/color cover photo; $100/b&w cover photo; $5 minimum/color inside photo; $5 minimum/b&w inside photo; $5/b&w page rate; $50-500/photo/text package. Pays on publication. Credit line given. Buys one-time rights or first N.A. serial rights. Simultaneous submissions and previously published work OK.

SUMMIT, The Mountain Journal, 1221 May St., Hood River OR 97031. Art Director: Adele Hammond. Circ. 25,000. Estab. 1990. Quarterly magazine. Features news related to the world of mountains. Readers are mostly male professionals, ages 35-45. Sample copy for $6 with 10 × 13 SAE and $2 postage.
Needs: Uses up to 40 photos/issue; all supplied by freelancers. Needs "landscape shots of mountains, flowers, mountain people, animals and mountain environments from all over the world. All imagery must have strong interpretative element as well as being graphically powerful. Both abstract and figurative photos welcome." Photos must be high-quality b&w or color only. Model release preferred (when applicable). Captions required.
Making Contact & Terms: Interested in receiving work from newer, lesser-known photographers. Query with list of stock photo subjects. Provide resume, business card, brochure, flyer or tearsheets to be kept on file for possible assignment. Reports in 3 weeks. Pays $250-300/color cover photo; $50-170/various page rates. Pays on publication. Credit line given. Buys one-time rights.

THE SUN, 107 N. Roberson, Chapel Hill NC 27516. (919)942-5282. Editor: Sy Safransky. Circ. 20,000. Estab. 1974. Monthly magazine. Sample copy $3 and 9 × 12 SAE with $1 postage. Photo guidelines free with SASE.
Needs: Uses about 6 photos/issue; all supplied by freelance photographers. Model release preferred.
Making Contact & Terms: Interested in receiving work from newer, lesser-known photographers. Send b&w prints by mail for consideration. SASE. Reports in 2 months. Pays $25-50/b&w cover and inside photo. Pays on publication. Credit line given. Buys one-time rights; negotiable. Previously published work OK.
Tips: Looks for "artful and sensitive photographs that are not overly sentimental. We use many photos of people. All the photographs we publish come to us as unsolicited submissions."

SUNDAY SCHOOL COUNSELOR, 1445 Boonville Ave., Springfield MO 65802. (417)862-2781. Editor: Sylvia Lee. Circ. 35,000. Monthly. Readers are local church school teachers and administrators.
Needs: Uses about 5 photos/issue; 3-4 supplied by freelance photographers. Needs photos of people, "babies to senior adults." Model release required. Free sample copy and photo guidelines.
Making Contact & Terms: Submit portfolio by mail for review. Send 5 × 7 or 8 × 10 b&w and color photos; 35mm, 2¼ × 2¼ or 4 × 5 color transparencies. SASE. Reports in 2 weeks. Pays $25-35/b&w photo; $35-100/color transparency. **Pays on acceptance.** Credit line given. Buys one-time rights. Simultaneous submissions and previously published work OK.

SURFING MAGAZINE, P.O. Box 3010, San Clemente CA 92672. (714)492-7873. Editor: Nick Carroll. Photo Editor: Larry Moore. Monthly. Circ. 120,000. Emphasizes "surfing and bodyboarding action and related aspects of beach lifestyle. Travel to new surfing areas covered as well. Average age of readers is 18 with 92% being male. Nearly all drawn to publication due to high quality, action packed photographs." Free photo guidelines with SASE. Sample copy free with legal size SAE and $2.25 postage.
Needs: Uses about 80 photos/issue; 35%+ supplied by freelance photographers. Needs "in-tight front-lit surfing and bodyboarding action photos as well as travel-related scenics. Beach lifestyle photos always in demand."
Making Contact & Terms: Send by mail for consideration 35mm or 2¼ × 2¼ transparencies; b&w contact sheet and negatives. SASE. Reports in 2-4 weeks. Pays $500/color cover photo; $30-125/color inside photo; $20-70/b&w inside photo; $500/color poster photo. Pays on publication. Credit line given. Buys one-time rights.
Tips: Prefers to see "well-exposed, sharp images showing both the ability to capture peak action as well as beach scenes depicting the surfing and bodyboarding lifestyle. Color, lighting, composition and proper film usage are important. Ask for our photo guidelines prior to making any film/camera/lens choices."

*TENNIS MAGAZINE, 5520 Park Ave., Trumbull CT 06611. (203)373-7000. Art Director: Lori Wendin. Circ. 800,000. Monthly magazine. Emphasizes instructional articles and features on tennis for hard core recreational tennis players and fans.
Needs: Freelancers supply 40% of photos. "We'll look at all photos submitted relating to the game of tennis. We use color action shots of the top athletes in tennis." Also uses some studio setups and instructional photography.
Making Contact & Terms: Send material by mail for consideration. Uses 35mm transparencies, Kodachrome 64 ASA preferred. SASE. Reports in 2 weeks. NPI; depends on space usage. Pays on publication. Credit line given. Buys first N.A. and overseas affiliates rights or on agreement with publisher.

TENNIS WEEK, 124 E. 40th St., New York NY 10016. (212)808-4750. Publisher: Eugene L. Scott. Managing Editors: Nina Talbot, Julie Tupper and Merrill Chapman. Circ. 62,000. Biweekly. Readers are "tennis fanatics." Sample copy $3.
Needs: Uses about 16 photos/issue. Needs photos of "off-court color, beach scenes with pros, social scenes with players, etc." Emphasizes originality. Subject identification required.
Making Contact & Terms: Send actual 8 × 10 or 5 × 7 b&w photos by mail for consideration. SASE. Reports in 2 weeks. Pays $25/b&w photo; $50/cover; $100/color cover. Pays on publication. Credit line given. Rights purchased on a work-for-hire basis.

TEXAS GARDENER, P.O. Box 9005, Waco TX 76714. (817)772-1270. Editor/Publisher: Chris S. Corby. Circ. 35,000. Bimonthly. Emphasizes gardening. Readers are "65% male, home gardeners, 98% Texas residents." Sample copy $1.
Needs: Uses 20-30 photos/issue; 90% supplied by freelance photographers. Needs "color photos of gardening activities in Texas." Special needs include "photo essays on specific gardening topics such as 'weeds in the garden.' Must be taken in Texas." Model release preferred. Captions required.
Making Contact & Terms: Query with samples. SASE. Reports in 3 weeks. Pays $100-200/color cover photo; $5-15/b&w inside photo; $10-200/color inside photo. **Pays on acceptance.** Credit line given. Buys all rights.
Tips: "Provide complete information on photos. For example, if you submit a photo of watermelons growing in a garden, we need to know what variety they are and when and where the picture was taken."

The Subject Index, located at the back of this book, can help you find publications interested in the topics you shoot.

TEXAS HIGHWAYS, P.O. Box 141009, Austin TX 78714. (512)483-3675. Editor: Jack Lowry. Photo Editor: Michael A. Murphy. Circ. 430,000. Monthly. *"Texas Highways* interprets scenic, recreational, historical, cultural and ethnic treasures of the state and preserves the best of Texas heritage. Its purpose is to educate and entertain, to encourage recreational travel to and within the state, and to tell the Texas story to readers around the world." Readers are 45 and over (majority); $24,000 to $60,000/year salary bracket with a college education. Sample copy and photo guidelines free.
Needs: Uses about 50 photos/issue; 50% supplied by freelance photographers. Needs "travel and scenic photos in Texas only." Special needs include "fall, winter, spring and summer scenic shots and wildflower shots (Texas only)." Captions required; include location, names, addresses and other useful information.
Making Contact & Terms: Interested in receiving work from newer, lesser-known photographers. Query with samples. Provide business card and tearsheets to be kept on file for possible future assignments. We take only color originals, 35mm or larger transparencies. No negatives. SASE. Reports in 1 month. Pays $120/half page color inside photo; $170/full-page color photo; $400/front cover photo. Pays on publication. Credit line given. Buys one-time rights. Simultaneous submissions OK.
Tips: "Know our magazine and format. Don't forget to caption and name names. We publish only photographs of Texas. We accept only high-quality, professional level work—no snapshots. Interested in a photographer's ability to edit their own material and the breadth of a photographer's work. Look at 3-4 months of the magazine. Query not just for photos but with ideas for new/unusual topics."

*TEXAS MONTHLY, PO Box 1569, Austin TX 78767. Works with a select group of photographers.

THANATOS, P.O. Box 6009, Tallahassee FL 32314. (904)224-1969. Fax: (904)224-7965. Editor: Jan Scheff. Circ. 6,000. Estab. 1975. Quarterly journal. Covers death, dying and bereavement. Readers include healthcare professionals, thanatologists, clergy, funeral directors, counselors, support groups, volunteers, bereaved family members, students, et al. Photo guidelines free with SASE.
Needs: Uses 8 photos/issue; all supplied by freelancers. Needs many b&w scenic and people shots to accompany articles. Also, full-color scenics to illustrate seasons for each quarterly edition. Model release required. Captions preferred.
Making Contact & Terms: Query with list of stock photo subjects. Provide resume, business card, brochure, flyer or tearsheets to be kept on file for possible assignment. Cannot return material. Reports in 4 weeks. Pays $100/color cover photo; $50/b&w inside photo. **Pays on acceptance.** Buys all rights; negotiable. Simultaneous submissions OK.

THIGH HIGH, 10th Floor, 801 Second Ave., New York NY 11217. (212)661-7878. Fax: (212)692-9297. Editor: Marc Medoff. Circ. 89,000. Estab. 1991. Quarterly magazine. Emphasizes leg and foot fetishism. Readers are young males, blue collar workers, over 18 years old. Sample copies free with 8½×11 SASE and 10 first class stamps. Photo guidelines free with SASE.
Needs: Uses 100-200 photos/issue; all supplied by freelancers. Needs photos of nude women with emphasis on legs and feet. Reviews photos with or without accompanying ms. Model/property release required; include copies of photo identification with date of birth over 18 years old.
Making Contact & Terms: Submit portfolio for review. Send unsolicited photos by mail for consideration. Provide resume, business card, brochure, flyer or tearsheets to be kept on file for possible future assignments. Send 35mm transparencies. Keeps samples on file. SASE. Reports in 1 month. Payment varies from $10/shot to $3,000/full set. **Pays on acceptance.** Credit line given. Buys one-time rights; negotiable. Simultaneous submissions and previously published work OK.
Tips: "We require technical perfection. Focus, lighting, composition, etc., must be 100% perfect. Look at our magazine and competing titles."

THRASHER MAGAZINE, P.O. Box 884570, San Francisco CA 94188-4570. (415)822-3083. Fax: (415)822-8359. Photo Editor: Bryce Kanights. Circ. 250,000. Estab. 1981. Monthly magazine. Emphasizes skateboarding, snowboarding and alternative music. Readers are primarily male between ages 12-24. Sample copy $3.25. Photo guidelines free with SASE.
Needs: Uses 55 photos/issue; 20 supplied by freelancers. Needs photos of skateboarding, snowboarding and alternative music. Reviews photos with or without a manuscript. Special needs are b&w action sequences. Model/property release preferred; release needed for minors. Captions preferred; include name of subject, location and date of shoot.
Making Contact & Terms: Send unsolicited photos by mail for consideration. Send 5×7, 8×10 b&w prints; 35mm, 2¼×2¼ transparencies. Keeps samples on file. SASE. Reports in 1-2 weeks. Pays $250/color cover photo; $200/b&w cover photo; $65/color inside photo; $50/b&w inside photo; $110/color page rate; $85/b&w page rate. Pays on publication. Credit line given. Buys all rights.
Tips: "Get to know the sports of skateboarding and snowboarding, the lifestyles and current trends."

*TIME, Time & Life Building, 1271 Avenue of the Americas, New York NY 10020. Prefers not to share information.

TODAY'S PHOTOGRAPHER INTERNATIONAL, (formerly *International Photographer*), P.O. Box 18205, Washington DC 20036. (919)945-9867. Photography Editor: Vonda H. Blackburn. Circ. 131,000. Estab. 1986. Bimonthly magazine. Emphasizes making money with photography. Readers are 90% male photographers. For sample copy, send 9 × 12 SAE. Photo guidelines free with SASE.
Needs: Uses 100 photos/issue; all supplied by freelance photographers. Model release required. Photo captions preferred.
Making Contact & Terms: Send 35mm, 2¼ × 2¼, 4 × 5, 8 × 10 b&w and color prints or transparencies by mail for consideration. SASE. Reports at end of the quarter. NPI; payment negotiable. Credit line given. Buys one-time rights, per contract. Simultaneous submissions and previously published work OK.
Tips: Wants to see "consistently fine quality photographs and good captions or other associated information. Present a portfolio which is easy to evaluate—keep it simple and informative. Be aware of deadlines. Submit early."

*TOTAL TV, 475 Fifth Ave., New York NY 10017. Photo Editor: Heather Alberts. Weekly magazine. Emphasizes movie and TV personalities, sports figures, musicians, nature.
Needs: Uses 30 photos/issue; all supplied by freelancers. Needs photos of personalities or TV and movie coverage. Reviews photos with or without ms. Model/property release preferred. Captions preferred.
Making Contact & Terms: Interested in receiving work from newer, lesser-known photographers. SASE. Reports in 1-2 weeks. Pays $35-2,000/job. **Pays on acceptance.** Credit line given. Simultaneous submissions and/or previously published work OK.

TOURING AMERICA, P.O. Box 6050, Mission Viejo CA 92690. (714)855-8822, ext. 410. Fax: (714)855-1850. Managing Editor: Gene Booth. Circ. 75,000. Estab. 1991. Bimonthly magazine. Emphasizes travel in US, Canada and Mexico. Readers are male and female, 30-55 primarily.
Needs: Uses 100-150 photos/issue; 99% supplied by freelancers. Needs travel photos, scenics with people in frame. "Our covers seem to be difficult to find." Model/property release preferred. Captions required; include "location, what's going on."
Making Contact & Terms: Query with list of stock photo subjects; "explain story idea." Keeps samples on file. Does not review unsolicited portfolios. SASE. Reports in 3 weeks. Pays $250 minimum/color cover photo; $50-150/color inside photo; $250-750/photo/text package, "preferred." Credit line given. Buys one-time rights; first N.A. serial rights for text; and anthology rights for text. Previously published work OK for photos only.
Tips: "We prefer story/photo packages. Writing must be excellent, with a lead that grabs the reader. Photos must have people in them, no Sierra Club scenics. Request our Authors' Guide which includes photo guidelines, then do what it says."

TOURS!, 546 E. Main St., Lexington KY 40508. (606)253-1036. Editor: Judy Hachey. Circ. 100,000. Estab. 1988. Quarterly magazine. Emphasizes escorted travel. Readers are 75% female and over age 50. Sample copy free with 9 × 12 SAE.
Needs: Cover photo usually supplied by freelancer. Need vertical slides/transparencies which include two or more people (50-plus) who look like they are engaged in a touring activity. North American destinations only! Model release required. Captions required.
Making Contact & Terms: Query with list of stock photo subjects. Send unsolicited photos by mail for consideration. Submit portfolio for review. Provide resume, business card, brochure, flyer or tearsheets to be kept on file for possible assignments. Send 35mm, 2¼ × 2¼, 4 × 5 transparencies. SASE. Reports in 1 month. Pays $200/color cover photo. **Pays on acceptance.** Credit line given. Buys one-time rights. Simultaneous submissions and previously published work OK.

TQ, P.O. Box 3512, Irving TX 75015. (214)570-7599. Managing Editor: Chris Lyon. Circ. 30,000. Estab. 1945. Monthly magazine. Emphasizes Christian living for Christian young people, ages 14-17. Free sample copy and photographer's guidelines with 9 × 12 SASE.
Needs: Buys 5-10 photos/issue. Photos of young people 14-17 years old in unposed, everyday activities. Scenic, sport, photo essay/photo feature, human interest, head shot, still life, humorous and special effects/experimental. Interested in photos of minorities. Current fashion. Model release preferred. Captions preferred.
Making Contact & Terms: Interested in receiving work from newer, lesser-known photographers. Send photos for consideration, or send contact sheet. Send contact sheet or color transparencies. Address to Art Director. SASE. Reports in 2-4 weeks. Pays $100 for most color photos. **Pays on acceptance.** Buys one-time rights; negotiable. Simultaneous submissions and previously published work OK.
Tips: "Close-up shots featuring moody, excited or unusual expressions needed. Would like to see more shots featuring unusual and striking camera and darkroom techniques. Looks for "wholesome youth 14-17 in fun situations, school, family: good-quality technical and creative work. We have a limited

budget but high standards. Also review your work and send only those pictures that have a shot at being printed. Limit your submissions."

TRACK AND FIELD NEWS, Suite 606, 2570 El Camino Real, Mountain View CA 94040. (415)948-8417. Fax: (415)948-9445. Associate Editor (Features/Photography): Jon Hendershott. Circ. 35,000. Estab. 1948. Monthly magazine. Emphasizes national and world-class track and field competition and participants at those levels for athletes, coaches, administrators and fans. Sample copy free with 9×12 SAE. Free photo guidelines.
Needs: Buys 10-15 photos/issue; 75% of freelance photos on assignment, 25% from stock. Wants on a regular basis photos of national-class athletes, men and women, preferably in action. "We are always looking for quality pictures of track and field action as well as offbeat and different feature photos. We always prefer to hear from a photographer before he/she covers a specific meet. We also welcome shots from road and cross-country races for both men and women. Any photos may eventually be used to illustrate news stories in *T&FN*, feature stories in *T&FN* or may be used in our other publications (books, technical journals, etc.). Any such editorial use will be paid for, regardless of whether material is used directly in *T&FN*. About all we don't want to see are pictures taken with someone's Instamatic or Polaroid. No shots of someone's child or grandparent running. Professional work only." Captions required; include subject name, meet date/name.
Making Contact & Terms: Interested in receiving work from newer, lesser-known photographers. Query with samples or send material by mail for consideration. Uses 8×10 glossy prints; contact sheet preferred; 35mm transparencies. SASE. Reports in 1 week. Pays $20/b&w inside photo; $50/color inside photo; $150/color cover photo. Payment is made bimonthly. Credit line given. Buys one-time rights.
Tips: "No photographer is going to get rich via *T&FN*. We can offer a credit line, nominal payment and, in some cases, credentials to major track and field meets to enable on-the-field shooting. Also we can offer the chance for competent photographers to shoot major competitions and competitors up close as well as the most highly regarded publication in the track world as a forum to display a photographer's talents."

*TRADE & CULTURE MAGAZINE, 7127 Harford Rd., Baltimore MD 21234. Magazine Design: Phil Jordan. Circ. 65,000. Estab. 1992. Bimonthly magazine. Emphasizes international business and culture. Readers are male and female executives actively engaged in global trade. Sample copy $2.90 with SASE.
Needs: Uses approximately 60-65 photos/issue; all supplied by freelancers. Needs head shots, travel, culture, business. Special photo needs include a lot of overseas work in all nations recognized by the U.N. Model release preferred. Property release preferred for headshots for feature stories. Captions required for subjects (if possible); include location, date.
Making Contact & Terms: Interested in receiving work from newer, lesser-known photographers. Provide resume, business card, brochure, flyer or tearsheets to be kept on file for possible future assignments. Keeps samples on file. Reports only when interested. NPI. Pays on publication. Credit line given. Buys all rights; negotiable. Previously published work OK.
Tips: "We look for shots that really give insight into the people of a particular culture. Be creative."

TRAILER LIFE, Dept. PM, 3601 Calle Tecate, Camarillo CA 93012. Publisher: Bill Estes. Editorial Director: Barbara Leonard. Monthly magazine. Emphasizes the why, how and how-to of owning, using and maintaining a recreational vehicle for personal vacation or full-time travel. Circ. 315,000. Send for editorial guidelines.
Needs: Human interest, how-to, travel and personal experience. The editors are particularly interested in photos for the cover; an RV must be included. Also accompanying ms related to recreational vehicles and ancillary activities.
Making Contact & Terms: Send material by mail for consideration or query with samples. Uses 8×10 b&w glossy prints; 35mm and 2¼×2¼ transparencies. SASE. Reports in 3 weeks. Pays $50-150/b&w photo; $75-300+/color photo. **Pays on acceptance.** Credit line given. Buys first N.A. rights.

TRANSITIONS ABROAD, 18 Hulst Rd., P.O. Box 344, Amherst MA 01004. (413)256-0373. Managing Editor: Lisa Aciukewicz. Circ. 15,000. Estab. 1977. Bimonthly magazine. Emphasizes travel. Readers are people interested in traveling, learning, living, or working abroad, all ages, both sexes. Sample copy $3.50. Photo guidelines free with SASE.
Needs: Uses 15 photos/issue; all supplied by freelancers. Needs photos of travelers in international settings or the people of other countries. Each issue has an area focus: Jan/Feb.—Asia and the Pacific Rim; Mar./Apr.—Europe and the former Soviet Union; May/June—The Mediterranean Basin and the Near East; Nov./Dec.—The Americas and Africa (South of the Sahara).
Making Contact & Terms: Query with list of stock photo subjects. Send unsolicited 8×10 b&w prints by mail for consideration. Prefers b&w; sometimes uses color photos; rarely uses transparencies. SASE. Reports in 4-6 weeks. Pays $25/inside photo; $125/b&w cover photo. Pays on publication. Credit

line given. Buys one-time rights. Simultaneous submissions and previously published work OK.

Tips: In freelance photographer's samples, wants to see "mostly people shots—travelers and people of other countries. We use very few landscapes or abstract shots."

TRAVEL & LEISURE, Dept. PM, 1120 Avenue of the Americas, New York NY 10036. (212)382-5600. Editor: Ila Stanger. Art Director: Lloyd Ziff. Picture Editor: Hazel Hammond. Circ. 1.2 million. Monthly magazine. Emphasizes travel destinations, resorts, dining and entertainment. Free photo guidelines with SASE.

Needs: Nature, still life, scenic, sport and travel. Model release required. Captions required.

Making Contact & Terms: Uses 8×10 semigloss b&w prints; 35mm, 2¼×2¼, 4×5 and 8×10 transparencies, vertical format required for cover. Pays $200-500/b&w photo; $200-500/color photo; $1,000/cover photo or negotiated. Sometimes pays $450-1,200/day; $1,200 minimum/complete package. Pays on publication. Credit line given. Buys first world serial rights, plus promotional use. Previously published work OK.

Tips: Seeing trend toward "more editorial/journalistic images that are interpretive representations of a destination."

*‡TRAVELLER, 45-49 Brompton Road, London SW3 1DC Great Britain. (071)581-4130. Fax: (071)581-1357. Managing Editor: Caroline Brandenburger. Circ. 35,000. Quarterly. Readers are predominantly male, professional, 35 years old and over. Sample copy £2.50.

Needs: Uses 30+ photos/issue; all supplied by freelancers. Needs photos of travel, wildlife. Reviews photos with or without ms. Captions preferred.

Making Contact & Terms: Interested in receiving work from newer, lesser-known photographers. Arrange personal interview to show portfolio. Submit portfolio for review. Provide resume, business card, brochure, flyer or tearsheets to be kept on file for possible future assignments. Send 35mm transparencies. Does not keep samples on file. SASE. Reports in 1 month. Pays £50/color cover photo; £25/color inside photo. Pays on publication. Buys one-time rights.

Tips: Looks for "original, quirky shots with impact, which tell a story."

TRUE WEST, P.O. Box 2107, Stillwater OK 74076. (405)743-3370. Fax: (405)743-3374. Editor: John Joerschke. Circ. 30,000. Estab. 1953. Monthly magazine. Emphasizes "history of the Old West (1830 to about 1915)." Readers are "people who like to read the history of the West, mostly male, age 45 and older." Sample copy $2 with 9×12 SAE. Photo guidelines free with SASE.

Needs: Uses about 50 or more photos/issue; almost all are supplied by freelance photographers. Needs "mostly Old West historical subjects, some travel, some scenic, (ghost towns, old mining camps, historical sites). We prefer photos with ms." Special needs include western wear; cowboys, rodeos, western events. Captions required; include name and location of site.

Making Contact & Terms: Interested in receiving work from newer, lesser-known photographers. Query with samples—b&w only for inside; color for covers. Query with stock photo list. Send unsolicited photos by mail for consideration. SASE. Reports in 1 month. Pays $100-175/color cover photo; $10-25/color inside photo; $10-25/b&w inside photo. **Pays on acceptance;** cover photos on publication. Credit line given. Buys first N.A. serial rights.

Tips: Prefers to see "transparencies of existing artwork as well as scenics for cover photos. Scenics should be free of modern intrusions such as buildings, powerlines, highways, etc. Inside photos need to tell story associated with the Old West. Most of our photos are used to illustrate stories and come with manuscripts; however, we will consider other work, scenics, historical sites, old houses. Even though we are Old West history, we do need current photos, both inside and for covers—so don't hesitate to contact us."

*TUFF STUFF, 2309 Hungary Road, Richmond VA 23228. (804)266-0140. Fax: (804)266-1145. Managing Editor: Tucker Freeman Smith. Circ. 250,000. Estab. 1984. Monthly magazine. Emphasizes sports collectibles. Readers are college educated males, ages 26-45, who collect sports memorabilia. Sample copy free with 8½×11 SASE and 9 first-class stamps.

Needs: Uses 15 photos/issue; all supplied by freelancers. Needs photos of sports and collecting-related materials. Reviews photos with or without ms. Model release preferred. Captions required; include name, age, etc.

Making Contact & Terms: Interested in receiving work from newer, lesser-known photographers. Provide resume, business card, brochure, flyer or tearsheets to be kept on file for possible future assignments. Keeps samples on file. SASE. Reports in 1 month. Pays $250-500/day; $400-1,000/color cover photo; $100-450/b&w inside photo. Pays on publication. Credit line given. Buys one-time rights; negotiable. Previously published work OK.

Tips: "You've got to have an eye for sports and know something about collecting sports memorabilia—hacks don't cut it."

TURN-ONS, LUSTY LETTERS, OPTIONS, BEAU, (*Lusty Letters* was formerly *Turn On Letters*), Box 470, Port Chester NY 10573. Photo Editor: Wayne Shuster. Circ. 60,000. Periodical magazines. Emphasizes "sexually oriented situations. We emphasize good, clean sexual fun among liberal-minded adults." Readers are mostly male; ages 18-65. Sample copy $2.95 with 6×9 SAE and $1 postage.

Needs: Uses approximately 20-30 b&w photos/issue, all stock. Black and white preferred, but will accept color sets for conversion to b&w. Pays $200/set. Needs a "variety of b&w photos depicting sexual situations of boy-girl, girl-girl, boy-boy, girl-boy-girl scenes. Also need color transparencies of single girls, girl-girl and single boys for cover; present in a way suitable for newsstand display." Model release required.

Making Contact & Terms: Query with samples. Send 8×10 glossy b&w prints or 35mm, 2¼×2¼, 4×5 transparencies by mail for consideration. SASE. Reports in 2 weeks. Pays $250/color cover photo and $20/b&w inside photo. Pays on publication. Buys one-time rights on covers, second rights OK for b&ws.

Tips: "Please examine copies of our publications before submitting work. In reviewing samples we consider composition of color photos for newsstand display and look for recent b&w photos for inside."

TV GUIDE, Four Radnor Corporate Center, Radnor PA 19088. Uses staff members to shoot photos.

TWINS MAGAZINE, Suite 155, 6740 Antioch, Merriam KS 66204. (913)722-1090. Fax: (913)722-1767. Editor: Barbara Unell. Art Director: Cindy Himmelberg. Circ. 55,000. Estab. 1984. Bimonthly magazine. Emphasizes parenting twins, triplets, quadruplets, or more and being a twin, triplet, quadruplet or more. Readers include the parents of multiples. Sample copy $4.50. Free photo guidelines with SASE.

Needs: Uses about 10 photos/issue; all supplied by freelance photographers. Needs family related— children, adults, family life. Usually needs to have twins, triplets or more included as well. Reviews photos with or without accompanying ms. Model release required. Property release preferred. Captions preferred.

Making Contact & Terms: Interested in receiving work from newer, lesser-known photographers. Query with resume of credits and samples. Provide resume, business card, brochure, flyer or tearsheets to be kept on file for possible assignments. SASE. Reports in 1 month. Pays $100 minimum/cover photo. Pays on publication. Credit line given. Buys all rights. Simultaneous submissions OK.

U—THE NATIONAL COLLEGE MAGAZINE, (formerly *U-The National College Newspaper*), Suite 820, 1800 Century Park E., Los Angeles CA 90067. (310)551-1381. Fax: (310)551-1659. Contact: Managing Editor. Circ. 1.5 million. Estab. 1988. Monthly magazine. Emphasizes college-oriented issues. Readers are 18-24 year-old college students and university faculty and staff. Sample copy free with SASE.

Needs: Uses 20-30 photos/issue; all supplied by college freelancers. Reviews photos with or without ms. Special photo needs include photos relating to recent college trends. Model release preferred. Captions required.

Making Contact & Terms: Interested in receiving work from newer, lesser-known photographers. Provide resume, business card, brochure, flyer or tearsheets to be kept on file for possible assignments. Keeps samples on file. Cannot return material. Reports in 1 month. Pays $25 minimum/photo. Pays on publication. Credit line given. Rights negotiable. Simultaneous submissions and/or previously published work OK.

Tips: "Must be a college-aged photographer. We don't use any b&w prints, only color negative and color slides. Call us for an assignment if you can shoot good color, are a college student and want to get a great clip."

UNITY, Unity Village MO 64065. Editor: Philip White. Associate Editor: Janet McNamara. Circ. 150,000. Estab. 1889. Monthly magazine. Emphasizes spiritual, metaphysical, self-help, poetry and inspirational articles. Free sample copy and photo guidelines.

Needs: Uses 14-18 photos/issue. Buys 200 photos/year, 20% from freelancers. Wants on a regular basis people and nature scenics for covers and 10-20 b&w scenics. Also human interest, nature, some still life and wildlife. Animal photos used sparingly. Model release required. Captions preferred, include location for scenics and ethnic clothed people. Stock numbers required.

Making Contact & Terms: Send insured material by mail for consideration. No calls in person or by phone. Uses 5×7 or 8×10 b&w semigloss prints; 4×5 or 2×2 color transparencies. Vertical format required for cover. Send SAE and check or money order for return postage. Do not send stamps or stamped envelopes. There is a 7-8 month lead time for seasonal material. Reports in 4-8 weeks. Pays $35/b&w photo; $200/cover, $65-125 inside color photo. **Pays on acceptance.** Credit line given. Buys first N.A. serial rights.

Tips: "Don't overwhelm us with hundreds of submissions at a time. We look for nature scenics, human interest, some still life and wildlife, photos of active people (although the primary interest of the photo is not on the person or persons). We are looking for photos with a lot of color and contrast."

🍁**UP HERE,** P.O. Box 1350, Yellowknife, Northwest Territories X1A 2N9 Canada. (403)920-4652. Fax: (403)873-2844. Editor: R. Allerston. Circ. 25,000. Estab. 1984. Bimonthly magazine. Emphasizes Canada's north. Readers are white collar men and women ages 30 to 60. Sample copy $3 and 9 × 12 SAE. Photo guidelines free with SASE.
Needs: Uses 20-30 photos/issue; 90% supplied by freelance photographers. Purchases photos with accompanying ms only. Captions required.
Making Contact & Terms: Provide resume, business card, brochure, flyer or tearsheets to be kept on file for possible assignments. SASE. Reports in 1-2 months. Pays $35-100/b&w photo; $50-150/ color photo; $150-500/cover. Pays on publication. Credit line given. Buys one-time rights.
Tips: "We are a *people* magazine. We need northern subjects—lots of faces. We're moving more into outdoor adventure—soft type, as they say in the industry—and wildlife. Few scenics as such. We approach local freelancers for given subjects, but are building a library. We can't always make use of photos alone, but a photographer could profit by sending sheets of dupes for our stock files." Wants to see "sharp, clear photos, good color and composition. We always need verticals to consider for the cover, but they usually tie in with an article inside."

UTAH HOLIDAY MAGAZINE, Dept. PM, Suite 200, 807 E. South Temple, Salt Lake City UT 84102. (801)532-3737. Art Director: Lisa Hildebrand. Monthly magazine. Emphasizes Salt Lake City and Utah in general. Readers are professional, business or self-employed people, 30-49 years of age. Circ. 18,000. Sample copy free with 9 × 12 SAE and 5 first-class stamps.
Needs: Uses 30-40 photos/issue; 100% supplied by freelance photographers. Needs photos of travel, scenics, people. Purchases photos with accompanying ms only. Model release and photo captions required.
Making Contact & Terms: Query with resume of credits and list of stock photo subjects. SASE. Reports in 1 month. Pays $300/color cover photo; $200/color inside photo; $100-150/b&w inside photo. Pays on publication. Credit line given. Buys one-time rights. Simultaneous submissions and previously published work OK.

***VANITY FAIR,** Conde Nast Building, 350 Madison Ave., New York NY 10017. Does not use freelancers.

***‡VAUHDIN MAAILMA,** Melkonkatu 10 C, Helsinki 00210 Finland. (+358)0-68261. Fax: (+358)0-6826206. Editorial Secretary: Patrik Ekman. Circ. 38,000. Estab. 1965. Monthly magazine. Emphasizes motorsport testing. Readers arc male, under 35 years of age, with good incomes. Sample copies available.
Needs: Uses 180-220 photos/issue; 80% supplied by freelancers. Needs photos of races, motorsports, exciting cars, bikes, drag race, etc. Reviews photos with or without ms.
Making Contact & Terms: Interested in receiving work from newer, lesser-known photographers. Send unsolicited photos by mail for consideration. Send 35mm transparencies. Keeps samples on file. SASE. Reports in 1-2 weeks. NPI. Pays on publication. Buys one-time rights.

VEGETARIAN TIMES, Dept. PM, P.O. Box 570, Oak Park IL 60303. (708)848-8100. Art Director: Dawn Fend. Published 12 times annually. Circ. 100,000. Sample copy $2.
Needs: Buys 80 photos/year; 90% specific, 10% stock. Primary: food (with styling) to accompany articles. Celebrity/personality (if vegetarians), sport, spot news, how-to (cooking and building), humorous. Model release and captions preferred.
Making Contact & Terms: Send material by mail for consideration. SASE. Reports in 6 weeks. Uses 8 × 10 glossy prints. Pays $40 minimum b&w/photos. Pays $300 up/(color slide) cover. Pays 30 days after acceptance. Rights vary. Credit line given. Simultaneous submissions OK.
Tips: "We consider composition, color usage, flair with food when reviewing photographer's samples."

VENTURE, P.O. Box 150, Wheaton IL 60189. (708)665-0630. Fax: (708)665-0372. Editor: Deborah Christensen. Art Director: Robert Fine. Circ. 20,000. Estab. 1959. Magazine published 6 times/year. "We seek to provide entertaining, challenging, Christian reading for boys 10-15." Sample copy $1.85 with 9 × 12 SAE and 98¢ postage. Photo guidelines available (SASE).
Needs: Buys 2-3 photos/issue; all from freelance stock. Photos of boys involved in sports, hobbies, camping, family life and just having fun. Also need photos of interest to boys: ecology, nature, adventure, occupations, etc.

 The maple leaf before a listing indicates that the market is Canadian.

Making Contact & Terms: Arrange a personal interview to show portfolio or send photos for consideration. Send 8×10 glossy b&w prints. SASE. Reports in 6 weeks. Pays $35/inside photo; $75-100/cover photo. Pays on publication. Buys first serial rights. Simultaneous submissions and previously published work OK.

VERMONT LIFE, 6 Baldwin St., Montpelier VT 05602. (802)828-3241. Editor: Tom Slayton. Circ. 95,000. Estab. 1946. Quarterly magazine. Emphasizes life in Vermont: its people, traditions, way of life, farming, industry and the physical beauty of the landscape for "Vermonters, ex-Vermonters and would-be Vermonters." Sample copy $4 with 9×12 SAE. Free photo guidelines.
Needs: Buys 30 photos/issue; 90-95% supplied by freelance photographers, 5-10% from stock. Wants on a regular basis scenic views of Vermont, seasonal (winter, spring, summer, autumn), submitted 6 months prior to the actual season; animal; documentary; human interest; humorous; nature; photo essay/photo feature; still life; travel; and wildlife. "We are using fewer, larger photos and are especially interested in good shots of wildlife, birds." No photos in poor taste, nature close-ups, cliches or photos of places other than Vermont. Model/property releases preferred. Captions required.
Making Contact & Terms: Interested in receiving work from newer, lesser-known photographers. Query first. Send 35mm or 2¼×2¼ color transparencies. SASE. Reports in 3 weeks. Pays $75-200/b&w photo; $75-200/color photo; $100-200/day; $400-800 job. Pays on publication. Credit line given. Buys one-time rights; negotiable. Simultaneous submissions OK.
Tips: "We look for clarity of focus; use of low-grain, true film (Kodachrome is best); unusual composition or subject."

VERMONT MAGAZINE, P.O. Box 288, 14 School St., Bristol VT 05443. (802)453-3200. Picture Editor: Julie Nordmeyer. Circ. 50,000. Estab. 1989. Bimonthly magazine. Emphasizes all facets of Vermont and nature, politics, business, sports, restaurants, real estate, people, crafts, art, architecture, etc. Readers are people interested in Vermont, including residents, tourists and summer home owners. Sample copy $3 with 9×12 SAE and 5 first-class stamps. Photo guidelines free with SASE.
Needs: Uses 30-40 photos/issue; 75% supplied by freelance photographers. Needs animal/wildlife shots, travel, Vermont scenics, how-to, portraits, products and architecture. Special photo needs include Vermont activities such as skiing, ice skating, biking, hiking, etc. Model release preferred. Captions required.
Making Contact & Terms: Interested in receiving work from newer, lesser-known photographers. Query with resume of credits and samples of work. Send 8×10 b&w prints or 35mm or larger transparencies by mail for consideration. Submit portfolio for review. Provide tearsheets to be kept on file for possible assignments. SASE. Reports in 1-2 months. Pays $450/color cover photo; $200/color page rate; $75-200/color or b&w photo; $275/day. Pays on publication. Credit line given. Buys one-time rights and first N.A. serial rights; negotiable. Previously published work OK, depending on "how it was previously published."
Tips: In portfolio or samples, wants to see tearsheets of published work, and at least 40 35mm transparencies. Explain your areas of expertise. Looking for creative solutions to illustrate regional activities, profiles and lifestyles. "We would like to see more illustrative photography/fine art photography where it applies to the articles and departments we produce."

VICTORIA MAGAZINE, 224 W. 57 St. New York NY 10019. (212)649-3732. Fax: (212)757-6109. Photography Editor: Charles Glaser. Circ. 900,000. Estab. 1987. Monthly magazine. Emphasizes women's interests, lifestyle. Readers are females, 70% married, average age 40. Photo guidelines free with SASE.
Needs: Uses "hundreds" of photos/issue; most supplied by freelancers. "We hire freelancers to shoot 99% of our stories. Occasionally a photographer will submit work that we consider exceptional and wish to publish. This is rare, and an exception to the rule." Needs beauty, fashion, home furnishings, lifestyle, children's corner, gardens, food, collections. Model/property release required.
Making Contact & Terms: Interested in receiving work from newer, lesser-known photographers. Submit portfolio for review. Provide tearsheets to be kept on file for possible future assignments. SASE. Reports in 1-2 weeks. Pays $650-750/day; $300/color page rate. **Pays on acceptance.** Credit line given. Buys one-time rights, all rights; negotiable. Previously published work OK.
Tips: Looking for beautiful photos, wonderful lighting, elegance of style, simplicity.

VIDEOMAKER MAGAZINE, P.O. Box 4591, Chico CA 95927. (916)891-8410. Editor: Stephen Muratore. Art Director: Sarah Ellis. Circ. 60,000. Estab. 1986. Monthly magazine. Emphasizes video production from hobbyist to low-end professional level. Readers are mostly male, ages 25-40. Sample copy free with 9×12 SAE.
Needs: Uses 50-60 photos/issue; 10-15% supplied by freelancers. Subjects include tools and techniques of consumer video production, videomakers in action. Reviews photos with or without ms. Model/property release required. Captions required.

Making Contact & Terms: Send unsolicited photos by mail for consideration; any size or format, color or b&w. Address photos to Art Director. SASE. Reports in 1 month. NPI. Pays on publication. Credit line given. Rights negotiable. Simultaneous submissions and previously published work OK.

VISTA, Suite 600, 999 Ponce, Coral Gables FL 33134. (305)442-2462. Fax: (305)443-7650. Editor: Renato Perez. Circ. 1.2 million. Estab. 1985. Monthly newspaper insert. Emphasizes Hispanic life in the US. Readers are Hispanic-Americans of all ages. Sample copy available.
Needs: Uses 10-50 photos/issue; all supplied by freelancers. Needs photos mostly of personalities with story only. No "stand-alone" photos. Reviews photos with accompanying ms only. Special photo needs include events in the Hispanic American communities. Model/property release preferred. Captions required.
Making Contact & Terms: Provide resume, business card, brochure, flyer or tearsheets to be kept on file for possible assignments. Keeps samples on file. SASE. Reports in 3 weeks. Pays $300/color cover photo; $150/color inside photo; $75/b&w inside photo; day assignments are negotiated. Pays on publication. Credit line given. Buys one-time rights. Previously published work OK.
Tips: "Build a file of personalities and events. Hispanics are America's fastest-growing minority."

*VOICE OF SOUTH MARION, P.O. Box 700, Belleview FL 32620. (904)245-3161. Editor: Jim Waldron. Circ. 1,700. Estab. 1969. Weekly tabloid. Readers are male and female, ages 12-65, working in agriculture and various small town jobs. Sample copy $1.
Needs: Uses 5-10 photos/issue; 2 supplied by freelance photographers. Features pictures that can stand alone with a cutline. Captions required.
Making Contact & Terms: Send 35mm and 2¼ × 2¼ transparencies; b&w prints by mail for consideration. SASE. Reports in 1-2 weeks. Pays $10/b&w cover photo; $5/b&w inside photo. Pays on publication. Credit line given. Buys one-time rights.

VOLLEYBALL MONTHLY, Dept. PM, P.O. Box 3137, San Luis Obispo CA 93401. (805)541-2294. Fax: (805)541-2438. Co-Publishers/Editors: Jon Hastings, Dennis Steers. Circ. 60,000. Estab. 1982. Monthly. Emphasizes volleyball. Readers are volleyball enthusiasts. Sample copy free with 9 × 12 SAE and $2 postage.
Needs: Model release preferred. Captions required.
Making Contact & Terms: Query with samples. Send b&w prints or transparencies by mail for consideration. SASE. Reports in 2 weeks. Pays $150/color cover photo; $25-50/b&w photo; $50-150/color photo; $150-300/day. Pays on publication. Credit line given. Buys one-time rights.

WASHINGTONIAN, Suite 200, 1828 L St. NW, Washington DC 20036. (202)296-3600. Fax: (202)785-1822. Photo Editor: Kathleen Hennessy. Monthly city/regional magazine emphasizing Washington metro area. Readers are 40-50, 54% female, 46% male and middle to upper middle professionals. Circ. 160,000. Estab. 1965.
Needs: Uses 75-150 photos/issue; 100% supplied by freelance photographers. Needs photos for illustration, portraits, reportage; tabletop of products, food; restaurants; nightlife; house and garden; fashion; and local and regional travel. Model release preferred; captions required.
Making Contact & Terms: Submit portfolio for review. Provide resume, business card, brochure, flyer or tearsheets to be kept on file for possible assignments. Pays $125-250/b&w photo; $150-300/color photo; $175-$350/day. Credit line given. Buys one-time rights ("on exclusive shoots we share resale").
Tips: "Read the magazine you want to work for. Show work that relates to its needs. Offer photo-story ideas. Send samples occasionally of new work."

WATERWAY GUIDE, 6151 Powers Ferry Rd. NW, Atlanta GA 30339. Fax: (404)618-0348. Editor: Judith Powers. Circ. 50,000. Estab. 1947. Quarterly cruising guide. Emphasizes recreational boating. Readers are men and women ages 25-65, management or professional, with average income $95,000 a year. Sample copy $31.95 and $3 shipping. Photo guidelines free with SASE.
Needs: Uses 10-15 photos/issue; all supplied by freelance photographers. Needs photos of boats, Intracoastal Waterway, bridges, landmarks, famous sights and scenic waterfronts. Expects to use more coastal shots from Maine to the Bahamas; also, more Great Lakes and Gulf of Mexico. Model release required. Captions required.
Making Contact & Terms: Send unsolicited photos by mail for consideration. Send b&w and color prints or 35mm transparencies. SASE. Reports in 2 months. Pays $600/color cover photo; $25/b&w inside photo; $50-500/color photo. Pays on publication. Credit line given. Buys first N.A. serial rights.

WEEKLY READER, US KIDS, READ, CURRENT SCIENCE, 245 Long Hill Rd., Middletown CT 06457. (203)638-2657. Fax: (203)638-2609. Photo Editor: Louise Augeri. Weekly, biweekly and monthly magazines; 8½ × 11 newspaper. Emphasizes news and education for children. Readers are male and female children, ages 4 thru 15. Combined circ. 10,000,000. Estab. 1928. Sample copy free with 8½ × 11 SASE.

Needs: Uses 5 photos/issue; yearly over 10,000 photos; all supplied by stock houses. Needs photos of animal/wildlife, travel, scenics, technology, personalities, how-to, etc. Special photo needs include more children in photos; regular events, e.g. Memorial Day Parades, Martin Luther King Day. Model release required for children. Captions required; include name of people, ages, date, location, etc.
Making Contact & Terms: Query with resume of credits. Query with list of stock photo subjects. Send unsolicited 11 × 14 (maximum) b&w and color prints; 35mm, 2¼ × 2¼, 4 × 5, 8 × 10 transparencies by mail for consideration. Provide business card, brochure, flyer or tearsheets to be kept on file for possible assignments. Keeps samples on file. SASE. Reports in 1 month. Pays $250/color and b&w cover or inside photo; $250/color or b&w page rate; $10-100/hour; $400-800/day. Pays on publication. Credit line given. Buys one-time rights; all rights at times; negotiable. Simultaneous submissions and previously published work OK.
Tips: In samples looks for "juvenile news photos. Be as professional and organized as possible."

WEIGHT WATCHERS, Dept. PM, 360 Lexington Ave., New York NY 10017. (212)370-0644. Editor: Lee Haiken. Art Director: Shelly Stansfield. Monthly magazine. For those interested in weight control, fitness, nutrition, inspiration and self-improvement. Circ. 1,000,000.
Needs: All on assignment: food and tabletop still life, beauty, health and fitness subjects, fashion, personality portraiture. All photos contingent upon editorial needs.
Making Contact & Terms: Photos purchased on assignment only. Portfolio—drop-off policy only. Buys approximately 12 photos/issue. Pays $300/single page; $500/spread; $700/cover. Credit line given. **Pays on acceptance.** Buys first rights.

WESTERN HORSEMAN, 3850 N. Nevada Ave., P.O. Box 7980, Colorado Springs CO 80933. (719)633-5524. Editor: Pat Close. Monthly magazine. Circ. 209,914. Estab. 1936. Readers are active participants in horse activities, including pleasure riders, ranchers, breeders and riding club members. Model/property release preferred. Captions required; include name of subject, date, location.
Needs: Articles and photos must have a strong horse angle, slanted towards the western rider—rodeos, shows, ranching, stable plans, training. "We also buy 35mm color slides for our annual cowboy calendar. Slides must depict ranch cowboys/cowgirls."
Making Contact & Terms: Interested in receiving work from newer, lesser-known photographers. Submit material by mail for consideration. Pays $15/b&w photo; $25-75/color photo; $400-500 maximum. "We buy mss and photos as a package." Payment for 1,500 words with b&w photos ranges from $100-400. Buys one-time rights; negotiable.
Tips: "For color, we prefer 35mm slides. For b&w, either 5 × 7 or 8 × 10 glossies. We can sometimes use color prints if they are of excellent quality. In all prints, photos and slides, subjects must be properly dressed. Baseball caps, T-shirts, tank tops, shorts, tennis shoes, bare feet, etc., are unacceptable."

WESTERN OUTDOORS, 3197-E Airport Loop, Costa Mesa CA 92626. Editor: Jack Brown. Circ. 138,000. Estab. 1961. Magazine published 9 times/year. Emphasizes hunting, fishing for 11 western states, Alaska, Western Mexico and Canada. Sample copy $1.75 with 10 × 12 SAE and $2 postage. Editorial and photo guidelines free with SASE.
Needs: Uses 21 photos/issue; 70 supplied by freelancers. Cover photos of hunting and fishing in the Western states. "We are moving toward 100% four-color books, meaning we will be buying only color photography in the near future. A special subject need will be photos of boat-related fishing, particularly small and trailerable boats and trout fishing cover photos." Most photos purchased with accompanying ms. Model/property release preferred for women and men in brief attire. Captions required.
Making Contact & Terms: Interested in receiving work from newer, lesser-known photographers. Query or send photos for consideration. Send 35mm Kodachrome II transparencies. SASE. Reports in 3 weeks. Pays $50-100/b&w photo; $50-100/color photo; $200-250/cover photo; $400-500 for text/photo package. **Pays on acceptance.** Buys one-time rights; negotiable.
Tips: "Submissions should be of interest to western fishermen or hunters, and should include a 1,120-1,500 word ms; a Trip Facts Box (where to stay, costs, special information); photos; captions; and a map of the area. Emphasis is on fishing and hunting how-to, somewhere-to-go. Submit seasonal material 6 months in advance. Make your photos tell the story and don't depend on captions to explain what is pictured. Avoid 'photographic cliches' such as 'dead fish with man,' dead pheasants draped over a shotgun, etc. Get action shots, live fish and game. We avoid the 'tame' animals of Yellowstone and other national parks. In fishing, we seek individual action or underwater shots. For cover photos, use

Can't find a listing? Check at the end of each market section for the " '93-'94 Changes" lists. These lists include any market listings from the '93 edition which were either not verified or deleted in this edition.

Photographer Stephen Fischer of Colorado Springs, Colorado, made a personal visit to show the editors of Western Horseman his photographic talent. Admiration for his work on Native American fashions turned into a sale of seven color photos, including this one, and a manuscript. The text-photo package has given him more national exposure and invitations to work with various Native American groups.

© Stephen Fischer

vertical format composed with action entering picture from right; leave enough left-hand margin for cover blurbs, space at top of frame for magazine logo. Add human element to scenics to lend scale. Get to know the magazine and its editors. Ask for the year's editorial schedule (available through advertising department) and offer cover photos to match the theme of an issue. In samples, looks for color saturation, pleasing use of color components; originality, creativity; attractiveness of human subjects as well as fish or game; above all—sharp, sharp, sharp focus! Send duplicated transparencies as samples, but be prepared to provide originals." Sees trend toward electronic imagery, computer enhancement and electronic transmission of images.

WESTWAYS, Dept. PM, P.O. Box 2890, Los Angeles CA 90051. (213)741-4850. Fax: (213)741-3033. Art Director: Don Letta. Estab. 1909. Emphasizes Western US and world travel, leisure time activities, people, history, culture and western events.
Making Contact & Terms: Interested in receiving work from newer, lesser-known photographers. Query first with sample of photography. Call for an appointment, show strong portfolio. Pays $50-200/ b&w or color photo; $75-200/hour; $300-700/day; $200-1,000/job. Buys one-time rights; negotiable.
Tips: "We like to get photos with every submitted manuscript. We take some photo essays (with brief text), but they must be unusual and of interest to our readers. All photos should be tack sharp originals for final reproduction and well captioned. Trends in our use of editorial photography include high drama and high photographic art."

WHEELINGS, P.O. Box 389, Franklin MA 02038. (508)528-6211. Editor: J.A. Kruza. Circ. 8,460. Tabloid magazine published 4 times a year. Emphasizes auto body shops, auto paint shops, auto dealers, auto paint manufacturers. Readers are auto industries with 8 or more employees. Photo guidelines free.
Needs: Uses 25 photos/issue; usually 10-15 supplied by freelance photographers. "We need news-type photos relating to the industry." Captions required.
Making Contact & Terms: Query with samples. SASE. Reports in 2 weeks. Pays $25 first photo, $10 for each additional photo; buys 3-5 photos in a series. **Pays on acceptance.** Credit line given. Prefers all rights; reassigns to photographer after use. Simultaneous submissions and previously published work OK.

WHERE CHICAGO MAGAZINE, 1165 N. Clark St., Chicago IL 60610. (312)642-1896. Fax: (312)642-5467. Editor: Margaret Doyle. Circ. 100,000. Estab. 1985. Monthly magazine. Emphasizes shopping, dining, nightlife and entertainment available in Chicago and its suburbs. Readers are male and female traveling executives and tourists, ages 25-55. Sample copy $3.

Needs: Uses 1 photo/issue; 90% supplied by freelancers. Needs scenic, seasonal shots of Chicago, must include architecture or landmarks that identify a photo as being shot in Chicago. Reviews photos with or without ms. "We look for seasonal shots on a monthly basis." Model/property release required. Captions required.

Making Contact & Terms: Send unsolicited photos by mail for consideration. Provide resume, business card, brochure, flyer or tearsheets to be kept on file for possible assignments. Send 35mm, 2¼×2¼, 4×5, 8×10 transparencies. SASE. Reports in 1 month. Pays $300/color cover photo. **Pays on acceptance.** Credit line given. Buys one-time rights; negotiable. Simultaneous submissions and previously published work OK.

Tips: "We only consider photos of downtown Chicago, without people in them. Shots should be colorful and current, in a vertical format. Keep our deadlines in mind. We look for covers two months in advance of issue publication."

WHERE MAGAZINE, 15th Floor, 600 Third Ave., New York NY 10016. (212)687-4646. Fax: (212)687-4661. Editor-in-Chief: Michael Kelly Tucker. Estab. 1936. Monthly. Emphasizes points of interest, shopping, restaurants, theater, museums, etc. in New York City (specifically Manhattan). Readers are visitors to New York staying in the city's leading hotels. Circ. 119,000/month. Sample copy available in hotels.

Needs: Buys cover photos only. Covers showing New York scenes; color photos only. Vertical compositions preferred. No mss. Model release and captions preferred.

Making Contact & Terms: Interested in receiving work from newer, lesser-known photographers. Arrange a personal interview to show portfolio. Does not return unsolicited material. Pays $300/color photo. Pays on publication. Credit line given. Rights purchased vary. Simultaneous submissions and previously published work OK.

WILDLIFE CONSERVATION MAGAZINE, Dept. PM, New York Zoological Park, Bronx NY 10460. (718)220-5121. Fax: (718)584-2625. Picture Consultant: Niki Barrie. Editor: Joan Downs. Circ. 140,000. Bimonthly. Emphasizes wildlife conservation and natural history, especially of endangered species. Readers include mature people (over 12), interested in wildlife and nature. Sample copy available for $2.95. Photo guidelines free with SASE.

Needs: Uses 60 photos/issue; supplied by freelance photographers, researchers and agencies. Needs wildlife photos. Model release required. Captions required.

Making Contact & Terms: Interested in receiving work from newer, lesser-known photographers. Query with list of stock photo subjects. Send ideas for photo essays but do not send unsolicited photos. Reports in 1 month. Pays $75-400/photo. Other rates are noted on guidelines. Pays on publication. Credit line given. Buys one-time rights.

Tips: To break in, compile a fairly specific list of species and geographic areas; get series of behavioral shots. Think in terms of photostories, or at least, "how could this photo be used in *Wildlife Conservation*?"

WINDSURFING, P.O. Box 2456, Winter Park FL 32790. (407)628-4802. Contact: Photo Editor. Monthly magazine. Emphasizes boardsailing. Readers are all ages and all income groups. Circ. 70,000. Sample copy free with SASE. Photo guidelines free with SASE.

• In 1992 this publication received a silver Charlie Award from the Florida Magazine Association for having the Best Overall Design for a circulation over 25,000.

Needs: Uses 80 photos/issue; 60% supplied by freelance photographers. Needs photos of boardsailing, flat water, recreational travel destinations to sail. Model release and captions preferred.

Making Contact & Terms: Query with samples. Send unsolicited photos by mail for consideration. Provide resume, business card, brochure, flyer or tearsheets to be kept on file for possible future assignments. Send 35mm, 2¼×2¼ and 4×5 transparencies by mail for consideration. Kodachrome and slow Fuji preferred. SASE. Reports in 3 weeks. Pays $20-100/b&w page; $30-350/color page. Credit line given. Buys one-time rights unless otherwise agreed on. Simultaneous submissions OK.

Tips: Prefers to see razor sharp, colorful images. The best guideline is the magazine itself. "Get used to shooting on, in or under water. Most of our needs are found there."

WISCONSIN TRAILS, Dept. PM, P.O. Box 5650, Madison WI 53705. (608)231-2444. Photo Editor: Nancy Mead. Circ. 35,000. Bimonthly magazine. For people interested in history, travel, recreation, personalities, the arts, nature and Wisconsin in general. Sample copy $3. Photo guidelines free with SASE.

Needs: Buys 300 photos/year. Seasonal scenics and photos relating to Wisconsin. Annual Calendar: uses horizontal and vertical formats; scenic photographs. Wants no color or b&w snapshots, color negatives, cheesecake, shots of posed people, b&w negatives ("proofs or prints, please") or "photos of things clearly not found in Wisconsin. We greatly appreciate caption info."

Making Contact & Terms: Query with resume of credits. Arrange a personal interview to show portfolio. Submit portfolio or submit contact sheet or photos for consideration. Provide calling card and flyer to be kept on file for possible future assignments. Send contact sheet or 5×7 or 8×10 glossy b&w prints. Send transparencies; "we use all sizes." Send 35mm, $2\frac{1}{4} \times 2\frac{1}{4}$ or 4×5 transparencies for cover; "should be strong seasonal scenics or people in action." Uses vertical format; top of photo should lend itself to insertion of logo; or a square to be boxed. Locations preferred and needed. SASE. Reports in 3 weeks. Pays $125/calendar and cover photos; $50/b&w photo. Pays on publication. Buys first serial rights or second serial (reprint) rights. Simultaneous submissions OK "only if we are informed in advance." Previously published work OK.

Tips: "Because we cover only Wisconsin and because most photos illustrate articles (and are done by freelancers on assignment), it's difficult to break into *Wisconsin Trails* unless you live or travel in Wisconsin." Also, "be sure you specify how you want materials returned. Include postage for any special handling (insurance, certified, registered, etc.) you request."

WITH, P.O. Box 347, Newton KS 67114. (316)283-5100. Co-editors: Eddy Hall, Carol Duerksen. Circ. 6,100. Estab. 1968. Magazine published eight times a year. Emphasizes "Christian values in lifestyle, vocational decision making, conflict resolution for US and Canadian high school students." Sample copy free with 9×12 SAE and 98¢ postage. Photo and writer's guidelines free with SASE.

Needs: Buys 75 photos/year; 8-10 photos/issue. Buys 35% of freelance photography from assignment; 65% from stock. Documentary (related to concerns of high school youth "interacting with each other, with family and in school environment; intergenerational"); fine art; head shot; photo essay/photo feature; scenic; special effects & experimental; how-to; human interest; humorous; still life; and travel. Particularly interested in action shots of teens, especially of ethnic minorities. We use some mood shots and a few nature photos. Prefers candids over posed model photos. Few religious shots, e.g., crosses, steeples, etc. Photos purchased with or without accompanying ms and on assignment. For accompanying mss wants issues involving youth—school, peers, family, hobbies, sports, community involvement, sex, dating, drugs, self-identity, values, religion, etc. Model release preferred.

Making Contact & Terms: Interested in receiving work from newer, lesser-known photographers. Send material by mail for consideration. Uses 8×10 glossy b&w prints. SASE. Reports in 8 weeks. Pays $20-35/b&w photo inside; $30-50/b&w cover photo; 4¢/word for text/photo packages, or on a per-photo basis. **Pays on acceptance.** Credit line given. Buys one-time rights. Simultaneous submissions and previously published work OK.

Tips: "Freelancers are our lifeblood. Candid shots of youth doing ordinary daily activities and mood shots are what we generally use. Photos dealing with social problems are also often needed. We rely greatly on freelancers, so we're interested in seeing work from a number of photographers. *With* is one of several periodicals published at this office, and we also publish Sunday school curriculum for all ages here, so there are many opportunities for photographers. Needs to relate to teenagers—either include them in photos or subjects they relate to; using a lot of 'nontraditional' roles, also more ethnic and cultural diversity, more emphasis on current global events. Use models who are average-looking, not obvious model-types. Teenagers have enough self-esteem problems without seeing 'perfect' teens in photos."

WOMAN ENGINEER, Equal Opportunity Publications, Inc., # 420, 150 Motor Parkway, Hauppage NY 11788-5145. (516)273-8743. Fax: (516)273-8936. Editor: Anne Kelly. Circ. 16,000. Estab. 1979. Quarterly magazine. Emphasizes career guidance for women engineers at the college and professional levels. Readers are college-age and professional women in engineering. Sample copy free with 9×12 SAE and 6 first-class stamps.

Needs: Uses at least one photo per issue (cover); planning to use freelance work for covers and possibly editorial; most of the photos are submitted by freelance writers with their articles. Model release preferred. Captions required.

Making Contact & Terms: Query with list of stock photo subjects or call to discuss our needs. SASE. Reports in 2 weeks. Pays $25/color cover photo; $15/b&w photo; $15/color photo. Pays on publication. Credit line given. Buys one-time rights. Simultaneous submissions and previously published work OK, "but not in competitive career-guidance publications."

Tips: "We are looking for strong, sharply focused photos or slides of women engineers. The photo should show a woman engineer at work, but the background should be uncluttered. The photo subject should be dressed and groomed in a professional manner. Cover photo should represent a professional woman engineer at work, convey a positive and professional image. Read our magazine, and find actual women engineers to photograph. We're not against using cover models, but we prefer cover subjects to be women engineers working in the field."

WOMAN'S WORLD, Dept. PM, 270 Sylvan Ave., Englewood Cliffs NJ 07632. (201)569-0006, Ext. 400. Editor-in-Chief: Dena Vane. Photo Editor: Stacy Pulsky. Weekly. Emphasizes women's issues. Readers are women 25-60 nationwide of low to middle income. Circ. 1,200,000. Sample copies available.
Needs: Uses up to 100 photos/issue; all supplied by freelancers and stock houses. Needs travel, fashion, crafts and celebrity shots. "For editorial pages we look for informative straightforward photos of women's careers, travel, people in everyday personal situations—couples arguing, etc., and medicine. Photographers should be sympathetic to the subject, and our straightforward approach to it." Photos purchased with or without accompanying ms. Model release and captions required. "Not responsible for any materials sent on spec. Please talk with someone at the magazine before sending anything."
Making Contact & Terms: Query with 8×10 b&w glossy prints or 35mm transparencies or provide basic background and how to contact. Prefers to see tearsheets of published work, or prints or slides of unpublished work, as samples. SASE. Reports in 1 month. Provide resume and tearsheets to be kept on file for possible future assignments. Pays $250/day plus expenses; $300/page for color and fashion; $150-200/day for b&w. **Pays on acceptance.** Credit line given. Buys one-time rights.

WOMEN'S SPORTS AND FITNESS MAGAZINE, Dept. PM, Suite 421, 1919 14th St., Boulder CO 80302. (303)440-5111. Photo Editor/Art Director: Laurie Jennings. Monthly. Readers are active women who are vitally interested in health and fitness. Recreational interests include participation in two or more sports, particularly cycling, running and swimming. Circ. 250,000. Sample copy and photo guidelines free with SASE.
Needs: 80% of photos supplied by freelance photographers. Call to receive photo schedule. Model release and captions preferred.
Making Contact & Terms: Call before submitting material. Provide resume, business card, brochure, flyer or tearsheets to be kept on file for possible future assignments. SASE. Reports in 1 month. Pays $400/color cover; $50-300/color inside; $200/color page. Pays on publication. Credit line given. Buys one-time rights.
Tips: Looks for "razor sharp images and nice light. Check magazine before submitting query. We look especially for photos of women who are genuinely athletic in active situations that actually represent a particular sport or activity."

*‡WOODTURNING. 166 High St., Lewes E. Sussex BN7 1XU United Kingdom. (0273)477374. Fax: (0273)478606. Editor: Nick Hough. Circ. 30,000. Estab. 1990. Bimonthly magazine. Emphasizes woodturning. Readers are mostly male 30+. Samples copy £2.75 (English currency), $6.50, £1, $2 (US) first-class stamps.
Needs: Reviews photos with accompanying ms only. "Photos nearly all sent by writers with articles." Some gallery photos of work, rest how-to with projects. Captions required.
Making Contact & Terms: Provide resume, business card, brochure, flyer or tearsheets to be kept on file for possible future assignments. Keeps samples on file sometimes. SASE. Reports in 1-2 weeks. Pays £50/color page rate; £50/per page. Pays on publication. Credit line given sometimes. Buys one-time rights. Consider simultaneous submission and/or previously published work (photos).
Tips: "We normally only consider articles with photos. Occasionally we use unusual photos with captions of woodturnings."

WORDSMITH, P.O. Box 891, Ft. Collins CO 80522-0891. (303)224-5218. Editor: Judith Kaufman. Estab. 1991. Annual magazine. Readers interested in poetry and fiction. Sample copy $5. Photo guidelines free with SASE.
Needs: Uses 1 photo/issue. "This is a literary magazine. We look at many different styles and subjects. We will consider submissions from all areas." Reviews photos with or without ms. Model/property release required.
Making Contact & Terms: Interested in receiving work from newer, lesser-known photographers. Send unsolicited photos by mail for consideration. Send 5×7 b&w, color prints. Keeps samples on file. SASE. Pays $25/color cover photo; $25/b&w cover photo; $10/b&w inside photo. Pays on publication. Credit line given. Buys one-time rights; negotiable.
Tips: "We look for visual art that will help to sell our magazine."

WORKBENCH MAGAZINE, Suite 310, 700 W. 47th St., Kansas City MO 64112. (816)531-5730. Fax: (816)531-3873. Editor: Robert N. Hoffman. Managing Editor: A. Robert Gould. Circ. 860,000. Estab. 1957. Bimonthly magazine. Emphasizes do-it-yourself projects for the woodworker and home remodeler. Free sample copy. Free photo guidelines and writer's guidelines.
Needs: Looks for residential architecture (interiors and exteriors of homes), wood crafts, furniture, wood toys and folk art. How-to; needs step-by-step shots. Photos are purchased with accompanying ms. "We also purchase photos to illustrate articles, including 'beauty' lead photographs." Model/property release required for product shots, homeowner's or craftspeople's projects and profile shots. Captions required; include people's names and what action is shown in photo.

Making Contact & Terms: Ask for guidelines, then send material by mail for consideration. Uses 5×7 or 8×10 glossy b&w prints; 2¼×2¼ or 4×5 transparencies and 8×10 glossy color prints; 4×5 color transparencies for cover, vertical format required. SASE. Reports in 4 weeks. Pay for b&w photos included in purchase price of ms; $125 minimum/color photo; $450 minimum/cover photo; $150-300/published page. **Pays on acceptance.** Credit line given with ms. Buys all rights; negotiable.
Tips: Prefers to see "sharp, clear photos; they must be accompanied by story with necessary working drawings. See copy of the magazine. We are happy to work with photographers in developing story ideas."

*THE WORLD & I, 2800 New York Ave. NE, Washington DC 20002. (202)635-4000. Fax: (202)269-9353. Photo Essay Editor: Adri de Groot. Contact department editors. Circ. 30,000. Estab. 1986. Monthly magazine. Sample copy $10. Photo guidelines free with SASE.
Needs: Uses 250 photos/issue; 50% supplied by freelancers. Needs news photos, head shots of important political figures; important international news photos of the month; scientific photos, new products, inventions, research; reviews of concerts, exhibitions, museums, architecture, photography shows, fine art; travel; gardening; adventure; food; human interests; personalities; activities; groups; organizations; anthropology, social change, folklore, Americana; Life and Ideals, unsung heroes doing altruistic work. Reviews photos with or without ms—depends on editorial section. Model release required for special features and personalities. Captions required.
Making Contact & Terms: Interested in receiving work from newer, lesser-known photographers. "Photographers should direct themselves to editors of different sections. If they have questions, they can ask the photo director or the photo essay editor for advice." For color, pays $75/¼ page, $125/½ page, $135/¾ page, $200/full page, $225/1¼ page, $275/1½ page, $330/1¾ page, $375/double page; for b&w, pays $45/¼ page, $95/½ page, $110/3/4 page, $150/full page, $165/1¼ page, $175/1½ page, $185/1¾ page; $200/double page. Pays on publication. Buys one-time rights. Previously published work OK.
Tips: "To break into the competitive Photo Essay department, study the guidelines well, and then make contact as described above. You must be a good and creative photographer who can tell a story with sufficient attention paid to details and the larger picture. Images must work well with the text, but all tell their own story and add to the story with strong captions. We will try to give you a quick reply, within 2 weeks. Do NOT submit travel pieces as Patterns photo essays, nor sentimental life stories as Life & Ideals photo essays."

WRESTLING WORLD, Lexington Library, Inc., 355 Lexington Ave., New York NY 10017. Fax: (212)986-5926. Editor: Stephen Ciacciarelli. Circ. 50,000. Bimonthly magazine. Emphasizes professional wrestling superstars. Readers are wrestling fans. Sample copy $2.95 with 9×12 SAE and 75¢ postage.
Needs: Uses about 60 photos/issue; all supplied by freelance photographers. Needs photos of wrestling superstars, action and posed, color slides and b&w prints.
Making Contact & Terms: Query with representative samples, preferably action. SASE. Reports ASAP. Pays $150/color cover photo; $75/color inside photo; $50-125/text/photo package. **Pays on acceptance.** Credit line given on color photos. Buys one-time rights.

YELLOW SILK: Journal of Erotic Arts, P.O. Box 6374, Albany CA 94706. (510)644-4188. Editor: Lily Pond. Circ. 16,000. Quarterly magazine. Emphasizes literature, arts and erotica. Readers are well educated, creative, liberal. Sample copy $7.50
Needs: Uses about 15-20 photos "by one artist" per issue. Have published the work of Judy Dater, Tee Corinne, Sandra Russell Clark, Stephen John Phillips and Jan Saudek. "All photos are erotic; none are cheesecake or sexist. No porn. We define 'erotic' in its widest sense; trees and flowers can be as erotic as humans making love. They are fine arts." Model release required.
Making Contact & Terms: Query with samples. Send prints, transparencies, contact sheets or photocopies by mail for consideration. Submit portfolio for review. SASE. Reports in 3 months. NPI; payment to be arranged. Pays on publication. Credit line given. Buys one-time rights; "use for promotional and/or other rights arranged."
Tips: "Get to know the publication you are submitting work to and enclose SASE in all correspondence. Interested in color work at this time."

YM, Dept. PM, 685 Third Ave., New York NY 10017. (212)878-8636. Photo Editor: Chantal Belsheim. Monthly magazine. Readers are girls from ages 17-21. Magazine emphasizes fashion/beauty. Circ. 1 million and growing. Sample copy free upon request. Photo guidelines available.
Needs: Needs "street photos of fashion, fashion, beauty and celebrities." Model release and captions preferred; "depending on subject."
Making Contact & Terms: Submit portfolio for review. Reports in 2 weeks, sometimes longer. Pays $300/color page rate or $200-250/b&w page rate. Buys all rights; non-negotiable. Simultaneous submissions and previously published work OK.

Tips: In portfolio or samples, looking for "good sense of color, light and composition." Also, photos that are "natural, fun, hip, well-styled and fairly unique." To break in, "send only your best and favorite work. Look at our magazine before contacting us."

YOUR HOME, Meridian Publishing, P.O. Box 10010, Ogden UT 84409. Editor/Publisher: Caroll Shreeve. Distributed to businesses to be used with their inserts, as their house magazine. "A monthly pictorial magazine with emphasis on home decor, buying, home construction, financing, landscaping and working with realtors. Send SASE for guidelines. Sample copy $1 plus 9 × 12 envelope.
Needs: "We prefer manuscripts (800 to 1,200 words) with color transparencies." No do-it-yourself pieces, emphasize using professionals. Model release required. Captions preferred.
Making Contact & Terms: Interested in receiving work from newer, lesser-known photographers. Responds to SASE within 1 month. Pays 15¢/word; $35 for color transparencies. Also needed are vertical transparencies for covers; pays $50/cover, negotiable for outstanding work. "These should have dramatic composition with sharp, contrasting colors." Six-month lead time. **Pays on acceptance.** Credit line given. Buys first N.A. rights.
Tips: Prefers to see "interior and exterior views of homes; good interior decor ideas; packages (photos with text) on home, garden, decorating and improvement ideas." Photos and text are commonly purchased as a package. About 50% of work is assigned. Send clear sharp pictures with contrasting colors for our review. The photo department is very strict about the quality of pictures chosen for the articles."

YOUR MONEY MAGAZINE, 5705 N. Lincoln Ave., Chicago IL 60659. (312)275-3590. Art Director: Beth Ceisel. Circ. 250,000. Estab. 1979. Bimonthly magazine. Emphasizes personal finance.
Needs: Uses 18-25 photos/issue, 130-150 photos/year; all supplied by freelance assignment. Considers all styles depending on needs. "Always looking for quality location photography, especially environmental portraiture." Model/property release required.
Making Contact & Terms: Interested in receiving work from newer, lesser-known photographers. Arrange a personal interview to show portfolio. Provide a business card, flyer or tearsheets to be kept on file. Transparencies, slides, proofs or prints returned after publication. Samples not filed are returned with SASE. Reports only when interested. Pays up to $1,200/color cover photo; $450/b&w page; $600/color page. **Pays on acceptance.** Credit line given.
Tips: "Show your best work. Include tearsheets in portfolio."

ZUZU'S PETALS QUARTERLY, P.O. Box 4476, Allentown PA 18105. (215)821-1324. Editor: T. Dunn. Circ. 300. Estab. 1992. Quarterly magazine. Emphasis on literature and the visual arts. Sample copies $5.
Needs: Uses 20 photos/issue; 50% supplied by freelancers. Needs photos of scenics (technological and natural), people and "artsy" shots. Reviews photos with or without accompanying ms. Model/property release preferred. Captions preferred; include location of subject.
Making Contact & Terms: Interested in receiving work from newer, lesser-known photographers. Send 8 × 10 or smaller glossy b&w prints by mail for consideration. Does not keep samples on file. SASE. Reports in 3 weeks. Pays in copies. Pays on publication. Credit line given. Buys one-time rights; negotiable. Simultaneous submissions and previously published work OK.
Tips: "We're looking for freshness, a different perspective on the everyday and the commonplace."

Consumer Publications/'93-'94 changes

The following markets appeared in the 1993 edition of *Photographer's Market* but are not listed in the 1994 edition. They may have been omitted for failing to respond to our request for updated information, they may have gone out of business or they may no longer wish to receive freelance work.

Arizona Literary Review (unable to locate)
Asia Pacific Travel and Health World (did not respond)
Best Wishes (asked to be deleted)
Billiards Digest (did not respond)
Bodyboarding Magazine (did not respond)
Bowlers Journal (did not respond)

Canadian Biker Magazine (few responses)
Careers & The Disabled, Equal Opportunity Publications, Inc. (did not respond)
Catholic Near East Magazine (did not respond)
Cheri (did not respond)
Chicago Parent News Magazine (did not respond)
Circle Track Magazine (did not respond)

Climbing Art (did not respond)
Collector Editions (not reviewing freelance work)
Country Woman (did not respond)
Crosscurrents (asked to be deleted)
Diver (did not respond)
Diver Magazine (not reviewing freelance work)
Dolls-The Collector's Magazine (not reviewing free-

lance work)
Down East Magazine (did not respond)
Duluth News-Tribune (did not respond)
E Magazine (did not respond)
East West Magazine (no longer published)
Easyriders Magazine (did not respond)
Ellery Queen's Mystery Magazine (did not respond)
Equal Opportunity (did not respond)
Fine Homebuilding (did not respond)
Finger Lakes Magazine (did not respond)
Florida Leader Magazine (did not respond)
Flying (asked to be deleted)
Four Wheeler Magazine (did not respond)
Fun in the Sun (did not respond)
Fun/West (did not respond)
Futurific Magazine (did not respond)
Gamut (suspended publication)
Golf Journal (did not respond)
Golf Traveler (did not respond)
Gospel Herald (did not respond)
Gun World (did not respond)
Guns & Ammo Magazine (did not respond)
Health World (did not respond)
Horse & Rider Magazine (did not respond)
Horse Illustrated (did not respond)
Illinois Magazine (suspended publication)
Income Plus (no longer needs photos)
Independent Living (did not respond)
Independent Senior (not reviewing freelance work)
Indianapolis Monthly (did not respond)
Insight (did not respond)

Jots (did not respond)
Karate/Kung Fu Illustrated (not reviewing freelance work)
Kidsports Magazine (did not respond)
Long Island Power & Sail (did not respond)
Louisiana Life Magazine (did not respond)
Marriage Partnership (did not respond)
Minority Engineer (did not respond)
Modern Bride (did not respond)
Moment (did not respond)
Motorhome (did not respond)
New Cleveland Woman Journal (unable to locate)
New Dominion Magazine (did not respond)
N.Y. Habitat (did not respond)
Northeast Outdoors (did not respond)
Ocean Navigator (unable to locate)
Opera News (unable to locate)
Orlando Magazine (did not respond)
Outlook (did not respond)
Overseas! (did not respond)
Paint Horse Journal (did not respond)
Pennsylvania Sportsman (did not respond)
Petersen's 4 Wheel (did not respond)
Petersen's Photographic Magazine (did not respond)
Practical Horseman (did not respond)
Primal Voices (did not respond)
Problems of Communism (did not respond)
Profitable Games (unable to locate)
Quilt World, Quick & Easy Quilting, Stitch 'N Sew Quilts (did not respond)
R&R Shoppers News (did not respond)
Review of Optometry (did not

respond)
Sail Magazine (did not respond)
St. Louis Magazine (did not respond)
Sea, The Magazine of Western Boating (did not respond)
Sheet Music Magazine (did not respond)
Skies America (did not respond)
Skiing Magazine (did not respond)
Skin Diver (did not respond)
Snow Week (did not respond)
Snowmobile Magazine (did not respond)
Snowmobile West (did not respond)
Soldiers of Fortune Magazine (did not respond)
Speedway Limited Edition (no longer published)
Sport Magazine (did not respond)
Straight (did not respond)
Swank (did not respond)
Tampa Review (did not respond)
Teens Today (did not respond)
Texas Fish & Game (did not respond)
Trailer Boats Magazine (did not respond)
Trajectories (unable to locate)
Triathlete Magazine (asked to be deleted)
Tropical Fish Hobbyist Magazine (did not respond)
Western Sportsman (not reviewing freelance work)
James White Review (did not respond)
Win Magazine (did not respond)
Woodenboat Magazine (inappropriate submissions)
Yellow Jersey Publications: Texas Bicyclist, Florida Bicyclist And California Bicyclist (did not respond)
Your Health (did not respond)

Newspapers & Newsletters

Photojournalists throughout the world are in for a wild and exciting ride over the next decade as leaders of the newspaper industry analyze and react to their changing field. Technological advances have made it possible for photographers to scan, edit and transmit their images from assignment locations to editorial desks within minutes. Because of these new systems, such as the Associated Press Leafdesks, the time from image creation to publication has been dramatically reduced.

Indianapolis, Indiana, photographer Mary Ann Carter says a Leafax system is essential for photographers who are pushing to meet deadlines during breaking news stories. Carter talks more about her field in our Insider Report beginning on page 350.

Such equipment not only makes it easier for photographers and editors, but readers benefit as well. They no longer have to wait an extra day to see photos of breaking news. Readers also won't have to rely on television to supply the visual aspect of a hot story.

The computer generation has forced publishers to consider different ways to provide information. Over the last couple years newspaper publishers have battled to keep readers and worked hard to overcome poor advertising sales during the recession. Profits have improved, but newspapers might never regain the 30-50 percent profit margins of the 1980s. In order to overcome slumping circulations and advertising revenues, publishers are examining the possibility of offering electronic services.

Because of this move toward computerization, photographers should become more familiar with computer software, such as Adobe Photoshop. Such software, which allows editors to easily perform sophisticated retouching of images, will become common at most newspapers and magazines.

Understand the business

A knowledge of computers, however, is not all you need to work with newspaper editors. You must understand the business. Always remind yourself that time is of the essence. Newspapers have various deadlines for each section that is produced. An interesting feature or news photo has a better chance of getting in the next edition if the subject is timely and has a local appeal. Most of the markets in this section are interested in regional coverage. Find publications near you and contact editors to get an understanding of their deadline schedules.

Also, ask editors if they prefer certain types of film or if they want color slides or b&w prints. Many smaller newspapers do not have the capability to run color images, so b&w prints are preferred. However, color slides can be converted to b&w. Editors who have the option of running color or b&w photos often prefer color film because of its versatility.

Although most newspapers rely on staff photographers, some hire freelancers as stringers for certain stories. Act professionally and build up an editor's confidence in you by supplying innovative images. For example, don't get caught in the trap of shooting "grip-and-grin" photos when a corporation executive is handing over a check to a nonprofit organization. Turn the scene into an interesting portrait. Capture some spontaneous interaction between the people receiving the money and the firm donating the funds. By planning ahead you can be creative.

When you receive assignments it is always good to think about the image before you snap your first photo. If you are scheduled to meet someone at a specific location, arrive early and scout around. Find a proper setting or locate some props to use in the shoot. Do whatever you can to show the editor that you are willing to make that extra effort to give him something unique.

Always try to retain resale rights to shots of major news events. High news value means high resale value, and strong news photos can be resold repeatedly. If you have an image with a national appeal search for those larger markets, possibly through the wire services. You also may find buyers among national news magazines, such as *Time* or *Newsweek*.

While most newspapers offer low payment for images, they are willing to negotiate if the image will have a major impact. Front page artwork often sells newspapers, so don't underestimate the worth of your images.

*ACA GUIDEPOST, 5999 Stevenson Ave., Alexandria VA 22304. (703)823-9800, ext. 357. Fax: (703)823-0252. Photo Editor: Siobhan McGowan. Circ. 60,000. Estab. 1952. Publication of the American Counseling Association. Monthly tabloid. Emphasizes mental health counseling. Readers are male and female mental health professionals, ages 25+. Sample copy $2.
Needs: Uses 5-10 photos/issue; 50% supplied by freelancers. Needs human interest shots (i.e., people in conversation or counseling situations, groups, children, medical professionals, students, people with disabilities). Reviews photos with or without ms. Special photo needs include people with disabilities, group therapy, counseling with professionals. Model/property release preferred. Captions preferred; include names of subjects, location, special circumstances.
Making Contact & Terms: Interested in receiving work from newer, lesser-known photographers. Query with stock photo list. Keeps samples on file. SASE. Reports in 1 month. Pays $75-150/color cover photo; $75-100/b&w cover photo; $50-75/b&w inside photo. Pays on publication. Credit line given. Buys one-time rights/negotiable. Simultaneous submissions and/or previously published work OK.
Tips: "We often write about current popular issues from a mental health angle—gays in the military, the gender and generation gap, familial abuse—and we need photos to accompany those articles. It is easiest for us to evaluate your work if you send a pamphlet with reproductions of your stock photos. We often choose directly from catalogs or pamphlets."

*THE ADVOCATE/PKA PUBLICATIONS, 301A Rolling Hills Park, Prattsville NY 12468. (518)299-3103. Art Editor: C.J. Karlie. Circ. 12,000. Estab. 1987. Bimonthly tabloid. Literary arts-oriented magazine geared toward the pre-professional. Readers are male and female, ages 12-90, all professions. Sample copy $3. Photo guidelines free with SASE.
Needs: Uses 3-6 photos/issue; 100% supplied by freelancers. Needs photos of animals, wildlife, scenics, humor. Reviews photos with or without ms. Model/property release required. Captions required; include where shot, people and subject of photo, location, anything which describes shot.
Making Contact & Terms: Interested in receiving work from newer, lesser-known photographers. Send unsolicited photos by mail for consideration. Send prints no longer than 8×10, color and b&w. Does not keep samples on file. SASE. Reports in 1 month. Pays contributor's copy and byline. Pays on publication. Credit line given. Buys one-time rights.
Tips: "Work should look good in black and white format. We do not print in color, but do accept both b&w and color prints. Just send prints with SASE, unpublished and not simultaneous submissions."

AGRI-TIMES NORTHWEST, 206 SE Court, Box 189, Pendleton OR 97801. (503)276-7845. Editor: Virgil Rupp. Circ. 5,500. Estab. 1983. Weekly newspaper. Emphasizes agriculture of eastern Oregon, eastern Washington and northern Idaho. Readers are agribusiness people and farmers, both men and women, of all ages. Sample copy free with 9×12 SAE and 4 first-class stamps. Photo guidelines free with SASE.
Needs: Uses 15-20 photos/issue; 70% supplied by freelance photographers. Uses all agriculturally related photos including crop production and animals such as cattle, hogs, horses and sheep. Request editorial calendar for special subject needs. Model release preferred. Photo captions required.
Making Contact & Terms: Query with list of stock photo subjects. Send unsolicited photos by mail for consideration. Send 5×7 or 8×10 glossy b&w prints. SASE. Reports in 1 month. "All b&w $10 per photo except 1 column photo, which is $5." Pays on publication. Credit line given. Buys one-time rights. Simultaneous submissions OK.

Tips: Especially looking for "photos of farmers and farming in our circulation area."

AMERICAN METAL MARKET, 825 7th Ave., New York NY 10019. (212)887-8550. Fax: (212)887-8520. Capital Cities/ABC, Inc. Diversified Publishing Group. Editor: Michael G. Botta. Circ. 13,000. Estab. 1882. Daily newspaper. Emphasizes metals production and trade. Readers are top level management (CEO's, chairmen, and presidents) in metals and metals related industries. Sample copies free with 10×13 SASE.
Needs: 90% of photos supplied by freelancers. Needs photos of press conferences, executive interviews, industry action shots and industry receptions. Photo captions required.
Making Contact & Terms: Provide resume, business card, brochure, flyer or tearsheets to be kept on file for possible assignments. Cannot return material. NPI. Credit line given. Buys all rights; negotiable. Simultaneous submissions OK.
Tips: "We tend to avoid photographers who are unwilling to release all rights. We produce a daily newspaper and maintain a complete photo file. We cover events worldwide and often need to hire freelance photographers. Best bet is to supply business card, phone number and any samples for us to keep on file. Keep in mind action photos are difficult to come by. Much of the metals industry is automated and it has become a challenge to find good 'people' shots."

AMERICAN SPORTS NETWORK, Box 6100, Rosemead CA 91770. (818)572-4727. President: Louis Zwick. Circ. 50,000-755,000. Publishes four newspapers covering "general collegiate, amateur and professional sports; i.e., football, baseball, basketball, track and field, wrestling, boxing, hockey, power-lifting and bodybuilding, etc."
Needs: Uses about 10-85 photos/issue in various publications; 90% supplied by freelancers. Needs "sport action, hard-hitting contact, emotion-filled photos. Have special bodybuilder annual calendar, collegiate and professional football pre- and post-season editions." Model release and captions preferred.
Making Contact & Terms: Send 8×10 glossy b&w prints and 4×5 transparencies by mail for consideration. Provide resume, business card, brochure, flyer or tearsheets to be kept on file for possible future assignments. SASE. Reports in 1 week. Pays $1,000/color cover photo; $250/inside b&w photo; negotiates rates by the job and hour. Pays on publication. Buys first N.A. serial rights. Simultaneous submissions and previously published work OK.

ANCHORAGE DAILY NEWS, Dept. PM, 1001 Northway Dr., Anchorage AK 99508. (907)257-4347. Editor: Howard Weaver. Photo Editor: Richard Murphy. Daily newspaper. Emphasizes all Alaskan subjects. Readers are Alaskans. Circ. 70,000. Estab. 1946. Sample copy free with 11×14 SAE and $2 postage.
Needs: Uses 10-50 photos/issue; 0-5% supplied by freelance photographers; most from assignment. Needs photos of all subjects, primarily Alaskan subjects. In particular, looking for freelance images for travel section; wants photos of all areas, especially Hawaii. Model release preferred. Captions required.
Making Contact & Terms: Contact photo editor with specific ideas. SASE. Reports in 1-3 weeks. Pays $25 minimum/b&w photo; $35 minimum/color photo: photo/text package negotiable. Pays on publication. Credit line given. Buys one-time rights. Simultaneous submissions OK.
Tips: "We, like most daily newspapers, are primarily interested in timely topics, but at times will use dated material." In portfolio or samples, wants to see "eye-catching images, good use of light and active photographs. More color is being used on a daily basis."

ARIZONA BUSINESS GAZETTE, Box 1950, Phoenix AZ 85001. (602)271-7300. Fax: (602)271-7363. General Manager: Mary Lou Bessette. Circ. 15,000. Estab. 1880. Weekly newspaper.
Needs: Business subjects. Model release preferred. Captions required, include name, title and photo description.
Making Contact & Terms: Interested in receiving work from newer, lesser-known photographers. Provide resume, business card, brochure, flyer or tearsheets to be kept on file for possible assignments. Cannot return unsolicited material. Reports when possible. Pays $100/color photo; $75/b&w photo; $125/day. Pays on publication. Buys one-time rights. Does not consider simultaneous submissions or previously published work.
Tips: Wants to see an "ability to shoot environmental portraits, creatively illustrate stories on business trends and an ability to shoot indoor, outdoor and studio work." Photographers should live in Arizona with some newspaper experience.

AVSC NEWS, 79 Madison Ave., New York NY 10016. (212)561-8000. Fax: (212)779-9439. Director of Communications: Pam Harper. Circ. 4,500. Estab. 1962. Publication of the Association for Voluntary Surgical Contraception. Quarterly newsletter. Emphasizes health care, contraception. Readers are health care professionals in the US and abroad. Sample copies for 4×9 SASE.

It is not uncommon for photographers to stumble upon interesting subjects when they are searching for other shots. Fairbanks, Alaska, photographer Genezaret Barron was searching for migrating caribou near the city when Barron came across this group of people fishing. "It was unusual to have this many people late in the year still fishing, and everyone has a 'secret' fishing spot," says Barron. The image sold for $60 to the Anchorage Daily News *and later* Alaska *magazine purchased one-time rights for $75.*

Needs: Uses 2-3 photos/issue; 1 supplied by freelancer. Needs photos of mothers and fathers with children in US and developing worlds. Photos only; does not accept mss. Special needs include annual report 15-20 photos; brochures throughout the year. Model release required. Captions preferred.

Making Contact & Terms: Interested in receiving work from newer, lesser-known photographers. Query with list of stock photo subjects. Reports in 2 weeks. Pays $100-200/b&w cover photo; $50-150/b&w inside photo. Pays on publication. Buys one-time rights. Previously published work OK.

Tips: Prefers to see a "sharp, good range of tones from white through all greys to black, and appealing pictures of people."

BAJA TIMES, P.O. Box 5577, Chula Vista CA 91912. General Manager: Carlos Chabert. Editor: John W. Utley. Circ. 65,000. Estab. 1978. Monthly. Emphasizes Baja California and Mexico travel and history. Readers are travelers to Baja California, Mexico and Baja aficionados from all over US and Canada. Free sample copy and writer/photographer guidelines with SAE (9×12) and 5 first-class stamps.

Needs: Uses about 12 photos/issue; most supplied by freelance photographers. Needs current travel, scenic, wildlife, historic, women, children, fishing, Baja fashions and beach photos. Photos purchased with or without accompanying ms. Special needs include: history of cities in Baja California and resorts, Baja shopping, sports and general recreation. Model/property release preferred. Captions required; include who, what, when, where and why.

Making Contact & Terms: Interested in receiving work from newer, lesser-known photographers. Send by mail for consideration b&w prints. Query with list of stock photo subjects. Now using full color photos for front cover. Avidly seeking outstanding Baja California, Mexico subjects. Will review color prints, but prefer transparencies for publication. Reports in 6 weeks. Pays $5-10/b&w photos; $45/color cover photo. Buys one-time rights.

Tips: "We need sharp photography with good definition. Photo essays are welcome, but please remember the basic subject matter is Baja California, Mexico."

*THE BUSINESS RECORD, #400, 708 Walnut St., Cincinnati OH 45202. (513)421-9300. Fax: (513)421-9212. Editor: Gail L. Paul. Circ. 12,000. Estab. 1988. Weekly tabloid. Emphasizes business news. Readers are male and female business people, ages 30-65. Sample copy free with SASE. Photo guidelines available.
Needs: Uses 10 photos/issue; all supplied by freelancers. Needs photos of business executives and businesses, new products, new developments (buildings/construction). Reviews photos with or without ms.
Making Contact & Terms: Interested in receiving work from newer, lesser-known photographers. Arrange personal interview to show portfolio. Pays $35-50/job. Pays on publication. Credit line given. Buys all rights.

CALIFORNIA SCHOOL EMPLOYEE, P.O. Box 640, San Jose CA 95106. (408)263-8000, ext. 298. Fax: (408)954-0948. Senior Designer: Lisa Yordy. Publication labor union, California School Employees Association (CSEA). Monthly (October-July) newspaper. Circ. 100,000+. Estab. 1932. Sample copy free upon request.
Needs: Uses freelance photos on assignment (70%) and from stock (30%). Needs photos of people. Special photo needs include school work sites, crowds, school and college related; wants to see facial emotion, action. Model release required; captions required including subject names.
Making Contact & Terms: Interested in receiving work from newer, lesser-known photographers. Provide resume, business card, brochure, flyer or tearsheets to be kept on file for possible assignments. SASE. NPI; payment negotiable. Pays on publication. Credit line given. Rights purchased are negotiable. Simultaneous submissions and previously published work OK.
Tips: "Know publisher's subject matter."

THE CAPITAL, 2000 Capital Dr., Annapolis MD 21401. (301)268-5000. Graphics Editor: Brian Henley. Circ. 45,000. Estab. 1877. Daily newspaper.
Needs: Uses 25 photos/issue; 1 supplied daily by freelancer; one monthly from freelance stock. Needs stock slides on boating, football, aging (senior citizens). Model release preferred. Captions preferred.
Making Contact & Terms: Query with list of stock photo subjects. Send unsolicited photos by mail for consideration. Submit portfolio for review. Uses b&w and color prints; 35mm transparencies. Reports in 1 week. Pays $50/color cover photo; $30/b&w cover photo; $20/color inside photo; $15/b&w inside photo. Pays on publication. Credit line given. Buys one-time rights.
Tips: "We use mostly spot news from freelancers."

CAPPER'S, Dept. PM, 1503 SW 42nd St., Topeka KS 66609-1265. (800)678-7741. Editor: Nancy Peavler. Estab. 1879. Biweekly tabloid. Emphasizes human-interest subjects. Readers are "mostly Midwesterners in small towns and on rural routes." Circ. 370,000. Sample copy 85¢.
Needs: Uses about 20-25 photos/issue, "one or two" supplied by freelance photographers. "We make no photo assignments. We select freelance photos with specific issues in mind." Needs "35mm color slides of human-interest activities, nature (scenic), etc., in bright primary colors. We often use photos tied to the season, a holiday or an upcoming event of general interest." Captions preferred.
Making Contact & Terms: Interested in receiving work from newer, lesser-known photographers. "Send for guidelines and a sample copy (SAE, 85¢ postage). Study the types of photos in the publication, then send a sheet of 10-20 samples with caption material for our consideration. Although we do most of our business by mail, a phone number is helpful in case we need more caption information. Phone calls to try to sell us on your photos don't really help." Reporting time varies. Pays $10-15/b&w photo; $30-40/color photo; only cover photos receive maximum payment. Pays on publication. Credit line given. Buys one-time rights.
Tips: "Generally, we're looking for photos of everyday people doing everyday activities. If the photographer can present this in a pleasing manner, these are the photos we're most likely to use. Season shots are appropriate for Capper's, but they should be natural, not posed. We steer clear of dark, mood shots; they don't reproduce well on newsprint. Most of our readers are small town or rural Midwesterners, so we're looking for photos with which they can identify. Although our format is tabloid, we don't use celebrity shots and won't devote an area much larger than 5×6 to one photo."

*❀CHILD CARE FOCUS, 364 McGregor St., Winnipeg, Manitoba R2W 4X3 Canada. (204)586-8587. Fax: (204)589-5613. Communication Officer: Debra Mayer. Circ. 2,000. Quarterly newspaper. Trade publication for the child care industry. Emphasizes anything pertaining to child care field. Readers are male and female, 18 years of age and up. Sample copy available. Photo guidelines available.
Needs: Uses 8-10 photos/issue; all supplied by freelancers. Needs photos of children, life shots, how-to, personalities. Reviews photos with or without a ms. Model release required. Captions required.
Making Contact & Terms: Interested in receiving work from newer, lesser-known photographers. Send unsolicited photos by mail for consideration. Provide resume, business card, brochure, flyer or tearsheets to be kept on file for possible future assignments. Uses 3×5 or larger b&w prints; 35mm transparencies. Keeps samples on file. SASE. Reports in 1 month. "We do not publish photos we

must pay for. We are non-profit and *may* print photos offered for free." Credit line given. Buys one-time rights. Previously published work OK.

*CRAIN'S CLEVELAND BUSINESS, Suite 310, 700 W. St. Clair, Cleveland OH 44113. (216)522-1383. Graphics Editor: Patric J. Hendrick. Circ. 26,000. Weekly tabloid emphasizing business. Readers are Northeast Ohio business and industry workers. Sample copy free for 9 × 12 SASE. Photo guidelines free with SASE.
Needs: Uses about 10 photos/issue; all supplied by freelancers. Needs photos of office environmentals, architecturals. Model release preferred. Captions required.
Making Contact & Terms: Arrange a personal interview to show portfolio. SASE. Reports in 2 weeks. Pays $50/job plus 27½¢/mile. **Pays on acceptance.** Credit line given. Buys all rights. Previously published work OK.
Tips: Prefers to see "work that shows an ability to interact with the person being photographed in order to obtain a natural, interesting image. Work which shows a sensitivity to 'playing angles' in architectural shots. Be prompt. Be available. Follow directions. After doing the assigned shot, try to find a new, imaginative angle that might offer the editor a more creative shot."

CRAIN'S DETROIT BUSINESS, 1400 Woodbridge, Detroit MI 48207. (313)446-6000. Graphics Editor: Nancy Kassen. Weekly tabloid. Emphasizes business. Estab. 1985. Sample copy for 11 × 14 SAE and 2 first-class stamps.
Needs: Uses 30 photos/issue; 9-10 supplied by freelancers. Needs environmental portraits of business executives illustrating product and/or specialty. Model release preferred; captions required.
Making Contact & Terms: Arrange a personal interview to show a portfolio. Submit portfolio for review. Provide resume, business card, brochure, flyer or tearsheets to be kept on file for possible assignments. SASE. Reports in 2 weeks. NPI. **Pays on acceptance.** Credit line given. Buys one-time rights.

CYCLE NEWS, Dept. PM, P.O. Box 498, Long Beach CA 90801. (310)427-7433. Publisher: Michael Klinger. Editor: Jack Mangus. Art Director: Ree Johnson. Weekly tabloid. Emphasizes motorcycle news for enthusiasts and covers nationwide races. Circ. 45,000. Estab. 1964.
Needs: Needs photos of motorcycle racing accompanied by written race reports; prefers more than one bike to appear in photo. Wants current material. Buys 1,000 photos/year. Buys all rights, but may revert to photographer after publication.
Making Contact & Terms: Send photos or contact sheet for consideration or call for appointment. "Payment on 15th of the month for issues cover-dated the previous month." Reports in 3 weeks. SASE. For b&w: send contact sheet, negatives (preferred for best reproduction) or prints (5 × 7 or 8 × 10, glossy or matte), captions required, pays $10 minimum. For color: send transparencies. captions required, pays $50 minimum. For cover shots: send contact sheet, prints or negatives for b&w; transparencies for color, captions required, payment negotiable.
Tips: Prefers sharp action photos utilizing good contrast. Study publication before submitting "to see what it's all about." Primary coverage area is nationwide.

THE DAILY NEWS, P.O. Box 189, Longview WA 98632. (206)577-2522. Fax: (206)577-2538. Photo Editor: Roger Werth. Company publication. Newspaper. Circ. 24,000.
Needs: Needs lifestyle shots, "newsy photos of people and sports." Reviews photos with accompanying ms only. Model/property release preferred. Captions required.
Making Contact & Terms: Provide resume, business card, brochure, flyer or tearsheets to be kept on file for possible assignments. Send b&w, color prints; 35mm transparencies. Reports in 1-2 weeks. Pays $35/all photos. Pays on publication. Buys one-time rights. Simultaneous submissions OK.

*DEKALB DAILY CHRONICLE, 2815 Barber Greene Rd., DeKalb IL 60115. (815)756-4841. Head Photographer: Robb Perea. Circ. 15,000. Estab. 1869. Daily newspaper. Emphasizes agriculture and features on DeKalb people. Sample copy for 50¢.
Needs: Feature pages run every week on Sunday—must pertain to DeKalb County. Photos purchased with accompanying manuscript only. Model release preferred; photo captions required.
Making Contact & Terms: Query with resume of credits. Send unsolicited 8 × 10 glossy b&w photos by mail for consideration. Also, call to query. Cannot return material. Reports in 1 month. NPI. **Pays on acceptance.** Credit line given. Buys one-time rights.

The maple leaf before a listing indicates that the market is Canadian.

Tips: "No 'set' pay scale per se; payment negotiable depending on several factors including quality of photo and need."

EAST BAY EXPRESS, 931 Ashby Ave., Berkeley CA 94710-2805. Photo Editor: Steve Aibel. Circ. 70,000. Estab. 1978. Weekly newspaper. Readers are students and professionals ages 18-45.
Needs: Uses 10 photos/issue; 100% supplied by freelancers. Needs environmental portraits. Model release preferred. Captions required.
Making Contact & Terms: Interested in receiving work from newer, lesser-known photographers. Arrange a personal interview to show portfolio. SASE. Reports in 2 weeks. Pays $250/color cover photo; $125-200/b&w cover photo; $60/b&w inside photo. Pays on publication. Credit line given. Buys one-time rights; negotiable.
Tips: Wants to see "b&w images where the photographer controls the subject. No 'street shooters.' Show a good strong portfolio with quality prints in a unique style and fill a 'photo-niche' that I don't have."

FISHING AND HUNTING NEWS, Dept. PM, 511 Eastlake Ave. E., Box C-19000, Seattle WA 98109. (206)624-3845. Managing Editor: Patrick McGann. Photo Editor: Dave Ellithorpe. Biweekly tabloid. Emphasizes how-to material, fishing and hunting locations and new products for hunters and fishermen. Circ. 133,000. Free sample copy and photo guidelines.
Needs: Buys 300 or more photos/year. Wildlife—fish/game with successful fishermen and hunters. Captions required.
Making Contact & Terms: Send samples of work for consideration. Uses 5×7 or 8×10 glossy b&w prints or negatives for inside photos. Uses color covers and some inside color photos—glossy 5×7 or 8×10 color prints, 35mm, 2¼×2¼ or 4×5 color transparencies. When submitting 8×10 color prints, negative must also be sent. SASE. Reports in 2 weeks. Pays $5-15 minimum/b&w print, $50-100 minimum/cover and $10-20 editorial color photos. Credit line given. **Pays on acceptance.** Buys all rights, but may reassign to photographer after publication. Submit model release with photo.
Tips: Looking for fresh, timely approaches to fishing and hunting subjects. Query for details of special issues and topics. "We need newsy photos with a fresh approach. Looking for near-deadline photos from Oregon, California, Utah, Idaho, Wyoming, Montana, Colorado, Texas, Alaska and Washington (sportsmen with fish or game)."

*THE FRONT STRIKER BULLETIN, P.O. Box 18481, Asheville NC 28814. (704)254-4487. Fax: (704)254-1066. Owner: Bill Retskin. Circ. 600. Estab. 1986. Publication of The American Matchcover Collecting Club. Quarterly newsletter. Emphasizes matchcover collecting. Readers are male, blue collar workers 55 years old and over. Sample copy $2.50.
Needs: Uses 2-3 photos/issue; none supplied by freelancers. Needs table top photos of match covers or related subjects. Reviews photos with accompanying ms only.
Making Contact & Terms: Interested in receiving work from newer, lesser-known photographers. Send unsolicited photos by mail for consideration. Send 5×7 matte b&w prints. Keeps samples on file. SASE. Reports in 1 month. NPI, negotiable. Pays on publication. Credit line given. Buys one-time rights; negotiable.

FULTON COUNTY DAILY REPORT, Dept. PM, 190 Pryor St. SW, Atlanta GA 30303. (404)521-1227. Art and Production Director: Chris Schroder. Daily newspaper, 5 times/week. Emphasizes legal news and business. Readers are male and female professionals age 25 up, involved in legal field, court system, legislature, etc. Sample copy $1, with 9½×12½ SAE and $1.50 postage.
Needs: Uses 5-10 b&w photos/issue; 30% supplied freelancers. Needs informal environmental photographs of lawyers, judges and others involved in legal news and business. Some real estate, etc. Especially wants to be able to get "a good freelancer in Georgia when I need one." Photo captions preferred; complete name of subject and date shot, along with other pertinent information. Two or more people should be identified from left to right.
Making Contact & Terms: Submit portfolio for review—call first. Query with list of stock photo subjects. Keeps samples on file. SASE. Reports in 1 month. "Freelance work generally done on an assignment-only basis." Pays $100/assignment. Credit line given. Simultaneous submissions and previously published work OK.
Tips: Wants to see ability with "casual, environmental portraiture, people—especially in office settings, urban environment, courtrooms, etc.; and photojournalistic coverage of people in law or courtroom settings." In general, needs "competent, fast freelancers from time to time around the state of

---

The asterisk before a listing indicates that the market is new in this edition. New markets are often the most receptive to freelance submissions.

Georgia who can be called in at the last minute. We keep a list of them for reference. Good work keeps you on the list." Recommends that "when shooting for FCDR, it's best to avoid law-book-type photos if possible, along with other overused legal cliches."

GLOBE, Dept. PM, 5401 NW Broken Sound Blvd., Boca Raton FL 33487. (407)997-7733. Photo Editor: Ron Haines. Circ. 2 million. Weekly tabloid. "For everyone in the family. *Globe* readers are the same people you meet on the street, and in supermarket lines—average, hard-working Americans."
Needs: Buys all photos from freelancers. Needs human interest photos, celebrity photos, humorous animal photos, anything unusual or offbeat. Captions required.
Making Contact & Terms: Send 8 × 10 b&w glossy transparencies or color prints for consideration. SASE. Reports in 1 week. Pays $75/b&w photo (negotiable); $125/color photo (negotiable); day and package rates negotiable. Buys first serial rights. Pays on publication unless otherwise arranged. Previously published work OK.
Tips: Advises beginners to look for the unusual, offbeat shots. "Do not write for photo guidelines. Study the publication instead. Tailor your submission to my market." Use of color is increasing.

GRIT, 1503 SW 42nd St., Topeka KS 66609. (913)274-4353. Contact: Editor. Circ. 400,000. Estab. 1882. Biweekly tabloid. Emphasizes "people-oriented material which is helpful, inspiring or uplifting. Readership is national." Sample copy $2.
Needs: Buys "hundreds" of photos/year. Needs on a regular basis "photos of all subjects, provided they have up-beat themes that are so good they surprise us. Human interest, sports, animals. Get action into shot, implied or otherwise, whenever possible. Be certain pictures are well composed, properly exposed and pin sharp. No cheesecake. No pictures that cannot be shown to any member of the family. No pictures that are out of focus or over/or under-exposed. No ribbon-cutting, check-passing or hand-shaking pictures. We use 35mm and up." Photos purchased with accompanying ms. Model release required. Captions required. "Single b&w photos that stand alone must be accompanied by 50-100 words of meaningful caption information."
Making Contact & Terms: Interested in receiving work from newer, lesser-known photographers if work is good. Send material by mail for consideration. Prefer b&w glossies or color slides/professional quality. Reports in 4-6 weeks. Pays $150 for cover photo; $75 for each color photo used; $40 for b&w. Uses much more color than b&w. Buys one-time rights; negotiable. SASE. **Pays on acceptance.**
Tips: Building network of freelance photographers nationwide for assignment. "Good major-holiday subjects seldom come to us from freelancers. For example, Easter, Fourth of July, Christmas or New Year. Remember that *Grit* publishes on newsprint and therefore requires sharp, bright, contrasting colors for best reproduction. Avoid sending shots of people whose faces are in shadows; no soft focus. When photo requires action make sure action is *in* photo."

INSIDE TEXAS RUNNING, Dept. PM, 9514 Bristlebrook, Houston TX 77083. (713)498-3208. Fax: (713)879-9980. Publisher/Editor: Joanne Schmidt. Circ. 10,000. Estab. 1977. Monthly tabloid. Emphasizes running and jogging with biking insert. Readers are Texas runners and joggers of all abilities. Sample copy $2.50
Needs: Uses about 20 photos/issue; 10 supplied by freelancers; 80% percent of freelance photography in issue comes from assignment from freelance stock. Needs photos of "races, especially outside of Houston area; scenic places to run; how-to (accompanying articles by coaches); also triathlon and bike tours and races." Special needs include "top race coverage; running camps (summer); variety of Texas running terrain." Captions preferred.
Making Contact & Terms: Interested in receiving work from newer, lesser-known photographers. Send glossy b&w or color prints by mail for consideration. SASE. Reports in 1 month. Pays $10-15/b&w or color photo; $25 per photo/text package. Pays on publication. Credit line given. Buys one-time rights; negotiable. Simultaneous submissions outside Texas and previously published work OK.
Tips: Prefers to see "human interest, contrast and good composition" in photos. Transparencies are now used for covers. "Look for the unusual. Race photos tend to look the same." Wants "clear photos with people near front; too often photographers are too far away when they shoot and subjects are a dot on the landscape." Wants to see road races in Texas outside of Houston area.

*ITS REVIEW, 109 McLaughlin Hall, Berkeley CA 94720. (510)642-3593. Fax: (510)642-1246. Editor: Betsy Wing. Circ. 5,000. Government publication: Univ. of California Institute of Transportation Studies. Quarterly newsletter. Emphasizes transportation—current issues, research in progress. Readers range from professors and transportation professionals to individuals with interest in transportation. Sample copy free, call for copy.
Needs: Uses 5-6 photos/issue; 2-3 supplied by freelancers. Needs photos of technology, people, events that illustrate certain stories. Reviews photos with or without ms. "We need good airport/aircraft/people during air travel photos." Model release required for any close-ups of faces in the foreground. Captions required; include type of aircraft, technology or airport being shown, plus names of any people in the foreground.

© Thad Allton

A true portrait of Americana, this photo by Topeka, Kansas, photographer Thad Allton was assigned as a cover photo for the weekly tabloid Grit. The shot, instead, was used inside as an illustration with a story on small town America. Editor-in-Chief Roberta Peterson says she likes working with Allton, whom she paid $150 for the shot, because he follows directions and captures the essence of any assignment.

Making Contact & Terms: Interested in receiving work from newer, lesser-known photographers. Call before submitting work. Does not keep samples on file. Cannot return material. Reports in 1 month. Pays $25-250/b&w cover photo; $10-100/b&w inside photo. **Pays on acceptance.** Credit line given. Buys one-time rights; all rights; negotiable. Simultaneous submissions and previously published work OK.

JEWISH EXPONENT, Dept. PM, 226 S. 16th St., Philadelphia PA 19102. (215)893-5740. Managing Editor: Al Erlick. Weekly newspaper. Emphasizes news of impact to the Jewish community. Circ. 70,000.
Needs: Buys 15 photos/issue. On a regular basis, wants news and feature photos of a cultural, heritage, historic, news and human interest nature involving Jews and Jewish issues. Query as to photographic needs for upcoming year. No art photos. Photos purchased with or without accompanying mss. Captions required. Uses 8 × 10 glossy prints; 35mm or 4 × 5 transparencies. Model release required "where the event covered is not in the public domain."
Making Contact & Terms: Query with resume of credits or arrange a personal interview. "Telephone or mail inquiries first are essential. Do not send original material on speculation." Provide resume, business card, letter of inquiry, samples, brochure, flyer and tearsheets to be kept on file. SASE. Reports in 1 week. Free sample copy. Pays $15-50/hour; $10-100/job. Also pays $10-35/b&w print; $10-75/color print or transparency; $10-75/cover photo. Credit line given. Pays on publication. Buys one-time, all, first serial, first North American serial and all rights. Rights are negotiable.
Tips: "Photographers should keep in mind the special requirements of high-speed newspaper presses. High contrast photographs probably provide better reproduction under newsprint and ink conditions."

THE JOURNAL OF LIGHT CONSTRUCTION, RR2, Box 146. Richmond VT 05477. (802)864-5495. Fax: (802) 434-4467. Editor: Don Jackson. Circ. 45,000. Estab. 1981. Monthly tabloid. Emphasizes light construction. Readers are architects, remodelers. Sample copy free. Photo guidelines free with SASE.
Needs: Uses 20 photos/issue; 5 supplied by freelancers. Needs photos of contruction work in progress. Model release preferred.
Making Contact & Terms: Interested in receiving work from newer, lesser-known photographers. Query with samples. Send unsolicited photos by mail for consideration. Provide resume, business card, brochure, flyer or tearsheets to be kept on file for possible future assignments. Uses 35mm, 2¼ × 2¼, 4 × 5 and 8 × 10 transparencies. SASE. Reports in 1 month. Pays $250/color cover photo; $40/b&w inside photo. **Pays on acceptance.** Credit line given. Buys first N.A. serial rights. Previously published work OK.

Tips: *"The Journal of Light Construction* has 12 themes for its issues. Covers reflect these themes. An editorial calendar is available by request."

*MARKETING HIGHER EDUCATION, Suite 114, 280 Easy St., Mountain View CA 94043-3736. (415)962-1105. Publisher: Bob Topor. Estab. 1986. Monthly newsletter. Emphasizes higher education. Readers are professionals working in higher education.
Needs: Uses 1-6 photos/issue. Needs photos of schools, community colleges, colleges, universities, people and facilities. Review photos with or without a ms. Special photo needs include b&w shots. Model release preferred. Captions preferred.
Making Contact & Terms: Interested in receiving work from newer, lesser-known photographers. Provide resume, business card, brochure, flyer or tearsheets to be kept on file for possible future assignments. Pays $10-25/b&w page rate. **Pays on acceptance.** Credit line given. Buys all rights.
Tips: Wants photos of good quality with strong composition.

MEDICAL TRIBUNE, Dept. PM, 257 Park Ave. S., New York NY 10010. (212)674-8500. Fax: (212)982-4398. Photo Editor: Mike Tamborrino. Tri-monthly broadsheet. Emphasizes medical news. Readers are physicians. Circ. 150,000. Estab. 1960. Sample copy free with 8×11 SAE and $1 postage.
Needs: Uses 40 photos/issue; 5 supplied by freelancers. Needs photos of doctors, medical devices to illustrate a specific story. Runs 6-8 color assignments/issue. Reviews photos with accompanying ms only. Model release preferred; captions required.
Making Contact & Terms: Provide resume, business card, brochure, flyer or tearsheets to be kept on file for possible future assignments. SASE. Reports in 1 week. Pays $200/b&w photo; $350/assignment. Pays on publication. Credit line given. Buys one-time rights; one-time rights include right to use in our foreign edition. Simultaneous submissions and previously published work OK.
Tips: Wants "versatility (close-up shots as well as over-all shots), good use of lighting, ability to shoot color. To contribute he/she should not be from NYC area. We do not hire photographers from here. Should be from areas in which we need photos."

METRO, 550 S. First St., San Jose CA 95113. (408)298-8000. Managing Editor: Sharan Street. Circ. 70,000. Alternative newspaper, weekly tabloid format. Emphasis on news, arts and entertainment. Readers are adults ages 25-44, in Silicon Valley. Sample copy $3.
Needs: Uses 15 photos/issue; 25% supplied by freelance photographers. Model release required for model shots. Captions preferred.
Making Contact & Terms: Query with resume of credits, list of stock photos subjects. Provide resume, business card, brochure, flyer or tearsheets to be kept on file for possible assignments. Does not return unsolicited material. Pays $75-100/color cover photo; $50-75/b&w cover photo; $25/b&w inside photo. Pays on publication. Credit line given. Buys one-time rights. Simultaneous submissions and previously published work OK "if outside of San Francisco Bay area."

MISSISSIPPI PUBLISHERS, INC., Dept. PM, 311 E. Pearl St., Jackson MS 39201. (601)961-7073. Photo Editors: Chris Todd and Scott Boyd. Daily newspaper. Emphasizes photojournalism: news, sports, features, fashion, food and portraits. Readers are very broad age range of 18-70 years; male and female. Circ. 100,000. Sample copy for 11×14 SAE and 54¢.
Needs: Uses 10-15 photos/issue; 1-5 supplied by freelance photographers. Needs news, sports, features, portraits, fashion and food photos. Special photo needs include food and fashion. Model release and captions required.
Making Contact & Terms: Provide resume, business card, brochure, flyer or tearsheets to be kept on file for possible assignments. Uses 8×10 matte b&w and color prints; 35mm, 2¼×2¼, 4×5, 8×10 transparencies. SASE. Reports 1 week. Pays $50-100/color cover photo; $25-50/b&w cover photo; $25/b&w inside photo; $20-50/hour; $150-400/day. Pays on publication. Credit line given. Buys one-time or all rights; negotiable.

*MODEL NEWS, 150 Fifth Ave., New York NY 10011. (212)645-8400. Publisher: John King. Circ. 250,000. Estab. 1975. Monthly newspaper. Emphasizes celebrities and talented models, beauty and fashion. Readers are male and female, ages 15-80. Sample copy $1.50, 8×10 SAE, 1 first-class stamp. Photo guidelines $1.50.

The First Markets Index preceding the General Index in the back of this book provides the names of those companies/ publications interested in receiving work from newer, lesser-known photographers.

Needs: Uses 1-2 photos/issue; 1-2 supplied by freelancers. Review photos with accompanying ms only. Special photo needs include new celebrities, famous faces, VIP's, old and young. Model release preferred. Captions preferred.

Making Contact & Terms: Interested in receiving work from newer, lesser-known photographers. Contact through rep. Arrange personal interview to show portfolio. Submit portfolio for review. Send unsolicited photos by mail for consideration. Provide resume, business card, brochure, flyer or tearsheets to be kept on file for possible future assignments. Send 8×10 b&w prints. Keeps samples on file. SASE. Reports in 3 weeks. Pays $60/b&w cover photo; $30/b&w inside photo. Pays on publication. Credit line given. Buys all rights. Considers simultaneous submissions.

MOM GUESS WHAT NEWSPAPER, 1725 L St., Sacramento CA 95814. (916)441-6397. Editor: Linda Birner. Circ. 21,000. Estab. 1978. Every two weeks tabloid. Gay newspaper that emphasizes political, entertainment, etc. Readers are gay and straight people. Circ. 21,000. Estab. 1978. Sample copy $1. Photo guidelines free with SASE.

Needs: Uses about 8-10 photos/issue; all supplied by freelancers, 80% from assignment and 20% from stock. Model release required. Captions required.

Making Contact & Terms: Interested in receiving work from newer, lesser-known photographers. Arrange a personal interview to show portfolio. Send 8×10 glossy b&w prints by mail for consideration. SASE. Pays $5-200/b&w photo; $10-15/hour; $25-50/day; $5-200 per photo/text package. Pays on publication. Credit line given. Buys one-time rights; negotiable. Previously published work OK.

Tips: Prefers to see gay related stories/human rights/civil rights and some artsy photos in portfolio; *no* nudes or sexually explicit photos.

*THE MOVING WORLD, 1611 Duke St., Alexandria VA 22314. Editor: Mike Hayes. Circ. 4,000. Estab. 1992. Publication of the American Movers Conference. Biweekly newspaper. Emphasizes the household goods moving industry. Readers are owners of businesses of all sizes associated with moving and transportation.

Needs: Uses 3-4 photos/issue. "I desperately need shots of moving vans, transportation and affiliated shots (i.e., roads, bridges, highway signs, maps, etc.)." Reviews photos with or without ms. Model/property release preferred.

Making Contact & Terms: Interested in receiving work from newer, lesser-known photographers. Send unsolicited photos by mail for consideration. Send 5×7 b&w prints. Keeps samples on file. SASE. Reports in 3 weeks. Pays $300-400/color cover photo; $50-100/b&w inside photo. Pays on publication. Credit line given. Buys one-time rights.

*NATIONAL ENQUIRER, 600 S. E. Coast Ave., Lantana FL 33464. (407)586-1111. Contact: Photo Editor. Weekly tabloid. Readers are mostly female, ages 18-45.

Needs: Uses 150-200 photos/issue; all supplied by freelancers. Needs celebrity shots, funny animal photos, spectacular stunt photos, human interest. Model release required. Captions preferred.

Making Contact & Terms: Interested in receiving work from newer, lesser-known photographers. Arrange personal interview to show portfolio. Submit portfolio for review. Query with resume of credits. Query with stock photo list. Provide resume, business card, brochure flyer or tearsheets to be kept on file for possible future assignments. Keeps samples on file. SASE. "Must have proper postage." Reports in 3 weeks. NPI. Payment varies according to photo. Credit line sometimes given. Buys one-time rights, first N.A. serial rights. If work is not published in competitive publication it will be considered.

NATIONAL EXAMINER, 5401 NW Broken Sound Blvd., Boca Raton FL 33487. (407)997-7733. Editor: Mike Irish. Photo Editor: Carole Moore. Weekly tabloid. General interest. Circ. 1 million.

Needs: Uses 80-100 photos/issue. Needs color and b&w: human interest, humorous animal/children pictures, action sequences, celebrities. Special photo needs include color photo stories related to women. Model release preferred. Captions required.

Making Contact & Terms: Query with samples or send photos for consideration. SASE. Pays $125/color and $50/b&w; some fees are negotiable. Pays on publication; assignments paid upon completion of work. Previously published work OK.

NATIONAL MASTERS NEWS, Box 2372, Van Nuys CA 91404. (818)785-1895. Fax: (818)782-1135. Editor: Al Sheahen. Circ. 5,600. Estab. 1977. Monthly tabloid. Official world and US publication for Masters (age 35 and over) track and field, long distance running and race walking. Sample copy free with 9×12 SASE.

Needs: Uses 25 photos/issue; 20% assigned and 80% from freelance stock. Needs photos of Masters athletes (men and women over age 35) competing in track and field events, long distance running races or racewalking competitions. Captions preferred.

Making Contact & Terms: Send any size matte or glossy b&w print by mail for consideration, "may write for sample issue." SASE. Reports in 1 month. Pays $20/b&w cover photo; $7.50-10/inside b&w photo. Pays on publication. Credit line given. Buys one-time rights. Simultaneous submissions and previously published work OK.

NATIONAL NEWS BUREAU, P.O. Box 43039, Philadelphia PA 19129. (215)546-8088. Editor: Andy Edelman. Circ. 300+ publications. Weekly syndication packet. Emphasizes entertainment. Readers are leisure/entertainment-oriented, 17-55 years old.
Needs: "Always looking for new female models for our syndicated fashion/beauty columns." Uses about 20 photos/issue; 15 supplied by freelance photographers. Captions required.
Making Contact & Terms: Arrange a personal interview to show portfolio. Query with sample. Submit portfolio for review. Send 8×10 b&w prints, b&w contact sheet by mail for consideration. SASE. Reports in 1 week. Pays $50-1,000/job. Pays on publication. Credit line given. Buys all rights.

*NEW HAVEN ADVOCATE, 1 Long Wharf Dr., New Haven CT 06511. (203)789-0010. Photographer: Kathleen Cei. Circ. 50,000. Estab. 1975. Weekly tabloid. Emphasizes general interest. Readers are male and female, educated, ages 20-50.
Needs: Uses 7-10 photos/issue; 0-1 supplied by freelancers. Needs photos of spot news and features. Reviews photos with or without ms. Model release required. Captions required.
Making Contact & Terms: Interested in receiving work from newer, lesser-known photographers. Provide resume, business card, brochure, flyer or tearsheets to be kept on file for possible assignments. Does not keep samples on file. SASE. Reports in 1 month. NPI. Pays on publication. Credit line given. Buys one-time rights. Simultaneous submissions and/or previously published work OK.

NEW YORK TIMES MAGAZINE, 229 W. 43 St., New York NY 10036. (212)556-3026. Photo Editor: Kathy Ryan. Weekly. Circ. 1,650,000.
● Ryan encourages smaller, but strong quality portfolios. She also will try to talk to photographers about their portfolios if she feels the work has potential. This publication also won numerous photo/cover awards in 1992 from the Sunday Magazine Editors Association.
Needs: The number of freelance photos varies. Model release and photo captions required.
Making Contact & Terms: Drop off portfolio for review. SASE. Reports in 1 week. Pays $250/b&w page rate; $300/color page rate; $225/half page; $350/job (day rates); $650/color cover photo. **Pays on acceptance.** Credit line given. Buys one-time rights.

✦NORTH ISLAND NEWS, P.O. Box 3013, Courtenay, British Columbia V9N 5N3 Canada. (604)334-4446. Fax: (604)334-4983. Editor: Jamie Bowman. Weekly newspaper. Emphasizes social issues, entertainment. Circ. 30,000. Estab. 1965. Sample copy free with SASE and $1 postage
Needs: Uses 4-5 photos/issue; 1-2 supplied by freelancers. Needs variety of photos especially of animal, action and illustrations for articles. Model release required. Captions preferred that include who, what, when, where and why.
Making Contact & Terms: Interested in receiving work from newer, lesser-known photographers. Send unsolicited photos by mail for consideration. Send any size b&w, color prints; 35mm, 2¼×2¼ tranparencies. Keeps samples on file. SASE. Pays $15/b&w cover photo; $10/b&w inside photo. Pays on publication. Credit line given. Buys one-time rights. Simultaneous submissions and previously published work OK.
Tips: "Call with idea, then for sample. Wants to see "action, local application or relevance. Clearly defined images with strong color."

NORTH TEXAS GOLFER, Suite 212, 9182 Old Katy Rd., Houston TX 77055. (713)464-0308. Editor: Steve Hunter. Monthly tabloid. Emphasizes golf in the northern areas of Texas. Readers average 48.5 years old, $72,406 income, upscale lifestyle and play golf 2-5 times weekly. Circ. 28,000. Sample copy free with SAE and $2 postage.
Needs: Uses about 20 photos/issue; none supplied by freelance photographers. "Photos are bought only in conjunction with purchase of articles." Photos purchased with accompanying ms only. Model release and captions preferred.
Making Contact & Terms: "Use the telephone." SASE. Reports in 2 weeks. NPI. Pays on publication. Credit line given. Buys one-time rights or all rights, if specified.

THE PATRIOT LEDGER, 400 Crown Colony Dr., Quincy MA 02169. (617)786-7084. Fax: (617)786-7025. Photo Editor: Joe Lippincott. Circ. 100,000. Estab. 1837. "Daily except Sunday" newspaper. General readership. Photo guidelines free with SASE.
Needs: Uses 15-25 photos/issue; most photos used come from staff; some freelance assigned. Needs general newspaper coverage photos—especially spot news and "grabbed" features from circulation area. Model release preferred. Captions required.

Journalism Provides Solid Foundation for Freelancers

Mary Ann Carter is equally at home snapping candid shots of political leaders or capturing on film the excitement of the NCAA's track and field championships. As a photojournalist whose work has appeared in this country's largest dailies, including the *New York Times*, *Los Angeles Times*, *Chicago Tribune*, and numerous national magazines such as *Time* and *Newsweek*, she's used to covering every type of story.

"The similarity in all of it is the fact you need to get a good story-telling image," says Carter of Indianapolis, Indiana. "The methods you use to do this may differ, but the goal is the same—to communicate."

Carter, who has a bachelor of arts in journalism from Indiana University, worked on the staff of a small paper in Virginia and then at the *Richmond*

Mary Ann Carter

News Leader before returning to Indiana as a stringer and fulltime freelancer. She says her journalism background has helped her in some unexpected ways.

"The main thing a journalism education does for you is teach you a code of ethics so you are prepared when you have to make important decisions," says Carter. "The best analogy I can make is that of what happens to a child in religion class. That child will probably not be immediately confronted with coveting a neighbor's goods, for instance, but it might happen later in life and he'll have an ethical basis on which to judge what to do."

Her background also helps when it comes to dealing with clients. "You know to be open with people and what to do if *Time* calls about a story and then *Newsweek* calls about it too. You know never to take the same assignment from competing publications."

Freelance photography is a difficult field to break into and the recent recession hit freelancers hard, especially in major cities like Chicago, says Carter. "For one thing, most newspapers outside the very big ones don't use freelancers much anymore. They tend to rely on the wire services."

Another problem is that fewer newspapers use documentary work or in-depth picture stories, and the few outlets open to such work, like *Life* magazine, are hard to crack, she says.

"I think in the future some of the more traditional markets for photojournalism are not going to be there. That's why we have to look more creatively for outlets." Freelancers should spend more time looking at less traditional markets such as catalog work and corporate clients, she says. "Land's End, for example, includes picture stories in their catalogs."

The economy has not been the only thing that has changed for photographers.

Advancements in technology have made it possible to transmit photographs almost instantly. Yet Carter says she still ships much of her film raw to the publication for processing.

Equipment that was once hard to come by, now is readily available from most local newspapers and branches of Associated Press. Carter says this helps tremendously when she is faced with pressing deadlines. Last year, for example, to meet a deadline, she had her film processed at a one-hour photomat, rented a hotel room and borrowed a Leafax transmitter, a device which will scan a negative and instantly transmit an image.

Carter advises beginning photojournalists to work on newspaper or magazine staffs before launching freelance careers. "Try to get experience as a staff photographer. It doesn't have to be the *Times* or even the largest newspaper in the state. Even at a small newspaper, you can get invaluable experience and you'll learn how newspapers work," she says. Experience at newspapers and stringing for the Associated Press also helped her learn to spot breaking news and identify major sporting events, she says.

"Do a lot of soul-searching," Carter warns. "You've got to look at the business side and decide how long you can live on a shoestring because it may be a long time before you turn the corner. If making big money is important to you, you might not want to become a freelance photojournalist."

—Robin Gee

As a photojournalist, Mary Ann Carter of Indianapolis, Indiana, is called upon to cover many different subjects. One day she may document auto racing at the Indianapolis 500, the next day she might cover a breaking news story, such as this situation of an angry client holding his mortgage banker hostage.

© Mary Ann Carter

Making Contact & Terms: Query with resume of credits. SASE. Reports as needed. Pays $15-75/ b&w inside photo or more if material is outstanding and especially newsworthy, $10-15/hour. Pays on publication. Credit line given. Rights negotiable. Simultaneous submissions and previously published work OK "depending on time and place."

Tips: Looks for "diversity in photojournalism: use NPPA pictures of the year categories as guidelines. Dynamite grabber qualities: unique, poignant images properly and accurately identified and captioned which concisely tell what happened. We want images we're unable to get with staff due to immediacy of events, shot well and in our hands quickly for evaluation and possible publication. To break in to our publication call and explain what you can contribute to our newspaper that is unique. We'll take it from there, depending on the results of the initial conversation."

*REGISTER CITIZEN, 190 Water St., Torrington CT 06790. (203)489-3121. Chief Photographer: John Murray. Circ. 17,000. Daily newspaper. Covers all Northwestern Connecticut.

Needs: Uses 10-12 photos/issue. Less than 10% supplied by freelance photographers. Needs photos of spot news, fires, accidents and rescues. Special photo needs include spot news. Captions required.

Making Contact & Terms: "Call when you have a 'hot' photo." Otherwise, send 8 × 10 b&w prints. SASE. Reports that day. NPI. Pays on publication. Credit line given. Buys one-time rights.

Tips: "Be in the right place at the right time and have film in your camera."

REVIEW NEWSPAPERS, Dept. PM, 100 N.E. 7th St., Miami FL 33132. (305)347-6638. Art Director: Michael Cole. Staff Photographers: Aixa Montero-Green, Melanie Bell and Ruth Cincotta. Circ. 11,000. Estab. 1926. Daily newspaper. Emphasizes law, business and real estate. Readers are 25-55 yrs., average net worth of $750,000, male and female. Sample copy for $1 with 9 × 11 SASE.

Needs: Uses 8-15 photos/issue; 20-40% supplied by freelance photographers. Needs mostly portraits, however we use live news events, sports and building mugs. Photo captions "an absolute must."

Making Contact & Terms: Arrange a personal interview to show portfolio. Submit portfolio for review. Send 35mm, 8 × 10 b&w and color prints. Accepts all types of finishes. Cannot return unsolicited material. If used, reports immediately. Pays $85 for most photos; pays more if part of photo/text package. Credit line given. Buys all rights; negotiable. Previously published work OK.

Tips: In photographer's portfolio, looks for "a good grasp of lighting and composition; the ability to take an ordinary situation and make an extraordinary photograph. We work on daily deadlines, so promptness is a must and extensive cutline information is needed."

ROLL CALL NEWSPAPER, Suite 107, 900 2nd St. NE, Washington DC 20002. (202)289-4900. Fax: (202)289-5337. Photo Editor: Laura Patterson. Circ. 18,000. Estab. 1955. Semi-weekly newspaper. Emphasizes U.S. Congress and politics. Readers are politicians, lobbyists and congressional staff. Sample copy free with 9 × 12 SAE with $1 postage.

Needs: Uses 20-30 photos/issue; up to 5 supplied by freelancers. Needs photos of anything involving current congressional issues, good or unusual shots of congressmen. Captions required.

Making Contact & Terms: Query with samples or list of stock photo subjects. Send unsolicited photos by mail for consideration. Uses 8 × 10 glossy b&w prints; 35mm transparencies. Does not return unsolicited material. Reports in 1 month. Pays $25-85/b&w photo; $30-300/color photo (if cover); $50-75/hour or job. Pays on publication. Credit line given. Buys one-time rights. Simultaneous submissions OK.

Tips: "We're always looking for unique candids of congressmen or political events. In reviewing photographer's samples, we like to see good use of composition and light for newsprint."

SENIOR VOICE OF FLORIDA, Suite E, 6281 39th St. North., Pinellas Park FL 34665. (813)521-3837. Managing Editor: Nancy Yost. Circ. 50,000. Estab. 1981. Monthly newspaper. Emphasizes lifestyles of senior citizens. Readers are Florida residents and tourists, 50 years old and older. Sample copy $1. Photo guidelines free with SASE.

Needs: Uses 6 photos/issue; 1-2 supplied by freelancers. Needs photos of recreational activities, travel, seasonal, famous persons (only with story). Reviews photos purchased with accompanying ms only. Model/property release required. Captions required.

Making Contact & Terms: Send photos with manuscript. Samples kept on file. SASE. Reports in 1-2 months. Pays $10/color cover photo; $5/color inside photo; $5/b&w inside photo. Pays on publication. Credit line given. Buys one-time rights; negotiable. Simultaneous submissions and previously published work OK.

Tips: "We look for crisp, clean, clear prints. Photos that speak to us rate special attention. We use photos only to illustrate manuscripts."

The Subject Index, located at the back of this book, can help you find publications interested in the topics you shoot.

*SERVICE REPORTER, 651 W. Washington, Chicago IL 60661. (312)993-0929. Editorial Director: Ed Schwenn. Circ. 48,000. Monthly tabloid. Emphasizes heating, air conditioning, ventilating and refrigeration. Sample copy $3.
Needs: Uses about 12 photos/issue; no more than one supplied by freelance photographers, others manufacturer-supplied. Needs photos pertaining to the field of heating, air conditioning, ventilating and refrigeration. Special needs include cover photos of personnel installing and servicing. Model release required. Captions required.
Making Contact & Terms: Query with stock photo list. Query on needs of publication. SASE. Reports in 2 weeks. Pays $50-100/color cover photo; $10/b&w photo; $25/color inside photo. Pays on publication. Credit line given. Buys one-time rights.

*SHOW BIZ NEWS, 150 Fifth Ave., New York NY 10011. (212)645-8400. Publisher: John King. Circ. 250,000. Estab. 1975. Monthly newspaper. Emphasizes model and talent agencies coast to coast. Readers are male and female, ages 15-80. Sample copy $1.50, 8×10 envelope. 1 first-class stamp. Photo guidelines $1.50.
Needs: Uses 1-2 photos/issue; 1-2 supplied by freelancers. Reviews photos with accompanying ms only. Needs photos of new celebrities, famous faces, VIP's, old and young. Model release preferred. Captions preferred.
Making Contact & Terms: Interested in receiving work from newer, lesser-known photographers. Contact through rep. Arrange personal interview to show portfolio. Submit portfolio for review. Send unsolicited photos by mail for consideration. Send 8×10 b&w prints. Keeps samples on file. SASE. Reports in 3 weeks. Pays $60/b&w cover photo; $30/b&w inside photo. Pays on publication. Gives credit line. Buys all rights. Considers simultaneous submissions.

SINGER MEDIA CORP., INC., Seaview Business Park, Unit #106, 1030 Calle Cordillera, San Clemente CA 92673. (714)498-7227. Fax: (714)498-2162. President: Kurt Singer. Worldwide circulation. Estab. 1940. Newspaper syndicate (magazine, journal, books, newspaper, newsletter, tabloid). Emphasizes books and interviews.
Needs: Needs photos for book covers, celebrities, movies, TV, rock/pop music pictures for advertising, jigsaw puzzles, posters, postcards, greeting cards, text features with transparencies (35mm, 2¼×2¼, 4×5). Reviews photos with accompanying ms only. Will use dupes only, cannot guarantee returns. No models. Usually requires releases on interview photos. Photo captions required.
Making Contact & Terms: Interested in receiving work from newer, lesser-known photographers, depending on subject. Query with list of stock photo subjects. Reports in 3 weeks. Pays $25-1,000/b&w photo; $50-1,000 plus royalties/color photo. Pays 50/50% of all syndication sales. Pays after collection. Credit line given. Buys one-time rights, foreign rights; negotiable. Previously published work OK.
Tips: "Worldwide, mass market, text essential. Trend is toward international interest. Survey the market for ideas."

SKIING TRADE NEWS, Dept. PM, 2 Park Ave., New York NY 10016. (212)779-5000. Editor: Iseult Devlin. Tabloid published 8 times/year. Emphasizes news, retailing and service articles for ski retailers. Circ. 16,000. Free sample copy with 12×24 SASE.
Needs: Uses 2-6 photos/issue. Celebrity/personality; photo essay/photo feature ("if it has to do with ski and skiwear retailing"); spot news; and humorous. Photos must be ski related. Model release and captions preferred.
Making Contact & Terms: Photos purchased with accompanying ms or caption. Uses 5×7 glossy prints; transparencies. Pays $25-35/b&w photo. Pays on publication. Buys one-time rights. Credit line given. Send material by mail for consideration. SASE. Reports in 1 month.

SKYDIVING, 1725 N. Lexington Ave., DeLand FL 32724. (904)736-4793. Fax: (904)736-9786. Editor: Sue Clifton. Circ. 9,700. Estab. 1979. Monthly newspaper. Readers are "sport parachutists worldwide, dealers and equipment manufacturers." Sample copy $3. Photo guidelines for SASE.
Needs: Uses 50 photos/issue; 5 supplied by freelancers. Selects photos from wire service, photographers who are skydivers and freelancers. Interested in anything related to skydiving—news or any dramatic illustration of an aspect of parachuting. Model release preferred. Captions preferred; include who, what, why, when, how.
Making Contact & Terms: Interested in receiving work from newer, lesser-known photogaphers. Send actual 5×7 or larger b&w or color photos or 35mm or 2¼×2¼ transparencies by mail for consideration. Keeps samples on file. SASE. Reports in 1 month. Pays $50-100/color cover photo; $25-50/color inside photo; $15-50/b&w inside photo. Pays on publication. Credit line given. Buys one-time rights.

THE SPORTING NEWS, 1212 N. Lindberg Blvd., St. Louis MO 63132. Prefers not to share information.

THE STAR NEWSPAPERS, Dept PM, 1526 Otto, Chicago Heights IL 60411. (708)755-6161. Fax: (708)755-0095. Photo Director: Max Ramirez. Publishes 19 weekly newspapers in south suburban Chicago. Circ. 100,000. Estab. 1920.

Needs: Buys 100 stock photos and offers 1,000 assignments annually. Uses photos for features, news, spot news and sports coverage. Captions required; include description of subject, especially of towns or events.

Making Contact & Terms: Arrange personal interview to show portfolio. Prefers b&w prints, any size over 5×7. Also uses 35mm and 2¼×2¼ transparencies. Works with local freelancers on assignment only. Does not keep samples on file. SASE. Pays $19-25/assignment. Credit line given. Buys one-time and all rights; negotiable.

Tips: Wants to see "variety of photojournalism categories." Also, show "ability both to utilize and supplement available light." To break in, "be ready to hustle and work lousy hours." Sees a trend toward more use of "a documentary style."

STREETPEOPLE'S WEEKLY NEWS (Homeless Editorial), (formerly Dorsey Advertising/PR.), P.O. Box 270942, Dallas TX 75227-0942. Newspaper publisher. Publisher: Lon G. Dorsey, Jr. Estab. 1977. For a copy of the paper send $2 to cover immediate handling (same day as received) and postage.

Needs: Uses photos for newspapers. Subjects include: photojournalists on articles about homeless or street people. Model/property release required. Captions required.

Making Contact & Terms: Interested in receiving work from newer, lesser-known photographers. Send unsolicited photos by mail for consideration with SASE for return of all materials. Reports promptly. Pays $5-10/b&w photo; $7-20/color photo; $20-500/job. Pays on acceptance or publication. Credit line sometimes given. Buys all rights; negotiable.

Tips: In freelancer's demos, wants to see "professionalism, clarity of purpose, without sex or negative atmosphere which could harm purpose of paper." The trend is toward "kinder, gentler situations, the 'let's help our fellows' attitude." To break in, "find out what we're about so we don't waste time with exhausting explanations. We're interested in all homeless situations. Inquires not answered without SASE."

SUN, 5401 NW Broken Sound Blvd., Boca Raton FL 33487. (407)997-7733, ext. 286. Photo Editor: Maureen Scozzaro. Weekly tabloid. Readers are housewives, college students, middle Americans. Sample copy free with extra large SAE and 55¢ postage.

Needs: Uses about 60 photos/issue; 50% supplied by freelance photographers. Wants varied subjects: action, unusual pets, offbeat medical, human interest, inventions, spectacular sports action; b&w human interest and offbeat pix and stories; and b&w celebrity photos. "Also—we are always in need of interesting, offbeat color photos for the center spread." Model release preferred. Captions preferred.

Making Contact & Terms: Query with stock photo list. Send 8×10 b&w prints, 35mm transparencies, b&w contact sheet or b&w negatives by mail for consideration. Send through mail with SASE. Reports in 2 weeks. Pays $100/b&w cover photo; $200/color cover photo; $75/b&w inside photo; $125/color inside photo. Pays on publication. Buys one-time rights. Simultaneous submissions and previously published work OK.

Tips: "We are specifically looking for the unusual, offbeat, freakish true stories and photos. *Nothing* is too far out for consideration. We would suggest you send for a sample copy and take it from there."

SUNSHINE: THE MAGAZINE OF SOUTH FLORIDA, 200 E. Las Olas Blvd., Ft. Lauderdale FL 33301-2293. (305)356-4685. Editor: John Parkyn. Art Director: Greg Carannante. "*Sunshine* is a Sunday newspaper magazine emphasizing articles of interest to readers in the Broward and Palm Beach counties region of South Florida." Readers are "the 800,000 readers of the Sunday edition of the *Sun-Sentinel.*" Sample copy and photo guidelines free with SASE.

Needs: Uses about 12-20 photos/issue; 30% supplied by freelancers. Needs "all kinds of photos relevant to a South Florida readership." Photos purchased with accompanying ms. Model release sometimes required. Captions preferred.

Making Contact & Terms: Query with samples. Provide resume, business card, brochure, flyer or tearsheets to be kept on file for possible future assignments. SASE. Reports in 1 month. "All rates negotiable; the following are as a guide only." Pays $200/color cover photo; $50-100/b&w photo; $75-100/color inside photo; $125-150/color page; $500-1,000 for text/photo package. Pays within 1 month of acceptance. Credit line given. Buys one-time rights. Simultaneous and previously published submissions OK.

*TECH TRANSFER, 109 McLaughlin Hall, Berkeley CA 94720. (510)642-3593. Fax: (510)642-1246. Editor: Betsy Wing. Circ. 3,500. Government publication. Quarterly newsletter. Emphsizes transportation, public works and technology. Readers work in transportation and public works departments of local governments. Sample copy for 9×12 SAE. "We pay postage."

Needs: Uses 2 or 3 photos/issue; all on assignment. Needs photos of state-of-the-art equipment being used by workers. Reviews photos with or without ms. Model release required. Captions required: include what technology is being used, in what location, and names of any people.

Making Contact & Terms: Interested in receiving work from newer, lesser-known photographers. Call editor to see if specific photo is of interest. Does not keep samples on file. Cannot return material. Reports in 1 month. Pays $50-200/b&w cover photo; $0-50/b&w inside photo. **Pays on acceptance.** Credit line given. Buys one-time rights, all rights; negotiable. Considers simultaneous submissions and/or previously published work.

*TEXAS AFFILIATED PUBLISHING COMPANY, 216 S. Madison Ave., Dallas TX 75208-4513. Publisher: Lon G. Dorsey Jr. Estab. 1990. Newspaper publisher.

Needs: Needs advertising-minded photojournalists for shooting supplemental advertorials for legal firms needing exposure in Texas.

Making Contact & Terms: Send sample copies of photo work, resume with addresses and phone numbers of references, brief work and salary (or fee payment) history. Also include $5 for Job Work Package. Due to the number of submissions received, the cost of operation and postage, the paper will not act upon any request for a Job Work Package omitting above postage and handling. No mail is answered without receipt of a self-addressed, stamped envelope. No unsolicited material is returned without SASE. Interested in hearing from advertising privy, photojournalists of a professional nature who have the capability of contacting law firms throughout Texas that want to receive establishment-type exposure in the Dallas/Tarrant County areas. Reports immediately. Pays $20-350/job. Pay is negotiable, and generally above scale due to the nature of the overall clientele transaction. Buys all rights.

Tips: "An unusually good opportunity for persons with the 'right stuff.' Receive a good fee and/or percentage of contract with client. Persons must be professional and responsible, given to exactness and timeliness. Executive studio or freelance photojournalist should be prepared to make an initial contact to establishments and smaller law firms in residential area about our opportunity. Some knowledge of the legal profession, college and telemarketing experience is a plus. Year round work is offered."

*TODAY'S MODEL, P.O. Box 205-454, Brooklyn NY 11220. (718)439-0889. Fax: (718)439-0226. Publisher: Sumit Arya. Circ. 100,000. Estab. 1993. Monthly newspaper. Emphasizes modeling and performing arts. Readers are male and female ages 13-28, parents of kids 1-12. Sample copy free with 9×12 SAE and $2.90 postage. Photo guidelines free with SASE.

Needs: Uses various number photos/issue. Needs photos of fashion—studio/on location/runway; celebrity models, performers, beauty and hair—how-to; photojournalism—modeling, performing arts. Reviews photos with or without ms. Needs models of all ages. Model/property release required. Captions preferred; include name and experience (resume if possible).

Making Contact & Terms: Interested in receiving work from newer, lesser-known photographers. Provide resume, business card, brochure, flyer or tearsheets to be kept on file for possible future assignments. Keeps samples on file. SASE. Reports only when interested. NPI. Pays on publication. Buys all rights; negotiable. Considers simultaneous submissions and/or previously published work.

TRAVEL NEWS, 15th Floor, 111 2nd Ave. NE, St. Petersburg FL 33701. (813)895-8241. Fax: (813)894-6318. Editor: Matthew Wiseman. Circ. 250,000. Estab. 1982. Monthly newspaper. Emphasizes travel. Readers are heads of households with middle- or upper-level income, ages 35 and up. Sample copy for 9×12 SASE. Photo guidelines available.

Needs: Uses 16 photos/issue; 6 supplied by freelancers. Needs photos of travel. Reviews photos with or without manuscript. Model/property release preferred. Captions required.

Making Contact & Terms: Query with stock photo list. Reports in 1-2 months. Pays $50/color cover photo; $10/b&w inside photo; $25/color page rate; $10/b&w page rate; $60-175/photo/text package. Pay on publication. Credit line given. Buys one-time rights; negotiable. Simultaneous submissions and previously published work OK.

Tips: Wants photos of "travelers enjoying themselves, nice destination shots."

*U.S. YOUTH SOCCER, Suite D-225, 3333 S. Wadsworth, Lakewood CO 80439. (303)987-3994. Fax: (303)987-3998. Editor: Jon DeStefano. Circ. 85,000. Estab. 1982. Publication of the United States Youth Soccer Association. Quarterly newspaper. Emphasizes soccer and kids. Readers are coaches.

The code NPI (no payment information given) appears in listings that have not given specific payment amounts.

Needs: Uses 40 photos/issue; 90% supplied by freelancers. Reviews photos with or without ms. Captions required; include names of players and teams.

Making Contact & Terms: Interested in receiving work from newer, lesser-known photographers. Send unsolicited photos by mail for consideration. Send color prints. Does not keep samples on file. Cannot return material. Reports in 1-2 weeks. NPI. Pays on publication. Buys one-time rights. Considers simultaneous submissions.

Tips: "Have fun, show emotion, humor or intensity."

VELONEWS, 1830 N. 55th, Boulder CO 80301-2700. (303)440-0601. Fax: (303)444-6788. Managing Editor: Tim Johnson. Paid circ. 35,000. The journal of competitive cycling. Covers road racing and mountain bike events on a national and international basis. Sample copy free with 9×12 SAE and $1.05 postage.

Needs: Bicycle racing and nationally important races. Looking for action shots, not just finish-line photos with the winner's arms in the air. No bicycle touring. Photos purchased with or without accompanying ms. Uses news, features, profiles. Captions and identification of subjects required.

Making Contact & Terms: Send samples of work or tearsheets with assignment proposal. Query first on mss. Send glossy b&w prints and transparencies. SASE. Reports in 3 weeks. Pays $16.50-50/b&w inside photo; $33-100/color inside photo; $75/b&w cover; $150/color cover; $15-100/ms. Credit line given. Pays on publication. Buys one-time rights.

Tips: "We're a newspaper; photos must be timely. Use fill flash to compensate for harsh summer light."

THE WASHINGTON BLADE, 1408 U St. NW, Washington DC 20009-3916. (202)797-7000. Fax: (202)797-7040. Senior Editor: Lisa M. Keen. Weekly tabloid. For and about the gay community. Readers are gay men and lesbians; moderate- to upper-level income; primarily Washington, DC metropolitan area. Circ. 34,000. Estab. 1969. Sample copy free with 9×12 SAE plus $1 postage.

Needs: Uses about 6-7 photos/issue; only out-of-town photos are supplied by freelance photographers. Needs "gay-related news, sports, entertainment events, profiles of gay people in news, sports, entertainment, other fields." Photos purchased with or without accompanying ms. Model release and captions preferred.

Making Contact & Terms: Interested in receiving work from newer, lesser-known photographers. Query with resume of credits. SASE. Reports in 1 month. Provide resume, business card and tearsheets to be kept on file for possible future assignments. Pays $25/inside photo. Pays within 45 days of publication. Credit line given. Buys all rights when on assignment, otherwise one-time rights. Simultaneous submissions and previously published work OK.

Tips: "Be timely! Stay up-to-date on what we're covering in the news and call us up if you know of a story about to happen in your city that you can cover. Also, be able to provide some basic details for a caption (*tell* us what's happening, too)." Especially important to "avoid stereotypes."

WATERTOWN PUBLIC OPINION, Dept. PM, Box 10, Watertown SD 57201. (605)886-6903. Fax: (605)886-4280. Editor: Gordon Garnos. Circ. 17,500. Estab. 1887. Daily newspaper. Emphasizes general news of this area or former area people. Sample copy 25¢.

Needs: Uses up to 8 photos/issue. Reviews photos with or without ms. Model release required. Captions required.

Making Contact & Terms: Send unsolicited photos by mail for consideration. Send b&w, color prints; 35mm, 2¼×2¼, 4×5, 8×10 transparencies. Does not keep samples on file. SASE. Reports in 1-2 weeks. Pays $5/b&w or color cover photo; $5/b&w or color inside photo; $5/color page rate. Pays on publication. Credit line given. Buys one-time rights; negotiable. Simultaneous submissions OK.

WESTART, Box 6868, Auburn CA 95604. (916)885-0969. Editor-in-Chief: Martha Garcia. Circ. 5,000. Emphasizes art for practicing artists, artists/craftsmen, students of art and art patrons, collectors and teachers. Free sample copy and photo guidelines.

Needs: Uses 20 photos/issue, 10 supplied by freelancers. "We will publish photos if they are in a current exhibition, where the public may view the exhibition. The photos must be b&w. We treat them as an art medium. Therefore, we purchase freelance articles accompanied by photos." Wants mss on exhibitions and artists in the western states. Captions required.

Making Contact & Terms: Send 5×7 or 8×10 b&w prints by mail for consideration. SASE. Reports in 2 weeks. Payment is included with total purchase price of ms. Pays $25 on publication. Buys one-time rights. Simultaneous and previously published submissions OK.

✱THE WESTERN PRODUCER, PO Box 2500, Saskatoon, Sasketchewan S7K 2C4 Canada. (306)665-3500. Fax: (306)653-1255. Editor: Garry Fairbairn. Circ. 105,000. Estab. 1923. Weekly newspaper. Emphasizes agriculture and rural living in western Canada. Photo guidelines free with SASE.

Needs: Buys up to 10 photos/issue; about 50-80% of photos supplied by freelancers. Livestock, nature, human interest, scenic, rural, agriculture, day-to-day rural life and small communities. Model/property release preferred. Captions required; include person's name and description of activity.
Making Contact & Terms: Interested in receiving work from newer, lesser-known photographers. Send material by mail for consideration. SASE. Reports in 2 weeks. Pays $20-40/photo; $35-100/color photo; $50-250 for text/photo package. Pays on publication. Credit line given. Buys one-time rights. Previously published work OK.
Tips: Needs current photos of farm and agricultural news. "Don't waste postage on abandoned, derelict farm buildings or sunset photos. We want modern scenes with life in them—people or animals, preferably both. Farm kids are always a good bet." Also seeks mss on agriculture, rural Western Canada, history, fiction and contemporary life in rural western Canada.

THE WICHITA EAGLE, Dept. PM, 825 E. Douglas, Wichita KS 67201. (316)268-6468. Director of Photography: Brian Corn. Daily newspaper. Emphasizes news. General readership. Circ. 190,000. Estab. 1900.
Needs: Occasionally needs freelance submissions. "We have our own staff, so we don't require much freelance work. What little we do want, however, has to do with Kansas people." Model release preferred. Captions required.
Making Contact & Terms: Query with list of stock photo subjects. Submit portfolio for review. Provide resume, business card, brochure, flyer or tearsheets to be kept on file for possible assignments. Send 35mm b&w and color prints, or transparencies by mail for consideration. SASE. Reports in 3 weeks. Pays $50/color cover photo; $30/b&w cover photo. Pays on publication. Credit line given. Buys one-time rights. Simultaneous and previously published work OK.
Tips: In photographer's portfolio or samples, wants to see "20 or so images that show off what the shooter does best, i.e., news spots, fashion." To break in with newspapers, "work hard, shoot as much as possible, and *never* give up!"

WISCONSIN, The Milwaukee Journal Magazine, P.O. Box 661, Milwaukee WI 53201. (414)224-2341. Fax: (414)224-2047. Editor: Alan Borsuk. Circ. 495,000. Estab. 1969. Weekly magazine. General-interest Sunday magazine focusing on the places and people of Wisconsin or of interest to Wisconsin-ites. Free sample copy with SASE.
Needs: Uses about 12 photos/issue; 1 supplied by freelancer. About 90% of photos are on assignment; very little stock. Needs "human-interest, wildlife, adventure, still life and scenic photos, etc." Model release preferred. Captions required.
Making Contact & Terms: Interested in receiving work from newer, lesser-known photographers. Query with samples. SASE. Reports in 3 months. Pays $125/color cover photo; $50-100/b&w inside photo, $50-125/color inside photo. Pays on publication. Buys one-time rights, "preferably first-time rights; negotiable."
Tips: "We're primarily interested in people and, to a lesser extent, nature. Our emphasis is strongly on Wisconsin themes."

WRITER'S FORUM, 1507 Dana Ave., Cincinnati OH 45207. (513)531-2222. Editor: Tom Clark. Circ. 13,000. Quarterly newsletter. Readers are students of Writer's Digest School. Emphasizes novel, short story and article writing techniques and marketing, student and faculty activities and interviews with freelance writers. Free sample copy.
Needs: Has not bought photos within the last two years, but "we will consider them." Celebrity/personality of well-known writers. Photos purchased with accompanying ms. No photos without related text of interest/help to writing students. Model release preferred; captions required.
Making Contacts & Terms: Send material by mail for consideration. Uses 8×10 glossy prints for inside or cover photos. SASE. Reports in 3 weeks. Pays $15/photo; $10-25/ms. **Pays on acceptance.** Credit line given. Buys one-time rights. Simultaneous submissions and previously published work OK. Accompanying mss include interviews with well-known writers on how they write and market their work; technical problems they overcame; people, places and events that inspired them, etc. 500-1,000 words.
Tips: "Get a sample if you are interested in working with our publication."

Newspapers & Newsletters/'93-'94 changes

The following markets appeared in the 1993 edition of *Photographer's Market* but are not listed in the 1994 edition. They may have been omitted for failing to respond to our request for updated information, they may have gone out of business or they may no longer wish to receive freelance work.

Auditioning (unable to locate)

Banjo Newsletter (did not respond)

Bear Essential News for Kids (unable to locate)

Catholic Health World (did not respond)

Chicago Tribune Magazine (did not respond)

CMD Profiles (did not respond)

Commercial Property News (did not respond)

Eyecare Business (did not respond)

Florida Grower and Rancher (did not respond)

General Aviation News &

Flyer (inappropriate submissions)

Gift and Stationery Business (did not respond)

Grain Matters (overstocked)

Guardian Newsweekly (unable to locate)

Gulf Coast Golfer (did not respond)

Intensive Caring Unlimited (did not respond)

Kane County Chronicle (did not respond)

Mercury (did not respond)

News-Gazette (did not respond)

On Track (did not respond)

Produce News (did not re-

spond)

Rubber and Plastics News (did not respond)

Sentinel, California (did not respond)

Sentinel, Florida (did not respond)

Southern Motoracing (did not respond)

Talent Management (did not respond)

Traverse City Record-Eagle (did not respond)

Ventura County & Coast Reporter (did not respond)

Voyager International (did not respond)

Yachtsman (did not respond)

Special Interest Publications

When concentrating on special interest publications it is important to be very specific in the types of samples you submit. These magazines are not filled with general material, as are consumer magazines. Normally these publications are affiliated with certain organizations that are trying to reach a clearly defined readership. If you know who those readers are you can supply editors with more appropriate samples, thus improving your sales potential.

Association publications in this section generally will be described with the phrase, "Publication of the (Name) Association." For company publications, the identifying phrase is "Company publication for the (Name) Co. or Corp." Some publications which are published by associations or companies but are intended for consumer or trade audiences may be found in the appropriate market sections.

Though the subject matter, readerships and circulation sizes of these publications vary, their photo editors do share a need for top-notch images. Photojournalist Mark Downey of Alameda, California, has found ways to meet the needs of editors and he discusses his methods as our Insider Report subject on page 378. You also should check the new Subject Index, located at the back of this book, to find markets for your work. The index tells you the types of images publications want from freelancers.

There are certain publications that are interested in text/photo packages and photographers who have an ability to write can benefit from these listings. Editors often turn down photo submissions because they do not have an article to coincide with the artwork. By providing the full package you can make work more attractive to editors. The key is to cover a topic that is unique and focuses on the magazine's audience. If you do not have talent as a writer, team up with writers who need artwork for their stories.

As with most publications, breaking in will probably happen in stages. You may be assigned smaller projects at first, but once you supply quality material—on time and within budget—you may become a regular contributor. In addition to shooting editorial work, you may also be offered additional, noneditorial opportunities as you become known within the parent company or organization. Among these would be shooting publicity materials, executive portraits, product advertising and documentation of company or organization events.

AAA MICHIGAN LIVING, 1 Auto Club Dr., Dearborn MI 48126. (313)336-1211. Fax: (313)336-1897. Executive Editor: Ron Garbinski. Managing Editor: Larry Keller. Monthly magazine. Emphasizes auto use, as well as travel in Michigan, US, Canada and foreign countries. Circ. 1,000,000. Estab. 1918. Free sample copy and photo guidelines.
Needs: Scenic and travel. "We buy photos without accompanying ms. Seeks mss about travel in Michigan, US and Canada. We maintain a file on stock photos and subjects photographers have available." Captions required.
Making Contact & Terms: Query with list of stock photo subjects. Uses 35mm, 2¼×2¼ or 4×5 transparencies. For covers in particular, uses 35mm, 4×5 or 8×10 color transparencies. SASE. Reports in 6 weeks. Pays up to $200/color photo depending on quality and size; $350/cover photo; $55-500/ms. Pays on publication for photos, on acceptance for mss. Buys one-time rights. Simultaneous submissions and previously published work not accepted.

AAA WORLD, Dept. PM, 1000 AAA Dr., Heathrow, FL 32746-5063. (407)444-8544. Editor/Associate Publisher: Doug Damerst. Circ. 2,553,000. Estab. 1981. Association publication of AAA (ABC member). Bimonthly magazine emphasizing how to drive, car care, how to travel and travel destinations. Readers are above average income and age. Sample copy free.
• In 1992 this publication received a silver Charlie Award from the Florida Magazine Association for having the Best Overall Magazine.
Needs: Uses 60 photos/issue; 20 supplied by freelancers. Needs photos of people enjoying domestic and international vacation settings. Model release required. Captions preferred.
Making Contact & Terms: Provide resume, business card, brochure, flyer or tearsheets to be kept on file for possible future assignments. Cannot return material. Reports in 3 weeks. Pays $75/color inside photo. **Pays on acceptance.** Credit line given. Buys one-time rights. Simultaneous submissions and previously published submissions OK.
Tips: "Our need is for travel photos, but not of places as much as of people enjoying travel."

ADVENTURE ROAD, Dept. PM, 200 E. Randolph Dr., Chicago IL 60601. (312)856-2583. Editor: Marilyn Holstein. Circ. 1,500,000. Estab. 1965. Publication of Amaco Motor Club. Bimonthly magazine. Emphasizes vacation travel. Readers are 60% male and 40% female, typically ages 48 and up. Sample copy free with SASE.
Needs: Uses 30-50 photos/issue; all supplied by freelance photographers. Model release required. Captions required.
Making Contact & Terms: Query with resume of credits. Pays $1,000/color cover photo; $200/color inside photo. Pays on publication. Credit line given. Buys one-time rights.

AI MAGAZINE, 445 Burgess Dr., Menlo Park CA 94025. (415)328-3123. Fax: (415)853-0197. Publishing Consultant: David Hamilton. Circ. 13,000. Estab. 1980. Publication of American Association of Artificial Intelligence (AAAI). Quarterly. Emphasizes artificial intelligence. Readers are research scientists, engineers, high-technology managers, professors of computer science. Sample copy $4 with 9×12 SAE and $2.40 postage.
Needs: Uses about 3-5 photos/issue; all supplied by freelancers. Needs photo of specialized computer applications. Model release required. Captions preferred.
Making Contact & Terms: Interested in receiving work from newer, lesser-known photographers. Arrange a personal interview to show portfolio. Query with list of stock photo subjects. Provide resume, business card, brochure, flyer or tearsheets to be kept on file for possible future assignments. SASE. Reports in 3 weeks. Pays $100-1,000/color cover photo; $25-250/color inside photo. Pays on publication. Credit line given. Buys one-time and first N.A. serial rights. Simultaneous submissions and previously published work OK.
Tips: Looks for "editorial content of photos, not artistic merit."

A bullet has been placed within some listings to introduce special comments by the editor of the Photographer's Market.

AIR LINE PILOT, 535 Herndon Parkway, Box 1169, Herndon VA 22070. (703)689-4171. Fax: (703)689-4370. Photography Associate: Barbara Sutliff. Circ. 65,000. Estab. 1933. Publication of Air Line Pilots Association. Monthly. Emphasizes news and feature stories for commercial airline pilots. Photo guidelines for SASE.

Needs: Uses 12-15 photos/issue; 25% comes from freelance stock. Needs dramatic 35mm Kodachrome transparencies of commercial aircraft, pilots and co-pilots performing work-related activities in or near their aircraft. Special needs include dramatic 35mm Kodachromes technically and aesthetically suitable for full-page magazine covers. Especially needs vertical composition scenes. Model release required. Captions required; include aircraft type, airline, location of photo/scene, description of action, date.

Making Contact & Terms: Interested in receiving work from newer, lesser-known photographers. Query with samples. Send unsolicited photos by mail for consideration. Uses 35mm transparencies. SASE. Pays $35/b&w photo; $35-350/color photo. **Pays on acceptance.** Buys one-time or all rights; negotiable. Simultaneous submissions and previously published work OK.

Tips: In photographer's samples, wants to see "strong composition, poster-like quality and high technical quality. Photos compete with text for space so they need to be very interesting to be published. Be sure to provide brief but accurate caption information and send in only top, professional quality work. For our publication, cover shots do not need to tie in with current articles. This means that the greatest opportunity for publication exists on our cover."

ALABAMA MUNICIPAL JOURNAL, 535 Adams Ave., P.O. Box 1270, Montgomery AL 36102. (205)262-2566. Fax: (205)263-0200. Publications Manager: Anne Roquemore. Circ. 4,500. Estab. 1945. Association publication of Alabama League of Municipalities. Monthly magazine. Emphasizes municipal government and its responsibilities. Readers are municipal officials—mayors, council members, judges, clerks, attorneys, male and female; ages 20-80; black and white, varied occupations besides municipal offices. Sample copy and guidelines free with 8½ × 11 SASE.

Needs: Uses 2-3 photos/issue (more depending on availability and appropriateness of subjects). Needs photos of daily operations of municipal government—police, fire, courts, sanitation, etc. Model release required. Captions preferred.

Making Contact & Terms: Interested in receiving work from newer, lesser-known photographers. Query with resume of credits and list of stock photo subjects. Provide resume, business card, brochure, flyer or tearsheets to be kept on file for possible assignments. Returns unsolicited material if SASE is enclosed. Reports in 1 month. Pays in copies (usually 3). Credit line given. Previously published work OK.

Tips: "Photos which grab the reader's attention and contribute to the story are most welcome. Don't strive for fanciness yet maintain some artistry in the photos."

ALFA OWNER, Suite E, 1371 E. Warner Ave., Tustin CA 92680. (714)259-8240. Editor: Elyse Barrett. Circ. 5,500. Publication of the Alfa Romeo Owners Club association. Monthly magazine. Emphasizes Alfa Romeo automobiles. Audience is upscale with median household income of $70,180. Majority hold executive, technical or professional positions. Average age is 35, with 75% male readership. Sample copy free with 9 × 12 SAE and 4 first-class stamps.

Needs: Uses 12 photos/issue; 50% supplied by freelancers. Needs shots of Alfa Romeos on the road, under-the-hood tech shots, photos of historical figures related to Alfa and "glamour" shots of Alfas. Model/property release preferred. Captions preferred.

Making Contact & Terms: Submit portfolio for review. Send a combination of color slides and/or 5 × 7 prints (if possible), plus some b&w prints. SASE. Reports in 2 weeks. Pays $75-100/color cover photo; $10/b&w inside photo. Negotiates hour and day rate. Pays on publication. Credit line given. Simultaneous submissions and previously published work OK.

Tips: "We would like to see the photographer's background in automotive photography. Experience in automotive photography is preferable, though such a background isn't crucial if the person's work is good enough. For *Alfa Owner*, knowledge of the tech aspects of automobiles is very valuable, as we need technical shots almost as much as we need glamour and 'on-the-road' photos. Focus and, for the cover, a vertical format are crucial."

AMERICAN BIRDS, Dept. PM, 950 3rd Ave., New York NY 10022. (212)979-3000. Editor-in-chief: Susan Roney Drennan. Circ. 13,000. Publication of National Audubon Society. Published 5 times/year. "Our major areas of interest are the changing distribution, population, migration and rare occurrence of the avifauna of North and South America, including Middle America and the West Indies. Readers are 'bird people only.' Of our 29,000 readers, 11% are professional ornithologists or zoologists, 79% serious amateurs, the rest novices." Sample copy $5. Photo guidelines free with SASE.

Needs: Uses one cover-quality shot, vertical format, color/issue. This most often supplied by freelancer. Also very interested in excellent color and b&w photos for inside use. Birds can be flying or perched, singly or in flocks, in any wild American habitat; picture essays on bird behavior. Avoid zoo or backyard shots. "Since we never know our needs too far in advance, best to send representative sampling."

Making Contact & Terms: Query with samples. Send transparencies by mail for consideration. Provide resume, business card, brochure, flyer or tearsheets to be kept on file for possible future assignments. SASE. Reports in 4 months. Pays up to $100/color cover photo. Pays on publication. Credit line given.

Tips: "We will probably be able to publish more photos this year than we have in the past. We look for very clear, easily identifiable birds. Diagnostic marks should be clearly visible, eyes open."

AMERICAN CRAFT, 72 Spring St., New York NY 10012. (212)274-0630. Editor: Lois Moran. Senior Editor: Pat Dandignac. Circ. 45,000. Estab. 1941. Bimonthly magazine of the American Craft Council. Emphasizes contemporary creative work in clay, fiber, metal, glass, wood, etc. and discusses the technology, materials and ideas of the artists who do the work. Free sample copy with 9×12 SAE and $1.25 postage.

Needs: Visual art. Shots of crafts: clay, metal, fiber, etc. Captions required.

Making Contact & Terms: Arrange a personal interview to show portfolio. Uses 8×10 glossy b&w prints; 4×5 transparencies and 35mm film; 4×5 color transparencies for cover, vertical format preferred. SASE. Reports in 1 month. Pays according to size of reproduction; $40 minimum/b&w and color photos; $175-350/cover photos. Pays on publication. Buys one-time rights. Previously published work OK.

AMERICAN FITNESS, Dept. PM, Suite 200, 15250 Ventura Blvd., Sherman Oaks CA 91403. (818)905-0040. Managing Editor: Rhonda J. Wilson. Circ. 25,100. Estab. 1983. Publication of the Aerobics and Fitness Association of America. Publishes 6 issues/year. Emphasizes exercise, fitness, health, sports nutrition, aerobic sports. Readers are fitness enthusiasts and professionals, 75% college educated, 66% female, majority between 20-45. Circ. 25,100. Sample copy $2.50.

Needs: Uses about 20-40 photos/issue; most supplied by freelancers. Assigns 90% of work. Needs action photography of runners, aerobic classes, especially high drama for cover: swimmers, bicyclists, aerobic dancers, runners, etc. Special needs include food choices, male and female exercises, people enjoying recreation, dos and don'ts. Model release required.

Making Contact & Terms: Query with samples or with list of stock photo subjects. Send b&w prints; 35mm, 2¼×2¼ transparencies; b&w contact sheets by mail for consideration. SASE. Reports in 2 weeks. Pays $10-35/b&w or color photo; $50-100 for text/photo package. Pays 4-6 weeks after publication. Credit line given. Buys first N.A. serial rights. Simultaneous submissions and previously published work OK.

Tips: Looks for "firsthand fitness experiences—we frequently publish personal photo essays." Fitness-oriented outdoor sports are the current trend (i.e. mountain bicycling, hiking, rock climbing). Over-40 sports leagues, youth fitness, family fitness and senior fitness are also hot trends. Wants high-quality, professional photos of people participating in high-energy activities—anything that conveys the essence of a fabulous fitness lifestyle. Also accepts highly stylized studio shots to run as lead artwork for feature stories. "Since we don't have a big art budget, freelancers usually submit piggyback pictures from their larger assignments."

AMERICAN FORESTS MAGAZINE, Dept. PM, 1516 P St. NW, Washington DC 20005. (202)667-3300. Editor: Bill Rooney. Circ. 30,000. Publication of American Forests (formerly American Forestry Association). Emphasizes use, enjoyment and management of forests and other natural resources. Monthly. Readers are "people from all walks of life, from rural to urban settings, whose main common denominator is an abiding love for trees, forests or forestry." Sample copy and free photo guidelines with magazine-size envelope and $1.25 postage.

Needs: Uses about 40 photos/issue, 35 of which are supplied by freelance photographers (most supplied by article authors). Needs woods scenics, wildlife, woods use/management and forestry shots. Model release preferred. Captions preferred.

Making Contact & Terms: Query with resume of credits. SASE. Reports in 6-8 weeks. $300/color cover photo; $40-75/b&w inside; $75-150/color inside; $350-800 for text/photo package. Pays on acceptance. Credit line given. Buys one-time rights.

Tips: Seeing trend away from "static woods scenics, toward more people and action shots." In samples wants to see "overall sharpness, unusual conformation, shots that accurately portray the highlights and 'outsideness' of outdoor scenes."

AMERICAN HUNTER, Suite 1000, 470 Spring Park Place, Herndon VA 22070. (703)481-3360. Editor: Tom Fulgham. Circ. 1.3 million. Monthly magazine. Sample copy and photo guidelines free with 9×12 SAE. Free writer's guidelines with SASE.

© Mike Chew

A company that produces knee and elbow pads hired freelancer Mike Chew of Sandy, Utah, to illustrate the need for their protective gear. This photo of an in-line skater going airborne goes far in portraying this message. Now one of Chew's stock shots, this image and two others on the sport were used to illustrate an article in American Fitness Magazine.

Needs: Uses wildlife shots and hunting action scenes. Photos purchased with or without accompanying ms. Seeks general hunting stories on North American game. Captions preferred.
Making Contact & Terms: Send material by mail for consideration. Uses 8 × 10 glossy b&w prints and 35mm color transparencies. (Uses 35mm color transparencies for cover). Vertical format required for cover. SASE. Reports in 1 month. Pays $25-75/b&w print; $40-275/color transparency; $300/color cover photo; $200-450 for text/photo package. Pays on publication for photos. Credit line given. Buys one-time rights.

AMERICAN LIBRARIES, 50 E. Huron St., Chicago IL 60611. (312)280-4216. Senior Production Editor: Edith McCormick. Circ. 53,000. Publication of the American Library Association. Magazine published 11 times/year. Emphasizes libraries and librarians. Readers are "chiefly the members of the American Library Association but also subscribing institutions who are not members." Sample copy free with SASE. General guidelines free with SASE.
Needs: Uses about 5-20 photos/issue; 1-3 supplied by freelance photographers. "Prefer vertical shots. Need sparkling, well-lit color prints or transparencies of beautiful library exteriors. Dramatic views; can be charming old-fashioned structure with character and grace or striking modern building. Library should be *inviting*. Added color enrichment helpful: colorful foliage, flowers, people engaged in some activity natural to the photo are examples." Special needs include "*color* photos of upbeat library happenings and events—must be unusual or of interest to sophisticated group of librarian-readers. Special need for school and academic library shots." All inside shots must be in color. "Supply possible cover photos of library exterior—as many views as possible of same subject."
Making Contact & Terms: Send transparencies or contact sheet by mail for consideration. SASE. Reports in 2-8 weeks. Pays $200-400/color cover photo; $75-150/color inside photo; $100-450/text/photo package. Credit line given. Buys first N.A. serial rights.
Tips: "Read or scan at least two issues thoroughly. We look for excellent, focused, well-lit shots, especially in color, of interesting events strongly related to library context—off-beat and upbeat occurrences in libraries of interest to sophisticated librarian audience. Also looking for rich color photos of beautiful library exteriors, both old-fashioned and charming and modern structures . . . people should be included in photos (e.g., one or two entering library building)."

AMERICAN MOTORCYCLIST, Dept. PM, P.O. Box 6114, Westerville OH 43081-6114. (614)891-2425. Vice President of Communication: Greg Harrison. Managing Editor: Bill Wood. Circ. 175,000. Publication of the American Motorcyclist Association. Monthly magazine. For "enthusiastic motorcyclists, investing considerable time in road riding or competition sides of the sport." "We are interested in

people involved in, and events dealing with, all aspects of motorcycling." Sample copy and photo guidelines for $1.50.
Needs: Buys 10-20 photos/issue. Subjects include: travel, technical, sports, humorous, photo essay/feature and celebrity/personality. Captions preferred.
Making Contact & Terms: Query with samples to be kept on file for possible future assignments. Reports in 3 weeks. SASE. Send 5×7 or 8×10 semigloss prints; transparencies. Pays $20-50/photo; $30-100/slide; $150 minimum/cover photo. Also buys photos in photo/text packages according to same rate; pays $6/column inch minimum for story. Pays on publication. Buys all rights.
Tips: Uses transparencies for covers. "The cover shot is tied in with the main story or theme of that issue and generally needs to be with accompanying ms. Show us experience in motorcycling photography and suggest your ability to meet our editorial needs and complement our philosophy."

THE AMERICAN MUSIC TEACHER, Suite 1432, 617 Vine St., Cincinnati OH 45202-2982. (513)421-1420. Art Director: Diane M. Devillez. Circ. 26,000. Publication of Music Teachers National Association. Bimonthly magazine. Emphasizes music teaching. Readers are music teachers operating independently from conservatories, studios and homes.
Needs: Uses about 4 photos/issue; 3 supplied by freelancers. Needs photos of musical subject matter. Model release preferred. Captions preferred.
Making Contact & Terms: Query with resume of credits. Query with samples. Query with list of stock photo subjects. Send unsolicited photos by mail for consideration. Provide resume, business card, brochure, flyer or tearsheets to be kept on file for possible future assignments. Uses 3×5 to 8×10 glossy b&w prints; 35mm, 2¼×2¼, 4×5 and 8×10 transparencies; b&w contact sheets. SASE. Pays $150 maximum/b&w photo; $250 maximum/color photo. **Pays on acceptance.** Credit line given. Buys one-time rights. Simultaneous submissions and previously published work OK.
Tips: In portfolio or samples, wants to see "teaching subjects, musical subject matter from classical to traditional, to computers and electronics, children and adults."

*AMERICAN SAILOR, P.O. Box 209, Newport RI 02840. (401)849-5200. Fax: (401)849-5208. Managing Editor: Pat Lussier. Circ. 30,000. Estab. 1986. Publication of the US Sailing Association. Publishes 10 issues/year. Magazine. Emphasizes sailing. Readers are male and female sailors ages 15-70. Sample copy free with SASE.
Needs: Uses 5 photos/issue; most supplied by freelancers. Needs photos of one-design, big boat, multihull and/or windsurfing. Reviews photos with or without ms. Captions preferred; include date, location of event, name(s) of boats pictured.
Making Contact & Terms: Interested in receiving work from newer, lesser-known photographers. Send unsolicited photos by mail for consideration. Provide resume, business card, brochure, flyer or tearsheets to be kept on file for possible future assignments. Send 5×7 or bigger color prints. Does not keep samples on file. SASE. Reports in 1 month. "No payment given. We are a non-profit organization." Credit line given.
Tips: Looks for "vertical, colorful shots. No technicals, no power boats, no bikini-clad women."

ANCHOR NEWS, 75 Maritime Dr., Manitowoc WI 54220. (414)684-0218. Editor: Isco Valli. Circ. 1,900. Publication of the Manitowoc Maritime Museum. Bimonthly magazine. Emphasizes Great Lakes maritime history. Readers include learned and lay readers interested in Great Lakes history. Sample copy free with 9×12 SAE and $1 postage. Guidelines free with SASE.
Needs: Uses 8-10 photos/issue; infrequently supplied by freelance photographers. Needs historic/nostalgic, personal experience and general interest articles on Great Lakes maritime topics. How-to and technical pieces and model ships and shipbuilding are OK. Special needs include historic photography or photos that show current historic trends of the Great Lakes. Photos of waterfront development, bulk carriers, sailors, recreational boating, etc. Model release required. Captions required.
Making Contact & Terms: Query with samples. Send 4×5 or 8×10 glossy b&w prints by mail for consideration. SASE. Reports in 1 month. Pays in copies only on publication. Credit line given. Buys first N.A. serial rights. Simultaneous submissions and previously published work OK.
Tips: "Besides historic photographs I see a growing interest in underwater archaeology, especially on the Great Lakes, and underwater exploration—also on the Great Lakes. Sharp, clear photographs are a must. Our publication deals with a wide variety of subjects; however, we take an historical slant with our publication. Therefore photos should be related to a historical topic in some respect. Also current trends in Great Lakes shipping. A query is most helpful. This will let the photographer know exactly what we are looking for and will help save a lot of time and wasted effort."

ANIMALS, Dept. PM, 350 S. Huntington Ave., Boston MA 02130. (617)522-7400. Fax: (617)522-4885. Publication of the Massachusetts Society for the Prevention of Cruelty to Animals. Circ. 100,000. Estab. 1868. Bimonthly. Emphasizes animals, both wild and domestic. Readers are people interested in animals, conservation, animal welfare issues, pet care and wildlife. Sample copy $2.50 with 9×12 SAE. Photo guidelines free with SASE.

Needs: Uses about 45 photos/issue; approx. 95% supplied by freelance photographers. "All of our pictures portray animals, usually in their natural settings, however some in specific situations such as pets being treated by veterinarians or wildlife in captive breeding programs." Needs vary according to editorial coverage. Special needs include clear, crisp shots of animals, wild and domestic, both close-up and distance shots with spectacular backgrounds, or in the case of domestic animals, a comfortable home or backyard. Model release required in some cases. Captions preferred.

Making Contact & Terms: Query with resume of credits; query with list of stock photo subjects. Provide resume, business card, brochure, flyer or tearsheets to be kept on file for possible future assignments. SASE. Reports in 4-6 weeks. Fees are usually negotiable; pays $50-150/b&w photo; $75-300/color photo; payment depends on size and placement. Pays on publication. Credit line given. Buys one-time rights.

Tips: Photos should be sent to Dietrich Gehring, Ten Eyck Photo Research, P.O. Box 740, Altamont NY 12009. Gehring does first screening. "Offer original ideas combined with extremely high-quality technical ability. Suggest article ideas to accompany your photos, but only propose yourself as author if you are qualified. We have a never-ending need for sharp, high-quality portraits of mixed-breed dogs and cats for both inside and cover use. Keep in mind we seldom use domestic cats outdoors; we often need indoor cat shots."

APA MONITOR, American Psychological Association, 750 First St. NE, Washington DC 20002. (202)336-6100. Editor: Laurie Denton. Managing Editors: John Bales and Kathleen McCarthy. Circ. 80,000. Monthly newspaper. Emphasizes "news and features of interest to psychologists and other behavioral scientists and professionals, including legislation and agency action affecting science and health, and major issues facing psychology both as a science and a mental health profession." Sample copy with $3 and 9×12 envelope.

Needs: Buys 60-90 photos/year. Photos purchased on assignment. Needs portraits, feature illustrations and spot news.

Making Contact & Terms: Arrange a personal interview to show portfolio or query with samples. Uses 5×7 and 8×10 glossy b&w prints; contact sheet OK. SASE. Pays by the job; $75/hour; $300-400/day. Pays on receipt of invoice. Credit line given. Buys first serial rights.

Tips: "Become good at developing ideas for illustrating abstract concepts and innovative approaches to cliches such as meetings and speeches. We look for quality in technical reproduction and innovative approaches to subjects."

APERTURE, Dept. PM, 20 E. 23rd St., New York NY 10010. (212)505-5555. Managing Editor: Michael Sand. Circ. 16,000. Publication of Aperture. Quarterly. Emphasizes fine art and contemporary photography, as well as social reportage. Readers include photographers, artists, collectors.

Needs: Uses about 60 photos/issue; issues are generally thematic—regular portfolio review. Model release required. Captions required.

Making Contact & Terms: Submit portfolio for review. SASE. Reports in one month. No payment. Credit line given.

Tips: "We are a nonprofit foundation and do not pay for photos."

APPALACHIAN TRAILWAY NEWS, Box 807, Harpers Ferry WV 25425. (304)535-6331. Fax: (304)535-2667. Editor: Judith Jenner. Circ. 26,000. Estab. 1939. Publication of the Appalachian Trail Conference. Bimonthly. Emphasizes the Appalachian Trail. Readers are conservationists, hikers. Sample copy $3 (includes postage and guidelines). Guidelines free with SASE.

Needs: Uses about 20-30 b&w photos/issue; 4-5 supplied by freelance photographers (plus 13 color slides each year for calendar). Needs scenes from/on the Appalachian Trail; specifically of people using or maintaining the trail. Special needs include candids—people/wildlife/trail scenes. Photo information required.

Making Contact & Terms: Interested in receiving work from newer, lesser-known photographers. Query samples. Send 5×7 or larger glossy b&w prints; b&w contact sheet; or 35mm transparencies by mail for consideration. SASE. Reports in 3 weeks. **Pays on acceptance.** Pays $100/b&w cover photo; $200 minimum/color slide calendar photo; $10-50/b&w inside photo. Credit line given. Rights negotiable. Simultaneous submissions and previously published work OK.

APPALOOSA JOURNAL, P.O. Box 8403, Moscow ID 83843. (208)882-5578. Editor: Debbie Moors. Circ. 17,000. Estab. 1946. Association publication of Appaloosa Horse Club. Monthly magazine. Emphasizes Appaloosa horses. Readers are Appaloosa owners, breeders and trainers, child through adult. Sample copy $3. Photo guidelines free with SASE.

The Subject Index, located at the back of this book, can help you find publications interested in the topics you shoot.

Needs: Uses 30 photos/issue; 20% supplied by freelance photographers. Needs photos (color and b&w) to accompany features and articles. Special photo needs include photographs of Appaloosas (high quality horses) in winter scenes. Model release required. Captions required.

Making Contact & Terms: Send unsolicited 8×10 b&w and color prints or 35mm and 2¼×2¼ transparencies by mail for consideration. Reports in 3 weeks. Pays $100-300/color cover photo; $50-100/color inside photo; $25-50/b&w inside photo. **Pays on acceptance.** Credit line given. Buys first N.A. serial rights. Previously published work OK.

Tips: In photographer's samples, wants to see "high quality color photos of high quality Appaloosa horses with people in outdoor environment. We often need a freelancer to illustrate a manuscript we have purchased. We need specific photos and usually very quickly."

ARMY RESERVE MAGAZINE, Room 501, 1815 N. Fort Myer Dr., Arlington VA 22209-1805. (703)696-3962. Fax: (703)696-3745. Editor: Lt. Col. James M. Nielsen. Circ. 665,000. Estab. 1955. Publication for U.S. Army Reserve. Quarterly magazine. Emphasizes training and employment of Army Reservists. Readers are ages 17-60, 60% male, 40% female, all occupations. No particular focus on civilian employment. Sample copy free with 9×12 SAE and 2 first-class stamps. Write for guidelines.

Needs: Uses 35-45 photos/issue; 85% supplied by freelancers. Needs photos related to the mission or function of the U.S. Army Reserve. Model release preferred (if of a civilian or non-affiliated person). Captions required.

Making Contact & Terms: Interested in receiving work from newer, lesser-known photographers. "Contact editor to discuss potential job before execution." Uses 5×7 b&w prints; 35mm or 2¼×2¼ transparencies. SASE. Reports in 1 month. "No pay for material; credit only since we are a nonprofit operation." Unable to purchase rights, but consider as "one-time usage." Simultaneous submissions and previously published work OK.

Tips: "High quality b&w prints of Army Reserve related training or community activities are in demand."

ASTA AGENCY MANAGEMENT MAGAZINE, Dept. PM, 1301 Carolina St., Greensboro NC 27401. (919)378-6065. Fax: (919)275-2864. Director of Art and Photography: Michael Robbins. Circ. 25,000. Estab. 1987. Publication of the American Society of Travel Agents (ASTA). Monthly magazine. Emphasizes the business of travel. Readers are male and female travel agents, owners and managers, ages 35-60. Sample copy free with 9×12 SAE and $3 postage.

Needs: Uses 20-25 photos/issue; 50% supplied by freelancers. Needs executive portraits, hotel properties, cruise ships, ports, airports, aircraft, business environment and equipment. Especially wants to see photos of South Pacific destinations, Caribbean and Mexican resorts and domestic travel. Model release preferred for collateral subjects that include "who, what, when, where."

Making Contact & Terms: Query with list of stock photo subjects. Provide resume, business card, brochure, flyer or tearsheets to be kept on file for possible assignments. Keeps samples on file. SASE. Reports in 1 month. Pays $350/color cover photo; $300/color inside photo; $200/b&w page rate; $300-350/day. Credit line given. Buys one-time rights, first N.A. serial rights. No submissions that other travel trade publications previously published.

Tips: Wants to see "everyday subject covered with imagination; use of light and color, variety of focal lengths, overalls, middle and long shots; portraits that show personality and dignity." Points out that "stock images must be current! I do not want 3-year-old pictures of hotels and resorts. The travel industry is everchanging. Know the trade and the issues."

AUTO TRIM NEWS, Suite 200, 6255 Barfield Rd., Atlanta GA 30328-4300. (404)252-8831. Fax: (404)252-4436. Editor: Gary Fong. Circ. 8,000. Estab. 1951. Publication of National Association of Auto Trim Shops. Monthly. Emphasizes automobile restoration and restyling. Readers are upholsterers for auto/marine trim shops; body shops handling cosmetic soft goods for vehicles.

Needs: Uses about 15 photos/issue; 6-10 supplied by freelance photographers, all on assignment. Needs "how-to photos; photos of new store openings; restyling showcase photos of unusual completed work." Special needs include "restyling ideas for new cars in the aftermarket area; soft goods and chrome add-ons to update Detroit." Captions required.

Making Contact & Terms: Interested in receiving work from newer, lesser-known photographers. Provide resume, business card, brochure, flyer or tearsheets to be kept on file for possible future assignments. Submit ideas for photo assignments in local area. Photographer should be in touch with a cooperative shop locally. SASE. Reports in 1 week. Pays $35/b&w cover photo; $75-95/job. **Pays on acceptance.** Credit line given if desired. Buys all rights; negotiable. Simultaneous submissions and previously published work OK.

Tips: "First learn the needs of a market or segment of an industry. Then translate it into photographic action so that readers can improve their business. In samples we look for experience in shop photography, ability to photograph technical subject matter within automotive and marine industries."

THE BIBLE ADVOCATE, P.O. Box 33677, Denver CO 80233. (303)452-7973. Fax: (303)452-0657. Editor: Roy A. Marrs. Circ. 16,000. Estab. 1863. Publication of the Church of God (Seventh Day). Monthly magazine; 11 issues/year. Emphasizes Christian and denominational subjects. Sample copy free with 9 × 12 SAE and 87¢ postage.
Needs: Needs scenics and some religious shots (Jerusalem, etc.). Captions preferred, include name, place.
Making Contact & Terms: Interested in receiving work from newer, lesser-known photographers. Submit portfolio for review. SASE. Reports as needed. No payment offered. Rights negotiable. Simultaneous submissions and previously published work OK.
Tips: Wants to see "b&w prints for inside and 35mm color transparencies for front cover—religious, nature, people." To break in, "be patient—right now we use material on an as-needed basis. We will look at all work, but please realize we don't pay for photos or cover art. Send samples and we'll review them. We are working several months in advance now. If we like a photographer's work, we schedule it for a particular issue so we don't hold it indefinitely."

BICYCLE USA, Suite 120, 190 W. Ostend St., Baltimore MD 21230. (410)539-3399. Fax: (410)539-3496. Editor: John W. Duvall. Circ. 22,000. Estab. 1965. Membership magazine of the League of American Wheelmen. Magazine published 8 times a year. Emphasizes bicycling. Audience consists of avid, well-educated bicyclists of all ages, occupations and sexes. Photo guidelines free with SASE.
Needs: Uses 15-20 photos/issue; all supplied by freelance photographers. Needs photos of travel, scenics and how-to. Cyclists must be shown with helmets. Prefers photos with accompanying manuscript, but will consider without. Model release preferred. Captions required.
Making Contact & Terms: Interested in receiving work from a newer, lesser-known photographers. Send unsolicited photos by mail for consideration. Uses b&w prints and 35mm transparencies. SASE. Reports in 1 month. Offers membership in the organization and sample copies as payment. Credit line given. Buys one-time rights. Previously published work OK.
Tips: "As an advocacy organization, we need photos of bicycle commuting, education and government relations in addition to general interest and travel photos."

BIKEREPORT, Box 8308, Missoula MT 59807. (406)721-1776. Editor: Dan D'Ambrosio. Circ. 25,000. Estab. 1974. Publication of Bikecentennial Association. Magazine published 9 times/year. Emphasizes bicycle touring. Readers are mid-30s, mostly male, professionals. Samples copy free with 9 × 12 SAE and $1 postage. Photo guidelines not available.
Needs: Uses 8 photos/issue; 50% supplied by freelancers. Needs scenics with bicycles. Photos purchased with accompanying ms only. Model release preferred. Captions required.
Making Contact & Terms: Submit portfolio for review. SASE. Reports in 3 weeks. Pays $100/color cover photo; $50/color page rate; $35/b&w page rate. Pays on publication. Credit line given. Buys one-time rights. Simultaneous submissions and previously published work OK.

THE BLACK WRITER, P.O. Box 1030, Chicago IL 60690. (312)995-5195. Editor: Mable Terrell. Publication of International Black Writers Association. Circ. 500. Estab. 1970. Quarterly magazine. Emphasizes current African-American writers. Readers are ages 15-75 and of various occupations. Sample copy free with 9½ × 12 SAE and 90¢ postage.
Needs: Uses 20 photos/issue; all supplied by freelancers. Needs photos of travel and personalities. Model release preferred. Captions required.
Making Contact & Terms: Provide resume, business card, brochure, flyer or tearsheets to be kept on file for possible assignments. SAE. Reports in 1 month. Pays $25/b&w cover photo; $20/b&w inside photo. **Pays on acceptance.** Credit line given. Buys one-time rights. Previously published work OK.
Tips: Looking for "quality photography."

BOWLING MAGAZINE, 5301 S. 76th St., Greendale WI 53129. (414)421-6400. Fax: (414)421-1194. Editor: Bill Vint. Circ. 120,000. Estab. 1938. Published by the American Bowling Congress. Bimonthly. Emphasizes bowling for readers who are bowlers, bowling fans or media. Free sample copy. Photo guidelines with SASE.
Needs: Uses about 20 photos/issue, 1 of which, on the average, is supplied by a freelancer. Provide calling card and letter of inquiry to be kept on file for possible future assignments. "In some cases we like to keep photos. Our staff takes almost all photos as they deal mainly with editorial copy published. Rarely do we have a photo page or need freelance photos. No posed action." Model/property release preferred. Captions required.
Making Contact & Terms: Interested in receiving work from new, lesser-known photographers. Send 5 × 7 or 8 × 10 b&w or color photos by mail for consideration. SASE. Reports in 2 weeks. Pays $20-25/b&w photo; $25-50/color photo. Pays on publication. Credit line given. Buys one-time rights, but photos are kept on file after use. No simultaneous submissions or previously published work.

BULLETIN OF THE ATOMIC SCIENTISTS, Dept. PM, 6042 S. Kimbark, Chicago IL 60637. (312)702-2555. Art Director: Paula Lang. Circ. 25,000. Monthly (except bimonthly in January-February, July-August, 10 issues/year). Emphasizes science and world affairs. "Our specialty is nuclear politics; we regularly present disarmament proposals and analysis of international defense policies. However, the magazine prints more articles on politics and the effects of technology than it does on bombs. The *Bulletin* is *not* a technical physics journal." Readers are "educated, interested in foreign policy, moderate-to-left politically; high income levels; employed in government, academe or research facilities; about 50% are scientists." Sample copy $3.
Needs: Uses about 7-10 photos/issue; "few if any" supplied by freelance photographers. "Our publication is so specialized that we usually must get photos from the insiders in government agencies. However, we are looking for freelance photographers in the Washington DC area."
Making Contact & Terms: Provide resume, business card, brochure, flyer or tearsheets to be kept on file for possible future assignments. "Don't send a manuscript or photos without a preliminary query." SASE. Reports in 2-4 weeks. Photographers are paid by the job; amount of payment is negotiable—pay range is $25-100/b&w photo; $50-200/color photo. Pays on publication. Credit line given. Buys one-time rights. Previously published work OK "on occasion."
Tips: "Make sure you examine several issues of any magazine you consider soliciting. This will save you time and money. Editors weary of reviewing photos and art from contributors with no knowledge of the publication. You'll make a better impression if you know what the magazine's about."

CALIFORNIA LAWYER, Dept. PM, Suite 1210, 1390 Market St., San Francisco CA 94102. (415)252-0500. Editor and Publisher: Ray Reynolds. Art Director: Gordon Smith. Circ. 138,000. Monthly. Emphasizes law/lawyers. Readers are mostly lawyers and judges.
Needs: Uses 12-18 photos/issue. Innovative photos to illustrate stories on topical legal issues. Needs artistic interpretations of lawyers/courts/related issues. Model release required. Captions preferred.
Making Contact & Terms: Query with samples. Send 8×10 glossy b&w prints or 35mm and 2¼×2¼ transparencies by mail for consideration. SASE. Reports in 2 weeks. Pays $650/color cover photo; $100-350 color inside; $75/b&w inside photo. **Pays on acceptance.** Credit line given. Buys one-time rights. Simultaneous submissions OK.
Tips: "We look for an artistic eye; dramatic lighting. Offer new and innovative ways to illustrate legal stories, not simply variations on the scales of justice."

CALIFORNIA NURSE, Suite 670, 1855 Folsom St., San Francisco CA 94103. Managing Editor: Catherine Direen. Circ. 28,000. Estab. 1904. Publication of California Nurses Association. Monthly tabloid. Emphasizes nursing. Readers are adults, male and female nurses. Sample copy free with SASE.
Needs: Uses 15-20 photos/issue; 10% supplied by freelancers. Needs photos of nurses, medical technology and populations served by health professionals, (e.g. elderly, infants, uninsured). Model release and photo descriptions required.
Making Contact & Terms: Send unsolicited 4×5 or 5×7 glossy b&w prints by mail for consideration. Provide resume, business card, brochure, flyer or tearsheets to be kept on file for possible assignments. Phone calls acceptable. SASE. Reports in 3 weeks. Pays $10-50/b&w cover photo; $10/b&w inside photo. Pays on publication. Buys one-time rights. Simultaneous submissions OK.
Tips: "Best choices are sensitive shots of people needing or receiving health care or RNs at work. Send sample photos, well-tailored to individual publication."

CALYPSO LOG, Suite 402, 870 Grumbrier Circle, Chesapeake VA 23320. (804)523-9335. Editor: Mary Batten. Circ. 260,000. Publication of The Cousteau Society. Bimonthly. Emphasizes expedition activities of The Cousteau Society; educational/science articles; environmental activities. Readers are members of The Cousteau Society. Sample copy $2 with 9×12 SAE and 65¢ postage. Photo guidelines free with SASE.
Needs: Uses 10-14 photos/issue; 1-2 supplied by freelancers; 2-3 photos per issue from freelance stock. Preference for underwater creature shots in natural habitats. We review duplicates only. Captions preferred.
Making Contact & Terms: Query with samples and list of stock photo subjects. Send unsolicited photos (duplicates) by mail for consideration. Uses color prints; 35mm and 2¼×2¼ transparencies (duplicates only). SASE. Reports in 5 weeks. Pays $50-200/color photo. Pays on publication. Buys one-time rights and translation rights for our French publication. Previously published work OK.
Tips: Send "sharp, clear images of underwater life/creatures in duplicate form only." In samples, wants to see "photos that tell a story of animals interacting with each other and/or the environment." Also sharp, clear, good composition and color; unusual animals or views of environmental features. Prefers transparencies over prints. "We look for ecological stories, food chain, prey-predator interaction and impact of people on environment. Please request a copy of our publication to familiarize yourself with our style, content and tone and then send samples that best represent underwater and environmental photography."

❦CANADA LUTHERAN, 1512 St. James St., Winnipeg, Manitoba R3H 0L2 Canada. (204)786-6707. Fax: (204)783-7548. Art Director: Darrell Dyck. Editor: Ferdy Baglo. Circ. 32,000. Estab. 1986. Publication of Evangelical Lutheran Church in Canada. Monthly. Emphasizes faith/religious content; Lutheran denomination. Readers are members of the Evangelical Lutheran Church in Canada. Sample copy for $1.50 with 9×12 SAE and $1 postage (Canadian).
Needs: Uses 4-10 photos/issue; most supplied though article contributors; 1 or 2 supplied by freelancers. Needs photos of people (in worship/work/play etc.); scenics.
Making Contact & Terms: Interested in receiving work from newer, lesser-known photographers. Send 5×7 glossy prints or 35mm transparencies by mail for consideration. SASE. Pays $15-50/b&w photo; $40-75/color photo. Pays on publication. Credit line given. Buys one-time rights.
Tips: "Trend toward more men and women in non-stereotypical roles. Do not restrict photo submissions to just the categories you believe the client needs. Give us a pile of shots that show your range. Let us keep them on file—then we will turn to that file each month when we need to illustrate something on short notice."

CEA ADVISOR, Dept. PM, Connecticut Education Association, 21 Oak St., Hartford CT 06106. (203)525-5641. Managing Editor: Michael Lydick. Circ. 30,000. Monthly tabloid. Emphasizes education. Readers are public school teachers. Sample copy free with $1.50 postage.
Needs: Uses about 20 photos/issue; 1 or 2 supplied by freelancers. Needs "classroom scenes, students, school buildings." Model release preferred. Captions preferred.
Making Contact & Terms: Send b&w contact sheet by mail for consideration. Provide resume, business card, brochure, flyer or tearsheets to be kept on file for possible future assignments. Cannot return material. Reports in 1 month. Pays $50/b&w cover photo; $25/b&w inside photo. Pays on publication. Credit line given. Buys all rights. Simultaneous submissions and previously published work OK.

CHESS LIFE, Dept. PM, 186 Route 9W, New Windsor NY 12553. (914)562-8350. Fax: (914)561-CHES. Editor-in-Chief: Glenn Petersen. Art Director: Jami Anson. Circ. 60,000. Publication of the U.S. Chess Federation. Monthly. *Chess Life* covers news of all major national and international tournaments; historical articles, personality profiles, columns of instruction, occasional fiction, humor . . . for the devoted fan of chess. Sample copy and photo guidelines free with SAE and 75¢ postage.
Needs: Uses about 10 photos/issue; 7-8 supplied by freelancers. Needs "news photos from events around the country; shots for personality profiles." Special needs include "Chess Review" section. Model release preferred. Captions preferred.
Making Contact & Terms: Query with samples. Provide business card and tearsheets to be kept on file for possible future assignments. SASE. Reports in "2-4 weeks, depending on when the deadline crunch occurs." Pays $100-200/b&w or color cover photo; $15-25/b&w inside photo; $15-30/hour; $150-250/day. Pays on publication. Credit line given. Buys one-time rights; "we occasionally purchase all rights for stock mug shots." Simultaneous submissions and previously published work OK.
Tips: Using "more color, and more illustrative photography. The photographer's name and date should appear on the back of all photos. 35mm color transparencies are preferred for cover shots." Looks for "clear images, good composition and contrast—with a fresh approach to interest the viewer. Increasing emphasis on strong portraits of chess personalities, especially Americans. Tournament photographs of winning players and key games are in high demand."

CHEVY OUTDOORS, 30400 Van Dyke Ave., Warren MI 48093. (313)574-9100. Art Director: Andrea Stork. Circ. 1,090,000. Publication of the Chevrolet company. Quarterly magazine. Emphasizes outdoor life and travel, recreational vehicles and fishing. Readership consists of men and women of all occupations, ages 20 to 70. Sample copy free with 9×12 SAE and $1.50 postage. Photo guidelines free with SASE.
Needs: Uses 80 photos/issue; 70% supplied by freelance photographers. Needs photos of animal/wildlife shots, travel, scenics. Model release required. Captions required.
Making Contact & Terms: Query with list of stock photo subjects. SASE. Reports in 2-6 weeks. Pays $350-600/b&w page. **Pays on acceptance.** Credit line given. Buys one-time rights. Simultaneous submissions and previously published work OK.
Tips: "Looking for intelligent, well-exposed and insightful outdoor photography. Photographers should have a genuine interest in subject."

The maple leaf before a listing indicates that the market is Canadian.

CHILDHOOD EDUCATION, Suite 315, 11501 Georgia Ave., Wheaton MD 20902. (301)942-2443. Director of Publications/Editor: Lucy Prete Martin. Assistant Editor: Anne Bauer. Circ. 15,000. Estab. 1924. Publication for the Association for Childhood Education International. Bimonthly journal. Emphasizes the education of children from infancy through early adolescence. Readers include teachers, administrators, day-care workers, parents, psychologists, student teachers, etc. Sample copy free with 9×12 SAE and $1.44 postage. Photo guidelines free with SASE.
Needs: Uses 5-10 photos/issue; 2-3 supplied by freelance photographers. Subject matter includes children infancy-14 years in groups or alone, in or out of the classroom, at play, in study groups; boys and girls of all races and in all cities and countries. Wants close-ups of children, unposed. Reviews photos with or without accompanying ms. Special needs include photos of minority children; photos of children from different ethnic groups together in one shot; boys and girls together. Model release required.
Making Contact & Terms: Interested in receiving work from newer, lesser-known photographers. Send unsolicited photos by mail for consideration. Uses 8×10 glossy b&w and color prints and color transparencies. SASE. Reports in 1 month. Pays $75-100/color cover photo; $25-50/b&w inside photo. Pays on publication. Credit line given. Buys one-time rights. Simultaneous submissions and previously published work are discouraged but negotiable.
Tips: "Send pictures of unposed children, please."

CHOSEN PEOPLE MAGAZINE, Dept. PM, 1300 Crossbeam Dr., Charlotte NC 28217. (704)357-9000. Communications Director: Andy Stebbins. Circ. 85,000. Estab. 1906. Publication of the Chosen People Ministries. Monthly. Emphasizes Jewish subjects, Israel. Readers are Christians interested in Israel and the Jewish people. Sample copy free with SASE.
Needs: Uses about 3-4 photos/issue; 3 supplied by freelancers. Needs "scenics of Israel, photos of Jewish customs and traditions." Model release required. Photo captions preferred.
Making Contact & Terms: Interested in receiving work from newer, lesser-known photographers. Query with samples or with list of stock photo subjects. Send 8×10 glossy b&w photos by mail for consideration. Provide resume, business card, brochure, flyer or tearsheets to be kept on file for possible future assignments. SASE. Reports in 3 weeks. Pays $50-100/b&w and color photo. **Pays on acceptance.** Credit line given. Buys one-time rights. Simultaneous submissions OK.
Tips: Wants to see photos of "Israel scenery, Jewish holidays and Jewish culture."

CHRISTIAN HOME & SCHOOL, 3350 E. Paris Ave. SE, Grand Rapids MI 49512. (616)957-1070. Senior Editor: Roger Schmurr. Circ. 51,000. Estab. 1922. Publication of Christian Schools International. Published 6 times a year. Emphasizes Christian family issues. Readers are parents who support Christian education. Sample copy free with 9×12 SAE with 4 first-class stamps. Photo guidelines free with SASE.
Needs: Uses 10-15 photos/issue; 7-10 supplied by freelancers. Needs photos of children, family activities, school scenes. Model release preferred.
Making Contact & Terms: Query with samples. Query with list of stock photo subjects. Send b&w prints or contact sheets by mail for consideration. SASE. Reports in 3 weeks. Pays $125-250/color cover photo; $30/b&w inside photo. Pays on publication. Credit line given. Buys one-time rights. Simultaneous submissions and previously published work OK.
Tips: Assignment work is becoming rare. Freelance stock most often used. "Photographers who allow us to hold duplicate photos for an extended period of time stand more chance of having their photos selected for publication than those who require speedy return of submitted photos."

CIVITAN MAGAZINE, P. O. Box 130744, Birmingham AL 35213-0744. (205)591-8910. Editor: Dorothy Wellborn. Circ. 36,000. Estab. 1920. Publication of Civitan International. Bimonthly magazine. Emphasizes work with mental retardation/developmental disabilities. Readers are men and women, college age to retirement and usually managers or owners of businesses. Sample copy free with 9×12 SAE and 2 first-class stamps. Photo guidelines not available.
Needs: Uses 8-10 photos/issue; 50% supplied by freelancers. Always looking for good cover shots (travel, scenic and how-to's). Model release preferred. Captions preferred.
Making Contact & Terms: Send unsolicited 2¼×2¼ or 4×5 transparencies or b&w prints by mail for consideration. Provide resume, business card, brochure, flyer or tearsheets to be kept on file for possible assignments. Reports in 1 month. Pays $50/color cover photo; $10 b&w inside photo. **Pays on acceptance.** Buys one-time rights. Simultaneous submissions and previously published work OK.

COAL VOICE, % National Coal Association, 1130 17th St. NW, Washington DC 20036. (202)463-2640. Editor: Aundrea Cika. Publication of the National Coal Association. Circ. 15,000. Estab. 1978. Bimonthly magazine. Covers coal and energy issues. Readers are coal producers, major coal consumers, industry representatives and allies, and state and local regulatory/legislature members. Sample copies free upon request.

Needs: Uses 5 photos/issue. Needs photos of technology, people and scenics.
Making Contact & Terms: Arrange personal interview to show portfolio. Query with list of stock photo subjects. Provide resume, business card, brochure, flyer or tearsheets to be kept on file for possible future assignment. NPI; payment varies according to use. Pays on publication. Credit line given. Rights purchased vary. Simultaneous submissions and previously published work OK.
Tips: "Looking for someone who can break through stereotypes and help enhance a misunderstood industry."

COMMERCIAL INVESTMENT REAL ESTATE JOURNAL, Dept. PM, Suite 600, 430 N. Michigan Ave., Chicago IL 60611. (312)321-4464. Fax: (312)321-4530. Editor: Lorene Norton Palm. Circ. 9,000. Estab. 1983. Publication of Commercial-Investment Real Estate Institute. Quarterly journal. Emphasizes commercial real estate brokerage and consulting. Readers are commercial real estate brokers, consultants, developers, mortgage bankers, attorneys. Sample copy free with 9 × 12 SAE and $1.45 postage.
Needs: Uses 3-6 photos/issue; all supplied by freelance photographers. Photo needs vary; may be office scenes, buildings, high-resolution close-ups for special effects, etc.
Making Contact & Terms: Provide resume, business card, brochure, flyer or tearsheets to be kept on file for possible assignments. Pays $800-900/b&w cover photo; $150-250/b&w inside photo. **Pays on acceptance.** Credit line given. Buys first N.A. serial rights. Previously published work OK.

COMMUNICATION WORLD, Suite 600, One Hallidie Plaza, San Francisco CA 94102. (415)433-3400. Editor: Gloria Gordon. Circ. 15,000. Estab. 1969. Publication of International Association of Business Communicators. Monthly magazine. Emphasizes public relations, business and organizational communications. Readers are members in corporate communication and consultants, ages 30+.
Needs: Uses 2-3 photos/issue; all supplied by freelancers. Needs photos that reflect communication in corporate atmosphere. Model release preferred. Captions required.
Making Contact & Terms: Arrange a personal interview to show portfolio. Query with resume of credits. Submit portfolio for review. Provide resume, business card, brochure, flyer or tearsheets to be kept on file for possible assignments. SASE. Pays $350/color cover photo; $250/b&w cover photo; $275+/color inside photo; $100/b&w inside photo; $250/color page rate. Pays on publication. Credit line given. Buys one-time rights. Simultaneous submissions and previously published work OK.

COMPANY: A MAGAZINE OF THE AMERICAN JESUITS, Dept. PM, 3441 N. Ashland Ave., Chicago IL 60657. (312)281-1534. Fax: (312)281-2667. Editor: E.J. Mattimoe. Circ. 128,000. Estab. 1983. Published by the Jesuits (Society of Jesus). Quarterly magazine. Emphasizes people; "a human interest magazine about people helping people." Sample copy free with 9 × 12 SAE and 95¢ postage. Photo guidelines free with SASE.
Needs: All photos supplied by freelancers. Needs photo-stories of Jesuit and allied ministries and projects, only photos related to Jesuit works. Photos purchased with or without accompanying ms. Model release required. Captions required.
Making Contact & Terms: Interested in receiving work from newer, lesser-known photographers. Query with samples. Provide resume, business card, brochure, flyer or tearsheets to be kept on file for possible future assignments. SASE. Reports in 1 month. Pays $300/color cover photo; $100-400/job. Pays on publication. Credit line given. Buys one-time rights; negotiable.
Tips: "Avoid large-group, 'smile-at-camera' photos. We are interested in people photographs that tell a story in a sensitive way—the eye-catching look that something is happening."

THE CONSTRUCTION SPECIFIER, Dept. PM, 601 Madison St., Alexandria VA 22314. (703)684-0300. Fax: (703)684-0465. Associate Editor: Kristine Kessler. Circ. 20,000. Estab. 1949. Publication of the Construction Specifications Institute. Monthly magazine. Emphasizes construction. Readers are architects and engineers in commercial construction. Sample copy free with 8½ × 11 SASE and 1 first-class stamp. Photo guidelines not available.
Needs: Uses 40 photos/issue; 15% supplied by freelance photographers; 85% from freelance stock. Needs architectural and construction shots. Model release required. Captions required.
Making Contact & Terms: Provide resume, business card, brochure, flyer or tearsheets to be kept on file for possible assignments. SASE. Pays $25-200/b&w photo; $50-400/color photo. Pays on publication. Credit line given. Buys one-time rights. Simultaneous submissions OK if in unrelated field. Previously published work OK.
Tips: Wants to see "photos depicting commercial construction: jobsite shots."

CURRENTS, Voice of the National Organization for River Sports, Box 6847, 314 N. 20th St., Colorado Springs CO 80904. (719)579-8759. Fax: (719)576-6238. Editor: Greg Moore. Circ. 10,000. Estab. 1979. Quarterly magazine. Membership publication of National Organization for River Sports, for canoeists, kayakers and rafters. Emphasizes river conservation and river access, also techniques of river running. Sample copy $1. Writer's and photographer's guidelines free with #10 SASE.

Martin McHugh, managing editor for Company Magazine, says this issue deals with the Jesuits' role in medicine and the cover photo tells viewers what the Jesuits are all about—compassion; professional care; healing of minds, hearts and bodies. The toy box in the background also adds to the photo by showing that the child is in caring hands.

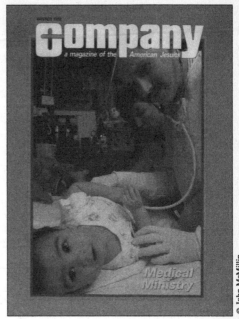

© John McMillin

Needs: Buys 10 photos/issue; 25% assigned, 75% unsolicited. Photo essay/photo feature (on rivers of interest to river runners). Need features on rivers that are in the news because of public works projects, use regulations, wild and scenic consideration or access prohibitions. Sport newsphotos of canoeing, kayaking, rafting and other forms of (whitewater) river paddling, especially photos of national canoe and kayak races; nature/river subjects, conservation-oriented; travel (river runs of interest to a nation-wide membership). Wants on a regular basis close-up action shots of whitewater river running and shots of dams in progress, signs prohibiting access. Especially needs for next year shots of whitewater rivers that are threatened by dams showing specific stretch to be flooded and dam-builders at work. No "panoramas of river runners taken from up on the bank or the edge of a highway. We must be able to see their faces, front-on shots. We always need photos of the twenty (most) popular whitewater river runs around the US." Photos purchased with or without accompanying ms. "We are looking for articles on whitewater rivers that are in the news regionally and nationally—for example, rivers endangered by damming; access is limited by government decree; rivers being considered for wild and scenic status; rivers offering a setting for unusual expeditions and runs; and rivers having an interest beyond the mere fact that they can be paddled. Also articles interviewing experts in the field about river techniques, equipment and history." Captions required.

Making Contact & Terms: Interested in receiving work from newer, lesser-known photographers. Send material or photocopies of work by mail for consideration. "We need to know of photographers in various parts of the country." Provide tearsheets or photocopies of work to be kept on file for possible future assignments. Uses 5×7 and 8×10 glossy b&w prints. Occasional color prints. Query before submitting color transparencies. SASE. Reports in 2 weeks. Pays $20-60/b&w print or color prints or transparencies; $50-150 text/photo package; $35 minimum/interview article. Credit line given. Buys one-time rights. Simultaneous submissions and previously published work OK if labeled clearly as such.

Tips: "Needs more squirt boating photos, photos of women and opening canoeing photos. Looks for close-up action shots of whitewater river runners in kayaks, rafts, canoes or dories. Little or no red. Show faces of paddlers. Photos must be clear and sharp. Tell us where the photo was taken—name of river, state and name of rapid, if possible."

❀ **CYCLING: BC**, Dept. PM, 332-1367 W. Broadway, Vancouver, British Columbia V6H 4A9 Canada. (604)737-3034. Fax: (604)738-7175. Office Manager: Betty Third. Circ. 2,600. Estab. 1974. Monthly newsletter. Publication of Bicycling Association of British Columbia. Emphasizes bicycling. Readers are 14-75 years old, male and female. Sample copy free with #10 SAE and IRC.

Needs: Uses 1 photo/issue; supplied by freelancer. Needs action photos of bicycling. Special photo needs include all photos for newsletters, promo materials.
Making Contact & Terms: Send b&w and color prints by mail for consideration. SAE and IRC. No payment. Reports in 2 weeks. Credit line given. Previously published work OK.
Tips: Bicycling Association of British Columbia asks for donations of photos. Will give photographer credit and send sample copy of publication.

DEFENDERS, 1244 19th St. NW, Washington DC 20036. (202)659-9510. Fax: (202)659-0680. Editor: James G. Deane. Circ. 73,000. Membership publication of Defenders of Wildlife. Quarterly magazine. Emphasizes wildlife and wildlife habitat. Sample copy free with 9 × 12½ SAE and $1.44 postage. Photo guidelines free with SASE.
Needs: Uses 35 or more photos/issue; "almost all" from freelancers. Captions required.
Making Contact & Terms: Query with list of stock photo subjects. In portfolio or samples, wants to see "wildlife group action and behaviorial shots in preference to static portraits. High technical quality." SASE. Reports ASAP. Pays $50-100/b&w photo; $75-450/color photo. Pays on publication. Credit line given. Buys one-time rights.
Tips: "*Defenders* focuses heavily on endangered species and destruction of their habitats, wildlife refuges and wildlife management issues, primarily North American, but also some foreign. Images must be sharp. Cover images usually must be vertical, able to take the logo up top, and be arresting and *simple*. Think twice before submitting anything but low speed (preferably Kodachrome) transparencies."

DIVERSION MAGAZINE, Dept. PM, 60 E. 42nd St., New York NY 10165. (212)297-9600. Fax: (212)808-9079. Photo Researcher: Michele Hadlow. Circ. 176,000. Monthly magazine. Emphasizes travel. Readers are doctors/physicians. Sample copy free with SASE.
Needs: Uses varying number of photos/issue; all supplied by freelancers. Needs a variety of subjects, "mostly worldwide travel. Hotels, restaurants and people." Model/property release preferred. Captions preferred; include precise locations.
Making Contact & Terms: Query with list of stock photo subjects. Keeps samples on file. SASE. Reports in 3 weeks. Pays $350/color cover photo; $135/quarter color page inside photo; $125/quarter page b&w inside; $225/color full page rate; $200/b&w full page; $200-250/day. Pays on publication. Credit line given. Buys one-time rights. Simultaneous submissions and previously published work OK.
Tips: "Send updated stock list and photo samples regularly."

THE DOLPHIN LOG, Suite 402, 870 Greenbrier Circle, Chesapeake VA 23320. (803)523-9335. Editor: Liz Foley. Circ. 105,000. Estab. 1981. Publication of The Cousteau Society, Inc., a nonprofit organization. Bimonthly magazine. Emphasizes "ocean and water-related subject matter for children ages 7 to 15." Sample copy $2 with 9 × 12 SAE and 75¢ postage. Photo guidelines free with SASE.
Needs: Uses about 20 photos/issue; 10 supplied by freelancers; 10% stock. Needs "selections of images of individual creatures or subjects, such as architects and builders of the sea, how sea animals eat, the smallest and largest things in the sea, the different forms of tails in sea animals, resemblances of sea creatures to other things. Also excellent potential cover shots or images which elicit curiosity, humor or interest." Model release required if person is recognizable. Captions preferred.
Making Contact & Terms: Query with samples or list of stock photos. Send 35mm transparencies or b&w contact sheets by mail for consideration. Send duplicates only. SASE. Reports in 2 months. Pays $50/b&w photo; $50-200/color photo. Pays on publication. Credit line given. Buys one-time rights and worldwide translation rights. Simultaneous and previously published submissions OK.
Tips: Prefers to see "rich color, sharp focus and interesting action of water-related subjects" in samples. "No assignments are made. A large amount is staff-shot. However, we use a fair amount of freelance photography, usually pulled from our files, approx. 45-50%. Stock photos purchased only when an author's sources are insufficient or we have need for a shot not in file. These are most often hard-to-find creatures of the sea." To break in, "send a good submission of dupes which are in keeping with our magazine's tone/content; be flexible in allowing us to hold slides for consideration."

DUCKS UNLIMITED, One Waterfowl Way, Memphis TN 38120. (901)758-3825. Production Coordinator: Diane Harvey. Circ. 520,000. Estab. 1937. Association publication of Ducks Unlimited. Bimonthly magazine. Emphasizes waterfowl conservation. Readers are professional males, ages 40-50. Sample copy $3. Guidelines free with SASE.
Needs: Uses 20-30 photos/issue; 70% supplied by freelance photographers. Needs wildlife shots (waterfowl/waterfowling), scenics and personalities. Special photo needs include dynamic shots of waterfowl interacting in natural habitat.
Making Contact & Terms: Send 20-40 35mm or larger transparencies with ideas for consideration. SASE. Reports in 1 month. Pays $350/color cover photo; $60-225/color inside photo; $150-300/day plus expenses for assignments; $500/photo essay. **Pays on acceptance.** Credit line given. Buys one-time

rights plus permission to reprint in our Mexican and Canadian publications. Previously published work OK.

*EASTERN CHALLENGE, P.O. Box 14866, Reading PA 19612-4866. (215)375-0300. Fax: (215)375-6862. Editor: Dr. Osborne Buchanan, Jr.. Circ. 20,000. Estab. 1967. Publications of the International Missions, Inc. Quarterly magazine. Emphasizes "Church-planting ministry in a number of countries." Sample copy free with SASE.
Needs: Uses 2 photos/issue. Needs photos of scenics and personalties. Reviews photos with or without accompanying ms. Model/property release preferred. Captions preferred.
Making Contact & Terms: Interested in receiving work from newer, lesser-known photographers. Send unsolicited photos by mail for consideration. Provide resume, business card, brochure, flyer or tearsheets to be kept on file for possible assignments. Keeps samples on file. SASE. Reports in 1 month. Pays "minimal or nominal amount; organization is nonprofit." Pays on publication. Credit line given. Buys all rights; negotiable. Simultaneous submissions and/or previously published work OK.
Tips: Looks for "color and contrast; relevance to program of organization."

THE ELKS MAGAZINE, 425 W. Diversey, Chicago IL 60614. (312)528-4500. Editor: Fred D. Oakes. Circ. 1.5 million. Estab. 1922. Publication of the B.P.O. Elks of the U.S. Publishes 10 times a year. Emphasizes general interest including travel, history, nostalgia, sports, business and self-improvement. Readers are 50+, 54% male, 46% female, broad occupational spectrum. Sample copy free with 9×12 SAE and 85¢ postage.
Needs: "We frequently use scenics for cover." Model release preferred. Captions preferred.
Making Contact & Terms: Interested in receiving work from newer, lesser-known photographers. SASE. Reports in 3 weeks. Pays $350-450/color cover photo. **Pays on acceptance.** Credit line given. Buys first N.A. serial rights. Simultaneous submissions OK.

ENVIRONMENTAL ACTION, Suite 600, 6930 Carroll Ave., Takoma Park MD 20910. (301)891-1106. Fax: (301)891-2218. Editor: Barbara Ruben. Circ. 14,000. Estab. 1970. Association publication of Environmental Action, Inc. Quarterly magazine. Emphasizes environmental subjects for activists of all ages. Sample copies $2.50.
Needs: Uses up to 10 photos/issue; 40% supplied by freelancers. Needs photos that "illustrate environmental problems and issues, including solid waste, toxic waste and energy." Model/property release preferred. Captions preferred.
Making Contact & Terms: Query with resume of credits. Send stock photo list. Provide resume, business card, brochure, flyer or tearsheet to be kept on file for possible assignments. Does not keep samples on file. Cannot return material. Reports in 1 month. Pays $40-150/b&w cover photo; $25-75/b&w inside photo. Pays on publication. Credit line given. Buys one-time rights. Simultaneous submissions and previously published work OK.
Tips: "We only publish in b&w, but we will consider both color and b&w original photos."

EXECUTIVE FEMALE, 4th Floor, 127 W. 24th St., New York NY 10011. (212)645-0770. Editor-in-Chief: Basia Hellwig. Art Director: Maxine Davidowitz. Circ. 250,000. Publication of National Association for Female Executives. Bimonthly. Emphasizes career advancement, problems/solutions in work place. Readers are "middle to upper level managers looking to move up in career. Also entrepreneurs and women starting or expanding small businesses."
Needs: Uses about 20 photos/issue; all assigned by the art director. Very rarely uses unsolicited work.
Making Contact & Terms: Send non-returnable samples of work to be kept on file for possible future assignments. Pays on publication. Credit line given. Buys one-time rights.
Tips: "Looks for very high quality, experienced portrait photographers throughout the country for assignment purposes only. Does not use generic stock photos of women in business settings."

FAMILY MOTOR COACHING, Dept. PM, 8291 Clough Pike, Cincinnati OH 45244. (513)474-3622. Editor: Pamela Wisby Kay. Circ. 95,000. Estab. 1963. Publication of Family Motor Coach Association. Monthly. Emphasizes motor homes. Readers are members of national association of motor home owners. Sample copy $2.50. Photo guidelines free with SASE.
Needs: Uses about 45-50 photos/issue; 40-45 supplied by freelance photographers. Each issue includes varied subject matter—primarily needs travel and scenic shots and how-to material. Photos purchased with accompanying ms only. Model release preferred. Captions required.
Making Contact & Terms: Query with resume of credits. SASE. Reports in 4-6 weeks. Pays $100-500/text/photo package. **Pays on acceptance.** Credit line given if requested. Prefers first N.A. rights, but will consider one-time rights on photos *only*.

FELLOWSHIP, Box 271, Nyack NY 10960. (914)358-4601. Fax: (914)358-4924. Contact: Editor. Circ. 8,500. Estab. 1935. Publication of the Fellowship of Reconciliation. Publishes 32-page b&w magazine 8 times/year. Emphasizes peace-making, social justice, nonviolent social change. Readers are religious peace fellowships—interfaith pacifists. Sample copy free with SASE.

Needs: Uses 8-10 photos/issue; 90% supplied by freelancers. Needs stock photos of monuments, civil disobedience, demonstrations—Middle East, South Africa, prisons, anti-nuclear, children, farm crisis, USSR. Also natural beauty and scenic; b&w only. Captions required.
Making Contact & Terms: Provide resume, business card, brochure, flyer or tearsheets to be kept on file for possible future assignments. "Call on specs." SASE. Reports in 3 weeks. Pays $25/b&w cover photo; $13.50/b&w inside photo. Pays on publication. Credit line given. Buys one-time rights. Simultaneous submissions and previously published work OK.
Tips: "You must want to make a contribution to peace movements. Money is simply token (our authors contribute without tokens)."

FFA NEW HORIZONS, 5632 Mount Vernon Memorial Hwy., Alexandria VA 22309-0160. (703)360-3600. Fax: (703)360-5524. Associate Editor: Lawinna McGary. Circ. 400,000. Estab. 1953. Publication of the National Future Farmers of America organization. Bimonthly magazine. Emphasizes agriculture, careers and youth interest. Readers are agriculture students, ages 14-21. Sample copy free. Photo guidelines free with SASE.
Needs: Uses 45 photos/issue; 18 supplied by freelancers. "We need exciting shots of our FFA members in action." Has continuing need for national coverage. Model/property release preferred. Photo captions required; include names, hometowns.
Making Contact & Terms: Provide resume, business card, brochure, flyer or tearsheets to be kept on file for possible assignments. Keeps samples on file. SASE. Reports in 1 month. Pays $100/color cover photo; $35/color inside photo; $20/b&w inside photo. **Pays on acceptance.** Credit line given. Buys one-time rights.
Tips: "We want to see energy and a sense that the photographer knows how to work with teenagers." Contact editor before doing any work. "We have specific needs and need good shooters."

FLORIDA WILDLIFE, 620 S. Meridian St., Tallahassee FL 32399-1600. (904)488-5563. Fax: (904)488-6988. Editor: Andrea Blount. Circ. 29,000. Estab. 1947. Publication of the Florida Game & Fresh Water Fish Commission. Bimonthly magazine. Emphasizes wildlife, hunting, fishing, conservation. Readers are wildlife lovers, hunters and fishermen. Sample copy $2.50. Photo guidelines free with SASE.
Needs: Uses about 20-40 photos/issue; 75% supplied by freelance photojournalists. Needs Florida fishing and hunting, all flora and fauna of southeastern US; how-to; covers and inside illustration. Do not feature products in photographs. No alcohol or tobacco. Special needs include hunting and fishing activities in Florida scenes; showing ethical and enjoyable use of outdoor resources. "Must be able to ID species and/or provide accurate natural history information with materials." Model release preferred. Captions required; include location and species.
Making Contact & Terms: Interested in receiving work from newer, lesser-known photographers. Query with samples. Send "35mm color transparencies, but we use some b&w enlarged prints" by mail for consideration. "Do not send negatives." SASE. Keeps materials on file, or will review and return if requested. Pays $50-75/color back cover; $100/color front cover; $20-50/b&w or color inside photo. Pays on publication. Credit line given. Buys one-time rights; "other rights are sometimes negotiated." Simultaneous submissions OK "but we prefer originals over duplicates." Previously published work OK but must be mentioned when submitted.
Tips: "Study back issues to determine what we buy from freelancers (no salt water species as a rule, etc.) Use flat slide mounting pages or individual sleeves. Show us your best. Annual photography contest often introduces us to good freelancers. Rules printed in March-April or May-June issue. Contest form must accompany entry; available in magazine or by writing/calling; winners receive honorarium and winning entries are printed in Sept.-Oct. and Nov.-Dec. issues."

FOCUS, Dept. PM, Owens-Corning Fiberglas, Toledo OH 43659. (419)248-8000. Fax: (419)241-5210. Editor: Bill Hamilton. Circ. 23,000. Estab. 1987. Monthly tabloid. For employees of Owens-Corning Fiberglas. Free sample copy.
Needs: Works with 12 photographers annually; 100% assigned. Captions required; include correctly spelled names. "We assign photo jobs based on our needs. We do not use unsolicited material. We use photojournalism; photography that tells a story. We do not use contrived, posed shots."

The First Markets Index preceding the General Index in the back of this book provides the names of those companies/publications interested in receiving work from newer, lesser-known photographers.

Making Contact & Terms: Query first with resume of credits. "Send photocopies of shots you think show your talent as a visual communicator." Uses 8×10 b&w glossy prints; must send negatives. NPI. Buys all rights.

GOLF COURSE MANAGEMENT, Dept. PM, 1421 Research Park Dr., Lawrence KS 66049-3859. (913)841-2240. Fax: (913)832-4490. Editor: Clay Loyd. Estab. 1926. Circ. 22,000. Publication of the Golf Course Superintendents Association of America. Monthly. Emphasizes "golf course maintenance/management." Readers are "golf course superintendents and managers." Sample copy free with 9×12 SAE and $4 postage. Photo guidelines free with SASE.
Needs: Uses about 25 photos/issue; 1-5 supplied by freelance photographers. Needs "scenic shots of famous golf courses, good composition, unusual holes dramatically portrayed." Also, golf course construction, maintenance, and renovation photos. Model release required. Captions preferred.
Making Contact & Terms: Query with samples. Provide business card, brochure, flyer or tearsheets to be kept on file for possible future assignments. SASE. Reports in 3 weeks. Pays $125-250/color cover photo. **Pays on acceptance.** Credit line given. Buys one-time rights.
Tips: Prefers to see "good color, unusual angles/composition for vertical format cover."

GREEN BAY PACKER YEARBOOK, P.O. Box 1773, Green Bay WI 54305. (414)435-5100. Publisher: John Wemple. Sample copy free with 9×12 SASE.
Needs: Needs photos of Green Bay Packer football action shots in NFL cities other than Green Bay. Captions preferred.
Making Contact & Terms: Query with resume of credits. Query with samples. Provide resume, business card, brochure, flyer or tearsheets to be kept on file for possible future assignments. Works with freelance photographers on assignment basis only. SASE. Reports in 2 weeks. Pays $50 maximum/color photo. Pays on acceptance or receipt of invoice. Credit line given on table of contents page. Buys all rights.
Tips: "We are looking for Green Bay Packer pictures when they play in other NFL cities—action photos. Contact me directly." Looks for "the ability to capture action in addition to the unusual" in photos.

THE GREYHOUND REVIEW, P.O. Box 543, Abilene KS 67410. (913)263-4660. Contact: Gary Guccione or Tim Horan. Circ. 7,000. Publication of the National Greyhound Association. Monthly. Emphasizes greyhound racing and breeding. Readers are greyhound owners and breeders. Sample copy with SAE and 2.50 postage.
Needs: Uses about 10 photos/issue; 2 supplied by freelance photographers. Needs "anything pertinent to the greyhound that would be of interest to greyhound owners." Captions required.
Making Contact & Terms: Query first. After response, send b&w or color prints and contact sheets by mail for consideration. Submit portfolio for review. Provide resume, business card, brochure, flyer or tearsheets to be kept on file for possible future assignments. Can return unsolicited material if requested. Reports within 1 month. Pays $75/color cover photo; $10-50/b&w; and $25-100/color inside photo. **Pays on acceptance.** Credit line given. Buys one-time and N.A. rights. Simultaneous submissions and previously published work OK.
Tips: "We look for human-interest or action photos involving greyhounds. No muzzles, please, unless the greyhound is actually racing. When submitting photos for our cover, make sure there's plenty of cropping space on all margins around your photo's subject; full bleeds on our cover are preferred."

GUERNSEY BREEDERS' JOURNAL, Dept. PM, P.O. Box 666, Reynoldsburg OH 43068-0666. (614)864-2409. Co-Editors: Becky Goodwin and Sheri Spelman. Circ. 2,200. Publication of American Guernsey Association. Magazine published 10 times a year. Emphasizes Guernsey dairy cattle, dairy cattle management. Readership consists of male and female dairymen, 20-70 years of age. Sample copy free with 8½×11 SASE.
Needs: Uses 40-100 photos/issue; uses less than 5% of freelance photos. Needs scenic photos featuring Guernsey cattle. Model release preferred. Captions preferred.
Making Contact & Terms: Query with resume of credits, business card, brochure, flyer or tearsheets to be kept on file for possible assignments. SASE. Reports in 1 month. Pays $100/color cover photo and $50/b&w cover photo. Pays on publication. Credit line given. Buys all rights; negotiable. Simultaneous submissions and previously published work OK.

HICALL, Church School Literature Department, 1445 Boonville Ave., Springfield MO 65802. (417)862-2781. Editor: Deanna S. Harris. Circ. 80,000. Estab. 1936. Publication of The General Council of the Assemblies of God. Thirteen weekly, 8-page issues published quarterly. Readers are primarily high school students (but also junior high). Sample copy free with 6×9 SAE and 50¢ postage. Photo guidelines free with SASE.

Needs: Uses 10-20 photos/quarter; 95% from freelance stock. Does not assign. Needs photos of teens in various moods (joy, loneliness, surprise). Some scenics used, including teens in the photo; high school settings and activities. Reviews photos with or without accompanying ms. Model release preferred.

Making Contact & Terms: Interested in receiving work from newer, lesser-known photographers. Send 8×10 glossy b&w prints; 35mm, 2¼×2¼ and 4×5 transparencies by mail for consideration. SASE. Pays $35-50/b&w photo; $50-100/color photo. **Pays on acceptance.** Credit line given. Buys one-time rights. Simultaneous submissions and previously published work OK.

Tips: Wants to see "sharp, clear, colorful, usually close-up shots of teens involved in various activities and with other people." For submission, wants good "composition and contrast of teens working, playing, eating, partying, relaxing, at school, home, church, etc. Also, mood shots, closeups." Be able to show emotion in subjects.

HISTORIC PRESERVATION, 1785 Massachusetts Ave. NW, Washington DC 20036. (202)673-4042. Art Director: Jeff Roth. Circ. 224,000. Publication of National Trust for Historic Preservation. Bimonthly. Emphasizes historic homes, towns, neighborhoods, restoration. Readers are upper income with an average age in the fifties. Also restoration professionals, architects, etc. Sample copy $2.50 with 9×12 SASE. Photo guidelines free with SASE.

Needs: Uses about 80 photos/issue; almost all supplied by freelancers. Assigns photos of historic homes, restoration in progress, exteriors and interiors. Needs strong photo portfolio ideas, b&w or color, relating to the preservation of buildings, craftspeople, interiors, furniture, etc. Using an increasing number of environmental portraits. "Last page department, 'Observed,' in each issue features a single, artful photo (color or b&w) of any subject that has something to do with historic preservation. Examples: a building that has since been razed; a special building saved from wrecking ball; a beautiful restoration; photographic record of some preservation controversy. The overriding requirement is that the photo be artful/stunning/thought-provoking." Model release required. Property release preferred. Captions preferred.

Making Contact & Terms: Arrange a personal interview to show portfolio. Query with samples. SASE. Reports in 1 month. Pays $50-200/b&w or color photo; $300-500/day. Other terms negotiable. **Pays on acceptance.** Credit line given. Buys first N.A. serial rights and one-time rights; negotiable.

Tips: Prefers to see "interestingly or naturally lit architectural interiors and exteriors. Environmental portraits, artfully done. Become familiar with our magazine. Suggest suitable story ideas. Will use stock when applicable."

HOOF BEATS, Dept. PM, 750 Michigan Ave., Columbus OH 43215. (614)224-2291. Fax: (614)228-1385. Executive Editor: Dean Hoffman. Design/Production Manager: Jenny Gilbert. Circ. 24,000. Estab. 1933. Publication of the US Trotting Association. Monthly. Emphasizes harness racing. Readers are participants in the sport of harness racing. Sample copy free.

Needs: Uses about 30 photos/issue; about 20% supplied by freelancers. Needs "artistic or striking photos that feature harness horses for covers; other photos on specific horses and drivers by assignment only."

Making Contact & Terms: Query with samples. SASE. Reports in 3 weeks. Pays $25-150/b&w photo; $50-200/color photo; $150 + /color cover photo; freelance assignments negotiable. **Pays on publication.** Credit line given if requested. Buys one-time rights. Simultaneous submissions OK.

Tips: "We look for photos with unique perspective and that display unusual techniques or use of light. Send query letter first. Know the publication and its needs before submitting. Be sure to shoot pictures of harness horses only, not Thoroughbred or riding horses." There is "more artistic use of b&w photography instead of color. More use of fill-flash in personality photos. We always need good night racing action or creative photography."

HORSE SHOW MAGAZINE, % AHSA, 220 E. 42nd St., New York NY 10017-5876. (212)972-2472, ext. 250. Fax: (212)983-7286. Editor: Kathleen Fallon. Circ. 57,000. Estab. 1937. Publication of National Equestrian Federation of US. Monthly magazine. Emphasizes horses and show trade. Majority of readers are upscale women, median age 31.

Needs: Uses up to 25 photos/issue; most are supplied by equine photographers; freelance 100% on assignment only. Needs shots of competitions. Reviews photos with or without accompanying ms. Especially looking for "excellent color cover shots" in the coming year. Model release required. Property release preferred. Captions required; include name of owner, rider, name of event, date held, horse and summary of accomplishments.

Making Contact & Terms: Interested in receiving work from newer, lesser-known photographers. Arrange personal interview to show portfolio. Cannot return material. Reports in 1-2 weeks. Pays $200/color or b&w cover photo; $20/color and b&w inside photo. **Pays on acceptance.** Credit line given. Buys one-time rights; negotiable. Previously published work OK.

Tips: "Get best possible action shots. Call to set up interview. Call to see if we need coverage of an event."

HR MAGAZINE, Dept. PM, 606 N. Washington St., Alexandria VA 22314. (703)548-3440. Publisher/ Editor: John T. Adams III. Art Director: Caroline Foster. Circ. 45,000. Estab. 1956. Association publication of SHRM. Monthly magazine. Emphasizes human resource management. Readers are human resource professionals. Sample copy $7.50.

Needs: Uses 10-25 photos/issue; 90% supplied by freelance photographers on assignment. Needs photos of worklife situations—software use, technology, work environments, human resource or personnel situations/issues. Model release preferred. Captions preferred.

Making Contact & Terms: Query with samples and list of stock photo subjects; provide resume, business card, brochure, flyer or tearsheets to be kept on file for possible future assignments. Cannot return material. Reports in 2 weeks. Pays $600/color cover photo. Also pays $300-800/day. **Pays on acceptance.** Credit line given. Buys one-time reproduction world rights. Previously published work OK.

Tips: SHRM also publishes a monthly newspaper that uses b&w photos, *HRNews.* Editor: Ceel Pasternak. Art Director: Caroline Foster. In samples, looks for corporate portraits on location.

HSUS NEWS, 700 Professional Dr., Gaithersburg MD 20879-3418. Art Director: T. Tilton. Circ. 500,000. Estab. 1954. Publication of The Humane Society of the US association. Quarterly magazine. Emphasizes animals. Sample copy free with 10×14 SASE.

Needs: Uses 60 photos/issue. Needs photos of animal/wildlife shots. Model release required.

Making Contact & Terms: Query with list of stock photo subjects. Send unsolicited transparencies by mail for consideration. Provide resume, business card, brochure, flyer or tearsheets to be kept on file for possible assignments. Reports in 3 weeks. Pays $300/color cover photo; $225/color inside photo; $150/b&w inside photo. **Pays on acceptance.** Credit line given. Buys one-time rights. Previously published work OK.

Tips: To break in, "don't pester us. Be professional with your submissions."

"IN THE FAST LANE", ICC National Headquarters, 2001 Pittston Ave., Scranton PA 18505. (717)347-5839. Editor: D.M. Crispino. Circ. 2,000+. Publication of the International Camaro Club. Bimonthly, 20-page newsletter. Emphasizes camaro car shows, events, cars, stories, etc. Readers are auto enthusiasts/Camaro exclusively. Sample copy $1.

Needs: Uses 20-24 photos/issue; 90% assigned. Needs Camaro-oriented photos only. "At this time we are looking for photographs and stories on the Camaro Pace cars 1967, 1969, 1982 and the Camaro 228's, 1967-1972." Reviews photos with accompanying ms only. Model release required. Captions required.

Making Contact & Terms: Send 3½×5 and larger b&w or color prints by mail for consideration. SASE. Reports in 2 weeks. Pays $5-20 for text/photo package. Pays on publication. Credit line given. Buys one-time rights. Previously published work OK.

Tips: "We need quality photos that put you at the track, in the race or in the midst of the show. Magazine is bimonthly; timeliness is even more important than with monthly."

INTERNATIONAL OLYMPIC LIFTER, Box 65855, 3602 Eagle Rock, Los Angeles CA 90065. (213)257-8762. Editor: Bob Hise II. Circ. 1,000. Estab. 1973. An international publication. Bimonthly magazine. Emphasizes Olympic-style weightlifting. Readers are athletes, coaches administrators enthusiasts of all ages. Sample copy $4.50 and 5 first-class stamps.

Needs: Uses 20 or more photos/issue; all supplied by freelancers. Needs photos of weightlifting action. Reviews photos with or without ms. Captions preferred.

Making Contact & Terms: Send unsolicited photos by mail for consideration. Send 5×7, 8×10 b&w prints. Does not keep samples on file. SASE. Reports in 1-2 weeks. Pays $25/b&w cover photo; $2-10/b&w inside photo. **Pays on acceptance.** Credit line given. Rights negotiable.

Tips: "Good, clear, b&w still and action photos of (preferably outstanding) olympic-style (overhead/ lifting) weightlifters. Must know sport of weightlifting, not bodybuilding or powerlifting."

*IPPL NEWS, P.O. Box 766, Summerville SC 29484. (803)871-2280. Chairwoman: Shirley McGreal. Circ. 13,000. Estab. 1973. Publication of International Primate Protection League. Quarterly magazine. Emphasizes non-human primates in wild and captivity. Readers are members of IPPL. Sample copy free with 9×12 SASE.

Needs: Uses 15-20 photos/issue; 50% supplied by freelancers. Primates covered in stories, and shots for cover. Reviews photos with or without ms. Captions preferred; include species, identification, location of shot.

Execution is Everything in a Competitive Market

In athletics, coaches look for players who want to take control when a game is tight—a baseball player who gets the hit when his team needs it or a basketball player who can score the winning basket as time runs out. Just as coaches want players who can execute, magazines are looking for the same thing from photographers. "I think one of the reasons people at *Time* like me is that they know they can depend on me," says photographer Mark Downey of Alameda, California.

Mark Downey

Downey has an impressive list of credits, which includes top magazines such as *Newsweek, National Geographic* and *U.S. News and World Report.* He has had numerous gallery exhibitions and published photo essays, and he often teaches photojournalism courses at California State University, Hayward.

As a professor, Downey tells students of his experiences with the hope that they can succeed in a very competitive marketplace. He often emphasizes the fact that they must have the drive to be photographers. "They really have to be very clear about that decision," he says. "There are so many more photographers than there were five years ago. Given the competition, I don't think you're going to be real successful if you don't have that passion and love what you do."

A passion for photography helps Downey maintain a schedule in which he travels across the globe on assignments for editors. He has spent time in the Philippines and Morocco, and in Guatemala, where it once took some fast talking and a little luck to complete an assignment for *Time.*

He was under a tight deadline and had to get unprocessed film from the Central American country to an editor in New York City. There was a flight embargo, and, in order to make deadline, he had to slip past immigration officials at the airport and convince a very suspicious American businessman to carry the film to the United States. "The film was in a clear plastic bag, but the guy was real nervous," recalls Downey, who had to assure the man that the canisters were not explosives. Although it was risky, Downey says his resourcefulness shows editors that he is willing to do what it takes to get the job done.

In such a competitive field, success often requires photographers to take those extra steps to come up with unique images, he says. In photojournalism, this means moving away from the "pack mentality" which often develops while photographers cover newsworthy events. "Always think for yourself. Just because there are a million photographers that doesn't mean that's the place you have to be," advises Downey. One of his best shots, in which a police officer is caught dive-tackling a demonstrator in San Francisco, California, came after Downey slipped away from the 25-30 photographers covering the event. His photo was purchased by Associated Press and picked up by national newspapers all over the United States.

He also preaches persistence with story ideas and does what he can to convince editors to use his material. "I think it's a good idea to keep in touch with writers," he says. "That's helped me sometimes when it's been a team effort on a story. There are very few magazines out there that are going to run photo essays anymore. It's a bit of a luxury." By doubling as a writer, or teaming up with one, a photographer can boost his chances of making sales, says Downey.

Downey encourages photographers to not only sharpen their photographic talents, but also develop their computer skills and knowledge of image altering software, such as Adobe Photoshop. "If I was starting today I would really learn computers. Don't see it as a threat to the industry, just see it as another aspect," he says.
—*Michael Willins*

Whether he is supplying images from Guatemala, the Philippines or Morocco, freelancer Mark Downey of Alameda, California, always tries to give editors something special. In this case, a Moroccan man struggles with a donkey he just purchased, but the apparent grin on his face makes you wonder if he is enjoying the tussle.

Making Contact & Terms: Interested in receiving work from newer, lesser-known photographers. Provide resume, business card, brochure, flyer or tearsheets to be kept on file for possible assignments. Keeps samples on file. Reports in 1 month. Pays $50/b&w cover; $25/b&w inside. Pays on publication. Buys one-time rights.

ITE JOURNAL, #410, 525 School St. SW, Washington DC 20024. (202)554-8050. Fax: (202)863-5486. Publications Director: Eduardo F. Dalere. Circ. 11,000. Estab. 1930. Publication of Institute of Transportation Engineers. Monthly journal. Emphasizes surface transportation, including streets, highways and transit. Readers are transportation engineers and professionals.
Needs: One photo used for cover illustration per issue. Needs "strikingly scenic shots of streets, highways, bridges, transit systems." Model release required. Captions preferred, include location, name or number of road or highway and details.
Making Contact & Terms: Interested in receiving work from newer, lesser-known photographers. Query with list of stock photo subjects. Send 35mm or 2¼ × 2¼ transparencies by mail for consideration. Provide resume, business card, brochure, flyer or tearsheets to be kept on file for possible assignments. Send originals; no dupes please. Pays $250/color cover photo; $50/b&w inside photo. Pays on publication. Credit line given. Buys one-time rights. Simultaneous submissions and previously published work OK.

JET SPORTS, Suite E, 1371 E. Warner Ave., Tustin CA 92680. (714)259-8240. Fax: (714)259-1502. Editor: Elyse Barrett. Circ. 41,000. Estab. 1983. Publication of the International Jet Sports Boating Association. Quarterly magazine. Emphasizes personal watercraft. Readers are male, aged 21-32. Sample copy free with 9 × 12 SASE. Photo guidelines free with SASE.
Needs: Uses 30-50 photos/issue; 70% supplied by freelancers, 50% on assignment, 20% from stock. Needs photos of personalities, race action, engines, girls, some scenics. Model/property release preferred. Captions preferred; include date, event, names, class.
Making Contact & Terms: Interested in receiving work from newer, lesser-known photographers. Send unsolicited 5 × 7 glossy b&w prints; 35mm or 2¼ × 2¼ transparencies by mail for consideration. Provide resume, business card, brochure, flyer or tearsheets to be kept on file for possible assignments. Does not keep samples on file. SASE. Reports in 2 months. Pays $250/color cover photo; $35-200/color inside photo; $10-20/b&w inside photo; $100/color page rate; $200-400/day. Pays on publication, or 30 days after mail date. Credit line given. Buys first N.A. serial rights or all rights; negotiable.
Tips: "As a quarterly, we need some guarantee of exclusivity, at least on some material." Looks for "different angles on race action and pan shots; reasonably tasteful girl pictures. More b&w will be needed: people pictures as well as action. More travel photography will be used: waterfront scenics (preferably with personal watercraft freatured)."

JOURNAL OF PHYSICAL EDUCATION, RECREATION & DANCE, American Alliance for Health, Physical Education, Recreation & Dance, Reston VA 22091. (703)476-3400. Managing Editor: Frances Rowan. Circ. 35,000. Estab. 1896. Monthly magazine. Emphasizes "teaching and learning in public school physical education, youth sports, youth fitness, dance on elementary, secondary or college levels (not performances; classes only), recreation for youth, children, families, girls and women's athletics and *physical* education and fitness." Sample copy free with 9 × 12 SAE and $1.80 postage. Photo guidelines free with SASE.
Needs: Freelancers supply cover photos only; 80% from assignment. Model release required. Captions preferred.
Making Contact & Terms: Interested in receiving work from newer, lesser-known photographers. Query with list of stock photo subjects. Buys 5 × 7 or 8 × 10 color prints; 35mm transparencies. Buys b&w by contract. SASE. Reports in 2 weeks. Pays $30/b&w photo; $250/color photo. Credit line given. Buys one-time rights. Previously published work OK.
Tips: "Innovative transparencies relating to physical education, recreation and sport are considered for publication on the cover—vertical format." Looks for "action shots, cooperative games, no competitive sports and classroom scenes. Send samples of *relevant* photos."

JOURNAL OF SOIL AND WATER CONSERVATION, 7515 NE Ankeny Rd., Ankeny IA 50021. (515)289-2331. Fax: (515)289-1227. Editor: Paula Porter. Circ. 11,000. Estab. 1946. Publication for the Soil and Water Conservation Society. Bimonthly journal. Emphasizes land and water conservation. Readers include a multidisciplinary group of academicians and professionals interested in the wise use of land and water resources. Free sample copy.

The asterisk before a listing indicates that the market is new in this edition. New markets are often the most receptive to freelance submissions.

Needs: Uses 15-30 photos/issue; 0-2 supplied by freelancers. Needs photos illustrating land and water conservation problems and practices used to solve those problems; including items related to agriculture, natural resources—i.e. water, land, soil, plants (particularly crops), reclamation, some "scenic" for cover shots, international agriculture techniques, third-world agriculture, urban resource issues. Reviews photos with or without accompanying ms. Model release required. Property release preferred. Captions preferred; include names, location (city, state, county).

Making Contact & Terms: Interested in receiving work from newer, lesser-known photographers. Send unsolicited photos by mail for consideration. Uses 5×7, 8×10 b&w prints; 35mm, 2¼×2¼, 4×5 and 8×10 color transparencies; b&w contact sheet. SASE. Reports in 2 weeks. Pays $50-100/color cover; $25-50 color inside; $10 up/b&w inside. **Pays on acceptance.** Credit line given. Buys one-time rights.

Tips: In samples wants to see "good quality photos of people involved in conservation-related activities."

JUDICATURE, Suite 1600, 25 E. Washington, Chicago IL 60602. (312)558-6900. Editor: David Richert. Circ. 20,000. Estab. 1917. Publication of the American Judicature Society. Bimonthly. Emphasizes courts, administration of justice. Readers are judges, lawyers, professors, citizens interested in improving the administration of justice. Sample copy free with 9×12 SAE and $1.45 postage.

Needs: Uses 2-3 photos/issue; 1-2 supplied by freelancers. Needs photos relating to courts, the law. "Actual or posed courtroom shots are always needed." Model/property releases preferred. Captions preferred.

Making Contact & Terms: Interested in receiving work from newer, lesser-known photographers. Send 5×7 glossy b&w prints by mail for consideration. Provide resume, business card, brochure, flyer or tearsheets to be kept on file for possible future assignments. SASE. Reports in 2 weeks. Pays $200/b&w cover photo; $125/b&w inside photo. Pays on publication. Credit line given. Buys one-time rights. Simultaneous submissions and previously published work OK.

KEYNOTER, Dept. PM, 3636 Woodview Trace, Indianapolis IN 46268. (317)875-8755. Art Director: Jim Patterson. Circ. 133,000. Publication of the Key Club International. Monthly magazine. Emphasizes teenagers, above average students and members of Key Club International. Readers are teenagers, ages 14-18, male and female, high GPA, college bound, leaders. Sample copy free with 9×12 SAE and 65¢ postage. Photo guidelines free with SASE.

Needs: Uses varying number of photos/issue; varying percentage supplied by freelancers. Needs vary with subject of the feature article. Reviews photos purchased with accompanying ms only. Model release required. Captions preferred.

Making Contact & Terms: Query with resume of credits. Pays $500/color cover photo; $350/b&w cover photo; $200/color inside photo; $100/b&w inside photo. **Pays on acceptance.** Credit line given. Buys first N.A. serial rights and first international serial rights.

KIWANIS MAGAZINE, 3636 Woodview Trace, Indianapolis IN 46268. (317)875-8755. Fax: (317)879-0204. Executive Editor: Chuck Jonak. Art Director: Jim Patterson. Circ. 285,000. Estab. 1915. Published 10 times/year. Emphasizes organizational news, plus major features of interest to business and professional men and women involved in community service. Free sample copy and writer's guidelines with SAE and five first-class stamps.

Needs: Uses photos with or without ms.

Making Contact & Terms: Send resume of stock photos. Provide brochure, business card and flyer to be kept on file for future assignments. Assigns 95% of work. Uses 5×7 or 8×10 glossy b&w prints; accepts 35mm but prefers 2¼×2¼ and 4×5 transparencies. Pays $50-700/b&w photo; $75-1,000/color photo; $400-1,000/text/photo package. Buys one-time rights.

Tips: "We can offer the photographer a lot of freedom to work *and* worldwide exposure. And perhaps an award or two if the work is good. We are now using more conceptual photos. We also use studio set-up shots. When we assign work, we want to know if a photographer can follow a concept into finished photo without on-site direction." In portfolio or samples, wants to see "studio work with flash and natural light."

LACMA PHYSICIAN, P.O. Box 3465, Los Angeles CA 90051-1465. (213)483-1581. Managing Editor: Janice M. Nagano. Circ. 10,000. Estab. 1875. Published 20 times/year—twice a month except January, July, August and December. Emphasizes Los Angeles County Medical Association news and medical issues. Readers are physicians and members of LACMA.

Needs: Uses about 1-12 photos/issue; from both freelance and staff assignments. Needs photos of association meetings, physician members, association events—mostly internal coverage. Photos purchased with or without accompanying ms. Model release required.

Making Contact & Terms: Arrange a personal interview to show portfolio. Does not return unsolicited material. Pays by hour, day or half day; negotiable. Pays $10/b&w photo; $15/color photo; $50-75/hour. Pays on publication with submission of invoice. Credit line given. Buys one-time rights or first N.A. serial rights "depending on what is agreed upon."
Tips: "We want photographers who blend in well, and can get an extraordinary photo from what may be an ordinary situation. We need to see work that demonstrates an ability to get it right the first time without a lot of set-up on most shoots."

LANDSCAPE ARCHITECTURE, Fifth Floor, 4401 Connecticut Ave. NW, Washington DC 20008. (202)686-2752. Managing Editor: Susan Waterman. Circ. 35,000. Estab. 1910. Publication of the American Society of Landscape Architects. Monthly magazine. Emphasizes "landscape architecture, urban design, parks and recreation, architecture, sculpture" for professional planners and designers. Sample copy $7. Photo guidelines free with SASE.
Needs: Uses about 50-75 photos/issue; 50% supplied by freelance photographers. Needs photos of landscape- and architecture-related subjects as described above. Special needs include aerial photography and portraits (head shots). "We also need international landscape photographs for our international section of the magazine." Model release required. Captions preferred.
Making Contact & Terms: Interested in receiving work from newer, lesser-known photographers. Query with samples or list of stock photo subjects. Provide resume, business card, brochure, flyer or tearsheets to be kept on file for possible future assignments. SASE. Reporting time varies. Pays $500/color cover photo; $50-300/color inside; $500/day; $250/half day. Pays on publication. Credit line given. Buys two-time rights. Previously published work OK.
Tips: "We don't want trite hackneyed, PR-type shots. We look for dramatic compositions, interesting/revealing details and a personal touch. We can only hope more landscape architects will hire professional photographs themselves to document their projects! There should be no flaw in any of the work shown in a portfolio. The compositions should be distinctive, not run-of-the-mill, not ordinary, not bloodless. Generally, it's a good idea to be available when called for the first time and not be late or overcharge if subsequent work is desired."

LAW PRACTICE MANAGEMENT, Box 11418, Columbia SC 29211-1418. (803)754-3563. Editor/Art Director: Delmar L. Roberts. Circ. 22,979 (BPA). Published 8 times/year. Publication of the Section of Law Practice Management, American Bar Association. For practicing attorneys and legal administrators. Sample copy $7 (make check payable to American Bar Association).
Needs: Uses 1-2 photos/issue; all supplied by freelance photographers. Needs photos of some stock subjects such as group at a conference table, someone being interviewed, scenes showing staffed office-reception areas; *imaginative* photos illustrating such topics as time management, employee relations, computers and word processing equipment, record keeping, filing, malpractice insurance protection, computer graphics of interest. Abstract shots or special effects illustrating almost anything concerning management of a law practice. "We'll exceed our usual rates for exceptional photos of this latter type." No snapshots or Polaroid photos. Model release required. Captions required.
Making Contact & Terms: Uses 5×7 glossy b&w prints; 35mm, 2¼×2¼, 4×5 transparencies. Send unsolicited photos by mail for consideration. They are accompanied by an article pertaining to the lapida "if requested." SASE. Reports in 1-3 months. Pays $150-200/color cover photo (vertical format); $50-60/b&w inside photo; $100-200/job. Pays on publication. Credit line given. Usually buys all rights, and rarely reassigns to photographer after publication.

THE LION, 300 22nd St., Oak Brook IL 60521-8842. (708)571-5466. Editor: Robert Kleinfelder. Circ. 600,000. Estab. 1918. For members of the Lions Club and their families. Monthly magazine. Emphasizes Lions Club service projects. Free sample copy and photo guidelines available.
Needs: Uses 50-60 photos/issue. Needs photos of Lions Club service or fundraising projects. "All photos must be as candid as possible, showing an activity in progress. Please, no award presentations, meetings, speeches, etc. Generally photos purchased with ms (300-1,500 words) and used as a photo story. We seldom purchase photos separately." Model release preferred for young or disabled children. Captions required.
Making Contact & Terms: Interested in receiving work from newer, lesser-known photographers. Works with freelancers on assignment only. Provide resume to be kept on file for possible future assignments. Query first with resume of credits or story idea. Send 5×7, 8×10 glossy b&w and color prints; 35mm transparencies. SASE. Reports in 2 weeks. Pays $10-25/photo; $50-600/text/photo package. **Pays on acceptance.** Buys all rights; negotiable.

LOYOLA MAGAZINE, 820 N. Michigan, Chicago IL 60611. (312)915-6157. Fax: (312)915-6215. Editor: William S. Bike. Circ. 90,000. Estab. 1971. Loyola University Alumni Publication. Magazine published 3 times/year. Emphasizes issues related to Loyola University of Chicago. Readers are Loyola University of Chicago alumni—professionals, ages 22 and up. Sample copy free with 9×12 SAE and 3 first-class stamps.

Needs: Uses 50 photos/issue; 40% supplied by freelancers. Needs Loyola-related or Loyola alumni-related photos only. Model release preferred. Captions preferred.
Making Contact & Terms: Send unsolicited photos by mail for consideration. Provide resume, business card, brochure, flyer or tearsheets to be kept on file for possible assignments. Send 8 × 10 b&w/color prints; 35mm and 2¼ × 2¼ transparencies. SASE. Reports in 3 months. Pays $300/b&w and color cover photo; $85/b&w and color inside photo; $50-150/hour; $400-1,200/day. **Pays on acceptance.** Credit line given. Buys one-time rights. Simultaneous submissions and previously published work OK.
Tips: "Send us information, but don't call."

THE LUTHERAN, 8765 W. Higgins Rd., Chicago IL 60631. (312)380-2546. Art Director: Jack Lund. Publication of Evangelical Lutheran Church in America. Circ. 1 million. Estab. 1988. Monthly magazine. Sample copy 75¢ with 9 × 12 SASE.
Needs: Assigns 35-40 photos/issue; 4-5 supplied by freelancers. Needs current news, mood shots. Model release required. Captions preferred.
Making Contact & Terms: Interested in receiving work from newer, lesser-known photographers. Query with list of stock photo subjects. Provide resume, brochure, flyer or tearsheets to be kept on file for possible future assignments. SASE. Reports in 3 weeks. Pays $35-100/b&w photo; $50-175/color photo; $175-300/day. Pays on publication. Credit line given. Buys one-time rights.
Tips: Trend toward "more dramatic lighting. Careful composition." In portfolio or samples, wants to see "candid shots of people active in church life, preferably Lutheran. Churches only have little chance of publication. Submit sharp well-composed photos with borders for cropping."

THE MAGAZINE FOR CHRISTIAN YOUTH!, Box 801, Nashville TN 37202. (615)749-6319. Fax: (615)749-6079. Editor. Circ. estimated 40,000. Estab. 1985. Publication of The United Methodist Church. Monthly. Emphasizes what it means to be a Christian teenager in the '90s—developing a Christian identity and being faithful. Readers are junior and senior high teenagers (Christian).
Needs: Uses about 25 photos/issue; 20 supplied by freelancers. Needs photos of teenagers. Special needs include "up-to-date pictures of teens in different situations—at school, at home, with parents, friends, doing activities, etc. Need photos of both white and ethnics." Model release required especially for "touchy social issues—AIDS, pregnancy, divorce, etc."
Making Contact & Terms: Interested in receiving work from newer, lesser-known photographers. Query with samples and list of stock photo subjects. Send 8 × 10 b&w prints; 35mm, 2¼ × 2¼ and 4 × 5 transparencies; b&w contact sheet by mail for consideration. SASE. Reports in 1 month. Pays $10-150/b&w photo and $35-300/color photo. **Pays on acceptance.** Credit line given. Buys one-time rights. Simultaneous submissions OK.
Tips: Prefers to see "quality photographs of teenagers in various situations, settings. Should appear realistic, not posed, and should be up-to-date in terms of clothing, trends, issues and fads. Photos of single teens plus some of teens with others. Don't give us photos that are blurry and/or have bad compositions. Give us pictures of *today's* teens." Interested in more color submissions. "We seldom assign photographers. We use approximately 90% stock and freelance. Submit work on speculation."

MAINSTREAM—ANIMAL PROTECTION INSTITUTE, P.O. Box 22505, Sacramento CA 95822, or 2831 Fruitridge Rd., Sacramento CA 95820. (916)731-5521. Fax: (916)731-4467. Contact: Art Department. Circ. 65,000. Estab. 1970. Official Publication of the Animal Protection Institute. Quarterly. Emphasizes "humane education toward and about animal issues and events concerning animal welfare." Readers are "all ages; people most concerned with animals." Sample copy and photo guidelines available with 9 × 12 SAE and $1.44 first class postage.
Needs: Uses approximately 30 photos/issue; 15 supplied by freelancers. Needs images of animals in natural habitats. Especially interested in "one of a kind" situational animal slides. All species, wild and domestic: marine mammals, wild horses, primates, companion animals (pets), farm animals, wildlife from all parts of the world, and endangered species. Animals in specific situations: factory farming, product testing, animal experimentation and their alternatives; people and animals working together; trapping and fur ranching; animal rescue and rehabilitation; animals in abusive situations (used/abused) by humans; entertainment (rodeos, circuses, amusement parks, zoos); etc. *API* also uses high quality images of animals in various publications besides its magazine. Submissions should be excellent quality—sharp with effective lighting. Prefer tight to medium shots with good eye contact. Vertical format required for *Mainstream* covers. Model release required for vertical shots and any recognizable faces.
Making Contact & Terms: Interested in receiving work from newer, lesser-known photographers. Query with resume, credits, stock list and sample submission of no more than 20 of best slides; originals are preferred unless dupes are *high quality*. Provide business card, brochure, flyer or tearsheets for *API* files for future reference. "We welcome all 'excellent quality' contacts with SASE." Black and white rarely used. However, will accept b&w images of outstanding quality of hard-to-get, issue-oriented situations: experimentation, product testing, factory farming etc. Original transparencies or high-quality dupes only; 35mm Kodachrome 64 preferred; larger formats accepted. Reports in 2-4

weeks. Pays $150/color cover; $35-50/b&w (from slide or photo) inside; $50-150/color inside. Pays on publication. Credit line given; please specify. Buys one-time rights. Simultaneous submissions and previously published work OK.

Tips: "The images used in *Mainstream* touch the heart. We see a trend toward strong subject, eye contact, emotional scenes, mood shots, inspirational close-ups and natural habitat shots."

MANAGEMENT ACCOUNTING, 10 Paragon Dr., Montvale NJ 07645. (201)573-9000. Fax: (201)573-0639. Editor: Robert Randall. Circ. 95,000. Estab. 1919. Publication of Instititue of Management Accountants. Monthly. Emphasizes management accounting. Readers are financial executives.

Needs: Uses about 25 photos/issue; 40% from stock houses. Needs stock photos of business, high-tech, production and factory. Model release required for identifiable people. Captions required.

Making Contact & Terms: Query with samples. Provide resume, business card, brochure, flyer or tearsheets to be kept on file for possible future assignments. Uses prints and transparencies. SASE. Reports in 2 weeks. Pays $100-200/b&w photo; $150-250/color photo. **Pays on acceptance.** Credit line given. Buys one-time rights. Simultaneous submissions and previously published work OK.

Tips: Prefers to see "ingenuity, creativity, dramatics (business photos are often dry), clarity, close-ups, simple but striking. Aim for a different slant."

✸THE MANITOBA TEACHER, 191 Harcourt St., Winnipeg, Manitoba R3J 3H2 Canada. (204)888-7961. Communications Officer: Janice Armstrong. Editorial Assistant/Advertising: Joy Montgomery. Publication of The Manitoba Teachers' Society. Emphasizes education in Manitoba—emphasis on teachers' interest. Readers are teachers and others in education. Circ. 16,800. Sample copy free with 10×14 SAE and Canadian stamps.

Needs: Uses approx. 4 photos/issue; 80% supplied by freelancers. Needs action shots of students and teachers in education-related settings. "Good cover shots always needed." Model release required. Captions required.

Making Contact & Terms: Send 8×10 glossy b&w prints by mail for consideration. Submit portfolio for review. Provide resume, business card, brochure, flyer or tearsheets to be kept on file for possible assignments. SASE. Reports in 1 month. Does not pay; only gives credit line.

Tips: "Always submit action shots directly related to major subject matter of publication and interests of readership of that publication."

MAP INTERNATIONAL, Dept. PM, P.O. Box 50, Brunswick GA 31520. (912)265-6010 or (800)-225-8550 (interstate toll free). Art Director: Michael Wilson. Publication of MAP International. Bi-monthly. Reports on the organization's annual distribution of $35 million in donated medicines and supplies to relief agencies in 75 countries in the developing world, as well as work in community health development projects. Sample copy and photo guidelines free with SASE.

Needs: "Specifically, we need photos depicting the health needs of people in the developing countries of Africa, Asia and Latin America, and the work being done to meet those needs. Also use photos of disaster situations like the war in Kuwait, *while situation is current*." Captions required.

Making Contact & Terms: Query with resume of credits. Query with samples. Query with list of stock photo subjects. Uses b&w 5×7 glossy prints; 35mm transparencies. SASE. Reports in 1 month. Pays $75/b&w cover photo; $25+/b&w inside photo; payment for color photos individually negotiated. **Pays on acceptance.** Credit line given. Buys one-time rights. Simultaneous submissions and previously published work OK, "depending on where they had been submitted or used."

Tips: "Photos should center on people: children, patients receiving medical treatment, doctors, community health workers with the people they are helping, hospitals, health development projects and informal health education settings. Our interest is much broader than crisis situations and emergency aid alone, and we try to show the hopeful side of what is being done. Care about people. We are a people-developing agency and if a photographer cares about the problems of people in developing nations it will come through in the work."

*MATERIALS PERFORMANCE, P.O. Box 218340, Houston TX 77218-8340. (713)492-0535, ext 207. Fax: (713)492-8254. Managing Editor: Theresa Baer. Circ. 16,000. Publication of National Association of Corrosion Engineers. Monthly magazine. Emphasizes corrosion control and prevention applications. Readers are male and female professionals, engineers to field technicians. Sample copy $10.

Needs: Uses at least 11 photos, cover and features/issue. Needs photos of materials technology: lab, field, office. Reviews photos with or without ms. Special photo needs include infrastructure, electronics, transportation, water distribution systems. Model/property release required. Captions required; include application and owner.

Making Contact & Terms: Query with stock photo list. Send unsolicited photos by mail for consideration. Send 4×5 color prints; 35mm transparencies. Does not keep samples on file. SASE. Reports in 1 month. NPI. Credit line given. Simultaneous submissions and/or previously published work OK.

THE MEETING MANAGER, 1950 Stemmons Freeway, Infomart, Dallas TX 75207. (214)746-5262. Art Director: Denise Blessing. Circ. 12,000 Estab. 1980. Publication of Meeting Planners International. Monthly magazine. Emphasizes planning meetings. Readers are ages 30-60, male and female. Sample copy available.
Needs: Uses 10-20 photos/issue; all supplied by freelancers. Needs various subjects for cover shots, other photos are specific events, some promotional material requiring photography. Special photo needs include cover photos and feature photos, some stock. Model/property release required. Captions preferred.
Making Contact & Terms: Interested in receiving work from newer, lesser-known photographers. Provide resume, business card, brochure, flyer or tearsheets to be kept on file for possible assignments. Reports as needed. Pays $50-150/b&w photo; $100-500/color photo; $200-400/job. Pays on publication. Credit line given. Rights negotiable. Previously published work OK.
Tips: Wants to see photographers "slicks or printed samples. Send samples of photography to be kept on file until matched with a specific job. Keep in mind MPI is a nonprofit organization and our budget keeps us limited."

✹MENNONITE BRETHREN HERALD, 3-169 Riverton Ave., Winnipeg, Manitoba R2L 2E5 Canada. (204)669-6575. Fax: (204)654-1865. Art Director: Fred Koop. Circ. 14,800. Publication of the Canadian Mennonite Brethren Church. Biweekly magazine. Publication emphasizes "issues of spiritual and social concern." Readers are primarily adult church members. Sample copy free with letter-size SASE (Canadian funds).
Needs: Uses 5-10 photos/issue; most supplied by freelancers. Approximately 85% purchased from stock; 15% on assignment. Looking for people-oriented shots. Some religious, some scenics, some abstract, but mostly people of all ages in activity of all sorts. Model release required. Captions preferred.
Making Contact & Terms: Send 5×7 or 8×10 glossy or matte b&w prints by mail for consideration. Letter-size SASE (Canadian funds). Pays $20-25 (Cdn.)/b&w cover; $15-20 (Cdn.)/b&w inside photo. Pays on publication. Credit line given. Buys one-time rights and first N.A. serial rights. Simultaneous submissions and previously published work OK.

THE MIDWEST MOTORIST, Dept. PM, Auto Club of Missouri, 12901 N. Forty Dr., St. Louis MO 63141. (314)523-7350. Editor: Michael Right. Circ. 385,000. Bimonthly. Emphasizes travel and driving safety. Readers are "members of the Auto Club of Missouri, ranging in age from 25-65 and older." Free sample copy and photo guidelines with SASE; use large manila envelope.
Needs: Uses 8-10 photos/issue, most supplied by freelancers. "We use four-color photos inside to accompany specific articles. Our magazine covers topics of general interest, historical (of Midwest regional interest), humor (motoring slant), interview, profile, travel, car care and driving tips. Our covers are full color mainly corresponding to an article inside. Except for cover shots, we use freelance photos only to accompany specific articles." Captions required.
Making Contact & Terms: Send by mail for consideration 5×7 or 8×10 b&w photos; 35mm, 2¼×2¼ or 4×5 color transparencies. Query with resume of credits. Query with list of stock photo subjects. SASE. Reports in 3-6 weeks. Pays $100-250/cover; $10-25/photo with accompanying ms; $10-50/b&w photo; $50-200/color photo; $75-200 text/photo package. Pays on publication. Credit line given. Rights negotiable. Simultaneous submissions and previously published work OK.
Tips: "Send an 8½×11 SASE for sample copies and study the type of covers and inside work we use."

MODERN MATURITY, 3200 E. Carson St., Lakewood CA 90712. (310)496-2277. Photo Editor: M.J. Wadolny. Circ. 20 million. Bimonthly. Readers are 50 years old and over. Sample copy free with 9×12 SASE. Guidelines free with SASE.
Needs: Uses about 50 photos/issue; 5 supplied by freelancers; 75% from assignment and 25% from stock. Needs nature, scenic, personality and travel photos. Model release preferred. Captions preferred.
Making Contact & Terms: Arrange a personal interview to show portfolio. SASE. Pays $50-200/b&w photo; $150-1,000/color photo; $350/day. **Pays on acceptance.** Credit line given. Buys one-time and first N.A. serial rights.

Can't find a listing? Check at the end of each market section for the " '93-'94 Changes" lists. These lists include any market listings from the '93 edition which were either not verified or deleted in this edition.

Tips: Prefers to see clean, crisp images on a variety of subjects of interest to people 50 or over. "Present yourself and your work in a professional manner. Be familiar with *Modern Maturity*. Wants to see creativity, ingenuity and perserverance."

THE MORGAN HORSE, P.O. Box 960, Shelburne VT 05482. (802)985-4944. Editor: Suzy Lucine. Circ. 8,500. Estab. 1941. Publication is official breed journal of The American Morgan Horse Association Inc. Monthly magazine. Emphasizes Morgan horses. Readers are all ages. Sample copy.
Needs: Uses 25 photos/issue; 50% supplied by freelancers. Needs photos of Morgan horses—farm scenes, "showing," trail riding, how-to and photos with owners. Special photo needs include covers and calendars. Model release preferred. Captions preferred.
Making Contact & Terms: Send unsolicited glossy b&w or color prints; 35mm, 2¼×2¼, 4×5, 8×10 transparencies by mail for consideration. SASE. Reports in 3 weeks. Pays $150/color cover photo; $25/color inside photo; $5/b&w inside photo. Pays on publication. Credit line given. Buys either one-time or all rights; negotiable.
Tips: "Artistic color photographs of Morgan horses in natural settings, with owners, etc., are needed for calendars and covers."

NACLA REPORT ON THE AMERICAS, Dept. PM, Rm 454, 475 Riverside Dr., New York NY 10115. (212)870-3146. Photo Editor: Deidre McFadyen. Circ. 11,500. Association publication of North American Congress on Latin America. Bimonthly journal. Emphasizes Latin American political economy; US foreign policy toward Latin America; and the Caribbean and domestic development in the region. Readers are academic, church, human rights, political activists, foreign policy interested. Sample copy $5 (includes postage).
Needs: Uses about 25 photos/issue; all supplied by freelancers. Model release preferred. Captions preferred.
Making Contact & Terms: Arrange a personal interview to show portfolio. Query with list of countries and topics covered. SASE. Reports in 2 weeks. Pays $30/b&w photo. Pays on publication. Credit line given. Buys one-time rights. Simultaneous submissions and previously published work OK.

*NATIONAL CATTLEMEN, Box 3469, Englewood CO 80155. (303)694-0305. Fax: (303)694-0305. Editor: Scott Cooper. Circ. 36,000. Estab. 1985. Publication of the National Cattlemen's Association. Monthly. Emphasizes all aspects of beef production. Readers are cattle ranchers and feedlot operators; most are male, median age 57. Sample copy free with 10×12 SASE.
Needs: Buys photos "as needed." Beef cattle shots, ranch shots, beef industry photography. Model/property release required. Captions preferred.
Making Contact & Terms: Arrange a personal interview to show portfolio. Query with list of stock photo subjects. Send prints or slides by mail for consideration. SASE. NPI. All rates negotiated; pricing structure in progress. Pays on publication. Credit line given. Buys one-time rights. Simultaneous submissions and previously published work OK.

NATIONAL GARDENING, Dept. PM, 180 Flynn Ave., Burlington VT 05401. (802)863-1308. Fax: (802)863-5962. Editor: Warren Schultz. Managing Editor: Vicky Congdon. Circ. 200,000. Estab. 1979. Publication of the National Gardening Association. Bimonthly. Covers fruits, vegetables, herb and ornamentals. Readers are home and community gardeners. Sample copy $2. Photo guidelines free with SASE.
Needs: Uses about 25 photos/issue; 20% supplied by freelancers. "Most of our photographers are also gardeners or have an avid interest in gardening or gardening research." Needs photos of "people gardening; special techniques; how to; specific varieties (please label); garden pests and diseases; soils; unusual gardens and food gardens in different parts of the country. We sometimes need someone to photograph a garden or gardener in various parts of the country for a specific story."
Making Contact & Terms: Interested in receiving work from newer, lesser-known photographers. Query with samples or list of stock photo subjects. SASE. Reports in 1 month. Pays $350/color cover photo; $30/b&w and $50-100/color inside photo. Also negotiates day rate against number of photos used. Pays on publication. Credit line given. Buys first N.A. serial rights.
Tips: "We're becoming more selective all the time, need top-quality work. Most photos used are color. We look for general qualities like sharp focus, good color balance, good sense of lighting and composition. Also interesting viewpoint, one that makes the photos more than just a record (getting down to ground level in the garden, for instance, instead of shooting everything from a standing position). Look at the magazine carefully and at the photos used. We work at making the stories friendly, casual and personal. When we write a story on growing broccoli, we love to have photos of people planting, harvesting or eating broccoli, not a formal shot of broccoli on a black background. We like to show process, step-by-step."

THE NATIONAL NOTARY, 8236 Remmet Ave., Box 7184, Canoga Park CA 91309-7184. (818)713-4000. Editor: Charles N. Faerber. Circ. 80,000. Bimonthly. Emphasizes "Notaries Public and notarization—goal is to impart knowledge, understanding and unity among notaries nationwide and internationally." Readers are employed primarily in the following areas: law, government, finance and real estate. Sample copy $5.

Needs: Uses about 20-25 photos/issue; 10 supplied by non-staff photographers. "Photo subject depends on accompanying story/theme; some product shots used." Unsolicited photos purchased with accompanying ms only. Model release required.

Making Contact & Terms: Query with samples. Provide business card, tearsheets, resume or samples to be kept on file for possible future assignments. Prefers to see prints as samples. Cannot return material. Reports in 4-6 weeks. Pays $25-300 depending on job. Pays on publication. Credit line given "with editor's approval of quality." Buys all rights. Previously published work OK.

Tips: "Since photography is often the art of a story, the photographer must understand the story to be able to produce the most useful photographs."

THE NATIONAL RURAL LETTER CARRIER, Dept. PM, 1630 Duke St., Alexandria VA 22314-3465 (703)684-5545. Managing Editor: RuthAnn Saenger. Circ. 70,000. Weekly magazine. Emphasizes Federal legislation and issues affecting rural letter carriers and the activities of the membership for rural carriers and their spouses and postal management. Sample copy 34¢. Photo guidelines free with SASE.

Needs: Photos purchased with accompanying ms. Buys 52 photos/year. Animal; wildlife; sport; celebrity/personality; documentary; fine art; human interest; humorous; nature; scenics; photo essay/photo feature; special effects and experimental; still life; spot news; and travel. Needs scenes that combine subjects of the Postal Service and rural America; "submit photos of rural carriers on the route." Model release required. Captions required.

Making Contact & Terms: Interested in receiving work from newer, lesser-known photographers. Send material by mail for consideration. Query with list of stock photo subjects. Uses 8×10 b&w or color glossy prints, vertical format preferred for cover. SASE. Reports in 4 weeks. Pays $60/photo. Pays on publication. Credit line given. Buys first serial rights. Previously published work OK.

Tips: "Please submit sharp and clear photos with interesting and pertinent subject matter. Study the publication to get a feel for the types of rural and postal subject matter that would be of interest to the membership. We receive more photos than we can publish, but we accept beginners' work if it is good."

NATIONAL TRUST FOR HISTORIC PRESERVATION, 1785 Massachusetts Ave. NW, Washington DC 20036. (202)673-4042. Fax: (202)673-4172. Art Director: Jeff Roth. Circ. 225,000. Estab. 1950. Bimonthly magazine. Emphasizes historic preservation. Readers are male and female with average income of $99,000, average age 50. Sample copy $2.50 and 9×12 SASE. Photo guidelines free with SASE.

Needs: Uses 75-100 photos/year; 90% supplied by freelancers. Needs photos of architecture, environmental portraits and travel. Reviews photos with or without accompanying ms. Always need unusual photos for picture page, "Observed"—write for guidelines for more specific description. Model/property release preferred. Captions preferred.

Making Contact & Terms: Interested in receiving work from newer, lesser-known photographers. Arrange personal interview to show portfolio. Submit portfolio for review. Provide brochure, flyer or tearsheets to be kept on file for possible assignments. Query with samples. SASE. Reports when interested. Pays up to $300/color stock inside photo; up to $300/b&w stock inside photo; $350-500/day. **Pays on acceptance.** Credit line given. Buys one-time rights.

Tips: "We want photographers who can shoot in natural, editorial style, producing artful and dramatic images."

THE NATURE CONSERVANCY MAGAZINE, 1815 N. Lynn St., Arlington VA 22209. (703)841-8742. Photo Editor: Maria Voles. Circ. 640,000. Estab. 1951. Publication of The Nature Conservancy. Bimonthly. Emphasizes "nature, rare and endangered flora and fauna, ecosystems in North and South America." Readers are the membership of The Nature Conservancy. Sample copy free with 9×12 SAE and $1.21 postage. Write for guidelines.

Needs: Uses about 20-25 photos/issue; 70% from freelance stock. The Nature Conservancy welcomes permission to make duplicates of slides submitted to the *Magazine* for use in slide shows only and internegs for proposals. Model release required. Property release preferred. Captions required; include location and names of flora and fauna. Proper credit should appear on slides.

Making Contact & Terms: Many photographers contribute the use of their slides. Uses color transparencies. Pays $200/color cover photo; $75-150/color inside photo; $50/b&w photo; $300/day. Pays on publication. Credit line given. Buys one-time rights; starting to consider all rights for public relations purposes; negotiable.

Tips: "Membership in the Nature Conservancy is only $25/year and the *Magazine* will keep photographers up to date on what the Conservancy is doing in your state. Many of the preserves are open to the public. We look for rare and endangered species, wetlands and flyways, including Latin America, South Pacific, Caribbean and Canada."

NETWORK for Public Schools, Suite 8, 900 2nd St. NE, Washington DC 20002. (202)408-0447. Fax: (202)408-0452. Editor: Susan Hlesciak Hall. Circ. 10,000. Estab. 1975. Publication of the National Committee for Citizens in Education. Published 6 times/year. Emphasizes "parent/citizen participation in public school." Readers are "parents, citizens, educators." Sample copy available.
Needs: Uses various number of photos/issue; 90% from freelance stock and 10% from assignment. Needs photos of "children (elementary and high school) in school settings or with adults (parents, teachers) shown in helping role; meetings of small groups of adults." Model release required. Captions preferred.
Making Contact & Terms: Interested in receiving work from newer, lesser-known photographers. Query with samples. Send glossy prints, contact sheets or good quality duplicator facsimiles by mail for consideration. SASE. Reports in 2 weeks. Pays $50/b&w cover photo; $35/b&w inside photo. **Pays on acceptance.** Credit line given. Rights negotiable. Simultaneous submissions and previously published work OK.
Tips: "In reviewing samples we look for appropriate subject matter—school-age children, often with helping adults (parents or teachers); good resolution, sharp focus of print; a picture conveying a mood and capturing expressions, telling a story with a message; picture must have focal point, good composition. Need to represent ethnic diversity among teachers and school children. Include full name, address and phone number on back of every print. Enclose return postage."

NEVADA FARM BUREAU AGRICULTURE AND LIVESTOCK JOURNAL, 1300 Marietta Way, Sparks NV 89431. (702)358-7737. Contact: Norman Cardoza. Circ. 4,700. Monthly tabloid. Emphasizes Nevada agriculture. Readers are primarily Nevada Farm Bureau members and their families; men, women and youth of various ages. Members are farmers and ranchers. Sample copy free with 10×13 SAE with 3 first-class stamps.
Needs: Uses 5 photos/issue; 30% occasionally supplied by freelancers. Needs photos of Nevada agriculture people, scenes and events. Model release preferred. Captions required.
Making Contact & Terms: Send b&w 3×5 and larger prints, any format and finish by mail for consideration. SASE. Reports in 1 week. Pays $10/b&w cover photo; $5/b&w inside photo. **Pays on acceptance.** Credit line given. Buys one-time rights.
Tips: "In portfolio or samples, wants to see newsworthiness, 50%; good composition, 20%; interesting action, 20%; photo contrast, resolution, 10%. Try for new angles on stock shots: awards, speakers, etc., We like 'Great Basin' agricultural scenery such as cows on the rangelands and high desert cropping. We pay little, but we offer credits for your resume."

NEW ERA MAGAZINE, 50 E. North Temple St., Salt Lake City UT 84150. (801)240-2951. Fax: (801)240-1727. Art Director: Lee Shaw. Circ. 200,000. Estab. 1971. Association publication of The Church Of Jesus Christ of Latter-day Saints. Monthly magazine. Emphasizes teenagers who are members of the Mormon Church. Readers are male and female teenagers, who are members of the Latter Day Saints Church. Sample $1 with 9×12 SAE and 2 first-class stamps. Photo guidelines free with SASE.
Needs: Uses 60-70 photos/issue; 35-40 supplied by freelancers. Anything can be considered for "Photo of the Month," most photos of teenage Mormons and their activities. Model/property release preferred. Captions preferred.
Making Contact & Terms: Arrange personal interview to show portfolio. Submit portfolio for review. Query with stock photo list. Send unsolicited photos by mail for consideration. Send any b&w or color print; 35mm, 2¼×2¼, 4×5 transparencies. Keeps samples on file. SASE. Reports in 6-8 weeks. Pays $150-300/day; "rates are individually negotiated, since we deal with many teenagers, non-professionals, etc." Credit line given. Buys all rights; negotiable.
Tips: "Most work consists of assignments given to photographers we know and trust, or of single item purchases for photo of the month."

THE NEW PHYSICIAN, 1890 Preston White Dr., Reston VA 22091. (703)620-6600. Editor: Richard Camer. Circ. 30,000. Publication of American Medical Student Association. Magazine published 9 times a year. Emphasizes medicine/health. Readers are medical students, interns, residents, medical educators. Sample copy free with SASE.
Needs: Needs freelance photos for about 6 stories per year. Needs photos usually on health, medical, medical training. Commissions photos to go with story or photo essay on above topics only. Model release required. Captions required.
Making Contact & Terms: Provide resume, business card, brochure, flyer or tearsheets to be kept on file for possible future assignments. NPI; pay negotiated. Pays 2-4 weeks after acceptance. Buys first N.A. serial rights.

NEW WORLD OUTLOOK, Dept. PM, Rm. 1351, 475 Riverside Dr., New York NY 10115. (212)870-3758/3765. Fax: (212)870-3940. Editor: Alma Graham. Circ. 33,000. Estab. 1910. Four-color magazine published 6 times/year. Features United Methodist mission and Christian involvement in evangelism, social concerns and problems around the world. Sample copy $2 with 9 × 12 SAE.

Needs: Interested in photographers who are planning trips to countries and regions in which there are United Methodist mission projects. Query first for interest and needs. Model release required for closeups and for "people in difficult situations." Captions required; include who, what, where, when, why.

Making Contact & Terms: Query first, by phone or letter. Cannot return material. If an appointment is made, bring samples of published photos, slides and b&w prints. Color preferred. Most photos used are by in-house or United Methodist-related photographers. Previously published work OK. Credit line given. Pays $25-75/b&w photo; $50-100/color photo; $150-250/color cover. Pays on publication. Buys one-time rights.

Tips: Wants to see strong images, good composition, human interest, geographic setting, religious themes. Follow current world events and religious trends for spotting photo opportunities.

NEWS PHOTOGRAPHER, Dept. PM, 1446 Conneaut Ave., Bowling Green OH 43402. (419)352-8175. Fax: (419)354-5435. Editor: James R. Gordon. Circ. 11,000. Estab. 1946. Publication of National Press Photographers Association, Inc. Monthly magazine. Emphasizes photojournalism and news photography. Readers are newspaper, magazine, television freelancers and photojournalists. Sample copy free with 9 × 12 SAE and 9 first-class stamps.

Needs: Uses 50 photos/issue. Needs photos of photojournalists at work; photos which illustrate problems of photojournalists. Special photo needs include photojournalists at work, assaulted, arrested; groups of news photographers at work, problems and accomplishments of news photographers. Captions required.

Making Contact & Terms: Send glossy b&w/color prints; 35mm, 2¼ × 2¼ transparencies by mail for consideration. Provide resume, business card, brochure, flyer or tearsheets to be kept on file for possible assignments; make contact by telephone. Reports in 3 weeks. Pays $75/color page rate; $50/b&w page rate; $50-150/photo/text package. **Pays on acceptance.** Credit line given. Buys one-time rights. Simultaneous submissions and previously published work OK.

NFPA JOURNAL, Dept. PM, 1 Batterymarch Park, Quincy MA 02169. (617)984-7566. Art Director: Jane Dashfield. Circ. 56,000. Publication of National Fire Protection Association. Bimonthly magazine. Emphasizes fire protection issues. Readers are fire professionals, engineers, architects, building code officials, ages 20-65. Sample copy free with 9 × 12 SAE.

Needs: Uses 25-30 photos/issue; 50% supplied by freelance photographers. Needs photos of fires and fire-related incidents. Especially wants to use more photos for Fire Fighter Injury Report and Fire Fighter Fatality Report. Model release preferred. Captions preferred.

Making Contact & Terms: Query with list of stock photo subjects, send unsolicited photos by mail for consideration. Provide resume, business card, brochure, flyer or tearsheets to be kept on file for possible assignments. Send color prints and 35mm transparencies in 3-ring slide sleeve with date. SASE. Reports in 3 weeks or "as soon as I can." NPI; payment negotiated. Pays on publication. Credit line given. Buys rights depending "on article and sensitivity of subject."

Tips: "Send cover letter, 35mm color slides preferably with manuscripts and photo captions."

*NORTH AMERICAN HUNTER, P.O. Box 3401, Minnetonka MN 55343. (612)936-9333. Fax: (612)936-9755. Publisher: Mark LaBarbera. Editor: Bill Miller. Associate Editor: Dan Dietrich. Circ. 500,000. Estab. 1978. Publication of North American Hunting Club. Bimonthly. Emphasizes hunting. Readers are all types of hunters with an eye for detail and an appreciation of wildlife. Sample copy $5.

Needs: Uses about 10 photos/issue; all supplied by freelance photographers. For covers, needs "action wildlife centered in vertical format. Inside, needs North American big game, small game, gamebirds and waterfowl only. Always looking for trophy white-tailed deer." Model release preferred. Captions preferred.

Making Contact & Terms: Interested in receiving work from newer, lesser-known photographers. Send 35mm, 2¼ × 2¼, 4 × 5 or 8 × 10 transparencies by mail for consideration or submit list of photos in your file. SASE. Reports in 1 month. Pays $350/color cover photo; $100/b&w photo; $100-350/color photo; and $325-400 for text/photo package. **"Pays promptly on acceptance."** Credit line given. Buys one-time rights; negotiable.

Tips: "We want top quality photos of North American big game that depict a particular behavior pattern that members of the North American Hunting Club might find useful in pursuing that animal. Action shots are especially sought. Get a copy of the magazine and check out the type of photos we are using."

NORTH AMERICAN WHITETAIL MAGAZINE, P.O. Box 741, Marietta GA 30061. (404)953-9222. Fax: (404)933-9510. Photo Editor: Gordon Whittington. Circ. 150,000. Estab. 1982. Published 8 times/year (July-Feb.) by Game & Fish Publications, Inc. emphasizing trophy whitetail deer hunting. Sample copy $3. Photo guidelines free with SASE.

Needs: Uses 20 photos/issue; 40% supplied by freelancers. Needs photos of large, live whitetail deer, hunter posing with or approaching downed trophy deer, or hunter posing with mounted head. Also use photos of deer habitat and sign. Model release preferred. Capitons preferred; include where scene was photographed and when.

Making Contact & Terms: Interested in receiving work from newer, lesser-known photographers. Query with resume of credits and list of stock photo subjects. Send unsolicited 8 × 10 b&w prints; 35mm transparencies (Kodachrome preferred). Will return unsolicited material in 1 month if accompanied by SASE. Pays $250/color cover photo; $75/inside color photo; $25/b&w photo. Tearsheets provided. Pays 75 days prior to publication. Credit line given. Buys one-time rights. Simultaneous submissions not accepted.

Tips: "In samples we look for extremely sharp, well composed photos of whitetailed deer in natural settings. We also use photos depicting deer hunting scenes. Please study the photos we are using before making submission. We'll return photos we don't expect to use and hold the remainder. Please do not send dupes. Use an 8× loupe to ensure sharpness of images and put name and identifying number on all slides and prints. Photos returned at time of publication or at photographer's request."

OAK RIDGE BOYS "TOUR BOOK" AND FAN CLUB NEWSLETTER, 329 Rockland Rd., Hendersonville TN 37075. (615)824-4924. Fax: (615)822-7078. Art Director: Kathy Harris. Circ. newsletter 15,000; tour book 50,000. Publication of The Oak Ridge Boys, Inc. Quarterly newsletter, tour book published "every 1-3 years." Tour book: 24 pages, full color. Emphasizes The Oak Ridge Boys (music group) exclusively. Readers are fans of Oak Ridge Boys and country music. Free sample copies available of newsletter; tourbook $10.

Needs: Uses 4-5 photos/issue of newsletter, 0-2 supplied by freelance photographers; 20-150/tour book, 1-50 supplied by freelance photographers. Needs photos of Oak Ridge Boys. Will review photos with or without accompanying ms; subject to change without notice. "We need *good* live shots or candid shots—not interested in just average shots." Model release required. Captions preferred.

Making Contact & Terms: Interested in receiving work from newer, lesser-known photographers. Send 8 × 10 or smaller color or b&w prints with any finish by mail for consideration. Samples kept on file. Sometimes returns material if SASE is enclosed. Reports vary, 6-8 weeks. Newsletter: Pays $50/photo. Tour Book: for color photos, pays $500/page; $250/half page; $125/quarter page. For b&w photos, pays $250/page; $125 half page; $60-70/quarter page. Price is negotiable depending on usage. Pays on publication. Credit line usually given. Buys all rights; negotiable. Simultaneous submissions and previously published work OK.

Tips: "We are interested in Oak Ridge Boys photos only! Send only a few good shots at one time—send prints only. No original slides or negatives please."

OKLAHOMA TODAY, Box 53384, Oklahoma City OK 73152. (405)521-2496. Fax: (405)521-3992. Editor: Jeanne M. Devlin. Circ. 45,000. Estab. 1956. Bimonthly magazine. "We cover all aspects of Oklahoma, from history to people profiles, but we emphasize travel." Readers are "Oklahomans, whether they live in-state or are exiles; studies show them to be above average in education and income." Sample copy $2.50. Photo guidelines free with SASE.

Needs: Uses about 50 photos/issue; 90-95% supplied by freelancers. Needs photos of "Oklahoma subjects only; the greatest number are used to illustrate a specific story on a person, place or thing in the state. We are also interested in stock scenics of the state." Model release required. Captions required.

Making Contact & Terms: Interested in receiving work from newer, lesser-known photographers. Query with samples. Send 8 × 10 glossy b&w prints; 35mm, 2¼ × 2¼, 4 × 5, 8 × 10 transparencies or b&w contact sheets by mail for consideration. No color prints. SASE. Reports in 6-8 weeks. Pays $50-200/b&w photo; $50-200/color photo; $50-750/job. Payment for text material on acceptance; payment for photos on publication. Buys one-time rights with a six-month from publication exclusive, plus right to reproduce photo in promotions for magazine, without additional payment with credit line. Simultaneous submissions and previously published work OK (on occasion).

Tips: To break in, "read the magazine. Subjects are normally activities or scenics (mostly the latter). I would like good composition and very good lighting. I look for photographs that evoke a sense of place, look extraordinary and say something only a good photographer could say about the image. Look at what Ansel Adams and Eliot Porter did and what Muench and others are producing and send me that kind of quality. We want the best photographs available and we give them the space and play such quality warrants."

❋THE ONTARIO TECHNOLOGIST, Suite 404, 10 Four Seasons Place, Etobicoke, Ontario M9B 6H7 Canada. (416)621-9621. Fax: (416)621-8694. Editor-in-Chief: Ruth M. Klein. Circ. 19,200. Publication of the Ontario Association of Certified Engineering Technicians and Technologists. Bimonthly. Emphasizes engineering technology. Sample copy free with SAE and IRC.

"The idea of an egg is perfection," says photographer Miji Doucet of Stringtown, Oklahoma. "(This photo) conveys the beauty of nature and life. It speaks of what is to come later in the future." Doucet says she received $100 for the image which appeared in a portfolio section of Oklahoma Today.

© Miji Doucet

Needs: Uses 10-12 photos/issue. Needs how-to photos—"building and installation of equipment; similar technical subjects." Model release preferred. Captions preferred.

Making Contact & Terms: Prefers business card and brochure for files. Send 5×7 glossy b&w or color prints for consideration. SASE. Reports in 1 month. Pays $25/b&w photo; $50/color photo. Pays on publication. Credit line given. Buys one-time rights. Previously published work OK.

OPASTCO ROUNDTABLE, Dept. PM, Suite 700, 21 Dupont Circle NW, Washington DC 20036. (202)659-5990. Fax: (202)659-4619. Public Relations Director: Linda M. Buckley. Circ. 3,200. Estab. 1988. Association publication of the Organization for the Protection and Advancement of Small Telephone Companies. Quarterly magazine. Covers news of small, rural, independent telephone companies. Readers are male and female owners and employees in small telephone companies. Sample copies free with 9×12 SAE and 8 first-class stamps.

Needs: Uses 20-30 photos/issue. Needs photos of small telephone company operators/business ventures and other general telecommunications subjects. Reviews photos with or without ms. "We would like to work with more photographers in rural areas where our members are located. Often we need a good photo to go with an article and have to rely on our member's own photography." Model/property release preferred. Captions required; include names and titles of subjects in photos.

Making Contact & Terms: Provide resume, business card, brochure, flyer or tearsheets to be kept on file for possible assignments. Send stock photo list. Send unsolicited photos by mail for consideration. Accepts both b&w and color photos; "we're very flexible." Keeps samples on file. SASE. Reports in 1 month. Pays $125-250/color cover photo; $45-85/b&w inside or color page photo. **Pays on acceptance.** Credit line given. Buys all rights; negotiable. Simultaneous submissions and previously published work OK.

OUTDOOR AMERICA, Level B, 1401 Wilson Blvd., Arlington VA 22209. (703)528-1818. Fax: (703)528-1836. Editor: Kristin Clarke. Circ. 59,000. Estab. 1922. Published quarterly. Emphasizes natural resource conservation and activities for outdoor enthusiasts, including hunters, anglers, hikers and campers. Readers are members of the Izaak Walton League of America and all members of Congress. Sample copy $1.50 with 9×12 envelope. Guidelines free with SASE.

Needs: Needs vertical wildlife or shots of anglers or hunters for cover. Buys pictures to accompany articles on conservation and outdoor recreation for inside. Model release preferred. Captions required; include date taken, model info, location and species.

Making Contact & Terms: Query with resume of photo credits. Send stock photo list. Tearsheets and non-returnable samples only. Uses 35mm and 2¼×2¼ slides. Not responsible for return of unsolicited material. SASE. Pays $200-250/color cover; $50-75/inside photo. Pays on publication. Credit line given. Buys one-time rights. Simultaneous and previously published work OK.

Tips: "*Outdoor America* seeks vertical photos of wildlife (particular game species); outdoor recreation subjects (fishing, hunting, camping or boating) and occasional scenics (especially of the Chesapeake Bay and Upper Mississippi river). We also like the unusual shot—new perspectives on familiar objects or subjects—for use on inside covers. We do not assign work. Approximately one half of the magazine's photos are from freelance sources." Points out that cover has moved from using a square photo format to full bleed.

PACIFIC DISCOVERY, Dept. PM, California Academy of Sciences, Golden Gate Park, San Francisco CA 94118. (415)750-7116. Fax: (415)750-7106. Art Director: Susan Schneider. Circ. 35,000. Estab. 1948. Publication of California Academy of Sciences. Quarterly magazine. Emphasizes natural history and culture of California, the western US, the Pacific and Pacific Rim countries. Sample copy $1.50 with 9×11 SASE. Photo guidelines free with SASE.

Needs: Uses 50 photos/issue; 40% supplied by freelance photographers. Scenics of habitat as well as detailed photos of individual species that convey biological information; wildlife, habitat, ecology, geology. "Scientific accuracy in identifying species is essential. We do extensive photo searches for every story." Current needs listed in Guilfoyle Reports, natural history photographers' newsletter published by AG Editions. Model release preferred. "Captions preferred, but captions are generally staff written."

Making Contact & Terms: Interested in receiving work from newer, lesser-known photographers. Query with list of stock photo subjects and file stock lists, but recommend consulting Guilfoyle Report and calling first. Uses color prints; 35mm, 2¼×2¼, or 4×5 transparencies. SASE. Reports in 1 month. Pays $200/color cover photo; $75-175/color inside photo; $100/color page rate; $125 color 1⅓ pages; $500-1,000 photo/text packages, but payment varies according to length of text and number of photos. Pays on panel selection. Credit line given. Buys one-time rights.

Tips: "*Pacific Discovery* has a reputation for high-quality photo reproduction and favorable layouts, but photographers must be meticulous about identifying what they shoot."

*PACIFIC UNION RECORDER, Box 5005, Westlake Village CA 91359. (805)497-9457. Editor: C. Elwyn Platner. Circ. 60,000. Estab. 1901. Company publication of Pacific Union Conference at Seventh-day Adventist. Biweekly magazine. Emphasizes religion. Readers are primarily age 18-90 church members. Sample copy free with 8½×11 SAE and 3 first-class stamps. Photo guidelines free with SASE.

Needs: Uses photos for cover only; 80% supplied by freelance photographers. Needs photos of animal/ wildlife shots, travel, scenics, limited to subjects within Nevada, Utah, Arizona, California and Hawaii. Model release required. Captions required.

Making Contact & Terms: Send unsolicited 35mm, 2¼×2¼, 4×5, 8×10 transparencies by mail for consideration. Limit of 10 transparencies or less/year per photographer. SASE. Reports in 1-2 months after contest. Pays $50/color cover photo. Pays on publication. Credit line given. Buys first one-time rights. Simultaneous submissions and previously published work not accepted.

Tips: "Avoid the trite, Yosemite Falls, Half Dome, etc." Holds Annual contest Nov. 1 each year; submit entries in October only.

PENNSYLVANIA ANGLER, Dept. PM, P.O. Box 67000, Harrisburg PA 17106-7000. (717)657-4518. Editor: Art Michaels. Circ. 53,000. Monthly. "*Pennsylvania Angler* is the Keystone State's official fishing magazine, published by the Pennsylvania Fish and Boat Commission." Readers are "anglers who fish in Pennsylvania." Sample copy and photo guidelines free with 9×12 SAE and 4 first-class stamps.

Needs: Uses about 25 photos/issue; 80% supplied by freelancers. Needs "action fishing and boating shots." Model release preferred. Captions required.

Making Contact & Terms: Query with resume of credits. Send 8×10 glossy b&w prints; 35mm or larger transparencies by mail for consideration. SASE. Reports in 2 weeks. Pays up to $200/color cover photo; $25-100/b&w inside photo; $25 up/color inside photo; $50-250 for text/photo package. **Pays on acceptance.** Credit line given. Buys variable rights.

Tips: "Crisp, well-focused action shots get prompt attention."

Market conditions are constantly changing! If you're still using this book and it's 1995 or later, buy the newest edition of **Photographer's Market** *at your favorite bookstore or order directly from* **Writer's Digest Books.**

PENNSYLVANIA HERITAGE, Dept PM, P.O. Box 1026, Harrisburg PA 17108-1026. (717)787-7522. Editor: Michael J. O'Malley, III. Circ. 10,000. Published by the Pennsylvania Historical & Museum Commission. Quarterly magazine. Emphasizes Pennsylvania history, culture and art. Readers are "varied—generally well-educated with an interest in history, museums, travel, etc." Sample copy free with SAE and 65¢ postage. Photo guidelines free with SASE.
Needs: Uses approximately 75 photos/issue; all supplied by freelance photographers; 60% on specific assignment, 40% from stock. Needs photos of "historic sites, artifacts, travel, scenic views, objects of material culture, etc." Photos purchased with accompanying ms only. "We are generally seeking illustrations for specific manuscripts." Captions required.
Making Contact & Terms: Query with samples and list of stock photo subjects. Provide resume, business card, brochure, flyer or tearsheets to be kept on file for possible future assignments. SASE. Reports in 1 month. Pays $5-50/b&w photo and $25-100/color photo. **Pays on acceptance.** Credit line given. Buys all rights. Simultaneous submissions OK.
Tips: "Send query *first* with sample and ideally, a list of Pennsylvania subjects that are available. Quality is everything. Don't bombard an editor or photo buyer with everything—be selective."

PENNSYLVANIAN MAGAZINE, Dept. PM, 2941 N. Front St., Harrisburg PA 17110. (717)236-9526. Fax: (717)236-8164. Editor: Patricia Hazur. Circ. 7,000. Estab. 1962. Monthly magazine of Pennsylvania State Association of Boroughs (and other local governments). Emphasizes local government in Pennsylvania. Readers are officials in small municipalities in Pennsylvania. Sample copy free with 9×12 SAE and 5 first-class stamps.
Needs: Number of photos/issue varies with inside copy. Needs "color photos of scenics (Pennsylvania), local government activities, Pennsylvania landmarks, ecology—for cover photos only; authors of articles supply their own photos." Special photo needs include photos of street and road maintenance work; wetlands scenic. Model release preferred. Captions preferred that include identification of place and/or subject.
Making Contact & Terms: Query with resume of credits. Query with list of stock photo subjects. Send unsolicited photos by mail for consideration. Provide resume, business card, brochure, flyer or tearsheets to be kept on file for possible assignments. Send color prints and 35mm transparencies. Does not keep samples on file. SASE. Reports in 1 month. Pays $25-50/color cover photo. Pays on publication. Buys one-time rights.

PENTECOSTAL EVANGEL, 1445 Boonville, Springfield MO 65802. (417)862-2781. Fax: (417)862-8558. Editor: Richard G. Champion. Managing Editor: John T. Maempa. Circ. 280,000. Official voice of the Assemblies of God, a conservative Pentecostal denomination. Weekly magazine. Emphasizes denomination's activities and inspirational articles for membership. Free sample copy and photographer's/writer's guidelines.
Needs: Uses 25 photos/issue; 5 supplied by freelance photographers. Human interest (very few children and animals). Also needs seasonal and religious shots. "We are interested in photos that can be used to illustrate articles or concepts developed in articles. We are not interested in merely pretty pictures (flowers and sunsets) or in technically unusual effects or photos. We use a lot of people and mood shots." Model release preferred. Captions preferred.
Making Contact & Terms: Send material by mail for consideration. Uses 8×10 b&w and color prints; 35mm or larger transparencies; color 2¼×2¼ to 4×5 transparencies for cover; vertical format preferred. SASE. Reports in 1 month. Pays $25/photo (minimum). **Pays on acceptance.** Credit line given. Buys one-time rights; all rights, but may reassign to photographer after publication; simultaneous rights; or second serial (reprint) rights. Simultaneous submissions and previously published work OK if indicated.
Tips: "Writers and photographers must be familiar with the doctrinal views of the Assemblies of God and standards for membership in churches of the denomination. Send seasonal material 6 months to a year in advance—especially color."

THE PENTECOSTAL MESSENGER, P.O. Box 850, Joplin MO 64802. (417)624-7050. Fax: (417)624-7102. Editor: Don Allen. Circ. 10,000. Estab. 1919. Official publication of the Pentecostal Church of God. Monthly magazine. Sample copy free with 9×12 SASE. Photo guidelines free with SASE.
Needs: Buys 10-12 photos/year; all from freelance stock. Scenic, nature, still life, human interest, Christmas, Thanksgiving, Bible and other religious groupings (Protestant). No photos of women or girls in shorts, pantsuits or sleeveless dresses. No men with cigarettes, liquor or shorts. Model/property release required.
Making Contact & Terms: Interested in receiving work from newer, lesser-known photographers. Send samples of work for consideration. Uses 3½×5 and 8×10 color prints and 2¼×2¼ transparencies. Vertical format required for cover. SASE. Reports in 1 month. Pays $5/inside; $25/outside cover (front). Pays on publication. Credit line given. Buys one-time rights and second serial rights. Simultaneous submissions and previously published work OK.

Tips: "We must see the actual print or slides (120 or larger). Do not write on back of picture; tape on name and address. Enclose proper size envelope and adequate postage. We need open or solid space at top of photo for name of magazine. We also print in the foreground often. Several seasonal photos are purchased each year. In selecting photos, we look for good composition, good color, sharp focus, interesting subject and detail. We anticipate the use of *more* photography (and less art) on covers. Most of our cover material comes from stock material purchased from freelance photographers. We are needing more photos of people related to issues of our day, e.g. abortion, AIDS, suicide, etc. Keep in mind our holiness requirements and look for subjects that would lend themselves to proclaiming the gospel and speaking out on the issues by which we are confronted in today's world."

PLANNING, American Planning Association, 1313 E. 60th St., Chicago IL 60637. (312)955-9100. Editor: Sylvia Lewis. Photo Editor: Richard Sessions. Circ. 30,000. Estab. 1972. Monthly magazine. "We focus on urban and regional planning, reaching most of the nation's professional planners and others interested in the topic." Free sample copy and photo guidelines with 9½×12½ SASE ($1.10 first class, 70¢ fourth class). Writer's guidelines included on photo guidelines sheet.
Needs: Buys 50 photos/year, 95% from freelance stock. Photos purchased with accompanying ms and on assignment. Photo essay/photo feature (architecture, neighborhoods, historic preservation, agriculture); scenic (mountains, wilderness, rivers, oceans, lakes); housing; and transportation (cars, railroads, trolleys, highways). "No cheesecake; no sentimental shots of dogs, children, etc. High artistic quality is very important. We publish high-quality nonfiction stories on city planning and land use. Ours is an association magazine but not a house organ, and we use the standard journalistic techniques: interviews, anecdotes, quotes. Topics include energy, the environment, housing, transportation, land use, agriculture, neighborhoods and urban affairs." Captions required.
Making Contact & Terms: Interested in receiving work from newer, lesser-known photographers. Query with samples. Uses 8×10 glossy and semigloss b&w prints; contact sheet OK; 4-color prints; 35mm or 4×5 transparencies. SASE. Reports in 1 month. Pays $50-100/b&w photo; $50-200/color photo; up to $350/cover photo; $200-600/ms. Pays on publication. Credit line given. Previously published work OK.
Tips: "Just let us know you exist. Eventually, we may be able to use your services. Send tearsheets or photocopies of your work, or a little self-promo piece. Subject lists are only minimally useful. How the work looks is of paramount importance."

POPULATION BULLETIN, Suite 520, 1875 Connecticut Ave., Washington D.C. 20009. (202)483-1100. Fax: (202)328-3937. Art/Production Manager: Aichin Jones. Circ. 15,000. Estab. 1929. Publication of the Population Reference Bureau. Quarterly journal. Publishes other population-related publications, including a monthly newsletter. Emphasizes demography. Readers are educators (both high school and college) of sociology, demography and public policy.
Needs: Uses 8-10 photos/issue; 70% supplied by freelancers. Needs vary widely with topic of each edition—people, families, young, old, all ethnic backgrounds—everyday scenes, world labor force, working people, minorities. Special photo needs include environmental related scenes with or without people. Everyday scenes, closeup pictures of locals in developing countries in S. America, Asia, Africa and Europe. Model/property release required. Captions preferred.
Making Contact & Terms: Interested in receiving work from newer, lesser-known photographers. Query with list of stock photo subjects. Send unsolicited photos by mail for consideration. Send b&w prints or photocopies. SASE. Reports in 1-2 weeks. Pays $25-75/b&w photo; $25-125/color photo. **Pays on acceptance.** Buys one-time rights. Simultaneous submissions and previously published work OK.
Tips: "Looks for subjects relevant to the topics of our publications, quality photographs, composition, artistic value and price."

✹PRESBYTERIAN RECORD, 50 Wynford Dr., Don Mills, Ontario M3C 1J7 Canada. (416)441-1111. Fax: (416)441-2825. Editor: Rev. John Congram. Circ. 68,000. Estab. 1875. Monthly magazine. Emphasizes subjects related to The Presbyterian Church in Canada, ecumenical themes and theological perspectives for church-oriented family audience. Photos purchased with or without accompanying ms. Free sample copy and photo guidelines with 9×12 SAE and $1 postage minimum.
Needs: Religious themes related to features published. No formal poses, food, nude studies, alcoholic beverages, church buildings, empty churches or sports. Captions preferred.
Making Contact & Terms: Interested in receiving work from newer, lesser-known photographers. Send photos. Uses prints only for reproduction; 8×10, 4×5 glossy b&w prints and 35mm and 2¼×2¼ color transparencies. Usually uses 35mm color transparency for cover or ideally, 8×10 transparency. Vertical format used on cover. SAE, IRCs for return of work. Reports in 1 month. Pays $5-25/b&w print; $50 up/cover photo; $20-50 for text/photo package. Pays on publication. Credit line given. Buys one-time rights; negotiable. Simultaneous submissions and previously published work OK.
Tips: "Unusual photographs related to subject needs are welcome."

PRESERVATION NEWS, Dept. PM, 1785 Massachusetts Ave. NW, Washington DC 20036. (202)673-4075. Executive Editor: Arnold Berke. Circ. 210,000. Estab. 1969. Publication of the National Trust for Historic Preservation. Monthly tabloid. Emphasizes historic preservation and building restoration. Readers are professional men and women, 20 years of age and older. Sample copy free with 9×12 SASE.
Needs: Uses 20 photos/issue; 15% supplied by freelancers. Needs photos of buildings, people with buildings, "event" shots (ceremonies, parties, openings, etc.) and scenics. Model release preferred. Captions preferred.
Making Contact & Terms: Query with list of stock photos. Provide resume, business card, brochure, flyer or tearsheets to be kept on file for possible assignments. SASE. Reports in 3 weeks. Pays $25-100/b&w cover or inside photo; $300-400/day. Pays on publication. Credit line given. Buys one-time rights. Previously published work OK.

PRINCETON ALUMNI WEEKLY, Dept. PM, 194 Nassau St., Princeton NJ 08542. (609)258-4885. Editor-in-Chief: J.I. Merritt. Photo Editor: Stacey Wszola. Circ. 52,000. Biweekly. Emphasizes Princeton University and higher education. Readers are alumni, faculty, students, staff and friends of Princeton University. Sample copy $1.50 with 8½×11 SAE and 37¢ postage.
Needs: Uses about 15 photos/issue; 10 supplied by freelance photographers. Needs b&w photos of "people, campus scenes; subjects vary greatly with content of each issue. Show us photos of Princeton." Captions required.
Making Contact & Terms: Arrange a personal interview to show portfolio. Provide brochure to be kept on file for possible future assignments. SASE. Reports in 1 month. Pays $100/b&w cover; $200/color cover; $25/b&w inside photo; $50/color inside photo; $45/hour. Pays on publication. Buys one-time rights. Simultaneous submissions and previously published work OK.

PRINCIPAL MAGAZINE, Dept. PM, 1615 Duke St., Alexandria VA 22314-3483. (703)684-3345. Editor: Lee Greene. Circ. 25,000. Estab. 1921. Publication of the National Association of Elementary School Principals. Bimonthly. Emphasizes public education—kindergarten to 8th grade. Readers are mostly principals of elementary and middle schools. Sample copy free with SASE.
 • This publication has received numerous awards for cover photography and overall design, including a silver Ozzie Award in 1992 from *Magazine Design & Production* and a 1st Place honor for content and design from the Washington Edpress Excellence in Print Awards.
Needs: Uses 5-10 b&w photos/issue; all supplied by freelancers. Needs photos of school scenes (classrooms, playgrounds, etc.), teaching situations, school principals at work, computer use and technology and science activities. The magazine sometimes has theme issues, such as back to school, technology and early childhood education. *No posed groups.* Close-ups preferred. Reviews photos with or without accompanying ms. Model release preferred. Captions preferred.
Making Contact & Terms: Interested in receiving work from newer, lesser-known photographers. Query with samples and list of stock photo subjects. Send b&w prints, b&w contact sheet by mail for consideration. SASE. Reports in 1 month. Pays $50/b&w photo. Pays on publication. Credit line given. Buys one-time rights; negotiable. Simultaneous submissions and previously published work OK.

PROCEEDINGS/NAVAL HISTORY, US Naval Institute, Annapolis MD 21402. (410)268-6110. Picture Editor: Charles Mussi. Circ. 110,000. Estab. 1873. Association publications. *Proceedings* is a monthly magazine and *Naval History* is a bimonthly publication. Emphasizes Navy, Marine Corps, Coast Guard. Readers are age 18+, male and female, naval officers, enlisted, retirees, civilians. Sample copy free with 9×12 SAE and 1 first-class stamp. Photo guidelines free with SASE.
Needs: Uses 50 photos/issue; 40% supplied by freelancers. Needs photos of foreign and US Naval, Coast Guard and Marine Corps vessels, personnel and aircraft. Captions required.
Making Contact & Terms: Send unsolicited photos by mail for consideration: 8×10 glossy or matte, b&w or color prints; 35mm transparencies. SASE. Reports in 1 month. Pays $200/color or b&w cover photo; $25/color inside photo; $25/b&w page rate; $250-500/photo/text package. Pays on publication. Credit line given. Buys one-time rights. Simultaneous submissions and previously published work OK.

PRORODEO SPORTS NEWS, Dept. PM, 101 Pro Rodeo Dr., Colorado Springs CO 80919. (719)593-8840. Editor: Kendra Santos. Circ. 30,000. Publication of Professional Rodeo Cowboys Association. Biweekly tabloid. Emphasizes professional rodeo. Sample copy $1.
Needs: Uses about 18 photos/issue; 5-6 supplied by freelancers. Needs action rodeo photos. Also uses behind-the-scenes photos, cowboys preparing to ride, talking behind the chutes—something other than action. Special needs include quality color prints from outdoor and indoor rodeos; also use b&w. Captions required.
Making Contact & Terms: Send 5×7, 8×10 glossy b&w and color prints by mail for consideration. SASE. Pays $50/color cover photo; $10/b&w and color inside photo. Other payment negotiable. Pays end of month. Credit line given. Buys all rights; negotiable.

© Robert Finken

The actions of each child on the playground equipment make this a fun photo, making it perfect for the pages of **Principal Magazine.** *Photographer Robert Finken, of Glendale, Arizona, says the image was used to illustrate an article entitled "Playground Reflections."*

Tips: In portfolio or samples, wants to see "the ability to capture a cowboy's character outside the competition arena, as well as inside. In reviewing samples we look for clean, sharp reproduction—no grain. Photographer should respond quickly to photo requests. I see more PRCA sponsor-related photos being printed."

PTA TODAY, 330 N. Wabash, Chicago IL 60611. (312)787-0977. Photo Editor: Moosi Raza Rizvi. Circ. 40,000. Estab. 1975. Published 7 times/year. Emphasizes parent education. Readers are parents living in the US—rural, urban, suburban and exurban. Sample copy $2.50 with 9×12 SASE.
Needs: Uses about 20-25 b&w photos/issue; all supplied by freelancers, 100% from stock. Needs "candid, not cutesy, shots of kids of all ages who live in the 1990s; their parents and teachers; anything to do with infancy through adolescence." Model release required "allowing photo to be used at the editor's discretion in *PTA Today* and other PTA publications."
Making Contact & Terms: Interested in receiving work from newer, lesser-known photographers. Send b&w prints only (any size) by mail for consideration. SASE. Reports within 2 weeks. Pays $50/b&w inside photo; $100/b&w cover each time used. Pays on publication. Credit line given on contents page. Simultaneous submissions and previously published work OK. Every photo should have the name and address of photographer.
Tips: "Our preference is for the dramatic, uncluttered, strong contrast, crisp and clean photos. Desperately need minority and mixed groups of children with each other or with parents, talking, discussing—all ages. Should be recent shots. Send SASE for schedule of topics to be covered in upcoming issues."

PUBLIC CITIZEN, 2000 P St. NW, Washington DC 20036. (202)833-3000. Editor: Peter Nye. Circ. 150,000. Bimonthly. "*Public Citizen* is the magazine of the membership organization of the same name, founded by Ralph Nader in 1971. The magazine addresses topics of concern to today's socially aware and politically active consumers on issues in consumer rights, safe products and workplaces, a clean environment, safe and efficient energy, and corporate and government accountability." Sample copy free with 9×12 SAE and 2 first-class stamps.

Needs: Uses 7-10 photos/issue; 2 supplied by freelancers. Needs photos to go along with articles on various consumer issues—assigns for press conference coverage or portrait shot of interview. Buys stock for other purposes.

Making Contact & Terms: Provide resume, business card, brochure, flyer or tearsheets to be kept on file for possible future assignments. Does not return unsolicited material. Pays $50-75/b&w inside photo. Pays on publication. Credit line given. Buys first N.A. serial rights. Simultaneous submissions and previously published work OK.

Tips: Prefers to see "good photocopies of photos and list of stock to keep on file. Common subjects: nuclear power, presidential administrations, health and safety issues, citizen empowerment, union democracy, etc."

PUBLIC POWER, Third Floor, 2301 M. St. NW, Washington DC 20037. (202)467-2948. Editor: Jeanne LaBella. Circ. 12,000. Publication of the American Public Power Association. Bimonthly. Emphasizes electric power provided by cities, towns and utility districts. Circ. 12,000. Sample copy and photo guidelines free.

Needs: "We buy photos on assignment only."

Making Contact & Terms: Query with samples. Provide resume, business card, brochure, flyer or tearsheets to be kept on file for possible future assignments. SASE. Reports in 1-2 weeks. Pay varies— $25-75/photo—more for covers. **Pays on acceptance.** Credit line given. Buys one-time rights. Simultaneous submissions and previously published work OK.

THE PULLER, Dept. PM, Suite L, 6969 Worthington-Galena Rd., Worthington OH 43085. (614)436-1761. Fax: (614)436-0964. Editor: Rhdawnda Bliss. Circ. 10,000. Estab. 1970. Publication of the National Tractor Pullers Association. Monthly magazine. Emphasizes tractor and truck pulling. Readers are mostly working class men and women, ages 18-36. Sample copies $2.50.

Needs: Uses up to 75 photos/issue; 60% supplied by freelancers. Needs photos of motorsport action and personalities in field. Reviews photos with or without ms. Especially wants to see coverage of NTPA's national pulling circuit in the coming year. Model release preferred. Captions required; include description of location, date, year and subject.

Making Contact & Terms: Send unsolicited 4×5 glossy b&w or color prints by mail for consideration. Also considers 35mm and 2¼×2¼ transparencies. Provide resume, business card, brochure, flyer or tearsheets to be kept on file for possible assignments. Keeps samples on file. SASE. Reports in 1 month. Pays $50/color cover; $15-50 inside photo. Pays on publication. Credit line given. Buys all rights; negotiable. Simultaneous submissions OK.

PURE–BRED DOGS/AMERICAN KENNEL GAZETTE, 51 Madison Ave., New York NY 10010. (212)696-8333. Photo Editor: David Savage. Circ. 58,000. Estab. 1889. Official publication of the American Kennel Club. Monthly. Emphasizes AKC pure-bred dogs. Readers are pure-bred dog fanciers and owners. Photo guidelines free with SASE.

Needs: Uses about 50 photos/issue; 50% supplied by freelancers. About "50% of covers are on assignment; most other work is submitted by professional and freelance 'dog' photographers." Needs photos of AKC pure-bred dogs (outdoor candids, excellent breed representatives). Model release preferred. Captions preferred.

Making Contact & Terms: Query with samples. Send 5×7 b&w and color prints; 35mm, 2¼×2¼ transparencies by mail for consideration (dupes only, no originals). SASE. Reports in 3 weeks. Pays $250/color cover photo; $25-100/color or b&w inside photo. Pays on publication. Buys first N.A. serial rights.

Tips: Prefers to see candids with attractive backgrounds. No show poses. Excellent show-quality representatives of AKC breeds, naturally posed or in action, "extremely sharp, with good contrast and lots of detail." Prefers duplicate transparencies. "Read the magazine and attend dog shows where quality dogs can be found as subjects." Trend is "more elegant rather than cute. No props or costumes. Simple backgrounds. Dog should be primary focus. Casual, not overly posed."

*REFORM JUDAISM, 838 Fifth Ave., New York NY 10021. (212)249-0100. Managing Editor: Joy Weinberg. Circ. 295,000. Estab. 1972. Publication of the Union of American Hebrew Congregations. Quarterly magazine. Emphasizes Reform Judaism. Readers are members of Reform congregations in North America. Sample copy $3.50.

The Subject Index, located at the back of this book, can help you find publications interested in the topics you shoot.

Needs: Uses 35 photos/issue; 10% supplied by freelancers. Needs photos relating to Jewish life or Jewish issues, Israel, politics. Captions required.

Making Contact & Terms: Provide resume, business card, brochure, flyer or tearsheets to be kept on file for possible assignments. Reports in 1 month. Pays on publication. Credit line given. Buys one-time rights; first N.A. serial rights. Simultaneous submissions and/or previously published work OK.

Tips: Wants to see "excellent photography: artistic, creative, evocative pictures that involve the reader."

RELAY MAGAZINE, P.O. Box 10114, Tallahassee FL 32302-2114. (904)224-3314. Editor: Stephanie Wolanski. Circ. 1,800. Estab. 1957. Association publication of Florida Municipal Electric. Monthly magazine. Emphasizes municipally owned electric utilities. Readers are city officials, legislators, public power officials and employees. Sample copy free with 9 × 12 SAE and 3 first-class stamps.

Needs: Uses various amounts of photos/issue; various number supplied by freelancers. Needs b&w photos of electric utilities in Florida (hurricane/storm damage to lines, utility workers, etc.). Special photo needs include hurricane/storm photos. Model/property release preferred. Captions required.

Making Contact & Terms: Send unsolicited photos by mail for consideration. Query with letter, description of photo. Send 5 × 7 or 8 × 10 b&w prints. Keeps samples on file. SASE. Reports in 1 month. Pays $20 and up/b&w cover photo; $10 and up/b&w inside photo. **Pays on acceptance.** Credit line given. Buys one-time rights, repeated use (stock); negotiable. Simultaneous submissions and/or previously published work OK.

Tips: "Must relate to our industry. Clarity and contrast important. Query first if possible."

THE RETIRED OFFICER MAGAZINE, 201 N. Washington St., Alexandria VA 22314. (800)245-8762. Fax: (703)838-8179. Contact: Associate Editor. Circ. 380,000. Estab. 1945. Monthly. Publication represents the interests of retired military officers from the seven uniformed services: recent military history (particularly Vietnam and Korea), travel, health, second-career job opportunities, military family lifestyle and current military/political affairs. Readers are officers or warrant officers from the Army, Navy, Air Force, Marine Corps, Coast Guard, Public Health Service and NOAA. Free sample copy and photo guidelines with 9 × 12 SAE and $1.25 postage.

Needs: Uses about 24 photos/issue; 8 (the cover and some inside shots) usually supplied by freelancers. "We're always looking for good color slides of active duty military people and healthy, active mature adults with a young 50s look—our readers are 55-65."

Making Contact & Terms: Interested in receiving work from newer, lesser-known photographers. Query with list of stock photo subjects. Provide resume, brochure, flyer to be kept on file. Do *not* send original photos unless requested to do so. Uses original 35mm, 2¼ × 2¼ or 4 × 5 transparencies. Pays $200/color cover photo; $20/b&w inside photo; $50-125 transparencies for inside use (in color); complimentary copies. Other payment negotiable. **Pays on acceptance.** Credit line given. Buys one-time rights.

Tips: "A photographer who can also write and submit a complete package of story and photos is valuable to us. Much of our photography is supplied by our authors as part of their manuscript package. We periodically select a cover photo from these submissions—our covers relate to a particular feature in each issue." In samples, wants to see "good color saturation, well-focused, excellent composition."

ROCKFORD REVIEW and TRIBUTARY, P.O. Box 858, Rockford IL 61105. Editor: David Ross. Association publications of Rockford Writers' Guild. *Review* is annual, *Tributary* quarterly magazine. Circ. 1,000. Estab. 1982. Emphasizes poetry and prose of all types. Readers are of all stages and ages who share an interest in quality writing and art. Sample copy $6 *Review*, $2.50 *Tributary*.

• These two publications are literary in nature and publish very few photographs.

Needs: Uses 1-5 photos/issue; all supplied by freelancers. Needs photos of scenics and personalities. Model/property release preferred. Captions preferred; include when and where of the photos and biography.

Making Contact & Terms: Interested in receiving work from newer, lesser-known photographers. Send unsolicited photos by mail for consideration. Send 8 × 10 or 5 × 7 glossy b&w prints. Does not keep samples on file. SASE. Reports in 4-6 weeks. Pays in one copy of magazine, but work is eligible for *Review*'s $50 Editor's Choice prize and *Tributary*'s $25 Readers' Poll prize. Pays on publication. Credit line given. Buys first N.A. serial rights. Simultaneous submissions OK.

Tips: "Experimental work with a literary magazine in mind will be carefully considered. Avoid the 'news' approach." Sees more opportunities for artsy photos.

THE ROTARIAN, 1560 Sherman Ave., Evanston IL 60201. (312)866-3000. Fax: (708)866-9732. Editor: Willmon L. White. Photo Editor: Judy Lee. Circ. 530,435. Estab. 1911. Monthly magazine. For Rotarian business and professional men and women and their families in 159 countries and geographic regions. Free sample copy and photo guidelines with SASE.

© photo by William Skutans

David Ross, editor-in-chief of the Rockford Review, says this image, "Solarized Homer," continues to haunt him because of its overpowering creative appeal. "That's what Rockford Review strives to do in its photos, illustrations, prose, poetry and drama," says Ross. Snapped by Will Skutans of Rockford, Illinois, the shot was used for the literary magazine's Volume X cover.

Needs: "Our greatest need is for the identifying face or landscape, one that says unmistakably, 'This is Japan, or Minnesota, or Brazil, or France or Sierra Leone,' or any of the other countries and geographic regions this magazine reaches." Captions preferred.

Making Contact & Terms: Interested in receiving work from newer, lesser-known photographers. Query with resume of credits or send photos for consideration. Uses 8 × 10 glossy b&w or color prints; contact sheet OK; 8 × 10 color glossy prints; for cover uses transparencies "generally related to the contents of that month's issue." SASE. Reports in 1-2 weeks. **Pays on acceptance.** NPI; payment varies. Buys one-time rights; occasionally all rights; negotiable.

Tips: "We prefer vertical shots in most cases. The key words for the freelance photographer to keep in mind are *internationality* and *variety*. Study the magazine. Read the kinds of articles we publish. Think how your photographs could illustrate such articles in a dramatic, story-telling way. Key submissions to general interest, art-of-living material." Plans special pre-convention promotion coverage of June 1994 Rotary International convention in Taipei, Taiwan.

SCIENCE AND CHILDREN, 3140 N. Washington Blvd., Arlington VA 22201. (703)243-7100. Circ. 24,000. Publication of the National Science Teachers Association. Monthly (September to May) journal. Emphasizes teaching science to elementary school children. Readers are male and female elementary science teachers and other education professionals.

Needs: Uses 40 photos/issue; 10 supplied by freelancers. Needs photos of "a variety of science-related topics, though seasonals, nature scenes and animals are often published. Also children." Special photo needs include children doing science in all settings, especially classroom. Model/property release required. Captions required.

Making Contact & Terms: Arrange personal interview to show portfolio. Send unsolicited b&w prints by mail for consideration. Pays $200/color cover photo; $50/color inside; $35 b&w inside. Pays on publication. Credit line given. Simultaneous submissions and previously published work OK.

Tips: "We can always use photographs of children and teachers working together."

THE SCIENCE TEACHER, NSTA, 3140 N. Washington Blvd., Arlington VA 22201. (703)243-7100. Fax: (703)243-7100. Managing Editor: Shelley Carey. Circ. 27,000. Estab. 1950s. Publication of the National Science Teachers Association. Publishes 9 monthly issues per year. Emphasizes high school science education. Readers are adult science teachers. Sample copy and photo guidelines free upon request.

Needs: Uses 5-10 photos/issue; assigns 35% of photos; uses less than 5% from stock. Needs color and b&w shots of high school students and teachers; no nature/scenics needed. Model release "required only if run with article on special education." Property release preferred. "No photo captions, please."

Making Contact & Terms: Interested in receiving work from newer, lesser-known photographers. Arrange personal interview to show portfolio. Query with stock photo list. Send 8 × 10 glossy b&w prints or 8 × 10 transparencies by mail for consideration. Provide resume, business card, brochure, flyer or tearsheets to be kept on file for possible assignments. SASE. "Often reports in 6 months for prints; sooner for queries." Pays $150/color cover; $50/b&w or color full page; or $35/b&w smaller page rate. Pays on publication. Credit line given. Buys one-time rights; rights negotiable. Simultaneous submissions and previously published work OK.

Tips: "Looking for a solid, basic style. We need photos of students and teachers in classroom and laboratory environments. The activities they are doing should not be too specific so we can use the photo in any article. We need more photos of women and minorities. Don't get too 'artsy.' "

SCOUTING MAGAZINE, Boy Scouts of America, 1325 Walnut Hill Lane, Irving TX 75062. Photo Editor: Brian Payne. Circ. 1 million. Bimonthly magazine. For adults within the Scouting movement. Free photo guidelines.

Needs: Assigns 90% of photos; uses 10% from stock. Needs photos dealing with success and/or personal interest of leaders in Scouting. Wants no "single photos or ideas from individuals unfamiliar with our magazine." Captions required.

Making Contact & Terms: "No assignments will be considered without a portfolio review by mail or in person." Call to arrange a personal appointment, or query with ideas. SASE. Reports in 10 working days. NPI. **Pays on acceptance.** Buys one-time rights.

Tips: Study the magazine carefully. In portfolio or samples, wants to see "diversity and ability to light difficult situations."

SCRAP PROCESSING AND RECYCLING, Suite 1000, 1325 G St. NW, Washington DC 20005. (202)466-4050. Fax: (202)775-9109. Editor: Elise Browne. Circ. 6,000. Estab. 1988. Publication of the Institute of Scrap Recycling Industries. Bimonthly magazine. Covers scrap recycling for owners and managers of private recycling operations worldwide. Sample copy $7.50.

Needs: Uses approx. 100 photos/issue; 15% supplied by freelancers. Needs operation shots of companies being profiled and studio concept shots. Model release required. Captions required.

Making Contact & Terms: Arrange personal interview to show portfolio. Query with list of stock photo subjects. Provide resume, business card, brochure, flyer or tearsheets to be kept on file for possible assignment. Reports in 1 month. Pays $500-800/day. Pays on publication. Credit line given. Rights negotiable. Previously published work OK.

Tips: Photographers must possess "ability to photograph people in corporate atmosphere as well as industrial operations; ability to work well with executives as well as laborers. We are always looking for good color photographers to accompany our staff writers on visits to companies being profiled. We try to keep travel costs to a minimum by hiring photographers located in the general vicinity of the profiled company. Other photography (primarily studio work) is usually assigned through freelance art director."

SEA FRONTIERS INC., UM Kinght Theater, 4th Floor, 400 SE Second Ave., Miami FL 33131. (305)375-8498. Fax: (305)375-9188. Editor: Bonnie Gordon. Art Director: Phoebe Diftler. Circ. 47,000. Estab. 1954. Bimonthly magazine. For anyone with an interest in any aspect of the sea, the life it contains and its conservation. Sample copy $5 postpaid. Photo guidelines free with SASE.
- In 1992 this publication received numerous Charlie Awards from the Florida Magazine Association, including honors for Best Overall Design, Best Use of Photography and Best Cover.

Needs: Buys 350 photos/year. Animal, nature, photo feature, scenic, wildlife, industry, vessels, structures and geological features. Ocean-related subjects only. Captions required.

Making Contact & Terms: Send photos for consideration. Send 35mm or 2¼×2¼ transparencies. Uses vertical format for cover. Allow space for insertion of logo. SASE. Reports in 1 month. Pays $30-50/color photo; $50/quarter page; $50/half page; $100/full page; $200/front cover; $75/back cover. Pays on publication. Credit line given. Buys one-time rights.

THE SECRETARY, Suite 706, 2800 Shirlington Rd., Arlington VA 22206. (703)998-2534. Publisher: Debra J. Stratton. Circ. 50,000. Estab. 1942. Association publication of the Professional Secretaries International. Published 9 times a year. Emphasizes secretarial profession—proficiency, continuing education, new products/methods and equipment related to office administration/communications. Readers include career secretaries, 98% women, in myriad offices, with wide ranging responsibilities. Sample copy free with SASE.

Needs: Uses 6 photos/issue; freelance photos 100% from stock. Needs secretaries (predominately women, but occasionally men) in appropriate and contemporary office settings using varied office equipment or performing varied office tasks. Must be in good taste and portray professionalism of secretaries. Especially interested in photos featuring members of minority groups. Reviews photos with or without accompanying ms. Model release preferred.

Making Contact & Terms: Interested in receiving work from newer, lesser-known photographers. Query with samples. Send unsolicited photos by mail for consideration. Uses 3½×4½, 8×10 glossy prints; 35mm, 2¼×2¼, 4×5 and 8×10 transparencies. SASE. Reports in 1 month. Pays $150 maximum/b&w photo; $500 maximum/color photo. Pays on publication. Credit line given. Buys first N.A. serial rights. Simultaneous submissions and previously published work OK.

THE SENTINEL, Industrial Risk Insurers, Dept. PM, 85 Woodland St., Hartford CT 06102. (203)520-7300. Editor: Anson Smith. Circ. 59,000. Quarterly magazine. Emphasizes industrial loss prevention for "insureds and all individuals interested in fire protection." Free sample copy and photo guidelines.

Needs: Uses 4-8 photos/issue; 2-3 supplied by freelance photographers. Needs photos of fires, explosions, windstorm damage and other losses at industrial sites. Prefers to see good industrial fires and industrial process shots, industrial and commercial fire protection equipment. No photos that do not pertain to industrial loss prevention (no house fires) but can use generic shots of natural disaster damage, e.g., floods, hurricanes, tornadoes. Model release preferred.

Making Contact & Terms: Send material by mail for consideration. Uses b&w or color glossy prints. Horizontal or vertical format for cover. Reports in 2 weeks. Pays $35/b&w photo; $100/color photo; $100/cover photo. **Pays on acceptance.** Credit line given. Buys one-time rights. Previously published work OK.

SERVICES, Dept. PM, Suite 225, 10201 Lee Highway, Fairfax VA 22030. (703)359-7090 or (800)368-3414. Editor: Patrick G. Johnstone. Circ. 15,000. Publication of the Building Service Contractors Association International. Monthly. Emphasizes building service contracting (janitorial mostly). Read-

A bullet has been placed within some listings to introduce special comments by the editor of the Photographer's Market.

ers largely consist of building service contractors, manufacturers and distributors of sanitary supplies, building owners and managers, and hospitals. Sample copy free with 9 × 12 SAE and $1.50 postage.

Needs: Needs photos of building maintenance services performed by outside contractors—office cleaning, floor and carpet care, window washing, lighting maintenance, exterior maintenance. Always needs good material on janitorial cleaning, floor and carpet care, upholstery and drapery care, water and fire damage restoration, window washing. Also needs photos for managerial articles—financial management, staff training, etc. Model release required. Captions required.

Making Contact & Terms: Arrange a personal interview to show portfolio. Send 8 × 10 matte b&w prints; 35mm transparencies; b&w contact sheets by mail for consideration. SASE. Reports in 1 week. Pays $350/color cover photo; $400-600/day. **Pays on acceptance.** Credit line given. Buys one-time rights. Simultaneous submissions and previously published work OK.

Tips: Prefers to see "strong communication values—photos that *tell me* something about the subject. Don't want something that looks like a set-up stock photo."

SHARING THE VICTORY, Publication of the Fellowship of Christian Athletes, Dept. PM, 8701 Leeds Rd., Kansas City MO 64129. Editor: John Dodderidge. Provides year-round outreach to athletes and coaches. "Best to study sample copy first. Send $1 plus 9 × 12 SASE."

Needs: Buys 12-15 photos/year. Photos used in magazines. Close-up and thoughtful or dramatic sports-related shots: "lots of high quality 35mm transparencies and color prints depicting the gamut of action and emotion in high-school-age team and individual sports; shots depicting camaraderie, sportsmanship, loyalty, humor etc., among both male and female athletes will be favorably considered." Model release preferred with close-ups but not necessary.

Making Contact & Terms: Query with samples. SASE. Reports in 2-3 weeks. Uses b&w and color prints, 35mm transparencies, b&w contact sheets. Pays $50-100/b&w photo and $100-200/color photo. Pays on publication. Credit line given. Buys one-time rights.

Tips: In reviewing samples looks for "technical excellence (clarity, density, etc.); creativity (freshness of angle, mood, etc); and applications to magazine's target audience (in this case high school male/female athletes)." Wants to see "35mm color slides of *Sports Illustrated* quality" in samples.

SHOOTING SPORTS USA, Dept. PM, 1600 Rhode Island Ave. NW, Washington DC 20036. (202)828-6000. Editor: Karen Elsner. Circ. 125,000. Publication of the National Rifle Association of America. Monthly. Emphasizes competitive shooting sports (rifle, pistol and shotgun). Readers are mostly NRA-classified competitive shooters including Olympic-level shooters. Sample copy free with 9 × 12 SAE with $1 postage. Editorial guidelines free with SASE.

Needs: Uses 1-10 photos/issue; about half or less supplied by freelance photographers. Needs photos of how-to, shooting positions, specific shooters. Photos preferred with ms, but will accept quality photos for covers. Model release required. Captions preferred.

Making Contact & Terms: Query with photo and editorial ideas by mail. Uses 8 × 10 glossy b&w prints. SASE. Reports in 2 weeks. Pays $150-250 for photo/text package; amount varies for photos alone. Pays on publication. Credit line given. Buys first N.A. serial rights. Previously published work OK when cleared with editor.

Tips: Looks for "generic photos of shooters shooting—obeying all safety rules—proper eye protection and hearing protection. If text concerns certain how-to advice, photos are needed to illuminate this. Always query first. We are in search of quality photos to interest both beginning and experienced shooters."

SIGNPOST MAGAZINE, Dept. PM, #512, 1305 Fourth Ave., Seattle WA 98101. (206)625-1367. Editor: Dan Nelson. Circ. 3,800. Estab. 1966. Publication of the Washington Trails Association. Monthly. Emphasizes "backpacking, hiking, cross-country skiing, all nonmotorized trail use, outdoor equipment and minimum-impact camping techniques." Readers are "people active in outdoor activities, primarily backpacking; residents of the Pacific Northwest, mostly Washington; age group: 9-90, family-oriented, interested in wilderness preservation, trail maintenance." Free sample copy. Photo guidelines free with SASE.

Needs: Uses about 10-15 photos/issue; 30% supplied by freelancers. Needs "wilderness/scenic; people involved in hiking, backpacking, canoeing, skiing, wildlife, outdoor equipment photos, all with Pacific Northwest emphasis." Captions required.

Making Contact & Terms: Send 5 × 7 or 8 × 10 glossy b&w prints by mail for consideration. SASE. Reports in 1 month. No payment for inside photos. Pays $25/b&w cover photo. Pays on publication. Credit line given. Buys one-time rights. Simultaneous submissions and previously published work OK.

Tips: "We are a b&w publication and prefer using b&w originals for the best reproduction. Photos must have a Pacific Northwest slant. Photos that meet our cover specifications are always of interest to us. Familiarity with our magazine would greatly aid the photographer in submitting material to us; a sample copy is free. Contributing to *Signpost* won't help pay your bills, but sharing your photos with other backpackers and skiers has its own rewards."

THE SINGLE PARENT, 8807 Colesville Rd., Silver Spring MD 20910. (301)588-9354. Fax: (301)588-9216. Contact: Editor. Circ. 90,000. Estab. 1957. Publication of Parents Without Partners, Inc. Published 6 times a year. Emphasizes "issues of concern to single parents: widowed, divorced, separated or never-married, and their children, from legal, financial, emotional, how-to, legislative or first-person experience." Readers are "parents mainly between 30-55, US and Canada." Sample copy free with SAE plus postage at 3 oz. rate.

Needs: Uses 4-7 photos/issue; all supplied by freelancers; 5-10% from assignment and 90-95% from stock. "We usually make assignments for a particular story. All photos relate to and illustrate articles in the magazine." Model release required. Property release preferred. Captions required.

Making Contact & Terms: Interested in receiving work from newer, lesser-known photographers. Query with samples. Send 8×10 b&w prints, b&w contact sheets and color slides/photos by mail for consideration. Provide resume, business card, brochure, flyer or tearsheets to be kept on file for possible future assignments. "35mm slides should be presented in multi-pocket, plastic slide pages, not jumbled loosely in an envelope. We're not interested in snapshots sent in by proud parents." SASE. Reports in 2 months. Pays $100/color cover photo; $35-50/b&w inside photo. Pays on publication. Credit line given. Buys one-time rights. Simultaneous submissions OK.

Tips: "We have received photo selections on long-term hold from several freelancers. Our first search for each issue is within these selections, and up to 6 photos in each issue are from these selections. We also have contact sheets and tearsheets from freelancers we query periodically for specific subjects and situations. Subjects we look for in samples are: children—happy, unhappy, angry, interacting; and children with one parent in all kinds of settings—reading, playing, working, *especially dads/kids*. Styles: abstract OK; sensitivity to mood, aesthetics. We occasionally need, and never find, children who are not on their best behavior. We usually look for a photo that easily relates to some aspect of the article to be illustrated. Often, this will establish a mood; sometimes it is symbolic of the theme of the article. Once in a great while, one will exactly match some situation portrayed in the article."

SOUTHERN CALIFORNIA BUSINESS, 404 S. Bixel St., Los Angeles CA 90017. (213)629-0671. Fax: (213)629-0611. Editor: Christopher Volker. Circ. 12,000. Estab. 1898. Association publication of L.A. Chamber of Commerce. Monthly newspaper. Emphasizes business. Readers are mostly business owners, male and female, ages 21-65. Sample copy $2. Photo guidelines not available.

Needs: Uses 10-20 photos/issue; 5-8 supplied by freelance photographers and public relations agencies. Needs photos of events, editorial, technology, business people and new products. Special photo needs include specialty shots on various subjects (mainly business-oriented).

Making Contact & Terms: Interested in receiving work from newer, lesser-known photographers. Query with list of stock photo subjects. Send b&w prints by mail for consideration. Provide resume, business card, brochure, flyer or tearsheets to be kept on file for possible assignments. SASE. Reports in 3 weeks. Pays $4-5/b&w photo; $100/b&w cover photo; $80-100/hour; $100-150/day; $100-250/photo/text package. Pays on publication. Credit line given. Buys first N.A. serial rights and all rights; negotiable. Model release required. Captions required. Simultaneous submissions OK.

Tips: In photographer's samples, wants to see "a variety of different subject matter but prefer people shots. Present new ideas, how photography could be more exciting. Send in detailed letter and description of work."

SPECTRUM, The Horace Mann Companies, One Horace Mann Plaza, Springfield IL 62715. (217)789-2500. Contact: Dave Waugh. Mail number L102. Monthly publication for employees. Includes articles on company programs, monthly employee honors and human interest features on employees and their families.

Needs: Uses about 35 photos/issue; 3-4 supplied by freelancers. "We need photos of our agents at work and with their families." Captions (at least names) preferred.

Making Contact & Terms: Provide resume, business card, brochure, flyer or tearsheets to be kept on file for possible future assignments. SASE. Reports "as soon as we would need a photographer from his/her area of the country." Pays $25-30/hour; $175 maximum/job. **Pays on acceptance.** Credit line given. Buys all rights and negatives. Simultaneous submissions and previously published work OK.

SPORTS CAR, Suite E, 1371 E. Warner, Tustin CA 92680. (714)259-8240. Editor: Rich McCormack. Circ. 50,000. Estab. 1944. Publication of the Sports Car Club of America. Monthly magazine. Emphasizes sports car racing and competition activities. Sample copy $2.95.

Needs: Uses 75-100 photos/issue; 75% from assignment and 25% from freelance stock. Needs action photos from competitive events, personality portraits and technical photos.

Making Contact & Terms: Query with resume of credits or send 5×7 color or b&w glossy/borders prints or 35mm or 2¼×2¼ transparencies by mail for consideration. Provide resume, business card, brochure, flyer or tearsheets to be kept on file for possible assignments. SASE. Reports in 1 month. Pays $25/color inside photo; $10/b&w inside photo; $250/color cover. Negotiates all other rates. Pays on publication. Credit line given. Buys first N.A. serial rights. Simultaneous submissions OK.

Tips: To break in with this or any magazine, "always send only the absolute best work; try to accommodate the specific needs of your clients. Have a relevant subject, strong action, crystal sharp focus, proper contrast and exposure. We need good candid personality photos of key competitors and officials."

STATE GOVERNMENT NEWS, Iron Works Pike, Box 11910, Lexington KY 40578. (606)231-1842. Executive Editor: Dag Ryen. Circ. 18,000. Estab. 1957. Publication of The Council of State Governments. Monthly. Emphasizes state government issues. Readers are state legislators and officials. Sample copy free with 9×12 SAE and $1 postage.
Needs: Uses about 12 photos/issue. Needs photos of state employees and decision makers in action. Model release required. Captions required.
Making Contact & Terms: Interested in receiving work from newer, lesser-known photographers. Query with list of stock photo subjects. Provide resume, business card, brochure, flyer or tearsheets to be kept on file for possible future assignments. SASE. Pays $150/color cover photo; $25/b&w inside photo. Pays on publication. Credit line not given. Buys one-time rights. Simultaneous submissions OK.
Tips: "Check with us for our current needs. Photograph people who are active and expressive. We may begin using more color."

*STL, 6996 Millbrook Blvd., St. Louis MO 63130. (314)726-7685. Fax: (314)726-0677. Art Director: Kathy Sewing. Circ. 52,000. Estab. 1991. City magazine published by KETC-TV (Channel 9). Monthly magazine. Emphasizes public television and local arts, history, education and culture. Readers are college educated; affluent men and women in Missouri and Illinois, primarily ages 50 and older. Sample copy free with 9×12 SAE and 4 first-class stamps.
Needs: Uses 16-20 photos/issue; 40% supplied by freelancers. Needs photos of people and nature; depends on editorial. Needs photos taken in Missouri or Illinois. 95% of time color photography preferred. Reviews photos with or without ms. Model release required. Property release preferred. Captions preferred; include name of person or object, location, date.
Making Contact & Terms: Interested in receiving work from newer, lesser-known photographers. Arrange personal interview to show portfolio. Provide resume, business card, brochure, flyer or tearsheets to be kept on file for possible assignments. Keeps samples on file. SASE. Reports in 4-6 weeks. NPI. Pays on publication. Credit line given. Buys one-time rights. Simultaneous submissions and/or previously published work OK.
Tips: "Don't look for subject and style as much as how well photos convey editorial message. Look for strong images that support editorial. We are a city magazine, feature local topics and prefer working with Missouri/Illinois photographers when possible."

STUDENT LAWYER, 750 N. Lake Shore Dr., Chicago IL 60611. Editor: Sarah Hoban. Managing Editor: Miriam R. Krasno. Circ. 35,000. Estab. 1972. Publication of the American Bar Association. Magazine published 9 times a school year. Emphasizes social and legal issues for law students. Sample copy $4.
Needs: Uses about 3-5 photos/issue; all supplied by freelancers. "All photos are assigned, determined by story's subject matter." Model release preferred. Captions required.
Making Contact & Terms: Interested in receiving work from newer, lesser-known photographers. Arrange a personal interview to show portfolio or send samples. SASE. Reports in 3 weeks. Pays $300/ color cover photo; $75-200/b&w; $100-250/color inside photo. **Pays on acceptance.** Credit line given. Buys one-time rights. Previously published work OK.

TANK TALK, 570 Oakwood Rd., Lake Zurich IL 60047. (708)438-TANK. Fax: (708)438-8766. Contact: Patti Schiele. Circ. 11,500. Publication of Steel Tank Institute. Bimonthly. Emphasizes matters pertaining to the underground and aboveground storage tank industry. Readers are tank owners, installers, government officials, regulators, manufacturers, engineers. Sample copy free with 9×12 SAE and 52¢ postage.
Needs: Uses about 4-6 photos/issue; 50-75% supplied by freelancers. Needs photos of installations, current developments in the industry, i.e., new equipment and features for tanks, author photos, fiberglass tank leaks. Photos purchased with accompanying ms only. Model/property release required. Captions required.
Making Contact & Terms: Interested in receiving work from newer, lesser-known photographers. "Call if you have photos of interest to the tank industry." Uses at least 5×7 glossy b&w prints. SASE. Reports in 2 weeks. NPI. Pays on publication. Buys all rights; negotiable. Simultaneous submissions and previously published work OK.

TEAM MAGAZINE, publication of the Young Calvinist Federation, Dept. PM, P.O. Box 7259, Grand Rapids MI 49510. (616)241-5616. Fax: (616)241-5558. Editor: Dale Dièleman. *Team* magazine is a quarterly digest for volunteer church youth leaders. It promotes shared leadership for holistic ministry with high school young people. Contributor's guidelines and sample issue of *Team* for SASE.

Needs: Buys 25-30 photos/year. Photos used in magazines and books—"we produce 1-2 books annually for youth leaders, an additional 5-25 pix." High school young people in groups and as individuals in informal settings—on the street, in the country, at retreats, at school, having fun; racial variety; discussing in two's, three's, small groups; studying the Bible; praying; dating; doing service projects; interacting with children, adults, the elderly.

Making Contact & Terms: Query with samples. Query with list of stock photo subjects. Send unsolicited photos by mail for consideration. "We like to keep those packages that have potential on file for 2 months. Others (with no potential) returned immediately." Uses 5×7 or 8×10 b&w glossy prints. Also uses color for cover. SASE. Pays $20-50/b&w photo; $50-150/color photo. Credit line given. Buys one-time rights.

Tips: In samples, looks for "more than just faces. We look for activity, unusual situations or settings, symbolic work. No out-of-date fashion or hair." To break in "Send us a selection of photos. We will photocopy and request as needed. We expect good contrast in b&w."

TEXAS ALCALDE MAGAZINE, P.O. Box 7278, Austin TX 78713. (512)471-3799. Fax: (512)471-8088. Editor: Ernestine Wheelock. Circ. 52,000. Estab. 1913. Publication of the University of Texas Ex-Students' Association. Bimonthly magazine. Emphasizes University alumni. Readers are graduates, former students and friends who pay dues in the Association. Sample copy free with 9×12 SAE and $1.30 postage.

Needs: Uses 65 photos/issue; 2-3 supplied by freelance photographers. Needs UT campus shots, professors, students, buildings, city of Austin, UT sports. Will review photos with accompanying ms only. Model release preferred. Captions required.

Making Contact & Terms: Interested in receiving work from newer, lesser-known photographers. Query with list of stock photo subjects. Send 5×7 or 8×10 glossy b&w and color prints; 35mm, 2¼×2¼ or 4×5 transparencies by mail for consideration. SASE. Reports in 1 month. Fee negotiable. Pays $100/color cover photo; $25/b&w and color inside photo. Pays on publication. Credit line given. Buys one-time rights. Simultaneous submissions and previously published work OK if details of use are supplied.

TEXAS REALTOR MAGAZINE, P.O. Box 2246, Austin TX 78768. (512)370-2286. Fax: (512)370-2390. Art Director: Lauren Levi. Circ. 45,000. Estab. 1972. Publication of the Texas Association of REALTORS. Monthly magazine. Emphasizes real estate sales and related industries. Readers are male and female realtors, ages 20-70. Sample copy free with SASE.

Needs: Uses 10 photos/issue; all supplied by freelancers. Needs photos of architectural details, business, office management, telesales, real estate sales, commercial real estate, nature, sales. Especially wants to see nature and beauty shots of private property for covers. Property release required.

Making Contact & Terms: Interested in receiving work from newer, lesser-known photographers. Pays $75-300/color photo; $1,500/job. Buys one-time rights; negotiable.

TEXTILE RENTAL MAGAZINE, Dept. PM, P.O. Box 1283, Hallandale FL 33008. (305)457-7555. Editor: Christine Seaman. Circ. 6,000. Publication of the Textile Rental Services Association of America. Monthly magazine. Emphasizes the "linen supply, industrial and commercial laundering industry." Readers are "heads of companies, general managers of facilities, predominantly male audience; national and international readers."

Needs: Photos "needed on assignment basis only." Model release preferred. Captions preferred or required "depending on subject."

Making Contact & Terms: "We contact photographers on an as-needed basis selecting from a directory of photographers." Cannot return material. Pays $350/color cover plus processing; "depends on the job." **Pays on acceptance.** Credit line given if requested. Buys all rights. Previously published work OK.

Tips: "Meet deadlines; don't charge more than $100-500 for a series of b&w photos that take less than half a day to shoot."

*TIKKUN, 5100 Leona St., Oakland CA 94619. (510)482-0805. Fax: (510)482-3379. Production Manager: Ann Flatté. Circ. 40,000. Estab. 1986. Bimonthly journal. Publication is a political, social and cultural Jewish critique. Readers are 75% Jewish, white, middle-class, literary people ages 30-60.

Needs: Uses 10 photos/issue; 50% supplied by freelancers. Needs political; social; commentary; middle eastern; U.S. photos. Reviews photos with or without ms.

Making Contact & Terms: Send unsolicited photos by mail for consideration. Uses b&w "or good photo copy" prints. Keeps samples on file. SASE. Reporting time varies. "Turnaround is 4 months, unless artist specifies other." Pays $25/b&w inside photo. Pays on publication. Credit line given. Buys all rights; negotiable. Simultaneous submissions and/or previously published work OK.

Tips: "Read or look at magazine before sending photos."

TOUCH, P.O. Box 7259, Grand Rapids MI 49510. (616)241-5616. Fax: (616)241-5558. Managing Editor: Carol Smith. Circ. 15,500. Estab. 1970. Publication of Calvinettes. Monthly. Emphasizes "girls 7-14 in action. The magazine is a Christian girls' publication geared to the needs and activities of girls in the above age group." Readers are "Christian girls ages 7-14; multiracial." Sample copy and photo guidelines free with 9×12 SASE. "Also available is a theme update listing all the themes of the magazine for six months."
Needs: Uses about 5-6 photos/issue; 50-75% from freelancers. Needs photos suitable for illustrating stories and articles: photos of girls aged 7-14 from multicultural backgrounds involved in sports, Christian service and other activities young girls would be participating in." Model/property release preferred.
Making Contact & Terms: Interested in receiving work from newer, lesser-known photographers. Send 5×7 glossy b&w prints by mail for consideration. SASE. Reports in 2 months. Pays $20-35/b&w photo; $50/cover. Pays on publication. Credit line given. Buys one-time rights. Simultaneous submissions OK.
Tips: "Make the photos simple. We prefer to get a spec sheet rather than photos and we'd really like to hold photos sent to us on speculation until publication. We select those we might use and send others back. Freelancers should write for our biannual theme update and try to get photos to fit the theme of each issue." Recommends that photographers "be concerned about current trends in fashions and hair styles and that all girls don't belong to 'families.'" To break in, "a freelancer can present a selection of his/her photography of girls, we'll review it and contact him/her on its usability."

TRANSPORT TOPICS, 2200 Mill Rd., Alexandria VA 22314. (703)838-1780. Fax: (703)548-3662. Chief Photographer: Michael James. Circ. 31,000. Estab. 1935. Publication of the American Trucking Association. Weekly tabloid. Emphasizes the trucking industry. Readers are male executives 35-65.
 • In 1991 this publication received several regional awards from the American Society of Business Press Editors, including two graphic awards for tabloid front page design.
Needs: Uses approximately 12 photos/issue; amount supplied by freelancers "depends on need." Needs photos of truck transportation in all modes. Model/property release preferred. Captions preferred.
Making Contact & Terms: Interested in receiving work from newer, lesser-known photographers. Send unsolicited 35mm or 2¼×2¼ transparencies by mail for consideration. Provide resume, business card, brochure, flyer or tearsheets to be kept on file for possible assignments. Does not keep samples on file. SASE. Reports in 2-4 weeks. NPI. Pays standard "market rate" for color cover photo. **Pays on acceptance.** Credit line given. Buys one-time rights; negotiable. Simultaneous submissions and previously published work OK.
Tips: "Trucks/trucking must be dominant element in the photograph—not an incidental part of an environmental scene."

TURKEY CALL, P.O. Box 530, Edgefield SC 29824. (803)637-3106. Fax: (803)637-0034. Publisher: National Wild Turkey Federation, Inc. (nonprofit). Editor: Gene Smith. Circ. 65,000. Estab. 1973. Bimonthly magazine. For members of the National Wild Turkey Federation—people interested in conserving the American wild turkey. Sample copy $3 with 9×12 SASE. Contributor guidelines free with SASE.
Needs: Buys at least 50 photos/year. Needs photos of "wild turkeys, wild turkey hunting, wild turkey management techniques (planting food, trapping for relocation), wild turkey habitat." Captions required.
Making Contact & Terms: Interested in receiving work from newer, lesser-known photographers. Send copyrighted photos to editor for consideration. Send 8×10 glossy b&w prints; color transparencies, any format. Uses some horizontal covers. SASE. Reports in 4 weeks. Pays $20/b&w photo; $50-75/inside color photo; cover negotiated. **Pays on acceptance.** Credit line given. Rights negotiable.
Tips: Wants no "poorly posed or restaged shots, mounted turkeys representing live birds, domestic turkeys representing wild birds or typical hunter-with-dead-bird shots. Photos of dead turkeys in a tasteful hunt setting are considered. Keep the acceptance agreement/liability language to a minimum. It scares off editors and art directors." Sees a trend developing regarding serious amateurs who are successfully competing with pros. Newer equipment is partly the reason. In good light and steady hands, full auto is producing good results. I still encourage tripods, however, at every opportunity."

V.F.W. MAGAZINE, 406 W. 34th St., Kansas City MO 64111. (816)756-3390. Fax: (816)968-1169. Editor: Richard Kolb. Managing Editor: Gary Bloomfield. Circ. 2.2 million. Monthly magazine, except July. For members of the Veterans of Foreign Wars (V.F.W.)—men and women who served overseas, and their families. Sample copy free with SAE and 50¢ postage.
Needs: Photos illustrating features on current defense and foreign policy events, veterans issues and, accounts of "military actions of consequence." Photos purchased with or without accompanying ms. Present model release on acceptance of photo. Captions required.

Making Contact & Terms: Interested in receiving work from newer, lesser-known photographers. Send 8×10 glossy b&w or color prints; transparencies. "Cover shots must be submitted with a ms. Price for cover shot will be included in payment of manuscript." SASE. Reports in 4 weeks. Pays $250 minimum. Pays $25-50/b&w photo; $35-250/color photo. **Pays on acceptance.** Buys one-time and all rights; negotiable.

Tips: "Go through an issue or two at the local library (if not a member) to get the flavor of the magazine." When reviewing samples "we look for familiarity with the military and ability to capture its action and people. We encourage military photographers to send us their best work while they're still in the service. Though they can't be paid for official military photos, at least they're getting published by-lines, which is important when they get out and start looking for jobs."

VIRGINIA TOWN & CITY, P.O. Box 12164, Richmond VA 23241. (804)649-8471. Fax: (804)343-3758. Editor: Christine Everson. Circ. 5,000. Estab. 1965. Monthly magazine of Virginia Municipal League concerning Virginia local government. Readers are state and local government officials in Virginia. Sample copy $1.50 with 9×12 SASE.

Needs: Wants photos of Virginia locations/topics only. "B&w photos illustrating scenes of local government and some color work for covers." Special photo needs include "illustrations of environmental issues, computer uses, development, transportation, schools, parks and recreation." Captions preferred.

Making Contact & Terms: Query with list of stock photo subjects. Send unsolicited photos by mail for consideration. Send b&w prints. Keeps samples on file. SASE. Report "when we can." Pays $60-100/color cover photo; $60-75/b&w cover photo. Pays on publication. Credit line given. Buys all rights; negotiable. Simultaneous submissions and previously published work OK.

VIRGINIA WILDLIFE, Dept. PM, P.O. Box 11104, Richmond VA 23230. (804)367-1000. Art Director: Emily Pels. Circ. 55,000. Monthly magazine. Emphasizes Virginia wildlife, as well as outdoor features in general, fishing, hunting and conservation for sportsmen and conservationists. Free sample copy and photo/writer's guidelines.

Needs: Buys 350 photos/year; about 95% purchased from freelancers. Photos purchased with accompanying ms. Good action shots relating to animals (wildlife indigenous to Virginia), action hunting and fishing shots, photo essay/photo feature, scenic, human interest outdoors, nature, outdoor recreation (especially boating) and wildlife. Photos must relate to Virginia. Accompanying mss: features on wildlife; Virginia travel; first-person outdoors stories. Pays 10¢/printed word. Model release preferred for children. Property release preferred for private property. Captions required; identify species and locations.

Making Contact & Terms: Send 35mm and 2¼×2¼ or larger transparencies. Vertical format required for cover. SASE. Reports (letter of acknowledgment) within 30 days; acceptance or rejection within 45 days of acknowledgement. Pays $30-50/color photo; $125/cover photo. Pays on publication. Credit line given. Buys one-time rights.

Tips: "We don't have time to talk with every photographer who submits work to us. We discourage phone calls and visits to our office, since we do have a system for processing submissions by mail. Our art director will not see anyone without an appointment. In portfolio or samples, wants to see a good eye for color and composition and both vertical and horizontal formats. We are seeing higher quality photography from many of our photographers. It is a very competitive field. Show only your best work. Name and address must be on each slide. Plant and wildlife species should also be identified on slide mount. We look for outdoor shots (must relate to Virginia); close-ups of wildlife."

VOCATIONAL EDUCATION JOURNAL, 1410 King St., Alexandria VA 22314. (703)683-3111. Fax: (703)683-7424. Managing Editor: Kathy Leftwich. Circ. 45,000. Estab. 1926. Monthly magazine for American Vocational Association. Emphasizes vocational education. Readers are teachers and administrators in high school and colleges. Sample copy free with 10×13 SASE.

Needs: Uses 15-20 photos/issue, 3-5 supplied by freelancers. "Students in classroom and job training settings; teachers; students in work situations." Model release preferred for children. Captions preferred; include location, explanation of situation.

Making Contact & Terms: Interested in receiving work from newer, lesser-known photographers. Query with list of stock photo subjects. Send unsolicited photos by mail for consideration. Provide resume, business card, brochure, flyer or tearsheets to be kept on file for possible assignments. Send 5×7 b&w prints and 35mm transparencies. Keeps samples on file. SASE. Reports as needed. Pays $400 up/color cover photo; $50 up/color inside photo; $30 up/b&w inside photo; $500-1,000/job. Pays

The asterisk before a listing indicates that the market is new in this edition. New markets are often the most receptive to freelance submissions.

on publication. Credit line given. Buys one-time rights; sometimes buys all rights; negotiable. Simultaneous submissions and previously published work OK.

THE WAR CRY, Dept. PM, The Salvation Army, 615 Slaters Lane, Alexandria VA 22313. (703)684-5500. Editor-in-Chief: Colonel Henry Gariepy. Circ. 300,000. Publication of The Salvation Army. Biweekly. Emphasizes the inspirational. Readers are general public and membership. Sample copy free with SASE.
Needs: Uses about 6 photos/issue. Needs "inspirational, scenic, general photos."
Making Contact & Terms: Send color or b&w glossy prints or color slides by mail for consideration. SASE. Reports in 2 weeks. Pays $35/b&w photo; up to $150/color photo; payment varies for text/photo package. **Pays on acceptance.** Credit line given "if requested." Buys one-time rights. Simultaneous submissions and previously published work OK.

THE WATER SKIER, 799 Overlook Dr., Winter Haven FL 33884. (813)324-4341. Fax: (813)325-8259. Managing Editor: Greg Nixon. Circ. 25,000. Estab. 1950. Publication of the American Water Ski Association. Magazine published 7 times a year. Emphasizes water skiing. Readers are male and female professionals 20-45 ages. Sample copy $2.50. Photo guidelines available.
Needs: Uses 25-35 photos/issue. 1-5 supplied by freelancers. Needs photos of sports action. Model/property release required. Captions required.
Making Contact & Terms: Interested in receiving work from newer, lesser-known photographers. Call first. SASE. Reports in 1 month. NPI. Pays on publication. Credit line given. Buys all rights.

♣WFCD COMMUNICATOR, Dept. PM, 934B Douglas St. E., Brandon, Manitoba R7A 7B2 Canada. (204)725-4236. Editor: Mike Jubinville. Circ. 2,700. Estab. 1980. Publication of the Western Fertilizer and Chemical Dealers Association. Quarterly magazine. Emphasizes fertilizer and chemicals, related equipment and products. Audience consists of independent fertilizer and chemical dealers who are primarily male (although this is changing) of various ages.
Needs: Uses approximately 10 photos/issue; 20% supplied by freelance photographers. Looking for agricultural shots related to fertilizer and chemical industry, e.g., application equipment and field work in progress. Written release and captions preferred.
Making Contact & Terms: Provide resume, business card, brochure, flyer or tearsheets to be kept on file for possible assignments. SASE. Reports in 1 month. Pays $25/b&w inside photo. Pays on publication. Credit line given. Buys one-time rights.
Tips: "Be very specific in the shots you take; match them exactly to the requirements of the publication. For example, a picture of a tractor and hay baler is useless to a publication that focuses on chemical application."

WILDLIFE PHOTOGRAPHY, P.O. Box 224, Greenville PA 16125. Editor: Bob Noonan. Circ. 3,000. Bimonthly. Emphasizes pursuit and capture of wildlife on film. Sample copy $2. Writer's guidelines free with SASE.
Needs: Uses about 20 photos/issue; 18 supplied by freelance photographers. Needs photos of wildlife, how-to. Photos purchased with accompanying ms only. Special needs include photographers in action under field conditions. Model release preferred. Captions required.
Making Contact & Terms: Preferably submit queried manuscript with photos. SASE. Reports in 6 weeks. Pays $20-75 for text/photo package. "But articles with more thought put into them, better writing, photos shot with us in mind and sidebars and sketches will have a payment ceiling at more than double the previous rate." Pays on publication. Credit line given. Buys one-time rights. Simultaneous submissions and previously published work OK.
Tips: "Select one photo challenge or species of wildlife and give us a ms/photo package which describes the photo target, the challenge and the methods used."

WOMAN BOWLER, 5301 S. 76th St., Greendale WI 53129. (414)421-9000. Fax: (414)421-3013. Editor: Jeffrey R. Nowak. Circ. 120,000. Estab. 1936. Publication of Women's International Bowling Congress. Magazine published 8 times a year. Emphasizes women's bowling. Sample copy free with 10 × 13 SAE and $2.50 postage. Photo guidelines free with SASE.
Needs: Uses 75 photos/issue; up to 70% supplied by freelancers; 30-50% on assignment. Needs photos of sports action, portraits in sports settings, competition and bowling interest shots. Use freelancers nationwide to help fill voids when staff members cannot travel." In near future, needs "available photographers nationwide for assignments in various areas." Model release preferred. Captions preferred.
Making Contact & Terms: Interested in receiving work from newer, lesser-known photographers. Provide resume, business card, brochure, flyer or tearsheets to be kept on file for possible assignments. Reports in 1-2 weeks. Pays $200-300/color cover photo; $100-300/b&w cover photo; $25/color or b&w inside photo; $75/color page rate; $50/b&w page rate; $75-300/photo/text package. **Pays on acceptance.**

Credit line given (if requested). Buys all rights. Simultaneous submissions and previously published work OK.

Tips: "Looking for '90s look to bowling. New treatments of sports photography welcome. *Woman Bowler* is an excellent opportunity for photographers looking for additional portfolio clips. Use 85-100% color photographs—very limited use of b&w. However, creative use of b&w welcomed. Prefer photographs that make lighting look natural, bowling center lighting poses many problems. Send letter of interest and samples of published work, tearsheets."

One mother's mess is another mother's photo opportunity. Photographer Terri Gonzalez of Beaverton, Oregon, shot this image of her sons playing in the mud and, in doing so, captured the fun and spontaneity of children. Young Children magazine paid Gonzalez $25 for one-time use of the photo.

© Terri Gonzalez

WOMENWISE, CFHC, Dept. PM, 38 S Main St., Concord NH 03104. (603)225-2739. Editor: Carol Porter. Circ. 3,000+. Estab. 1978. Publication of the Concord Feminist Health Center. Quarterly tabloid. Emphasizes women's health from a feminist perspective. Readers are women, all ages and occupations. Sample copy $2.95.

Needs: All photos supplied by freelancers; 80% assignment; 20% or less stock. Needs photos of primarily women, women's events and demonstrations, etc. Model release required. Captions preferred.

Making Contact & Terms: Interested in receiving work from newer, lesser-known photographers, "if it's excellent quality and supports our editorial stance." Arrange a personal interview to show portfolio. Send b&w prints. Pays $15/b&w cover photo; sub per b&w inside photo. Pays on publication. Credit line given. Buys first N.A. serial rights.

Tips: "We don't publish a lot of 'fine-arts' photography now. We want photos that reflect our commitment to empowerment of all women. We prefer work by women. Do not send originals to us, even with SASE. We are small (staff of three) and lack the time to return original work."

WOODMEN OF THE WORLD, Dept. PM, 1700 Farnam St., Omaha NE 68102. (402)342-1890. Assistant Editor: Billie Jo Foust. Circ. 495,000. Estab. 1890. Official publication for Woodmen of the World Life Insurance Society. Bimonthly magazine. Emphasizes American family life. Free sample copy and photo/writer's guidelines.

Needs: Buys 25-30 photos/year. Historic, animal, celebrity/personality, fine art, photo essay/photo feature, scenic, special effects and experimental, how-to, human interest, humorous; nature, still life, travel and wildlife. Accompanying mss: "material of interest to the average American family." Model release required. Captions preferred.

Making Contact & Terms: Send material by mail for consideration. Uses 8 × 10 glossy b&w prints; 35mm, 2¼ × 2¼ and 4 × 5 transparencies; glossy b&w prints and 4 × 5 transparencies for cover, vertical format preferred. SASE. Reports in 1 month. Pays $50/b&w inside photo; $50 minimum/cover inside photo; $100-300/cover photo; 10¢/word for ms. **Pays on acceptance.** Credit line given on request. Buys one-time rights. Previously published work OK.

Tips: "Submit good, sharp pictures that will reproduce well. Our organization has local lodges throughout America. If members of our lodges are in photos, we'll give them more consideration."

YOUNG CHILDREN, 1509 16th St., NW, Washington DC 20036. (202)232-8777. Photo Editor: Julie Andrews. Circ. 83,000. Bimonthly journal. Emphasizes education, care and development of young children and promotes education of those who work with children. Read by teachers, administrators, social workers, physicians, college students, professors and parents. Free photo and writer's guidelines.

Needs: Buys photos on continuing basis. Also publishes 8 books/year with photos. Children (from birth to age 8) unposed, with/without adults. Wants on a regular basis "children engaged in educational activities: dramatic play, scribbling/writing, playing with blocks—typical nursery school activities. Especially needs photos of minority children and children with disabilities." No posed, "cute" or stereotyped photos; no "adult interference, sexism, unhealthy food, unsafe situations, old photos, children with workbooks, depressing photos, parties, religious observances. Must provide copies of model releases for all individuals in photos." Accompanying mss: professional discussion of early childhood education and child development topics.

Making Contact & Terms: Interested in receiving work from newer, lesser-known photographers. Query with samples. Send glossy b&w and color prints; transparencies. SASE. Pays $25/inside photo; $75/posters and covers; no payment for ms. Pays on publication. Credit line given. Buys one-time rights; negotiable. Simultaneous submissions and previously published work OK.

Tips: "Write for our guidelines. We are using more photos per issue and using them in more creative ways, such as collages and inside color." Looks for "photos that depict children actively learning through interactions with the world around them; sensitivity to how children grow, learn and feel."

Special Interest Publications/'93-'94 changes

The following markets appeared in the 1993 edition of *Photographer's Market* but are not listed in the 1994 edition. They may have been omitted for failing to respond to our request for updated information, they may have gone out of business or they may no longer wish to receive freelance work.

Academe: Bulletin of the AAUP (not reviewing freelance work)

AG Alert (not reviewing freelance work)

American Bar Association Journal (did not respond)

Angus Journal (overstocked)

Archaeology Magazine (out of business)

B.C. Professional Engineer (not reviewing freelance work)

Computer Magazine (asked to be deleted)

Confident Living (out of business)

Contact Magazine (not reviewing freelance work)

Dealer Progress Magazine (needs too specialized)

Discovery Magazine (out of business)

Florida Foliage Magazine (publication sold)

Ford Times (out of business)

Futurist (not using photos)

Journal of the National Technical Association (asked to be deleted)

Mature Years (asked to be deleted)

Motorland Magazine (inappropriate submissions)

Persimmon Hill (did not respond)

Public Employee Magazine (did not respond)

Real Estate Finance Today (asked to be deleted)

Soaring (did not respond)

Soccer America (did not respond)

Surgical Technologist (did not respond)

Traffic Safety (did not respond)

Trot (needs too specific)

Trout (did not respond)

Volkswagen World (asked to be deleted)

Waste Age Magazine (asked to be deleted)

Trade Publications

Just as special interest publications fill a specific need, so too do trade magazines. Most trade publications are directed toward the business community in an effort to keep readers abreast of the everchanging trends and events in their specific professions. For photographers, covering these professions can be financially rewarding and can serve as a stepping stone toward acquiring future jobs.

As often happens with this category, the number of trade publications produced increases or decreases as professions develop or deteriorate. In recent years, for example, many in-flight magazines for airlines corporations have been discontinued due to the industry's financial setbacks. On the flip side, magazines involving computers have flourished as the technology continues to grow. In this year's edition of *Photographer's Market* there are numerous trade publication listings covering a variety of professions.

Primarily, photos in trade publications, as in other publication markets, serve to attract the reader to the articles and illustrate the text in an informative way. Trade publication readers are usually well-educated and very knowledgeable about their businesses or professions. The editors and photo editors, too, are often experts in their particular fields. So, with both the readers and the publications' staffs, you are dealing with a much more discriminating audience. To be taken seriously, your photos must not be merely technically good pictures but also communicate a solid understanding of the subject and reveal greater insights.

In particular, photographers who can communicate their knowledge in both verbal and visual form will often find their work more in demand. If you have such expertise, you may wish to query about submitting a photo/text package that highlights a unique aspect of working in that particular profession or that deals with a current issue of interest to that field.

One photographer who often works with corporations and has sold work to trade magazines is Donna Jernigan of Charlotte, North Carolina. Jernigan is featured in our Insider Report on page 418.

Many of the photos purchased by these publications come from stock—both that of freelance inventories and of stock photo agencies. Generally, these publications are more conservative with their freelance budgets and use stock as an economical alternative. For this reason, listings in this section will often advise sending a stock list as an initial method of contact. Some of the more established publications with larger circulations and advertising bases will sometimes offer assignments as they become familiar with a particular photographer's work. For the most part, though, stock remains the primary means of breaking in and doing business with this market.

*AAP NEWS, P.O. Box 927, Elk Grove IL 60007. Editor: Elizabeth Oplatka. Circ. 45,500. Estab. 1985. Publication of of the American Academy of Pediatrics. Monthly tabloid. Emphasizes children's advocacy and health care. Readers are primarily physicians and childrens advocates in US and Canada. Sample copy available.
Needs: Uses 10-30 photos/issue; all supplied by freelancers. Needs photo journalistic shots. Reviews photos purchased with or without ms. Model/property released required. Captions required; include time, date, place, identification.
Making Contact & Terms: Interested in receiving work from newer, lesser-known photographers. Provide resume, business card, brochure, flyer or tearsheets to be kept on file for possible assignments. Send 35mm transparencies. Keeps samples on file. Cannot return material. Reports in 1 month or more. Pays. $35-65/hour; $0-100/color cover photo; $0-100/b&w inside photo. Pays on billing. Rights negotiable. Simultaneous submissions and/or previously published work OK.

ABA BANKING JOURNAL, 345 Hudson St., New York NY 10014. (212)620-7256. Art Director: Jeff Menges. Circ. 30,000. Estab. 1909. Monthly magazine. Emphasizes "how to manage a bank better. Bankers read it to find out how to keep up with changes in regulations, lending practices, investments, technology, marketing and what other bankers are doing to increase community standing."
Needs: Buys 12-24 photos/year; freelance photography is 50% assigned, 50% from stock. Personality, and occasionally photos of unusual bank displays or equipment. "We need candid photos of various bankers who are subjects of articles." Photos purchased with accompanying ms or on assignment.
Making Contact & Terms: Query with samples. For b&w: contact sheet preferred; uses 8 × 10 glossy prints "if prints are ordered." For color: uses 35mm transparencies and 2¼ × 2¼ transparencies. For cover: uses color transparencies, square format required. SASE. Reports in 1 month. Pays $100-500/photo; $100 minimum/job; $200/printed page for photo/text package. **Pays on acceptance.** Credit line given. Buys one-time rights.
Tips: "I look for the ability to take a portrait shot in a different and exciting way—not just 'look at the camera and smile.' "

ACROSS THE BOARD MAGAZINE, published by The Conference Board, Dept. PM, 845 Third Ave., New York NY 10022-6601. (212)759-0900. Picture Editor: Marilyn Stern. Estab. 1974. Trade magazine with 10 monthly issues (January/February and July/August are double issues). Readers are upper-level managers in large corporations. Recent articles have covered pollution in Eastern Europe, working conditions in Korea, US design, healthcare.
Needs: Use 15-20 photos/issue; some supplied by freelancers. Wide range of needs, including location portraits, industrial, workplace, social topics, environmental topics, government and corporate projects, foreign business (especially east and west Europe, former USSR and Asia). Needs striking, unusual or humorous photos with newsworthy business themes for "Sightings" department. Captions required.
Making Contact and Terms: Query *by mail only* with resume of credits, list of stock photo subjects and clients, and brochure or tearsheets to be kept on file. Cannot return material. "No phone queries please. We buy one-time rights, or six-month exclusive rights if we assign the project. We pay $100-275 inside, up to $500 for cover or $350 per day for assignments."
Tips: "Our style is journalistic. We sometimes assign locally around the USA and internationally. We keep a regional file of photographers."

🍁**ALUMI-NEWS**, Dept. PM, P.O. Box 400, Victoria Station, Westmount, Quebec H3Z 2V8 Canada. (514)489-4941. Editor: Nachml Artzy. Circ. 18,000. Bimonthly magazine. Emphasizes renovation, construction. Readers are constructors/renovators. Circ. 18,000. Sample copy free with SAE and IRC.
Needs: Uses 20 photos/issue; 25-50% supplied by freelance photographers. Needs photos of construction and renovations. Model release preferred. Captions preferred.
Making Contact & Terms: Query with list of stock photo subjects. SASE. Reports in 2 weeks. Pays $300/color cover photo; $100-200/color inside photo and $300-500/day. Pays in 30 days. Credit line given. Buys one-time rights; negotiable. Simultaneous submissions and previously published work OK.
Tips: "We prefer 'people on the job' photos as opposed to products/buildings."

AMERICAN AGRICULTURIST, Suite 202, 2333 N. Triphammer Rd., Ithaca NY 14850. (607)257-8670. Fax: (607)257-8238. Editor: Eleanor Jacobs. Circ. 53,000. Estab. 1842. Monthly. Emphasizes agriculture in the Northeast—specifically New York, New Jersey and New England. Photo guidelines free with SASE.
Needs: Occasionally photos supplied by freelance photographers; 90% on assignment, 25% from stock. Needs photos of farm equipment, general farm scenes, animals. Geographic location: only New York, New Jersey and New England. Reviews photos with or without accompanying ms. Model release required. Captions preferred.
Making Contact & Terms: Interested in receiving work from newer, lesser-known photographers. Query with samples and list of stock photo subjects. Send 35mm transparencies by mail for consideration. SASE. Reports in 3 months. Pays $200/color cover photo and $75-150/inside color photo. **Pays on acceptance.** Credit line given. Buys one-time rights.
Tips: "We need shots of modern farm equipment with the newer safety features. Also looking for shots of women actively involved in farming and shots of farm activity. We also use scenics. We send out our editorial calendar with our photo needs yearly."

 The maple leaf before a listing indicates that the market is Canadian.

AMERICAN BANKER, Dept. PM, 1 State St. Plaza, New York NY 10004. (212)943-6700. Fax: (212)943-2984. Art Director: Pamela Budz. Circ. 17,000. Estab. 1835. Daily tabloid. Emphasizes banking industry. Readers are male and female, senior executives in finance, ages 35-59.

• This publication has made several changes recently that affect photographers! *American Banker* switched from b&w to color on its front page; it expanded sections for b&w photos inside; and it has introduced a twice-monthly, full color glossy magazine that incorporates large displays of creative portraits of bankers in the technology field.

Needs: Uses varying number of photos/issue; 2 supplied by freelancers. Needs environmental portraits. Captions required; include name of subject, company, date and location of shoot, name and telephone number of photographer.

Making Contact & Terms: Interested in receiving work from newer-lesser-known photographers. Arrange a personal interview to show portfolio. Send unsolicited b&w or color prints by mail for consideration. Provide resume, business card, brochure, flyer or tearsheets to be kept on file for possible assignments. Keeps samples on file. SASE. Reports in 1-2 weeks. Pays $500-700/color cover photo; $100-225/color or b&w inside photo; also pays for film, processing and mileage "where applicable." **Pays on acceptance.** Credit line given. Buys one-time rights. Simultaneous submissions and previously published work OK.

Tips: "We look for photos that offer a creative insight to corporate portraiture and technically proficient photographers who can work will with stuffy businessmen in a limited amount of time – 30 minutes or less is the norm. Photographers should send promo cards that indicate their style and ability to work with executives. Portfolio should include 5-10 samples either slides or prints, with well-presented tearsheets of published work. Portfolio reviews by appointment only. Samples are kept on file for future reference."

AMERICAN BEE JOURNAL, Dept. PM, 51 S. 2nd St., Hamilton IL 62341. (217)847-3324. Editor: Joe M. Graham. Circ. 13,000. Monthly trade magazine. Emphasizes beekeeping for hobby and professional beekeepers. Sample copy free with SASE.

Needs: Uses about 25 photos/issue; 1-2 supplied by freelance photographers. Needs photos of beekeeping and related topics, beehive products, honey and cooking with honey. Special needs include color photos of seasonal beekeeping scenes. Model release preferred. Captions preferred.

Making Contact & Terms: Query with samples. Send 5 × 7 or 8½ × 11 b&w and color prints by mail for consideration. SASE. Reports in 2 weeks. Pays $50/b&w color cover photo; $10/b&w inside photo. Pays on publication. Credit line given. Buys all rights.

*AMERICAN BREWER MAGAZINE, Box 570, Hayward CA 94541. (510)538-9500 (AM only). President: Bill Owens. Circ. 10,000. Estab. 1986. Quarterly magazine. Emphasizes micro-brewing and brewpubs. Readers are males ages 25-35. Sample copy $5.

Needs: Uses 5 photos/issue; 5 supplied by freelancers. Reviews photos with accompanying ms only. Captions required.

Making Contact & Terms: Contact by phone. Reports in 1-2 weeks. NPI; pays per job. **Pays on acceptance.** Credit line given. Buys one-time rights; negotiable. Simultaneous submissions OK.

AMERICAN FARRIERS JOURNAL, P.O. Box 624, Brookfield WI 53008-0624. (414)782-4480. Fax: (414)782-1252. Editor: Frank Lessiter. Circ. 7,000 (paid). Estab. 1974. Magazine published 7 times/year. Emphasizes horseshoeing and horse health for professional horseshoers. Sample copy free with SASE.

Needs: Looking for horseshoeing photos, documentary, how-to (of new procedures in shoeing), photo/essay feature, product shot and spot news. Photos purchased with or without accompanying ms. Captions required.

Making Contact & Terms: Interested in receiving work from newer, lesser-known photographers. Query with printed samples. Uses 4-color transparencies for covers. Vertical format. Artistic shots. SASE. Pays $25-50/b&w photo; $30-100/color photo; up to $150/cover photo. Pays on publication. Credit line given.

AMERICAN OIL & GAS REPORTER, Dept. PM, P.O. Box 343, Derby KS 67037. (316)788-6271. Publisher: Charlie Cookson. Circ. 12,000. Estab. 1957. "A monthly business publication serving the domestic exploration, drilling and production markets within the oil/gas industry. The editorial pages are designed to concentrate on the domestic independent oilman. Readers are owners, presidents and other executives." Sample copy free with SASE.

Needs: Uses 1 color photo for cover/issue; virtually all from stock. Needs "photos dealing with oil and gas drilling and production. We prefer to use only independent oil and gas photos; we discourage anything that would have to do with a major oil company, i.e., Standard, Exxon, Shell, etc." Property release preferred. Captions required; include company name, description and location.

Making Contact & Terms: Interested in receiving work from newer, lesser-known photographers. Send 35mm transparencies and unsolicited photos by mail for consideration. Returns unsolicited material with SASE. Pays $50-100/color cover photo. Pays on publication. Credit line given. Buys one-time rights. Simultaneous submissions OK.

Tips: Prefers to see "any picture that depicts a typical or picturesque view of the domestic oil and gas industry." Prefers shots depicting "drilling rigs at work and working well sites, not abandoned well sites or equipment 'graveyards.' Wants to show active industry, people in the shots. Do not have special assignments. Need stock photos that match editorial material in issue." Prefers action shots with people as opposed to scenics.

APARTMENT NEWS PUBLICATIONS, INC., 3220 E. Willow St., Long Beach CA 90806. (310)424-8674. Fax: (213)636-8353. Art Director: Marci Post. Circ. 60,000. Estab. 1958. Monthly magazine. Emphasizes apartment ownership and management. Readers are male and female apartment owners, ages 35-55. Sample copy free. Photo guidelines available.

Needs: Uses 1-5 photos/issue; 1 supplied by freelancers. Needs cover shots of apartment buildings, photos geared toward the apartment owner/manager. Model/property release preferred. Captions preferred.

Making Contact & Terms: Send unsolicited photos by mail for consideration. Provide resume, business card, brochure, flyer or tearsheets to be kept on file for possible assignments. Send 35mm transparencies. Keeps samples on file. Reports only when interested. Pays $100/color cover photo. **Pays on acceptance.** Buys all rights; negotiable. Simultaneous submissions and/or previously published work OK.

Tips: Looks for "clean, balanced work showing ability to shoot outdoor subject matter properly providing depth and vibrant color. We mainly use slides of buildings in different architectural styles and periods, and also prefer blue sky at top of frame and use of flowers."

ART DIRECTION, 6th Floor, 10 E. 39th St., New York NY 10016. (212)889-6500. Fax: (212)889-6504. Contact: Soshanna Summer. Circ. 11,000. Monthly magazine. Emphasis is on advertising design for art directors of ad agencies. Sample copy $4.50 and $1 postage.

Needs: Buys 5 photos/issue. Photos purchased with accompanying mss only.

Making Contact & Terms: Works with freelance photographers on assignment only basis. Provide tearsheets to be kept on file for possible future assignments. SASE. Reports in 2 weeks. Pays $50/b&w photo. Pays on publication. Credit line given. Buys one-time rights.

ATHLETIC MANAGEMENT, (formerly College Athletic Management), 438 W. State St., Ithaca NY 14850. (607)272-0265. Fax: (607)273-0701. Managing Editor: Eleanor Frankel. Circ. 28,000. Estab. 1989. Bimonthly magazine. Emphasizes the management of athletics. Readers are managers of high school and college athletic programs.

Needs: Uses 6-10 photos/issue; 50% supplied by freelancers. Needs photos of athletic events and athletic equipment/facility shots. Model release preferred.

Making Contact & Terms: Interested in receiving work from newer, lesser-known photographers. Submit portfolio for review. Keeps samples on file. SASE. Reports in 1-2 weeks. Pays $150-300/color cover photo; $100-150/b&w cover or color inside photo; $50-100/b&w inside photo. Pays on publication. Credit line given. Buys first N.A. serial rights; negotiable. Previously published work OK.

✹ATLANTIC SALMON JOURNAL, P.O. Box 429, St. Andrews, New Brunswick E0G 2X0 Canada. (506)529-1026. Fax: (506)529-4985. Contact: Larry Taylor. Circ. 20,000. Estab. 1952. Publication of the Atlantic Salmon Federation. Quarterly magazine. Emphasizes Atlantic Salmon Conservation and fishing. Readers are males and females, ages 15-25. Sample copy free with 8½×11 SAE and $2.85 Canadian postage.

Needs: Uses 9-10 photos/issue; 4-5 supplied by freelancers. Needs action shots of Atlantic salmon fishing.

Making Contact & Terms: Interested in receiving work from newer, lesser-known photographers. Provide resume, business card, brochure, flyer or tearsheets to be kept on file for possible assignments. Send 8½×10 matte color or b&w prints; 35mm, 2¼×2¼, 4×5, 8×10 transparencies. Does not keep samples on file. SASE (Canadian postage or US equivalent). Will not report if photos are not wanted. Pays $75-200 color cover photo; $50-150/b&w inside photo; $25-75/color page rate. Pays on publication. Credit line given. Buys all rights; negotiable.

Tips: "We look for unique Atlantic salmon shots or flyfishing in Northeastern rivers or scenic river shots."

AUTOMATED BUILDER, Dept. PM, P.O. Box 120, Carpinteria CA 93014. (805)684-7659. Editor and Publisher: Don Carlson. Circ. 26,000. Estab. 1964. Monthly. Emphasizes home and apartment construction. Readers are "factory and site builders and dealers of all types of homes, apartments and commercial buildings." Sample copy free with SASE.

Needs: Uses about 40 photos/issue; 10-20% supplied by freelance photographers. Needs in-plant and job site construction photos and photos of completed homes and apartments. Photos purchased with accompanying ms only. Captions required.
Making Contact & Terms: Interested in receiving work from newer, lesser-known photographers. "Call to discuss story and photo ideas." Send 35mm or 2¼×2¼ transparencies by mail for consideration. Will consider dramatic, preferably vertical cover photos. Send color proof or slide. SASE. Reports in 2 weeks. Pays $300/text/photo package; $150/cover photo. Credit line given "if desired." Buys first time reproduction rights.
Tips: "Study sample copy. Query editor on story ideas related to industrialized housing industry."

*AVIONICS MAGAZINE, 7811 Montrose Rd., Potomac MD 20854. (301)340-2100. Fax: (301)340-0542. Editor: David Robb. Circ. 24,000. Estab. 1978. Monthly magazine. Emphasizes aviation electronics. Readers are avionics engineers, technicians, executives. Sample copy free with 9×12 SASE.
Needs: Uses 15-20 photos/issue; 10% supplied by freelancers. Reviews photos with or without ms. Captions required.
Making Contact & Terms: Interested in receiving work from newer, lesser-known photographers. Send unsolicited photos by mail for consideration. Provide resume, business card, brochure, flyer or tearsheets to be kept on file for possible assignments. Send 8½×11 glossy color prints; 35mm, 2⅜×2⅜, 4×5, 8×10 transparencies. Keeps samples on file. SASE. Reports in 1-2 months. Pays $150-200/color cover photo. **Pays on acceptance.** Credit line given. Rights negotiable. Simultaneous submissions OK.

*BARTENDER MAGAZINE, P.O. Box 158, Liberty Corner NJ 07938. (908)766-6006. Fax: (908)766-6607. Art Director: Bill Miller. Circ. 140,000. Estab. 1979. Quarterly magazine. *Bartender Magazine* serves full-service drinking establishments (full-service means able to serve liquor, beer and wine). "We serve single locations including individual restaurants, hotels, motels, bars, taverns, lounges and all other full-service on-premises licensees." Sample copy $2.50.
Needs: Number of photos/issue varies. Number supplied by freelancers varies. Needs photos of liquor related, drinks, bars/bartenders. Reviews photos with or without ms. Model/property release required. Captions preferred.
Making Contact & Terms: Interested in receiving work from newer, lesser-known photographers. Provide resume, business card, brochure, flyer or tearsheets to be kept on file for possible assignments. SASE. NPI. Pays on publication. Credit line given. Buys all rights; negotiable. Previously published work OK.

BEEF, 3rd Floor, 7900 International Dr., Minneapolis MN 55425. (612)851-4668. Editor: Paul D. Andre. Circ. 107,000. Monthly magazine. Emphasizes beef cattle production and feeding. Readers are feeders, ranchers and stocker operators. Sample copy and photo guidelines free with SASE.
Needs: Uses 35-40 photos/issue; "less than 1%" supplied by freelance photographers. Needs variety of cow-calf and feedlot scenes. Model release required. Captions required.
Making Contact & Terms: Send 8×10 glossy b&w prints and 35mm transparencies by mail for consideration. SASE. Reports in 1 month. Pays $25/b&w inside photo; $50/color inside photo. **Pays on acceptance.** Buys one-time rights.
Tips: "We buy few photos, since our staff provides most of those needed."

BEEF TODAY, Farm Journal Publishing, Inc., Suite 100, 6205 Earle Brown Dr., Brooklyn Center MN 55430. (612)561-0300. Photo Editor: Greg Lamp. Circ. 220,000. Monthly magazine. Emphasizes American agriculture. Readers are active farmers, ranchers or agribusiness people. Sample copy and photo guidelines free with SASE.
Needs: Uses 20-30 photos/issue; 75% supplied by freelance photographers. "We use studio-type portraiture (environmental portraits), technical, details, scenics." Model release preferred. Captions required.
Making Contact & Terms: Arrange a personal interview to show portfolio. Query with resume of credits along with business card, brochure, flyer or tearsheets to be kept on file for possible assignments. SASE. Reports in 2 weeks. NPI. "We pay a cover bonus." **Pays on acceptance.** Credit line given. Buys one-time rights. Simultaneous submissions OK.
Tips: In portfolio or samples, likes to "see about 20 slides showing photographer's use of lighting and photographer's ability to work with people. Know your intended market. Familiarize yourself with the magazine and keep abreast of how photos are used in the general magazine field."

The asterisk before a listing indicates that the market is new in this edition. New markets are often the most receptive to freelance submissions.

*BEVERAGE AISLE, 150 Great Neck Rd., Great Neck NY 11021. (516)829-9210. Fax: (516)829-3591. Editor: Hank Behar. Circ. 20,000. Estab. 1992. Monthly magazine. Emphasizes beverage retailing. Readers are male and female executives, ages 35-55.
Needs: Uses 50 photos/issue; 10 supplied by freelancers. Needs photos of humans, foodstore interiors.
Making Contact & Terms: Keeps samples on file. Cannot return material. Pays $250 minimum/job. **Pays on acceptance.** Buys all rights.
Tips: Looks for ability to shoot in fluorescent light.

BEVERAGE WORLD, Dept. PM, 150 Great Neck Rd., Great Neck NY 11021. (516)829-9210. Fax: (516)829-5414. Editor: Larry Jabbonsky. Managing Editor: Paul Leone. Circ. 32,000. Estab. 1881. Monthly. Emphasizes the beverage industry. Readers are "bottlers, wholesalers, distributors of beer, soft drinks, wine and spirits." Sample copy $3.50.
Needs: Uses 25-50 photos/issue; many supplied by freelance photographers. Needs "freelancers in specific regions of the U.S. for occasional assignments."
Making Contact & Terms: Query with samples. Provide resume, business card, brochure, flyer or tearsheets to be kept on file for possible assignments. Pays $100/day; fees paid per assignment; payment range varies according to nature of assignment. Pays on publication or per assignment contract. Rights purchased varies.
Tips: Prefers to see "interesting angles on people, products. Provide affordable quality."

BRAKE & FRONT END, Dept. PM, 11 S. Forge St., Akron OH 44304. (216)535-6117. Fax: (216)535-0874. Editor: Doug Kaufman. Circ. 30,000. Estab. 1931. Monthly magazine. Emphasizes automotive maintenance and repair. Readers are automobile mechanics and repair shop owners. Sample copy $1.
Needs: May buy up to 6 covers annually. Needs "color photos for use on covers. Subjects vary with editorial theme, but basically they deal with automotive or truck parts and service." Wants no "overly commercial photos which emphasize brand names" and no mug shots of prominent people. Model release required. Captions required.
Making Contact & Terms: Send contact sheet for consideration. Uses 5×7 b&w glossy prints. For cover: send contact sheet or transparencies. Study magazine then query. Lead time for cover photos is 2 months before publication date. Reports immediately. Pays $8.50 minimum. "Price is negotiable depending on what is needed." Pays on publication. Credit line given. Buys first N.A. serial rights. Simultaneous submissions OK.
Tips: Send for editorial schedules. Looks for "new, fresh ideas for technical automotive subjects."

BUILDING SUPPLY HOME CENTERS, Dept. PM, 1350 E. Touhy, P.O. Box 5080, Des Plaines IL 60017. Fax: (708)635-8800. Editor: Ed Fitch. Art Director: Glen Luensman. Circ. 47,000. Estab. 1917. Monthly magazine. Emphasizes lumberyards, home center retailing, residential construction. Readers are owners and managers of lumberyards and home centers. Sample copy $10.
Needs: Uses 100+ photos/issue; freelance usage varies widely; most is stock, couple issues per year are all assignment. Needs photos of retail and construction. Model release preferred. Captions preferred.
Making Contact & Terms: Query with list of stock photo subjects. SASE. Report time varies. Pays $100-300/color cover photo; $50-150/color inside photo; $300-600/day. Pays on publication. Credit line given. Buys one-time rights. Simultaneous submissions and previously published work OK.
Tips: Wants to see "application to our industry, uniqueness and clean, sharp look. We're using more symbolic work for covers and lead feature. Make it applicable to market."

BUILDINGS: The Facilities Construction and Management Magazine, Dept. PM, P.O. Box 1888, 427 6th Ave. SE, Cedar Rapids IA 52406. (319)364-6167. Fax: (319)365-5421. Editor: Linda Monroe. Circ. 42,000. Estab. 1906. Monthly magazine. Emphasizes commercial real estate. Readers are building owners and facilities managers. Sample copy $5.
Needs: Uses 50 photos/issue; 10% supplied by freelancers. Needs photos of concept, building interiors and exteriors, company personnel and products. Model and/or property release preferred. Captions preferred.
Making Contact & Terms: Provide resume, business card, brochure, flyer or tearsheets to be kept on file for possible assignments. Send 3×5, 8×10, b&w, color prints; 35mm, 2¼×2¼, 4×5 transparencies. SASE. Reports as needed. Pays $350/color cover photo; $200/color inside photo. Pays on publication. Credit line given. Rights negotiable. Simultaneous submissions OK.

BUSINESS ATLANTA, 6151 Powers Ferry Rd. NW., Atlanta GA 30339. (404)955-2500. Editor: John Sequerth. Art Director: Betsy Jenniges. Circ. 36,000. Estab. 1980. Monthly. Emphasizes "general magazine-style coverage of business and business-related issues in the metro Atlanta area." Readers are "everybody in Atlanta who can buy a house, office building or Rolls Royce." Sample copy $3.25.
Needs: Uses about 40 photos/issue; 35-40 supplied by freelance photographers. Needs "good photos mostly of business-related subjects if keyed to local industry." Model release required. Captions required.

Making Contact & Terms: Interested in receiving work from newer, lesser-known photographers. Arrange a personal interview to show portfolio. SASE. Reports in 1 month. Pays $75/b&w photo; $500-800/color cover photo; $100-400/color inside photo; $200 minimum/job; $100-1,000/package. Pays on publication. Credit line given. Buys one-time rights and reprint rights.

Tips: "Photographers must be based in Atlanta. Study the publication for the feel we strive for and don't bring us something either totally off the wall or, at the other extreme, assume that business means boring and bring us something duller than ditchwater. People in the business community are becoming more willing to do unusual things for a photo. We need the ability to work on location with subjects who have little time to spend with a photographer. Anybody can shoot a perfume bottle in a studio. Study *Business Atlanta* to see the types of work we use. Then show me something better."

*BUSINESS FOR CENTRAL NJ, P.O. Box 201, Princeton NJ 08542. (908)329-0003. Fax: (908)329-0252. Editor: George M. Taber. Circ. 11,000. Estab. 1988. Publication of Network of City Business Journals. Bimonthly tabloid. Emphasizes business news. Readers are male and female executives, ages 35-55. Sample copy $1.25.

Needs: Uses 20-30 photo/issue; 50% supplied by freelancers. Needs photos of companies, staffers, etc. Reviews photos with accompanying ms only. Model release preferred. Property release required. Captions preferred.

Making Contact & Terms: Interested in receiving work from newer, lesser-known photographers. Provide resume, business card, brochure, flyer or tearsheets to be kept on file for possible assignments. Send 8×10 prints. Keeps samples on file. SASE. Reports in 1-2 weeks. NPI. **Pays on acceptance.** Credit line given. Buys all rights; negotiable. Simultaneous submissions and/or previously published work OK.

BUSINESS NEW HAMPSHIRE MAGAZINE, #201, 404 Chestnut St., Manchester NH 03101. (603)626-6354. Fax: (603)626-6359. Art Director: Nikki Bonenfant. Circ. 13,000. Estab. 1984. Monthly magazine. Emphasizes business. Readers are male and female – top management, average age 45. Sample copy free with 9×12 SASE and $1.25 postage.

 • In 1991 this publication received a second place award, the Graniteer Award, for outstanding cover photography. The honor was given by the Ad Club of New Hampshire.

Needs: Uses 3-6 photos/issue. Needs photos of people, high-tech, software and locations. Model/property release preferred. Captions required; include names, locations, contact phone number.

Making Contact & Terms: Interested in receiving work from newer, lesser-known photographers. Arrange personal interview to show portfolio. Provide resume, business card, brochure, flyer or tearsheets to be kept on file for possible assignments. Keeps samples on file. SASE. Reports in 3 weeks. Pays $1,000/color cover photo; $60/color inside photo; $40/b&w inside photo. Pays on publication. Credit line given. Buys one-time rights.

Tips: Looks for "people in environment shots, interesting lighting, lots of creative interpretations, a definite personal style. If you're just starting out and want excellent statewide exposure to the leading executives in New Hampshire, you should talk to us."

CALIFORNIA BUSINESS, Dept. PM, Suite 700, 221 Main St., San Francisco CA 94105. (415)543-8290. Fax: (415)543-8232. Art Director: Lisa Burnett. Circ. 140,000. Estab. 1965. Monthly magazine. Emphasizes business. Readers are male and female executives, ages 35-55. Sample copy free with SASE.

Needs: Uses 40-45 photos/issue; all supplied by freelancers. Needs photos of "portraiture, on-location accounts for 80% events (news-related). Architecture makes up the other 20%." Model release preferred. Captions required; include name and title.

Making Contact & Terms: Contact through rep. Arrange personal interview to show portfolio. Provide resume, business card, brochure, flyer or tearsheets to be kept on file for possible assignments. Cannot return material. Reports in 1-2 weeks. Pays $850/color or b&w cover photo; $375/color or b&w page rate. **Pays on acceptance.** Credit line given. Buys first N.A. serial rights. Previously published work OK.

*CAREER PILOT MAGAZINE, 4959 Massachusetts Blvd., Atlanta GA 30337. (404)997-8097. Fax: (404)997-8111. Graphic Designer: Patrick Carlson. Circ. 19,000. Estab. 1983. Monthly magazine. Emphasizes career advancement for pilots. Sample copy available.

A bullet has been placed within some listings to introduce special comments by the editor of the Photographer's Market.

Build a Solid Rapport with Subjects

Photographer Donna Jernigan of Charlotte, North Carolina, understands her personality. She is often bubbly and personable with just a trace of saleswoman mixed in. These characteristics are essential, not only in her dealings with clients, but also in establishing a rapport with her subjects. "I find that I work best when there is a real partnership between the editor and me, and then I create a partnership between myself and the subjects. My relationship with the subjects is very important to me," says Jernigan.

A true "people person," Jernigan concentrates on human values in her photography and tries to get the shot she wants without being overbearing. Predominately a corporate photographer who instructs her subjects to "just have fun and ignore me." Her list of clients includes NationsBank, American Express and

Donna Jernigan

Allstate Insurance. These and other clients appreciate the sense of realism she creates. "Sometimes less is more. I make very simple pictures and try to get very little into them," she says.

Jernigan continually finds editors to be more and more receptive to her work, even though she didn't seriously consider selling images until 1981. In that year, she attended a Writer's Digest photo workshop given by top stock photographers Jim Pickerell and Carl Purcell. While there, she sat at the same table with photographer Phil Douglis, who quickly turned into her mentor. "He changed my life," she says. It was during one of Douglis' workshops in 1986 that she learned why her images worked. The seminar also gave her some direction which led to assignments in the corporate world. "I didn't know how to network into businesses. I was a babe in the woods and it took me a long time to learn," she says.

Marketing is a big weakness for many photographers, and they must learn the business aspects of the industry in order to make their work more attractive, she says. They must realize that there is a difference between pretty photos and those that will sell.

While creating images Jernigan often finds it helpful to ask herself two very important questions: Does it look natural? How does the person feel? "Be true to yourself and then just find the markets that work. If you're trying to fit into someone else's vision, you will find yourself fighting them psychologically," she says.

It also has been helpful for Jernigan to study her subjects and search for repeated gestures that she can capture on film. This adds a sense of realism that is lacking in many corporate publications. "A lot of the things I see in annual reports and a lot of commercial work is slick stuff that is technically perfect, but it's missing a human element. And that really bothers me," says Jernigan.

Often a photographer can capture the human element by using wide angle lenses to move in close for strong compositions. The important thing is to feel at ease with your subjects, because eventually the strong rapport comes through in your work. "Some photographers are afraid to invade other people's spaces, but if you're comfortable doing it, they don't mind," she says.
— *Michael Willins*

A mysterious harvest moon along the waterfront in Savannah, Georgia, is not the typical subject matter for freelancer Donna Jernigan of Charlotte, North Carolina, but the scene works well on the cover of Insights, *published by The Harleysville Insurance Companies. Usually Jernigan finds clients who are attracted to her photojournalistic approach to people photography.*

Needs: Uses 10 photos/issue; 3 supplied by freelancers. Needs photos of lifestyle, financial and health related topics. Model/property release required.

Making Contact & Terms: Interested in receiving work from newer, lesser-known photographers. Provide resume, business card, brochure, flyer or tearsheets to be kept on file for possible assignments. No phone calls. Keeps samples on file. SASE. Reports in 1-2 weeks. Pays $100-500/job; $300-400/color cover photo; $100-200/color inside photo. Pays on publication. Buys one-time rights. Previously published work OK.

Tips: "No fashion photography, wildlife or scenics. Still-lifes preferred. Send professional promo package. Attention to detail is very important."

CHEMICAL ENGINEERING, 1221 Avenue of the Americas, New York NY 10020. Phone: (212)512-3377. Fax: (212)512-4762. Art Director: Maureen Gleason. Circ. 80,000. Estab. 1903. Monthly magazine. Emphasizes equipment and technology of the chemical process industry. Readers are mostly male, median age 38. Sample copies available for $7, postage included.

• This publication has received several awards, including honors for having a creative cover and overall outstanding design. In 1991 this publication received an Ozzie honorable mention award.

Needs: Occasionally works with freelancers. Needs composite images, CAD (computer-aided design) images, shots of plant personnel at work, high-tech effects, shots of liquids, tanks, drums, sensors, toxic waste, landfills and remediation. Especially wants to see photos of environmental clean up, recycling, plant staff handling bulk solids, thermoplastic pumps, cyclone selection, batch process plants, corrosive gases, valves, flowmeters and strainers. Model/property release required. Captions required; include "when, where and whom."

Making Contact & Terms: Interested in receiving work from newer, lesser-known photographers. Submit portfolio for review. Send stock photo list. Provide, resume, business card, brochure, flyer or tearsheets to be kept on file for possible assignments. Keeps samples on file. SASE. Reports in 3 weeks. Pays $700/color cover photo; $200/color inside photo; $100/b&w inside photo; $200/color page rate; $100/b&w page rate. Pays on publication. Credit line given. Buys one-time rights; negotiable. Simultaneous submissions and previously published work OK.

Tips: "Please respond ONLY if you are familiar with the chemical processing industry." Points out that "after technology, our focus is on engineers at work. We want to feature a diversity of ages, ethnic types and both men and women in groups and individually. Pictures must show *current* technology, and identify location with permission of subject. Also, photos must be clean, crisp and have good color saturation for excellent reproduction."

THE CHRISTIAN MINISTRY, 407 S. Dearborn St., Chicago IL 60605-1150. (312)427-5380. Fax: (312)427-1302. Managing Editor: Mark Halton. Circ. 12,000. Estab. 1969. Bimonthly magazine. Emphasizes religion—parish clergy. Readers are 30-65 years old, 80% male, 20% female, parish clergy and well-educated. Sample copy free with 9×12 SAE and 98¢ postage. Photo guidelines free with SASE.

Needs: Uses 8 photos/issue; all supplied by freelancers. Needs photos of clergy (especially female clergy), church gatherings, school classrooms and church symbols. Future photo needs include social gatherings and leaders working with groups. Model release preferred. Captions preferred.

Making Contact & Terms: Interested in receiving work from newer, lesser-known photographers. Send 8×10 b&w prints by mail for consideration. SASE. Reports in 3 weeks. Pays $50/b&w cover photo; $25/b&w inside photo. Pays on publication. Credit line given. Buys one-time rights. Will consider simultaneous submissions.

Tips: "We're looking for up-to-date photos of clergy, engaged in preaching, teaching, meeting with congregants, working in social activities. We need photos of women, African-American and Hispanic clergy."

THE CHRONICLE OF PHILANTHROPY, Suite 775, 1255 23rd St. NW, Washington DC 20037. (202)466-1205. Fax: (202)466-2078. Art Director: Sue LaLumia. Circ. 28,000. Estab. 1988. Biweekly tabloid. Readers come from all aspects of the nonprofit world such as charities (large or small grant maker/giving), foundations and relief agencies such as the Red Cross. Sample copy free.

Needs: Uses 20 photos/issue; 50-75% supplied by freelance photographers. Needs photos of people (profiles) making the news in philanthropy and environmental shots related to person(s)/organization. Most shots arranged with freelancers are specific. Model release required. Captions required.

Making Contact & Terms: Arrange a personal interview to show portfolio. Send unsolicited photos by mail for consideration. Send 35mm, 2¼×2¼ transparencies and prints by mail for consideration. Provide resume, business card, brochure, flyer or tearsheets to be kept on file for possible assignments. Will send negatives back via certified mail. Reports in 1-2 days. Pays (color and b&w) $225 + expenses/half day; $350 + expenses/full day; $75/reprint. Pays on publication. Buys one-time rights. Previously published work OK.

CITY & STATE, Dept. PM, 740 N. Rush St., Chicago IL 60611. (312)649-5200. Fax: (312)649-5228. Assistant Managing Editor Graphics: Dan Wassmann. Circ. 50,000. Estab. 1984. Biweekly tabloid. Emphasizes state and local government and current events. Readers are male government executives, average age 44. Sample copy $2.50. To request, call (313)446-1634.
Needs: Uses 1-5 photos/issue; all supplied by freelancers. Needs personality profiles of government people (mayors, governors), current events photos and "anything relating to the business of government including environmental issues, recycling etc." Especially wants to see "healthcare photos, economic development photos and anything to do with recycling." Captions preferred; include "who, what, where and when."
Making Contact & Terms: Arrange a personal interview to show portfolio. Submit portfolio for review. Provide resume, business card, brochure, flyer or tearsheets to be kept on file for possible assignments. Does not keep samples on file. Cannot return material. Pays $150-185/color cover photo; $85-125/b&w cover, color inside or b&w inside photo; $350/day. Pays on publication. Credit line given. Rights negotiable. Simultaneous submissions and previously published work OK.
Tips: Wants to see "good quality, well-thought-out pictures, environmental (people) photos: positioning the subject in an area with good lighting that gives the reader a sense of who that person is and what they do." To break in, "present your work in an organized, professional manner and be willing to take direction."

CLAVIER, Dept. PM, 200 Northfield Rd., Northfield IL 60093. (708)446-5000. Editor: Kingsley Day. Circ. 20,000. Estab. 1962. Magazine published 10 times/year. Readers are piano and organ teachers. Sample copy $2.
Needs: Human interest photos of keyboard instrument students and teachers. Special needs include synthesizer photos and children performing.
Making Contact & Terms: Send material by mail for consideration. Uses glossy b&w prints. For cover: Kodachrome, glossy color prints or 35mm transparencies. Vertical format preferred. SASE. Reports in 1 month. Pays $100-150/color cover; $10-25/b&w inside photo. Pays on publication. Credit line given. Buys all rights.
Tips: "We look for sharply focused photographs that show action and for clear color that is bright and true. We need photographs of children and teachers involved in learning music at the piano. We prefer shots that show them deeply involved in their work rather than posed shots. Very little is taken on specific assignment except for the cover. Authors usually include article photographs with their manuscripts. We purchase only one or two items from stock each year."

CLEANING MANAGEMENT MAGAZINE, 13 Century Hill Dr., Latham NY 12110. (518)783-1281. Editor: Tom Williams. Circ. 45,000. Estab. 1963. Monthly. Emphasizes management of cleaning/custodial/housekeeping operations for commercial buildings, schools, hospitals, shopping malls, airports, etc. Readers are middle to upper-middle managers of in-house cleaning/custodial departments, and managers/owners of contract cleaning companies. Sample copy free (limited) with SASE.
Needs: Uses 10-15 photos/issue. Needs photos of cleaning personnel working on carpets, hard floors, tile, windows, restrooms, large buildings, etc. Model release preferred. Captions required.
Making Contact & Terms: Provide resume, business card, brochure, flyer or tearsheets to be kept on file for possible assignments. Query with specific ideas for photos related to our field. SASE. Reports in 1-2 weeks. Pays $25/b&w inside photo. Credit line given. Rights negotiable. Simultaneous submissions and previously published work OK.
Tips: "Query first and shoot what the publication needs."

CLIMATE BUSINESS MAGAZINE, Dept. PM, P.O. Box 13067, Pensacola FL 32501. (904)433-1166. Fax: (904)435-9174. Publisher: Elizabeth A. Burchell. Circ. 24,000. Estab. 1990. Quarterly magazine. Emphasizes business. Readers are executives, ages 35-54, with average annual income of $68,000. Sample copy $4.75.
Needs: Uses 50 photos/issue; 20 supplied by freelancers. Needs photos of Florida topics: technology, government, ecology, global trade, finance, travel and life shots. Model/property release required. Captions preferred.
Making Contact & Terms: Send unsolicited photos by mail for consideration. Provide resume, business card, brochure, flyer or tearsheets to be kept on file for possible assignments. Send 5×7 b&w or color prints; 35mm, 2¼×2¼ transparencies. Keeps samples on file. SASE. Reports in 3 weeks. Pays $75/color cover photo; $25/color inside photo; $25/b&w inside photo; $75/color page. Pays on publication. Buys one-time rights.
Tips: "Don't overprice yourself and keep submitting work."

COLLISION, Box M, Franklin MA 02038. (508)528-6211. Editor: Jay Kruza. Circ. 20,000. Magazine published every 5 weeks. Emphasizes "technical tips and management guidelines" for auto body repairmen and dealership managers in eastern US. Sample copy $3. Photo guidelines free with SASE.

Needs: Buys 100 photos/year; 12/issue. Photos of technical repair procedures, association meetings, etc. A regular column called "Stars and Cars" features a national personality with his/her car. Prefer at least 3 b&w photos with captions as to why person likes this vehicle. If person has worked on it or customized it, photo is worth more. Special needs include: best looking body shops in US, includes exterior view, owner/manager, office, shop, paint room and any special features (about 6-8 photos). Captions required

Making Contact & Terms: Query with resume of credits and representational samples (not necessarily on subject) or send contact sheet for consideration. Send b&w glossy or matte contact sheet or 5×7 prints. SASE. Reports in 3 weeks. Pays $135; $25 for first photo; $10 for each additional photo in the series; pays $50 for first photo and $25 for each additional photo for "Stars and Cars" column. Prefers to buy 5 or 7 photos per series. Extra pay for accompanying mss. **Pays on acceptance.** Buys all rights, but may reassign to photographer after publication. In created or set-up photos, which are not direct news, requires photocopy of model release with address and phone number of models for verification. Simultaneous submissions OK.

Tips: "Don't shoot one or two frames; do a sequence or series. It gives us choice, and we'll buy more photos. Often we reject single photo submissions. Capture how the work is done to solve the problem."

COMMERCIAL CARRIER JOURNAL, Dept. PM, Chilton Way, Radnor PA 19089. (215)964-4513. Editor-In-Chief: Gerald F. Standley. Managing Editor: Carole A. Smith. Circ. 79,000. Estab. 1911. Monthly magazine. Emphasizes truck and bus fleet maintenance operations and management.
Needs: Spot news (of truck accidents, Teamster activities and highway scenes involving trucks). Photos purchased with or without accompanying ms, or on assignment. Model release required. *Detailed* captions required. For color photos, uses prints and 35mm transparencies. For covers, uses color transparencies. Uses vertical cover only. Needs accompanying features on truck fleets and news features involving trucking companies.
Making Contact & Terms: Send material by mail for consideration. SASE. Reports in 3 weeks. NPI; payment varies. Pays on a per-job or per-photo basis. **Pays on acceptance.** Credit line given. Buys all rights.

*COMPRESSED AIR MAGAZINE, 253 E. Washington Ave., Washington NJ 07882-2495. (201)850-7818. Editor: S.M. Parkhill. Circ. 149,000. Monthly. Emphasizes "industrial subjects, technology, energy." Readers hold middle to upper management positions in Graad SIC range. Sample copy free.
Needs: Uses about 20 photos/issue; "very few" supplied by freelance photographers. Model release preferred. Captions preferred.
Making Contact & Terms: Provide resume, business card, brochure, flyer or tearsheets to be kept on file for possible future assignments. Cannot return material. NPI. Previously published work OK.
Tips: "We look for high quality color shots, and have increased use of 'symbolic' photos to supplement industrial shots."

CONNSTRUCTION MAGAZINE, Dept. PM, Suite 211, 62 LaSalle Rd., West Hartford CT 06107. (203)523-7518. Fax: (203)231-8808. Editor: Tracy E. McHugh. Circ. 5,500. Estab. 1962. Quarterly magazine. Emphasizes horizontal construction. Readers are 21-60, male and female, construction company owners and managers. Sample copy free with 9×12 SAE and 5 first-class stamps. No photo guidelines.
Needs: Uses 80 photos/issue; 10% supplied by freelance photographers. Photo types include trade, on-site and personalities. Model release required. Captions required.
Making Contact & Terms: Query with resume of credits. Provide resume, business card, brochure, flyer or tearsheets to be kept on file for possible assignments. SASE. Reports in 1-2 weeks. Most rates negotiable. Pays $200-400 color cover photo. Pays on publication. Credit line given. Buys first N.A. serial rights.
Tips: "We generally use everything from event coverage to detailed, cover studio shots. But everything is issue specific. Always best to contact us to discuss a shot first."

❄CONSTRUCTION COMMENT, Dept. PM, 6th Floor, 920 Yonge St., Toronto, Ontario M4W 3C7 Canada. (416)961-1028. Fax: (416)924-4408. Executive Editor: Gregory Kero. Circ. 5,000. Estab. 1970. Semiannual magazine. Emphasizes construction and architecture. Readers are builders, contractors, architects and designers. Sample copy and photo guidelines available.
Needs: Uses 25 photos/issue; 50% supplied by freelance photographers. Needs "straightforward, descriptive photos of buildings and projects under construction, and interesting people shots of workers at construction sites." Model release preferred. Captions preferred.
Making Contact & Terms: Arrange a personal interview to show portfolio. Query with resume of credits or list of stock photo subjects. Provide resume, business card, brochure, flyer or tearsheets to be kept on file for possible assignments. SASE. Reports in 1 month. Pays $200/color cover photo; $100/b&w cover photo; $25/color or b&w inside photo. Pays on publication. Credit line given. Buys all

rights to reprint in our other publications; rights negotiable. Simultaneous submissions and previously published work OK.

Tips: Looks for "representative photos of building projects and interesting construction-site people shots."

CORPORATE CASHFLOW, 6151 Powers Ferry Rd., Atlanta GA 30339. (404)256-9800. Editor: Dick Gamble. Circ. 40,000. Estab. 1980. Monthly magazine. Emphasizes corporate treasury management. Readers are senior financial officers of large and mid-sized US corporations. Sample copy available.

Needs: Uses 1 or 2 photos/issue; all supplied by freelancers.

Making Contact & Terms: Provide resume, business card, brochure, flyer or tearsheets to be kept on file for possible assignments. "Atlanta photographers only." Pays $400/color cover photo. **Pays on acceptance.** Credit line given. Buys one-time rights.

CORPORATE CLEVELAND, Dept. PM, 1720 Euclid Ave., Cleveland OH 44115. (216)621-1644. Fax: (216)621-5918. Art Director: J.R. Weber. Circ. 30,000. Estab. 1977. Monthly magazine. Emphasizes "all types of business within northeast Ohio." Readers are executives and business owners. Sample copy $2.

Needs: Uses 20-25 photos/issue; 95% supplied by freelancers. Needs photos of "people and industrial processes within articles." Captions required.

Making Contact & Terms: Provide resume, business card, brochure, flyer or tearsheets to be kept on file for possible assignments. SASE. Reports in 2 weeks. Pays $200+/color cover photo; $25+/ b&w inside photo; $50+/color inside photo. **Pays on acceptance.** Credit line given. Buys one-time rights. Simultaneous submissions and previously published work OK.

CORPORATE DETROIT MAGAZINE Dept. PM, Suite 303, 26111 Evergreen, Southfield MI 48076. (313)357-8300. Fax: (313)357-8308. Editor: Gary Hoffman. Circ. 36,000. Monthly independent circulated to senior executives. Emphasizes Michigan business. Readers include top-level executives. Sample copy free with 9×12 SASE. Call editor for photo guidelines.

Needs: Uses variable number of photographs; most supplied by freelance photographers. Needs photos of business people, environmental, feature story presentation, mug shots, etc. Reviews photos with accompanying ms only. Special needs include photographers based around Michigan for freelance work on job basis. Model release preferred. Captions required.

Making Contact & Terms: Arrange a personal interview to show portfolio. Query with resume of credits and samples. SASE. Reports in 2 weeks. NPI; pay individually negotiated. Pays on publication. Credit line given. Buys all rights.

DAIRY TODAY, Farm Journal Publishing, Inc., Suite 100, 6205 Earle Brown Dr., Brooklyn Center MN 55430. (612)561-0300. Photo Editor: Greg Lamp. Circ. 111,000. Monthly magazine. Emphasizes American agriculture. Readers are active farmers, ranchers or agribusiness people. Sample copy and photo guidelines free with SASE.

Needs: Uses 20-30 photos/issue; 75% supplied by freelancers. "We use studio-type portraiture (environmental portraits), technical, details, scenics." Model release preferred. Captions required.

Making Contact & Terms: Arrange a personal interview to show portfolio. Query with resume of credits along with business card, brochure, flyer or tearsheets to be kept on file for possible assignments. SASE. Reports in 2 weeks. NPI. "We pay a cover bonus." **Pays on acceptance.** Credit line given. Buys one-time rights. Simultaneous submissions OK.

Tips: In portfolio or samples, likes to "see about 20 slides showing photographer's use of lighting and ability to work with people. Know your intended market. Familiarize yourself with the magazine and keep abreast of how photos are used in the general magazine field."

DANCE TEACHER NOW, 3020 Beacon Blvd., W. Sacramento CA 95691-3436. (916)373-0201. Fax: (916)373-0232. Editor: K.C. Patrick. Circ. 6,000. Estab. 1979. Magazine published 9 times per year. Emphasizes dance, business, health and education. Readers are dance instructors and other related professionals, ages 15-80. Sample copy free with 9×12 SASE. Guidelines free with SASE.

Needs: Uses 20 photos/issue; all supplied by freelancers. Needs photos of action shots (teaching, etc.). Reviews photos with accompanying ms only. Model/property release preferred. Captions preferred.

Making Contact & Terms: Provide resume, business card, brochure, flyer or tearsheets to be kept on file for possible assignments. Keeps samples on file. SASE. Pays $50+/color cover photo; $20/color inside photo; $20/b&w inside photo. Pays on publication. Credit line given. Buys one-time rights plus publicity rights; negotiable. Simultaneous submissions and/or previously published work OK.

The Subject Index, located at the back of this book, can help you find publications interested in the topics you shoot.

DARKROOM & CREATIVE CAMERA TECHNIQUES, Dept. PM, Preston Publications, P.O. Box 48312, 7800 Merrimac Ave., Niles IL 60714. (708)965-0566. Fax: (708)965-7639. Publisher: Seaton T. Preston. Editor: David Alan Jay. Circ. 45,500. Estab. 1979. Bimonthly magazine. Covers darkroom techniques, creative camera use, photochemistry and photographic experimentation/innovation — particularly in photographic processing, printing and reproduction — plus general user-oriented photography articles aimed at advanced amateurs and professionals. Lighting and optics are also very important. Sample copy $4.50. Free photography and writer's guidelines free with SASE.
Needs: "The best way to publish photographs in *Darkroom Techniques* is to write an article on photo or darkroom techniques and illustrate the article. Except for article-related pictures, we publish few single photographs. The two exceptions are: cover photographs — we are looking for strong poster-like images that will make good newsstand covers; and Professional Portfolio — exceptional, professional photographs of an artistic or human nature; most of freelance photography comes from what is currently in a photographer's stock." Model/property release preferred. Captions required if photo is used.
Making Contact & Terms: Interested in receiving work from newer, lesser-known photographers. "To submit for cover or Professional Portfolio, please send a selected number of superior photographs of any subject; however, we do not want to receive more than 10 or 20 in any one submission. We ask for submissions on speculative basis only. Except for portfolios, we publish few single photos that are not accompanied by some type of text." Prefers color transparencies over color prints. B&w submissions should be 8×10. For cover submissions, 4×5 transparencies are preferable. Pays $300/covers; $100/page for text/photo package; negotiable. Pays on publication only. Credit line given. Buys one-time rights.
Tips: "We are looking for exceptional photographs with strong, graphically startling images. We look for colorful graphic images with room at top and on one side for covers; technically accurate, crisp, clear images for portfolios. No run-of-the-mill postcard shots please. We are the most technical general-al-interest photographic publication on the market today. Authors are encouraged to substantiate their conclusions with experimental data. Submit samples, article ideas, etc. It's easier to get photos published with an article."

DATA COMMUNICATIONS MAGAZINE, 41st Floor, 1221 Avenue of the Americas, New York NY 10020. (212)512-2639. Fax: (212)512-6833. Art Director: Ken Surabian. Circ. 70,000. Estab. 1972. Monthly magazine. Emphasizes data communications. Readers are men in middle management positions.
Needs: Uses 4 photos/issue; 40-50% supplied by freelance photographers. Needs photos of people, still life, industry-related equipment or processes. Model release required. Captions required.
Making Contact & Terms: Interested in receiving work from newer, lesser-known photographers. Provide resume, business card, brochure, flyer or tearsheets to be kept on file for possible assignments. Cannot return material. Reports in 2 weeks. Pays $1,000/color cover photo; $650/color inside photo; $650/color page rate; $150/b&w photo; $250-350/day. **Pays on acceptance.** Credit line given. Buys one-time and international one-time rights.
Tips: Wants photographers who work well with high-tech concepts.

***■DELTA DESIGN GROUP, INC.**, Box 112, 409 Washington Ave., Greenville MS 38702. (601)335-6148. Fax: (601)378-2826. President: Noel Workman. Publishes magazines dealing with cotton marketing, dentistry, health care, travel and Southern agriculture.
Needs: Photos used for text illustration, promotional materials and slide presentations. Buys 25 photos/year; offers 10 assignments/year. Southern agriculture (cotton, rice, soybeans, sorghum, forages, beef and dairy, and catfish); California and Arizona irrigated cotton production; all aspects of life and labor on the lower Mississippi River; Southern historical (old photos or new photos of old subjects); recreation (boating, water skiing, fishing, canoeing, camping). Model release required. Captions preferred.
Making Contact & Terms: Query with samples or list of stock photo subjects or mail material for consideration. SASE. Reports in 1 week. Pays $50 minimum/job. Credit line given, except for photos used in ads or slide shows. Rights negotiable. Simultaneous submissions and previously published work OK.
Tips: "Wide selections of a given subject often deliver a shot that we will buy, rather than just one landscape, one portrait, one product shot, etc."

***DENTAL ECONOMICS**, Box 3408, Tulsa OK 74101. (918)835-3161. Editor: Dick Hale. Circ. 10,000. Monthly magazine. Emphasizes dental practice administration — how to handle staff, patients and bookkeeping and how to handle personal finances for dentists. Free sample copy. Photo and writer's guidelines free with SASE.
Needs: Buys 20 photos/year. Celebrity/personality, head shot, how-to, photo essay/photo feature, special effects/experimental and travel. No consumer-oriented material. "We use an occasional 'lifestyle' article, and the rest of the mss relate to the business side of a practice: scheduling, collections,

consultation, malpractice, peer review, closed panels, capitation, associates, group practice, office design, etc." Also uses profiles of dentists. Photos purchased with or without accompanying ms, or on assignment.

Making Contact & Terms: Send material by mail for consideration. Uses 8×10 b&w glossy prints; 35mm or 2¼×2¼ transparencies. "No outsiders for cover." SASE. Reports in 2-4 weeks. Pays $50-150/job; $75-400 for text/photo package; $5-15/b&w photo; $35-50/color photo. Pays in 30 days. Credit line given. Buys all rights but may reassign to photographer after publication.

Tips: "Write and think from the viewpoint of the dentist—not as a consumer or patient. If you know of a dentist with an unusual or very visual hobby, tell us about it. We'll help you write the article to accompany your photos. Query please."

DESIGN & COST DATA, Dept. PM, 8602 N. 40th St., Tampa FL 33604. (813)989-9300. Fax: (813)980-3982. Managing Editor: Mary Rector. Marketing Director: Robert Rizzi. Circ. 10,000. Estab. 1958. Quarterly magazine. Covers architecture and architectural design. Readers are architects, specifiers, designers, builders; male and female; students and professionals. Sample copy free with 11×14 SAE and $2 postage.

Needs: Uses 15-20 photos/issue; 30% supplied by freelancers. Needs architectural photos, including newly completed buildings and newly renovated structures. Permissions and names of architect and building owner required. Captions required.

Making Contact & Terms: Send unsolicited glossy b&w or color prints any format; also send any format transparencies. SASE. Reports in 1 month. Pays $100/color cover photo; $75/color inside photo; $35/b&w inside photo. Pays on publication. Credit line given. Buys one-time rights. Simultaneous submissions and previously published work OK.

Tips: Photographers "must have contact with architects. We feature photography of only the projects that have been chosen for our magazine."

EDUCATION WEEK, Dept. PM, Suite 250, 4301 Connecticut Ave. NW, Washington DC 20008. (202)364-4114. Fax: (202)364-1039. Editor-in-Chief: Ronald A. Wolk. Photo Editor: Benjamin Tice Smith. Circ. 65,000. Estab. 1981. Weekly. Emphasizes elementary and secondary education.

Needs: Uses about 20 photos/issue; all supplied by freelance photographers; 90% on assignment, 10% from stock. Model/property release preferred. Model release usually needed for children (from parents). Captions required; include names, ages, what is going on in the picture.

Making Contact & Terms: Interested in receiving work from newer, lesser-known photographers. Query with samples. Provide resume and tearsheets to be kept on file for possible future assignments. Cannot return material. Reports in 2 weeks. Pays $50-150/b&w photo; $100-300/day; $50-250/job; $50-300 for text/photo package. **Pays on acceptance.** Credit line given. Buys all rights; negotiable. Simultaneous submissions and previously published work OK.

Tips: "When reviewing samples we look for the ability to make interesting and varied images from what might not seem to be photogenic. Show creativity backed up with technical polish."

ELECTRICAL APPARATUS, Barks Publications, Inc., 400 N. Michigan Ave., Chicago IL 60611-4198. (312)321-9440. Associate Publisher: Elsie Dickson. Circ. 16,000. Monthly magazine. Emphasizes industrial electrical machinery maintenance and repair for the electrical aftermarket. Readers are "persons engaged in the application, maintenance and servicing of industrial and commercial electrical and electronic equipment." Sample copy $4.

Needs: "Assigned materials only. We welcome innovative industrial photography, but most of our material is staff-prepared." Photos purchased with accompanying ms or on assignment. Model release required "when requested." Captions preferred.

Making Contact & Terms: Query with resume of credits. Contact sheet or contact sheet with negatives OK. SASE. Reports in 3 weeks. Pays $25-100/b&w or color. Pays on publication. Credit line given. Buys all rights, but exceptions are occasionally made.

ELECTRONIC BUSINESS, Dept. PM, 275 Washington St., Newton MA 02158. (617)964-3030. Fax: (617)964-7136. Art Director: Michael Roach. Assistant Art Director: Martha Abdella. Circ. 75,000. Estab. 1974. Biweekly. Emphasizes the electronic industry. Readers are CEOs, managers and top executives.

Needs: Uses 25-30 photos/issue; 25% supplied by freelancers, most on assignment. Needs corporate photos and people shots. Model/property release preferred. Captions required.

Making Contact & Terms: Interested in receiving work from newer, lesser-known photographers. Arrange a personal interview to show portfolio; provide resume, business card, brochure, flyer or tearsheets to be kept on file for possible future assignments. Cannot return material. Pays $50-250/b&w photo; $200-400/color photo; $50-100/hour; $400-800/day; $200-500/photo/text package. **Pays on acceptance.** Credit line given. Buys one-time rights. Simultaneous submissions and previously published work OK.

Tips: In photographer's portfolio looks for informal business portrait, corporate atmosphere.

ELECTRONICS NOW MAGAZINE, (formerly *Radio-Electronics Magazine*), 500 B Bi-County Blvd., Farmingdale NY 11735. (516)293-3000. Fax: (516)293-3115. Editor: Brian C. Fenton. Circ. 171,679. Estab. 1929. Monthly magazine. Emphasizes electronics. Readers are electrical engineers and technicians, both male and female, ages 25-60. Sample copy free with 9×12 SAE.

Needs: Uses 25-50 photos/issue; 2-3 supplied by freelance photographers. Needs photos of how-to, computer screens, test equipment and digital displays. Purchases photos with accompanying ms only. Model release required. Captions preferred.

Making Contact & Terms: Submit portfolio for review. Provide resume, business card, brochure, flyer or tearsheets to be kept on file for possible assignments. SASE. Reports in 2 weeks. Pays $400/color cover photo. **Pays on acceptance.** Credit line given. Buys all rights; negotiable. Simultaneous submissions OK.

EMERGENCY, The Journal of Emergency Services, Dept. PM, 6300 Yarrow Dr., Carlsbad CA 92009. (619)438-2511. Fax: (619)931-5809. Editor: Rhonda Foster. Circ. 26,000. Monthly magazine. Emphasizes pre-hospital emergency medical and rescue services for paramedics, EMTs and firefighters to keep them informed of latest developments in the emergency medical services field. Sample copy $5.

Needs: Buys 50-75 photos/year; 5 photos/issue. Documentary, photo essay/photo feature and spot news dealing with pre-hospital emergency medicine. Needs shots to accompany unillustrated articles submitted and cover photos; year's calendar of themes forwarded on request with #10 SASE. "Try to get close to the action; both patient and emergency personnel should be visible." Photos purchased with or without accompanying ms. Model and property releases preferred. Captions required; include the name, city and state of the emergency rescue team and medical treatment being rendered in photo. Also needs color transparencies for "Action," a photo department dealing with emergency personnel in action. Accompanying mss: instructional, descriptive or feature articles dealing with emergency medical services.

Making Contact & Terms: Interested in receiving work from newer, lesser-known photographers. Uses 5×7 or 8×10 b&w glossy prints; 35mm or larger transparencies. For cover: Prefers 35mm; 2¼×2¼ transparencies OK. Vertical format preferred. Send material by mail for consideration, especially action shots of EMTs/paramedics in action. SASE. Pays $30/inside photo; $100/color cover photo; $100-300/ms. Pays for mss/photo package, or on a per-photo basis. **Pays on acceptance.** Credit line given. Buys all rights, "nonexclusive."

Tips: Wants well-composed photos with good overall scenes and clarity that say more than "an accident happened here. We're going toward single-focus, uncluttered photos." Looking for more color photos for articles. "Good closeups of actual treatment. Also, sensitive illustrations of the people in EMS— stress, interacting with family/pediatrics etc. We're interested in rescuers, and our readers like to see their peers in action, demonstrating their skills. Make sure photo is presented with treatment rendered and people involved. Prefer model release if possible."

EUROPE, (formerly *Europe Magazine*), Suite 700, 2100 M St. NW, Washington DC 20037. (202)862-9557. Editor-in-Chief: Robert J. Guttman. Managing Editor: Peter Gwin. Photo Editor: Anne Alvarez. Circ. 25,000. Magazine published 10 times a year. Covers the European Community with "in-depth news articles on topics such as economics, trade, US-EC relations, industry, development and East-West relations." Readers are "business people, professionals, academics, government officials." Free sample copy.

Needs: Uses about 20-30 photos/issue, most of which are supplied by stock houses and freelance photographers. Needs photos of "current news coverage and sectors, such as economics, trade, small business, people, transport, politics, industry, agriculture, fishing, some culture, some travel. No traditional costumes. Each issue we have an overview article on one of the 12 countries in the European Community. For this we need a broad spectrum of photos, particularly color, in all sectors. If a photographer queries and lets us know what he has on hand, we might ask him to submit a selection for a particular story. For example, if he has slides or b&w's on a certain European country, if we run a story on that country, we might ask him to submit slides on particular topics, such as industry, transport or small business." Model release preferred. Captions preferred; identification necessary.

Making Contact & Terms: Interested in receiving work from newer, lesser-known photographers. Query with list of stock photo subjects. Initially, a list of countries/topics covered will be sufficient. SASE. Reports in 3-4 weeks. Pays $75-150/b&w photo; $100 minimum/color transparency for inside; $400/cover; per job negotiable. Pays on publication. Credit line given. Buys one-time rights. Simultaneous submissions and previously published work OK.

Tips: "For certain articles, especially the Member Reports, we are now using more freelance material than previously. We need good photo and color quality, but not touristy or stereotypical. We want to show modern Europe growing and changing. Feature business or industry if possible."

FARM CHEMICALS, Dept. PM, 37733 Euclid Ave., Willoughby OH 44094. (216)942-2000. Fax: (216)942-0662. Editorial Director: Charlotte Sine. Editor: Dale Little. Circ. 32,000. Estab. 1896. Monthly magazine. Emphasizes application and marketing of fertilizers and protective chemicals for crops for those in the farm chemical industry. Free sample copy and photo guidelines with 9 × 12 SAE.
Needs: Buys 6-7 photos/year; 5-30% supplied by freelancers. Photos of agricultural chemical and fertilizer application scenes (of commercial – not farmer – applicators). Model release preferred. Captions required.
Making Contact & Terms: Query first with resume of credits. Uses 8 × 10 glossy b&w and color prints or transparencies. SASE. Reports in 3 weeks. Pays $25-50/b&w photo; $50-100/color photo. **Pays on acceptance.** Buys one-time rights. Simultaneous submissions and previously published work OK.

FARM JOURNAL, INC., 230 W. Washington Sq., Philadelphia PA 19105. (215)829-4865. Editor: Earl Ainsworth. Photo Editor: Tom Dodge. Circ. 800,000. Monthly magazine. Emphasizes the business of agriculture: "Good farmers want to know what their peers are doing and how to make money marketing their products." Free sample copy upon request.
Needs: Freelancers supply 60% of the photos. Photos having to do with the basics of raising, harvesting and marketing of all the farm commodities. People-oriented shots are encouraged. Also uses human interest and interview photos. All photos must relate to agriculture. Photos purchased with or without accompanying ms. Model release required. Captions required.
Making Contact & Terms: Arrange a personal interview or send photos by mail. Provide calling card and samples to be kept on file for possible future assignments. Uses 8 × 10 or 11 × 14 glossy or semigloss color or b&w prints; 35mm or 2¼ × 2¼ transparencies, all sizes for covers. SASE. Reports in 1-4 weeks. Pays by assignment or photo; $25-100/b&w photo; $100-200/color photo, depending on size; pays more for covers. **Pays on acceptance.** Credit line given. Buys one-time rights; negotiable. Simultaneous submissions OK.
Tips: "Be original, take time to see with the camera. Be more selective, take more shots to submit. Take as many different angles of subject as possible. Use fill where needed. We also publish five titles – *Farm Journal, Top Producer* (photo editor is Tom Dodge), *Hogs Today, Beef Today, Dairy Today* (photo editor is Greg Lamp – (612)631-3151)."

FIREHOUSE MAGAZINE, Suite 21, 445 Broad Hollow Rd., Melville NY 11747. (516)845-2700. Fax: (516)845-7109. Editor-in-Chief: Barbara Dunleavy. Art Director: Tina Sheely. Circ. 110,000. Estab. 1973. Monthly. Emphasizes "firefighting – notable fires, techniques, dramatic fires and rescues, etc." Readers are "paid and volunteer firefighters, EMT's." Sample copy $3 with 9 × 12 SAE and approximately $1.65 postage. Photo guidelines free with SASE.
Needs: Uses about 30 photos/issue; 20 supplied by freelance photographers. Needs photos in the above subject areas. Model release preferred.
Making Contact & Terms: Send 8 × 10 matte or glossy b&w or color prints; 35mm, 2¼ × 2¼, 4 × 5, 8 × 10 transparencies or b&w or color negatives with contact sheet by mail for consideration. "Photos must not be more than 30 days old." SASE. Reports ASAP. Pays $200/color cover photo; $15-45/b&w photo; $15-75/color photo. Pays on publication. Credit line given. Buys one-time rights.
Tips: "Mostly we are looking for action-packed photos – the more fire, the better the shot. Show firefighters in full gear, do not show spectators. Fire safety is a big concern. Much of our photo work is freelance. Try to be in the right place at the right time as the fire occurs."

*FLORIDA UNDERWRITER, Dept. PM, Suite 213, 9887 Gandy Blvd. N, St. Petersburg FL 33702. (813)576-1101. Editor: James E. Seymour. Circ. 10,000. Estab. 1984. Monthly magazine. Emphasizes insurance. Readers are insurance professionals in Florida. Sample copy free with 9 × 12 SASE.
Needs: Uses 10-12 photos/issue; 1-2 supplied by freelancers; 80% assignment and 20% freelance stock. Needs photos of insurance people, subjects, meetings and legislators. Captions preferred.
Making Contact & Terms: Query first with list of stock photo subjects. Send b&w prints, 35mm, 2¼ × 2¼, 4 × 5, 8 × 10 transparencies by mail for consideration. Provide resume, business card, brochure, flyer or tearsheets to be kept on file for possible assignments. SASE. Reports in 3 weeks. Pays $50-150/b&w cover photo; $15-35/b&w inside photo; $5-20/color page rate. Pays on publication. Credit line given. Buys all rights; negotiable. Simultaneous submissions and previously published work OK (admission of same required).
Tips: "Like the insurance industry we cover we are cutting costs. We are using fewer freelance photos (almost none at present)."

*FOOD DISTRIBUTION MAGAZINE, #104, 912 Drew St., Clearwater FL 34615. (813)443-2723. Fax: (813)446-1750. Art Director: Amy Wagner. Circ. 40,000. Estab. 1959. Monthly magazine. Emphasizes gourmet and specialty foods. Readers are male and female executives, ages 30-60. Sample copy $5.
Needs: Uses 20+ photos/issue; 3 supplied by freelancers. Needs photos of food, still-life, human interest, people. Reviews photos with accompanying ms only. Model release required for models only. Captions preferred; include photographer's name, subject.

Making Contact & Terms: Send unsolicited photos by mail for consideration. Send any size color prints and 4×5 transparencies. SASE. Reports in 1-2 weeks. Pays $100 minimum/color cover photo; $50 minimum/color inside photo. Pays on publication. Credit line given. Buys all rights. Simultaneous submissions OK.

*FOOD PRODUCT DESIGN MAGAZINE, Suite 202, 601 Skokie Blvd., Northbook IL 60062. (708)559-0385. Fax: (708)559-0389. Executive Editor: Debra Kronowitz. Circ. 26,000. Estab. 1991. Monthly. Emphasizes food development. Readers are research and development people in food industry.
Needs: Needs food shots (4-color). Special photo needs include food shots — pastas, cheese, reduced fat, sauces, etc.; as well as group shots of people, lab shots, focus group shots.
Making Contact & Terms: Interested in receiving work from newer, lesser-known photographers. Query with stock photo list. Send unsolicited photos by mail for consideration. Send color prints; 35mm, 4×5, 8×10 transaparecies. SASE. Reports in 1-2 weeks. Pays $300 minimum/job; negotiable based on job, time, etc. "Depends on job and way photo will be used." Pays on publication. Credit line given. Buys all rights for use in magazine. Simultaneoussubmissions and/or previously published work OK.
Tips: "Know your stuff. Submit work or call me — I keep in very close contact with my photographers, food stylists and writers."

FOODSERVICE EQUIPMENT & SUPPLIES SPECIALIST, 1350 E. Touhy Ave., Des Plaines IL 60018. (708)635-8800. Editor: Greg Richards. Circ. 20,000. Monthly magazine. Emphasizes "the foodservice equipment distribution business; stories focus on kitchen design and management profiles. Readers are equipment distributor sales and management personnel, kitchen designers. Sample copy free with 9×12 SASE.
Needs: Uses 8-16 photos/issue. Assigns photos of business management settings, plus restaurant and institutional kitchens. Model release required.
Making Contact & Terms: Provide resume, business card, brochure, flyer or tearsheets to be kept on file for possible assignments. SASE. Reports in 2 weeks. Pays $600-800/day; frequently makes day assignments. **Pays on acceptance.** Credit line given. Buys all rights; negotiable. Previously published work OK.
Tips: "Study the magazine carefully and determine whether you would have both the desire and the ability to shoot the types of photos you see."

FORD NEW HOLLAND NEWS, Dept. PM, P.O. Box 1895, New Holland PA 17557. (717)355-1276. Editor: Gary Martin. Circ. 400,000. Estab. 1960. Published 8 times a year. Emphasizes agriculture. Readers are farm families. Sample copy and photo guidelines free with 9×12 SASE.
Needs: Buys 30 photos/year. 50% freelance photography/issue from assignment and 50% freelance stock. Needs photos of scenic agriculture relating to the seasons, harvesting, farm animals, farm management and farm people. Reviews photos with accompanying ms only. Model release required. Captions required.
Making Contact & Terms: "Show us your work." SASE. Reports in 2 weeks. "Collections viewed and returned quickly." Pays $50-500/color photo, depends on use and quality of photo; $400-$1,500/photo/text package; $500/cover. Payment negotiable. **Pays on acceptance.** Buys first N.A. serial rights. Previously published work OK.
Tips: Photographers "must see beauty in agriculture and provide meaningful photojournalistic caption material to be successful here. It also helps to team up with a good agricultural writer and query us on a photojournalistic idea."

FURNITURE RETAILER, 1301 Carolina St., Greensboro NC 27401. (919)378-6065. Fax: (919)275-2864. Editor: Patricia Bowling. Monthly magazine. Emphasizes retail home furnishings stores. Readers are primarily male and female retail company executives. Sample copy and photo guidelines free with SASE.
Needs: Uses 15-20 photos/issue; 50% supplied by freelancers. Needs personality photos, shots of store interiors.
Making Contact & Terms: Query with resume of credits. Provide resume, business card, brochure, flyer or tearsheets to be kept on file for possible assignments. Reports only when interested. Pays $500/color cover photo; $250/color inside photo. **Pays on acceptance.** Credit line given. Buys first N.A. serial rights.
Tips: Looks for "ability to capture personality in business subjects for profiles; ability to handle diverse interiors."

FUTURES MAGAZINE, Dept. PM, Suite 1150, 250 S. Wacker Dr., Chicago IL 60606. (312)977-0999. Managing Editor: Diane Glaser. Editor: Ginger Szala. Circ. 70,000. Monthly magazine. Emphasizes futures and options trading. Readers are individual traders, institutional traders, brokerage firms, exchanges. Sample copy $4.50.

Needs: Uses 12-15 photos/issue; 80% supplied by freelance photographers. Needs mostly personality portraits of story sources, some mug shots, trading floor environment. Model release required. Captions preferred.

Making Contact & Terms: Arrange a personal interview to show portfolio. Query with list of stock photo subjects. Provide resume, business card, brochure, flyer or tearsheets to be kept on file for possible future assignments. SASE. Reports in 2 weeks. Pays $150/half day minimum. Pays on publication. Credit line given. Buys all rights.

Tips: All work is on assignment. Be competitive on price. Shoot good work without excessive film use.

*GEOTECHNICAL FABRICS REPORT, Suite 800, 345 Cedar St., St. Paul MN 55101. (612)222-2508. Fax: (612)222-8215. Editor: Danette. R. Fettig. Circ. 14,000. Estab. 1983. Published 9 times/year. Emphasizes geosynthetics in civil engineering application. Readers are male and female civil engineers, professors and consulting engineers. Sample copies available. Photo guidelines available.

Needs: Uses 6 photos/issue; various number supplied by freelancers. Needs photos of finished applications using geosynthetics, photos of the application process. Reviews photos with or without ms. Model release required. Captions required; include project, type of geosynthetics used and location.

Making Contact & Terms: Interested in receiving work from newer, lesser-known photographers. Send unsolicited photos by mail for consideration. Send any size color and b&w prints. Keeps samples on file. SASE. Reports in 1 month. NPI. Credit line given. Buys all rights; negotiable. Simultaneous submissions OK.

Tips: "Contact manufacturers in the geosynthetics industry and offer your services."

GRAIN JOURNAL, Dept. PM, 2490 N. Water St., Decatur IL 62526. (217)877-9660. Editor: Mark Avery. Circ. 11,822. Bimonthly. Also produces monthly newsletter. Emphasizes grain industry. Readers are "elevator managers primarily as well as suppliers and others in the industry." Sample copy free with 10×12 SAE and 85¢ postage.

Needs: Uses about 6 photos (but we want more)/issue. We need photos concerning industry practices and activities. Captions preferred.

Making Contact & Terms: Query with samples and list of stock photo subjects. SASE. Reports in 1 week. Pays $100/color cover photo; $30/b&w inside photo. Pays on publication. Credit line given. Buys all rights; negotiable.

*GROUND WATER AGE, 13 Century Hill Dr., Latham NY 12110. (518)783-1281. Fax: (518)783-1386. Editor: Roslyn Dahl. Monthly magazine. Circ. 17,000. Estab. 1966. Emphasizes management, marketing and technical information. Readers are water well drilling contractors, water pump specialists and monitoring well contractors. Free sample copy and photo guidelines.

Needs: Buys 5-10 photos/year. Needs picture stories and photos of water well drilling activity and pump installation.

Making Contact & Terms: Send 5×7 matte b&w prints; 8×10 matte color prints; transparencies; negatives. Uses vertical format for covers. SASE. Reports in 3 weeks. NPI; payment negotiable. **Pays on acceptance.** Buys all rights, but may reassign to photographer after publication. Simultaneous submissions and previously published work OK.

Tips: "There is a need for quality photos of on-site, job-related activity in our industry. Many photo sites are outdoors. Some familiarity with the industry would be helpful, of course." In photographer's samples, wants to see "an ability to capture a water well contractor, pump installer or monitoring well contractor in action. We have been improving our color cover shots. We'd appreciate more contributions from freelancers."

THE GROWING EDGE, 215 SW 2nd St., P.O. Box 1027, Corvallis OR 97333. (503)757-2511. Fax: (503)757-0028. Editor: Don Parker. Circ. 40,000. Estab. 1989. Published quarterly. Emphasizes "new and innovative techniques in gardening, indoors, outdoors and in the greenhouse—hydroponics, artificial lighting, greenhouse operations/control, water conservation, new and unusual plant varieties." Readers are serious amateurs to small commercial growers.

Needs: Uses about 20 photos per issue; most supplied with articles by freelancers. Occasional assignment work (5%); 80% from freelance stock. Model release required. Captions preferred; include plant types, equipment used.

Market conditions are constantly changing! If you're still using this book and it's 1995 or later, buy the newest edition of Photographer's Market *at your favorite bookstore or order directly from Writer's Digest Books.*

Making Contact & Terms: Send query with samples. Accepts b&w or color prints; transparencies (any size); b&w or color negatives with contact sheets. SASE. Reports in 4-6 weeks or will notify and keep material on file for future use. Pays $175/cover photos; $25-50/inside photos; $75-400/text/photo package. Pays on publication. Credit line given. Buys first world and one-time anthology rights; negotiable. Simultaneous submissions and previously published work OK.

Tips: "Most photographs are used to illustrate processes and equipment described in text. Some photographs of specimen plants purchased. Many photos are of indoor plants under artificial lighting. The ability to deal with tricky lighting situations is important." Expects more assignment work in the future.

HEAVY DUTY TRUCKING, P.O. Box W, Newport Beach CA 92658-8910. (714)261-1636. Editor: Deborah Whistler. Circ. 96,000. Monthly magazine. Emphasizes trucking. Readers are mostly male—corporate executives, fleet management, supervisors, salesmen and drivers—ages 30-65. Photo guidelines free with SASE.

Needs: Uses 30 photos/issue; 30-100% supplied by freelancers. Needs photos of scenics (trucks on highways), how-to (maintenance snapshots). Model release is "photographer's responsibility." Captions preferred.

Making Contact & Terms: Query with resume of credits. Send unsolicited photos by mail for consideration. Send 35mm transparencies. SASE. Pays $150/color cover photo; $75/color or b&w inside photo. Pays on publication; sends check when material is used. Buys one-time rights.

HEAVY TRUCK SALESMAN, P.O. Box W, Newport Beach CA 92658-8910. (714)261-1636. Managing Editor: Deborah Whistler. Circ. 15,000. Bimonthly magazine. Emphasizes trucking. Readers are mostly male truck dealers and salesmen, ages 30-65. Photo guidelines free with SASE.

Needs: Uses 30 photos/issue; 30-100% supplied by freelancers. Needs photos of truck dealerships, truck salesmen with customers, scenics (trucks on highways), how-to (maintenance snapshots). Model release is "photographer's responsibility." Captions preferred.

Making Contact & Terms: Query with resume of credits. Send unsolicited photos by mail for consideration. Send 35mm transparencies. SASE. Pays $150/color cover photo; $75/color or b&w inside photo. Pays on publication; sends check when material is used. Buys one-time rights.

‡HELICOPTER INTERNATIONAL, 75 Elm Tree Rd., Locking, Weston-S-Mare, Avon BS248EL England. (934)822524. Editor: E. apRees. Circ. 22,000. Bimonthly magazine. Emphasizes helicopters and autogyros. Readers are helicopter professionals. Sample copy $4.50 and A4 SAE.

Needs: Uses 25-35 photos/issue; 50% supplied by freelance photographers. Needs photos of helicopters, especially newsworthy subjects. Model release preferred. Captions required.

Making Contact & Terms: Send unsolicited photos by mail for consideration. Send 8×10 or 4×5 glossy b&w or color prints. Cannot return material. Reports in 1 month. Pays $20/color cover photo; $5/b&w inside photo. Pays on publication. Credit line given. Buys one-time rights. Simultaneous submissions or previously published work OK.

Tips: Magazine is growing. To break in, submit "newsworthy pictures. No arty-crafty pix; good clear shots of helicopters backed by newsworthy captions, e.g., a new sale/new type/new color scheme/accident, etc."

HIGH VOLUME PRINTING, Dept. PM, P.O. Box 368, Northbrook IL 60065. (708)564-5940. Fax: (708)564-8361. Editor: Catherine M. Stanulis. Circ. 30,000. Bimonthly. Emphasizes equipment, systems and supplies; large commercial printers: magazine and book printers. Readers are management and production personnel of high-volume printers and producers of books, magazines and periodicals. Sample copy $5 plus $1.41 postage. Photo guidelines free with SASE.

Needs: Uses about 30-35 photos/issue. Model release required. Captions preferred.

Making Contact & Terms: Query with samples or with list of stock photo subjects. Send b&w and color prints (any size or finish); 35mm, 2¼×2¼, 4×5 or 8×10 transparencies; b&w or color contact sheet or negatives by mail for consideration. SASE. Reports in 1 month. Pays $200 maximum/color cover photo; $50 maximum/b&w or color inside photo; $200 maximum text/photo package. Pays on publication. Credit line given. Buys one-time rights with option for future use. Previously published work OK "if previous publication is indicated."

HISPANIC BUSINESS, Dept. PM, Suite 300, 360 S. Hope Ave., Santa Barbara CA 93105. (805)682-5843. Senior Editor: Hector Cantu. Circ. 150,000. Estab. 1979. Monthly publication. Emphasizes Hispanics in business (entrepreneurs and executives), the Hispanic market. Sample copy $3.50. Photo guidelines available.

Needs: Uses 25 photos/issue; 10% supplied by freelancers. Needs photos of personalities and action shots. No mug shots. Model and/or property release required. Captions required; include name, title.

Making Contact & Terms: Query with resume of credits. Keeps samples on file. Reports in 1-2 weeks. Pays $450/color cover photo; $200/color inside photo; $150/b&w inside photo. Pays on publication. Credit line given. Rights negotiable.

Tips: Wants to see "unusual angles, bright colors, hand activity. Photo tied to profession."

HOGS TODAY, Farm Journal Publishing, Inc., Suite 100, 6205 Earle Brown Dr., Brooklyn Center MN 55430. (612)561-0300. Photo Editor: Greg Lamp. Circ. 125,000. Monthly magazine. Sample copy and photo guidelines free with SASE.
Needs: Uses 20-30 photos/issue; 75% supplied by freelancers. "We use studio-type portraiture (environmental portraits), technical, details, scenics." Model release preferred. Captions required.
Making Contact & Terms: Arrange a personal interview to show portfolio. Query with resume of credits along with business card, brochure, flyer or tearsheets to be kept on file for possible assignments. SASE. Reports in 2 weeks. NPI. "We pay a cover bonus." **Pays on acceptance.** Credit line given. Buys one-time rights. Simultaneous submissions OK.
Tips: In portfolio or samples, likes to "see about 20 slides showing photographer's use of lighting and ability to work with people. Know your intended market. Familiarize yourself with the magazine and keep abreast of how photos are used in the general magazine field."

IB (INDEPENDENT BUSINESS): AMERICA'S SMALL BUSINESS MAGAZINE, #211, 875 S. Westlake Blvd., Westlake Village CA 91361. (805)496-6156. Fax: (805)496-5469. Editor: Daniel Kehrer. Editorial Director: Don Phillipson. Circ. 600,000. Estab. 1990. Bimonthly magazine. Emphasizes small business. All readers are small business owners throughout the US. Sample copy $4. Photo guidelines free with SASE.
Needs: Uses 25-35 photos/issue; all supplied by freelancers. Needs photos of "exclusively people (men and women) who are small business owners. All pix are by assignment. No spec photos." Special photo needs include dynamic, unusual photos of offbeat businesses and their owners. Model/property release required. Captions required; include correct spelling on name, title, business name, location.
Making Contact & Terms: Query with resume of credits. Provide resume, business card, brochure, flyer or tearsheets to be kept on file for possible assignments. Keeps samples on file. SASE. Reports in 6 weeks. Pays $300/color inside photo; $300-700/day. **Pays on acceptance.** Credit line given. Buys first plus non-exclusive reprint rights.
Tips: "We want colorful, striking photos of small business owners that go well above-and-beyond the usual business magazine. Capture the essence of the business owner's 'native habitat.' "

*IGA GROCERGRAM, 1301 Carolina St., Greensboro NC 27401. (919)378-6065. Fax: (919)275-2864. Managing Editor: Mickey McLean. Publication of the Independent Grocers Alliance. Circ. 16,000. Estab. 1926. Monthly magazine, plus special issues. Emphasizes food industry. Readers are IGA retailers, mainly male. Sample copy $2 plus postage.
Needs: Uses 10 photos/issue; all supplied by freelancers. Needs in-store shots, food (appetite appeal). Model/property release preferred. Captions preferred.
Making Contact & Terms: Send unsolicited 35mm transparencies by mail for consideration. Provide resume, business card, brochure, flyer or tearsheets to be kept on file for possible assignments. Keeps samples on file. Reports in 3 weeks. Pays $300/color cover photo; $250/b&w cover photo; $75/color inside photo; $25/b&w inside photo; $100/color page rate; $50/b&w page rate. **Pays on acceptance.** Credit line given. Buys one-time rights. Simultaneous submissions and previously published work OK.

ILLINOIS LEGAL TIMES, Dept. PM, Suite 1513, 222 Merchandise Mart Plaza, Chicago IL 60654. (312)644-4378. Associate Editor: Kelly Fox. Circ. 13,162. Estab. 1987. Monthly trade publication, tabloid format. Covers law. Readers are Illinois-based lawyers of various ages and backgrounds. Sample copy free with 10×13 SASE.
Needs: Uses 30-35 photos/issue; most supplied by freelancers. Needs photos of personalities in the profession.
Making Contact & Terms: Query with resume of credits. Provide resume, business card, brochure, flyer or tearsheets to be kept on file for possible assignment. SASE. Reports in 3 weeks. Pays $100/color or b&w cover photo; $35/color or b&w inside photo. Pays on 15th of month of cover date in which photos appear. Credit line given. Buys all rights; negotiable.

*INDEPENDENT BANKER, P.O. Box 267, Sault Centre MN 56310. (612)352-6546. Editor: Dave Bordewyk. Circ. 10,000. Estab. 1950. Publication of Independent Bankers Association of America. Monthly magazine. Emphasizes independent commercial banking. Readers are male and female chief executives, ages 35-65. Sample copy $3.
Needs: Uses 15 photos/issue; 5 supplied by freelancers. Needs shots of bankers at work in the bank with fellow bankers or customers, shots of bank buildings. Reviews photos with or without accompanying ms. Model release preferred. Captions preferred.
Making Contact & Terms: Interested in receiving work from newer, lesser-known photographers. Provide resume, business card, brochure, flyer or tearsheets to be kept on file for possible assignments. Keeps samples on file. Cannot return material. Reports in 1 month. Pays $50-150/job; $50-100/color cover photo; $40 minimum/color inside photo; $25 minimum/b&w inside photo. **Pays on acceptance.**

Buys one-time rights; negotiable. Simultaneous submissions and/or previously published work OK.
Tips: "Get to know our publication first—what our needs are, etc."

INDUSTRIAL PHOTOGRAPHY, PTN Publications, Dept. PM, 445 Broad Hollow Rd., Melville NY 11747. (516)845-2700. Publisher: George Schaub. Managing Editor: Steve Shaw. Circ. 46,000. Monthly magazine. "Our emphasis is on the industrial photographer who produces images (still, cine, video) for a company or organization (including industry, military, government, medical, scientific, educational, institutions, R&D facilities, etc.)." Free sample copy and writer's/photo guidelines.
Needs: All mss and photos must relate to the needs of industrial photographers. Photos purchased with accompanying ms. Seeks mss that offer technical or general information of value to industrial photographers, including applications, techniques, case histories of in-plant departments, etc. Model/property release required. Captions required.
Making Contact & Terms: Query with story/photo suggestion. Provide letter of inquiry and samples to be kept on file for possible future assignments. Uses 4×5, 5×7 or 8×10 glossy b&w and color prints or 35mm transparencies; allows other kinds of photos. SASE. Reports in 1 month. Pays $150 minimum/ms, including all photos and other illustrations. Pays on publication. Credit line given. Buys first N.A. serial rights except photo with text.
Tips: Trend toward "photo/text packages only." In samples wants to see "technical ability, graphic depiction of subject matter and unique application of technique." To break in, "link up with a writer" if not already a writer as well as photographer. "We also are looking for top cover shots."

INDUSTRIAL SAFETY AND HYGIENE NEWS, Dept. PM, 1 Chilton Way, Radnor PA 19089. (215)964-4057. Editor: Dave Johnson. Circ. 60,000. Monthly magazine. Emphasizes industrial safety and health for safety and health management personnel in over 36,000 large industrial plants (primarily manufacturing). Free sample copy.
Needs: Occasionally use freelance photography for front covers. Magazine is tabloid size, thus front cover photos must be powerful and graphic with the dramatic impact of a poster.
Making Contact & Terms: Send material by mail for consideration. Uses color, 35mm and 2¼×2¼ transparencies. Photographer should request editorial schedule and sample of publication. SASE. Reports in 2 weeks. Pays $300-400/color photo. Credit line given. Pays on publication. Buys all rights on a work-for-hire basis. Previously published work OK.

IN-PLANT PRINTER AND ELECTRONIC PUBLISHER, Dept. PM, P.O. Box 1387, Northbrook IL 60065. (708)564-5940. Editor: Andrea Cody. Circ. 41,000. Bimonthly. Emphasizes "in-plant printing; print and graphic shops housed, supported, and serving larger companies and organizations and electronic publishing applications in those locations." Readers are management and production personnel of such shops. Sample copy $5. Photo guidelines free with SASE.
Needs: Uses about 5-10 photos/issue. Needs "working/shop photos, atmosphere, interesting equipment shots, how-to." Model release required. Captions preferred.
Making Contact & Terms: Query with samples or with list of stock photo subjects. Send b&w and color (any size or finish) prints; 35mm, 2¼×2¼, 4×5, 8×10 slides, b&w and color contact sheet or b&w and color negatives by mail for consideration. SASE. Reports in 1 month. Pays $200 maximum/b&w or color cover photo; $25 maximum/b&w or color inside photo; $200 maximum text/photo package. Pays on publication. Credit line given. Buys one-time rights with option for future use. Previously published work OK "if previous publication is indicated."
Tips: "Good photos of a case study—such as a printshop, in our case—can lead us to doing a follow-up story by phone and paying more for photos. Photographer should be able to bring out the hidden or overlooked design elements in graphic arts equipment." Trends include artistic representation of common objects found in-plant—equipment, keyboard, etc.

INSTANT AND SMALL COMMERCIAL PRINTER, Dept. PM, P.O. Box 368, Northbrook IL 60065. (708)564-5940. Fax: (708)564-8361. Editor: Jeanette Clinkunbroomer. Circ. 55,000. Estab. 1982. Published 10 times/year. Emphasizes the "instant and retail printing industry." Readers are owners, operators and managers of instant and smaller commercial (less than 20 employees) print shops. Sample copy $3. Photo guidelines free with SASE.
Needs: Uses about 15-20 photos/issue. Needs "working/shop photos, atmosphere, interesting equipment shots, some how-to." Model release required. Captions preferred.
Making Contact & Terms: Interested in receiving work from newer, lesser-known photographers. Query with samples or with list of stock photo subjects or send b&w and color (any size or finish) prints; 35mm, 2¼×2¼, 4×5 or 8×10 slides; b&w and color contact sheet or b&w and color negatives by mail for consideration. SASE. Reports in 1 month. Pays $300 maximum/b&w and color cover photo; $50 maximum/b&w and color inside photo; $200 maximum text/photo package. Pays on publication. Credit line given. Buys one-time rights with option for future use; negotiable. Previously published work OK "if previous publication is indicated."

THE INSTRUMENTALIST, 200 Northfield Rd., Northfield IL 60093. (708)446-5000. Fax: (708)446-6263. Senior Editor: Ann Rohner. Circ. 20,000. Estab. 1946. Monthly magazine. Emphasizes instrumental music education. Readers are school band and orchestra directors and performers. Sample copies $2.50.
Needs: Buys 1-5 photos/issue, mostly color. Needs headshots and human interest photos. "All photos should deal with instrumental music in some way." Especially needs photos for Photo Essay section.
Making Contact & Terms: Send unsolicited photos by mail for consideration. Uses 5×7 or 8×10 glossy b&w and color prints; 35mm and 2¼×2¼ transparencies. Vertical format preferred. SASE. Reports in 2-4 weeks. Pays $15-25/photo. Pays on publication. Credit line given. Buys all rights.
Tips: Request sample copy to review. "We look for shots that capture a natural expression of a player or that zoom in on an instrument to show it in a new perspective. We receive more marching band shots than we can use. We are always looking for closeups of people or classical instruments (no rock or folk instruments). Be sure to take into account logo placement, vertical format and room for cropping. The cover and an occasional inside shot come from assignments. Many covers are provided by freelancers introducing themselves to us for the first time."

✸THE JOURNAL, Addiction Research Foundation, 33 Russell St., Toronto, Ontario M5S 2S1 Canada. (416)595-6053. Fax: (416)595-6036. Editor: Anne MacLennan. Managing Editor: Elda Hauschildt. Circ. 12,000. Estab. 1972. Bimonthly tabloid. Readers are professionals in the alcohol and drug abuse field: doctors, teachers, social workers, enforcement officials and government officials. Free sample copy and photo guidelines.
Needs: Buys 4-10 photos/issue. Photos relating to alcohol and other drug abuse and smoking. No posed shots. Model release. Captions preferred.
Making Contact & Terms: Interested in receiving work from newer, lesser-known photographers. Send photos or contact sheet for consideration. Send 5×7 glossy b&w prints. Not copyrighted. Reports ASAP. Pays $35-85/photo. Pays on publication. Buys one-time rights.
Tips: "We are looking for action shots, street scenes, people of all ages and occupations. Shots should not appear to be posed."

JOURNAL OF EXTENSION, Dept. PM, 432 N. Lake St., Madison WI 53706. (608)262-1974. Assistant Editor: Colleen L. Schuh. Circ. 12,000. Estab. 1963. Quarterly journal. A professional journal for adult educators. Readers are adult educators, extension personnel.
Needs: Uses 1 cover photo/issue; all supplied by freelancers. "Each issue we try to highlight the lead article, so the subject matter varies each time." Model release required.
Making Contact & Terms: Send 4×6 or 5×7 b&w prints by mail for consideration. Call to check on current needs. SASE. Reports in 1 month. Pays $75-100/b&w cover photo. **Pays on acceptance.** Credit line given. Buys one-time rights.

JOURNAL OF PROPERTY MANAGEMENT, 7th Floor, 430 N. Michigan Ave., Chicago IL 60611. (312)329-6058. Managing Editor: Marilyn Evans. Circ. 19,600. Estab. 1934. Bimonthly magazine. Emphasizes real estate management. Readers are mid- and upper-level managers of investment real estate. Sample copy free with SASE. Photo guidelines available.
Needs: Uses 6 photos/issue; 50% supplied by freelancers. Needs photos of buildings, building operations and office interaction. Model/property release preferred.
Making Contact & Terms: NPI.

✳LAND LINE MAGAZINE, 311 R.D. Mize Rd., Grain Valley MO 64029. (816)229-5791. Fax: (816)229-0518. Managing Editor: Sandi Laxson. Circ. 80,000. Estab. 1975. Publication of Owner Operator Independent Drivers Association. Bimonthly magazine. Emphasizes trucking. Readers are male and female independent truckers, with an average age of 44. Sample copy $2.
Needs: Uses 18-20 photos/issue; 50% supplied by freelancers. Needs photos of trucks, highways, truck stops, truckers, etc. Reviews photos with or without ms. Model/property release preferred for company trucks, drivers. Captions preferred.
Making Contact & Terms: Interested in receiving work from newer, lesser-known photographers. Provide resume, business card, brochure, flyer or tearsheets to be kept on file for possible assignments. Send glossy color or b&w prints; 2¼×2¼ transparencies. Pays $100/color cover photo; $50/b&w cover photo; $50/color inside photo; $30/b&w inside photo. Credit line given. Buys one-time rights. Previously published work OK.

LLAMAS MAGAZINE, P.O.Box 100, Herald CA 95638. (209)223-0469. Fax: (209)223-0466. Circ. 5,500. Estab. 1979. Publication of The International Camelid Journal. Magazine published 8 times a year. Emphasizes llamas, alpacas, vicunas, gunacos and camels. Readers are llama and alpaca owners and ranchers. Sample copy $5.75. Photo guidelines free with SASE.

Needs: Uses 30-50 photos/issue; all supplied by freelancers. Wants to see "any kind of photo with llamas, alpacas, camels in it. Always need good verticals for the cover. Always need good action shots." Model release required. Captions required.

Making Contact & Terms: Send unsolicited b&w or color 35mm prints or 35mm transparencies by mail for consideration. Provide resume, business card, brochure, flyer or tearsheets to be kept on file for possible assignments. Reports in 1-2 weeks. Pays $100/color cover photo; $25/color inside photo; $15/b&w inside photo. Pays on publication. Credit line given. Buys one-time rights. Simultaneous submissions and previously published work OK.

Tips: "You must have a good understanding of llamas and alpacas to submit photos to us. It's a very specialized market. Our rates are modest, but our publication is a very slick 4-color magazine and it's a terrific vehicle for getting your work into circulation. We are willing to give photographers a lot of free tearsheets for their portfolios to help publicize their work."

MARINE BUSINESS JOURNAL, 1766 Bay Rd., Miami Beach FL 33139. (305)538-0700. Fax:(305)532-8657. Editorial Director: Andree Conrad. Bimonthly. Emphasizes recreational marine industry. Readers are people employed in the boating industry, mostly males, age 30-65. Sample copy $5. Photo guidelines free with SASE.

Needs: Uses 5-10 photos/issue; all supplied by freelancers. "Needs photo stringers on-call nationwide for occasional event/product photography." Reviews photos with accompanying ms only. Model release required when appropriate. Captions required.

Making Contact & Terms: Query with resume of credits. Query with stock photo list. Provide resume, business card, brochure, flyer or tearsheets to be kept on file for possible assignments. Reports in 1 month. Pays $50/color inside photo; $25/b&w inside photo. Pays on publication. Credit line given. Buys one-time rights.

Tips: "Not interested in photos without story, but we are interested in compiling a good list of reliable photojournalists around the country. So write in with samples and resumes."

MARKETERS FORUM, 383 E. Main St., Centerport NY 11721. (516)754-5000. Fax: (516)754-0630. Publisher: Martin Stevens. Circ. 70,000. Estab. 1981. Monthly magazine. Readers are entrepreneurs and retail store owners. Sample copy $3.

Needs: Uses 3-6 photos/issue; all supplied by freelancers. "We publish trade magazines for retail variety goods stores and flea market vendors. Items include: jewelry, cosmetics, novelties, toys, etc. (five and dime type goods). We are interested in creative and abstract impressions—not straight-on product shots. Humor a plus" Model/property release required.

Making Contact & Terms: Send unsolicited photos by mail for consideration. Send color prints; 35mm, 4×5 transparencies. Does not keep samples on file. SASE. Reports in 1-2 weeks. Pays $100/ color cover photo; $50/color inside photo. **Pays on acceptance.** Buys one-time rights. Simultaneous submissions and/or previously published work OK.

*MEMBERS MAGAZINE, 5822 W. 74th St., Indianapolis IN 46278. (317)328-4356. Fax: (317)328-4354. Publication Account Manager: Sharron Hoke. Circ. 20,000. Estab. 1991. Monthly magazine. Emphasis on the retail hardware industry. Readers are owners of True Value Hardware and V&S variety stores. Sample copy free with 9×12 manila SAE and 5 first-class stamps. Photo guidelines free with SASE.

Needs: Uses 30-40 photos/issue; 5 supplied by freelancers. Needs portrait photos of store owners shot on location. "We do not need stock photography."

Making Contact & Terms: Interested in receiving work from newer, lesser-known photographers. Provide resume, business card, brochure, flyer or tearsheets to be kept on file for possible assignments. Keeps samples on file. SASE. Reports in 1-2 weeks. Pays $600-800/day, plus expenses; $300-400/½ day, plus expenses. Pays on receipt of invoice, net 30 days. Credit line given. Buys all rights; negotiable.

Tips: "Must have experience with fluorescent lighting, own lighting equipment, and have an ability to make subjects feel at ease and look 'unposed.' Must have short turn-around time. This is ideal for someone building a portfolio."

*MEXICO UPDATE, P.O. Box 188037, Carlsbad CA 92009. (619)929-0707. Fax: (619)929-0714. Art Director: Jim Crandall. Circ. 40,000. Estab. 1992. Bimonthly magazine. Emphasizes travel to Mexico for travel professionals. Readers are travel agents and travel industry people. Sample copy $2. Photo guidelines free with SASE.

Needs: Uses 30-40 photos/issue; 10 supplied by freelancers. Needs travel industry shots—hotels, resorts, tourism officials, etc. in Mexico for US travel pros. Model/property release preferred. Captions required; include correct spelling of people's names, location, time of day/year.

Making Contact & Terms: Interested in receiving work from newer, lesser-known photographers. Call. Does not keep samples on file. SASE. Reports in 1 month. Pays $100/color cover photo; $20-100/color inside photo. Pays on publication. Buys one-time rights. Previously published work OK.

Tips: Wants technically sound, inventive, creative shots.

MINORITY BUSINESS ENTREPRENEUR, 924 N. Market St., Inglewood CA 90302. (310)673-9398. Fax: (310)673-0170. Executive Editor: Jeanie Barnett. Circ. 35,000. Estab. 1984. Bimonthly magazine. Emphasizes minority, small, disadvantaged businesses. Sample copy free with 9½ × 12½ SAE and 5 first-class stamps. "We have editorial guidelines and calendar of upcoming issues available."
Needs: Uses 5-10 feature photos/issue. Needs "good shots for cover profiles and minority features of our entrepreneurs." Model release preferred. Property release required. Captions preferred; include name, title and company of subject, and proper photo credit.
Making Contact & Terms: Interested in receiving work from newer, lesser-known photographers. Query with resume of credits. Provide resume, business card, brochure, flyer or tearsheets to be kept on file for possible assignments. "Never submit unsolicited photos." SASE. Reports in 5 weeks. NPI; payment negotiable. Pays on publication. Credit line given. Buys first N.A. serial rights; negotiable.
Tips: "We're starting to run color photos in our business owner profiles. We want pictures that capture them in the work environment. Especially interested in minority and women photographers working for us. Our cover is an oil painting composed from photos. It's important to have high quality b&ws which show the character lines of the face for translation into oils. Read our publication and have a good understanding of minority business issues. Never submit photos that have nothing to do with the magazine."

MODERN BAKING, Dept. PM, Suite 418, 2700 River Rd., Des Plaines IL 60018. (708)299-4430. Fax: (708)296-1968. Editor: Ed Lee. Circ. 27,000. Estab. 1987. Monthly. Emphasizes on-premise baking, in supermarkets, foodservice establishments and retail bakeries. Readers are owners, managers and operators. Sample copy for 9 × 12 SAE with $2.90 postage.
Needs: Uses 30 photos/issue; 1-2 supplied by freelancers. Needs photos of on-location photography in above-described facilities. Model/property release preferred. Captions required; include company name, location, contact name and telephone number.
Making Contact & Terms: Interested in receiving work from newer, lesser-known photographers. Provide resume, business card, brochure, flyer or tearsheets to be kept on file for possible future assignments. SASE. Reports in 2 weeks. Pays $50 minimum; negotiable. **Pays on acceptance.** Credit line given. Buys all rights; negotiable.
Tips: Prefers to see "photos that would indicate person's ability to handle on-location, industrial photography."

MODERN OFFICE TECHNOLOGY, 1100 Superior Ave., Cleveland OH 44114. (216)696-7000. Fax: (216)696-7658. Editor: Lura K. Romei. Circ. 150,000. Estab. 1957. Monthly magazine. Emphasizes office automation, data processing. Readers are middle and upper management and higher in companies of 100 or more employees. Sample copy free with 11 × 14 SAE and 44¢ postage.
Needs: Uses 15 photos/issue; 1 supplied by freelancers. Needs office shots, office interiors, computers, concept shots of office automation and networking; "any and all office shots are welcome." Model/property release preferred. Captions required; include non-model names, positions.
Making Contact & Terms: Provide resume, business card, brochure, flyer or tearsheets to be kept on file for possible future assignments. Reports in 3 weeks. Pays $500/color cover photo; $50-100/b&w or color inside photo. Pays on publication. Credit line given. Buys one-time rights.
Tips: "Good conceptual (not vendor-specific) material about the office and office supplies is hard to find. Crack that and you're in business." In reviewing a photographer's samples, looks for "imagination and humor."

*MODERN PLASTICS, 1221 6th Ave., New York NY 10020. (212)512-3491. Art Director: Bob Barravecchia. Circ. 65,000. Monthly magazine. Readers are male buyers in the plastics trade.
Needs: Needs photos of how-to, etc. Purchases photos with accompanying ms only. Model release required. Property release preferred. Captions required; include manufacturer's name and model number.
Making Contact & Terms: Interested in receiving work from newer, lesser-known photographers. Arrange a personal interview to show portfolio. Cannot return material. Reports in 1 week. Pays $500/color cover photo and $100/color inside photo. **Pays on acceptance.** Credit line given. Buys first N.A. serial rights.
Tips: In portfolio or samples looks for concept covers.

MUSHING MAGAZINE, P.O. Box 149, Ester AK 99725. (907)479-0454. Publisher: Todd Hoener. Circ. 6,000. Estab. 1987. Bimonthly magazine. Readers are dog drivers, all-season mushing enthusiasts, dog lovers, outdoor specialists, innovators and history lovers. Sample copy $4 in US. Photo guidelines free with SASE.

The code NPI (no payment information given) appears in listings that have not given specific payment amounts.

Needs: Uses 15 photos/issue; most supplied by freelancers. Needs action photos: all-season and wilderness; also still and close-up photos: specific focus (sledding, carting, equipment, etc). Special photo needs include skijoring, feeding, caring for dogs, summer carting or packing, 1-3 dog-sledding and kids mushing. Model release preferred. Captions preferred.

Making Contact & Terms: Interested in receiving work from newer, lesser-known photographers. Send unsolicited photos by mail for consideration. Submit portfolio for review. Reports in 2 months. Pays $150 maximum/color cover photo; $100 maximum/color inside photo; $15-30/b&w inside photo. Pays on publication. Credit line given. Buys first N.A. serial rights and second reprint rights.

Tips: Wants to see work that shows "the total mushing adventure/lifestyle from environment to dog house." To break in, one's work must show "simplicity, balance and harmony. Strive for unique, provocative shots that lure readers and publishers."

*MUSIC EDUCATORS JOURNAL, 1902 Association Dr., Reston VA 22091. (703)860-4000. Contact: Graphic Designer. Circ. 60,000. Monthly magazine. Emphasizes music. Readers are music teachers.

Needs: Uses about 35 photos/issue; all supplied by freelancers. Needs photos of music students, music classroom situations, K-12 and college and music teachers. Model release preferred.

Making Contact & Terms: Send 5×7 or 8×10 b&w and color prints; 35mm, 2¼×2¼ transparencies by mail for consideration. Provide resume, business card, brochure, flyer or tearsheets to be kept on file for possible future assignments. SASE. Reports in 1 month. Pays $20/b&w inside photo. **Pays on acceptance.** Credit line given. Buys one-time rights. Simultaneous submissions and previously published work OK.

NATIONAL BUS TRADER, 9698 W. Judson Rd., Polo IL 61064-9049. (815)946-2341. Fax: (815)946-2347. Editor: Larry Plachno. Circ. 5,600. Estab. 1977. "The Magazine of Bus Equipment for the United States and Canada—covers mainly integral design buses in the United States and Canada." Readers are bus owners, commercial bus operators, bus manufacturers, bus designers. Sample copy free (no charge—just write or call).

Needs: Uses about 30 photos/issue; 22 supplied by freelance photographers. Needs photos of "buses; interior, exterior, under construction, in service." Special needs include "photos for future feature articles and conventions our own staff does not attend."

Making Contact & Terms: "Query with specific lists of subject matter that can be provided and mention whether accompanying mss are available." SASE. Reports in 1 week. Pays $3-5/b&w photo; $100-3,000/photo/text package. **Pays on acceptance.** Credit line given. Buys rights "depending on our need and photographer." Simultaneous submissions and previously published work OK.

Tips: "We don't need samples, merely a list of what freelancers can provide in the way of photos or ms. Write and let us know what you can offer and do. We often use freelance work. We also publish *Bus Tours Magazine*—a bimonthly which uses many photos but not many from freelancers; *The Bus Equipment Guide*—infrequent, which uses many photos; and *The Official Bus Industry Calendar*—annual full-color calendar of bus photos. We also publish historical railroad books and are looking for historical photos on midwest interurban lines and railroads. Due to publication of historical railroad books, we are purchasing many historical photos. In photos looks for subject matter appropriate to current or pending article or book. Send a list of what is available with specific photos, locations, bus/interurban company and fleet number."

NATIONAL FISHERMAN, Dept. PM, 120 Tillson Ave., Rockland ME 04841. (207)594-6222. Fax: (207)594-8978. Art Director: Marydale Abernathy. Circ. 50,000. Estab. 1960. Monthly magazine. Emphasizes commercial fishing, boat building, marketing of fish, fishing techniques and fishing equipment. For amateur and professional boatbuilders, commercial fishermen, armchair sailors, bureaucrats and politicians. Free sample copy with 11×15 SAE and $2 postage.

Needs: Buys 5-8 photo stories monthly; buys 4-color action cover photo monthly. Action shots of commercial fishing, work boats, traditional sailing fishboats, boat building, deck gear. No recreational, caught-a-trout photos.

Making Contact & Terms: Query. Reports in 8 weeks. Pays $10-25/inside b&w print; $250/color cover transparency. Pays on publication.

Tips: "We seldom use photos unless accompanied by feature stories or short articles—i.e., we don't run a picture for its own sake. Even those accepted for use in photo essays must tell a story—both in themselves and through accompanying cutline information. However, we do use single, stand-alone photos for cover shots. We need sharp b&w glossy photos—5×7s are fine. For cover, please send 35mm transparencies; dupes are acceptable. We want high-quality b&w images for inside that will hold detail on newsprint. Send slide samples."

NATION'S BUSINESS, U.S. Chamber of Commerce, 1615 H St. NW, Washington DC 20062. (202)463-5447. Photo Editor: Laurence L. Levin. Assistant Photo Editor: Frances Borchardt. Circ. 850,000. Monthly. Emphasizes business, especially small business. Readers are managers, upper management and business owners. Sample copy free with 9×12 SASE.

Needs: Uses about 30-40 photos/issue; 65% supplied by freelancers. Needs portrait-personality photos, business-related pictures relating to the story. Foreign scenics. Model release preferred. Captions required.

Making Contact & Terms: Arrange a personal interview to show portfolio. Submit portfolio for review. SASE. Reports in 3 weeks. Pays $200/b&w or color inside photo; $175-300/day. Pays on publication. Credit line given. Buys one-time rights.

Tips: In reviewing a portfolio, "we look for the photographer's ability to light, taking a static situation and turning it into a spontaneous, eye-catching and informative picture."

*NEVADA CASINO JOURNAL, #205, 3100 W. Sahara Ave., Las Vegas NV 89102. (702)253-6230. Fax: (702)253-6804. Editor: Adam Fine. Circ. 35,000. Estab. 1990. Monthly journal. Emphasizes casino operations. Readers are casino executives, employees and vendors. Sample copy free with 11 × 14 SAE and $2.50 postage.

Needs: Uses 40-60 photos/issue; 5-10 supplied by freelancers. Needs photos of gaming tables and slot machines, casinos and portraits of executives. Model release required for gamblers, employees. Captions required.

Making Contact & Terms: Interested in receiving work from newer, lesser-known photographers. Query with resume of credits. Query with stock photo list. Reports in 2-3 months. Pays $100 minimum/color cover photo; $10-35/color inside photo; $10-25/b&w inside photo. Pays on publication. Credit line given. Buys all rights; negotiable.

Tips: "Read and study photos in current issues."

*NEW JERSEY CASINO JOURNAL, 2524 Arctic Ave., Atlantic City NJ 08401. (609)344-9000. Fax: (609)345-3469. Photo Editor: Rick Greco. Circ. 25,000. Estab. 1985. Monthly. Emphasizes casino operations. Readers are casino executives, employers and vendors. Sample copy free with 11 × 14 SAE and $2.50 postage.

Needs: Uses 40-60 photos/issue; 5-10 supplied by freelancers. Needs photos of gaming tables and slot machines, casinos and portraits of executives. Model release required for gamblers, employees. Captions required.

Making Contact & Terms; Interested in receiving work from newer, lesser-known photographers. Query with resume of credits. Query with stock photo list. Reports in 2-3 months. Pays $100 minimum/color cover photo; $10-35/color inside photo; $10-25/b&w inside photo. Pays on publication. Credit line given. Buys all rights; negotiable.

Tips: "Read and study photos in current issues."

NEW METHODS, P.O. Box 22605, San Francisco CA 94122-0605. (415)664-3469. Art Director: Ronald S. Lippert, AHT. Monthly. Emphasizes veterinary personnel, animals. Readers are veterinary professionals and interested consumers. Circ. 5,600. Estab. 1976. Sample copy $2.90 (20% discount on 12 or more). Photo guidelines free with SASE.

Needs: Uses 12 photos/issue; 2 supplied by freelance photographers. Assigns 95% of photos. Needs animal, wildlife and technical photos. Most work is b&w. Model/property releases preferred. Captions preferred.

Making Contact & Terms: Interested in receiving work from newer, lesser-known photographers. Arrange a personal interview to show portfolio. Query with resume of credits, samples or list of stock photo subjects. Provide resume, business card, brochure, flyer or tearsheets to be kept on file for possible assignments. SASE. Reports in 2 months. Payment is rare, negotiable; will barter. Pays on publication. Credit line given. Buys one-time rights. Simultaneous submissions and previously published work OK.

Tips: Ask for photo needs before submitting work. Prefers to see "technical photos (human working with animal(s) or animal photos (*not cute*)" in a portfolio or samples. On occasion, needs photographer for shooting new products and local area conventions.

911 MAGAZINE, P.O. Box 11788, Santa Ana CA 92711. (714)544-7776. Fax: (714)838-9233. Editor: Alan Burton. Circ. 25,000. Estab. 1988. Bimonthly magazine. Emphasizes emergency response — police, fire, paramedic, dispatch, utilities, etc. Readers are ages 20-65, mostly male. Sample copy free with 9 × 12 SAE and 7 first-class stamps. Photo guidelines free with SASE.

Needs: Uses up to 25 photos/issue; 75% supplied by freelance photographers. "From the Field" department photos are needed of incidents involving emergency agencies in action from law enforcement, fire suppression, paramedics, dispatch, etc., showing proper techniques and attire. Model release preferred. Captions required; include incident location by city and state, agencies involved, duration, dollar cost, fatalities and injuries.

Making Contact & Terms: Query with list of stock photo subjects. Send unsolicited photos by mail for consideration. Provide resume, business card, brochure, flyer or tearsheets to be kept on file for possible assignments. Uses 35mm, 2¼ × 2¼, 4 × 5, 8 × 10 glossy contacts, b&w or color prints; 35mm, 2¼ × 2¼, 4 × 5, 8 × 10 transparencies. SASE. Reports in 3 weeks. Pays $100-300/color cover photo;

$50-150/b&w cover photo; $25-75/color inside photo; $20-50/b&w inside photo. Pays on publication. Credit line given. Rights are negotiable. Simultaneous submissions and previously published work OK.
Tips: "We need photos for unillustrated cover stories and features appearing in each issue. Topics include rescue, traffic, communications, training, stress, media relations, crime prevention, etc. Calendar available. Assignments possible."

OCEANUS, Woods Hole Oceanographic Institution, Woods Hole MA 02543. (508)457-2000 ext. 2386. Fax: (508)457-2182. Editor: Vicky Cullen. Circ. 15,000. Estab. 1952. Quarterly. The purpose of *Oceanus* is to serve as a forum for international perspectives on our ocean environment.
Needs: Uses about 60 photos/issue; 5-25% supplied by freelancers. "All four issues per year are thematic, covering marine subjects." Captions required.
Making Contact & Terms: Query with resume of credits or with list of stock photo subjects. Provide resume, business card, brochure, flyer or tearsheets to be kept on file for possible assignments. Cannot return material. Prefer to trade/negotiate photo use in exchange for caption credits and possible complimentary advertising to our parallel key source market as *Oceanus* is part of a nonprofit research insitition with limited funding.
Tips: "The magazine uses b&w and color photos. Color slides are preferred. Send us high-contrast b&w or color slides with strong narrative element (scientists at work, visible topographic, atmospheric alterations or events). Increasingly we are broadening our scope to cover all aspects of the ocean, from their scientific to artistic perspectives."

OCULAR SURGERY NEWS, Dept. PM, 6900 Grove Rd., Thorofare NJ 08086. (609)848-1000. Editor: Keith Croes. Circ. 18,000. Biweekly newspaper. Emphasizes ophthalmology, medical and eye care. Readers are ophthalmologists in the US. Sample copy free with 9 × 12 SAE and 10 first-class stamps.
Needs: Uses 30 photos/issue; less than 10% supplied by freelancers. Needs photos of medical subjects—tie in with special issues. Plans 6 special issues each year; contact for needs. Model release preferred. Captions preferred.
Making Contact & Terms: Query with list of stock photo subjects. Provide resume, business card, brochure, flyer or tearsheets to be kept on file for possible assignments. SASE. Reports in 2 weeks. Pays $300/color cover photo; $150/color inside photo; $150-250/day. Pays on publication. Credit line given. Buys one-time rights.

PACIFIC BOATING ALMANAC, Dept. PM, P.O. Box 341668, Los Angeles CA 90034. (213)287-2831. Contact: Peter L. Griffes. Circ. 20,000. Estab. 1965. Annual publication. Emphasizes West Coast Boating Almanac. Readers are "boat owners who cruise the coast." Circ. 20,000. Estab. 1965. Sample copy $16.95.
Needs: Uses 100 photos/issue; 30% supplied by freelancers. Needs only boating-related photos of the boats and marinas—as well as coastline and aerial scenes. Captions preferred.
Making Contact & Terms: Send unsolicited color prints by mail for consideration. Keeps samples on file. SASE. Reports in 3 weeks. Pays $100-200/color cover photo; $20-50/b&w inside photo. **Pays on acceptance.** Credit line given. Buys all rights "only for use in the Almanac." Simultaneous submissions and previously published work OK.
Tips: Wants to see crisp images.

PACIFIC FISHING, 1515 NW 51st, Seattle WA 98107. (206)789-5333. Fax: (206)784-5545. Editor: Steve Shapiro. Circ. 11,000. Estab. 1979. Monthly magazine. Emphasizes commercial fishing on West Coast—California to Alaska. Readers are 80% owners of fishing operations, primarily male, ages 25-55; 20% processors, marketers and suppliers. Sample copy free with 11 × 14 SAE and $2 postage. Photo guidelines free with SASE.
Needs: Uses 15 photos/issue; 10 supplied by freelancers. Needs photos of *all* aspects of commercial fisheries on West Coast of US and Canada. Special needs include "high-quality, active photos and slides of fishing boats and fishermen working their gear, dockside shots and the processing of seafood." Model/property release preferred. Captions required; include names and locations.
Making Contact & Terms: Query with resume of credits. Query with list of stock photo subjects. Keeps samples on file. SASE. Reports in 2-4 weeks. Pays $150/color cover photo; $50-100/color inside photo; $25-50/b&w inside photo. Pays on publication. Credit line given. Buys one-time rights, first N.A. serial rights. Previously published work OK "if not previously published in a competing trade journal."
Tips: Wants to see "clear, close-up and active photos."

*PCI-PAINT & COATINGS INDUSTRY MAGAZINE, Suite 100, 755 W. Big Beaver, Troy MI 48084. (313)244-6494. Fax: (313)362-0317. Art Director: Amy Turunen. Circ. 17,115. Magazine published 11 months a year. Emphasizes paint, coatings, adhesives and printing inks. Readers are mainly men who are manufacturers of paint and coatings and buyers of materials, equipment and supplies. Sample copy free with 9 × 12 envelope and 3 or 4 first-class stamps.

Needs: Uses 12 photos/issue; currently none supplied by freelancers. Needs photos of technology, industry or conceptual. Special photo needs include "fun stuff" — graphic presentation of paint and coatings. Model release required. Property release preferred. Captions required; include general description of what is in photo.

Making Contact & Terms: Interested in receiving work from newer, lesser-known photographers. Query with stock photo list. Provide resume, business card, brochure, flyer or tearsheets to be kept on file for possible assignments. Keeps samples on file. SASE. Reports in 1-2 weeks. Pays $300-400/color cover photo; $300-350/b&w cover photo; $50-200/color inside photo; $50-150/b&w inside photo. Pays on publication. "Photo credits are always given next to image if published." Buys one-time rights or all rights; negotiable. Simultaneous submissions and/or previously published work.

Tips: Wants to see a "creative, bold, graphic, artful depiction of straight forward subject matter. We do not have huge budgets. As art director, I'm trying to do the most creative designs with a limited budget. Any photographer willing to work within these constraints is most welcome. It's a good opportunity for those just starting who want to see their work published for their portfolios."

PEDIATRIC ANNALS, Dept. PM, 6900 Grove Rd., Thorofare NJ 08086. (609)848-1000. Editor: Mary L. Jerrell. Circ. 36,000. Monthly journal. Emphasizes "the pediatrics profession." Readers are practicing pediatricians. Sample copy free with SASE.

Needs: Uses 1-4 photos/issue; all supplied by freelance photographers. Needs photos of "children in medical settings, some with adults." Written release required. Captions preferred.

Making Contact & Terms: Query with samples. Provide resume, business card, brochure, flyer or tearsheets to be kept on file for possible future assignments. Reports in 6 weeks. Pays $350/color cover photo; $25/inside photo; $50/color inside photo. Pays on publication. Credit line given. Buys all rights. Simultaneous submissions and previously published work OK.

*PERSONAL SELLING POWER, INC., Box 5467, Fredericksburg VA 22405. (703)752-7000. Editor-in-Chief: Laura B. Gschwandtner. Magazine for sales and marketing professionals. Uses photos for magazine covers and text illustration. Recent covers have featured leading personalities such as Malcolm Forbes, Ed McMahon and Larry King.

Needs: Buys about 35 freelance photos/year; offers about 6 freelance assignments/year. Business, sales, motivation, etc. Subject matter and style of photos depend on the article. Most photos are business oriented, but some can also use landscape.

Making Contact & Terms: Query with resume of credits, samples and list of stock photo subjects. Uses transparencies, or in some cases b&w; formats can vary. Report time varies according to deadlines. NPI. Payment and terms negotiable. **Pays on acceptance.** Credit line given. Buys one-time rights. Previously published work OK.

Tips: Photographers should "send only their best work. Be reasonable with price. Be professional to work with. Also, look at our magazine to see what types of work we use and think about ways to improve what we are currently doing to give better results for our readers." As for trends, "we are using more and better photography all the time, especially for cover stories."

PET BUSINESS, 5400 NW 84th Ave., Miami FL 33166. Editor: Elizabeth McKey. Circ. 17,000. Estab. 1964. Monthly news magazine for pet industry professionals. Sample copy $3. Guidelines free with SASE.

Needs: Photos of well-groomed pet animals (preferably purebred) of any age in a variety of situations. Identify subjects. Animals: dogs, cats, fish, birds, reptiles, amphibians, small animals (hamsters, rabbits, gerbils, mice, etc.) Also, can sometimes use shots of petshop interiors — but must be careful not to be product-specific. Good scenes would include personnel interacting with customers or caring for shop animals. Model/property release preferred. Captions preferred; include essential details regarding animal species.

Making Contact & Terms: Interested in receiving work from newer, lesser-known photographers. Submit photos for consideration. Reports within 3 months with SASE. Pays $20/b&w glossy; $20/color print or transparency. Pays on publication. Credit line given. Buys all rights; negotiable.

Tips: Uncluttered background. Portrait-style always welcome. Close-ups best. News/action shots if timely. "Make sure your prints have good composition, and are technically correct, in focus and with proper contrast. Avoid dark pets on dark backgrounds! Send only 'pet' animal, not zoo or wildlife, photos."

*PET PRODUCT NEWS & PSM MAGAZINE, P.O. Box 6050, Mission Viejo CA 92690. (714)855-8822. Fax: (714)855-3045. Associate Editor: Lisa Hanks. Estab. 1950. Monthly tabloid. Emphasizes pets and business subjects. Readers are pet store owners and managers. Sample copy $4.50. Photo guidelines free with SASE.

Needs: Uses 15-25 photos/issue; 75-100% supplied by freelancers. Needs photos of people interacting with pets, pets doing "pet" things, pet stores and vets examining pets. Reviews photos with or without ms. Model/property release preferred. Captions preferred; include type of animal, name of pet store, name of well-known subjects, any procedures being performed on an animal that are not self-explanatory.

Making Contact & Terms: Interested in receiving work from newer, lesser-known photographers. Send unsolicited photos by mail for consideration. Send 5×7 or 8×10 glossy color and b&w prints; 35mm transparencies. SASE. Reports in 2 months. Pays $50-75/color cover photo; $50 minimum/b&w cover photo; $35 minimum/color inside photo; $35 minimum/b&w inside photo; $150-250/photo/text package. Pays on publication. Credit line given; must appear on each slide or photo. Buys one-time rights. Previously published work OK.

Tips: Looks for "appropriate subjects, clarity and framing, sensitivity to the subject. No avant garde or special effects. We need clear, straight-forward photography. Definitely no 'staged' photos, keep it natural. Read the magazine before submission. We are a trade publication and need business-like, but not boring, photos that will add to our subjects."

PETROGRAM, 209 Office Plaza, Tallahassee FL 32301. (904)877-5178. Fax: (904)877-5864. Editor: Tara Boyter. Circ. 700. Estab. mid-1970s. Association publication. Monthly magazine. Emphasizes the wholesale petroleum industry. Readers are predominantly male, increasingly female, ages 30-60. Sample copy free with 9×12 SAE and 4 first-class stamps.

Needs: Uses 3-15 photos/issue; 1 supplied by freelancer. Needs photos of petroleum equipment, convenience store settings, traffic situations and environmental protection (Florida specific). Reviews photos with or without a ms. Model/property release preferred. Captions preferred; include location and date.

Making Contact & Terms: Interested in receiving work from newer, lesser-known photographers. Submit portfolio for review. Query with stock photo list. Send unsolicited photos by mail for consideration. Provide resume, business card, brochure, flyer or tearsheets to be kept on file for possible assignments. Send 5×7, 8×10 glossy b&w or color prints. Keeps samples on file. SASE. Reports in 3 weeks. Pays $100/color cover photo; $75/b&w cover photo; $50/color inside photo; $25/b&w inside photo. Pays on publication. Credit line given. Rights negotiable.

Tips: "We are new at considering freelance. We've done our own up to now except very occasionally when we've hired a local photographer. We are a good place for 'non-established' photographers to get a start."

PHOTOELECTRONIC IMAGING, 1090 Executive Way, Des Plaines IL 60018. (708)299-8161. Fax: (708)299-2685. Editor-in-Chief: Kimberly Brady. Art Director: Debbie Todd. Circ. 50,000. Estab. 1957. Monthly magazine. Emphasizes industrial imagemaking by the in-house (captive) visual communicator and corporate/commercial photographer. Covers all media of visual communications including traditional silver-halide still and motion pictures, still and motion video, audiovisuals, computergraphics, etc. Readers work in industry, military, government, medicine, scientific research, evidence, police departments. Photo guidelines free with SASE.

Needs: Images must relate to some aspect of "industrial" imaging. Model release required. Captions required; include technical shooting details.

Making Contact & Terms: Query with resume of credits, samples or dupe photos for consideration. Original photos or slides sent at contributor's risk. Prefers photo/article packages. Uses glossy, unmounted b&w prints, color prints or any size transparencies. SASE. Reports in 5 weeks. Payment based on published page rate of $150. Pays on publication. Credit line given.

PIPELINE AND UTILITIES CONSTRUCTION, P.O. Box 219368, Houston TX 77218-9368. (713)558-6930. Fax: (713)558-7029. Editor: Robert Carpenter. Circ. 27,000. Estab. 1945. Monthly. Emphasizes construction of oil and gas, water and sewer underground pipelines and cable. Readers are contractor key personnel and company construction managers. Sample copy $3.

Needs: "Uses photos of pipeline construction, but must have editorial material on project with the photos." Reviews photos with accompanying ms only.

Making Contact & Terms: Send unsolicited photos by mail for consideration. Uses 4×5 or 8×10 color or b&w prints. SASE. Reports in 1 month. Pays $100-300 for text/photo package. Buys one-time rights. Simultaneous submissions OK.

Tips: "We rarely use freelance photography. Freelancers are competing with staff as well as complimentary photos supplied by equipment manufacturers. Subject matter must be unique, striking and 'off the beaten track' (i.e., somewhere we wouldn't travel ourselves to get photos)."

PIZZA TODAY, Dept. PM, P.O. Box 1347, New Albany IN 47151. (812)949-0909. Managing Editor: Danny Bolin. Circ. 52,000. Estab. 1983. Monthly. Emphasizes pizza trade. Readers are pizza shop owner/operators. Sample copy free with 9½×12½ SAE.

Needs: Uses 80 photos/issue; 20 supplied by freelancers; 100% from assignment. Needs how-tos of pizza making, product shots, profile shots. Special needs include celebrities eating pizza, politicians eating pizza. Captions required.

Making Contact & Terms: Provide resume, business card, brochure, flyer or tearsheets to be kept on file for possible assignments. SASE. Reports in 1 month. Pays $5-15/b&w photo; $20-30/color photo (prefer 35mm slides); all fees are negotiated in advance. Pays on publication. Credit line given. Buys all rights. Will negotiate with photographer unwilling to sell all rights. Previously published work OK.
Tips: Accept samples by mail only. "Team up with writer/contributor and supply photos to accompany article. We are not looking for specific food shots—looking for freelancers who can go to pizza shops and take photos which capture the atmosphere, the warmth and humor; 'the human touch.' "

PLANTS SITES & PARKS MAGAZINE, #201, 100 W. Sample Rd., Coral Springs FL 33065-3938. (800)753-2660. Fax: (305)755-7048. Art Director: David Lepp. Circ. 40,000. Estab. 1973. Bimonthly magazine. Emphasizes economic development and business. Readers are executives involved in selecting locations for their businesses.
Needs: Uses 15-20 photos/issue; 5-10 supplied by freelancers. General business subjects, locations, industrial, food processing and people. Model and/or property release required. Captions preferred.
Making Contact & Terms: Query with list of stock photo subjects. Provide resume, business card, brochure, flyer or tearsheets to be kept on file for possible assignments. Keeps samples on file. Reports in 3 weeks. Pays $500/color cover photo; $100-150/color inside photo. Pays on acceptance and publication; negotiable. Buys one-time rights; negotiable. Simultaneous submissions and previously published work OK.
Tips: Wants to see "only very good quality work. Original slides, *no* dupes; no research fees."

POLICE MAGAZINE, 6300 Yarrow Dr., Carlsbad CA 92009. (619)438-2511. Fax: (619)931-9809. Managing Editor: Dan Burger. Estab. 1976. Monthly. Emphasizes law enforcement. Readers are various members of the law enforcement community, especially police officers. Sample copy $2 with $9 × 12$ SAE and 6 first-class stamps. Photo guidelines free with SASE.
Needs: Uses about 15 photos/issue; 99% supplied by freelance photographers. Needs law enforcement related photos. Special needs include photos relating to daily police work, crime prevention, international law enforcement, police technology and humor. Model release required. Property release preferred. Captions preferred.
Making Contact & Terms: Interested in receiving work from newer, lesser-known photographers. Arrange a personal interview to show portfolio. Send b&w prints, 35mm transparencies, b&w contact sheet or color negatives by mail for consideration. SASE. Pays $100/color cover photo; $30/b&w photo; $30 (negotiable)/color inside photo; $150-300/job; $150-300/text/photo package. **Pays on acceptance.** Buys all rights; rights returned to photographer 45 days after publication. Simultaneous submissions OK.
Tips: "Send for our editorial calendar and submit photos based on our projected needs. If we like your work, we'll consider you for future assignments. A photographer we use can grasp the conceptual and the action shots."

POLICE TIMES/CHIEF OF POLICE, 3801 Biscayne Blvd., Miami FL 33137. (305)573-0070. Editor-in-Chief: Jim Gordon. Circ. 50,000+. Bimonthly magazines. Readers are law enforcement officers at all levels. Sample copy $2.50. Photo guidelines free with SASE.
Needs: Buys 60-90 photos/year. Photos of police officers in action, civilian volunteers working with the police and group shots of police department personnel. Wants no photos that promote other associations. Police-oriented cartoons also accepted on spec. Model release preferred. Captions preferred.
Making Contact & Terms: Send photos for consideration. Send glossy b&w and color prints. SASE. Reports in 3 weeks. Pays $5-10 upwards/inside photo; $25-50 upwards/cover photo. **Pays on acceptance.** Credit line given if requested; editor's option. Buys all rights, but may reassign to photographer after publication. Simultaneous submissions and previously published work OK.
Tips: "We are open to new and unknowns in small communities where police are not given publicity."

POLLED HEREFORD WORLD, 11020 NW Ambassador Dr., Kansas City MO 64153. (816)891-8400. Editor: Ed Bible. Circ. 10,000. Estab. 1947. Monthly magazine. Emphasizes Polled Hereford cattle for registered breeders, commercial cattle breeders and agribusinessmen in related fields.
Making Contact & Terms: Query. Uses b&w prints and color transparencies and prints. Reports in 2 weeks. Pays $5/b&w print; $100/color transparency or print. Pays on publication.
Tips: Wants to see "Polled Hereford cattle in quantities, in seasonal and/or scenic settings."

*POWERLINE MAGAZINE, Suite B, 10251 W. Sample Rd., Coral Springs FL 33065-3939. (305)755-2677. Fax: (305)755-2679. Editor: James McMullen. Photos used in trade magazine of Electrical Generating Systems Association and PR releases, brochures, newsletters, newspapers and annual reports.

Needs: Buys 40-60 photos/year; gives 2 or 3 assignments/year. "Cover photos, events, award presentations, groups at social and educational functions." Model release required. Property release preferred. Captions preferred; include identification of individuals only.
Making Contact & Terms: Interested in receiving work from newer, lesser-known phorographers. Provide resume, business card, brochure, flyer or tearsheets to be kept on file for possible future assignments. Solicits photos by assignment only. Uses 5×7 glossy b&w and color prints; b&w and color contacts sheets; b&w and color negatives. SASE. Reports as soon as selection of photographs is made. NPI. Buys all rights; negotiable.
Tips: "Basically a freelance photographer working with us should use a photojournalistic approach, and have the ability to capture personality and a sense of action in fairly static situations. With those photographers who are equipped, we often arrange for them to shoot couples, etc., at certain functions on spec, in lieu of a per-day or per-job fee."

THE PREACHER'S MAGAZINE, Dept. PM, E. 10814 Broadway, Spokane WA 99206. (509)226-3464. Editor: Randal E. Denny. Circ. 18,000. Estab. 1925. Quarterly professional journal for ministers. Emphasizes the pastoral ministry. Readers are pastors of large to small churches in 5 denominations; most pastors are male. No sample copy available. No photo guidelines.
Needs: Uses 1 photo/issue; all supplied by freelancers. Large variety needed for cover, depends on theme of issue. Model release preferred. Captions preferred.
Making Contact & Terms: Send 35mm b&w/color prints by mail for consideration. Reports ASAP. Pays $60/color cover photo. **Pays on acceptance.** Credit line given. Buys one-time rights. Simultaneous submissions and previously published work OK.
Tips: In photographer's samples wants to see "a variety of subjects for the front cover of our magazine. We rarely use photos within the magazine itself."

PRO SOUND NEWS, 2 Park Ave., New York NY 10016. (212)213-3444. Editor: Debra Pagan. Managing Editor: Tom Di Nome. Circ. 21,000. Monthly tabloid. Emphasizes professional recording and sound and production industries. Readers are recording engineers, studio owners and equipment manufacturers worldwide. Sample copy free with SASE.
Needs: Uses about 24 photos/issue; all supplied by freelance photographers. Needs photos of recording sessions, sound reinforcement for concert tours, permanent installations. Model release required. Captions required.
Making Contact & Terms: Query with samples. Send 8×10 glossy color prints by mail for consideration. SASE. Reports in 2 weeks. NPI; pays by the job or for text/photo package. Pays on publication. Credit line given. Buys one-time rights. Simultaneous submissions and previously published work OK.

PROFESSIONAL PHOTOGRAPHER, 1090 Executive Way, Des Plaines IL 60018. (708)299-8161. Fax: (708)299-2685. Editor: Alfred DeBat. Senior Editor: Deborah Goldstein. Art Director: Debbie Todd. Circ. 32,000+. Estab. 1907. Monthly. Emphasizes professional photography in the fields of portrait, wedding, commercial/advertising, corporate and industrial. Readers include professional photographers and photographic services and educators. Approximately half the circulation is Professional Photographers of America members. Sample copy $5 postpaid. Photo guidelines free with SASE.
  • Images sent to this publication should be technically perfect and photographers should include information about how the photo was produced.
Needs: Uses 25-30 photos/issue; all supplied by freelancers. "We only accept material as illustration that relates directly to photographic articles showing professional studio, location, commercial and portrait techniques. A majority are supplied by Professional Photographers of America members." Reviews photos with accompanying ms only. "We always need commercial/advertising and industrial success stories. How to sell your photography to major accounts, unusual professional photo assignments. Also, photographer and studio application stories about the profitable use of electronic still imaging for customers and clients." Model release preferred. Captions required.
Making Contact & Terms: Query with resume of credits. "We want a story query, or complete ms if writer feels subject fits our magazine. Photos will be part of ms package." Uses 8×10 glossy unmounted b&w or color prints; 35mm, 2¼×2¼, 4×5 and 8×10 transparencies. SASE. Reports in 8 weeks. NPI. "PPA members submit material unpaid to promote their photo businesses and obtain recognition." Credit line given. Previously published work OK.

Can't find a listing? Check at the end of each market section for the " '93-'94 Changes" lists. These lists include any market listings from the '93 edition which were either not verified or deleted in this edition.

PROPERTY MANAGEMENT, (formerly *Property Management Monthly*), Suite 400, 8601 Georgia Ave., Silver Spring MD 20910. (301)588-0681. Fax: (301)588-6314. Editor: Ms. Jayson H. Nuhn. Circ. 12,000+. Estab. 1984. Monthly tabloid. Emphasizes management of commercial real estate (offices, apartments, retail, industrial). Readers are males and females involved in the property management/ real estate industry. Sample copy free with SASE.
Needs: Uses 30 photos/issue; "almost all" supplied by freelancers. Needs photos of architectural, technical and people. Special photo needs include architectural photos and "grip and grin" people shots at industry functions. Model and/or property release is required. Captions preferred; include name and location.
Making Contact & Terms: Query with resume of credits. Provide resume, business card, brochure, flyer or tearsheets to be kept on file for possible assignments. Keeps samples on file. SASE. Reports in 1 month. Pays $250 per half-day; $500 per all day shoot, plus expenses/color cover; $75 per hour, expenses; $6 per print/b&w inside photo. **Pays on acceptance.** Credit line given. Buys one-time rights.
Tips: Looks for "good use of light/shadows and background shoots. Creativity in posing portrait shots." Photographers "should live in the metropolitan area because our photo needs are met on assignment in this area. Must be able to get names of subjects accurately when photographing industry event."

*PUBLIC WORKS MAGAZINE, 200 S. Broad St., Ridgewood NJ 07451. (201)445-5800. Contact: Edward B. Rodie. Circ. 52,000+. Monthly magazine. Emphasizes the planning, design, construction, inspection, operation and maintenance of public works facilities (bridges, roads, water systems, landfills, etc.) Readers are predominately male civil engineers, ages 20 and up. Some overlap with other planners, including consultants, department heads, etc. Sample copy free upon request. Photo guidelines available, but for cover only.
Needs: Uses dozens of photos/issue. "Most photos are supplied by authors or with company press releases." Purchases photos with accompanying ms only. Captions required.
Making Contact & Terms: Provide resume, business card, brochure, flyer or tearsheets to be kept on file for possible assignments. SASE. Reports in 2 weeks. NPI; payment negotiated with editor. Credit line given "if requested." Buys one-time rights.
Tips: "Nearly all of the photos used are submitted by the authors of articles (who are generally very knowledgeable in their field). They may occasionally use freelancers. Cover personality photos are done by staff and freelance photographers." To break in, "learn how to take good clear photos of public works projects that show good detail without clutter. Prepare a brochure and pass around to small and mid-size cities, towns and civil type consulting firms; larger (organizations) will probably have a staff photographers."

QUALITY DIGEST, P.O. Box 1503, Red Bluff CA 96080. (916)527-8875. Fax: (916)527-6983. Editor: Scott M. Paton. Circ. 20,000. Estab. 1981. Monthly digest. Emphasizes quality improvement. Readers are mainly mid-level and senior-level managers in large corporations. Sample copy $6.25. No photo guidelines.
Needs: Uses 10-12 photos/issue; 50% supplied by freelancers. Needs photos of training sessions, meetings in progress, office situations and factory scenes. Special photo needs include service quality. Model release required. Captions required.
Making Contact & Terms: Send b&w prints by mail for consideration. Reports in 1 month. Pays $300/color cover photo; $50/b&w inside photo. **Pays on acceptance.** Credit line given. Buys all rights; negotiable. Simultaneous submissions OK.

QUICK FROZEN FOODS INTERNATIONAL, Suite 305, 2125 Center Ave., Fort Lee NJ 07024-5898. (201)592-7007. Fax: (201)592-7171. Editor: John M. Saulnier. Circ. 13,000. Quarterly magazine. Emphasizes retailing, marketing, processing, packaging and distribution of frozen foods around the world. Readers are international executives involved in the frozen food industry: manufacturers, distributors, retailers, brokers, importers/exporters, warehousemen, etc. Review copy $8.
Needs: Buys 20-30 photos/year. Plant exterior shots, step-by-step in-plant processing shots, photos of retail store frozen food cases, head shots of industry executives, product shots, etc. Captions required.
Making Contact & Terms: Query first with resume of credits. Uses 5×7 glossy b&w prints. SASE. Reports in 1 month. NPI. **Pays on acceptance.** Buys all rights, but may reassign to photographer after publication.
Tips: A file of photographers' names is maintained; if an assignment comes up in an area close to a particular photographer, he may be contacted. "When submitting names, inform us if you are capable of writing a story, if needed."

THE RANGEFINDER, 1312 Lincoln Blvd., Santa Monica CA 90401. (310)451-8506. Fax: (310)395-9058. Editor: Arthur Stern. Circ. 50,000. Estab. 1952. Monthly magazine. Emphasizes topics, developments and products of interest to the professional photographer. Readers are professionals in all phases of photography. Sample copy free with 11×14 SAE and 2 first-class stamps. Photo guidelines free with SASE.

Needs: Uses 20-30 photos/issue; 70% supplied by freelancers. Needs all kinds of photos; almost always run in conjunction with articles. "We prefer photos accompanying 'how-to' or special interest stories from the photographer." No pictorials. Special needs include seasonal cover shots (vertical format only). Model release required. Property release preferred. Captions preferred.
Making Contact & Terms: Interested in receiving work from newer, lesser-known photographers. Query with resume of credits. Keeps samples on file. SASE. Reports in 1 month. Pays $60 minimum/ printed editorial page with illustrations. Pays on publication. Credit line given. Buys first N.A. serial rights; negotiable. Previously published work occasionally OK; give details.

RECOMMEND WORLDWIDE, Dept. PM, Suite 120, 5979 NW 151st St., Miami Lake FL 33014. (305)828-0123. Art Director: Linda Eouthat. Managing Editor: Roger Vance. Monthly. Emphasizes travel. Readers are travel agents, meeting planners, hoteliers, ad agencies. Sample copy free with 8½×11 SAE and 10 first-class stamps.
Needs: Uses about 40 photos/issue; 70% supplied by freelance photographers. "Our publication divides the world up into 7 regions. Every month we use destination-oriented photos of animals, cities, resorts and cruise lines. Features all types of travel photography from all over the world." Model release preferred. Captions preferred; identification required.
Making Contact & Terms: "We prefer a resume, stock list and sample card or tearsheets with photo review later." SASE. Pays $150/color cover photo; $25/color inside photo; $50/color page. Pays 30 days upon publication. Credit line given. Buys one-time rights. Simultaneous submissions and previously published work OK.
Tips: Prefers to see "transparencies—either 2¼×2¼ or 35mm first quality originals, travel oriented."

REFEREE, P.O. Box 161, Franksville WI 53126. (414)632-8855. Fax: (414)632-5460. Editor: Tom Hammill. Circ. 35,000. Estab. 1976. Monthly magazine. Readers are mostly male, ages 30-50. Sample copy free with 9×12 SAE and 5 first-class stamps. Photo guidelines free with SASE.
Needs: Uses up to 50 photos/issue; 75% supplied by freelancers. Needs action officiating shots—all sports. Photo needs are ongoing. Model release preferred. Captions preferred.
Making Contact & Terms: Send unsolicited photos by mail for consideration. Any format is accepted. Reports in 1-2 weeks. Pays $100/color cover photo; $75/b&w cover photo; $35/color inside photo; $20/ b&w inside photo. Pays on publication. Credit line given. Rights purchased negotiable. Simultaneous submissions and previously published work OK.
Tips: Prefers photos which bring out the uniqueness of being a sports official. Need photos primarily of officials at high school level in baseball, football, basketball, soccer, volleyball and softball in action. Other sports acceptable, but used less frequently. "When at sporting events, take a few shots with the officials in mind, even though you may be on assignment for another reason." Address all queries to Tom Hammill, Editor. "Don't be afraid to give it a try. We're receptive, always looking for new freelance contributors. We are constantly looking for offbeat pictures of officials/umpires. Our needs in this area have increased."

REGISTERED REPRESENTATIVE, Suite 280, 18818 Teller Ave., Irvine CA 92715. (714)851-2220. Art Director: Chuck LaBresh. Circ. 80,000. Estab. 1976. Monthly magazine. Emphasizes stock brokerage industry. Magazine is "requested and read by 90% of the nation's stock brokers." Sample copy for $2.50.
Needs: Uses about 8 photos/issue; 5 supplied by freelancers. Needs environmental portraits of financial and brokerage personalities, and conceptual shots of financial ideas, all by assignment only. Model/ property release preferred. Captions required.
Making Contact & Terms: Interested in receiving work from newer, lesser-known photographers. Provide brochure, flyer or tearsheets to be kept on file for possible future assignments. Cannot return material. Pays $250-600/b&w or color cover photo; $100-250/b&w or color inside photo. Pays 30 days after publication. Credit line given. Buys one-time rights. Simultaneous submissions and previously published work OK.
Tips: "I look for something unusual in styling, lighting, camera lenses, whatever. I don't want a straight head shot, but I don't want it totally wacked-out either. I want something that is a little unusual (to provide interest) but not so weird that the concept/subject can't be identified."

REMODELING, 655 15th St. NW, Washington DC 20005. (202)737-0717. Managing Editor: Leslie Ensor. Circ. 95,000. Published 12 times/year. "Business magazine for remodeling contractors." Readers are "small contractors involved in residental and commercial remodeling." Sample copy free with 8×11 SASE.
Needs: Uses 10-15 photos/issue; number supplied by freelancers varies. Needs photos of remodeled residences, both before and after. Reviews photos with "short description of project, including architect's or contractor's name and phone number. We have three regular photo features: *Double Take* is photo caption piece about an architectural photo that fools the eye. *Ideas* is a photo caption showing architectural details. *Before and After* describes a whole-house remodel."

Tension on the referee's face and his body language show that he has reached a boiling point as he ejects NBA star Karl Malone of the Utah Jazz in a game against the Los Angeles Lakers. Photographer Mary Crandall of Salt Lake City, Utah, says it was a frustrating day for Malone, whose wife was in labor. Earlier that day former Laker star Magic Johnson announced he was retiring because he tested HIV positive. Crandall sold the shot for $50 to Referee magazine, which used the image as a two-page spread illustrating a feature story.

Making Contact & Terms: Interested in receiving work from newer, lesser-known photographers. Provide resume, business card, brochure, flyer or tearsheets to be kept on file for possible future assignments. Reports in 1 month. Pays $100/color cover photo; $25/b&w inside photo; $50/color inside photo; $300 maximum/job. **Pays on acceptance.** Credit line given. Buys one-time rights.

Tips: Wants "interior and exterior photos of residences that emphasize the architecture over the furnishings."

RESCUE MAGAZINE, Dept. PM, Jems Communications, P.O. Box 2789, Carlsbad CA 92018. (619)431-9797. Fax: (619)431-8176. Director of Design and Production: Harriet Wilcox. Circ. 25,000. Estab. 1988. Bimonthly. Emphasizes techniques, equipment, action stories with unique rescues; paramedics, EMTs, rescue divers, fire fighters, etc. Rescue personnel are most of our readers. Sample copy free with 9×12 SAE and $2 postage. Photo guidelines free with SASE.

Needs: Uses 20-25 photos/issue; 5-10 supplied by freelance photographers. Needs rescue scenes, transport, injured victims, equipment and personnel, training. Special photo needs include strong color shots showing newsworthy rescue operations, including a unique or difficult rescue/extrication, treatment, transport, personnel, etc. b&w showing same. Model release preferred. Captions required.

Making Contact & Terms: Interested in receiving work from newer, lesser-known photographers. Query with samples. Send 5×7 or larger glossy b&w or color prints, 35mm or 2¼×2¼ transparencies or b&w or color contacts sheets by mail for consideration. Don't send originals. SASE. Pays $150-200/color cover photo; $50-75/b&w inside photo; $75-125/color inside photo; $400-600/day. Pays on publication. Credit line given. Buys one-time rights. Previously published work OK (must be labeled as such).

© photo by Jeffrey Dodge

Photographer Jeffrey Dodge of New York, New York, says he was working on a new portfolio of polaroid transfers when a photo assignment from Registered Representative came about. "It gave me the opportunity to showcase my experiments with cross processing and polaroid transfers," says Dodge, who received $600 for the job. Art Director Chuck LaBresh says Dodge went way beyond the original assignment to come up with a much better shot.

Tips: "Ride along with a rescue crew or team. This can be firefighters, paramedics, mountain rescue teams, dive rescue teams, and so on. Get in close." Looks for "photographs that show rescuers in action, using proper techniques and wearing the proper equipment. Submit timely photographs that show the technical aspects of rescue."

RESOURCE RECYCLING, P.O. Box 10540, Portland OR 97210. (503)227-1319. Editor: Meg Lynch. Circ. 15,000. Estab. 1982. Monthly. Emphasizes "the recycling of post-consumer waste materials (paper, metals, glass, plastics etc.)" Readers are "recycling company managers, local government officials, waste haulers and environmental group executives." Circ. 14,000. Estab. 1982. Sample copy free with $2 postage plus 9 × 12 SASE.
Needs: Uses about 5-15 photos/issue; 1-2 supplied by freelancers. Needs "photos of recycling facilities, curbside recycling collections, secondary materials (bundles of newspapers, soft drink containers), etc." Model release preferred. Captions required.
Making Contact & Terms: Send glossy b&w prints and contact sheet. SASE. Reports in 1 month. NPI; payment "varies by experience and photo quality." Pays on publication. Credit line given. Buys first N.A. serial rights. Simultaneous submissions OK.
Tips: "Because *Resource Recycling* is a trade journal for the recycling industry, we are looking only for photos that relate to recycling issues."

RESTAURANT HOSPITALITY, 1100 Superior Ave., Cleveland OH 44114. (216)696-7000. Fax: (216)696-0836. Editor-in-Chief: Michael DeLuca. Circ. 100,000. Estab. 1919. Monthly. Emphasizes "restaurant management, hotel food service, cooking, interior design." Readers are "restaurant owners, chefs, food service chain executives."
Needs: Uses about 30 photos/issue; 50% supplied by freelancers. "We buy from stock more often than on assignment." Needs "people with food, restaurant and foodservice interiors and occasional food photos." Special needs include "spectacular food and/or beverage shots; query first." Model release preferred. Captions preferred.
Making Contact & Terms: Send resume of credits or samples, or list of stock photo subjects. Provide resume, business card, brochure, flyer or tearsheets to be kept on file for possible future assignments. Pays $50-500/b&w or color photo; $350/half day; $150-450/job plus normal expenses. **Pays on acceptance.** Credit line given. Buys one-time rights plus reprint rights. Previously published work OK "if exclusive to foodservice press."
Tips: "Let us know you exist. We can't assign a story if we don't know you. Send resume, business card, samples, etc. along with introductory letter."

ROOFER MAGAZINE, Dept. PM, Suite 214, 6719 Winkler Rd., Ft. Myers FL 33919. (813)275-7663. Associate Publisher: Angela M. Williamson. Art Director: Jimmy Veralli. Circ. 17,000. Estab. 1981. Monthly. Emphasizes the roofing industry and all facets of the roofing business. Readers are roofing contractors, manufacturers, architects, specifiers, consultants and distributors. Sample copy free with 9×12 SAE and $1.75 postage.
Needs: Uses about 25 photos/issue; few are supplied by freelancers. Needs photos of unusual roofs or those with a humorous slant (once published a photo with a cow stranded on a roof during a flood). Needs several photos of a particular city or country to use in photo essay section. Also, photographs of buildings after major disasters, showing the destruction to the roof, are especially needed. "Please indicate to us the location, time and date taken, and cause of destruction (i.e., fire, flood, hurricane)." Model release required. Captions preferred; include details about date, location and description of scene.
Making Contact & Terms: Query with samples. Provide resume, brochure and tearsheets to be kept on file for possible future assignments. Cannot return material. Reports in 1 month. Pays $25 maximum/b&w photo; $50 maximum/color photo. Pays maximum $125 per page for photo essays. Pays on publication. Usually buys one-time rights, "exclusive to our industry."
Tips: "Good lighting is a must. Clear skies, beautiful landscaping around the home or building featured add to the picture. Looking for anything unique, in either the angle of the shot or the type of roof. Humorous photos are given special consideration and should be accompanied by clever captions or a brief, humorous description. No photos of reroofing jobs on your home will be accepted. Most of the photos we publish in each issue are contributed by our authors. Freelance photographers should submit material that would be useful for our photographic essays, depicting particular cities or countries. We've given assignments to freelance photographers before, but most submissions are the ideas of the freelancer."

SALOME: A JOURNAL FOR THE PERFORMING ARTS, Dept. PM, 5548 N. Sawyer, Chicago IL 60625. (312)539-5745. Editor: Effie Mihopoulos. Estab. 1975. Quarterly. Emphasizes performing arts. Sample copy $4. Photo guidelines free with SASE.
Needs: Uses approx. 500 photos/issue; 50% supplied by freelance photographers; 10% freelance assignment; 5-25% stock. Needs photos of performing arts subjects. Model release preferred. Captions preferred; identification of subject (if person) necessary.
Making Contact & Terms: Send b&w prints by mail for consideration. SASE. Reports in 2 weeks. Pays in copy of magazine. Pays on publication. Credit line given. Buys one-time rights. Simultaneous submissions and previously published work OK (must state with submission).
Tips: Looks for "good composition and a striking image that immediately grabs your attention." There is a trend of "more good photographers creating fiercer competition. Send an overview of photos; examine previous issue of magazine to prepare a sample portfolio."

*****SAN DIEGO BUSINESS JOURNAL**, Suite 200, 4909 Murphy Cyn. Rd., San Diego CA 92123. (619)277-6359. Fax: (619)277-2149. Creative Director: Steven Parker. Circ. 20,000. Estab. 1981. Weekly tabloid. Emphasizes business. Readers are 75% male 25% female executives, 75% top management, San Diego's affluent and influential business leaders. Sample copy free with 12×15½ SASE.
Needs: Uses 20 photos/issue; 2 supplied by freelancers. Needs photos of high-tech, commercial real estate, international trade, health care, fitness, financial, automotive, environmental, executive travel. Reviews photos with or without ms. Special photo needs include fitness, automotive, environmental (business), travel. Model/property release required. Captions preferred; include location, subject, date shot.
Making Contact & Terms: Interested in receiving work from newer, lesser-known photographers. Provide resume, business card, brochure, flyer or tearsheets to be kept on file for possible assignments. Keeps samples on file. SASE. Reports in 1-2 weeks. Pays $75-175/color cover photo; $50-150/b&w cover photo; $50-100/color inside photo; $25-75/b&w inside photo. Pays on publication. Credit line given. Buys one-time rights, all rights; negotiable. Simultaneous submissions and/or previously published work OK.
Tips: "Looking for dynamic, high-impact, simple images shot by a photographer willing to experiment with style and technique. All business related subjects. Be willing to try new styles and techniques. Offer suggestions to publications that can push them beyond standard photojournalistic layouts to intriguing, compelling ones."

The First Markets Index preceding the General Index in the back of this book provides the names of those companies/publications interested in receiving work from newer, lesser-known photographers.

THE SCIENTIST, Dept. PM, 3501 Market St., Philadelphia PA 19104. (215)386-0100, ext. 1503. Design Coordinator: Stephen Iwanczuk. Circ. 30,000. Biweekly tabloid. Emphasizes science. Readers are mostly scientists or science administrators.

Needs: Uses 30-40 photos/issue; 30-50% supplied by freelance photographers. Uses photos of "mostly people in labs or with work." Model release preferred. Captions preferred.

Making Contact & Terms: Provide resume, business card, brochure, flyer or tearsheets to be kept on file for possible assignments. SASE. Reports in 1 month. Pays $125/b&w cover or inside photo. Pays on publication. Credit line given. Buys one-time rights. Previously published work OK.

Tips: "We only use b&w photographs. Since this publication is people oriented, I'm looking for unusual portraits."

SEAFOOD LEADER, 850 NW 46th St., Second Floor, Seattle WA 98107. (206)547-6030. Fax: (206)548-9346. Photo Editor: Carolyn Cox. Published bimonthly. Emphasizes seafood industry, commercial fishing. Readers are buyers and brokers of seafood. Circ. 16,000. Estab. 1981. Sample copy $5 with 9 × 12 SASE.

Needs: Uses about 40 photos/issue; 50% supplied by freelance photographers, most from stock. Needs photos of international seafood harvesting and farming, supermarkets, restaurants, shrimp, Alaska, many more. Model release preferred. Captions preferred; include name, place, time.

Making Contact & Terms: Interested in receiving work from newer, lesser-known photographers. Query with list of stock photo subjects. Send photos on subjects we request. SASE. "We only want it on our topics." Reports in 1 month. Pays $100/color cover photo; $50/color inside photo; $25/b&w photo. Pays on publication. Credit line given. Buys one-time rights. Previously published work OK.

Tips: "Send in slides relating to our needs—request editorial calendar." Looks for "aesthetic shots of seafood, shots of people interacting with seafood in which expressions are captured (i.e. not posed shots); artistic shots of seafood emphasizing color and shape. We want clear, creative, original photography of commercial fishing, fish species, not sports fishing."

SECURITY DEALER, Dept. PM, Suite 21, 445 Broad Hollow Rd., Melville NY 11747. (516)845-2700. Fax: (516)845-7109. Editor: Susan Brady. Circ. 22,000. Estab. 1967. Monthly magazines. Emphasizes security subjects. Readers are blue collar businessmen installing alarm, security, CCTV and access control systems. Sample copy free with SASE.

Needs: Uses 2-5 photos/issue; none at present supplied by freelance photographers. Needs photos of security-application-equipment. Model release preferred. Captions required.

Making Contact & Terms: Interested in receiving work from newer, lesser-known photographers. Send b&w and color prints by mail for consideration. SASE. Reports "immediately." Pays $25-50/b&w photo; $200/color cover photo; $50-100/inside color photos. Pays 30 days after publication. Credit line given. Buys one-time rights in security trade industry. Simultaneous submissions and previously published work OK.

Tips: "Do not send originals, dupes only, and only after discussion with editor."

SERVISTAR'S *SUCCESSFUL CONTRACTOR, 5822 W. 74th St., Indianapolis IN 46278. (317)328-4356. Fax: (317)328-4354. Publication Account Manager: Sharron Hoke. Circ. 30,000. Estab. 1992. Quarterly magazine. Readers are contractors, remodelers and professional builders. Sample copy free with 9 × 12 manila SAE and 5 first-class stamps. Photo guidelines free with SASE.

Needs: Uses 10-15 photos/issue; 5-10 supplied by freelancers. Needs photos of construction workers, building sites, on-the-job shots. Reviews photos with or without ms. Special photo needs include environmental and economic issues within this industry. Model/property release preferred.

Making Contact & Terms: Interested in receiving work from newer, lesser-known photographers. Query with stock photo list. Send unsolicited photos by mail for consideration. Send 2¼ × 2¼ transparencies. Keeps samples on file. SASE. Reports in 3 weeks. Pays $200-600/color cover photo; $100-300/color inside photo. **Pays on acceptance.** Credit line given. Buys all rights; negotiable.

Tips: Looks for "four-color, vertical composition, for cover photo. Focus is on the general contractor/construction worker being a successful businessman. We're always looking for new and creative ways to depict this industry, which means we will consider both figurative and metaphorical subjects . . . think lumber and construction as it relates to current environmental and economic issues."

SHEEP! MAGAZINE, Dept. PM, W. 2997 Market Rd., Helenville WI 53137. (414)593-8385. Fax: (414)593-8384. Editor: Dave Thompson. Circ. 13,000. Estab. 1982. Monthly tabloid. Emphasizes sheep and wool. Readers are sheep and wool producers across the US and Canada. Sample copy $1. Photo guidelines available.

Needs: Uses 30 photos/issue; 50% supplied by freelancers. Needs photos of sheep, lambs, sheep producers, wool, etc. Model release preferred. Captions preferred.
Making Contact & Terms: Send unsolicited photos by mail for consideration. Provide resume, business card, brochure, flyer or tearsheets to be kept on file for possible assignments. Uses b&w and color prints; 35mm transparencies. SASE. Reports in 3 weeks. Pays up to $200/color cover photo; $100-150/b&w cover photo; $100/color inside photo; $50/b&w inside photo. Credit line given. Buys one-time and all rights; negotiable. Previously published work OK.

SHELTER SENSE, Humane Society of the US, 2100 L St. NW, Washington DC 20037. (202)452-1100. Editor: Geoffrey Handy. Circ. 3,500. Estab. 1978. Monthly newsletter. Emphasizes animal protection. Readers are animal control and shelter workers, men and women, all ages. Sample copy free with 9×12 SAE and 2 first-class stamps.
Needs: Uses 15 photos/issue; 35% supplied by freelance photographers. Needs photos of domestic animals interacting with people/humane workers; animals during the seasons; animal care, obedience; humane society work and functions, other companion animal shots. "We do not pay for manuscripts." Model release required for cover photos only. Captions preferred.
Making Contact & Terms: Interested in receiving work from newer, lesser-known photographers. Provide resume, business card, brochure, flyer or tearsheets to be kept on file for possible assignments. SASE. Reports in 3 weeks. Pays $45/b&w cover photo; $35/b&w inside photo. **Pays on acceptance.** Credit line given. Buys one-time rights.
Tips: "We almost always need good photos of people working with animals in an animal shelter, in the field, or in the home. We do not use photos of individual dogs, cats and other companion animals as much as we use photos of people working to protect, rescue or care for dogs, cats and other companion animals."

SHOOTER'S RAG—A PRACTICAL PHOTOGRAPHIC GAZETTE, P.O. Box 8509, Asheville NC 28814. (704)254-6700. Editor: Michael Havelin. Circ. 1,000-1,500. Estab. 1992. Quarterly. Emphasizes photographic techniques, practical how-tos and electronic imaging. Readers are male and female professionals, semi-professionals and serious amateurs. Sample copy $3 with 10×13 SAE and 75¢ postage. Photo guidelines free with SASE.
Needs: Uses 3-10 photos/issue; 50-75% supplied by freelancers. "Single photos generally not needed. Photos with text and text with photographs should query." Special photo needs include humorous b&w cover shots with photographic theme and detailed description of how the shot was done with accompanying set up shots. Model/property release preferred. Captions required.
Making Contact & Terms: Interested in receiving work from newer, lesser-known photographers. Query with resume of credits, ideas for text/photo packages. Do not send portfolios. Does not keep samples on file. Cannot return material. Reports in 1 month. Pays $50/b&w cover photo; $25/b&w inside photo; $50-200/photo text package. Pays on publication. Credit line given. Buys one-time rights; negotiable. Simultaneous submissions and/or previously published work OK. Electronic submissions preferred via CIS or Land O'Sky BBS (704)254-7800.
Tips: "Writers who shoot and photographers who write well should query. Develop your writing skills as well as your photography. Don't wait for the world to discover you. Announce your presence."

SIGNCRAFT MAGAZINE, P.O. Box 06031, Fort Myers FL 33906. (813)939-4644. Editor: Tom McIltrot. Circ. 21,000. Estab. 1980. Bimonthly magazine. Readers are sign artists and sign shop personnel. Sample copy $5. Photo guidelines free with SASE.
Needs: Uses over 100 photos/issue; few at present supplied by freelancers. Needs photos of well-designed, effective signs. Model release preferred. Captions preferred.
Making Contact & Terms: Query with samples. Send b&w or color prints; 35mm, 2¼×2¼ transparencies; b&w, color contact sheet by mail for consideration. SASE. Reports in 1 month. NPI. Pays on publication. Credit line given. Buys first N.A. serial rights. Previously published work possibly OK.
Tips: "If you have some background or past experience with sign making, you may be able to provide photos for us."

SOCIAL POLICY, Room 620, 25 W. 43rd St., New York NY 10036. (212)642-2929. Managing Editor: Audrey Gartner. Circ. 3,500. Estab. 1970. Quarterly. Emphasizes "social policy issues—how government and societal actions affect people's lives." Readers are academics, policymakers, lay readers. Sample copy $2.50.
Needs: Uses about 9 photos/issue; all supplied by freelance photographers. Needs photos of social consciousness and sensitivity. Model release preferred.
Making Contact & Terms: Arrange a personal interview to show portfolio. Query with samples. Provide resume, business card, brochure, flyer or tearsheets to be kept on file for possible future assignments. Send 8×10 glossy b&w prints or b&w contact sheets by mail for consideration. SASE. Reports in 2 weeks. Pays $75/b&w cover photo; $25/b&w inside photo. Pays on publication. Credit line given. Buys one-time rights. Simultaneous submissions and previously published work OK.

Tips: "Be familiar with social issues. We're always looking for relevant photos."

SOUNDINGS TRADE ONLY, 35 Pratt St., Essex CT 06426. (203)767-3200. Editor: David Eastman. Circ. 32,000. Estab. 1978. Coated-stock tabloid. Monthly national trade paper for the recreational boating industry. Sample copy free with 12×18 SAE and $2 postage.
Needs: Uses one or two large color photos on page one; 90% by freelance photographers. Subjects: People at work in any setting related to the business (not the sport) of boating—boatyards, marinas, dealerships, boat or accessory manufacturing plants. Captions required; include what is going on, where (name of company and location), when and who (name and title of anyone featured in photo). Answer the "what" in detail.
Making Contact & Terms: Send unsolicited color transparencies by mail for consideration. Prefers large variety to pick from. No stock or file photos. SASE. Reports in 2 months. Pays $200 for lead photo on page one; $175 for second photo on page one; $125 for color photo used inside. Also uses b&w spot photos inside; pays $50. Sometimes makes assignments at $200/half day; send resume for file. Credit line given. Buys first-time rights.
Tips: "Photos are played large as free-standing art elements. Selection is based on vivid color and geometry. High visual impact is more important than subject matter; striking or unusual subject is a bonus."

SOUTHERN LUMBERMAN, Suite 116, 128 Holiday Ct., P.O. Box 681629, Franklin TN 37068-1629. (615)791-1961. Fax: (615)790-6188. Managing Editor: Nanci Gregg. Circ. 12,000. Estab. 1881. Monthly. Emphasizes forest products industry—sawmills, pallet operations, logging trades. Readers are predominantly owners/operators of midsized sawmill operations nationwide. Sample copy $2 with 9×12 SAE and $1.25 postage. Photo guidelines free with SASE.
Needs: Uses about 4-5 photos/issue; 50% supplied by freelancers. "We need b&ws of 'general interest' in the lumber industry. We need photographers from across the country to do an inexpensive b&w shoot in conjunction with a phone interview. We need 'human interest' shots from a sawmill scene— just basic 'folks' shots—a worker sharing lunch with the company dog, sawdust flying as a new piece of equipment is started; face masks as a mill tries to meet OSHA standards, etc." Looking for photo/ text packages. Model release required. Captions required.
Making Contact & Terms: Interested in receiving work from newer, lesser-known photographers. Query with samples. Send 5×7 or 8×10 glossy b&w prints; 35mm, 4×5 transparencies, b&w contact sheets or negatives by mail for consideration. SASE. Reports in 4-6 weeks. Pays minimum $20/b&w photos; $25-50/color photo; $125-175/photo/text package. Pays on publication. Credit line given. Buys first N.A. serial rights.
Tips: Prefers b&w capture of close-ups in sawmill, pallet, logging scenes. "Try to provide what the editor wants—call and make sure you know what that is, if you're not sure. Don't send things that the editor hasn't asked for. We're all looking for someone who has the imagination/creativity to provide what we need. I'm not interested in 'works of art'—I want and need b&w feature photos capturing essence of employees working at sawmills nationwide. I've never had someone submit anything close to what I state we need—try that. *Read* the description, shoot the pictures, send a contact sheet or a couple 5×7's."

SOYBEAN DIGEST, 540 Maryville Centre Dr., St. Louis MO 63141-1007. (314)576-2788. Fax: (314)576-2786. Editor: Gregg Hillyer. Circ. 230,000. Estab. 1940. Monthly. Emphasizes production and marketing of soybeans for high-acreage soybean growers. Sample copy $3.
Needs: Buys 75 photos/year; 40% from freelance assignment, 10% from freelance stock. Soybean production and marketing photos of modified equipment. Photos purchased with or without accompanying ms and on assignment. Accompanying mss: grower techniques for soybean production and marketing. Prefers photos with ms. Model release required for recognizable persons. Property release preferred. Captions preferred; include name, phone number, address (for people), location, season. No static, posed or outdated material.
Making Contact & Terms: Interested in receiving work from newer, lesser-known photographers. Send material by mail for consideration. Query with list of stock photo subjects, resume, business card, brochure and samples. Uses 5×7 or 8×10 b&w prints; 35mm or 2¼×2¼ transparencies; 35mm, 2¼×2¼, 4×5 and 8×10 transparencies for cover, vertical format preferred. SASE. Reports in 3 weeks. Pays $200-400/text/photo package or on a per-photo basis. **Pays on acceptance.** Credit line given. Buys all rights, but may reassign after publication. Previously published work possibly OK.
Tips: "In portfolio or samples we look for soybean, corn and cotton production and related subjects; environmental and conservational corn, soybean and cotton production images; photo journalistic style, saturated color, correct (or bracketed) exposures, a sense of composition, sharp focus, variety of shooting conditions, i.e. weather, light, lenses, formats, angles of view. With continued advances in photographic film and magazine printing we are seeing higher quality images being reproduced. Let us know where you're located. Become familiar with types of photos that are being used in crop production magazines. Be aware that we have a stock photo library ourselves, so you will be 'competing'

with a potential client. Your photography has to be fresh, out of the ordinary with reader-appeal. That's not easy to accomplish."

SPEEDWAY SCENE, P.O. Box 300, North Easton MA 02356. (508)238-7016. Editor: Val LeSieur. Circ. 70,000. Estab. 1970. Weekly tabloid. Emphasizes auto racing. Sample copy free with 8½ × 11 SAE and 4 first-class stamps.
Needs: Uses 200 photos/issue; all supplied by freelancers. Needs photos of oval track auto racing. Reviews photos with or without ms. Captions required.
Making Contact & Terms: Send unsolicited photos by mail for consideration. Send b&w, color prints. Reports in 1-2 weeks. NPI. Credit line given. Buys all rights. Simultaneous submissions and/or previously published work OK.

SPORTING GOODS DEALER, 6th Floor, 2 Park Ave., New York NY 10016. (212)779-5556. Editor-in-Chief: Michael Jacobsen. Circ. 29,000. Monthly magazine. Emphasizes news and merchandising ideas for sporting goods dealers. Sample copy $2 with 9 × 12 SAE and 2 first-class stamps (refunded with first accepted photo).
Needs: Photos purchased with or without accompanying ms or on assignment. Spot news relating to the merchandising of sporting goods. Outdoor (fishing, hunting, camping, water sports)-related photos (color preferred). Seeks mss on the merchandising of sporting goods through trade channels. Free writer's guidelines. Captions required.
Making Contact & Terms: Send material by mail for consideration. Uses 5 × 7 b&w glossy prints; transparencies, standard sizes. Pays $3-6/photo; $200-300/full-page color photo; 2¢/word for ms. Pays on publication. Buys all rights. Simultaneous submissions and previously published work OK if not published in a sporting goods publication.

STAGE DIRECTIONS, 3020 Beacon Blvd., W. Sacramento CA 95691. (916)373-0201. Fax: (916)373-0232. Editor: Stephen Peithman. Circ. 2,000. Estab. 1988. Journal published ten times per year. Emphasizes drama, stage production and theater administration. Sample copy free with SASE. Photo guidelines free with SASE.
Needs: Uses 10 photos/issue; all supplied by freelancers. Needs photos of action or close-up product shots. No talking heads. Model/property release preferred. Captions preferred.
Making Contact & Terms: Provide resume, business card, brochure, flyer or tearsheets to be kept on file for possible assignments. Keeps samples on file. SASE. Reports in 1 month. Pays $20/color and b&w cover photo; $20/color and b&w inside photo. Pays on publication. Credit line given. Buys one-time rights plus publicity rights; negotiable. Simultaneous submissions and/or previously published work OK.

STEP-BY-STEP GRAPHICS, Dept. PM, 6000 N. Forest Park Dr., Peoria IL 61614-3592. (309)688-2300. Managing Editor: Catharine Fishel. Circ. 45,000. Estab. 1985. Bimonthly. Emphasizes the graphic communications field. Readers are graphic designers, illustrators, art directors, studio owners, photographers. Sample copy $7.50.
Needs: Uses 130 photos/issue; all supplied by freelancers. Needs how-to shots taken in artists' workplaces. Assignment only. Model release required. Captions required.
Making Contact & Terms: Query with samples. Provide resume, business card, brochure, flyer or tearsheets to be kept on file for possible future assignments. SASE. Reports in 1 month. NPI; pays by the job on a case-by-case basis. **Pays on acceptance.** Credit line given. Buys one-time rights or first N.A. serial rights.
Tips: In photographer's samples looks for "color and lighting accuracy particularly for interiors." Recommend letter of inquiry plus samples.

SUNSHINE ARTISTS, (formerly *Sunshine Artists USA*), Dept. PM, 1736 N. Highway 427, Longwood FL 32750. (407)332-4944. Editor: Jeff Prutsman. Circ. 50,000. Monthly. Emphasizes arts and crafts in malls and outdoors. Readers are mainly professional artists and craftsmen making a living at mall and outdoor shows. Sample copy $2.50.
Needs: Uses 25-30 photos/year; mainly submitted by readers. Also 3-4 (35mm slides) of artist's work on cover each month. Needs 5 × 7 b&w photos of artist's work with article. Photos purchased with accompanying ms only. Special needs include unusual artwork or craft from successful artisans on the show circuit. Model release required. Captions preferred.
Making Contact & Terms: Query with resume of credits. Cannot return material. Reports in 2 weeks. Pays $10/b&w inside photo; $15-35/text/photo package. Pays on publication. Credit line given. Buys first N.A. serial rights.

✱**TEACHING TODAY,** 49 Primrose Blvd., Sherwood Park, Alberta T8H-1G1 Canada. (403)467-5273. Fax: (403)467-5273. Editor: Max Coderre. Circ. 12,000. Estab. 1983. Magazine published 5 times a year. Emphasizes professional development of teachers. Readers are primarily educators, from preschool through university level. "Sample copy sent if request accompanied with 9×12 envelope and $3 check or money order. (In US, send US funds.)"

Needs: Uses 3-5 photos/issue; 100% supplied by freelancers; 1% freelance assignment; 99% freelance stock. Needs photos of teachers and/or students in kindergarten to university level to enhance articles. Model release required.

Making Contact & Terms: Interested in receiving work from newer, lesser-known photographers. Send unsolicited photos by mail for consideration. Send b&w or color prints, any size or format. "Enclose envelope with check/money order to cover cost of return mailing or at least 4 IRCs." Reports in 2 months. Pays $5-25/b&w photo; $15-100/color photo. Pays on publication. Credit line given. Buys one-time rights. Simultaneous submissions OK.

Tips: "For color photos for front cover—simple, uncluttered, vivid colors—most photos used are of 1 or 2 people, usually "subjects" pertain to educational field. B&w or small photographs also used for inside purposes (e.g., to enhance articles). When sending work, give suggestion, reason of where, how, why photos could be (should be) used in educational publication."

TECHNICAL ANALYSIS OF STOCKS & COMMODITIES, Dept. PM, 3517 SW Alaska St., Seattle WA 98126-2700. (206)938-0570. Art Director: Christine Morrison. Circ. 27,500. Estab. 1982. Monthly magazine. Emphasizes stocks, bonds, futures, commodities, options and mutual funds. Sample copy $5.

Needs: Uses 6 photos/issue; all supplied by freelancers. Needs photos of security instruments (paper) or trading floor. Model/property release preferred. Captions preferred.

Making Contact & Terms: Send unsolicited photos by mail for consideration. Send 5×7 glossy color prints; 35mm, 2¼×2¼ or 4×5 transparencies. Keeps samples on file. SASE. Reports in 1 month. Pays $150/color cover photo; $100/color inside photo; $50/b&w inside photo. Pays on publication. Credit line given. Buys one-time and reprint rights; negotiable. Simultaneous submissions and/or previously published work OK.

TECHNOLOGY & LEARNING, 330 Progress Rd., Dayton OH 45449. (513)847-5900. Editor: Holly Brady. Art Director: Ellen Wright. Circ. 82,000. Monthly. Emphasizes computers in education. Readers are teachers and administrators, grades K-12. Sample copy $3.

Needs: Uses about 7-10 photos/issue; 2 or more supplied by freelance photographers. Photo needs "depend on articles concerned. No general categories. Usually photos used to accompany articles in a conceptual manner. Computer screen shots needed often." Model release required.

Making Contact & Terms: Contact Ellen Wright to arrange a personal interview to show portfolio. Query with nonreturnable samples. Provide resume, business card, brochure, flyer or tearsheets to be kept on file for possible future assignments. SASE. Reports in 3 weeks. Pays $300-700/color cover photo; $50-100/b&w inside photo; $100-300/color inside photo. **Pays on acceptance.** Credit line given. Buys one-time rights. Previously published work OK.

TENNIS INDUSTRY, Dept. PM, 1156 Avenue of the Americas., New York NY 10036. (212)921-3783. Vice President, Manufacturing: James Kukar. Circ. 30,000. Published 11 times/year. Emphasizes tennis trade. Sample copy $1 and 9×12 SASE.

Needs: Uses 10-30 photos/issue, all supplied by freelance photographers. Model release preferred. Captions required.

Making Contact & Terms: Query with list of stock photo subjects. Submit portfolio for review. SASE. Reports in 1 month. Pays $350/color cover photo; $150/color inside photo. Buys one-time and all rights; negotiable. Simultaneous submissions and previously published work OK.

THOROUGHBRED TIMES, Suite 101, 801 Corporate Dr., Lexington KY 40503. (606)223-9800. Editor: Mark Simon. Circ. 17,000. Estab. 1985. Weekly newspaper. Emphasizes thoroughbred breeding and racing. Readers are wide demographic range of industry professionals. No photo guidelines.

Needs: Uses 18-20 photos/issue; 40-60% supplied by freelancers. "Looks for photos only from desired trade (thoroughbred breeding and racing)." Needs photos of specific subject features (personality, farm or business). Model release preferred. Captions preferred.

Making Contact & Terms: Provide resume, business card, brochure, flyer or tearsheets to be kept on file for possible assignments. SASE. Reports in 1 month. Pays $25/b&w cover or inside photo; $25/b&w page rate; $150/day. Pays on publication. Credit line given. Buys one-time rights. Previously published work OK.

TOP PRODUCER, Farm Journal Publishing, Inc., 230 W. Washington Square, Philadelphia PA 19105. (215)829-4865. Photo Editor: Tom Dodge. Circ. 250,000. Monthly. Emphasizes American agriculture. Readers are active farmers, ranchers or agribusiness people. Sample copy and photo guidelines free with SASE.

Needs: Uses 20-30 photos/issue; 75% supplied by freelance photographers. "We use studio-type portraiture (environmental portraits), technical, details and scenics." Model release preferred. Captions required.

Making Contact & Terms: Arrange a personal interview to show portfolio. Query with resume of credits along with business card, brochure, flyer or tearsheets to be kept on file for possible assignments. SASE. Reports in 2 weeks. NPI. "We pay a cover bonus." **Pays on acceptance.** Credit line given. Buys one-time rights. Simultaneous submissions and previously published work OK.

Tips: In portfolio or samples, likes to "see about 20 slides showing photographer's use of lighting and photographer's ability to work with people. Know your intended market. Familiarize yourself with the magazine and keep abreast of how photos are used in the general magazine field."

TRADESWOMAN MAGAZINE, Dept. PM, P.O. Box 40664, San Francisco CA 94140. (415)821-7334. Editors: Janet Scoll Johnson and Robin Murphy. Circ. 1,500. Estab. 1981. Quarterly. Emphasizes women in nontraditional blue collar trades work (carpenters, electricians, etc.). Readers are highly skilled specialized women in crafts jobs with trade unions, and self-employed women such as contractors. Women doing work which is currently considered nontraditional. Sample copy $3.

Needs: Uses about 10-15 photos/issue; one-third supplied by freelance photographers. Needs "photos of women doing nontraditional work—either job site photos or inshop photos. Occasionally we just use photos of tools." Special needs include cover quality photos—b&w only.

Making Contact & Terms: Send unsolicited photos by mail for consideration. Send high contrast b&w prints; b&w contact sheet. SASE. Reports in 1 month. Pays $25/b&w photo; negotiable. **Pays on acceptance.** Credit line given. Rights negotiable. Simultaneous submissions and previously published work OK.

Tips: "We are looking for pictures of strong women whom we consider pioneers in their fields. Since we are nonprofit and do not have a lot of money, we often offer write-ups about authors and photographers in addition to small payments."

TRUCKERS NEWS, P.O. Box W, Newport Beach CA 92658-8910. (714)261-1636. Managing Editor: Deborah Whistler. Circ. 200,000. Monthly magazine. Emphasizes trucking. Readers are over-the-road truck drivers, mostly male, ages 30-65. Photo guidelines free with SASE.

Needs: Uses 20 photos/issue; 50% supplied by freelancers. Needs photos of scenics (trucks on highways), drivers at work. Model release is "photographer's responsibility." Captions preferred.

Making Contact & Terms: Query with resume of credits. Send unsolicited photos by mail for consideration. Send 35mm transparencies. SASE. Pays $150/color cover photo; $75/color or b&w inside photo. Pays on publication. Sends check when material is used. Buys one-time rights. Simultaneous submissions or previously published work not accepted.

TRUCKSTOP WORLD, P.O. Box W, Newport Beach CA 92658-8910. (714)261-1636. Managing Editor: Deborah Whistler. Circ. 12,000. Quarterly magazine. Emphasizes trucking. Readers are truckstop managers, mostly male, ages 30-65. Photo guidelines free with SASE.

Needs: Uses 10 photos/issue; 30-100% supplied by freelancers. Needs photos of truckstops. Model release is "photographer's responsibility." Captions preferred.

Making Contact & Terms: Query with resume of credits. Send unsolicited photos by mail for consideration. Send 35mm transparencies. SASE. Pays $150/color cover photo; $75/color or b&w inside photo. Pays on publication. Sends check when material is used. Buys one-time rights.

U.S. NAVAL INSTITUTE PROCEEDINGS, U.S. Naval Institute, Annapolis MD 21402. (301)268-6110. Picture Editor: Charles Mussi. Circ. 119,790. Monthly magazine. Emphasizes matters of current interest in naval, maritime and military affairs—including strategy, tactics, personnel, shipbuilding and equipment. Readers are officers in the Navy, Marine Corps and Coast Guard; also for enlisted personnel of the sea services, members of other military services in this country and abroad and civilians with an interest in naval and maritime affairs. Free sample copy.

Needs: Buys 15 photos/issue. Needs photos of Navy, Coast Guard and merchant ships of all nations; military aircraft; personnel of the Navy, Marine Corps and Coast Guard; and maritime environment and situations. No poor quality photos. Captions required.

Making Contact & Terms: Query first with resume of credits. Uses 8×10 glossy, color and b&w prints or slides. SASE. Reports in 2 weeks on pictorial feature queries; 6-8 weeks on other materials. Uses 8×10 glossy prints or slides, color and b&w. Pays $10 for official military photos submitted with articles; $250-500 for naval/maritime pictorial features; $200/color cover photo; $50 for article openers; $25/inside editorial. Pays on publication. Buys one-time rights.

Market conditions are constantly changing! If you're still using this book and it's 1995 or later, buy the newest edition of Photographer's Market at your favorite bookstore or order directly from Writer's Digest Books.

Tips: "These features consist of copy, photos and photo captions. The package should be complete, and there should be a query first. In the case of the $25 shots, we like to maintain files on hand so they can be used with articles as the occasion requires. Annual photo contest—write for details."

UNITED ARTS, Suite 6D, 141 Wooster, New York NY 10012. (212)473-6695. Publisher: Larry Qualls. Circ. 3,000. Estab. 1988. Quarterly journal. Emphasizes theatre, dance and art. Readers are in the university community. Sample copy available.
Needs: Needs photos of dance, theatre and art. Special photo needs include art photos of sculpture and theater production shots. Model release required. Captions required.
Making Contact & Terms: Query with resume of credits. Reports in 3 weeks. NPI. Credit line given. Simultaneous submissions and previously published work OK.

*UTILITY AND TELEPHONE FLEETS, P.O. Box 183, Cary IL 60013. (708)639-2200. Fax: (708)639-9542. Editor & Associate Publisher: Alan Richter. Circ. 18,000. Estab. 1987. Magazine published 8 times a year. Emphasizes equipment and vehicle management and maintenance. Readers are fleet managers, maintenance supervisors, generally 35 + in age and primarily male. Sample copy free with SASE. No photo guidelines.
Needs: Uses 30 photos/issue; 3-4% usually supplied by a freelance writer with an article. Needs photos of vehicles and construction equipment. Special photo needs include alternate fuel vehicles and eye-grabbing colorful shots of utility vehicles in action as well as utility construction equipment. Model release preferred. Captions required; include person's name, company and action taking place.
Making Contact & Terms: Interested in receiving work from newer, lesser-known photographers. Provide resume, business card, brochure, flyer or tearsheets to be kept on file for possible assignments. SASE. Reports in 1-2 weeks. Pays $50/color cover photo; $10/b&w inside photo; $50-200/photo/text package ($50/published page). Pays on publication. Credit line given. Buys one-time rights; negotiable.
Tips: "Be willing to work cheap and be able to write; the only photos we have paid for so far were part of an article/photo package." Looking for shots focused on our market with workers interacting with vehicles, equipment and machinery at the job site.

*UTILITY CONSTRUCTION AND MAINTENANCE, P.O. Box 183, Cary IL 60013. (708)639-2200. Fax: (708)639-9542. Editor: Alan Richter. Circ. 25,000. Estab. 1990. Quarterly magazine. Emphasizes equipment and vehicle management and maintenance. Readers are fleet managers, maintenance supervisors, generally 35 + in age and primarily male. Sample copy free with SASE. No photo guidelines.
Needs: Uses 80 photos/issue; 1-2% usually supplied by a freelance writer with an article. Needs photos of vehicles and construction equipment. Special photo needs include eye-grabbing colorful shots of utility construction equipment. Model release preferred. Captions required.
Making Contact & Terms: Provide resume, business card, brochure, flyer or tearsheets to be kept on file for possible assignments. SASE. Reports in 1-2 weeks. Pays $50/color cover photo; $10/b&w inside photo; $50-200/photo/text package ($50/published page). Pays on publication. Credit line given. Buys one-time rights.
Tips: "Be willing to work cheap and be able to write as the only photos we have paid for so far were part of an article/photo package."

*☀UTU NEWS CANADA, Suite 750, 1595 Telesat Ct., Gloucester, Ontario K1B 5R3 Canada. (613)747-7979. Fax: (613)747-2815. Editor: J. Michael Hone. Circ. 12,000. Publication of United Transportation Union. Quarterly tabloid. Emphasizes trade union and transportation issues. Primarily male rail employees—bus operators, age 20-65. Sample copy available.
Needs: Uses 2 photos/issue. Needs photos of technology, personalities. Special photo needs include transportation technology and steam engine (rail). Model/property release required. Captions required.
Making Contact & Terms: Interested in receiving work from newer, lesser-known photographers. Submit portfolio for review, Send unsolicited photos by mail for consideration. Uses b&w and color prints. Keeps samples on file. SASE. Reports in 1-2 weeks. NPI; payment varies. **Pays on acceptance.** Buys one-time rights. Simultaneous submissions and/or previously published work OK.

VM & SD (VISUAL MERCHANDISING AND STORE DESIGN), 407 Gilbert Ave., Cincinnati OH 45202. Fax: (513)421-5144. Editor: Janet Groeber. Circ. 20,000. Estab. 1922. Monthly magazine. Emphasizes store design and store display (all types of stores). Readers are visual merchandisers and store designers, architects, store owners, presidents and chief executive officers. Sample copy free.
Needs: Number of freelance photos used varies considerably. About 20% assigned. Needs architectural shots of stores and photos of displays. Captions preferred.
Making Contact & Terms: Interested in receiving work from newer, lesser-known photographers. Query with resume of credits. Provide business card, brochure, flyer or tearsheets to be kept on file for possible assignments. Send unsolicited photos by mail for consideration. Send color 35mm, 2¼ × 2¼ or

4×5 transparencies. SASE. Reports in 3 weeks. Pays $150/color cover photo; $50/color inside photo; $20/b&w inside photo. Pays on publication. Credit line given. Buys one-time rights. Simultaneous submissions and previously published work OK.
Tips: Trend in publication toward "excellent facade shots of stores and more shots concentrating on architectural detail." In samples, wants to see "an excellent sense of composition in interior photographs depicting not only the design of the space, but also the integration of merchandise presentation." To break in, "submit 4×5 or 2¼×2¼ transparencies showing imaginative window displays as well as unusual store interiors. With interiors, try to convey the store from several vantage points."

WALLS & CEILINGS MAGAZINE, 8602 N. 40th St., Tampa FL 33604. (813)989-9300. Editor: Lee Rector. Circ. 19,500. Monthly magazine. Emphasizes wall and ceiling construction, drywall, lath, plaster, stucco and exterior specialty finishes. Readership consists of 98% male, wall and ceiling contractors. Sample copy $4.
Needs: Uses 15-20 photos/issue; 30% supplied by freelancers. Needs photos of interior/exterior architectural shots, contractors and workers on job (installing drywall and stucco). Model release required.
Making Contact & Terms: Query with resume of credits. Send unsolicited photos by mail for consideration. Send glossy b&w or color prints, any size, or 35mm, 2¼×2¼ or 4×5 transparencies. SASE. Reports in 1 month. Pays $150/color cover photo; $50/color inside photo; $25/b&w inside photo; $50-150/photo/text package. Pays on publication. Credit line given. Buys exclusive, one-time and "our industry" rights. Simultaneous submissions and previously published work OK, provided not submitted to or published by competitors.

WARD'S AUTO WORLD, Dept. PM, 28 W. Adams St., Detroit MI 48226. (313)962-4433. Fax: (313)962-4456. Editor-in-Chief: David C. Smith. Circ. 92,00. Estab. 1965. Monthly. Emphasizes the automotive industry. Sample copy free with 9×12 SAE and $2 postage.
Needs: Uses about 40 photos/issue, mainly color transparencies; 10-30% supplied by freelancers; 100% assignment. Subject needs vary. "Most photos are assigned. We are a news magazine—the news dictates what we need." Model release preferred. Captions required.
Making Contact & Terms: Arrange a personal interview to show portfolio. Query with samples. Provide resume, business card, brochure, flyer or tearsheets to be kept on file for possible future assignments. SASE. Reports in 2 weeks. Pays $50-100/b&w photo; $60-125/color photo; $10-20/hour; $350-500/day. Pays on publication. Credit line given. Buys all rights.
Tips: In reviewing a photographer's portfolio or samples, looks for "creativity, originality and quality." Also looks for "ability to capture news subjects in good candid poses. We need photographers to accompany reporters on interviews, plant tours, etc. More photos are being printed of people; fewer on cars themselves. *Do not* send us photos of cars. We have all we need. We want freelancers with proven work abilities (who can accompany a reporter on assignment)."

WATER CONDITIONING & PURIFICATION MAGAZINE, Suite 101, 4651 N. First Ave., Tucson AZ 85718. (602)293-5446. Fax: (602)887-2383. Editor: Darlene Scheel. Circ. 15,446, international. Estab. 1959. Monthly magazine. Emphasizes water treatment. Readers are water treatment professionals. Sample copy free with 9×12 SASE.
Needs: Uses 20-30 photos/issue; 60% supplied by freelancers. Most photos are used for cover illustrations. "Cover shots vary from water scenes to technology involving water treatment." Wants to see "mainly cover shots" in the coming year. Model/property release preferred. Captions preferred.
Making Contact & Terms: Send unsolicited color prints or 35mm, 2¼×2¼, 4×5 or 8×10 transparencies by mail for consideration. Provide resume, business card, brochure, flyer or tearsheets to be kept on file for possible assignments. SASE. Reports as needed. Pays $150/color or b&w cover photo; $100/b&w inside photo. Pays on publication. Credit line given. Buys one-time rights.
Tips: "Looking for active water shots—cascading brooks, etc."

WATER WELL JOURNAL, 6375 Riverside Dr., Dublin OH 43017. (614)761-3222. Fax: (614)761-3446. Associate Editor: Gloria Swanson. Circ. 28,490. Estab. 1946. Monthly. Emphasizes construction of water wells, development of ground water resources and ground water cleanup. Readers are water well drilling contractors, managers, suppliers and ground water scientists. Sample copy $3 (US); $6 (foreign).
Needs: Uses 1-3 freelance photos/issue plus cover photos. Needs photos of installations and how-to illustrations. Model release preferred. Captions required.
Making Contact & Terms: Contact with resume of credits; inquire about rates. "We'll contact." Pays $10-50/hour; $200/color cover photo; $50/b&w inside photo; "flat rate for assignment." Pays on publication. Credit line given "if requested." Buys all rights.

***WILSON LIBRARY BULLETIN,** 950 University Ave., Bronx NY 10452. (718)588-8400. Fax: (718)681-1511. Editor: Grace Anne A. DeCandido. Circ. 14,000. Estab. 1914. Monthly (except July and August) magazine. Emphasizes the issues and the practice of librarianship. For librarians and information professionals.

Needs: Buys 10-15 photos/year; 2-5 photos assigned. Needs photos of library interiors, people reading in all kinds of libraries—school, public, university, community college, etc. No posed shots, dull scenics or dated work.
Making Contact & Terms: Interested in receiving work from newer, lesser-known photographers. Send photos for consideration with SASE for return. Provide business card and brochure to be kept on file for possible future assignments. Send 5×7 or 8×10 glossy b&w prints, color slides or transparencies. Reports in 4-6 weeks. Pays $10-15/b&w photo; $25-50/color photo; $300/color cover or text/photo package. Pays on publication. Credit line given. Buys one-time rights.
Tips: Looks for "interesting subjects portrayed creatively and high quality. Send a brochure or business card with samples to be kept on file."

*WINES & VINES, 1800 Lincoln Ave., San Rafael CA 94901. (415)453-9700. Contact: Philip E. Hiaring. Circ. 5,000. Estab. 1919. Monthly magazine. Emphasizes winemaking in the US for everyone concerned with the wine industry, including winemakers, wine merchants, suppliers, consumers, etc. Wants color cover subjects on a regular basis.
Making Contact & Terms: Interested in receiving work from newer, lesser-known photographers. Query or send material by mail for consideration. Provide business card to be kept on file for possible future assignments. SASE. Reports in 5 weeks to 3 months. Pays $10/b&w print; $50-100/color cover photo. Pays on publication. Credit line given. Buys one-time rights. Previously published work OK.

*WISCONSIN ARCHITECT, 321 S. Hamilton St., Madison WI 53703. (608)257-8477. Advertising/Production Manager: Cheryl Seurinck. Circ. 3,400. Estab. 1931. Publication of Wisconsin Society of Architects/American Institute of Architects. Bimonthly magazine. Emphasizes architecture. Readers are design and construction industry professionals.
Needs: Uses approximately 35 photos/issue. "Photos are almost exclusively supplied by architects who are submitting projects for publication. Of these approximately 65% are professional photographers hired by the architect."
Making Contact & Terms: Contact us through architects. Keeps samples on file. SASE. Reports in 1-2 weeks when interested. Pays $50-100/color cover photo when photo is specifically requested. Pays on publication. Credit line given. Rights negotiable. Simultaneous submissions and/or previously published work OK.

THE WISCONSIN RESTAURATEUR, #300, 31 S. Henry, Madison WI 53703. Editor: Jan LaRue. Circ. 4,200. Monthly magazine, except combined issue in November and December. Trade magazine for the Wisconsin Restaurant Association. Emphasizes the restaurant industry. Readers are "restaurateurs, hospitals, schools, institutions, cafeterias, food service students, chefs, etc." Free sample copy and photo and writer's guidelines with 9×12 SAE and $1.85 postage.
Needs: Buys 12 photos/year. Animal; celebrity/personality; photo essay/photo feature; product shot; scenic; special effects/experimental; how-to; human interest; humorous; nature; still life; and wildlife. Wants on a regular basis unusual shots of normal restaurant activities or unusual themes. Photos should relate directly to food service industry or be conceived as potential cover shots. No restaurants outside Wisconsin; national trends OK. No nonmember material except the very unusual. Ask for membership list for specific restaurants. Photos purchased with or without accompanying ms. Uses accompanying mss related to the food service industry—how-to, unusual concepts, humorous and "a better way." No cynical or off-color material. Model release required. Captions preferred.
Making Contact & Terms: Send material by mail for consideration. Provide photocopies of previously submitted work. Uses 5×7 glossy b&w prints, vertical format required for cover. SASE. Reports in 1 month. Pays $7.50-15/b&w inside photo; $10-25/b&w cover photo; $15-50 for text/photo package, or on a per-photo basis. **Pays on acceptance.** Credit line given. Buys one-time rights. Simultaneous submissions and previously published work OK.

WOODSHOP NEWS, 35 Pratt St., Essex CT 06426. (203)767-8227. Senior Editor: Thomas Clark. Circ. 100,000. Estab. 1986. Monthly tabloid. Emphasizes woodworking. Readers are male, 20's-60's, furniture makers, cabinetmakers, millworkers and hobbyist woodworkers. Sample copy and photo guidelines free with 11×13 SAE.
Needs: Uses 40 photos/issue; up to 10% supplied by freelancers. Needs photos of people working with wood. Model release required. Captions required.
Making Contact & Terms: Provide resume, business card, brochure, flyer or tearsheets to be kept on file for possible assignments. SASE. Reports in 1 month. Pays $250/color cover photo; $30/b&w inside photo. Pays on publication. Credit line given. Buys one-time rights.

WORLD FENCE NEWS, Dept. PM, Suite M, 6301 Manchaca Rd., Austin TX 78745. (800)231-0275. Fax: (512)445-3496. Managing Editor: Rick Henderson. Circ. 13,000. Estab. 1983. Monthly tabloid. Emphasizes fencing contractors and installers. Readers are mostly male fence company owners and employees, ages 30-60. Sample copy free with 10×12 SASE.

Needs: Uses 35 photos/issue; 20 supplied by freelancers. Needs photos of scenics, silhouettes, sunsets which include all types of fencing. Also, installation shots of fences of all types. "Cover images are a major area of need." Model and/or property release preferred mostly for people shots. Captions required; include location, date.

Making Contact & Terms: "If you have suitable subjects, call and describe." SASE. Reports in 3 weeks. Pays $100/color cover photo; $25/b&w inside photo. **Pays on acceptance.** Credit line given. Buys one-time rights. Previously published work OK.

WRITER'S DIGEST/WRITER'S YEARBOOK, 1507 Dana Ave., Cincinnati OH 45207. (513)531-2222. Fax: (513)531-2902. Managing Editor: Peter Blocksom. Circ. 250,000. Estab. 1921. Monthly magazine. Emphasizes writing and publishing. Readers are "writers and photojournalists of all description: professionals, beginners, students, moonlighters, bestselling authors, editors, etc." Sample copy $3. Guidelines free with SASE.

Needs: Buys 15 photos/year. Uses about 10% freelance material each issue. Purchases about 75% of photos from stock or on assignment; 25% of those with accompanying ms. Primarily celebrity/personality ("to accompany profiles"); some how-to, human interest and product shots. All must be writer-related. Submit model release with photo. Captions required.

Making Contact & Terms: Query with resume of credits, list of photographed writers, or contact sheet. Provide brochure and samples (print samples, not glossy photos) to be kept on file for possible future assignments. "We never run photos without text." Uses 8 × 10 glossy prints; send contact sheet. "Do *not* send negatives." Pays $50-75. "Freelance work is rarely used on the cover." Pays on acceptance. Credit line given. Buys first N.A. serial rights, one-time use only. Simultaneous submissions OK if editors are advised. Previously published work OK.

Tips: "We most often use photos with profiles of writers; in fact, we won't buy the profile unless we can get usable photos. The story, however, is always our primary consideration, and we won't buy the pictures unless they can be specifically related to an article we have in the works. We sometimes use humorous shots in our Writing Life column. Shots should not *look* posed, even though they may be. Photos with a sense of place, as well as persona, preferred. Have a mixture of tight and middle-distance shots of the subject. Study a few back issues. Avoid the stereotyped writer-at-typewriter shots; go for an array of settings. Move the subject around, and give us a choice. We're also interested in articles on how a writer earned extra money with photos, or how a photographer works with writers on projects, etc."

Trade Publications/'93-'94 changes

The following markets appeared in the 1993 edition of *Photographer's Market* but are not listed in the 1994 edition. They may have been omitted for failing to respond to our request for updated information, they may have gone out of business or they may no longer wish to receive freelance work.

American Bookseller (did not respond)
American Fire Journal (did not respond)
Apparel Industry Magazine (did not respond)
Aquatics International (did not respond)
Athletic Business (did not respond)
AVC (did not respond)
Beverage Dynamics (did not respond)
Butter Fat Magazine (asked to be deleted)
CFO Magazine (did not respond)
Chemicalweek (asked to be deleted)
Computers in Healthcare Magazine (did not respond)
Cranberries (did not respond)
Datamotion Magazine (did not respond)
Dairy Herd Management (asked to be deleted)

Direct Marketing Magazine (did not respond)
Employee Assistance (did not respond)
Entertainment Express International (did not respond)
Farm Store Merchandising (ceased publication)
Fleet Owner Magazine (did not respond)
Flooring (no longer using photos)
Florida Specifier (did not respond)
Footwear Plus (did not respond)
General Aviation News & Flyer (did not respond)
Golf Industry (did not respond)
Graphis (did not respond)
Hearth and Home (did not respond)
Indiana Business Magazine (not reviewing freelance work)
Insurance Week (did not re

spond)
Jems (did not respond)
Jobber Retailer Magazine (did not respond)
Journal of Psychoactive Drugs (did not respond)
Journal of Psychosocial Nursing (did not respond)
Kalis' Shopping Center Leasing Directory (did not respond)
Maintenance Supplies (did not respond)
MD Magazine (did not respond)
Medical Economics Magazine (inappropriate submissions)
Meeting News (not reviewing freelance work)
Middle Eastern Dancer (sold magazine)
Music & Computer Educator (out of business)
New England Business (unable to locate)
Northern Logger & Timber Processor (asked to be

deleted)
OH&S Canada (did not respond)
Oregon Business Magazine (did not respond)
Plant (uses too few photos)
Plastics Technology (did not respond)
Plumbing, Heating, Piping (did not respond)
Press (did not respond)
Professional Agent (not reviewing freelance work)

Progressive Architecture (did not respond)
Seafood Business Magazine (did not respond)
Small World (did not respond)
Sports Car International (did not respond)
Sportstyle (did not respond)
Successful Farming (did not respond)
Tech Directions (asked to be deleted)
Telecommunications (did not

respond)
Today's Trucking (inappropriate submissions)
Travel Agent Magazine (asked to be deleted)
Veterinary Economics (asked to be deleted)
Wang in the News (asked to be deleted)
Work Boat (inappropriate submissions)
World Trade Magazine (did not respond)

Record Companies

If you are excited about the possibility of working within the record company market you should be prepared to offer clients a variety of skills. At times you will be asked to take a photojournalistic approach to your work, especially when called upon to supply action-packed concert footage. You also should have the ability to coordinate group or individual portraits, and often studio shots require strong, innovative concepts.

Record companies have numerous responsibilities as they work to record and release records, cassettes and CDs. They sign artists to recording contracts, decide what songs those artists will record and determine which songs to release. They also oversee the manufacturing, distribution and promotion of new releases.

As you work with record companies you will be asked to supply images for all kinds of uses. Some assignments are made for album, cassette or CD covers. Frequently images are used in promotional pieces to sell the work of recording artists. As always, you should try to retain rights to images for future sales and the usage should help you establish a fair price during negotiations.

Building your portfolio

A good portfolio for record companies shows off your skills and style in an imaginative way, but especially illustrates your ability to solve creative problems facing art directors. Such problems may include coming up with fresh concepts for record art, working within the relatively limited visual format of the 5-inch compact disc liner sheet or assembling a complex shot on a limited budget. If you have not worked for a record company client, you still can study the needs of various companies in this section and shoot a series of self-assignments which clearly show your problem-solving abilities.

When photographer Paul Natkin, of Chicago, Illinois, began shooting musical acts he used small clubs and unknown bands to build his portfolio. Years of hard work, and a lot of trial and error, have turned him into one of the industry's top photographers and he discusses the field in our Insider Report on page 468.

Natkin's success proves that photographers should build on their successes. Shooters who go on to long-term, high-profile success often start working with smaller, independent music companies, or "indies." Larger companies typically rely on stables of photographers who are either on staff or work through art studios that deal with music companies. Because of this tendency, it can be difficult for newcomers to break in when these companies already have their pick of talented, reliable photographers. Start out slowly and develop a portfolio of outstanding images. Eventually the larger companies will become familiar with your work and they will seek you out when looking for images or handing out assignments.

Freelancers also must be alert when dealing with the independent market. Some newer companies have not learned the various aspects of professionalism and ethics in doing business, and, in a few cases, companies deliberately deceive freelancers in terms of payment and copyright. When trying to attract new clients in this field, query prospective companies and request copies of their various forms and contracts for photographers. Seeing the content of such material can tell you a great deal about how well organized and professional a company is. Also talk to people within the music industry to get a better understanding of the company with which you want to do business.

*■AFTERSCHOOL PUBLISHING COMPANY, P.O. Box 14157, Detroit MI 48214. (313)571-0363. President: Herman Kelly. Estab. 1978. Handles all forms of music. Freelancers used for portraits, in-concert shots, studio shots and special effects for publicity, brochures, posters and print advertising.
Needs: Buys 5-10 images annually. Offers 5-10 assignments annually. Interested in animation, love. Reviews stock photos. Model release required. Captions required.
Audiovisual Needs: Uses videotape, prints, papers for reproductions. Subjects include: love, fun, comedy, life.
Specs: Uses prints, all sizes and finishes, and videotape, all sizes.
Making Contact & Terms: Interested in receiving work from newer, lesser-known photographers. Submit portfolio for review. Keeps samples on file. SASE. Reports in 1 month. NPI; payment negotiable. Credit line given. Rights negotiable.

ALPHA INTERNATIONAL RECORD CO., 1080 N. Delaware Ave., Philadelphia PA 19125. (215)425-8682. Fax: (215)425-4376. Production Manager: Arthur Stoppe. Estab. 1989. Handles pop, urban, dance and alternative music. Freelancers used for portraits, in-concert shots and studio shots for cover/liner, publicity, posters and print advertising.
Needs: Offers 6-8 assignments annually. Needs "good environmental portraits" (b&w and color) of people for album-cover type use and press/publicity use. The types of photos used for record album and single art have a lot more in common with contemporary fashion and even fine art photographs than they may have had in the past. Model/property release required.
Specs: Uses 8×10 glossy color prints; 35mm and 2¼×2¼ transparencies.
Making Contact & Terms: Interested in receiving work from newer, lesser-known photographers. Provide resume, business card, self-promotion piece or tearsheets to be kept on file for possible future assignments. Works on assignment only. Keeps samples on file. SASE. Reports in 1-2 weeks. Pays $500-1,500/job; $50-250/color photo; $50-250/b&w photo. **Pays on acceptance.** Credit line given. Buys all rights.

‡ALPHABEAT, Box 12 01, D-6980 Wertheim/Main, West Germany. Phone: 9342-841 55. Managing Director: Stephan Dehn. Handles disco, dance, pop, soft ballads, wave, synth-pop, electro-disco and funk. Photographers used for portraits, studio shots and special effects for album covers, publicity, brochures, posters and product advertising.
Specs: Uses color prints.
Making Contact & Terms: Send unsolicited photos by mail for consideration. Submit portfolio for review. Provide resume, business card, brochure, flyer or tearsheets to be kept on file for possible future assignments. Works with freelancers on assignment only. SAE, IRC. Reports in 2 weeks. NPI. Pays according to type of order. Credit line given. Buys all rights; negotiable.

 The double dagger before a listing indicates that the market is located outside the United States and Canada.

APON RECORD COMPANY, INC., Steinway Station, P.O. Box 3082, Long Island NY 11103. (212)721-5599. President: Andre M. Poncic. Handles classical, folklore and international. Photographers used for portraits and studio shots for album covers and posters.
Needs: Offers 50+ assignments/year.
Specs: Uses b&w prints and 4×5 transparencies.
Making Contact & Terms: Send photos by mail for consideration. Provide brochure and samples to be kept on file for possible future assignments. Cannot return material. Reports in 3 months. NPI; payment negotiable. Credit line given. Buys all rights.

ART ATTACK RECORDINGS/CARTE BLANCHE RECORDS, Dept. PM, Fort Lowell Station, P.O. Box 31475, Tucson AZ 85751. (602)881-1212. President: William Cashman. Handles rock, pop, country, and jazz. Photographers used for portraits, in-concert shots, studio shots and special effects for album covers, inside album shots, publicity and brochures.
Needs: Offers 10-15 assignments/year.
Specs: "Depends on particular project."
Making Contact & Terms: Arrange a personal interview to show portfolio. Provide resume, business card, brochure, flyer or tearsheets to be kept on file for possible future assignments. Works with freelancers on assignment only. "We will contact only if interested." NPI; payment negotiable. Credit line given.
Tips: Prefers to see "a definite and original style—unusual photographic techniques, special effects" in a portfolio. "Send us samples to refer to that we may keep on file."

AZRA RECORDS, Dept. PM, P.O. Box 459, Maywood CA 90270. (213)560-4223. Fax: (213)560-1240. President: David Richards. Estab. 1980. Handles rock, heavy metal, novelty and seasonal. Photographers used for special effects and "anything unique and unusual" for picture records and shaped picture records.
Needs: Model release required. Property release preferred. Captions preferred.
Specs: Uses 8×10 b&w or color glossy prints and 35mm transparencies.
Making Contact & Terms: Interested in receiving work from newer, lesser-known photographers. Query with resume of credits or send "anything unique in photo effects" by mail for consideration. Works with freelancers on assignment only; "all work is freelance-assigned." SASE. Reports in 2 weeks. Pays $50-250/b&w; $50-1,000/color photo; payment "depends on use of photo, either outright pay or percentages." Credit line given. Buys one-time rights; negotiable.
Tips: Wants to see unique styles or photo angles. "Query first. We have a wide variety of projects going at all times."

ROBERT BATOR & ASSOCIATES, Dept. PM, 51 Lakeside Dr., Lake Paradise, Monson MA 01057. (413)267-3537. Fax: (413)267-3538. Art Director: Joan Bator. Estab. 1969. Handles rock and country. Photographers used for in-concert shots and studio shots for album covers, inside album shots, publicity and posters.
Needs: Buys 5,000 photos/year. Offers 400 assignments/year. Model release preferred. Captions preferred.
Specs: Uses 4×5 and 8×10 glossy ("mostly color") prints.
Making Contact & Terms: Send unsolicited photos by mail for consideration. Provide resume, business card, brochure, flyer or tearsheets to be kept on file for possible future assignments. "You can submit female suggestive photos for sex appeal, or male, but in good taste." Works with freelancers on assignment only. SASE. Reports in 1 week. Pays $100-150/b&w photo; $150-250/color photo; $150-189/hour; $400-500/day; $375-495/job. Credit line given. Buys one-time rights; other rights negotiable.
Tips: Looks "for good clear photos of models. Show some imagination. Would like some sexually-oriented prints—because advertising is geared for it. Also fashion shots—men's and women's apparel, especially swim suits and casual clothing."

BOUQUET-ORCHID ENTERPRISES, 204 Crestview St., Minden LA 71055-2020. (318)377-2538. President: Bill Bohannon. Photographers used for live action and studio shots for publicity flyers and brochures.
Making Contact & Terms: Provide brochure and resume to be kept on file for possible future assignments. Works with freelancers on assignment only. SASE. Reports in 1 month. Pays $200 minimum/job.
Tips: "We are using more freelance photography in our organization. We are looking for material for future reference and future needs."

*■CORNELL ENTERTAINMENT GROUP, Suite 210, 80 St. Michael St., Mobile AL 36602. (205)694-7500. Handles R&B, gospel, pop and rock. Freelancers used for cover/liner shots, inside shots, publicity, posters, event/convention coverage and print advertising.

Needs: Reviews stock photos for video purposes. Model/property release required.
Audiovisual Needs: Uses slides and videotape.
Making Contact & Terms: Interested in receiving work from newer, lesser-known photographers. Arrange personal interview to show portfolio. Submit portfolio for review. Works on assignment only. Keeps samples on file. SASE. Reports in 4-6 weeks. NPI.

COSMOTONE RECORDS, Suite 412, 3350 Highway 6, Houston TX 77478. Record Producer: Rafael Brom. Handles all types of records. Photographers used for portraits, studio shots and special effects for album covers, inside album shots, brochures, posters and product advertising.
Needs: Offers 1-3 assignments/year.
Specs: Uses all sizes, all finish b&w and color photos.
Making Contact & Terms: Works on assignment only. Cannot return material. Will contact only if interested. Pays $30-200/b&w photo; $50-350/color photo; $30-1,000/job. Credit line given. Buys one-time rights and all rights; negotiable.

*■CREATIVE NETWORK, INC., P.O. Box 2818, Newport Beach CA 92659. (714)494-0181. Fax: (714)494-0982. Manager: Joseph Nicoletti. Estab. 1976. Handles all types of records. Freelancers used in all situations. "Many formats are used, depending on our clients' needs."
Needs: Buys "hundreds" of images annually; about 70% supplied by freelancers. Offers 30 to 100 assignments annually. Reviews stock photos; any type of subject is welcome. Model/property release preferred for pictures of faces. Captions preferred; include description of subject matter.
Audiovisual Needs: Uses videotape of all subjects.
Specs: Uses 8×10 maximum glossy color and b&w prints; 35mm transparencies; VHS videotape format only.
Making Contact & Terms: Interested in receiving work from newer, lesser-known photographers. Provide resume, business card, self-promotion pieces or tearsheets to be kept on file for possible future assignments. Works with local freelancers only. Keeps samples on file. SASE. Reports in 1-2 weeks. NPI. Buys all rights; negotiable.
Tips: "Creativity is very important, as well as style."

*■CURTISS UNIVERSAL RECORD MASTERS, P.O. Box 1622, Hendersonville TN 37077. (615)822-1044. Manager: Dick Derwald. Estab. 1970. Handles all kinds of music. Freelancers used for in-concert shots, studio shots, special effects for cover/liner shots, inside shots, publicity, brochures, posters, event/convention coverage, print advertising.
Needs: Buys various number of images annually; all supplied by freelancers. Offers various number of assignments annually. Interested in photos and slides. Reviews stock photos of all subjects. Model/property release preferred.
Audiovisual Needs: Uses videotape.
Specs: Uses 5×7 color and b&w prints; videotape (10 to 30 minutes long).
Making Contact & Terms: Interested in receiving work from newer, lesser-known photographers. Submit portfolio for review. Query with resume of credits. Query with samples. Query with stock photo list. Provide resume, business card, self-promotion pieces or tearsheets to be kept on file for possible future assignments. Works on assignment only. Does not keep samples on file. SASE. Reports in 3 weeks. NPI. **Pays on acceptance** and invoice. Credit line given. Rights negotiable.

*‡EFA-MEDIEN-GMBH, Mousonstr. 12, 6000 Frankfurt Germany. (69)495099. Fax: (69)445092. A&R Manager: Ulrich Vormehr. Estab. 1982. Handles rock, jazz, avant garde and pop for the Houses in Motion label. Photographers used for portraits, in-concert shots, studio shots and special effects for album covers. Also, inside album shots, publicity, brochures, posters and product advertising.
Needs: Buys 10-12 photos/year. Model release required. Property release preferred. Captions preferred.
Specs: Uses color prints.
Making Contact & Terms: Interested in receiving work from newer, lesser-known photographers. Send unsolicited photos by mail for consideration or submit portfolio for review. SAE, IRC. Reports in 1 month. Credit line given. Buys one-time rights; negotiable. Pays $100-250/b&w photo, $50-250/color photo.

FINER ARTISTS RECORDS, Suite 115, 2170 S. Parker Rd., Denver CO 80231. (303)755-2546. President: R.J. Bernstein. Estab. 1960. Handles rock, classical and country. Uses portraits, in-concert shots, studio shots and special effects for album covers, inside album shots, publicity, brochures and posters.
Needs: Uses 6 freelancers/year.
Making Contact & Terms: Query with resume of credits. Send unsolicited photos by mail for consideration. Submit portfolio for review. Provide resume, business card, brochure, flyer or tearsheets to be kept on file for possible future assignments. Works with freelancers on assignment only. Reports in 1 month. NPI; payment negotiable. Credit line given. Buys one-time or all rights; negotiable.

FOX FARM RECORDING, 2731 Saundersville Ferry Road, Mt. Juliet TN 37122. (615)754-2444. Owner: Kent Fox. Estab. 1970. Handles bluegrass and gospel. Photographers used for portraits, studio shots, special effects for album covers, inside album shots and publicity.
Specs: Uses b&w/color.
Making Contact & Terms: Send unsolicited photos by mail for consideration. Works with freelancers on assignment only. SASE. Reports in 1 month. Pays $100-2,000/job. Credit line sometimes given. Buys all rights.

*GLOBAL PACIFIC RECORDS, 270 Perkins St., Sonoma CA 95476. (707)996-2748. Fax: (707)996-2658. Senior Vice President: Howard L. Morris. Handles jazz, World, New Age, modern rock. Photographers used for portraits, in-concert shots, studio shots and special effects for album covers, inside album shots, publicity, brochures, posters and product advertising.
Needs: Buys 12-18 images annually.
Specs: Uses 8×10 glossy b&w and color prints or transparencies.
Making Contact & Terms: Submit portfolio for review. Provide resume, business card, brochure, flyer or tearsheets to be kept on file for possible future assignments. SASE. Reports in 2 weeks. NPI. Buys all rights; negotiable.
Tips: Prefers "technically excellent (can be blown up, etc.), excellent compositions, emotional photographs. Be familiar with what we have done in the past. Study our music, album packages, etc., and present material that is appropriate."

HARD HAT RECORDS & CASSETTES, 519 N. Halifax Ave., Daytona Beach FL 32118. (904)252-0381. Fax: (904)252-0381. CEO: Bobby Lee Cude. Estab. 1978. Handles country, pop, disco, gospel, MOR, Broadway. Photographers used for portraits, in-concert shots, studio shots, special effects for album covers, inside shots, publicity, brochures, posters and event/convention coverage.
Needs: Offers varied number of assignments/year. Examples of recent uses: "Daytona Beach's Sand In My Shoes," cover montage; "Don't Blow;" and "Blow Blow Stereo."
Specs: Uses 8×10 glossy b&w prints.
Making Contact & Terms: Interested in receiving work from newer, lesser-known photographers. Provide resume, business card, brochure, flyer or tearsheets to be kept on file for possible future assignments. Works on assignment only. SASE. Does not return unsolicited material. Reports in 1 month. NPI. Pays on a contract basis. Credit line sometimes given. Buys all rights; negotiable.
Tips: "Submit credentials as well as work done for other record companies as a sample; also price, terms. Read *MIX/MUSICIAN* magazines."

*HIGHER OCTAVE MUSIC, Suite 41, 8033 Sunset Blvd., Los Angeles CA 90046. (213)856-0039. Vice President, Creative Services: Dee Westlund. Handles New Age. Photographers used for studio shots and special effects for album covers, inside album shots, publicity and brochures.
Specs: Uses b&w and color prints.
Making Contact & Terms: Submit portfolio for review. Provide resume, business card, brochure, flyer or tearsheets to be kept on file for possible future assignments. SASE. Reports in 3-4 weeks. NPI. Credit line given. Buys all rights; negotiable.
Tips: "New Age album covers are finally getting away from lovely landscapes and into a more progressive look—I look for clean elegance for our covers. Freelancers are in demand with small independent record companies that don't have lots of money to spend, but have the time to work with the photographer—for the right shot at the right price."

JODY RECORD INC., 2557 E. 1st St., Brooklyn NY 11223. (718)339-8047. VP-Sales: Tom Bosco. A&R Director: Vince Vallis. Handles rock, jazz, country, pop. Photographers used for portraits, in-concert shots, studio shots and special effects for album covers, publicity, brochures and posters.
Specs: Uses b&w prints.
Making Contact & Terms: Send unsolicited photos by mail for consideration. Works on assignment only. Reports in 2 weeks. NPI. Credit line given. Buys all rights; negotiable.
Tips: Looks for something unusual in photos.

*■KAIZAN MUSIC, c/o Jacobson & Colfin, Suite 434, 156 Fifth Ave., New York NY 10010. (212)691-5630. Fax: (212)645-5038. Attorney: Bruce E. Colfin. Estab. 1981. Handles jazz, classical, New Age. Freelancers used for portraits for cover/liner.

The solid, black square before a listing indicates that the market uses various types of audiovisual materials, such as slides, film or videotape.

Needs: Buys 12 images annually; 12 supplied by freelancers. Interested in all types of subjects. Reviews stock photos. Model release required. Captions required.
Audiovisual Needs: Uses videotape. Subjects include entertainment (music).
Making Contact & Terms: Interested in receiving work from newer, lesser-known photographers. Send cover letter and SASE. Keeps samples on file. Reports in 3 weeks. NPI. Credit line given. Rights negotiable.

KIMBO EDUCATIONAL, P.O. Box 477, 10 N. Third Ave., Long Branch NJ 07740. (908)229-4949. Production Manager: Amy Laufer. Handles educational — early childhood movement oriented records, tapes and videocassettes. General entertainment songs for young children. Physical fitness programs for all ages. Photographers used for album and catalog covers, brochures and product advertising.
Needs: Offers 5 assignments/year.
Specs: Uses transparencies.
Making Contact & Terms: Provide resume, business card, brochure, flyer or tearsheets to be kept on file for possible future assignments. Cannot return material. "We keep samples on file and contact photographer if in need of their services." Payment for each job is different — small advertising job, $75 minimum; album covers, $200-400." Buys all rights; negotiable.
Tips: "We are looking for top quality work but our budgets do not allow us to pay New York City prices (need reasonable quotes). Prefer local photographers — communication easier. We are leaning a little more toward photography, especially in our catalog. In the educational marketplace, it's becoming more prevalent to actually show our products being used by children."

K-TEL INTERNATIONAL (USA), INC., 15535 Medina Rd., Plymouth MN 55447. (612)559-6800. Director of Creative Services: John Dittrich. Estab. 1969. Handles rock, classical, country, jazz, rap, oldies and gospel. Photographers used for portraits, studio shots and special effects for album covers, inside album shots, publicity, brochures, posters, event/convention coverage, and product advertising.
Needs: Assigns 12 jobs/year. Examples of recent uses: The Wood Brothers (CD and cassette cover); The Country Music Classics Series (CD and cassette cover). Model release required. Captions preferred.
Specs: Uses b&w and color.
Making Contact & Terms: Interested in receiving work from newer, lesser-known photographers. Query with resume of credits. Send by mail for consideration promotional pieces that can be filed for future reference. Provide resume, business card, brochure, flyer or tearsheets to be kept on file for possible future assignments. Cannot return material. Reports in 1 month. NPI; negotiable according to project budget. Credit line given. Buys all rights; negotiable.
Tips: In reviewing samples looks for "creativity, dramatic lighting and unusual contemporary techniques."

L.R.J. RECORDS, Box 3, Belen NM 87002. (505)864-7441. Fax: (505)864-7442. President: Little Richie Johnson. Estab. 1959. Handles country and bilingual records. Photographers used for record album photos.
Making Contact & Terms: Send material by mail for consideration. NPI; payment negotiable. Pays on receipt of completed job. Credit line given. Buys all rights, but may reassign to photographer.

LIN'S LINES, Suite 434, 156 Fifth Ave., New York NY 10010. (212)691-5630. Fax: (212)645-5038. President: Linda K. Jacobson. Estab. 1983. Handles all types of records. Uses photos for portraits, in-concert shots, studio shots for album covers, inside album shots, publicity, brochures, posters and product advertising.
Needs: Offers 6 assignments/year.
Specs: Uses 8×10 prints; 35mm transparencies.
Making Contact & Terms: Query with resume of credits. Provide resume, business card, brochure, flyer or tearsheets to be kept on file for possible future assignments. "Do not send unsolicited photos." Works on assignment only. SASE. Reports in 1 month. Pays $50-500/b&w photo; $75-750/color photo; $10-50/hour; $100-1,500/day; $75-3,000/job. Credit line given. Buys one-time rights; all rights, but may reassign to photographer.
Tips: Prefers unusual and exciting photographs such as holograms and 3-D images. "Send *interesting* material, initially in postcard form."

LOCONTO PRODUCTIONS & RECORDING STUDIOS, P.O. Box 16540, Plantation FL 33318. (305)741-7766. Executive Vice President: Phyllis Loconto. Handles "all types" of records. Photographers used for portraits, studio shots, album covers, inside album shots, publicity, brochures, posters, event/convention coverage and product advertising.
Specs: Varied.
Making Contact & Terms: NPI. Pays/job; negotiated. Credit line given. Buys all rights.
Tips: "I manage 'events' promotions — always interested in creative photography."

The solitary life of a cowboy, portrayed in this photo taken by Joe Treleven, of Minneapolis, Minnesota, serves as a perfect cover for a country music compact disc. The shot was purchased by K-Tel International (USA), Inc., which hired Treleven for the assignment.

LUCIFER RECORDS, INC., P.O. Box 263, Brigantine NJ 08203. (609)266-2623. President: Ron Luciano. Photographers used for portraits, live action shots and studio shots for album covers, record sleeves, publicity flyers, brochures and posters.
Needs: Freelancers supply 50% of photos.
Making Contact & Terms: Provide brochure, calling card, flyer, resume and samples. Submit portfolio for review. SASE. Reports in 2-6 weeks. NPI; payment negotiable. Buys all rights.

*LUKE RECORDS INC., 8400 NE 2nd Ave., Miami FL 33138. (305)757-1969. Fax: (305)757-3456. Production Manager: Frank Tabino. Estab. 1980. Handles rap and rhythm and blues. Freelancers used for portraits, in-concert shots, studio shots and special effects for cover/liner shots, inside shots, publicity, brochures, posters and print advertising.
Needs: Offers 30 assignments annually. Reviews stock photos. Model release required. Captions preferred.
Specs: Uses prints and 2¼ × 2¼ transparencies.
Making Contact & Terms: Query with stock photo list. Provide resume, business card, self-promotion pieces or tearsheets to be kept on file for possible future assignments. Works with freelancers on assignment only. Keeps samples on file. Cannot return material. Reports in 1-2 weeks. Pays $350-750/job. Pays 30 days after acceptance. Credit line given. Buys all rights.

JACK LYNCH MUSIC GROUP, (Nashville Country Productions/Nashville Bluegrass/Jalyn & Nashville Country Recording Companies), 306 Millwood Dr., Nashville TN 37217-1604. (615)366-9999. CEO: Col. Jack Lynch. Estab. 1963. Handles country, bluegrass and gospel. Photographers used for portraits, in-concert shots and studio shots for album covers.
Needs: Offers 1-10 assignments/year.
Specs: Uses various size b&w and color prints/transparencies.
Making Contact & Terms: Provide resume, business card, brochure, flyer or tearsheets to be kept on file for possible future assignments. Works with freelancers on assignment only. SASE. Reports in 1 month. Pays variable rates; $50-100/b&w photo; $100-200/color photo; $50-100/hour; $500-1,000/

day; and $500-1,000/job. Credit line usually given. Buys exclusive product rights.
Tips: Call or write for information. Looks for good service, quality work and reasonable fees.

LEE MAGID, P.O. Box 532, Malibu CA 90265. (213)463-5998. President: Lee Magid. Operates under Grass Roots Records label. Handles R&B, jazz, C&W, gospel, rock, blues, pop. Photographers used for portraits, in-concert shots, studio shots and candid photos for album covers, publicity, brochures, posters and event/convention coverage.
Needs: Offers about 10 assignments/year.
Specs: Uses 8×10 buff or glossy b&w or color prints and 2¼×2¼ transparencies.
Making Contact & Terms: Send print copies by mail for consideration. Works with freelancers on assignment only. SASE. Reports in 2 weeks. NPI. Credit line given. Buys all rights.

MARICAO RECORDS/HARD HAT RECORDS, 519 N. Halifax Ave., Daytona Beach FL 32118. (904)252-0381. Fax: (904)252-0381. CEO: Bobby Lee Cude. Handles country, MOR, pop, disco and gospel. Photographers used for portraits, in-concert shots, studio shots and special effects for album covers, inside album shots, publicity, brochures, posters, event/convention coverage and product advertising.
Needs: Offers 12 assignments/year. Model/property release required. Captions required.
Specs: Uses b&w and color photos.
Making Contact & Terms: Interested in receiving work from newer, lesser-known photographers. Submit portfolio for review. Provide resume, business card, brochure, flyer, tearsheets or samples to be kept on file for possible future assignments. Works with freelancers on assignment only. SASE. Reports in 2 weeks. NPI; pays "standard fees." Credit line sometimes given. Buys all rights.
Tips: "Submit sample photo with SASE along with introductory letter stating fees, etc. Read *Mix Music* magazine."

*MAUI ARTS & MUSIC-SURVIVOR RECORDS, Suite 661, 880 Front St., Lahaina HI 96761. (808)661-5151. Public Relations: Diane Christopher. Estab. 1974. Handles rock, jazz, country, R&B, easy listening, New Age. Freelancers used for portraits, in-concert shots and studio shots.
Needs: Buys 1-15 images annually. Offers 1-15 assignments annually. Interested in beautiful sensual visuals. Reviews stock photos. Model release and photo captions preferred.
Specs: Uses matte, color and/or b&w prints; 35mm, 2¼×2¼, 4×5, 8×10 transparencies.
Making Contact & Terms: Interested in receiving work from newer, lesser-known photographers. Query with samples. Provide resume, business card, brochure, self-promotion pieces or tearsheets to be kept on file for possible future assignments. Works with freelancers on assignment only. Keeps samples on file. Reports in 1 month. Pays $25-125/hour; $100-1,200/day; $100-3,000/job; $100-1,000/color photo; $100-1,000/b&w photo. Rights negotiable.

*■MIRAMAR PRODUCTIONS, 200 2nd Ave. W., Seattle WA 98119. (206)284-4700. Fax: (206)286-4433. Production Manager: David Newsom. Estab. 1985. Handles rock and New Age. Freelancers used for portraits, in-concert shots and studio shots for cover/liner, inside shots, publicity, brochure, posters and print advertising.
Needs: Buys 10-20 images annually; 10-20 supplied by freelancers. Offers 10-20 assignments annually. Reviews stock photos. Model/property release required. Captions preferred.
Audiovisual Needs: Uses slides, film and videotape.
Specs: Uses 35mm, 2¼×2¼, 4×5 transparencies; 35mm, 16mm film; no less than Betacam videotape.
Making Contact & Terms: Interested in receiving work from newer, lesser-known photographers. Query with samples. Works on assignment only. Keeps samples on file. SASE. Pays $100-2,500/job.
Pays on acceptance. Credit line given. Buys all rights; negotiable.

*■MUST ROCK RSNY PRODUCTIONZ, c/o Jacobson & Colfin, Suite 434, 156 Fifth Ave., New York NY 10010. (212)691-5630. Fax: (212)645-5038. Attorney: Bruce Colfin. Estab. 1987. Handles rap and others. Freelancers used for in-concert shots and studio shots for cover/liner shots.
Needs: Buys few images annually. Model release required. Captions preferred.
Audiovisual Needs: Uses videotape. Subjects include entertainment.
Making Contact & Terms: Interested in receiving work from newer, lesser-known photographers. Send cover letter with SASE. Keeps samples on file. Reports in 3 weeks. NPI. Credit line given. Rights negotiable.

*NARADA PRODUCTIONS, 1845 N. Farwell Ave., Milwaukee WI 53202. (414)272-6700. Image Coordinator: Michele Frane. Estab. 1980. Produces adult contemporary instrumentals and New Age music. Photographers used for album covers and booklets.
Needs: Uses 20+ freelance photos/year. Captions preferred, especially if location is involved.
Specs: Uses all formats of color and b&w photographs.
Making Contact & Terms: Interested in receiving work from newer, lesser-known photographers. Send unsolicited photos. Send a limited number of your best pieces. Provide resume, business card, brochure, flyer, duplicate slides/transparencies, promotional pieces or tearsheets to be kept on file

for future reference. NPI; payment "varies depending on usage." Credit line given. Buys one-time, worldwide rights.

Tips: Images should be simple, graphic, powerful and dynamic. "Generally, work should be evocative of places and experiences and be something we've never seen before. We also need portraiture of artists. Send us unique work in a wide range of subject matter."

NEXT PLATEAU RECORDS, INC., Suite 1103, 1650 Broadway, New York NY 10019. (212)541-7640. Executive Vice President: Jenniene Leclereq. Estab. 1979. Handles R&B, dance, rap and crossover/ pop. Photographers used for portraits, in-concert shots, studio shots and video shoot shots for album covers, publicity and posters.

Needs: Offers 8-12 assignments/year. Wants to see "photos which could easily translate to an album cover (musicians/conceptual)."

Specs: Uses 8 × 10 glossy b&w prints.

Making Contact & Terms: Interested in receiving work from newer, lesser-known photographers. Send unsolicited photos by mail for consideration. Works with freelance photographers on assignment only. Cannot return unsolicited material. Photographers should follow up in 2-4 weeks. Pays $800-1,500/job for album work; pays less for promo shots. Buys all rights; negotiable.

NUCLEUS RECORDS, P.O. Box 111, Sea Bright NJ 07760. (201)823-8718. President: Robert Bowden. Estab. 1979. Handles rock, country. Photographers used for portraits, studio shots for publicity, posters and product advertising.

Needs: Send still photos of people for consideration. Model release preferred. Captions preferred.

Making Contact & Terms: Interested in receiving work from newer, lesser-known photographers. Works with freelance photographers on assignment basis only. SASE. Reports in 3 weeks. Pays $25-50/b&w photo; $75-150/color photo; $50-75/hour; $100-200/day; $500-1,000/job. Credit line given. Buys one-time rights and all rights; negotiable.

*■ONE STEP TO HAPPINESS MUSIC, c/o Jacobson & Colfin P.C., Suite 434, 156 Fifth Ave., New York NY 10010. (212)691-5630. Fax: (212)645-5038. Estab. 1987. Handles rock. Freelancers used for in-concert shots for cover/liner shots.

Needs: Buys 12 images annually; 12 supplied by freelancers. Offers 12 assignments annually. Interested in any type of material. Reviews stock photos. Model release required. Captions required.

Audiovisual Needs: Uses videotape. Subjects include entertainment.

Making Contact & Terms: Interested in receiving work from newer, lesser-known photographers. Send cover letter with SASE. Keeps samples on file. Reports in 3 weeks. NPI. Credit line given. Rights negotiable.

*■PDS COMMUNICATIONS, INC., P.O. Box 412477, Kansas City MO 64141. (800)473-7550. Public Relations Director: Carla Griffin. Estab. 1990. Handles R&B, jazz, pop, rap, house and others. Freelancers used for portraits, in-concert shots, studio shots, promotional and corporate for cover/liner, posters and event/convention coverage.

Needs: Buys 300-400 images annually; 200 supplied by freelancers. Offers 20-30 assignments annually. Interested in creative, conceptual. Model/property release preferred.

Audiovisual Needs: Uses slides, film and videotape for public relations, corporate, instructional.

Specs: Uses 8 × 10 glossy color and/or b&w prints; ¾" or VHS videotape.

Making Contact & Terms: Interested in receiving work from newer, lesser-kinown photographers. Query with resume of credits. Works with freelancers on assignment only. Does not keep samples on file. Cannot return material. Reports in 1 month. NPI. Pays upon usage. Credit line given. Buys all rights.

Tips: Photographers should be interested in "enhancing style and creativity while working within industry standards." Sees a trend toward "studio-style portraits with layout designs creating effects."

*PLAYBACK RECORDS/GALLERY II RECORDS, INC., P.O. Box 630755, Miami FL 33163. (305)935-4880. Fax: (305)933-4007. President: Jack Gale. Estab. 1983. Handles country. Uses portraits and in-concert shots for album covers, inside album shots, publicity and posters.

Specs: Uses b&w and color prints.

Making Contact & Terms: Send unsolicited photos by mail for consideration. Provide resume, business card, brochure, flyer or tearsheets to be kept on file for possible future assignments. Send 8 × 10 glossy color prints and poster album cover images. Cannot return material. Reports whenever need

The asterisk before a listing indicates that the market is new in this edition. New markets are often the most receptive to freelance submissions.

INSIDER REPORT

Success Within Music Industry Hinges on Access to the Stars

For Chicago-based photographer Paul Natkin, the entertainment industry has been a mixed bag. There are days of complete frustration, such as the day he had a public relations person standing beside him while he photographed actress Elizabeth Taylor. He was limited to 10 shots of Taylor and every time he snapped the shutter he was reminded what shot he was on. Talk about pressure to produce.

© Jol Dantzig

Paul Natkin

Then there are the good times, such as when a publicist for musician Prince asked Natkin to shoot photos during the recording star's birthday celebration in Minneapolis, Minnesota. Natkin fretted over the idea of spending money on an airplane ticket for the party, but eventually agreed to attend. "I figured if they were calling me they were calling everybody. It wasn't until I got there that I found out I was the only one," he says.

The event turned into a gold mine for Natkin because it took place right before Prince's album *Purple Rain* hit record stores, and before a movie by the same name appeared in theaters. At the party Natkin photographed the star while he performed wearing many of the outfits from the movie. He did not wear the clothes again during ensuing concerts. Whenever a magazine called Prince's agent to get shots of the star in those outfits they were directed to Natkin. "It was just luck," he says, remembering the incident.

Luck may have helped, but years of perseverance and dedication have led to Natkin's success. Since 1986 he has been staff photographer for The Oprah Winfrey Show, and in 1989 he served as official photographer during the Rolling Stones Steel Wheels Tour. He has shot album covers for various recording artists, such as Ozzy Osbourne, Johnny Winter and Styx, and his work often appears in top magazines, including *Rolling Stone, Newsweek* and *Parade*.

Natkin, who specializes in concert footage and studio and location portraiture, began his photography career in 1976. Over the years he has seen the music industry change in the way it deals with photographers. When he began, approaching performers was easy. Now, gaining adequate access has become a battle. "The main reason is they just don't want to be bothered and the easiest way not to be bothered is to not let anybody in, or give them really limited access and then get rid of them," he says.

Often such limitations mean that photographers only get a few minutes with recording artists. In order to overcome this problem Natkin spends a lot of time preparing for the shoot, picking out the proper location and using assistants to test lighting and exposures. Then, when the performer appears for the shoot, everything is ready.

For photographers who want to work with record companies, Natkin suggests they start out with smaller bands, rather than big stars to whom access is difficult. Record companies also respond to images that are published in magazines, he says. "When the magazine calls you up and asks you to shoot a band, more than likely you're going to have to call the publicist from the record company to get access," says Natkin. "Once you've done that, and they see your pictures in the magazine, especially if it is a reputable magazine, then it's going to be much easier to call them. At some point it's going to turn around. You're going to call them asking for access and they're going to say, 'Listen, we really need a new publicity shot of this guy. So think about it when you're shooting and if you get something we like, we'll buy it.'"

It's also very important to keep your files current. Musicians constantly change their physical appearance, both in the clothes they wear and the way they style their hair. Photographers also must be thick-skinned. "You're going to get turned down 90 percent of the time, but if you get something good the other 10 percent of the time, that's how you build a career."

— *Michael Willins*

© Paul Natkin

In recent years, photographer Paul Natkin of Chicago, Illinois, has seen a trend developing in the music industry, away from concert footage and toward portraiture. He has tried to capitalize on this movement with photos like this one of guitarist Keith Richards of the Rolling Stones.

arises. Pays per b&w or color photo or by the job. Credit line given. Buys one-time rights or all rights; negotiable.

THE PRESCRIPTION CO., 70 Murray Ave., Port Washington NY 11050. (516)767-1929. President: David F. Gasman. VP (A&R): Kirk Nordstrom. Tour Coordinator: Bill Fearn. Executive Vice President: John Bradley. Handles rock, soul and country & western. Uses photos for portraits, in-concert/studio shots and special effects for album covers, inside album shots, publicity flyers, brochures, posters, event/convention coverage and product advertising.
Specs: Uses b&w/color prints.
Making Contact & Terms: Arrange interview to show portfolio. "Send a flyer or tearsheets to be kept on file. Works on assignment only. Cannot return material. "We want no original photos submitted." NPI; payment negotiable. Rights negotiable.
Tips: "We're only a small company with sporadic needs. If interested we will set up an in-person meeting. There is always need for good photography in our business, but like most fields today, competition is growing stiffer. Art and technique are important, of course, but so is a professional demeanor when doing business."

PRO/CREATIVES, 25 W. Burda Pl., New City NY 10956-7116. President: David Rapp. Handles pop and classical. Photographers used for record album photos, men's magazines, sports, advertising illustrations, posters and brochures.
Making Contact & Terms: Query with examples, resume of credits and business card. SASE. Reports in 1 month. NPI. Buys all rights.

‡R.T.L. MUSIC/SWOOP RECORDS, Stewart House, Hill Bottom Rd., Sands-IND-EST, Highwycombe, Bucks, HP124HJ England. (063)064-7374. Fax: (063)064-7612. Owner: Ron Lee. Estab. 1970. Uses portraits, in-concert shots, studio shots and special effects for album covers, inside album shots, publicity, brochures, posters, event/convention coverage and product advertising.
Needs: Wants to see all types of photos. Examples of recent uses: "Nightmare" (front cover); "Daniel Boone" (front/back cover); and "Orphan" (front cover). Model release required. Photo captions required.
Specs: Uses 8×10 glossy or matte, b&w or color prints.
Making Contact & Terms: Interested in receiving work from newer, lesser-known photographers. Reports in 3 weeks. NPI. Credit line given. Buys all rights; negotiable.
Tips: Depending on the photographer's originality, "prospects can be very good."

RAPP PRODUCTIONS including RR & R Records, Rapp Records and Rapture and Ready Records, 1422 Meadow Ave., E. Lansing MI 48823 or RR & R Music Inc., # 204, 23 Music Sq. East, Nashville TN 37203. Publicity Coordinator: Beverly Bell. Estab. 1966. Handles Rapp Records, commercial all types; RR & R, all categories; Rapture Records, Christian music, all categories and Ready Records, promotional. Photographers used for portraits, in-concert shots, studio shots, special effects for album covers, publicity, brochures, posters, event/convention, product advertising.
Needs: Number of photos bought from freelancers per year varies. Subject matter varies. No fantasy or abstracts, porno, New Age or sadistic shots. Model/property release preferred. Captions required.
Specs: Uses all formats and sizes.
Making Contact & Terms: Rights negotiable. Send unsolicited photos by mail for consideration. Submit portfolio for review. SASE. Pays $50/b&w or color photo; $10/hour; $50/day; $10/job. Payment varies according to usage; negotiable. Buys one-time, exclusive product and all rights; negotiable.
Tips: "I'm not trying to promote art – only need promotional shots for music business, advertisement, photos of artist and album covers."

*ROADRUNNER RECORDS, Suite 407, 225 Lafayette Street, New York NY 10012. (212)219-0077. Director of Publicity: Susan Marcus. Estab. 1986. Handles heavy metal, hard rock, alternative, industrial. Photographers used for portraits, in-concert shots, studio shots and special effects for album covers, inside album shots and publicity.
Needs: Buys 20-30 photos/year.
Specs: Varies.
Making Contact & Terms: Provide resume, business card, brochure, flyer or tearsheets to be kept on file for possible future assignments. Does not return material. Reports in 3 weeks. Pays $200-1,000/job. Credit line given. Buys all rights, but may reassign to photographer.
Tips: Editor is looking for "variety, good composition and unique shots. Pay attention to both photo quality and creativity."

ROBBINS RECORDS, INC., HC80, Box 5B, Leesville LA 71446. National Representative: Sherree Angel. Estab. 1972. Handles religious, gospel and country. Photographers used for studio shots and special effects for album covers and publicity.

Needs: Offers variable assignments/year. Uses religious or gospel material for album covers.
Specs: Uses various size b&w or color prints.
Making Contact & Terms: Send material by mail for consideration. Provide resume, business card, brochure, flyer or tearsheets to be kept on file for possible future assignments. Works on assignment only. Cannot return material. Report time varies. NPI; pays agreed amount/job. Buys all rights; negotiable.
Tips: "Freelancers have a fair chance of working with record companies. Some special effects photography is being used."

*ROCK-A-BILLY RECORDS, P.O. Box 1622, Hendersonville TN 37077. (615)822-1044. Manager: S.D. Neal. Estab. 1975. Handles rock, jazz, New Age, rock-a-billy music. Freelancers used for in-concert shots, studio shots and special effects for cover/liner shots, inside shots, publicity, brochures, posters, event/convention coverage and print advertising.
Needs: Buys various number of images annually; all supplied by freelancers. Offers various number of assignments annually. Reviews stock photos. Model/property release preferred. Captions required.
Audiovisual Needs: Uses videotape.
Specs: Uses 3×5 color and b&w prints; videotape (5 minutes to 1 hour long).
Making Contact & Terms: Interested in receiving work from newer, lesser-known photographers. Submit portfolio for review. Query with resume of credits. Query with samples. Query with stock photo list. Provide resume, business card, self-promotion pieces or tearsheets to be kept on file for possible future assignments. Works on assignment only. Keeps samples on file. SASE. Reports in 3 weeks. NPI. **Pays on acceptance.** Credit line given. Rights negotiable.

ROCKIT RECORDS/SATELLITE MODELING STUDIOS, Suite 306, 35918 Union Lake Rd., Harrison Twp. MI 48045. (313)792-8452. Marketing Director: Joseph Trupiano. Estab. 1980. Handles rock, pop, pop/rock, country, heavy metal, r&b, rap, new age, jazz, dance. Freelancers used for portraits, in-concert shots, studio shots, special effects, seascape and landscape **with female models** for inside album shots, publicity, brochures, posters, event/convention coverage, product advertising, creative set.
Needs: Examples of recent uses: "Staying Power Vol 2" CD (photo used in insert); "Power Source Vol 3" CD (photo used in insert) and "Prelude to Power Vol 4" CD (photo used in insert). Model/property release required. Photo captions preferred.
Specs: Uses 8×10 glossy b&w and color prints.
Making Contact & Terms: Interested in receiving work from newer, lesser-known photographers. Send samples of best work, resume, portfolio if possible. SASE. Reports in 1 month. NPI; pays by the job, amount depends on client negotiation. Credit line given. Buys one-time rights; negotiable.
Tips: "We solicit poster companies, record companies, advertisers, magazines. Our requirements are female models in: tropical scenes, beach scenes, exotic scenes, sensual looks, etc. Be creative with your set design. Use lots of satin backdrops, floor coverings (satin), pillows (African props such as zebra, leopard, tiger, type of pillows and fabrics). Color up your lighting by using yellows, reds, greens, etc. More and more uses for innovative and creative shots are in demand. These type photos will always assist in the sales of our products. The more appealing it is to the consumer, the better the chances of making that sale. We presently are accepting photos of 'female models' for our record company products (compact disc inserts) released by our affiliate record label, Rockit Records, Inc. Should your photo be accepted it will gain recognition for the photographer on a 'worldwide level.' "

ROCKWELL RECORDS, P.O. Box 1127, Haverhill MA 01831. (508)373-5677. President: Bill Macek. Produces top 40 and rock 'n' roll records. Photographers used for live action shots, studio shots and special effects for album covers, inside album shots, publicity, brochures and posters. Photos used for jacket design and artist shots.
Needs: Buys 1-2 photos and offers 1-2 assignments/year. Freelancers supply 100% of photos. Interested in seeing all types of photos. "No restrictions. I may see something in a portfolio I really like and hadn't thought about using."
Making Contact & Terms: Arrange a personal interview. Submit b&w and color sample photos by mail for consideration. Submit portfolio for review. Provide brochure, calling card, flyer or resume to be kept on file for possible future assignments. Local photographers preferred, but will review work of photographers from anywhere. SASE. NPI; payment varies.

ROLL ON RECORDS®, 112 Widmar Pl., Clayton CA 94517. (510)672-8201. Owner: Edgar J. Brincat. Estab. 1986. Handles country, rock, R&B, pop/soul, gospel, middle of the road, easy listening. Photographers used for portraits, in-concert shots, studio shots and special effects for album covers, inside album shots and publicity.

Needs: Offers 2-4 assignments/year.

Specs: Uses various sizes, glossy b&w or color prints.

Making Contact & Terms: Query with resume of credits. Provide resume, business card, brochure, flyer or tearsheets to be kept on file for possible future assignments. Works with freelancers on assignment only. SASE. Reports in 2 weeks. Pays $300-1,500/b&w photo; $400-2,000/color photo; negotiable. Credit line given. Buys all rights.

Tips: "We expect an itemized contract and a price that does not change" when working with freelancers. The future outlook is "very good" for freelancers.

SIRR RODD RECORD & PUBLISHING CO., 2453 77th Ave., Philadelphia PA 19150-1820. President/ A&R: Rodney Jerome Keitt. Handles R&B, jazz, top 40, rap, pop, gospel and soul. Uses photographers for portraits, in-concert shots, studio shots and special effects for album covers, inside album shots, publicity, posters, event/convention and product advertising.

Needs: Buys 10 (minimum) photos/year.

Specs: Uses 8×10 glossy b&w or color prints.

Making Contact & Terms: Submit portfolio for review. Provide resume, business card, brochure, flyer or tearsheets to be kept on file for possible future assignments. SASE. Reports in 1 month. Pays $40-200/b&w photo; $60-250/color photo; $75-450/job. Credit line given. Buys all rights, negotiable.

Tips: "We look for the total versatility of the photographer. Of course, you can show us the more common group photos, but we like to see new concepts in group photography. Remember that you are freelancing. You do not have the name, studio, or reputation of 'Big Time' photographers, so we both are working for the same thing—exposure! If your pieces are good and the quality is equally good, your chances of working with record companies are excellent. Show your originality, ability to present the unusual, and what 'effects' you have to offer."

*‡SOUND CEREMONY RECORDS, 23 Selby Rd E11, London, England. (08)15031687. Managing Director: Ron Warren Ganderton. Handles rock. Uses photographers for portraits, in-concert shots, studio shots and glamour shots promotion for album covers, inside album shots, publicity, posters and product advertising.

Needs: Buys up to 75 photos/year. "Any interest welcomed. All types of material will be considered as we are involved in diverse, versatile events."

Specs: Uses various sizes; b&w and color prints.

Making Contact & Terms: Query with resume of credits. Send unsolicited photos by mail for consideration. Provide resume, business card, brochure, flyer or tearsheets to be kept on file for possible future assignments. Does not return unsolicited material. Reports in 2 weeks; international, 3 weeks. NPI. "All pay depends on negotiation." Credit line given. Buys one-time rights, all rights; negotiable.

Tips: Prefers to see diverse samples.

*‡SPHEMUSATIONS, 12 Northfield Rd., One house, Stomarket Suffolk 1P14 3HF England. 0449-613388. General Manager: James Butt. Handles classical, country and western. Photographers used for portraits, in-concert shots, studio shots, special effects and ensemble portraits for album covers, inside album shots, publicity, brochures, posters, event/convention coverage and product advertising.

Needs: Gives 2-6 assignments/year. "Prefers to see good portraits of artists, and album cover to which the photographer has contributed work. Especially wants to see pictures which show a sense of character and culture."

Specs: Uses glossy b&w or color prints.

Making Contact & Terms: Send unsolicited photos by mail for consideration. Submit portfolio for review. Provide resume, business card, brochure, flyer or tearsheets to be kept on file for possible future assignments. Works with freelance photographers on assignment basis only. SAE, IRC. Reports in 1 month. Pays $10-1,000/b&w photo; $50-2,000/color photo; $5-25/hour; $30-175/day; $25-2,500/job. Credit line given. Buys all rights but may reassign rights; negotiable.

Tips: Chances of working with record companies are many, varied, and excellent. There is a trend toward visually sensitive, perceptive photography, which reveals something more than simple surface— values.

Market conditions are constantly changing! If you're still using this book and it's 1995 or later, buy the newest edition of Photographer's Market *at your favorite bookstore or order directly from Writer's Digest Books.*

*STRADER ENTERTAINMENT, Suite 203, 920 N. Wilcox Ave., Los Angeles CA 90038. (213)463-3209. President/CEO: James Strader. Estab. 1985. Handles rock, acid jazz and rhythm and blues. Freelancers used for portraits, in-concert shots and studio shots for publicity, brochures, posters and print advertising.
Needs: Buys 4 images annually; offers 24 assignments annually. Reviews stock photos. Model release required.
Specs: Uses 8×10 matte b&w prints, 8×10 transparencies.
Making Contact & Terms: Provide resume, business card, self-promotion pieces or tearsheets to be kept on file for possible future assignments. Keeps samples on file. Reports in 1 month. Pays $50-125/hour; $350-1,200/day; $50-300/color photo; $50-200/b&w photo. Pays on acceptance; credit line depends on usage. Buys all rights.
Tips: "We provide personal management for actors, comedians and musicians. We are using more innovative pieces that are eye-catching for posters, calendars and point-of-purchase."

SUSAN RECORDS, P.O. Box 1622, Hendersonville TN 37077-1622. Manager: S.D. Neal. Estab. 1970. Handles rock and country. Uses in-concert shots, studio shots and special effects for album covers, inside album shots, publicity, brochures, posters, event/convention coverage and product advertising.
Specs: Uses any size or format b&w/color.
Making Contact & Terms: Send unsolicited photos by mail for consideration. Submit portfolio for review. Works with freelance photographers on assignment only. SASE. Reports in 3 weeks. NPI; payment negotiable. Pays per b&w photo and per color photo. Credit line given. Buys one-time rights.
Tips: Observes that opportunities are good. Sees trend toward use of many concert shots.

*■MICK TAYLOR MUSIC, % Jacobson & Colfin, P.C., Suite 434, 156 Fifth Ave., New York NY 10010. (212)691-5630. Fax: (212)645-5038. Attorney: Bruce E. Colfin. Estab. 1986. Handles rock. Freelancers used for portraits for cover/liner.
Needs: Buys 12 images annually; 12 supplied by freelancers. Offers 12 assignments annually. Interested in all types of music-related material. Reviews stock photos. Model release required. Captions required.
Audiovisual Needs: Uses videotape. Subjects include entertainment (music).
Making Contact & Terms: Interested in receiving work from newer, lesser-known photographers. Send cover letter with SASE. Keeps samples on file. Reports in 3 weeks. NPI. Credit line given. Rights negotiable.

TEROCK RECORDS, P.O. Box 1622, Hendersonville TN 37077. Secretary: S.D. Neal. Handles rock, soul and country records. Uses photographers for in-concert and studio shots for album covers, inside album shots, publicity flyers, brochures, posters and product advertising.
Making Contact & Terms: Send material by mail for consideration. SASE. Reports in 3 weeks. NPI. Pays per job. "Photographers have to set a price." Credit line given.

*TIME-LIFE MUSIC, 777 Duke St., Alexandria VA 22314. (703)838-6916. Fax: (703)838-6915. Photo Editor: Eleanor Kask. Estab. 1960. Handles rock, jazz, hit parade and classical. Freelancers used for portraits, in-concert shots, studio shots, special effects for CD covers, inside booklet and as art reference.
Needs: Buys "a lot" of images annually. Wants to see Xerox copies. Model/property release preferred. Captions preferred.
Specs: Uses 8×10 glossy color and/or b&w prints; 35mm, 4×5 transparencies.
Making Contact & Terms: Interested in receiving work from newer, lesser-known photographers. Query with samples. Keeps samples on file. SASE. Reports after publication. NPI. Pays upon usage. Credit line given. Buys one-time rights.

*UAR RECORDS, P.O. Box 1264, Peoria IL 61654. (309)673-5755. Fax: (309)673-5755. Owner: Jerry Hanlon. Estab. 1968. Handles country, country rock, Christian. Freelancers used for portraits for cover/liner shots and publicity.
Needs: Reviews stock photos. Scenery (country scenes, water scenes), churches.
Specs: Uses color and/or b&w prints; 4×5 transparencies.
Making Contact & Terms: Interested in receiving work from newer, lesser-known photographers. Submit portfolio for review. Provide resume, business card, self-promotion pieces or tearsheets to be kept on file for possible future assignments. Works with freelancers on assignment only. Keeps samples on file. Cannot return material. Reports in 1 month. NPI. Pays upon usage.

Record Companies/'93-'94 changes

The following markets appeared in the 1993 edition of *Photographer's Market* but are not listed in the 1994 edition. They may have been omitted for failing to respond to our request for updated information, they may have gone out of business or they may no longer wish to receive freelance work.

Antone's Records (did not respond)
Brentwood Music (did not respond)
Camex (did not respond)
DOVentertainment (did not respond)
Dynamite Records (did not respond)
Four Winds Record Productions (did not respond)
Geffen Records (did not respond)
Invasion/GNA Records (did not respond)
IRS Records (did not respond)
Island Records (did not respond)
Landmark Communications Group (did not respond)
Laser Records & Music Pty (did not respond)
Legs Records-A.J. Promotions (did not respond)
Lone Wolf (did not respond)
Mr. Wonderful Productions (did not respond)
Nightstar Records (did not respond)
Northeastern Records (did not respond)
Original Sound Record Co. (did not respond)
Relativity Records (did not respond)
Solar Records (did not respond)
Sound Achievement Group (did not respond)
Sparrow Corporation (did not respond)
Storyville Records AB (did not respond)
Transworld Records (did not respond)
Mike Vaccaro Productions (did not respond)
Windham Hill Productions (did not respond)

Stock Photo Agencies

Whether you are a well-established photographer who has built up a strong client base or a newcomer trying to find beginning markets, stock can become an important source of income for you. Year after year more corporations are finding out about stock and, instead of hiring photographers to tackle assignments, they are turning to stock agencies for images. This trend will continue and it's up to you to take advantage of such business practices and make them work for you.

Stock agencies are blossoming all over the world, supplying clients with images for advertisements, editorial work, brochures or annual reports. In this section you will find around 200 different agencies, some with very specific collections of work, others with more general topics, such as people, fashion, sports and industrial locations. Whatever your specialty, there is an agency out there for you.

As you begin to build your stock files there are a number of ways to go about it. First, take every situation or event and consider it a viable subject for a stock photo. This could mean your child's dance classes or baseball games, birthday parties or normal social gatherings. The important thing is to shoot often and edit the work before you submit images to an agency.

Rebecca Taylor, of FPG International Stock Agency in New York City, says quite often photographers do not realize how much stock they need to shoot to be successful. Taylor provides more thoughts regarding the stock industry as the subject of our Insider Report on page 498.

In each listing we have tried to include information regarding submissions. Most agencies require a photographer to supply a certain number of images as an initial submission, and then provide more photos at various intervals. This information is usually shown in the phrase, "Expects minimum initial submission of (#) images with periodic submissions of at least (#) images."

When working with stock agencies it is imperative that your images have model or property releases. Photos with releases have more earning potential than those without. For that reason, most agencies require releases for all images they keep on file. If you do not know when such forms are necessary check out the information regarding releases on page 21 in the Business of Photography.

The computer revolution

On the whole, the industry is in the middle of a revolution as computer technology makes it easier to store, manipulate and display images. Software

Ethical guidelines for stock

Before a photographer signs a contract with a stock photo agency, he needs some guarantee of fair treatment. The Picture Agency Council of America (PACA) has established a set of ethical guidelines to which all members in the council must adhere in order to retain their memberships. These guidelines are a good check list for the photographer to use when prospecting for an agency or negotiating his contract.

PACA members will openly and freely discuss with photographers:
- *Ownership of agency, and/or change thereof.*
- *Editing, inventory and refiling procedures.*
- *Disposition of any suit or settlement pertaining to a specific photographer's work, including documentation if requested.*
- *International representation policies.*
- *Policies regarding free or reduced rate usages for charitable organizations.*
- *Sub agency or franchise representation policies.*

Membership agencies should also offer photographers a fair and straightforward written contract, which should address such items as:
- *Payment schedule.*
- *Right to inspect agency records as they pertain to the individual photographer.*
- *Contract period and renewal.*
- *Charges, deductions or assessments related to the photographer's account.*
- *Procedure and schedule for return of photographs upon termination of contract.*

Also royalty statements should include:
- *An adequate photo description.*
- *A description or code for the usage.*
- *The amount of the photographer's share.*
- *An itemization of any deductions that are made.*

such as Adobe Photoshop (which now caters to users of Macintosh and IBM PC computers), Aldus PhotoStyler and Micrografix Picture Publisher provide photographers with a variety of imaging enhancement options. Introduced in 1992, the Kodak Photo CD also has become a viable way for photographers to market their images to corporations, advertising firms or design studios. CDs will hold dozens of images and can be marketed to clients who can buy a disk for a one-time fee. For more on computer technology, see the Business of Photography section at the front of this book.

Although there are many photographers who are finding ways to benefit from such technological changes, others are afraid that the industry will suffer from unethical practices. For example, photos now can be scanned into computers and altered through digital manipulation into something unrecognizable, even to the original photographer. Numerous images can be combined into one. Such technology will make it more difficult to catch copyright infringers.

There also is concern that clients who purchase CDs at rather low prices will use the images over and over again without having to pay extra for the work. There is no way to tell which images are used, and a handful of images out of 100 may be used over and over again. However, photographers receive payment based on the images they have on the disks, not based on the number of times their images are used.

One organization which hopes to combat some of these potential problems is the American Society of Media Photographers. ASMP has formed a copyright collective designed to work with CD-ROM producers in creating disks at a reasonable profit for photographers. The collective, known as the Media Photographers' Copyright Agency, also will work to protect copyrights.

Much of this technology is being adapted by stock photo agencies, which want to stay competitive in a very busy marketplace. For example, Gamma Liaison, an agency based in New York City, has begun storing images on videodisks that are linked to a database. The move is designed to improve the efficiency of photo searches and distribution. Other agencies are digitally storing their images.

Keep in touch

Because of all these changes you should study agency contracts, request copies of their guidelines and find out how they plan to market your work. For example, some agencies are willing to place images on clip art disks while others have campaigned against such practices. Most firms are reputable, but some are either unethical in their practices or have not yet acquired proper organization and professionalism. By understanding how various agencies operate you will know which ones you want to have marketing your work. You can find more information on choosing a stock agency in the Business of Photography section.

There are a number of helpful references and organizations that will assist you in learning more about the stock industry and its standard practices. The following sources also can help you stay in touch with industry trends: *Taking-Stock*, a newsletter published six times a year by stock photo expert Jim Pickerell (301)251-0720; the *ASMP Stock Photography Handbook,* published by the

American Society of Media Photographers (212)889-9144; and the Picture Agency Council of America, contact PACA President Paul Henning at (800)457-7222.

*■★AAA IMAGE MAKERS, Suite 301, 337 W. Pender St., Vancouver, British Columbia V6B 1T3 Canada. (604)688-3001. Owner: Reimut Lieder. Art Director: Trina Holt. Estab. 1981. Stock photo agency. Has 150,000 photos. Clients include: advertising agencies, public relations firms, audiovisual firms, businesses, book/encyclopedia publishers, magazine and textbook publishers, postcard publishers, calendar companies and greeting card companies.
Needs: People, families, business, travel and "much more. We provide our photographers with a current needs list on a regular basis."
Specs: Uses 8×10 glossy or pearl b&w prints; 35mm, 2¼×2¼, 4×5 and 8×10 transparencies.
Payment & Terms: Pays 50% commission on color and b&w. Average price per image: $300-500/b&w; $400/color. Enforces minimum prices. Offers volume discount to customers; terms specified in photographer's contract. Discount sales terms not negotiable. Works on contract basis only. Offers limited regional exclusivity, guaranteed subject exclusivity. Charges 50% duping fee, 50% catalog insertion. Statements issued quarterly. Payment made quarterly. Photographers allowed to review account records. Rights negotiated by client needs. Does not inform photographer or allow him to negotiate when client requests all rights. Model release preferred. "All work must be marked 'MR' or 'NMR' for model release or no model release. Photo captions required.
Making Contact: Interested in receiving work from newer, lesser-known photographers. Arrange personal interview to show portfolio. Submit portfolio for review. Query with resume of credits. Query with samples. Send SASE with letter of inquiry, resume, business card, flyer, tearsheets or samples. Samples kept on file. Expects minimum initial submission of 200 images. Reports in 2-3 weeks. Photo guideline sheet free with SASE. Market tips sheet distributed quarterly to all photographers on contract; free with SASE.
Tips: "As we do not have submission minimums, be sure to edit your work ruthlessly. We expect quality work to be submitted on a regular basis. Research your subject completely and shoot shoot shoot!!"

AAA STOCK PHOTOGRAPHY, 32 Spring St., Wallington NJ 07057. (201)773-7966. Fax: (201)773-7966. "Call before faxing." Reviewer: Jeff Greenberg. Estab. 1988. Picture library. Has 100,000 photos. Clients include: textbook publishers, magazine publishers, religious publishing houses and travel industry.
Needs: Images used by magazine publishers and religious publishing houses. Slides that usually sell well include: candids of people of all ages, all colors, all cultures and countries in daily activities at home, school, work, play, pray, etc. Also inspirational and moody scenics, nature, symbolic images. "AAA supplies photos mainly to religious publishers."
Specs: Uses 35mm transparencies.
Payment & Terms: Pays 60% commission and passes on documentation and samples of published work "if provided by publisher." Publishers pay ranges from $50-250/slide for one-time use. Payment passed on immediately. Buys one-time and electronic media rights.
Making Contact: Interested in receiving work from newer, lesser-known photographers. "By sending your slides to AAA, you agree: that AAA and the publishers are never responsible for your slides or their value in any way and that these slides will circulate permanently and never return to you. AAA keeps no records other than your name and address, so correspondence will occur only when AAA sends you payment or when you send more surplus slides in 20-count slides sheets to AAA."
Tips: "We are the only agency in the world that gives photographers a way to make money from surplus slides. Surplus slides are outtakes, extras, duplicates, and other slides which take up space and are not as important to you as your better slides. Send them in 20-count slide sheets with your name on each slide. AAA will circulate all your slides in their slide sheets from publisher to publisher continuously and permanently. We accept all photographers."

‡ACTION PRESS, Kollaustr. 64-66, 2000 Hamburg 54 Germany. (040)55-49-000. Fax: (040)580-888. Contact: Renate Meier. Estab. 1970. Stock photo agency. News/feature syndicate. Has 8 million photos. Has branch office in 3 other cities. Clients include: book/encyclopedia publishers, magazine publishers and newspapers.
Needs: Actual events, people, movies, show-biz and landscapes.
Specs: Uses 35mm transparencies.
Payment & Terms: Pays 40-60% commission on color photos. Average price per image (to clients): $80-100/b&w; $100-200/color. Negotiates fees below standard minimum prices. Offers volume discounts to customers; inquire about specific terms. Photographer can choose not to sell images on discount terms. Works with or without a contract; limited regional exclusivity. Statements issued

monthly. Payment made monthly. Offers one-time rights. Model/property release required. Captions required.
Making Contact: Query with samples. Query with stock photo list. Samples kept on file. Expects minimum initial submission of 100 images with periodic submission of about 400-800 images/month. Reports in 1 month. Market tips sheet distributed quarterly upon request.

ADVENTURE PHOTO, Suite 202, 56 E. Main St., Ventura CA 93001. (805)643-7751. Fax: (805)643-4423. Estab. 1987. Stock agency. Member of Picture Agency Council of America (PACA). Has 125,000 photos. Clients include: advertising agencies, public relations firms, businesses, magazine publishers, calendar and greeting card companies.
Needs: Adventure Photo offers its clients 5 principle types of images: Adventure Sports (sailing, windsurfing, rock climbing, skiing, mountaineering, mountain biking, etc.), Adventure Travel (all fifty states as well as third world and exotic locations.), Landscapes, Environmental and Wildlife.
Specs: Uses 35mm, 2¼ × 2¼ and 4 × 5 transparencies.
Payment & Terms: Pays 50% commission on color photos. Works on contract basis only. Offers nonexclusive contract. Contracts renew automatically with each submission; time period not specified. Statements issued monthly. Payment made monthly. Photographers allowed to review sales figures. Offers one-time rights; occasionally negotiates exclusive and unlimited use rights. "We notify photographers and work to settle on acceptable fee when client requests all rights." Model release required. Captions required, include description of subjects, locations and persons.
Making Contact: Write to photo editor for copy of submission guidelines. SASE. Reports in 1 month. Photo guidelines free with SASE.
Tips: In freelancer's portfolio or samples, wants to see "well-exposed, well-lit transparencies (reproduction quality). Unique outdoor sports, travel and wilderness images. We love to see shots of this subject matter that portray metaphors commonly used in ad business (risk taking, teamwork, etc.)." To break in, "we request new photographers send us 2-4, 20-image sheets they feel are representative of their work. Then when we sign a photographer, we pass ideas to them regularly about the kinds of shots our clients are requesting, and we pass them any ideas we get too. Then we counsel our photographers always to look at magazines and advertisements to stay current on the kinds of images art directors and agencies are using."

■**AMERICAN STOCK PHOTOGRAPHY**, Dept. PM, Suite 716, 6255 Sunset Blvd., Hollywood CA 90028. (213)469-3900. President: Christopher C. Johnson. Manager: Darrell Presho. Stock photo agency. Has 2+ million photos. Clients include: advertising agencies, public relations firms, audiovisual firms, businesses, book/encyclopedia publishers, magazine publishers, newspapers, postcard companies, calendar companies, greeting card companies and TV and movie production companies.
Needs: General stock, all categories. Special emphasis upon California scenics and lifestyles.
Specs: Uses 35mm, 2¼ × 2¼, 4 × 5 transparencies; b&w contact sheets; b&w negatives.
Payment & Terms: Buys photos outright; pays $5-20. Pays 50% commission. General price range: $100-750. Offers one-time rights. Model release required. Captions required.
Making Contact: Contact Camerique Inc., 1701 Skippack Pk., P.O. Box 175, Blue Bell, PA 19422. (215)272-4000. SASE. Reports in 1 week. Photo guidelines free with SASE. Tips sheet distributed quarterly to all active photographers with agency; free with SASE.

■‡**THE ANCIENT ART & ARCHITECTURE COLLECTION**, 6 Kenton Rd., Harrow-on-the-Hill, Middlesex HA1 2BL London, England. (81)422-1214. Contact: The Librarian. Picture library. Has 200,000 photos. Clients include: public relations firms, audiovisual firms, book/encyclopedia publishers, magazine publishers and newspapers.
Specs: Uses 35mm, 2¼ × 2¼, 4 × 5 or 8 × 10 transparencies.
Payment & Terms: Pays 50% commission. Works with photographers on contract basis only. Offers non-exclusive rights. Contracts renew automatically with additional submissions. Statements issued quarterly. Payment made quarterly. Offers one-time rights. Fully detailed captions required.
Making Contact: Query with samples and list of stock photo subjects. SASE. Reporting time not specified.
Tips: "Material must be suitable for our specialist requirements. We cover historical and archeological periods from 25,000 BC to the 19th century AD, worldwide. All civilizations, cultures, religions, objects and artifacts as well as art are includable. Pictures with tourists, cars, TV aerials, and other modern intrusions not accepted."

The double dagger before a listing indicates that the market is located outside the United States and Canada.

■‡ANDES PRESS AGENCY, 26 Padbury Ct., London E2 7EH England. (071)739-3159. Director: Carlos Reyes. Picture library and news/feature syndicate. Has 500,000 photos. Clients include: audiovisual firms, book/encyclopedia publishers, magazine publishers and newspapers.

Needs: "We have a large collection of photographs on social, political and economic aspects of Latin America, Africa, Asia, Europe and Britain, specializing in contemporary world religions."

Specs: Uses 8×10 glossy b&w prints; 35mm and 2¼×2¼ transparencies; b&w contact sheets and negatives.

Payment & Terms: Pays 50% commission for b&w and color photos. General price range: £50-200/ b&w photo; £50-300/color photo; (British currency). Enforces minimum prices. Works on contract basis only. Offers nonexclusive contract. Statements issued quarterly. Payment made quarterly. Photographers allowed to review account records to verify sales figures. Offers one-time rights. Informs photographer and allows him to negotiage when client requests all rights. "We never sell all rights, photographer has to negotiate if interested." Model/property release preferred. Captions required.

Making Contact: Interested in receiving work from newer, lesser-known photographers. Query with samples. Send stock photo list. SASE. Reports in 1 week. Photo guidelines free with SASE.

Tips: "We want to see that the photographer has mastered one subject in depth. Also, we have a greater market for photo-features as opposed to stock photos only."

■ANIMALS ANIMALS/EARTH SCENES, 17 Railroad Ave., Chatham NY 12037. (518)392-5500. Branch office: Suite 1111, 580 Broadway, New York NY 10012. (212)925-2110. President: Eve Kloepper. Member of Picture Agency Council of America (PACA). Has 850,000 photos. Clients include: ad agencies, public relations firms, businesses, audiovisual firms, book publishers, magazine publishers, encyclopedia publishers, newspapers, postcard companies, calendar companies and greeting card companies.

Needs: "We specialize in nature photography with an emphasis on all animal life."

Specs: Uses 8×10 glossy or matte b&w prints; 35mm and some larger format color transparencies.

Payment & Terms: Pays 50% commission. Offers one-time rights; other uses negotiable. Model release required if used for advertising. Captions required, include Latin names, and "they must be correct!"

Making Contact: Send material by mail for consideration. SASE. Reports in 1-2 months. Free photo guidelines with SASE. Tips sheet distributed regularly to established contributors.

Tips: "First, pre-edit your material. Second, know your subject."

ANTHRO—PHOTO FILE, 33 Hurlbut St., Cambridge MA 02138. (617)868-4784, 497-7227. President/ Owner: Nancy S. DeVore. Stock photo agency. Has approximately 10,000 color photos, 2,000 b&w photos. Clients include: book/encyclopedia publishers, magazine publishers and newspapers; *Primate Societies* by Smuts, U.Chicago Press (photos of monkeys and apes); *Discover* magazine, article on chimpanzees; and *Cultural Anthropology*, by Haviland, Holt, Rinehart, Winston (photos of various peoples).

Needs: Anthropology and biology.

Specs: Uses 8×10 glossy b&w prints; 35mm and 2¼×2¼ transparencies.

Payment & Terms: Pays 40% commission to agency, 60% to photographer. Pays $125-600/b&w photo; $160-800/color photo. Works with or without signed contract, negotiable. Offers guaranteed subject exclusivity within files. Contracts renew automatically with each submission; time period not specified. Charges duping fee at cost/image. Statements issued annually. Payment made annually, within one month of end of cycle. Photographers allowed to review account records to verify sales figures. Buys one-time rights. Informs photographer and allows him to negotiate when client requests all rights. Model/property release preferred for US people close-up. Captions required; include description of action, people and place.

Making Contact: Query with samples; "send 25 dupes labeled with name and caption." SASE.

Tips: Prefers to see behavioral/anthropological emphasis. "Send duplicates or prints labeled and captioned with emphasis on the important topics for anthrotexts and biology texts; sociology texts; geography and social studies texts. Look at the current best selling texts. There is an increasing need for illustratiing culture change and environmental pollution."

*■‡APL ARGUS PHOTOLAND, Room 2106 Goldmark, 502 Hennessy Rd., Hong Kong. (852)890-6970. Fax: (852)881-6979. Director: Joan Li. Estab. 1992. Stock photo agency. Has 120,000 photos. Has one branch office. Clients include: advertising agencies, public relations firms, audiovisual firms, businesses, book/encyclopedia publishers, magazine publishers, postcard publishers, calendar companies, greeting card companies and mural printing companies.

Needs: "We handle general subject matters. Our specific needs are people in all situations, including people in business/sport. We also look for beautiful natural scenics and cityscapes, wildlife and computer graphics. All in high quality."

Specs: Uses 35mm, 2¼×2¼ and 4×5 transparencies.
Payment & Terms: Pays 50-60% commission. Offers volume discounts to customers; inquire about specific terms. Photographers can choose not to sell images on discount terms. Works on contract basis only. Offers limited regional exclusivity. Contracts renew automatically with additional submissions. Charges 100% duping fees. Statements issued monthly. Payment made monthly. Photographers allowed to review account records. Offers one-time rights. Informs photographer and allows him to negotiate when client requests all rights. Model/property releases preferred. Photo captions required; include name of event(s), name of building(s), location and geographical area.
Making Contact & Terms: Interested in receiving work from newer, lesser-known photographers. Submit portfolio for review. Samples not kept on file. SASE. Expects minimum initial submission of 500-1,000 pieces with periodic submission of at least 500 images quarterly. Reports in 1-2 weeks. Photo guidelines free with SASE. Market tips sheet distributed upon request; free with SASE.

*APPALIGHT, Box 89-C, Griffith Run Rd., Spencer WV 25276. (304)927-2978. Fax: (304)927-3650. Director: Chuck Wyrostok. Estab. 1988. Stock photo agency. Has 20,000 photos. Clients include advertising agencies, public relations firms, businesses, book/encyclopedia publishers, magazine publishers, calendar companies, greeting card companies and graphic designers.
Needs: General subject matter with emphasis on child development, inspirational, city scapes, travel. Special need for African-American and Hispanic people/lifestyles, active seniors, teens, handicapped people coping, US vacation spots. "Presently we're building comprehensive sections on the entire Pacific region and on positive solutions to environmental problems of all kinds."
Specs: Uses 8×10, glossy b&w prints; 35mm, 2¼×2¼, 4×5 transparencies.
Payment & Terms: Pays 50% commission on b&w and color photos. General price range: $150 and up. Works on contract basis only. Offers nonexclusive rights. Charges 100% duping rate. Statements issued quarterly. Payment made quarterly. Photographers allowed to review account records during regular business hours or by appointment. Offers one-time rights, electronic media rights. "When client requests all rights photographer is contacted for his consent, but we handle all negotiations." Model release preferred. Captions required; include who, what, where and Latin names when needed.
Making Contact: Query with stock photo list. Samples not kept on file. SASE. Expects minimum initial submission of 300-500 images with periodic submissions of 200-300 several times/year. Reports in 1 month. Photo guidelines sheet free with SASE. Market tips sheet distributed "periodically" to contracted photographers.
Tips: "We look for a solid blend of topnotch technical quality, style, content and impact contained in images that portray metaphors applying to ideas, moods, business, endeavors, risk-taking, teamwork and winning."

*■ART RESOURCE, 9th Floor, 65 Bleecker St., New York NY 10012. (212)505-8700. Fax: (212)420-9286. Permissions Director: Joanne Greenbaum. Estab. 1970. Stock photo agency specializing in fine arts. Member of the Picture Agency Council of America (PACA). Has access to 3 million photos. Clients include: advertising agencies, public relations firms, audiovisual firms, businesses, book/encyclopedia publishers, magazine publishers, newspapers, postcard publishers, calendar companies, greeting card companies and all other publishing and scholarly businesses.
Needs: Painting, sculpture, architecture only.
Specs: Uses 8×10 b&w prints; 35mm, 4×5, 8×10 transparencies.
Payment & Terms: NPI. Average price per image: $75-500/b&w; $185-10,000/color. Negotiates fees below standard minimum prices. Offers volume discounts to customers; terms specified in photographer's contract. Discount sales terms not negotiable. Offers exclusive only or nonexclusive rights. Contracts renew automatically with additional submissions. Statements issued quarterly. Payment made quarterly. Photographers allowed to review account records. Offers one-time rights, electronic media rights, agency promotion and other negotiated rights. Does not inform photographer or allow him to negotiate when client requests all rights. Photo captions required.
Making Contact: Query with stock photo list. "Only fine art!" Cannot return material.
Tips: "We only represent European fine art archives and museums in US and Europe, but occasionally represent a photographer with a specialty in certain art."

ATLANTA STOCK ASSOCIATES, P.O. Box 723093, Atlanta GA 31139. (404)434-8363. Fax: (404)435-7835. President: Betsy Harbison. Photo Editor: Don Holebrooks. Estab. 1987. Southeastern regional stock photo agency. Southeastern Agency Rep. for Ewing Galloway, New York. Has over 1 million slides. Clients include: ad agencies, public relations firms, audiovisual firms, corporate clients, book/ encyclopedia publishers, magazine publishers, trade show/exhibit manufacturers.
Needs: Specializes in Southeastern images, but "general practitioner. We want to see a photographer's view of the world around him." People and their lifestyles, occupations, industry, transportation, plants and animals, major cities and travel destinations, abstracts, scenics and still lifes. "Each image must be able to stand alone if necessary." Critically needs model-released shots of ordinary people, all ages, all races in a variety of daily activities as a single, in family structure, corporate, and in peer

group portrait model-released shots of ethnics, including African-American, hispanic, oriental. Major issues include wellness, health, nutrition, ecology, pollution and recycling worldwide, city skylines, historic locations, area festivals, education at any level and holiday scenics.

Specs: "Tack sharp" images, simple backgrounds void of unrelated material. Successful shots have proper placement in frame for subject and effective use of dead space for copy. Verticals with various angles and distances from the same subject are best. 35mm transparencies are base format; larger formats acceptable, "but must be individually mounted with protection covering film."

Payment & Terms: Pays 50% commission on use fees ranging from $125 and up. Requires exclusivity within Southeastern US. Statements issued quarterly. Payment made quarterly if under $300, at time of sale if over $300. Offers one-time rights; CD-ROM rights and exclusivity "only on photographer's written permission." Model/property release preferred. Captions required. Wants 300 acceptable original images as minimum to start contract and 300 each succeeding year. Contracts renew for three years with additional submissions.

Making Contact: Query with letter stating photographer's interest and photo background to request guidelines. SASE for return invitation to submit portfolio for review. "When you have been invited to send a submission you must remit $5 for administrative fees, 100 slides for review and return postage and shipping materials for your submission. Professional status is not required for acceptance, however, materials must compete with material in agency for the client's choice. We are looking for strong volume shooters. If the 300 minimum taxes your capacity then save yourself and don't respond."

Tips: "ASA has a very close working relationship with its photographers. You will be one of maximum 50-75 photographers in our files. Your professional status is not a concern; your eye and how you capture images on film are paramount."

‡AUSTRALIAN PICTURE LIBRARY, 2 Northcote St., St. Leonards NSW 2065 Australia, (02)438-3011. Fax: (02)439-6527. Managing Director: Jane Symons. Estab. 1979. Stock photo agency and news/feature syndicate. Has 750,000 photos. Clients include: advertising agencies, public relations firms, audiovisual firms, businesses, book/encyclopedia publishers, magazine publishers, newspapers, postcard publishers, calendar companies and greeting card companies.

Needs: Photos of Australia, sports, people, industry, personalities.

Specs: Uses 8×10 b&w prints; 35mm, 2¼×2¼ and 6×7cm transparencies.

Payment & Terms: Pays 50% commission. Offers volume discounts to customers. Works on contract basis only; offers exclusive contracts. Statements issued quarterly. Payment made quarterly. Offers one-time rights. Informs photographer and allows him to negotiate when client requests all rights. Model/property release required. Captions required.

Making Contact: Submit portfolio for review. Expects minimum initial submission of 400 images with minimum yearly submissions of at least 1,000 images. Reports in 1 month. Photo guidelines free with SASE. Catalog available. Market tips sheet distributed quarterly to agency photographers.

Tips: Looks for formats larger than 35mm in travel, landscapes and scenics with excellent quality. "There must be a need within the library that doesn't conflict with existing photographers too greatly."

■‡BARNABY'S PICTURE LIBRARY, Barnaby House, 19 Rathbone St., London WIP 1AF England. (071)636-6128. Fax: (071)637-4317. Contact: Mrs. Ruth Turner. Stock photo agency and picture library. Has 4 million photos. Clients include: ad agencies, public relations firms, audiovisual firms, businesses, book/encyclopedia publishers, magazine publishers, newspapers, film production companies, BBC, all TV companies, record companies, etc.

Specs: Uses 8×10 b&w prints; 35mm, 2¼×2¼, 4×5 and 8×10 transparencies.

Payment & Terms: Pays 50% commission on b&w and color photos. Works on contract basis only. Offers nonexclusive rights. Statements issued semi-annually. Payment made semi-annually. Offers one-time rights. "The photographer must trust and rely on his agent to negotiate best price!" Model release required. Captions required.

Making Contact: Interested in receiving work from newer, lesser-known photographers. Arrange a personal interview to show portfolio. Send unsolicited photos by mail for consideration. Submit portfolio for review. SASE. "Your initial submission of material must be large enough for us to select a minimum of 200 pictures in color or b&w and they must be your copyright." Reports in 3 weeks. Photo guidelines free with SASE. Tips sheet distributed quarterly to anyone for SASE.

‡BAVARIA BILDAGENTUR GMBH, Postfach 1160, 8035 Gauting, West Germany. (089)850-8044. Fax: (089)850-8043. Director: Anton Dentler. Stock photo agency and picture library. Has 800,000 photos. Clients include: ad agencies, public relations firms, audiovisual firms, businesses, book/encyclopedia publishers, magazine publishers, newspapers, postcard companies, calendar companies and greeting card companies.

Placed as a stock shot in the files of Barnaby's Picture Library, this photo by freelancer David Hodgson is one of many humorous animal images he has snapped. Mary Buckland, managing director at Barnaby's, says a trade magazine paid $50 to use this light-hearted image.

© David Hodgson/Barnaby's Picture Library

Needs: All subjects.

Specs: Uses 35mm, 2¼ × 2¼, 4 × 5 and 8 × 10 transparencies.

Payment & Terms: Pays 50% commission on color photos. Charges filing fee. Statements issued quarterly. Payment made quarterly. Photographers allowed to review account records. Offers one-time rights and first rights. Informs photographer and allows him to negotiate when client requests all rights. Model/property release required. Captions required.

Making Contact: Interested in receiving work from newer, lesser-known photographers. Query with samples. Send unsolicited photos by mail for consideration. Submit portfolio for review. SASE. Reports in 2 weeks. Photo guidelines sheet for SASE.

■**ROBERT J. BENNETT, INC.**, 310 Edgewood St., Bridgeville DE 19933. (302)337-3347, 270-0326. Fax: (302)337-3444. President: Robert Bennett. Estab. 1947. Stock photo agency.

Needs: General subject matter.

Specs: Uses 8 × 10 glossy b&w prints; 35mm, 2¼ × 2¼ and 4 × 5 transparencies.

Payment & Terms: Pays 50% commission US; 40-60% foreign. Pays $5-50/hour; $40-400/day. Pays on publication. Works on contract basis only. Offers limited regional exclusivity. Charges filing fees and duping fees. Statements issued monthly. Payment made monthly. Photographers allowed to review account records to verify sales figures. Buys one-time, electronic media and agency promotion rights. Informs photographer and allows him to negotiate when client requests all rights. Model/property release required. Captions required.

Making Contact: Interested in receiving work from newer, lesser-known photographers. Query with resume of credits. Query with stock photo list. Provide resume, business card, brochure or tearsheets to be kept on file for possible future assignments. Works on assignment only. Keeps samples on file. Reports in 1 month.

The solid, black square before a listing indicates that the market uses various types of audiovisual materials, such as slides, film or videotape.

BIOLOGICAL PHOTO SERVICE, P.O. Box 490, Moss Beach CA 94038. (415)726-6244. Photo Agent: Carl W. May. Stock photo agency. Has 80,000 photos. Clients include: ad agencies, businesses, book/encyclopedia publishers and magazine publishers.

Needs: All subjects in the life sciences, including agriculture, natural history and medicine. Stock photographers must be scientists. Subject needs include: color enhanced scanning electron micrographs; photographic coverage of contemporary medical problems; MRI, CAT scan, PET scan, ultrasound, and X-ray images; minor phyla of invertebrates; animal behavior; and biological conservation. All aspects of general and pathogenic microbiology. All aspects of normal human biology and the basic medical sciences, including anatomy, histology, human embryology and human genetics. Computer-generated images of molecules.

Specs: Uses 4×5 through 11×14 glossy, high-contrast b&w prints; 35mm, $2\frac{1}{4} \times 2\frac{1}{4}$, 4×5, 8×10 transparencies. "Dupes acceptable for rare and unusual subjects, but we prefer originals."

Payment & Terms: Pays 50% commission on b&w and color photos. General price range: $90-500, sometimes higher for advertising uses. Statements issued quarterly. Payment made quarterly; "one month after end of quarter." Photographers allowed to review account records to verify sales figures "by appointment at any time." Offers one-time rights; negotiable. Informs photographer and allows him to negotiate when client requests all rights. "Photographer is consulted during negotiations for 'buyouts,' etc." Model release required for photos used in advertising and other commercial areas. Photo captions required; include complete identification of subject and location.

Making Contact: Query with list of stock subjects and resume of scientific and photographic background. SASE. Reports in 2 weeks. Photo guidelines free with query, resume and SASE. Tips sheet distributed intermittently to stock photographers only.

Tips: "When samples are requested, we look for proper exposure, maximum depth of field, adequate visual information and composition, and adequate technical and general information in captions. Requests fresh light and electron micrographs of traditional textbook subjects; applied biology such as bio-engineering, agriculture, industrial microbiology, and medical research; biological careers; field research. We avoid excessive overlap among our photographer/scientists. We are experiencing an ever-growing demand for photos covering environmental problems of all sorts—local to global, domestic and foreign. Tropical biology, marine biology, and forestry are hot subjects. Our three greatest problems with potential photographers are: 1) inadequate captions; 2) inadequate quantities of *good* and *diverse* photos; 3) poor sharpness/depth of field/grain/composition in photos."

BLACK STAR PUBLISHING CO., INC., 116 E. 27th St., New York NY 10016. (212)679-3288. President: Benjamin V. Chapinck. Stock agency. Has 4 million color transparencies, 1 million b&w prints. Clients include: magazines, ad agencies, book/encyclopedia publishers, corporations, poster companies, graphic design firms, TV and card companies.

Specs: Send at least 300 color transparencies. All formats accepted. "Our tastes and needs are eclectic. We do not know from day to day what our clients will request. Submissions should be made on a trial and error basis. Our only demand is top quality. Mark slides with 'MR' for those that are model released."

Payment & Terms: Pays 50% commission. Offers first N.A. serial rights; "other rights can be procured on negotiated fees." Model release, if available, should be submitted with photos. "Especially need model-released photos of business, lifestyle and medicine."

Making Contact: Call to arrange an appointment or to get additional info. Also send submissions or porfolios with SASE. Reports in 1-2 weeks, sooner if requested. SASE. Free photo guidelines.

Tips: Black Star's files are international and topical, and also include a broad-based, model-released subject file for sales to advertising agencies. Requires exclusive worldwide contracts.

‡JOHN BLAKE PICTURE LIBRARY, The Georgian House, 6 The Plain, Thornbury, Bristol BS12 2AG United Kingdom. (0454)418321/413240. Fax: (0454)416636. Proprietor: John Blake. Picture library. Has 50,000 photos. Clients include: ad agencies, businesses, book/encyclopedia publishers, magazine publishers, postcard and calendar companies.

Needs: "The general topography of Britain, Europe and the rest of the world, in all format transparencies and b&w. Constantly expanding stock includes landscapes, countryside, churches, architecture, cities, towns, villages, gardens, people at work and play. Comprehensive collection on the Cotswolds."

Specs: Uses 6×8 glossy b&w prints; $2\frac{1}{4} \times 2\frac{1}{4}$ and 4×5 transparencies.

Payment & Terms: Pays 50% commission for b&w and color photos. General price range: $50-250. Works with or without a signed contract, negotiable. Offers nonexclusive contract. Statements issued monthly. Payment made monthly. Photographers allowed to review account records to verify sales figures. Offers one-time rights. Informs photographer and allows him to negotiate when client requests all rights. Model release required. Captions required.

Making Contact: Query with list of stock photo subjects. Solicits photos by assignment only. SASE. Reports in 1 month. Photo guidelines free for SASE.

Tips: Prefers to see "sharp and accurate focusing, good composition, good color saturation: ability to take less than obvious view of a commonly-seen tourist attraction. We require color shots of businesses, office situations, where VDTs, keyboards, faxes etc. are in use. Business people meeting, ancillary services such as secretarial needs are always in demand. We are always on the lookout for topical features on the USA (crime, environmental issues, etc.) which we would also need copy for. Good composition is becoming less important as ad agencies and publishers seek to achieve eye-catching effects with logos and graphics in pictures. We often need to find images with blank areas to one side to get this effect for clients."

■**D. DONNE BRYANT STOCK PHOTOGRAPHY,** P.O. Box 80155, Baton Rouge LA 70898. (504)387-1620. Fax: (504)383-2951. President: Douglas D. Bryant. Stock photo agency. Currently represents 60 professional photographers. Has 250,000 photos. Clients include: ad agencies, audiovisual firms, book/encyclopedia publishers and magazine publishers.

Needs: Specializes in picture coverage of Latin America with emphasis on Mexico, Central America, South America, the Caribbean Basin and the Southern USA. Eighty percent of picture rentals are for editorial usage. Important subjects include agriculture, anthropology/archeology, art, commerce and industry, crafts, education, festivals and ritual, geography, history, indigenous people and culture, museums, parks, religion, scenics, sports and recreation, subsistence, tourism, transportation, travel and urban centers.

Specs: Uses 8×10 glossy b&w; 35mm, 2¼×2¼ and 4×5 color transparencies.

Payment & Terms: Pays 50% commission on b&w and color photos. General price range: $85-1,600. Works with or without a signed contract, negotiable. Offers nonexclusive contracts. Statements issued monthly. Payment made monthly. Does not allow photographers to review account records to verify sales figures. Offers one-time rights. Offers $1,500 per image for all rights. Model release preferred for people. Captions required; include location and brief description.

Making Contact: Interested in receiving work from newer, lesser-known photographers. Query with resume of credits and list of stock photo subjects. SASE. Reports in 1 month. Photo guidelines free with SASE. Tips sheet distributed every 3 months to agency photographers.

Tips: Prefers to see "developed picture stories related to one of the subjects listed above. Would like to see more coverage of commerce and industry, as well as better coverage of the modern urban environment in Latin American countries. There is a decreasing interest in Latin American Indians and ruins and an increasing interest in the modern and dynamic urban Latin culture. A photographer interested in shooting Latin scenics will make sales through the DDB Stock Agency, but a photographer who is willing to photograph inside modern schools, factories and hospitals will make far more. We would like to improve our coverage of Mexico, especially Mexico City and the other larger cities. We also want to increase coverage of Cuba, the Dominican Republic, Lima, Caribbean Isles, tropical rainforest destruction/colonization and illegal aliens/INS activity along the US/Mexico border. We are seeing an increased demand for Hispanic culture in the US. All these areas are receiving increasing interest and our files are weak in these subject areas. Freelancers interested in working successfully with DDB Stock should visit Latin America two or more times a year to shoot stock pictures. These self assignments should be coordinated with the agency to assure saleable subjects. Successful agency photographers submit 500-1,000 new images each year. Most successful agency photographers speak Spanish and understand Latin culture. The photographers who earn the most money at DDB Stock are those who would rather tour a Mexican steel mill or hospital than relax on the beach at Cancun. Our ideal photographer is a cultural geographer with an artist's eye and world class photography talent. We have several of these individuals and value them highly."

✹**BRYCE FINLEY, INC.,** P.O. Box 553, Christina Lake, British Columbia V0H 1E0 Canada. (604)447-6106. CEO: Bryce Finley. Estab. 1987. Stock photo agency. Has 5 million photos. Clients include: advertising agencies, public relations firms, book/encyclopedia publishers, magazine publishers, postcard companies, calendar companies and greeting card companies.

Needs: Handles all subjects, expecially model-released people engaged in all activities, for advertising. Especially needs people photographs, sports, leisure.

Specs: Uses 35mm transparencies and larger formats.

Payment & Terms: Pays 50% commission. Statements issued quarterly. Payment made quarterly. Offers one-time rights. Model/property release required. Captions required.

Making Contact: Interested in receiving tearsheets. Query with samples of published material. Cannot return samples. Reports in 2 weeks only when interested.

■**CALIFORNIA VIEWS/Pat Hathaway Historical Collection,** 171 Forest Ave., Pacific Grove CA 93990. (408)373-3811. Photo Archivist: Pat Hathaway. Picture library; historical collection. Has 60,000 b&w images, 2,000 35mm color. Clients include: ad agencies, public relations firms, audiovisual firms, businesses, book/encyclopedia publishers, magazine publishers, newspapers, postcard companies, cal-

endar companies, greeting card companies, television and video and historical exhibition.
Needs: Historical photos of California from 1860-1990.
Specs: Uses 8×10 b&w prints.
Payment & Terms: Buys photos outright; pays $10-100 per b&w photo. General price range: $100-150, $175-200. Offers one-time rights.
Making Contact: Deals with local freelancers only. Buys only historical photos. Does not return unsolicited material. Reports in 1 month.

*■‡CAMERA PRESS LTD., 21 Queen Elizabeth Street, London SE1 2PD England. (071)378-1300. Fax: (071)278-5126. Telex 21654. Operations Director: Roger Eldridge. Picture library, news/feature syndicate. Clients include: ad agencies, public relations firms, audiovisual firms, book/encyclopedia publishers, magazine publishers, newspapers, postcard companies, calendar companies, greeting card companies and TV stations. Clients principally press, but also advertising, publishers, etc.
Needs: Documentary, features, world personalities, i.e. politicians, athletes, statesmen, artists.
Specs: Uses prints; 35mm, 2¼×2¼ and 4×5 transparencies; b&w contact sheets and negatives.
Payment & Terms: Pays 50% commission for color or b&w photos. "Top rates in every country." Offers one-time rights. Model release required. Captions required.
Making Contact: SASE. Reports in 1 month.
Tips: Prefers to see "lively, colorful (features) series which tells a story and individual portraits of up-and-coming world personalities. Exhibit photographic excellence and originality in every field. We specialize in worldwide syndication of news stories, human interest features, show business personalities 'at home' and general portraits of celebrities. Good accompanying text and/or interviews are an advantage. Remember that subjects which seem old-hat and clichéd in America may have considerable appeal overseas. Try to look at the US with an outsider's eye."

■CAMERIQUE INC. INTERNATIONAL, Main office: Dept. PM, 1701 Skippack Pike, P.O. Box 175, Blue Bell PA 19422. (215)272-4000. Fax: (215)272-7651. Representatives in Boston, Los Angeles, Chicago, New York City, Montreal, Sarasota FL, and Tokyo. Photo Director: Mildred Johnson. Estab. 1973. Has 300,000 photos. Clients include: advertising agencies, public relations firms, audiovisual firms, businesses, book/encyclopedia publishers, magazine publishers, newspapers, postcard companies, calendar companies, greeting-card companies.
Needs: General stock photos, all categories. Emphasizes people activities all seasons. Always need large format color scenics from all over the world. No fashion shots. All people shots, including celebrities, must have releases.
Specs: Uses 35mm, 2¼, 4×5 transparencies; b&w contact sheets; b&w negatives; "35mm accepted if of unusual interest or outstanding quality."
Payment & Terms: Sometimes buys photos outright; pays $10-25/photo. Also pays 50% commission on b&w/color. General price range: $150-500. Works on contract basis only. Offers limited regional exclusivity and nonexclusive contracts. Contracts are valid "indefinitely until cancelled in writing." Charges $100-150 catalog insertion fee; $30 duping fee. Also charges advertising fees; not specified. Statements issued monthly. Payment made monthly; within 10 days of end of month. Offers one-time rights. Model/property release required for people, houses, pets. Captions required; include "any descriptive information that would help to market photos."
Making Contact: Query with list of stock photo subjects. Send unsolicited photos by mail for consideration. "Send letter first, we'll send our questionnaire and spec sheet." SASE. Reports in 2 weeks. "You must include correct return postage for your material to be returned." Tips sheet distributed periodically to established contributors.
Tips: Prefers to see "well-selected, edited color on a variety of subjects. Well-composed, well-lighted shots, featuring contemporary styles and clothes. Be creative, selective, professional and loyal. Communicate openly and often."

CATHOLIC NEWS SERVICE, 3211 Fourth St. NE, Washington DC 20017-1100. (202)541-3252. Photos/Graphics Manager: Barbara Stephenson. Photos/Graphics Researcher: Sarah Davis. Wire service transmitting news, features and photos to Catholic newspapers.
Needs: News or feature material related to the Catholic Church or Catholics; head shots of Catholic newsmakers; close-up shots of news events, religious activities. Especially interested in photos aimed toward a general family audience and photos depicting modern lifestyles, e.g., family life, human interest, teens, poverty, active senior citizens, families in conflict, unusual ministries, seasonal and humor.
Specs: Uses 8×10 glossy prints.
Payment & Terms: Pays $25/photo; $75-200/job. Offers one-time rights. Captions required.
Making Contact: Send material by mail for consideration. SASE.
Tips: Submit 10-20 good quality prints covering a variety of subjects. Some prints should have relevance to a religious audience. "Knowledge of Catholic religion and issues is helpful. Read a Diocesan newspaper for ideas of the kind of photos used. Photos should be up-to-date and appeal to a general

family audience. No flowers, no scenics, no animals. As we use more than 1,000 photos a year, chances for frequent sales are good. Send only your best photos."

‡CEPHAS PICTURE LIBRARY, 20 Bedster Gardens, East Molesey, Surrey KT8 9SZ United Kingdom. Tel. & Fax: (081)979-8647. Director: Mick Rock. Picture library. Has 50,000 photos. Clients include: ad agencies, public relations firms, businesses, book/encyclopedia publishers, magazine publishers, postcard companies and calendar companies.
Needs: "We are a general picture library covering all aspects of all countries. Wine and vineyards a major speciality."
Specs: Prefers 2¼×2¼ transparencies, 35mm accepted.
Payment & Terms: Pays 50% commission for color photos. General price range: £50-500+ (English currency). Offers one-time rights. Model release preferred. Captions required.
Making Contact: Send unsolicited photos by mail for consideration. SASE. Reports in 1 week. Photo guidelines for SASE.
Tips: Looks for "transparencies in white card mounts with informative captions and names on front of mounts. Only top-quality, eye-catching transparencies required. Our sales of transparencies relating to wine and vineyards are expanding rapidly. We need more from the USA, the less well-known areas, as well as California: Mexico, Chile, Argentina and Brazil. Show us more city scenes and National Parks. Also required are pictures of Americans in everyday situations, showing the American way of life, etc. — especially teenagers."

■BRUCE COLEMAN PHOTO LIBRARY, 117 E. 24th St., New York NY 10010. (212)979-6252. Fax: (212)979-5468. Photo Director: Marta Serra-Jovenich. Estab. 1970. Stock photo agency. Member of Picture Agency Council of America (PACA). Has 900,000 photos. Clients include: advertising agencies, public relations firms, audiovisual firms, businesses, book/encyclopedia publishers, magazine publishers, newspapers, postcard publishers, calendar companies, greeting card companies, zoos (installations), T.V.
Needs: Nature, travel, science, people, industry.
Specs: Uses 35mm, 2¼×2¼, 4×5 color transparencies.
Payment & Terms: Pays 50% commission on color film. Average price per image (to clients): color $175-975. Works on exclusive contract basis only. Contracts renew automatically for 5 years. Statements issued quarterly. Payment made quarterly. Does not allow photographer to review account records; any deductions are itemized. Offers one-time rights. Informs photographer and allows him to negotiate when client requests all rights. Model/property release preferred for people, private property. Captions required; location, species, genus name, Latin name, points of interest.
Making Contact: Query with resume of credits. Samples kept on file. SASE. Expects minimum initial submission of 300 images with annual submission of 2,000. Reports in 3 months on completed submission; 1 week acknowledgement. Photo guidelines free with SASE. Catalog available. Markets tips sheet distributed bi-monthly to most active photographers. Also quarterly newsletter, "Norman's News," given to all current photographers.
Tips: "We look for strong dramatic angles, beautiful light, sharpness. No gimmicks (prism, color, starburst filters, etc.). We like photos that express moods/feelings and show us a unique eye/style. We like work to be properly captioned. Caption labels should be typed or computer generated and they should contain all vital information regarding the photograph." Sees a trend "toward a journalistic style of stock photos. We are asked for natural settings, dramatic use of light and/or angles. Photographs should not be contrived and should express strong feelings toward the subject. We advise photographers to shoot a lot of film, photograph what they really love and follow our want lists."

■‡COLORIFIC PHOTO LIBRARY, Visual House, 1 Mastmaker Rd., London E14 9WT England. (071)515-3000. Fax: (071)538-3555. Editorial Director: Christopher Angeloglou. Estab. 1970. Picture library, news/feature syndicate. Has 300,000+ photos. Clients include: advertising agencies, public relations firms, audiovisual firms, book/encyclopedia publishers, magazine publishers, newspapers, calendar companies.
Specs: Uses 35mm, 2¼×2¼ transparencies.
Payment & Terms: Pays 50% commission on color photos. Average price per image (to clients): $150-350/color photo. Enforces minimum prices. "Prices vary according to type of market." Photographers have option of not allowing their work to be discounted. Works with or without contract. Offers limited regional exlusivity and nonexclusive contracts. Contracts renew automatically with additional submissions every three-five years. Statements issued quarterly. Payment made quarterly. Offers one-time rights. Informs photographer and allows him to negotiate when client requests all rights. Model/property release preferred. Captions required.
Making Contact: Query with resume of credits. SASE. Expects minimum initial submission of 250 images. Review held after first submission received. Reports as needed. Photo guidelines free with SASE.

■‡**COLOTHEQUE S.P.R.L.**, Avenue Paul Hymans, 103 (bte 23), 1200 Brussels Belgium. (02)762-48-07. Fax: (02)770-39-67. Manager: René J. Mertens von der Becke. Stock photo agency and picture library. Has 200,000 photos. Clients include: advertising agencies, public relations firms, audiovisual firms, businesses, book/encyclopedia publishers, magazine publishers, postcard companies, calendar and greeting card companies, and tour operators.

Specs: Uses 35mm, 2¼ × 2¼ and 4 × 5 transparencies.

Payment & Terms: Pays 60% commission on color photos. General price range: 3,000-60,000 (Belgian currency). Enforces minimum prices. Offers volume discounts to customers; terms specified in photographer's contract. Photographers can choose not to sell images on discount terms. Works on contract basis only. Offers limited regional exclusivity. Contracts renew automatically for unlimited time period. Statements issued monthly or quarterly depending on sales. Payments made monthly or quarterly. Photographers allowed to review account records to verify sales figures. Offers one-time rights. Model/property release required. Captions required.

Making Contact: Interested in receiving work from newer, lesser-known photographers. Arrange a personal interview to show a portfolio. Send unsolicited photos by mail for consideration. SASE.

Tips: Stock photography business is "growing in quality and quantity." To break in, "furnish excellent material."

‡**EDUARDO COMESANA-AGENCIA DE PRENSA**, Casilla de Correo 178 (Suc.26), Buenos Aires 1426 Argentina. (541)771-9418, 773-5943. Fax: (541)771-9418. Director: Eduardo Comesana. Stock photo agency, picture library and news/feature syndicate. Has 300,000 photos. Clients include: ad agencies, book/encyclopedia publishers, magazine publishers and newspapers.

Needs: Personalities, entertainment, politics, science and technology, expeditions, archeology, travel, industry, nature, human interest, education, medicine, foreign countries, agriculture, space, ecology, leisure and recreation, couples, families and landscapes. "We have a strong demand for science-related subjects like shown in *Discover, Smithsonian* and *National Geographic* magazines."

Specs: Uses 8 × 10 glossy b&w prints; 35mm, 2¼ × 2¼ and 4 × 5 transparencies.

Payment & Terms: Pays $80/b&w photo; $100-300/color photo; 60% commission. Works with or without contract; negotiable. Offers limited regional exclusivity. Contracts continue "indefinitely unless terminated by either party with not less than 90 days written notice." Statements issued quarterly. Payment made quarterly. Photographers allowed to review account records to verify sales figures. Offers one-time and electronic media rights. Informs photographer and allows him to negotiate when client requests all rights. Model/property release preferred. Photo captions required; include "who, what, where, when, why and how."

Making Contact: "Send introductory letter or fax stating what photographer wants to syndicate. Do not send unsolicited material without previous approval. We would like to know as much as possible about the prospective contributor. A complete list of subjects will be appreciated." Include IRCs or check for postage in US dollars. Reports in 1 month.

Tips: Represents Black Star in South America; Woodfin Camp & Associates, Outline Press Syndicate from New York City; and Shooting Star from Los Angeles. "We would like to review magazine-oriented stories with a well-written text and clear captions. In case of hot news material, please fax or phone before sending anything. Freelancer should send us an introductory letter stating the type of photography he intends to sell through us. In our reply we will request him to send at least 5 stories of 10 to 20 colors each, for review. We would like to have some clippings of his photography."

*****COMPIX PHOTO AGENCY**, 3621 NE Miami Court, Miami FL 33137. (305)576-0102. Fax: (305)576-0064. President: Alan J. Oxley. Estab. 1986. News/feature syndicate. Has 1 million photos. Clients include: advertising agencies, public relations firms, book/encyclopedia publishers, magazine publishers and newspapers.

Needs: Wants photos for news/feature picture stories, human interest, celebrities and stunts.

Specs: Uses 35mm, 2¼ × 2¼, 4 × 5, 8 × 10 transparencies.

Payment & Terms: Pays 50% commission. Average price per image $175-up. Will sometimes negotiate fees below standard minimum, "if client is buying a large layout." Works with or without contract. Statements issued monthly. Payment made monthly. Photographers allowed to review account records "if showing those records does not violate privacy of other photographers." Offers one-time or negotiated rights based on story, quality and exclusivity. Photographer will be consulted when client wants all rights, but agency does negotiating. Photo captions required; include basic journalistic info.

Making Contact: "Show us some tearsheets." Reports in 3 weeks. Photo guidelines free with SASE.

Tips: "This is an agency for the true picture journalist, not the ordinary photographer. We are an international news service which supplies material to major magazines and newspapers in 30 countries and we shoot hard news, feature stories, celebrity, royalty, stunts, animals and things bizarre. We offer guidance, ideas and assignments but prefer to work with experienced, aggressive photojournalists who have good technical skills and can generate at least some of their own material."

■**COMSTOCK, INC.**, 30 Irving Place, New York NY 10003. (212)353-8600. Senior Editor: Thomas Wear. Member of Picture Agency Council of America (PACA). Has 4 million photos. Clients include: ad agencies, public relations and audiovisual firms, businesses, book/encyclopedia and magazine publishers, newspapers, and postcard, calendar and greeting card companies.
Needs: Write for subject guidelines.
Specs: Uses 35mm (preferred), 2¼×2¼, 4×5 or 8×10 transparencies; 8×10 b&w double-weight fiber-based prints.
Payment & Terms: Pays 50% of stock sale; 25% commission to agency on assignments. General price range: $150-20,000. Works on contract basis only. Offers exclusive contract only. Contracts renew automatically with each submission for one year after first 5-year base period. Charges filing fee of $2/image. Charges duping fee of $3.50 per 4×5; $1.75 per 35mm. Statements issued monthly. Payment made monthly. Photographers allowed to review account records to verify sales figures or account for various deductions, but "during normal business hours, and for their accounts only." Offers one-time rights and nonexclusive rights. "We do not sell all rights and discourage the practice. If client does ask, the photographer is informed." Model and/or property release preferred; "must have model releases for commercial files." Photo captions required; include "who, what, when, where, why."
Making Contact: Contact Thomas Wear, Senior Editor. Query with resume of credits or list of stock photo subjects. SASE. Reports in 3 weeks.
Tips: "We represent very few photographers all of whom are extremely productive, most of whom make their living from stock photography. We could use more coverage in the science and hi-tech areas and in child-development from birth to full adulthood. We look for creativity, originality, a recognizable point of view, consistent technical excellence. Have an area of specialty and expertise. Present a scrupulously *edited* portfolio. Know and understand what stock is and what competition is out there; have a specialty that you care about passionately."

■**CUSTOM MEDICAL STOCK PHOTO**, Dept. PM, 3819 N. Southport Ave., Chicago IL 60613. (312)248-3200 or (800)373-2677. Fax: (312)248-7427. Medical Archivist: Mike Fisher. Member of Picture Agency Council of America (PACA). Clients include: ad agencies, magazines, textbook publishers, design firms, audiovisual firms and hospitals. All commercial and editorial markets that express interest in medical and scientific subject area. Clients include: Scott, Foresman & Co., editorial, drug abuse, psychological testing, pathology; Foote, Cone, Belding, commerical.
Needs: Biomedical, scientific, healthcare environmentals and general biology for advertising illustrations, textbook and journal articles, annual reports, editorial use and patient education.
Specs: Uses 35mm, 2¼×2¼ and 4×5 transparencies. Negatives for electron microscopy. 4×5 copy transparencies of medical illustrations.
Payment & Terms: Pays per shot or commission. Per-shot rate depends on usage. Commission: 50% on domestic leases; 30-40% on foreign leases. Works on contract basis only. Credit line given if applicable, client discretion. Offers one-time rights; other rights negotiable.
Making Contact: Query with list of stock photo subjects and request current want list and submission packet. "PC captioning disk available for database inclusion, please request. Do not send uncaptioned unsolicited photos by mail. SASE. Reports in average 4 weeks. Monthly want list available by US Mail, and by Fax. Model and property release copies required.
Tips: "Our past want lists are a valuable guide to the types of images requested by our clients. Past want lists are available. Environmentals of researchers hi-tech biomedicine, physicians, nurses and patients of all ages in situations from neonatal care to mature adults are requested frequently. Almost any image can qualify to be medical if it touches an area of life: breakfast, sports, etc. Trends also follow newsworthy events found on newswires. Photos should be good clean images that portray a single idea whether it is biological, medical or scientific. Photographers should possess the ability to recognize the newsworthiness of subjects. Put together a minimum of 100 images for submission. Call before shipping to receive computer disk and caption information and return information. Contributing to our agency can be very profitable if a solid commitment can exist."

CYR COLOR PHOTO AGENCY, Box 2148, Norwalk CT 06852. (203)838-8230. Contact: Judith A. Cyr. Has 125,000 transparencies. Clients include: ad agencies, businesses, book publishers, magazine publishers, encyclopedia publishers, calendar companies, greeting card companies, poster companies and record companies.

 The asterisk before a listing indicates that the market is new in this edition. New markets are often the most receptive to freelance submissions.

Needs: "As a stock agency, we are looking for all types. There has been a recent interest in family shots (with parents and children) and people in day-to-day activities. Also modern offices with high-tech equipment and general business/professional settings. Mood shots, unusual activities, etc. are always popular—anything not completely 'standard' and common. Photos must be well-exposed and sharp, unless mood shots."

Specs: Uses 35mm to 8×10 transparencies.

Payment & Terms: Pays 50% commission. Works on contract basis only. Offers nonexclusive contract. Payment made upon payment from client. Offers one-time rights, all rights, first rights or outright purchase; price depending upon rights and usage. Informs photographer and allows him to negotiate when client requests all rights. Model release preferred. Captions preferred.

Making Contact: Send material by mail for consideration. SASE. "Include postage for manner of return desired." Reports in 4 weeks. Distributes tips sheet periodically to active contributors; "usually when returning rejects."

Tips: Each submission should be accompanied by an identification sheet listing subject matter, location, etc. for each photo included in the submission. All photos should be properly numbered, with photographer's initials; also using vinyl sheets is a great time-saver in reviewing photos. "We have received more requests from clients to use 35mm in a slide presentation only (i.e. one time) and/or in a video presentation. Thus, there are more uses of a photo with limited copyright agreements."

■‡**DAS PHOTO**, Domaine de Bellevue, 181, Septon 6940 Belgium. (086)32 24 26. Director: David Simson. Stock photo agency. Has 50,000 photos. Clients include: advertising agencies, public relations firms, audiovisual firms, book/encyclopedia publishers, magazine publishers, calendar companies and greeting card companies. Previous/current clients include: Stern and Oggi, Oxford University Press; *Vogue*; Geographical Magazine; Spectator; Guardian; BBC; *Penthouse* and Times.

Needs: Handles "mainly reportage—suitable for publishers and magazines although we do deal with most subjects. We are specialists in selling photo material in all European countries."

Specs: Uses 8×10 glossy b&w prints; 35mm, 2¼×2¼, 4×5 and 8×10 transparencies.

Payment & Terms: Pays 50% commission. Pays $40-500/b&w photo; $60-1,000/color photo; $350/day plus expenses. Works on contract basis only. Offers limited regional exclusivity contract. Guarantees subject exclusivity within files. Contracts renew automatically for 3 years with additional submissions. Charges duping fee of $2/image. Statements issued quarterly. Payment made quarterly, when sales are made. Photographers allowed to review account records to verify sales figures. Offers one-time, electronic media and agency promotion rights; exclusive rights only after consulting photographer. Informs photographers and allows them to negotiate when a client requests all rights. Model release preferred. Photo captions required; include description of location, country and subject matter.

Making Contact: Interested in receiving work from newer, lesser-known photographers. Query with samples. Send unsolicited photos by mail for consideration. SASE. Reports in 1 week. Photo guideline sheet and tips sheet free with SASE.

Tips: "We take a large variety of material but it has to be saleable, sharp and good color saturation. Send 100-500 good saleable images for selection."

■**LEO DE WYS INC.**, 1170 Broadway, New York NY 10001. (212)689-5580. Fax: (212)545-1185. President: Leo De Wys. Office Manager: Laura Diez. Member of Picture Agency Council of America (PACA). Has 350,000 photos. Clients include: ad agencies, public relations and AV firms; business; book, magazine and encyclopedia publishers; newspapers, calendar and greeting card companies; textile firms; travel agencies and poster companies.

Needs: Travel and destination (over 2,000 categories); and released people pictures in foreign countries (i.e., Japanese business people, German stockbrokers, English nurses, Mexican dancers, exotic markets in Asia, etc.).

Specs: Uses 35mm, medium format and 4×5 transparencies.

Payment & Terms: Price depends on quality and quantity. Usually pays 50% commission; 33⅓% for foreign sales. General price range: $125-6,500. Works with photographers on contract basis only. Offers exclusive and limited regional exclusive contracts; prefers to offer exclusive contract. Contracts renew automatically for five years. Offers to clients "any rights they want to have; payment is calculated accordingly." Charges 50% catalog insertion fee. "Company advances duping cost and deducts after sale has been made." Statements issued bimonthly and quarterly. Payment made bimonthly and quarterly. Photographers allowed to review account records to verify their sales figures. Offers one-time rights. Informs photographers and permits them to negotiate when client requests all rights; some conditions. Model release required; "depends on subject matter." Captions preferred.

Making Contact: Query with samples—"(about 40 pix) is the best way." Query with list of stock photo subjects or submit portfolio for review. SASE. Reporting time depends; often the same day. Photo guidelines free with SASE.

Tips: "Photos should show what the photographer is all about. They should show technical competence—photos that are sharp, well-composed, have impact, if color they should show color. Company now uses bar coded computerized filing system." Seeing trend toward more use of food shots tied in with travel such as "key lime pie for Key West and Bavarian beer for Germany. Also more shots of people—photo-released and in local costumes. Currently, the destinations most in demand are the USA, Canada, Mexico and the Caribbean."

DEVANEY STOCK PHOTOS, Suite 306, 755 New York Ave., Huntington NY 11743. (516)673-4477. Fax: (516)673-4440. President: William Hagerty. Photo Editor: Ruth Fahlbusch. Has over 1 million photos. Clients include: ad agencies, book publishers, magazines, corporations and newspapers. Previous/current clients: Young & Rubicam, BBD&O, Hallmark Cards, *Parade* Magazine, MacMillan Publishing, Harcourt Brace & Jovanovich, *Newsday*.
Needs: Accidents, animals, education, medical, artists, elderly, scenics, assembly lines—auto and other, entertainers, schools, astronomy, factory, science, automobiles, family groups, aviation, finance, babies, fires, shipping, movies, shopping, flowers, food, beaches, oceans, skylines, foreign, office, birds, sports, gardens, operations, still life, pets, business, graduation, health, police, teenagers, pollution, television, children, history, hobbies, travel, churches, holidays, cities, weddings, communications, houses, women, writing, zoos, computers, housework, recreation, religion, couples, crime, crowds, dams, industry, laboratories, law, lawns, lumbering, restaurants, retirement, romance, etc.—virtually all subjects.
Specs: Uses 8×10 glossy b&w prints; uses all sizes of transparencies.
Payment & Terms: Does not buy photos outright. Pays 50% commission on color; 30% on b&w. Works with photographers with or without a signed contract, negotiable. Contracts automatically renew for a 3-year period. Offers nonexclusive contract. Statements issued upon sale. Payment made monthly. Offers one-time rights. Model release preferred. Captions required.
Making Contact: Interested in receiving work from newer, lesser-known photographers. Query with list of stock photo subjects or send material by mail for consideration. SASE. Reports in 1 month. Free photo guidelines with SASE. Distributes monthly tips sheet free to any photographer. Model/property release preferred. Captions required. "Releases from individuals and homeowners are most always required if photos are used in advertisements."
Tips: "An original submission of 200 original transparencies in vinyl sheets is required. We will coach."

‡DIANA PHOTO PRESS AB, Box 6266, S-102 34, Stockholm Sweden. (46)8 314428. Fax: (46)8 314401. Manager: Diana Schwarcz. Estab. 1973. Clients include: magazine publishers and newspapers.
Needs: Personalities and portraits of well-known people.
Specs: Uses 18×24 b&w prints; 35mm transparencies.
Payment & Terms: Pays 30% commission on b&w and color photos. Average price per image (to clients): $150/b&w and color image. Enforces minimum prices. Works on contract basis only. Statements issued monthly. Payment made in 60-90 days. Offers one-time rights. Informs photographer and allows him to negotiate when client requests all rights. Captions required.
Making Contact: Query with samples. Samples kept on file. SASE. Does not report; "Wait for sales report."

■‡DINODIA PICTURE AGENCY, 13 Vithoba Ln., Vithalwadi, Kalbadevi, Bombay India 400 002. (91)22-318572. Fax: (91)22-2067675. Owner: Jagdish Agarwal. Estab. 1987. Stock photo agency. Has 200,000 photos. Clients include: advertising agencies, public relations firms, audiovisual firms, businesses, book/encyclopedia publishers, magazine publishers, newspapers, postcard companies, calendar companies and greeting card companies.
Needs: "We specialize in photos on India—people and places, fairs and festivals, scenic and sports, animals and agriculture."
Specs: Uses 35mm, 2¼×2¼ and 4×5 transparencies.
Payment & Terms: Pays 50% commission on b&w and color photos. General price range: US $50-250. Negotiate fees below stated minimum prices. Offers volume discounts to customers; inquire about specific terms. Discount sales terms not negotiable. Works on contract basis only. Offers limited regional exclusivity. "Prefers exclusive for India." Contracts renew automatically with additional submissions for 5 years. Statement issued monthly. Payment made monthly. Photographers permitted to review sales figures. Informs photographer and allows him to negotiate when client requests all rights. Offers one-time rights. Model release preferred. Captions required.
Making Contact: Interested in receiving work from newer, lesser-known photographers. Query with resume of credits, samples and list of stock photo subjects. SASE. Reports in 1 month. Photo guidelines free with SASE. Market tips sheet distributed monthly to contracted photographers.
Tips: "We look for style, maybe in color, composition, mood, subject-matter; whatever, but the photos should have above average appeal." Sees trend that "market is saturated with standard documentary-type photos. Buyers are looking more often for stock that appears to have been shot on assignment."

DR. STOCK INC., Dept. PM, 9439 Battle Point Dr. NE, Bainbridge Island WA 98110. (206)780-0211. CEO: Peter Berndt, MD. Estab. 1990. Stock photo agency. Has 5,000 photos. Clients include: advertising agencies, public relations firms, businesses, book/encyclopedia pubilshers, magazine publishers, newspapers.

Needs: Handles biomedical, biological, scientific images only.

Specs: Uses 35mm, 2¼×2¼ transparencies.

Payment & Terms: Pays 40% commission on color photos. General price range: $50 up. Statements issued quarterly. Payment made monthly on receipt of our payment. Photographers allowed to review account records to verify sales figures. Offers one-time rights. Model release required for recognizable subjects. Captions required.

Making Contact: Interested in receiving work from newer, lesser-known photographers. Query with samples. Query with list of stock photo subjects. SASE. Reports in 1 month. Photo guidelines free with SASE. Market tips sheets free with SASE.

Tips: This firm is in a heavy recruitment stage and seeks new photographers; recruiting very selectively. "We need a steady supply of high quality medical, biological, scientific subjects; prefer the images on slow (fine grained film). We see an increasing demand for scientific images of all kinds. The market seems unlimited, but competition is certainly noticeable."

■**DRK PHOTO**, 265 Verde Valley School Rd., Sedona AZ 86336. (602)284-9808. Fax: (602)284-9096. President: Daniel R. Krasemann. "We handle only the personal best of a select few photographers—not hundreds. This allows us to do a better job aggressively marketing the work of these photographers." Member of Picture Agency Council of America (PACA) and A.S.P.P. Clients include: ad agencies; PR and AV firms; businesses; book, magazine, textbook and encyclopedia publishers; newspapers; postcard, calendar and greeting card companies; branches of the government, and nearly every facet of the publishing industry, both domestic and foreign.

Needs: "Especially needs marine and underwater coverage." Also interested in S.E.M.'s, African, European and Far East wildlife, and good rainforest coverage.

Specs: Uses 35mm, 2¼×2¼ and 4×5 transparencies.

Payment & Terms: Pays 50% commission on color photos. General price range: $75-"into thousands." Works on contract basis only. Offers nonexclusive contracts. Contracts renew automatically. Statements issued quarterly. Payment made quarterly. Offers one-time rights; "other rights negotiable between agency/photographer and client." Model release preferred. Captions required.

Making Contact: "With the exception of established professional photographers shooting enough volume to support an agency relationship, we are not soliciting open submissions at this time. Those professionals wishing to contact us in regards to representation should query with a brief letter of introduction and tearsheets."

■**DYNAMIC GRAPHICS INC., CLIPPER & PRINT MEDIA SERVICE**, 6000 N. Forrest Park Dr., Peoria IL 61614. (309)688-8800. Photo Editor: Samantha M. Wick. Clients include: ad agencies, printers, newspapers, companies, publishers, visual aid departments, TV stations, etc.

Needs: Generic stock photos (all kinds). "Our needs are somewhat ambiguous and require that a large number of photos be submitted for consideration. We will send a 'photo needs list' and additional information if requested."

Specs: Majority of purchases are b&w. Send 8×10 prints, contact sheets and high contrast conversions. Minimal use of 35mm and 4×5 transparencies.

Payment & Terms: Pays $50 and up/b&w photo; $100 and up/color photo. **Pays on acceptance.** Rights are specified in contract. Model release required.

Making Contact: Interested in receiving work from newer, lesser-known photographers. Send tearsheets or folio of 8×10 b&w photos by mail for consideration; supply phone number where photographer may be reached during working hours. Reports in 6-8 weeks.

*****ECHO IMAGE**, 1317 NW Prospect Ave., Grants Pass OR 97526-1263. (503)474-9649. Fax: (503)474-9649. Director of Photography: Catherine Davis. Estab. 1992. Stock photo agency. Has about 30,000 photos. Clients include: advertising agencies, businesses, magazine publishers and graphic design firms.

Needs: Up-to-date model-released people and lifestyles, especially active seniors; business and finance; travel; agriculture; industry.

Specs: Uses 35mm, 2¼×2¼, 4×5, 8×10 transparencies.

Payment & Terms: Pays 50% commission on color domestic sales. Average price per image: $300-800/color. May offer volume discounts to customers. Statements issued quarterly. Payment made quarterly. Payment made within 10 days after end of calendar quarter. Photographers allowed to review account records. Offers one-time rights; "rights are negotiated based upon client's needs." Informs photographer and allows him to negotiate when client requests all rights. Model/property release preferred for identifiable people and private property. Captions required. "Captions should be thorough, indicating at the very least the photo subject matter (if not obvious), location, and date. Type on separate sheet."

Making Contact: Interested in receiving work from newer, lesser-known photographers. Send unsolicited photos in slide pages by mail for consideration. Be sure to include a separate typed sheet with detailed caption information and SASE for return of your material. "To get an overview of your work, we'd like to see about 100 color images." Samples are kept on file. Reports in 3 weeks. Photo guidelines free with SASE.

Tips: "Take the time to carefully edit your work, and show us your best. Competition in stock photography is ferocious, so only the best is good enough. Photos must be tack sharp (use a 12x loupe) and reflect good composition and technical control. We prefer Kodachrome or Fuji professional films, and all images submitted must be originals. Submit your photos to us in pages — not in little boxes. We do not require a minimum number of images in an initial submission, nor do we require a minimum number of images to be submitted thereafter. However, a few pictures, no matter how good, cannot generate much income. Successful stock photography is based on a long-term commitment and prolific, high-quality submissions."

■**ELITE PHOTOGRAPHY, INC.**, Box 2789, Toledo OH 43606. Director: David Thompson. Clients include: advertising agencies, public relations firms, audiovisual firms, businesses, magazine publishers, postcard companies, calendar and greeting card companies, book/encyclopedia publishers, video distributors.

Needs: "We are a stock agency that is specializing in photography of women, be it pretty pictures, cheesecake, nude, exotic, or erotic. Although we are strict on such rules as focusing and exposures, our needs are as varied as the marketplace — if it is salable, we will sell it."

Specs: Uses 35mm and 2¼ × 2¼ transparencies. "Don't send larger transparencies or b&w unless she is a special subject."

Payment & Terms: Rarely buys photos/film outright. Pays 50% commission on b&w and color photos. General price range: $150-1,500, complete sets higher. Works on contract basis only. Contracts renew automatically with additional submissions; all for one-year extensions. Statements issued after sales within 45 days of receiving payment. Buys "any rights the photographers will sell." Model release required. Captions preferred.

Making Contact: Interested in receiving work from newer, lesser-known photographers. Query with samples. Send unsolicited photos by mail for consideration. "Send a professional looking package certified to us. Make sure it is sent requesting a return receipt." SASE. Reports in 2 weeks. Photo guidelines, tip sheet free with SASE *and* samples. (No phone calls please.)

Tips: "Be able to compose, focus and expose a photograph properly. Remember that we specialize in photographs of women, with cheesecake and nude/erotic the biggest and fastest sales. Show us you can produce marketable images, and we'll do the rest. Almost all of our magazine buyers are screaming for cover shots — shoot them! In addition, we also direct market sets overseas to publishers. This creates a very lucrative market for those with sets that have already sold in the US. We can still market them to the rest of the world. For those with such talent, Elite now deals in video and is interested in seeing sample VHS tapes that fall within our subject guidelines. We are very interested in seeing much more photography involving women working in all career fields and in various forms of play such as sports and other leisure activities. We also want more mother and child photography."

■**ENVISION**, 220 W. 19th St., New York NY 10011. (212)243-0415. Director: Sue Pashko. Estab. 1986. Stock photo agency. Has 200,000 photos. Clients include: advertising agencies, audiovisual firms, book/encyclopedia publishers, magazine publishers, postcard companies, calendar and greeting card companies and graphic design firms.

Needs: Professional quality photos of food, commercial food processing, fine dining, American cities (especially the Midwest), crops, Third World lifestyles, marine mammals, European landmarks, tourists in Europe and Europe in winter looking lovely with snow, and anything on Africa and African-Americans.

Specs: Uses 35mm, 2¼ × 2¼, 4 × 5 or 8 × 10 transparencies.

Payment & Terms: Pays 50% commission on b&w and color photos. General price range: $200 and up. Offers one-time rights; "each sale individually negotiated — usually one-time rights." Model/property release required. Captions required.

Making Contact: Query with resume of credits "on company/professional stationery." SASE. Reports in 1 month.

Tips: "We are looking for the *very* best quality photographs. Clients expect the very best in professional quality material. Photos that are unique, taken with a very individual style. Demands for traditional subjects *but* with a different point of view; African- and Hispanic-American lifestyle photos are in great demand."

■‡**GREG EVANS PHOTO LIBRARY**, 91 Charlotte St., London W1P ILB England. (071)636-8238. Fax: (071)637-1439. Manager: Greg Evans. Picture library. Has 250,000 photos. Clients include: ad agencies; public relations and audiovisual firms; businesses; book/encyclopedia and magazine publishers; newspapers; and postcard, calendar, greeting card and travel companies.
Specs: Uses 35mm, 2¼ × 2¼, 4 × 5, 2¼ × 2¾ and 8 × 10 transparencies.
Payment & Terms: Buys photos outright. Pays 50% commission on color photos. Offers one-time rights. Model release required.
Making Contact: Arrange a personal interview to show portfolio. Send unsolicited photos by mail for consideration. SASE. Reports in 1 week. Quarterly tips sheet free with SASE.
Tips: Wants to see "creativity, sharpness, clarity, perfect exposure, precise captions."

■**EWING GALLOWAY**, 100 Merrick Rd., Rockville Centre NY 11570. (516)764-8620. Photo Editor: Tom McGeough. Estab. 1920. Stock photo agency. Member of Picture Agency Council of America (PACA). Has 3 million photos. Clients include: advertising agencies, public relations firms, audiovisual firms, businesses, book/encyclopedia publishers, magazine publishers, newspapers, postcard companies, calendar companies, greeting card companies and religious organizations.
• This agency has expanded its agent base by setting up an agreement with Atlanta Stock Associates. ASA will now represent Ewing Galloway in the Atlanta area.
Needs: General subject library. Does not carry personalities or news items. Lifestyle shots (model released) are most in demand.
Specs: Uses 8 × 10 glossy b&w prints; 35mm, 2¼ × 2¼ and 4 × 5 transparencies.
Payment & Terms: Pays 30% commission on b&w photos; 50% on color photos. General price range: $400-450. Charges catalog insertion fee of $400/photo. Statements issued monthly. Payment made monthly. Offers one-time rights; also unlimited rights for specific media. Model/property release required. Photo captions required; include location, specific industry, etc.
Making Contact: Interested in receiving work from newer, lesser-known photographers. Query with samples. Send unsolicited photos by mail for consideration; must include return postage. SASE. Reports in 3 weeks. Photo guidelines free with SASE. Market tips sheet distributed monthly; free with SASE.
Tips: Wants to see "high quality—sharpness, subjects released, shot only on best days—bright sky and clouds. Medical and educational material is currently in demand. We see a trend toward photography related to health and fitness, high-tech industry, and mixed race in business and leisure."

■**FASHIONS IN STOCK**, Dept. PM, 23-68 Steinway St., Long Island City NY 11105. (718)721-1373. President: Nicasio Sanchez. Estab. 1987. Stock photo agency. Has 60,000 photos. Clients include: advertising agencies, public relations firms, businesses, magazine publishers and calendar companies.
Needs: "We specialize in stock photos that tell a story, illustrate a scenario, be it in the area of business, leisure, family, friendships, etc. Many of our stock photos are fashion-oriented. Our photos also deal with current controversial issues. The photos all include people against a backdrop of unique regional interest or interesting architecture, exotic locales. People also shown participating in sports of all kinds, in business settings, at family holidays, shopping, and in academic environments."
Specs: Uses 8 × 10 fiber base, b&w prints; 35mm, 2¼ × 2¼, 4 × 5 transparencies; b&w contact sheets; b&w negatives; 16mm film; VHS videotape.
Payment & Terms: Pays 50% commission on b&w/color photos. Offers one-time rights; other rights negotiable. Model release required. Captions preferred.
Making Contact: Arrange a personal interview to show portfolio "if photographer's location is permanent." Submit portfolio for review. SASE. Reports in 1 week. Tips sheet distributed to photographers with fashions in stock.
Tips: "We are looking for current, fashionable stock photography that can convey an idea or sell a product or service. The photos must have flexibility, universality, a keen insight into people's feelings. We also look for unique locations in different areas of the United States as a background. Our focus is mostly on commercial print advertising." Stock is being used instead of assignment work by many advertising agencies. "They are looking for casual, upscale types of people of all ages. I notice a large request for young women (20s to early 30s) in professional scenarios, different ethnic groups (Asian, African-American, Hispanic) working and playing together, and elderly people involved in work or exercise. The photographer working with FIS would grow rapidly and would save considerable processing and model expenses. We also push for assignment work for our photographers. We are currently establishing an office in Manhattan."

FERN-WOOD DESIGNS AND PHOTO MARKETING AGENCY, (A Division of Fern-Wood Enterprises, Inc.), P.O. Box 948, Wrightsville Beach NC 28480. (919)256-2897. Fax: (919)256-3299. President: Carol G. Wood. Estab. 1990. Stock photo agency and greeting card publisher. Clients include: advertising agencies, public relations firms, businesses, postcard companies and calendar companies.

Needs: "Coastal beach scenes, boats, birds, flowers, historical landmarks, old barns and buildings, landscapes and people worldwide, specializes in photos with natural settings rather than posed settings, unusual and interesting subject matter."

Specs: Uses 4×6 glossy b&w or color prints; 35mm, 2¼×2¼ and 4×5 transparencies.

Payment & Terms: Buys photos outright. Pays $50 minimum; higher fees negotiable. Pays 50% commission on color photos. General price range: average $250. Offers volume discounts to customers; terms specified in photographer's contract. Photographers can choose not to sell images on discount terms. Works on contract basis only; offers limited regional exclusivity and guaranteed subject exclusivity. Contracts renew automatically for one year. Charges $25 filing fee with contract. Statements issued quarterly. Payment made monthly. Photographers permitted to review account records to verify sales figures or account for various deductions. Offers one-time rights; rights negotiated depending on photographer. Informs photographers and allows them to participate in negotiations when client requests all rights. Model release required if subject is identifiable. Captions preferred.

Making Contact: Interested in receiving work from newer, lesser-known photographers. Arrange a personal interview to show portfolio. Query with list of stock photo subjects. Send unsolicited photos by mail for consideration. Keeps samples on file. SASE. Reports in 3 weeks. Market tips sheet distributed monthly to photographers and clients; free with SASE.

Tips: Looks for style, composition, subject matter and originality. Sees trend toward natural shots of coastal regions, golf courses, candid shots of people in their own environment, historical landmarks and environmental subject matter.

■**FINE PRESS SYNDICATE**, Box 22323, Ft Lauderdale FL 33335. Vice President: R. Allen. Has 49,000 photos and 100+ films. Clients include: ad agencies, public relations firms, businesses, audiovisual firms, book publishers, magazine publishers, postcard companies and calendar companies worldwide.

Needs: Nudes, figure work and erotic subjects (female only).

Specs: Uses glossy color prints; 35mm, 2¼×2¼ transparencies; 16mm film; videocasettes: VHS and Beta.

Payment & Terms: Pays 50% commission on color photos and film. Price range "varies according to use and quality." Enforces minimum prices. Works on contract basis only. Offers exclusivity only. Statements issued monthly. Payment made monthly. Offers one-time rights. Does not inform photographer or permit him to negotiate when client requests all rights. Model/property release preferred.

Making Contact: Interested in receiving work from newer, lesser-known photographers. Send unsolicited material by mail for consideration or submit portfolio for review. SASE. Reports in 2 weeks.

Tips: Prefers to see a "good selection of explicit work. Currently have European and Japanese magazine publishers paying high prices for very explicit nudes. Clients prefer 'American-looking' female subjects. Send as many samples as possible. Foreign magazine publishers are buying more American work as the value of the dollar makes American photography a bargain. More explicit poses are requested."

FIRST IMAGE WEST, INC., (formerly Visual Images West, Inc.), 921 W. Van Buren #201, Chicago IL 60607. (812)733-3239. Contact: Tom Neiman. Estab. 1985. Stock photo agency. Member of Picture Agency Council of America (PACA). Clients include: advertising agencies, public relations firms, businesses, book/encyclopedia publishers, magazine publishers, and newspapers. Clients include Bank of America, Wrangler Jeans, Jeep, America West Airlines.

Needs: Needs photos of Southwestern lifestyles and scenics. Also general travel and model-released lifestyles.

Specs: Uses 2¼×2¼ up to 4×5 transparencies; "scenics in large format only."

Payment & Terms: Pays 50% commission on domestic photos. General price range: editorial, $185 and up; advertising, $230 base rate. Works on contract basis only. Offers limited regional exclusive and catalog exclusive contracts. Statements issued when payment is due. Payment made monthly. Photographers allowed to review account records to verify sales figures. Offers one-time rights and specific print and/or time usages. When client requests all rights, "we inform photographer and get approval of 'buyout' but agency is sole negotiator with client." Model/property release required for people, homes, vehicles, animals. Photo captions required.

Making Contact: Contact by telephone for photographer's package. SASE. Reports in 1 month. Photo guidelines free with SASE. Tips sheet distributed quarterly to contract photographers.

Tips: Trend among clients is "toward medium and large format." Looks for "professional quality, sharp focus, proper exposure, simple design and a direct message. When sending work to review make sure the submission is tightly edited. Include subject list of what work is available."

■✸**FIRST LIGHT ASSOCIATED PHOTOGRAPHERS**, Suite 204, 1 Atlantic Ave., Toronto, Ontario M6K 3E7 Canada. (416)532-6108. President: Pierre Guevremont. Estab. 1984. Stock and assignment agency. Has 450,000 photos. Clients include: advertising agencies, public relations firms, audiovisual firms, businesses, book/encyclopedia publishers, magazine publishers, newspapers, postcard companies, calendar companies and greeting card companies.

Needs: Natural history, international travel, commercial imagery in all categories. Special emphasis upon model-released people, high tech, industry and business. "Our broad files require variety of subjects."
Specs: Uses 35mm, 2¼×2¼ and 4×5 transparencies.
Payment & Terms: Pays 50% commmission. General price range: $150-5,000. Works on contract basis only. Offers limited regional exclusivity. Charges variable catalog insertion fees. Statements issued monthly. Payment made monthly. Offers one-time rights. Informs photographers and permits them to negotiate when client requests all rights. Model release preferred. Captions required.
Making Contact: Query with list of stock photo subjects. SASE. Reports in 1 month. Photo guidelines free with SASE. Tips sheet distributed every 6 weeks.
Tips: Wants to see "tight, quality edit and description of goals and shooting plans."

*FOLIO, INC., 3417½ M St., Washington DC 20007. President: Susan Soroko. Estab. 1983. Stock photo agency. Types of clients: newspapers, textbooks, education, industrial, retail, fashion, finance.
Needs: Works with 30-50 photographers/month. Photos used for billboards, consumer magazines, trade magazines, direct mail, P-O-P displays, catalogs, posters, signage and newspapers.
Specs: Uses 35mm, 2¼×2¼ and 4×5 transparencies.
Payment & Terms: Pays "50% of sales." Pays on publication or on receipt of invoice. Works on contract basis only. Offers one-time rights. Model release required. Photo captions required.
Making Contact: Arrange a personal interview to show portfolio. Provide resume, business card, brochure, flyer or tearsheets to be kept on file for possible future assignments. SASE. Reports in 3 weeks. Credit line given.
Tips: "Call first, send in requested information."

■🍁FOTO EXPRESSION INTERNATIONAL (Toronto), Box 1268, Station "Q", Toronto, Ontario M4T 2P4 Canada. (416)841-1065. Fax: (416)841-2283. Photo Editor: Mrs. Veronika Kubik. Selective archive of photo, film and audiovisual materials. Clients include: ad agencies; public relations and audiovisual firms; TV stations and networks; film distributors; businesses; book, encyclopedia, trade and news magazine publishers; newspapers; postcard, calendar and greeting card companies.
Needs: City views, aerial, travel, wildlife, nature/natural phenomena and disasters, underwater, aerospace, weapons, warfare, industry, research, computers, educational, religions, art, antique, abstract, models, sports. Worldwide news and features, personalities and celebrities.
Specs: Uses 8×10 b&w; 35mm and larger transparencies; 16mm, 35mm film; VHS, Beta and commercial videotapes (AV). Motion picture, news film, film strip and homemade video.
Payment & Terms: Sometimes buys transparencies outright. Pays 40% for b&w; 50% for color and 16mm, 35mm films and AV (if not otherwise negotiated). Offers one-time rights. Model release required for photos. Captions required.
Making Contact: Submit portfolio for review. The ideal portfolio for 8×10 b&w prints includes 10 prints; for transparencies include 60 selections in plastic slide pages. With portfolio you must send SASE with return postage (out of Canada—either money-order or International Reply Coupon). Reports in 3 weeks. Photo guidelines free with SASE. Tips sheet distributed twice a year only "on approved portfolio."
Tips: "We require photos, slides, motion picture films, news film, homemade video and AV that can fulfill the demand of our clientele." Quality and content is essential. Photographers, cameramen, reporters, writers, correspondents and representatives are required worldwide by FOTOPRESS, Independent News Service International, (416-841-4486/Fax: 416-841-2283), a division of the FOTO expPRESS-ion in Toronto. Contact Mr. Milan J. Kubik, Director, International section.

FOTOCONCEPT INC., Dept. PM, 18020 SW 66th St., Ft. Lauderdale FL 33331. (305)680-1771. Fax: (305)680-8996. Vice President: Aida Bertsch. Estab. 1985. Stock photo agency. Member of Picture Agency Council of America (PACA). Has 150,000 photos. Clients include: magazines, advertising agencies, newspapers and publishers.
Needs: General worldwide travel, medical and industrial.
Specs: Uses 35mm, 2¼×2¼, 4×5 transparencies.
Payment & Terms: Pays 50-55% commission for color photos. Works on contract basis only. Offers nonexclusive contract. Contracts renew automatically with each submission for one year. Statements issued quarterly. Payment made quarterly. Photographers allowed to review account records to verify sales figures. Offers one-time rights. Informs photographer and allows him to negotiate when client requests all rights. Model release required. Captions required.

The maple leaf before a listing indicates that the market is Canadian.

Making Contact: Query with samples. Query with list of stock photo subjects. SASE. Reports in 1 month. Photo guidelines free with SASE. Tips sheet distributed annually to all photographers.

Tips: Wants to see "clear, bright colors and graphic style." Points out that they are "looking for photographs with people of all ages with good composition, lighting and color in any material for stock use. Send 200 transparencies which best represent work with a SASE, for consideration."

■‡**FOTO-PRESS TIMMERMANN,** Speckweg 34A, D-8521 Moehrendorf, West Germany. 9131/42801. Fax: 9131/450528. Contact: Wolfgang Timmermann. Stock photo agency. Has 100,000 slides. Clients include: ad agencies, audiovisual firms, businesses, book/encyclopedia publishers, magazine publishers, newspapers and calendar companies.

Needs: All themes: landscapes, countries, towns, people, business, nature.

Specs: Uses 35mm, 2¼×2¼, 4×5 and 8×10 transparencies.

Payment & Terms: Pays 50% commission on color prints. Average price per image to clients: $130-300. Enforces strict minimum prices. Works on nonexclusive contract basis only. First period: three years, automatically renewed for one year. Offers one-time rights. Model/property release preferred. Captions required, include state, country, city, subject, etc.

Making Contact: Interested in receiving work from newer, lesser-known photographers. Query with list of stock photo subjects. Send unsolicited photos by mail for consideration. SASE. Reports in 2 weeks.

■**FOTOS INTERNATIONAL,** 4230 Ben Ave., Studio City CA 91604. (818)508-6400. Fax: (818)762-2181. Manager: Max B. Miller. Has 4 million photos. Clients include: ad agencies, public relations firms, businesses, book publishers, magazine publishers, encyclopedia publishers, newspapers, calendar companies, TV and posters.

Needs: "We are the world's largest entertainment photo agency. We specialize exclusively in motion picture, TV and popular music subjects. We want color only! The subjects can include scenes from productions, candid photos, rock, popular or classical concerts, etc., and must be accompanied by full caption information."

Specs: Uses 35mm color transparencies only.

Payment & Terms: Buys photos outright; no commission offered. Pays $5-200/photo. Offers one-time rights and first rights. Model release optional. Captions required.

Making Contact: Query with list of stock photo subjects. SASE. Reports in 1 month.

FPG INTERNATIONAL CORP., 32 Union Square E., New York NY 10003. (212)777-4210. Director of Photography: Rebecca Taylor. A full service agency with emphasis on images for the advertising, corporate, design and travel markets. Member of Picture Agency Council of America (PACA).

Needs: High-tech industry, model-released human interest, foreign and domestic scenics in medium formats, still life, animals, architectural interiors/exteriors with property releases.

Specs: Minimum submission requirement per year—1,000 original color transparencies, exceptions for large format, 250 b&w full-frame 8×10 glossy prints.

Payment & Terms: Pays 50% commission upon licensing of reproduction rights. Works on contract basis only. Offers exclusive contract only. Contracts renew automatically upon contract date; 5-year contract. Charges catalog insertion fee; rate not specified. Statements issued monthly. Payment made monthly. Photographers allowed to review account records to verify sales figures. Licenses one-time rights; negotiable. "We sell various rights as required by the client." When client requests all rights, "we will contact a photographer and get his permission"; some conditions.

Making Contact: "Initial approach should be by mail. Tell us what kind of material you have, what your plans are for producing stock and what kind of commercial work you do. Enclose reprints of published work." Photo guidelines and tip sheets provided for affiliated photographers. Model/property releases required and must be indicated on photograph. Captions required.

Tips: "Submit regularly; we're interested in committed, high-caliber photographers only. Be selective and send only first-rate work. Our files are highly competitive."

FRANKLIN PHOTO AGENCY, 85 James Otis Ave., Centerville MA 02632. (508)428-4378. President: Nelson Groffman. Has 35,000 transparencies. Clients include: publishers, advertising and industrial.

Needs: Scenics, animals, horticultural subjects, dogs, cats, fish, horses, antique and classic cars, and insects.

Specs: Uses 35mm, 2¼×2¼ and 4×5 color transparencies. "More interest now in medium size format—2¼×2¼."

Payment & Terms: Pays 50% commission. General price range: $100-300; $60/b&w photo; $100/color photo. Works with or without contract, negotiable. Offers nonexclusive contract. Statements issued semi-annually. Payment made when client pays. Offers one-time and one-year exclusive rights. Informs photographer and allows him to negotiate when client requests all rights. Model/property release required for people, houses; present release on acceptance of photo. Photo captions preferred.

Clients, Agencies Expect More Than Generic Stock

The call for impressive stock photographs has never been louder, as more and more businesses discover the value of picture agencies. Rebecca Taylor, director of photography for FPG International Corporation in New York City, says many businesses are using stock as a first choice rather than hiring photographers for assignments. As a result, many photographers are turning to stock as a way of improving yearly profits.

© Michael Goldman

Rebecca Taylor

"For many years stock photos tended to have a very generic, fairly straightforward look. All agencies represented that kind of material," says Taylor, who has been with FPG for over 10 years. Although traditional stock is still very popular, buyers are searching for images that are unique and fit in with specific concepts they want to convey.

FPG's files include a wide range of images, from industrial shots and high-technology to animals, still lifes and special effects. In order to supply such diverse topics, the agency works with 150-200 photographers worldwide. "We look for photographers who want to explore creative avenues through stock, who are interested in trying new kinds of work," says Taylor. Newcomers chosen to work with FPG generally have very specific areas of expertise. "We don't bring on many new photographers. We are very selective. We have a lot of good photographers now and we want to make sure that the photographers we've got are doing everything they can do before we bring in additional material."

Taylor says she receives 20-30 portfolios each month from photographers eager to work with her agency. Whether a photographer will receive a response depends on the type of images he provides and the way he presents himself and his work. "Obviously we're interested in photographers who have high technical capabilities and really bring some kind of personal vision to their work. We're not just looking for run-of-the-mill, straight stock photographs," she says. Unprofessional queries, or letters from photographers who obviously don't understand what a stock agency is, will not get answered, she adds.

Taylor initially likes to see actual portfolios because they show how photographers are presenting themselves to the market. Then, based upon what she sees, she will ask for additional samples, anywhere from "a couple hundred to five hundred." Once photographers sign contracts they should be prepared to shoot a lot of film and provide top-notch images on a regular basis.

Taylor says freelancers often fail to provide enough material, which hurts their chances of success and the income potential for the agency. "I don't think they quite understand it until they get into it. And the people who really, really succeed are very committed to producing on a regular basis," she says. The number of submissions depends on the subjects a photographer shoots. A sports photographer, for example, will shoot a lot more film than someone shooting photos of automobiles.

In recent years Taylor has seen an increasing number of photographers using computers to alter images. She sees this as both a help and a hindrance. "Sometimes I think it works very well," she says. "There are people who are very skilled at creating and combining or retouching images on a computer; they can maintain a photographic integrity and make it look very good. It all depends on the skill of the people doing it and, fortunately, we have very good people doing it."

On the flip side, however, there are many photographers who have the equipment to alter images, but don't have the talent. "I think it is very easy to put two pictures together, but a photographer should bring to it an eye for light and shadow, and a balance amongst the elements they're bringing in," she says.

In spite of the technological changes, it's still crucial that the photographer create excellent, marketable photographs. To do this it helps to know how an agency's files are set up and what formats are preferred. It also is important to let the subject matter dictate the format you use. Then find agencies that suit your style. "If you are a 35mm shooter and you are competing against the larger formats, that may be to your detriment," says Taylor, pointing out that clients often tend to prefer larger transparencies.

— *Michael Willins*

66 We look for photographers who want to explore creative avenues through stock, who are interested in trying new kinds of work. **99**

— Rebecca Taylor

Making Contact: Interested in receiving work from newer, lesser-known photographers. Query first with resume of credits. SASE. Reports in 1 month.
Tips: Wants to see "clear, creative pictures—dramatically recorded."

■**FROZEN IMAGES, INC.**, Suite 512, 400 First Ave. N., Minneapolis MN 55401. (612)339-3191. Director: Lonnie Schroeder. Stock photo agency. Has approximately 175,000 photos. Clients include: ad agencies, public relations firms, audiovisual firms, graphic designers, businesses, book/encyclopedia publishers, magazine publishers, newspapers and calendar companies.
Needs: All subjects including abstracts, scenics, industry, agriculture, US and foreign cities, high tech, businesses, sports, people and families.
Specs: Uses transparencies.
Payment & Terms: Pays 50% commission on color photos. Works on contract basis only. Offers limited regional exclusivity. Contracts renew automatically with each submission; time period not specified. Charges catalog insertion fee; rate not specified. Statements issued monthly. Payment made monthly; within 10 days of end of month. Photographers allowed to review account records to verify sales figures "with notice and by appointment." Offers one-time rights. Informs photographers when client requests all rights, but agency negotiates terms. Model/property release required for people and private property. Photo captions required.
Making Contact: Query with resume of credits. Query with list of stock photo subjects. SASE. Reports in 1 month or ASAP (sometimes 6 weeks). Photo guidelines free with SASE. Tips sheet distributed quarterly to photographers in the collection.
Tips: Wants to see "technical perfection, graphically strong, released (when necessary) images in all subject areas."

FUNDAMENTAL PHOTOGRAPHS, Dept. PM, 210 Forsyth St., New York NY 10002. (212)473-5770. Fax: (212)228-5059. Partner: Kip Peticolas. Estab. 1979. Stock photo agency. Applied for membership into the Picture Agency Council of America (PACA). Has 50,000 photos. Clients include: advertising agencies, book/encyclopedia publishers.
Needs: Science related topics.
Specs: Uses 35mm, 2¼×2¼, 4×5 and 8×10 transparencies.
Payment & Terms: Pays on commission basis; b&w 40%, color 50%. General price range: $100-500/b&w photo; $150-1,200/color photo, depends on rights needed. Enforces minimum prices. Offers volume discount to customers. Does not inform photographer or allow him to negotiate when client requests all rights. Works on contract basis only. Offers guaranteed subject exclusivity. Contracts renew automatically with additional submissions. Charges duping fees $25/4×5 dupe. Payment made quarterly. Photographers allowed to review account records. Offers one-time and electronic media rights. "We request permission and lowest fee from photographer." Model release preferred. Captions required.
Making Contact: Interested in receiving work from newer, lesser-known photographers. Arrange a personal interview to show portfolio. Submit portfolio for review. Query with resume of credits, samples or list of stock photo subjects. Keeps samples on file. SASE. Expects minimum initial submission of 100 images. Reports in 1-2 weeks. Photo guidelines free with SASE. Tips sheet distributed.
Tips: "We are looking for science subjects ranging from nature and rocks to industrials, medicine, chemistry and physics; macrophotography, stroboscopic, well lit still life shots are desirable. The biggest trend that affects us is the increased need for images that relate to the sciences and ecology."

■**GAMMA LIAISON**, 11 E. 26th St., New York NY 10010. (212)447-2525. Executive Vice President/Director: Jennifer Coley. Photographer Relations: Florence Nash. Has 5 million plus photographs. Extensive stock files include news (reportage), human interest stories, movie stills, personalities/celebrities. Clients include: newspapers and magazines, book publishers, audiovisual producers and encyclopedia publishers.
Needs: People, sports, scenics, travel, industry, medical, special effects, food and still life.
Specs: Uses 35mm or 2¼×2¼ transparencies.
Payment & Terms: Pays 50% commission. Works on contract basis only. Offers exclusive and non-exclusive contracts. Contracts renew automatically with each submission; time period not specified. Statements issued monthly. Payment made monthly. Leases one-time rights. Model release required. Captions required.
Making Contact: Submit portfolio with description of past experience and publication credits.
Tips: Involves a "rigorous trial period for first 6 months of association with photographer." Prefers previous involvement in publishing industry. Also has second division, Liaison International, which specializes in corporate assignment work and stock files for advertising agencies and graphic designers.

■‡**GEOSCIENCE FEATURES PICTURE LIBRARY**, 6 Orchard Dr., WYE, Kent TN25 5AU United Kingdom. (0233)812707 (UK). Fax: (0233)812707. Contact: Dr. Basil Booth. Stock photo agency, earth sciences and natural history picture library. Has 160,000 photos; approximately 10,000 feet 16mm film, mainly volcanic eruptions. Clients include: ad agencies, public relations firms, audiovisual firms, businesses, book/encyclopedia publishers, magazine publishers, newspapers, calendar companies and television companies.

Needs: Zoology (all aspects, particularly animal behavior, portrait shots of mammals, birds, reptiles, etc. are required but action pictures are being requested more these days; no zoo shots). Botany (all aspects, plants, for example, should include flower close-up, entire flower head and entire plant, plant adaptations, trees, etc.). Microbiology. Earth sciences, particularly violent weather (tornados), volcanic eruptions and northern lights. General subjects.

Specs: Uses 8×10 glossy b&w prints; 35mm, 2¼×2¼, 6×7cm, 4×5 and 8×10 transparencies; b&w and color contact sheets, 16mm film, and VHS videotape. "No filtration material; we will add at duping stage."

Payment & Terms: Pays 55% commission for b&w photos; 60% commission for color photos; 50% for film. General price range: £20-50/b&w photo; £30-500/color photo. Works on contract basis only. Statements issued on receipt of check from purchasing client. "Examination of account records by qualified accountant only and with respect to information concerning that photographer only. The photographer will be responsible for any charges made by his/her appointed accountant." Offers one-year exclusive and occasionally 3-year exclusive rights; mostly nonexclusive, one-time only, one-edition and territory rights. Model release preferred. Captions required (brief).

Making Contact: Interested in receiving work from newer, lesser-known photographers. Arrange a personal interview to show portfolio. Query with resume of credits, samples and list of stock photo subjects. SASE. Expects minimum initial submission of 200 images. Reports in 2 weeks to 1 month, depending on work load. Photo guidelines free with SASE. Distributes tips sheet twice a year to all our photographers. "Concentrate in fields most familiar to you—i.e., bird photographers should specialize in birds, and so on, and improve technique, especially with difficult subjects."

Tips: Prefers to see "images that are razor sharp. Full color saturation. No filter gimmicks. Good composition (artistic where relevant). Where possible each picture should tell a story (except landscape, etc). Action shots. High speed flash. No posed wild animals. No domestic animals. Several themes to show photographer's versatility. Photographers should remember that we cannot supply any images unless such images are specifically requested by a client. It can take 6 months to 2 years before results come in. Images should be factual and well-composed, but not arty."

■‡**GEOSLIDES & GEO AERIAL (Photography)**, 4 Christian Fields, London SW16 3JZ England. Tel. and Fax: (081)764-6292. Library Directors: John Douglas (Geoslides); Kelly White (Geo Aerial). Picture library. Has approximately 100,000 photos. Clients include: ad agencies, public relations firms, audiovisual firms, businesses, book/encyclopedia publishers, magazine publishers, newspapers, calendar companies and television.

Needs: Only from: Africa (South of Sahara); Asia; Arctic and Sub-Arctic; Antarctic. Anything to illustrate these areas. Accent on travel/geography and aerial (oblique) shots.

Specs: Uses 8×10 glossy b&w prints; 35mm and 2¼×2¼ transparencies.

Payment & Terms: Pays 50% commission. General price range $70-1,000. Works with or without contract; negotiable. Offers nonexclusive contract. Statements issued monthly. Payment made upon receipt of client's fees. Offers one-time rights and first rights. Does not inform photographer or allow him to negotiate when client requests all rights. Model release required. Photo captions required; include description of location, subject matter and sometimes the date.

Making Contact: Query with resume of credits and list of stock photo subjects. SASE. Reports in 1 month. Photo guidelines for SASE (International Reply Coupon). No samples until called for. Leaflets available.

Tips: Looks for "technical perfection, detailed captions, must suit lists (especially in areas). Increasingly competitive on an international scale. Quality is important. Need for large stocks with frequent renewals." To break in, "build up a comprehensive (i.e. in subject or geographical area) collection of photographs which are well documented."

JOEL GORDON PHOTOGRAPHY, 112 4th Ave., New York NY 10003. (212)254-1688. Picture Agent: Joel Gordon. Stock photo agency. Clients include: ad agencies, designers and textbook/encyclopedia publishers.

Specs: Uses 8×10 b&w prints, 35mm transparencies, b&w contact sheets and b&w negatives.

Payment & Terms: "Usually" pays 50% commission on b&w and color photos. Offers volume discounts to customers; terms specified in contract. Photographers can choose not to sell images on discount terms. Offers nonexclusive contract. Payment made after customer's check clears. Photographers allowed to review account records to verify sales figures. Does inform photographer and allow him to negotiate when client requests all rights. Offers one-time rights. Model/property release and photo captions preferred.

Making Contact: Interested in receiving work from newer, lesser-known photographers.

*■AL GROTELL UNDERWATER PHOTOGRAPHY, #15D, 170 Park Row, New York NY 10038. (212)349-3165. Fax: (212)349-4363. Owner: Al Grotell. Estab. 1971. Stock photo agency. Has 12,000 photos. Clients include: advertising agencies, audiovisual firms, businesses, book/encyclopedia publishers, magazine publishers, newpapers, calendar companies.

Needs: All underwater subjects.

Specs: Color prints; 35mm transparencies.

Payment & Terms: Pays 50% commission on color. Offers volume discounts to customers; terms specified in photographer's contract. Discount sales terms not negotiable. Works with or without a signed contract, negotiable. No statements issued. Payment made immediately after payment from client. Buys one-time rights. Informs photographer and allows him to negotiate when client requests all rights. Model release preferred. Captions required.

Making Contact: Interested in receiving work from newer, lesser-known photographers. Query with stock photo list. SASE. Reports in 1-2 weeks.

Tips: Looking for material not currently in stock.

■HIGH COUNTRY IMAGES, 631 Lupfer Ave., Whitefish MT 59937. (406)862-6622 or (406)862-6617. Manager: Alan T. Thompson. Estab. 1990. Stock photo agency. Has 10,000-20,000 slides; 8,000-12,000 negatives. Clients include: advertising agencies, businesses, book/encyclopedia publishers, magazine publishers, calendar companies, greeting card companies.

Needs: "All subject matter except nude or obscene. Prefer shots of people doing things, mixed races, travel, hobbies, pets, children, farm, etc."

Specs: Uses 8 × 10 glossy b&w or color prints; 35mm or 2¼ × 2¼ transparencies; 8mm, super 8, 16mm, 35mm film; VHS videotape.

Payment & Terms: Pays 50% commission on b&w and color photos; 80% commission on films and videos. General price range: $75-100 b&w; $100-300 color. Photographers can choose not to sell images on discount terms. Works on contract basis only. Offers nonexclusive contract. Contract renews automatically with additional submissions. Charges $1 catalog insertion fee. Statements issued quarterly. Payment made monthly. Photographers permitted to review account records to verify sales figures or account for various deductions. Offers one-time rights. Informs photographer and allows him to negotiate when client requests all rights. Model/property release required. Photo captions required; include "when, what, where, etc."

Making Contact: Interested in receiving work from newer, lesser-known photographers. Send for free information. SASE. Reports in 1 month. Photo guidelines free with SASE. Market tips sheet distributed quarterly to contracted photographers; details free with SASE.

Tips: Query first, then send best work (3 × 5) print sample. Do not send originals or negatives. "We use a lot of shots with people doing things and mixed races working together."

■HILLSTROM STOCK PHOTO, INC., Dept. PM, 5483 N. Northwest Hwy., (Box 31100), Chicago IL 60630 (60631 for Box No.). (312)775-4090, 775-3557. President: Ray F. Hillstrom, Jr. Stock photo agency. Has 1 million color transparencies; 50,000 b&w prints. "We have a 22-agency network." Clients include: ad agencies, public relations firms, audiovisual firms, businesses, book/encyclopedia publishers, magazine publishers, newspapers, calendar companies, greeting card companies and sales promotion agencies.

Needs: "We need hundreds of 35mm color model-released sports shots (all types); panoramic 120mm format worldwide images. Model-released: heavy industry, medical, high-tech industry, computer-related subjects, family-oriented subjects, foreign travel, adventure sports and high-risk recreation, Midwest festivals (country fairs, parades, etc.), the Midwest. We need more color model released family, occupation, sport, student, senior citizen, high tech and on-the-job shots."

Specs: Uses 8 × 10 b&w prints; 35mm, 2¼ × 2¼ and 4 × 5 transparencies.

Payment & Terms: Pays $50-5,000/b&w and color photo. Pays 50% commission on b&w and color photos. Works with or without contract, negotiable. Offers limited regional exclusivity. Statements issued periodically; time period not specified. Payment made monthly; within 30 days. Photographers allowed to review account records to verify sales figures. Offers one-time rights. Informs photographer and allows him to negotiate when client requests all rights. Model/property release required for people and private property. Captions required; include location, subject and description of function.

Making Contact: Send unsolicited photos by mail for consideration. Include three business cards and detailed stock photo list. SAE and check for postage for return of submitted material; make check payable to Hillstrom Stock Photo. Reports in 3 weeks. Photo guidelines free with SASE.

Tips: Prefers to see good professional images, proper exposure, mounted, and name IDs on mount. In photographer's samples, looks for "large format, model and property release, high-tech, people on the job, worldwide travel and environment. Show us at least 200 different images with 200 different subjects."

■‡HOLT STUDIOS INTERNATIONAL, LTD., The Courtyard, 24 High St., Hungerford, Berkshire, RG17 0NF United Kingdom. 0488-683523. Director: Nigel D. Cattlin. Picture library. Has 50,000 photos. Clients include: ad agencies, public relations firms, audiovisual firms, businesses, book/encyclopedia publishers, magazine publishers and newspapers.
Needs: Photographs of world agriculture associated with crop production and crop protection including healthy crops and relevant weeds, pests, diseases and deficiencies. Farming, people and machines throughout the year including good landscapes. Livestock and livestock management. Worldwide assignments undertaken.
Specs: Uses 35mm, 2¼ × 2¼ and 4 × 5 transparencies.
Payment & Terms: Occasionally buys photos outright. Pays 50% commission. General price range: $100-1,500. Offers guaranteed subject exclusivity. Contracts renew automatically with additional submissions; for three years. Offers one-time rights. Model release preferred. Captions required.
Making Contact: Interested in receiving work from newer, lesser-known photographers. Send unsolicited photos by mail for consideration. SASE. Reports in 2 weeks. Photo guidelines free with SASE. Distributes tips sheets every 3 months to all associates.
Tips: "Holt Studios looks for high quality technically well-informed and fully labeled color transparencies of subjects of agricultural interest." Currently sees "expanding interest particularly conservation and the environment."

■✦HOT SHOTS STOCK SHOTS, INC., 341 Lesmill Rd., Toronto, Ontario M3B 2V1 Canada. (416)441-3281. Fax: (416)441-1468. Attention: Editor. Member of Picture Agency Council of America (PACA). Clients include: advertising and design agencies, publishers, major printing houses and product manufacturers.
Needs: People and human interest/lifestyles, commerce and industry, wildlife, historic and symbolic Canadian.
Specs: Color transparency material any size, b&w contacts only.
Payment & Terms: Pays 50% commission, quarterly upon collection; 30% for foreign sales through sub-agents. Price ranges: $200-2,000. Pays $100-500/b&w photo; $100-3,000/color photo. Works on contract basis only. Offers exclusive, limited regional exclusivity and nonexclusive contracts. Most contracts renew automatically for 3-year period with each submission. Charges catalog insertion fee of 50% of separation costs. Statements issued quarterly. Payment made quarterly. Photographers allowed to review account to verify sales figures. Offers one-time, electronic media, and other rights to clients. Allows photographer to negotiate when client requests all rights. Requests agency promotion rights. Model/property release preferred. Photo captions required, include where, when, what, who, etc.
Making Contact: Must send a minimum of 300 images. Unsolicited submissions must have return postage. Reports in 1 week. Photo guidelines free with business SASE.
Tips: "Submit colorful, creative, current, technically strong images with negative space in composition." Looks for people, lifestyles, variety, bold composition, style, flexibility and productivity. "People should be model released for top sales. Prefer Kodachrome and medium format." Photographers should "shoot for business, not for artistic gratification; tightly edited, good technical points (exposure, sharpness etc.) professionally mounted, captioned/labeled and good detail."

■‡THE HUTCHISON LIBRARY, 118B Holland Park Ave., London W11 4UA England. (071)229-2743. Director: Michael Lee. Stock photo agency, picture library. Has around 500,000 photos. Clients include: ad agencies, public relations firms, audiovisual firms, businesses, book/encyclopedia publishers, magazine publishers, newspapers, postcard companies, calendar companies, television and film companies.
Needs: "We are a general, documentary library (no news or personalities, no modeled 'set-up' shots). We file mainly by country and aim to have coverage of every country in the world. Within each country we cover such subjects as industry, agriculture, people, customs, urban, landscapes, etc. We have special files on many subjects such as medical (traditional, alternative, hospital etc.), energy, environmental issues, human relations (relationships, childbirth, young children, etc. but all *real people*, not models). We are principally a color library though we hold a very small collection of b&w 'back-up.' "
Specs: Uses 8 × 10 b&w prints and 35mm transparencies.
Payment & Terms: Pays 50% commission for b&w and color photos. Statements issued semiannually. Payment made semiannually. Sends statement with check in June and January. Offers one-time rights. Model release preferred. Captions required.

Market conditions are constantly changing! If you're still using this book and it's 1995 or later, buy the newest edition of Photographer's Market at your favorite bookstore or order directly from Writer's Digest Books.

Making Contact: Arrange a personal interview to show portfolio. Send letter with brief description of collection and photographic intentions. Reports in about 2 weeks, depends on backlog of material to be reviewed. "We have letters outlining working practices and lists of particular needs (they change)." Distributes tips sheets to photographers who already have a relationship with the library.

Tips: Looks for "collections of reasonable size (rarely less than 1,000 transparencies) and variety, well captioned (or at least well indicated picture subjects, captions can be added to mounts later), sharp pictures (an out of focus tree branch or whatever the photographer thinks adds mood is not acceptable, clients must not be relied on to cut out difficult areas of any picture), good color, composition and informative pictures, prettiness is rarely enough . . . our clients want information, whether it is about what a landscape looks like or how people live, etc. We only very occasionally accept a new collection. The general rule of thumb is that we would consider a collection which had a subject we did not already have coverage of or a detailed and thorough specialist collection."

■‡**I.C.P. INTERNATIONAL COLOUR PRESS**, Via Alberto Da Giussano 15, Milano Italy 20145. (02)4696459 or 48008493. Fax: (02)48195625. Marketing Assistant: Alessandro Bissocoli. Estab. 1970. Stock photo agency. Has 1.2 million transparencies. Clients include: advertising agencies, public relations firms, audiovisual firms, businesses, book/encyclopedia publishers, magazine publishers, postcard publishers, calendar companies and greeting card companies.

Specs: Uses 35mm, 2¼×2¼, 4×5 and 8×10 transparencies only.

Payment & Terms: Pays 50% commission on color photos. Average price per image (to clients): $400/color image. Offers volume discounts to customers; terms specified in photographer's contract. Discount sales terms not negotiable. Works on exclusive contract basis only. Contracts renew automatically with additional submissions, for three years. Charges 100% duping, postage and packing fees. Statements issued monthly. Payment made monthly. Photographers permitted to review account records to verify sales figures or deductions. Offers one-time, first and sectorial exclusive rights. Model/property release required. Captions required.

Making Contact: Arrange personal interview to show portfolio. Query with samples and stock photo list. Works on assignment only. SASE. No fixed minimum for initial submission. Reports in 3 weeks.

*‡**THE IMAGE FACTORY**, 7 Green Walks, Prestwich, Manchester M25 5DS England. (061)798-0435. Fax: (061)224-0893. Principal: Jeff Anthony. Estab. 1988. Picture library. Has 200,000 photos. Has 2 branch offices. Clients include: advertising agencies, public relations firms, audiovisual firms, businesses, book/encyclopedia publishers, magazine publishers, newspapers, postcard publishers, calendar companies and greeting card companies.

Needs: Needs photos from all over the world.

Specs: Uses 35mm, 2¼×2¼, 4×5, 8×10 transparencies.

Payment & Terms: Pays 60% commission. Works on contract basis only. Offers guaranteed subject exclusivity. Contracts renew automatically with additional submissions; originally for 3 years and then annually. Statements issued annually. Photographers allowed to review account records. Offers one-time rights. Informs photographer and allows him to negotiate when client requests all rights. Model/property release preferred. Captions required, include as many details as possible.

Making Contact: Interested in receiving work from newer, lesser-known photographers. Submit portfolio for review. SASE. Expects minimum initial submission of 100 images. Reports in 1 month. Photo guidelines free with SASE. Market tips sheet distributed annually; free with SASE.

Tips: Looks for "good color saturation, clarity and good description. We will look at anything if the quality is good."

■✳**IMAGE FINDERS PHOTO AGENCY, INC.**, 7th Floor, 134 Abbott St., Vancouver, British Columbia V6B 2K4 Canada. (604)688-9818. General Manager: Pindar Azad. Has 300,000 photos of all subjects. Clients include: ad agencies, graphic designers, public relations firms, businesses, audiovisual firms, book publishers, magazine publishers, encyclopedia publishers, newspapers, postcard companies, calendar companies and greeting card companies.

Needs: Business, education, medical, hospitality, service and industrial, and general worldwide stock.

Specs: Uses transparencies only.

Payment & Terms: Pays 50% commission. General price range: $200+, more for ad campaigns. Works on contract basis only. Offers limited regional exclusivity. Some contracts renew automatically with each submission; time periods of 1 and 2 years according to contract. Charges duping fee of 50%/image; takes out of commissions. Charges variable catalog insertion fee; takes out of commissions. Statements issued quarterly. Payment made quarterly. Offers one-time rights, all rights or first rights. Informs photographer and allows him to negotiate when client requests all rights; "requires photographer's written approval." Model/property release required for people and houses. Captions required; include description, technical data, etc.

Making Contact: "Send SASE for questionnaire and description of agency. Please do not send unsolicited material. Tearsheets OK." Photo guidelines free with SAE and International Reply Coupons. *"Please no foreign stamps—stamps must be Canadian."* Distributes quarterly want list to established contributors.

Tips: "Show the very best work. Ask lots of questions, and review monthly magazine and stock catalogs."

■**THE IMAGE WORKS**, P.O. Box 443, Woodstock NY 12498. (914)246-8800. Directors: Mark Antman and Alan Carey. Stock photo agency. Member of Picture Agency Council of America (PACA). Has 350,000 photos. Clients include: ad agencies, audiovisual firms, book/encyclopedia publishers, magazine publishers and newspapers.

Needs: "We specialize in documentary style photography of worldwide subject matter. People in real life situations that reflect their social, economic, political, leisure time and cultural lives." Topic areas include health care, education, business, family life and travel locations.

Specs: Uses 8×10 glossy/semi-glossy b&w prints; 35mm and 2¼×2¼ transparencies.

Payment & Terms: Pays 50% commission on b&w and color photos. General price range: $135-900. Works on contract basis only. Offers nonexclusive contract. Charges duping fee of $1.75. Charges catalog insertion fee of 50%. Statements issued monthly. Payment made monthly. Photographers allowed to review account records to verify sales figures by appointment. Photographer must also pay for accounting time. Offers one-time and electronic media rights. Informs photographer and allows him to negotiate when client requests all rights. Model release preferred. Captions required.

Making Contact: Query with list of stock photo subjects or samples. SASE. Reports in 1 month. Tips sheet distributed monthly to contributing photographers.

Tips: "We want to see photographs that have been carefully edited, that show technical control and a good understanding of the subject matter. All photographs must be thoroughly captioned and indicate if they are model released. The Image Works is known for its strong multicultural coverage in the United States and around the world. Photographs should illustrate real-life situations, but not look contrived. They should have an editorial/photojournalistic feel, but be clean and uncluttered with strong graphic impact for both commercial and editorial markets. We are actively expanding our collection of humor photographs and are interested in seeing new work in this area. Photographers who work with us must be hard workers. They have to want to make money at their photography and have a high degree of self-motivation to succeed. As new digital-based photographic and design technology forces changes in the industry there will be a greater need for experienced photo agencies who know how to service a broad range of clients with very different needs. The agency personnel must be versed, not only in the quality and subject matter of its imagery, but also in the various new options for getting photos to picture buyers. As new uses of photography in new media continue to evolve, the need for agencies from the perspective of both photographers and picture buyers will continue to grow."

■**IMAGERY UNLIMITED**, P.O. Box 2878, Alameda CA 94501. (510)769-9766. President: Jordan Coonrad. Estab. 1981. Stock photo agency. Has 50,000+ photos. Clients include: advertising agencies, public relations firms, designers, audiovisual firms, businesses, book/encyclopedia publishers, magazine publishers, newspapers, and postcard and calendar companies.

Needs: Needs photos of "military, aviation, aerials, computers, business situations, travel and high-tech industry."

Specs: Uses 35mm, 2¼×2¼, 4×5, 8×10 transparencies.

Payment & Terms: Sometimes buys photos outright. Pays 30-60%; "50% is average." General price range: $200-5,000. Works with or without contract, negotiable. Charges various fees; types and amounts not specified. Statements issued monthly. Payment made monthly. Photographers allowed to review account records to verify sales figures. Offers one-time rights, electronic media rights and various negotiable rights. "Rights are negotiated based on client needs." Informs photographer and allows him to negotiate when client requests all rights. Model release preferred for "people in advertising or corporate use." Photo captions are required; include description of subject and noteworthy facts.

Making Contact: Query with resume of credits. Query with samples. Send stock photo list. Also "send photos when requested after initial contact." SASE. Reports in 1 month. Photo guidelines not available. Tips sheet sometimes distributed.

Tips: In freelancer's samples, wants to see high quality, sharp, graphic images. "Prefer Kodachrome. Other film OK in 2¼ and larger formats. Submit 100-200 well-edited images in pages. *No yellow boxes.*" Sees trend toward "increased use of stock photos."

IMAGES PRESS SERVICE CORP., Dept. PM, 7 E. 17th St., New York NY 10003. (212)675-3707. Fax: (212)243-2308. Managers: Peter Gould and Barbara Rosen. Has 100,000+ photos. Clients include: public relations firms, book publishers, magazine publishers and newspapers.

© Voller Ernst/Image Works

Dogs often chase cars, but ships? The humor in this photo is obvious. It's almost as if the dog has completed a mission and is now happily on his way. Mark Antman, co-director of the Image Works, says his agency received this image from one of its foreign affiliates, Voller Ernst, in Berlin, Germany.

Needs: Current events, celebrities, feature stories, pop music, pin-ups and travel.
Specs: Uses b&w prints, 35mm transparencies, b&w contact sheets and b&w negatives.
Payment & Terms: Pays 50% commission on b&w and color photos. General price range: $50-1,000. Offers one-time rights or first rights. Captions required.
Making Contact: Query with resume of credits or with list of stock photo subjects. Also send tearsheets or photocopies of "already published material, original story ideas, gallery shows, etc." SASE. Reports in 2 weeks.
Tips: Prefers to see "material of wide appeal with commercial value to publication market; original material similar to what is being published by magazines sold on newsstands. We are interested in ideas from freelancers that can be marketed and assignments arranged with our clients and subagents." Wants to see "features that might be of interest to the European or Japanese press, and that have already been published in local media. Send copy of publication and advise rights available." To break in, be persistent and offer fresh perspective.

■**IMPACT VISUALS PHOTO & GRAPHIC, INC.**, Suite 901, 28 W. 27th St., New York NY 10001. (212)683-9688. Co-Editors: Donna Binder and Robert Fox. News/feature syndicate. Has 500,000 images in archive. Clients include: public relations firms, audiovisual firms, businesses, book/encyclopedia publishers, magazine publishers, newspapers, progressive organizations, churches, unions and nonprofit organizations.
Needs: Needs "b&w and color transparency work . . . news and documentary photos on issues of social concern: especially poverty, workers, environment, racism, gay/lesbian, anti-intervention, government, Latin America, Africa, Asia; also economics, education, health, etc.
Specs: Uses 8×10 glossy or matte b&w prints; 35mm transparencies.
Payment & Terms: Does not buy outright. Pays 50% commission on b&w and color photos to members, 40% to contributors. Pays $25-2,500; most in $75-225 range. Works with or without contract; negotiable. Offers exclusive contract only. Contracts renew automatically with each submission for 1 year period after initial term of 2 years. Charges duping fee of 100%/image. Statements issued bi-

monthly. Payment made bimonthly. Photographers allowed to review account records to verify sales figures; "by appointment for full members." Offers one-time rights; other rights negotiable. Informs photographer and allows him to negotiate when client requests all rights; "handled through the agency on a separate percentage." Model release preferred. Captions required; include "date, place, who and what."

Making Contact: Write for intro brochure for "new members." SASE. Reports in 1 month. Photo guidelines free with SASE. Tip sheet distributed bi-monthly to members only.

Tips: In portfolio or samples, especially looks for "20-30 b&w prints, captioned, and/or 40-60 color slides, captioned. Should show news or documentary from a progressive perspective, with strong composition and excellent technique on 'issues of social concern.' Also include resume and note about interests and political perspectives broadly speaking."

■**INDEX STOCK PHOTOGRAPHY**, 126 Fifth Ave., New York NY 10011. (212)929-4644. Fax: (212)633-1914. Photo Editor: Lindsey Nicholson. Has 500,000 tightly edited photos. Clients include: ad agencies; corporate design firms; graphic design and in-house agencies; direct mail production houses; magazine publishers; audiovisual firms; calendar, postcard and greeting card companies.

Needs: Up-to-date, model-released, people photos. Also: business executives and activities in general, industry, technology (science & research) and computers, family, mature adults, sports, US and general scenics, major cities and local color, foreign/travel, and animals.

Specs: Uses 35mm, 2¼×2¼, 4×5 and 8×10 transparencies. "All images must be sleeved."

Payment & Terms: Pays 50% commission on back-up material; 25% on catalog shots. General price range: $125-5,000. Works on contract basis only. Offers exclusive only, few nonexclusive rights. Contracts renew automatically with additional submissions. Charges 25% catalog insertion fee. Statements issued quarterly. Payment made quarterly. "We pay when we issue an invoice, regardless of when we are paid by our customers." Photographers allowed to review account records. Sells one-time rights plus some limited buyouts (all rights) and exclusives. Informs photographer but does not allow him to negotiate when client requests all rights. Model/property releases required. Captions required.

Making Contact: Interested in receiving work from newer, lesser-known photographers "if they are members of some professional organization such as ASMP." Query with list of stock photo subjects. Reports in 2 weeks with submission guidelines and general information.

Tips: "Index has grown rapidly over the past three years. We are highly-automated and service-oriented. We have expanded our Far Eastern representation to include Korea, Taiwan and Hong Kong and our European representation to include Portugal, Austria, and Czechoslovakia. Educate yourself to the demands and realities of the stock photography marketplace, find out where your own particular style and expertise fit in, and edit unmercifully. The demands for new images increase daily as more ad people become comfortable using stock images that rival assignment work." Looks for "technically perfect samples of that photographer's personal expertise; different examples/compositions of the same subject. Submit 200-500 originals (in person or by mail) that are representative of your work."

INTERNATIONAL COLOR STOCK, INC., Dept. PM, Suite 1502, 555 NE 34th St., Miami FL 33137. (305)573-5200. Contact: Dagmar Fabricius or Randy Taylor. Estab. 1989. Stock photo syndicate. Clients include: foreign agencies distributing to all markets.

Needs: "We serve as a conduit, passing top-grade, model-released production stock to foreign agencies. We have no US sales and no US archives."

Specs: Uses 35mm, 2¼×2¼ transparencies.

Payment & Terms: Pays 80% commission. Works on contract basis only. Offers exclusive foreign contract only. Contracts renew automatically on annual basis. Charges duping fee of 100%/image. Also charges catalog insertion fee of 100%/image. Statements issued monthly. Payment made monthly. Photographers allowed to review account records to verify sales figures "upon reasonable notice, during normal business hours." Offers one-time rights. Requests agency promotion rights. Informs photographer and allows him to negotiate when client requests all rights; "if notified by subagents." Model/property release required. Captions preferred; include "who, what, where, when, why and how."

Making Contact: Query with resume of credits. Reports "only when photographer is of interest" to them. Photo guidelines sheet not available. Tips sheet not distributed.

Tips: Has strong preference for experienced photographers. "Our percentages are extremely low. Because of this, we deal only with top shooters seeking long-term success. If you are not published 20 times a month or have not worked on contract for two or more photo agencies or have less than 15 years experience, please do not call us."

INTERNATIONAL PHOTO NEWS, Dept. PM, 193 Sandpiper Ave., Royal Palm Beach FL 33411. (407)793-3424. Photo Editor: Jay Kravetz. News/feature syndicate. Has 50,000 photos. Clients include: newspapers, magazines and book publishers. Previous/current clients include: *Lake Worth Herald*, *S. Florida Entertainment Guide* and *Prime-Time*; all three celebrity photos with story.

Needs: Celebrities of politics, movies, music and television at work or play.
Specs: Uses 5×7, 8×10 glossy b&w prints.
Payment & Terms: General price range: $5. Pays $5/b&w photo; $10/color photo; 25% commission. Offers one-time rights. Captions required.
Making Contact: Query with resume of credits. Solicits photos by assignment only. SASE. Reports in 1 week.
Tips: "We use celebrity photographs to coincide with our syndicated columns. Must be approved by the celebrity."

INTERNATIONAL STOCK, Dept. PM, 113 E. 31st St., New York NY 10016. (212)696-4666. Fax: (212)725-1241. Managing Director: Donna Sickels. Estab. 1982. Stock photo agency. Member of Picture Agency Council of America (PACA). Has 1 million photos. Clients include: advertising agencies, public relations firms, audiovisual firms, businesses, book/encyclopedia publishers, magazine publishers, newspapers, postcard companies, calendar companies, greeting card companies.
Needs: Model-released people/lifestyle photos for advertising, worldwide travel, industry, corporate and computer scenes, medicine and health, food, fashion, special effects, sports, scenics and animals.
Specs: Uses b&w and color prints; 35mm, 2¼×2¼, 4×5 and 8×10 transparencies.
Payment & Terms: Pays 50% commission on b&w and color photos. General price range: $350-500. Offers one-time rights and all rights. Model release preferred. Captions required.
Making Contact: Query with list of stock photo subjects. SASE. Reports in 2 weeks. Photo guidelines free with SASE. Market tips sheet distrubuted to contracted photographers.

INTERPRESS OF LONDON AND NEW YORK, 400 Madison Ave., New York NY 10017. Editor: Jeffrey Blyth. Has 5,000 photos. Clients include: magazine publishers and newspapers.
Needs: Offbeat news and feature stories of interest to European editors. Captions required.
Specs: Uses 8×10 b&w prints and 35mm color transparencies.
Payment & Terms: NPI. Offers one-time rights.
Making Contact: Send material by mail for consideration. SASE. Reports in 1 week.

JEROBOAM, INC., 120-D 27th St., San Francisco CA 94110. (415)824-8085. Contact: Ellen Bunning. Has 150,000 b&w photos, 100,000 color slides. Clients include: text and trade books, magazine and encyclopedia publishers and editorial.
Needs: "We want people interacting, relating photos, artistic/documentary/photojournalistic images, especially minorities and handicapped. Images must have excellent print quality—contextually interesting and exciting, and artistically stimulating." Need shots of school, family, career and other living situations. Child development, growth and therapy, medical situations. No nature or studio shots.
Specs: Uses 8×10 double weight glossy b&w prints with a ¼" border. Also uses 35mm transparencies.
Payment & Terms: Works on consignment only; pays 50% commission. Works without a signed contract. Statements issued monthly. Payment made monthly. Photographers allowed to review account records to verify sales figures. Offers one-time rights. Informs photographer and allows him to negotiate when client requests all rights. Model/property release preferred for people in contexts of special education, sexuality, etc. Captions preferred; include "age of subject, location, etc."
Making Contact: Interested in receiving work from newer, lesser-known photographers. Call if in the Bay area; if not, query with samples; query with list of stock photo subjects; send material by mail for consideration or submit portfolio for review. "We look at portfolios the first Wednesday of every month." SASE. Reports in 2 weeks.
Tips: "The Jeroboam photographers have shot professionally a minimum of 5 years, have experienced some success in marketing their talent and care about their craft excellence and their own creative vision. Jeroboam images are clear statements of single moments with graphic or emotional tension. We look for people interacting, well exposed and printed with a moment of interaction. New trends are toward more intimate, action shots even more ethnic images needed. Be honest in regards to subject matter (what he/she *likes* to shoot)."

■**JOAN KRAMER AND ASSOCIATES, INC.**, Suite 605, 10490 Wilshire Blvd., Los Angeles CA 90024. (310)446-1866. Fax: (310)446-1856. President: Joan Kramer. Member of Picture Agency Council of America (PACA). Has 1 million b&w and color photos dealing with travel, cities, personalities, animals, flowers, lifestyles, underwater, scenics, sports and couples. Clients include: ad agencies, maga-

---

Can't find a listing? Check at the end of each market section for the " '93-'94 Changes" lists. These lists include any market listings from the '93 edition which were either not verified or deleted in this edition.

zines, recording companies, photo researchers, book publishers, greeting card companies, promotional companies and AV producers.

Needs: "We use any and all subjects! Stock slides must be of professional quality."

Specs: Uses 8×10 glossy b&w prints; any size transparencies.

Payment & Terms: Pays 50% commission. Offers all rights. Model release required.

Making Contact: Query or call to arrange an appointment. Do not send photos before calling. SASE.

HAROLD M. LAMBERT STUDIOS, INC., Dept. PM, P.O. Box 27310, Philadelphia PA 19150. (215)885-3355. Vice President: Raymond W. Lambert. Has 1.5 million b&w photos and 400,000 transparencies of all subjects. Clients include: ad agencies, publishers and religious organizations.

Needs: Farm, family, industry, sports, robotics in industry, scenics, travel and people activities. No flowers, zoo shots or nudes.

Specs: Uses 35mm, 2¼×2¼ or 4×5 transparencies.

Payment & Terms: Buys photos outright—"rates depend on subject matter, picture quality and film size"; or pays 50% commission on color. Works on contract basis only. Offers nonexclusive contract. Offers one-time rights. Under some conditions, informs photographer and allows him to negotiate when client requests all rights. Model/property release required for people (single person and very small groups), domestic animals and real property. Captions preferred. Present model release on acceptance of photo. Submit material by mail for consideration. Reports in 2 weeks. SASE. Free photo guidelines.

Making Contact & Terms: Send negatives or contact sheet. Photos should be submitted in blocks of 100.

Tips: "We return unaccepted material, advise of material held for our file, and supply our photo number." Also, "We have 7 selling offices throughout the US and Canada."

LANDMARK STOCK EXCHANGE, Dept. PM, 51 Digital Dr., Novato CA 94949. (415)883-1600. 1-800-288-5170. Fax: (415)883-6725. Contact: Director. Estab. 1989. Stock photo agency and licensing agents. Clients include: advertising agencies, design firms, book publishers, magazine, postcard, greeting card, poster publishers, T-shirts, design firms and "many" gift manufacturers.

Needs: Scenics, model-released people (women/men in swimsuits, children), cars, still-life, illustration, unique photographs i.e. abstracts, hand-colored, b&w images.

Specs: Uses 35mm, 2¼×2¼, 4×5 transparencies.

Payment & Terms: Pays 50% commission for licensed photos. Enforces minimum prices. "Prices are based on usage." Payment made monthly. Offers one-time rights. Model/property release required. Captions preferred for scenics and animals.

Making Contact: Arrange personal interview to show portfolio. Submit portfolio for review. Query with samples. Query with stock photo list or phone call. Samples kept on file. SASE. Photo guidelines free on request.

Tips: "We are always looking for innovative, creative, images in all subject areas, and strive to set trends in the photo industry. Many of our clients are gift manufacturers. We look for images that are suitable for publication on posters, greeting cards, etc. We consistently get photo requests for outstanding scenics, swimsuit shots (men and women) and wildlife."

■LGI PHOTO AGENCY, Dept. PM, 241 W. 36th St., New York NY 10018. (212)736-4602. Vice President: Laura Giammarco. Estab. 1978. Stock photo agency and news/feature syndicate. Has 1 million photos. Clients include: advertising agencies, public relations firms, audiovisual firms, book/encyclopedia publishers, magazine publishers, newspapers and calendar companies.

Needs: "We handle news events which relate to personalities in TV, music, film, sports, politics etc. We also represent special studio and at-home sessions with these people."

Specs: Uses mostly photos, some film.

Payment & Terms: Pays 50% commission on b&w/color photos; percentage on film varies. General price range: minimum $125/b&w, $175/color. Offers one-time rights.

Making Contact: Arrange a personal interview to show portfolio. Non-local photographers can phone for advice submitting work for review. Works on assignment only. Cannot return material. Reports as needed.

LIAISON INTERNATIONAL, 11 E. 26th St., New York NY 10010. (212)447-2514. Vice President: Lisa Papel. Photographer Relations: Susan Carolonza. Corporate and stock division of Gamma Liaison. Extensive stock material with the following categories: people, scenic/nature, animals, food, sports, travel, industry, abstract/art. Clients include: corporations, graphic designers, advertising agencies.

Specs: Uses 35mm or 2¼×2¼ transparencies.

Payment & Terms: Pays 50% commission. Works on contract basis only. Offers exclusive contract only; works on assignment. Contracts renew automatically with each submission; time period not specified. Statements issued monthly. Payment made monthly. Offers all rights on assigned stock.

Making Contact: Submit portfolio with description of past experience and publication credits.
Tips: Involves a "rigorous trial period for first 6 months of association with photographer." Previous experience with corporate assignments or stock photography requested. (For editorial photography, see also listing for Gamma Liaison in this section).

LIGHT SOURCES STOCK, 23 Drydock Ave., Boston MA 02210. (617)261-0346. Fax: (617)261-0358. Editor: Sonja L. Rodrigue. Estab. 1989. Stock photo agency. Has 50,000 photos. Clients include: advertising agencies, book/encyclopedia publishers, magazine publishers, calendar companies, greeting card companies.
Needs: Children, families, educational, medical and scenics (travel).
Specs: Uses 35mm and 2¼×2¼ transparencies.
Payment & Terms: Pays 50% commission. Average price per image (to clients): $100-250/b&w photo; $100-450/ color photo. Enforces minimum prices. Offers volume discounts to customers; inquire about specific terms. Photographers can choose not to sell images on discount terms. Works on contract basis only. Offers nonexclusive contracts. Contracts renew automatically with additional submissions. Statements issued semiannually. "Payment is made when agency is paid by the client." Offers one-time rights. Informs photographer and allows him to negotiate when client requests all rights. Model/property release preferred. Captions required.
Making Contact: Interested in receiving work from newer, lesser-known photographers. Arrange personal interview to show portfolio. Samples kept on file. SASE. Expects minimum initial submission of 200 images with periodic submission of at least 100 images every six months. Reports in 1-2 weeks. Photo guidelines available.

LIGHTWAVE, Suite 306-114, 1430 Massachusetts Ave., Cambridge MA 02138. (617)628-1052. (800)628-6809 (outside 617 area code). Fax: (617)623-7568. Contact: Paul Light. Has 250,000 photos. Clients include: ad agencies and textbook publishers.
Needs: Candid photos of people in everyday activities in the U.S., France, Japan and Spain.
Specs: Uses color transparencies.
Payment & Terms: Buys photos outright; pays $190/photo. 50% commission. Works on contract basis only. Offers nonexclusive contract. Contracts renew automatically with each submission for one year. Statements issued annually. Payment made "after each usage." Offers one-time rights. Informs photographer and allows him to negotiate when client requests all rights. Model/property release preferred. Captions preferred.
Making Contact: Interested in receiving work from newer, lesser-known photographers. Send SASE for guidelines.
Tips: "Photographers should enjoy photographing people in everyday activities. Work should be carefully edited before submission. Shoot constantly and watch what is being published. We are looking for photographers who can photograph daily life with compassion and originality."

■**M.A. PHOTRI,** (formerly Marilyn Gartman Agency, Inc.), Dept. PM, 40 E. 9th St., Chicago IL 60605. (312)987-0078. Fax: (312)987-0134. President/Manager: John Ford. Stock photo agency. Has 500,000 photos. Clients include: ad agencies, public relations firms, audiovisual firms, businesses, book/encyclopedia publishers, magazine publishers and calendar companies.
Needs: Geographic (world wide) general categories going from subjects like abstracts to zoos.
Specs: Uses b&w prints, 35mm, 2¼×2¼, 4×5 and 8×10 transparencies.
Payment & Terms: Pays 50% commission for b&w and color photos. Offers one-time rights. Model release required. Captions required.
Making Contact: Query with resume of credits, samples and list of stock photo subjects. Do not send unsolicited material. Distributes tips sheet every few months to contracted photographers.
Tips: "We will speak to the individual photographer and request portfolio or samples—at that time we will tell the photographer what we desire to see."

🍁**MACH 2 STOCK EXCHANGE LTD.,** #204-1409 Edmonton Tr NE, Calgary, Alberta T2E 3K8 Canada. (403)230-9363. Fax: (403)230-5855. Manager: Pamela Varga. Estab. 1986. Stock photo agency. Member of Picture Agency Council of America (PACA). Clients include: advertising agencies, public relations firms, audiovisual firms and businesses.
Needs: Corporate, high-tech, lifestyle, industry. In all cases, prefer people-oriented images.
Specs: Uses 35mm, 2¼×2¼, 4×5, 8×10 transparencies.
Payment & Terms: Pays 50% commission on color photos. Average sale $300. Works on contract basis only. Offers limited regional exclusivity. Contracts renew automatically with additional submissions. Charges 50% duping and catalog insertion fees. Statements issued monthly. Payment made monthly. "All photographers' statements are itemized in detail. They may ask us anything concerning their account." Offers one-time and 1-year exclusive rights; no electronic media rights for clip art type CD's. Informs photographer and allows him to negotiate when client requests all rights. "We generally do not sell buy-out." Model/property release required. Captions required.

Making Contact: Query with samples and list of stock photo subjects. SASE. Reports in 1 month. Market tips sheet distributed 4 times/year to contracted photographers.

Tips: "Please call first. We will then send a basic information package out. If terms are agreeable between the two parties then original images can be submitted pre-paid." Sees trend toward more photo requests for families, women in business, the environment and waste management. Active vibrant seniors. High-tech and computer-generated or manipulated images, minorities (Asians mostly).

MEDICAL IMAGES INC., 26 W. Shore Pl., Salisbury CT 06068. (203)824-7858. President: Anne Darden. Estab. 1990. Stock photo agency. Has 30,000 photos. Clients include: advertising agencies, public relations firms, corporate accounts, book/encyclopedia publishers, magazine publishers and newspapers.

Needs: Medical and health-related material, including commercial-looking photography of generic doctor's office scenes, hospital scenarios and still life shots. Also, technical close-ups of surgical procedures, diseases, high-tech colorized diagnostic imaging, microphotography, nutrition, exercise and preventive medicine.

Specs: Uses 8×10 glossy b&w prints; 35mm, 2¼×2¼, 4×5 and 8×10 transparencies.

Payment & Terms: Pays 50% commission on b&w and color photos. Average price per image: $175-3,500. Enforces minimum prices. Works with or without contract. Offers non-exclusive contract. Contracts renew automatically. Statements issued quarterly. Payment made bimonthly. "If client pays within same period, photographer gets check right away; otherwise, in next payment period." Photographer's accountant may review records with prior appointment. Offers one-time rights. Model/property release preferred. Captions required; include medical procedures, diagnosis when applicable, whether model released or not, etc.

Making Contact: Interested in receiving work from newer, lesser-known photographers. Query with list of stock photo subjects or telephone with list of subject matter. SASE. Reports in 2 weeks. Photo guidelines available. Market tips sheet distributed quarterly to contracted photographers.

Tips: Looks for "quality of photograph—focus, exposure, composition, interesting angles; scientific value; and subject matter being right for our markets." Sees trend toward "more emphasis on editorial or realistic looking medical situations. Anything too 'canned' is much less marketable."

■**MEDICHROME**, 232 Madison Ave., New York NY 10016. (212)679-8480. Manager: Ivan Kaminoff. Has 500,000 photos. Clients include: publications firms, businesses, book/encyclopedia and magazine publishers, newspapers and pharmaceutical companies.

Needs: Needs "everything that is considered medical or health-related, such as: stock photos of doctors with patients and other general photos to very specific medical shots of diseases and surgical procedures; high-tech shots of the most modern diagnostic equipment; exercise and diet also." Special needs include organ transplants, home health care, counseling services and use of computers by medical personnel.

Specs: Uses 8×10 b&w prints; and 35mm, 2¼×2¼, 4×5 and 8×10 transparencies.

Payment & Terms: Pays 50% commission on b&w and color photos. General price range: "$150 and up. All brochures are based on size and print run. Ads are based on exposure and length of campaign." Offers one-time or first rights; all rights are rarely needed—very costly. Model release preferred. Captions required.

Making Contact: Query by "letter or phone call explaining how many photos you have and their subject matter." SASE. Reports in 2 weeks. Distributes tips sheet every 6 months to Medichrome photographers only.

Tips: Prefers to see "loose prints and slides in 20-up sheets. All printed samples welcome; no carousel, please. Lots of need for medical stock. Very specialized and unusual area of emphasis, very costly/difficult to shoot, therefore buyers are using more stock."

■**MEGA PRODUCTIONS, INC.**, 1714 N. Wilton Place, Los Angeles CA 90028. (213)462-6342. Fax: (213)462-7572. Director: Michele Mattei. Estab. 1974. Stock photo agency and news/feature syndicate. Has "several million" photos. Clients include: book/encyclopedia publishers, magazine publishers, television, film and newspapers.

Needs: Needs television, film, studio, celebrity, paparazzi, feature stories (sports, national and international interest events, current news stories). Written information to accompany stories needed. "We do not wish to see fashion and greeting card-type scenics."

Specs: Uses 35mm, 2¼×2¼ transparencies.

Payment & Terms: Pays 50% commission on color photos. General price range: $100-20,000; 50% commission of sale. Offers one-time rights. Model release preferred. Captions required.

Making Contact: Query with resume of credits. Query with samples. Query with list of stock photo subjects. Works with local freelancers. Occasionally assigns work.

Tips: "Studio shots of celebrities, and home/family stories are frequently requested." In samples, looking for "marketability, high quality, recognizable personalities and current newsmaking material. Also, looks for paparazzi celebrity at local and national events. We deal mostly in Hollywood entertainment stories. We are interested mostly in celebrity photography and current events. Written material on personality or event helps us to distribute material faster and more efficiently."

MOTION PICTURE AND TV PHOTO ARCHIVE, Dept. PM, 11821 Mississippi Ave., Los Angeles CA 90025. (310)478-2379. Fax: (310)477-4864. President: Ron Avery. Estab. 1988. Stock photo agency. Member of Picture Agency Council of America. Has 60,000 photos. Has eight branch offices. Clients include: advertising agencies, book/encyclopedia publishers, magazine publishers, newspapers, postcard publishers, calendar companies, greeting card companies.
Needs: Color shots of current stars.
Specs: Uses 8×10 b&w/color prints; 35mm, 2¼×2¼, 4×5 and 8×10 transparencies.
Payment & Terms: Buys photos/film outright. Pays 50% commission on b&w and color photos. Average price per image (to clients): $180-1,000/b&w image; $180-1,500/color image. Enforces minimum prices. Offers volume discounts to customers; terms specified in photographer's contract. Works with or without a signed contract, negotiable with limited regional exclusivity. Contracts renew automatically with additional submissions.
Making Contact: Reports in 1-2 weeks.

■**MOUNTAIN STOCK PHOTO & FILM**, P.O. Box 1910, Tahoe City CA 96145. (916)583-6646. Fax: (916)583-5935. Manager: Meg deVré. Estab. 1986. Stock photo agency. Member of Picture Agency Council of America (PACA). Has 60,000+ photos; minimal films/videos. Clients include: advertising agencies, public relations firms, audiovisual firms, businesses, book/encyclopedia publishers, magazine publishers, newspapers, calendar companies, greeting card companies.
Needs: "We specialize in and always need action sports, scenic and lifestyle images."
Specs: Uses 35mm, 2¼×2¼, 4×5, transparencies.
Payment & Terms: Pays 50% commission on color photos. Enforces minimum prices. "We have a $100 minimum fee." Offers volume discounts to customers; inquire about specific terms. Discount sales terms not negotiable. Works on contract basis only. Offers guaranteed subject exclusivity (within files). Some contracts renew automatically. Charges 50% catalog insertion fee. Statements issued quarterly. Payment made quarterly. Photographers are allowed to review account records with due notice. Offers unlimited and limited exclusive rights. Informs photographer and allows him to negotiate when client requests all rights. Model/property release required. Captions required.
Making Contact: Interested in receiving work from newer, lesser-known photographers. Query with resume of credits. Query with samples. Query with stock photo list. Samples kept on file. SASE. Expects minimum initial submission of 500 images. Reports in 1 month. Photo guidelines free with SASE. Market tips sheet distributed quarterly to contracted photographers; upon request.
Tips: "I see the need for images, whether action or just scenic, that evoke a feeling or emotion."

NATIONAL NEWS BUREAU, P.O. Box 43039, Philadelphia PA 19129. (215)546-8088. Photo Editor: Andy Edelman. Clients include: book, magazine and newspaper publishers. Distributes/syndicates to over 300 publications.
Needs: "All feature materials, fashion, celebrity."
Specs: Uses 8×10 b&w and color prints, and b&w and color contact sheets.
Payment & Terms: Buys photos outright; pays $50-1,000. Offers all rights. Model release required. Captions required.
Making Contact: Query with samples. Send photos by mail for consideration. Submit portfolio for review. SASE. Reports in 2 weeks.
Tips: Needs photos of "new talent—particularly undiscovered female models." Points out that "European magazine market is a major outlet for female photos."

■‡**NATURAL SCIENCE PHOTOS**, 33 Woodland Dr., Watford, Hertfordshire WD1 3BY England. 0923-245265. Fax: 0923-246067. Partners: Peter and Sondra Ward. Estab. 1969. Stock photo agency and picture library. Members of British Association of Picture Libraries and Agencies. Has 100,000 photos. Clients include: ad agencies, public relations firms, audiovisual firms, businesses, book/encyclopedia publishers, magazine publishers, newspapers, postcard companies, calendar companies, greeting card companies and television.
Needs: Natural science of all types, including wildlife (terrestrial and aquatic), habitats (including destruction and reclamation), botany (including horticulture, agriculture, pests, diseases, treatments and effects), ecology, pollution, geology, primitive peoples, astronomy, scenics (mostly without artifacts), climate and effects (e.g. hurricane damage), creatures of economic importance, (e.g. disease carriers and domestic animals and fowl). "We need all areas of natural history, habitat and environment from South and Central America, also high quality marine organisms."
Specs: Uses 35mm, 2¼×2¼ original color transparencies.
Payment & Terms: Pays 66% commission for color photos. General price range: $55-1,400. "We have minimum fees for small numbers, but negotiate bulk deals sometimes involving up to 200 photos at a time." Works on contract basis only; offers nonexclusive contract. Statements issued quarterly or

semiannually depending on volume of sales made (if large, pay more frequently). Offers one-time rights, exclusive on calendars. Informs photographers and permits them to negotiate when a client requests all rights. Copyright not sold without written permission. Model release preferred. Captions required.

Making Contact: Arrange a personal interview to show a portfolio. Submit portfolio for review. Query with samples. Send unsolicited photos by mail for consideration. Samples kept on file. SASE. Reports in 1-4 weeks, according to pressure on time.

Tips: "We look for all kinds of living organisms, accurately identified and documented, also habitats, environment, weather and effects, primitive peoples, horticulture, agriculture, pests, diseases and etc. Animals, birds, etc. showing action or behavior particularly welcome. We are not looking for 'arty' presentation, just straightforward graphic images, only exceptions being 'moody' scenics. There has been a marked increase in demand for really good images with good color and fine grain with good lighting. Pictures that would have sold a few years ago that were a little 'soft' or grainy are now rejected, particularly where advertising clients are concerned."

NAWROCKI STOCK PHOTO, P.O. Box 16565, Chicago IL 60616. (312)427-8625. Fax: (312)427-0178. Director: William S. Nawrocki. Stock photo agency, picture library. Member of Picture Agency Council of America (PACA). Has over 300,000 photos and 500,000 historical photos. Clients include: ad agencies, public relations firms, editorial, businesses, book/encyclopedia publishers, magazine publishers, newspapers, postcard companies, calendar companies and greeting card companies.

Needs: Model-released people, all age groups, all types of activities; families; couples; relationships; updated travel, domestic and international; food.

Specs: Uses 35mm, 2¼ × 2¼, 2¼ × 2¾, 4 × 5 and 8 × 10 transparencies. "We look for good composition, exposure and subject matter; good color." Also, finds large format work "in great demand." Medium format and professional photographers preferred.

Payment & Terms: Buys only historical photos outright. Pays variable percentage on commission according to use/press run. Commission depends on agent-foreign or domestic 50%/40%/35%. Works on contract basis only. Offers limited regional exclusivity and nonexclusivity. Charges duping and catalog insertion fees. Statements issued monthly. Payment made monthly. Offers one-time media rights; other rights negotiable. Requests agency promotion rights. Informs photographer and allows him to negotiate when client requests all rights. Model release required. Captions required.

Making Contact: Interested in receiving work from newer, lesser-known photographers. Arrange a personal interview to show portfolio. Query with resume of credits, samples and list of stock photo subjects. Submit portfolio for review. Provide return Federal Express. SASE. Reports ASAP. Allow 2 weeks for review. Photo guidelines free with SASE. Tips sheet distributed "to our photographers." Suggest that you call first—discuss your photography with the agency, your goals, etc. "NSP prefers to help photographers develop their skills. We tend to give direction and offer advice to our photographers. We don't take photographers on just for their images. NSP prefers to treat photographers as individuals and likes to work with them." Label and caption images. Has network with domestic and international agencies.

Tips: "A stock agency uses just about everything. We are using more people images, all types—family, couples, relationships, leisure, the over 40's group. Looking for large format—variety and quality. More images are being custom shot for stock with model releases. Model releases are very, very important—a key to a photographer's success and income. Model releases are the most requested for ads/brochures."

NEW ENGLAND STOCK PHOTO, Box 815, Old Saybrook CT 06475. (203)388-1741. President: Betty Rogers Johansen. Stock photo agency. Has 100,000 photos in files. Clients include: ad agencies; public relations firms; businesses; book/encyclopedia publishers; magazine publishers, postcard, calendar and greeting card companies.

Needs: "We are a general interest agency with a wide variety of clients and subject matter. Always looking for good people shots—workplace, school, families, couples, children, senior citizens—engaged in everyday life situations, including recreational sports, home life, vacation and outdoor activities. We also get many requests for animal shots—horses, dogs, cats and wildlife (natural habitat). Special emphasis on New England—specific places, lifestyle and scenics, but have growing need for other US and international subject matter. Also use setup shots of flowers, food, nostalgia."

 The double dagger before a listing indicates that the market is located outside the United States and Canada.

Specs: Uses 8×10 glossy b&w prints; 35mm, 2¼×2¼, 4×5 transparencies. "We are especially interested in more commercial/studio photography, such as food and interiors, which can be used for stock purposes. Also, we get many requests for particular historical sites, annual events, and need more coverage of towns/cities, mainstreets and museums."

Payment & Terms: Pays 50% commission for b&w and color photos; 75% to photographer on assignments obtained by agency. Average price per image: $100-1,000/b&w photo; $100-3,000/color photo. Works with photographers on contract basis only. Offers nonexclusive contract. Charges catalog insertion fee. Statements issued monthly. Payments made monthly. Photographers allowed to review account records to verify sales figures. Offers one-time rights; postcard, calendar and greeting card rights. Informs photographer and allows him to negotiate when client requests all rights. Model/property release preferred (people and private property). Captions required.

Making Contact: Interested in receiving work from newer, lesser-known photographers. Query with list of stock photo subjects or send unsolicited photos by mail for consideration. SASE. Reports in 3 weeks. Guidelines free with SAE and .98¢ postage. Distributes monthly tip sheet to contributing photographers.

Tips: "Do a tight edit. Do not send overexposed or unmounted transparencies. We provide one of the most comprehensive photo guideline packages in the business, so write for it before submitting. Send a cross section of your best work. There has been an increased use of stock, but a demand for only top quality work. Images must have balanced lighting, great color saturation and strong focal point mood. Social issues and family situations, with an ethnic mix, are still at the top of our list of needs. Also travel (with people) and outdoor leisure activities."

■**THE NEW IMAGE STOCK PHOTO AGENCY INC.**, Suite 200, 38 Quail Ct., Walnut Creek CA 94596. (510)934-2405. President: Tracey Prever. Estab. 1986. Stock photo agency. Has 50,000 photos. Clients include: advertising agencies, public relations firms, audiovisual firms, businesses, book/encyclopedia publishers, magazine publishers, newspapers, calendar companies and greeting card companies.

Needs: "We mainly deal with commercial clients in advertising. We look for model-released people images in all different situations . . . lifestyles, corporate, people working, etc. Also, industry, travel, technology and medical."

Payment & Terms: Pays 50% commission on color photos. General price range: $200-2,000. Offers limited regional exclusivity contract. Statements issued bimonthly. Payment made bimonthly. Offers one-time rights. Informs photographer and allows him to negotiate when client requests all rights. Model release required. Captions required.

Making Contact: Arrange a personal interview to show portfolio. SASE. Reports in 1 month. Photo guidelines free with SASE. Tips sheet distributed quarterly to contracted photographers.

Tips: Wants to see "technical quality as well as salable subject matter, variety, model-released people images." Individual style is especially desired.

*■**NEWS FLASH INTERNATIONAL, INC.**, Division of Observer Newspapers, 2262 Centre Ave., Bellmore NY 11710. (516)679-9888. Editor: Jackson B. Pokress. Has 25,000 photos. Clients include: ad agencies, public relations firms, businesses and newspapers.

Needs: "We handle news photos of all major league sports: football, baseball, basketball, boxing, wrestling, hockey. We are now handling women's sports in all phases including women in boxing, basketball, softball, etc." Some college and junior college sports. Wants emphasis on individual players with dramatic impact. "We are now covering the Washington DC scene. There is currently an interest in political news photos."

Specs: Super 8 and 16mm documentary and educational film on sports, business and news; 8×10 glossy b&w prints or contact sheet; transparencies.

Payment & Terms: Pays 40% commission/photos and films. Pays $5 minimum/photo. Offers one-time or first rights. Model release required. Captions required.

Making Contact: Query with samples. Send material by mail for consideration or make a personal visit if in the area. SASE. Reports in 1 month. Free photo guidelines and tips sheet on request.

Tips: "Exert constant efforts to make good photos—what newspapers call grabbers—make them different than other photos, look for new ideas. There is more use of color and large format chromes." Special emphasis on major league sports. "We cover Mets, Yankees, Jets, Giants, Islanders on daily basis. Rangers and Knicks on weekly basis. We handle bios and profiles on athletes in all sports. There is an interest in women athletes in all sports."

‡**OKAPIA K.G.**, Michael Grzimek & Co., 6 Frankfurt/Main, Roderbergweg 168 Germany; or Constanze Presse Haus, Kurfürstenstr. 72 -74 D1000 Berlin 30 Germany. 030 2640018 1. Fax: 030 2640018 2. President: Grzimek. Stock photo agency and picture library. Has 350,000 photos. Clients include: ad agencies, book/encyclopedia publishers, magazine publishers, newspapers, postcard companies, calendar companies, greeting card companies and school book publishers.

Needs: Natural history, science and technology, and general interest.

Specs: Uses 13×18cm minimum b&w prints; 35mm, 2¼×2¼, 4×5 and 8×10 transparencies.

Payment & Terms: Buys photos outright; pays $40. Pays 50% commission on b&w and color photos. Offers one-time rights. Model release required. Captions required.

Making Contact: Send unsolicited material by mail for consideration. SASE. Expects minimum initial submission of 200 slides. Distributes tips sheets on request.

Tips: "We need every theme which can be photographed." For best results, "send pictures continuously." Work must be of "high standard quality."

OMEGA NEWS GROUP/USA, P.O. Box 30167, Philadelphia PA 19103-8167. (215)763-1152. Fax: (215)763-4015. Managing Editor: A.S. Rubel. Stock photo and press agency. Clients include: ad agencies, public relations firms, businesses, book publishers, magazine publishers, encyclopedia publishers, newspapers, calendar and poster companies.

Needs: "All major news, sports, features, society shots, shots of film sets, national and international personalities and celebrities in the news as well as international conflicts and wars."

Specs: Uses 8×10 glossy b&w prints; 35mm, 2¼×2¼ or 4×5 transparencies. Photos must be stamped with name only on mounts and back of prints; prints may be on single or double weight but unmounted.

Payment & Terms: Pays 50% commission. NPI; price depends upon usage (cover, inside photo, etc.). Offers first North American serial rights; other rights can be procured on negotiated fees. Releases required on most subjects; captions a must.

Making Contact: Submit material by mail for consideration. SASE. Send resume, including experience, present activities and interests, and range of equipment. Supply phone number where photographer may be reached during working hours.

Tips: Should have experience in news and/or commercial work on location. "We always welcome the opportunity to see new work. We are interested in quality and content, not quantity. Comprehensive story material welcomed."

OMNI-PHOTO COMMUNICATIONS, 5 E. 22nd St., New York NY 10010. (212)995-0805. Fax: (212)995-0895. President: Roberta Guerette. Estab. 1979. Stock photo agency. Has 100,000 photos. Clients include: advertising agencies, public relations firms, audiovisual firms, businesses, book/encyclopedia publishers, magazine publishers, postcard publishers, calendar companies, greeting card companies.

Needs: Travel, multicultural and people.

Specs: Uses 8×10 b&w prints; 35mm, 2¼×2¼, 4×5, 8×10 transparencies.

Payment & Terms: Pays 50% commission on b&w and color photos. Works on contract basis only. Offers limited regional exclusive contracts. Contracts renew automatically with additional submissions. Model/property release required. Captions required.

Making Contact: Interested in receiving work from newer, lesser-known photographers. Query with resume of credits. Query with samples. SASE. Expects minimum initial submission of 200-300 images. Photo guidelines free with SASE.

Tips: "Spontaneous-looking, yet professional quality photos of people interacting with each other. Carefully thought out backgrounds, props and composition, commanding use of color. Stock photographers must produce high quality work at an abundant rate. Self-assignment is very important, as is a willingness to obtain model releases, caption thoroughly and make submissions regularly."

‡ORION PRESS, 1-13 Kanda-Jimbocho, Chiyoda-ku, Tokyo Japan 101. (03)3295-1400. Fax: (03)3295-0227. Manager: Mr. Mitsuo Nagamitsu. Estab. 1952. Stock photo agency. Has 700,000 photos. Has 3 branch offices. Clients include: advertising agencies, public relations firms, businesses, book/encyclopedia publishers, magazine publishers, newspapers, postcard publishers, calendar companies, greeting card companies.

Needs: All subjects, especially wish to have images of people.

Specs: Uses 35mm, 2¼×2¼, 6×6 cm., 4×5, 8×10 transparencies.

Payment & Terms: Pays 50% commission on b&w and color photos. Average price per image (to clients): $175-290/b&w photo; $290-500/color photo. Negotiates fees below standard minimum prices. Offers volume discounts to customers; inquire about specific terms. Photographers can choose not to sell images on discount terms. Works with or without a signed contract. Offers limited regional exclusivity; negotiable. Contracts renew automatically with additional submissions. Statements issued monthly. Payment made 2½ months after sales report. Offers one-time rights. Model/property release required. Captions required.

Making Contact: Query with samples. SASE. Expects minimum initial submission of 100 images with periodic submission of at least 100-200 images. Photo guidelines free on request.

■OUTLINE, (formerly Outline Press Syndicate Inc.), Dept. PM, 11th Floor, 596 Broadway, New York NY 10012. (212)226-8790. President: Jim Roehrig. Personality/Portrait. Has 250,000 photos. Clients include: advertising agencies, public relations firms, magazine publishers, newspapers and production/film co.

Needs: Heavy emphasis on personalities, film, TV, political feature stories.

Payment & Terms: General price range: negotiable. Rights negotiable. Model release preferred. Captions required.

Making Contact: Query with resume of credits. Works with local freelancers by assignment only. Cannot return material. Reports in 3 weeks.

Tips: Prefers a photographer that can create situations out of nothing. "The market seems to have a non-ending need for celebrities and the highest quality material will always be in demand."

■‡OXFORD SCIENTIFIC FILMS, Lower Road, Long Hanborough, Witney, Oxfordshire OX8 8LL England. (0993)881881. Photo Library Manager: Sandra Berry. Film Library: Jane Mulleneux. Film unit and stills and film libraries. Has 250,000 photos; over one million feet of stock footage on 16mm, and 40,000 feet on 35mm. Clients include: ad agencies, design companies, audiovisual firms, book/encyclopedia publishers, magazine and newspaper publishers, calendar, postcard and greeting card companies.

Needs: Natural history: animals, plants, behavior, close-ups, life-histories, histology, embryology, electron microscopy. Scenics, geology, weather, conservation, country practices, ecological techniques, pollution, special-effects, high speed, time-lapse.

Specs: Uses 35mm and larger transparencies; 16 and 35mm film and videotapes.

Payment & Terms: Pays 50% commission on b&w and color photos. Enforces minimum prices. Offers volume discounts to customers; inquire about specific terms. Discount sale terms not negotiable. Works on contract basis only; prefers exclusivity, but negotiable by territory. Contracts renew automatically with additional submissions. "All contracts reviewed after 24 months initially, either party may then terminate contract, giving 3 months notice in writing." Statements issued quarterly. Payment made quarterly. Photographers permitted to review sales figures. Informs photographer and allows him to negotiate when client requests all rights. Photo captions required.

Making Contact: Interested in receiving work from newer, lesser-known photographers. Query with stock photo list. SASE. Reports in 1 month. Distributes want lists quarterly to all photographers.

Tips: Prefers to see "good focus, composition, exposure, rare or unusual natural history subjects."

PACIFIC STOCK, P.O. Box 90517, Honolulu HI 96835. (808)735-5665. Fax: (808)735-7801. Owner/President: Barbara Brundage. Estab. 1987. Stock photo agency. Member of Picture Agency Council of America (PACA). Has 100,000+ photos. Clients include advertising agencies, public relations firms, audiovisual firms, businesses, book/encyclopedia publishers, magazine publishers, postcard companies, calendar companies and greeting card companies. Previous/current clients: American Airlines, *Life* magazine (cover), Eveready Battery (TV commercial).

Needs: "Pacific Stock is the *only* stock photo agency worldwide specializing in Pacific-related photography. Locations include North American West Coast, Hawaii, Pacific Islands, Australia, New Zealand, Far East, etc. Subjects include: people, travel, culture, sports, marine science and industrial."

Specs: Uses 35mm, 2¼ × 2¼, 4 × 5 and 8 × 10 (all formats) transparencies.

Payment & Terms: Pays 50% commission on color photos. Works on contract basis only. Offers limited regional exclusivity. Charges catalog insertion rate of 50%/image. Statements issued monthly. Payment made monthly. Photographers allowed to review account records to verify sales figures. Offers one-time or first rights; additional rights with photographer's permission. Informs photographer and allows him to negotiate when client requests all rights. Model and property release required for all people and certain properties, i.e. homes and boats. Photo captions are required; include: "who, what, where."

Making Contact: Query with resume of credits and list of stock photo subjects. SASE. Reports in 2 weeks. Photo guidelines free with SASE. Tips sheet distributed quarterly to represented photographers; free to interested photographers with SASE.

Tips: Looks for "highly edited shots preferrably captioned in archival slide pages. Photographer must be able to supply minimum of 1,000 slides (must be model released) for initial entry and must make quarterly submissions of fresh material from Pacific area destinations from areas outside Hawaii." Major trends to be aware of include: "Increased requests for 'assignment style' photography so it will be resellable as stock. The two general areas (subject) requested are: tourism usage and economic development. Looks for focus, composition and color. As the Pacific region expands, more people are choosing to travel to various Pacific destinations, while greater development occurs, i.e. tourism, construction, banking, trade, etc. Be interested in working with our agency to supply what is on our want lists."

*PAINET, #1, 466 Loring Pl., El Paso TX 79927. (915)852-4840. Owner: Mark Goebel. Estab. 1985. Picture library. Has 40,000 photos. Clients include: advertising agencies and magazine publishers.
Needs: "We publish catalogs to market our photos. Our primary emphasis is on 'people' pictures. However, we would review animals and graphic scenics."
Specs: Uses 35mm transparencies.
Making Contact: Interested in receiving work from newer, lesser-known photographers. Query with samples. Samples not kept on file. SASE. Submit 20 of your best dupes in a 35mm slide preserver sheet. Include return postage. Reports in 1-2 weeks. Catalog available for $19.
Tips: Wants to see "high quality depictions of life's diverse moments and emotions, not just 'pretty' pictures."

■PANORAMIC IMAGES, #3700, 230 N. Michigan Ave., Chicago IL 60601. (312)236-8545. Fax: (312)704-4077. Contact: Doug Segal (Panoramics only) or Tim Potter (Illustrative only). Estab. 1986. Stock photo agency. Member of Picture Agency Council of America (PACA). Has 50,000 photos. Clients include: advertising agencies, audiovisual firms, businesses, magazine publishers, newspapers, postcard companies, calendar companies, corporate design firms, graphic designers and corporate art consultants.
Needs: Works only with *panoramic formats* (2:1 aspect ratio or greater). Subject include: cityscapes/skylines, landscape/scenics, travel, conceptual and backgrounds (puffy clouds, sunrises/sunsets, water, trees, etc.) Also accepts medium and large formats. "No 35mm."
Specs: Uses 2¼×5, 2¼×7 and 2¼×10 (6×12cm, 6×17cm and 6×24cm). "2¼ formats (chromes only) preferred; will accept 70mm pans, 5×7, 4×10, 4×5 and 8×10 horizontals and verticals."
Payment & Terms: Pays 50% commission on color photos. Average price: $700. Offers one-time rights and limited exclusive usage. Model release preferred "and/or property release, if necessary." Captions required. Please read our submission guidelines before sending photos.
Making Contact: Arrange a personal interview to show portfolio. Query with samples. Query with list of stock photo subjects. SASE. Reports in 1 month; also sends "response postcard immediately to all photo submissions." Photo guidelines free with SASE. Tips sheet distributed 3-4 times yearly to agencies and prospective photographers, free with SASE.
Tips: Wants to see "well-exposed chromes. Panoramic portraiture of well-known locations nationwide and worldwide. Also, generic beauty panoramics. Use of panoramic point of view is exponentially increasing in lucrative advertising and corporate design areas. PSI has doubled in gross sales, staff and number of contributing photographers over the past months and we expect strong growth to continue. We've also added a library featuring illustrative stock with a strong sense of design and a fine-art bent; shapes and colors, moods and feelings from cities and everyday life; the elements of nature and seasons in color and b&w."

DOUGLAS PEEBLES PHOTOGRAPHY, 445 Iliwahi Loop, Kailua, Oahu HI 96734. (808)254-1082. Fax: (808)254-1267. Owner: Douglas Peebles. Estab. 1975. Stock photo agency. Has 50,000 photos. Clients include: advertising agencies, public relations firms, businesses, magazine publishers, newspapers, postcard companies and calendar companies.
Needs: South Pacific and Hawaii.
Specs: Uses 35mm, 2¼×2¼, 4×5 color transparencies.
Payment & Terms: Pays 50% commission on color photos. General price range: $100-5,000; $100-5,000/color photo. Works on contract basis only. Offers nonexclusive contract. Charges 50% duping fee. Statements issued quarterly. Payment made quarterly. Photographers allowed to review account records to verify sales figures. Offers one-time rights. Model/property release required. Captions preferred.
Making Contact: Interested in receiving work from newer, lesser-known photographers. Contact by telephone. SASE. Reports in 1 month. Photo guideline sheet not available.
Tips: Looks for "strong color, people in activities and model released. Call first."

PHOTO ASSOCIATES NEWS SERVICE, #1636, 3421 M. St. NW, Washington DC 20007. (202)965-4428. Fax: (202)337-1969 or (703)659-0896. Bureau Manager: Peter Heimsath. Estab. 1970. News/feature syndicate. Has 15,000 photos. Clients include: public relations firms, book/encyclopedia publishers, magazine publishers, newspapers.
Needs: Needs feature and immediate news for worldwide distribution, also celebrities doing unusual things.
Specs: Uses 8×10 glossy or matte b&w or color prints; 35mm transparencies.
Payment & Terms: Pays $100-750/color photo; $50-100/b&w photo. Pays 50-60% commission on b&w and color photos. Average price per image (to clients): $75-750/b&w photo; $100-500/color photo. Negotiates fees at standard minimum prices depending on subject matter and need, reflects monies to be charged. Offers volume discounts to customers; terms specified in photographer's contract. Photographers can choose not to sell images on discount terms. Works on contract basis only. Statements issued monthly. Payment made "as we are paid. Photographers may review records to verify

sales, but don't make a habit of it. Must be a written request." Offers one-time rights. Informs photographer and allows him to negotiate when client requests all rights. Photo Associates News Service will negotiate with client request of all rights purchase. Model/property release preferred. Captions required; include name of subject, when taken, where taken, competition and process instructions.
Making Contact: Interested in receiving work from newer, lesser-known photographers. Query with resume of credits, samples or stock photo list. Samples kept on file. SASE. Expects minimum initial submission of 100 images with periodic submission of at least 100 images every two months. Reports in 1 month. Photo guidelines free with SASE. Market tips sheet distributed to those who make serious inquiries with SASE.
Tips: "Put yourself on the opposite side of the camera, to grasp what the moment has to say. Are you satisfied with your material before you submit it? More and more companies seem to take the short route to achieve their visual goals. They don't want to spend real money to obtain a new approach to a possible old idea. Too many times, photographs lose their freshness, because the process isn't thought out correctly."

■‡PHOTO INDEX, 2 Prowse St., West Perth Western Australia 6005. (09)481-0375. Fax: (09)481-6547. Manager: Lyn Woldendorp. Estab. 1979. Stock photo agency. Has 80,000 photos. Clients include: advertising agencies, public relations firms, audiovisual firms, businesses, book/encyclopedia publishers, magazine publishers, postcard publishers, calendar companies.
Needs: Needs generic stock photos, especially lifestyle, sport and business with people.
Specs: Uses 35mm, 2¼×2¼, 4×5 transparencies.
Payment & Terms: Pays 50% commission on color photos. Average price per image (to clients): $150-200/color photo. Offers volume discounts to customers; inquire about specific terms. Discount terms not negotiable. Works on exclusive contract basis only. Five-year contract renewed automatically. Statements issued quarterly. Payment made quarterly. Photographers permitted to review account records to verify sales figures or account for various deductions "within reason." Offers one-time rights. Informs photographer and allows him to negotiate when client requests all rights. Model/property release required. Captions required that include what industry and work.
Making Contact: Interested in receiving work from newer, lesser-known photographers. Query with samples. Expects minimum initial submission of 1,000 images with periodic submission of at least several hundred, quarterly. Reports in 1-2 weeks. Photo guidelines free with SASE. Catalog available. Market tips sheet distributed quarterly to contributing photographers.
Tips: "A photographer working in the stock industry should treat it professionally. Observe what sells of his work in each agency, as one agency's market can be very different to another's. Take agencies' photo needs lists seriously. Treat it as a business."

‡THE PHOTO LIBRARY (Photographic Library of Australia, Ltd.), Suite 1, No. 7 Ridge St., North Sydney 2060 N.S.W. Australia. (02)929-8511. Editor: Lucette Moore. Picture library. Has over 400,000 photos. Clients include: advertising agencies, public relations firms, magazines, businesses, book/encyclopedia publishers, postcard companies, calendar companies, greeting card companies, designers and government departments.
Needs: From abstracts to zoos. "We especially are looking for people pictures (families, couples, business), industrial and high tech."
Specs: Uses 35mm, 2¼×2¼, and 4×5 transparencies.
Payment & Terms: Pays 50% commission for color photos. Offers limited regional exclusivity contract following expiration of agreement: continues until photographer wants to withdraw images. Statements issued quarterly. Payment made quarterly; 10 days after end of quarter. Photographer allowed to review his own account, once per year to verify sales figures. Offers one-time rights, all rights and limited rights. Informs photographer and allows him to negotiate when client requests all rights. Requires model release (held by photographer) and photo captions.
Making Contact: Interested in receiving work from newer, lesser-known photographers. Send unsolicited photos by mail for consideration to Lucette Moore, Box 121, Cammeray N.S.W. Works with local and overseas freelancers. SASE. Reports in 10 days. Guidelines free with SASE. Distributes tips sheet quarterly to photographers on file.
Tips: Prefers to see top quality commercial usage and good graphic images. "We see an increase in stock usage by advertising agents as they recognize a higher level of creative excellence in stock compared to previous years."

*■‡PHOTO LIBRARY INTERNATIONAL, Box 75, Leeds LS7 3NZ United Kingdom 0532-623005. Managing Director: Kevin Horgan. Picture library. Clients include ad agencies, public relations firms, audiovisual firms, businesses, book/encyclopedia publishers, magazine publishers, newspapers, postcard companies, calendar companies and greeting card companies.

Needs: Most contemporary subjects, excluding personalities or special news events, i.e. industry, sport, travel, transport, scenics, animals, commerce, agriculture, people, etc.
Specs: Uses 35mm, 2¼×2¼ and 4×5 transparencies.
Payment & Terms: 50% commission.

■**PHOTO NETWORK,** Dept. PM, 1541J Parkway Loop, Tustin CA 92680. (714)259-1244. Owner: Cathy Aron. Stock photo agency. Member of Picture Agency Council of America (PACA). Has 500,000 photos. Clients include: ad agencies, AV producers, textbook companies, graphic artists, public relations firms, newspapers, corporations, magazines, calendar companies and greeting card companies.
Needs: Needs shots of personal sports and recreation, industrial/commercial, high-tech, families, couples (all ages), animals, travel and lifestyles. Special subject needs include people over 55 enjoying life, medical shots (patients and professionals), children and animals.
Specs: Uses 35mm, 2¼×2¼, 4×5 transparencies.
Payment & Terms: Pays 50% commission. Works on contract basis only. Offers limited regional exclusivity. Contracts automatically renew with each submission for 3 years. Charges catalog insertion fee; rate not specified. Statements issued monthly. Payment made monthly. Photographers allowed to review account records to verify sales figures. Offers one-time rights. Informs photographer and allows him to negotiate when client requests all rights. Model/property release preferred. Captions preferred; include places—parks, cities, buildings, etc. "No need to describe the obvious, i.e., mother with child."
Making Contact: Query with list of stock photo subjects. Send a sample of 200 images for review. SASE. Reports in 1 month.
Tips: Wants to see a portfolio "neat and well-organized and including a sampling of photographer's favorite photos." Looks for "clear, sharp focus, strong colors and good composition. We'd rather have many very good photos rather than one great piece of art. Would like to see photographers with a specialty or specialties and have it covered thoroughly. You need to supply new photos on a regular basis and be responsive to current trends in photo needs. Contract photographers are supplied with quarterly 'want' lists and information about current trends."

PHOTO OPTIONS STOCK AGENCY, 1432 Linda Vista Dr., Birmingham AL 35226. (205)533-4331, (205)979-8412. President: Elaine Fredericksen. Estab. 1983. Stock photo agency. Has 40,000 photos. Clients include: advertising agencies, public relations firms, businesses, book/encyclopedia publishers, magazine publishers.
Needs: "Our specialty is photos of the Southeast, but we also stock all general areas: corporate, life style, sports, etc."
Specs: Uses 35mm, 2¼×2¼, 4×5, 8×10 transparencies.
Payment & Terms: Pays 50% commission on color photos. Works on contract basis only. Offers non-exclusive contract. Issues statement with each check. Payment made monthly at end of month payment is received. Photographer is allowed to review account records. Offers one-time rights. Informs photographer and allows him to negotiate when client requests all rights. Model release required for people, especially children. Property release preferred. Captions required. "Good captions sell photos."
Making Contact: Arrange a personal interview to show portfolio. Submit portfolio for review. Query with samples. Samples not kept on file. Expects minimum initial submission of 200-500 images. "Regular submissions of photos increase sales." Reports in 3 weeks. Photo guidelines free with SASE. Market tips sheet distributed quarterly to agency photographers; free with SASE. Samples available upon request.
Tips: In samples looks for "dynamic, professional-quality images, commercial as well as artistic; good, thorough captions and appropriate model releases. Best sellers are photos of the Southeast and images of people, especially business, corporate, medical situations. Commit yourself to providing a continuous supply of stock to an agency. Fresh images sell. If you are not friendly and cooperative, don't call us. We're a down-home, personal service agency."

PHOTO RESEARCHERS, INC., 60 E. 56th St., New York NY 10022. (212)758-3420. Fax: (212)355-0731. President: Robert Zentmaier. Stock agency representing hundreds of photographers. Includes the National Audubon Society and Science Source Collection. Member of Picture Agency Council of America (PACA). Clients include: ad agencies and publishers of textbooks, encyclopedias, filmstrips, trade books, magazines, newspapers, calendars, greeting cards, posters, and annual reports in US and foreign markets.

The solid, black square before a listing indicates that the market uses various types of audiovisual materials, such as slides, film or videotape.

Needs: All aspects of natural history and science; human nature (especially children and young adults 6-18 engaged in everyday activity); industry; "people doing what they do"; and pretty scenics to informational photos, particularly needs model-released people photos and property photos such as houses, cars and boats.

Specs: Uses 8×10 matte doubleweight b&w prints and any size transparencies.

Payment & Terms: Rarely buys outright; works on 50% stock sales and 30% assignments. General price range: $150-7,500. Offers one-time and one-year exclusive rights. Indicate model release on photo.

Making Contact: Query with description of work, type of equipment used and subject matter available. Send to Bug Sutton, Creative Director. Follow up to arrange a personal interview to show portfolio. Submit portfolio for review. SASE. Reports in 1 month maximum.

Tips: "When a photographer is accepted, we analyze his portfolio and have consultations to give the photographer direction and leads for making sales of reproduction rights. We seek the photographer who is highly imaginative or into a specialty, enthusiastic and dedicated to technical accuracy. We are taking very few photographers—unlike the old days. We are looking for serious photographers who have many hundreds of photographs to offer for a first submission and who are able to contribute often. More advertisers are using stock. Many editorial textbook publishers are turning to color only. Electronic imaging systems for showing and selling stock will be in place before we know it."

■✿**PHOTO SEARCH LTD.**, #2002, 9909 104 St., Edmonton, Alberta T5K 2G5 Canada. (403)425-3766. Fax: (403)425-3766. Photo Editor: Gerry Boudrias. Estab. 1991. Stock photo agency. Has 75,000 photos. Clients include: advertising agencies, public relations firms, audiovisual firms, businesses, book/encyclopedia publishers, magazine publishers, newspapers, postcard publishers, calendar companies, graphic designers, government agencies.

Needs: "We always need good people photos showing, among other things, multi-culturalism, seniors leading active, healthy lives, and women in nontraditional work roles. Especially needed for next year will be: environmental issues, natives, lifestyle photos of couples, high-tech industrial, business people, travel in Southeast Asia, wildlife, nightlife, and outdoor recreation activities."

Specs: Uses 35mm, 2¼×2¼, 4×5 color transparencies.

Payment & Terms: Pays 50% commission on color photos. Average price per image (to clients): $80-400/color photo; editorial work ranges from $80-200; advertising work ranges from $200-500. Negotiates fees below standard minimum prices. Offers volume discounts to customers; terms specified in photographer's contract. Photographers can choose not to sell images on discount terms. Works on limited regional exclusivity contract basis only. "All contracts are automatically renewed for a one-year period, unless either party provides written notice." Statements issued quarterly. Payment made quarterly. Photographers permitted to review account records to verify sales figures or account for various deductions. Offers one-time and electronic media rights. Informs photographer and allows him to negotiate when client requests all rights. "While we reserve the right to final judgment, we confer with photographers about all-right sales. We insist on doing what we feel is right for the agency and the photographer." Model/property release required. "Model releases are imperative for photographers who wish to make sales in the advertising field." Captions required. "Point out information that could be important that may not be evident in the image."

Making Contact: Interested in receiving work from newer, lesser-known photographers who have adequate size collections. Submit portfolio for review. Query with samples. Query with stock photo list. SASE. Expects minimum initial submission of 200 images. Reports in 1 month. Photo guidelines free with SASE. Send international postage for mailings to U.S. "General list for anybody on request."

Tips: "Photographers should contact several agencies in the hope of finding one that can meet their needs and financial expectations. Who you sign with is a *very* important decision that could affect your career for many years to come. Marketing methods are constantly changing, due in part to the advent of electronic imaging. The way we serve our clientele, their needs, and the way we supply our images and services will continue to change in the near future."

■**PHOTOBANK**, Suite B, 17952 Skypark Circle, Irvine CA 92714. (714)250-4480. Fax: (714)752-5495. Photo Editor: Kristi Bressert. Stock photo agency. Has 750,000 transparencies. Clients include: ad agencies, public relations firms, audiovisual firms, book/encyclopedia publishers, magazine publishers, postcard companies, calendar publishers and greeting card companies.

Needs: Emphasis on active couples, lifestyle, medical, family and business. High-tech shots are always needed. These subjects are highly marketable, but model releases are a must.

Specs: Uses all formats: 35mm, 2¼×2¼, 4×5, 6×7 and 8×10; color only.

Payment & Terms: Pays 50% commission. Average price per image: $275-500/color photo. Negotiates fees below minimum prices. Offers volume discounts to customers; terms specified in photographer's contract. Photographers can choose not to sell images on discount terms. Works with or without contract. Offers exclusive, limited regional exclusive nonexclusive and guaranteed subject exclusivity contracts. Contracts renew automatically with additional submissions. Statements issued quarterly. Payment made quarterly. Photographers permitted to review account records to verify sales figures or account for various deductions. Offers one-time rights, electronic media rights and agency promotion rights. Informs photographer and allows him to negotiate when client requests all rights. Offers one-time rights. Model/property release required. Captions preferred.

Making Contact: Query with samples and list of stock photos. SASE. Reports in 2 weeks. Photo guidelines free with SASE.

Tips: "Clients are looking for assignment quality and are very discerning with their selections. Only your best should be considered for submission. Please tightly edit your work before submitting. Model-released people shots in lifestyle situations (picnic, golf, tennis, etc.) sell."

PHOTOEDIT, 6056 Corbin Ave., Tarzana CA 91356. (818)342-2811. Fax: (818)343-9548. President: Leslye Borden. Estab. 1987. Stock photo agency. Member of Picture Agency Council of America (PACA). Has 250,000 photos. Clients include: advertising, public relations firms, businesses, book/encyclopedia publishers, magazine publishers.

Needs: People—seniors, teens, children, families, minorities.

Specs: Uses 35mm transparencies.

Payment & Terms: Pays 50% commission on color photos. Average price per image (to clients): $185/quarter page textbook only, other sales higher. Works on contract basis only. Offers nonexclusive contract. Charges catalog insertion fee of $400/per image. Statements issued quarterly; monthly if earnings over $1,000 per month. Payment made monthly or quarterly at time of statement. Photographers are allowed to review account records. Offers one-time rights; limited time use. Consults photographer when client requests all rights. Model preferred for people.

Making Contact: Arrange a personal interview to show portfolio. Submit portfolio for review. Query with samples. Samples not kept on file. SASE. Expects minimum initial submission of 1,000 images with additional submission of 1,000 per year. Reports in 1 month. Photo guidelines free with SASE.

Tips: In samples looks for "drama, color, social relevance, inter-relationships, current (*not* dated material), tight editing. We want photographers who have easy access to models (not professional) and will shoot actively and on spec."

PHOTOLINK STOCK PHOTOGRAPHY, Dept. PM, 141 The Commons, Ithaca NY 14850. (607)272-0642. Fax: (607)272-8634. Director: Jon Reis. Estab. 1988. Stock photo agency. Has 50,000 photos. Clients include: advertising agencies, public relations firms, businesses, book/encyclopedia publishers, magazine publishers.

Needs: Up-to-date model released photos of families, children, business people; recreational sports; aviation; travel/scenics including upstate New York.

Specs: Uses 8×10 (off-beat pics), b&w prints; 35mm transparencies.

Payment & Terms: Pays 50% commission on b&w and color photos. Average price per image (to clients): b&w $150-200; color $150-200. Works on contract basis only. Offers guaranteed subject exclusivity (within files). Issues annual statements. Payment made bimonthly. Photographers are allowed to review account records. Offers one-time rights. Informs photographer and allows him to negotiate when client requests all rights. Model/property release preferred. Captions required; include what, where.

Making Contact: Interested in receiving work from newer, lesser-known photographers. Query with stock photo list. Samples not kept on file. SASE. Expects minimum initial submission of 80 images with additional submissions of at least 30-40 every 3 months. Reports in 1-2 weeks. Photo guidelines free with SASE. Market tips sheet distributed quarterly to contracted photographers.

Tips: Looks for "diversity of work with 3-5 subjects extensively covered; detailed captions and model released; strong initial editing before we see the work—just your best. It's hard to sell photos which are unreleased or uncaptioned. Get out there with model releases and then clearly caption your slides!"

■**PHOTOPHILE,** Dept. PM, Suite B-203, 6150 Lusk Blvd., San Diego CA 92121. (619)453-3050. Fax: (619)452-0994. Director: Kelly Nelson. Clients include: publishers (trade, text, reference, periodical, etc.), advertisers, broadcasters, etc.

Needs: Lifestyle, vocations, sports, industry, entertainment, business and computer graphics.

Specs: Uses 35mm, 2¼×2¼, 4×5 and 6×7 original transparencies.

Payment & Terms: Pays 50% commission. NPI. Works on contract basis only. Offers limited regional exclusivity. Statements issued monthly. Payment made monthly; photographers are paid the first week of the month upon payment from client. Photographers are allowed to review account records to verify sales figures. Rights negotiable; usually offers one-time rights. Informs photographer and allows him to negotiate when client requests all rights. Model/property release required. Captions preferred; include location or description of obscure subjects; travel photos should be captioned with complete destination information.

Making Contact: Write with SASE for photographer's information. "Professionals only, please." Expects a minimum submission of 500 salable images and a photographer must be continuously shooting to add new images to files.

Tips: "Specialize, and shoot for the broadest possible sales potential. Get releases!" Points out that the "greatest need is for model-released people subjects; sharp-focus and good composition are important." If photographer's work is salable, "it will sell itself."

PHOTOREPORTERS, INC., Dept. PM, 875 6th Ave., New York NY 10001. (212)736-7602. General Manager: Roberta Boehm. Estab. 1958. Stock photo agency, news/feature syndicate. Clients include: public relations firms, book/encyclopedia publishers, magazine publishers and newspapers.
Needs: Celebrities, politics and photo stories such as human interest.
Specs: Uses 35mm transparencies.
Payment & Terms: Pays 50% commission on b&w and color photos. General price range: $175/quarter page color; $125/quarter page b&w. Enforces minimum prices. Photographers can choose not to sell images on discount terms. Works with or without contract. Statements issued monthly. Payment made monthly. Offers one-time and electronic media rights. Model release preferred. Captions preferred.
Making Contact: Contact by telephone. SASE. Reports in 3 weeks.

■**PHOTOTAKE, INC.,** Dept. PM, 4523 Broadway, New York NY 10040. (212)942-8185. Fax: (212)942-8186. Director: Leila Levy. Stock photo agency; "fully computerized photo agency specializing in science and technology in stock and on assignment." Has 200,000 photos. Clients include: ad agencies, businesses, newspapers, public relations and AV firms, book/encyclopedia and magazine publishers, and postcard, calendar and greeting card companies.
Needs: General science and technology photographs, medical, high-tech, computer graphics, special effects for general purposes, health-oriented photographs, natural history, people and careers.
Specs: Uses 8×10 prints; 35mm, 2¼×2¼, 4×5 or 8×10 transparencies; contact sheets or negatives.
Payment & Terms: Pays 50% commission on b&w and color photos. Offers one-time or first rights (world rights in English language, etc.). Model release required. Captions required.
Making Contact: Arrange a personal interview to show portfolio. Query with samples or with list of stock photo subjects. Submit portfolio for review. *SASE.* Reports in 1 month. Photo guidelines "given on the phone only." Tips sheet distributed monthly to "photographers that have contracted with us at least for a minimum of 500 photos."
Tips: Prefers to see "at least 100 color photos on general photojournalism or studio photography and at least 5 tearsheets—this, to evaluate photographer for assignment. If photographer has enough in medical, science, general technology photos, send these also for stock consideration." Using more "illustration type of photography. Topics we currently see as hot are: general health, computers, news on science. Photographers should always look for new ways to illustrate concepts generally."

■**PHOTRI INC.,** Suite C2 North, 3701 S. George Maxon Dr., Falls Church VA 22041. (703)931-8600. President: Jack Novak. Member of Picture Agency Council of America (PACA). Has 1 million b&w photos and color transparencies of all subjects. Clients include: book and encyclopedia publishers, ad agencies, record companies, calendar companies, and "various media for AV presentations."
Needs: Military, space, science, technology, romantic couples, people doing things, humor, picture stories. Special needs include calendar and poster subjects. Needs ethnic mix in photos. Has subagents in 10 foreign countries interested in photos of USA in general.
Specs: Uses 8×10 glossy b&w prints; 35mm and larger transparencies.
Payment & Terms: Seldom buys outright; pays 50% commission. Pays: $45-65/b&w photo; $100-1,500/color photo; $50-100/film/ft. Negotiates fees below standard minimums. Offers volume discounts to customers; term's specified in photographer's contract. Discount sale terms not negotiable. Work with or without contract; offers non-exclusivity. Charges $150 catalog insertion fee. Statements issued quarterly. Payment made quarterly. Photographers allowed to review records to verify sales figures or account for various deductions. Offers one-time rights. Model release required if available and if photo is to be used for advertising purposes. Property release required. Captions required.
Making Contact: Call to arrange an appointment or query with resume of credits. SASE. Reports in 2-4 weeks.
Tips: "Respond to current needs with good quality photos. Take, other than sciences, people and situations useful to illustrate processes and professions. Send photos on energy and environmental subjects. Also need any good creative 'computer graphics.' Subject needs include major sports events."

■**THE PICTURE CUBE INC.,** Dept. PM, Suite 1131, 89 Broad St., Boston MA 02110. (617)367-1532. Fax: (617)482-9266. President: Sheri Blaney. Member of Picture Agency Council of America (PACA). Has 300,000 photos. Clients include: ad agencies, public relations firms, businesses, audiovisual firms, textbook publishers, magazine publishers, encyclopedia publishers, newspapers, postcard companies, calendar companies, greeting card companies and TV. Guidelines available with SASE.
Needs: US and foreign coverage, contemporary images, agriculture, industry, energy, high technology, religion, family life, multicultural, animals, transportation, work, leisure, travel, ethnicity, communications, people of all ages, psychology and sociology subjects. "We need lifestyle, model-released images

of families, couples, technology and work situations. We emphasize New England/Boston subjects for our ad/design and corporate clients."

Specs: Uses 8×10 prints; 35mm, 2¼×2¼, 4×5 and larger slides. "Our clients use both color and b&w photography."

Payment & Terms: Pays 50% commission. General price range: $125-300/b&w; $160-400/color photo. "We negotiate special rates for nonprofit organizations." Offers volume discounts to customers; inquire about specific terms. Discount sales terms not negotiable. Works on nonexclusive contract basis only. Contracts renew automatically for three years. Charges catalog insertion fee. Statements issued monthly. Payment made bimonthly. Photographers allowed to review account records to verify sales figures. Offers one-time rights. Informs photographer and allows him to negotiate when a client requests all rights. Model/property release preferred. Captions required; include event, location, description, if model released.

Making Contact: Request guidelines before sending any materials. Arrange a personal interview to show portfolio. SASE. Reports in 1 month.

Tips: "B&w photography is being used more and we will continue to stock it. Serious freelance photographers "must supply a good amount (at least a thousand images per year, sales-oriented subject matter) of material, in order to produce steady sales. All photography submitted must be high quality, with needle-sharp focus, strong composition, correctly exposed. All of our advertising clients require model releases on all photos of people, and often on property (real estate)."

PICTURE GROUP, INC., 830 Eddy St., Providence RI 02905. (401)461-9333. Managing Editor: Philip Hawthorne. Estab. 1979. Stock photo agency, news/feature syndicate. Has 500,000+ photos. Clients include: editorial, corporate, magazine and book publishers.

Needs: Needs photos of "topical, contemporary issues and news, including industry, science, health, environment, politics, lifestyles and people in the news."

Specs: Uses 35mm and 2¼×2¼ transparencies; b&w occasionally.

Payment & Terms: NPI; commission negotiable. Offers one-time rights. Model release preferred. Captions required.

Making Contact: Contact by phone before sending work. SASE. Reports ASAP. Photo guidelines available to contract photographers. Tips distributed occasionally to contract photographers.

Tips: In freelancer's samples, wants to see professionalism, originality, intelligence, relevance, integrity and hard work. "The demand for released material is growing, also for most up-to-date, distinctive, well-informed material with complete captions."

■PICTURE PERFECT STOCK PHOTOS, 159 Main St., P.O. Box 15760, Stamford CT 06901-0760. (203)967-9952. Fax: (203)975-1119. Director: Andres Aquino. Stock photo agency, picture library. Has 300,000+ photos. Clients include: advertising agencies, public relations firms, audiovisual firms, businesses, book/encyclopedia publishers, magazine publishers, newspapers, postcard publishers, calendar companies, greeting card companies.

Needs: Photos of all subjects; heavy on people, travel, glamour, beauty, fashion, medical, science, business and technology.

Specs: Uses b&w prints; 35mm, 2¼×2¼, 4×5, 8×10 transparencies; VHS and ¾", videotape.

Payment & Terms: Pays 50% commission on b&w and color photos. Also buys photographs in bulk. Average price per image (to clients): b&w $150-2,000; and color $150-3,000. Enforces minimum prices. Offers volume discounts to customers; terms specified in photographer's contract. Photographers can choose not to sell images on discount terms. Works on contract basis only. Offers exclusive and nonexclusive contracts. Charges filing fee of $4/shipment; catalog insertion fee of 15%, 30% or 50%, "based on royalty desired by photographer." Statements issued bimonthly. Payment made monthly. Photographer is allowed to review account records pertaining to his/her sales only. Offers one-time rights. Informs photographer and permits him to negotiate when client requests all rights. Model/property release required. Captions required; include description and location.

Making Contact: Interested in receiving work from newer, lesser-known photographers. Query with samples. Query with stock photo list. Samples kept on file. SASE. Expects minimum initial submission of 20-100 images, with additional submission of 20/month or more. Reports in 3 weeks. Photo guidelines free with SASE. Market tips sheet distributed from time to time in the form of newsletter. Send $4 for sample requests and guidelines.

Tips: "We prefer sharp, carefully edited images in your area of specialization. Trends: images with specific commercial applications; images with senior citizens enjoying outdoor activities or engaged in activities with younger people; and images that evoke emotions and intellectual responses."

PICTURE THAT, INC., Dept. PM, 880 Briarwood Rd., Newtown Square PA 19073. (215)353-8833. Stock Librarian: Lili Etezady. Estab. 1978. Stock photo agency. Clients include: advertising agencies, public relations firms, businesses, book/encyclopedia publishers, magazine publishers, postcard companies, calendar companies and greeting card companies.

Needs: Handles all subjects: nature, scenics, sports, people of all types and activities, animals, some abstracts and art, and travel (especially East Coast and Pennsylvania).
Specs: Uses 35mm and 2¼ × 2¼ transparencies and others..
Payment & Terms: Pays 50% commission on photos. General price range: varies with usage and circulation. Works with or without contract. Offers limited regional exclusivity and guaranteed subject exclusivity in contracts. Charges 100% duping fees. Statements issued monthly. Payment made "within 10 days from when we get paid." Offers one-time rights. Informs photographer and allows him to negotiate when client requests all rights. "We negotiate for them if they agree." Model release preferred. Captions required.
Making Contact: Query with list of stock photo subjects. SASE. Call for info.
Tips: Likes to see good color and good exposure. Send images in plastic sheets with captions and photographer's name on slides. "We encourage new photographers as we build our stock. We are receiving more and more requests for lifestyle photos, people in all situations, especially active and sports shots; also senior citizens. They must be model-released."

PICTURES INTERNATIONAL, P.O. Box 470685, Tulsa OK 74147-0685. (918)664-1339. Picture Editor: Jim Wray. Has 50,000 images. Clients include: ad agencies, public relations firms, magazine publishers, and paper product (calendars, postcards, greeting cards) companies.
Specs: Uses 2¼ × 2¼ and larger transparencies; also 8 × 10 glossy b&w and color prints. Will consider stereo (3-D) images; see separate listing under "Advertising in Three-Dimension."
Payment & Terms: Pays 50% commission on b&w and color photos. Model releases required. Captions required.
Making Contact: Submit photos by mail for consideration. SASE. Photo guidelines and tip sheet free upon request.

■**PICTURESQUE STOCK PHOTOS**, 1520 Brookside Drive #3, Raleigh NC 27604. (919)828-0023. Manager: Syd Jeffrey. Estab. 1987. Stock photo agency. Member of Picture Agency Council of America (PACA). Has 300,000 photos. Clients include: advertising agencies, design firms, corporations, book/encyclopedia publishers and magazine publishers.
Needs: Travel/destination, model-released people, lifestyle, business, industry and general topics.
Specs: Uses 35mm, 2¼ × 2¼, 4 × 5 and 8 × 10 transparencies.
Payment & Terms: Pays 40-50% commission. Works on contract basis only. Contracts renew automatically. Payment made monthly. Photographers allowed to review account records. Offers various rights depending on client needs. Model/property release required. Captions required.
Making Contact: Interested in receiving work from newer, lesser-known photographers. Contact by telephone for submissions guidelines. SASE. Reports in 1 month. Tips sheet distributed quarterly to member photographers.
Tips: Submission requirements include 200-300 original transparencies; wide range of subjects.

■‡**PLANET EARTH PICTURES/SEAPHOT LTD**, 4 Harcourt St., London W1H IDS England. 071-262-4427. Fax: 071-706-4042. Managing Director: Gillian Lythgoe. Has 200,000 photos. Clients include: ad agencies, public relations and audiovisual firms, businesses, book/encyclopedia and magazine publishers, and postcard and calendar companies.
Needs: "Marine—surface and underwater photos covering all marine subjects, including water sports, marine natural history, seascapes, ships, natural history. All animals and plants: interrelationships and behavior, landscapes, natural environments, pollution and convervation." Special subject needs: polar and rainforest animals and scenery.
Specs: Uses any size transparencies.
Payment & Terms: Pays 50% commission on color photos. General price range: £50 (1 picture/1 AV showing), to over £1,000 for advertising use. Prices negotiable according to use. Works with or without a signed contract, negotiable. Statements issued quarterly. Payment made quarterly. Photographers allowed to review account records to verify sales figures. Offers one-time rights. Informs photographer and allows him to negotiate when client requests all rights. Model release preferred. Captions required.
Making Contact: Arrange a personal interview to show portfolio. Send photos by mail for consideration. SASE. Reports ASAP. Distributes tips sheet every 6 months to photographers.
Tips: "We like photographers to receive our photographer's booklet that gives details about photos and captions. In reviewing a portfolio, we look for a range of photographs on any subject—important for the magazine market—and the quality. Trends change rapidly. There is a strong emphasis that photos taken in the wild are preferable to studio pictures. Advertising clients still like larger format photographs. Exciting and artistic photographs used even for wildlife photography, protection of environment."

■‡**PRO-FILE,** 2B Winner Commercial Building, 401-403 Lockhart Rd., Wanchai Hong Kong. (852)574-7788. Fax: (852)574-8884. Director: Neil Farrin. Stock photo agency. Has 100,000+ photos. Clients include: advertising agencies, public relations firms, audiovisual firms, businesses, book/encyclopedia publishers, magazine publishers and calendar companies.
Needs: General stock, worldwide, emphasis on Asia.
Specs: Uses 35mm, 2¼×2¼ and 4×5 transparencies.
Payment & Terms: Pays 50% commission. Works on contract basis only. Guarantees subject exclusivity within files and limited regional exclusivity. Charges duping and catalog insertion fees. Statements issued quarterly. Payment made quarterly. Photographers allowed to review account records to verify sales figures. Offers one-time and electronic media rights. Requests agency promotion rights. Informs photographer and allows him to negotiate when client requests all rights. Model/property release required. Captions required.
Making Contact: Interested in receiving work from newer, lesser-known photographers. Query with resume of credits and list of stock photo subjects. SASE. Reports in 3 months. Distributes tips sheet "as necessary" to current photographers on file.
Tips: Has second office in Singapore; contact main office for information.

■**PROFILES WEST,** Dept. PM, 210 E. Main St., P.O. Box 1199, Buena Vista CO 81211. (719)395-8671. Fax: (719)395-8840. President, Photographer Representative: Allen Russell. Estab. 1987. Stock photo agency. Member of Picture Agency Council of America (PACA). Has 200,000 photos. Clients include: advertising agencies, public relations firms, audiovisual firms, businesses, book/encyclopedia publishers, magazine publishers, postcard companies, calendar companies and greeting card companies.
Needs: "Our specialty is the American West and its people at work and play. We are very strong in leisure sports and lifestyles, people at work and Western scenes."
Specs: Uses 35mm, medium and large format transparencies.
Payment & Terms: Pays 50% commission on color photos. General price range: $125+. Works on contract basis only. Offers nonexclusive contract and guarantees subject exclusivity within files. Contracts renew automatically with each submission for 1 year. Charges catalog insertion of varying rate. Statements issued bimonthly. Payment made bimonthly. Photographers allowed to review account records to verify sales figures or account for various deductions. Offers one-time and electronic media rights. "A wide range of rights is offered but one-time dominates." Informs photographer and allows him to negotiate when client requests all rights. Model and/or property release preferred.
Making Contact: Query with list of stock photo subjects. Submit portfolio for review. SASE. Photo guidelines free with SASE. Tips sheet distributed to contract photographers.
Tips: In photographer's portfolio, wants to see "an organized style which shows people and their environment in a manner which looks unposed, even when it often is. A commitment to developing a series of subjects rather than only random shots." The trend is towards "a desire for images which go beyond the limits of what has come to be expected from stock: more emotion, realism, etc. There is a tremendous need for stock photographers to accept that they are small business people and act accordingly. Most need to tighten their scope of subject and find where they can best compete."

■**RAINBOW,** Dept. PM, P.O. Box 573, Housatonic MA 01236. (413)274-6211. Fax: (413)274-6689. Director: Coco McCoy. Estab. 1976. Stock photo agency. Member of Picture Agency Council of America (PACA). Has 195,000 photos. Clients include: public relations firms, design agencies, audiovisual firms, book/encyclopedia publishers, magazine publishers and calendar companies. 20% of sales come from overseas.
● In the near future this agency plans to offer its own CD-ROM discs with around 2,000 images.
Needs: Although Rainbow is a general coverage agency, it specializes in high technology images and is continually looking for talented coverage in fields such as alternative energy computer graphics, pathology research, medicine, DNA, communications, lasers and space. "We are also looking for graphically strong and colorful images in such areas as macro and microphotography, illustrations of physics, biology and earth science concepts; also active children, teenagers and elderly people. Worldwide travel locations are always in demand, showing people, culture and architecture. Our rain forest file is growing but is never big enough!"
Specs: Uses 35mm and larger transparences.
Payment & Terms: Pays 50% commission. General price range: $165-$1,000. Works with or without contract, negotiable. Offers limited regional exclusivity contract. Contracts renew automatically with each submission; no time limit. Charges duping fee of 50%/image. Statements issued quarterly. Payment made quarterly. Photographers allowed to review account records to verify sales figures. Offers one-time rights. Informs photographer and allows him to negotiate when client requests all rights. Model release is required for advertising, book covers or calendar sales. Photo captions required for scientific photos or geographic locations, etc.; include simple description if not evident from photo and Latin and common names for plants and insects.

Making Contact: Interested in receiving work from newer, lesser-known photographers. "Photographers may write or call us for more information. We may ask for an initial submission of 150-300 chromes." Arrange a personal interview to show portfolio or query with samples. SASE. Published professionals only. Reports in 2 weeks. Guidelines sheet for SASE. Distributes a tips sheets twice a year.

Tips: "The best advice we can give is to encourage photographers to better edit their photos before sending. No agency wants to look at grey rocks backlit on a cloudy day! With no caption!" Looks for well-composed, well-lit, sharp focused images with either a concept well illustrated or a mood conveyed by beauty or light. "Clear captions help our researchers choose wisely and ultimately improve sales. As far as trends in subject matter go, strong, simple images conveying the American Spirit . . . families together, farming, scientific research, winning marathons, hikers reaching the top, are the winners. And include females doing 'male' jobs, black scientists, Hispanic professionals, Oriental children with a blend of others at play, etc. The importance of model releases for editorial covers, selected magazine usage and always for advertising/corporate clients cannot be stressed enough!"

■❋**REFLEXION PHOTOTHEQUE**, Suite 1000, 1255 Square Phillips, Montreal PQ H3B 3G1 Canada. (514)876-1620. President: Michel Gagne. Estab. 1981. Stock photo agency. Has 100,000 photos. Clients include: advertising agencies, public relations firms, audiovisual firms, businesses, book/encyclopedia publishers, magazine publishers, newspapers, postcard companies, calendar companies and greeting card companies.

Needs: Model-released people of all ages in various activities. Also, beautiful homes, recreational sports, North American wildlife, industries, U.S. cities, antique cars, hunting and fishing scenes, food, and dogs and cats in studio setting.

Specs: Uses 35mm, 2¼×2¼, 4×5, 8×10 transparencies.

Payment & Terms: Pays 50% commission on color photos. Average price per image: $150-500. Enforces minimum prices. Offers volume discounts to customers; inquire about specific terms. Discount sales terms not negotiable. Works on contract basis only. Offers limited regional exclusive and non-exclusive contracts. Contracts renew automatically for five years. Charges 100% duping fee and 75% catalog insertion fee. Statements issued quarterly. Payment made monthly. Photographers allowed to review account records to verify sales figures. Offers one-time rights. Informs photographer and allows him to negotiate when client requests all rights. Model/property release preferred. Photo captions required; include country, place, city, or activity.

Making Contact: Interested in receiving work from newer, lesser-known photographers. Arrange a personal interview to show portfolio. Query with list of stock photo subjects. Submit portfolio for review. "We deal with local freelancers only." SASE. Reports in 1 month. Photo guidelines available.

Tips: "Limit your selection to 100 images. Images must be sharp and well exposed. Send only if you have high quality material on the listed subjects."

*****RETNA LTD.**, Third Floor, 18 E. 17th St., New York NY 10013. (212)255-0622. Manager: Julie Grahame. Estab. 1979. Stock photo agency, assignment agency. Has 1 million photos. Clients include advertising agencies, public relations firms, book/encyclopedia publishers, magazine publishers, newspapers and record companies.

Needs: Handles photos of musicians (pop, rock, jazz, contemporary, rap, R&B) and celebrities (movie, film and television and politicians).

Specs: Uses 8×10 b&w prints; 35mm and 2¼×2¼ transparencies; b&w contact sheets; b&w negatives.

Payment & Terms: Pays 50% commission on b&w and color photos. General price range: $125-1,500. Works on contract basis only. Contracts renew automatically with additional submissions all-for five years. Statements issued monthly. Payment made monthly. Offers one-time rights; negotiable. When client requests all rights photographer will be consulted, but Retna will negotiage. Model/property release required. Captions required.

Making Contact: Works on contract basis only. Arrange a personal interview to show portfolio. Works on assignment only. SASE. Reports in 2 weeks. Does not publish "tips" sheets, but makes regular phone calls to photographers.

Tips: Wants to see "a clean presentation of chromes and prints (color and b&w). Prints must be excellent." Observes that current trends include "mostly color; some b&w personality shots. Mostly sessions etc."

A bullet has been placed within some listings to introduce special comments by the editor of the Photographer's Market.

■REX USA LTD (incorporating RDR), 351 W. 54th St., New York NY 10019. (212)586-4432. Fax: (212)541-5724. Bureau Chief: April Sandmeyer. Estab. 1935. Stock photo agency, news/feature syndicate. Affiliated with Rex Features in London. Member of Picture Agency Council of America (PACA). Has 1,500,000 photos. Clients include: advertising agencies, public relations firms, audiovisual firms, businesses, book/encyclopedia publishers, magazine publishers, newspapers, postcard companies, calendar companies, greeting card companies and TV, film and record companies.

Needs: Primarily editorial material: celebrities, personalities (studio portraits, candid, paparazzi), human interest, news features, movie stills, glamour, historical, geographic, general stock, sports and scientific.

Specs: Uses all sizes and finishes of b&w and color prints; 35mm, 2¼×2¼, 4×5, and 8×10 transparencies; b&w and color contact sheets; b&w and color negatives; VHS videotape.

Payment & Terms: NPI; payment varies depending on quality of subject matter and exclusivity. "We obtain highest possible prices, starting at $100-100,000 for one-time sale." Pays 50% commission on b&w and color photos. Works with or without contract. Statements issued monthly. Payment made monthly. Photographers allowed to review account records. Offers one-time rights, first rights and all rights. Informs photographer and allows him to negotiate when client requests all rights. Model release preferred. Captions preferred.

Making Contact: Interested in receiving work from newer, lesser-known photographers. Arrange a personal interview to show portfolio. Query with samples. Query with list of stock photo subjects. SASE. Reports in 1-2 weeks.

CHRIS ROBERTS REPRESENTS, Dept. PM, P.O. Box 7218, Missoula MT 59807. (406)728-2180. Owner/ Art Director: Chris Roberts. Photographer's representative company, stock photo agency. Has 3,000 photos.

Needs: "We are building a specialty in images from the Western and Southwestern US, people, animals, nature, scenics, architecture, industry and livelihoods (cowboys, Indians, loggers, fishermen). **Specs:** Uses 35mm and 4×5 transparencies.

Payment & Terms: Pays 50% on color photos. General price range: $45 minimum. Works on contract basis only. Offers nonexclusive contract. Payment made upon receipt of payment from client. Photographers allowed to review account records to verify sales figures. Offers one-time and limited rights. Informs photographer and allows him to negotiate when client requests all rights. Model releases (for recognizable faces) required. Captions required.

Making Contact: Interested in receiving work from newer, lesser-known photographers. Query with SASE. Arrange a personal interview to show portfolio. Send unsolicited photos by mail for consideration. Submit portfolio for review. Provide resume, business card, brochure, flyer or tearsheets to be kept on file for possible future assignments. SASE. Reports in 3 weeks. Submission guidelines available.

Tips: "If you've got a scenic or good location spot, put people doing something in it." In reviewing portfolio looks for "simplicity, composition, clarity, technical expertise."

■RO-MA STOCK, 3101 W. Riverside Dr., Burbank CA 91505-4741. (818)842-3777. Fax: (818)566-7380. Owner: Robert Marien. Estab. 1989. Stock photo agency. Member of Picture Agency Council of America (PACA). Has 80,000 photos. Clients include: advertising agencies; public relations firms; multimedia firms; corporations; textbook and magazine publishers; postcard, calendar, greeting card, design and film/video production companies.

Needs: Animals, plants, wildlife, underwater scenes, landscapes, micro/macro photos of organisms and environmental subjects. Also, adults, elderly and children involved with nature, outdoor leisure, and outdoor sports involving every age range. Also looking for outer-space fictional images of the planets and the universe and sciences (botany, ecology, geology, astronomy, weather, natural history, medicine).

Specs: Primarily uses 35mm, 2¼×2¼, 4×5 and 70mm dupes. Prefers medium format mounted in 4×5 cardboard mounts. Also 8×10 b&w prints, contact sheets and negatives.

Payment & Terms: Pays 50% commission on b&w and color; international sales, 40% of gross. General price range: $200+. Offers volume discounts to customers; terms specified in photographer's contract. Contract renews automatically with each submission for one year. Charges 100% duping fees; 50% catalog insertion fee. Statements issued quarterly. Payments made quarterly; within 30 days of end of quarter. Photographers allowed to review account records to verify sales figures. Offers one-time rights and first rights. Informs photographer when client requests all rights to obtain permission to proceed with negotiation. Model/property release required for recognizable people and private places. Captions required for animals/plants, include common name, scientific name, habitat, photographer's name; for others include subject, location, photographer's name.

Making Contact: Interested in receiving work from newer, lesser-known photographers. Query with resume of credits, tearsheets or samples and list of specialties. No unsolicited original work. Responds with tips sheet, agency profile and questionnaire for photographer with SASE. Photo guidelines and tips distributed periodically to contract photographers.

Tips: Wants photographers with "ability" to produce excellent competitive photographs for the stock photography market on specialized subjects and be willing to learn, listen and improve agency's file contents. Looking for well-composed subjects, high sharpness and color saturation. Emphasis on exotic animals and plants, action outdoor sports, people involved with the environment (including destruction or salvation, manufacturing and industry). Also, patterns in nature, in art and in architecture are welcome."

© photo by Robert Marien/RO-MA Stock

Robert Marien, photographer/president of RO-MA Stock, says his interest and knowledge of nature and ecology led to this rare and interesting shot. The image was purchased several times by magazines and was used here in a religious publication.

■‡S & I WILLIAMS POWER PIX, Castle Lodge, Wenvoe, Cardiff CF5 6AD Wales, United Kingdom. (0222) 595163. Fax: (0222)593905. President: Steven Williams. Picture library. Has 100,000 photos. Clients include: ad agencies, public relations firms, audiovisual firms, businesses, book/encyclopedia publishers, magazine publishers, postcard companies, calendar companies, greeting card companies and music business, i.e. records, cassettes and CDs.
Specs: Uses 35mm, 2¼×2¼, 4×5 and 8×10 transparencies.
Payment & Terms: Pays 50% commission on b&w and color photos. General price range: £50-£500 (English currency). Model release required. Captions required.
Making Contact: Arrange a personal interview to show portfolio. Query with resume of credits, samples or stock photo list. SASE. Reports in 1-2 weeks. Photo guidelines available for SASE. Distributes a tips sheet every 3-6 months to photographers on books.
Tips: Prefers to see "a photographer who knows his subject and has done his market research by looking at pictures used in magazines, record covers, books, etc.—bright colorful images and an eye for something just that little bit special."

*■S.K. STOCK, 117 S. 11th St., Garland TX 75040. (214)272-1561. Photo Manager: Sam Copeland. Estab. 1985. Stock photo agency. Has 1,500 photos. Clients include: public relations firms, book/encyclopedia publishers, magazine publishers, calendar companies and greeting card companies.
Needs: Wants to see nudes, flowers, sunsets, animals, all subjects.
Specs: Uses 4×6, 4×4, color and/or b&w prints; 35mm 2¼×2¼, 4×5 and 8×10 transparencies; film; VHS videotape.
Payment & Terms: Buys photos outright; pays $50/color photo; $50/b&w photo; $80/minute of videotape footage. Pays 50% commission on b&w, color, film and videotape. Average price per image: $100-300/b&w; $75-150/color; $100-400/film. Negotiates fees below standard minimum prices. Works on contract basis only. Offers nonexclusive contract. Charges 10% insertion fee. Statements issued bimonthly. Payment made "as soon as we get payed, photographers do too." Photographers allowed to

review account records "so that they can see they are not being cheated." Offers one-time rights. Informs photographer and allows him to negotiate when client requests all rights "as long as I get 10 percent." Model/property release required. Captions required; include title, and send a list of all work.
Making Contact: Interested in receiving work from newer, lesser-known photographers. Query with samples. Query with stock photo list. Keeps samples on file. SASE. Expects minimum initial submission of 30 images with periodic submission of at least 30 images every other month. Reports in 3 weeks. Photo guidelines free with SASE. Market tips sheet distributed every 3 months; free with SASE upon request.
Tips: "Your work must be sharp. We need people who will submit work all the time, clear and sharp. No out of range pictures."

■‡SCIENCE PHOTO LIBRARY, LTD., 112 Westbourne Grove, London W2 5RU England. (071)727-4712. Fax: (071)727-6041. Research Director: Rosemary Taylor. Stock photo agency. Has 100,000 photos. Clients include: ad agencies, public relations firms, audiovisual firms, businesses, book/encyclopedia publishers, magazine publishers, newspapers, postcard companies, calendar companies and greeting card companies.
Needs: SPL specializes in all aspects of science, medicine and technology. "Our interpretation of these areas is broad. We include earth sciences, landscape, and sky pictures; animals up to the size of insects (but not natural history pictures of birds, mammals etc.). We have a major and continuing need of high-quality photographs showing science, technology and medicine *at work*: laboratories, high-technology equipment, computers, lasers, robots, surgery, hospitals, etc. We are especially keen to sign up American freelance photographers who take a wide range of photographs in the fields of medicine and technology. We like to work closely with photographers, suggesting subject matter to them and developing photo features with them. We can only work with photographers who agree to our distributing their pictures throughout Europe, and preferably elsewhere. We duplicate selected pictures and syndicate them to our agents around the world."
Specs: Uses color prints; and 35mm, 2¼×2¼, 4×5, 6×7, 6×5 and 6×9 transparencies.
Payment & Terms: Pays 50% commission for b&w and color photos. General price range: $80-1,000; varies according to use. Only discount below minimum for volume or education. Offers volume discounts to customers; inquire about specific terms. Discount sales terms not negotiable. Works on contract basis only. Offers exclusivity; exceptions are made; subject to negotiation. Agreement made for four years; general continuation is assured unless otherwise advised. Statements issued quarterly. Payment made quarterly. Photographers allowed to review account records to verify sales figures; fully computerized accounts/commission handling system. Offers one-time and electronic media rights. Model release required. Captions required.
Making Contact: Interested in receiving work from newer, lesser-known photographers. Query with samples or query with list of stock photo subjects. Send unsolicited photos by mail for consideration. Returns material submitted for review. Reports in 3 weeks. Photo guidelines sheet for SASE. "Distribute a tip sheet to our photographers."
Tips: Prefers to see "a small (20-50) selection showing the range of subjects covered and the *quality*, style and approach of the photographer's work. Our bestselling areas in the last 2 years have been medicine and technology. We see a continuing trend in the European market towards very high-quality, carefully-lit photographs. This is combined with a trend towards increasing use of medium and large-format photographs and decreasing use of 35mm (we make medium-format duplicates of some of our best 35mm); impact of digital storage/manipulation; problems of copyright and unpaid usage. The emphasis is on an increasingly professional approach to photography."

SHARPSHOOTERS, INC., Suite 114, 4950 SW 72 Ave., Miami FL 33155. (305)666-1266. Manager, Photographer Relations: Edie Tobias. Estab. 1984. Stock photo agency. Member of Picture Agency Council of America (PACA). Has 500,000 photos. Clients include: advertising agencies.
Needs: Model-released people for advertising use. Well-designed, styled photographs that capture the essence of life: children; families; couples at home, at work and at play.
Specs: Uses transparencies only, all formats.
Payment & Terms: Pays 50% commission on color photos. General price range: $275-15,000. Works on contract basis only. Offers exclusive contract only. Statements issued monthly. Payments made monthly. Photographers allowed to review account records; "monthly statements are derived from computer records of all transactions and are highly detailed." Offers one-time rights usually, "but if clients pay more they get more usage rights. We never offer all rights on photos." Model/property release required. Photo captions preferred.
Making Contact: Interested in receiving work from newer, lesser-known photographers. Query along with nonreturnable printed promotion pieces. Cannot return unsolicited material. Reports in 1 week.
Tips: Wants to see "technical excellence, originality, creativity and design sense, excellent ability to cast and direct talent and commitment to shooting stock." Observes that "photographer should be in control of all elements of his/her production: casting, styling, props, location, etc., but be able to make a photograph that looks natural and spontaneous."

*SHASHINKA PHOTO LIBRARY, Suite 2108, 501 Fifth Ave., New York NY 10017-6165. (212)490-2180. Fax: (212)490-2187 (23). Estab. 1973. Picture library. Clients include: advertising agencies, public relations firms, textbook/encyclopedia publishers, magazine publishers, newspapers, postcard publishers, calendar companies.
Needs: Specializing in Japan and Asia.
Specs: Uses 35mm, 2¼×2¼, 4×5 transparencies.
Payment & Terms: Buys photos only if offered as a photo story. Pays 50% commission on b&w and color photos. Average minimum price per image: $75/b&w; $150/color. "Some publishers or users have a very low print run such as 3,000-4,000 books. In such cases we prefer to sell rather than pass. That's our philosophy. However, this is infrequent." Offers volume discounts to customers; inquire about specific terms. Works with or without contract. Offers nonexclusive contract. "Frankly, we don't use formal contracts. Just a letter of understanding concerning holding time, etc." Statements issued only when images are sold. Photographers paid upon payment from user. Offers one-time rights. Does not inform photographer when client requests all rights. Model release preferred for nudes and close-ups that can invite lawsuits. Captions preferred; include subject, circumstances, if applicable, and date.
Making Contact: Submit portfolio for review. Send selections with SASE. Keeps samples on file "if good prospects." SASE. Expects minimum initial submission of 20-25 images in one plastic sheet. Reports in 1 month. Photo guidelines available free on request. Catalog available free with SASE.
Tips: "Other than Japan and Asia, we also have need for natural and physical science illustrated stories for children's science magazines/books. However, contents don't differentiate whether for children or adults. Children (4-12 yrs.) in photos favored."

SILVER IMAGE PHOTO AGENCY, INC., Dept. PM, 5128 NW 58th Court, Gainesville FL 32606. (904)373-5771. President/Owner: Carla Hotvedt. Estab. 1988. Stock photo agency. Assignments in Florida/S. Georgia. Has 20,000 color/b&w photos. Clients include: public relations firms, book/encyclopedia publishers, magazine publishers and newspapers.
Needs: Florida-based travel/tourism, Florida cityscapes and people, nationally oriented topics such as drugs, environment, recycling, pollution, etc. Humorous people and animal photos.
Specs: Uses 8×10 glossy b&w prints; 35mm transparencies.
Payment & Terms: Pays 50% commission on b&w/color photos. General price range: $25-600. Works on contract basis only. Offers nonexclusive contract. Statements issued monthly. Payment made monthly. Offers one-time rights. Informs photographer and allows him to negotiate when client requests all rights. Model release preferred. Captions required: include name, year shot, city, state, etc.
Making Contact: Query with list of stock photo subjects. SASE; will return if query first. Reports on queries in 2 weeks; material up to 2 months. Photo guidelines free with SASE. Tips sheets distributed as needed. SASE. Do not submit material unless requested first.
Tips: Looks for ability to tell a story in one photo. "I will look at photographer's work if they seem to have images outlined on my stock needs list which I will send out after receiving a query letter with SASE. Because of my photojournalistic approach my clients want to see people-oriented photos, not just pretty scenics. I also get many calls for drug-related photos and unique shots from Florida."

*■SIPA PRESS/SIPA IMAGE, 30 W. 21st St., New York NY 10010. (212)463-0150. Fax: (212)463-0160. Managing Editor: Jody Potter. Estab. 1969. Stock photo agency and news/feature syndicate. Has 15 million photos. Has 1 branch office. Clients include: advertising agencies, audiovisual firms, businesses, book/encyclopedia publishers, magazine publishers, newspapers.
Needs: Travel, people, education, business, industry, science, medicine, wildlife, sports.
Specs: Uses b&w prints, 35mm, 2¼×2¼, 4×5, 8×10 transparencies.
Payment & Terms: Pays 50% commission on b&w and color photos. Offers one-time rights. Model release required. Captions required.
Making Contact: Submit portfolio for review. Query with samples. Samples not kept on file. SASE. Reports in 3 weeks. Photo guidelines free with SASE.
Tips: "Always interested in images representing contemporary themes and emotional concepts."

‡THE SLIDE FILE, 79 Merrion Square, Dublin 2 Ireland. (0001)766850. Fax: (0001)608332. Director/Picture Editor: George Munday. Stock photo agency and picture library. Has 50,000 photos. Clients include: ad agencies, public relations firms, businesses, book/encyclopedia publishers, magazine publishers, newspapers and designers.
Needs: Overriding consideration is given to Irish or Irish-connected subjects. Has limited need for overseas locations, but is happy to accept material depicting other subjects, particularly people.
Specs: Uses 35mm, 2¼×2¼ and 4×5 transparencies.
Payment & Terms: Pays 50% commission on color photos. General price range: £60-1,000 English currency ($75-900). Works on contract basis only. Offers exclusive contracts and limited regional exclusivity. Contracts renew automatically with additional submissions. Statements issued quarterly. Payment made quarterly. Photographers allowed to review account records. Offers one-time rights.

Informs photographer when client requests all rights, but "we take care of negotiations." Model release preferred. Captions required.

Making Contact: Interested in receiving work from newer, lesser-known photographers. Query with list of stock photo subjects. Works with local freelancers only. Does not return unsolicited material. Expects minimum initial submission of 250 transparencies; 1,000 images annually. "A return shipping fee is required: important that all similars are submitted together. We keep our contributor numbers down and the quantity and quality of submissions high. Send for information first." Reports in 1 month.

Tips: "Apart from growing sales of Irish-oriented material, the trend seems to indicate increasing use of people shots—executives, families, couples, etc. particularly on medium format."

*■THE SOURCE STOCK FOOTAGE LIBRARY, INC., 738 N. Constitution Dr., Tucson AZ 85748. (602)298-4810. Fax: (602)290-8831. Manager: John Willwater. Film production company and film/video stock footage library. Has 40 hours of select film/video stock footage. Clients include: advertising agencies, public relations firms, audiovisual firms, corporations (internal, marketing video communication programs).

Needs: Specializes in scenics, nature, environmental, destination (foreign and US), industrial and certain archival footage.

Specs: Uses 16/35mm film; all formats of videotape.

Payment & Terms: Pays 40% commission on film and videotape. Negotiates fees below standard minimum prices. "Most work is done in corporate communications market. Rates are often tied to budgets." Offers volume discounts to customers; terms specified in photographer's contract. Photographers can choose not to sell images on discount terms. Works with or without contract. Offers nonexclusive contract. Statements issued quarterly. Payments made quarterly. Photographers allowed to review account records. Offers one-time rights. Informs photographers and allows them to negotiate when client requests all rights. Model release preferred.

Making Contact: Interested in receiving work from newer, lesser-known photographers. Query with samples. Keeps samples on file. SASE. Reports in 1-2 weeks. Photo guidelines free with SASE. Catalog free with SASE. Market tips sheet available free upon request.

Tips: "At the moment producers want high production value with lots of camera moves, spectacular shots. Documentary style is not highly sought."

■SOUTHERN STOCK PHOTO AGENCY, Suite 33, 3601 W. Commercial Blvd., Ft. Lauderdale FL 33309. (305)486-7117. Fax: (305)486-7118. Contact: Victoria Ross. Estab. 1976. Stock photo agency. Member of Picture Agency Council of America (PACA). Has 750,000 photos. Clients include: advertising agencies, design firms, businesses, book/encyclopedia publishers, magazine publishers, newspapers, calendar and greeting card companies.

Needs: Needs photos of "southern U.S. cities, Bahamas, Caribbean, South America, and model-released lifestyle photos with young families and active seniors."

Specs: Uses color, 35mm, 2¼ × 2¼, 4 × 5 transparencies.

Payment & Terms: Pays 50% commission on color photos. General price range: $225-5,000. Works on contract basis only. Offers nonexclusive contract. Contracts renew automatically. Statements issued bimonthly. Payment made bimonthly. Photographers allowed to review account records. Offers one-time rights, first time rights and all rights. Informs photographer and allows him to negotiate when client requests all rights. Model release and photo captions required.

Making Contact: Interested in receiving work from newer, lesser-known photographers. Query with samples. SASE. Reports in 1 month. Photo guidelines free with SASE.

Tips: In portfolio or samples, wants to see approximately 200 transparencies of a cross section of work. Photographers "must be willing to submit regular new work."

■SOVFOTO/EASTFOTO, INC., Suite 1505, 225 W 34th St., New York NY 10122. (212)564-5485. Fax: (212)564-4249. Director: Victoria Edwards. Estab. 1935. Stock photo agency. Has 800,000 photos. Clients include: audiovisual firms, book/encyclopedia publishers, magazine publishers, newspapers.

Needs: Interested in photos of Eastern Europe, Russia, China, CIS republics.

Specs: Uses 8 × 10 glossy b&w and color prints; 35mm, 2¼ × 2¼ transparencies.

Payment & Terms: Pays 50% commission. Average price per image to clients $150-250/b&w photo; $150-250/color photo. Negotiates fees below standard minimum prices. Bulk sales are negotiable. Offers volume discounts to customers. Offers exclusive contracts, limited regional exclusivity and non-exclusivity. Statements issued quarterly. Payment made quarterly. Photographers permitted to review account records to verify sales figures or account for various deductions. Offers one-time, electronic media and nonexclusive rights. Model/property release preferred. Captions required.

Making Contact: Arrange personal interview to show portfolio. Query with samples. Query with stock photo list. Samples kept on file. SASE. Expects minimum initial submission of 50-100 images. Reports in 1-2 weeks.

Tips: Looks for "news and general interest photos (color) with human element."

SPECTRUM PHOTO, 3127 W. 12 Mile Rd., Berkley MI 48072. Phone: (313)398-3630. Fax: (313)398-3997. Manager: Corinne Bolton. Estab. 1990. Stock photo agency. Has 250,000 images. Clients include: ad agencies, public relations firms, businesses, magazine publishers, postcard publishers, calendar companies and display companies.
Needs: All subjects, but especially "high-tech, business, industry, lifestyles, food and backgrounds."
Specs: Uses 8 × 10 glossy b&w prints; 35mm, 2¼ × 2¼, 4 × 5 transparencies, 70mm and panoramic.
Payment & Terms: Pays 50% commission on b&w and color film. General price range: $50-300/b&w photo; $150-1,500/color photo. Works on contract basis only. Offers limited regional exclusivity. Contracts renew automatically with each submission; time period not specified. Charges duping fee of 50%/image. Statements issued monthly. Payment made bimonthly. Photographers allowed to review account records to verify sales figures. Offers one-time and electronic media rights. Requires agency promotion rights. Informs photographer and permits negotiation when client requests all rights, with some conditions. Model/property release required. Captions required.
Making Contact: Query with samples. Does not keep samples on file. SASE. Submit minimum of 50-100 images in initial query. Expects periodic submissions of 300-600 images each year. Reports in 3 weeks. Photo guidelines sheet free with SASE. Tips sheet available periodically to contracted photographers.
Tips: Wants to see "creativity, technical excellence and marketability" in submitted images. "We have many requests for business-related images, high-tech, and lifestyle photos. Shoot as much as possible and send it to us."

■‡SPORTING PICTURES (UK), LTD., 7A Lambs Conduit Passage, London, WC1R 4RG England. (071)405-4500. Fax: (071)831-7991. Picture Editor: Steve Brown. Estab. 1972. Stock photo agency, picture library. Has 3 million photos. Clients include: advertising agencies, public relations firms, audiovisual firms, businesses, book/encyclopedia publishers, magazine publishers, newspapers, postcard companies, calendar companies and greeting card companies.
Needs: Sport photos: gridiron, basketball, baseball, ice hockey, boxing and athletics.
Specs: Uses 35mm transparencies.
Payment & Terms: Pays 50-60% commission. Enforces minimum prices. Works with or without a signed contract, negotiable; offers guaranteed subject exclusivity. Statements issued quarterly. Payment made quarterly. Does not inform photographer or allow him to negotiate when client requests all rights. Model/property release preferred. Captions preferred.
Making Contact: Interested in receiving work from newer, lesser-known photographers. Submit portfolio for review. Samples kept on file "if pictures are suitable." SASE. Expects minimum initial submission of 50 images. Reports ASAP.

*SPORTS FILE, P.O. Box 449, Route 100, Waitsfield VT 05673. (802)496-9300. Fax: (802)496-9302. Estab. 1985. Stock photo agency. Has approximately 75,000 photos. Works with other agencies in Austria, Sweden, Italy, Germany, France. Clients include: advertising agencies, book/encyclopedia publishers, magazine publishers, newspapers, sports card companies.
Needs: Interested in winter and summer mountain sports.
Specs: Uses 35mm transparencies.
Payment & Terms: Pays 50% commission on color photos. Enforces minimum prices. "Almost never" offers volume discounts to customers; inquire about specific terms. Discount sales terms not negotiable. Works with or without contract. Offers exclusive and non-exclusive contracts. Charges 5% filing fee, 5% duping fee. Statements issued quarterly. Offers all rights. Informs photographer and allows him to negotiate when client requests all rights, "but negotiation with client would occur through sports file." Model/property release preferred. Captions preferred, include where, what, when.
Making Contact: Interested in receiving work from newer, lesser-known photographers. Query with samples. Keeps samples on file. SASE. Reports in 1 month. Catalog card available with SASE. Market tips sheet distributed twice a year to anyone interested in receiving it; free with SASE.
Tips: "We are looking for dynamic sports photography, especially when it has a unique perspective. Anything 'artistic' in sports photography is also sought." Wants to see eye-catching colors, action and perspective.

■SPORTS LENS, INC., 570 H Grand St.-H-1102, New York NY 10002. (212)979-0873. President: Tony Furnari. Stock photo agency. Has 50,000 photos. Clients include: advertising agencies, public relations firms, audiovisual firms, businesses, book/encyclopedia publishers, magazine publishers, newspapers, calendar companies, greeting card and sports related companies.
Needs: All sports: pro golf, strobed basketball and track and field.
Specs: Uses 35mm, 2¼ × 2¼ transparencies.
Payment & Terms: Pays 50% commission on b&w and color photos. Average price per image (to clients): $75-150/b&w photo; $125-500/color photo. Enforces minimum prices. Offers volume discounts to customers; terms specified in photographer's contract. Discount sales terms not negotiable. Works with or without a signed contract, negotiable. Statements issued per usage of slide. Payment

made ASAP, pending client payment. Photographers permitted to review account records to verify sales figures or account for various deductions "upon request." Offers one-time rights. Model/property release required with generic sports photos or leisure sports activities. Captions required.

Making Contact: Interested in receiving work from newer, lesser-known photographers. Query with resume of credits. Expects minimum initial submission of 100 slides. Reports in 1-2 weeks. Market tips sheet free on request, distributed when needed to Sports Lens, Inc. photographers only.

Tips: Looks for "professional quality, sharp images, action, head shots. No dupes ever used. Originals only."

SPORTSLIGHT PHOTO, Suite 800, 127 W. 26 St., New York NY 10001. (212)727-9727. Director: Roderick Beebe. Stock photo agency. Has 250,000 photos. Clients include: ad agencies, public relations firms, businesses, book/encyclopedia publishers, magazine publishers, newspapers, postcard companies, calendar companies, greeting card companies and design firms.

Needs: "We specialize in every sport in the world. We deal primarily in the recreational sports such as skiing, golf, tennis, running, canoeing, etc., but are expanding into pro sports, and have needs for all pro sports, action and candid close-ups of top athletes. We also handle adventure-travel photos, e.g., rafting in Chile, trekking in Nepal, dogsledding in the Arctic, etc."

Specs: Uses 35mm transparencies.

Payment & Terms: Pays 50% commission. General price range: $70-3,000. Contract negotiable. Offers limited regional exclusivity. Contract is of indefinite length until either party (agency or photographer) seeks termination. Statements issued quarterly. Payment made quarterly. Photographers allowed to review account records to verify sales figures "when discrepancy occurs." Offers one-time rights, rights depend on client, sometimes exclusive rights for a period of time. Informs photographer and allows him to negotiate when client requests all rights. Model release required for corporate and advertising usage. (Obtain releases whenever possible.) Strong need for model-released "pro-type" sports. Captions required.

Making Contact: Interested in receiving work from newer, lesser-known photographers. Query with list of stock photo subjects, "send samples *after* our response." SASE must be included. Cannot return unsolicited material. Reports in 2-4 weeks. Photo guideline sheet free with SASE.

Tips: In reviewing work looks for "range of sports subjects that show photographer's grasp of the action, drama, color and intensity of sports, as well as capability of capturing great shots under all conditions in all sports. Well edited, perfect exposure and sharpness, good composition and lighting in all photos. Seeking photographers with strong interests in particular sports. Shoot variety of action, singles and groups, youths, male/female—all combinations. Plus leisure, relaxing after tennis, lunch on the ski slope, golf's 19th hole, etc. Clients are looking for all sports these days. All ages, also. Sports fashions change rapidly, so that is a factor. Art direction of photo shoots is important. Avoid brand names and minor flaws in the look of clothing. Attention to detail is very important. Shoot with concepts/ideas such as teamwork, determination, success, lifestyle, leisure, cooperation and more in mind. Clients look not only for individual sports, but for photos to illustrate a mood or idea. There is a trend toward use of real-life action photos in advertising as opposed to the set-up slick ad look. More unusual shots are being used to express feelings, attitude, etc."

■**TOM STACK & ASSOCIATES**, Suite 212, 3645 Jeannine Dr., Colorado Springs CO 80917. (719)570-1000. Contact: Jamie Stack. Member of the Picture Agency Council of America (PACA). Has 1.5 million photos. Clients include: ad agencies, public relations firms, businesses, audiovisual firms, book publishers, magazine publishers, encyclopedia publishers, postcard companies, calendar companies and greeting card companies.

Needs: Wildlife, endangered species, marine-life, landscapes, foreign geography, people and customs, children, sports, abstract/art and mood shots, plants and flowers, photomicrography, scientific research, current events and political figures, Indians, etc. Especially needs women in "men's" occupations; whales; solar heating; up-to-date transparencies of foreign countries and people; smaller mammals such as weasels, moles, shrews, fisher, marten, etc.; extremely rare endangered wildlife; wildlife behavior photos; current sports; lightning and tornadoes; hurricane damage. Sharp images, dramatic and unusual angles and approach to composition, creative and original photography with impact. Especially needs photos on life science flora and fauna and photomicrography. No run-of-the-mill travel or vacation shots. Special needs include photos of energy-related topics—solar and wind generators, recycling, nuclear power and coal burning plants, waste disposal and landfills, oil and gas drilling, supertankers, electric cars, geo-thermal energy.

Specs: Uses 35mm transparencies.

Payment & Terms: Pays 60% commission. General price range: $150-200/color; as high as $7,000. Offers one-time rights, all rights or first rights. Model release preferred. Captions preferred.

Making Contact: Query with list of stock photo subjects or send at least 800 transparencies for consideration. SASE or mailer for photos. Reports in 2 weeks. Photo guidelines with SASE.

Tips: "Strive to be original, creative and take an unusual approach to the commonplace; do it in a different and fresh way." Have "more action and behavioral requests for wildlife. We are large enough to market worldwide and yet small enough to be personable. Don't get lost in the 'New York' crunch—

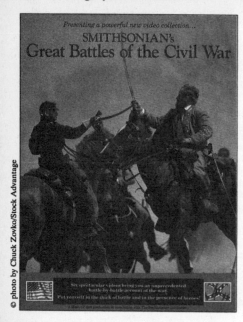

SMITHSONIAN's
Great Battles of the Civil War

© photo by Chuck Zovko/Stock Advantage

A battle re-enactment between soldiers in the U.S. Civil War produced this action-packed image that was used on the cover of a video promotion piece, "Smithsonian's Great Battles of the Civil War." The photo is one of many Civil War battlefield shots in the files at The Stock Advantage.

try us. Shoot quantity. We try harder to keep our photographers happy. We attempt to turn new submissions around within 2 weeks. We take on only the best so we can continue to give more effective service."

■THE STOCK ADVANTAGE, 213 N. 12th St., Allentown PA 18102. (215)776-7381. Fax: (215)776-1831. Director of Marketing: James Gallucci. Estab. 1986. Stock photo agency. Has 100,000 photos; 3,500 feet of film. Clients include: advertising agencies, public relations firms, businesses, book/encyclopedia publishers, magazine publishers, newspapers and TV, video/film producers.
Needs: Regional, lifestyle, new technology and business photos.
Specs: Uses 35mm, 2¼×2¼, 4×5 transparencies; all types of film/video.
Payment & Terms: Pays 50% commission. Average price per image to clients $350-450/color photo. Enforces minimum prices. Offers volume discounts to customers; inquire about specific terms. Discount sales terms not negotiable. Works on contract basis only; offers nonexclusive contracts. Contracts renew automatically after two-year period has elapsed. Charges shipping and handling. Statements issued quarterly. Payment made quarterly. Offers one-time and electronic media rights; negotiable. Model/property release preferred. Captions required.
Making Contact: Arrange personal interview to show portfolio. Query with samples. SASE. Expects minimum initial submission of 500 images with bimonthly submissions of at least 200. Reports in 1-2 weeks. Photo guidelines free with SASE. Free catalog available. Market tips sheet distributed to agency members and nonmembers upon request.
Tips: "Subjects vary based on photographer's interests. Images are accepted on most formats, all must be of good composition, high resolution, film of fine grain and correct exposure."

■STOCK BOSTON INC., Dept. PM, 36 Gloucester St., Boston MA 02115. (617)266-2300. Manager of Editing: Jean Howard. Estab. 1970. Stock photo agency. Member of Picture Agency Council of America (PACA). Clients include: advertising agencies, public relations firms, audiovisual firms, businesses, book/encyclopedia publishers, magazine publishers, newspapers, postcard companies, calendar companies and greeting card companies.
Needs: "We seek pictures of real people in their everyday lives. Technical quality must be excellent, model releases are preferred."
Specs: Uses 8×10 b&w prints; 35mm, 2¼×2¼, 4×5, 8×10 transparencies.
Payment & Terms: Pays 50% on b&w and color photos. General price range: $175 up. Offers one-time rights. Model release preferred. Captions preferred.
Making Contact: Send SASE for information. Reports in 1 week. Photo guidelines available on

acceptance. Tips sheet distributed quarterly to contributors.
Tips: In freelancers' portfolios or samples, wants to see "a representative sample of the type of work they typically shoot: 50-100 b&w prints, 100-200 transparencies. Please request more information." Trends in stock include "a swing away from the bland, over-lit studio set-up and move towards a realistic approach. B&w still does quite well at Stock Boston, particularly in the editorial market."

■**THE STOCK BROKER,** Dept. PM, Suite 110, 450 Lincoln St., Denver CO 80203. (303)698-1734. Contact: Jeff Cook. Estab. 1981. Stock photo agency. Member of Picture Agency Council of America (PACA). Has 200,000 photos. Clients include: advertising agencies, public relations firms, audiovisual firms, businesses, book/encyclopedia publishers, magazine publishers and calendar companies.
Needs: Recreational and adventure sports, travel, nature, business/industry and people.
Specs: Uses 8×10 glossy b&w prints; 35mm, 2¼×2¼, 4×5 or 8×10 transparencies.
Payment & Terms: Pays 50% commission on color and b&w photos. General price range: $200-4,000. Offers one-time rights. Model release required.
Making Contact: Query with samples. SASE. Reports in 1 month. Photo guidelines free with SASE. Market tips sheet distributed to contract photographers.
Tips: "Since we rarely add new photographers we look for outstanding work both asthetically and technically. Photos that are conceptual, simple, graphic, and bright and work well for advertising are selected over those that are simply documentary, busy or subtle. Clients are getting more daring and creative and expect better quality. Each year this has caused our standards to go up and our view of what a stock photo is to expand."

STOCK IMAGERY, INC., 711 Kalamath, Denver CO 80204. (303)592-1091. (800)288-3686. Fax: (303)592-1278. Contact: Les Voorhis. Estab. 1980. Stock photo agency. Member of Picture Agency Council of America (PACA). Has 150,000+ photos. "We also deal with a network of sub-agents in 15 countries around the world." Clients include: advertising agencies, public relations firms, audiovisual firms, businesses, book/encyclopedia publishers, magazine publishers, newspapers, postcard publishers, calendar companies, greeting card companies, TV.
Needs: All subjects.
Specs: Uses 35mm, 2¼×2¼, 4×5, 8×10 transparencies.
Payment & Terms: Pays 50% commission on color photos. Average price per image (to clients): color $300+. "We have set prices, but under special circumstances we contact photographer prior to negotiations." Works on contract basis only. Offers exclusive, guaranteed subject exclusivity or nonexclusive contracts. Contracts run 5 years and renew for 3 additional years. Charges vary for promotions/catalogs; 100% for file dupes. "Duplicates and catalog fees are deducted from photographers' commissions at a rate not to exceed 50% in any one quarter." Statements issued quarterly. Payment made quarterly. Photographers allowed to review account records by appointment only. Offers one-time rights or unlimited, exclusive rights (1 year). Informs photographer and allows him to negotiate when client requests all rights. Model/property release required. Captions required.
Making Contact: Interested in receiving work from newer, lesser-known photographers. Arrange personal interview to show portfolio. Query with samples. Query with stock photo list. Samples kept on file. SASE. Minimum number of images in initial submission varies. "Photographer must have 250 images on file to be put under contract." Photo guidelines free with SASE. Market tips sheet distributed quarterly. Sent with photographer's commission reports or free with SASE.
Tips: In samples looks for "high-caliber, natural style of work. Growing trend in environmental photography (pro and con), and natural, 'average' people instead of slickly posed models. Abstract and computer-graphics-type work is growing also. Present a well edited sample of your work. Selection must be a good representation of the type of work that you can supply on a regular basis."

■**THE STOCK MARKET,** Dept. PM, 360 Park Ave. South, New York NY 10010. (212)684-7878. Contact: Sally Lloyd, Kelly Foster or Gerry Thies. Estab. 1981. Stock photo agency. Member of Picture Agency Council of America (PACA). Has 1,600,000 photos. Clients include: advertising agencies, public relations firms, corporate design firms, book/encyclopedia publishers, magazine publishers, newspapers, postcard companies, calendar companies and greeting card companies.
Needs: Topics include lifestyle, corporate, industry, nature and travel.
Specs: Uses color, all formats.
Payment & Terms: Pays 50% gross sale on color photos. Works on exclusive contract basis only. Charges catalog insertion fee of 50%/image for US edition only. Statements issued bimonthly. Payment made bimonthly. Photographers allowed to review account records to verify sales figures. Offers one-time rights and first rights. When client requests to buy all rights, "we ask permission of photographer, then we negotiate." Model and property release preferred for all people, private homes, boats, cars, property. Captions are required; include "what and where."
Making Contact: Arrange a personal interview to show portfolio. Query with samples. Submit portfolio of 250 transparencies in vinyl sheets. SASE. Reports in 2-3 weeks. Tips sheet distributed as needed to contract photographers only.

■**STOCK MONTAGE**, (formerly Historical Pictures), Dept. PM, Room 201, 921 W. Van Buren, Chicago IL 60607. (312)733-3239. Fax: (312)733-2844. Sales Research: Shirley Neiman. Picture library. Clients include: ad agencies, audiovisual firms, book/encyclopedia publishers and magazine publishers and corporate clients.

Needs: Topics from pre-history through current times worldwide.

Specs: Uses any size, any finish b&w and color prints; also transparencies and b&w negatives.

Payment & Terms: Buys photos outright. Pays 50% commission. Works on contract basis only (nonexclusive). Offers one-time rights. Photo captions required.

Making Contact: Query with list of stock photo subjects. Will return material submitted for review. Reports in 1 month.

Tips: Most sales are to editorial clients such as book and magazine publishers and corporate clients.

■**STOCK OPTIONS**, Dept. PM, 4602 East Side Ave., Dallas TX 75226. (214)826-6262. Fax: (214)826-6263. Owner: Karen Hughes. Estab. 1985. Stock photo agency. Member of Picture Agency Council of America (PACA). Has 50,000 photos. Clients include: advertising agencies, public relations firms, audiovisual firms, corporations, book/encyclopedia, magazine publishers, newspapers, postcard companies, calendar and greeting card companies. "We are a subsidiary for Camerarique Ave. Int'l."

Needs: Emphasizes the southern US. Files include Gulf Coast scenics, wildlife, fishing, festivals, food, industry, business, people, etc. Also western folklore.

Specs: Uses 35mm, 2¼ × 2¼ and 4 × 5 transparencies and 70mm.

Payment & Terms: Pays 50% commission on b&w or color photos. General price range: $300-1,500. Works on contract basis only. Offers nonexclusive contract. Contract automatically renews with each submission to 5 years from expiration date. Charges catalog insertion fee of $300/image and marketing fee of $5/hour. Statements issued upon receipt of payment. Payment made immediately. Photographers allowed to review account records to verify sales figures. Offers one-time and electronic media rights. "We will inform photographers for their consent only when a client requests all rights, but we will handle all negotiations." Model and property release is preferred for people, some properties, all models. Captions are required; include subject and location.

Making Contact: Interested in receiving work from newer, lesser-known photographers. Arrange a personal interview to show portfolio. Query with list of stock photo subjects. Contact by "query and submit 200 sample photos." Works with local freelancers only. SASE. Reports in 1 month. Tips sheet distributed annually to all photographers.

Tips: Wants to see "clean, in focus, relevant and current materials." Current stock requests include: industry, environmental subjects, people in up-beat situations, food, Texas cities and rural scenics.

■‡**STOCK PHOTOS**, Carbonero y Sol, 30, Madrid 28006 Spain. (1)564-4095. Fax: (1)564-4353. Director: Marcelo Brodsky. Estab. 1988. Stock photo agency and news/feature syndicate. Has 150,000 photos. Clients include: advertising agencies, audiovisual firms, businesses, book/encyclopedia publishers, magazine publishers and newspapers.

Needs: Stock photography for advertising with model-released people, top quality magazine stories with short text and people.

Specs: "We specialize in advertising in our ad section and we also handle magazine photography in our editorial section." Uses 35mm b&w prints; 35mm, 2¼ × 2¼, 4 × 5, 8 × 10 transparencies.

Payment & Terms: Pays 50% commission on color photos. General price range: Minimum $90-1,500. Offers one-time rights. Model release required for advertising materials.

Making Contact: Query with samples. Reports in 3 weeks. Tips sheet distributed once a year to working photographers; free with SASE.

Tips: Looks for "transparencies of technical excellence, professionalism in producing stock and knowledge of the needs of this market, whether editorial or advertising. We need high-tech imagery, high-tech stories/reportage for magazines, pictures with models, teenagers, people consuming, people working at their professions, medicine, etc. Portraits of celebrities have another area of the market and we also sell them very well in Spain."

■**STOCK PILE, INC.**, Main office: Dept. PM, 2404 N. Charles St., Baltimore MD 21218. (301)889-4243. Branch: Box 15384, Rio Rancho NM 87174. (505)892-7288. Vice President: D.B. Cooper. Picture library. Has 28,000 photos. Clients include: ad agencies, art studios, slide show producers, etc.

Needs: General agency looking for well-lit, properly composed images that will attract attention. Also, people, places and things that lend themselves to an advertising-oriented marketplace.

Specs: Transparencies, all formats. Some b&w 8 × 10 glossies.

Payment & Terms: Pays 50% commission on b&w and color photos. Works on contract basis only. Contracts renew automatically with additional submissions. Payment made monthly. Offers one-time rights. Informs photographer and permits him to negotiate when client requests all rights. Model release preferred. Captions required.

Making Contact: Interested in receiving work from newer, lesser-known photographers. Inquire for guidelines, submit directly (minimum 100) or call for personal interview. All inquiries and submissions must be accompanied by SASE. *Send all submissions to New Mexico address.* Periodic newsletter sent to all regular contributing photographers.

THE STOCK SHOP, 232 Madison Ave., New York NY 10016. (212)679-8480. Fax: (212)532-1934. President: Barbara Gottlieb. Estab. 1975. Member of Picture Agency Council of America (PACA). Has 2 million photos. Clients include: advertising agencies, public relations firms, businesses, book/encyclopedia publishers, magazine publishers, postcard companies, calendar companies and greeting card companies.
Needs: Needs photos of travel, industry and medicine. Also model-released lifestyle including old age, couples, babies, men, women, families.
Specs: Uses 35mm, 2¼×2¼, 4×5 and 8×10 transparencies.
Payment & Terms: Pays 50% commission on color photos. General price range: $150 and up. Works on exclusive contract basis only. Contracts renew automatically with each submission for length of original contract. Charges catalog insertion fee of 7½%/image. Statements issued monthly. Payment made monthly. Offers one-time rights. Does not inform photographer of client's request for all rights. Model release required. Captions required.
Making Contact: Arrange a personal interview to show portfolio. Submit portfolio for review. SASE. Tips sheet distributed as needed to contract photographers only.
Tips: Wants to see "a cross section of the style and subjects the photographer has in his library. 200-300 samples should tell the story. Photographers should have at least 1,000 in their library. Photographers should not photograph people *before* getting a model release. The day of the 'grab shot' is over."

THE STOCK SOLUTION, 307 W. 200 South, #3004, Salt Lake City UT 84101. (801)363-9700. Fax: (801)363-9707. President: Royce Bair. Stock photo agency. Member of Picture Agency Council of America (PACA). Has 150,000 photos. Clients include: ad agencies, businesses, book/encyclopedia and magazine publishers, calendar companies and design studios.
Needs: Leisure, outdoor recreation, business, finance, industry, health/medical, education, family/children, national parks, major cities, commerce, transportation. Nature and scenics only on a limited basis.
Specs: Uses 35mm, 2¼×2¼, 4×5 and 8×10 transparencies; also 8×10 b&w prints.
Payment & Terms: Pays 50% commission on color photos. General price range: $250-500; "minimum usually $150, maximum is unlimited." Works on contract basis only. Offers nonexclusive contract. Statements issued quarterly. Payment made periodically. "Photos with net sales of $500/month or more are paid monthly." Photographers may review account records to verify sales. Offers one-time rights; occasionally, one-year exclusives for advertising or calendar. Informs photographer and allows him to negotiate when client requests all rights. Model/property release is preferred, "but required for advertising use sales." Photo captions are preferred; include: "who (I.D. person(s) in photo and give model release info), and *where* (state or country and city or what mountain range or what national park, etc.)."
Making Contact: Query with resume of credits, samples, list of stock photo subjects. Submit portfolio for review. SASE. Reports in 2 weeks. Photo guidelines free with SASE. Tips sheet sent quarterly free to contract photographers; $3 for inquiring, noncontract photographers.
Tips: "We can usually determine with a portfolio of only 100 slides if we want to represent a photographer. We actively seek photographers who photograph people in real-life situations of home, family and work, but who are willing to make the extra effort necessary to prop and light the scene in order to make it more salable to today's demanding clients in advertising and publishing." Does not require exclusive contract, but offers worldwide representation if requested. Recommends reading the *ASMP Stock Photography Handbook*.

■**STOCK SOUTH**, Dept. PM, Suite K-2, 75 Bennett St. NW, Atlanta GA 30309. (404)352-0538. Fax: (404)352-0563. President: David Perdew. Estab. 1989. Stock photo agency. Has 150,000 photos; color and b&w. Clients include: advertising agencies, public relations firms, audiovisual firms, businesses, book/encyclopedia publishers, magazine publishers and newspapers. Holds photographs on consignment.

The First Markets Index preceding the General Index in the back of this book provides the names of those companies/publications interested in receiving work from newer, lesser-known photographers.

Needs: Lifestyles, corporate, leisure, travel (southeastern particularly). All should be model- and property-released.
Specs: Uses 8×10 glossy b&w prints; 35mm, 2¼×2¼, and 4×5 transparencies.
Payment & Terms: Pays 50% commission on b&w and color photos. General price range: $250-1,000. Rights negotiable. Model/property release required.
Making Contact: Query with samples. SASE. Reports in 3 weeks. Photo guidelines free with SASE. Market tips sheet distributed monthly to contracted photographers.
Tips: Wants to see photos that are "model-released, clean, dramatic and graphic. In all situations, we're looking for outstanding photographs that are better than anything we've seen. Edit tightly."

■**THE STOCKHOUSE, INC.**, Box 540367, Houston TX 77254-0367. (713)942-8400. Fax: (713)526-4634. Sales and Marketing Director: Celia Jumonville. Stock photo agency. Member of Picture Agency Council of America (PACA). Has 500,000 photos. Clients include: advertising agencies, public relations firms, audiovisual firms, businesses, book/encyclopedia publishers, magazine publishers, newspapers, postcard companies, calendar companies and greeting card companies.
Needs: Needs photos of general topics from travel to industry, lifestyles, nature, US and foreign countries. Especially interested in Texas and petroleum and medical.
Specs: Uses 35mm, 2¼×2¼, 4×5, 8×10 transparencies; "originals only."
Payment & Terms: Pays 50% commission on color photos. General price range: $200-1,000. Works on contract basis only. Offers limited regional exclusivity. Statements issued monthly. Payment made following month after payment by client. Photographers allowed to review account records to verify sales figures by appointment. Offers one-time rights; other rights negotiable. Informs photographer and allows him to negotiate when client requests all rights; must be handled through the agency only. Model/property release preferred for people and personal property for advertising use; photographer retains written release. Photo captions required; include location, date and description of activity or process.
Making Contact: Interested in receiving work from newer, lesser-known photographers. Query with samples; request guidelines and tipsheet. Send submissions to 3301 W. Alabama, Houston TX 77254. SASE. Photo guidelines free with SASE. Tips sheet distributed quarterly to contract photographers.
Tips: In freelancers' samples, wants to see "quality of photos—color saturation, focus and composition. Also variety of subjects and 200-300 transparencies on the first submission. Trends in stock vary depending on the economy and who is needing photos. Quality is the first consideration and subject second. We do not limit the subjects submitted since we never know what will be requested next. Industry and lifestyles and current skylines are always good choices."

■**TONY STONE IMAGES, INC.**, (formerly Tony Stone Worldwide Ltd.), #1250, 6100 Wilshire Blvd., Los Angeles CA 90048. (213)938-1700. (Offices in 15 locations worldwide). Director of Photography: Sarah Stone. Estab. in U.S. 1988, Worldwide 1968. Stock photo agency. Member of Picture Agency Council of America (PACA). Clients include: advertising agencies, public relations firms, audiovisual firms, businesses, book/encyclopedia publishers, magazine publishers, newspapers, calendar, greeting card and travel companies.
• This agency has established a photographer's advisory committee that will give agency photographers a stronger voice in marketing images.
Needs: Very high quality, technically and creatively excellent stock imagery on all general subjects for worldwide and US distribution.
Specs: Uses b&w prints; 35mm, 2¼×2¼, 4×5 and 8×10 transparencies.
Payment & Terms: Pays 50% commission on b&w and color photos. Price ranges vary according to usage. "Minimum price is $100 unless very exceptional circumstances, e.g., very specialized, low-level usage or limited exposure of imagery." Offers volume discounts to customers, "but *maximum* 10% and then rarely"; inquire about specific terms. Works on contract basis only. "We ask for exclusivity on a photographer's best work only." Charges catalog insertion fee. Statements and payment issued monthly. Offers various rights. "When client requests all rights, we ask photographer's permission and negotiate accordingly." Model/property release required. Photo captions required with as much detail as possible.
Making Contact: "Please do not send unsolicited images. Call our Creative Department for free submission guidelines."
Tips: Wants to see "technical ability, creativity. Commitment to high standards." Sees increased demand for high quality. "If you can't shoot better imagery than that already available, don't bother at all."

■**SUPERSTOCK INC.**, Dept. PM, 11 W. 19th St., New York NY 10011. (212)633-0708. Director of Photographer Relations: Jane Stoffo. Stock photo agency. Has more than 300,000 photos in file. Clients include: ad agencies, public relations firms, audiovisual firms, businesses, book/encyclopedia publishers, magazine publishers, newspapers, postcard companies, calendar companies, greeting card companies and major corporations.

Needs: "We are a general stock agency involved in all markets, our files are comprised of all subject matter."

Specs: Uses 35mm, 2¼×2¼, 4×5 and 8×10 transparencies.

Payment & Terms: "We work on a contract basis." Contracts renew automatically with each submission for five years. Statements issued monthly. Payment made monthly. Photographers allowed to review account records to verify sales figures. Rights offered "varies, depending on client's request." Informs photographer and allows him to negotiate when client requests all rights. Model release required. Captions required.

Making Contact: Query with resume of credits. Query with tearsheets only. Query with list of stock photo subjects. Submit portfolio for review "when requested." SASE. Reports in 3 weeks. Photo guidelines sheet free with SASE or sent if requested via phone. Newsletter distributed monthly to contracted photographers.

Tips: "The use of catalogs as a buying source is a very effective means of promoting photographs, and a continuing trend in the industry is the importance of bigger, comprehensive catalogs. We produce the SuperStock Photo Catalog in the US. Space is available to professional photographers regardless of any of their other photographic affiliations. Participation in this catalog provides an excellent opportunity for photographers to take advantage of the growing international market for stock, and receive the highest royalty percentage for internationally distributed photographs."

■❋**TAKE STOCK INC.,** 516 15th Ave. SW, Calgary, Alberta T2R 0R2 Canada. (403)229-3458. Fax: (403)541-9104. Vice President: Helen Grenon. Estab. 1987. Stock photo agency. Clients include: advertising agencies, public relations firms, audiovisual firms, corporate, book/encyclopedia publishers, magazine publishers, newspapers, postcard companies, calendar companies and greeting card companies.

Needs: Model-released people (all ages), Canadian images, arts/recreation, industry/occupation, business, high-tech.

Specs: Uses 35mm, 2¼×2¼, 4×5, 8×10 transparencies. Prefers medium to large format.

Payment & Terms: Pays 50% commission on transparencies. General price range: $80-600. Works on contract basis only. Offers limited regional exclusivity. Contracts renew automatically with additional submissions with "1-year review then every 3 years." Charges 100% duping fees. Statements issued monthly. Payment made monthly. Photographers allowed to review account records to verify sales figures, "anytime by appointment." Offers one-time rights, exclusive rights. Informs photographer and allows him to negotiate when client requests all rights. Model/property release required. Captions required.

Making Contact: Query with list of stock photo subjects. SASE. Reports in 3 weeks. Photo guidelines free with SASE. Tips sheet distributed monthly to photographers on file.

■‡**TANK INCORPORATED,** Box 212, Shinjuku, Tokyo 160-91, Japan. T81-3-3239-1431. Telex: 26347 PHTPRESS. Fax: T81-3-3230-3668. President: Masayoshi Seki. Has 500,000 slides. Clients include: advertising agencies, encyclopedia/book publishers, magazine publishers and newspapers.

Needs: "Women in various situations, families, special effect and abstract, nudes, scenic, sports, animal, celebrities, flowers, picture stories with texts, humorous photos, etc."

Specs: Uses 8×10 b&w prints; 35mm, 2¼×2¼ and 4×5 slides; b&w contact sheets; videotape.

Payment & Terms: Pays 40% commission on b&w and color photos. "As for video, we negotiate at case by case basis." General price range: $70-1,000. Works on contract basis only. Offers limited regional exclusivity within files. Contracts renew automatically with each submission for 3 years. Statements issued monthly. Payment made monthly; within 45 days. Photographers allowed to review account records to verify sales figures. Offers one-time rights. Informs photographer and allows him to negotiate when client requests all rights. Model and property release is required for glamour/nude sets. Photo captions required.

Making Contact: Interested in receiving work from newer, lesser-known photographers. Query with samples, with list of stock photo subjects or send unsolicited material by mail for consideration. SASE. Reports in 1 month. Photo guidelines free with International Reply Coupons.

Tips: "We need some pictures or subjects which strike viewers. Pop or rock musicians are very much in demand. If you want to make quick sales, give us some story ideas with sample pictures which show quality, and we will respond to you very quickly. Also, give us brief bio. Color transparencies with sample stories to accompany—no color prints at all. Stock photography business requires patience. Try to find some other subjects than your competitors. Keep a fresh mind to see salable subjects." Remarks that "photographers should have eyes of photo editor. Try to take photos which make editors use them easily. Also, give a little background of these photos."

TERRAPHOTOGRAPHICS/BPS, Box 490, Moss Beach CA 94038. (415)726-6244. Photo Agent: Carl May. Stock photo agency. Has 25,000 photos on hand; 70,000 on short notice. Clients include: ad agencies, businesses, book/encyclopedia publishers and magazine publishers.

Needs: All subjects in the earth sciences: paleontology, volcanology, seismology, petrology, oceanography, climatology, mining, petroleum industry, civil engineering, meteorology, astronomy. Stock photographers must be scientists. "Currently, we need more on energy resource conservation, natural and cut gems, economic minerals, recent natural disasters and severe weather." Environmental issues are hot topics. Much more needed from the Third World, formerly Communist countries and the Middle East.

Specs: Uses 8×10 glossy b&w prints; 35mm, 2¼×2¼, 4×5 and 8×10 transparencies.

Payment & Terms: Pays 50% commission on all photos. General price range: $90-500. Works with or without a signed contract, negotiable. Offers exclusive contract only. Contracts have automatic renewal clauses; time period not specified. Statements issued quarterly. Payment quarterly within one month of end of quarter. Photographers allowed to review account records to verify sales figures. Offers one-time rights; other rights negotiable. However, "this rarely happens at our agency." Informs photographer and allows him to negotiate when client requests all rights. Model release required for any commercial use, but not purely editorial. Photo captions required; include "all information necessary to identify subject matter and give geographical location."

Making Contact: Query with list and resume of scientific and photographic background. SASE. Reports in 2 weeks. Photo guidelines free with query, resume and SASE. Tips sheet distributed intermittently only to stock photographers.

Tips: Prefers to see proper exposure, maximum depth of field, interesting composition, good technical and general information in caption. Natural disasters of all sorts, especially volcanic eruptions, storms and earthquakes; scientists at work using modern equipment. "We are a suitable agency only for those with both photographic skills and sufficient technical expertise to identify subject matter. We only respond to those who provide a rundown of their scientific and photographic background and at least a brief description of coverage. Captions must be neat and contain precise information on geographical locations. Don't waste your time submitting images on grainy film. Our photographers should be able to distinguish between dramatic, compelling examples of phenomena and run-of-the-mill images in the earth and environmental sciences. We need more on all sorts of weather phenomena; the petroleum and mining industries from exploration through refinement; problems and management of toxic wastes; environmental problems associated with resource development; natural areas threatened by development; and oceanography."

■**THIRD COAST STOCK SOURCE**, P.O. Box 92397, Milwaukee WI 53202. (414)765-9442. Director: Paul Henning. Managing Editor: Mary Ann Platts. Sales and Research Manager: Paul Butterbrodt. Support Services Manager: J.P. Slater. Member of Picture Agency Council of America (PACA). Has over 125,000 photos. Clients include: ad agencies, public relations firms, audiovisual firms, corporations, book/encyclopedia publishers, magazine publishers, newspapers, calendar companies and greeting card companies.

Needs: People in lifestyle situations, business, industry, sports and recreation, medium format scenics (domestic and foreign), traditional stock photo themes with a new spin.

Specs: Uses 35mm, 2¼×2¼, 4×5 and 8×10 transparencies (slow and medium speed color tranparency film preferred).

Payment & Terms: Pays 50% commission on b&w and color photos. General price range: $200 and up. Enforces minimum prices. Works on contract basis only. Offers various levels of exclusivity. Contracts with photographers renew automatically for 3 or 5 years. Charges duping and catalog insertion fee. Statements issued bimonthly. Payment made bimonthly. Photographers allowed to review account records to verify sales figures. Offers one-time rights. Informs photographer when client requests all rights. Model release required. Captions required.

Making Contact: Interested in receiving work from any photographer with professional-quality material. Submit 200-300 images for review. SASE. Reports in 1 month. Photo guidelines free with SASE. Tips sheet distributed 4 times/year to "photographers currently working with us."

Tips: "We are looking for technical expertise; outstanding, dramatic and emotional appeal. We are anxious to look at new work. Learn what stock photography is all about. Our biggest need is for photos of model-released people: couples, seniors, business situations, recreational situations, etc. Also, we find it very difficult to get great winter activity scenes (again, with people) and photos which illustrate holidays: Christmas, Thanksgiving, Easter, etc."

■‡**TROPIX PHOTOGRAPHIC LIBRARY**, 156 Meols Parade, Meols, Merseyside L47 6AN England. Tel: 51-632-1698. Fax: 51-632-1698. Director: Veronica Birley. Picture library specialist. Has 25,000 transparencies. Clients include: book/encyclopedia publishers, magazine publishers, newspapers, ad agencies, public relations firms, audiovisual firms, businesses, television/film companies and travel agents.

Needs: "All aspects of the developing world and the natural environment. Detailed and accurate captioning is essential. Tropix documents the Third World from its power stations to its peanut growers, from its rain forests to its refugees. Education, medicine, agriculture, industry, technology and other Third World topics. Plus the full range of environmental topics worldwide."

Specs: Uses 35mm, 2¼ × 2¼, 4 × 5 transparencies and, rarely, 8 × 10 glossy (with borders) b&w prints.
Payment & Terms: Pays 50% commission. General price range: £50-175 (English currency). Works on contract basis only. Guarantees subject exclusivity within files. Charges cost of returning photographs by insured/registered post, if required. Statements issued quarterly. Payment made quarterly. Photographers allowed to have qualified auditor review account records to verify sales figures in the event of a dispute but not as routine procedure. Offers one-time rights. Other rights only by special written agreement. Informs photographer when a client requests all rights but agency handles negotiation. Model release preferred. Photo captions required; include accurate, detailed data, preferably on disk. Guidelines are available from agency.
Making Contact: Interested in receiving work from both established and newer, lesser-known photographers. Query with list of stock photo subjects; *no* unsolicited photographs, please. Reports in 1 month, sooner if material is topical. Photo guidelines free with SASE. "On receipt of our leaflets, a very detailed reply should be made by letter. Photographs are requested after receipt of this letter, if the photographer appears suitable. When submitting photographs, always screen out those which are technically imperfect."
Tips: Looks for "special interest topics, accurate and informative captioning, sharp focus always, correct exposure, strong images and an understanding of and involvement with specific subject matters. Travel scenes, views and impressions, however artistic, are not required except as part of an informed, detailed collection. Not less than 200 saleable transparencies per country photographed should be available." Sees a trend toward electronic image grabbing and development of a pictorial data base.

UNICORN STOCK PHOTO LIBRARY, 7809 NW 86th Terrace, Kansas City MO 64153-1769. (816)587-4131. Fax: (816)741-0632. President/Owner: Betts Anderson. Has 170,000 color slides. Clients include: ad agencies, corporate accounts, textbooks, magazines, calendars and religious publishers.
Needs: Ordinary people of all ages and races doing everyday things: at home, school, work and play. Current skylines of all major cities; tourist attractions, historical; wildlife; seasonal/holiday; and religious subjects. "We particularly need images showing 2 or more races represented in one photo and family scenes with BOTH parents. There is a critical need for more minority shots including hispanics, orientals and blacks. We also need ecology illustrations such as recycling, pollution and people cleaning up the earth."
Specs: Uses 35mm color slides.
Payment & Terms: Pays 50% commission. General price range: $50-400. Works on contract basis only. Offers nonexclusive contract. Contracts renew automatically with additional submissions for 3 years. Charges duping fee; rate not specified. Statement issued monthly. Payment made monthly. Offers one-time rights. Informs photographer and allows him to negotiate when client requests all rights. Model release preferred; increases sales potential considerably. Photo captions required; include: location, ages of people, dates on skylines.
Making Contact & Terms: Write first for guidelines. "We are looking for professionals who understand this business and will provide a steady supply of top-quality images. At least 300 images are required to open a file. Contact us by letter including $10 for our 'Information for Photographers' package."
Tips: "We keep in close, personal contact with all our photographers. Our monthly newsletter is a very popular medium for doing this. Our biggest need is for minorities and interracial shots. If you can supply us with this subject, we can supply you with checks. Because UNICORN is in the Midwest, we have many requests for farming/gardening/agriculture/winter and general scenics of the Midwest."

*■U.S. NAVAL INSTITUTE, 118 Maryland Ave., Annapolis MD 21402. (410)268-6110. Fax: (410)269-7940. Photo Archivist: Mary Beth Straight. Picture library. Has 450,000 photos. Clients include: advertising agencies, public relations firms, audiovisual firms, businesses, book/encyclopedia publishers, magazine publishers, newspapers, calendar companies, greeting card companies. "Anyone who may need military photography. We are a publishing press, as well."
Needs: US and foreign ships, aircraft, equipment, weapons, personalities, combat, operations, etc. Anything dealing with military.
Specs: Uses 5 × 7, 8 × 10 color and/or b&w prints; 35mm transparencies.
Payment & Terms: Buys photos outright. Works with or without contract. Offers contracts on a case-by-case basis. Offers rights on a case-by-case basis. Informs photographer and allows him to negotiate when client requests all rights, "if requested in advance by photographer." Captions required; include date taken, place, description of subject.
Making Contact: Interested in receiving work from newer, lesser-known photographers. Query with samples. Samples kept on file. SASE and Social Security number. Expects minimum initial submission of 5 images. Reports in 1 month. Photo guidelines free with SASE.
Tips: "We do not look for posed photography. Want dramatic images or those that tell story. The U.S. Naval Institute is a nonprofit agency and purchases images outright on a very limited basis. However, we do pay for their use within our own books and magazines. Prices are somewhat negotiable, but lower than what the profit-making agencies pay."

‡UNIVERSAL-STOCK AGENCY, Friedrich Lau Str. 26, 4000 Düsseldorf 30 Germany. (211)431-1557. Fax: (211)454 1631. Director: Ralf Dietrich. Estab. 1953. Stock photo agency. Has 1 million photos. Clients include: advertising agencies, public relations firms, businesses, book/encyclopedia publishers, magazine publishers, newspapers, postcard publishers, calendar companies, greeting card companies, TV industry.

Needs: "We handle all topics apart from well known personalities and politics. Our needs are: people, business, industry and geography worldwide."

Specs: Uses 35mm, 2¼×2¼, 4×5, 8×10 transparencies.

Payment & Terms: Pays 50% commission color photos. Average price per image (to clients): $100-150. Offers volume slide discounts to customers; terms specified in photographer's contract. Discount sales terms not negotiable. Works on contract basis only; offers guaranteed subject exclusivity. Statements issued quarterly. Payment made quarterly. Photographers allowed to review account records. Offers one-time rights. Informs photographer and allows him to negotiate when client requests all rights. Model/property release required. Captions required.

Making Contact: Interested in receiving work from newer, lesser-known photographers. Submit portfolio for review. Samples kept on file. SASE. Expects minimum initial submission of not less than 100 images with about 600 to 1,000 slides annually. "Send original slides for review." Reports in 4 months. Photo guidelines free with SASE. Market tips sheet distributed upon request.

Tips: "Look at the way advertisements are made in magazines. Sales are more likely in mid-size formats. Read books with motives of cities, landscapes, etc. Look for postcards to get an idea of how to take photos and what to take photos of."

*VIESTI ASSOCIATES, INC., P.O. Box 20424, New York NY 10028. (212)787-6500. Fax: (212)595-6303. President: Joe Viesti. Estab. 1986. Stock photo agency. Has "several hundred reels." Has 6 branch offices. Clients include: advertising agencies, businesses, book/encyclopedia publishers, magazine publishers, newspapers, postcard publishers, calendar companies, greeting card companies, design firms.

Needs: "We are a full service agency."

Specs: Uses 35mm, 2¼×2¼, 4×5, 8×10 transparencies; 35mm film; all formats videotape.

Payment & Terms: Pays 60% commission on b&w and color photos; 60% commission on films. Average price per image: $500/b&w; $500/color; $1,500/min. of film; $1,500/min. of videotape. "We negotiate fees above our competitors on a regular basis." Works on contract basis only. Offers non-exclusive contract; "catalog photos are exclusive." Contract renews automatically with additional submissions. Charges duping fees "at cost." Catalog insertion rate varies. Statements issued monthly. "Payment is made the month after payment is received." Photographers and accountants allowed to review account records. Rights vary. Informs photographer and allows him to negotiate when client requests all rights. Model/property release preferred. Captions required.

Making Contact: Interested in receiving work from newer, lesser-known photographers as well as from established photographers. Arrange personal interview to show portfolio. Query with samples. Send no originals, dupes or tearsheets only; include return postage if return desired. Samples kept on file. Expects minimum submissions of 500 edited images. 100 edited images per month is average. Reports in 1-2 weeks. Catalog available. "Price varies according to which catalog. Market tips sheet distributed upon request from our photographers."

Tips: There is an "increasing need for images and video from interactive, multimedia clients. No need to sell work for lower prices to compete with low ball competitors. Our clients regularly pay higher prices if they value the work."

■VISUALS UNLIMITED, Dept. PM, P.O. Box 146, Hale Hill Rd., East Swanzey NH 03446-0146. (603)352-6436. President: Dr. John D. Cunningham. Stock photo agency and photo research service. Has 500,000+ photos. Clients include: ad agencies, public relations firms, audiovisual firms, businesses, book/encyclopedia publishers, magazine publishers, postcard companies, calendar companies and greeting card companies.

Needs: All fields: (biology, environmental, medical, natural history, geography, history, scenics, chemistry, geology, physics, industrial, astronomy and "general."

Specs: Uses 5×7 or larger b&w prints; 35mm, 2¼×2¼, 4×5 and 8×10 transparencies; b&w contact sheets; and b&w negatives.

Payment & Terms: Pays 50% commission for b&w and color photos. Negotiates fees based on use, type of publication, user (e.g., nonprofit group vs. publisher). Average price per image (to clients): $30-90/b&w photo; $50-190/color photo. Offers volume discounts to customers; terms specified in contract. Photographers can choose not to sell images on discount terms. Works on contract basis only. Offers non-exclusive contract. Contracts renew automatically for an indefinite time unless return of photos is requested. Statements issued per project. Payment made 1-2 days after completion of project. Photographers not allowed to review account records to verify sales figures; "All payments are exactly 50% of fees generated." Offers one-time rights. Informs photographer and allows him to negotiate when client requests all rights. Model release preferred. Captions required.

Making Contact: Interested in receiving work from newer, lesser-known photographers. Query with samples or send unsolicited photos for consideration. Submit portfolio for review. SASE. Reports in 1 week. Photo guidelines sheet is free with SASE. Distributes a tip sheet several times/year as deadlines allow, to all people with files.

Tips: Looks for "focus, composition and contrast, of course. Instructional potential (e.g., behavior, anatomical detail, habitat, example of problem, living conditions, human interest). Increasing need for exact identification, behavior, and methodology in scientific photos; some return to b&w as color costs rise. Edit carefully for focus and distracting details; submit anything and everything from everywhere that is geographical, biological, geological, environmental, and people oriented."

WEST STOCK, INC., Suite 400, 2013 4th Ave., Seattle WA 98121. (206)728-7726. Fax: (206)728-7638. Chairman: Mark Karras. President: Rick Groman. Project Director: Stephanie Webb. Files contain over 500,000 transparencies. Clients include: ad agencies, design firms, major corporations, magazines, book publishers, calendar and greeting card companies.
- This agency has been a proponent of clip art disks and it offers photographers contracts which allow their work to be marketed via CD-ROM disks. The contracts are separate from the normal operating contract.

Needs: "Our files are targeted to meet the needs of advertising, corporate communications and publishing. We need strong imagery of virtually all subjects, especially people involved in business, leisure activities, sports and recreation. Model-released people and property essential."

Specs: Only original transparencies accepted, 35mm and larger.

Payment & Terms: Pays 50% commission. General price range: $200-15,000. Except for slide shows and multi-media presentations, we generally do not go below $200/range. Works on contract basis only. Offers nonexclusive contracts. Standard contract is 3 years with automatic renewal for additional 3 years. Charges catalog insertion fee of $145/image. Statements issued monthly. Payment made monthly. "Our contracts have an audit provision." Photographers allowed to review account records. Offers one-time, electronic media, agency promotion and other rights. Informs photographer and allows him to negotiate when client requests all rights. Model/property releases required. Captions required.

Making Contact: Very interested in receiving work from newer, lesser-known photographers. Send letter outlining qualifications along with tearsheets to receive guidelines. "Please, no telephone calls or portfolios sent without our request."

Tips: "We expect photographers to have a thorough understanding of stock photography prior to contacting us. There are many differences between agencies. Inform yourself as to business practices, types and amounts of photography needed and anticipated trends. We do not represent amateur photographers. The stock photography market is competitive and sophisticated. In order to stay ahead of the crowd we demand nothing but the finest in professional photography. We see a trend toward more and more photography. Electronics in the photo business is here to stay."

■WESTLIGHT, 2223 S. Carmelina Ave., Los Angeles CA 90064. (310)820-7077. Owner: Craig Aurness. Estab. 1978. Stock photo agency. Member of Picture Agency Council of America (PACA). Has 2 million photos. Clients include: advertising agencies, public relations firms, audiovisual firms, corporations, book/encyclopedia publishers, magazine publishers, newspapers, postcard companies, calendar companies, greeting card companies and TV.
- Westlight is working with Kodak's Photo CD technology to produce Photo CD cartridges.

Needs: Needs photos of all top quality subjects.

Specs: Uses 35mm, 2¼×2¼, 4×5 transparencies.

Payment & Terms: Pays 50% commission; international sales, 40% of gross. General price range: $600+. Offers exclusive contract. Contracts renew automatically for 1 year at the end or 5 years if no notice is given. Charges duping fees of 100%/image. Also charges catalog insertion fee 50%/image. Statements issued quarterly. Payment made quarterly; within 45 days of end of quarter. Photographers allowed to review account records to verify sales figures. Offers one-time rights, electronic media and agency promotion rights. Informs photographer and allows him to negotiate when client requests all rights. Model/property release required for recognizable people and private places. Captions required.

Making Contact: Query with resume of credits. Query with tearsheet samples. Query with list of stock photo subjects; show a specialty. Cannot return material. Reports in 1 month. Photo guidelines free with SASE. Tips sheet distributed monthly to contract photographers. Send tearsheets only, no unsolicited photos.

Tips: Photographer must have "ability to regularly produce the best possible photographs on a specialized subject, willingness to learn, listen and fill agency file needs. Photographers must request application in writing only. All other approaches will not be answered."

■‡DEREK G. WIDDICOMBE, Worldwide Photographic Library, Oldfield, High Street, Clayton West, Huddersfield, Great Britain HD8 9NS. (011)44 484 862638. Fax: (011)44 484 862638. Proprietor: Derek G. Widdicombe. Picture library. Has over 100,000 photos. Clients include: ad agencies, public relations firms, audiovisual firms, businesses, book/encyclopedia publishers, magazine publishers, newspapers, postcard companies, calendar companies, greeting card companies, television, packaging, exhibition and display material, posters, etc.

Needs: "The library covers many thousands of different subjects from landscape, architecture, social situations, industrial, people, moods and seasons, religious services, animals, natural history, travel subjects and many others. We have some archival material. These subjects are from worldwide sources."

Specs: Uses 20.3 × 24.4 cm. glossy b&w prints. Also, all formats of transparencies; 35mm preferred.

Payment & Terms: Pays 50% commission for b&w and color photos. General price range: reproduction fees in the range of £25-200 (English currency); pays $52-333 or higher/b&w photo; $73-500 or higher/color photo. Works with or without contract; negotiable. Offers limited regional exclusivity and nonexclusive contract. Statements issued quarterly. Payment made quarterly. Photographers not allowed to review account records to verify sales figures. Offers one-time and electronic media rights. Requests agency promotion rights. Does not inform photographer or allow him to negotiate when client requests all rights. Model/property release required for portraits of people and house interiors. Photo captions required.

Making Contact: "Send letter first with details on what you have to offer." Send small selection at own risk with return postage/packing. SASE.

Tips: Looks for "technical suitability (correct exposure, sharpness, good tonal range, freedom from defects, color rendering [saturation] etc.). Subject matter well portrayed without any superfluous objects in picture. Commercial suitability (people in pictures in suitable dress, up-to-date cars—or none, clear-top portions for magazine/book cover titles). Our subject range is so wide that we are offering the whole spectrum from very traditional (almost archival) pictures to abstract, moody, out-of-focus shots. Send material in small batches—normally a hundred images at a time, and let us know what you have to send."

THE WILDLIFE COLLECTION, a division of Cranberry Press Inc., 69 Cranberry St., Brooklyn NY 11201. (718)935-9600. Fax: (718)935-9031. Director: Sharon A. Cohen. Estab. 1987. Stock photo agency. Has 150,000 photos. Clients include: advertising agencies, public relations firms, businesses, book/encyclopedia publishers, magazine publishers, newspapers, postcard companies, calendar companies, greeting card companies, zoos and aquariums.

Needs: "We handle anything to do with nature—animals, scenics, vegetation, underwater. We are in particular need of coverage from the Galapagos, Everglades, India, South America, Europe and Antarctica, as well as endangered animals, in particular chimpanzees and bonobos."

Specs: Uses 35mm, 2¼ × 2¼, 4 × 5 transparencies.

Payment & Terms: Pays 50% commission on color photos. General price range: $100-6,000. Works on contract basis only. Offers limited regional exclusivity. Contracts renew automatically "until either party wishes to terminate." Statements issued monthly. Payment made monthly. Photographers permitted to review sales figures. Offers one-time rights. Informs photographers and allows them to negotiate when client requests all rights, "but they can only negotiate through us—not directly." Model release "not necessary with nature subjects." Photo captions required; include common, scientific name and region found.

Making Contact: Interested in receiving work from newer, lesser-known photographers, as well as more established photographers. Query with samples. Printed samples kept on file. SASE. Expects minimum initial submission of 200 images. "We would like 2,000 images/year; this will vary." Reports in 2 weeks. Photo guidelines and free catalog with 6½ × 9½ SAE with 75¢ postage. Market tips sheet distributed quarterly to signed photographers only.

Tips: In samples wants to see "great lighting, extreme sharpness, *non-stressed* animals, large range of subjects, excellent captioning, general presentation. Care of work makes a large impression. The effect of humans on the environment is being requested more often as are unusual and endangered animals."

■‡**WORLD VIEW-HOLLAND BV,** (formerly World View-Fotoheek BV), A.J. Ernststraat 181, Amsterdam, Holland 1083 GV. 31-20-6420224. Fax: 31-20-6611355. Managing Director: Bert Blokhuis. Estab. 1985. Stock photo agency. Has over 150,000 transparencies. Clients include: advertising agencies, audiovisual firms, businesses, calendar companies and corporations.
Needs: Wants to see "sizes bigger then 35mm, only model-released commercial subjects."
Specs: Uses 2¼×2¼, 4×5, 8×10 transparencies only.
Payment & Terms: Pays 40-60% commission on transparencies. General price range: US $300/color photos, minimum $100. Offers volume discounts to customers; inquire about specific terms. Discount sales terms not negotiable. Works on contract basis only. Offers limited regional exclusivity. Contracts renew automatically for 4 years. Statements issued monthly. Payment made quarterly. Photographers permitted to review sales figures. Offers one-time rights. Informs photographer and allows him to negotiate when client requests all rights. Model release required. Captions required.
Making Contact: Interested in receiving work from newer, lesser-known photographers. Query with samples. SASE. Reports in 3 weeks.
Tips: In freelancer's samples, wants to see "small amount of pictures (20 or 30) plus a list of subjects available and list of agents." Work must show quality.

WORLDWIDE IMAGES, (formerly Worldwide Photo Images), Suite 112, 805 E St., San Rafael CA 94901. (415)485-4212. Owner: Norman Buller. Estab. 1988. Stock photo agency. Has 4,000 photos. Clients include: advertising agencies, businesses, book/encyclopedia publishers, magazine publishers, postcard companies, calendar companies, greeting card companies and men's magazines, foreign and domestic.
Needs: Nudes, animals, people, celebrities, rock stars, amateur and X-rated videos and all pro sports.
Specs: Uses b&w and color prints; also 35mm, 2¼×2¼ transparencies.
Payment & Terms: Pays 50% commission on all sales. Works with or without a signed contract, negotiable. Offers nonexclusive contract. Payment made immediately upon payment from client. Photographers allowed to review account records to verify sales figures. Offers one-time or first rights and all rights. Informs photographer and allows him to negotiate when client requests all rights but handles all negotiation. Model release required.
Making Contact: Interested in receiving work from newer, lesser-known photographers. Query with samples and list of stock photo subjects. Send unsolicited photos by mail for consideration. Reports immediately.
Tips: "Work must be good. Buyers are incredibly picky! Getting harder to please every day. We have worldwide clientele, don't edit too tightly, let me see 90% of your material on hand and critique it from there!"

‡**WORLDWIDE PRESS AGENCY,** Box 579, 1000 Buenos Aires, Argentina. (54)962-3182 and (54)952-9927. Director: Victor Polanco. Stock photo agency and picture library. Clients include: ad agencies, book/encyclopedia publishers, magazine publishers, newspapers, postcard companies, calendar companies and greeting card companies.
Needs: Handles picture stories, fashion, human interest, pets, wildlife, film and TV stars, pop and rock singers, classic musicians and conductors, sports, interior design, architectural and opera singers.
Specs: Uses 8×12 glossy b&w prints; 35mm and 2¼×2¼ transparencies.
Payment & Terms: Pays 40% commission for b&w and color photos. General price range: "The Argentine market is very peculiar. We try to obtain the best price for each pic. Sometimes we consult the photographer's needs." Offers one-time rights. Model release preferred. Captions preferred.
Making Contact: Query with list of stock photo subjects. Does not return unsolicited material. Reports "as soon as possible."

■**ZEPHYR PICTURES,** Suites D & U, 2120 Jimmy Durante Blvd., Del Mar CA 92014. (619)755-1200. Fax: (619)755-3723. Owner: Leo Gradinger. Estab. 1982. Stock photo agency. Member of Picture Agency Council of America (PACA). Also commercial photo studio. Has 200,000+ photos. Clients include: advertising agencies, public relations firms, audiovisual firms, businesses, book/encyclopedia publishers, magazine publishers, newspapers, postcard and calendar companies, developers, corporate, finance, education, design studios and TV stations.
Needs: "We handle everything from A to Z. We specialize in people (model-released) for advertising. New material is shot on a weekly basis. We also have lots of great material for the textbook and editorial markets."
Specs: Uses 35mm, 2¼×2¼, 4×5, 8×10, 6×7 transparencies.
Payment & Terms: Pays 50% commission for b&w and color photos. Average price per image: $250-650. Enforces minimum prices. Sub agency agreement 50-50 domestic, 40% to photographer on foreign sales. Offers volume discounts to customers; inquire about specific terms. Discount sales terms not negotiable. Works on contract basis only. Offers limited regional exclusivity. Contracts renew automatically for three years, auto-renewal each year thereafter. Charges 25% catalog insertion fee. Statements issued monthly. Payment made monthly. Photographers allowed to review account records to

verify sales figures. Offers one-time rights; other rights negotiable. Model/property release and photo captions required.

Making Contact: Interested in receiving work from newer, lesser-known photographers. Arrange a personal interview to show portfolio. Query with list of stock photo subjects. SASE. Reports in 2-3 weeks, according to time demands. Photo guidelines available occasionally. Tips sheet distributed twice a year to any photographers who are contracted for submissions.

Tips: "I am looking for a photographer who *specializes* in one maybe two areas of expertise. Be professional. Call or write to let us know who you are and what you specialize in. If we are interested, we ask you to send 20 to 40 of your very best images with a SAE and return postage. We are shooting at the highest level of sophistication for stock since our beginning 10 years ago. The market demands it and we will continue to try and provide a high level of creativity in our images."

Stock Agencies/'93-'94 changes

The following markets appeared in the 1993 edition of *Photographer's Market* but are not listed in the 1994 edition. They may have been omitted for failing to respond to our request for updated information, they may have gone out of business or they may no longer wish to receive freelance work.

Ace Photo Agency (did not respond)

Amwest Picture Agency (out of business)

Arquivo Internacional De Cor (did not respond)

Frank Driggs Collection (did not respond)

Focus Tony Stone Worldwide (asked to be deleted)

Focus-Stock Fotografico (did not respond)

F/Stop Pictures (not reviewing freelance work)

Havelin Communications (not reviewing freelance work)

Image Bank/West (did not respond)

Journalism Services (did not respond)

Keystone Pressedienst GMBH (did not respond)

Lifestyles Stock Photo Agency (unable to locate)

Mauritius Die Bildagentur GMBH (did not respond)

National Baseball Library (no longer using freelance photos)

Natural Selection Stock Photography (asked to be deleted)

Out of This World Photography (out of business)

Photo Images (did not respond)

Photographic Game (asked to be deleted)

Photo/Nats (overstocked)

Pictor International (did not respond)

H. Armstrong Roberts (did not respond)

Roca-Sastre, Agencia Aci (did not respond)

Silver Visions (did not respond)

Travel Image (not reviewing freelance work)

Weatherstock (not reviewing freelance work)

Resources

Contests

You have been camped out for days in early spring, hidden by your blind and waiting for caribou or some other wildlife to plop down in your sights for that perfect shot. You have scouted out the surroundings and the early morning sun makes this watering hole glisten—if only the animals would cooperate. Finally, it happens. Three bear cubs come bounding out of the woods and begin playing in the water. Snap. You're certain the shot is an award winner. Maybe you're right.

Filling this section is a group of 66 contest listings that are excellent for aspiring photographers who want to measure their talent and progress. There are numerous wildlife contests, for those of you who might follow the above scenario as nature photographers. There also are competitions for film and video, still lifes, fine art and others. Whatever your specialty, this section has a contest for you.

Several symbols appear before listings in this section for a variety of reasons. Over a dozen contests appear with an asterisk (*) before them to indicate they are new in this year's edition. We are pleased to announce that *Photographer's Market*, holding its first annual cover photo contest, is one of those first-time listings.

You might also find a solid, black square (■) before a listing, indicating that a contest accepts audiovisual material. International contests appear with a double-dagger (‡).

The listings contain only the basic information needed to make contact with the sponsoring organization and a brief description of the styles or media open for consideration. This year we have tried to acquire new cost/entry fee information and these amounts are included whenever possible.

Before entering a contest here are a couple suggestions you might want to consider: First, check with contest officials to see what types of images won in previous years. By reviewing winning photos from former contests you might discover a trend in judging that could help you when submitting entries. If you can't see the images, ask what style and subject matter have been popular. Every little bit helps.

Some of this information can be found by reading through the listings to find out which ones will accept your work. Once you have examined the listings, write to the sponsors for complete, up-to-date entry information.

When entering contests be especially alert for any which require the surrender or transfer of "all rights" to images, either upon entry or upon winning the contest. While you can benefit greatly from the publicity and awards connected with some of the more prestigious contests, you do not want to unknowingly forfeit your copyright. Granting limited rights for publicity is reasonable, but you should never assign rights of any kind without adequate financial compensation or without a written agreement. In your request for entry guidelines, be sure to request clear information about such terms.

■**AMERICAN INTERNATIONAL FILM/VIDEO FESTIVAL**, P.O. Box 4034, Long Beach CA 90804. Festival Chairman: George Cushman. Sponsored by the American Motion Picture Society. Sponsors worldwide annual competition in its 64th consecutive year for film and videotape. Closing date September 30, 1993.

ANACORTES ARTS & CRAFTS FESTIVAL, P.O. Box 6, Anacortes WA 98221. (206)293-6211. Director: Joan Tezak. Two-day festival, first weekend in August. Over 225 booths plus juried show with prizes.

ART SHOW AT THE DOG SHOW, 11301 West 37 North, Wichita KS 67205. (316)722-6181. Chairman: Joe Miller. Entry fee of $20 for up to 3 entries. A national juried fine arts competition devoted to canine art. All entries must include a dog.

ARTIST FELLOWSHIP GRANTS, c/o Oregon Arts Commission, 550 Airport Rd. SE, Salem OR 97310. (503)378-3625. Assistant Director: Vincent Dunn. Offers cash grants to Oregon photographers in odd-numbered years.

■**BALTIMORE ANNUAL INDEPENDENT FILM & VIDEO MAKERS' COMPETITION**, % The Baltimore Film Forum, 10 Art Museum Dr., Baltimore MD 21218. (410)889-1993. Annual international competition. Applications available in summer, entries due in fall. Winners screened in April during International Film Festival.

*****BEST IN THE WEST**, Suite 302, 251 Post St., San Francisco CA 94108. (415)421-6867. Vice President: Janet Kennedy. Sponsor: American Advertising Federation. Annual competition for advertising and design work created in the 13 Western states only.

CAMERA BUG INTERNATIONAL, Camera Bug World Headquarters, 2106 Hoffnagle St., Philadelphia PA 19152. (215)742-5515. Contest Chairman: Nicholas M. Friedman. Annual contest open to all photographers. Provide SASE or 29¢ postage for submission guidelines.

COUNTERPOINT: ANNUAL NATIONAL JURIED DRAWING, PHOTOGRAPHY, AND PRINTMAKING EXHIBITION, P.O. Box 176, Ingram TX 78025. Art Director: Betty Vernon. Send SASE to Hill Country Arts Foundation, P.O. Box 176PM, Ingram TX 78025 for prospectus. Cost: Handling fee to enter competition $22 for 3 slides. Awards $2,200.

■**THE CREATIVITY AWARDS SHOW**, 6th Floor, 10 E. 39th St., New York NY 10016. (212)889-6500. Show Director: Dan Barron. Sponsor: *Art Direction* magazine. Annual show for photos and films published for worldwide distribution.

*****EAST TEXAS INTERNATIONAL PHOTOGRAPHY CONTEST**, P.O. Box 4104, East Texas Station, Commerce TX 75429. (214)886-5234. Advisor: Stan Godwin. Sponsors: East Texas State University Photographic Society; Eastman Kodak Co., Prof. Photo Div.; Canon, USA; and General Fire Extinguisher. Annual contest in April for still photos/prints. Three main divisions: commercial, fine-art and photojournalism. Over $10,000 in awards annually. Send long SASE to above address for prospectus.

ECLIPSE AWARDS, Thoroughbred Racing Associations, Suite 1, 420 Fair Hill Dr., Elkton MD 21921-2573. (410)392-9200. Fax: (410)398-1366. Director of Services: Kennith R. Knelly. Sponsor: Thoroughbred Racing Associations, Daily Racing Form and National Turf Writers Association. Annual event for photographers. Given for outstanding achievement in the coverage of thoroughbred racing.

*EYE GALLERY — SELECTIONS '93, 1151 Mission St., San Francisco CA 94103. (415)431-6911. Director: Lynette Molnar. Annual juried photography exhibition. Rotating nationally recognized jurors. Purchase Awards. March deadline.

FINE ARTS WORK CENTER IN PROVINCETOWN, P.O. Box 565, Provincetown MA 02657. (508)487-9960. Contact: Visual Coordinator. Seven-month residency program for artists and writers. Housing, monthly stipend and materials allowance provided from October 1 through May 1. Send SASE for application. Deadline February 1.

*SAMUEL S. FLEISHER ART MEMORIAL, 709-721 Catharine St., Philadelphia PA 19147. (215)922-3456. Gallery Coordinator: Lanny Bergner. Sponsors challenge competition for avant-garde and fine art photography. Applicants must live within 50 miles of Philadelphia. Cost: $10.

44th INTERNATIONAL EXHIBITION OF PHOTOGRAPHY, 2260 Jimmy Durante Blvd., Del Mar CA 92014-2216. (619)755-1161. Sponsor: Del Mar Fair (22nd District Agricultural Association). Annual event for still photos/prints. May 8 deadline. Send #10 SASE for brochure.

GALLERY MAGAZINE, 401 Park Ave. S., New York NY 10016-8802. Contest Editor: Judy Linden. Sponsors monthly event for still photos of nudes. Offers monthly and annual grand prizes. Write for details or buy magazine.

GEORGIA COUNCIL FOR THE ARTS INDIVIDUAL ARTISTS GRANT PROGRAM, 530 Means St. NW, Suite 115, Atlanta GA 30318. (404)651-7926. Visual Arts Manager: Richard Waterhouse. Open to individual artists, who must have been legal residents of Georgia for at least one year prior to the application date. To be eligible for funding, the artist must submit a specific project proposal for completion during the 1995 fiscal year. Deadline: April 1, 1994.

GOLDEN ISLES ARTS FESTIVAL, Box 673, Saint Simons Island GA 31522. (912)638-8770. Contact: Registration Chairman. Sponsor: Coastal Alliance for the Arts. Annual competition for still photos/prints; all fine art and craft.

GREATER MIDWEST INTERNATIONAL IX, CMSU Art Center Gallery, Warrensburg MO 64093. (816)543-4498. Gallery Director: Billi R.S. Rothove. Sponsor: CMSU Art Center Gallery/Missouri Arts Council. Sponsors annual competition for all media. Send SASE for current prospectus.

*HAWAII VISITORS BUREAU TRAVEL JOURNALISM AWARDS, Suite 801, Waikiki Business Plaza, 2270 Kalakaua Ave., Honolulu HI 96815. (808)923-1811. Communications Specialist: Cari Costanzo. Cost: $10/entry. Write for guidelines.

IDAHO WILDLIFE, P.O. Box 25, Boise ID 83707. (208)334-3748. Editor: Diane Ronayne. Annual contest; pays cash prizes of $20-150. Rules in summer and fall issues of *Idaho Wildlife* magazine. Deadline October 1. Winners published.

INDIVIDUAL ARTIST FELLOWSHIP PROGRAM, % Montana Arts Council, P.O. Box 202201, 316 N. Montana, Helena MT 59620. (406)444-6430. Director of Artists Services: Martha Sprague. Offers several annual awards of $2,000 in all visual arts, including photography. *Open to Montana residents only.*

‡INTERNATIONAL DIAPORAMA FESTIVAL, Auwegemvaart 79, B-2800 Mechelen, Belgium. President: J. Denis. Sponsor: Koninklijke Mechelse Fotokring. Competition held every other year (even years) for slide/sound sequences.

INTERNATIONAL WILDLIFE PHOTO COMPETITION, 280 E. Front St., Missoula MT 59802. (406)728-9380. Chairman: Noreen Rebich. Professional and amateur catagories, color and b&w prints, color slides accepted; $1,700 in cash and prizes. Entry deadline mid-March 1994. Co-sponsored by the 17th Annual International Wildlife Film Festival and the Rocky Mountain School of Photography.

*JURIED PHOTOGRAPHY EXHIBITION, 5601 South Braeswood, Houston TX 77096. (713)729-3200. Cultural Arts Director: Marilyn Hassid. Sponsor: Jewish Community Center of Houston. Competition held every other year for still photos/prints (slide entry format) in the spring in conjunction with Houston Fotofest. For next exhibition, write for information.

MAYFAIR 1994 JURIED PHOTOGRAPHY EXHIBITION, 2020 Hamilton St., Allentown PA 18104. (215)437-6900. Maximum 3 entries, $10 non-refundable fee to enter. May juried exhibition open to all types of original photographs by artists within 75-mile radius of Allentown. Send for prospectus; entry deadline March 1.

■THE "MOBIUS"™ ADVERTISING AWARDS, 841 N. Addison Ave., Elmhurst IL 60126-1291. (708)834-7773. Fax: (708)834-5565. Chairman: J.W. Anderson. Executive Director: Patricia Meyer. Sponsor: The United States Festivals Association. Annual international awards competition for print advertising, package design, TV and radio commericals. Annual October 1st entry deadline. Awards in early February each year.

*MOTHER JONES INTERNATIONAL FUND FOR DOCUMENTARY PHOTOGRAPHY AWARDS, 1663 Mission St., San Francisco CA 94103. Contact: Bethany Schoenfeld. Sponsors awards programs for in-depth (1+ years) in-progress social documentary projects. Awards five grants of $7,000 each. Write for guidelines or fax (415)863-5136.

NATURAL WORLD PHOTOGRAPHIC COMPETITION & EXHIBITION, The Carnegie Museum of Natural History, 4400 Forbes Ave., Pittsburgh PA 15213. (412)622-3283. Contact: Division of Education. Held each fall, contest accepts color and b&w prints depicting the "natural world." Prizes totalling $1,300 are awarded and a juried show is selected for exhibition in the museum.

NEW YORK STATE FAIR PHOTOGRAPHY COMPETITION AND SHOW, New York State Fair, Syracuse NY 13209. (315)487-7711. Program Manager: Janet J. Edison. Fee: $5 per entrant for one or two works. Open to amateurs and professionals in both b&w and color. Two prints may be entered per person. Prints only, no transparencies. Entry deadline August 1.

NEW YORK STATE YOUTH MEDIA ARTS SHOWS, New York State Summer Institutes, The State Education Department, Room 685 EBA, Albany NY 12234. (518)474-8773. Funded by the state legislature and administered by the New York State Education Department. Annual exhibition for still photos, film, videotape and computer arts. *Open to New York state elementary and secondary grade students only.*

NIKON SMALL WORLD COMPETITION, 1300 Walt Whitman Rd., Melville New York 11747. (516)547-8500. Advertising Manager: B. Loechner. International contest for photography through the microscope, 35mm—limit 3 entries. First prize $4,000.

1994 PHOTOGRAPHY ANNUAL, 410 Sherman, P.O. Box 10300, Palo Alto CA 94303. (415)326-6040. Executive Editor: Jean A. Coyne. Sponsor: *Communication Arts* magazine. Annual competition for still photos/prints.

■NORTH AMERICAN OUTDOOR FILM/VIDEO AWARDS, Suite 101, 2017 Cato Ave., State College PA 16801. (814)234-1011. Sponsor: Outdoor Writers Association of America. $75 fee/entry. Annual competition for films/videos on conservation and outdoor recreation subjects. Two categories: Recreation/Promotion and Conservation/Natural History.

PHOTO EXHIBIT '94, P.O. Box 614, Park Forest IL 60466-0614. (708)474-9194. Exhibit Director: Kare Lindell. Sponsor: Park Forest Photography Club. Annual competition held in April for color and b&w prints and slides. Seven categories. Open to amateur photographers residing in the United States. March 6 deadline.

PHOTO METRO MAGAZINE ANNUAL CONTEST, 17 Tehama St., San Francisco CA 94105. (415)243-9917. Photography contest with cash prizes, publication and exhibition. Send SASE for information.

*PHOTO REVIEW ANNUAL COMPETITION, 301 Hill Ave., Langhorne PA 19047. (215)757-8921. Editor: Stephen Perloff. Cost: $18 for up to three prints, $4 each for up to two more. National annual photo competition; all winners reproduced in summer issue of *Photo Review* magazine. Ten entrants selected for group exhibition at the Corcoran Gallery of Art, Washington, DC. One entrant selected for one-person show at the Print Club, Philadelphia, PA.

*PHOTOGRAPHER'S MARKET, 1507 Dana Ave., Cincinnati OH 45207. (513)531-2690, ext. 286. Editor: Michael Willins. Cost: $10/image for professionals; $5/image for students. Annual cover photo contest. Work must be submitted by August 31. Call or write for guidelines.

PHOTOGRAPHIC ALLIANCE U.S.A., 1864 61st St., Brooklyn NY 11204-2352. President: Henry Mass. Sole US representative of the International Federation of Photographic Art. Furnishes members with entry forms and information regarding worldwide international salons as well as other information regarding upcoming photographic events.

PHOTOGRAPHIC COMPETITION ASSOCIATION QUARTERLY CONTEST, P.O. Box 53550-B, Philadelphia PA 19105. (215)828-2773. Contact: Competition Committee. Sponsor: Photographic Competition Association (PCAA). Quarterly competition for still photos/prints.

PHOTOGRAPHY NOW, % the Center for Photography at Woodstock, 59 Tinker St., Woodstock NY 12498. (914)679-9957. Sponsors annual competition. Call for entries. Juried annually by renowned photographers, critics, museums. Call or write for prospectus in December and March.

PHOTOSPIVA 94, Spiva Art Center, 3950 Newman Rd., Joplin MO 64801. (417)623-0183. Director: V.A. Christensen. National photography competition. Send SASE for prospectus.

PHOTOWORK 94, Barrett House Galleries, 55 Noxon St., Poughkeepsie NY 12601. (914)471-2550. Associate Director: Fran Smulcheski. National photography exhibition judged by New York City curator. Deadline for submissions December 1993. Send SASE in September for prospectus.

PICTURE PERFECT, P.O. Box 15760, Stamford CT 06901. (203)967-2512. Publisher: Andres Aquino. Ongoing photo contest in 31 subjects. Offers publishing opportunities, cash prizes and outlet for potential stock sales. Send SAE with 2 first-class stamps for details.

PICTURES OF THE YEAR, 27 Neff Annex, 9th and Elm, Columbia MO 65201. (314)882-4442. Coordinator: Marilyn Upton. Photography competition for professional magazine, newspaper and freelance photographers.

PULITZER PRIZES, 702 Journalism, Columbia University, New York NY 10027. (212)854-3841 or 3842. Annual competition for still photos/prints published in American newspapers. February 1 deadline for work published in the previous year.

*WILLIAM REAGH LOS ANGELES PHOTOGRAPHY CENTER'S ANNUAL CONTEST & EXHIBITION, (formerly Los Angeles Photography Center's Annual Contest and Exhibition), 412 S. Park View St., Los Angeles CA 90057. (213)383-7342. Competition open to all photographers. Categories are also open. Offering prizes in 1st, 2nd, 3rd and honorable mention. Juried show with exhibition from June-August.

SAN FRANCISCO SPCA PHOTO CONTEST, SF/SPCA, 2500 16th St., San Francisco CA 94103. (415)554-3000. Coordinator: Frank Burtnett. Entry fee $5 per image, no limit. Photos of pet(s) with or without people. Color slides, color or b&w prints, no larger than 8 × 12 (matte limit 11 × 14). Make check payable to SF/SPCA. Three best images win prizes. Deadline for entry December 15 each year; include return postage and phone number.

SELECTIONS, 1151 Mission St., San Francisco CA 94103. Executive Director: Lynette Molnar. Offers annual juried photography exhibition with Eye Gallery. March deadline. Send SASE for prospectus.

■SINKING CREEK FILM/VIDEO FESTIVAL, 402 Sarratt, Vanderbilt University, Nashville TN 37240. (615)322-2471. Director: Meryl Truett. Sponsors annual competition for 16mm film and ¾" videotape. Offers workshops in film and video production and seminars in media analysis. Holds screening of winners from its national film/video competition. Festival held in June at Vanderbilt University, Nashville, TN. April deadline; $8,000 in cash awards.

■SPRINGFIELD INTERNATIONAL COLOR SLIDE EXHIBIT, Box 255P, Wilbraham MA 01095. Sponsor: Springfield Photographic Society. Sponsors annual event for 35mm color slides in January.

The solid, black square before a listing indicates that the market uses various types of audiovisual materials, such as slides, film or videotape.

TAYLOR COUNTY FAIR PHOTO CONTEST, P.O. Box 613, Grafton WV 26354-0613. Co-Chairman: K.M. Bolyard. Entry fee: $5 for two prints; $3 each thereafter. Color and b&w.

*■TEN BEST OF THE WEST FILM/VIDEO FESTIVAL, 2746 Tyler St., Long Beach CA 90810. Festival Chairman: Gordon Campbell. Open to motion picture makers in the Western United States and Canada. Sponsored by the motion picture clubs in the Western United Sates and Canada.

31ST ANNUAL INTERNATIONAL UNDERWATER PHOTOGRAPHIC COMPETITION, P.O. Box 2401, Culver City CA 90231. (310)421-2295. Competition Chairperson: Bill Brush. Cost: $7.50 per image, maximum 4 images per category. Offers annual competition in 8 categories (7 underwater, 1 ocean related). Deadline October 15.

33RD ANNUAL NAVAL AND MARITIME PHOTO CONTEST, U.S. Naval Institute, 118 Maryland Ave., Annapolis MD 21402. (410)268-6110. Picture Editor: Charles Mussi. Sponsors annual competition for still photos/prints and 35mm slides. December 31 deadline.

*■THREE RIVERS ARTS FESTIVAL, 207 Sweetbriar St., Pittsburgh PA 15211. (412)481-7040. Publications Assistant: Carrie L. Sutilla. Annual competition for still photos/prints and videotape. Early February deadline.

■U.S. INTERNATIONAL FILM AND VIDEO FESTIVAL, (formerly U.S. Industrial Film & Video Festival), 841 N. Addison Ave., Elmhurst IL 60126-1291. (708)834-7773. Fax: (708)834-5565. Chairman: J.W. Anderson. Executive Director: Patricia Meyer. Sponsor: The United States Festivals Association. Annual international awards competition for film and video. Founded 1968. Annual March entry deadline.

UNLIMITED EDITIONS INTERNATIONAL JURIED PHOTOGRAPHY COMPETITIONS, % Competition Chairman, P.O. Box 4144, Friendly Station, Greensboro NC 27404-4144. (704)696-3269. President/ Owner: Gregory Hugh Leng. Sponsors juried photography contests offering cash and prizes. Also offers opportunity to sell work to Unlimited Editions.

WESTCHESTER INTERNATIONAL SALON, P.O. Box 248, Larchmont NY 10538. (914)834-1555. Color slide competition worldwide, pictorial, nature, photo-travel, photo-journalism divisions. Held annually in March.

WESTERN HERITAGE AWARDS, 1700 NE 63rd St., Oklahoma City OK 73111. (405)478-2250. Public Relations Director: Dana Sullivant. Sponsor: National Cowboy Hall of Fame. Annual competition for film and videotape held the 3rd week of March in Oklahoma City.

‡WORLD PRESS PHOTO, Van Baerlestraat 144, Amsterdam The Netherlands 1071 BE. 31(20)6766096. Fax: 31(20)6764471. Annual contest open to photojournalists and press photographers. Covers press photographs in b&w and color taken during 1993. Deadline January 31, 1994.

■WORLDFEST–HOUSTON INTERNATIONAL FILM & TV FESTIVAL AND FILM MARKET, P.O. Box 56566, Houston TX 77256. (713)965-9955. Fax: (713)965-9960. Executive Director: J.H. Todd. Sponsor: City of Houston, Kodak, others. Annual festival for film, videotape and screenplays held in April in Houston. Request entry fee and additional information by mail or phone. All winning entries are automatically submitted to more than 200 international film festivals.

YOSEMITE RENAISSANCE, P.O. Box 313, Yosemite CA 95389. (209)372-4775. Director: Kay Pitts. Annual all media exhibit. Cash awards of $4,500. September 10 deadline for slide entry. Send for entry form.

YOUR BEST SHOT, % *Popular Photography*, 1633 Broadway, New York NY 10019. Monthly photo contest, 2-page spread featuring 5 pictures: first ($300), second ($200), third ($100) and two honorable mention ($50 each).

Workshops

Unless you have had your head buried in the sand you certainly have noticed that photography is headed in a new direction, one filled with computer manipulation and compact discs. Technological advances are no longer the wave of the future—they're here. Even if you haven't invested a lot of time and money into electronic cameras, computers or software, you certainly must understand what you're up against if you plan to succeed as a professional photographer.

Although outdoor and nature photography still are popular with instructors, some of the technological advances are examined closely in the workshops listed in this section. There also are numerous tours listed which provide special photographic experiences, such as cruises, river raft trips and backpacking in remote areas.

As you peruse these pages remember to take a good look at the quality of the workshop and the level of photographers that the sponsors want to attract. It is important to know if the workshop is for beginners, advanced amateurs or professionals and information from the workshop organizer can help you make that determination. Nothing is worse for a professional than attending a workshop that deals with the basics of capturing images. On the other hand, a beginner does not want to attend a workshop in which everyone is talking way over his head. Know what you want to get out of the workshop and know what will be covered while you are there.

These workshop listings contain only the basic information needed to make contact with sponsors and a brief description of the styles or media covered in the programs. This year, however, we have tried to include more information on workshop costs, and this information has been added whenever possible.

The workshop experience can be whatever the photographer wishes it to be—a holiday from his working routine, or an exciting introduction to new skills and perspectives on the craft. Some photographers who start out by attending someone else's workshops come away so inspired that sooner or later they establish their own. Maybe you, too, can learn enough to become a workshop instructor.

ANSEL ADAMS GALLERY PHOTOGRAPHY WORKSHOPS, P.O. Box 455, Yosemite National Park CA 95389. (209)372-4413. Contact: Workshop Coordinator. Offers workshops in fine art photography within Yosemite National Park.

ALASKA UP CLOSE, P.O. Box 32666, Juneau AK 99803. (907)789-9544. Contact: Judy Shuler. Offers photography tours and workshops in nature and wildlife subjects.

*ALSEK/TATSHENSHINI RIVER WILDERNESS PHOTOGRAPHY WORKSHOP, (formerly Alsek River Wilderness Photography Workshop), % Mountain Travel●Sobek 6420 Fairmount Ave., El Cerrito CA 94530. (800)227-2384. Offers 10-day river trips through spectacular glacial and mountain areas of Alaska.

AMBIENT LIGHT WORKSHOPS, 5 Tartan Ridge Rd., Burr Ridge IL 60521. (708)325-5464. Contact: John J. Mariana. $45-85/day. In-the-field and darkroom. One-week travel workshops.

AMERICAN SOUTHWEST PHOTOGRAPHY WORKSHOP, P.O. Box 220450, El Paso TX 79913. (915)757-2800. Director: Geo. B. Drennan. Offers intense field workshops for the serious black-and-white photographer.

🍁AMPRO PHOTO WORKSHOPS, 636 E. Broadway, Vancouver BC V5T 1X6 Canada. (604)876-5501. Fax: (604)876-5502. Course tuition ranges from under $100 for part-time to $5,500 for full-time. Approved trade school. Offers part-time and full-time career courses in commercial photography and photofinishing technician. "Twenty-nine different courses in camera, darkroom and studio lighting— from basic to advanced levels. Special seminars with top professional photographers."

ANCHELL PHOTOGRAPHY WORKSHOPS, 2067 18th Ave., San Francisco CA 94116-1249. (415)566-9868. Director: Steve Anchell. Tuition: $395-525. Offers workshops in fine art figure photography and landscape techniques.

ANDERSON RANCH ARTS CENTER, P.O. Box 5598, Snowmass Village CO 81615. (303)923-3181. Fax: (303)923-3871. Cost: $225 and up. One- and two-week workshops run from May through October with such recognized photographers/teachers as Jim Bones, Chris Burkett, Tom Carabasi, Judy Dater, Ralph Gibson, Cherie Green Hiser, Jay Maisel, Judy Natal, Chris Rainier, Meridel Rubenstein, John Sexton, Philip Trager and Jerry Uelsmann. Program highlights include documentary, portrait, dance and landscape photography; photojournalism and advanced techniques. Special field expeditions offer trips to the Green and Colorado rivers and the Rocky Mountains.

BALLENGER-TULLEY PHOTO WORKSHOPS, P.O. Box 457, La Canada CA 91012. (818)954-0933 or (818)564-9086. Contact: Noella Ballenger or Jalien Tulley. Three-day travel and nature photo workshops in California. Individual instruction in small groups emphasizes visual awareness and problem solving in the field.

AL BELSON PHOTOGRAPHY WORKSHOPS, 3701 W. Moore Ave., Santa Ana CA 92704. (714)432-7070, ext. 608. Director: Al Belson. Workshops throughout the year covering portraiture, landscape and fine art.

BLOCK ISLAND PHOTOGRAPHY WORKSHOPS, 319 Pheasant Dr., Rocky Hill CT 06067. (203)563-9156. Directors: Stephen Sherman and Jack Holowitz. Workshops take place on Block Island, Rhode Island and also in the deserts of California and the canyons of Arizona. Offers workshop programs in black-and-white zone system, portraiture and landscapes.

*HOWARD BOND WORKSHOPS, 1095 Harold Circle, Ann Arbor MI 48103. (313)665-6597. Owner: Howard Bond. Offers 1-day workshop: View Camera Techniques; and two 2-day workshops: Zone System for all formats and refinements in b&w printing. Also offers b&w field workshops: 4 days at Lake Superior Provincial Park and 3 days at Colorado's Great Sand Dunes.

MATT BRADLEY PHOTOGRAPHY WORKSHOPS, 15 Butterfield Ln., Little Rock AR 72212. (501)224-0692. Workshop Director: Marcia Hartmann. *National Geographic* photographer teaches his "Creative Image" workshop three times a year at various Arkansas state parks.

THE BROOKFIELD/SoNo PHOTOGRAPHIC WORKSHOP, 127 Washington St., Norwalk CT 06854. (203)853-6155. Director: John Russell. Community darkroom with school offering classes and workshops for all levels and interests.

 The maple leaf before a listing indicates that the market is Canadian.

*NANCY BROWN HANDS-ON WORKSHOPS, 6 W. 20 St., New York NY 10011. (212)924-9105. Contact: Nancy Brown. $950 for week, breakfast and lunch included. Offers three one-week workshops in New York City studio; workshops held one week each month in July, August and September.

CALIFORNIA WILDLIFE PHOTOGRAPHIC SAFARIS, P.O. Box 30694, Santa Barbara CA 93130. (805)569-3731. Contact: Sharon Peterson. Offers 5-day photo safaris to photograph and study the biology of California's unspoiled wildplaces and treasured wildlife. Five-person limit per safari. Photographic instructor: B. "Moose" Peterson.

CAMERA-IMAGE WORKSHOPS, P.O. Box 1501, Downey CA 90240. Instructors: Craig Fucile and Jan Pietrzak. Offers 3- and 4-day workshops during winter, spring and fall in California desert, Sierra Nevada Mountains and the California central coast. Workshop fees are approximately $55/day and cover tuition only. Instruction in color, b&w techniques, exposure, filtration, equipment use, Cibachrome and hand-coated printmaking.

*CANYONLANDS FIELD INSTITUTE PHOTO WORKSHOPS, P.O. Box 68, Moab UT 84532. (801)259-7750. Contact: Director of Programs. Program fees range from $265-415. Offers programs in landscape photography in Canyonlands & Arches National Parks.

■CAPE MAY PHOTOGRAPHIC WORKSHOP, 1511 New York Ave., Cape May NJ 08204. (609)884-7117 ext. 16. Contact: Bill Deering. Offers workshops (including international workshops in Paris, Israel and Italy) in wide range of disciplines for beginners to advanced photographers, including: photojournalism, portrait, advertising, fine art, documentary design, still life, corporate, stock, business, computers, color printing (Ciba), b&w printing, wildlife and nature, video and film.

VERONICA CASS ACADEMY OF PHOTOGRAPHIC ARTS, 7506 New Jersey Ave., Hudson FL 34667. (813)863-2738. President: Veronica Cass Weiss. Price per week ranges from $450-525. Offers 8 one-week workshops in photo retouching techniques.

CENTER FOR PHOTOGRAPHY, 59 Tinker St., Woodstock NY 12498. (914)679-9957. Contact: Director. Offers monthly exhibitions, a summer and fall workshop series, annual call for entry shows, library, darkroom, fellowships, memberships, and photography magazine, classes, lectures. Has interns in workshops and arts administration.

*CHEESEMANS' ECOLOGY SAFARIS, 20800 Kittredge Rd., Saratoga CA 95070. (800)527-5330. Contact: Doug and Gail Cheeseman. Cost is $2,650. Offers two-week photo and sound recording tour to Trinidad and Tobago. 4 leaders for 12 members of the group. Tour runs June 27-July 10.

CHINA PHOTO WORKSHOP TOURS, #211, 22111 Cleveland, Dearborn MI 48124-3461. (313)561-1842. Director: D.E. Cox. Offers annual photo tours to China's major cities and scenic countryside; includes meetings with top Chinese photographers.

CLOSE-UP EXPEDITIONS, 1031 Ardmore Ave., Oakland CA 94610. (510)465-8955. Guide and Outfitter: Donald Lyon. Sponsored by the Photographic Society of America. Worldwide, year-round travel and nature photography expeditions, 10-25 days. Professional photographer guides put you in the right place at the right time to create unique marketable images.

CORY NATURE PHOTOGRAPHY WORKSHOPS, 1629 Rustic Homes Lane, Signal Mountain TN 37377. (615)886-1004. Contact: Tom or Pat Cory. Small workshops featuring individual attention in Chattanooga, the Smoky Mountains of Tennessee, the Blue Ridge area of North Carolina and the High Sierras of California. Fees for Chattanooga 1- to 1¼-day workshops including lunch, $45 to $75. Smoky Mountain workshops run Friday night through 1 p.m. on Sundays, include meals and lodging, $255 single occupancy, $225 double occupancy. Week-long High Sierras field trip includes lodging and transportation from Reno airport, $1,245 single occupancy, $1,095 double occupancy. Write for other workshop prices and more details about workshops.

CREATIVE ADVENTURES, 67 Maple St., Newburgh NY 12550. (914)561-5866. Contact: Richie Suraci. Photographic adventures into "exotic, sensual, beautiful international locations." Send SASE.

*CREATIVE ARTS WORKSHOP, 80 Audubon St., New Haven CT 06511. (203)562-4927. Photography Department Head: Harold Shapiro. Offers advanced workshops and courses and beginning classes.

*THE CREATIVE IMAGE WORKSHOP, 37 Midland Ave., Elmwood Park NJ 07407. (800)346-3007. Contact: Drew DeGrado. Offers training in special effects and techniques of advertising photography.

CREATIVE VISION WORKSHOPS IN COLORADO HIGH COUNTRY, 317 E. Winter Ave., Danville IL 61832-1857. (217)442-3075. Director: Orvil Stokes. Tuition: $475. Offers workshops in the color zone system, previsualization, contrast control, image design, selling your photographs and modified b&w zone system for roll film.

CUMMINGTON COMMUNITY OF THE ARTS, Cummington Community of the Arts, RR#1, Box 145, Cummington MA 01026. (413)634-2172. Executive Director: Rick Reiken. Residences for artists of all disciplines from 1-3 months.

DEERFIELD AT STONINGTON, 701 Elm Street, Essexville MI 48732. (800)882-8458. Director: Chuck McMartin. Offers wildlife photo workshops in the Hiawatha National Forest in Michigan's Upper Peninsula.

CHARLENE FARIS WORKSHOPS, #A, 9524 Guilford Dr., Indianapolis IN 46240. (317)848-2634. Director: Charlene Faris. Offers one-day programs for beginners in marketing and learning to shoot marketable photos. Seven-week courses taught two or three times annually at IU-PUI Continuing Studies Division. Send SASE for schedule and information.

FOCUS ADVENTURES, P.O. Box 771640, Steamboat Springs CO 80477. (303)879-2244. Fax: (303)879-9022. Owner: Karen Schulman. Workshops in the art of seeing, nature photography, hand coloring photographs, light, creativity and self-promotion. Customized private and small group lessons available.

FOCUS SEMINAR IN HYBRID IMAGING AND NEW TECHNOLOGIES, 5210 Photo/Lansing Community College, P.O. Box 40010, Lansing MI 48901-7210. (517)483-1673. A three-day series of workshops, seminars, forums and demonstrations related to hybrid imaging, new technologies in photography, imaging and computer graphics.

FRIENDS OF ARIZONA HIGHWAYS PHOTO WORKSHOPS, (formerly Friends of Arizona Highways Photo Adventures), P.O. Box 6106, Phoenix AZ 85005-6106. (602)271-5904. Travel Coordinator: Laura Reeves. Offers photo adventures to Arizona's spectacular locations with top professional photographers whose work routinely appears in *Arizona Highways*.

*FRIENDS OF PHOTOGRAPHY, 250 Fourth St., San Francisco CA 94103. (415)495-7000. Director of Education: Deborah Klochko. Short-term workshops in documentary and architectural work to landscape and portraiture.

OLIVER GAGLIANI ZONE SYSTEM WORKSHOP, 35 Yosemite Rd., San Rafael CA 94903. (415)472-4010. Contact: Barry Lee Marris. Cost is $850. Offers two-week workshop in Zone System techniques in Virginia City, Nevada.

*JOHN & BARB GERLACH NATURE PHOTOGRAPHY SEMINARS, P.O. Box 206, Lapeer MI 48446. (313)664-3362. President: John Gerlach. Tuition for the one-day seminar is $65. Offers seminars titled "How to Shoot Beautiful Nature Photographs for Fun and Profit" in various locations throughout the US.

GLOBAL PRESERVATION PROJECTS, (formerly Fine Art Workshop Series), P.O. Box 30866, Santa Barbara CA 93105. (805)682-3398. Director: Thomas I. Morse. Offers workshops promoting the preservation of environmental and historic treasures. Produces international photographic exhibitions and publications.

GREAT SMOKY MOUNTAINS PHOTOGRAPHY WORKSHOPS, 205 Wayah Road, Franklin NC 28734. (704)369-6044. Instructors: Tim Black/Bill Lea. Cost is $285 per participant (includes lodging). Offers programs which emphasize the use of natural light in creating quality scenic, wildflower and wildlife images.

HEART OF NATURE PHOTOGRAPHY WORKSHOPS, (formerly Heart of Nature Inspirational Workshops), 14618 Tyler Fte Rd., Nevada City CA 95959. (916)292-3839. Contact: Robert Frutos. Cost: $145/weekend workshop. "Explores your personal vision, offers discovery techniques for visualizing and creating powerful images and the technical skills to render your unique vision."

*HILL COUNTRY ARTS FOUNDATION, P.O. Box 176PM, Ingram TX 78025. (210)367-5121. Art Director: Betty Vernon. Cost: "Understanding T-Max 3200 Film," $100 plus material and lab fees; "Platinum/Palladium Printing," $175 plus material fee. Both workshops are held in July.

HORIZONS: The New England Craft Program, 374 Old Montague Rd., Amherst MA 01002. (413)549-4841. Director: Jane Sinauer. Two 3-week summer sessions in b&w for high school students each summer plus 1-week adult workshop in Oaxaca, Mexico in February.

INFRARED WORKSHOP, Photocentral, P.O. Box 3998, Hayward CA 94540. (510)278-7705. Coordinators: Geir and Kate Jordahl. Cost: $150/intensive two-day workshop. Workshops dedicated to seeing more through photography.

INTERNATIONAL CENTER OF PHOTOGRAPHY, 1130 5th Ave. at 94th St., New York NY 10128. (212)860-1776. Contact: Education Department. Offers programs in b&w photography, non-silver printing processes, color photography, still life, photographing people, large format, studio, color printing, editorial concepts in photography, zone system, the freelance photographer, etc.

INTERNATIONAL PHOTO TOURS (VOYAGERS INTERNATIONAL), P.O. Box 915, Ithaca NY 14851. (607)257-3091. Managing Director: David Blanton. Emphasizes techniques of nature photography.

IRISH PHOTOGRAPHIC & CULTURAL EXCURSIONS, (formerly Irish Photographic Workshop), Voyagers, P.O. Box 915, Ithaca NY 14851. (607)257-3091. Cost: $1,890 (land). Offers two-week trip in County Mayo in the west of Ireland.

*LAKE POWELL PHOTOGRAPHIC WORKSHOP, Wahweap Lodge and Marina, Page AZ 86040. (602)645-1001. Director: Steven Ward. Offers opportunities to live on houseboats while photographing Lake Powell and surrounding topography.

JOE McDONALD'S WILDLIFE PHOTOGRAPHY WORKSHOPS AND TOURS, Rt. 2, Box 1095., McClure PA 17841. (717)543-6423. (215)433-7025, answering machine and messages. Owner: Joe McDonald. Offers small groups, quality instruction with emphasis on wildlife.

*■THE MacDOWELL COLONY, 100 High St., Peterborough NH 03458. (603)924-3886 or (212)966-4860. Offers studio space to writers, composers, painters, sculptors, printmakers, photographers and filmmakers competitively, based on talent. Residency up to 2 months. Artists are asked to contribute toward cost of their residency according to financial resources. Application deadline: January 15 for summer; April 15 for fall/winter; September 15 for winter/spring. Call or write for application, guidelines and brochure.

McNUTT FARM II/OUTDOOR WORKSHOP, 6120 Cutler Lake Rd., Blue Rock OH 43720. (614)674-4555. Director: Patty L. McNutt. Outdoor shooting of livestock, pets, wildlife and scenes in all types of weather.

*MACROTOURS PHOTO WORKSHOPS, P.O. Box 460041, San Francisco CA 94114. (415)826-1096. Director Bert Banks. Fees range from $45-1,595. Offers travel workshops for wildflowers, scenics, wildlife to Alaska, Southwest and Western National Parks. Brochure available; call or write.

MENDOCINO COAST PHOTOGRAPHY SEMINARS, P.O. Box 1629, Mendocino CA 95460. (707)937-2805. Program Director: Hannes Krebs. Offers a variety of workshops, including a foreign expedition to Chile.

MESSANA PHOTO WORKSHOP, 22500 Rio Vista, St. Clair Shores MI 48081. (313)773-5815. Joseph P. Messana. Offers on-location photographic workshops—architecture, nature, scenics, models and sculpture—in various cities. Send SASE for information on locations and fees.

MICHIGAN PHOTOGRAPHY WORKSHOPS, MPW INTERNATIONAL, 28830 W. 8 Mile Rd., Farmington Hills MI 48336. Fax: (313)542-3441. Directors/Instructors: Alan Lowy and C.J. Elfont. Workshops, seminars and lectures dealing with Classical Nude Figures (Victorian House), Nude Figure in the Environment (Ludington Dunes), Boudoir and Fashion photography, Nature photography on location, and Still-life and Product photography.

*MISSISSIPPI VALLEY WRITERS CONFERENCE, Augustana College, Rock Island IL 61265. Director: David R. Collins. Registration $25, plus individual workshop expenses. Open to the basic beginner or polished professional, the MVWC provides a week-long series of workshops, including five daily sessions in photography.

MISSOURI PHOTOJOURNALISM WORKSHOP, 27 Neff Annex, 9th and Elm, Columbia MO 65201. (314)882-4442. Coordinator: Marilyn Upton. Workshop for photojournalists. Participants learn the fundamentals of documentary photo research, shooting, editing and layout.

*NATIONAL INSTITUTE FOR EXPLORATION, Suite 2A, 277 W. 11th St., New York NY 10014. (212)243-5547. Director: Norman Isaacs. N/E is an organization made up of photographers of all skill levels and backgrounds dedicated to producing publishable photographic projects which document the continuing evolution of people with their environment. Offers opportunities for photographers of all skill levels to become published in magazines and travel adventure books.

NATURE IMAGES, INC., P.O. Box 2037, West Palm Beach FL 33402. (407)586-7332. Director: Helen Longest-Slaughter. Photo workshops offered in Yellowstone National Park, Wisconsin's northwoods and Everglades National Park.

*NATURE PHOTOGRAPHY EXPEDITIONS, 418 Knottingham Dr., Twin Falls ID 83301. (800)574-2839. Contact: Douglas C. Bobb. Cost: $1,200/person, includes room, meals and transportation during the tour; requires a $300 deposit. Offers several workshops in the spring, summer and fall in the Yellowstone Ecosystem.

*NATURE PHOTOGRAPHY WORKSHOPS, % The Glacier Institute, P.O. Box 7457PM, Kalispell MT 59904. (406)756-3911. Program Director: Lee Christianson. Offers variety of workshops including Winter Photography, Black & White Photography, and Spring Photography in Glacier National Park with Marshall Noice; Nature Photography with Diane Ensign and Adv. Nature Photography with John Hooton.

*NEVER SINK PHOTO WORKSHOP, P.O. Box 641, Woodbourne NY 12788. (212)929-0008; (914)434-0575. Owner: Louis Jawitz. Offers weekend workshops in scenic, travel, location and stock photography from late July through early September in Catskill Mountains.

NEW ENGLAND SCHOOL OF PHOTOGRAPHY, 537 Commonwealth Ave., Boston MA 02215. (617)437-1868. Academic Director: Martha Hassell. Instruction in professional and creative photography.

NEW YORK CITY COLOR PRINTING WORKSHOPS, 230 W. 107th St., New York NY 10025. (212)316-1825. Contact: Joyce Culver. Offers two-day weekend, color print workshop making prints from color negatives or internegatives in a professional New York City lab. Call or write for brochure.

1994 PHOTOGRAPHIC EDUCATION SERIES, St. Charles Parks & Recreation, 1900 West Randolph, St. Charles MO 63301. (314)949-3372. Program Administrator: Patrick Zarrick. Comprehensive photography series featuring out-of-state photo tours and workshops, regional weekend field workshops and seminars featuring "finest photographers" in U.S. and weekly "how-to" programs.

*NORTH LIGHT WORKSHOPS, 1416 Farmington Ave., Farmington CT 06032. (203)673-7179. Owner: Mark G. Harutunian. Offers workshops on black and white Zone System Photography.

*NORTHEAST PHOTO ADVENTURE SERIES WORKSHOPS, 55 Bobwhite Dr., Glemont NY 12077. (518)432-9913. President: Peter Finger. Price ranges from $99 for a weekend to $600 for a week-long workshop. Offers over 20 weekend and week-long photo workshops, held in various locations. Recent locations have included: Cape Cod, Maine, Acadia National Park, Vermont, The Adirondacks, The Catskills, Block Island, Martha's Vineyard, Nantucket, Prince Edward Island, Nova Scotia and New Hampshire. "Small group instruction from dawn 'til dusk." Write for additional information.

*NORTHERN KENTUCKY UNIVERSITY SUMMER PHOTO WORKSHOP, Highland Heights KY 41099-1002. (606)572-5423. Professor of Art: Barry Andersen. Offers programs by a series of visiting photographers.

NUDE PHOTOGRAPHY, THE PLUM TREE SUMMER PROGRAM, (formerly Photography Before 1900), Box A-1, State Road 68, Pilar NM 87531. (800)678-7586. Instructor: Cecelia Portal. Cost: $250 plus model fee. Black and white, male and female nude photography.

The First Markets Index preceding the General Index in the back of this book provides the names of those companies/ publications interested in receiving work from newer, lesser-known photographers.

∎**THE OGUNQUIT PHOTOGRAPHY SCHOOL,** Box 2234, Ogunquit ME 03907. (207)646-7055. Director: Stuart Nudelman. Offers programs in photographic sensitivity, marketing photos, photodocumentation and creativity, and nature photography with guest instructors, AV symposiums for educators and traveling workshops.

∎**OHIO INSTITUTE OF PHOTOGRAPHY AND TECHNOLOGY,** 2029 Edgefield Rd., Dayton OH 45439. (513)294-6155. Education Coordinator: Helen Morris. Convenient, affordable, intense weekend workshops in Adobe Photoshop, QuarkXPress and Video Toaster. Summer weekend workshops in still photography offer a variety of topics including nature, fashion/glamour, studio portraiture, photographing people, large format, color printing, darkroom effects and more.

OKLAHOMA FALL ARTS INSTITUTES, P.O. Box 18154, Oklahoma City OK 73154. (405)842-0890. Fax: (405)848-4538. Tuition: $350 for 4 days. October photography workshop at Quartz Mountain Arts and Conference Center in Southwest Oklahoma.

ON LOCATION SEMINARS, (formerly Visual Departures Photographic Workshops), P.O. Box 1653, Ross CA 94957. (415)927-4579. President: Brenda Tharp. Offers multi-day photography tours and workshops in exciting locations worldwide. Destinations include: Southwest US; California — Wildflowers, Death Valley, Joshua Tree, Redwoods, Sierra; Galapagos, Costa Rica and others. Specializes in creative outdoor and travel photography with emphasis on low-impact travel and unique cultural experiences.

OREGON PHOTO TOURS, 745 E. 8th, Coquille OR 97423. (503)396-5792. Owner: Tony Mason. Offers one-on-one photographic tours throughout Oregon and the American West.

OREGON SCHOOL OF ARTS AND CRAFTS, 8245 SW Barnes Rd., Portland OR 97225. (503)297-5544. Offers workshops and classes in photography throughout the year, b&w, color and alternative processes. Call or write for a schedule.

*****OUTBACK PHOTO TOURS AND WORKSHOPS,** % Bob Grytten, Inc., P.O. Box 8792, St. Petersburg FL 33738. (813)397-3013. President: Bob Grytten. Offers weekend tours and workshops in 35mm nature photography, emphasizing Florida flora and fauna. Also offers programs on marketing one's work.

OZARK PHOTOGRAPHY WORKSHOP FIELDTRIP, 40 Kyle St., Batesville AR 72501. (501)793-4552. Conductor: Barney Sellers. Cost: two-day trip, $100; participants furnish own food, lodging and transportation. Limited to 12 people. Offers opportunities for all-day, outdoor subject shooting. No slides shown, fast moving, looking at subjects through the camera lens.

PACIFIC NORTHWEST FIELD SEMINARS, #212, 83 S. King, Seattle WA 98104. (206)553-2636. Coordinator: Jean Tobin. Averate cost is $40/day. Nature photography seminars of 1-4 days, from May to October, in areas such as Mt. Rainier National Park, Crater Lake National Park, Mount St. Helens, Oregon Dunes and the Columbia Gorge. Write for catalog.

PETERS VALLEY CRAFT CENTER, 19 Kuhn Rd., Layton NJ 07851. (201)948-5200. Fax: (201)948-0011. Offers workshops June, July and August, 3-5 days long. Offers instruction in a wide range of photographic disciplines. Located in Delaware Water Gap National Recreation Area, 1½ hours west of New York City. Write, call or fax for catalog.

PHOTO ADVENTURE TOURS, 2035 Park St., Atlantic Beach NY 11509-1236. (516)371-0067. Manager: Pamela Makaea. Offers photographic tours to Iceland, India, Nepal, Russia, China, Scandinavia and domestic locations such as New Mexico, Navajo Indian regions, Hawaiian Islands, Michigan, Albuquerque Balloon Festival and New York.

PHOTO FOCUS/COUPEVILLE ARTS CENTER, P.O. Box 171 MP, Coupeville WA 98239. (206)678-3396. Director: Judy Lynn. Offers variety of workshops with nationally recognized instructors.

*****PHOTO METRO MAGAZINE AND DIGITAL WORKSHOPS,** 17 Tehama St., San Francisco CA 94105. (415)243-9917. Publisher: Henry Brimmer. Computer workshops for Adobe Photoshop, QuarkXPress, Illustrator, etc. For brochure, dates and prices, send SASE.

PHOTO TOURS: IN FOCUS WITH MICHELE BURGESS, 20741 Catamaran Lane, Huntington Beach CA 92646. (714)536-6104. President: Michele Burgess. Tour prices range from $3,000 to $4,500 from US. Offers overseas tours to photogenic areas with expert photography consultation, at a leisurely pace and in small groups (maximum group size 20).

PHOTOGRAPHIC ARTS WORKSHOPS, P.O. Box 1791, Granite Falls WA 98252. (206)691-4105. Director: Bruce Barnbaum. Offers wide range of workshops across US, Mexico and Canada. Workshops feature instruction in composition, exposure, development, printing and photographic philosophy. Includes critiques of student portfolios. Sessions are intense, held in field, darkroom and classroom with various instructors. Ratio of students to instructor is always 8:1 or fewer.

PHOTOGRAPHY AT THE SUMMIT: JACKSON HOLE, (formerly Photography at the Summit), Suite 650, 3200 Cherry Creek Dr. S., Denver CO 80209. (303)744-2538 or (800)745-3211. Administrator: Chip Garofalo. A week-long workshop and weekend conferences with top journalistic, fine art and illustrative photographers and editors.

PHOTOGRAPHY WORKSHOPS, 8410 Madeline Drive, St. Louis MO 63114. (314)427-6311. Instructors: Ed and Lee Mason. Offers customized workshops for one, three or five days, and for 3 weeks at your location.

PHOTOGRAPHY WORKSHOPS, % Pocono Environmental Education Center, RD2, Box 1010, Dingmans Ferry PA 18328. (717)828-2319. Attention: Dan Hendey. Offers weekend workshops throughout the year focusing on subjects in the natural world.

PHOTO-NATURALIST WORKSHOPS, P.O. Box 377, Terlingua TX 79852. (800)359-4138. President: Steve Harris. Offers rafting/photo tours with Jim Bones through various canyons in the Southwest.

*PT. REYES FIELD SEMINARS, Pt. Reyes National Seashore, Pt. Reyes CA 94956. (415)663-1200. Director: Julie Milas. Fees range from $35-140. Offers weekend photography seminars taught by recognized professionals.

PRATT MANHATTAN, 295 Lafayette Ave., New York NY 10012. (212)925-8481. Assistant Dean (School of Professional Studies): Karen Miletsky. Tuition ranges from $75-300. Offers courses on intro to the camera, architectural photography, photographic lighting and beginner through advanced photography.

PROFESSIONAL PHOTOGRAPHER'S SOCIETY OF NEW YORK PHOTO WORKSHOPS, 121 Genesee St., Avon NY 14414. (716)226-8351. Director: Lois Miller. Cost is $475. Offers week-long, specialized, hands-on workshops for professional photographers.

REDWOOD NATIONAL PARK FIELD SEMINARS, 1111 Second St., Crescent City CA 95531. (707)464-6101. Contact: Field Seminar Coordinator. Fees range from $25-200. One- to five-day workshops in the redwoods and along coastline, beginning and advanced seminars.

ROCKY MOUNTAIN PHOTO WORKSHOPS, % Latigo Ranch, Box 237, Kremmling CO 80459. (800)227-9655. (303)724-9008. Director: Jim Yost. Cost (1993): $1,075 (wildflower workshop), $900 (round-up workshop); price includes meals, lodging and instructions. Offers workshops in photography featuring western cattle round-ups and wildflowers.

ROCKY MOUNTAIN SCHOOL OF PHOTOGRAPHY, P.O. Box 7605, Missoula MT 59807. (406)543-0171 or (800)394-7677. Vice President: Jeanne Chaput de Saintonge. Offers workshops throughout US and abroad and a 10-week career training program each summer in Montana.

SAN JUAN MAJESTY WORKSHOP, 412 Main St., Grand Junction CO 81501. (303)245-6700. Director: Steve Traudt. Current cost of $595; includes lodging and most meals. Offers annual photography workshops in the scenic Rocky Mountain area of Ouray, Colorado in late July.

RON SANFORD, P.O. Box 248, Gridley CA 95948. (916)846-4687. Contact: Ron or Nancy Sanford. Travel and wildlife workshops and tours.

PETER SCHREYER PHOTOGRAPHIC TOURS, P.O. Box 533, Winter Park FL 32790. (407)671-1886. Tour Director: Peter Schreyer. Specialty photographic tours to the American West, Europe and the backroads of Florida. Travel in small groups of 10-15 participants.

*"SELL & RESELL YOUR PHOTOS" SEMINAR, by Rohn Engh, Pine Lake Farm, Osceola WI 54020. (715)248-3800. Seminar Coordinator: Sue Bailey. Offers day-long workshops in major cities. Workshops cover principles based on methods outlined in author's best-selling book of the same name.

JOHN SEXTON PHOTOGRAPHY WORKSHOPS, 291 Los Agrinemsors, Carmel Valley CA 93924. (408)659-3130. Director: John Sexton. Managing Director: Victoria Bell. Offers a selection of intensive workshops with master photographers.

SIERRA PHOTOGRAPHIC WORKSHOPS, 3251 Lassen Way, Sacramento CA 95821. (800)925-2596. In Canada, phone: (916)974-7200. Contact: Sierra Photographic Workshops. Offers week-long workshops in various scenic locations for "personalized instruction in outdoor photography, technical knowledge useful in learning to develop a personal style, learning to convey ideas through photographs."

*SILVER LIGHT PHOTOGRAPHY WORKSHOPS, P.O. Box 723, Moorpark CA 93020. (805)529-8155. Co-founders/Directors: James Ponder and David Whittemore. Cost: Varies depending on length of workshops (six-days average: $385). "Exciting, hands-on field sessions in visually stimulating and historically interesting locations. Top-quality instruction in b&w, color and alternative processes. Fine arts orientation."

BOB SISSON'S MACRO/NATURE PHOTOGRAPHY, %Katherine L. Rowland, P.O. Box 35187, Sarasota FL 34242-5187. (813)349-1714. Coordinator: Katherine L. Rowland. Cost: $400/course. "You will be encouraged to take a closer look at nature through the lens, to learn the techniques of using nature's light correctly and to think before exposing film."

SISTER KENNY INSTITUTE INTERNATIONAL ART SHOW BY DISABLED ARTISTS, 800 E. 28th St., Minneapolis MN 55407-3799. (612)863-4482. Director: Nanette Boudreau. Show is held once a year usually in April and May for disabled artists only. Deadline for entries, Feb. 28.

*SITKA CENTER FOR ART AND ECOLOGY, P.O. Box 65, Otis OR 97368. (503)994-5485. Contact: Executive Director. Offers one- to five-day workshops during summer months. July 30-Aug. 2: Gary Braasch Workshop "Patterns in Nature" (35mm transparencies).

THE 63 RANCH PHOTO WORKSHOPS, P.O. Box 979, Livingston MT 59047. (406)222-0570. Director: Laurance B. Aiuppy. Contact: Sandra Cahill. Workshop in June and September including field day in Yellowstone National Park for intermediate to advanced amateur (or beginning professional) photographers.

*SOUTHAMPTON MASTER PHOTOGRAPHY WORKSHOP, % Long Island University-Southampton Campus, Southampton NY 11968-9822. (516)283-4000, ext 349. Contact—Summer Director: Carla Caglioti. Offers a diverse series of one-week photo workshops through the month of July.

*SOUTHEASTERN CENTER FOR THE ARTS, INC., (SCA), 1935 Cliff Valley Way, Atlanta GA 30329. (404)633-1990. Co-Directors: Jeanne and Neil Chaput de Saintonge. Offers professional career program and adult education classes.

*SOUTHERN SHORT COURSE IN NEWS PHOTOGRAPHY, P.O. Box 4154, Asheboro NC 27204-4154. (919)419-6794. Chairman: Mark Dolejs. Offers annual seminar and contest for news photography.

SOUTHWEST PHOTOGRAPHIC WORKSHOPS, INC., P.O. Box 19272, Houston TX 77224. (713)496-2905. Contact: Jay Forrest. Location photographic workshops in Texas, New Mexico and Latin America.

*SPECIAL EFFECTS FOR BACKGROUNDS, P.O. Box 1745, San Marcos TX 78667. (512)353-3111. Director of Photography: Jim Wilson. Offers three-day programs in background projection techniques.

SPIRIT WALKER EXPEDITIONS, P.O. Box 240, Gustavus AK 99826. (907)697-2266. President: Nathan Borson. Cost: approximately $200/day, everything included. Offers guided wilderness sea kayaking tours in Southeastern Alaska.

SPLIT ROCK ARTS PROGRAM, University of Minnesota, 306 Wesbrook Hall, 77 Pleasant St. SE, Minneapolis MN 55455. (612)624-6800. Registrar: Vivien Oja. One-week, intensive summer residential workshops; nature and documentary photography as well as other arts. Duluth campus on Lake Superior.

*SPORTS PHOTOGRAPHY WORKSHOP, Suite 650, 3200 Cherry Creek Dr. S., Denver CO 80209. (303)744-2538 or (800)745-3211. Administrator: Chip Garofalo. There is a tuition fee of $600 and a $250 deposit must accompany your application. Balance is due upon acceptance into workshop. A week-long workshop in sports photography with photographers and editors from *Sports Illustrated*. Held in conjunction with the US Olympic Festival.

STONE CELLAR DARKROOM WORKSHOPS, 51 Hickory Flat Rd., Buckhannon WV 26201. (304)472-1669. Photographer/Printmaker: Jim Stansbury. Master color printing and color field work, small classes with Jim Stansbury. Work at entry level or experienced level.

SUMMIT PHOTOGRAPHIC WORKSHOPS, P.O. Box 24571, San Jose CA 95154. (408)265-4627. Owner and Instructor: Barbara Brundege. Nature, wildlife and outdoor photographic seminars and tours lasting up to one week in California, U.S. National Parks and wilderness areas.

SUPERIOR/GUNFLINT PHOTOGRAPHY WORKSHOPS, P.O. Box 19286, Minneapolis MN 55419. Director: Layne Kennedy. Prices range from $585-650. Write for details. Fee includes all meals/lodging and workshop. Offers wilderness adventure photo workshops three times yearly. Winter session includes dogsledding. Fall session includes canoe trips into border waters of Canada-Minnesota. Summer session treks into Badlands/Black Hills. Workshop stresses how to shoot effective magazine photos.

*TOUCH OF SUCCESS PHOTO SEMINARS, P.O. Box 194, Lowell FL 32663. (904)867-0463. Director: Bill Thomas. Costs vary from $250-895 US to $5,000 for safaris. Offers workshops on nature scenics, plants, wildlife, stalking, building rapport and communication, composition, subject selection, lighting, marketing and business management. Workshops held at various locations in US. Photo safaris led into upper Amazon, Andes, Arctic, Alaska, Africa and Australia. Writer's workshops for photographers who wish to learn to write.

*TOUCHSTONE CENTER FOR THE CRAFTS, P.O. Box 2141, Uniontown PA 15401. (412)438-2811. Office Manager: Julie Greene. Offers week-long and weekend photography workshops featuring master level photographers as instructors.

TRAVEL PHOTOGRAPHY WORKSHOP in Santa Fe with Lisl Dennis, P.O. Box 2847, Santa Fe NM 87504-2847. (505)982-4979. Cost is $1,150 (includes lodging, some meals and day trips). One-week workshops in 35mm color photography in May and September.

TRINITY ALPS PHOTOGRAPHY WORKSHOPS, 216 Marquis Place, Santa Maria CA 93454. (805)928-3386. Instructors: Charles Krebs and Mary Ellen Schultz. Offers programs in all aspects of nature photography. Makes trips to California, Washington, Maine and Canada.

*TWIN FALLS NATURE PHOTOGRAPHY WORKSHOPS, Twin Falls State Park, P.O. Box 1023, Mullens WV 25882. (304)294-4000. Park Superintendent: Scott Durham. Offers spring and fall nature workshops.

*UNIVERSITY OF CALIFORNIA EXTENSION PHOTOGRAPHY WORKSHOPS, Suite 155, 740 Front Street, Santa Cruz CA 95060. (408)427-6620. Contact: Photography Program. Ongoing program of workshops in photography throughout California, also international study tours in photography.

UNIVERSITY OF WISCONSIN SCHOOL OF THE ARTS AT RHINELANDER, 727 Lowell Hall, 610 Langdon St., Madison WI 53703. (608)263-3494. Coordinator: Kathy Berigan. One-week interdisciplinary arts program held during July in northern Wisconsin.

JOSEPH VAN OS PHOTO SAFARIS, INC., P.O. Box 655, Vashon Island WA 98070. (206)463-5383. Director: Randy Green. Offers photo tours and workshops worldwide.

VENTURE WEST, P.O. Box 7543, Missoula MT 59807. (406)825-6200. Owner: Cathy Ream. Offers various photographic opportunities, including wilderness pack and raft trips, ranches, and fishing and hunting.

*THE VIRGINIA WORKSHOP, 864 Locust Ave., Charlottesville VA 22902. (804)977-8069. Contact: Glenn Showalter. Workshops for the beginning, intermediate and advanced photographer. Emphasizes the art of seeing composition, visual communication and camera work for the productive professional businessperson and the artist. Emphasis on landscape/nature areas and photographic design.

*VISITING ARTISTS WORKSHOPS, (formerly Location Portraiture), % Southwest Craft Center, 300 Augusta, San Antonio TX 78205. (512)224-1848. Public Relations Director: Tracey Ramsey Bennett. Workshops range from $150-200. Approximately four photography workshops are offered during the spring and fall sessions.

PETE VOGEL PHOTO WORKSHOPS, P.O. Box 229, Winchester OR 97495. (503)672-2453. Instructor: Pete Vogel. Offers 3-day workshops at Wildlife Safari, a 600-acre drive-thru wild animal park.

MARK WARNER NATURE PHOTO WORKSHOPS, P.O. Box 142, Ledyard CT 06339. (203)376-6115. Offers 1-4 day workshops on nature and wildlife photography by nationally published photographer and writer at various East Coast locations.

WFC ENTERPRISES, P.O. Box 5054, Largo FL 34649. (813)581-5906. Owner: Wayne F. Collins. Cost: $300. Photoworkshops (glamour), January through November, all on weekend. Free brochure on request.

WHITE MAGIC UNLIMITED, P.O. Box 5506, Mill Valley CA 94942-5506. (415)381-8889. President: Jack Morison. Offers specialty travel and photo safaris worldwide.

WILD HORIZONS, INC., P.O. Box 5118-PM, Tucson AZ 85703. (602)622-0672. President: Thomas A. Wiewandt. Average costs: domestic travel $1,400/week; foreign travel $2,000/week. Offers workshops in field techniques in nature/travel photography at vacation destinations in the American Southwest selected for their outstanding natural beauty and wealth of photographic opportunities. Customized learning vacations for small groups are also offered in E. Africa and Ecuador/Galápagos.

WILDERNESS PHOTOGRAPHY EXPEDITIONS, 402 S. 5th, Livingston MT 59047. (406)222-2302. President: Tom Murphy. Offers programs in wildlife and landscape photography in Yellowstone Park and Montana.

WOODSTOCK PHOTOGRAPHY WORKSHOPS, 59 Tinker, Woodstock NY 12498. (914)679-9957. Fax: (914)679-6337. Offers annual lectures and workshops in creative photography from June through October. Faculty includes numerous top professionals in fine art and commercial photography. Topics include still life, landscape, portraiture, lighting, alternative processes. Offers 1-, 2- and 3-day events as well as travel workshops in the US and overseas.

WORKSHOPS IN THE WEST, P.O. Box 1261, Manchaca TX 78652. (512)295-3348. Contact: Joe Englander. Costs: $185-5,000. Photographic instruction in beautiful locations throughout the world, all formats, color and b&w, darkroom instruction.

YELLOWSTONE INSTITUTE, P.O. Box 117, Yellowstone National Park WY 82190. (307)344-2294. Registrar: Jeanne Peterman. Offers workshops in nature, wildlife and close-up photography during the summer, fall and winter. Custom courses can be arranged.

YOSEMITE FIELD SEMINARS, P.O. Box 230, El Portal CA 95318. (209)379-2646. Seminar Coordinator: Penny Otwell. Costs: $95-250. Offers workshops in outdoor field photography throughout the year. Write or call for free brochure.

Recommended Books & Publications

Photographer's Market recommends the following additional reading material to stay informed of market trends as well as to find additional names and addresses of photo buyers. Most are available either in a library or bookstore or from the publisher. To insure accuracy of information, use copies of these resources that are no older than a year.

ADVERTISING AGE, *740 Rush St., Chicago IL 60611-2590. Weekly advertising and marketing tabloid.*

ADWEEK, *A/S/M Communications,Inc., 49 E. 21st St., New York NY 10010. Weekly advertising and marketing magazine.*

AMERICAN PHOTO, *43rd Floor, 1633 Broadway, New York NY 10019. Monthly magazine, emphasizing the craft and philosophy of photography.*

ART CALENDAR, *P.O. Box 199, Upper Fairmont MD 21867-0199. Monthly magazine listing galleries reviewing portfolios, juried shows, percent-for-art programs, scholarships and art colonies, among other art-related topics.*

ART DIRECTION, *6th Floor, 10 E. 39th St., New York NY 10016-0199. Monthly magazine featuring art directors' views on advertising and photography.*

ART DIRECTORS ANNUAL, *Art Directors Club, 250 Park Ave. South, New York NY 10003. Annual showcase of work selected by the organization.*

ASMP BULLETIN, *monthly newsletter of the American Society of Media Photographers, 419 Park Ave. South, New York NY 10016. Subscription comes with membership in ASMP.*

COMMUNICATION ARTS, *410 Sherman Ave., Box 10300, Palo Alto CA 94306. Magazine covering design, illustration and photography. Published 8 times a year.*

THE DESIGN FIRM DIRECTORY, *Wefler & Associates, Inc., Box 1167, Evanston IL 60204. Annual directory of design firms.*

EDITOR & PUBLISHER, *The Editor & Publisher Co., Inc., 11 W. 19th St., New York NY 10011. Weekly magazine covering latest developments in journalism and newspaper production. Publishes an annual directory issue listing syndicates and another directory listing newspapers.*

ENCYCLOPEDIA OF ASSOCIATIONS, *Gale Research Co., 835 Penobscot Building, Detroit MI 48226-4094. Annual directory listing active organizations.*

FOLIO, *Box 4949, Stamford CT 06907-0949. Monthly magazine featuring trends in magazine circulation, production and editorial.*

GREEN BOOK, *% AG Editions, 41 Union Square, #523, New York NY 10003. Annual directory of nature and stock photographers for use by photo editors and researchers.*

GREETINGS MAGAZINE, *MacKay Publishing Corp., 309 Fifth Ave., New York NY 10016. Monthly magazine featuring updates on the greeting card and stationery industry.*

GUIDE TO TRAVEL WRITING & PHOTOGRAPHY, *by Ann and Carl Purcell, published by Writer's Digest Books, 1507 Dana Ave., Cincinnati OH 45207.*

GUILFOYLE REPORT, *% AG Editions, 41 Union Square, #523, New York NY 10003. Quarterly market tips newsletter for nature and stock photographers.*

HOW TO SHOOT STOCK PHOTOS THAT SELL, *by Michal Heron, published by Allworth Press, distributed by Writer's Digest Books, 1507 Dana Ave., Cincinnati OH 45207.*

HOW YOU CAN MAKE $25,000 A YEAR WITH YOUR CAMERA, *by Larry Cribb, published by Writer's Digest Books, 1507 Dana Ave., Cincinnati OH 45207. Newly revised edition of the popular book on finding photo opportunities in your own hometown.*

INDUSTRIAL PHOTOGRAPHY, *% PTN Publishing, 445 Broad Hollow Rd., Melville NY 11747. (516)845-2700. Monthly magazine for photographers in various types of staff positions in industry, education and other institutions.*

INTERNATIONAL STOCK PHOTOGRAPHY REPORT, *by Craig Aurness, % Westlight Stock Photo Agency, 2223 S. Carmelina Ave., Los Angeles CA 90064. Annual report on trends and issues affecting photographers and agencies in the stock photo industry.*

LIGHTING SECRETS FOR THE PROFESSIONAL PHOTOGRAPHER, *by Alan Brown, Tim Grondin and Joe Braun, published by Writer's Digest Books, 1507 Dana Ave., Cincinnati OH 45207.*

LITERARY MARKET PLACE, *R.R. Bowker Company, 121 Chanlon Rd. New Providence NJ 07974.*

MADISON AVENUE HANDBOOK, *Peter Glenn Publications, 17 E. 48th St., New York NY 10017. Annual directory listing advertising agencies, audiovisual firms and design studios in the New York area.*

NEGOTIATING STOCK PHOTO PRICES, *by Jim Pickerell. Available through American Society of Media Photographers, 419 Park Ave. South, New York NY 10016. Hardbound book which offers pricing guidelines for selling photos through stock photo agencies.*

NEWS PHOTOGRAPHER, *Suite 306, 3200 Croasdaile Dr., Durham NC 27705. (919)383-7246. Monthly news tabloid published by the National Press Photographers Association.*

NEWSLETTERS IN PRINT, *Gale Research Co., 835 Penobscot Building, Detroit MI 48226-4094. Annual directory listing newsletters.*

1994 GUIDE TO LITERARY AGENTS & ART/PHOTO REPS, *published by Writer's Digest Books, 1507 Dana Ave., Cincinnati OH 45207.*

O'DWYER DIRECTORY OF PUBLIC RELATIONS FIRMS, *J.R. O'Dwyer Company, Inc., 271 Madison Ave., New York NY 10016. Annual directory listing public relations firms, indexed by specialties.*

OUTDOOR PHOTOGRAPHER, *Suite 1220, 12121 Wilshire Blvd., Los Angeles CA 90025. Monthly magazine emphasizing equipment and techniques for shooting in outdoor conditions.*

THE PERFECT PORTFOLIO, *by Henrietta Brackman, published by Amphoto Books, % Watson-Guptill Publishing, 1515 Broadway, New York NY 10036.*

PETERSEN'S PHOTOGRAPHIC MAGAZINE, *8490 Sunset Blvd., Los Angeles CA 90069. Monthly magazine for beginning and semi-professional photographers in all phases of still photography.*

PHOTO DISTRICT NEWS, *49 East 21st St., New York NY 10010. Monthly trade magazine for the photography industry.*

THE PHOTOGRAPHER'S BUSINESS & LEGAL HANDBOOK, *by Leonard Duboff, published by Images Press, distributed by Writer's Digest Books, 1507 Dana Ave., Cincinnati OH 45207. A guide to copyright, trademarks, libel law and other legal concerns for photographers.*

PHOTOGRAPHER'S SOURCE, *by Henry Horenstein, published by Fireside Books, % Simon & Schuster Publishing, Rockefeller Center, 1230 Avenue of the Americas, New York NY 10020.*

PRINT, *RC Publications Inc., 3200 Tower Oaks Blvd., Rockville MD 20852. Bimonthly magazine focusing on creative trends and technological advances in illustration, design, photography and printing.*

PROFESSIONAL PHOTOGRAPHER, *published by Professional Photographers of America (PPA), 1090 Executive Way, Des Plaines IL 60018. Monthly magazine, emphasizing technique and equipment for working photographers.*

PROFESSIONAL PHOTOGRAPHER'S GUIDE TO SHOOTING & SELLING NATURE & WILDLIFE PHOTOS, *by Jim Zuckerman, published by Writer's Digest Books, 1507 Dana Ave., Cincinnati OH 45207.*

PROFESSIONAL PHOTOGRAPHER'S SURVIVAL GUIDE, *by Charles E. Rotkin, published by Writer's Digest Books, 1507 Dana Ave., Cincinnati OH 45207. A guide to becoming a professional photographer,* *making the first sale, completing assignments and earning the most from photographs.*

PUBLISHERS WEEKLY, *Cahners Publications/Div. of Reed Publishing USA, 249 W. 17th St., New York NY 10011. Weekly magazine covering industry trends and news in book publishing, book reviews and interviews.*

PUBLISHING NEWS, *Hanson Publishing Group, Box 4949, Stamford CT 06907-0949. Bimonthly news-magazine of the publishing industry.*

THE RANGEFINDER, *1312 Lincoln Blvd., Santa Monica CA 90406. Monthly magazine on photography technique, products and business practices.*

SELL & RESELL YOUR PHOTOS, *by Rohn Engh, published by Writer's Digest Books, 1507 Dana Ave., Cincinnati OH 45207. Newly revised edition of the classic volume on marketing your own stock images.*

SHUTTERBUG, *5211 S. Washington Ave., Titusville FL 32780. Monthly magazine of photography news and equipment reviews.*

STANDARD DIRECTORY OF ADVERTISING AGENCIES, *National Register Publishing Co., Inc., 3002 Glenview Rd., Wilmette IL 60091. Annual directory listing advertising agencies.*

STANDARD RATE AND DATA SERVICE, *3002 Glenview Rd., Wilmette IL 60091. Annual directory listing magazines, plus their advertising rates.*

STOCK PHOTOGRAPHY HANDBOOK, *by Michal Heron, published by American Society of Media Photographers, 419 Park Ave. South, New York NY 10016.*

STOCK PHOTOGRAPHY: The Complete Guide, *by Ann and Carl Purcell, published by Writer's Digest Books, 1507 Dana Ave., Cincinnati OH 45207.*

THE STOCK WORKBOOK, *published by Scott & Daughters Publishing, Inc., Suite A, 940 N. Highland Ave., Los Angeles CA 90038. (213)856-0008. Annual directory of stock photo agencies.*

SUCCESSFUL FINE ART PHOTOGRAPHY, *by Harold Davis, published by Images Press, distributed by Writer's Digest Books, 1507 Dana Ave., Cincinnati OH 45207.*

TAKING STOCK, *published by Jim Pickerell, Suite A, 110 Frederick Ave., Rockville MD 20850. Newsletter for stock photographers; includes coverage of trends in business practices such as pricing and contract terms.*

WRITER'S MARKET, *Writer's Digest Books, 1507 Dana Ave., Cincinnati OH 45207. Annual directory listing markets for freelance writers. Lists names, addresses, contact people and marketing information for book publishers, magazines, greeting card companies and syndicates. Many listings also list photo needs and payment rates.*

Glossary

Absolute-released images. Any images for which signed model or property releases are on file and immediately available. For working with stock photo agencies that deal with advertising agencies, corporations and other commercial clients, such images are absolutely necessary to sell usage of images. Also see Model release, Property release.

Acceptance (payment on). The buyer pays for certain rights to publish a picture at the time he accepts it, prior to its publication.

Agency promotion rights. In stock photography, these are the rights that the agency requests in order to reproduce a photographer's images in any promotional materials such as catalogs, brochures and advertising.

Agent. A person who calls upon potential buyers to present and sell existing work or obtain assignments for his client. A commission is usually charged. Such a person may also be called a *photographer's rep*.

All rights. A form of rights often confused with work for hire. Identical to a buyout, this typically applies when the client buys all rights or claim to ownership of copyright, usually for a lump sum payment. This entitles the client to unlimited, exclusive usage and usually with no further compensation to the creator. Unlike work for hire, the transfer of copyright is not permanent. A time limit can be negotiated, or the copyright ownership can run to the maximum of 35 years.

All reproduction rights. See all rights.

All subsidiary rights. See all rights.

ASMP member pricing survey. These statistics are the result of a national survey of the American Society of Media Photographer's (ASMP) compiled to give an overview of various specialties comprising the photography market. Though erroneously referred to as "ASMP rates", this survey is not intended to suggest rates or to establish minimum or maximum fees.

Assignment. A definite OK to take photos for a specific client with mutual understanding as to the provisions and terms involved.

Assignment of copyright, rights. The photographer transfers claim to ownership of copyright over to another party in a written contract signed by both parties. Terms are almost always exclusive, but can be negotiated for a limited time period or as a permanent transfer.

Assign (designated recipient). A third-party person or business to which a client assigns or designates ownership of copyrights that the client purchased originally from a creator, such as a photographer.

Audiovisual. Materials such as filmstrips, motion pictures and overhead transparencies which use audio backup for visual material.

Automatic renewal clause. In contracts with stock photo agencies, this clause works on the concept that every time the photographer delivers an image, the contract is automatically renewed for a specified number of years. The drawback is that a photographer can be bound by the contract terms beyond the contract's termination and be blocked from marketing the same images to other clients for an extended period of time.

AV. See Audiovisual.

Betacam. A videotape mastering format typically used for documentary/location work. Because of its compact equipment design allowing mobility and its extremely high-quality for its size, it has become an accepted standard among TV stations for news coverage.

Bimonthly. Every two months.

Biweekly. Every two weeks.

Bleed. In a mounted photograph it refers to an image that extends to the boundaries of the board.

Blurb. Written material appearing on a magazine's cover describing its contents.

Body copy. Text used in a printed ad.

Bounce light. Light that is directed away from the subject toward a reflective surface.

Bracket. To make a number of different exposures of the same subject in the same lighting conditions.

Buyout. A form of work for hire where the client buys all rights or claim to ownership of copyright, usually for a lump sum payment. Also see All rights, Work for hire.

Capabilities brochure. In advertising and design firms, this type of brochure—similar to an annual report—is a frequent request from many corporate clients. This brochure outlines for prospective clients the nature of a company's business and the range of products or services it provides.

Caption. The words printed with a photo (usually directly beneath it) describing the scene or action. Synonymous with *cutline*.

Catalog work. The design of sales catalogs is a type of print work that many art/design studios and advertising agencies do for retail clients on a regular basis. Because the emphasis in catalogs is upon selling merchandise, photography is used heavily in catalog design. Also there is a great demand for such work, so many designers, art directors and photographers consider this to be "bread and butter" work, or reliable source or income.

Cibachrome. A photo printing process that produces fade-resistant color prints directly from color slides.

Clips. See Tearsheets.

Collateral materials. In advertising and design work, these are any materials or methods used to communicate a client's marketing identity or promote its product or service. For instance, in corporate identity designing, everything from the company's trademark to labels and packaging to print ads and marketing brochures is often designed at the same time. In this sense, collateral design—which uses photography at least as much as straight advertising does—is not separate from advertising but supportive to an overall marketing concept.

Commission. The fee (usually a percentage of the total price received for a picture) charged by a photo agency or agent for finding a buyer and attending to the details of billing, collecting, etc.

Composition. The visual arrangement of all elements in a photograph.

Copyright. The exclusive legal right to reproduce, publish and sell the matter and form of a literary or artistic work.

C-print. Any enlargement printed from a negative. Any enlargement from a transparency is called an R-print.

Credit line. The byline of a photographer or organization that appears below or beside published photos.

Crop. To omit unnecessary parts of an image when making a print or copy negative in order to focus attention on the important part of the image.

Cutline. See Caption.

Day rate. A minimum fee which many photographers charge for a day's work, whether a full day is spent on a shoot or not. Some photographer's offer a half-day rate for projects involving up to a half-day of work. This rate typically includes mark-up but not additional expenses, which are usually billed to the customer.

Demo(s). A sample reel of film or sample videocassette which includes excerpts of a filmmaker's or videographer's production work for clients.

Disclaimer. A denial of legal claim used in ads and on products.

Dry mounting. A method of mounting prints on cardboard or similar materials by means of heat, pressure, and tissue impregnated with shellac.

EFP. Abbreviation for Electronic Field Processing equipment. Trade jargon in the news/video production industry for a video recording system that is several steps above ENG in quality. Typically, this is employed when film-like sharpness and color saturation are desirable in a video format. It requires a high degree of lighting, set-up and post-production. Also see ENG.

ENG. Abbreviation for Electronic News Gathering equipment. Trade jargon in the news/video production industry for professional-quality video news cameras which can record images on videotape or transmit them by microwave to a TV station's receiver.

Exclusive property rights. A type of exclusive rights in which the client owns the physical image, such as a print, slide, film reel or videotape. A good example is when a portrait which is shot for a person to keep, while the photographer retains the copyright.

Exclusive rights. A type of rights in which the client purchases exclusive usage of the image for a negotiated time period, such as one, three or five years. Can also be permanent. Also see All rights, Work for Hire.

Fee-plus basis. An arrangement whereby a photographer is given a certain fee for an assignment—plus reimbursement for travel costs, model fees, props and other related expenses incurred in filling the assignment.

First rights. The photographer gives the purchaser the right to reproduce the work for the first time. The photographer agrees not to permit any prior publication of the work elsewhere for a specified amount of time.

Format. The size, shape and other traits giving identity to a periodical.

Four-color printing, four-color process. A printing process in which four primary printing inks are run in four separate passes on the press to create the visual effect of a full-color photo, as in magazines, posters and various other print media. Four separate negatives of the color photo—shot through filters—are placed identically (stripped) and exposed onto printing plates, and the images are printed from the plates in four ink colors.

Gaffer. In motion pictures, the person who is responsible for positioning and operating lighting equipment, including generators and electrical cables.

Grip. A member of a motion picture camera crew who is responsible for transporting, setting up, operating, and removing support equipment for the camera and related activities.

Holography. Recording on a photographic material the interference pattern between a direct coherent light beam and one reflected or transmitted by the subject. The resulting hologram gives the appearance of three dimensions, and, within limits, changing the viewpoint from which a hologram is observed shows the subject as seen from different angles.

In perpetuity. A term used in business contracts which means that once a photographer has sold his copyrights to a client, the client has claim to ownership of the image or images forever. Also see All rights, Work for hire.

Internegative. An intermediate image used to convert a color transparency to a black-and-white print.

IRC. Abbreviation for International Reply Coupon. IRCs are used instead of stamps when submitting material to foreign buyers.

Leasing. A term used in reference to the repeated selling of one-time rights to a photo; also known as *renting*.

Logo. The distinctive nameplate of a publication which appears on its cover.

Model release. Written permission to use a person's photo in publications or for commercial use.

Ms, mss. Manuscript and manuscripts, respectively. These abbreviations are used in *Photographer's Market* listings.

Multi-image. A type of slide show which uses more than one projector to create greater visual impact with the subject. In more sophisticated multi-image shows, the projectors can be programmed to run by computer for split-second timing and animated effects.

Multimedia. A generic term used by advertising, public relations and audiovisual firms to describe productions using more than one medium together—such as slides and full-motion, color video—to create a variety of visual effects. Usually such productions are used in sales meetings and similar kinds of public events.

News Release. See Press release.

No right of reversion. A term in business contracts which specifies once a photographer sells his copyrights to an image or images, he has surrendered his claim to ownership. This may be unenforceable, though, in light of the 1989 Supreme Court decision on copyright law. Also see All rights, Work for hire.

NPI. An abbreviation used within listings in *Photographer's Market* that means "no payment information given." Even though we request specific dollar amounts for payment information in each listing, the information is not always provided.

Offset. A printing process using flat plates. The plate is treated to accept ink in image areas and to reject it in nonimage areas. The inking is transferred to a rubber roller and then to the paper.

One-time rights. The photographer sells the right to use a photo one time only in any medium. The rights transfer back to the photographer on his request after the photo's use.

On spec. Abbreviation for "on speculation." Also see Speculation, Assignment.

PACA. See Picture Agency Council of America.

Page rate. An arrangement in which a photographer is paid at a standard rate per page. A page consists of both illustrations and text.

Panoramic Format. A camera format which creates the impression of peripheral vision for the viewer. It was first developed for use in motion pictures and later adapted to still formats. In still work, this format requires a very specialized camera and lens system.

Pans. See Panoramic format.

Picture Agency Council of America. A trade organization consisting of stock photo agency professionals established to promote fair business practices in the stock photo industry. The organization monitors its member agencies and serves as a resource for stock agencies and stock photographers.

Point-of-purchase, point-of-sale. A generic term used in the advertising industry to describe in-store marketing displays which promote a product. Typically, these colorful and highly-illustrated displays are placed near check out lanes or counters, and offer tear-off discount coupons or trial samples of the product.

P-O-P, P-O-S. See Point-of-purchase.

Portfolio. A group of photographs assembled to demonstrate a photographer's talent and abilities, often presented to buyers.

Press Release. A form of publicity announcement which public relations agencies and corporate communications staff people send out to newspapers and TV stations to generate news coverage. Usually this is sent in typewritten form with accompanying photos or videotape materials. Also see Video News Release.

Property release. Written permission to use a photo of private property and public or government facilities in publications or commercial use.

Publication (payment on). The buyer does not pay for rights to publish a photo until it is actually published, as opposed to payment on acceptance.

Release. See Model release, Property release.

Rep. Trade jargon for sales representative. Also see Agent.

Query. A letter of inquiry to an editor or potential buyer soliciting his interest in a possible photo assignment or photos that the photographer may already have.

Resume. A short written account of one's career, qualifications and accomplishments.

Royalty. A percentage payment made to a photographer/filmmaker for each copy of his work sold.

R-print. Any enlargement made from a transparency. Any enlargement from a negative is called a C-print.

SAE. Self-addressed envelope. Rather than requesting a self-addressed, stamped envelope, market listings may advise sending a SAE with the proper amount of postage to guarantee safe return of sample copies.

SASE. Abbreviation for self-addressed stamped envelope. Most buyers require SASE if a photographer wishes unused photos returned to him, especially unsolicited materials.

Self-assignment. Any photography project which a photographer shoots to show his abilities to prospective clients. This can be used by beginning photographers who want to build a portfolio or by photographers wanting to make a transition into a new market.

Self-promotion piece. A printed piece which photographers use for advertising and promoting their businesses. These pieces usually use one or more examples of the photographers' best work, and are professionally designed and printed to make the best impression.

Semigloss. A paper surface with a texture between glossy and matte, but closer to glossy.

Semimonthly. Twice a month.

Serial rights. The photographer sells the right to use a photo in a periodical. Rights usually transfer back to the photographer on his request after the photo's use.

Simultaneous submissions. Submission of the same photo or group of photos to more than one potential buyer at the same time.

Speculation. The photographer takes photos on his own with no assurance that the buyer will either purchase them or reimburse his expenses in any way, as opposed to taking photos on assignment.

Stock photo agency. A business that maintains a large collection of photos which it makes available to a variety of clients such as advertising agencies, calendar firms, and periodicals. Agencies usually retain 40-60 percent of the sales price they collect, and remit the balance to the photographers whose photo rights they've sold.

Stock Photography. Primarily the selling of reprint rights to existing photographs rather than shooting on assignment for a client. Some stock photos are sold outright, but most are rented for a limited time period. Individuals can market and sell stock images to individual clients from their personal inventory, or stock photo agencies can market a photographer's work for them. Many stock agencies hire photographers to shoot new work on assignment which then becomes the inventory of the stock agency.

Stringer. A freelancer who works part-time for a newspaper, handling spot news and assignments in his area.

Stripping. A process in printing production where negatives are put together to make a composite image or prepared for making the final printing plates, especially in four-color printing work. Also see Four-color printing.

Subagent. See Subsidiary agent.

Subsidiary agent. In stock photography, this is a stock photo agent which handles marketing of stock images for a primary stock agency in certain US or foreign markets. These are usually affiliated with the primary agency by a contractual agreement rather than by direct ownership, as in the case of an agency which has its own branch offices.

SVHS. Abbreviation for Super VHS. A videotape equipment format utilizing standard VHS format tape but which is a step above consumer quality in resolution. The camera system separates the elements of the video signal into two main components of sharpness and color which can be further enhanced in post-production and used for TV broadcast.

Table-top. Still-life photography; also the use of miniature props or models constructed to simulate reality.

Tabloid. A newspaper that is about half the page size of an ordinary newspaper, and which contains many photos and news in condensed form.

Tearsheet. An actual sample of a published work from a publication.

Trade journal. A publication devoted strictly to the interests of readers involved in a specific trade or profession, such as doctors, writers, or druggists, and generally available only by subscription.

Transparency. A color film with positive image, also referred to as a slide.

Tungsten light. Artificial illumination as opposed to daylight.

U-Matic. A trade name for a particular videotape format produced by the Sony Corporation.

Unlimited use. A type of rights in which the client has total control over both how and how many times an image will be used. Also see All rights, Exclusive rights, Work for hire.

VHS. Abbreviation for Video Home System. A standard videotape format for recording consumer-quality videotape. This is the format most commonly used in home videocassette recording and portable camcorders.

Video news release. A videocassette recording containing a brief news segment specially prepared for broadcast on TV new programs. Usually, public relations firms hire AV firms or filmmaker/videographers to shoot and produce these recordings for publicity purposes of their clients.

Videotape. Magnetic recording tape similar to that used for recording sound but which also records moving images, especially for broadcast on television.

Videowall. An elaborate installation of computer-controlled television screens in which several screens create a much larger moving image. For example, with 8 screens, each of the screens may hold a portion of a larger scene, or two images can be shown side by side, or one image can be set in the middle of a surrounding image.

VNR. See Video news release.

Work for hire, Work made for hire. Any work that is assigned by an employer and the employer becomes the owner of the copyright. Copyright law clearly defines the types of photography which come under the work-for-hire definition. An employer can claim ownership to the copyright only in cases where the photographer is a fulltime staff person for the employer or in special cases where the photographer negotiates and assigns ownership of the copyright in writing to the employer for a limited time period. Stock images cannot be purchased under work-for-hire terms.

GET YOUR WORK INTO
THE RIGHT BUYERS' HANDS!

You work hard... and your hard work deserves to be seen by the right buyers. But with the constant changes in the industry, it's not always easy to know who those buyers are. That's why you'll want to keep up-to-date and on top with the most current edition of this indispensable market guide.

Keep ahead of the changes by ordering *1995 Photographer's Market* today. You'll save the frustration of getting manuscripts returned in the mail, stamped MOVED: ADDRESS UNKNOWN. And of NOT submitting your work to new listings because you don't know they exist. All you have to do to order the upcoming 1995 edition is complete the attached post card and return it with your payment or charge card information. Order now, and there's one thing that won't change from your *1994 Photographer's Market* - the price! That's right, we'll send you the 1995 edition for just $22.95. *1995 Photographer's Market* will be published and ready for shipment in September 1994.

Don't let another opportunity slip by...get a jump on the industry with the help of *1995 Photographer's Market*. Order today! You deserve it!

(See other side for more books to help you sell your photos)

More Books To Help You Sell Your Photos...

*SAVE UP TO
$3.75 ON THESE
GREAT TITLES!*

Sell & Re-Sell Your Photos
This indispensable guide by Rohn Engh will help you
set up a profitable, home-based business selling to all photo markets. Includes
important information on tax laws, current pricing guidelines, plus info on
today's equipment and film. 368 pages/$14.95 $12.75/paperback

How You Can Make $25,000 a Year With Your Camera
You'll find hundreds of ideas for selling your photos in your own community–
no matter where you live! Includes info on pricing and negotiating rights, a
special section on glamour photography, plus how to use a computer to manage your photo business. 224 pages/$12.95 $11.00/paperback

Professional Photographer's Survival Guide
(*REVISED & UPDATED*)
Learn how to survive in the photography field! This guide shows you the ropes, from making the
first sale to successfully completing assignments to get the most from your photographs. 368
pages/$16.95 $14.50/paperback

NEW! Outstanding Special Effects Photography on a Limited Budget
How to create a variety of dramatic special effects with inexpensive equipment and techniques —
plus how to come up with ideas, practical techniques to translate them into reality, and where to
market those images. 144 pages/$24.95 $21.20/paperback

Use coupon on other side to order today!

World rights. A type of rights in which the client buys usage of an image in the international marketplace. Also see All rights.

Worldwide exclusive rights. A form of world rights in which the client buys exclusive usage of an image in the international marketplace. Also see All rights.

Zone System. A system of exposure which allows the photographer to previsualize the print, based on a gray scale containing nine zones. Many workshops offer classes in Zone System.

Zoom lens. A type of lens with a range of various focal lengths.

First Markets Index

The following index contains hundreds of markets which are interested in receiving work from newer, lesser-known photographers. While some of these listings are lower paying markets, many are at the top-end of the pay scale. The index has been divided up into categories which coincide with the sections in this book.

Advertising, Public Relations and Audiovisual Firms
Barksdale Ballard and Co
Baron Advertising, Inc.
Bramson & Associates
Brower, Lowe & Hall Advertising, Inc.
Butwin & Associates Advertising, Inc.
Epstein & Walker Associates
Everett, Brandt & Bernauer, Inc.
Fraser Advertising
GGH&M Advertising
Grant/Garrett Communications
Group 400 Advertising
Harrington Associates Inc.
Harris & Love, Inc.
HP Communications
HP Direct, Inc.
Image Associates
January Productions
Kollins Communications Inc.
Kopf, Zimmermann, Schultheis
Kranzler, Kingsley Communications Ltd.
McAndrew Advertising Co.
Mizerek Advertising
Molino + Associates, Inc.
MSR Advertising
Olson and Gibbons, Inc.
Paragon Advertising
Paton Public Relations, Pat/ Paton & Associates, Inc.
Photec
Porras & Lawlor Associates
Prather & Associates Inc.
Red Hots Entertainment
Redgate Communications Corporation
Roggen Advertising and Public Relations, Ted
Sanoski Company, Inc., Sandra
Selz, Seabolt And Associates
Smith Advertising & Associates
Southshore Advertising Inc

Spencer Productions, Inc.
Thomas & James Advertising
Tri Video Teleproduction — Lake Tahoe
Varon & Associates, Inc.
Watt, Roop & Co.
White Productions, Inc., Dana
Zelman Studios, Ltd.

Art/Design Studios
A.T. Associates
Aliman Design Inc., Elie
Bachman Design Group
Berson, Dean, Stevens
Boeberitz Design, Bob
Brainworks Design Group
Burchett Design Concept, Carla S.
Canetti Design Group The Photo Library
Carew Design
Csoka/Benato/Fleurant, Inc.
Duck Soup Graphics, Inc.
Elliot Hutkin, Inc.
Graphic Design Concepts
Hammond Design Associates
Hirsch Design Group, Inc., David
Hoffman Design, John
Hulsey Graphics
James Design Studio, Peter
Jensen Communications Group, Inc.
Jones Medinger Kindschi Bushko Inc.
Lieber Brewster Corporate Design
Mauck & Associates
Miranda Designs Inc.
Mitchell Studios Design Consultants
Nicholson Associates Inc., Tom
O'Mara Design Group, Inc.
Pike And Cassels, Inc.
Saks Associates, Arnold
Schecterson Associates, Jack
Signature Design
Tribotti Designs
Unit One, Inc.

California Museum of Photography
Camera Obscura Gallery, The
Center for Exploratory and Perceptual Art
Concept Art Gallery
Eleven East Ashland (I.A.S.)
Focal Point Gallery
Foster Goldstrom
Freeport Art Museum
Galesburg Civic Art Center
Gallery One
Gallery 614
Gallery Ten
Galman Lepow Associates, Inc.
Gill Gallery, Stephen
Gold Gallery, Fay
Hillwood Art Museum
Hughes Fine Arts Center
Imagery
Kendall Campus Art Gallery—Miami-
   Dade Community College
Lite Rail Gallery
Lysographics Fine Art
Minot Art Gallery
Museum of Contemporary Photography,
   Columbia College, The
Neikrug Photographica Ltd.
New Ground Gallery
Northern Illinois University Art Gallery in
   Chicago
Nye Gomez Gallery
Open Space Arts Society
Orlando Gallery
Photographic Resource Center
Red Mountain Gallery
Rockridge Cafe
Rossi Gallery, The
Shapiro Gallery, Michael
South Shore Art Center, Inc.
Spirit Square Center for the Arts
Sunprint Cafe & Gallery
SUNY Plattsburgh Art Museum
Union Square Gallery/Ernst Haas Viewing
   Room
Viridian Gallery
Washington Project for the Arts
Wustum Museum of Fine Arts, Charles A.

Paper Products
Acme Graphics, Inc.
Alaska Wild Images
Art Resource International Ltd./Bon Art
Atlanta Market Center
Beautyway
Bokmon Dong Communications
Cedco Publishing Co.
Comstock Cards
Dayspring Greeting Cards (formerly Out-

reach Publications: Dayspring & Joy-
   fully Yours Cards
DeBos Publishing Company
Diebold Designs
Flashcards, Inc.
Galison Books
McCleery-Cumming Company, Inc.
Northword Press Inc.
Product Centre-S.W. Inc., The Texas Post-
   card Co.
Rockshots, Inc.
Sunrise Publications, Inc.
West Graphics

Publications
AAP News
ACA Guidepost
Accent on Living
Advocate/PKA Publications, The
AI Magazine
Air Line Pilot
Alabama Literary Review
Alabama Municipal Journal
Alaska Geographic
American Agriculturist
American Banker
American Cage-Bird Magazine
American Dane Magazine
American Farriers Journal
American Horticulturist
American Oil & Gas Reporter
American Sailor
American Skating World
American Survival Guide
Amiga Format
Appalachian Trailway News
Arizona Business Gazette
Army Reserve Magazine
Athletic Management
Atlantic Salmon Journal
Auto Trim News
Automated Builder
Automobile Magazine
Avionics Magazine
AVSC News
Back Home in Kentucky
Baja Times
Ball Magazine
Balloon Life
Ballstreet News Journal
Bartender Magazine
Bible Advocate, The
Bicycle USA
Bike Journal International
Bow & Arrow
Bowling Magazine
Brigade Leader
Brown's Probasketball, Hubie

Shout! Magazine
Show Biz News
Simply Seafood
Singer Media Corp., Inc.
Single Parent, The
680 Magazine
Sky
Skydiving
Soap Opera Digest
Southern Accents
Southern California Business
Southern Lumberman
Soybean Digest
Sport Fishing
Spur
STL
Storm Magazine
Streetpeople's Weekly News (Homeless Editorial)
Summit
Sun, The
Tank Talk
Teaching Today
Tech Transfer
Texas Alcalde Magazine
Texas Highways
Texas Realtor Magazine
Today's Model
Total TV
Touch
TQ
Track and Field News
Trade and Culture Magazine
Transport Topics
Traveller
True West
Tuff Stuff
Turkey Call
Twins Magazine
U—The National College Magazine
U.S. Youth Soccer
Utility and Telephone Fleets
UTU News Canada
V.F.W. Magazine
Vauhdin Maailma
Vermont Life
Vermont Magazine
Victoria Magazine
VM & SD (Visual Merchandising and Store Design)
Vocational Education Journal
Washington Blade, The
Water Skier, The
Western Horseman
Western Outdoors
Western Producer, The
Westways
Where Magazine

Wildlife Conservation Magazine
Wilson Library Bulletin
Wines & Vines
Wisconsin
With
Woman Bowler
Womenwise
Wordsmith
World & I, The
Young Children
Your Home
Your Money Magazine
Zuzu's Petals Quarterly

Record Companies
Afterschool Publishing Company
Alpha International Record Co.
Azra Records
Cornell Entertainment Group
Creative Network, Inc.
Curtiss Universal Record Masters
EFA-Medien-GmbH
Hard Hat Records & Cassettes
Kaizan Music
K-tel International (USA), Inc.
Maricao Records/Hard Hat Records
Maui Arts & Music-Survivor Records
Miramar Productions
Must Rock RSNY Producionz
Narada Productions
Next Plateau Records, Inc.
Nucleus Records
One Step To Happiness Music
PDS Communications, Inc.
Rapp Productions
Rock-A-Billy Records
Rockit Records/Satellite Modeling Studios
R.T.L. Music/Swoop Records
Sphemusations
Taylor Music, Mick
Time-Life Music
Uar Records

Stock Photo Agencies
Aaa Image Makers
AAA Stock Photography
Andes Press Agency
APL Argus Photoland
Barnaby's Picture Library
Bavaria Bildagentur GmbH
Bennett, Inc., Robert J.
Bryant Stock Photography, D. Donne
Das Photo
Devaney Stock Photos
Dinodia Picture Agency
Dr. Stock Inc.
Dynamic Graphics Inc., Clipper & Print Media Service

Echo Image
Elite Photography, Inc.
Ewing Galloway, Inc.
Fern-Wood Designs and Photo Marketing
    Agency
Fine Press Syndicate
Franklin Photo Agency
Fundamental Photographs
Geoscience Features Picture Library
Gordon Photography, Joel
Grotell Underwater Photography, Al
High Country Images
Image Factory, The
Index Stock Photography
Jeroboam, Inc.
Light Sources Stock
Lightwave
Medical Images Inc.
Mountain Stock Photo & Film
Nawrocki Stock Photo
Omni-Photo Communications
Painet
Peebles Photography, Douglas
Photo Index
Photo Library, The
Photo Network
Photo Search Ltd.
Photolink Stock Photography
Picture Perfect Stock Photos
Picturesque Stock Photos

Pro-File
Rainbow
Reflexion Phototheque
Rex USA Ltd.
Roberts Represents, Chris
Ro-Ma Stock
S.K. Stock
Science Photo Library, Ltd.
Sharpshooters, Inc.
Slide File, The
Source Stock Footage Library, Inc., The
Southern Stock Photo Agency
Sporting Pictures (UK), Ltd.
Sports File
Sports Lens, Inc.
Sportslight Photo
Stock Imagery, Inc.
Stock Options
Stock Pile, Inc.
Stockhouse, Inc., The
Tank Incorporated
Third Coast Stock Source
Tropix Photographic Library
U.S. Naval Institute
Universal-Stock Agency
Viesti Associates, Inc.
West Stock, Inc.
Wildlife Collection, The
World View-Holland BV
Worldwide Images
Zephyr Pictures

Subject Index

New to this edition of *Photographer's Market*, this index can help you find editors who are searching for the kinds of images you are producing. Consisting of markets from the Publications section, this index is broken down into 24 different subjects. If, for example, you shoot sports photos and want to find out which publishers purchase sports material, turn to that category in this index.

Memorabilia/Hobbies

Outdoors/Environmental

People

Political

Portraits

Product Shots/Still Lifes

General Index

Can't find a listing? Check at the end of each market section for the " '93-'94 Changes" lists. These lists include any market listings from the '93 edition which were either not verified or deleted in this edition.

Can't find a listing? Check at the end of each market section for the " '93-'94 Changes" lists. These lists include any market listings from the '93 edition which were either not verified or deleted in this edition.

Cushman and Associates, Inc., Aaron D. 67
Custom Medical Stock Photo 489
Cycle News 343
Cycle World Magazine 253
Cycling: BC 371
Cyr Color Photo Agency 489

D
D Magazine 253
Daily News, The 343
Dairy Today 423
Dakota Outdoors 253
Dallas Life Magazine, Dallas Morning News 253
Daloia Design 157
Dance Magazine 253
Dance Teacher Now 423
Darkroom & Creative Camera Techniques 424
Das Photo 490
Data Communications Magazine 424
Davidson & Associates 69
Dayspring Greeting Cards 208
De Havilland Fine Art 181
De Wys Inc., Leo 490
Death Valley Natural History Association 126
DeBos Publishing Company 209
Deer and Deer Hunting 254
Deerfield at Stonington 556
Defenders 372
DeKalb Daily Chronicle 343
Delta Design Group, Inc. 424
Dental Economics 424
Design & Cost Data 425
Design Design, Inc. 209
Devaney Stock Photos, 491
Diana Photo Press AB 491
Diebold Designs 209
Diegnan & Associates 73
Dinodia Picture Agency 491
Dir Communications 254
Dirt Wheels 255
Discovery Productions 52
Diversion Magazine 372
Dr. Stock Inc. 492
Dog Fancy 255
Dolphin Log, The 372
Donahue Advertising & Public Relations, Inc. 52

Down Beat Magazine 255
Doyle Assoc., Inc., Richard L. 79
DRK Photo 492
Duck Soup Graphics, Inc. 105
Ducks Unlimited 372
Dudley Zoetrope Productions 91
Dutton Children's Books 126
Dykeman Associates Inc. 93
Dynamic Graphics Inc., Clipper & Print Media Service 492

E
East Bay Express 344
East Coast Publishing 126
East Texas International Photography Contest 548
Eastern Challenge 373
Echo Image 492
Eclipse Awards 548
Edelman Gallery, Catherine 181
Education Week 425
Educational Images Ltd. 75
Educational Video Network 93
EFA-Medien-GmbH 462
EGD & Associates, Inc. 57
Electrical Apparatus 425
Electronic Business 425
Electronics Now Magazine 426
Eleven East Ashland (I.A.S.) 181
Elite Photography, Inc. 493
Elite Video, Inc. 86
Elks Magazine, The 373
Elle 255
Elliot Hutkin, Inc. 106
Elliott & Clark Publishing 126
Elysium Growth Press 127
EMC Publishing 127
Emergency, The Journal of Emergency Services 426
Emmerling Inc., John (see Emmerling Post Inc., Advertising 79)
Emmerling Post Inc., Advertising 79
Entrepreneur 255
Entry Publishing, Inc. 127
Environment 256
Environmental Action 373
Envision 493
Epconcepts 209
Epic Products Inc. 158
Eples Associates 84
Epstein & Walker Associates 80

Can't find a listing? Check at the end of each market section for the " '93-'94 Changes" lists. These lists include any market listings from the '93 edition which were either not verified or deleted in this edition.

Can't find a listing? Check at the end of each market section for the " '93-'94 Changes" lists. These lists include any market listings from the '93 edition which were either not verified or deleted in this edition.

Can't find a listing? Check at the end of each market section for the " '93-'94 Changes" lists. These lists include any market listings from the '93 edition which were either not verified or deleted in this edition.

Can't find a listing? Check at the end of each market section for the " '93-'94 Changes" lists. These lists include any market listings from the '93 edition which were either not verified or deleted in this edition.

Can't find a listing? Check at the end of each market section for the " '93-'94 Changes" lists. These lists include any market listings from the '93 edition which were either not verified or deleted in this edition.

Can't find a listing? Check at the end of each market section for the " '93-'94 Changes" lists. These lists include any market listings from the '93 edition which were either not verified or deleted in this edition.

**Can't find a listing? Check at the end of each market section for the " '93-'94 Changes"
lists. These lists include any market listings from the '93 edition which were either not
verified or deleted in this edition.**

**Can't find a listing? Check at the end of each market section for the " '93-'94 Changes"
lists. These lists include any market listings from the '93 edition which were either not
verified or deleted in this edition.**

Other Books of Interest

Professional Photographer's Survival Guide, by Charles E. Rotkin—A comprehensive guide on becoming a professional photographer, making the first sale, successfully completing assignments and earning the most from your photographs. 368 pages/$16.95/paperback

Outstanding Special Effects Photography on a Limited Budget, by Jim Zuckerman—How to create a wide variety of dramatic special effects with inexpensive equipment and techniques—plus how to come up with ideas, practical techniques to translate them into reality, where and how to market those images, and much more. 144 pages/175+ color illus./$24.95/paperback

Guide to Literary Agents & Art/Photo Reps, edited by Roseann Shaughnessy—This new directory provides thorough and accurate listings of 400 reps and agents across North America. 240 pages/$18.95/paperback

Achieving Photographic Style, by Michael Freeman—You'll learn how to achieve the same special effects the pros use by examining the work of 100 great professionals, including Cartier-Bresson and Ansel Adams. 224 pages/$21.95/paperback

APA #2: Japanese Photography—A comprehensive collection of over 1,200 color photographs, representing the work of Japan's top commercial photographers. 616 pages/$69.95/hardcover

Expert Techniques for Creative Photography, by Michael Busselle—Top photographer and author of more than 20 books, Michael Busselle shows you how to achieve professional photographic results by applying some traditional-and some not-so-traditional-photographic techniques. 192 pages/95 color, 37 b&w illus./$24.95/paperback

Creative Techniques for Photographing Children, by Vik Orenstein—Proven techniques for creating beautiful portraits and candid shots of children, whether the photographer is a professional, amateur or parent. 144 pages/$24.95/paperback

Profitable Model Photography, by Art Ketchum—Any photographer-from beginner to experienced—will learn how to set up a model photography business, and how to keep their business growing. 128 pages/$18.95/paperback

How to Start & Run a Successful Photography Business, by Gerry Kopelow—In this practical, easy-to-implement guide, aspiring professional photographers will find everything they need to start and run their own successful photography business. 160 pages/$19.95/paperback

Sell & Re-Sell Your Photos, by Rohn Engh—This consistent bestseller—now in its tenth year of publication—has been revised and updated to continue helping you sell your photos, again and again, to nationwide markets by phone and mail. 368 pages/40 b&w illus/$14.95/paperback

A Guide to Travel Writing & Photography, by Ann & Carl Purcell—This book introduces you to the colorful and appealing opportunities that allow you to explore your interest in travel while making a living. 144 pages/80 color photos/$22.95/paperback

The Professional Photographer's Guide to Shooting & Selling Nature & Wildlife Photos, by Jim Zuckerman—A professional photographer shows you how to take fabulous wildlife and nature photos—and the best ways to reach the right markets for those photos. 144 pages/250 color photos/$24.95/paperback

Photo Gallery & Workshop Handbook, by Jeff Cason—This book offers the most current, accurate and up-to-date U.S. and international and workshop info. 192 pages/$19.95/paperback

Nikon System Handbook, by Moose Peterson—You'll find everything "you ever needed to know" about the Nikon system, from lenses to flashes. 144 pages/$19.95/paperback

Photographer's Publishing Handbook, by Harold Davis—This book provides insight into the variety of options for selling your photos and/or getting them published, including self-publishing. 160 pages/$19.95/paperback

Photo Marketing Handbook, by Jeff Cason—The perfect *international* companion to *Photographer's Market*! Now you sell your photos worldwide! 160 pages/$21.95/paperback.

Lighting Secrets for the Professional Photographer, by Alan Brown, Tim Grondin, & Joe Braun—A "problems/solutions" approach to special lighting tricks and techniques for creating more dynamic photographs, complete with 4-color illustrations and step-by-step explanations. 144 pages/300 color illus/$24.95/paperback

Stock Photography: The Complete Guide, by Ann and Carl Purcell—Everything photographers need to know to succeed in the profitable stock photography market-from what to shoot for stock to organizing an inventory of photos—from two highly successful professional photographers. 144 pages/$19.95/paperback

How to Shoot Stock Photos That Sell, by Michal Heron—Includes 25 step-by-step assignments to help photographers build an integrated file of stock subjects that fill the current gaps in stock. 192 pages/30 b&w illus/$16.95/paperback

How to Sell Your Photographs & Illustrations, by Elliott & Barbara Gordon-This book offers proven techniques, procedures, and formulas to help photographers and illustrators increase their freelance income. 128 pages/24 b&w illus/$15.99/ paperback

How You Can Make $25,000 a Year with Your Camera (No Matter Where You Live), by Larry Cribb—Revised and Updated! Scores of ideas for photographers who want to sell photographs in their own communities. 224 pages/Illustrated/$12.95/paperback

To order books directly from the publisher, include $3.00 postage and handling for one book, $1.00 for each additional book. Allow 30 days for delivery.

Send to: Writer's Digest Books
1507 Dana Avenue, Cincinnati, Ohio 45207
Credit card orders
Call TOLL-FREE
1-800-289-0963
Prices subject to change without notice.

Points to review when researching agencies: _____

- *Avoid agencies that sell usage rights at substantial discounts. This sometimes develops when photographers accept small commissions from sales. A typical commission is around 50 percent.*

- *Watch out for agencies that charge unreasonable fees. It is not uncommon for agencies to split promotional or duping fees with photographers, however some agencies take advantage of such agreements.*

- *Steer clear of agencies that play favorites. In order to get top-notch photographers to sign contracts, some stock companies offer financial guarantees.*